lonely planet

W9-AHL-574

Germany

Andrea Schulte-Peevers, Sarah Johnstone, Etain O'Carroll,
Jeanne Oliver, Tom Parkinson, Nicola Williams

Contents

Highlights	6	Rhineland-Palatinate	491
Getting Started	9	Saarland	528
Itineraries	13	Hesse	536
The Authors	19	North Rhine-Westphalia	566
Snapshot	21	Bremen	619
History	23	Lower Saxony	631
The Culture	44	Hamburg	682
Environment	69	Schleswig-Holstein	709
Food & Drink	74	Directory	734
Berlin	87	Transport	755
Brandenburg	142	Health	773
Saxony	163	World Time Zones	775
Thuringia	202	Language	776
Saxony-Anhalt	236	Glossary	784
Harz Mountains	262	Behind the Scenes	788
Mecklenburg-Western Pomerania	283	Index	795
Bavaria	317	Legend	816
Baden-Württemberg	423		

Schleswig-Holstein (p709)
Hamburg (p682)
Bremen (p619)
Mecklenburg-Western Pomerania (p283)
Lower Saxony (p631)
Berlin (p87)
Saxony-Anhalt (p236)
Brandenburg (p142)
North Rhine-Westphalia (p566)
Harz Mountains (p262)
Saxony (p163)
Hesse (p536)
Thuringia (p202)
Rhineland-Palatinate (p491)
Saarland (p528)
Bavaria (p317)
Baden-Württemberg (p423)

Destination: Germany

Germany. The land of bratwurst and beer halls, lederhosen and autobahns, right? Right. But that's just scratching the surface. Europe's most populous nation is much too complex and interesting to be described using mere stereotypes. Its capital, Berlin, is one of the most exciting cities on the continent. Since being awakened, Sleeping Beauty–style, from the deep slumber of division, it has abandoned its lassitude and dour look, and replaced them with infectious energy, creativity and bold new architecture. For travellers, the world-class museums and legendary nightlife here are just part of the allure.

And there are many more reasons to come to Germany, including the astonishing, unforgettable landscapes that lift the spirit and demand exploration. Majestic panoramas of jagged, snow-draped peaks unfold above flowering meadows in the Bavarian Alps. Mighty rivers flow past cities that have shaped the country's history. Forest-fringed lakes, windswept islands, bizarre rock formations, fields of golden wheat – they're all part of the unique quilt stitched by nature in Germany.

But first and foremost, Germany is about culture. Museums, churches and palaces are veritable treasure chests overflowing with art from across the globe. Architectural highlights range from the best-preserved Roman ruins north of the Alps to the latest visions of world-class architects. Gourmet food and wine satisfy the choosiest connoisseur. An impressive musical heritage thrives in the myriad opera houses and concert halls. And where else can you retrace the footsteps of some of the greatest minds ever to have walked the earth, from Martin Luther to Goethe and Bach to Einstein? 'Old Europe' it may be, but that's just what makes Germany so appealing.

JON DAVISON

RÜGEN ISLAND (p311)
Explore the many faces of this fascinating island, including its rugged chalk cliffs, windswept beaches, Romantic-era spa architecture and tree-lined country roads

BERLIN (p87)
Visit world-class museums by day and bustling bars, pubs and clubs by night

LÜBECK (p714)
Catch the Hanseatic spirit in this Unesco-recognised town known for its delicious marzipan confections

HAMBURG (p702)
Let your hair down on a tour of this vibrant city's eclectic bar and pub scene

DENMARK

POLAND

NETHERLANDS

NORTH SEA

BALTIC SEA

SCHLESWIG-HOLSTEIN

MECKLENBURG-WESTERN POMERANIA

BRANDENBURG

LOWER SAXONY

SAXONY-ANHALT

NORTH RHINE-WESTPHALIA

100 km
60 miles

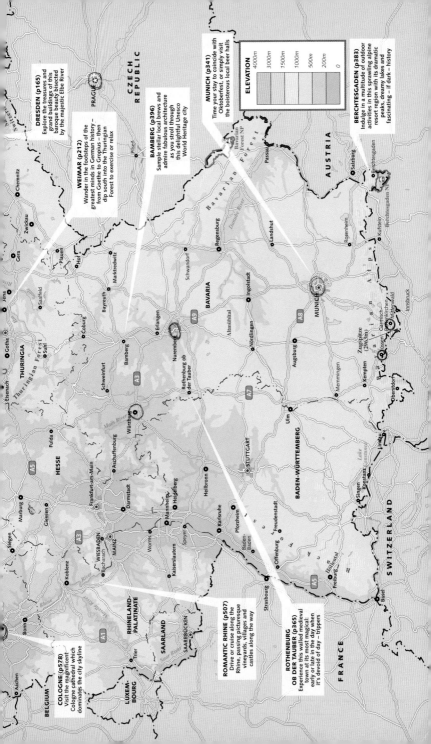

DRESDEN (p165)
Explore the treasures and grand buildings of this baroque beauty bisected by the majestic Elbe River

WEIMAR (p212)
Wander in the footsteps of the greatest minds in German history – from Goethe to Gropius – then dip south into the Thuringian Forest to exercise or relax

BAMBERG (p396)
Sample stellar local brews and admire fabulous architecture as you stroll through this delightful Unesco World Heritage city

MUNICH (p341)
Time your stay to coincide with Oktoberfest, or simply visit the boisterous local beer halls

ELEVATION
4000m
3000m
1500m
1000m
500m
200m
0

BERCHTESGADEN (p383)
Indulge in a multitude of outdoor activities in this sprawling alpine resort region with its dramatic peaks, dreamy lakes and fascinating – if dark – history

COLOGNE (p578)
Visit the magnificent Cologne cathedral which dominates the city skyline

ROMANTIC RHINE (p507)
Drive or cruise along the Rhine, passing picturesque vineyards, villages and castles along the way

ROTHENBURG OB DER TAUBER (p365)
Experience this walled medieval town at its most magical: early or late in the day when it's devoid of day – trippers

Half-timbered houses between crooked lanes paved with weathered cobble-stones – Germany's Alstadts (old towns) are places of great beauty and romance. Some are even Unesco World Heritage sites, including **Goslar** (p265), **Stralsund** (p305), **Quedlinburg** (p277) and those pictured below. **Lüneburg** (p651) and **Celle** (p646) have well-preserved medieval looks. Towns partly enclosed by ancient fortifications – such as **Rothenburg ob der Tauber** (p365) and **Bacharach** (p513) along the Romantic Rhine – also exude a special charm. **Erfurt's** Alstadt is anchored by a towering Dom (cathedral; p207), while neighbouring **Weimar** (p212), is practically an outdoor museum.

MARK AVELLINO

Take a stroll through the World Heritage site of Bamberg (p396)

Admire the stunning medieval Altstadt in Lübeck (p714)

DAVID PEEVERS

Experience the baroque splendour of the Zwinger (p172) in Dresden, faithfully restored after WWII

ANDREA SCHULT

Germany is a land of great physical beauty with vastly divergent landscapes, many of them protected as national or nature parks. Watch the disappearing water expose the muddy ocean floor in the Wattenmeer (Wadden Sea) surrounding the **East Frisian Islands** (p678). Boaters and birders are drawn to the placid lakes of **Müritz National Park** (p294), while the craggy formations of **Saxon Switzerland** (p178) are popular with climbers and hikers. The Black Forest is a fine region for a ramble with the **Wutachschlucht** (Wutach Gorge; p477) and the **Höllental** (p473) offering dramatic scenery, as do the areas pictured below.

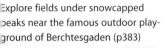

Explore fields under snowcapped peaks near the famous outdoor playground of Berchtesgaden (p383)

MARTIN MOOS

MARTIN MOOS

Meander through the more peaceful regions of the Bavarian Alps (p378)

DAVID PEEVERS

Contemplate the beauty of Rügen Island (p311)

From rock bands to opera, cosy pubs to high-tech lounges, village discos to urban techno temples – come sundown, the Germans certainly know how to party. Beyond the diverse experiences pictured below, you'll need serious stamina to keep up with the intense, nonstop and often weird scene in **Berlin** (p87). **Hamburg** (p682), where the Beatles cut their musical teeth, is (in)famous for its Reeperbahn district. **Leipzig** (p184) and **Rostock** (p294) have the most buzzing after-dark scenes in eastern Germany. Nightlife is also good in student towns, including hilly **Marburg** (p558).

DAVID PEEVERS

Let your hair down in Düsseldorf (p568)

Experience the *joie de vivre* of the Rhineland people in the Altstadt of Cologne (p577)

DAVID PEEVERS

Celebrate Oktoberfest at night in the traditional beer halls and gardens of Munich (p319)

Getting Started

After centuries of practice, Germany has come quite close to perfecting its tourism infrastructure, making travelling around the country a great pleasure. From backpackers to jetsetters, all will find their needs and expectations met. Room and travel reservations are a good idea during peak season (summer and around holidays), but otherwise you can keep your advance planning to a minimum.

WHEN TO GO

Germany is a fine destination year-round, but most people visit between May and September when sunny skies are most likely and much of life moves outdoors. Beer gardens and cafés bustle at all hours; outdoor events and festivals enliven cities and villages; and hiking, cycling and swimming are popular pursuits – at least as long as the weather plays along. Remember that rain is a possibility in any month. The flipside of summer travel is, of course, larger crowds at museums and other attractions. Accommodation needn't be hard to come by unless you're drawn to beach and mountain resorts popular with German holiday-makers.

See Climate Charts (p740) for more information.

The shoulder seasons (from March to May and from October to early November) bring fewer tourists and often surprisingly pleasant weather. In April and May, when flowers and fruit trees are in bloom, it can be mild and sunny. Indian summers that stretch well into autumn are not uncommon.

With the exception of winter sports, activities between November and early March are likely to focus more on culture and city life. In these months, skies tend to be gloomy and the mercury often drops below freezing. On the plus side, there are fewer visitors and shorter queues (except in the winter resorts). Just pack the right clothes and keep in mind that there are only six to eight hours of daylight. In December the sun (if there is any) sets around 3.30pm.

The ski season usually starts in early to mid-December, moves into full swing after the New Year and closes down again with the onset of the snowmelt in March.

For related information, see School Holidays (p746).

COSTS & MONEY

Germany is fairly inexpensive and you can stretch the euro even further by taking advantage of various discounts. For about €80 to €100 a day you can live quite comfortably; double that and you'll be living it up. For mere survival, you'll need to budget from €40 to €50 for your activities, transport and accommodation.

DON'T LEAVE HOME WITHOUT...

- Valid travel insurance (p747)
- Your ID card or passport and visa if required (p753)
- Towel and soap if staying in hostels, private rooms or cheap pensions
- Foul-weather gear
- This book and an open mind

Comfortable mid-range accommodation starts at about €80 for a double room with breakfast in the cities, and €60 in the countryside. Many hostels and hotels have special 'family' rooms with three or four beds, or they can supply sleeping cots for a small extra fee. In some places, children under a certain age pay nothing if staying in their parents' room without requiring extra bedding. Holiday flats with kitchens are ideal for trimming food costs.

A full restaurant meal with wine or beer will cost you from €20 to €30. Drinks prices (even non-alcoholic ones) can run surprisingly high even in basic eateries. Eating out doesn't have to take a huge bite out of your budget, however, as long as you stick to cafés and casual restaurants where you'll get meals for under €10. Generally, prices in supermarkets are a bit lower than in the UK, USA and Australia.

Museum admission ranges from €0.50 for small local history museum to €8 for international-calibre art museums. Some sights and museums are free, or have 'free' days, and discounts are offered for children, teens, students and seniors. Tourist-geared discount cards (often called Welcome Cards) cost around €9 a day. They offer free public transport and discounts on admissions, tours and the like.

Car-hire costs vary; expect to pay around €45 a day for a medium-sized, new car. It is perhaps the most comfortable and convenient mode of transport, although in cities parking may be elusive and expensive; however, if there are three or more of you travelling together, it may be the most economical way of getting around. In cities, buying day or other passes for public transport almost always gleans cheaper fares than single tickets. If you're travelling by train, consider a rail pass or take advantage of Deutsche Bahn's special promotions or tickets (p771).

TRAVEL LITERATURE

To get you in the mood for your trip, consider reading some of these titles written by travellers who have visited Germany before you:

A Tramp Abroad by Mark Twain is a literary classic that includes keen and witty observations about Germany garnered by the author during two visits in the 1880s. Twain's postscript 'The Awful German Language' is a hilarious read.

Three Men on the Bummel by Jerome K Jerome, the sequel to the even funnier *Three Men in a Boat*, is a classic comic tale that follows three English gentlemen on their cycling trip through the Black Forest in the 1890s.

Deutschland: A Winter's Tale by Heinrich Heine is a poetic travelogue about the author's journey from Paris to Hamburg. It also packs a satirical punch and strong criticism of Germany's mid-19th-century political landscape. It was censored immediately.

Mr Norris Changes Trains and *Goodbye to Berlin* are by Christopher Isherwood, who lived in Berlin during the Weimar years and whose stories inspired the movie *Cabaret*. The books brilliantly and often entertainingly chronicle the era's decadence and despair.

The Temple by Stephen Spender is an autobiographical novel by one of Britain's most celebrated 20th-century poets, based on his travels to Germany in the late 1920s and his encounters with, among others, Isherwood.

In a German Pension by Katherine Mansfield is a collection of satirical short stories written after Mansfield's stay in Bavaria as a young women. Her ability to inject meaning into vignettes makes it an especially worthwhile read.

TOP 10S
MUST-SEE GERMAN MOVIES

Planning and dreaming about your trip to Germany is best done in a comfy living room with a bowl of popcorn in one hand and a remote in the other. Head down to your local video store to pick up these flicks, from silent-era classics to the latest Academy Award winner. Look for brief reviews of some of them on p64.

- *Das Boot* (1981)
  Director: Wolfgang Petersen
- *Metropolis* (1927)
  Director: Fritz Lang
- *Die Blechtrommel*
  (The Tin Drum, 1979)
  Director: Volker Schöndorff
- *Der Blaue Engel* (The Blue Angel, 1930)
  Director: Josef von Sternberg
- *Goodbye, Lenin!* (2003)
  Director: Wolfgang Becker

- *Die Ehe der Maria Braun*
  (The Marriage of Maria Braun, 1979)
  Director: Rainer Werner Fassbinder
- *Nirgendwo in Afrika* (Nowhere in Africa, 2001)
  Director: Caroline Link
- *Lola rennt* (Run Lola Run, 1998)
  Director: Tom Tykwer
- *Der Himmel über Berlin* (Wings of Desire, 1987)
  Director: Wim Wenders
- *Der Bewegte Mann* (Maybe, Maybe Not, 1994)
  Director: Sönke Wortman

TOP READS

One of the best ways to learn about a country's culture and grasp a sense of a people is to immerse yourself in a good book. The following Top 10 – from classics to contemporary works – have won kudos and critical acclaim in Germany and abroad. See p62 for reviews of some of them.

- *Berlin Alexanderplatz* (1929)
  Alfred Döblin
- *Das Urteil* (The Trial, 1912)
  Franz Kafka
- *Der geteilte Himmel*
  (Divided Heaven, 1963)
  Christa Wolf
- *Der Mauerspringer* (The Wall Jumper, 1982)
  Peter Schneider
- *Die Blechtrommel* (The Tin Drum, 1959)
  Günter Grass

- *Im Westen nichts Neues*
  (All Quiet on the Western Front, 1929)
  Erich Maria Remarque
- *Jakob der Lügner* (Jacob the Liar, 1968)
  Jurek Becker
- *Lagerfeuer* (2003)
  Julia Franck
- *Simple Stories* (2001)
  Ingo Schulze
- *Zonenkinder* (2002)
  Jana Hensel

OUR FAVOURITE FESTIVALS & EVENTS

Contrary to popular prejudice, the Germans really know how to let their hair down, and there's almost always something interesting on around the country. The following list is our Top 10, but for additional festivals and events throughout Germany and the year, see the various destination chapters. For an overview of national and major regional festivals, see p745.

- Internationale Filmfestspiele
  (Berlin Film Festival)
  (Berlin) February (p119)
- Cannstatter Volkfest
  (Stuttgart) September/October (p430)
- Carnival/Fasching
  Various regions: (Cologne),
  February (p581); (Munich), February (p340)
- Frankfurt Book Fair
  (Hesse) September–October (p546)
- Hamburger Dom
  (Hamburg) March (p696)

- Kieler Woche
  (Schleswig-Holstein)
  June (p712)
- Leipzig Bach Festival
  (Saxony) Around Ascension Day (p190)
- Love Parade
  (Berlin) July (p119)
- Munich Oktoberfest
  (Bavaria) September–October (p340)
- Rhine in Flames
  (Rhineland-Palatinate)
  May–September (p508)

The German Way by Hyde Flippo is organised alphabetically into 70 snappy, easy-to-read topics. It is an insightful book that mixes practical information (eg money, shopping) with background (education, fashion) to familiarise readers with the complexity of the German society and psyche.

From Berlin is by Armando, a Dutch writer, artist and (since 1979) Berlin resident, who has turned his observations about the city and the people who lived through WWII into a collection of snappy vignettes – from humorous to touching to heart-wrenching.

INTERNET RESOURCES

Hunt down bargain air fares, book hotels, check on weather conditions or chat with locals and other travellers about the best places to visit (or avoid!) by surfing the electronic waves. Start with Lonely Planet's website (www.lonelyplanet.com), where you'll find travel news, links to useful resources and the Thorn Tree bulletin board.

CIA World Fact Book – Germany (www.cia.gov/cia/publications/factbook/geos/gm.html) Frequently updated data about geopolitical, demographic, economic and other aspects of Germany.

Expatica (www.expatica.com) Geared toward expats living in Germany but filled with information of interest to travellers as well.

German Information Center (www.germany-info.org) Government-issued information on German politics, business and culture; offers the option to subscribe to a weekly newsletter.

German National Tourist Office (www.germany-tourism.de) Official site packed with information on all aspects of travel to and within Germany.

Goethe Institut (www.goethe.de) Interesting background articles on the state of German society, media, the arts, science, research and other topics.

Map 24 (www.map24.de) Interactive map and route planner for Germany.

Online German Course (www.deutsch-lernen.com) Free language lessons for absolute beginners and moderately advanced students.

Itineraries
CLASSIC ROUTES

ESSENTIAL GERMANY
Two Weeks / Berlin to Cologne

Kick off in **Berlin** (p87), Germany's dynamic capital. You'll need three or four days to admire its great art and architecture, grasp its complex history and frolic in its nice-to-naughty nightlife. From here it's south to **Dresden** (p165), a city literally risen from the ashes of WWII, sitting pretty in its baroque splendour right on the Elbe River. Next stop is **Munich** (p319), capital of Bavaria, where you can cap off a day of touring palaces and museums in a lively beer hall or beer garden. Spend two or three days here before venturing northwest to **Heidelberg** (p440), Germany's oldest university town. Its great Altstadt (Old Town) is lorded over by a romantic castle, a fitting overture for your next destination: the **Romantic Rhine** (p507). Stop briefly in **Worms** (p497) and **Mainz** (p493) for a look at their fantastic Romanesque cathedrals before plunging on into this lovely region. Steeped in legend and lore, it is dotted with medieval castles plucked straight from the world of fairy tales. Allow a couple of days to savour the sights and crisp riesling wines before heading to **Cologne** (p577), where you'll be charmed by the easy-going locals, a landmark cathedral, and happening restaurant and bar scene.

So you want bragging rights to your 'Big German Adventure'? This 1250km route delivers you to all the major hot spots, from the fast-paced capital of Berlin to clichéd Bavarian *Gemütlichkeit* and Rhenish charm and exuberance.

THE GRAND CIRCLE

Four Weeks / Berlin to Berlin

Berlin (p87) is again our starting point, but before moving south to **Dresden** (p165), take a side trip to **Potsdam** (p144) to explore the masterful Sanssouci Park and Palace. From Dresden, it's west to **Weimar** (p212), the cradle of the German Enlightenment, and one-time home of Goethe, Schiller and other German greats. Continue south to picture-perfect **Bamberg** (p396), with its pristine Altstadt and excellent breweries. Spend a few days in **Munich** (p319), then head on to world-famous **Neuschwanstein** (p375), the sugary castle built by King Ludwig II of Bavaria. **Freiburg** (p467) your next stop, is a bustling university town and gateway to the **Southern Black Forest** (p466).

Work your way north through cuckoo-clock country to historic **Heidelberg** (p440) and the castle-studded **Romantic Rhine** (p507) between Mainz and Koblenz. Then follow the meandering **Moselle** (p516) to **Trier** (p518), with the best-preserved Roman ruins north of the Alps. Cross the gentle Eifel mountain range to arrive in lively **Cologne** (p577), from where it's an easy day trip to **Aachen** (p594), with its splendid Dom (cathedral) founded by Charlemagne. Plunge on to **Hamburg** (p682), a bustling port city with a kicking nightlife and first-rate museums. Wind down your tour by comparing the charms of the Hanseatic cities of **Lübeck** (p714) and **Schwerin** (p286) before travelling south again, back to Berlin.

Our 1800km Grand Circle tour expands on Essential Germany and provides a more thorough introduction to the country's hugely diverse regions, and their historical, cultural and natural assets.

ROADS LESS TRAVELLED

MID-GERMAN MEANDERINGS   Two Weeks / Düsseldorf to Dessau

Bustling **Düsseldorf** (p568) is a magnet for fans of art, shopping and a good time. This is especially true in the Altstadt, fittingly nicknamed the 'world's longest bar'. Those with a penchant for the offbeat will be spoiled by their choices in the adjacent **Ruhrgebiet** (p598). Here you'll find such quirky delights as Gasometers housing cutting-edge art, an ex-colliery turned artists' colony, and blast furnaces doubling as concert venues; all intriguing stops on its Industrial Heritage Trail. Continue east to **Kassel** (p561), which merits a stop to explore the Wilhelmshöhe, a rambling nature park with waterfalls, castles and the towering Herkules monument.

From here it's not far to the remote and densely forested **Kyffhäuser** (p222) region, with its spooky monument to Emperor Wilhelm I and bizarre GDR-period Panorama Museum. For a little rest and relaxation spend a couple of days taking in the natural splendours and fresh air of the **Harz Mountains** (p262). Don't leave without stopping in delightful **Quedlinburg** (p277), a well-preserved symphony in half-timbered houses. **Eisleben** (p256), the birthplace of Protestant reformer Martin Luther, is only a short drive south, or make a beeline straight for **Dessau** (p243), synonymous with the Bauhaus, the 20th century's most influential school of architecture.

Don't like the tourist hordes? Already 'done' Berlin, Munich and Cologne? Then try this 550km route, which cuts straight through the middle of Germany and takes you to places with great appeal and smaller crowds.

BALTIC DELIGHTS

Though no stranger to domestic tourism, Germany's towns and resorts fringing the Baltic Sea rarely make it onto international travellers' itineraries – undeservedly so.

The first stop is **Flensburg** (p724), easily reached by train or autobahn from Hamburg, which is Germany's northernmost town and beckons with a handsome Altstadt. **Schleswig** (p721), a quick hop south, embraces a huge fjord, and boasts the intriguing Viking Museum and art-filled Schloss Gottdorf. Next up is **Lübeck** (p714), a highlight on this route, largely because of its Unesco-protected town centre crammed with medieval merchants' homes and churches. East of here, Swedish-flavoured **Wismar** (p301) is a pleasant place to explore and is also the gateway to **Poel Island** (p304), which often drowns in water-sports devotees.

En route to Rostock stop in **Bad Doberan** (p301), with its great red-brick Minster and kid-friendly narrow-gauge train. **Rostock** (p294) itself may not be so pretty but it does have some interesting sights and serves as the region's nightlife hub. **Stralsund** (p305), by contrast, has a very attractive Altstadt and is also the gateway to **Rügen Island** (p311), with its tree-lined country roads, long sandy beaches and mysterious chalk cliffs. Back on the mainland, **Greifswald** (p308) is an old university town close to beach-fringed **Usedom Island** (p310), a popular holiday island that Germany shares with Poland.

This 480km route traces the coastline from the country's borders with Denmark to where it rubs shoulders with Poland.

TAILORED TRIPS

CASTLES & PALACES

Until unification in 1871, Germany was a mosaic of fiefdoms whose over-seers ruled from the comfort of their Schloss (palace) or Burg (castle). A sentimental favourite among Germans is the **Wartburg** (p224) in Eisenach, most famous as the site where Martin Luther translated the Bible while in hiding. Less well known is **Schloss Weesenstein** (p177) near Dresden, which has its own brewery and 'upstairs-downstairs' exhibits about life at court.

Schloss Sanssouci (p145) in Potsdam is a perennial crowd pleaser, not least because of its charming gardens. You'll find a similar setup at the baroque **Schloss Charlottenburg** (p113) in Berlin, home of the Prussian Hohenzollern clan. The family's ancestral seat – **Burg Hohenzollern** (p439) – is some 700km southwest near Tübingen. From a distance, it looks medieval and mysterious, but it's actually a 19th-century neo-Gothic confection, the original long having been destroyed. A similar fate befell **Schloss Heidelberg** (p443), although much of it survives as a romantic ruin. For more romance, visit the robber barons' hang-outs along the Romantic Rhine, especially the labyrinthian **Burg Rheinfels** (p512) and the pristine **Marksburg** (p511) which, like the

Burg Eltz (p525), has never been destroyed. Other must-sees include King Ludwig II's delightful **Schloss Linderhof** (p381) and **Schloss Schwerin** (p288).

CATHEDRALS & CHURCHES

Germany has a wealth of houses of worship, the most magnificent of which lift the spirit with their beauty and priceless treasures. One of these is the amazing cathedral (Dom) in **Aachen** (p594), which was Charlemagne's private palace chapel and is also his burial place. Nearby in Cologne, the soaring spires of its **Dom** (p578), built over six centuries, dominate the skyline. Also on the Rhine stands the great trio of Romanesque cathedrals in **Mainz** (p494), **Worms** (p498) and **Speyer** (p500). The size and symmetry of the

latter especially is awesome, as is the crypt with its striped arches. In the deepest Black Forest, the Dom in **St Blasien** (p476) is a rare neoclassical gem lidded by the third-largest dome in Europe. Bavaria brims with baroque churches; the **Asamkirche** (p335) in Munich and the **Wieskirche** (p378) in Steingaden are among the finest examples of the style. North of here in Ulm, its **Münster** (p451) has the world's tallest steeple. Saxony's landmark **Frauenkirche** in Dresden (p171), levelled during WWII, is set to reopen in 2006. Churches with amazing carved altars include the **Jakobskirche** (p366) in Rothenburg ob der Tauber, the **St Nikolaikirche** (p577) in Kalkar and the **Petrikirche** (p603) in Dortmund.

WINE

Wine lovers can build an entire itinerary around their favourite libation Throughout Germany's 13 growing regions, they can tour estates, explore musty cellars stocked with vintage barrels and meet vintners during wine tastings. They can hike along vineyard trails, drink a toast to Bacchus in cosy wine taverns, then retire to their room on a wine estate.

Germany's most famous grape is the noble riesling. The best vintages hail from the tiny Rheingau area, with tourist-ridden **Rüdesheim** (p515) at its heart, and from the Middle Rhine region (between Koblenz and Bingen), where **Bacharach** (p513), with its amazing half-timbered main street, is the most appealing of the many wine towns. Fans of red wines

should head to the **Ahr Valley** (p504), where you can hike from vineyard to vineyard along the signposted Rotweinwanderweg (Red Wine Hiking Trail). In southwestern Germany, near the French border, is the Baden region, whose **Kaiserstuhl** area (p472) produces exceptional late burgundies and pinot gris. In and around **Würzburg** (p360) is the Franken region, whose vintners make excellent dry and earthy wines bottled in curvy green flagons called *Bocksbeutel*. Germany's, and indeed Europe's, northernmost growing region is **Saale-Unstrut** (p257), with Freyburg at its centre. Its sparkling wine, called Rotkäppchen (Little Red Riding Hood), was a favourite in GDR days.

WORLD HERITAGE SITES

Germany has nearly 30 places recognised by Unesco for their historical and cultural importance. Wander the warren of lanes of well-preserved medieval towns such as **Quedlinburg** (p277), **Goslar** (p265), **Bamberg** (p396) and **Lübeck** (p714). Look at the lifestyles of the rich and powerful, at the baroque palaces of **Sanssouci** (p145) in Potsdam and **Augustusburg** (p588) in Brühl, or the medieval castles along the **Romantic Rhine** (p507). The bulging coffers of the Church financed some treasures, including the cathedrals of **Aachen** (p595), **Cologne** (p578), **Hildesheim** (p655) and **Speyer** (p500), the monasteries in **Reichenau Island** (p482) and **Lorsch** (p555), the **Würzburg Residence** (p360) and **Wieskirche** (p378) in Steingaden. Sites honouring Protestant reformer

Martin Luther, including **Wartburg** (p224) in Eisenach and memorials in **Eisleben** (p256) and **Lutherstadt Wittenberg** (p249) – humble by comparison. Places prominent in more recent history include **Weimar** (p212), which drew a who's who of German thinkers in the 18th century and is also the birthplace of the Bauhaus. Bauhaus buildings in **Dessau** (p243) are also on Unesco's list. Recent additions include **Berlin's Museumsinsel** (p105), while the well-preserved Roman ruins in **Trier** (p518), were among the first five sites to make the cut. For a change of pace visit Essen's **Zollverein Colliery** (p599) and the Völklingen's **Völklinger Hütte** (p534), both considered outstanding 'cathedrals of industry'.

The Authors

ANDREA SCHULTE-PEEVERS

**Coordinating Author,
Berlin, Rhineland-Palatinate,
Saarland & North Rhine-Westphalia**

Andrea was born and raised in Germany, educated in London and at UCLA and has made a career out of writing about her native country for the past 14 years. She's been involved in writing every edition of this book and has also written Lonely Planet's *Berlin* and *Bavaria* guides. This trip allowed her to (over)indulge in good food and wine in Rhineland-Palatinate and Saarland, sample great culture and dizzying nightlife in Berlin and revisit her roots in North Rhine-Westphalia.

My Favourite Trip

Truth be told, I've never had a bad time travelling in Germany, but some places occupy a special place in my heart. Berlin (p87) I find irresistible for a number of reasons including its new architecture, nightlife and creative spirit. The majesty of the Dom (cathedral) in Cologne (p578) never fails to enthral me. My encounter with tiny, half-timbered Bacharach (p513) on the Romantic Rhine was definitely love at first sight. Strolling the streets of Weimar (p212), where a pantheon of German thinkers made their home, makes me proud of this country. And finally, I always find plenty to feed my cravings for the off-beat in the Ruhrgebiet (p598), whose people display an unlimited knack for turning former industrial sites into cutting-edge venues of creativity.

○ Berlin

○ Ruhrgebiet
○ Cologne ○ Weimar

○ Bacharach

SARAH JOHNSTONE

**Saxony-Anhalt, Bremen,
Lower Saxony, Hamburg & Schleswig-Holstein**

Having worked for Reuters, Virgin Atlantic's former in-flight magazine, *Hot Air*, and *Business Traveller*, Sarah Johnstone also has a long history of murdering the German language – at school, at university, among German friends and on many visits to the country for work, study and pleasure since 1990. It was only the concentrated effort of travelling for this guidebook that finally convinced her that maybe her amateur linguistic adventures hadn't been a total waste. Sarah's from Queensland but (nominally) based in London. Her writing has also appeared in the *Times*, the *Independent on Sunday* and the *Face*.

ETAIN O'CARROLL

Bavaria

Plagued by a bad case of itchy feet from an early age, Etain now works as a travel writer and photographer, and has published with a variety of magazines and papers worldwide. Her first visit to Germany was as a student, soaking up a culture and attitudes very different from those in her native Ireland. Later stints living and working in Germany fuelled further exploration off the beaten track and many good friendships. Work on this book allowed her the privilege of returning to explore some of Germany's most interesting territory – from a taste of brisk air in the glorious Alps to a near overdose of lavish churches and incredible medieval towns.

JEANNE OLIVER
Baden-Württemberg

Jeanne is a freelance travel writer based in the south of France. She grew up in New Jersey before moving to New York for a degree in English and then law. The travel bug bit hard, however, and she spun off to ever more far-flung destinations before finally landing in Paris to begin her writing career. She's been with Lonely Planet since 1996 and tackled the colder regions of Germany for the previous edition. Besides *Germany*, Jeanne has also authored and/or helped update guides to *Croatia*, *France*, *Normandy* and *Greece*.

TOM PARKINSON
Harz Mountains, Mecklenburg-Western Pomerania, Hesse, Brandenburg, Saxony & Thuringia

Tom first visited Germany at the tender age of three, and was promptly involved in a road accident. Undeterred, he started learning the language at school and has been coming back ever since, eventually completing a German degree before striking out as a dictionary editor and freelance journalist. Tom explored former East Germany for this book, braving witches in the Harz Mountains, culture overdose in Thuringia, thick accents in Saxony, and crowded waterways in Brandenburg, balanced with a healthy dose of Western capitalism in Hesse.

NICOLA WILLIAMS
History, The Culture, Environment, Food & Drink

France-based travel writer Nicola Williams made her first trip to Germany in the back of a lorry with 10 Welsh policemen – kipping for the night at Bonn police station and discovering the fine German art of prising open one beer bottle with another. Nicola has travelled extensively in both the Rhineland and eastern Germany since then. She still can't open a bottle of beer like Germans do.

CONTRIBUTORS

The Health chapter is based on material supplied by **Dr Caroline Evans**. Having studied medicine at the University of London, Caroline completed general practice training in Cambridge. She is the medical adviser to Nomad Travel Clinic, a private travel-health clinic in London, and is also a GP specialising in travel medicine. Caroline has acted as expedition doctor for Raleigh International and Coral Cay expeditions.

Snapshot

Change is afoot in Germany, and Germans don't quite know what to make of it. If Chancellor Schröder has his way, their generous social welfare system will soon be a thing of the past. The government's ambitious Agenda 2010 reform package seeks to revamp everything from health care to state pensions to employment benefits. The goal: to restore competitiveness and economic prosperity to a country still trying to understand the new rules of the Age of Globalism.

According to financial analysts, reform couldn't happen too soon. Germany, once Europe's powerhouse and its economic engine, has lost much of its steam, and has been mired in recession and zero growth since 2000. While September 11 and the general global downtown can partly be blamed, these experts insist that the root causes lie within the country itself. Among them: an inflexible labour market, high non-wage labour costs (eg health care and pension contributions), a lack of incentives for the unemployed to return to work, and an entrenched – and costly – bureaucracy.

All this has led to Germany becoming the current 'sick man of Europe'. Schröder's reforms seek to heal, but he can't do it without doling out some bitter pills in the form of benefit cuts, higher health-care contributions, and a call for sacrifice and greater self-determination. He's sweetening the medicine by lowering income taxes, but Germans – used to the government taking care of basic needs from womb to tomb – are wary. They know change is inevitable, but they're horrified by the prospect of it. Many worry that reforms will be carried out on the back of the 'little man'. Opposition is especially strong among labour unions, retirement groups and left-wing parties, such as the Party of Democratic Socialism (PDS), the successor party to the communist GDR-era Sozialistische Einheitspartei Deutschlands (SED).

And as if economic woes weren't enough, Germans are still reeling from the realisation that their once proud education system is also no longer up to snuff. A 2002 comparative study called the Program for International Student Assessment (PISA) ranked German students 25th out of 32 industrialised nations, instantly creating collective embarrassment in the land of 'poets and thinkers'. *Mein Gott*, even the American and Italian kids scored better!

Perhaps it's because German children don't spend all that much time in school compared with kids from other nations. Most are home by lunchtime, which may have been fine in the days of stay-at-home mums who could help with homework in the afternoon. But it's out of step with today's reality, where women, including many mothers, make up nearly half of the country's workforce.

So, will more all-day schools improve Germany's educational report card? The government certainly hopes so and has allocated €4 billion towards creating 10,000 more of them (up from the current 1800) over the next few years. At least some of that money has been earmarked for counselling and remedial training for the kids that scored especially poorly: students from low-income and immigrant families.

Which leads to another conversational minefield currently being explored around German dinner tables: multiculturalism (see also p50). There's no denying that German society is becoming increasingly diverse, especially in the cities, and it's a trend that's likely to continue.

FAST FACTS

Area: 356,970 sq km

Population: 82,536,700

GDP: €526.2 billion (2002)

Inflation: 0.8% (Nov 2003)

Unemployment: 11.3% (Nov 2003)

Land use: 54.7% farming, 29.2% forest, 5.8% built-up areas

Life expectancy: women 80.6 years, men 74.4 years

Passenger cars: 44.7 million

Fat factor: 47% overweight, 11% obese

Museums: 4570

The country needs to welcome as many as half a million newcomers each year to sustain current population levels. And the recent immigration law reforms have created a whole new set of German citizens with surnames like Ozdemir or Kucuk and skin tones in shades of sandalwood to chocolate.

Social integration, both of new immigrants and long-term foreign residents, remains an uncomfortable challenge. Germans expect their immigrants to assimilate, speak the language and respect, and preferably adapt to, national values. Many immigrants, though, cling to their own traditions and cultural identities, and are often unaware of German sensibilities. This leads to conflict and resentment. And more than anything, an ethnically diverse society is confusing to Germans, though it's certainly no reason to suspect intrinsic racism – as many are quick to assume. A federal programme offering classes in German history, culture, law and language is intended to help remedy this needless lack of understanding, but there's also a realisation that true integration must happen at all levels of society.

> 'Social unification between the two former Germanys remains a work in progress, some 15 years after the fall of the Wall'

These things take time, after all. Even social unification between the two former Germanys remains a work in progress, some 15 years after the fall of the Wall. The one thing people in both parts of the country seem to share is frustration over how long it's taking to bring the Eastern half up to par with the West. West Germans continue to pay a so-called Solidarity tax, which still pumps billions of euro into the East, yet unemployment remains at a moribund 20% to 25% in many towns, around twice the national average.

Few want to turn back the clock to pre-1989, but a general unhappiness with the status quo has certainly strengthened the support among *Ossies* (East Germans) for the PDS. It has also spurred a trend called Ostalgie – a hybrid word for *Ost* (east) and *Nostalgie* (nostalgia) – a sentimental yearning for GDR products and cultural icons (see also p47).

Its many domestic woes aside, Germany remains a strong supporter of European integration and was a driving force behind the expansion of the EU to include 10 Eastern European nations. It is also fiercely committed to the international community and does its part in fighting the war on terrorism. Its military commitment is limited to peacekeeping under UN or NATO command, which has led to German troops being stationed in such places as Afghanistan and Kosovo.

Most Germans, however, possess a strong pacifist streak, which fuelled the country's intense opposition to the war in Iraq. There's widespread disregard (to put it mildly) for the policies of the US government under President George W Bush, who is perceived as an 'arrogant bully' with a 'cowboy mentality'. Criticism extends not only to the war but also to the US's refusal to work within the framework of the UN and to adhere to such international agreements as the Kyoto Protocol. Schröder's willingness to side with France against the US in the Iraqi war debate was widely supported by the German people.

History

Germany's long and complex roots are entwined in the actions of a bunch of tribal Teutons who merrily wandered around northern Europe, eventually setting up barbarian camp in the region around 500 BC. It was only with the division of the Frankish Reich in the 9th century, however, that regions east of the mighty Rhine River formed their own cultural identity to create a distinct German history. A newly centralised Germany belatedly shook off the yoke of regional dynastic rule in the 19th century – only to wildly spiral along a heady course of feudalism, unification, fascism, occupation, division, reunification, recession and European integration.

THE CELTS & THE ROMANS

Celts, then Germanic tribes from the north, were the first inhabitants of Germany. Bronze Age humans populated an area stretching southwards from Sweden and Denmark to the North German plains and Harz Mountains. By AD 100, six broad settlement groups had formed, roughly scattered between present-day Denmark in the north, Kaliningrad in the northeast, the Danube in the southeast and the Rhine region in the west.

Germanic tribes clashed with conquering Romans from the 1st century BC, only to be pushed back eastwards across the Rhine. In 71 BC the area of today's North Rhine-Westphalia and other regions west of the Rhine were seized by Atovius, a powerful tribal leader hailing from the north; the area was grabbed back by Julius Caesar in 58 BC.

The Teutoburg Forest (Teutoburger Wald) in North Rhine-Westphalia was believed until recently to have been the site of the crushing defeat of Roman legions by Arminius in AD 9 and the liberation of the greater part of Germany from Roman domination (see the boxed text The Varus Disaster p24). After the 'Battle of Teutoburg Forest' the Romans stopped extending their control further and consolidated southern fortifications instead. In AD 1 they started building what is today central Europe's largest archaeological site – a wall running 568km from Koblenz on the Rhine to Regensburg on the Danube. Some 900 watchtowers and 60 forts studded this frontier line, dubbed Der Limes (The Limes). A 280km-long route linking Detmold with Xanten takes cyclists past the remains of many today.

The industriousness of the Romans who founded Germany's first cities is evoked in the thermal baths and amphitheatre of Augusta Treverorum (Trier today), and in other Roman relics in Aachen, Xanten, Cologne, Bonn, Mainz (where 4th-century Roman shipwrecks can be viewed), Bingen (prized for its Roman surgical instruments), Koblenz, Augsburg and Regensburg. The Rhine and Moselle vineyards are a lasting tribute to the Romans' penchant for a tipple or two.

The Great Migration throughout Europe in the 4th century, triggered by Hun horsemen galloping in from Central Asia, saw Germanic tribes pack their bags and run to southern Europe. The threat ended in 453 when Attila, leader of the Huns, died. In 486 the Western Empire collapsed and the Romans sought protection among resettled Germanic tribes. By

For more information on the ancient Germanic world, follow the link on Ancient Worlds at www.ancientsites.com.

The Roman Empire and Its Germanic Peoples by Herwig Wolfram & Thomas Dunlap (translator) is an authoritative history spanning five centuries of Germanic tribe migrations and the foundations of the Roman Empire.

Discover tourist sights along the German Limes Road (Deutsche Limesstrasse) at www.limesstrasse.de.

TIMELINE	900–500 BC	100–58 BC
	Celts, then Germanic tribes, move into the area called Germany today	Germanic tribes clash with conquering Romans

this time the Germanic population had adopted Roman administrative, fi
nancial and political structures, from which the Frankish Reich evolved.

The Frankish Reich

For a comprehensive overview of German history, see the broad-based German Culture website www.germanculture .com.ua.

Based on the Rhine's western bank, the Frankish Reich became Europe'
most important political power in medieval times. This was due, in part
to the Merovingian king, Clovis (r. 482–511), who united diverse population groups. In its heyday the Reich included present-day France, Ger
many, the Low Countries and half the Italian peninsula. After converting
to Christianity, missionaries like St Boniface (675–754) – the considered
father of German Christianity – crossed the Rhine to convert pagans.

When fighting broke out among aristocratic clans in the 7th century
the Merovingians were replaced by the Carolingians who introduced
hierarchical Church structures. From his grandiose residence in Aachen
Charlemagne (r. 768–814) – the Reich's most important king – conquered Lombardy, won territory in Bavaria, waged a 30-year war against
the Saxons in the north and was crowned Kaiser by the pope in 800. The
cards were reshuffled in the 9th century when attacks by Danes, Saracens
and Magyars threw the eastern portion of Charlemagne's empire into
turmoil and saw the emergence of four main tribal duchies – Bavaria
Franconia, Swabia and Saxony.

Two Lives of Charlemagne by Betty Radice (ed) is a striking Charlemagne biography, beautifully composed by a monk and a courtier who spent 23 years in Charlemagne's court.

Charlemagne's burial in Aachen Cathedral turned a court chapel into
a major pilgrimage site (and it remains so today). The Treaty of Verdun
(843) saw a gradual carve-up of the Reich and when Louis the Child
(r. 900–11) – a grandson of Charlemagne's brother – died heirless, the
East Frankish (ie German) dukes elected a king from their own ranks
Thus, the first German monarch was created.

DYNASTY: SAXONS TO HOHENSTAUFENS

Charlemagne's grandson, Louis the German (r. 843–76) and Konrad I
(r. 911–18) both promoted a distinctly German cultural identity. The
next ruler, Saxon dandy 'Henry the Fowler' Heinrich I (r. 919–36) was
out trapping finches in Quedlinburg when he learnt of his forthcoming
regentship – a reign that saw the bird-catching king establish hegemony
over French-speaking Lorraine in 925.

Aachen Cathedral hosted the coronation (and burial) of dozens of German kings for 600 years from 936. The first to be crowned there, Heinrich's

THE VARUS DISASTER

The Battle of Teutoburg Forest, the Romans' most crushing defeat, was dubbed the *Clades Variana* (Varus Disaster) after the Roman general Varus who killed himself after losing all three of his legions (20,000 soldiers) to the Teutons. However, it seems it didn't take place in Teutoburg Forest (northeastern North Rhine-Westphalia) at all, despite a statue of a victorious Arminius, built in 1875 atop Mount Grotenburg near Detmold, that marks the supposed battleground.

In fact, historians had absolutely no idea where the bloody ambush took place until the 1990s when archaeologists dug up Roman face helmets, breast shields, bone deposits and other bat-tle remains in Kalkriese, north of Osnabrück in Lower Saxony; the Museum und Park Kalkriese (www.mupk.de) marks the spot today.

AD 9

Roman expansion is halted with the Roman defeat at the Battle of Teutoburg Forest

486

The Western Empire collapses and the Romans seek protection among resettled Germanic tribes

on Otto I (r. 936–73), followed in Charlemagne's footsteps of assimilating Church figures into civil administration and revitalised the Reich's power over Italy as far south as Rome. On the eastern border he consolidated administrative buffer regions that gradually turned into duchies.

In 962 Otto renewed Charlemagne's pledge to protect the papacy, prompting a reciprocal papal pledge of loyalty to the Kaiser. The subsequent mutual dependence (without the pope, a king could not be crowned Kaiser) caused numerous power struggles over the centuries and created the Holy Roman Empire, a nebulous state that survived until 1806 (see the boxed text below).

Under the Salian dynasty, the Investiture Conflict occurred when the papacy tried to stamp out the practice of simony (selling religious pardons and relics). Heinrich IV (r. 1056–1106) opposed the change, and as a result was excommunicated in 1076. The king was only absolved after marching from Speyer, on the Rhine's left bank, to Canossa in northern Italy where he stood barefoot in the snow for three days begging the pope's forgiveness. Heinrich's enemies rebelled on the issue, and 20-year civil war ensued to control bishoprics and their wealth.

The issue of simony was finally resolved in the small Rhineland town of Worms where the Treaty of Worms (1122) granted local bishops independence from the Reich. Salian monarchs were buried in Speyer Cathedral (in Rhineland-Palatinate). Following the death of the heirless Heinrich V (r. 1106–25), the *Kurfürsten* (prince electors) chose the Saxon noble Lothar II (r. 1125–37) and later, Hohenstaufen Konrad III (r. 1138–52), to rule.

Aachen assumed the role of Reich capital under Friedrich I Barbarossa (r. 1152–89) who granted the town its rights of liberty in 1165 – the year Charlemagne was canonised. Reich fortunes improved until Friedrich fell foul of the pope. Meanwhile, Heinrich der Löwe (Henry the Lion), a Welf interested in Saxony and Bavaria, extended influence eastwards in campaigns to Germanise and convert the Slavs. But when he, too, fell foul

DID YOU KNOW?

The use of the title Kaiser was a direct legacy of Roman times (from 'Caesar').

WHAT WAS THE HOLY ROMAN EMPIRE?

It was an idea, mostly, and not a very good one. It grew out of the Frankish Reich, which was seen as the legitimate successor state to the defunct Roman Empire. When Charlemagne's father, Pippin, helped a beleaguered pope (Charlemagne would later do the same), he received the title *Patricius Romanorum*, or Protector of Rome, virtually making him Caesar's successor. Having retaken the extensive papal territories from the Lombards, he presented them to the Church (the last of these territories is the modern Vatican state). Charlemagne's reconstituted 'Roman Empire' then passed into German hands.

The empire was known by various names throughout its lifetime. It formally began (for historians, at least) in 962 with the crowning of Otto I as Holy Roman Emperor and finally collapsed in 1806, when Kaiser Franz II abdicated. From 1508, Maximilian I and his successors favoured 'Emperor-Elect', a title that evolved as 'King of the Romans' under the Habsburgs.

The empire sometimes included Italy as far south as Rome. Sometimes it didn't – the pope usually had a say in that. It variously encompassed present-day Netherlands, Belgium, Switzerland, Lorraine and Burgundy (in France), Sicily, Austria and an eastern swathe of land that lies in the Czech Republic, Poland and Hungary. It was also known as the 'First Reich' (not to be confused with Otto von Bismarck's Second Reich or Adolf Hitler's Third Reich).

The Merovingian dynasty is replaced by the Carolingians who introduce hierarchical Church structures and rule until 919

768–814

The Frankish Reich reaches its zenith under the rule of Charlemagne who is crowned Kaiser by the pope

of Friedrich, his Saxon interests were carved up and given to the Reich Bavaria fell into the hands of the powerful Wittelsbach family.

Under Heinrich VI (r. 1190–97), the Reich married into Sicily (caus ing another papal nervous attack). But Heinrich's unexpected deat prompted a fight for the crown between Welfs and Hohenstaufen: leading to the election of both a king and (pope-backed) anti-king i Phillip von Schwaben and Heinrich der Löwe's son, Otto IV.

TERRIBLE TIME

Electing rulers turned monarchs into lackeys of the Kurfürsten an prevented a unified Reich. When Friedrich II (r. 1212–50), a papa nominated replacement for the unfortunate Phillip von Schwaber flexed muscle in Italy, he was nullified by Pope Innocent IV, leading t the Great Interregnum (Terrible Time). The Reich, flush with kings, los all central authority.

But dynastic rivalry didn't thwart eastward expansion. Land east of th Oder River in Silesia and Moravia had been settled by German peasant and city-dwellers in the mid-12th century. In the 13th century Teutoni Knights pushed eastwards, establishing fortresses that later grew int towns such as Königsberg (present-day Kaliningrad). The eventual uni fied state of the knights stretched, at its peak, from the Oder to Estonia (In 1525 the reduced area controlled by the knights became the Duch of Prussia, a vassal state of Poland until the rise of Brandenburg-Prussi around the 17th century.)

The coronation of a Habsburg in 1273 ended the Terrible Time.

THE HOUSE OF HABSBURG

This dynasty dominated European affairs well into the 20th century thanks to Rudolf (r. 1273–91) who strengthened his dynasty throug territorial expansion and marriage, and shifted the focus of the Reich t Austria, the traditional Habsburg stamping ground.

The Declaration of Rense (1338) dispensed with the pope's confirmatio of elected kings, thus making the Holy Roman Empire a separate entity fror the papacy and ending centuries of built-in conflict. The Imperial Die of Nuremberg and Metz (1355–56) established the Golden Bull (1356), document that laid down rules for the election of Kaisers and regulated th relationship between the Kaiser and the princes. But Kaisers still danced t the merry tune of the princes, who retained the power to elect their ruler: leaving the way open for weak central authority until the 19th century.

The (Ger)man on the street battled with panic lynching, pogrom against Jews and labour shortages – all sparked off by the plagu (1348–50) that wiped out about 25% of Europe's population. In th southwest, Heidelberg University opened in 1386. Between 1414 an 1418 the Council of Constance met in the lakeside town to resolve th Great Schism (1378–1417), which saw three popes elected at the sam time (the council dumped all three and elected another).

Through a clutch of glittering arranged marriages (of his children an grandchildren), Maximilian I (r. 1493–1519) assured Habsburg control c the German Reich until 1806 and ascendancy in much of central Europe The Diet of Worms (1495) established a supreme court to handle dispute

DID YOU KNOW?

The name Habsburg (Hapsburg) originates from *Habichts Burg* (literally 'Hawk Castle'), the spot on the Rhine (in present-day Switzerland, immediately across the border from Germany) from where the great Swabian family first hailed.

Louis the Child dies heirless, prompting Germany's first monarch to be elected	Saxon and Salian emperors rule Germany, creating the Holy Roma Empire in 962

THE HANSEATIC LEAGUE

From about the mid-11th century, a swelling population, land pressure and greater mobility encouraged the growth of cities. Some were imperial (controlled by the Reich before being granted autonomy by crown charter), while others were free cities (those that had shaken off their clerical rulers). The main difference was that imperial cities retained military and financial obligations to the Reich. Laws in cities were more liberal than in the countryside, which was often under the thumb of oppressive feudal lords. Any peasant who managed to flee to a city and stay there for one year and one day could become a resident. This gave rise to the expression *Stadtluft macht frei* (city air liberates).

The Hanseatic League, whose origins lay in guilds and associations formed by out-of-town merchants, was the most important league. Formed in 1358, it was dominated by Lübeck (see the boxed text League of Gentlemen p716), which controlled a large slice of European shipping trade. At its zenith, the league had over 150 member cities. It earned a say in the choice of Danish kings after the Danes inspired its wrath by sinking a flotilla of the league's ships off Gotland in 1361. The resulting Treaty of Stralsund turned the league into northern Europe's most powerful economic and political entity.

As well as Lübeck, the league included such cities as Riga and Danzig (now Gdansk) on the Baltic Sea, Hamburg and Bremen on the North Sea, and inland cities like Cologne, Dortmund and Hildesheim. By the 15th century, however, competition from Dutch and English shipping companies, internal disputes and a shift in the centre of world trade from the North and Baltic Seas to the Atlantic had caused decline. Hamburg, Bremen, Rostock, Lübeck and Stralsund are still known as Hanse cities.

---

between princes – an admirable move yet one that proved wholly insufficient in the face of religious revolution.

A QUESTION OF FAITH

In the university town of Wittenberg in 1517, German theology professor Martin Luther (1483–1546) launched the Reformation with his 95 theses that questioned the papal practice of selling indulgences to exonerate sins. Church authorities gave Luther a hearing in Augsburg and threatened him with excommunication. But Luther refused to repudiate his theses, broke from the Catholic Church and was banned by the Reich, only to be hidden in Wartburg Castle (Thuringia) where he translated his New Testament from Latin into German. His death mask is in Halle.

It was not until 1555 that the Catholic and Lutheran churches were ranked as equals, thanks to Karl V (r. 1520–58) who signed the Peace of Augsburg (1555), allowing princes to decide the religion of their principality. The more secular northern principalities adopted Lutheran teachings, while the clerical lords in the south, southwest and Austria stuck with Catholicism.

But the religious issue did not die. Rather, it degenerated into the bloody Thirty Years' War, which Sweden and France had joined by 1635. Calm was restored with the Peace of Westphalia (1648) but left the Reich – embracing over 300 states and about 1000 smaller territories – nominal, impotent state. Switzerland and the Netherlands gained independence, France won chunks of Alsace and Lorraine, and Sweden helped itself to the mouths of the Elbe, Oder and Weser Rivers.

DID YOU KNOW?

The first Bible was printed in Latin in 1456 using a revolutionary technique – hand-set type cast in moveable moulds – by the Mainz-born inventor of moveable type, Johannes Gutenberg (1397–1468).

152–89

Aachen becomes Reich capital under Friedrich I Barbarossa

1273

The House of Habsburg takes the Reich reins

ENLIGHTENMENT

Grand palaces were built by the rabble of autocratic princes who control
led the Reich's fortunes in the 17th century. Composers Johann Sebastia
Bach and Georg Friedrich Händel were ushered on stage by the Enlight
enment and a wave of *Hochkultur* (high culture) swept through society'
top sliver. The masses remained illiterate.

Brandenburg-Prussia became an entity to be reckoned with, kick-starte
by the acquisition of former Teutonic Knights' territories and assisted b
Hohenzollern king Friedrich Wilhelm I (the Soldier King) and his son
Friedrich II (r. 1740–86). After the Seven Years' War (1756–63) with Aus
tria, Brandenburg-Prussia annexed Silesia and sliced up Poland.

Between 1801 and 1803 an imperial deputation secularised and recon
stituted German territory, much at the behest of Napoleon Bonaparte. I
1806 the Rhine Confederation eradicated about 100 principalities. Sniffin
the end of the Holy Roman Empire, Kaiser Franz II (r. 1792–1806) packe

JEWS IN GERMANY

The first Jews arrived in present-day Germany with the conquering Romans, settling in important
Roman cities on or near the Rhine, such as Cologne, Trier, Mainz, Speyer and Worms. As non-
Christians, Jews had a separate political status. Highly valued for their trade connections, they
were formally invited to settle in Speyer in 1084, granted trading privileges and the right to build
a wall around their quarter. A charter of rights granted to the Jews of Worms in 1090 by Henry
IV allowed local Jews to be judged according to their own set of laws.

The First Crusade (1095–99) resulted in a wave of pogroms in 1096, usually against the will of
local rulers and townspeople. Many Jews resisted the attacks before committing suicide once their
situation became hopeless. This, the *Kiddush ha-shem* (martyr's death), established a precedent
of martyrdom that became a tenet of European Judaism in the Middle Ages. But the attacks also
set the tone for persecution by mobs during troubled times. Jews fared better in the Second
Crusade (1147–49), taking refuge in castles until the danger had passed.

In the 13th century Jews were declared crown property by Frederick II, an act that afforded
protection but exposed them to royal whim. Rabbi Meir of Rothenburg, whose grave lies in
Europe's oldest Jewish cemetery in Worms (see p498) fell foul of King Rudolph of Habsburg
in 1293 for leading a group of would-be emigrants to Palestine; he died in prison. The Church
also prescribed distinctive clothing for Jews at this time, which later meant that in some towns
Jews had to wear badges.

Things deteriorated with the arrival of the plague in the mid-14th century, when Jews were
accused of having poisoned Christians' drinking wells. Persecution, including trials and burn-
ings, was now sanctioned by the state. Political fragmentation meant Jews were financially
exploited by both the Kaiser and local rulers, and libellous notions circulated throughout the
Christian population. The 'blood libel' accused Jews of using the blood of Christians in rituals.
The even more bizarre 'ost-desecration libel' accused Jews of desecrating or torturing Christ by,
among other dastardly deeds, sticking pins into communion wafers, which then wept tears or
bled.

Money lending was the main source of income for Jews in the 15th century. Expulsions
remained commonplace, with large numbers emigrating to Poland, where Yiddish developed.
The Reformation marked another low point, with Martin Luther calling at various times for the
confiscation of Jewish religious texts, expulsion of Jews, serfdom and the destruction of Jewish
homes. Deeper fragmentation after the Thirty Years' War again exposed Jews to the whims of

1338

Centuries of conflict between popes and kings ends as the Holy
Roman Empire breaks away from the Vatican

1356

Germany's first constitutional document, the Golden Bull, is
adopted

is bags for Austria, renamed himself Franz I of Austria and abdicated in 1806. The same year Brandenburg-Prussia fell to the French, the humilia-tion of defeat prompting reforms that brought it closer to civil statehood: Jews were granted equality and bonded labour was abolished.

In 1813, with French troops driven back by the Russians, Leipzig witnessed one of Napoleon's most significant defeats. At the Congress of Vienna (1815), Germany was reorganised into a confederation of 35 states and an ineffective *Reichstag* was established in Frankfurt, an un-satisfactory solution that only minimally improved on the Holy Roman Empire. The *Reichstag* poorly represented the most populous states, however, and failed to rein in Austro-Prussian rivalry.

> A communist vision of a classless and stateless society is portrayed in *The Communist Manifesto*, written in exile by Trier-born Karl Marx and Friedrich Engels. Capitalism will be toppled by a new working class, the pair warns readers.

THE RISE OF THE PROLETARIAT

Feudal structures decayed and an industrial, urban proletariat emerged in the early 19th century to fuel nationalist calls for a centralised state.

---

competing territorial and central authorities, but by the 17th century they were valued again for their economic contacts.

Napoleon granted Germany's Jews equal rights, but reforms were repealed by the 1815 Congress of Vienna. Anti-Jewish feelings in the early 19th century coincided with German nation-alism and a more vigorous Christianity. Pressure was applied on Jews to assimilate. Famous as-similated Jews, such as the Düsseldorf-born poet Heinrich Heine (1797–1856) – who claimed 'Christ rode on an ass, but now asses ride on Christ' – often exerted a liberal influence on society.

With unification in 1871, Jews enjoyed almost equal status in Germany, but they were still barred from government and could not become army officers. In the late-19th century Germany became a world centre of Jewish cultural and historical studies. There was a shift to large cities such as Leipzig, Cologne, Breslau (now Wroclaw in Poland), Hamburg, Frankfurt-am-Main and to the capital, Berlin, where one-third of German Jews lived.

The Weimar Republic meant emancipation for the 500,000-strong Jewish community. Many assumed a direct political role in democratic and socialist parties (Hugo Preuss drafted Germany's first democratic constitution). But economic disasters in the 1920s soon brought a backlash. Despite over 100,000 Jews serving Germany in the armed forces during WWI, they became scapegoats for Germany's defeat, the humiliating peace and ensuing economic woes.

Many unassimilated Eastern European Jews immigrated to Germany in the 1920s. Meanwhile, German Jews continued to assimilate. Germany also became an important centre for Hebrew literature after Russian writers and academics fled the revolution of 1917.

After Hitler came to power, the fate of German Jewry was sealed by new race laws. Increasing persecution led many to emigrate, and by 1939 less than half the 1933 population figure (530,000) remained in Germany. By 1943 Germany was declared *Judenrein*, or clean of Jews. This ignored the hundreds of thousands of Eastern European Jews incarcerated on 'German' soil. Around six million Jews died in Europe as a direct result of Nazism and its barbarity.

Germany's Jewish community currently numbers around 100,000 and is the third largest in Europe. In 2003 a historic agreement was signed between the Central Council of Jews in Germany and Germany's federal government, granting the Jewish organisation the same legal status in Germany as the Catholic and Lutheran churches. In mid-2003, high-profile member of Germany's Jewish community Michel Friedman resigned from his post as vice president of the Central Council of Jews after admitting to dabbling in cocaine; see p66 for more.

There are particularly informative Jewish museums in Berlin (p111) and Frankfurt (p545).

The Hanseatic League is born

The Great Schism in the Catholic Church is resolved at the Council of Constance in southern Germany

Workers' movements were banned as a result. Dresden and Leipzig in Saxony were linked by railway in 1837 and the Young Germany movement of satirists lampooned the powerful of the day.

Berlin, along with much of the southwest, erupted in riots in 1848 prompting German leaders to call together Germany's first ever parliamentary delegation in Frankfurt's Paulskirche. Austria, meanwhile, broke away from Germany, came up with its own constitution and promptly relapsed into monarchism. As revolution fizzled, Prussian king Friedrich Wilhelm IV drafted his own constitution in 1850, which would remain in force until 1918.

AND THE FALL OF 'HONEST OTTO' BISMARCK

The creation of a unified Germany with Prussia at the helm was the ambition of Otto von Bismarck (1815–98), a former member of the Bundestag and Prussian prime minister. An old-guard militarist, he waged war against Denmark (with Austria his ally) over Schleswig-Holstein in 1864, and in 1866 fought the Seven Weeks' War against Austria to unify northern Germany. In 1870 he isolated France, manoeuvred it into declaring war on Prussia in 1870, then surprised Napoleon III by securing the support of most southern German states. War with France resulted in Bismarck's annexation of Alsace-Lorraine.

Berlin stood as the proud capital of a unified Germany by 1871. Western Europe's largest state, it extended from Memel (Klaipėda in present-day Lithuania) to the present-day Dutch border, including Alsace-Lorraine (southwest) in present-day France and Silesia (southeast) in present-day Poland. The Prussian king was crowned Kaiser of the Reich – a bicameral constitutional monarchy – at Versailles on 18 January 1871 and Bismarck became its 'Iron Chancellor'. Suffrage was limited to men in the new Reich and the national colours were black, white and red.

Bismarck's power was based on the support of merchants and *Junker* a noble class of nonknighted landowners. His achievements were largely based on a dubious 'honest Otto' policy, whereby he acted as a broker between European powers, encouraging colonial vanities to divert attention from his own deeds. He created alliances to cover his back against Russia, Austria-Hungary, France, Italy and Britain. Germany began to catch up with Britain industrially and the number of Germans emigrating tailed off substantially from the peak levels of the 1840s and 1850s. Bismarck belatedly graced the Reich of Kaiser Wilhelm I with a few African jewels after 1880, acquiring colonies in central, southwest and east Africa as well as numerous Pacific paradises, such as Tonga, where a weary Prussian prince might one day lay down his steel helmet and relax in the sun.

But antagonists (such as social democrat August Bebel whose call for universal suffrage and economic equality won him a two-year prison sentence in 1872) were at hand. In 1875 the Socialist Workers' Party formed, changing its name to its current one, the German Social Democratic Party (Sozialdemokratische Partei Deutschlands; SPD) in 1890. When Wilhelm II became Kaiser in 1888, divisions arose between the Kaiser, who wanted to extend the social security system, and Bismarck who enacted his stricter antisocialist laws. Finally, in March 1890, the Kaiser's scalpel excised Bismarck from the political scene.

Bismarck to the Weimar Republic is the focus of Hans-Ulrich Wehler's *The German Empire 1871-1918*, a translation of an authoritative German work. For a revealing study of the Iron Chancellor himself, read *Bismarck, the Man and the Statesman* by Gordon Craig.

'Laws are like sausages. It's better not to see them being made.'
BISMARCK

1517	1555
Martin Luther launches the Reformation with his 95 theses in the east German town of Wittenburg	The Peace of Augsburg allows princes to decide their principality's religion, equalising Catholicism and Protestantism

The legacy of Bismarck's brilliant diplomacy slowly unravelled during the pre-WWI period, which saw a wealthy and unified, industrially advanced Germany paddle towards the new century with incompetent leaders at its helm.

THE GREAT WAR

Technological advances and the toughening of Europe into colonial power blocs made WWI far from 'great'. The conflict began with the assassination of the heir to the Austro-Hungarian throne, Archduke Franz-Ferdinand, in Sarajevo in 1914, for which Serbia was wrongly blamed. Russia prepared to come to Serbia's defence in the ensuing Serbia–Austria-Hungary conflict. Germany, in turn, came to the defence of Austria-Hungary against Russia, while declaring war on France to protect its western borders. Belgium's unfortunate geographic location – bang in Germany's line of attack against France – dragged Britain, Belgium's ally, into the war and within days it had escalated into a European and Middle Eastern affair: Germany, Austria-Hungary and Turkey against Britain, France, Italy and Russia. In 1915 a German submarine attack on a British passenger liner killed 120 US citizens. By 1917 the USA had also entered the war. In Germany, meanwhile, hunger fuelled widespread pessimism.

PEACE

The communist revolution at home forced the Russians to accept peace with Germany through the humiliating Treaty of Brest-Litovsk (1918). Then Germany's military failures on the western front lead to a cease-fire and the acceptance of US president Woodrow Wilson's 14-point peace plan. To facilitate negotiations, Prince Max von Baden, a liberal, took over leadership of the government and the constitution was changed to make the chancellor responsible to parliament – creating Germany's first truly parliamentary party system.

The Treaty of Versailles (1919) made Germany responsible for all losses incurred by its enemies. It also forced Germany to relinquish its colonies, to cede Alsace-Lorraine to France and territory in western Poland, and to pay high reparations.

The peace treaty paved the way for the League of Nations, a commendable attempt to create international order (Germany joined in 1926, the USSR in 1934), although its power was undermined by the USA never joining.

In Kiel in 1919 a mutiny by sailors triggered off a workers' revolt, culminating in revolution in Berlin and the abdication of Kaiser Wilhelm II. This ended monarchical rule in Germany.

THE RISE OF HITLER

The end of the war did not create stability – or peace – in Germany. Socialist and democratic socialist parties fought tooth and nail, while the radical Spartacus League (joined by other groups in 1919 to form the German Communist Party; KPD) sought to create a republic based on Marx' theories of proletarian revolution. Following the bloody quashing of an uprising in Berlin, Spartacus founders 'Red' Rosa Luxemburg (1871–1919) and Leipzig-born Karl Liebknecht (1871–1919) were arrested and murdered en route to prison by *Freikorps* soldiers (war volunteers). Their

WWI: Trenches on the Web provides dozens of hot links to other Great War-related websites www.worldwar1.com.

Marc Ferro's *The Great War 1914-18* is a compelling account of WWI.

The Thirty Years' War sweeps through Bavaria and leaves the Reich a disempowered region of 300-plus states	Brandenburg-Prussia becomes a mighty European power under Frederick the Great

bodies were dumped in Berlin's Landwehr canal, only to be recovered several months later and buried in Berlin.

Meanwhile, in July 1919, in the Thuringian city of Weimar (where the constituent assembly briefly sought refuge during the Berlin chaos the federalist constitution of a new democratic republic was adopted. I granted women suffrage and established basic human rights, but it also gave the president the right to rule by decree – a right that would later prove instrumental in Hitler's rise to power.

This so-called Weimar Republic (1919–33) was governed by a coalition of left and centre parties headed by President Friedrich Ebert of the SPI until 1925 and then by Field Marshal Paul von Hindenburg, a gritty 78-year old monarchist. The republic, however, pleased neither communists no monarchists. In 1920 right-wing militants forcibly occupied the government quarter in Berlin. This 'Kapp Putsch', prompted the government to flee to Dresden. Workers' strikes followed, but the *Putsch* (revolt) failed.

A new currency, the *Rentenmark*, was introduced in 1923 to curb hyperinflation and cure the country's economic ills, but for many it was too late. The same year Adolf Hitler (1889–1945), an Austrian-born volunteer in the German army during WWI, launched the Munich Putsch in another bid to topple the republic. Hitler and other members of his National Socialist German Workers' Party (NSDAP) marched through Munich, were arrested and their party banned. Hitler wound up in jail for two years, writing *Mein Kampf* – a nationalist, anti-Semitic work – while inside. Once out, he set about rebuilding the party.

Hitler's NSDAP gained 18% of the vote in the 1930 elections, prompting Hitler to run against Hindenburg for the presidency in 1932, when he won 37% of a second-round vote. A year later, faced with failed economic reforms and persuasive right-wing advisors, Hindenburg appointed Hitler chancellor, with a coalition cabinet of Nationalists (conservatives, old aristocrats and powerful industrialists) and National Socialists (Nazis). Hitler consolidated his power by appointing his supporters to newly created ministries. When the *Reichstag* mysteriously burnt down in Berlin in March 1933, Hitler had the excuse he needed to request emergency powers to arrest all communist and liberal opponents.

Parliament met a week later in Berlin's Kroll Opera House to vote on Hitler's proposed Enabling Law, and intimidating Nazi state police officers – the *Sturmabteilung* (SA; see the boxed text The Night of the Long Knives opposite) – only allowed Nationalist and Nazi politicians to enter. Hitler thus secured the power to decree laws and change the constitution without consulting parliament. The Nazi dictatorship had begun. When Hindenburg died a year later, Hitler fused the offices of president and chancellor to become Führer and chancellor of the Third Reich.

NAZIS IN POWER

Local governments were taken over by Nazi officials, trade unions were outlawed, all competing political parties banned and the SA stepped up its terror campaign. Intellectual and artistic activity was suppressed, sparking the burning of 'un-German' books on 10 May 1933 by students in Berlin and university towns across the country. Membership of the Hitlerjugend (Hitler Youth) was obligatory for anyone aged between 10

DID YOU KNOW?

In 1923 a postage stamp cost 50 billion marks, a loaf of bread cost 140 billion marks and US$1 was worth 4.2 trillion marks. In November, the new *Rentenmark* was traded in for one trillion old marks.

DID YOU KNOW?

Adolf Hitler's *Mein Kampf* (My Struggle) sold over nine million copies in 1925 when it was first published and has been translated into numerous languages.

William Shirer's definitive 100-page plus *The Rise & Fall of the Third Reich* remains a powerful reportage. His Berlin of those times is the literary equivalent of the brutal north face of the Eiger.

Brandenburg-Prussia falls to the French and the Holy Roman Empire collapses

The Congress of Vienna redraws the map of Europe and divides Germany into 35 states

THE NIGHT OF THE LONG KNIVES

Conceived to police public meetings and enforce law, the brown-shirted Nazi state police – the *Sturmabteilung* (SA) – had become a troublesome bunch by 1934 – for Germans and their dictator alike. So much so, that on the night of 30 June 1934, Hitler ordered SS troops to round up and kill high-ranking SA officers. Their leader, Ernst Röhm, was shot and 76 others were knifed to death.

Hitler hushed up the gruesome night (dubbed 'The Night of the Long Knives') until 13 July when he announced to the *Reichstag* that, henceforth, the SA (which numbered two million, easily outnumbering the army) would serve under the command of the army, which, in turn, would swear an oath of allegiance to Hitler. Justice would be executed by himself and the black-shirted *Schutzstaffel* (SS) under the leadership of former chicken-farmer Heinrich Himmler, effectively giving the SS unchallenged power and making its Nazi Germany's most powerful – and feared – force.

and 18, and other youth organisations were disbanded except those of the Catholic Church.

In April 1933 Joseph Goebbels, head of the well-oiled Ministry of Propaganda, announced a boycott of Jewish businesses. Soon after, Jews were expelled from public service and non-Aryans (incorrectly defined by Hitler as Roma or Sinti – gypsies, nonwhites and Jews) were banned from many professions, trades and industries. The Nuremberg Laws (1935) deprived non-Aryans of German citizenship and forbade them to marry or have sexual relations with Aryans – anyone who broke these race laws faced the death penalty (and had to pay their own trial and execution costs to boot).

Hitler's successful economic policy won him phenomenal support among the middle and lower-middle classes. He had achieved this success by pumping large sums of money into employment programmes, and encouraging employers to adopt military principles. At the same time conscription was introduced to build up Germany's air force. In 1936 he started rearming Germany and developing heavy industry. Industries established by the SS relied on a compulsory 'volunteer workforce' of all women and men aged 18 to 25. In Wolfsburg, Lower Saxony, economical cars for the people started rolling out of Germany's first Volkswagen factory, founded in 1938.

The same year Hitler's troops were welcomed into Austria. Foreign powers, in an attempt to avoid another bloody war, accepted the Anschluss (annexation) of Austria. Then, following this same policy of appeasement, the Munich Agreement was signed in September 1938 by Hitler, Mussolini, Britain's Neville Chamberlain and France's Eduardo Daladier. In it, the largely ethnic-German Sudetenland of Czechoslovakia was relinquished to Hitler. By March 1939, he also had annexed Moravia and Bohemia.

WWII
Early Victories

A nonaggression pact was signed between Hitler and Stalin's USSR in August 1939, whereby the Tokyo–Berlin–Rome axis (Hitler had already signed agreements with Italy and Japan) was expanded to include Moscow.

For an insightful look at Hitler's speeches, public addresses and letters, look no further than www.hitler.org.

A detailed history of WWII with Nazi leader biographies, a Holocaust timeline with over 150 images, and a special focus on the pre-WWII years in Nazi Germany make this website stand out – www.historyplace.com.

1848	1864–71
The first parliamentary delegation *(Nationalversammlung)* meets in Frankfurt	Prussian chancellor Bismarck's brilliant diplomacy creates a unified Germany with Prussia at its helm and Berlin as its capital

THE NIGHT OF BROKEN GLASS

Nazi horror escalated on 9 November 1938 with the Reichspogromnacht (often called *Kristallnacht* or the 'Night of Broken Glass'). In retaliation for the assassination of a German consular official by a Polish Jew in Paris, synagogues and Jewish cemeteries, property and businesses across Germany were desecrated, burnt or demolished. About 90 Jews died that night. The next day another 30,000 were incarcerated, and Jewish businesses were transferred to non-Jews through forced sale at below-market prices.

Listen to news reports of the 1936 BBC Olympics, Hitler announcing Germany's WWII attack on Poland or the fall of the Wall on the BBC News website (follow the Europe/Country Profile links) at http://news.bbc.co.uk.

Chester Wilmot presents an interesting account of WWII in his *The Struggle for Europe*, told from the perspective of an Australian journalist slap-bang in the thick of things.

One of a clutch of fabulous films by Germany's best-known female director, Margarethe von Trotta, *Rosenstrasse* (2003) is a portrayal of a 1943 protest against the deportation of their Jewish husbands by a group of non-Jewish women.

Soviet neutrality was assured by a secret Soviet–German protocol that divided up Eastern Europe into spheres of interest.

In late August an SS-staged attack on a German radio station in Gleiwitz (Gliwice), Poland, gave Hitler the excuse to march into Poland. This proved the catalyst for WWII; three days later, on 3 September 1939 France and Britain declared war on Germany.

Poland was no match for Hitler's army. Jews were driven into ghettos and forced to wear the yellow Star of David, and ethnic Germans were resettled (about 900,000 up to 1944) in west Poland from areas occupied by the USSR under the terms of the secret protocol. The SS, under the leadership of Heinrich Himmler (1900–45), provided the war machine with elite troops, ran concentration camps and organised the Gestapo (secret police). At home, war meant food shortages and increased political oppression.

Belgium, the Netherlands and France quickly fell to Germany. In June 1941 Germany broke its nonaggression pact with Stalin by attacking the USSR. Though successful at first, Operation Barbarossa soon ran into problems and Hitler's troops retreated. With the defeat of the German 6th army at Stalingrad (today Volgograd) the following winter, morale flagged at home and on the fronts.

The Final Solution

At Hitler's request, a conference in January 1942 on Berlin's Wannsee came up with a protocol clothed in bureaucratic jargon that laid the basis for the murder of millions of Jews. The Holocaust was a systematic, bureaucratic and meticulously documented genocidal act carried out by about 100,000 Germans, but with the tacit agreement of a far greater number.

Jewish populations in occupied areas were systematically terrorised and executed by SS troops. Having abandoned vague plans to resettle European Jewry on the African island of Madagascar, Hitler deported Jews to concentration camps in east Germany (those in Sachsenhausen Buchenwald and Mittelbau Dora), and Eastern Europe. Roma, political opponents, priests, homosexuals, resistance fighters and habitual criminals were also incarcerated in a network of 22 camps, mostly in Eastern Europe. Another 165 work camps (such as Auschwitz-Birkenau in Poland) provided labour for big industry, including IG Farbenindustrie AG, producer of the cyanide gas Zyklon B that was used in gas chambers to murder over three million Jews. Of the estimated seven million people sent to camps, 500,000 survived.

The mass extermination of Jews and other Nazi atrocities were outlined in the anti-Nazi leaflets distributed in Munich and other cities by

1914–18	1919
WWI: Germany, Austria-Hungary and Turkey go to war against Britain, France, Italy and Russia; Germany is defeated	Monarchical rule ends; under the Weimar Republic, women are granted suffrage and basic human rights are embedded in law

The White Rose, a group of Munich university students whose resistance attempts cost most of them their lives (see the boxed text The White Rose p332). Resistance to Hitler was rare indeed, especially after the failed attempt by Claus Graf Schenk von Stauffenberg and other high-ranking army officers to assassinate Hitler on 20 July 1944, which subsequently saw the SS arrest more than 7000 people and execute most of them.

The Tables Turn

Systematic air raids on German cities followed the invasion of Normandy in France in June 1944, and the return of the Allies to the European mainland. The brunt of the bombings was suffered by the civilian population; Dresden's Frauenkirche, Germany's greatest Protestant church, was destroyed during a British raid in February 1945 that killed 35,000 people, many of them refugees. (Today it is being painstakingly reconstructed to be completed for Dresden's 800th anniversary.) From the east the Russians advanced.

A defeated and paranoid Führer and his new bride Eva Braun committed suicide on 30 April 1945 in a Berlin bunker (which was unearthed during construction work in 1999, but not preserved for fear of turning the Hitler hideaway into a neo-Nazi shrine). Two days later Berlin fell to the Soviets. Red Army soldiers stormed and set alight the *Reichstag*, showering it with bullet holes and scrawling its walls with triumphant anti-Nazi graffiti – both preserved during the reconstruction of the 19th-century parliament building in the late 1990s. On 7 May 1945, Germany capitulated and peace was signed at the US headquarters in Rheims and again in Berlin in what is now the Museum Berlin-Karlshorst (a German–Soviet history museum).

OCCUPATION

In Schloss Cecilienhof in Potsdam (Brandenburg), the Potsdam Conference (1945) carved up a ruined Germany into four occupation zones, with regions east of the Oder and Neisse Rivers going to Poland as compensation for earlier territorial losses to the USSR. Agreements reached at Potsdam and the earlier Yalta Conference (1944) split Berlin into 12 administrative areas under British, French, US control and Soviet control; the Soviets controlled eight of the 12.

Reviving Germany's devastated economy was the Allies' immediate concern. Their economic aid package, the Marshall Plan (1948), provided the basis for West Germany's *Wirtschaftswunder* (economic miracle). It rebuilt cities such as Cologne, Hamburg, Dortmund and Kiel where 50% to 70% of homes had been bombed; removed Hitler's ban on political parties; and set up regional and state administrative bodies. In 1946–47, Allied-zone populations voted in Germany's first free elections since 1933, resulting in elected state parliaments.

These advances only widened the rift between Allied and Soviet zones (where inflation still strained local economies, food shortages affected the population, and the Communist and Social Democrat parties were made to unite as the Socialist Unity Party; Sozialistische Einheitspartei Deutschlands; SED).

The showdown came in June 1948 when the Allies introduced the Deutschmark (DM) in their zones. Furious at the lack of consultation,

The Colditz Story (1954), directed by Guy Hamilton, is a gripping if sobering watch. Based on the book *The Colditz Story* (1957) by prison escapee Pat Reid, it portrays the escapes of Allied POWs during WWII from the Nazi's legendary high-security prison in Western Saxony.

Of the dozens of books covering Nazi concentration camps, *I Never Saw Another Butterfly: Children's Drawings and Poems from Terezin Concentration Camp 1942-1944* by Yana Volakova (ed) says it all. *This Way for the Gas, Ladies and Gentlemen* by Tadeusz Borowski is equally chilling.

For an uncomfortable reminder that the Allies were far-from-innocent occupiers, read *Crimes & Mercies: The Allies' Policy of Occupation in Germany after 1945* by James Bacque. Squirm, you will.

Adolf Hitler winds up in jail and writes *Mein Kampf* after leading an abortive coup in Munich

Hitler becomes chancellor of Germany and creates a dictatorship

GERMANY'S CHANGING BORDERS

HOLY ROMAN EMPIRE AT THE END OF THE THIRTY YEARS' WAR (PEACE OF WESTPHALIA, 1648)

GERMAN EMPIRE 1871-1918

GERMANY AFTER THE TREATY OF VERSAILLES (1919-38)

GERMANY 1945-89

the USSR issued its own currency and promptly announced a full-scale economic blockade of West Berlin. During the remarkable Berlin Blockade that ensued for almost a year, some 300,000 flights supplied the west of the city to compensate for blocked supplies from the east. At the height of the airlift, American, Canadian, British and several Australian air crews flew in the equivalent of 22 freight trains of 50 carriages daily, at intervals of 90 seconds. These flights earned the name *Rosinenbomber* (raisin bombers) because they carried so much dried fruit.

A NEW EAST & WEST GERMANY

In this frosty East–West climate, the Rhineland town of Bonn hosted West German state representatives in September 1948 who met to ham-

---

1939–45

WWII: Hitler invades Poland, France and Britain to declare war on Germany; Jews are exterminated en masse during the Holocaust

1945

Hitler kills himself in a Berlin bunker while a defeated Germany surrenders; Germany is split into occupied Allied zones

ner out a draft constitution for a new Federal Republic of Germany (FRG, or BRD by its German initials). A year later, 73-year-old Konrad Adenauer, a Cologne mayor during the Weimar years, was elected West Germany's first chancellor. Bonn – Adenauer's hometown – was the natural candidate for the FRG's provisional capital.

East Germany reciprocated by adopting its own constitution for the German Democratic Republic (GDR; DDR by its German initials). On paper, it guaranteed press and religious freedoms and the right to strike. In reality, such freedoms were limited and no-one dared strike. In its chosen capital of Berlin, a bicameral system was set up (one chamber was later abolished) and Wilhelm Pieck became the country's first president. From the candidate, however, the Socialist Unity Party led by party boss Walter Ulbricht dominated economic, judicial and security policy.

In keeping with centralist policies, the East German states of Saxony, Mecklenburg-Western Pomerania, Saxony-Anhalt and Thuringia were divided into 14 regional administrations and the notorious Ministry for State Security (Ministerium für Staatssicherheit) was created in 1950 to ensure SED loyalty (see the boxed text Stasi Secrets, p38). Workers became economically dependent on the state through the collectivisation of farms and the implementation (in 1948 and 1950 respectively) of two- and five-year plans, aimed at creating a broad production base in industrial sectors. GDR companies such as the car factory in Zwickau near Leipzig (which produced Trabants as the GDR answer to the West Germany's Volkswagen) were nationalised.

In Soviet zones the task of weeding out Nazis tended to be swift and harsh. In the west the Allies held war-crimes trials in courtroom 600 of Nuremberg's Court House (open to visitors today). The Nuremberg trials set a precedent in international justice, although Cold War politics and adverse public reaction led to their abandonment in 1948. The Nuremberg sentences were never recognised by the West German government.

THE 1950S

The economic vision of Bavarian-born, cigar-puffing Ludwig Erhard unleashed West Germany's *Wirtschaftswunder*. Between 1951 and 1961 the economy averaged a yet-to-be-repeated annual growth rate of 8%.

Erhard was economic minister and later vice-chancellor in Konrad Adenauer's government. His policies encouraged investment, sparked off economic activity to promote welfare-state capitalism and beckoned guest workers from southern Europe (mainly Turkey, Yugoslavia and Italy) to resolve the labour shortage in the FRG. He created the European Coal and Steel Community to regulate coal and steel production with France, Italy, West Germany and the Benelux countries, and in 1958 West Germany joined the European Economic Community (the EU today). Adenauer's deep-rooted fear of the USSR saw him pursue a ruthless policy of integration with the West. In 1952 he flatly rejected a proposal by Stalin to establish a joint council to pave the way for a unified, neutral Germany with its own defence policy.

In East Germany, Stalin's death in 1953 raised hopes of reform – but brought nothing. Extreme poverty and economic tensions merely

German Boy: A Child In War by Wolfgang Samuel is the true tale of a German family, told through the eyes of the young Wolfgang, who fled Berlin as the Red Army approached.

Interviews with former Stasi men in the mid-1990s forms the basis of Australian journalist Anna Funder's *Stasiland* – crammed with fresh and alternative insights into what the men of the Stasi are doing now.

A Train of Powder by Rebecca West ranks as one of the most informative books on the Nuremberg trials.

1948	1950s
British-, French- and US-occupied West Germany becomes the FRG; Soviet-occupied East Germany becomes the GDR	West Germany witnesses an 'economic miracle' and becomes an EEC and NATO member; East Germany joins the Warsaw Pact

persuaded the government to set production goals higher. Smouldering discontent erupted in violence on 17 June 1953 when 10% of GDR workers took to the streets. Soviet troops quashed the uprising, with scores of deaths and the arrest of about 1200 people.

Meanwhile, the FRG thrived. It achieved military integration into the West in May 1955 by joining NATO, changed its constitution to allow German-based armed forces and introduced conscription. East Germany's response was to join the Warsaw Pact defence alliance and the Eastern bloc trade organisation Comecon.

The first call for West Germany to arm with nuclear weapons - opposed by the man on the street but supported by several leading West German political figures, as well as the USA – reared its fearful head in 1957. The same year, a proposal was put forward by Poland to ban all nuclear weapons on German, Polish and Czechoslovakian soil and   failed – for no other reason than Warsaw Pact troops easily outnumbered NATO's.

STASI SECRETS

The Ministry of State Security, commonly called the Stasi, was based on the Soviet KGB and served as the 'shield and sword' of the SED. Almost a state within the state, it boasted an astonishing spy network of about 90,000 full-time employees and 180,000 inoffizielle Mitarbeiter (unofficial co-workers) by 1989. Since 1990, only 250 Stasi agents have been prosecuted and since the 10-year limit ended in 2000, future trials are unlikely.

When it came to tracking down dissidents, there were no limits. One unusual collection of files found in its Berlin archive kept a record of dissidents' body odour. Some dissidents who had been hauled in for interrogation were made to deliver an odour sample, usually taken with a cotton wool pad from the unfortunate victim's crotch. The sample was then stored in an hermetic glass jar for later use if a dissident suddenly disappeared. To track down a missing dissident by odour, Stasi sniffer dogs were employed. These specially trained groin-sniffing curs were euphemistically known as 'smell differentiation dogs'.

What happened to the dogs after the Stasi was disbanded is unclear. What happened to the six million files the Stasi accumulated in its lifetime is a greater cause for concern. In January 1990, protestors stormed the Stasi headquarters in Berlin (today a museum, memorial and research centre – see p116 for details), demanding to see the files. Since then, the controversial records have been assessed and safeguarded by the Gauck Commission (Gauck Behörde), a Berlin-based public body. In mid-2000, 1000-odd information-packed CDs, removed by the CIA's Operation Rosewood immediately after the fall of the wall in 1989, were returned to Germany. A second batch of CIA files (apparently acquired by the CIA from a Russian KGB officer in 1992) were handed over in July 2003. The files, for the first time, matched code names with real names – making many people very nervous.

The Stasi spied on some 2.4 million people, amassing thousands of pages of information on public figures such as Helmut Kohl (who went to court in 2001 to prevent the public release of his records, only for a new law to be passed in September 2003 allowing files on public figures to be opened).

Since 2002, Stasi files on an ordinary person can only be opened with the consent of that person. Information on public figures obtained through eavesdropping, phone tapping etc and other means that violate basic human rights cannot be released. In 2002 alone, 94,000 applied to see their files.

1961	1969
The GDR government builds the Berlin Wall between East and West Germany and turns East Germany into an industrial power	In West Germany, an East-friendly Ostpolitik policy is adopted by new Social Democrat chancellor Willy Brandt

THE WALL

The exodus of young, well-educated and employed East German refugees seeking a better fortune in West Germany strained the troubled GDR economy to such a degree that the GDR government – with Soviet consent – built a wall to keep them in. The Berlin Wall, the Cold War's most potent symbol, went up between East and West Berlin on the night of 12 August 1961. The inner-German border was fenced off and mined.

Having walled in what was left of the miserable population (330,000 East Germans fled to the west in 1953 alone), the East German government launched a new economic policy in a bid to make life better. And it did. The standard of living rose to the highest in the Eastern bloc and East Germany became its second-largest industrial power (behind the USSR). Unemployment was unheard of.

The appointment of Erich Honecker (1912–94) in 1971 opened the way for *rapprochement* with the West and enhanced international acceptance of the GDR. Although Honecker fell in line with Soviet policies (replacing reunification clauses in the East German constitution with a declaration of irrevocable alliance to the USSR in 1974), he rode out world recession and an oil crisis in the early 1970s, and oversaw a period of housing construction, pension rises and help for working mothers. Economic stagnation nonetheless took root by the late 1980s.

ON THE WESTERN SIDE

In the 1950s the foundation of contemporary Germany's multicultural society was laid when West Germany signed treaties with several countries to import foreign workers. The first was signed with Italy in 1955, followed by others with Greece, former Yugoslavia, Portugal, Spain, Morocco, Tunisia and Turkey. By the 1960s, some 1.6 million *Gastarbeiter* (guest workers) were living and working in Germany (peaking at 2.3 million in 1973, when the oil crisis and economic recession cut the programme short).

By the end of 1956, the USSR had released the last German internee and the West German government had banned the German Communist Party. 'Love your friends, don't recognise your enemies' was the policy of Adenauer who signed a friendship treaty with France (1963) and refused to recognise East Germany. The same year he was ousted by his vice-chancellor, Ludwig Erhard, who did little to address the troubled economy of 1960s West Germany.

The absence of parliamentary opposition fuelled radical demands by the student movement to reform West Germany's antiquated university system (many textbooks either ignored Nazism or took a soft line), encourage open discussion of the Hitler years, and adopt a more flexible policy towards the Eastern bloc. Emergency acts passed to protect the current political system evoked public outrage.

The turning point came in 1969 when the SPD formed a new government with the FDP under Willy Brandt (1913–92). The Lübeck-born, 1971 Nobel Peace Prize winner spent the Hitler years working in exile as a journalist in Scandinavia, where he was stripped of German citizenship for anti-Nazi writings. Normalising relations with East Germany (his East-friendly policy was known as *Ostpolitik*) was his priority and in December 1972 the two Germanys signed the Basic Treaty, paving the

Berlin and the Wall by Ann Tusa is a saga about the events, trials and triumphs of the Cold War, the building of the wall and its effects on the people and the city of Berlin.

A Concrete Curtain: The Life & Death of the Berlin Wall is a stunning and informative online presentation of the wall by the Deutsches Historisches Museum (German History Museum) in Berlin. See www.wall-berlin.org.

1972	1974
The two Germanys sign the Basic Treaty, paving the way for both countries to join the United Nations	Brandt is replaced as West German chancellor by Helmut Schmidt, who continues *Ostpolitk*

way for both to join the United Nations in 1973. The treaty guaranteed sovereignty in international and domestic affairs (but fudged formal recognition since it was precluded by the West German constitution).

A legend in his own time, Brandt was replaced by Helmut Schmidt (b. 1918) in 1974 after a scandal (one of Brandt's close advisers turned out to be a Stasi spy). The 1970s saw antinuclear and green issues move onto the agenda, opposed by Schmidt and ultimately leading to the election of Greens party representatives to the Bonn parliament in 1979. In 1974 West Germany joined the G8 group of industrial nations.

Terrorism increased during the '70s and several prominent business and political figures were assassinated by the anti-capitalist Red Army Faction: a group that disbanded after the suicide of two of their leaders in prison.

Brandt's vision of East–West cordiality was borne out by Chancellor Helmut Kohl (b. 1930) who, with his conservative coalition government from 1982, groomed relations between East and West while dismantling parts of the welfare state at home. In the West German capital in 1987, Kohl received East German counterpart Erich Honecker with full state honours.

REUNIFICATION

German reunification surprised the world.

View B&W photographs – including one of Walter Ulbricht announcing there 'would be no wall' and the subsequent graffiti-clad Wall – and map out your own Wall tour at www.the-berlin-wall.de.

The so-called *Die Wende* (turning point) came in September 1989 when East Germans started flocking to the West after Hungary opened its border with Austria. Despite the East German government tightening travel restrictions, nothing could stop the flow of people flocking to seek refuge in West German consulates and embassies in East Berlin, Warsaw Prague and Budapest. In the East German town of Leipzig, demonstrators attending traditional Monday church services swelled throughout October to more than 250,000, safe in the knowledge that the church supported their calls for improved human rights and an end to SED political monopoly. By November, East Germany was losing its citizens at a rate of about 10,000 per day.

The replacement of Honecker by Egon Krenz (b.1937) did not stave off the day of reckoning. On 9 November 1989, in a televised press conference by SED boss Günter Schabowsky, GDR citizens were told they could travel to the West. When asked when exactly this move would take effect, Schabowsky mistakenly said 'right away'. Tens of thousands rushed through border points in Berlin, watched by perplexed guards, who knew nothing about this new regulation but did not intervene. Wild partying accompanied the fall of the Wall.

After the Wall by Marc Fisher is an account of German society, with emphasis on life after the *Wende* (fall of communism). Fisher was bureau chief for the Washington Post in Bonn and presents some perceptive social insights.

Round-table talks were held to hammer out a course. In March 1990 free elections in the GDR saw an alliance headed by Lothar de Maizière of the CDU assume power. The old SED administrative regions were abolished and the original (pre-1952) states (Brandenburg, Mecklenburg-Western Pomerania, Saxony, Saxony-Anhalt and Thuringia) revived. The new united Berlin became a separate city-state. Economic union took force in mid-1990, and in August 1990 the Unification Treaty was signed. Postwar occupation zones were abolished by the Two-Plus-Four Treaty and on 2 December 1990, Germany's first unified post-WWII elections were held, marking the end of 45 years of occupation by the USSR and the Allies in a divided Germany.

1982	1989
A conservative coalition government is formed in West Germany under Christian Democrat Helmut Kohl	Hungary opens its border with Austria and East Germans are allowed to travel to the West – prompting the fall of the Berlin Wall

On 21 July 1990 – in one of those incredible moments in music history – Pink Floyd performed their original 1980s *The Wall* tour to a crowd of 200,000 (and TV audience of millions worldwide) on Berlin's Potsdamer Platz. The Eighties icons Bryan Adams and Van Morrison, the Marching Band of the Combined Soviet Forces and the East German symphony orchestra were in Roger Walters' star-studded cast. One year previously, just four months before the Wall fell, West Berlin DJ Dr Mottte had spawned Berlin's famous Love Parade with his Friede, Freude, Eierkucken (Peace, Happiness, Pancakes) rally of some 150 fellow music heads.

TOWARDS A NEW MILLENNIUM

The enormous task of truly uniting the two Germanys formed the bulk of an era dominated by one figure, Chancellor Helmut Kohl – often dubbed the 'Unification Chancellor'. Under Kohl Germany became the world's third largest economic power (after the USA and Japan).

Economic integration topped Kohl's list of things to do. By privatising East German assets through the Treuhandanstalt (Trust Agency), he tackled the rampant problems inherent in the GDR's overstaffed and over-subsidised state industries, in which 80% of the East German workforce was engaged in 1989. Initial efforts in modernising eastern Germany's infrastructure produced a boom, but the pace of growth slackened as West German companies proved reluctant to invest in industries where productivity was less than 70% of West German levels.

Kohl brought former East German functionaries to justice, notably Erich Honecker who died in Chile in 1994 after spells in the USSR, in the Chilean embassy in Moscow, and in Germany itself where his court case was abandoned due to his ill health. In foreign policy, Kohl soothed neighbours where German unification hurt, made friends with Yeltsin, and advocated an expanded EU as vital for eastern Germany's integration. Kohl was also a driving force behind the decision to move the seat of parliament in 1999 from Bonn back to Berlin. The same year, Germany's current president, former SPD chairman Johannes Rau (b. 1931), took up his largely ceremonial office in a spanking new building, steps away from his official residence in Prince Ferdinand's Schloss Bellevue (1785).

Germany's longest-serving chancellor (16 years) was voted out of office in 1998, when his coalition of Christian Democrat and Liberals (CDU/CSU and FDP) was replaced by a coalition of the SPD and Bündnis 90/Die Grünen (Alliance 90/Green parties), headed by Chancellor Gerhard Schröder (b. 1944). A year on, Kohl's golden reputation lay in ruins after revelations that the CDU had maintained slush funds over several decades, flaunting the German constitution. Allegations of party kickbacks during the privatisation of the East German Leuna company also surfaced. Kohl was stripped of his lifelong position as CDU honorary chairman and fined around €150,000.

For Germany's Greens, the 1998 election victory was historic. It was not only the first time that the Bündis 90/Die Grünen party had co-governed federally, it also marked the first time anywhere in the world that a 'green' party had formed part of a national government.

Countrywide millennium celebrations marking 10 years of unification were a sober and reflective occasion, heavily underscored by the disturbing

Behind-the-scene footage, interviews, an account of the Wall's fall and shots of the 2500-brick wall rebuilt during the show is included on *The Wall: Live in Berlin*, the much-awaited 2003-released DVD of Pink Floyd's electrifying concert in Berlin in 1990.

DID YOU KNOW?

Germany is a constitutional democracy with a president and bicameral system based on the *Bundestag* (popularly elected lower house of 598 members) and the *Bundesrat* (upper house of delegates nominated by 16 states).

The Unification Treaty is signed, postwar occupation zones are abolished and Germany's first unified post-WWII elections are held

Berlin becomes capital of the new Germany; Kohl's government charts a rigorous course towards east–west economic integration

rise that year of violent neo-Nazi racist attacks on foreigners. Natural disaster struck in August 2002 when the worst floods of the century wreaked havoc across central Europe, claiming 21 lives and causing €15 billion of damage in southern and eastern Germany as the Elbe River burst its banks. Dresden was particularly badly hit.

... AND A NEW EUROPE

Keep abreast with current affairs at www.dw-world.de.

While Germany is accused by some of trying to dominate an expanded European Union, its enormous contribution to the continent-wide debate on the future of a new Europe is unquestionable. This is thanks to German chancellor Gerhard Schröder who, having secured a second term in office with his SPD-Greens coalition in late 2002, has very much led the (at-times heated) debate on Europe. For Germany, restored to its position at the heart of Europe, its future is strongly bound within an eastward-looking EU.

Keep on top of German politics with www.germany-info.org.

As Europe lapsed into recession in 2001, so Germany's giant-sized economy received a sharp slap in the moneybelt. Economic ills were further exacerbated by the steady fall in value of the euro – in circulation in Germany to replace the Deutschmark from January 2002 – and the US-led 2003 war with Iraq, which saw a German chancellor publicly oppose the US for the first time in 50 years.

By 2003 unemployment in Germany ranked the highest in Europe (11.3% nationally), while annual GDP growth and inflation hovered at a shameful 0.1% and 0.8% respectively. The government's 2002 budget deficit exceeded the 3% of GDP ceiling set by the European Union's Maastricht Treaty, putting it under enormous pressure from the EU to buck up. Eastern Germany remains particularly burdensome on government resources; since 1989 the government has poured more than €600 billion into eastern Germany and will have to continue injecting grants of several billion euros into the region over the next few years if it wants to avoid a social revolution.

Discover stat after stat on the Germany of a new Europe on the website of the Federal Statistical Office (Statistisches Bundesamt Deutschland) – www.destatis.de.

For Schröder reform is the only way out – and up – for the stagnant German economy. In March 2003, both the coalition parties and the opposition Christian Social Union (CSU) and Christian Democratic Union (CDU) backed Agenda 2010, a reform initiative aimed at shaking up an old and inflexible social welfare system that does not square up to the country's new needs in a changing Europe. Personal health service contributions will increase; income tax will be cut; the social security will be reorganised; and a more flexible, partly private pension scheme will be implemented to meet the needs of an ageing population. In eastern Germany, hundreds of thousands of publicly subsidised jobs will be created to alleviate extreme unemployment, which hovers at a miserable 18% (up to 26% in cities like Neu-Brandenburg). Unemployment did not exist in the GDR.

Strikes by East German engineering union workers calling for a 35-hour (rather than 38) working week in line with their west German counterparts in mid-2003 temporarily paralysed Germany's car industry. (Interestingly, the strikes failed, throwing the unions in disarray.) Automobile production by big names such as Volkswagen, Audi, BMW and DaimlerChrysler has steadily fallen in the past four years and accounts for 10% of total industrial output. Manufacturing, the traditional mainstay

THINK GREEN

Germans either love or hate the Greens.

A peace movement that grew out of the 1979 NATO decision to station Pershing II and Cruise missiles in Western Europe, the Greens (die Grünen; www.gruene.de) has been a real political party since 1980. In the heady days of reunification it gained its current double-banger name – Bündnis 90/Die Grünen – after teaming up with Alliance 90 (Bündnis 90), a former GDR civil-rights group. Fame came in 1998 when the Greens won 47 seats in the *Bundestag* and joined forces with the Schröder-driven SPD to form a coalition government. While Schröder is said to have ridden on the back of a 'No to war with Iraq' stance to get re-elected in 2002, the Greens were credited with a down-to-earth and coherent, policy-driven campaign. The party went on to gain 9% of the national vote. 'The red–green coalition got back in...not despite the Greens, but despite the SPD and because of the Greens' is how one newspaper summed up the victory that saw 12% of all first-time voters back the Greens.

Active and moderately successful on economic and environment issues, the Greens have clinched a deal with the powerful energy industry to wean Germany off nuclear power by around 2030; championed Germany's same-sex marriage law (2001); fought tooth and nail for a change in agricultural policy; secured compensation for victims of forced or slave labour during the Nazi era; and revamped Germany's archaic citizenship laws, which dated from 1913 and decided nationality by blood rather than birthplace or residency. During the Kosovo war, however, the party threw pacifism out the window through its support for German forces to fight in the conflict.

As interesting and contentious as the party itself are the political figures that define it. Maverick Green leader Joschka Fischer (b. 1948), a former taxi driver and son of a Hungarian butcher, has been minister of foreign affairs and vice-chancellor since 1998. He is no means a saint (or pacifist); Fischer's days looked numbered in 2001 when snaps of him beating up a policeman as a bearded left-wing militant member of a *Putzgruppe* (clean-up mob) in 1970s Frankfurt-am-Main made headline news. But the country's most popular politician, stayed the course – and went on to woo voters with his wit and charismatic demeanour. Stars in his party include Environment Minister Jürgen Trittin who first turned heads in the mid-1980s as press speaker for the Green Party representatives; Minister for Consumer Protection Renate Künast who admirably grabbed the bull by the horns in 2001 as Germany lapsed into hysteria about mad cow disease; and 19-year-old Anna Lührmann – the world's youngest MP who is one of 55 Greens sitting in Germany's *Bundestag*.

of German economy, employs about 33% of the workforce, while export industries employ another 20% – Germany is the world's second largest exporter, trading primarily with other EU countries and the Asia-Pacific region. On the cutting edge, albeit it a green one, is the country's environmental technology industry, which corners 18% of the world market.

Racial violence remains a grave problem. Attempts by the government to ban the neo-Nazi National Democratic Party (NPD) failed in March 2003 when the constitutional court refused to support the ban. The NPD – along with the German People's Party (DVU) and Republikaner – was one of three far-right political parties that failed to gain the obligatory 5% of the national vote required to be represented in the *Bundestag*.

In January 2004, Germany enthusiastically embraced the inclusion of 10 new Eastern and Central European countries into the (traditionally western European) EU – a move that shifted the centre of Europe eastwards and a step closer to Berlin.

2002	2003
The German mark is replaced by the euro; floods devastate cities in eastern and southern Germany	Unemployment reaches an all-time high; Schröder introduces the Agenda 2010 reform initiative to revive the stagnant economy

The Culture

THE NATIONAL PSYCHE

Germans have an image problem – a brutal fact spelt out in the European Parliament in July 2003 when Italian prime minister Silvio Berlusconi likened a German politician to a Nazi concentration-camp guard.

But Germans are tired of being stereotyped; two world wars, a Cold War, Hitler, the Holocaust, Sauerkraut, road-clogging campervans, sunbed snaggers and a bevy of other not-yet-exhausted tags have been tolerated by Germans for decades. In the run-up to Germany's 2002 World Cup qualifier football match against England, Britain's tabloid press oozed anti-German jingoism. In response to complaints from Germans living in Britain about the use of the word *kraut* in an advertisement ('The Krauts are Coming!'), Britain's Advertising Standards Agency defended the term as 'a light-hearted reference to a national stereotype unlikely to cause serious or widespread offence'. Coined during WWI to denote its cabbage-eating enemy, the term is old hat and one that Germans no longer want to hear.

Contemporary Germans are generally liberal, forward thinking and open to an enlarged Europe. Most embraced the euro with zeal when it was introduced, many travel, an astonishing number of people (of all generations) speak one or two foreign languages, and protecting the environment is paramount.

Many feel a new sense of confidence in their country thanks to its position at the heart of an eastward-bound Europe. Yet most remain low-key towards nationalism, albeit for historical reasons that cast shadows over the means by which nationhood was won. This dichotomy is reflected in their ambiguous relationship with the national anthem, composed around an obscure Croatian folk song in 1797. Prior to unification, only fools or hard-core nationalists sang it, while the Nazis tagged the ditty *Die Fahne Hoch* (Raise the Flag) onto it. By 1945 when the original was readopted, the first two verses mentioned defunct borders, wine and women – and had to be slashed.

Much soul-searching goes into what it means to be German: to say one is 'proud to be German' only raises eyebrows (neo-Nazis roar this catchphrase at nationalist rallies). Perhaps an overriding reason for nationalist nonchalance is, quite simply, the lack of devotion some Germans feel towards Germany. While daily life for West Germans remained unaltered after the fall of the Wall, life for East Germans changed so dramatically that equating reunified Germany with the country they grew up in can be problematic. Stripped of their socialist clothing, many older eastern Germans feel done out of both country and identity. Even younger and more critical East Germans regard certain aspects of their former country with nostalgia; see the Ostalgie boxed text (p47).

On the western side of today's cultural and social *Mauer in den Köpfen* (literally 'wall in the head'), a chunk of people question what east brought to west (beyond enormous government expenditure). Many slam *Ossis* (a nickname for former East Germans) as lazy, unmotivated and culturally backward; while *Ossis* see *Wessis* (a nickname for former West Germans) as arrogant, materialistic and far too cocksure for their own good.

Germans in general are blunt and straightforward. They correct you if you are wrong, don't praise you if you are right, and spend little (or no) time exchanging civilities. They face each other squarely in conversation,

The German embassy in Washington provides useful cultural insights online at www.germany-info.org.

Günter Grass' tour-de-force, *Die Blechtrommel* (The Tin Drum, 1959), humorously traces recent German history – including Nazism – through the eyes of Oskar, a child who refuses to grow up. *Ein weites Feld* (Too Far Afield, 1992) addresses 'unification without unity' after the Wall falls.

THE CULTURE •• Lifestyle 45

although such a direct stance can seem overbearing. A solid handshake is common among men and women; younger people kiss on the cheek. Contrary to popular belief, Germans do have a sense of humour – as the German tabloid *Bild* proved after the Berlusconi blunder when it offered its readers a free flight to Italy (to show Italians just how great German tourists are), published various useful Italian phrases (Can I offer you my deck chair?) and reportedly paid for a bunch of topless models to beach-party in front of the Italian embassy in Berlin.

Not to be thought of as clichéd is the Germans' strong sense of tradition. Hunters still wear green and master chimney sweeps march around in pitch-black suits and top hats; apprentice carpenters roam the country on *Wanderschaft*, a 16th-century tradition once obligatory so tradespeople became familiar with foreign skills of the trade. Some Bavarian women don the *Dirndl* (skirt and blouse), and Bavarian menfolk occasionally sport *Lederhosen* (leather trousers), a *Loden* (short jacket) and felt hat.

Germans are not prudish. Nude bathing on beaches and mixed saunas (in the nude) are commonplace, although many women prefer single-sex saunas. Donning a swimsuit or covering your private bits with a towel in a sauna is frowned upon.

Berlin as it really is leaps off the pages of Vladimir Kaminer's highly readable and humorous short stories in *Russen Disko* (Russian Disco, 2002).

LIFESTYLE

A quick pry into the apartment of Herr Otto Normalverbraucher (Mr Otto Average Consumer) is an instant eye-opener: He puts condensed milk in his coffee-filter machine coffee, splits his rubbish between four bins and detests doors being left open. He drinks fizzy mineral water, takes showers (not baths), and is Mr Casual in dress code. His mobile phone is a *Handy*, his bicycle is a Dutch Gazelle and his car is love itself (521 in every 1000 Germans are car owners, compared to 419 in the UK and 469 in the EU). At the shops, he rarely pays by credit card – this *is* the predominantly cash society that insisted on the €500 bill being issued – and always takes along his own cloth bag when shopping.

Flirting, fashion, fun and everything else you need to gen up on culturally to study and live in Germany is on the net at www.campus-germany.de.

Normalverbraucher has a landlord: with a longstanding tradition of renting rather than buying (32% of tenants bring in a monthly household income of €3200 or more, yet still rent), home ownership remains low in Germany. In 2002, 42.2% of people owned their own homes. Monthly rents are substantially lower in eastern Germany – a two-child household pays almost 25% less (€419 a month) than its west-German counterpart.

German households on both sides of the old wall are pretty wired up: around 55% have a PC, 35% have Internet access and almost 70% have a

---

DOS & DON'TS

- Germans draw a fat line between *Sie* and *du* (both meaning 'you'). Addressing an acquaintance with the formal *Sie* is a must, unless invited to do otherwise. Muttering a familiar *du* (reserved for close friends and family) to a shop assistant will only incite wrath and bad service, although *du* is often acceptable in young people-packed bars. If in doubt, use *Sie*.

- Mention the war, but use tact and relevance when doing so. Beware of implying that fascist ideas are intrinsically German.

- Push firmly but politely with German bureaucracy; shouting will only slam down the shutters. Germans lower (rather than raise) their voices when mad.

- Give your name at the start of a phone call, even when calling a hotel or restaurant to book a room or table.

WHEN NAKED VEGETARIANS PUMP IRON

The idea of strapping young Germans frolicking unselfconsciously naked in the healthy outdoors is not new. A German *Körperkultur* (physical culture) first took shape in the late-19th century to remedy industrial society's so-called 'physical degeneration'. Out of this, Germany's modern *Freikörper* (naturist) movement was born.

The early movement was something of a right-wing, anti-Semitic animal, whose puritanical members were scorned by some outsiders as 'the lemonade bourgeoisie'. Achieving total beauty was the name of the game. Anathema to the movement, for example, was someone with a las-civious 'big-city lifestyle' that included smoking, fornicating, eating meat, drinking, and wearing clothes made of synthetic fibres, or anyone with predilections for artificial light. Early naturism also sprouted Germany's first vegetarian *Reform* restaurants and shops.

The most interesting characters to develop out of this odd era were bodybuilders – predominantly vegetarian and naturist but internationalist in spirit. Some achieved fame abroad under pseudonyms. Others were immortalised in Germany by sculptors, who employed them as models for their works.

Famous pioneers of the movement in Germany include Kaliningrad-born Eugene Sandow (1876–1925) who died trying to pull a car out of a ditch; Berlin-born Hans Ungar (1878–1970), who became famous under the pseudonym Lionel Strongfort; and Theodor Siebert (1866–1961), from Alsleben, near Halle, in eastern Germany.

DID YOU KNOW?

The GDR's so-called *Das Tal der Ahnungslosen* (Valley of the Ignorants) covered an area of some 1.5 million East Germans in the Elbe Valley around Dresden. TV viewers here had the misfortune of not receiving West German stations as well as the regular *Ostsender* (East German TV) and *Zonenfunk* (Soviet-occupation zone TV).

Women's issues are lob-bied by the 52-member association Deutscher Frauenrat (German Women's Council) at www.deutscher -frauenrat.de.

Handy. Practically every household has at least one TV set (which 40% of Germans claim they cannot live without).

Traditional family dynamics are shifting. People are marrying later, with women and men marrying at the average age of 28 and 31 respectively, while an increasing number don't marry (26% of babies born in 2002 were born out of wedlock and 20% of families are single-parent) or don't have children (40% of female graduates aged between 35 and 39 in western Germany are childless). And so the country's birth rate – already one of Europe's lowest – continues to tumble.

Since 2001, parents have enjoyed equal rights to maternity and paternity leave, and the right to work part-time. In addition to child benefits (paid across the board until a child is at least 16 and, in some circumstances, up to 27), many parents receive a means-tested child-rearing benefit (€307 a month) for the first two years of a child's life. Childcare remains under-funded and incompatible with German school hours (8am to 1pm), which see pupils finish their school day at lunchtime. Working parents have yet to reap the benefits of the government's €4 billion Future Education & Care package, launched in 2003 to fund 10,000 new all-day schools.

Reunification had a tremendous impact on GDR lifestyle. Not only did it shut childcare centres, end free contraception, cut health pro-grammes and push many women back into more traditional roles, but it also ushered in unemployment. Those that are employed work longer hours and earn less than western Germans – prompting engineering union workers in eastern Germany in mid-2003 to strike in a failed bid to bring their 38-hour working week in line with that of their western counterparts (who only work 35 hours). Germany's official working week is 37.2 hours. Gross monthly earnings in production industries averaged €2759 in eastern Germany and €3716 in western Germany in 2002.

Women form 42% of the national workforce, but earn less than men (women grossed an average €2789 a month in 2002 compared with €3946 by men). In parliament, around 30% of MPs are women (compared with less than 10% in 1980). Rita Süssmuth (b. 1937) served as first female president of the *Bundestag* from 1988 until 1998.

Abortion is illegal (except when medical or criminal indications exist), but since 1995 unpunishable if carried out within 12 weeks of conception and after compulsory counselling. Rape within marriage has been a constitutional offence since 1997.

Same-sex marriages have been legal since 2001. Gays and lesbians walk with ease in most cities, especially Berlin, Hamburg, Cologne and Frankfurt-am-Main, although homosexuals do encounter discrimination in certain eastern German areas (eg Magdeburg, Frankfurt an der Oder and parts of eastern Berlin). See p746 for more.

Germans retire by the age of 63, but if current plans go through parliament, Normalverbraucher won't be allowed to retire until he is 64 and could well work until the ripe old age of 67.

DID YOU KNOW?

The country's first gay publication, *Der Eigene*, went to press in 1906.

OSTALGIE

'Once upon a time there was a land, and I lived there, and if I am asked how it was, I say it was the best time of my life – because I was young and in love.'

Sonnenallee (Sun Alley, 1999) *directed by Leander Haussmann*

When the Wall came tumbling down, no-one in their right mind ever imagined that one day, someone, somewhere, might hark after a Soviet-produced East German fork, a scrap of drab beige wallpaper or a Club Cola. But a decade on, *Ostalgie* – nostalgia for all things east – is precisely what is happening.

Sentimental nostalgia for the former GDR (DDR in German) has simmered on the fringe of Berlin trends since the late 1990s. But with the release of the box-office smash hit *Goodbye Lenin!* (2003), O*stalgie* rocketed into the mainstream. Jars of East German *Spreewaldgurken* (pickled cucumbers) now assume cult status, Florena hand cream is the only hand cream to use, and the *Ampelmännchen* – the little green man that helped East German pedestrians cross the street – has been sweetly revived in lollipop-size.

Trabis and Wartburgs – as the two main cars driven in East Germany were called in GDR-speak – are being dragged off the scrapheap of history and given pride of place in the many kitsch GDR-inspired bars suddenly springing up. GDR memorabilia is filling museums and second-hand shops, while songs once sung by the blue-shirted *Jungpioniere* (Young Pioneers, the GDR youth organisation) star at *Ossi* parties thrown by young hip things in the capital.

On German TV, GDR-inspired chat shows (see p66) have resurrected a host of former East German celebrities. The Young Pioneer salute opened the first such show, which saw East German boxer Axel Schulz reminisce about the Schwalbe moped and WM66 washing machine; 1980s East German rapper Birger Lars Dietrich don a pair of black East German army NVA tracksuit bottoms, now the height of retrospective chic; and TV presenter Victoria Herrmann demonstrate how to cook *Tempo-bohnen* (white fast-cook beans). Frank Schöbel – the first to appear on East German TV in a pair of jeans (1964) and the first East German singer to have a pop hit in West Germany (1971) – was also there.

Online *Ostalgie* is huge. GDR border signs are sold for €99 at www.grenzschild.de/index2.htm, the best English-language site with links to most other *Ostalgie*-related sites. At www.ddr-all tagskultur.de surfers click through images of Sprachlos (East German cigarettes) and other GDR iconography; send *Ampelmännchen* e-cards; and test their Eastern prowess with an *Ossi* quiz. You can tune into GDR music at www.musik-der-ddr.de, while www.ddr-woerterbuch.de is an online GDR dictionary, and 500-odd GDR jokes raise a giggle at www.ddr-witz.de.

But there is a bittersweet edge to this rose-tinted land of retro bell-bottoms and flower-power shirts. Critics say the darker side of the GDR should not be forgotten and that a land where people were spied on and denied basic freedom should not be glamorised – whatever the cost. The crux will be if Berlin entrepreneur Peter Massine gets the green light to cash in on *Ostalgie* with a GDR theme park, a €1.2 million project proposed in 2003 for East Berlin's industrial Oberschöneweide district.

POPULATION

Germany is densely populated – 230 people are packed into every sq km (compared with 116 per sq km in the EU), although a far greater wedge is crammed into western Germany. The most densely populated areas are Greater Berlin, the Ruhr region, the Frankfurt-am-Main area, Wiesbaden and Mainz, and another region taking in Mannheim and Ludwigshafen. In eastern Germany, about 20% of the national population lives on 33% of the country's overall land.

Most people inhabit villages and small towns, and German cities are modest by world standards: Berlin aside, the biggest cities are Hamburg (1.7 million), Munich (1.3 million) and Cologne (one million).

East Germany's population dropped to below the 1906 level after reunification as easterners moved to the more lucrative west. Oddly, Berlin's postreunification population boom has been offset by the exodus of young families from the capital to the surrounding countryside.

In keeping with European trends, the overall population of Germany is ageing; fewer people are having children, and even they are having fewer children than before, meaning Germany will need to welcome some 500,000 immigrants a year if it wants to prevent its population sinking to 74 million by 2050.

For an analysis of Germany's foreign population, see p50.

SPORT

Germany has always given sport a sporting chance. The Nazis (albeit for propagandist reasons) hosted the Olympics in Berlin in 1936, televising the spectacular event for the first time. During the Cold War era, the GDR invested a fortune in world-class athletes. In anticipation of its role as the 12-city host of soccer's 2006 World Cup, Germany is pouring billions of euros into revamping old stadiums and designing new state-of-the-art stadiums, much to the joy of German sport enthusiasts who will reap the benefits long after the last medallist has stepped off the podium.

Football

Football incites passion in the most mild-mannered of Germans and is one field where British–German rivalry can be unpleasantly strong.

Germany has played in more World Cups than any other nation and has won the title three times to boot. Its first victory in 1954 against Hungary in Bern, Switzerland, was unexpected and miraculous for a country slumbering deep in post-WWII depression. The 'miracle of Bern' – as the winning goal by Helmut Rahn (1929–2003) was dubbed – turned the Essen-born right-winger into a sporting icon and sent national morale soaring.

West Germany won the 1974 World Cup in the home town of Munich's Franz Beckenbauer (b. 1945), dubbed 'Kaiser' and 'Emperor Franz' for his outstanding flair and elegance. Beckenbauer kicked off his career in 1965 as a midfielder with Bayern München, captained West Germany from 1971, won European Player of the Year in 1972 and 1976, and led Bayern to a hat trick of European Cups between 1974 and 1976. He is credited with revolutionising the role of sweeper and turning Bayern München into Germany's top club. In 1990 he led Germany to World Cup victory as manager, making him the only footballer to win the cup as both player and manager.

This time Beckenbauer is chairman of the World Cup organising committee. Matches will be held at stadiums in Berlin, Cologne, Dortmund,

Frankfurt-am-Main, Gelsenkirchen (10km north of Essen), Hamburg, Hanover, Kaiserslautern, Leipzig, Munich, Nuremberg and Stuttgart.

Top German sides to play in Germany's premier league, the *Bundesliga*, include Werder Bremen, VfB Stuttgart, Bayer Leverkusen and Borussia Dortmund. Bayern München has won the league championship 18 times. Saturday afternoon matches are shown on TV sports channel DSF.

Tennis

German tennis was unknown until 1985 when the unseeded 17-year-old Boris Becker (b. 1967), from Leimen near Heidelberg, became Wimbledon's youngest-ever men's singles champion. The red-head, known for his power play, won five more Grand Slam titles in a career that ended in 1999.

As intense off-court as on-court, Becker still thrills: His marriage to black model and actress, Barbara, in 1993 was pounced on as confirmation that a country not known for its tolerance of interracial marriages was at last loosening up (three years later he threatened to quit Germany because of racist threats). The pair divorced in 2001 after it emerged that Becker had fathered the child of a Russian model, following five minutes of hanky-panky in the broom cupboard of a London restaurant. In 2002 Becker was given a two-year suspended prison sentence for tax evasion. Promoting tennis in Germany and commentating at the annual Masters Series in Hamburg entertains the tennis whiz today. The other German male players of note are one-time Wimbledon champion (1991), Michael Stich (b. 1968) and 2003 Australian Open finalist Rainer Schuttler (b. 1976).

Mannheim-born Steffi Graf (b. 1969) dominated women's tennis in the 1990s, winning her first Grand Slam title in 1987 and scooping 21 more (including seven Wimbledons) before her retirement in 1999. These days she markets her own line of designer handbags, puts her face on Deutsche Telekom TV commercials with tennis-playing husband Andre Agassi and chairs a Hamburg-based charity for children. Anke Huber (b. 1976), ranked No 11 in the world in 2000, showed initial promise but has yet to serve any real aces.

Hamburg hosts the men's German Open tournament each May; women play in Berlin in June.

Other Sports

Germans like cycling – to get around and for sport. On the professional circuit, East German Jan Ullrich (b. 1973), who won the 1997 Tour de France and finished second in 2003, is the German star.

Michael Schumacher (b. 1969) dominates motor racing. By far the best (and highest-paid) racing driver in the world, he became the youngest double Formula 1 World Champion in 1995, has driven for Ferrari since 1996, and has won more than 50 Grand Prix races. Younger brother Ralf (b. 1975) drives for Williams. In Germany both race at the Hockenheim circuit, host to the German Grand Prix since 1976. The European Grand Prix rips around Nürburgring.

Home-grown winter-sport legends include luger Georg Hackl, born in the Bavarian Alps in 1966, whose gold in the singles luge event at the 2002 Winter Olympics made him the first luger to win an Olympic medal in the same event five consecutive times. In the 2002 Four Hills Tournament, ski-jumper Sven Hannawald (b. 1974) clinched all four jumping events, recalling the success of former East German Jens Weissflog (b. 1964) who won the title four times. Weissflog and retired downhill/

West Germany's 1954 World Cup victory provides the impetus for Sönke Wortmann's *Das Wunder von Bern* (The Miracle of Bern, 2003), a powerful family drama about a WWII prisoner of war returning to a football-crazy son he no longer recognises.

Bundesliga scoreboards, rankings and fixtures are online at www.germansoccer.net (English) and www.bundesliga.de (German).

DID YOU KNOW?

Outdoor handball was invented in Germany around 1895 to keep football players on their toes out of season. Berlin hosted the first official 11-a-side handball match (1917) and its Olympic debut (1936).

slalom skier Rosi Mittermaier (b. 1950), triple medallist at the 197
Winter Olympics, are today TV commentators in their respective field
Former East German figure skating champion, Katrina Witt (b. 1965) i
another Olympic medallist to turn her hand to TV.

American football clubs in Berlin, Frankfurt-am-Main and Düsseldor
compete in the National Football League: Europe league (NFL Europe
www.nfleurope.com), with Frankfurt Galaxy clinching the 2003 NFl
Europe championships (making Frankfurt Europe's premier America
football club).

German golfer Bernhard Langer, captain of the European team i
the 2004 Ryder Cup, has popularised golfing. The son of a Russia
POW who jumped off a Siberia-bound train to land in Bavaria, Lange
has twice won the Masters Tournament, and boasts 42 victories on th
European Tour.

MULTICULTURALISM

Multicultural Germany has always drawn immigrants, be it French Hu
guenots escaping religious persecution (about 30% of Berlin's populatio
in 1700 was Huguenot), 19th-century Polish miners who settled in the
Ruhr region, post-WWII asylum seekers, or foreign *Gastarbeiter* (gues
workers) imported during the 1950s and 1960s to resolve labour short
ages. After reunification, the foreign population soared (from 4.5 millio
in the 1980s to 7.3 million in 2002) as emigrants from the collapsed USSF
and then war-ravaged former Yugoslav republics dashed in. Each yea
some 100,000 *Spätaussiedler* (people of German heritage, mainly from
Eastern Europe and Kazakhstan) arrive at the border.

Such a legacy would suggest the whole issue of multiculturalism to have
been done and dusted long ago. But no: Never has multiculturalism beer
such a hot potato in Germany as it is today. Foreigners form 9% (7.3
million) of the national population, the largest ethnic communities being
Turks (26% of foreigners), Italians, Greeks, Yugoslavs, Poles and Croats.

Germany only passed its first immigration law in 2003, a sequel to a
new nationality law (2000) that finally gave automatic German citizenship to anyone born in Germany to long-term resident foreign parents.
(Prior to this, nationality was defined by blood.) Approximately 180,000
'foreigners' have been naturalised each year since, although dual nationality remains a pipe dream.

DID YOU KNOW?

Slavonic Sorbs live in
pockets of Saxony and
Brandenburg, and a small
Danish minority can be
found around Flensburg
(Schleswig-Holstein) on
the Danish border.

A desire to control (and limit) the immigration flow, coupled with a
shortage of highly skilled labour and a crying need to better integrate
its foreign population, was the inspiration behind the immigration law.
Applicants are assessed according to several strict criteria, including age,
education and language skills. German history, culture, law and language
classes will be available to foreigners already living in Germany, the latter
being compulsory for those who don't speak German. The federal budget
for language courses for foreigners in 2003 was €16.8 million.

A controversial clause in the immigration law also gives permanent
residency to a limited number of highly qualified foreign workers. In a
country where unemployment ranks among Europe's highest, it is hardly
surprising that this gets under some people's skin. A fear of foreigners
taking those jobs that there are accounts for a lot of antiforeigner senti-
ment in Germany today.

Distrust between immigrants (be it recent arrivals or Turks who have
been living in Germany for two generations) and a certain fraction of
German society has increased since reunification. This has manifested
itself most brutally in racial violence – an alarming trend. Forty-five

ercent more xenophobic, right-wing and anti-Semitic crimes were ommitted in 2000 than 1999. In the early 1990s a spate of nasty attacks n foreigners (a firebombing in Mölln in 1992 killed three Turks, another n Solingen a year later left five Turks dead) saw the government crack lown on far-right violence. Yet it continues. In 2002 a 16-year-old boy in astern Germany was mutilated and murdered by two neo-Nazis youths ecause 'he looked like a Jew' and in late 2003 a plot to bomb a Jewish entre in Munich during a presidential visit was uncovered. Despite the anning of more prominent neo-Nazi skinhead groups, an extreme-right outh subculture has a certain hold in eastern German towns where un-mployment is particularly high.

Germany's asylum laws are among Europe's toughest. Refugees arriv-ng in Germany from a country where human rights are protected are not ntitled to asylum, meaning anyone who arrives by land won't be granted sylum. Victims of nonstate persecution (civil war, natural disaster etc) re likewise excluded. Just over 90,000 asylum seekers applied for asylum n Germany in 2002; no more than 3% will be recognised.

MEDIA

Private broadcasters have competed with public broadcasters in Ger-many since 1987, creating one of Europe's most competitive and packed TV broadcasting markets. All but 10% of the country's 34 million TV households have the pick of scores of private channels, many received free by cable or satellite.

German companies dominated the market until August 2003 when Los Angeles–based Israeli billionaire, Haim Saban, bought a 72% stake in Germany's largest free-to-air broadcaster, ProSiebenSat1, following the collapse of its parent company, Kirch Gruppe, in 2002. Bids were also made by media tycoons Rupert Murdoch and Silvio Berlusconi, turning the whole deal into a political wrangle. The bankrupted group also owned Premiere, Germany's only pay TV channel (albeit horribly unprofitable) with 2.4 million subscribers.

Founded by Bavarian entrepreneur Leo Kirch, Kirch Gruppe had been Europe's most powerful media empire, comprising over 150 subsidiary companies, which, among other things, owned a 40% stake in Germany's biggest publishing house, German dubbing rights for thousands of films, plus broadcasting rights for Formula 1 racing, the German football league *Bundesliga* and the 2006 World Cup. Management bought out the daugh-ter company owning the football rights (and the sports channel DSF) and appointed 1970s West German football player and current TV football commentator Günter Netzer to run it.

Public licence fees subsidise the country's two public broadcasters ARD (known as the 1st channel) and ZDF (the so-called 2nd channel). Unlike Mainz-based ZDF, Munich-headquartered ARD groups together several regional public stations, which contribute to the nationwide programmes shown on the 1st channel as well as the wholly regional shows transmitted on the so-called 3rd channel. Both have broken into digital broadcasting, with Berlin and its surrounds becoming Europe's first metropolitan area to go digital in August 2003. Saxony, Saxony-Anhalt, Thuringia and North Rhine-Westphalia will follow in 2004, and the country's analogue transmitters will be switched off by 2010.

Print media has a strong regional bias, with few publications being available nationally. Axel Springer and Bertelsmann are the largest publishers. Both the press and broadcasters are independent and free of censorship.

DID YOU KNOW?

The Bambi Awards – Germany's annual media awards – sees national celebrities such as Düsseldorf-born supermodel Claudia Schiffer proffer statuettes of fawns to showbiz stars and celebrities.

RELIGION

The constitution guarantees religious freedom, the main religions being Catholicism and Protestantism, each with about 26.6 million adherents (around one-third of the country's total population each). Religion is stronger in western Germany.

Unlike the Jewish community, which has increased in Germany (from 82,000 in 1999 to 100,000 in 2003) due to immigration from the former Soviet Union, the Catholic and Protestant churches are losing worshippers. This drop in congregation is attributed partly to the obligatory church tax (about 9% of income) that those belonging to a recognised denomination have to pay – Catholics, Protestants and Jews pay, but Muslims (which number around 3.2 million and are predominantly Turkish) do not.

Most German Protestants are Lutheran, headed by the Evangelische Kirche (Protestant Church), an official grouping of a couple of dozen Luthern churches with Hanover headquarters. Lutherans don't deem Methodists, Jehovah's Witnesses or other non-Catholic Christians to be proper Protestants.

The largest Jewish communities are in Berlin, Frankfurt-am-Main and Munich. Countrywide, there are 83 congregations, represented by the Bonn-based umbrella organisation, the Zentralrat der Juden in Deutschland (Central Council of Jews in Germany). The latter was granted equal federal status with the Catholic and Protestant churches in 2003.

ARTS
Visual Arts
FRESCOES TO EXPRESSIONISTS

Trier's St Maximin crypt and the Stiftskirche St Georg on Reichenau Island are rare reminders of the intricate fresco work that dominated Carolingian art (c. 800). Depicting biblical scenes, they lit up church ceilings (such as in Hildesheim's Michaeliskirche) from the 12th century and stained glass emerged as an art form. Central Europe's earliest cycle lights up Augsburg cathedral. As church windows grew larger, so stained glass became more important, as pieces in the Cologne and Limburg cathedrals demonstrate.

In 15th-century Gothic churches Cologne artists dropped the usual gold background on religious panels in favour of rudimentary landscapes. The finest examples can be seen in Hamburg's Kunsthalle.

Human elements shaped Renaissance art – a period dubbed the *Dürerzeit* (Age of Dürer) in Germany after the first German to seriously grapple with the theory and practice of Italian Renaissance art, Nuremberg-born Albrecht Dürer (1471–1528). View his work in the Alte Pinakothek in Munich. In Wittenberg, Dürer influenced Franconian-born court painter Lucas Cranach the Elder (1472–1553) whose *Apollo und Diana in waldiger Landschaft* (Apollo and Diana in a Forest Landscape, 1530) hangs in Berlin's Gemäldegalerie (Picture Gallery). Cranach idealised beauty and scrapped some of the Renaissance's naturalist elements, as did other artists of his southern German school of mannerism.

Sculptor Tilman Riemenschneider (1460–1531) chipped away at all mediums, abandoning colour for monochrome pieces and sculpting stone so it resembled wood. Two centuries later, sculpture became integrated into architectural design and gardens, creating the inspiration for Andreas Schlüter's (1660–1714) imposing *Reiterdenkmal des Grossen Kurfürsten* (Horseman's Monument of the Great Prince Elector) in front of Berlin's Schloss Charlottenburg. The four-horse chariot with Victoria

COLLECTIVE MEMORY

Unesco's 'Memory of the World' programme safeguards the world's most precious documentary heritage. German contributions include:

- a unique collection of 145,000 pieces of worldwide music (excluding Western art and pop) in Berlin's Ethnologisches Museum, recorded between 1893 and 1952 (listed 1999; see p115)

- Goethe's literary estate, stashed in the Goethe & Schiller Archives in Weimar's Stiftung Weimarer Klassik (2001; see p213)

- Beethoven's 9th Symphony, the score of which is kept in the Alte Staatsbibliothek (Old National Library in Berlin (2001; see p104)

- the negative of the reconstructed version of Fritz Lang's silent film, *Metropolis* (1927), pieced together in 2001 from a fragmented original (2001)

- the 1282-page Gutenberg Bible – Europe's first book to be printed with moveable type – is one of four of the original 30 to survive. Learn about the digital version at www.gutenberg digital.de (2001); the original cannot be viewed

on Berlin's Brandenburg Gate is the work of Germany's leading neoclassical sculptor, Johann Gottfried Schadow (1764–1850).

During this baroque period, palace walls were frescoed to create the illusion of more space. In Bavaria, Johann Baptist Zimmermann (1680–1758) worked with typical rococo pastels. In the mid-18th century, neoclassicism brought back the human figure and an emphasis on Roman and Greek mythology, seen in the work of German theorist Johann Winckelmann (1717–68). Hesse-born Johann Heinrich Tischbein (1751–1829) painted Goethe at this time in a classical landscape surrounded by antique objects. View *Goethe in der Campagna* (1787) in Frankfurt-am-Main's Städelsches Kunstinstitut (Städel Art Institute).

For a comprehensive lowdown of Germany's contemporary art scene and events see www.art-in.de (German only).

Religious themes, occasionally mystic, dominated 19th-century Romanticism. Caspar David Friedrich's (1774–1840) painting of Christ's crucifixion, *Das Kreuz im Gebirge* (Cross in the Mountains), set for the first time in a purely natural landscape, caused a sensation. It hangs in the Kunstmuseum Düsseldorf. Northern Germany is portrayed in many of Friedrich's symbolic landscapes.

In Hamburg, the Kunsthalle showcases works by the founder of the German Romantic movement, Philipp Otto Runge (1777–1810), as well as intensely religious works by the Nazarener (Nazareths). The art museum also displays the later realistic works of painters including Cologne-born Wilhelm Leibl (1844–1900) who specialised in painting Bavarian folk. Adolph Menzel (1815–1905), who ranked alongside Leibl as one of the best realist painters, went unnoticed until he began works based on the life of Friedrich I. View his 1852 *Das Flötenkonzert* (The Flute Concert) in Berlin's Alte Nationalgalerie (Old National Gallery).

Dip into cutting-edge German art with www.haschult.de, www.kunst-werke -berlin.de and www.eigen-art.com.

German impressionists are well represented in the Moderne Galerie of Saarbrücken's Saarland Museum. Key exponents of the late-19th-century movement include Max Liebermann (1847–1935), often slammed as 'ugly' and 'socialist' on canvas; Fritz von Uhde (1848–1911); and Lovis Corinth (1858–1925) whose later work, *Die Kindheit des Zeus* (Childhood of Zeus, 1905) – a richly coloured frolic in nature with intoxicated, grotesque elements – is housed in Bremen's Kunsthalle.

The Dresden art scene spawned Die Brücke (The Bridge) in 1905, a movement that played with bright, dynamic surfaces and strove for a direct and true representation of creative force. Its expressionist members – Ernst Kirchner (1880–1936), Erich Heckel (1883–1971) and Karl Schmidt-Rottluff (1884–1976) – employed primitivist and cubist elements, lived in artists' communes and turned their studios into exhibition space. Germany's best expressionist painter, Emil Nolde (1867–1956), an artistic lone wolf, only fleetingly belonged to Die Brücke and was forbidden from working by the Nazis in 1941.

A vivid picture of mid-19th-century German society is painted in Heinrich Heine's *Deutschland: Ein Wintermärchen* (Germany: A Winter's Tale), based on a trip the writer took from Aachen to Hamburg.

A second group of Munich-based expressionists, Der Blaue Reiter (Blue Rider), saw Wassily Kandinsky (1866–1944), Gabrielle Münter (1877–1962), Paul Klee (1879–1940) and Franz Marc (1880–1916) strive for a purer, freer spirit through colour and movement. See the end result in Munich's Städtische Galerie im Lenbachhaus.

MODERN VISUAL ARTS

Postwar angst gave a new aggression to art, evident in the work of German expressionist Otto Dix (1891–1969) who expressed the horror he had seen fighting in WWI. This represented a move towards Dadaism, a movement mocking the bourgeoisie that developed briefly in Germany around 1916. The effect that war had on women was evoked by Käthe Kollwitz (1867–1945) who worked her way through naturalism and expressionism to arrive at agitprop and socialist realism; see her work in the Käthe Kollwitz museums in Berlin and Cologne.

Berlin Alexanderplatz: The Story of Franz Biberkopf by Alfred Döblin (translated by Eugene Jolas) is a masterful 600-odd-page epic set in the seedy Alexanderplatz district of 1920s Berlin (filmmaker Rainer Fassbinder made a 15-hour version of it).

Social criticism also inspired Berlin's George Grosz (1893–1959) who took pencil and brush to society in the 1920s with witty, skilful caricatures. He escaped execution by the skin of his teeth after a military court sentenced him to death in 1918, and was received by Lenin on a 1922 trip to Russia. Another painter and sculptor, Rhineland graphic artist Max Ernst (1891–1976), moved from Dadaism to grotesque surrealism at this time.

New Objectivity, the umbrella term for these post-WWI realist-driven styles, reached its zenith in the early 20th century alongside the architecture-driven Bauhaus movement (see p57). Berlin's Bauhaus Archive/Museum of Design brilliantly displays paintings by Kandinsky, Münter and Klee, and sculptures by Gerhard Marcks (1889–1981).

Art turned black with WWII, often portraying silence and death: *Die Saat des Todes* (The Seed of Death, 1937) by Berlin's John Heartfield (1891–1968) depicts a skeleton in a wasteland sprinkled with swastikas. In the capital, many artists, Grosz included, were classified as 'degenerate' (see opposite) and forced into exile (Grosz went to New York). Others were murdered, retreated from public life or threw in art altogether. Artists that did paint could only produce Nazi art – Hitler-approved didactic pieces portraying Nazi ideology – on which little value is placed.

Post-1945 revived respected prewar expressionists including Nolde, Schmidt-Rottluff and Kandinsky; and a new abstract expressionism took root in the work of Stuttgart's Willi Baumeister (1889–1955) and Ernst-Wilhelm Nay (1902–68) in Berlin.

In the 1950s and 1960s, Düsseldorf-based Gruppe Zero (Group Zero) plugged into Bauhaus, using light and space to create a harmonious whole. Otto Piene (b. 1928) used projection techniques to create 'light ballets', while Heinz Mack (b. 1931) rolled out metal sculptures. In 1970s Donaueschingen, Anselm Kiefer (b. 1945) went for size with satirical monumental paintings constructed from symbolic photographic images. East German-born Sigmar Polke (b. 1941) remains a leading figure in German pop art, parodying modern politics and social convention in his work. View his thoughts at Essen's Museum Folkwang, Hamburg's Kunsthalle and the Kunstmuseum in Bonn.

DEGENERATE ART

Abstract expressionism, surrealism and Dadaism – 'Jewish subversion' and 'artistic bolshevism' in Nazi eyes – were definitely not Hitler's favourite movements . In fact, by 1937, such forms of expression fell under the axe of *Entartung* (degeneracy), a German biological term borrowed by the Nazis to describe virtually all modern movements. The same year, paintings by Klee, Beckmann, Dix and others – all supposedly spawned by the madness of 'degenerates' – were exhibited in Munich and promptly defaced in protest. Ironically, the exhibition drew a daily scornful yet curious crowd of 20,000-odd.

A year later, a law was passed allowing for the forced removal of degenerate works from private collections. While many art collectors saved their prized works from Nazi hands, the fate of many other artists' works was less fortunate. Many works were sold abroad to rake in foreign currency and in 1939 about 4000 paintings were publicly burned in Berlin.

New-wave music and visual arts were fused with the early 1980s Neue Wilde (New Wild Ones) movement – Cologne, Berlin and Hamburg being its main hubs. Survivor Markus Lüpertz (b. 1941) remains active in Berlin and Düsseldorf.

The environment-driven action art of HA Schult (b. 1939) amazes. His *Trash People* – 1000 life-sized people sculpted from rubbish – has been on world tour since 1996 (star appearances include Moscow's Red Square, atop the Matterhorn in Switzerland, and astride the Great Wall near Peking, while Antarctica is planned for 2006). In 1999 Schult created the world's largest trash sculpture at Cologne-Bonn airport, while *LoveLetters* (2001) saw the artist smother an old post office façade in Berlin-Mitte in love letters.

'Every man is an artist' claimed another eco-friendly artist, Düsseldorf's Joseph Beuys (1921–86). A greasy bathtub and *7000 Oaks* (1982), an art project that saw 7000 oak trees planted over a period of several years in the German town of Kessel, rank among his most outstanding outlandish works.

Sexuality and human fragility crop up in the multimedia work of Rebecca Horn (b. 1944) who makes sculptures to perform in film. Big shots in contemporary photography include Leipzig-born, Düsseldorf-based Andreas Gursky (b. 1955), whose work can be seen in Cologne's Museum Ludwig; and Candida Höfer (b. 1944), who has images in permanent collections at the Kunsthalle in Hamburg and at Karlsruhe. London-based Bavarian Jürgen Teller (b. 1964) is a darling of fashion photography and has shot Björk and a pregnant Kate Moss, among others.

Germany remains a fertile breeding ground for cutting-edge art. Its capital has been a showcase since 1990 when Berlin artists started exhibiting their work in an abandoned liqueur factory in run-down Berlin-Mitte, charting the birth of the contemporary art institute Kunst-Werke (since moved to a former margarine factory). The pioneering Galerie Eigen+Art has exhibition spaces in Berlin and Leipzig. Video art is nurtured at New Media schools in Karlsruhe and Frankfurt-am-Main, while Cologne's art collection (covering all periods) is among Europe's strongest. Venues as exciting as the art they display include the 1920s Gasometer in Oberhausen in the Ruhrgebiet – Europe's highest plate gas container to boot!

Architecture

Architecture fiends will get a kick out of Germany, from its booty of prewartime (unbombed) buildings to its wealth of extraordinary cutting-edge creations designed by the world's greatest contemporary architects.

WORLD CUP ART

'Think big' is the clear inspiration behind two artistic plots hatched to celebrate the forthcoming 2006 World Cup.

Between now and 2006, a 20m-tall black-and-white football is touring Germany's 12 host cities. Inside the so-called World Cup Globe, multimedia games, virtual installations and panoramic video screens promote German culture and give football fans a chance to digitally test their penalty shoot-out skills, blow the referee's whistle etc. To find out where the world's biggest football is (complete with 20 hexagonal and 12 pentagonal panels), visit the 2006 World Cup website at www.fifaworldcup.com. Guaranteed fixtures include Munich (for the opening match) in early June 2006 and Berlin (for the final) a month later.

An events manager in Cologne meanwhile plans to rebuild the Berlin Wall for the World Cup – in white plastic. A screen showing historic images of the stone wall would be embedded in a floating chunk above Potsdamer Platz, while international artists would paint the plastic wall during the two months it would stand in Berlin in summer 2006. The project is estimated to cost €25 million.

CAROLINGIAN TO ART NOUVEAU

Aachen, with its Byzantine-inspired cathedral, kicks off this architectural tour. Built for Charlemagne to use as a court chapel from 805, the Pfalzkapelle was inspired by San Vitale in Ravenna and is typical of the grand buildings of the Carolingian period, which were loosely based on styles and techniques used in Italy. A century on, architects drew on Carolingian, Christian (Roman) and Byzantine influences but aimed for a more proportional interior and integrated columns, as reflected in the elegant Stiftskirche St Cyriakus in Gernrode (Harz Mountains) and the Romanesque cathedrals in Worms, Speyer and Mainz.

Early Gothic architecture, slow to reach Germany from its northern-French birthplace, retained many Romanesque elements, as the cathedral in Magdeburg (Saxony-Anhalt) illustrates. Subsequent structures exhibited purely Gothic traits – ribbed vaults, pointed arches and flying buttresses to allow greater height and larger windows, as the fine examples in Cologne's cathedral (Kölner Dom), Marburg (Elisabethkirche), Trier (Liebfrauenkirche), Freiburg (Münster) and Lübeck (Marienkirche) testify. From the 15th century, elaborately patterned vaults and hall churches emerged. Munich's Frauenkirche and Michaelskirche are typical of this late Gothic period.

The Renaissance took its time to flower in Germany, but when it did (around the mid-16th century) it bestowed southern Germany and trade routes along the Rhine with stone heads of Hermes placed on structural features, ornate leaf work and columns sculptured like human figures. Heidelberg boasts some good examples. In northern Germany, the secular Weser Renaissance style flourished: Visit the ducal palace (Schloss) in Celle (Lower Saxony) to see the multiple-wing castle with winding staircases ascending a tower that this period ushered in.

From the early 17th century to the mid-18th century, feudal rulers asserted their importance through baroque residences. Ornate and excessive structures, usually incorporating sculpture and painting into their design, dominated their surroundings with grand portals, wide staircases and wings that created enclosed courtyards. In Baden-Württemberg, the residential retreat of Karlsruhe was dreamt up, while Italian architect Barelli started work on Munich's Schloss Nymphenburg. In northern Germany, buildings were less ornamental, as the work of baroque architect Johann Conrad Schlaun (1695–1773) in Münster or Dresden's treas-

DID YOU KNOW?

Jugendstil – an alternative name in German for Art Nouveau – takes its name from the arts magazine *Jugend* (Jugend meaning youth), first published in Munich in 1896.

re trove of baroque architecture demonstrates. Late baroque ushered in
otsdam's rococo Schloss Sanssouci.

Berlin's Brandenburg Gate, based on a Greek design, is a brilliant
howcase of neoclassicism. This late-18th-century period saw baroque
olly and exuberance fly out the window – and strictly geometric col-
mns, pediments and domes fly in. The colonnaded Altes Museum, Neue
Vache and Schauspielhaus – all designed by leading architect Karl Frie-
lrich Schinkel (1781–1841) – are other pure forms of neoclassicism still
racing the capital. In Bavaria, Leo von Klenze (1784–1864) chiselled his
vay through virtually every ancient civilisation, with eclectic creations
uch as the Glyptothek and Propyläen on Munich's Königsplatz.

A wave of derivative architecture based on old styles swept through
ate-19th-century Germany. A German peculiarity was the so-called rain-
ow style, which blended Byzantine with Roman features. Renaissance
evivalism found expression in Georg Adolph Demmler's (1804–86)
chloss in Schwerin, while sections of Ludwig II's fairy-tale concoction
n Neuschwanstein (Bavaria) are neo-Romanesque.

In Frankfurt Paul Wallots competed against 188 other German archi-
ects to design Berlin's Wilhelmian style (neobaroque) Reichstag building
1894), restored with a stunning glass-and-steel cupola (inspired by the
original) by internationally acclaimed British architect Norman Foster.
Vallots' use of steel to create a greater span and large glass surface was
ubsequently adopted by the early-20th-century Art Nouveau move-
nent, which created some of the country's most impressive industrial
rchitecture: Look no further than Berlin's Wertheim bei Hertie depart-
nent store.

*Erich Mendelsohn and the
Architecture of German
Modernism by Kathleen
James zooms in on
Mendelsohn's expression-
ist buildings in Berlin and
Frankfurt.*

MODERN DESIGN

No architectural movement has had greater influence on modern design
han Bauhaus, which was spearheaded by the son of a Berlin architect,
Walter Gropius (1883–1969). Through his founding in 1919 of the
taatliches Bauhaus – a modern art and design institute in Weimar –
Bauhaus pushed the industrial forms of Art Nouveau to their functional
imit and sought to unite architects, painters, furniture designers and
culptors in their art. Critics claimed Bauhaus was too functional and
mpersonal, relying too heavily on cubist and constructivist forms. But
ny visit to the Bauhaus Building in Dessau (where the institute was based
fter 1925) or the nearby Meisterhäuser (Master Craftsmen's Houses),
vhere teachers from the school (such as painters Kandinsky and Klee)
ved, instantly reveals just how much the avant-garde movement pioneered modern architecture. In Berlin, the Bauhaus Archive/Museum of
Design (Gropius designed the building himself in 1964) is a must-see.
Also see Design for Life (p246).

*For an informative and
illustrated dip into Berlin
architecture – past,
present and future – visit
the Senate Department of
Urban Development at
www.stadtentwicklung
.berlin.de.*

The Nazis shut down the Bauhaus school in 1932, frightening away
talented young architects like Aachen-born Bauhaus director Mies van
der Rohe (1886–1969) who fled to the USA in 1938. Nazi architecture
revelled in pomposity and oppressed all individual talent, although it
did produce Werner March's lavishly embellished Olympisches Stadion
1934) for the 1936 Berlin Olympics. A reinforced concrete roof topped
•y a transparent membrane is one of the startling features planned by
contemporary architects who are revamping the stadium for the 2006
World Cup while taking care to preserve its historical architectural
eatures.

Postwar reconstruction demanded cheap soulless buildings that could
•e erected quickly. Architecture in the GDR continued to lean towards

monumentalism – in Berlin look no higher than the 361.5m-tall TV towe (1969) or Frankfurter Allee. East Germany also inadvertently created on of the world's most potent architectural symbols in the Berlin Wall.

Experimental design took off in the 1960s in Düsseldorf with Hube Petschnigg's 26-storey high-rise Thyssenhaus (1960)and Der Neue Zol hof (New Customs House; p571) by Frank Gehry (who returned in 198 to design the Vitra Design Museum in Weil am Rhein and again in 199 to grace Hanover with some fish-shaped bus stops). The 1970s saw th unveiling of Munich's Olympisches Stadion (1972), with its enormou transparent tentlike roof that visitors can scale (with the aid of rope an snap hook) for an alternative architectural tour (see www.olympiapar -muenchen.de/english/zeltdach_tour).

Destined to outshine all other stadiums worldwide is Munich's ne €280 million stadium, designed by Swiss architects Jacques Herzog an Pierre de Meuron for the 2006 World Cup and already acclaimed as th

---

UNESCO WORLD HERITAGE SITES IN GERMANY

Among Germany's fabulous treasures and the dates their Unesco status was declared are:

- Aachen Dom (Cathedral, 1978; see p595)
- Bamberg (1993; see p396)
- Berlin's Museumsinsel (Museum Island, 1999; see p105)
- Augustusburg and Falkenlust castles in Brühl (1984; see p588)
- Cologne Dom (Cathedral, 1996; see p578)
- Garden kingdom of Dessau-Wörlitz (2000; see p247)
- Luther memorials in Eisleben and Lutherstadt Wittenberg (1996; see p256 and p248)
- Zollverein Pit XII coal mine industrial complex in Essen (2001; see p599)
- Goslar and mines of Rammelsberg (1992; see p265 and p266)
- Hildesheim's Cathedral and St Michaeliskirche (1985; see p655 and p656)
- Lorsch Abbey and Altenmünster (1991; see p555)
- Lübeck (1987; see p714)
- Messel Pit fossil site (1995; see p555)
- Potsdam's palaces and parks (1990; see p145)
- Quedlinburg (1994; see p277)
- Reichenau Island (2000; see p482)
- Speyer's Kaiserdom cathedral (1981; see p500)
- Trier's Roman monuments, Dom and Liebfrauen Kirche (1986; see p519)
- Upper Middle Rhine Valley (2000; see p507)
- Völklinger Hütte ironworks (1994; see p534)
- Wartburg castle (1999; see p224)
- Classical Weimar (1998; see p216)
- Bauhaus sites in Weimar and Dessau (1996; see p216 and p244)
- Wieskirche, Wies' pilgrimage church (1983; see p378)
- Wismar and Stralsund historic centres (2002; see p301 and p305)
- Würzburg's Residence and Court Gardens (1981; see p360)

orld's most unusual – and high-tech. Bearing an uncanny resemblance
o a rubber dinghy, its bubblelike translucent exterior will shimmer in a
ainbow of changing colours.

The extraordinary building boom that hit Berlin in the 1990s saw the
orld's top architects create a new cityscape for the capital. On Pots-
amer Platz Italian architect Renzo Piano designed DaimlerCity (1998)
nd Nuremberg-born Helmut Jahn (b. 1940) turned a playful hand to
ie glass-and-steel Sony Center (2000). The minimalist and edgy Neues
ranzler Eck (2000) is also a Jahn creation. American Daniel Libeskind
esigned the zinc-clad zigzag building of Berlin's Jüdisches Museum
2001), and New York contemporary Peter Eisenman dreamt up 2700
oncrete pillars for Europe's most haunting Holocaust Memorial
2005).

Of particular note on the home-grown architect front is Hamburg-
ased firm von Gerkan, Marg und Partner, whose bursting portfolio
icludes Berlin's new central train station (Lehrter Hauptbahnhof; to
pen in 2006) and Swissôtel-Kudamm-Eck (2001) with its eye-catching
J-sq-metre video screen (also in Berlin). Oswald Matthias Ungers of
Cologne (b. 1926) housed his city's Wallraf-Richartz-Museum (2001) in
cube, while Dresden-born Axel Schultes (b. 1943) and Kiel's Charlotte
rank (b. 1959), both Berlin-based, teamed up to create the capital's white
oncrete New Chancellery (2001; dubbed 'the washing machine' by many
erliners). Munich architect Stefan Braunfels (b. 1950) masterminded
1unich's modernist Pinakothek der Moderne (2002).

1usic
OVE BALLADS TO 20TH-CENTURY CLASSICAL

jerman music found its voice in the church and later in court when val-
ant 12th-century knights wooed women through love ballads. Modern
rtists have rerecorded some of these by minstrel Walther von der Vo-
elweide (c. 1170–1230) who produced lyrical works with a political and
hilosophical edge. Two centuries on, burghers adopted the troubadour
radition to create strict musical forms.

Martin Luther sparked off Protestant-hymn singing during the Ren-
issance, collaborating with Johann Walther (1496–1570) to publish the
irst book of hymns sung in German. The Enlightenment brought in
iisenach-born Johann Sebastian Bach (1685–1750) who walked several
undred kilometres to Lübeck to hear play baroque organist-of-the-day,
Dietrich Buxtehude (1637–1707): Bach's legacy is there to explore at the
3ach Museum in Leipzig (where he died). His contemporary, Georg
riedrich Händel (1685–1759) hailed from Halle in Saxony-Anhalt (his
iouse is now a museum), but lived and worked almost exclusively in
ondon from 1714.

The influence of Austrians Joseph Haydn (1732–1809) and Wolfgang
Amadeus Mozart (1756–91) on German music in the late-18th century
vas immeasurable. In Vienna, Haydn taught Bonn-born Ludwig van
3eethoven (1770–1827) whose work reflects the Enlightenment. Other
iotable German composers were Carl Philipp Emanuel Bach (1714–88),
ne of 20 children fathered by JS Bach, and Christoph Willibald Gluck
1714–87) who dabbled with Italian opera styles before switching to a
impler, classical style.

Romantic composers of the 19th century continued the tradition,
stablished in Beethoven's time, of living from their work. This fitted
n well with the ideology of free (if sometimes hungry) Hamburg-born
rtist, Felix Mendelssohn-Bartholdy (1809–47), who composed his first

Fourteen informative
essays bring the vibrant
musical age of Luther et
al alive in the 300-page-
plus *Music in the German
Renaissance* by John
Kmetz (ed).

overture at the age of 17 and later dug up works by JS Bach to give th latter the fame he enjoys today. Germanic myths were idealised in th compositions of Carl Maria von Weber (1786–1826) whose summe home in Dresden is now a museum.

A summer music festival in Bayreuth celebrates the life and works c Richard Wagner (1813–83), who balanced all the components of operati form to produce the *Gesamtkunstwerk* (complete work of art). He wa strongly influenced by Weber, Beethoven and Mozart; see p400 for mor about this Nazi-favoured composer.

Hamburg also produced Johannes Brahms (1833–97) and his flurr of influential symphonies, chamber and piano works. Bonn hosted depressed Robert Schumann (1810–56) who checked into an asylur there two years before he died. And his wife, Clara Wieck (1819–96 a gifted pianist in her own right, are buried in Bonn. Bavarian Richar Strauss (1864–1949) – often said to have been born in the wrong plac (Munich) at the wrong time – worked in the late Romantic tradition c Wagner, only to delve into a style reminiscent of Mozart at the end c his career.

Pulsating 1920s Berlin ushered in Vienna-born Arnold Schönber (1874–1951), inventor of a new tonal relationship, who exerted an enor mous influence on German classical music. One of his pupils, Hann Eisler (1898–1962), went into exile in 1933 but returned to East Berlin t teach in 1950. Among his works was the East German national anthem *Auferstanden aus Ruinen* (Resurrected from Ruins), lyric-less from 196 when its pro-unification words fell out of favour with party honchos.

Hamburg-born composer and conductor Paul Dessau (1894–1979 caused a political stink among GDR officials with the anti–social real ist music he composed for Brecht's *The Trail of Lucullus* in 1951. Hi contemporary, Hanau-born Paul Hindemith (1895–1963), was banne by the Nazis and composed his most important orchestral composition outside his homeland. The Hindemith Institute in Frankfurt-am-Mai (www.hindemith.org) promotes his music and safeguards his estate.

German classical music thrives. One of the country's oldest orchestras the Berlin Philharmonic Orchestra (1882), plays on stages worldwide as does the Dresden Opera Orchestra and the Leipzig Orchestra. Th young Kammersymphonie Berlin, established in 1991, recaptures th multifaceted music scene of 1920s Berlin through its focus on less com mon orchestral works. Acclaimed (and glamorous) German violinist Anne-Sophie Mutter (b. 1963), gave her first solo performance with th Berlin Symphony Orchestra (founded 1966) at the age of 14 and mad her first recording with the Berlin Philharmonic a year later.

CONTEMPORARY

German jazz in the 1950s oozed rebellion. Frankfurter trombonis Albert Mangelsdorff (b. 1928) soared to stardom as one of the world' best exponents of free jazz, fusing sounds with saxophonist Heinz Saue (b. 1932) to create the Albert Mangelsdorff Quintetts. Another great 1950 sax player, Klaus Doldinger (b. 1936) formed the legendary fusion ban Passport in 1970, producing some 50 records in a career that made hin the considered master of jazz-rock fusion. JazzFest Berlin brings the bes of German and European jazz to the capital each November (see p119).

German rock rolled from 1969 with psychedelic band Amon Düü (who were back on tour in 2002); Cologne-based experimental group Can; and the better-known Tangerine Dream. Kraftwerk – hailed as th 'mother of techno' and electronic pop music with its chart-hitting albun

The tempestuous Schumanns inspired filmmakers worldwide: Katherine Hepburn played Clara in Clarence Brown's *Song of Love* (1947), and Berlin-born Nastassja Kinski starred alongside pop idol Herbert Grönemeyer in Peter Schamoni's *Fruehlingssinfonie* (Spring Symphony, 1999).

For more information, practical and historical, on the Berlin Philharmonic Orchestra tune into www.berlin-philharmonic .com.

utobahn (1974) – made a massive comeback in 2003 with the release
f a new album. These early bands spawned Berlin's techno-orientated
egendary Love Parade (see p119) in 1989.

Recent electronica names to look for include techno kings Sven Väth,
Dr Motte (godfather of Berlin's Love Parade) and Westbam. Paul van
Dyk and Ian Pooley dominate today's house and trance scene; while the
Berlin-based producer collective, Jazzanova (which includes the Jazza-
ova DJ team), produces a breathtaking fusion of deep jazz, breakbeat,
riphop, funk and other new and retro sounds. Berlin's techno and
ouse label, Studio K7, draws top-shelf artists and is another name to
ook for.

Watch the video and hear the music of Germany's most influential techno band at www.kraftwerk.com.

Nena, the 1980s pioneer of Neue Deutsche Welle along with bands
ke Extrabreit, DAF (Deutsch-Amerikanische-Freundschaft) and Hubert
Kah, was another former pop star to reappear in 2003 with a platinum-
elling album *(Nena feat. Nena)*, featuring a duo (released as the single
Anyplace, Anywhere, Anytime') with Kim Wilde. The pop artist hit
No 1 in the UK charts and No 2 in the USA in 1984 with her playful
99 Luftballons' (released in Britain, Australia and the USA as '99 Red
Balloons').

Not to be confused with Nena, East German-born Nina Hagen fol-
owed her foster father (the writer Wolf Biermann) to West Germany
fter he was stripped of East German citizenship, thus turning herself into
Germany's ultimate 1980s punk girl. Punk still kicks in the capital where

A HISTORY OF GERMAN MUSIC IN 10 CDS

Stack your CD player with the following, sit back and take a whirlwind tour through German musical history:

- *Crusaders: In Nomine Domini & German Choral Song around 1600* by various composers (Christophorus label) – a couple of ballads by Walther von der Vogelweide feature on this 1996 compilation of medieval courtly music. The second CD reflects Luther's age.
- *Brandenburg Concertos* by JS Bach – six concertos, considered the lighter of his many works.
- 'Water Music' by Handel – music for wind and strings, written to woo King George I during a Thames river party in London in 1717.
- *Beethoven: Nine Symphonies* performed by Berlin Philharmonic Orchestra – of the nine, it's Symphony No 9 in D minor that stands out. Beethoven's use of song in the last movement marked the first time a voice had been used in a symphony.
- *Tannhäuser und der Sägerkrieg auf dem Wartburg* (Tannhäuser and the Song Contest of the Wartburg) by Richard Wagner – three-act opera set in 13th-century Thuringia; composed 1843–45.
- *Brahms: Violin Concerto, Double Concerto* performed by Anne-Sophie Mutter, Antonio Meneses and the Berlin Philharmonic Orchestra – combine Brahms with violinist virtuoso Mutter for a spot of armchair soul-soaring.
- *Ataraxia* by Passport – the 2002 album by warm-sax-and-other-jazzy-stuff legend.
- *Tour de France Soundtracks* by Kraftwerk – cycling inspires two-wheeler tracks, written around the 1983 single, *Tour de France*, upon which the album is based. Track No 9 is about a heart monitor.
- *In Between & The Remixes: 1997-2000* by Jazzanova – the first gives a rundown of the six-piece band's mixing skills; the second is the breakbeat-jazz lounge act's own debut album.
- *99 Cents* by Chicks on Speed – punk, funk and fashion fused; released on the girls' own label.

Die Ärzte remain strong. All-girl feminist punk band, Chicks on Speed
a trio of gals from Munich, New York and rural Australia – merge musi
with art and fashion in Berlin as their own cheeky fashion label calle
Sell-Out testifies.

Herbert Grönemeyer (the German Springsteen) achieved success wit
Bochum (1984), which stayed in the charts for 79 weeks. His straine
vocal style is not everyone's cup of tea, but his lyrics exhibit an appealin
irony as his latest album, *Mensch* (2002), demonstrates.

German hip-hop booms. Early 1990s band, Die Fantastischen Vier
remains one of the most popular modern bands, as shown by its album
4:99 (1999) and stunning performance in a subsequent MTV Unplugge
concert series. ASD, Böhse Onkelz, Terranova and Hamburg's Fettes Bro
and Beginner (formerly Die Absoluten Beginner) are also worth listenin
to. German artist Xavier Naidoo, who scooped Best German Act in th
2002 MTV Europe awards following the European success of his 199
album *Nicht von dieser Welt* (Not from this World), enjoyed worldwid
exposure with American hip-hop artist RZA (from the Wu-Tang Clan
in the compilation album, *The World According to RZA* (2003).

One of Germany's most noted mainstream rock bands, Fury in th
Slaughterhouse, joined forces with rapper Scorpio to make the rap-roc
track, *Are You Real. Brilliant Thieves* (2001) is their latest album. Berlin
longstanding Element of Crime meanwhile have released a new compila
tion album (2002) of their 1991–96 hits. Otherwise, mainstream pop i
dominated by young bands and artists spawned by Germany's TV realit
shows, pop-star quests and soap operas.

Traditional nondescript, thigh-slapping pop songs are known a
Schlager by Germans. In Berlin, the Paris-imported 19th-century tradi
tion of cabaret thrives.

Literature
EARLY LITERATURE

Educated clerical figures wrote down what remained of a tribal ora
tradition during Charlemagne's reign (c. 800), while knights performe
secular epics in court in the 12th century.

DID YOU KNOW?

Luther said, 'Look at their gobs to find out how they speak, then translate so they understand and see you're speaking to them in German.'

Luther's 16th-century translation of the Bible revolutionised the liter
ary language into common German. A century on, attempts to groom
the German language spawned a dose of literary absolutism: Martin
Opitz (1597–1639) created the basis for a new German poetry with hi
theoretical work *Buch der deutschen Poeterey* (Book of German Poetry
and poet Andreas Gryphius (1616–64) ushered politics into the literar
arena with his exploration of the horrors of the Thirty Years' War in th
sonnet, *Tränen des Vaterlandes* (Tears of the Fatherland). *Geschichte de
Agathon* (Agathon, 1766–67) by Christoph Martin Wieland (1733–1813
is considered Germany's first *Bildungsroman* (a novel showing the devel
opment of the hero). This Württemberg-born man of letters was also th
first to translate Shakespeare into German.

The 18th century ushered in Sturm und Drang (literally 'Storm an
Stress'). Johann Wolfgang von Goethe (1749–1832), unusually from
Frankfurt's upper class, earned fame with his early work *Götz von Ber
lichingen* (1773) and followed it up with the movement's first novel, *Di
Leiden des jungen Werthers* (The Sorrows of Young Werther, 1774). I
Württemberg, dramatist Friedrich von Schiller (1759–1805) was makin
heads turn on stage (see p67).

Neoclassicism cultivated the idea of the 'beautiful soul', with writer
harking to ancient Greece and Rome for inspiration. Goethe's *Italienisch

Read *Simplicissimus* (Adventures of a Simpleton) by Hans Jacob Christoffel von Grimmelshausen as an appetiser to the German novel.

Reise (Italian Journey, 1786) heralded a move towards classicism as he depicted a writer's inner struggle towards harmony through the means of travel. Between 1794 and 1805, he wrote the novel *Wilhelm Meisters Lehrjahre* (Wilhelm Meister's Apprenticeship).

Early Romanticism took the individual deeper into fancy and imagination. Germany's best Romantic poet (another Württemberg chap), Friedrich Hölderlin (1770–1843), strove for perfect balance and rhythm in his work. Unfortunately, the onset of madness cut short his career. Saxony's Novalis (b. Georg Friedrich Philipp von Hardenburg; 1772–1801) created the symbol of Romantic yearning, the blue flower, in one of his early novels, and tackled death and grief in his best work, the poems *Hymnen an die Nacht* (Hymns to the Night, 1800).

A 600km-long Fairy-Tale Road (see p564) leads literary travellers around Germany in the footsteps of the Grimm brothers, Jakob (1785–1863) and Wilhelm (1786–1859). Serious academics who wrote *German Grammar* and *History of the German Language*, they're best known for their collection of fairy tales, myths and legends.

Harsh censorship in the 1830s caused many writers of the Junges Deutschland (Young Germany) movement to turn to satire. In Düsseldorf, Heinrich Heine's (1797–1856) politically scathing *Deutschland: Ein Wintermärchen* (Germany: A Winter's Tale) contributed to his work being banned in 1835. His earlier *Buch der Lieder* (Book of Songs) is one of Germany's finest love-poem collections.

With the onset of realism around 1840, the novel dominated. Many, like those by Schleswig-Holstein native Theodor Storm (1817–88), evoked regional flavours. Writer and illustrator Wilhelm Busch (1832–1908), from near Hanover, continues to delight adults and children with his illustrated – if somewhat twisted – *Max und Moritz* (1858). Dripping with wit and irony, Busch provided a light relief to the grimier and more descriptive works that naturalism produced.

20TH CENTURY TO PRESENT DAY

The 20th century opened with lyrical poet, Rainer Maria Rilke (1875–1926), whose mother called him Sophia and dressed him in frocks for the first five years of his life. The Prague-born son of a railway official worker debuted as a poet at the age of 19 and spent much of his most productive years in France and Switzerland.

The Weimar years witnessed the flowering of Lübeck-born Thomas Mann (1875–1955), recipient of the Nobel Prize for Literature in 1929, whose greatest novels focus on the society of his day. For Mann, 'Germany's first lady' was writer and poet Ricarda Huch (1864–1947), a courageous opponent of Nazism. Mann's older brother, Heinrich (1871–1950), adopted a stronger political stance than Thomas in his work; his *Professor Unrat* (1905) provided the raw material for the Marlene Dietrich film *Der blaue Engel* (see p64).

Berlin's underworld during the Weimar Republic served as a focus for Alfred Döblin's (1878–1957) big novel *Berlin Alexanderplatz* (1929). Hermann Hesse (1877–1962), another Nobel Prize winner, adopted the theme of the outsider in *Steppenwolf* (1927) and imbued New Romantic spirituality into his work after a journey to India in 1911. Osnabrück-born Erich Maria Remarque's (1898–1970) antiwar novel *Im Westen nichts Neues* (All Quiet on the Western Front, 1929) was banned in 1933 and remains one of the most widely read German books. The angst of an exile cries out in Kurt Tucholsky's (1890–1935) *Schloss Gripsholm* (Castle Gripsholm, 1931), a short, dreamlike story published two years

The Complete Fairy Tales by Jacob and Wilhelm Grimm is a beautiful collection of 210 fairy tales, passed orally between generations and collected by German literature's most magical brothers.

Meaty Thomas Mann starters include *Buddenbrooks*, a look at declining bourgeois values; *Der Zauberberg* (The Magic Mountain), which links personal and social illness around the time of WWI; and the menacing *Doktor Faustus* in which the central character exchanges health and love for creative fulfilment.

Find reviews for the latest contemporary German titles to be translated into English at www.new-books-in -german.com.

before Tucholsky was stripped of his citizenship. Exiled in Sweden, th
pacifist writer killed himself.

Post-WWII social questions and the German psyche were the focu
of the political Gruppe 47 circle of writers to emerge after 1945. Amon
them were two later Nobel Prize winners, Cologne-born Heinrich Bö
(1917–85) and Günter Grass (b. 1927). Both fought in WWII. Grass – a
immediate household name after the publication of his first novel, *D*
Blechtrommel (The Tin Drum, 1959) – used Berlin as the backdrop fo
several works and ghost-wrote for Social Democrat Willy Brandt in th
early 1970s.

East Germany spawned several literary aces, including the controver
sial but sparkling Christa Wolf (b. 1929), who comments on east–wes
relations in her contemporary works; highly respected poet Sarah Kirsc
(b. 1935), who emigrated from East Germany; Chemnitz-born Kersti
Hensel (b. 1961); and the politically concerned Stefan Heym (b. 1913)
whose collection of stories, *Auf Sand gebaut* (Built on Sand), looks at th
situation of East Germans around 1990. More recently, eastern German
produced the satirical Thomas Brussig (b. 1965) whose phallic-drive
novel, *Helden wie wir* (Heroes Like Us, 1996), has been made into a filn
(see opposite).

A trio of leading literary figures was born in 1944 – the strongly mys
tic Botho Strauss, crime novelist and Berlin professor Bernard Schlink
and novelist WG Sebald (1944–2001) who assured his place as one o
Germany's best writers with his powerful portrayal of four exiles in *Di*
Ausgewanderten (The Emigrants). Sebald died at the height of his caree
in a car accident. Munich-based writer and playwright, Patrick Süskinc
(b. 1949), was another German writer to win international acclaim witl
Das Parfum (Perfume), his extraordinary tale of a psychotic 18th-century
perfume-maker.

Vladimir Kaminer (b. 1967) represents a new wave of young Berli
writers. Moscow-born, the Jewish emigrant settled in the capital after th
fall of the Wall and sketches Berlin's multicultural face with wit, insigh
and satire in his short stories. Reunified Berlin is painted in vibran
colour by Judith Hermann (b. 1970) whose pop-literature work appeal
to 30-somethings. Dresden-born Ingo Schulze (b. 1962) landed a coupl
of literary prizes with his first short-story collection, *33 Augenblicke de*
Glücks (33 Moments of Happiness, 1995) and was hailed by critics a
having produced 'the long awaited unification novel' with *Simple Storie*
(2001). Michael Kumpfmüller (b. 1961) is another Berlin big gun.

Cinema & Television
CINEMA

It was only when shooting started at the UFA film studios in Babelsberg
(Potsdam) in 1912 that German filmmakers were noticed. The studio
produced a clutch of low-budget expressionist films followed by surrea
silent-movie epics in the 1920s, notably Fritz Lang's ambitious classic
Die Nibelungen (The Nibelungen, 1922–24) and *Metropolis* (1927). Witl
the stunning performance of actress Marlene Dietrich (see p66) in the
talking film *Der blaue Engel* (The Blue Angel, 1930), directed by Jose
von Sternberg, the world pricked up its ears to what was now a thriving
industry.

In 1932 the Nazis forced Lang to premiere his first talkie, *Das Tes-*
tament des Dr Mabuse (The Testament of Dr Mabuse), a film about a
psychiatric patient devising plans to take over the world, in Austria
Nazi domination of the UFA film studios followed and Germany's mos

DID YOU KNOW?

Frankfurt has hosted
the world's largest
literary marketplace, the
international book fair
(www.frankfurt-book
-fair.com), since 1949
when centuries-old East
German host, Leipzig, had
its door slammed shut by
Soviet occupiers.

Pick up *Der geteilte*
Himmel (Divided Heaven)
by East German writer,
Christa Wolf, to discover
the fate of a woman's
love for a man who fled
to West Germany.

DID YOU KNOW?

Germany awards a rash
of prizes for literature,
the Joseph Breitbach
Prize yielding the
juiciest financial reward
(€120,000). Many are
awarded by the State
Academy of Arts in Berlin
(www.adk.de).

alented actors and directors moved to Hollywood, including Berlin-born Conrad Veidt (1893–1943), known as Major Strasser in *Casablanca* and for his menacing Nazi roles. Exiled film director Wilhelm Thiele (1890–1975) wound up making *Tarzan* movies.

In Nazi Germany, Leni Riefenstahl (1902–2003) made Nazi propaganda films. In *Olympia* (1936), a film of the 1936 Olympics, she revolutionised sports filming techniques. Briefly imprisoned after WWII for her Nazi involvement, the fearless filmmaker released her last film – *Impressionen unter Wasser* (Impressions Under Water, 2002), based on 200 scuba dives she did in her 70s – on her 100th birthday.

Sapped of talent and bankrupt, Germany's postwar film industry produced little beyond Trümmerfilme (rubble films) dealing with Nazism or war. The UFA studios became Soviet-driven, although the talents of individual directors such as Cannes award-winning Konrad Wolf (1925–82) somehow managed to shine.

'Papa's cinema is dead' was the philosophy of the Oberhausener Gruppe, a bunch of 1960s directors who called for change in an industry that – with the advent of television – still hadn't picked up. Vesely's *Das Brot der frühen Jahre* (The Bread of Early Years, 1962) pre-empted the new lease of life breathed into German film by the German New Wave movement (Der junge deutsche Film). This dynamic group used film to evoke pertinent moral questions and social commentary.

Terrorism and society's threat to self-identity dominated film in the 1970s and 1980s. The eclectic, at times grotesque, exploration of society, sexuality and the human psyche by Rainer Werner Fassbinder (1946–82) won him nine awards in Germany alone. The *enfant terrible* of New German Cinema, Fassbinder made 41 films in a cocaine-spiked career that spanned 14 years and ended in a fatal overdose. His contemporary, Wim Wenders (b. 1945), Golden Palm winner at Cannes for *Paris, Texas* (1984), pushed narrative-cinema style to its limit in *Der Himmel über Berlin* (Wings of Desire, 1987), a portrayal of two angels moving through divided Berlin. In the early 1990s, relationship themes dominated. Lola's quest to raise US$100,000 in 20 minutes to save her lover's life in Tony

The Wonderful, Horrible Life of Leni Riefenstahl (1993), directed by Ray Muller, is a stunning three-hour biographical epic of Hitler's most famous filmmaker. Highlights include pieces to camera by a 90-year-old Riefenstahl.

Fritz Lang's *Metropolis* (1927) stands out as an ambitious cinema classic. A silent science-fiction film, it depicts the revolt of a proletarian class that lives underground (see also p148).

Read what the critics say about 500+ more German films at www.german-cinema.de.

GDR RETRO FILMS – TOP FIVE

- Leander Haussmann's *Sonnenallee* (Sun Alley, 1999) is set in a fantastical wall-clad East Berlin in the 1970s, and evokes everything nostalgic for the former GDR.
- *Helden wie wir* (Heroes like Us, 1999) directed by Sebastian Peterson, based on the novel by Thomas Brussig, sees the protagonist (who claims to have been Erich Honecker's personal blood donor) recount the story of his life, including how his penis allegedly leads to the collapse of the Berlin Wall.
- Dull lives are led in dull Frankfurt an der Oder in dull East Germany – until Ellen and Chris are caught doing it. Laughs abound in *Halbe Trepe* (Grill Point, 2001), directed by East German-born Andreas Dresen.
- The Wall falls the day the bar-tending lead actor hits 30 in West Berlin's bohemian Kreuzberg district. Haussmann's humorous *Herr Lehmann* (Berlin Blues, 2003) is based on a cult book by the Element of Crime lead singer Sven Regener.
- *Goodbye Lenin!* (2003), the box-office smash hit by Wolfgang Becker, has cult status as a son tries to re-create the GDR for a bedridden ailing mother whose health can't stand the shock of a fallen Wall.

For more on *Ostalgie*, see p47.

MARLENE DIETRICH

Marlene Dietrich (1901–92), born into a good middle-class family in Berlin by the name of Marie Magdalena von Losch, was the daughter of a Prussian officer. After acting school, she worked in the silent film industry in the 1920s, stereotyped as a hard-living, libertine flapper. But she soon carved a niche in the film fantasies of lower middle-class men as the dangerously seductive *femme fatale*, best typified by her 1930 talkie *Der blaue Engel* (The Blue Angel), which turned her into a Hollywood star.

The film was the start of a five-year collaboration with director Josef von Sternberg, during which time she built on her image of erotic opulence – dominant and severe, but always with a touch of self-irony. Dressed in men's suits for *Marocco* in 1930, she lent her 'sexuality is power' attitude bisexual tones, winning a new audience overnight.

Dietrich stayed in Hollywood after the Nazi rise to power, though Hitler, no less immune to her charms, reportedly promised perks and the red-carpet treatment if she moved back to Germany. She responded with an empty offer to return if she could bring Sternberg – a Jew and no Nazi favourite. She took US citizenship in 1937 and sang on the front to Allied GIs.

After the war, Dietrich retreated slowly from the public eye, making occasional appearances in films, but mostly cutting records and performing live. Her final years were spent in Paris, bedridden and accepting few visitors, immortal in spirit as mortality caught up with her.

Der blaue Engel (The Blue Angel, 1930) tells the tragic tale of a pedantic professor who is hopelessly infatuated with a sexy cabaret singer. Watch this to see the vamp image that Marlene Dietrich enjoyed all her life.

Tykwer's electric-paced *Lola Rennt* (Run Lola Run, 1998) made a big impact worldwide.

Home-grown filmmakers are rewarded with annual prize money of €3 million, funded by the government. From 2005, the prizes will be awarded by the star-studded German Film Academy, set up in 2003 to give German film an industry-wide backbone. Generous state subsidies typically account for 10% to 30% of a film's budget (box-office hits then repay the cash).

New millennium directors outdare all others in the issues they tackle. At the 2003 Cannes film festival, Max Färberböck raised eyebrows with *September,* a look at life in Germany after the 11 September 2001 terrorist attacks in New York, while Kurdish German filmmaker Yüksel Yasav hit audiences with his no-holds-barred portrayal of life on Hamburg's prostitute-laden Reeperbahn for two asylum seekers in *Kleine Freiheit* (Small Freedom). Caroline Link's tale of a German-Jewish family's pre-WWII flight to Kenya, *Nirgendwo in Afrika* (Nowhere in Africa, 2001) won an Oscar for Best Foreign Film (2003), while a hilarious attempt at reconstructing the GDR for a bedridden mother made Wolfgang Becker's *Goodbye Lenin!* (2003) a box-office smash hit.

Read what's on the box this week with the online German TV programme guide at www.tvtv.de (German only).

TELEVISION

For a rundown of TV rulings, channels and so on, see p51.

Every German knows you don't phone your friends at 8pm, so sacred is *Tagesschau* (the 8pm evening news) on ARD. Watch this 15-minute national newsreel to witness one TV broadcast where the presenter still reads the news from a pile of on-screen papers (rather than off-screen cue cards). The 10-minute news slot, broadcast on ZDF at 7pm, is less popular.

Watch the news (follow the Mediathek link) with ZDF at www.zdf.de or ARD at www.ard.de (German only).

Long-running cop show *Derrick*, first made in Germany in 1974 and sold to 94 countries since, is a TV classic. *Tatort* is the other cult crime series to watch. Once seen, never forgotten is *Dinner for One* (see opposite).

Sabine Christiansen hosts Germany's most popular current affairs talk show. Interestingly, a cocaine-and-call-girl scandal in mid-2003 surrounding Germany's other big chat show host, Central Council of

---

SAME PROCEDURE AS EVERY YEAR

Eccentric as it might seem, it is a 1920s British cabaret sketch that Germans traditionally sit down to watch on New Year's Eve.

Filmed (in English) for German television in 1963, the B&W cult classic *Dinner for One*, also called *Der 90. Geburtstag* (The 90th Birthday), sees the 90-year-old Miss Sophie (played by May Warden in the original 1960s German TV production) get increasingly sloshed during a formal dinner party with her butler James (played by British actor Freddie Frinton) and a bunch of imaginary friends – all long since dead and buried.

Jews vice-president Michel Friedman, prompted its public broadcasters to immediately axe his show, *Vorsicht! Friedman* (Watch Out! Friedman). Friedman was known for his hard-hitting, controversial style.

GDR nostalgia remains the inspiration behind a rash of East German–oriented chat shows (see p47). Reality TV shows (get your parents to pick your date with *Family Date* etc) are the other big trend, with Germany's *Big Brother* one of the most successful European franchises.

> Tune into current affairs in English with international German broadcaster Deutsche Welle at www.dw-world.de.

Theatre

The curtain didn't rise on German theatre until the 18th century when enlightened dramatists Lessing, Goethe and Schiller stepped on-stage.

Saxony's Gotthold Ephraim Lessing (1729–81) rejected the French inclinations of his Leipzig contemporary, Johann Christoph Gottsched (1700–66), in favour of Shakespearian dramatic forms. Digging up the Greek idea that tragedy employed empathy and fear to evoke the audience's passion, Lessing wrote several fables and tragedies, including *Miss Sara Samson* (1755) and *Emilia Galotti* (1772).

> Read up-to-date reviews of the latest plays running by German playwrights at www.goethe.de /enindex.htm.

In 1796 August Wilhelm Iffland (1759–1814) took the lead at Berlin's Royal National Theatre, becoming noted for his natural yet sophisticated productions, particularly of plays by Friedrich von Schiller (1759–1805) from Württemberg whose works, *Die Räuber* (1781, The Robbers) and *Kabale und Liebe* (Cabal and Love), proved invaluable. In 1808, Schiller encouraged Goethe to publish the first part of his two-part *Faust*. Based on a pact with the devil, Goethe's play explores the human struggle for ultimate power and knowledge.

Georg Büchner's (1813–37) *Woyzeck* anticipated the Theatre of the Absurd. He lent his characters – in *Woyzeck*'s case a simple hero caught up in hostile social forces – a complex psychology in his works.

In 1894 the director of Berlin's Deutsches Theater hired a young actor, Max Reinhardt (1873–1943), who became German theatre's most influential expressionist director, working briefly with dramatist Bertolt Brecht (1898–1956). Both men went into exile under Nazism.

Brecht's epic theatre was loosely Marxist, rejecting Lessing's Greek leanings for political, didactic forms. His *Leben des Galilei* (Life of Galileo) and *Die Dreigroschenoper* (The Threepenny Opera, 1928) are his most popular dramatic works. After WWII the Augsburg-born dramatist (his birthplace is a pilgrimage site today) ended up in East Berlin where he could count on a sympathetic audience. In the 1950s, Brecht created the Berliner Ensemble, a place that produced his plays and became one of the capital's most vibrant theatres. The reputation still stands. See p107 for more details about Brecht.

After WWII, postmodern theatre provoked strong debate with its non-linear, fragmented structure. Staunch Marxist Heiner Müller (1929–95) was unpalatable in both Germanys in the 1950s. An apprentice under

The definitive read for anyone interested in a more detailed account of the rise of German theatre is Michael Patterson's hard-to-find but worth-the-search *The First German Theatre: Schiller, Goethe, Kleist and Buchner in Performance*.

Brecht at the Berliner Ensemble, his early plays tackled political issues in East Germany in a conventional manner. In the 1980s existential work such as *Quartet* (1980) earned him an avant-garde label. In the 1960s Berlin director Rudolf Noelte (1921–2002) took centre stage as the master of German postwar theatre.

Directors like Peter Stein (b. 1937) have earned contemporary German theatre its reputation for producing classic plays in an innovative and provocative manner. One of the Jungen Wilden (Young Wilds) in the 1970s and 1980s, Stein founded Berlin's Schaubühne theatre as a collective in 1970 (even the cleaner had a say as to what went on) and built it into one of Germany's leading theatre companies (it remains so). In the 1990s, artistic director Andrea Breth (b. 1952) lent Schaubühne productions a feminist touch.

Eye-catching contemporary playwrights include Munich-born, Berlin based Rainald Goetz (b. 1954) whose prize-winning *Jeff Koons* (1999) premiered at the Deutsches Schauspielhaus in Hamburg (see p705) and opens with the third act first; Wener Fritsch (b. 1960), whose dark plays portray a violent world, occasionally veering on the obscene; and Simone Schneider (b. 1962) who addresses contemporary inertia and restlessness in her theatre and radio plays. The witty Moritz Rinke (b. 1967) stunned audiences with his *Der Mann, der noch keiner Frau Blösse entdeckte* (The Man Who Never Saw Women's Nakedness, 1999) when it was premiered at Stuttgart's Staattheater and London's Royal Court Theatre.

Environment

THE LAND

Germany – 356,866 sq km hugged by Poland, Czech Republic, Austria, Switzerland, France, Belgium, the Netherlands, Luxembourg and Denmark – is flat in the north and mountainous in the south. Zugspitze, its biggest peak, rises to 2962m near the Austrian border.

The Rhine River is Germany's most potent national symbol, starting its 1320km-long northbound journey in the Swiss Alps and draining into the North Sea coast. Most other German rivers – except the eastward-flowing Danube – likewise spill into the North or Baltic Seas.

Coastline and lowlands characterise northern Germany. The North Sea coast consists partly of drained land and dykes, and peers out at the East Frisian Islands, which – at low tide – can be reached on foot. Schleswig-Holstein's Baltic Sea coast is riddled with bays and fjords, giving way to sandy inlets, spits and occasional cliffs. Chalk cliffs make Rügen, Germany's largest Baltic Sea island, famous. Inland, the Northern Lowlands – pocked by marsh, heath and glacial lakes – embrace a broad expanse of low-lying land that sweeps about one-third of the country. The Spreewald, a holiday area southeast of Berlin, is a picturesque wetland with narrow, navigable waterways.

The Black Forest, Sauerland (near Cologne), Elbsandsteingebirge (southwest of Dresden) and Bavarian Forest form the Central Uplands – a complicated patchwork of mountain ranges, rifts and valleys. Germany's most memorable vineyards and hiking areas can be found in the warmer valleys around the Moselle River. North of the river, the volcanic Eifel Upland is known for its crater lakes (Maare).

South of the Danube, the Alpine Foothills proffer moorland, low rolling hills and subalpine plateaus. There are several large glacial lakes in the area, such as the Chiemsee and Ammersee, as well as hundreds of small ones. The German Alps themselves lies wholly within Bavaria, from Lake Constance (Germany's largest lake) to Berchtesgaden in the east. Many peaks are well above 2000m.

WILDLIFE

Wildlife watchers will enjoy Germany, although few areas have escaped human impact. Of the 76 German mammals studied for the 'Red List' of endangered or extinct species, 16% are in danger of dying out, including the Eurasian otter and white whale. One-third of its 3000 native fern and flowering plants species are also endangered.

Animals

The pesky but sociable racoon, a common non-native, scoots about eastern Germany, and soon lets hikers know if it has been disturbed with its shrill whistle-like sound. Beavers can be found beavering around wetlands near the Elbe River.

In the Alps, the alpine marmot inhabits the area below the tree line, while the wild goat lives in the area above. The snow hare, whose fur is white in winter, is fairly common in this neck of the woods, as is the chamois, which also populates pockets of the Black Forest, the Swabian Alps and Elbsandsteingebirge (south of Dresden). A rare but wonderful Alpine treat for bird-watchers with patience is the sighting of a golden eagle – Berchtesgaden National Park staff might be able to help you spot

Owls of the World: Their Lives, Behaviour and Survival by James R Duncan makes the ideal companion for wildlife enthusiasts out to spot Germany's eagle-owl, Eurasian pygmy owl and other owl species.

one. The jay, with its darting flight patterns and calls imitating othe
species, is easy to sight in the foothills; look for flashes of blue on it
wings.

Lynx died out in Germany in the 19th century. They were reintroduce
in the 1980s, only to be illegally hunted to extinction again. Today, a fe
populate the Bavarian Forest national park, although chances of seein
one in the wild are virtually zero. They have also been sighted in uplan
regions of eastern Germany. The wild cat, another indigenous feline
has returned to forest regions, including the Harz Mountains. Wild cat
often breed with domestic cats, making it hard for the untrained eye t
distinguish between the two.

Seals on the North Sea and Baltic Sea coasts are common, especiall
on sandbanks in northern Germany's Wattenmeer. The Wattenmee
also lures migratory birdlife, particularly from March to May and from
August to October when several species stopover to feed on the region'
rich marine life. Summertime sandpipers can be identified by their rust
brown back and dark stripes on a white breast, while the shelduck has a
green head, a broad white stripe around the neck and a red beak. Marsh
geese and eider are other frequent visitors.

Sea eagles, practically extinct in western Germany, are becoming mor
plentiful in eastern Germany, as are falcons, white storks and cranes
The east of the country also sees wolves, which regularly cross the Ode
River from Poland, and European moose, which occasionally appear o
moors and in mixed forests. Forests everywhere provide a habitat for a
wide variety of songbirds, as well as woodpeckers.

Plants

German forests – studded with beech, oak, birch, chestnut (mostly th
nonedible horse-chestnut variety), lime, maple and ash trees – are beau
tiful places to escape the madding crowds and relax. Mixed deciduou
forest carpets river valleys at lower altitudes, and coniferous species grow
thicker as you ascend.

Waldfrüchte (berries) are particularly colourful and, for the most part
poisonous. The same applies to mushrooms, which are essential for the
development of healthy root systems in trees, especially in deciduous
forests. Chanterelle (*Pfifferlinge*) mushrooms are one of the seasonal
culinary delights.

Alpine regions burst with wildflowers – orchids, cyclamen, gentians
pulsatilla, alpine roses, edelweiss and buttercups. Meadow species colou
spring and summer, and great care is taken these days not to cut pastures
until plants have seeded. Visitors should stick to paths, especially in al
pine areas and coastal dunes where ecosystems are fragile. In late August
heather blossom is the particular lure of Lüneburg Heath, northeast o
Hanover.

NATIONAL PARKS

The country's vast and varied natural scapes are protected to varying
degrees by 90 nature parks, 13 biosphere reserves and 13 national parks
although only 0.04% of land is fully protected. In western Germany, the
Upper Middle Rhine Valley is safeguarded as a Unesco World Heritage
Area to prevent further damage.

ENVIRONMENTAL ISSUES

Germans are acutely aware of what needs to be done to protect their
fragile environment. They are fanatical recyclers, true cycling fiends

The highly unlikely title
*Animals in the Third
Reich: Pets, Scapegoats
& the Holocaust* by Klaus
P Fischer and Boria Sax
looks at the treatment
of animals under Hitler's
Third Reich and Nazism's
symbolic use of nature for
its own twisted means.

*Flora and Vegetation of
the Wadden Sea Islands
and Coastal Areas* by
KS Diikema (ed) and
WJ Wolff (ed), remains
indispensable for anyone
spending time in any of
the three Wattenmeer
(Wadden Sea) national
parks.

For comprehensive
national park details
and hot links to park
websites, surf
www.germany-tourism.de.

National Park	Features	Activities	Best Time to Visit	Page
Bavarian Forest	mountain forest & upland moors near the Czech border (243 sq km): deer, hazel grouse, fox, otter, eagle-owl, Eurasian pygmy owl	walking, mountain biking, cross-country skiing, botany	spring & winter	421
Berchtesgaden	lakes, subalpine spruce stands, salt mine & ice cave (210 sq km): eagle, golden eagle, marmot, blue hare, alpine salamander	wildlife watching, walking, skiing	spring & winter	384
Hainich	Europe's largest mixed deciduous forest (76 sq km): beech trees, black storks, wild cats, rare bats	walking	spring	223
Hamburg Wadden Sea	three-island mud-flat park with meadows & sand dunes (120 sq km): sea swallows, arctic terns, sandwich terns	mud-flat walking, bird-watching	spring & autumn (bird-watching), late spring & early autumn (walking)	708
Harz	mountainous granite terrain (158 sq km): deer, red deer, wild boar, black woodpecker, fox, wild cat	walking	spring, summer & autumn	269
Hochharz	caves & spectacular rock formations (58 sq km): black kite, kingfisher, wild cat	walking	any time but weekends (too jam-packed)	273
Jasmund	cretaceous landscape of chalk cliffs, forest, creeks & moors (30 sq km): white-tailed eagle	walking, cycling	not summer (paths like ant trails)	315
Lower Saxony Wadden Sea	salt-marsh & bog landscape (2780 sq km): seal, shell duck	swimming, walking, bird-watching	August & September (bird-watching), late spring & early autumn (walking)	678
Müritz	beech, bogs & lakes galore (318 sq km): sea eagles fish-hawk, crane, white-tailed eagle, Gothland sheep	cycling, canoeing, water hiking, walking, bird-watching	spring, summer & autumn	294
Saxon Switzerland	spectacular sandstone & basalt rock formations (93 sq km): eagle-owl, otter, fat dormouse	walking, climbing, rock climbing	not summer (throngs with Dresden day-trippers)	178
Schleswig-Holstein Wadden Sea	dramatic seascape of dunes, salt marshes & mud flats (4410 sq km): sea life, migratory birds	bird-watching, tidal watching, mud-flat walking, swimming	spring & autumn (bird-watching), late spring & early autumn (walking)	728
Lower Oder Valley	river meadows astride the Oder (165 sq km): black stork, sea eagle, beaver, aquatic warbler, crane	walking, cycling, bird-watching	winter (bird-watching), spring (other activities)	161
Vorpommersche Boddenlandschaft	dramatic Baltic seascape (805 sq km): crane, red deer, wild boar	bird-watching, water sports, walking	autumn (crane watching), summer (water sports)	304

For information on Germany's 90-odd nature parks see www.naturparke.de (German only).

and, since 1998, have given the green-fingered Greens (Die Grünen) a chance to have their say in national policy making as junior partner in Germany's coalition government. See p43 for a Green party lowdown.

Smog alerts are commonplace on the road. Petrol vehicles sport advanced catalysers, and diesel vehicles will be fitted with soot filters by 2005, reducing exhaust emissions by 90%. The government stepped up an ecological tax on petrol, diesel, heating oil, natural gas and electricity in 2002 as part of its ongoing campaign to save energy, cut down on carbon-dioxide emissions and further reduce other forms of pollution. The same year it pledged to reduce Germany's 1990 level of greenhouse gas emissions by 21% between 2008 and 2012 – by 2002, its emissions were already 18.7% down on those notched up 12 years previously.

In forests, measures have been taken to reduce the effects of acid rain (around 65% of forest stands are affected to some degree by acid rain with damage slightly higher in eastern Germany) such as applying lime to reduce unnaturally high acidity levels in the soil. Forests in Germany are, unusually, on the increase as farmland is reafforested.

Germany will shut all 19 of its nuclear energy plants (current generators of 30% of the country's energy needs) by 2020; the first, Stade plant, was closed in mid-November 2003. Until that time, nuclear waste must be stored in interim facilities on the reactor sites and damage caused by plants will be covered by a €2.5 billion pot put in reserve by the government. From 2005, spent-fuel processing will be banned, making storage in sealed castor containers the only option. Much of Germany's 450 tonnes of annual radioactive waste is currently reprocessed in France (La Hague) and Britain (Sellafield).

The issue of nuclear-waste transport and storage was especially sticky in the 1990s when rail transports of waste to storage facilities in Gorleben (Lower Saxony) and Ahaus (North Rhine-Westphalia) were protected from Greenpeace protestors by thousands of police.

Research into renewable energies is underway, with the government investing €30 million into geothermal and solar-power generation programmes, as well as hydroelectricity and biomass research projects. In 2002 around 2.9% of energy (10% of electricity) was generated in an eco-friendly manner by the wind, sun, water and biomass (wood, plants, animal wastes etc). By 2025 the government hopes offshore wind farms alone will provide 15% of electricity. The first pilot project – an 80-turbine farm

DID YOU KNOW?

The green car of the future – an ecofriendly machine that runs more than 150km on a 3L tank of petrol – is being developed by Germany's auto industry.

HOW TO RECYCLE A TEABAG

It might be something of a national joke, but recycling a teabag really does require all four rubbish bins found in Germans homes, at airports and in dozens of other public places.

Germans are Europe's biggest recyclers. Biodegradable waste – garden rubbish, potato peelings, food leftovers, coffee granules and used tea bags (minus metal clip, string and paper tag) – goes in a bio-bin. Recyclable paper, waxed cardboard, cardboard and teabag paper tags go in a second bin, while recyclable plastics – including packaging materials, margarine tubs, empty food tins, cans and teabag clips – go in a third. Everything that is left (including the synthetic string on a teabag) – except glass, batteries and anything else physically capable of being recycled – goes in the fourth 'residuary waste' bin.

Then there are the empty mineral water bottles (plastic and glass), beer cans etc to dispose of. Cunningly, these yield a returnable deposit (look for *Mehrwegflasche* or *Pfandflasche* on the label) of as much as €0.50 per bottle – persuading the laziest of consumers to return their empties to one of 100,000 specified shops and points of sale countrywide.

Germans produce 10kg of rubbish per capita, daily.

ENVIRONMENT: THE BIG PICTURE

Germany hosts a couple of ground-breaking environmental film festivals. In them, hundreds of environment-based films and documentaries by home-grown and international filmmakers are shown on a green screen.

Freiberg hosts the annual Ökomedia International Environmental Film Festival (www.oeko media-institut.de) each year in late October or early November, and Berlin stages the Festival of Environmental Film Festivals (www.ecomove.de) at the end of November.

In 2003 the Agriculture Ministry honoured filmmakers for the first time with Organic Farm Filming Awards – part of a government campaign to up the percentage of organic farms from 4% of all farms to 20% by 2010.

34km west of the Frisian island of Sylt in the North Sea – was given the green light in 2002, with construction to start no later than 2005.

Bavaria now boasts the world's largest solar power plant. Constructed in a former ammunition depot in Hernau, near Regensburg, the €18.4 million project generates enough electricity for 4500 people (over 3.5 million kWh a year).

The Rhine Action Programme (1987–2000) cleaned up the Rhine in what is seen as Europe's environmental turnaround of the century. Declared well and truly dead by 1970, the Upper Rhine was spawning salmon and sea trout again by 1997 – for the first time in 50 years. The transformation was all the more remarkable given that some 15% of the world's chemical industry plants are settled along the river banks. Since the catastrophic chemical spill from a Swiss factory in 1986, chemical pollutants have been reduced by 90%. The longer-term Action Plan High Water, in place until 2020, is working on restoring river banks and important adjoining meadows in a bid to stave off damaging floods such as those witnessed by the Elbe in 2002.

Greenpeace is active in Germany, successfully opposing controversial plans by Shell to sink the Brent Spar oil platform in the North Sea in the 1990s. Coastal shipping and off-shore oil drilling nonetheless remain a serious hazard to both the North and Baltic Seas, and the fragile marine ecosystem supported found by the ever-shifting East Frisian Islands. Environmentalists are as yet unable to determine what impact underwater cable-lines for the proposed offshore wind farms will have on indigenous marine life. An artificial reef, afloat off Nienhagen near Rostock since 2002, will remain there until 2006 in the hope of luring colonies of algae, starfish, mussels and other species back to the Baltic.

Flick through the Global Directory for Environmental Technology for a green listing of German organisations and action groups at www.eco-web.com.

Green information galore, including daily ozone readings from 370 points in Germany, is posted on the Federal Environment Agency's (Umwelt Bundes Amt) website, www.umweltbundes amt.de.

Food & Drink

German cuisine is rooted in a land of meat, pickled cucumbers and potato dumplings – and is hearty. Contemporary German cooking is a lighter, less meaty affair, yet portions can still be giant enough to dwarf the beefiest of appetites.

Beer is king of the drinks cabinet, with wine ranking very much a paltry second. Their wines were mocked for years as cringingly sweet and unfashionable; now Germany's winemakers have been shedding their Liebfraumilch-rules skin and gaining a newfound respect among wine critics worldwide, especially with their startling riesling.

STAPLES & SPECIALITIES

Be it in a German backwater or Berlin's busy heart, bread and sausage (*Brot und Wurst*) reign supreme on the kitchen table. The proof of the pudding? There are no fewer than 200 different bread types and a mind-boggling 1500 sausage species.

Bread

German bread is moist, strong tasting (due to its whole rye grain) and comes in all shapes and sizes: *Weissbrot* is white, *Schwarzbrot* (also called *Vollkornbrot*) is black and like corkboard, while *Bauernbrot* is brown and sour. Sprinkle *Bauernbrot* with sunflower seeds to get *Sonnenblumenbrot*. *Bauernbrot*, *Roggenbrot* and *Pumpernickel* are typical rye breads.

A traditional *Frühstück* (breakfast) is built from bread – smear the centuries-old staple with butter and jam, top it with cheese, salami or other meat, or accompany it with a soft- or hard-boiled egg. Bread isn't dished up with lunch (the main meal of the day), but is served again with a light snack in the evening. A slice of bread buttered with dripping is called *Schmalzbrot*.

Fresh bread rolls (*Semmel* in Bavaria, *Wecken* in the rest of southern Germany, *Brötchen* in the north and *Schrippe* in Berlin) come in dozens of varieties – coated in melted cheese (*Käsesemmel* or *Käsebrötchen*), covered in caraway (*Kümmelsemmel*) or poppy seeds (*Mohnbrötchen*), cooked with sweet raisins (*Rosininbrötchen* or *Rosinenstuten*), studded with sesame seeds (*Sesamsemmel*), sprinkled with sugar (*Salzstangel*) or covered in nuts and grains (several types).

Brezeln are traditional pretzels, covered in rock salt and made to munch on the move or with a beer or three.

GERMANY'S TOP EATS

Germany's 'best' in the conventional sense they might not be, but we followed our stomachs to nose out – several hundred meals later – this tasty cross-section of tastebud ticklers.

Maxwell Edgy urban flair in Berlin (p125).

Im Füchschen Boisterous beer-hall fun and fodder in Düsseldorf (p573).

Auerbachs Keller Faustian classicism in Leipzig (p191).

La Vela Riverfront bustle and dramatic views in Hamburg (p702).

Rosenpalais Bavaria at its best in Regensburg (p414).

Lorenz Minimalist design and fusion fodder in Nuremberg (p392).

Sausage

Throw Germany's primary staple together with its indisputable other and you get what many a German would die for – a *Heisses Würstchen* (hot dog). A staple since the Middle Ages, thanks to the ease with which peasants could use the less appetising bits of the animal that would otherwise be wasted, the sausage *(Wurst)* today is a noble and highly respected part of German cuisine. Strict rules determine the authenticity of sausage types and, in cases such as the Nuremberg sausage, ensure animals' innards remain well away from the cooking pot. Sausage skins are traditionally made from salt-preserved animal intestines, but are more often synthetic today – requiring the sausage to be skinned before eating.

Sausages are commonly served with a slice of bread and a sweet *(süss)* or spicy *(scharf)* mustard *(Senf)*. *Bratwurst* – a generic spiced sausage built from minced pork and veal meat – is cooked up countrywide and can be boiled in beer, baked with apples and cabbage, stewed in a casserole or simply flung on a barbecue. Dozens more sausages, though originating in particular regions, can be tasted throughout Germany: *Blutwurst* is blood sausage (not to be confused with black pudding, which is *Rotwurst* in German), *Leberwurst* is liver sausage and a *Wiener* is what hot-dog fiends worldwide call a Frankfurter. A *Thüringer* is long, thin and spiced, while a *Knackwurst* is lightly tickled with garlic. Juicy regional favourites include Saxony's brain sausage *(Bregenwurst)* and Munich's white rubbery *Weisswurst*, a white veal sausage best downed with a froth-topped *Weissbier* (see p77).

When served as a main course, sausages are best accompanied with a mountain of pickled cabbage, otherwise known as *Sauerkraut* (if it is white) or *Blaukraut* or *Rotkohl* (if the cabbage is red). Preparing this quintessential German side dish entails shredding the cabbage, drowning it in white wine vinegar and slowly cooking it. Braising the cabbage with sliced apples and wine turns it into *Bayrischkraut* or *Weinkraut*. *Sauerkraut* is served with dozens of other standard German item menus too, including *Schnitzel* (a pork, veal or chicken breast pounded flat, coated in egg, dipped in breadcrumbs and pan-fried), pickled pork knuckles *(Eisbein)*, roast chicken *(Rosthähnchen)*, turkey breast *(Putenbrust)* and *Sauerbraten* (marinated and roasted beef swimming in a tangy gravy).

Potatoes, Pasta & Dumplings

It was not until the 16th century that the potato arrived in Germany, but when it did, it arrived with a vengeance. Potatoes can be mashed, fried, grated and then fried, chopped into French fries, or served cold in a potato salad. *Himmel und Erde* (Heaven and Earth) is a side dish of mashed potatoes and stewed apples, frequently served for children or with black pudding. *Pellkartoffeln* come in their jackets, capped with a dollop of quark (a typical German curd cheese). Northerners use potatoes to thicken caraway seed soup *(Kirtagsuppe)*, while Westphalians fry up them into pan-sized pancakes, served with salted fish or sweet jam.

In southern Germany, grains rule over root vegetables. In Baden-Württemberg, potatoes are replaced by *Spätzle* (literally 'little sparrows'), a type of noodle pasta dished up as a main meal or used to dress meat or fish. Thuringians and Bavarians both make *Klösse*, dumplings bound together with pounded flour and potato or bread, while semolina dumplings float in *Griessklösschensuppe* (dumpling soup). Sweeter in all respects than these stomach-pounding bullets are sweet *Knödel* (dumplings) conjured up for dessert in households countrywide. *Dampfnudeln* are hot yeast dumplings coated in a vanilla sauce, and Bavarian

Shop for *Brot und Wurst* as in Germany at www.germandeli.com.

Pickled Herring and Pumpkin Pie: A Nineteenth-century Cookbook for German Immigrants to America by Henriette Davids and Louis Pitschmann was first published in the 19th century to help German emigrants adapt their palate without losing that traditional German taste.

Senfknödel come dunked in milk. Quark, flour and eggs are key ingredients of all these sweet dumplings, which, like their savoury counterparts, are poached in water.

Cooking the German Way by Helga Parnell is one of the simpler German cookbooks on the market, ideal for those seeking a basic culinary background of the region. It includes a history as well as recipes for basic German dishes.

Sugar & Spice

Dumplings aside, dessert *(Nachspeise* or *Nachtisch)* usually consists of something light such as custard (often served with fruit), *Rote Grütze* (a tart fruit compote topped with vanilla sauce), ice cream or a fruit salad.

But the sweet toothed are not left aching. Germans eat the most delectable cakes with vigour during *Kaffee und Kuchen,* an afternoon ritual that sees Germans sit down to coffee and cakes around 3pm. For a sweet list of cakes you can expect to wrap your tongue around, see p85.

Christmas brings its own sweeter-than-sweet array of delectable delights (see the boxed text below).

Regional Dishes

Northern German cuisine is heavier and meatier (read: lots of root vegetables) than that of the south where lighter grains and dairy products dominate. (Health fiends note that 'dairy' tends to translate as 'greasy' in Bavaria.) Fish swims in on the Frisian islands and Germany's northern coast, while subtle French influences (snail soup and the like) find their way into kitchens in Saarland and Baden-Württemberg. Cosmopolitan Berlin is so sophisticated these days that it's hard-pushed to drum up any dishes it can call its own beyond the *Berliner Boulette* (fried meat patty) and *Currywurst* (curried sausage).

No two dishes better sum up northern Germany's winter-warming seafaring fodder than *Labskaus,* a thick fish, meat and potato stew originally from Hamburg and usually made with herring and salted beef, topped with a fried egg; and *Grünkohl mit Pinkel,* another feisty concoction combining steamed kale with pork belly, bacon and *Pinkelwurst* (a pork, beef, oat and onion sausage from Bremen). Eel soup *(Aalsuppe)* and herring in all its guises (raw, smoked, pickled or rolled in sour cream) are favourites in Schleswig-Holstein and Lower Saxony.

In eastern Germany, Leipzig's *Leipziger Allerlei,* a colourful vegetarian creation that sees carrots, cauliflower, peas, green beans and mushrooms share the same plate, makes a refreshing change from the carnivorous norm.

Spices and herbs play an important role in northern and eastern German cuisine, due no less to the region's strategic location on the North and Baltic Seas coupled with its proximity to Scandinavian and Eastern

---

...AND ALL THINGS NICE

German Christmas, with its sweet and spicy cookies and cakes, is a fiesta of all things nice. *Christstollen* is a spiced cake loaded with sultanas, raisins and candied peel, sprinkled with icing sugar and occasionally spruced up inside with a ball of marzipan. Germany's Christmas cake is rarely baked in German homes today, but sold in abundance in Christmas markets – *Stollen* from Dresden is the best.

Cookies, by contrast, are cooked in every home countrywide, with age-old family recipes being passed between generations. *Leckerli* (honey-flavoured ginger biscuits), *Spekulatius* (almond biscuits), *Lebkuchen* (gingerbread), *Nürnberger Lebkuchen* (soft cookies with nuts, fruit peel, honey and spices from Nuremberg) and Florentines (candied fruit and nut-studded biscuits topped with chocolate) are but some of the dozens of types. Little balls of *Lübecker Marzipan* (marzipan from Lübeck) are equally sweet.

European countries. Caraway seeds, juniper berries, dill and marjoram dominate.

Roast beef marinated in spiced vinegar and dressed on the plate in a dark gravy *(Rheinischer Sauerbraten)* is a Rhineland favourite, while Palatinates eats stuffed pork belly *(Saumagen)*. Neighbouring Hesse and Westphalia produce outstanding cured and smoked hams. Meat-stuffed pasta cushions *(Maultaschen)* and *Geschnetzeltes* (veal slices with mushrooms and onions baked in a white wine and cream sauce) are dishes worth nibbling in Baden-Württemberg. Quark, the German equivalent of cottage cheese, accounts for 50% of total cheese consumption in Germany.

No part of the pig is safe from Bavarian chefs who cook up its knuckles *(Schweinshax'n)*, ribs *(Rippchen)*, tongue *(Züngerl)* and belly *(Wammerl)*. *Pfälzer Saumagen* (stuffed stomach of pork) is Helmut Kohl's old-time favourite. Pork meat is minced to make Liver Cheese *(Leberkäs)*, a meatloaf that has nothing to do with liver or cheese. Cows suffer a similar fate: *Tellerfleisch* translates as slices of lean boiled beef accompanied by horseradish or mustard, but some might find Bavarian *Kronfleisch* (beef diaphragm) less appealing.

> Discover 101 things to do with a pig with Olli Leeb's *Bavarian Cooking*, jam-packed with cultural and culinary insight into one of Germany's tastiest regional cuisines.

DRINKS

Beer and wine are Germany's staple drinks (see below). Schnapps is the German tippler's delight. Actually a generic term for any spirit or hard liquor, Schnapps is drunk as an aperitif or digestive rather than as a means of getting blotto. It is best served at room temperature, tipped back in shots, and can be made from apples *(Apfelschnapps)*, pears *(Birnenschnapps)*, plums *(Pflaumenschnapps; Zwetschgengeist* in Bavaria), raspberries *(Himbeergeist)* or wheat *(Kornschnapps)*.

Coffee is usually served fresh, strong and accompanied by condensed milk and sugar. The American bottomless cup has yet to hit Germany, but the French-style milky breakfast coffee has: in fashionable Berlin, trendies hang over bowls of *Milchkaffee* (milk coffee/café latte), containing large amounts of hot milk. Tea comes as an empty cup and teabag.

No table is properly laid without a bottle of sparkling mineral water *(Mineralwasser)*, with loads of bubbles *(mit Kohlensäure)* or a modest sprinkling *(wenig Kohlensäure)*. In bars and cafés, flavoured fizzy mineral water *(Mineralwasser mit Aroma)* is fashionable. Truly still mineral water is an expensive rarity, and drinking tap water is rarely done.

> **DID YOU KNOW?**
>
> Germans are the third biggest fizzy water drinkers in Europe – they downed 113.7L per capita of the stuff in 2002 (compared with 94L and 19.4L per capita drank by the French and British respectively).

Beer

Few countries match Germany beer-wise: be it bottom or top fermented, heavily malted or hoppy, drunk out of a 0.2L glass or served in a traditional Stein, accompanied by *Wurst* under chestnut trees in the Bavarian Alps or cooked up with pickled herring in a northern coastal resort, German beer is must-sup when in Germany.

Long ago, Germanic tribes incorporated beer into their sacrificial rituals, using herbs and spices to make the brew. German monks came up with a tastier hop-made brew by AD 1000 and quickly turned brewing into a lucrative sideline, free of taxes imposed on private secular breweries by local rulers. With the clampdown on the sale of monastical-made beer by Kaiser Sigismund (r. 1410–37) in the 15th century, beer brewing fell into the hands of secular city governments – the Benedictine monastery in Andechs near Munich is one of 11 monasteries to still brew beer; see p357.

Stringent laws govern how beer is made in Germany (prompting an EU ruling to the effect that European beers must not be excluded from Germany's lucrative beer market). Passed in Bavaria in 1516, the German

> Horst Dornbusch's *Prost!: The Story of German Beer* is exactly that.

Anyone wanting to tour the Bavarian capital's hundreds of beer gardens, halls and bars – with intent to drink – would do well to invest in the 200-odd page *The Beer Drinker's Guide to Munich* by Larry Hawthorne.

DID YOU KNOW?

What did Germany's first railway line carry when it opened between Nuremberg and Fürth in 1835? Beer.

Everything else about beer is at www.allaboutbeer.com.

Reinheitsgebot (purity law) applies countrywide today and demands that German breweries use just four ingredients to brew beer – malt, yeast, hops and water. To make beer, barley is cooked in a kiln to malt it; it's then mashed, soaked in water and strained to make wort. Hop flowers are boiled up with the wort, releasing bitter resins and hop oils to give beer its distinctive taste. The beer is then cooled, left to ferment with yeast to produce the alcohol, separated from the yeast, then aged and carbonated. Top and bottom fermenting techniques refer to the type of yeast used, and where the yeast prefers to live while it does its work – at the top or bottom of the brewing vessel. Bottom brewing is the traditional method and is used to produce older-style beers like ales, porters, stouts and wheat beers, while top brewing is used for lagers, pilsners, Dortmunders and Bocks.

The distinctive tastes of Germany's 5000 different beer labels are derived from simple variations in this basic production process. Low-alcohol beer contains up to 2.8% alcohol, *Schankbier* (draught beer) contains 2.8% to 4.6% alcohol, *Vollbier* (literally 'full beer') has an alcohol content of 4.6% to 5.6%, and the potent *Starkbier* (strong beer) is over 5.5% alcohol.

Many beers are regional, meaning a Saxon Rechenberger cannot be found in Cologne, where the locally brewed Päffgen Kölsch is the tastier choice. Many beer fiends believe the earthy, monk-brewed Andechs Doppelbock Dunkel (see p357), to be among the world's best beers. Mainstream varieties include Pils (Pilsener), a hoppy beer with a creamy head and alcohol content of around 4.8%; the less bitter Helles Lagerbier, a pale-coloured lager found in Bavaria, Baden-Württemberg and the Ruhr region and containing 4.6% to 5% alcohol, strong malt aromas and a slightly sweet taste; and Weizenbier/Weissbier (wheat beer), which is made from wheat (rather than barley) and contains 5.4% alcohol. A Hefeweizen has a stronger shot of yeast, whereas Kristallweizen is clearer with more fizz. Beer lovers rank the filtered Traunstein Hofbräu Weisse, with its spicy vanilla and banana overtones, as one of Bavaria's best wheat beers; Hofbräuhaus Traunstein in Traunstein brews it.

German beer is brewed by 1279 breweries (almost 75% of all those in the EU) in Germany. Yet the country is not a leader in the global market. A sharp fall in beer consumption in Germany in the past decade (from 142L per head in the early 1990s to 121.5L in 2002) has forced hundreds of traditionally family-run breweries to shut up shop, merge with others or be swallowed up by the big-boy brewers to stay afloat. Bremen-based Beck's, brewer of one of Germany's best-known beers since 1873, was bought out by Belgian beer giant Interbrew in 2002, while Hamburg's Holsten (founded

---

BREWERY TOURS

Touring a brewery is enlightening. Holsten (www.holsten.de) runs breweries in Hamburg, Braunschweig in Lower Saxony, Dresden in Central Saxony and Görlitz in Eastern Saxony, as well as a beer museum in Lüneburg in lower Saxony – all of which can be visited (details are on its website).

Beck's Brewery (Bremen), Warsteiner in the gentle Sauerland mountains (Warstein, North Rhine-Westphalia) and Friesisches Brauhaus zu Jever (Jever, Lower Saxony), where Jever beer has been brewed since 1848, are other big-name breweries that run tours. Originally a family business, the latter was bought up by Brau und Brunnen – a German brewer of 19 regional beer brands including Rostocker, Berliner Pilsner, Frankfurter Pilsner and Dortmunder Union – in 1994. The art of 19th-century beer making is unravelled at Maisel's Brauerei- und Büttnerei-Museum in Bayreuth (Bavaria), the world's most comprehensive beer museum (or so says the *Guinness Book of Records*). Tour details are included in the regional chapters.

1879), 48%-owned by a New York-born son of German émigrés, has its roots firmly embedded in the USA. Since 2000, German brewers have lost 18% of annual sales to other international beer giants, while beer brewed by German microbreweries (family-run breweries with an annual production of less than 500,000L) accounts for just 2% of national production.

Bavarian beer gardens and beer halls are easily the most atmospheric spots to swill – see the respective regional chapters for recommendations. Local drinking culture also can be lapped up in abundance at one of Germany's many beer festivals: Munich's Oktoberfest (see p341) is Europe's most legendary.

BEER GLOSSARY

Alkoholfreies Bier – Nonalcoholic beer.

Alt (old) – A dark, top-fermented full beer with malted barley from the Düsseldorf area.

Berliner Weisse – With around 2.8% alcohol, draught or Schankbier is mostly brewed in and around Berlin. It contains lactic acid, giving it a slightly sour taste, and a blend of malted wheat and barley. Top-fermented, it's often drunk *mit Grün* (with green), which is with woodruff syrup, or *mit Schuss*, which is with raspberry syrup.

Bockbier/Doppelbock – These two strong beers have around 7% alcohol, but Doppelbock is slightly stronger. Though usually bottom-fermented, both Weizenbock and Weizendoppelbock are two top-fermented wheat beers produced in the south. There's a 'Bock' for almost every occasion: Maibock (usually drunk in May/spring), Weihnachtsbock (brewed for Christmas) etc. All Bock beers originate from Einbeck, near Hanover. Eisbock (ice Bock) is dark and more aromatic.

Dampfbier (steam beer) – Originating from Bayreuth in Bavaria, it's top-fermented and has a fruity flavour.

Dunkles Lagerbier (dark lager) – Dunkel (dark) is brewed throughout Germany, but especially in Bavaria. With a light use of hops, it's full-bodied with a strong malt aroma. Malt is dried at a high temperature, lending it a dark colour, and it's bottom-fermented.

Export – Traditionally with higher alcohol to help it survive a long journey, this beer is closely associated today with Dortmund, and is often dry to slightly sweet.

Helles Lagerbier (pale lager) – Helles (pale or light) refers to the colour, not alcohol content, which is still around 4.6% to 5%. Brewing strongholds are in Bavaria, Baden-Württemberg and in the Ruhr region. Bottom-fermented, it has strong malt aromas and is slightly sweet.

Hofbräu – This is a brewery belonging to a royal court for Hof – for some time in Bavaria only a few nobles enjoyed the right to brew wheat beer.

Klosterbräu – This type of brewery belongs to a monastery.

Kölsch – By law, this top-fermented beer can only be brewed in or around Cologne. It has about 4.8% alcohol, a solid hop flavour and pale colour, and is served in glasses (0.2L) called *Stangen* (literally 'sticks').

Leichtbier (light beer) – These low-alcohol beers have about 2% to 3.2% alcohol.

Malzbier (malt beer) – A sweet, aromatic, full-bodied beer, it is brewed mainly in Bavaria and Baden-Württemberg.

Märzen (March) – Full-bodied with strong malt aromas, it's traditionally brewed in March. Today, it's associated with the Oktoberfest.

Obergäriges Bier – Top-fermented beer.

Pils (pilsener) – This bottom-fermented full beer with pronounced hop flavour and a creamy head has an alcohol content of around 4.8% and is served throughout Germany.

Rauchbier (smoke beer) – This dark beer has a fresh, spicy or 'smoky' flavour.

Schwarzbier (black beer) – Slightly stronger, this dark, full beer has an alcohol content of about 4.8% to 5%. Full-bodied, it's bottom fermented using roasted malt.

Untergäriges Bier – Bottom-fermented beer.

Weizenbier/Weissbier (wheat beer) – Predominating in the south, especially in Bavaria, it has around 5.4% alcohol. A Hefeweizen has a stronger shot of yeast, whereas Kristallweizen is clearer with more fizz. Fruity and spicy, it's sometimes served with a slice of lemon, which ruins the head and, beer purists say, also the flavour.

For more bare beer facts, statistics, beer-cooking tips and more, surf with German Federation of Brewers at www.brauer-bund.de.

DID YOU KNOW?

Germany only produces 10% of the world's beer output; 89% of German beer is drunk in Germany.

German Wheat Beer by Eric Warner provides an insightful history of wheat-beer brewing, as well as tips, tricks and recipes for home- and microbrewers.

Wine

Wine and wine-making techniques were brought to Germany by the Romans and elaborated upon by monks in monasteries – until the early 19th century when Napoleon carved up the church vineyards and sold them to private interests.

Today's southern-facing vineyards carpet an area of 100,000 hectares on the Rhine and Moselle riverbanks in southwest Germany. White-wine varieties predominate and tend to be medium-dry *(halbtrocken)* or sweet *(lieblich)* rather than dry *(trocken)*. The most widely planted grape variety in Germany, the Müller-Thurgau or Rivaner grape, has a slight muscat flavour and is less acidic than its sister riesling or Kerner grape varieties. The Gewürztraminer produces spicy wines with an intense bouquet, while 2% of German vineyards are planted with the robust, soft and full-bodied Ruländer (Grauburgunder), known to the rest of the world as Pinot Gris.

German reds are light and lesser known. Spätburgunder, also known as Pinot Noir, is the best of the bunch and goes into some velvety, full-bodied reds with an occasional (and much welcome) almond taste. The hearty and fruity Trollinger grape, grown in Württemberg, and the light and mild Portugieser of Austrian origin are two other red grape varieties.

Apple wine *(Ebbelwei* or *Ebbelwoi)* from southern Hesse (see p549) can be drunk pure, with a shot of mineral water or with lemonade, and is a fine alternative to a straightforward red or white. *Glühwein*, a cinnamon-spiced hot and mulled wine drink, is served countrywide during the crisp and cold weeks preceding Christmas.

WINE REGIONS

If you buy just one bottle of wine, make it a Moselle-Saar-Ruwer riesling from the Mosel-Saar-Ruwer region, one of the 13 wine-growing regions in Germany. It is here, on some of the world's steepest vineyards where grapes are still hand-picked, that some of the best German wines are grown. Slate soil contributes a flinty taste to these racy fragrant wines with a fruity bouquet, which are made from the Riesling grape and drunk young or old. Chalkier riverside soils are planted with the Elbing grape, an ancient Roman variety.

East of the Moselle, the Nahe region produces fragrant, fruity and full-bodied wines with a fairly neutral nose using Müller-Thurgau and Silvaner grapes as well as Riesling. Riesling grape harvests form the mainstay of Rheingau and Mittelrhein (Middle Rhine), which are two other highly respected wine-growing pockets whose fragrant and lively rieslings easily challenge neighbouring Mosel-Saar-Ruwer as 'best German wine' for many aficionados. Rheingau Spätburgunder reds are also excellent.

Germany's much-mocked Liebfraumilch wine was born in the Rhein-hessen, a valley south of Rheingau. Various grapes flourish both here (rieslings from Nierstein rate among Germany's finest) and in Pfalz (Palatinate), Germany's most productive wine-growing region one hop south near the French border. Mellow and fiery reds from Ahr, one of Germany's smallest wine-growing regions along the Ahr River, are rarely sold outside the region.

Heading into Baden-Württemberg on the Rhine's eastern bank, wine lovers can get tipsy on local wine festivals in pinprick-sized Hess-ische Bergstrasse (try Heppenheim in late June) or enjoy a tipple or three in the Baden wine region, which runs south from Heidelberg to the northern shore of Lake Constance and produces fine whites, full-

Germany's wine market, from medieval times to present, is the fascinating focus of *The Wines of Germany* by Stephen Brook who, among other things, addresses the question of why German wine has long been mocked.

Want to see what the wine critics say? Don't know what wine to serve with braised rabbit? Go to www.germanwineusa.org.

The Atlas of German Wines and *Traveller's Guide to the Vineyards* by Hugh Johnson is an informative and practical companion for travellers interested in touring and tasting the vineyards and wines of southern Germany.

bodied and racy Spätburgunder reds, as well as the popular Spätburgunder Weissherbst rosé wine. Loads more fruity reds can be sniffed and
spat next door in Württemberg, Germany's largest red-wine producing
region around Stuttgart.

Dry earthy whites from around Würzburg in the Franken region are
sold in a small green flagon known as a *Bocksbeutel*; for several historic
wine-tasting opportunities, see p360. In Saale/Unstrut, Germany's
northernmost wine area, medium whites and the GDR's legendary
Rotkäppchen (Little Red Riding Hood) sparkling wine can be tasted at
the Landesweingut Kloster Pforta in Schulpforte, a stunning estate with
a 1000-year-old vineyard (see p260).

Elbtal (Elbe Valley) sparkling wines are the mainstay of the Sachsen
vineyards, further east around Dresden and Meissen.

For more information on
German wine-growing
regions, grape varieties,
wine tours and courses,
visit the German Wine
Institute (Deutsches
Weininstitut)
www.deutscheweine.de.

WINE GLOSSARY

Auslese – A 'selected harvest', it is usually intense and sweet.

Beerenauslese (BA) – Grapes are picked overripe, and it's usually a dessert wine.

Deutscher Landwein (country wine) – Landwein is usually dry or semi-dry.

Deutscher Tafelwein (table wine) – This is the lowest category of wine and mostly poor
quality.

Eiswein – Grapes are picked and pressed while frozen (very sweet).

QbA (Qualitätswein bestimmter Anbaugebiete) – The lowest category of quality wine.

QmP (Qualitätswein mit Prädikat) – 'Quality wine of distinction'.

Qualitätswein – Wine from one of the 13 defined wine-growing regions, which has to pass a
tasting test.

Sekt – Sparkling wine.

Spätauslese – Literally 'selected late-harvest', this type of wine has concentrated flavours,
but is not necessarily sweet.

Trockenbeerenauslese (TBA) – The grapes are so overripe they are shrivelled (intensely
sweet) and resemble raisins.

A region-based book,
*All Along the Rhine:
Recipes, Wine & Lore*
from Germany, France,
Switzerland, Austria,
Liechtenstein & Holland
by Kay Shaw Nelson,
provides a mouth-
watering choice for trav-
ellers with a penchant for
fine food and wine.

WHERE TO EAT & DRINK

German restaurants are formal places touting uniformed waiters, menus
the length of your arm, linen tablecloths, good service and high prices.
Diners seeking authentic local cuisine in an atmospheric setting should
steer clear of restaurants tucked in local town-hall basements (*Ratskeller*) –
traditional German dishes might well by dished up in these tourist-
orientated imitators and the atmosphere will buzz (with tourists) all right,
but prices are high and food quality is low. Old town squares are other
hot spots for over-rated, overpriced places to dine.

Surveying those already munching before committing your own palate
is one way of sorting out the good from the bad; restaurants filled with
smiling Germans are usually choice spots. German-only (rather than
English) menus (*Speisekarte*) displayed outside an establishment are another good sign; you might well end up with pig trotters on your plate,
but the cuisine and atmosphere will most surely be authentic.

Diners seeking somewhere less formal can opt for a *Gaststätte*, a relaxed and often more 'local' place to eat with a large menu, daily specials
and a beer garden out the back. Equally inviting are small bistros calling
themselves *Weinkeller* or *Bierkeller* (cellars serving wine or beer), which
cook up light meals as well as serving glasses of wine or beer. Most cafés
and bars serve coffee and light snacks as well as alcohol.

Bills are paid directly at the table and always include a service charge of
around 15%. Most people still leave a tip nonetheless – unless of course
the place has left them vowing never to return again.

Quick Eats

A *Stehcafé* is a stand-up café where sweet cravers can indulge in coffee an cakes at speed and on the cheap. Stand-up food stalls (*Schnellimbiss* or sim ply *Imbiss*) around town make handy speed-feed stops for savoury fodde In Berlin and other cities, some stalls cook up quick Greek, Italian, Middl Eastern and Chinese bites. Pizza joints are a dime a dozen countrywide.

Germany's Turkish population has donated the doner kebab to it snack repertoire. Kiosks and takeaway restaurants in every city and tow sell slices of roasted beef, chicken or lamb sandwiched inside pitta brea with onions, tomato, tahini and spices for around €3. Most kebab joint also do veggie versions, as well as salads, sandwiches smothered wit *caçik*, the Turkish equivalent to Greek *tzatziki* (a garlic, cucumber an yogurt sauce) and *lahmacun* (Turkish pizza comprising salad vegetable piled onto a pancake-shaped bread, topped with a spicy red sauce, driz zled with *tzatziki* and rolled up like a burrito).

Other street offerings include pizza slices (€1 to €2.50), hot dogs an sandwiches. In the north, herring and other marinated fish abound while fresh-fish sandwiches are a speciality of Nordsee – a countrywid quick-eat chain.

Bavarian beer gardens typically serve light snacks such as fresh warn pretzels *(Brez'n)*, Bavarian-style meat loaf *(Leberkäs)* and radishes *(Radi* to their beer-swilling clientele.

VEGETARIANS & VEGANS

While vegetarians will have few tummy grumbles in Berlin and other cit ies where budget eateries, cafés and restaurants dedicated to the land o vegetables do exist, provincial Germany might raise a rumble. Vegetable cooked with meat are often considered meat-free, while many so-called vegetarian places serve fish or chicken.

But all is not lost in this carnivorous land. Most city-based Thai, Viet namese and other Asian eateries cook up dishes suitable for vegetarians and a couple of regional dishes do not – miraculously – contain meat *Leipziger AllerLei* (see p76) is a safe vegetarian option in Western Saxony while vegetarians in Frankfurt can feast on *Grüne Sosse* – a tasty gree sauce eaten as a main dish on top of boiled potatoes or hard-boiled eggs Fresh basil, chives, cress, dill, sorrel, parsley and tarragon (estragon are among the wealth of herbs to be found in this green, cream-based sauce – a seasonal dish available early spring to early autumn. Vegetable or cheese-stuffed strudel (*Gemüsestrudel* or *Topfenstrudel*), potato pancakes (*Kartoffelpuffer*) and potato and semolina dumplings (*Erdäp felknödel*) are more widespread veg-inspired offerings.

Vegans will certainly suffer hunger pangs. Most salads come with cheese and/or a mayonnaise-based salad dressing, and many 'vegetarian pizzas contain eggs.

The New German Cookbook: More than 230 Contemporary and Trad-itional Recipes by Lamar Elmore, Jean Anderson and Hedy Wuerz, and *The German Cookbook: a Complete Guide to Mastering Authentic German Cooking* by Mimi Sgeraton are two other handy little recipe numbers to have on your kitchen shelf.

For a list of wholly-vegetarian and veg-friendly dining spots in Berlin, Hamburg, Frankfurt, Heidelberg and other towns in Germany see www.vegdining.com.

EATING ATLAS

Stuck for somewhere to eat? The *Schlemmer Atlas* (www.schlemmer-atlas.de) is the Michelin of Germany. Published annually, the restaurant listings guide reviews hundreds of restaurants throughout Germany, ranging from one-star joints serving 'ambitious cuisine with particularly recommended regional cuisine' to palatial five-star palaces known for their gourmet cooking. Reviews are in German but there are explanations to the many symbols – that indicate if qual-ity beer is available on tap, if the sommelier serves exceptional wine vintages, and the like – in English. Bookshops sell it.

WHINING & DINING

Dining with kids is by no means a whining affair in Germany. High chairs are a permanent fixture in restaurants – upmarket and budget alike – and, if you're lucky, the waiter will come clad with damp cloth at the end of your meal to wipe sticky little fingers clean. Most *Gaststätte* and less formal restaurants offer a small choice of *Kindermenü* (children's menu) and dishes for children (*Kinderteller* or *Für unsere kleinen Gäste*) and those that don't will most certainly try to meet any special small-appetite requirements. Asking for a glass of water for the little one will only yield an expensive bottle of fizzy mineral water. Eating establishments are not equipped with nappy-changing facilities, and some fast-food and quick-eat places have a fold-down changing table in the women's loo.

Supermarkets sell a vast range of ready-made baby food and toddler meals – predominantly organic – as well as formula milk, organic fruit juices and teas.

HABITS & CUSTOMS

Germans eat three square meals a day – breakfast (*Frühstück*), lunch (*Mittagessen*) and dinner (*Abendessen*) – in addition to coffee and cakes (see p76).

Breakfast at home is served on a wooden board (rather than plate). Great animal-shaped boards, complete with a hollowed-out eye to prop up a hard-boiled egg, can often be found at markets. Yogurt, quark, muesli, cereal and fruit salad, as well as the typical breakfast staples (see p74), feature in hotel buffets.

Traditionally lunch is the main meal of the day. Many restaurants tout lunchtime dishes or a fixed lunch menu (*Gedeck* or *Tagesmenü*) of the day (usually a salad, soup or starter, a main course and occasionally a drink, for a fixed price). Dinner is dished up at home about 7pm and in restaurants from around 5pm to 11pm. Both meals are relaxed and require few airs and graces beyond the obligatory *Guten Appetit* (literally 'good appetite'), exchanged between diners before eating. German workers lunching at shared tables exchange a courtesy *Mahlzeit* (literally 'mealtime') before tucking in.

Restaurants in large cities on weekend nights get crowded, so it's best to book a table. Few slot in more than two seatings per evening, making diners feel more than welcome to linger over coffee or a digestive liqueur (*Magenbitter*). *Jägermeister* is a popular digestive, often served on the house. The bill is presented when you request it. An astonishing number of restaurants do not accept credit cards.

When ordering coffee or tea, specify whether you want a cup or pot. After-dinner coffee drinkers wanting a small strong black coffee (rather than a big cup of filter coffee) should ask for an espresso. At home most Germans make coffee using a coffee-filter machine. A highly irritating custom, particularly prevalent in tourist resorts, is the refusal to serve a solitary cup of coffee on the outdoor terrace of a café or restaurant. Tea drinkers with a penchant for milk will have to ask for milk.

Prost (cheers!) is the toast used for alcoholic drinks and requires everyone at the table to raise a full glass and chink it lightly against those of their fellow drinkers. Several toasts can be made during a meal.

Soft drinks come in cans (*Dosen*) or bottles (from 33cL to 2L) and are widely available, although the diet versions less so. German tap water is drinkable, but few Germans indulge in it. Asking for a glass or jug of tap water in a restaurant is a grave social blunder.

A Culinary Voyage through Germany by the former chancellor's wife, Hannelore Kohl, takes travellers on a voyage of German culinary regions, with recipes by the good wife herself and commentary by Helmut.

Kerry Stewart's *The Hungry Traveller* appeases the feistiest of appetites with its practical eat-your-way-around Germany approach. Eating customs, shopping tips, markets and key German-English culinary terms are among its contents.

See how traditional central European cuisine has influenced German fodder in *From Stroganov to Strudel* by Lesley Chamberlain (ed), a great recipe book weighed down with sauerkraut, dumpling, stew and other traditional German, Austrian, Hungarian and Czech recipes.

EAT YOUR WORDS

Pronunciation guidelines are included in the Language chapter (p776).

Useful Phrases

Can you recommend ...? — *Können Sie ... empfehlen?*
ker-nen zee ... emp-*fay*-len

... a restaurant — *... ein Restaurant*
ain res-to-*rang*

... a bar/pub — *... eine Kneipe*
ai-ne *knai*-pe

Where would you go for ...? — *Wo kann man hingehen, um ...?*
vaw kan man *hin*-gay-en um ...

... local specialities — *... örtliche Spezialitäten zu essen*
ert-li-khe shpe-tsya-li-*tay*-ten tsoo e-sen

... a cheap meal — *... etwas Billiges zu essen*
et-vas *bi*-li-ges tsoo e-sen

... a celebration — *... etwas zu feiern*
et-vas tsoo *fai*-ern

I would like to reserve a table for ... — *Ich möchte einen Tisch für ... reservieren.*
ikh *merkh*-te ai-nen tish für ... re-zer-*vee*-ren

... (two) people — *(zwei) Personen*
(tsvai) per-*zaw*-nen

... (eight) o'clock — *(acht) Uhr*
(akt) oor

I'm starving! — *Ich bin am Verhungern!*
ikh bin am fer-*hung*-ern

Are you still serving food? — *Gibt es noch etwas zu essen?*
gipt es nokh *et*-vas tsoo e-sen

Do you have ...? — *Haben Sie ...?*
hah-ben zee

... a menu in English? — *... eine englische Speisekarte*
ai-ne *eng*-li-she shpai-ze-kar-te

... kosher food — *... koscheres Essen*
kaw-she-res e-sen

... vegetarian food — *... vegetarisches Essen*
ve-ge-*tah*-ri-shes e-sen

What would you recommend? — *Was empfehlen Sie?*
vas emp-*fay*-len zee

What's in that dish? — *Was ist in diesem Gericht?*
vas ist in *dee*-zem ge-*rikht*

Is it cooked in meat stock? — *Ist es in Fleischbrühe?*
ist es in *flaish*-brü-e

Does it take long to prepare? — *Dauert das lange?*
dow-ert das *lang*-e

I'd like a local speciality. — *Ich möchte etwas Typisches aus der Region.*
ikh *merkh*-te *et*-vas tü-pi-shes ows dair re-*gyawn*

That was delicious! — *Das hat hervorragend geschmeckt!/Das war sehr lecker!*
das hat her-*fawr*-rah-gent ge-*shmekt*/das vahr zair *le*-ker

My compliments to the chef! — *Mein Kompliment an den Koch!*
main kom-pli-*ment* an dayn kokh

would like ... , please.   *Ich möchte ... , bitte.*
ikh *merkh*-te ... *bi*-te
.. a cup of tea/coffee   *eine Tasse Tee/Kaffee*
ai-ne *ta*-se tay/*ka* fay
... with (milk)   *... mit (Milch)*
mit (milkh)
The bill, please.   *Die Rechnung, bitte.*
dee *rekh*-nung, *bi*-te

Menu Decoder
STARTERS
Bauernsuppe (*bow*-ern-zu-pe) – cabbage and sausage 'Farmer's soup'
Fleischbrühe (*flaish*-brü-e) – bouillon
Frühlingssuppe/Gemüsesuppe (*frü*-lings-zu-pe/ge-*moo*-ze-zu-pe) – vegetable soup
Graupensuppe (*grow*-pen-zu-pe) – barley soup
Kieler Sprotten (*kee*-ler *shpro*-ten) – small smoked herring
Kohlroulade (*kawl*-ru-lah-de) – minced meat stuffed cabbage leaves
Vorspeisen (*fawr*-shpai-zen) – starters

MAIN COURSES
Brathuhn (*braht*-hoon) – roast chicken
Eintopf (*ain*-topf) – one-pot meat and veg stew
Hackbraten (*hak*-brah-ten) – meatloaf
Hauptgerichte (*howpt*-ge-rikh-te) – main courses
Holsteiner Schnitzel (*hol*-shtai-ner *shni*-tsel) – veal with fried egg, served with seafood
Rheinischer Sauerbraten (*rai*-ni-sher *zow*-er-brah-ten) – marinated meat, slightly sour and roasted
Schweinshaxen (*shvains*-hak-sen) – crispy Bavarian pork leg with potato dumplings

DESSERTS & CAKES
Aachener Printen (*ah*-khe-ner *prin*-ten) – cakes with chocolate, nuts, fruit peel, honey and spices
Apfelstrudel (*ap*-fel-shtroo-del) – apple strudel
Eis (ais) – ice cream
Cremespeise (*kraym*-shpai-ze) – mousse
Eierkuchen (*ai*-er-koo-khen) – pancake
Frankfurter Kranz (*frank*-fur-ter krants) – sponge cake with rum, butter cream and cherries
(Frankfurt)
Gebäck (ge-*bek*) – pastries
Kompott (kom-*pot*) – stewed fruit
Kuchen (*koo*-khen) – cake
Nachspeisen (*nahkh*-shpai-zen) – desserts
Obatzter (*aw*-bats-ter) – Bavarian soft cheese mousse
Obstsalat (*awpst*-za-laht) – fruit salad
Torte (*tor*-te) – layer cake

Glossary
BASICS

bread	*Brot*	brawt
bread roll	*Brötchen*	bret-khen
butter	*Butter*	bu-ter
cheese	*Käse*	kay-ze
egg(s)	*Ei(er)*	ai(-er)
mustard	*Senf*	zenf
milk	*Milch*	milkh
noodles	*Nudeln*	noo-deln
pepper	*Pfeffer*	pfe-ffer

rice	*Reis*	rais
salt	*Salz*	zalts
sugar	*Zucker*	*tsu*-ker

FISH

carp	*Karpfen*	karp-fen
cod	*Dorsch*	dorsh
eel	*Aal*	ahl
fish	*Fisch*	fish
herring	*Hering*	*hay*-ring
prawn	*Garnele*	gar-*nay*-le
trout	*Forelle*	fo-*re*-le

MEAT

beef	*Rindfleisch*	rint-flaish
chicken	*Hähnchen or Huhn*	hayn-khen or hoon
chopped or minced meat	*Hackfleisch*	hak-flaish
duck	*Ente*	en-te
filet, tenderloin	*Filet*	fi-*lay*
ham	*Schinken*	shing-ken
game	*Wild*	vilt
goose	*Gans*	gans
lamb	*Lammfleisch*	lam-flaish
meat	*Fleisch*	flaish
pheasant	*Fasan*	fa-zahn
poultry	*Geflügel*	ge-flü-gel
pork	*Schweinefleisch*	shvai-ne-flaish
salmon	*Lachs*	laks
veal	*Kalbfleisch*	kalp-flaish

FRUIT & VEGETABLES

apple	*Apfel*	ap-fel
artichoke	*Artischocke*	ar-ti-*sho*-ke
beans	*Bohnen*	baw-nen
cabbage	*Kohl*	kawl
cucumber; gherkins	*Gurke*	gur-ke
garlic	*Knoblauch*	knawp-lowkh
orange	*Apfelsine*	ap-fel-*zee*-ne
potato	*Kartoffel*	kar-*to*-fel
red cabbage	*Rotkohl*	rawt-kawl

DRINKS

apple cider	*Apfelwein*	ap-fel-*vaine*
beer	*Bier*	beer
coffee	*Kaffee*	ka fay
juice	*Saft*	zaft
mulled wine	*Glühwein*	glü vaine
water	*Wasser*	va-ser
white/red wine	*Weisswein/Rotwein*	vais vaine/rawt-vaine

Berlin

CONTENTS

History 89
Orientation 91
Information 92
Dangers & Annoyances 103
Sights 103
Activities 116
Berlin for Children 117
Tours 118
Festivals & Events 119
Sleeping 119
Eating 124
Drinking 129
Entertainment 132
Shopping 136
Getting There & Away 138
Getting Around 139

Berlin, once languishing as a city divided, has become a synonym for urbanity in the 21st century, a magnet for creative types of all stripes and a hub of European youth culture. Since the demise of the Wall, the German capital has been a city frantically on the move, imbued with an infectious dynamism that has drawn the world's best and brightest, from artists to scientists to architects, not to mention scores of visitors curious about what's cooking in this laboratory of creativity.

Berlin can keep you busy 24/7. In the daytime, there are amazing museums to explore, bold new architecture to admire and stately palaces to visit. Browse stylish boutiques for that edgy urban look created by fashion-forward designers, get an eyeful of progressive art in the many galleries and observe locals at leisure over a steaming mug of Milchkaffee in one of the countless cafés.

But for many, Berlin's true spirit doesn't reveal itself until the sun goes down. The city's justly famous for its unbridled and often boundary-pushing nightlife. Quasi-legal squat clubs to chic jet-set hang-outs, you're sure to find a bar, pub, lounge or club to suit your mood. Those after a highbrow culture fix have plenty of opera, classical music, cabaret and theatre to enjoy.

The world has always looked to this most dramatic city – sometimes in fascination, sometimes in horror and sometimes even in deep sympathy. At once repellent and seductive, light-hearted and brooding, one thing is certain: Berlin rocks.

HIGHLIGHTS

- **Dining**
  Pig out at Sunday brunch at such buzzy neighbourhood cafés as Tomasa in Schöneberg (p128)
- **Views**
  Take in the panorama from the Reichstag cupola (p108) or the Fernsehturm (TV Tower; p106)
- **Bargain**
  Explore all of Berlin's essential sights by hopping aboard Bus 100 or 200 at Bahnhof Zoo (p140)
- **Sleeping**
  Spend a night amid the fantasy of the Propeller Island Lodge (p122)
- **Architecture**
  Confront Daniel Libeskind's stunning Jewish Museum (p111)
- **Chill-Out Spot**
  Soak up the sounds at Liquidrom (p133)
- **Offbeat Experience**
  Tour the city's underground with Berliner Unterwelten (p118)

Reichstag ★ ★ Fernsehturm (TV Tower)
★ Bahnhof Zoo
Tomasa
Propeller ★ ★ ★ ★ Jewish Museum
Island Lodge   Liquidrom

■ TELEPHONE CODE: 030 ■ POPULATION: 3.39 MILLION ■ AREA: 889 SQ KM

HISTORY

By German standards, Berlin entered the stage of history relatively late and puttered long in relative obscurity for centuries. Founded in the 13th century as a trading post, it merged with its sister settlement Cölln across the Spree River in 1307. The town achieved a modicum of prominence after the powerful Hohenzollern clan from southern Germany took charge in 1411, in east until the 17th century when it was ravaged during the Thirty Years' War (1618–48) with only 6000 people surviving the pillage, plunder and starvation.

Ironically, the war's aftermath gave Berlin its first taste of cosmopolitanism. Keen on quickly raising the number of his subjects, Elector Friedrich Wilhelm (called the 'Great Elector'; r. 1640–88) shrewdly invited foreigners to settle in Berlin. Some Jewish families arrived from Vienna, but the bulk of the new settlers were Huguenot refugees from France. By 1700, one in five locals was of French descent.

Elector Friedrich III, the Great Elector's son, presided over a lively and intellectual court, but was also a man of great political ambition. In 1701, he simply promoted himself to become King Friedrich I of Prussia, making Berlin a royal residence and capital of the new state of Brandenburg-Prussia.

His son, Friedrich Wilhelm I (r. 1713–40), laid the groundwork for Prussian military might. Soldiers were this king's main obsession and he dedicated much of his life to building an army of 80,000, partly by instituting the draft (highly unpopular even then) and by persuading his fellow rulers to trade him men for treasure. History quite appropriately knows him as the *Soldatenkönig* (Soldier King).

These soldiers, however, never saw action until Friedrich II (aka Frederick the Great; r. 1740–86) succeeded his father to the throne in 1740. Friedrich fought tooth and nail for two decades to wrest Silesia from Austria and Saxony. When not busy on the battlefield, 'Old Fritz', as he was also called, sought greatness through building (much of Unter den Linden dates back to his reign) and embracing the ideals of the Enlightenment. With some of the day's leading thinkers in town (Gotthold Ephraim Lessing and Moses Mendelssohn among them), Berlin blossomed into a great cultural centre some even called 'Athens on the Spree'.

Old Fritz's death sent Prussia on a downward spiral, culminating in a serious trouncing of its army by Napoleon in 1806. The French marched triumphantly into Berlin on October 27 and left two years later, their coffers bursting with gold. The post-Napoleonic period saw Berlin caught up in the reform movement sweeping through Europe. Since all this ferment brought little change from the top, Berlin joined with other German cities, in 1848, in a bourgeois democratic revolution. Alas, the time for democracy wasn't yet ripe and the status quo was quickly restored.

Meanwhile, the Age of Industrialisation had snuck up on Berliners, with companies like Siemens and Borsig vastly spurring the city's growth and spawning a new working class and political parties like the Social Democratic Party (SPD) to represent them. Berlin boomed politically, economically and culturally, especially after becoming capital of the German Reich in 1871. By 1900 the population had reached the two million mark.

Once again war, WWI in this case, stifled Berlin's momentum. In its aftermath, it found itself at the heart of a power struggle between monarchists, Spartacists and democrats. Though the democrats won out, the Weimar Republic only brought instability, corruption and inflation. Berliners responded like there was no tomorrow and made their city as much a den of decadence as a cauldron of creativity. Artists of all stripes flocked to this city of cabaret, Dada and jazz.

Hitler's rise to power put an instant halt to the fun. Berlin suffered heavy bombing in WWII and an invasion of 1.5 million Soviet soldiers during the final, decisive Battle of Berlin in April 1945. During the Cold War, it became ground zero for hostilities between the US and the USSR. The Berlin Blockade of 1948 and the construction of the Berlin Wall in 1961 were major milestones in the standoff. For 40 years, East and West Berlin developed as two completely separate cities.

With reunification, Berlin once again became the German capital in 1990 and the seat of government in 1999. Initial euphoria quickly gave way to disillusionment

BERLIN

GREATER BERLIN

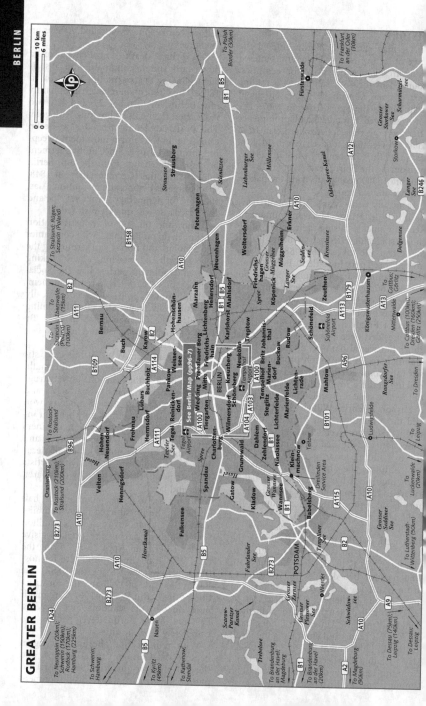

0 ——— 10 km
0 ——— 6 miles

See Berlin Map (pp96-7)

To Neuruppin (120km);
Schwerin (150km);
Rostock (170km);
Hamburg (225km)

To Rostock;
Stralsund

To Schwerin;
Hamburg

To Szczecin,
Eberswalde (15km)
To Poland (100km)

To Stralsund; Rügen;
Szczecin (Poland)

To Polish
Border (30km)

To Frankfurt
an der Oder
(30km)

To Cottbus (100km);
Dresden (160km);
Görlitz (250km)

To Cottbus;
Görlitz

To Dresden

To Leipzig

To Luckenwalde
(20km)

To Lutherstadt-
Wittenberg (50km)

To Dessau;
Leipzig

To Dessau (75km);
Leipzig (140km)

To Magdeburg
(90km)

To Brandenburg
an der Havel
(20km)

To Brandenburg
an der Havel;
Magdeburg

To Kyritz
(45km)

To Rathenow;
Stendal

Oranienburg

Nauen

POTSDAM

Werder

Havelkanal

Havel

Spree

Sacrow-Paretzer
Kanal

Grosser
Zernsee

Grosser
Plessower
See

Treblinsee

Fahrlander
See

Grosser
Wannsee

Grosser
Müggelsee

Langer
See

Seddin-
see

Zeuthener
See

Rangsdorfer
See

Grosser
Seddiner
See

Tegeler
See

Teupitz

Storkow

Grosser
Storkower
See

Langer
See

Dolgensee

Oder-Spree-Kanal

Liebenberger
See

Seelenbinder
See

Müllensee

Strausee

Fürstenwalde

Erkner

Krossinsee

Königswusterhausen

Mittenwalde

Schönefeld
Airport

Tegel
Airport

Tempelhof
Airport

Dreilinden
Service Area

Teltow

Ludwigsfelde

Mahlow

Schwielow-
see

Babelsberg

Kleinmachnow

Wannsee

Kladow

Gatow

Nikolassee

Zehlendorf

Dahlem

Grunewald

Spandau

Falkensee

Hennigsdorf

Velten

Hohen
Neuendorf

Frohnau

Hermsdorf

Lübars

Reinicken-
dorf

Buchholz

Buch

Karow

Pankow

Weissen-
see

Hohenschön-
hausen

Bernau

Marzahn

Karlshorst

Mahlsdorf

Lichtenberg

Friedrichs-
hain

Prenzlauer Berg

BERLIN

Wedding

Tiergarten

Mitte

Kreuzberg

Schöneberg

Wilmersdorf

Charlotten-
burg

Treptow

Neukölln

Johannis-
thal

Britz

Buckow

Rudow

Schönefeld

Marien-
dorf

Tempelhof

Steglitz

Lichterfelde

Marienfelde

Lichten-
rade

Mariendorf

Köpenick

Friedrichs-
hagen

Woltersdorf

Neuenhagen

Hellersdorf

Petershagen

Strausberg

Strausee

Storkow

Zeuthen

Hundrichssee

Müggelheim

Road labels

A24, A10, B273, B5, B96, A11, B2, B109, B158, A10, B5, B1, B158, A10, B1, B101, A115, B1, A9, A2, B1, A10, A13, A113, A96, A10, A12, B246, B179, B5, B1, B5, B4, A103, A104, A100, A111, A114, A100

rejoining the two city halves proved to be ainful and costly. Mismanagement, excesve spending and corruption sent the city's ebt soaring to nearly €40 billion in 2002. lready in 2001, a €1.6 billion bail-out of ae Bankgesellschaft Berlin had led to the ollapse of the centre-right government and ae election of Klaus Wowereit, an openly ay Social Democrat, as governing mayor. is agenda of eliminating the debt, low-ing unemployment and attracting new usiness has ushered in a new period of scal conservatism with painful spending ats for popular social programmes and altural institutions.

RIENTATION

erlin is a city-state surrounded by the undesland (federal state) of Brandenurg. Parks, forests, lakes and rivers make p about one third of it. The Spree River ends its way across the city for over 0km, from the Grosser Müggelsee, the aty's largest lake, in the east, to Spandau a the west. North and south of Spandau, ae Havel River widens into a series of lakes, om Tegel to below Potsdam. A network f canals links the waterways to each other

and to the Oder River in the east on the Polish border.

Berlin is made up of 12 administrative districts, of which the central ones of Schöneberg, Charlottenburg-Wilmersdorf, Prenzlauer Berg, Kreuzberg-Friedrichshain and Mitte are of most interest to visitors. Mitte, formerly in East Berlin, is the city's historic core and packs in most landmark sights, including the **Brandenburg Gate**, the **Reichstag** and new **government district**, **Unter den Linden** boulevard, **Potsdamer Platz**, **Museumsinsel** and the **TV Tower** on Alexanderplatz. Its Scheunenviertel area, anchored by the **Hackesche Höfe**, is jammed with bars, restaurants, galleries and quirky boutiques. It segues into Prenzlauer Berg to the north, a newly gentrified and largely residential district with nightlife centred on Käthe-Kollwitz-Platz and Helmholtzplatz.

South of Mitte, Kreuzberg counts **Checkpoint Charlie** and the **Jewish Museum** among its highlights. Eastern Kreuzberg, around Kottbusser Tor, has been nicknamed 'Little Istanbul' for its large Turkish population. The watering holes lining Oranienstrasse still reflect some of the district's anarchic spirit, although a new generation of students

---

BERLIN IN...

One Day

Start your day early to beat the crowds to the dome of the **Reichstag** (p108), then head south to the **Brandenburg Gate** (p103) to start a classic stroll along **Unter den Linden** (p104) with a detour to **Gendarmenmarkt** (p104) and the glamorous shops along Friedrichstrasse. After lunch, take a peek into the **Berliner Dom** (Berlin Cathedral; p105) before being awed by the antiquities at the **Pergamon Museum** (p105), then conclude the day in the **Scheunenviertel** (p106) with its many cafés, galleries, shops and classic Berlin courtyards like the Hackesche Höfe.

Two Days

Follow the one-day itinerary, then revisit Cold War history at **Checkpoint Charlie** (p111) and the nearby Haus am Checkpoint Charlie museum. Spend the rest of the morning at the amazing **Jewish Museum** (p111) before heading off to Berlin's showcase of urban renewal, the **Potsdamer Platz** (p110). Make a stop here at the **Filmmuseum** (p110) or walk a few steps west to the Kulturforum and the superb **Gemäldegalerie** (p109). At night, sample the cuisine and bar scene of Prenzlauer Berg.

Three Days

Follow the two-day itinerary, then make **Schloss Charlottenburg** (p113) and the area museums, especially the **Ägyptisches Museum** (p114), the focus of your third day. Once you've had your cultural fill, follow up with some leisurely shopping along the **Ku'damm** (p114) and at the **KaDeWe** (p136) department store. Have an early dinner around **Savignyplatz** (p127), then catch some live jazz at **Quasimodo** (p135) or the latest show at the **Wintergarten-Das Varieté** (p133).

BERLIN

and nonconformists now prefers the cheap rents in Friedrichshain (sometimes called 'F-Town' by the hipper-than-thou) across the Spree River. This is also where you'll find the **East Side Gallery**, the longest surviving section of the Wall.

The vast Tiergarten park links Mitte with Charlottenburg, the hub of western Berlin. Sights here cluster around Bahnhof Zoo, including the war-ruined **Kaiser-Wilhelm Memorial Church**, the **Ku'damm** shopping mile and the historic **Berlin Zoo**. Further west is **Schloss Charlottenburg** (Charlottenburg Palace), one of the city's must-see sights, and still beyond, the Nazi-era **Olympic Stadium**. Much of Charlottenburg, though, is upmarket residential, as are adjoining Wilmersdorf and Schöneberg. The latter also has a throbbing gay and lesbian scene around Nollendorfplatz.

For details about Berlin's airports and train stations, see Getting There & Away (p138) and Getting Around (p139).

Maps

The maps in this book should suffice unless you're planning on doing detailed explorations of the outlying suburbs. An even more detailed map is Lonely Planet's *Berlin* city map, which covers Berlin and Vicinity (1:60,000), Central Berlin (1:34,500) and Zoo, Tiergarten and Mitte (1:20,000), as well as an index to all the streets and sights.

Falkplan also makes good maps that come either as the standard sheet map or the Falk Megaplan with a patented folding system, and ADAC and the RV Verlag Euro City aren't bad either. Maps are available from newsagents and the bookshops listed later in this chapter and cost from €4.50 to €7.50.

INFORMATION
Bookshops

Berlin Story (Map pp98-9; ☎ 2045 3842; Unter den Linden 10) Berlin-related books, maps, videos and magazines, many in English.
Books in Berlin (Map p102; ☎ 313 1233; Goethestrasse 69) New and used English-language books.
East of Eden International Bookshop (Map pp96-7; ☎ 423 9362; Schreinerstrasse 10) Large selection of used English-language books.
Fair Exchange (Map pp100-1; ☎ 694 4675; Dieffenbachstrasse 58) Used books.

Hugendubel Charlottenburg (Map p102; ☎ 214 060; Tauentzienstrasse 13); Potsdamer Platz (Map p100-1; ☎ 253 9170; Potsdamer Platz Arkaden) Excellent chain shop with comfortable sofas for previewing.
St George's Bookshop (Map p126; ☎ 8179 8333; Wörtherstrasse 25) Used English books; reading lounge.

Cultural Centres
British Council (Map pp98-9; ☎ 311 0990; Hackescher Markt 1) Well-stocked library with books, videos and periodicals, plus Internet access and events.
Goethe Institut (Map pp98-9; ☎ 259 063; Neue Schönhauser Strasse 20)
Institut Français (Map p102; ☎ 885 9020; Kurfürstendamm 211)

Discount Cards
Berlin WelcomeCard (€21) Entitles one adult and up to three children under 14 to 72 hours of public transport within the Berlin-Potsdam area and free or discounted admission to museums, shows, attractions, sightseeing tours and boat cruises. It's available at the BTM tourist offices (see Tourist Information, p103) and many hotels.
Clubbing Berlin (€10) Great bargain for night owls with admission vouchers to 12 clubs, including Sage and Casino. Sold at BTM offices and A&O hostels.
SchauLust Museen Berlin (€10) Amazing bargain for museum lovers. Valid on three consecutive days, this pass gives unlimited admission to 50 of Berlin's museums, including blockbusters like the Pergamon and the Egyptian. Sold at the BTM tourist offices.
SMB Museum Pass (Tagskarte adult/concession €10/5; Dreitagskarte adult/concession€12/6) Tagskarte means day pass; Dreitagskarte three-day pass. Good for unlimited admission to all museums run by the Staatliche Museen zu Berlin (State Museums Berlin). Museums where this pass is valid are indicated throughout this chapter where admission price is mentioned. Admission is free for under 16s and for four hours before close Thursdays.

Emergency
ADAC Roadside Assistance (☎ 0180-222 2222)
BVG Public Transport Lost & Found (Map p129; ☎ 2562 3040; Potsdamer Strasse 180/182)
Drug hotline (☎ 192 37)
Emergency numbers (☎ 110 police, ☎ 112 fire brigade & ambulance)
Gay Advice Hotline (☎ 194 46)
International Helpline (☎ 4401 0607; ☯ 6pm-midnight)
Lesbian Advice Hotline (☎ 215 2000)
Municipal Lost & Found (Map pp100-1; ☎ 756 00; Platz der Luftbrücke 6) At Tempelhof airport.
Rape Crisis Hotline (☎ 251 2828)
Wheelchair Breakdown Service (☎ 8431 0910)

Internet Access

Hamra (Map p126; ☎ 4285 0095; Raumerstrasse 16; per 15 min; ☼ 10am-varies) Surfing goes exotic with waterpipes and cocktails.

Alpha Café (Map p126; ☎ 447 9067; Dunckerstrasse 72; per 20 min; ☼ noon-midnight)

Internet (Map pp100-1; ☎ 2977 6270; 1st fl, main hall, Ostbahnhof; €1 per hr; ☼ 10am-10pm)

Netz Galaxie (Map p102; ☎ 7870 6446; Joachimsthaler Strasse 19; €1 per hr; ☼ 11am-2am)

Surf & Sushi (Map pp98-9; ☎ 2838 4898; Oranienburger Strasse 17; €2.50 per 30 min; ☼ noon-varies, from 4pm Sun) Berlin's only 'wired' sushi bar.

Internet Resources

www.berlin.de Official website of the Berlin government with comprehensive information on culture, transport, economy, politics etc (English and German).

www.berlin-tourist-information.de Official site of the BTM, Berlin's official tourist office, with information, hotel reservation system, links and historical information (English and German).

www.berlin-info.de Plenty of information – some excellent, some sketchy – about hotels, sightseeing and Berlin generally (English and German).

www.berlinfo.com English-language site packed with interesting topics, but could benefit from an update.

Laundry

Berlin has plenty of places to wash your smalls. The dominant chain is **Schnell und Sauber** with many outlets across town, including at Uhlandstrasse 53 in Charlottenburg (Map p102), Bergmannstrasse 109 in Kreuzberg (Map pp100-1) and Torstrasse 115 in Mitte (Map pp98-9). A load of laundry usually costs €3 to €3.50, plus €0.50 for each 10 minutes of dryer time. All are open from 6am to 11pm daily.

Left Luggage

Major railway stations, such as Zoo and Ostbahnhof, have coin lockers that cost from €1 to €2 for 24 hours, and left-luggage offices that charge €2 per item per day. The central bus station ZOB also has a left-luggage station, as does Tegel airport. Schönefeld and Tempelhof have lockers only.

Libraries

America Memorial Library (Map pp100-1; ☎ 902 260; Blücherplatz 1)

Berliner Stadtbibliothek (Map pp98-9; ☎ 9022 401; Breite Strasse 30-36)

Media

For listings magazines, see p133.

Berliner Zeitung Left-leaning German-language daily most widely read in the eastern districts.

Der Tagesspiegel Local German-language daily with centre-right political orientation, solid news and foreign section, and decent cultural coverage.

Ex-Berliner English-language magazine for expats and visitors, with listings and irreverent yet informative articles about the city.

Tageszeitung (taz) Founded in 1970s Kreuzberg, this once boldly alternative German-language daily is struggling to keep afloat.

Medical Services

The US and UK consulates can provide lists of English-speaking doctors.

Charité Hospital (Map pp98-9; ☎ 2802 4766, emergencies 280 20; Schumannstrasse 20-21) The most central major hospital.

Uniklinikum Benjamin Franklin (☎ 8445 3015, emergencies 844 50; Hindenburgdamm 30; S1 to Botanischer Garten) In the Steglitz district, in the southwest of the city.

Virchow Klinikum (Map pp96-7; ☎ 4505 2000, 450 50 emergencies; Augustenburger Platz 1) In the Wedding district, take the U9 to Amrumer Strasse.

Zahnklinik Medeco (Medeco Dental Clinic; Map pp100-1; ☎ 2309 5960; Stresemannstrasse 121; ☼ 7am-midnight)

Money

American Express (Map pp98-9; ☎ 2045 5721; Friedrichstrasse 172)

Cash Express (Map pp98-9; ☎ 2045 5096; Bahnhof Friedrichstrasse; ☼ 7am-8pm Mon-Fri, 8am-8pm Sat & Sun)

Reisebank Bahnhof Zoo (Map p102; ☎ 881 7117; ☼ 7.30am-10pm); Ostbahnhof (Map pp100-1; ☎ 296 4393; ☼ 7am-10pm Mon-Fri, 8am-8pm Sat & Sun)

Post

Post offices abound throughout Berlin. The **main post office** (Joachimstaler Strasse; ☼ 8am-midnight Mon-Sat, 10am-midnight Sun) is near Bahnhof Zoo. To receive poste restante mail, have letters clearly marked 'Postlagernd' and addressed to you at 10612 Berlin.

Telephone

Most public pay phones no longer accept coins but operate with phonecards available at post offices, tourist offices and newstands. Reisebank (above) sells phonecards with especially good rates for international calls.

(Continued on page 103)

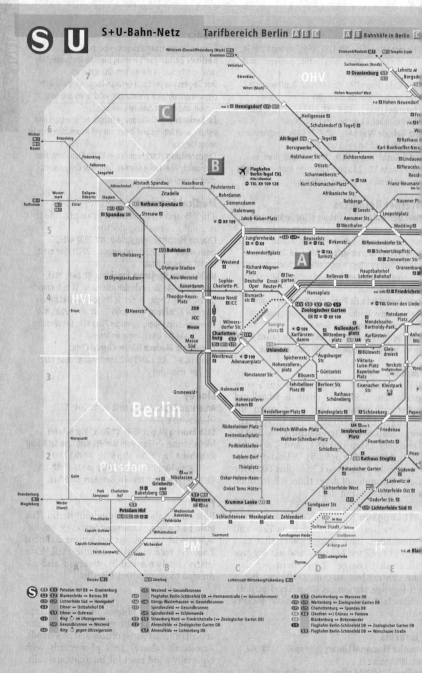

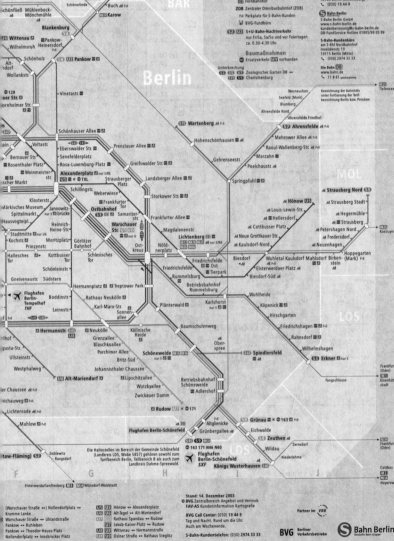

INFORMATION
East of Eden International Bookshop..1 H3
Lesbenberatung.................................2 D5
Virchow Klinikum...............................3 C2

SIGHTS & ACTIVITIES (pp103-17)
Ägyptisches Museum...........................4 A3
Altes Schloss....................................5 A3
Bauhaus Archive/Museum of Design.6 D4
Belvedere...7 A3
Berggruen Collection...........................8 A3
Bröhan Museum.................................9 A3
Erika-Hess-Eisstadion.........................10 D2
Mausoleum......................................11 A3
Museum of Pre- and Early History.....12 A3
Neuer Flügel....................................13 A3
Neuer Pavillon..................................14 A3
Schloss Charlottenburg......................15 A3
Soviet War Memorial – Treptow......16 H5
Tiergarten.......................................16 D4
Zucker Museum................................18 C1

SLEEPING (pp119-24)
Generator Berlin...............................19 H3
Gold Hotel am Wismarplatz...............20 H4
NH Berlin-Alexanderplatz...................21 G3

EATING (pp124-9)
Café am Neuen See............................22 C4
Hitit..23 A4
Luisen-Bräu.....................................24 A3
Umspannwerk Ost............................25 G3

DRINKING (pp129-32)
Bar am Lützowplatz...........................26 D4
Begine..27 D5

ENTERTAINMENT (pp130-36)
Kino International..............................28 G3
Wintergarten-Das Varieté...................29 D5

SHOPPING (pp136-8)
Flohmarkt am Arkonaplatz.................30 F2

TRANSPORT
Tour Boat Landing – Charlottenburg..31 A3
ZOB...32 A4

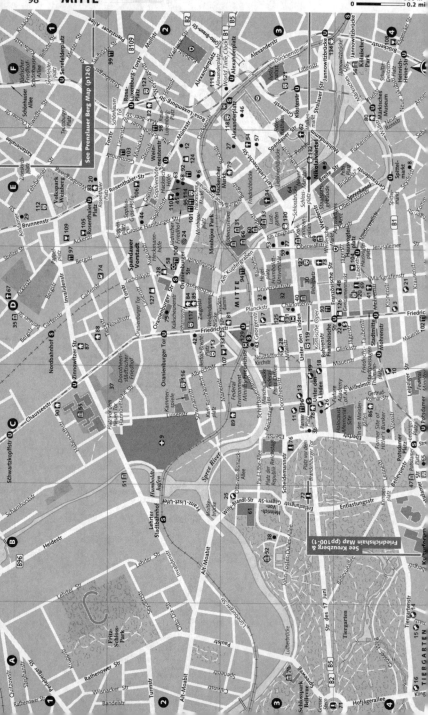

INFORMATION
American Express...1 D4
Australian Embassy...2 D4
Austrian Embassy...3 D4
Berlin Story...4 D3
Berliner Stadtbibliothek...5 E2
British Council...6 E2
BTM Tourist Office...(see 36)
BTM Tourist Office...(see 46)
Canadian Embassy...7 D3
Cash Express...(see 129)
Cedok...8 E4
Charité Hospital...9 C3
Czech Republic Embassy...10 C4
Dutch Embassy...(see 7)
French Embassy...11 C3
Goethe Institute...12 E2
Hugendubel...(see 91)
Hungarian Embassy & Consulate...13 C3
Irish Embassy...(see 2)
Italian Embassy...14 A4
Japanese Embassy...15 A4
Mexican Embassy...16 A4
New Zealand Embassy...(see 3)
Nordic Embassies...17 A4
Russian Consulate...18 D3
Russian Embassy...19 C3
Schnell und Sauber Laundrette...20 E1
Slovakian Embassy...21 D4
South African Embassy...(see 3)
Sputnik Travel...22 H4
STA Travel...23 D3
Surf & Sushi...24 E2
Swiss Embassy...25 B3
UK Embassy...26 C3
Ungarn Tours...27 E3
USA Embassy...28 D3

SIGHTS & ACTIVITIES (pp103-11)
ADFC Bicycle Club...29 E1
Alte Königliche Bibliothek...30 D3
Alte Nationalgalerie...31 E3
Alte Staatsbibliothek...32 D3

Altes Museum...33 E3
Berliner Dom...34 E3
Berliner Mauer Dokumentationszentrum...35 D1
Brandenburg Gate...36 C3
Brecht-Weigel Gedenkstätte...37 D2
Carillon...38 B3
Centrum Judaicum...(see 58)
DaimlerChrysler Contemporary at Haus Huth...39 C4
Deutsche Guggenheim...40 D3
Deutscher Dom...41 D4
Fahrradservice Kohnke...42 D2
Fahrradstation - Friedrichstrasse...43 D3
Fahrradstation Auguststrasse...44 D2
Fahrradstation Hackesche Höfe...45 E2
Fernsehturm...46 F3
Filmmuseum Berlin...(see 91)
Französischer Dom...47 C4
Friedrichwerdersche Kirche...48 D4
Gedenkstätte Deutscher Widerstand...49 B4
German Historical Museum...50 B4
German Parliament Exhibit...(see 41)
Hamburger Bahnhof...51 C1
Haus der Kulturen der Welt...52 B3
Hugenottenmuseum...(see 47)
IM Pei Bau...53 E3
Marienkirche...54 E3
Museum für Naturkunde...55 C1
Neptunbrunnen...57 E3
Neue Synagoge...58 D2
Neue Wache...59 D3
New Federal Chancellery...60 B3
Neues Museum (under reconstruction)...61 E3
Nikolaikirche...62 E3
Otto Weidt Workshop...63 E2
Palast der Republik...64 E3
Panorama Observation Deck...65 C4
Pergamon Museum...66 D3
Reconciliation Chapel...67 D1
Rosenhöfe...68 E2
Schiller Statue...69 D4

Schloss Bellevue...70 A3
Siegessäule...71 A4
Soviet War Memorial...72 B3
St-Hedwigskirche...73 D3
Stadtbad Mitte...74 D1
Tacheles...75 D2
Wall Victims Memorial...76 C3
Zeughaus...77 E3

SLEEPING (pp120-1)
Adlon Hotel Kempinski...78 C3
Alexander Plaza Berlin...79 E3
art'otel berlin mitte...80 F4
Artist Hotel Riverside...81 D3
Circus – The Hostel...82 F2
Circus – The Hostel...83 E1
Clubhouse Hostel...84 D2
Dietrich-Bonhoeffer-Haus...85 D2
Frauenhotel Intermezzo...86 C4
Honigmond Garden Hotel...87 D1
Kinder-Hotel...88 C3
Künstlerheim Luise...89 C3
Mitte's Backpacker Hostel...90 C1

EATING (pp124-6)
Asia Pavilion...91 C4
Bagels & Bialys...(see 48)
Borchardt...92 E2
Die Zwölf Apostel...93 D3
Gosch...94 C1
Hasir...(see 65)
Margaux...95 E2
Maxwell...96 D4
Milagro...97 D1
Monsieur Vuong...(see 75)
Noct Vagus...98 F2
Oren...99 F2
Piccola Italia...100 F2
Schlotzsky's Deli...101 C4
Unsicht-Bar...102 D4
...103 E2

DRINKING (pp129-34)
925 Lounge Bar...104 D4

Ackerkeller...105 E1
B-flat...106 E2
Broker's Bier Börse...107 D3
Café Podewil...(see 84)
Kalkscheune...108 F4
Sage Club...109 E1
Seven Lounge...110 D2
Sophienklub...111 F2
Sternradio

ENTERTAINMENT (pp132-6)
Acud...112 E1
Arsenal Cinema...(see 47)
Berliner Ensemble...113 D2
Chamäleon Varieté...114 D2
Cinemaxx...115 C4
Deutsches Theater...116 C2
Friedrichstadtpalast...117 D2
Hackesche Höfe Cinema...(see 114)
Hackesches Hof-Theater...118 F3
Hekticket...119 D3
Komische Oper Box Office...120 D4
Konzerthaus...121 F3
Podewil...122 D3
Staatsoper Unter den Linden...91 C4
Volksbühne am Rosa-Luxemburg-Platz...123 F2

SHOPPING (pp136-8)
Buttenheim Levi's Store...124 E2
Dussmann...125 D3
Galeries Lafayette...126 D4
Lisa D...(see 114)
Nix...127 D2
Sterling Gold...128 D2

TRANSPORT
Bahnhof Friedrichstrasse...129 E3
Berliner Wassertaxi Service...130 E3
Tempelhofer Bus Tour Departures...131 D3
Tour Boat Landing - Nikolaviertel...132 D4
Tour Boat Landing Friedrichsstrasse...133 D3
Tour Boat Landing Jannowitzbrücke...134 F3

See Mitte Map (pp98-9)

KREUZBERG 61

INFORMATION
@Internet..1 F1
America Memorial Library.........2 C3
Fair Exchange...............................3 E4
Hugendubel....................................4 A2
Municipal Lost & Found..........5 B5
Reisebank..................................(see 1)
Schnell + Sauber Laundrette....6 F5
Zahnklinik Medeco....................7 B2

SIGHTS & ACTIVITIES   (pp111-13)
Abgeordnetenhaus.........................8 B2
Berlin Wall Remnant.................(see 25)
Checkpoint Charlie.........................9 C2
Deutsches Technikmuseum......10 A3
East Side Gallery...........................11 G2
Fahrradstation..............................12 B4
Gemäldegalerie............................13 A2
Haus am Checkpoint Charlie....14 C2
Jüdisches Museum.......................15 C2
Kunstgewerbemuseum..............16 A1
Kupferstichkabinett....................17 A2
Martin-Gropius-Bau....................18 B2
Musical Instruments Museum....19 A1
Neue Nationalgalerie................20 A2
Neue Staatsbibliothek...............21 A2
Pedal Power..................................22 B4
Schwules Museum.......................23 B4

Spectrum..(se
Stadtbad Neukölln..........................
Topography of Terror.....................

SLEEPING      (pp1
Bax Pax Hostel..................................
City Hostel Meininger 12............
Die Fabrik Hostel............................
East-Side Hotel.................................
Hotel am Anhalter Bahnhof.3
Hotel Riehmers Hofgarten..
Juncker's Hotel-Garni......(se
Odyssee Globetrotter
    Hostel....................................
Pegasus Hostel.................................
Wohnagentur am
    Mehringdamm.........................

EATING   (pp1
Abendmahl...
Altes Zollhaus..................................
Bar Centrale......................................
Chandra Kumari...............................
Gasthaus Dietrich Herz....
Morgenland......................................
Osteria No 1......................................
Papaya...
Schlotzsky's Deli.............................

DRINKING 🍸 (p132–35)
90° Grad.....................44 A3
Ankerklause................45 E3
Astro Bar...................(see 47)
Casino......................46 G2
Dachkammer................47 H1
Die Busche.................48 G2
Goldfisch..................(see 42)
Golgatha....................49 B4
Haifischbar.................50 C4
Junction Bar...............51 C4
Konrad Tönz................52 G3
Kumpelnest.................53 A2
Maria am Ufer.............54 F1
Melitta Sundström Café...(see 23)
Roses......................55 E3
SchwuZ Disco..............(see 23)
SO36.......................56 E3
Würgeengel.................57 E3

ENTERTAINMENT 🎭 (pp132–6)
Babylon Cinema............58 E3
Berliner Philharmonie &
  Kammermusiksaal.........59 A1
Eiszeit Cinema.............60 F3
Friends of Italian Opera...61 B4
Neues Tempodrom &
  Liquidrom................62 B2

SHOPPING 🛍 (pp136–8)
Colours Kleidermarket......63 B4
Flohmarkt am Moritzplatz..64 D2
Hallentrödelmarkt Treptow.65 H3
O-Ton Keramik.............66 E3
Outdoor....................67 B4
Space Hall.................68 C4
Turkish Market............69 E3

TRANSPORT (pp138–41)
CityNetz Mitfahrzentrale...70 D4
Classic Bike Harley-Davidson.71 E3
Mitfahr2000...............72 A4
Robben & Wientjes.........73 D2
V2-Moto...................74 G3

INFORMATION
Alternativ Tours.................................. 1 B3
Books in Berlin.................................... 2 B2
BTM Tourist Office.............................. 3 D2
BVG Information Kiosk........................ 4 D2
Darpol.. 5 A1
Euraide.. 6 D2
French Consulate..........................(see 8)
Hugendubel... 7 D2
Institut Français.................................. 8 C3
Netz Galaxie Internet Cafe................ 9 D3
Reisebank... 10 D3
Schnell und Sauber Laundrette....... 11 C3
STA Travel.. 12 C1

SIGHTS & ACTIVITIES   (pp113-15)
Aquarium.. 13 D2
Berlin Zoo... 14 D2
Erotik Museum................................... 15 D2
Horst-Dohm-Eisstadion...................... 16 A5
Kaiser-Wilhelm-Gedächtniskirche... 17 D2
Käthe-Kollwitz-Museum.................... 18 C3
Stadtbad Charlottenburg.................. 19 B1
Story of Berlin.................................... 20 C3

SLEEPING   (pp122-3)
A&O Hostel am Zoo............................ 21 D2
Art Nouveau Hotel.............................. 22 B2
Erste Mitwohnzentrale....................... 23 A3
Hecker's Hotel.................................... 24 C2
Home Company................................... 25 D3
Hotel Askanischer Hof....................... 26 B3

Hotel Bleibtreu.................................. 27 C3
Hotel Bogota...................................... 28 C3
Hotel Gates.. 29 C1
Hotel-Pension Augusta...................... 30 C3
Hotel-Pension Castell........................ 31 B3
Hotel-Pension Fischer....................... 32 D3
Hotel-Pension Funk........................... 33 C3
Hotel-Pension Korfu II....................... 34 D2
Hotel-Pension München..................... 35 D4
Propeller Island Lodge....................... 36 A3

EATING   (pp127-8)
Alt-Luxemburg.................................... 37 A2
Arche Noah & Jewish
  Community House............................. 38 C2
Café Wintergarten im
  Literaturhaus.................................... 39 C3
Die Zwölf Apostel............................. 40 C2
First Floor......................................(see 3)
Good Friends...................................... 41 C2
Gosch... 42 C2
La Caleta.. 43 B3
Mar y Sol... 44 C2
Schwarzes Café.................................. 45 C2
Tomasa... 46 D4
YVA-Suite... 47 C2

DRINKING   (p132-35)
A-Trane... 48 C2
Bar de Paris Bar................................ 49 C2
Bar Jeder Vernunft............................ 50 C3
Dicke Wirtin...................................... 51 C2

Far Out... 52
Gainsbourg..................................(see 48)
Galerie Bremer.................................. 53
Quasimodo... 54

ENTERTAINMENT   (pp132-
Deutsche Oper Berlin........................ 55
Hekticket... 56
Theaterkasse Centrum...................... 57
Zaubertheater Igor Jedlin................. 58

SHOPPING   (pp136-
Flohmarkt am Tiergarten................... 59
Wertheim bei Hertie Department
  Store... 60

TRANSPORT   (pp138-4
CityNetz Mitfahrzentrale............(see 2
Europcar.......................................(see 62
Hertz & Avis...................................... 61
Mitfahr2000................................(see 2
Sixt Budget.. 62

OTHER
Berolina Sightseeing
  Departures...................................... 63 C
BVB Tour Bus Departures................. 64 D
BVG Top Tour Departures................. 65 D
Severin + Kühn Bus Tour
  Departures...................................... 66 C
Tempelhofer Bus Tour
  Departures...................................... 67 D

Continued from page 93)

Tourist Information

Berlin Tourismus Marketing (BTM; www.berlin-tourist
nformation.de) Operates three tourist offices and a **call
centre** (☎ 250 025; ⊙ 8am-7pm Mon-Fri, 9am-6pm
Sat & Sun) whose multilingual staff can answer general
questions and make hotel and event bookings. When not
staffed, you can listen to recorded information or order
brochures.
BTM Tourist Office Brandenburg Gate (Map pp98-9;
south wing; ⊙ 10am-6pm)
BTM Tourist Office Europa-Center (Map p102;
Budapester Strasse 45; ⊙ 10am-7pm Mon-Sat,
10am-6pm Sun)
BTM Tourist Office TV Tower (Map pp98-9;
Alexanderplatz; ⊙ 10am-6pm)
Euraide (Map p102; www.euraide.de; Bahnhof Zoo;
⊙ 8.30am-noon Mon-Sat, 1-4.30pm Mon-Fri) Behind
the Reisezentrum, this helpful office provides advice and
information on trains, lodging, tours and other travel-related
subjects, in English.

Travel Agencies

Travel agencies offering cheap flights adver-
tise in the 'Reisen' classified section (Klein-
anzeigen), part of the popular city magazines
Zitty and Tip (p133).
Alternativ Tours (Map p102; ☎ 881 2089;
Wilmersdorfer Strasse 94)
Cedok (Map pp98-9; ☎ 204 4644; Seydelstrasse 27)
Czech Republic specialist.
Darpol (Map p102; ☎ 342 0074; Kaiser-Friedrich-Strasse
19) Poland specialist.
Sputnik Travel (Map pp98-9; ☎ 2030 2246; Friedrich-
strasse 176) Russia specialist.
STA Travel Charlottenburg (Map p102; ☎ 310 0040;
Hardenbergstrasse 9); Mitte (Map pp98-9; ☎ 2016 5063;
Dorotheenstrasse 30); Prenzlauer Berg (Map p126; ☎ 2859
8264; Gleimstrasse 28) Student- and youth-oriented; issues
ISIC cards.
Ungarn Tours (Map pp98-9; ☎ 247 8296; Karl-
Liebknecht-Strasse 9) Hungary specialist.

DANGERS & ANNOYANCES

By all accounts, Berlin is among the safest
and most tolerant of European cities. Walking alone at night is not usually dangerous,
although of course there's always safety in
numbers as in any urban environment.

Despite some bad press, racial attacks are
quite infrequent in Berlin. Having said that,
while people of any skin colour are usually
safe in the central districts, prejudice towards foreigners and gays is more likely
to rear its ugly head in the outlying eastern
districts like Marzahn and Lichtenberg,
where unemployment and general dissat-
isfaction with postreunification society are
higher. No matter the colour of your skin,
if you see any 'white skins' (skinheads wearing jackboots with white boot laces), walk
the other way – and fast.

Drugs should be avoided for obvious reasons, but in particular because a lot of the
stuff is distributed by Mafialike organisations and is often dangerously impure.

Most U/S-Bahn stations are equipped with
electronic information and emergency devices labelled 'SOS/Notruf/Information' and
are indicated by a large red bell. If you require
emergency assistance simply push the 'SOS'
button. The Information button allows you
to speak directly with the stationmaster.

SIGHTS

Each of Berlin's districts has its own appeal, although must-see sights concentrate
in Mitte in the historic city centre. The
Jewish Museum and Checkpoint Charlie in
Kreuzberg and Schloss Charlottenburg also
rank high on the list of major attractions,
while the charms of Prenzlauer Berg and
Schöneberg lie mostly in their relaxed, leafy
streets and laid-back nightlife. Of the outer
districts, the one of greatest appeal is Zehlendorf, home of fabulous museums, and
lush parks and lakes offering all kinds of
recreation options.

Mitte

Mitte (Middle) is Berlin's birthplace and,
throughout its history, has always been
the city's nexus of politics, culture and
commerce. Packed with blockbuster sights,
museums, entertainment and hotel options,
this is where Berlin visitors spend most of
their time.

BRANDENBURG GATE & PARISER PLATZ   Map pp98-9

A symbol of division during the Cold War,
the recently restored landmark **Brandenburg
Gate** (Brandenburger Tor), now epitomises
German reunification. Its history, however,
began in the 18th century as the most beautiful of Berlin's 18 city gates. The Quadriga
statue, a horse-drawn chariot piloted by the
winged goddess of victory, perches triumphantly on top. In the northern wing is the

Raum der Stille (Room of Silence), where the weary and frenzied can sit and contemplate peace.

The gate flanks **Pariser Platz**, now again framed by embassies and bank buildings as it was during its 19th-century heyday as the 'emperor's reception hall'. Also here is the faithfully rebuilt **Hotel Adlon** (now called the Adlon Hotel Kempinski, also see p121), the *grande dame* of Berlin caravanserais, which has sheltered Charlie Chaplin, Greta Garbo, Bill Clinton and many other celebrity guests. Famous names or deep pockets continue to be a requirement for spending the night with front-row viewing over the Brandenburg Gate.

Just south of the gate, construction finally began in August 2003 of the **Memorial to the Murdered European Jews**, colloquially known as Holocaust Memorial. New York architect Peter Eisenman's vision consists of a vast grid of concrete pillars of varying heights, making it resemble an abstract field of wheat in the wind. Visitors will be able to access this maze at any point and make their individual journey through it. An underground information centre will be part of the complex. Its inauguration is planned for 8 May 2005, the 60th anniversary of the end of WWII.

UNTER DEN LINDEN   Map pp98-9

Berlin's most splendid boulevard extends for about 1.5km east of the Brandenburg Gate. First up on your right is the hulking **Russian Embassy** (Unter den Linden 63-65), a white marble behemoth built in Stalin-era 'wedding cake' style. Further on, at Charlottenstrasse, the **Deutsche Guggenheim** (☎ 202 0930; Unter den Linden 13-15; adult/concession €3/2, free Mon; ☾ 11am-8pm Fri-Wed, 11am-10pm Thu) presents changing exhibits, mostly featuring top names in contemporary art, in stark, high-ceilinged galleries. It's a joint venture between the Deutsche Bank and the Guggenheim foundation, hence the name.

Opposite the gallery is the **Alte Staatsbibliothek** (Old National Library; Unter den Linden 8), which has amassed an astonishing archive since its founding in 1661, including the original sheet music of Beethoven's 9th Symphony. Next up is the **Humboldt Universität** (1753), originally a palace of Heinrich, brother of King Friedrich II whose pompous equestrian statue occupies a prime spot on Unter

den Linden outside the university. Marx and Engels studied here, while Albert Einstein and the Brothers Grimm are on the long list of illustrious former faculty members.

Bebelplatz, across the street, was the site of the first big official Nazi book-burning in May 1933, an event commemorated by a poignant below-ground memorial by Micha Ullmann consisting of empty bookshelves. Buildings framing the square include the baroque **Alte Königliche Bibliothek** (Old Royal Library; 1780), now part of the university; the **Staatsoper Unter den Linden** (1743); and the domed **St Hedwigskirche** (1783), partly modelled on Rome's Pantheon and Berlin's only Catholic church until 1854.

Just east of here is the **Friedrichswerdersche Kirche** (☎ 208 1323; Werderscher Markt; adult/concession €3/1.50, SMB pass valid; ☾ 10am-6pm Tue-Sun), which houses a permanent exhibit on the architecture and sculpture of Karl Friedrich Schinkel. Admission is included in the price of the Museumsinsel ticket (see p105).

For more Schinkel return to Unter den Linden and the 1818 **Neue Wache** (admission free; ☾ 10am-6pm). Originally a Prussian guardhouse, it is now a memorial to the 'victims of war and tyranny'. An enlarged version of Käthe Kollwitz's emotional sculpture *Mother and her Dead Son* dominates the austere room.

The pink building next door is the baroque **Zeughaus**, a former armoury designed by Andreas Schlüter in 1806 that usually houses the **German Historical Museum**, which is set to reopen in late 2004 following a complete makeover. Already in business, though, is the brand-new **IM Pei Bau** (☎ 203 040; Unter den Linden 2; admission prices vary; ☾ 10am-10pm Thu, 10am-6pm Fri-Tue), an extravagant museum extension designed by the 'Mandarin of Modernism', star architect IM Pei. Built for temporary exhibits, it's a truly awesome space, starkly geometric, yet imbued with a sense of lightness achieved through an airy atrium and generous use of glass.

GENDARMENMARKT   Map pp98-9

A short walk southwest of Bebelplatz, the Gendarmenmarkt ranks as Berlin's most elegant square. The twin churches of Deutscher Dom and Französischer Dom combine with Schinkel's **Konzerthaus** (also see p135) to form a superbly harmonious architectural trio.

BERLIN

Inside the **Deutscher Dom** is a free but hopelessly academic exhibit on German parliamentarianism that has bored thousands of school children to tears. The **Französischer Dom** was built for the French Huguenots who fled to Berlin following their expulsion from France in 1685. Their story is chronicled in the **Hugenottenmuseum** (☎ 2016 6883; adult/concession €2/1; ☒ noon-5pm Tue-Sat, 11-5pm Sun), located in the **tower** (☒ 9am-7pm), which offers sweeping views of Mitte's main sights.

MUSEUMSINSEL   Map pp98-9
East of the Zeughaus, the sculpture-studded **Schlossbrücke** (Palace Bridge) leads to the island in the Spree River where Berlin's settlement began in the Middle Ages. Its northern half is 'Museum Island' – a more appropriate moniker might be 'Treasure Island'. A Unesco World Heritage Site since 1999, the complex is undergoing a complete overhaul until at least 2010. In the meantime, three of the five museums are open; the **Museumsinsel ticket** (€8/4) allows admission to all three and to Friedrichswerdersche Kirche (p104).

Alte Nationalgalerie
A sensitively restored Greek-temple building by August Stüler, the **Alte Nationalgalerie** (Old National Gallery; ☎ 2090 5801; Bodestrasse 1-3; adult/concession €8/4, SMB pass valid; ☒ 10am-6pm Tue-Sun, 10am-10pm Thu), represents a stylish setting for the museum's 19th-century European art. The collection ranges from Romantics like Caspar David Friedrich to sculptors like Gottfried Schadow. The gorgeous upstairs rotunda showcases the emotional sculptures of Reinhold Begas, while the marble stairwell is decorated with a frieze of German greats by Otto Geyers.

Pergamon Museum
If you only have time for one museum while in Berlin, make it the **Pergamon Museum** (☎ 2090 5555; Am Kupfergraben; adult/concession €8/4, includes audio guide, SMB pass valid; ☒ 10am-6pm Tue-Sun, 10am-10pm Thu). A feast of classical Greek, Babylonian, Roman, Islamic and Middle Eastern art and architecture, it will amaze and enlighten you. The three sections (Collection of Classical Antiquities, Museum of Near Eastern Antiquities and Museum of Islamic Art) are all worth seeing at leisure, but if you're pressed for time, make a beeline to the following.

The museum's namesake and main draw, the **Pergamon Altar** from Asia Minor (165 BC, in today's Turkey), is a gargantuan raised marble shrine with a 120m frieze of the gods doing battle with the giants. The next room features the immense **Gate of Miletus**, a masterpiece of Roman architecture, which leads straight into another culture and century: Babylon during the reign of Nebuchadnezzar II (604–562 BC). The top billing here goes to the brilliant **Ishtar Gate**, sheathed in glazed brick tiles in a luminous cobalt blue and ochre. The reliefs of striding lions, horses, dragons and unicorns are so strident, you can almost hear the fanfare.

Upstairs, major highlights include the fortresslike 8th-century **Caliph's palace** from Mshatta in today's Jordan and the 17th-century **Aleppo Room**, whose walls are entirely sheathed in immensely intricate wooden panelling.

Altes Museum
More art and sculpture from ancient Rome and Greece are on view at the **Altes Museum** (☎ 2090 5254; enter from Lustgarten; adult/concession €8/4, SMB pass valid; ☒ 10am-6pm Tue-Sun). An imposing neoclassical edifice (1830) by Karl Friedrich Schinkel, it was the first building on Museum Island and has a famed rotunda featuring sculptures of Zeus and his celestial entourage.

Berliner Dom
Overlooking Museumsinsel is the great 1905 neo-Renaissance **Berliner Dom** (☎ 202 690; Am Lustgarten; adult/concession €5/3; ☒ church 9am-8pm Mon-Sat, noon-8pm Sun Apr-Sep, to 7pm Oct-Mar; viewing gallery 9am-8pm Apr-Sep, 9am-5pm Oct-Mar; crypt 9am-6pm Mon-Sat, noon-6pm Sun), the former court church of the royal Hohenzollern family, members of which are buried in its crypt. The views from the gallery are well worth it. Free organ recitals take place at 3pm daily.

SCHLOSSPLATZ   Map pp98-9
Nothing of today's Schlossplatz evokes memory of the magnificent edifice that stood here from 1451 to 1951: the Berliner Stadtschloss. Despite international protests, the GDR government demolished the barely war-damaged structure, which it considered a 'symbol of Prussian militarism', in 1951. The only section saved was

the triumphal-arch from which Karl Lieb-knecht had proclaimed a Socialist German Republic in 1918; it was incorporated into the Staatsratsgebäude (State Council Building) on the square's south side.

In the 1970s, to further drive home the point, the Honecker regime built its **Palast der Republik** on the former Schloss site. Nicknamed 'Erich's Lampenladen' (Erich's lamp shop) because of the many suspended ceiling lamps in the foyer, it served as home of the GDR parliament (the Volkskammer) until 1989. Shortly thereafter it was closed for a costly asbestos clean-up. In 1993, one step ahead of Christo and his wrapped Reichstag, a French artist clad the structure with plastic sheets designed to look like the old Schloss, sparking a movement to rebuild the historic landmark. The idea gathered steam for a while, but for now a prohibitive price tag has put plans on ice and the fate of the GDR's 'palace' remains uncertain.

ALEXANDERPLATZ & AROUND   Map pp98-9

Former East Berlin's main commercial hub, **Alexanderplatz** – 'Alex' for short – was named in honour of Tsar Alexander I who visited Berlin in 1805. Today it's a mere shadow of the low-life district Alfred Döblin called 'the quivering heart of a cosmopolitan city' in his 1929 novel *Berlin Alexanderplatz*. Rebuilt numerous times, its current socialist look dates from the 1960s. On 4 November 1989 some 700,000 people gathered here to rally against the GDR regime. They were vociferous but peaceful and they were heard: five days later, the Wall came tumbling down.

The main sight here is the 365m-tall **Fernsehturm** (TV Tower; ☎ 242 3333; adult/child €5/2.50; ☼ 9am-1am Mar-Oct, 10am-midnight Nov-Feb). If it's a clear day and the queue isn't too long, it's worth paying for the elevator ride to the top. Just below the antenna is a shiny steel sphere which, when hit by sunlight, produces the reflection of a huge cross, a phenomenon that caused much consternation among the atheist GDR honchos. West Berliners promptly dubbed it 'the Pope's revenge'.

Dwarfed by the TV Tower is the nearby brick **Marienkirche** (☎ 242 4467; Karl-Liebknecht-Strasse 8; admission free; ☼ 10am-4pm Mon-Thu, noon-4pm Sat & Sun), Berlin's second-oldest church, built in 1270. Eye-catching features include

a marble pulpit by Andreas Schlüter and a Dance of Death fresco. The epic **Neptunbrunnen** (Neptune Fountain; 1891) nearby is by Reinhold Begas; the female figures symbolise the rivers Rhine, Elbe, Oder and Weichsel. The hulking building just south is the 1860 **Rotes Rathaus** (Red Town Hall; ☎ 902 60; Rathausstrasse 15; admission free; ☼ 9am-6pm Mon-Fri), a neo-Renaissance structure where Berlin's governing mayor and his Senate keep their offices. It's nicknamed Red Town Hall because of the colour of the bricks used in its construction.

Just behind the town hall is the twee Nikolaiviertel (Nicholas Quarter), a not entirely unsuccessful attempt by GDR architects to re-create a medieval town in celebration of Berlin's 750th anniversary in 1988. The result is a maze of narrow alleys lined by diminutive houses and lorded over by the spindly twin spires of the **Nikolaikirche** (☎ 2472 4529; admission €1.50; ☼ 10am-6pm Tue-Sun), Berlin's oldest church (1230), which has a moderately interesting exhibit on the city's history until 1648.

For a more in-depth look at local history up to modern times, head southeast to the **Märkisches Museum** (March of Brandenburg Museum; ☎ 308 660; Am Köllnischen Park 5; adult/concession €4/2, free on Wed; ☼ 10am-6pm Tue-Sun). Housed in a red-brick, cathedral-like pile, its thematic highlights include music and literature, theatre, glass, art and crafts. Best of all are the quirky Automatophones, which are 18th-century mechanical musical instruments that are wound up and launched on their cacophonous journeys on Sundays at 3pm (adult/concession €2/1 extra). Since 9 November 2003 seven especially artistic sections of the Wall have also been on display here.

SCHEUNENVIERTEL   Map pp98-9

North of Alexanderplatz, the Scheunenviertel (sometimes also known as Spandauer Vorstadt) is one of Berlin's liveliest areas, teeming with nightclubs, bars and restaurants along Oranienburger Strasse and its side streets. Since reunification it has also reprised its historical role as the centre of the city's Jewish community. The gleaming gold dome of the rebuilt **Neue Synagoge** on Oranienburger Strasse stands as a beacon of this development. Built in Moorish-Byzantine style, it was Germany's largest synagogue with 3200 seats when it opened in 1866. During the 1938 Kristallnacht pogroms, a local police chief prevented SA thugs from setting it on fire, an act of courage commemorated by a plaque. The Nazis still managed to desecrate it, though it wasn't destroyed until hit by bombs in 1943.

Today the New Synagogue contains a community and research centre called **Centrum Judaicum** (☎ 2840 1250; Oranienburger Strasse 28-30; adult/concession €3/2; ☼ 10am-8pm Sun & Mon, 10am-6pm Tue-Thu, 10am-2pm Fri May-Oct; reduced hours Nov-Apr) with a permanent exhibit about the history of the building and Jewish life and culture in Berlin and Brandenburg.

The crumbling building just up the street is the **Tacheles** (☎ 282 6185; Oranienburger Strasse 54-56), a former department store that became an art squat after reunification and has since evolved into an edgy cultural centre. It's still a chaotic, graffiti-covered warren of artists' studios, galleries, a cinema, café and beer garden, but now it also houses a fancy restaurant named Milagro (p125).

Another tourist magnet is the Hackesche Höfe, eight linked courtyards filled with cafés, galleries, boutiques and theatres. The best is Hof 1, whose façades are emblazoned with intricately patterned Art Nouveau tiles. The concept worked so well that there are now several more restored courtyard complexes in the area. Right next to the Hackesche Höfe is the brand-new **Rosenhöfe**, which features a sunken rose garden and sculpted filigree metal balustrades intended to resemble flowers and botanical tendrils. A hop and a skip away, between Sophienstrasse and Gipsstrasse, are the quiet and dignified **Sophie-Gips-Höfe** courtyards with artistic light installations. The nicest courtyards for our money, though, are the breezy **Heckmannhöfe** between Oranienburger Strasse and Auguststrasse, where benches and a pretty fountain invite lingering.

ORANIENBURGER TOR AREA
Map pp98-9

Oranienburger Strasse eventually merges with Friedrichstrasse at Oranienburger Tor. The area south of here has traditionally been Berlin's premier **theatre district**. Major venues include the flashy **Friedrichstadtpalast**, the well-respected **Deutsches Theater & Kammerspiele** and the **Berliner Ensemble**, founded by Bertolt Brecht after WWII (p136).

Brecht, in fact, lived just a short walk north of Oranienburger Tor in what is now the **Brecht-Weigel Gedenkstätte** (Brecht-Weigel Memorial House; ☎ 283 057 044; Chausseestrasse 125; tours adult/concession €3/1.50; guided tours half-hourly

---

BERTOLT BRECHT

Bertolt Brecht (1898–1956), the controversial poet and playwright who spent the last seven years of his life in East Berlin, wrote his first play, *Baal*, while studying medicine in Munich in 1918. His first opus to reach the stage, *Trommeln in der Nacht* (Drums in the Night; 1922), won the coveted Kleist Prize, and two years later he moved to the Deutsches Theater in Berlin to work with the Austrian director Max Reinhardt.

Over the next decade, in plays like *Die Dreigroschenoper* (The Threepenny Opera; 1928), Brecht developed his theory of 'epic theatre', which, unlike 'dramatic theatre', forces its audience to detach itself emotionally from the play and its characters and to reason intellectually.

A staunch Marxist, Brecht went into exile during the Nazi years, surfaced in Hollywood as a scriptwriter, then left the USA after being called in to explain himself during the communist witch-hunts of the McCarthy era. The exile years produced many of his best plays: *Mutter Courage und ihre Kinder* (Mother Courage and Her Children; 1941), *Leben des Galilei* (The Life of Galileo; 1943), *Der gute Mensch von Sezuan* (The Good Woman of Sezuan; 1943) and *Der kaukasische Kreidekreis* (The Caucasian Chalk Circle; 1948).

Brecht returned to East Berlin in 1949 where he founded the Berliner Ensemble with his wife, the actress Helene Weigel, who directed it until her death in 1971. During his lifetime Brecht was both suspected in the East for his unorthodox aesthetic theories and scorned (and often boycotted) in much of the West for his communist principles. A staple of left-wing directors throughout the 1960s and 1970s, Brecht's plays are now under reassessment, though his influence in freeing the theatre from the constraints of a 'well made play in three acts' is undeniable. The superiority of Brecht's poetry, so little known in English, remains undisputed.

10-11.30am Tue-Fri, 5-6.30pm Thu, 9.30am-1.30pm Sat & hourly 11am-6pm Sun). A half-hour tour takes in Brecht's relatively modest office, library and bedroom, as well as the cluttered quarters of his actress wife Helene Weigel who lived here until her death in 1971. Call ahead about English-language tours. The basement restaurant serves food prepared from Weigel's recipes (mains €9 to €14).

The couple is buried in the adjacent **Dorotheenstädtischer Friedhof** (8am-sunset) along with other German luminaries including the architect Schinkel, the philosopher Hegel and the writer Heinrich Mann. Look for the chart with names and grave locations at the end of the walkway leading to the cemetery.

North of here is the Humboldt University's **Museum für Naturkunde** (Natural History Museum; ☎ 2093 8591; Invalidenstrasse 43; adult/concession €3.50/2; 9.30am-5pm Tue-Fri, 10am-6pm Sat & Sun), a vast repository with a world-famous dinosaur hall featuring a gigantic brachiosaurus skeleton. Other star exhibits include a rare specimen of an archaeopteryx, the prehistoric species that forms the evolutionary link between reptiles and birds.

Further west, the **Hamburger Bahnhof** (☎ 3978 3412; Invalidenstrasse 50-51; adult/concession €6/3, SMB pass valid; 10am-6pm Tue-Fri, 11am-6pm Sat & Sun) is Berlin's premier contemporary art museum. It's housed in a former train station centred on a vaulted hall with the loftiness of a Gothic cathedral. Besides high-calibre temporary exhibits, the museum displays selections from its permanent collection, with Andy Warhol, Anselm Kiefer, Robert Rauschenberg and especially Joseph Beuys all well represented. Admission is included in the Kulturforum ticket price (see p109).

NEW GOVERNMENT QUARTER
Map pp98-9

The decision to move the federal government from Bonn to Berlin in 1991 sparked a frenzied building boom in the area northwest of the Brandenburg Gate that lasted throughout the 1990s. The main anchor of Berlin's new government quarter, though, actually has quite a bit of history already: the 1894 **Reichstag** (Platz der Republik 1), which has been the seat of the *Bundestag*, the German parliament, since 1999. Its most striking contemporary feature is the glistening glass dome, designed by Sir Norman Foster who also supervised the renovation. A trip

on the **lift** (elevator; admission free; 8am-midnight, last entry 10pm) and up a spiralling ramp to the top is one of the highlights of any Berlin visit, as much for the views of the city as for the mind-bending close-ups of the mirror-clad funnel at the dome's centre. Come early or expect to queue.

The Reichstag has often been at the heart of momentous events in German history. After WWI, Philipp Scheidemann proclaimed the German Republic from one of its windows. The Reichstag fire on the night of 27 February 1933 allowed Hitler to blame the communists and seize power. A dozen years later, bombs and the victorious Soviets nearly obliterated the building. Restoration – without the dome – wasn't finished until 1972. At midnight on 2 October 1990 the reunification of Germany was enacted here. In summer 1995, the artist Christo and his wife, Jeanne-Claude, wrapped the edifice in fabric for two weeks. Sir Norman set to work shortly thereafter.

West of the Reichstag, the **New Federal Chancellery** (Neues Kanzleramt; Willy-Brandt-Strasse 1) is a sparkling, modern design by Axel Schultes that Berliners have nicknamed 'washing machine'. A central white cube containing the chancellor's office and residence is flanked by two long office blocks, giving the complex an 'H' shape if viewed from above. It's not accessible to the public but you'll get a sense of its dimensions when viewing it from Moltkebrücke or the northern Spree bank.

TIERGARTEN PARK
Map pp98-9

The new government quarter occupies the northernmost reaches of the Tiergarten, Europe's largest metropolitan park, which sweeps westward from Brandenburg Gate all the way to Bahnhof Zoo in Charlottenburg. Originally a hunting ground for Prussian rulers, its shady trees, groomed paths, lakes and meadows now invite a jog, picnic or stroll. Chime concerts ring out at noon and 6pm daily from the huge **carillon** (mapon John-Foster-Dulles-Allee, just south of the New Chancellery.

Nearby, the **Haus der Kulturen der Welt** (House of World Cultures; ☎ 397 870; John-Foster-Dulles-Allee 10; admission varies; 10am-9pm Tue-Sun) seeks to foster global dialogue through a series of art exhibits, lectures, seminars and performances. This swooping, free-form building, which Berliners have dubbed the 'pregnant oyster',

as the American contribution to the 1957 International Building Exposition.

Strasse des 17 Juni, named after the date of the 1953 workers' uprising in East Berlin, cuts east–west through the park. Along here, near the Brandenburg Gate, is the **Soviet War Memorial** flanked by two Russian tanks, allegedly the first to enter the city in 1945. The reddish-brown marble is said to have come from Hitler's chancellery. More of this recycled marble made it into the **Sowjetisches Ehrenmal** (Soviet Memorial) in Treptower Park (p116).

Further west looms the landmark **Siegessäule** (Victory Column; adult/concession €1.50/1; 9.30am-6.30pm Mon-Thu, 9.30am-7pm Fri-Sun), which commemorates 19th-century Prussian military exploits and is crowned by a gilded statue of Victoria (locals call her Gold-Else'). You can climb to the top, but the views are only so-so. The column has become a symbol of Berlin's gay community (the largest of Berlin's gay publications is named after it) and marks the terminus of the annual Christopher Street Parade. The park around here is a pick-up area, especially around the Löwenbrücke.

North of here, **Schloss Bellevue**, a white neoclassical palace from 1785, is the official residence of the German president.

SOUTH OF TIERGARTEN PARK

The area south of the Tiergarten, also called the Diplomats Quarter, is home to several spectacular new embassy buildings. Standouts include the **Nordic embassies** (Map pp98-9; Rauchstrasse 1), a joint complex of the Scandinavian countries distinguished by a shimmering turquoise façade, and the **Mexican embassy** (Map pp98-9; Klingelhöferstrasse 27), a boldly modern concrete and glass edifice.

Just south of here, on the Landwehrkanal, the **Bauhaus Archive/Museum of Design** (Map pp96-7; ☎ 254 0020; Klingelhöferstrasse 14; adult/concession €4/2; 10am-5pm Wed-Mon) is devoted to the artists of the Bauhaus School (1919–33), who laid the basis for much contemporary architecture and design. It's housed in a striking white building designed by the school's founder, Walter Gropius. The exhibits present furniture, blueprints, models and graphic prints by Gropius, Klee, Kandinsky and other Bauhaus practitioners. For more on the Bauhaus School, see the boxed text Design for Life (p246).

Further east is the **Gedenkstätte Deutscher Widerstand** (Map pp98-9; ☎ 2699 5000; Stauffenbergstrasse 13-14; admission free; 9am-6pm Mon-Wed & Fri, 9am-8pm Thu, 10am-6pm Sat & Sun) with an exhibit detailing German resistance efforts against the Nazis, with emphasis on the assassination attempt of Hitler on 20 July 1944 led by Graf von Stauffenberg. He and his co-conspirators were killed in the courtyard.

Follow the canal east to the **Neue Nationalgallerie** (New National Gallery; Map pp100-1; ☎ 266 2651; Potsdamer Strasse 50; adult/concession €6/3, SMB pass valid; 10am-6pm Tue-Fri, 10am-10pm Thu, 11am-6pm Sat & Sun), Berlin's main repository of work by 20th-century European artists until 1960. Klee, Kirchner, Munch, Picasso, Miró and many others grace the walls, but it's the German expressionists who steal the show: the warped works of Otto Dix, the 'egghead' figures by George Grosz and Kirchner's Potsdamer Platz are all stunners. The gallery is housed in a futuristic glass-and-steel cube designed by Mies van der Rohe in 1968. Admission is included in the Kulturforum ticket price (see below).

KULTURFORUM
Map pp100-1

This cluster of top-notch museums and concert venues off the southeastern edge of Tiergarten park was master-planned in the 1950s by Hans Scharoun, one of the era's premier architects, although most buildings weren't completed until the 1980s. The **Kulturforum ticket** (adult/concession €6/3) allows entry to all the museums here as well as the Neue Nationalgallerie (above) and the Hamburger Bahnhof (p108).

If you only see one museum here, make it the **Gemäldegalerie** (Picture Gallery; ☎ 266 2951; Stauffenbergstrasse 40; adult/concession €6/3, SMB pass valid; 10am-6pm Tue-Sun, 10am-10pm Thu). Set in a gloriously designed building, it's a spectacular showcase of European painting from the 13th to the 18th centuries. Highlights include work by masters such as Rembrandt, Rubens, Cranach, Dürer, Holbein, Botticelli, Raphael, Titian, de la Tour, Gainsborough, Reynolds, Goya and Velázquez. The galleries are accessed from the football-field-sized and pillared Great Hall, lavishly lit by circular skylights. Admission includes audio-guides with commentary (German or English) on selected paintings.

North of here, the cavernous **Kunstgewerbemuseum** (☎ 266 2951; adult/concession €6/3, SMB pass valid; ⊙ 10am-6pm Tue-Fri, 11am-6pm Sat & Sun) brims with decorative arts from the Middle Ages to the present. The vast collections range from gem-encrusted reliquaries to Art Deco ceramics and modern appliances. Don't miss Carlo Bugatti's crazy suite of furniture (1885) blending elements of Islamic, Japanese and Native American design.

Across the plaza, the **Kupferstichkabinett** (Copperplate Etchings Gallery; ☎ 266 2951; Matthäikirchplatz 8; adult/concession €6/3, SMB pass valid; ⊙ 10am-6pm Tue-Fri, 11am-6pm Sat & Sun) displays one of the world's largest and finest collections of graphic art, including exceptional works by Dürer, Rembrandt, Picasso and many other top artists.

The honey-coloured building east of here is Berlin's premier classical concert venue, the Hans Scharoun-designed **Berliner Philharmonie** (1961) with otherworldly acoustics achieved through a complicated layout of three pentagonal floors twisting and angling around the central orchestra pit (see p135).

Also built to plans by Scharoun were the adjacent **Kammermusiksaal** (Chamber Music Hall; 1987) and the 1978 **Neue Staatsbibliothek** (New National Library; ☎ 2660; Potsdamer Strasse 33; ⊙ reading rooms 9am-9pm Mon-Fri, 9am-7pm Sat) across Potsdamer Strasse, as well as the **Musical Instruments Museum** (☎ 2548 1178; Tiergartenstrasse 1; adult/concession €6/3; ⊙ 9am-5pm Mon-Fri, 10am-5pm Sat & Sun). The latter's collection of harpsichords, medieval trumpets and shepherds' bagpipes may not start a stampede for tickets, but the museum displays them in a unique and wonderful way. A highlight is the mighty **Wurlitzer**, an organ with more buttons and keys than a troop of Beefeater guards. Demonstrations take place at noon on Saturday.

POTSDAMER PLATZ   Map pp98-9

A showcase of urban renewal and perhaps the most visible symbol of the 'New Berlin', **Potsdamer Platz** is a major tourist attraction. The historic place was a busy traffic hub that became synonymous with metropolitan life and entertainment in the early 20th century. In 1924, Europe's first (hand-operated) traffic light was installed here, a replica of which was recently hoisted in the same spot. World War II sucked all life out of Potsdamer Platz and the area soon plunged into a coma, bisected by the Wall until reunification.

In the 1990s, the city tapped an international cast of the finest minds in contemporary architecture, including Arata Isozaki, Rafael Moneo, Richard Rogers and Helmut Jahn, to design Potsdamer Platz – The Sequel based on a master plan by Renzo Piano. Hamstrung by city-imposed building guidelines, the final product, while certainly far from avant-garde, is nevertheless a pleasant and above all human-scale cityscape.

Berliners and visitors have by and large embraced the new development, which consists of two sections: **DaimlerCity**, which celebrated its fifth anniversary in 2003, and the **Sony Center**, inaugurated in 2000. Part of the appeal certainly lies in its entertainment value. Aside from two multiplex cinemas – including two IMAX theatres – the arty Arsenal Cinema, a couple of nightclubs, a casino and a musical theatre bring in decent crowds. In 2000 the International Film Festival moved here from Charlottenburg. The central plaza of the Sony Center, with its dramatic tentlike glass roof, and the steps adjoining an artificial pond within DaimlerCity have become popular spots for hanging out and people-watching.

A multimedia journey through German film history and a behind-the-scenes look at special effects are what await visitors to the **Filmmuseum Berlin** (☎ 300 9030; Potsdamer Strasse 2; adults/concession €6/4; ⊙ 10am-6pm Tue-Sun, 10am-8pm Thu). The museum kicks off with appropriate theatricality as it sends you through a warped mirror room straight from *The Cabinet of Dr Caligari*. Major themes include pioneers and early divas, Fritz Lang's silent epic *Metropolis*, Leni Riefenstahl's awe-inspiring *Olympia*, and post-WWII movies. As she did in real life, though, it is femme fatale Marlene Dietrich who steals the show with selections from her private collection of costumes, personal finery, photographs and documents.

Fans of 20th-century abstract, conceptual and minimalist art should pop into the **DaimlerChrysler Contemporary** (Haus Huth; admission free; ⊙ 11am-6pm), a gallery space in the only surviving historic structure on Potsdamer Platz. Changing exhibits are drawn from the corporation's permanent collection, which ranges from Bauhaus artists like Oscar Schlemmer and Max Bill to international hotshots like Andy Warhol and Jeff Koons.

For a bird's-eye view of Potsdamer Platz, you can take what is billed as the world's astest elevator to the **Panorama Observation eck** (Potsdamer Platz 1; adult/concession €3.50/2.50; 11am-8pm Tue-Sun).

Kreuzberg

South of Mitte, Kreuzberg has a split personality. Its eastern end, bordering the Spree River, has largely preserved the free-spirited, grungy vibe that drew scores of students, punks, hippies and anyone in search of an alternative lifestyle long before reunification. Some of the edginess may since have worn off, but the area still teems with no-nonsense bars, clubs and alternative cinemas along Oranienstrasse and its side streets. This is also the hub of Berlin's Turkish community with an excellent Turkish Market along the canal (p137).

Kreuzberg's western half around Viktoriapark, by contrast, has a gentrified air about it and is mostly residential. Northern Kreuzberg has the district's two major sights: the Jewish Museum and Checkpoint Charlie.

JÜDISCHES MUSEUM

The history of German Jews and their contributions to culture, art, science and other fields is creatively chronicled at the **Jüdisches Museum** (Jewish Museum; Map pp98-9; 2599 3300; Lindenstrasse 9-14; adult/concession €5.50/2.75; 10am-10pm Mon, 10am-8pm Tue-Sun, closed Jewish holidays & Christmas Eve), one of Berlin's must-do sights. It's the largest Jewish Museum in Europe. The horrors of the Holocaust are commemorated most poignantly through a series of 'voids' – empty spaces intended to symbolise the loss of humanity, culture and people.

The museum itself, a stunning work of art by Daniel Libeskind, is a metaphor for the torturous history of the Jewish people. Zinc-clad walls rise skyward in a sharply angled zigzag ground plan that's an abstract interpretation of a star. Instead of windows, irregular gashes pierce the building's gleaming skin. It's one of the most daring examples of the architecture of the New Berlin.

Tickets include admission to the **Otto Weidt Workshop** (Map pp98-9; 2859 9407; Rosenthaler Strasse 39; workshop only €1.50; noon-8pm Mon-Fri, 11am-8pm Sat & Sun) near the Hackesche Höfe (p107). Between 1941 and 1943 Weidt, a brush and broom maker, employed scores of deaf and blind Jews in his workshop, thereby saving them from deportation and death.

CHECKPOINT CHARLIE

Checkpoint Charlie, at the intersection of Friedrichstrasse and Zimmerstrasse, was the main gateway for non-Germans between the two Berlins during the Cold War. A reconstructed US Army guardhouse now stands at the site (the original being in the Allied Museum; see p115), as does the famous sign: 'You are now leaving the American sector.'

The period is engagingly chronicled in the **Haus am Checkpoint Charlie** (Map pp100-1; 253 7250; Friedrichstrasse 43-45; adult/concession €9.50/5.50; 9am-10pm), with a strong emphasis on the history and horror of the Berlin Wall. The exhibit is strongest when documenting the amazing feats of courage and ingenuity some GDR citizens displayed in their escapes to the West in home-made hot-air balloons, tunnels, concealed compartments in cars and even a one-man submarine.

TOPOGRAPHIE DES TERRORS & AROUND

West of Checkpoint Charlie, along Niederkirchner Strasse, once stood some of the most feared institutions of the Third Reich: the Gestapo headquarters, the SS central command, the SS Security Service and, after 1939, the Reich Security Main Office. None of these buildings exist anymore, but since 1997 a harrowing open-air exhibit called **Topography of Terror** (Topographie des Terrors; Map pp100-1; 2548 6703; Niederkirchnerstrasse 8; admission free; 10am-8pm May-Sep, 10am-dusk Oct-Apr) documents the historical importance of this site and the brutal institutions that occupied it. It's in German, but a free audioguide in English is available from the information kiosk. Note that some of the exhibit's photographs may be too graphic for children.

The beautiful building overlooking the grounds is the **Martin-Gropius-Bau** (Map pp100-1; 254 860; Niederkirchner Strasse 7; admission & hrs vary), now used for large-scale exhibits of international stature. Designed by the uncle of Bauhaus founder Walter Gropius, it's an Italian Renaissance-style cube with a spacious atrium and façades adorned with mosaics and terracotta reliefs. The stately building across the street is the **Abgeordnetenhaus** (Map pp100-1), the seat of Berlin's parliament.

THE BERLIN WALL

Shortly after midnight of 13 August 1961 construction began on a barrier that would divide Berlin for almost three decades. The Berlin Wall was a desperate measure by a GDR government on the verge of economic and political collapse to stem the exodus of its own people, 2.6 million of whom had left for the West since 1949.

Euphemistically called 'Anti-Fascist Protection Barrier', this grim symbol of oppression stretched for 160km, turning West Berlin into an island of democracy within a sea of socialism. Continually reinforced and refined over time, its cold concrete slabs – which you could touch or paint on the western side – ultimately backed up against a dangerous no-man's land of barbed wire, mines, attack dogs and watchtowers staffed by loyal border guards ready to gun down anyone trying to escape.

Of the over 5000 people who attempted escape only about 1600 made it across; most were captured and 191 were killed, the first only a few days after 13 August. The full extent of the cruelty of the system became blatantly clear on 17 August 1962 when 18-year-old Peter Fechtner was shot during his attempt to flee and was then left to bleed to death while the East German guards looked on.

This potent symbol of the Cold War scarred the city – and indeed the world – for just over 28 years. The countdown to its demise began in early 1989 when thousands of GDR citizens fled the country via Hungary, while even more staged massive protests against the Honecker regime at home. On 9 November 1989 the GDR government finally caved in: amid cheers, champagne and fireworks, the Wall was history. Memento seekers chiselled away much of it and entire sections ended up in museums around the world. Most of it, though, was unceremoniously recycled for use in road construction.

Today little more than 1.5km of the Wall is left, but throughout Berlin segments, memorial sites, museums and signs commemorate this horrifying but important chapter in German history. Besides the places mentioned below, the Haus am Checkpoint Charlie (p111) also chronicles this period.

East Side Gallery

This is the longest, best-preserved and most interesting surviving stretch of Wall and the one to see if you're pressed for time. Paralleling Mühlenstrasse in Friedrichshain (pp100-1), the 1300m-long section is an open-air gallery created by international artists in 1990; some freshened up their work in 2000.

Berliner Mauer Dokumentationszentrum

The events leading up to 13 August 1961 and the early days of the barrier construction are chronicled at the small but high-tech **Berliner Mauer Dokumentationszentrum** (Map pp98-99; Berlin Wall Documentation Centre; pp97-9; ☎ 464 1030; Bernauer Strasse 111; admission free; ☒ 10am-5pm Wed-Sun) through archival documents, photographs and listening stations playing eyewitnesses' testimonies and speeches. Climb the tower for a look at the memorial across the street, an artistic rendition of the death strip behind an original section of the Wall. To get to the centre, take the U8 to Bernauer Strasse. A short walk east along Bernauer Strasse is the **Reconciliation Chapel** (pp98-9; ☒ 10am-5pm Wed-Sun), a place of remembrance also noteworthy for its simple but radiant design.

Wall Victims Memorial

Just south of the Reichstag, on the eastern end of Scheidemannstrasse, is this sad memorial to the 191 people who died trying to scale the Wall – the last only nine months before it tumbled (Map pp98-9).

DEUTSCHES TECHNIKMUSEUM

The giant **Deutsches Technikmuseum** (German Museum of Technology; Map pp100-1; ☎ 902 540; Trebiner Strasse 9; adult/concession €3/1.50; ☒ 9am-5.30pm Tue-Fri, 10am-6pm Sat & Sun) is loaded with interactive stations, demonstrations and exhibits and is a fantastic place to keep the kids entertained for hours. This is even more true at the adjacent **Spectrum science centre** (enter from Möckernstrasse 26; admission included), where visitors can participate in about 250 experiments that explain various scientific principles, and the **Museumspark** with wind and watermills, railway systems and a historic brewery. A new ship-shaped addition, which opened in December 2003, appropriately houses the museum's renowned navigation exhibits.

Charlottenburg

This western district, Berlin's main visitor magnet until the fall of the Wall, may no longer get all of its former attention, but it's still worthy of exploration. The area south of Bahnhof Zoo, including Kurfürstendamm and its southern extension Tauentzienstrasse (home of the famous KaDeWe department store; see Shopping p136), has excellent mainstream shopping. New architecture, including Helmut Jahn's edgy glass office and retail complex called the **Neues Kranzler Eck** (Kurfürstendamm 23), has added much-needed contemporary flair, although it's the splendour of baroque Schloss Charlottenburg and its cluster of superb museums that continue to dazzle visitors the most.

SCHLOSS CHARLOTTENBURG   Map pp96-7

Charlottenburg Palace is one of the few remaining sites in Berlin reflecting the former grandeur of the royal Hohenzollern clan. Commissioned by Elector Friedrich III (later King Friedrich I) as a summer residence for his wife, Queen Sophie-Charlotte (1668–1705), it's on Spandauer Damm, about 3km northwest of Bahnhof Zoo. Each of the palace buildings charges separate admission (see details following). A special ticket, the Kombinationskarte (adult/concession €7.50/5.50), is good for admission to the Neuer Flügel (including audio-guide), Neuer Pavillon, Mausoleum, Belvedere and the upper floors of the Altes Schloss. At weekends and during summer holidays, demand for tickets is high, so show up early.

The palace's central – and oldest – section is the **Altes Schloss** (☎ 3209 1440; adult/concession €8/5; tours 9am-4pm Tue-Fri, 10am-4pm Sat & Sun), designed by Nering Eosander and containing the former royal living quarters. It must be visited on a 50-minute tour in German (ask for an English-language pamphlet). Each of the rooms is an extravaganza in stucco, brocade, gilt and overall opulence. Highlights include the Hall of Mirrors; the Oval Hall with views of the French gardens and distant Belvedere, the wind gauge in Friedrich I's bedchamber, the Porcelain Chamber smothered in Chinese blueware and figures, and the Eosander Chapel with its trompe l'oeil arches. After the tour you're free to explore the upper floor, with more paintings, silverware, vases, tapestries, weapons, Meissen porcelain and other items essential to the royal lifestyle. Admission to the upper floor is adult/concession €2/1.50.

The reign of King Friedrich II saw the addition, in 1746, of a new wing, the **Neuer Flügel** (☎ 320 911; adult/concession €5/4, includes audio guide; ☒ 10am-6pm Tue-Fri, 11am-6pm Sat & Sun). You'll find some of the palace's most beautiful rooms, including the frilly White Hall, the former dining hall, with its elaborate concave ceiling; the Golden Gallery, a rococo extravaganza of mirrors and gilding; and the Concert Hall. To the right of the staircase are the comparatively austere Winterkammern (Winter Chambers) of Friedrich Wilhelm II.

In the palace's west wing, the **Museum of Pre- and Early History** (☎ 3267 4811; adult/concession €6/3, SMB pass valid; ☒ 9am-5pm Tue-Fri, 10am-5pm Sat & Sun) has an outstanding collection of archaeological artefacts from the Stone Age to the Middle Ages of European and Middle Eastern cultures. Top billing goes to the antiquities unearthed in Troy (in today's Turkey) in 1871. The museum was under renovation at the time of writing, but should be open by the time you read this. Admission is included in the Charlottenburg ticket price (see p114).

A stroll through the sprawling **Charlottenburg Schlossgarten** (Charlottenburg Palace Garden; admission free) makes for a nice respite from all that sightseeing, although there's still more of it right in the park. The 1824 **Neuer Pavillon** (adult/concession €2/1.50; ☒ 10am-5pm

Tue-Sun), also known as Schinkel Pavilion after its architect, contains paintings, sculpture and crafts from the early 19th century. The 1788 rococo **Belvedere** (adult/concession €2/1.50; ☉ 10am-5pm Tue-Sun Apr-Oct, noon-4pm Tue-Fri, noon-5pm Sat & Sun Nov-Mar) is a folly that contains an impressive collection of porcelain from the royal manufacturer, KPM. Queen Luise (1776–1810) and her husband, Friedrich Wilhelm III (1770–1840) are among those resting in the neoclassical **Mausoleum** (adult/concession €1; ☉ 10am-5pm Tue-Sun Apr-Oct).

SCHLOSS AREA MUSEUMS   Map pp96-7

A **Charlottenburg ticket** (adult/concession €6/3) allows admission to these three museums and the Museum of Pre- and Early History (p113).

The undisputed star of Berlin's **Ägyptisches Museum** (Egyptian Museum; ☎ 3435 7311; Schlossstrasse 70; adult/concession €6/3, SMB pass valid; ☉ 10am-6pm Tue-Sun) – and the item everyone comes to see – is the bust of **Queen Nefertiti**, she of the long graceful neck and stunning looks (even after all these years – about 3300, give or take a century or two). This was among the many treasures German archaeologists unearthed during the 1912 excavations of a site in the Nile city of Amarna. Also on display are busts of other royal family members, as well as statues, reliefs, totemic animal figures and everyday items. Highlights from later periods include the 'Berlin Green Head' (500 BC) and the monumental Kalabsha Gate (around 20 BC).

Across the street awaits the **Berggruen Collection** (☎ 3269 5815; Schlossstrasse 1; adult/concession €6/3, SMB pass valid; ☉ 10am-6pm Tue-Sun), a delicacy for fans of Pablo Picasso. It showcases works from all of the major creative phases of this Catalan artist, ranging from the Blue and Rose to the Cubist periods and the more mellow canvases of his later years. Upstairs, the emphasis shifts to Paul Klee, along with paintings by Cézanne, Gauguin and Braque, and sculptures by Giacometti.

Art Nouveau, Art Deco and Functionalism take centre stage at the adjacent **Bröhan Museum** (☎ 3269 0600; Schlossstrasse 1a; adult/concession €6/3; ☉ 10am-6pm Tue-Sun). This vast collection of glass, porcelain, silver, furniture and lamps created between 1889 and 1939 is most effectively displayed in the fully furnished and decorated period rooms, including those by Hector Guimard, Émile Ruhlmann and Henry van de Velde.

KURFÜRSTENDAMM & AROUND   Map p1•

Originally a riding path leading to th royal hunting palace in the Grunewald fo est, Kurfürstendamm (Ku'damm for shor received its current look in the 1880s cou tesy of Bismarck who had it widened, pave and lined with fancy residential building On Breitscheidplatz, its southern terminu the landmark **Kaiser-Wilhelm-Gedächtniskirch** (Kaiser Wilhelm Memorial Church; 189 stands quiet and dignified amid the roarin commercialism. Allied bombs left only th husk of the west tower intact; it now con tains a **Gedenkhalle** (Memorial Hall; ☉ 10am-4p or 5pm Mon-Sat) with original ceiling mosaic marble reliefs, liturgical objects and photo from before and after the bombing. Th adjacent octagonal **hall of worship** (☉ 9am 7.30pm) with its intensely midnight-blu windows was added in 1961.

Northeast of the church, the exotic Ele phant Gate marks the entrance to the **Berli Zoo** (☎ 254 010; Hardenbergplatz 8; zoo or aquariur adult/student/child €9/7/4.50, for both €14/11/7; ☉ zo 9am-6.30pm Apr-Sep, closes earlier Oct-Mar, ☉ aquariur 9am-6pm year-round), Germany's oldest anima park dating back to 1844. Some 14,00 animals representing 1500 species make their home here, including endangere rhinoceroses and rare giant pandas o loan from China. The adjacent Aquarium has three floors of fish, amphibians, reptile and other creatures. A highlight here is the crocodile hall.

West of Breitscheidplatz, the **Erotik Museum** (☎ 8862 6613; Joachimstaler Strasse 4; adult/concession €5/4; ☉ 9am-midnight) displays erotic sculptures, drawings and objects from around the world. It is the brainchild of Beate Uhse, Germany's porno and sex toy marketing equivalent of Martha Stewart. And, yes, you must be at least 18 to get in.

Appealing to a different kind of sensibility is the exquisite **Käthe-Kollwitz-Museum** (☎ 882 5210; Fasanenstrasse 24; adult/concession €5/2.50; ☉ 11am-6pm Wed-Mon) in a side street off Ku'damm. Dedicated to one of the greatest woman artists of the 20th century, its extensive collection of graphics, lithographs, woodcuts, sculptures and drawings shows the socialist artist's work in all its versatility and complexity. Audio-guides (in English too) are available.

Further west on Ku'damm, the **Story of Berlin** (☎ 8872 0100; Ku'damm Karree mall, Kurfürstenmm 207-208; adult/student/child €9.30/7.50/3.50; 10am-8pm, last admission 6pm) presents city history with a high-tech twist. Outfitted with space-age headphones whose commentary in English or German activates automatically as you enter a room, you time-travel through the history of Berlin from its founding in 1237 to today. Admission also includes a tour of the fully functional atomic bunker underneath the building. Budget at least two hours for this museum.

OLYMPIA STADION
Commissioned by Hitler for the 1936 Olympic Games, the **Olympia Stadion** (Olympic Stadium; ☎ 301 1100; tours €5 by appointment only, 10-person minimum), lies about 6km west of Bahnhof Zoo. Today the stadium is still very much in use for soccer, track and other sporting events. Sections of it remain closed, though, while it is being preened and modernised for the 2006 World Cup (soccer). For a preview of what the revamped stadium will look like, visit the multimedia exhibit **Olympia-Stadion-Die Ausstellung** (adult/concession €2.50/1.50; 10am-6pm Wed & Sun) with its cool computer-animated panoramas. To get to the stadium, take the U2 to Olympia-Stadion Ost or the S5 to Olympiastadion.

The **Maifeld**, a vast field west of the stadium, was used for Nazi mass rallies. It's overlooked by the 77m-high **Glockenturm** (Clock Tower; ☎ 305 8123; adult/concession €2.50/1; 9am-5pm Apr-Oct, call for winter hours), which offers views over the stadium, the city and the Havel River. Northwest of here, the **Waldbühne** is a lovely amphitheatre used for summer concerts, film screenings and other cultural events.

Southwestern Berlin
The southwestern area of Berlin is one of the greenest, with about half of the land covered by forest, rivers and lakes. The villa-studded suburbs of Dahlem and Wannsee contribute greatly to its small-town character. Dahlem especially has a lot to offer visitors. Besides the **Freie Universität** and the **Botanical Garden** (☎ 8385 0027; Königin-Luise-Strasse 6-8; adult/concession €4/2; 9am-dusk), you'll find several world-class museums here.

ETHNOLOGISCHES MUSEUM
The **Dahlem ticket** (adult/concession €4/2) allows admission to the museums here and the Museum of Europäischer Kulturen (p116).

It's impossible to describe fully the extraordinary collection of the **Ethnologisches Museum** (Museum of Ethnology; ☎ 830 1438; Lansstrasse 8; SMB pass valid; 10am-6pm Tue-Fri, 11am-6pm Sat & Sun). It has one of the world's largest and most outstanding collections of preindustrial non-European art and objects. Budget at least two hours to walk through its labyrinth of halls – it's an eye-opening journey of discovery that'll fly by in no time. Note that some sections may be closed while receiving a gradual overhaul. The Africa exhibit is particularly impressive with its wealth of masks, ornaments, vases, musical instruments and other objects of ceremonial and everyday life, most hailing from Cameroon, Nigeria and Benin. The high level of craftsmanship is especially evident in a beaded throne that was a gift from King Njoya of Cameroon to Emperor Wilhelm II. The South Seas halls are another crowd-pleaser, with cult objects from New Guinea, Tonga, Melanesia and other islands, as well as a vast space displaying outriggers and other boats.

Under the same roof, the **Museum für Indische Kunst** (Museum of Indian Art) presents fine and applied art from India, Southeast Asia and Central Asia from the 2nd century BC to the present. Keep an eye out for exquisite terracottas, stone sculptures and bronzes, as well as wall paintings and sculptures scavenged from Buddhist cave temples along the Silk Route.

Also here is the **Museum für Ostasiatische Kunst** (Museum of East Asian Art), which features ceramics, bronzes, lacquerware, jade objects and graphics from China, Japan and Korea. A highlight is a full-sized Japanese tea room.

To get to here, take the U1 to Dahlem-Dorf.

ALLIIERTENMUSEUM
Housed in the former Outpost cinema for US troops, the **AlliiertenMuseum** (Allied Museum; ☎ 818 1990; Clayallee 135; admission free; 10am-6pm Thu-Tue) is an engaging multimedia exhibit that documents the history and challenges faced by the Western Allies during the Cold War. The original guard cabin from Checkpoint Charlie is here, as is a piece of the Wall and a GDR guard tower. Inside, highlights include the documentation of the Berlin Airlift and the partly re-created

Berlin Spy Tunnel, built by the CIA to tap into the central Soviet phone system. Take U1 to Oskar-Helene-Heim, then any bus or a 10-minute walk north on Clayallee.

HAUS DER WANNSEEKONFERENZ GEDENKSTÄTTE

In January 1942, a group of elite Nazi officials met in a stately villa on Lake Wannsee to discuss the so-called 'Final Solution', the systematic deportation and annihilation of the European Jews. The same building now houses the **Haus der Wannseekonferenz Gedenkstätte** (Wannsee Conference Memorial Exhibit; ☎ 805 0010; Am Grossen Wannsee 56-58; admission free; ☺ 10am-6pm Mon-Fri, 2-6pm Sat & Sun). You can stand in that fateful room, study the minutes of the meeting and look at photographs of the Nazi thugs. The other rooms chronicle, in a thorough and graphic fashion, the horrors leading up to and perpetrated during the Holocaust. English-language pamphlets may be borrowed from the desk. Take the S1 or S7 to Wannsee, then bus No 114.

BRÜCKE MUSEUM

In 1905 Karl Schmidt-Rottluff, Erich Heckel and Ernst Ludwig Kirchner founded an artist group that sought to break away from the staid traditions taught at conventional art schools. Calling themselves Die Brücke (The Bridge), they were soon joined by Emil Nolde, Max Pechstein and others in developing a ground-breaking approach that paved the way for German expressionism. Their works are the focus of the small but worthwhile **Brücke Museum** (☎ 831 2029; Bussardsteig 9; adult/concession €4/2; ☺ 11am-5pm Wed-Mon). Take the U1 to Oskar-Helene-Heim, then bus No 115 to Pücklerstrasse.

MUSEUM EUROPÄISCHER KULTUREN

The main exhibit at the **Museum Europäischer Kulturen** (Museum of European Cultures; ☎ 8390 1295; Im Winkel 6-8; adult/concession €4/2, SMB pass valid; ☺ 10am-6pm Tue-Fri, 11am-6pm Sat & Sun) is based on a fairly abstract and heady concept: it seeks to show how cultural cross-fertilisation has shaped the heritage and identity of European countries in the context of the production, exhibition and use of images. Fortunately, on the exhibition floor this translates into more tangible – and often quite interesting – displays of furniture, tiles, carpets, paintings, photography, film,

TV and wherever else images play a role people's daily lives. Admission is includ in the Dahlem ticket price (see p115).

Eastern Districts

The outlying districts – eg Lichtenber Treptow, Marzahn – in eastern Berlin a of limited interest to visitors, with a fe notable exceptions.

In Lichtenberg, the one-time Stasi hea quarters now houses the so-called **Sta Museum** (☎ 553 6854; Ruschestrasse 103 (House adult/concession €3/2; ☺ 11am-6pm Tue-Fri, 2-6pm Sat Sun), where you can see the office of longtim Stasi chief Erich Mielke, cunning survei lance devices and communist parapherna lia. Take the U5 to Magdalenenstrasse.

Southeast of here, the **Museum Berli Karlshorst** (☎ 5015 0841; Zwieseler Strasse 4, c Rheinsteinstrasse; admission free; ☺ 10am-6pm Tue-Su is filled with documents, objects, uniform and photographs chronicling every stage o the often difficult German–Soviet relation ship from 1917 to reunification. It's house in the villa where German commander signed the unconditional surrender of th Wehrmacht on 8 May 1945. Take the S3 t Karlshorst.

Treptow's main attraction is the monu mental **Soviet War Memorial** (Map pp96-7; Sow jetisches Ehrenmal; ☺ 24hr) in Treptower Park which attests both to the immensity o WWII's losses and to the overblown self importance of the Stalinist state. From the S-Bahn station Treptower Park, head south wards for about 750m on Puschkinallee, then enter the park through the stone gate.

ACTIVITIES
Cycling

The German bicycle club **ADFC** (Map pp98-9; ☎ 448 4724; www.adfc-berlin.de; Brunnenstrasse 28; ☺ noon-8pm Mon-Fri, 10am-4pm Sat) publishes an excellent guide showing all the bike routes in the city. It's available at their office/shop and also in bookshops and bike stores.

Several agencies in town hire out bicycles with costs ranging from €10 to €25 per day and €35 to €85 per week, depending on the model. A minimum deposit of €50 and/or ID is required.

Fahrradservice Kohnke (Map pp98-9; ☎ 447 6666; Friedrichstrasse 133; ☺ 9am-midnight Mon-Fri)
Fahrradstation (☎ 0180-510 8000 information & booking); Scheunenviertel (Map pp98-9; ☎ 2838 4848; Hof

ll, Hackesche Höfe; 10am-7pm Mon-Fri, 10am-4pm at); Scheunenviertel (☎ 2859 9661; Auguststrasse 29a; 10am-7pm Mon-Fri, 10am-3pm Sat); Bahnhof Fried- chstrasse (Map pp98-9; ☎ 2045 4500; Friedrichstrasse 41/142; 8am-8pm Mon-Fri, 10am-4pm Sat & Sun); Kreuzberg (Map pp100-1; ☎ 215 1566; Bergmannstrasse ; 10am-7pm Mon-Fri, 10am-3pm Sat)

Pedal Power (Map pp100-1; ☎ 5515 3270; Gross-beerenstrasse 53; 10am-7pm Mon-Fri, 10am-2pm Sat) Specialises in tandems (per day/week €20/79).

Prenzlberger Orange Bikes (Map p126; ☎ 442 8122; Kollwitzstrasse 35; 2.30-7pm Mon-Fri, 1-7pm Sat, 6-7pm) The opening hours shown here for Sundays are for the return of bikes only.

Ice Skating
Berlin's municipal indoor ice rinks are open from mid-October to early March. The cost is €3.60/1.65 per two-hour skating session, plus €3.60 per hour to hire skates. Call for specific hours, although 9am to 9pm is a good general guideline.

Erika-Hess-Eisstadion (Map pp96-7; ☎ 4575 5555; Müllerstrasse 185, Wedding) Take the U6 to Reinickendorfer Strasse.

Horst-Dohm-Eisstadion (Map p102; ☎ 823 4060; Fritz-Wildung-Strasse 9, Wilmersdorf) Take the U1 to Heidelberger Platz.

Running
Berlin is great for running because of its many parks. By far the most popular jogging ground is the Tiergarten, although the Tegeler Forst in Tegel and the Grunewald in Wilmersdorf/Zehlendorf are even more scenic. The trip around the scenic Schlachtensee is 5km. The park of Schloss Charlottenburg is another nice spot. Or else just hit the city streets.

Swimming
Berlin has lots of indoor and outdoor public pools. Some are closed on certain mornings when school groups take over. Others are restricted to specific groups – women only, men only, nudists, seniors – at certain times of the week. Unless noted otherwise, pool admission is adult/concession €4/2.50; saunas (all nude, usually mixed) generally cost adult/concession €14/10. Opening hours vary greatly by day, pool and season. For specifics, either call the facility or the hotline at ☎ 01803-102 020, or check the website (German only) at www.berlinerbaeder betriebe.de.

Blub Badeparadies (☎ 609 060; www.blub-berlin.de; Buschkrugallee 64; 4hr admission adult/concession €9/8, day pass €12/10; 10am-11pm) Fun indoor/outdoor pool with waterfall, 120m slide, saltwater pool, Jacuzzis, sauna and wave pool. Take the U7 to Grenzallee in the southeast of the city.

Stadtbad Charlottenburg (Map p102; Krumme Strasse 10); Alte Halle (☎ 3438 3860); Neue Halle (☎ 3438 3865) Alte Halle is a beautiful Art Nouveau pool with colourful tiles; Neue Halle is modern with 50m lap pool; sauna. Popular with gay men on nude bathing nights.

Stadtbad Neukölln (Map pp100-1; ☎ 6824 9812; Ganghoferstrasse 3) Two-pool bathing temple adorned with mosaics, columns, frescoes and marble; sauna. Take the U7 to Rathaus Neukölln.

Stadtbad Mitte (Map pp98-9; ☎ 3088 0910; Gartenstrasse 5) Modernised 1928 Bauhaus structure with 50m lap pool. Take S1 or S2 to Nordbahnhof.

Strandbad Wannsee (☎ 803 5612; Wannseebadweg 25, Zehlendorf) Possibly Europe's largest lakeside lido with 1km of sandy beach and plenty of infrastructure on the city's southwestern edge. Take the S1, S3 or S7 to Nikolassee, then bus No 513.

BERLIN FOR CHILDREN
Travelling to Berlin with the tots in tow is not a problem, especially if you don't keep the schedule too packed, and involve the kids in the day-to-day planning. Lonely Planet's *Travel with Children* by Cathy Lanigan gives good general advice on the subject. There's certainly no shortage of things to see and do around Berlin.

Kids love animals, of course, making the huge **Berlin Zoo & Aquarium** (p114), with its giant pandas, cuddly koalas and fearsome crocodiles, a sure winner. Dinosaur fans should stop in at the **Natural History Museum** (p108) for close-ups of the largest dino skeleton on display anywhere. The **German Museum of Technology** (p113) has hundreds of interactive stations where kids can learn why the sky is blue or how a battery works. In the southwestern suburb of Zehlendorf is the **Domäne Dahlem** (☎ 832 5000; Königin-Luise-Strasse 49), which illustrates the daily working life on a 17th-century farm (take the U1 to Dahlem Dorf), and the **Düppel Museum Village** (☎ 802 6671; Clauertstrasse 11), a re-created medieval village with Sunday demonstrations of old-time crafts (take the S1 to Zehlendorf or U1 to Oskar-Helene-Heim, then bus 115 from either to Ludwigsfelder Strasse).

Aspiring Harry Potters will like the magic shows presented by **Zaubertheater Igor Jedlin**

(Map p102; ☎ 323 3777; Roscherstrasse 7). Another fun diversion is the antics of **Cabuwazi** (☎ 530 0040), a nonprofit circus troupe of children aged 10 to 17 that performs at venues around town. Call or check the listings magazines for upcoming shows. Puppet shows are also big with the pre-teen set and are enjoyable even without German language skills. Of the many venues the **Puppentheater Berlin** (Map p126; ☎ 423 4314; Greifswalder Strasse 81-84) enjoys the best reputation.

On hot summer days, a few hours spent at the **Blub Badeparadies** or the lakeside beach of the **Strandbad Wannsee** (p117) will go a long way towards keeping tempers cool.

It's perfectly acceptable to bring your kids along to all but the fanciest restaurants, some of which even have special menus. But if you're up for a romantic night for two, try the following babysitter services or ask at your hotel for a recommendation:

Aufgepasst (☎ 851 3723; www.aufgepasst.de) English-speaking babysitters, nannies and day care.

Biene Maja (☎ 344 3973; www.babysitteragentur -berlin.de)

Kinder-Hotel (Map pp98-9; ☎ 4171 6928; www .kinderinsel.de; Eichendorffstrasse 17) Children-only hotel with 24-hour day care in 12 languages.

TOURS
Bus Tours
Most city sightseeing tours operate on the 'get-on, get-off as often as you wish' principle and there's very little difference between operators. The main competitors take in the major sights – including Kurfürstendamm, Brandenburg Gate, Schloss Charlottenburg, Berliner Dom and Alexanderplatz – on loops that take about two hours without getting off. Unless noted taped commentary comes in – count 'em – eight languages. Buses leave roughly every half-hour, with the first tour usually around 10am, and stop running around 6pm (earlier in winter). The cost is around €16 to €18. Children under 13 get a 50% discount.

Berolina Sightseeing (Map p102; ☎ 8856 8030) Starts at Kurfürstendamm 220.

BVB (Map p102; ☎ 683 8910) Tours originate at Kurfürstendamm 225.

BVG Top Tour (Map p102; ☎ 2562 6570; adult/child 6-14 €20/15) Open-top double-decker buses depart daily from mid-April to October from Kurfürstendamm 18. Live German/English commentary.

Severin + Kühn (Map p102; ☎ 880 4190) Tours start at Kurfürstendamm 216.

Tempelhofer (Map p102; ☎ 752 4057) Tours leave from Kurfürstendamm 231 (Map p102) and Unter den Linden 14 (Map pp98-9).

Cruises
A lovely way to experience Berlin on a warm summer day is from the deck of a tour boat cruising along the city's rivers, canals and lakes. Narration is provided in English and German. Tours range from one-hour spins around Museumsinsel taking in the main historic sights (from €4) to leisurely three-hour trips into the green suburbs (from €10) and night-time dinner cruises. Food and drink are sold on board, or bring along your own picnic. Small children usually travel free, while those under 14 and seniors can expect a 50% discount.

QUIRKY BERLIN

Sure, Berlin wouldn't be the same without the Pergamon, Reichstag and Unter den Linden, but the city also has plenty in store for those tired of the lemming routine. Catch that authentic GDR vibe while venturing into the city's 'wild east' behind the wheel of your own **Trabi** (Trabi Safari; ☎ 2759 2273) or explore **Berlin's underbelly** (Berliner Unterwelten; ☎ 4991 0518) on a tour of its dark and dank canals, abandoned subway tunnels and air-raid shelters.

For an even more disorienting experience, book a table at **Unsicht-Bar** (p125) or **Nocti Vagus** (Map pp98-9; ☎ 7474 9123; Saarbrücker Strasse 36-38), where you'll be dining in complete darkness, although probably not on the grasshopper stew or giant mealworm pasta served at **Soda** (p125).

Even Berlin's museum scene gets into the bizarre business with such entries as the **Zucker Museum** (Sugar Museum; Map p96-7; ☎ 3142 7574; Amrumer Strasse 32), dedicated to the sweeter things in life. Another hoot is the **Gründerzeit Museum** (☎ 567 8329; Hultschiner Damm 333), a collection of late-19th-century period rooms amassed by Charlotte von Mahlsdorf (born Lothar Bergfelde), a transvestite and icon of the gay movement in the GDR, who died in 2002.

Departure points vary by company but include the Nikolaiviertel (Map pp98-9), Friedrichsstrasse (Map pp98-9), Jannowitzbrücke (Map pp98-9) and Schloss Charlottenburg (Map pp96-7).

Berliner Wassertaxi (Map pp98-9; ☎ 6588 0203) One-hour tours aboard original Amsterdam canal boats.

Reederei Bruno Winkler (☎ 3499 5933; www.reederei winkler.de)

Reederei Riedel (☎ 691 3782; www.reederei-riedel.de)

Stern und Kreis Schifffahrt (☎ 536 3600; www .sternundkreis.de)

Walking Tours

Three companies offer guided English-language tours of Berlin, all of them excellent with well-informed and affable guides who provide a lively commentary and are eager to answer your questions. If time is limited and all you want is Berlin in a nutshell, take either the Famous Insider Walk with Insider Tour, the Discover Berlin tour with Original Berlin Walks, or Brewer's Classic Berlin, all of which last about four hours. If you have more time to play with or want to soak up as much information as possible, put on your most comfortable walking shoes and sign up for the all-day Brewer's Best of Berlin tour. It can take anything from six to 11 hours, depending on your group's stamina. Various thematic tours are also available. For details, pick up the companies' flyers at the tourist offices, hostels and many hotels.

Brewer's Best of Berlin (www.brewersberlin.de; tours €10) Tour options: Best of Berlin, Classic Berlin, Best of Potsdam. Tours pick up from the Circus Hostel (p120) at Rosenthaler Platz, the Clubhouse Hostel (p120) and the Odyssee Globetrotter Hostel (p121) and also leave from the New Synagogue (p106).

Insider Tour (☎ 692 3149; www.insidertour.com; tours €10-12, bike tour €20 includes bicycle; discounts apply for students, under 26, seniors and WelcomeCard holders) Tour Options: Famous Insider Tour, Berlin by Bike, Red Star (communist Berlin), Third Reich, Berlin by Night and Bar & Club Crawl.

Original Berlin Walks (☎ 301 9194; www.berlinwalks .com; tours €10-15, discounts if under 26 or with WelcomeCard) Tour options: Discover Berlin, Infamous Third Reich Sites, Jewish Life in Berlin, Sachsenhausen Concentration Camp, Potsdam.

For those preferring to go at their own pace, the **Hear We Go audio-guides** (€7; 90 minutes) are an alternative. A tour of the new government district is available from the BTM tourist office at the Brandenburg Gate (Map pp98-9), while the Haus am Checkpoint Charlie (Map pp100-1) hires out tours that follow in the footsteps of the Berlin Wall.

FESTIVALS & EVENTS

Berlin's calendar is loaded with annual fairs, festivals, concerts and parties. This website www.berlin.de/eventkalender has complete listings, but the tourist offices are a good source as well. The following is just a small sample:

Internationale Filmfestspiele (☎ 259 200; www .berlinale.de) The world's second-largest film festival (after Cannes), also called Berlinale; in February.

Internationale Tourismusbörse (☎ 303 80; www .itb-berlin.com) The world's largest travel show with exhibitors from everywhere; open to the public at the weekend; in April.

Festtage in der Staatsoper (☎ 203 540; www .staatsoper-berlin.org) An annual series of gala concerts and operas under the auspices of the Staatsoper Unter den Linden, it brings renowned conductors, soloists and orchestras to Berlin; late March/early April.

Theatertreffen Berlin (☎ 254 890; www.berlinerfes tspiele.de/theatertreffen) Three weeks of new productions by emerging and established German-language ensembles from Germany, Austria and Switzerland; May.

Karnival der Kulturen (☎ 6097 7022; www.karneval -berlin.de) Berlin's answer to London's Notting Hill Carnival, this is a raucous street festival with a parade of wacky, costumed people dancing and playing music on floats; late May/early June.

Christopher Street Day (☎ 2362 8632; www.csd -berlin.de) The biggest annual gay event with a big parade and nonstop partying; late June.

Love Parade (☎ 284 620; www.loveparade.de) Berlin's top annual techno event held in mid-July still attracts around one million people. The parade is followed by nonstop partying in clubs and the streets; mid-July.

JazzFest Berlin (☎ 254 890; www.jazzfest-berlin.de) Four-day jazz festival at various venues; early November.

Christmas Markets These are held daily from late November to around Christmas Eve on Breitscheidplatz (Map p102), Alexanderplatz (Map pp98-9) and outside the Opernpalais on Unter den Linden (Map pp98-9). In 2003, a nostalgic market premiered on Gendarmenmarkt (Map pp98-9).

SLEEPING

Berlin is busiest between May and September when room reservations are a good idea, especially if you're keen about a particular place. New hotels crop up all the time, with 'art hotels' (artist-designed boutique hotels) being the latest rage. Berlin also has many excellent independent hostels, which all seem to outdo each other in terms of comfort, décor and services. In addition to dorms, most now offer private rooms, often with en suite facilities, and even small apartments catering for couples and families.

Mitte is a great area to stay if you like being within walking distance of the major sights and burgeoning nightlife, although you'll pay a premium for the privilege. But Berlin's excellent public transportation system means you're never far from the action, no matter where you unpack your suitcase.

Charlottenburg and Wilmersdorf, for instance, generally offer better rates and more mid-priced options than other neighbourhoods. This is where you'll still find ambience-laden traditional pensions occupying graceful late-19th-century apartment buildings complete with birdcage lifts. Many have recently been spruced up, although you'll still find cheaper rooms with shared facilities. Some are not staffed all day, so ring ahead.

With its vibrant street life and relaxed bar and café scene, Kreuzberg makes for another fun and reasonably priced Berlin base, as does Friedrichshain, whose gritty GDR aesthetic sets it apart from heavily gentrified Mitte and Prenzlauer Berg. The latter, though, is a lovely neighbourhood, still central yet quieter than Mitte, but so far lodging options are surprisingly thin.

Unless mentioned otherwise, rates listed below include breakfast.

Mitte & Prenzlauer Berg
BUDGET
Circus – The Hostel Weinbergsweg (Map pp98-9; ☎ 2839 1433; www.circus-hostel.de; Weinbergsweg 1a; dm €15-20, s/d €32/48, 2-/4-person apartment with 2-night minimum €75/130; ☒ ☐); Rosa-Luxemburg-Strasse (Map pp98-9; Rosa-Luxemburg-Strasse 39-41) Beg, borrow and/or steal to secure a bed at this hostel, now in two excellent locations with easy access to sights and nightlife. Clean, cheerfully painted rooms, excellent showers, free lockers and competent and helpful staff are just a few factors that make these places winners. The penthouse apartments at the Weinbergsweg location, with private facilities, a full kitchen and killer views, are a bargain. The downstairs café serves breakfast, drinks and

small meals, and the basement bar has different activities nightly.

Generator Berlin (Map pp96-7; ☎ 417 2400 www.the-generator.co.uk; Storkower Strasse 160; dm €12-16.50, s/tw/tr/q with private bathroom per person €40/27/24/21, with shared bathroom €35/23/19/18 ☒ ☐) This slick 854-bed hostel scores big for its clean and spacious rooms, free breakfast, in-room lockers, linen and towel and youthful party atmosphere. The liberal use of psychedelic blue neon light adds an intriguing touch, and the hip circular bar is great for striking up friendships. Its 'deep east' location, though, means you'll be riding the train a lot (S4, S8 to Storkower Strasse).

Frauenhotel Intermezzo (Map pp98-9; ☎ 224 9096; www.hotelintermezzo.de; Gertrud-Kolmar-Strasse 5 s €45, d €70-80) Run by a trio of young women this man-free hotel has largish rooms with Scandinavian furnishings. Triples and quads also available. Breakfast is €5.50 per person

Hotel Transit Loft (Map p126; ☎ 789 0470; www .transit-loft.de; Greifswalder Strasse 219; dm/s/d €19/59/69 ℗) Occupying the 3rd and 4th floors o a former warehouse, this place is a hybrid hostel/hotel. All of the well-lit and functionally furnished rooms have private bathrooms and there's also a large dorm for backpackers Rates include a big breakfast buffet.

Mitte's Backpacker Hostel (Map pp98-9; ☎ 283 0965; www.baxpax.de; Chausseestrasse 102; dm €15-18 s/d/tr/q €30/46/63/80, discounts Oct-Apr; ☐) Quite a bit of imagination has gone into the décor of this well-established hostel where you'll sleep in such intriguingly themed digs a. the Arabic Room or the Underwater Room Other welcome features include a communal kitchen, bike hire and women-only dorms.

Other recommendations:

Helter Skelter (Map pp98-9; ☎ 2804 4997; www .helterskelterhostel.com; Kalkscheunenstrasse 4-5; shared bathroom dm €14-20, s/d €46/32; ☐) In the same building as the Kalkscheune, a major party and music location (p134), this place is also central to sights, theatre and restaurants. Breakfast is €3.

Lette 'm Sleep (Map p126; ☎ 4473 3623; www.back packers.de; Lettestrasse 7; shared bathroom dm €13-18, d €44) Central Prenzlauer Berg location, with 24-hour check-in, free Internet access and coffee, and a freshly spruced-up kitchen and common room.

MID-RANGE
Honigmond Garden Hotel (Map pp98-9; ☎ 284 5577; www.honigmond-berlin.de; Invalidenstrasse 122

€85-95, d €112-142; P ⊠) Never mind the location on a busy thoroughfare: this place, in a carefully restored 1845 building, is absolutely enchanting. Relax in the lush garden at the back, then retreat to pretty rooms, some with stucco ceilings, four-poster beds and polished wood floors.

Künstlerheim Luise (Map pp98-9; ☎ 284 480; www.kuenstlerheim-luise.de; Luisenstrasse 19; s €82-95, d €121-139; P ⊠) The only problem about this unique hotel is that you may not want to leave your amazing artist-designed room. Sure, take time to admire and even be inspired, but then tear yourself away and explore the city. Breakfast €7 per person.

Artist Hotel Riverside (Map pp98-9; ☎ 284 900; www.artist-hotels.de; Friedrichstrasse 106; r €90-130) Flea-market finds and movie props decorate the lobby lounge, which, like many of the 20 rooms, has views of the Spree River. For the romantically inclined, the 'wedding suite' – complete with waterbed and whirlpool bath – is the ticket. In-room champagne breakfast is €12 per person.

Hotel Kastanienhof (Map p126; ☎ 443 050; hotel-kastanienhof-berlin.de; Kastanienallee 65; s €73-83, d €98-118, ste €118-128; P ⊠) Staff are quick with a smile at this popular place right between Mitte and Prenzlauer Berg, one of the first area hotels after reunification. Those in need of more elbow space should book one of the good-value suites or apartments.

Dietrich-Bonhoeffer-Haus (Map pp98-9; ☎ 284 670; www.hotel-dbh.de; Ziegelstrasse 30; s €85-115, d €125-150; P ⊠) Named after the German theologian and resistance fighter who was killed by the Nazis, this church-affiliated hotel offers a central location, warm atmosphere and pleasantly furnished modern rooms.

Myer's Hotel (Map p126; ☎ 440 140; www.myers hotel.de; Metzer Strasse 26; s €80-130, d €100-165; ⊠) In a stately 19th-century building on a quiet street, yet close to Käthe-Kollwitz-Platz, Myer's has comfortable rooms that differ widely in terms of size and amenities. The lobby bar, tea room with bold red walls, garden and rooftop terrace are all great for kicking back between sightseeing forays.

TOP END
Adlon Hotel Kempinski (Map pp98-9; ☎ 226 10; www.hotel-adlon.de; Unter den Linden 77; s €280-440, d €330-490; P ⊠ ⊠ ⊠ ⊠) With front-row vistas of the Brandenburg Gate and a sumptuous 'restored-historical' ambience, this elegant full-service hotel leaves no desire unfulfilled. There's a high celebrity quotient. Rooms are wired for connectivity and even have 110V for American appliances. Breakfast buffet €24 per person.

art'otel berlin mitte (Map pp98-9; ☎ 240 620; www.artotel.de; Wallstrasse 70-73; s €128-168, d €158-198; P ⊠ ⊠ ⊡) One of the first-generation Berlin art hotels, this one fuses a modernist wing with an 18th-century patrician townhouse via a dramatic atrium. Rooms and public areas abound with works by contemporary German artist Georg Baselitz.

Alexander Plaza Berlin (Map pp98-9; ☎ 240 010; www.alexander-plaza.com; Rosenstrasse 1; s €150-180, d €160-190; P ⊠ ⊠ ⊡) At this delightful boutique hotel, 19th-century glamour meets New Millennium comforts. Natural colours, parquet floors and big windows are hallmarks. Nice inner courtyard.

Kreuzberg & Friedrichshain
BUDGET
City Hostel Meininger 12 (Map pp100-1; ☎ 7871 7414; www.meininger12.com; Hallesches Ufer 30; dm €13.50, s/d/tr/q €49/66/78/100; P ⊠ ⊡) Close to Potsdamer Platz and the Jewish Museum, this well-run hostel has friendly design and 71 rooms with private shower and toilet, including some suited for families and the disabled. The bar and rooftop terrace are great for kicking back, and there's lots of free stuff, including an all-you-can-eat breakfast buffet, parking, linen, towels and lockers.

Odyssee Globetrotter Hostel (Map pp100-1; ☎ 2900 0081; www.globetrotterhostel.de; Grünberger Strasse 23; dm €13-19, s/d with shared bathroom €35/45; ⊡) This funky and energetic hostel is a perfect base for those keen on making an in-depth study of Friedrichshain's nightlife. Rooms are artily decorated, clean and have lockers. Other perks include free breakfast buffet and linen, late checkout and a happening bar-lounge.

BaxPax (Map pp100-1; ☎ 6951 8322; www.baxpax .de; Skalitzer Strasse 104; dm €15-18, s/d/tr €30/46/60, discounts Oct-Apr; ⊡) Sister property to Mitte's Backpacker Hostel, this place in a former factory also has quirky themed rooms, including one where you can sleep in a VW Beetle and another decked out in GDR paraphernalia. There's also a large well-equipped kitchen with terrace.

Pegasus Hostel (Map pp100-1; ☎ 2935 1810; www.pegasushostel.de; Strasse der Pariser Kommune 35;

dm €13-15, s/d/tr/q with shared bathroom €30/46/57/64, discounts Nov-Mar; 💻) In a former Jewish girls' school, this large hostel has a beautiful backyard that's great for chilling and socialising, as are the well-equipped kitchen and on-site restaurant. Rooms have sinks and cheerful colours, and there are even doubles with private bathrooms and TV for €60.

Other recommendations:

A&O Hostel Friedrichshain (☎ 2900 7365, toll-free 0800-222 5722; www.aohostels.com; Boxhagener Strasse 73; dm €10-13, s/d/q with bathroom €49/56/88, discounts Nov-Feb; 🅿 ✗ 💻) Full-service hostel in a quiet area inside a former lift (elevator) factory with 24-hour bar, beer garden, kitchen, laundry and other services. Also see A&O Am Zoo (below).

Die Fabrik (Map pp100-1; ☎ 611 7116; www.diefabrik .com; Schlesische Strasse 18; dm €18, s/d/tr/q €36/49/66/ 80; 💻) In a former telephone factory, this hostel has a more grown-up ambience and an all-day café.

MID-RANGE

Hotel Riehmers Hofgarten (Map pp100-1; ☎ 7809 8800; www.riehmers-hofgarten.de; Yorckstrasse 83; s €98, d €123-138) Near Viktoriapark, this intimate 20-room hotel is part of a protected 1891 building complex with a lush inner courtyard certain to delight romantics. Rooms are decked out in custom-made classical-modern furniture; original art adds splashes of colour throughout. Gourmet restaurant.

East-Side Hotel (Map pp100-1; ☎ 293 833; www .eastsidehotel.de; Mühlenstrasse 6; s €60-80, d €70-100; 🅿) One of the first Friedrichshain hotels, the East-Side has comfortable rooms although the décor could use a little imagination. Singles all face the East Side Gallery, the longest remaining stretch of the Wall. Rates include an à la carte breakfast.

Gold Hotel am Wismarplatz (Map pp96-7; ☎ 293 3410; www.gold-hotel-berlin.de; Weserstrasse 24; s €53-68, d €73-103; ✗) The flowery bedspreads and curtains may be a bit dated, but otherwise this renovated hotel within easy access to the Friedrichshain bar scene is not a bad choice.

Juncker's Hotel Garni (Map pp100-1; ☎ 293 3550; www.junckers-hotel.de; Grünberger Strasse 21; s/d €59/73; 🅿) The carpeted rooms with small TV and desk won't win style awards, but since they're facing away from the street, they're great for sleeping with the windows open. Breakfast is €6 per person.

Hotel am Anhalter Bahnhof (Map pp100-1; ☎ 251 0342; www.hotel-anhalter-bahnhof.de; Strese-

mannstrasse 36; s €50-75, d €75-105; 🅿 ✗) This older place is a decent standby thanks to its friendly staff and relatively central location. An innovative computerised check-in system allows you to check in 24/7. Cheaper rooms share facilities.

TOP END

NH Berlin-Alexanderplatz (Map pp96-7; ☎ 422 6130; fax 422 613 300; Landsberger Allee 26-32; s €113-213, d €146-246; 🅿 ✗ ✗ 💻) Despite the name, this large, full-service hotel is actually opposite the Volkspark Friedrichshain. Rooms are contemporary and comfortable, if a touch generic with their easy-on-the-eye natural colour scheme. Bonus facilities include a fitness centre with sauna and steam room.

Charlottenburg & Wilmersdorf

BUDGET

Hotel-Pension Korfu II (Map p102; ☎ 212 4790; www .hp-korfu II.de; Rankestrasse 35; s/d with private bathroom from €53/67, with shared bathroom €33/47) Right by the Gedächtniskirche, this pension is a great bargain base for exploring Berlin. The pleasantly bright, carpeted rooms sport Scandinavian-style furniture and a surprising range of amenities.

A&O Hostel Am Zoo (Map p102; ☎ 297 7810; www .aohostel.com; Joachimstaler Strasse 1-3; dm €10-17, s/d with private bathroom €65/68; ✗ 💻) Opposite Bahnhof Zoo, this is one of the few new hostels in the western city. Rooms are bright,

---

THE AUTHOR'S CHOICE

Propeller Island Lodge (Map p102; ☎ 891 9016; www.propeller-island.de; Albrecht-Achilles-Strasse 58; s €75-125, d €90-140; ✗) Hands-down Berlin's most eccentric hotel, this is the brainchild of artist/musician Lars Stroschen who designed and handcrafted every accessory and piece of furniture in the 30 rooms. The result is a series of unique, warped and wicked environments perfect for those with imagination and a sense of adventure. How about a night in the 'Flying Bed' room with slanted walls and a bed seemingly hovering above the floor? Or the one called 'Gallery' with a rotating round bed and upstairs viewing platform? This is no conventional hotel, so don't expect the usual amenities. Lars does serve breakfast, though (€7 per person).

with neat laminate flooring, metal-frame beds and large lockable cabinets. Fill up at the breakfast buffet (€4) or grab a bag lunch available any time for €2. It's also a Bus About pick-up location (see Bus p138).

Hotel-Pension Castell (Map p102; ☎ 882 7181; www hotel-castell.de; Wielandstrasse 24; s/d €65/85) Most rooms here are plain and the furniture is getting a bit long in the tooth, but all are clean and have their own shower and toilet

Hotel-Pension Fischer (Map p102; ☎ 2191 5566; hotelpensionfischer@t-online.de; Nürnberger Strasse 24a; s €35-80, d €60-115; P ✕) The owners have seriously slicked up this place, bringing the décor and furniture into the new millennium. Seven of the 10 rooms now have their own shower and toilet.

Hotel-Pension München (Map p102; ☎ 857 9120; www.hotel-pension-muenchen-in-berlin.de; Güntzelstrasse 62; s/d €60/80, apartment €75-105; P) This small and quiet pension is owned by artist Renate Prasse, whose drawings, paintings and sculptures add aesthetic touches to the entrance area and rooms. Furnishings are rather ordinary but are coupled with modern amenities, including private bathrooms, cable TV and telephone.

MID-RANGE

Art Nouveau Hotel (Map p102; ☎ 327 7440; www .hotelartnouveau.de; Leibnizstrasse 59; s/d/ste €95/110/160; ✕) A rickety birdcage lift drops you off on the 4th floor leading to one of Berlin's best pensions. The owners have made creative use of colour and furnished each room with stylish antiques and new, comfortable beds. Expect plenty of attention to detail.

Hotel Gates (Map p102; ☎ 311 060; www.hotel-gates .com; Knesebeckstrasse 8-9; r from €80; P ▯) If you're a serious surfer dude (of the Internet, that is), this is the place for you. Rates include unlimited round-the-clock high-speed access on your in-room flat-screen PC. Room sizes vary but all are comfortable if a tad functional. Breakfast is €10 per person.

Hotel-Pension Funk (Map p102; ☎ 882 7193; www.hotel-pension-funk.de; Fasanenstrasse 69; s/d €69/89) Stucco ceilings, Art Nouveau windows, old-fashioned wallpaper and 1920s furniture are among the authentic retro touches of this charming pension in the former home of silent movie star Asta Nielsen. It's very popular, so early reservations are advised.

Hotel Bogota (Map p102; ☎ 881 5001; www.hotel bogota.de; Schlüterstrasse 45; s/d €72/98, with shared bath-room €44/69; P ✕) Step back in time in this delightful hotel, which offers historical ambience and friendly service at no-nonsense prices. It was the one-time home and studio of YVA, a 1930s fashion photographer and mentor of Helmut Newton (who, incidentally, began life as Helmut Neustadter in 1920s Berlin). Children stay free in their parents' room.

Hotel-Pension Augusta (Map p102; ☎ 883 5028; www.hotel-augusta.de; Fasanenstrasse 22; s €75-95, d €125-175 Apr-Oct; s €55-85 d €75-150 Nov-Mar; ✕ ✕) Rooms here have been subjected to a rigorous face-lift and now sparkle in cheerful colours and décor ranging from romantic to modern. Some have balconies or cosy alcoves. Ask about the brand-new suites.

Hotel Askanischer Hof (Map p102; ☎ 881 8033; www.askanischer-hof.de; Kurfürstendamm 53; s €95-115, d €117-145; ✕) Ornately carved doors open up to good-sized rooms decked out in the nostalgic style of the 1920s. Expect eclectic furniture, draped windows, chandeliers and oriental carpets coupled with the usual range of modern comforts.

TOP END

Hecker's Hotel (Map p102; ☎ 889 00, www.heckers -hotel.de; Grolmannstrasse 35; s €120-210, d €140-210; P ✕ ✕) Blue light envelops the cutting-edge cool lobby of this stylish hotel. Rooms, by contrast, feature soothing colours and some are like minisuites with walk-in closets, sitting areas, large desks and spacious marble bathrooms.

Hotel Bleibtreu (Map p102; ☎ 884 740; www .bleibtreu.de; Bleibtreustrasse 31; s €102-182, d €112-292; ✕) In a pretty side street off Ku'damm, the Bleibtreu flaunts an edgy, urban feel tempered by the warmth of Italian design and natural materials. Rooms are small but stylish, and extras include a steam room and on-site restaurant. Breakfast is €15 per person.

Long-Term Rentals

If you're planning to stay in Berlin for a month or longer, consider renting a room or an apartment through a *Mitwohnzentrale* (flat-sharing agency), which matches people willing to let their digs to those needing a temporary home. Accommodation can be anything from rooms in shared student flats to furnished apartments. Agencies to try include:

Erste Mitwohnzentrale (Map p102; ☎ 324 3031; www.mitwohn.com; Sybelstrasse 53)

HomeCompany (Map p102; ☎ 194 45; www.homecompany.de; Joachimstaler Strasse 17)

Wohnagentur am Mehringdamm (Map pp100-1; ☎ 786 2003; www.wohnung-berlin.de; Mehringdamm 66)

Camping

Camping facilities in Berlin are neither plentiful nor particularly good. All are far from the city centre and cumbersome to reach by public transport. Still, most fill up quickly, with many spaces taken up by caravans, so be sure to call ahead to inquire about availability. Charges are around €5.10 per person, plus €3.80 for a small tent site to €6.60 for a larger tent with car space; showers are €0.50.

Campingplatz Breithorn (☎ 365 3408; Breithorn-weg, Spandau; ⊗ Apr-Sep) Private Havel beach, grassy spots. Take U7 to Spandau, then bus No 136 to Kraftwerk Oberhavel.

Campingplatz Bürgerablage (☎ 335 4584; Zum Jagen 11, Spandau; ⊗ Apr-Sep) Also riverside. Take U7 to Spandau, then bus No 134 or 137 to the camp sites.

Campingplatz Dreilinden (☎ 805 1201; Albrechts-Teerofen, Zehlendorf; ⊗ Mar-Oct) Canalside camping about 30 minutes on foot from the Griebnitzsee S-Bahn station (S7), or take S1 to Wannsee, then bus No 118, then 20 minutes' walk.

EATING

Berlin's traditional reputation as a culinary wasteland is no longer deserved as a new generation of chefs, many with international experience, has given fresh impetus to the cuisine scene. Dishes have become lighter, healthier and more interesting. Fresh ingredients, low-fat cooking techniques and seasonal menus are increasingly commonplace.

Asian restaurants, especially, have proliferated and although spice levels and ingredients are usually calibrated to match conservative local tastes, you can still find a decent *pad thai*, madras curry or tuna roll. Vegetarians will be glad to find that tofu, tempeh and seitan have finally entered the local culinary vernacular. And even those finicky Michelin testers have awarded precious stars to several establishments.

One of life's little luxuries is a leisurely breakfast, and Berliners have just about perfected the art, especially on Sundays

when many cafés dish out lavish buffe where you can seriously pig out. Speak ing of pig: as elsewhere in Germany, it' a staple of traditional Berlin cooking an you may not want to leave town withou having sunk your teeth into *Eisbein m Sauerkraut* (pork knuckle with sauerkraut or at least a classic *Currywurst* (sausag slices doused in a tangy curried sauce) o *boulette* (meat patties) at the local *Imbis* (snack bar). Berlin's most popular fast food by the way, is the *döner* (a pita sandwic stuffed with slivered roasted meat, salad and a garlicky yogurt sauce), introduced here some 20-odd years ago by a Turkish immigrant.

Unless mentioned, restaurants below serve lunch and dinner and stay open unti at least midnight. German-reading foodie might like to pick up the annual restauran guides published by *Zitty* and *Tip*, availabl at newsstands for around €5.

Mitte & Prenzlauer Berg
BUDGET

Monsieur Vuong (Map pp98-9; ☎ 3087 2643; Alte Schönhauser Strasse 46; mains €6.40) Despite its stylish red walls, good-looking clientele and beauti-ful dishware, this bustling eatery only looks expensive. The Vietnamese fare – soups and two or three main courses daily – is uni-formly delicious, as are the fresh fruit cock-tails and the exotic teas. No reservations, so be prepared to queue.

Piccola Italia (Map pp98-9; ☎ 283 5843; Oranien-burger Strasse 6; dishes €3-7; ⊗ until 1am Sun-Thu, until 3am Fri & Sat) This tiny take-away-only pizze-ria around the corner from the Hackesche Höfe is always packed with snackers hungry for its tasty, toothsome fare. Mini-pizzas start at €1.50.

Rice Queen (Map p126; ☎ 4404 5800; Danziger Strasse 13; mains €5-9) Cheerfully painted walls and modernist furniture form the backdrop for chef Garry Chan's inspired pan-Asian cuisine. Expect intriguing flavour bombs that draw from the cuisines of Malaysia, China, Thailand and Indonesia.

Bagels & Bialys (Map pp98-9; ☎ 283 6546; Rosenthaler Strasse 46-48; dishes €2-5; ⊗ until 5am) Office workers, tourists, night owls – every-one comes to this hole-in-the-wall to fuel up on bagels, salads, soups, *shwarma* (spicey meat) and other pick-me-ups. Most of it is made to order.

THE AUTHOR'S CHOICE

Unsicht-Bar (Map pp98-9; 2434 2500; Gormannstrasse 14; 3-/4-course menu €40/45; dinner only;) Dinner at this boundary-pushing restaurant is a delicious treat for all the senses but one: sight. The dining room is bathed in pitch-black, can't-see-the-end-of-your-nose darkness. Cell phones, cigarettes and any light source, however small, are banished. After choosing from several menus in the (lighted) reception area, you're led to your table by a sight-impaired server who'll take care of you throughout the evening. After dinner, catch a show at the attached theatre, the Dunkelbühne, which presents readings, talk shows and concerts, yes, in the dark. Perfect for blind dates...

Other recommendations:

Konnopke Imbiss (Map p126; 442 7765; Schönhauser Allee 44a; sausage €1-2; 5.30am-8pm Mon-Fri) This Berlin institution makes what many say is the best *Currywurst* in town.

Asia Pavillon (Map pp98-9; Potsdamer Platz Arkaden mall; meals €2.50-7) Chinese fast food, hot, cheap and heaps of it.

MID-RANGE

Mao Thai (Map p126; 441 9261; Wörther Strasse 30; mains €10-18, lunch under €10;) The menu is as intriguing as the carved statuettes and original Asian art at this classy classic. The sublime Thai cuisine has complex flavouring that tends to be on the spicy side.

Frida Kahlo (Map p126; 445 7016; Lychener Strasse 37; mains €10-15) The look of this lively restaurant-bar was inspired by the eponymous painter's house in Mexico City. In the Berlin version, you'll be noshing on delicious Mexican classics, from enchiladas to fajitas.

Gugelhof (Map p126; 442 9229; Knaackstrasse 37; mains €8-14) Bill Clinton was here and Berlin mayor Klaus Wowereit likes the joint too. Cheese fondue, *choucroute* (a sauerkraut-based dish) and tarte flambé top a menu of Alsatian soul food. Also serves breakfast and lunch specials under €8.

Die Zwölf Apostel (Map pp98-9; 201 0222; Georgenstrasse; mains €8-16) Cap off a day of culture on the nearby Museumsinsel with pizzas the size of manta rays delivered straight from the wood-fire oven. A flock of cher-

ubs looks on from the vaulted ceiling. The Charlottenburg branch at Bleibtreustrasse 49 is open 24 hours (Map p102).

Soda (Map p126; 4405 6071; Schönhauser Allee 36-39; mains €8-15) This fashionable restaurant-bar-club combo right amid the red-brick romance of the Kulturbrauerei (p135) has a menu that travels around the world. You can even get into *Survivor* mode and order the grasshopper curry with couscous. Enjoy...

Miro (Map p126; 4473 3013; Raumerstrasse 29; mains €8-12) Miro, which means 'hero' in Turkish, does indeed serve heroic portions of delicious dishes from the eastern province of Anatolia. The cooking is focused on grilled or fried meats, although meatless options abound as well. Killer appetiser platter.

Milagro (Map pp98-9; 2758 2330; Oranienburger Strasse 54-56; mains €7-15) Those who remember the Tacheles as an anarchic artists' squat will do a double-take at this street-level restaurant with its nifty green leather banquettes, oversized mirrors and gilded ceiling. The food's mostly Mediterranean with nouveau German touches. Nice garden.

Other recommendations:

Oren (Map pp98-9; 282 8228; Oranienburger Strasse 28; mains €6-12) Jewish and Israeli cuisine; the Orient-Express appetiser platter is recommended.

Café Belluno (Map p126; 441 0548; Kollwitzstrasse 66; mains €6-10) *Dolce vita* with a view of Kollwitzplatz.

Hasir (Map pp98-9; 2804 1616; Oranienburger Strasse 4; mains €11-15) Flagship branch of this quality Turkish restaurant chain.

TOP END

Maxwell (Map pp98-9; 280 7121; Bergstrasse 22; mains €16.50-20; dinner only) Lou Reed, Oliver Stone and Damien Hirst, whose art graces this sublime restaurant, are among the celeb patrons of this gorgeously restored red-brick exbrewery. Fortunately, the chef puts substance before culinary pyrotechnics. International food, top wine list and idyllic courtyard.

Margaux (Map pp98-9; 2265 2611; Unter den Linden 78; mains €24-40; closed Mon) It took Michael Hoffmann only one year to garner a coveted Michelin star for his breathtaking concoctions of classic French cuisine infused with avant-garde touches. Gilded ceilings, marble floors and cheery canvases form a suitably grand backdrop. Top wine list, too.

Borchardt (Map pp98-9; 2039 7117; Französische Strasse 47; mains €10-20) This classy haunt of the

BERLIN

famous, rich and fabulous has ceilings supported by marble columns as lofty as the chef's ambitions. The Franco-German food changes daily, but is sometimes served with an unnecessary dollop of attitude towards mere mortals.

Kreuzberg & Friedrichshain
BUDGET
Gasthaus Dietrich Herz (Map pp100-1; ☎ 693 7043; Marheinekeplatz 15; mains €3.50-8.50) If you think a schnitzel is a schnitzel is a schnitzel (with apologies to Gertrude Stein), come to this old-fashioned Kreuzberg institution to find a dozen varieties all costing €6. The breakfast for €2.50, including coffee, is a steal as well. In summer tables spill out on the square with its children's playground.

Morgenland (Map pp100-1; ☎ 611 3183; Skalitzer Strasse 35; mains €5-9) This place is great for breakfast, especially at weekends when it's an all-you-can-eat affair for €8. Otherwise the food's pan-European – pasta to lamb to fried fish.

Schlotzsky's Deli (Map pp100-1; ☎ 2233 8899; Friedrichstrasse 200; sandwiches €4; ☒ 10am-7pm) It's

touristy, sure, but the Berlin branch of this American franchise near Checkpoint Charlie makes fresh, honest-to-goodness sandwiches and even offers free refills on soft drinks.

MID-RANGE
Papaya (Map pp100-1; ☎ 2977 1231; Krossener Strasse 11; mains €6-12) While the minimalist décor won't transport you to faraway places, the competently prepared Thai food will. All the classics are here, from tom ka soups to pad thai noodles and complex curries.

Umspannwerk Ost (Map pp96-7; ☎ 4280 9497; Palisadenstrasse 48; mains €8-16) This historic transformer station has literally been transformed into an industrial-chic restaurant whose chefs prepare German-Mediterranean cuisine in an open show kitchen. It's intimately lit and has a long bar and upstairs gallery seating with bird's-eye views. Get on the U5 to Weberwiese to find it.

Osteria No 1 (Map pp100-1; ☎ 786 9162; Kreuzbergstrasse 71; mains €7-16) This kid-friendly Italian restaurant (there's a playground in the lush garden) is a foodie's delight and even appears on the radar screen of celebs like Wim

INFORMATION	
Al Hamra Internet Café	1 B2
Alpha Café	2 B1
St George's Bookshop	3 C3
STA Travel	4 A1

SIGHTS & ACTIVITIES	(pp103–17)
Max-Schmeling-Halle	5 A1
Prenzlberger Orange Bikes	6 B3

SLEEPING	(pp120–1)
Hotel Kastanienhof	7 A3
Hotel Transit Loft	8 C3
Lette 'm Sleep	9 B1
Myer's Hotel	10 B3

EATING	(pp124–6)
Café Amsterdam	11 A1
Café Belluno	12 B3
Frida Kahlo	13 B1
Gugelhof	14 B3
Konnopke Imbiss	15 A2
Mao Thai	16 B3
Miro	17 B2
Rice Queen	18 B2
Schall und Rauch	19 A1
Soda	20 A2

DRINKING	(pp129–32)
Flax	21 C3
Greifbar	22 B1
La Bodeguita del Medio	23 B2
Magnet Club	24 C3
Stiller Don	25 C1
X-Bar	26 B2

ENTERTAINMENT	(pp132–6)
Kulturbrauerei	27 A2
Puppentheater Berlin	28 D2

SHOPPING	(pp136–8)
Eisdieler	29 A2
Schönhauser Allee Arcaden	30 B1
Thatchers	31 A2

TRANSPORT	(pp138–41)
Mitfahr2000	32 A2
Robben & Wientjes Prenzlauer Allee 96	33 C1

Wenders and Nastassja Kinski. Antipasti to pasta to meats and fish, it's all good.

Chandra Kumari (Map pp100–1; ☎ 694 1203; Gneisenaustrasse 4; mains €5-13) The food at this Sri Lankan restaurant is so perky, it may get you off your Prozac. Only organically grown vegetables and hormone-free meats make it into the richly flavoured curries and rice dishes.

Abendmahl (Map pp100–1; ☎ 612 5170; Muskauer Strasse 9; mains €9-16) Vegetarians come to worship at this upmarket restaurant (whose name translates as 'Last Supper'), although fish also makes an appearance on the menu. Watched over by religious paraphernalia, you'll be treated to cleverly named dishes like Hot Venus on Earth (pasta shells stuffed with spinach-ricotta mix) or Flaming Inferno (a Thai fish curry).

TOP END
Bar Centrale (Map pp100–1; ☎ 786 2989; Yorckstrasse 82; appetisers & pastas €9-12, mains €13-20) Creative

Italian (not a pizza in sight) is the name of the game here. Most of the imagination goes into the antipasti menu, which may feature grilled scallops, shrimp in lobster sauce with arugula, or duck fillet with pine nut sauce. Hungry yet?

Altes Zollhaus (Map pp100–1; ☎ 692 3300; Carl-Herz-Ufer 20; menus €25-39) A customs house in an earlier incarnation, this elegantly restored half-timbered jewel of a restaurant, right on the canal in Kreuzberg, is the perfect setting for the upmarket and updated German cuisine prepared by chef Günter Beyer. First-timers can't go wrong with the roast duck.

Charlottenburg & Wilmersdorf
BUDGET
Gosch (Map p102; ☎ 8868 2800; Kurfürstendamm 212; sandwiches €2-3.50, mains €6-15) Only the brisk North Sea wind is missing from this stylish fish bistro, a clone of the original branch on the Frisian island of Sylt. Come here for a quick takeaway sandwich or pick your 'poisson' at the counter, then wait while it's turned into a delicious meal. Also on Alte Potsdamer Strasse 1 in Mitte (Map pp98–9).

Luisen-Bräu (Map pp96–7; ☎ 341 9388; Luisenplatz 1; mains €6-15) This low-key microbrewery with solid German food is ideal for restoring energies after a day in and around Schloss Charlottenburg.

Schwarzes Café (Map p102; ☎ 313 8038; Kantstrasse 148; dishes €4.50-9; ☯ 24hr; ☒) This café classic was founded in 1978 by 15 women who charged men DM1 (€0.50) 'admission' to benefit a women's shelter (a practice since abandoned). Breakfast is served any time. It's also famous for its – ahem! – creatively designed toilets.

MID-RANGE
Mar y Sol (Map p102; ☎ 313 2593; Savignyplatz 5; tapas €2-4, mains €10-18; ☯ dinner only) Grab a table on a balmy night in the palm-studded garden and feel yourself transported to Seville while munching on *manchego* (cheese), *chorizo* (sausage), *jamón Serrano* (ham), gambas, *albondigas* (meatballs) and other tastebud-tickling tapas.

YVA-Suite (Map p102; ☎ 8872 5573; Schlüterstrasse 52; mains €9-18; ☯ 6pm-3am Sun-Thu, 6pm-5am Fri & Sat) This hip bar-lounge-restaurant combo is a sophisticated retreat for the rich and fabulous. Nibble on dishes inspired by the cuisines of Europe in the seductively lit dining room or choose from over 1000 whiskeys in the bar. YVA, by the way, was a 1930s fashion photographer killed by the Nazis (see also Hotel Bogota, p123).

Hitit (Map pp96-7; ☎ 322 4557; Knobelsdorffstrasse 35; mains €7.50-15) Wall reliefs and fountains create a stylish yet relaxed ambience at this popular Turkish restaurant. The appetiser platter is a winner, though main courses of grilled meat, as well as the meatless casseroles, are good choices too.

Café Wintergarten im Literaturhaus (Map p102; ☎ 882 5414; Fasanenstrasse 23; mains €10-16) Book rats, artists and shoppers gather at this lovely Art Nouveau villa for the international fare, which includes some choices for waist-watchers and vegetarians. Sit in the idyllic garden or the stylish interior with black furniture and stucco ceilings.

Good Friends (Map p102; ☎ 313 2659; Kantstrasse 30; mains €7-19) The dangling ducks in the window hint at the authenticity of the Cantonese food served at this classic eatery that's always bustling despite being low on ambience. Choose from a menu as long as the Great Wall of China or just ask your Chinese table neighbours for a recommendation.

Other recommendations:

Arche Noah (Map p102; ☎ 882 6138; Fasanenstrasse 79; mains €10-17) Berlin's oldest certified kosher restaurant inside the Jewish Community House with legendary 30-item hot and cold buffet on Tuesday nights (€18).

La Caleta (Map p102; ☎ 8862 7475; Wielandstrasse 26a; mains €10-18) Spanish-run romantic restaurant with interesting tapas, fresh fish and Spanish vino.

TOP END

First Floor (Map p102; ☎ 2502 1020; 1st fl, Palace Hotel, Budapester Strasse 45; mains €30-38; ⊗ closed Sat lunch) Top ingredients and classic techniques translate into superb French cuisine at this den of fine dining. For his efforts, chef Michael Buchholz has garnered the attention of serious foodies, not to mention the crew from Michelin who lauded him with a star.

Alt-Luxemburg (Map p102; ☎ 323 8730; Windscheidstrasse 31; mains €24-28; ⊗ dinner only, closed Sun) A gourmet mainstay for over 20 years, this elegant but unpretentious restaurant wows diners with classic fare, mostly of a Franco-German bent, and swift and attentive service.

Schöneberg
BUDGET
Rani (Map p129; ☎ 215 2673; Goltzstrasse 32; dishes €3.50-7) This self-service eatery stands out from the Indian restaurants south of Winterfeldtplatz. In summer, the pavement tables and tangy lassis (yogurt drinks) are coolest.

Baharat Falafel (Map p129; ☎ 216 8301; Winterfeldtstrasse 37; dishes €2-5; ⊗ until 2am) The humble falafel goes gourmet at this unassuming little take-away place. Service is fast and friendly.

MID-RANGE
Café am Neuen See (Map pp96-7; ☎ 254 4930; Lichtensteinallee 2; mains €7-12) This huge lakeside beer garden in Tiergarten park is a picturesque place to while away a warm summer night. For sustenance there's Bavarian sausage, pretzels and pizza, and you can even hire a boat to take your sweetie for a spin.

Tim's Canadian Deli (Map p129; ☎ 2175 6960; Maassenstrasse 14; mains €5-17) When the sun's out, there are few better places for breakfast than this corner café's convivial outdoor tables with a view of the Winterfeldtplatz. At other times, it's the veggie burgers, bagels, steaks and other feel-good food that keep the cash register ringing.

Café Einstein (Map p129; ☎ 261 5096; Kurfürstenstrasse 58; breakfast €4-13, mains €10-20) Schnitzels with noodles and warm apple strudels – you'll find them at this classic Viennese coffee house in a gorgeous villa with garden. Marble table-tops, jumbo-sized mirrors and red upholstered banquettes add to the stylish look, although the staff and clientele can be a bit on the snooty side.

Trattoria á Muntagnola (Map p129; ☎ 211 6642; Fuggerstrasse 27; mains €8-17; ⊗ dinner only) Fresh pasta and flavour-packed sauces form the main ingredients of the southern Italian country cooking at this neighbourhood Italian eatery. The décor – think Chianti bottles, garlic strings and red-and-white tablecloths – is clichéd but comfortable. Kids are welcome, of course.

Other recommendations:

Tomasa (Map p102; ☎ 213 2345; Motzstrasse 60; breakfasts €5-15) Original branch of the small breakfast/brunch emporium with unusual selections, big portions and pleasantly unobtrusive service.

Ousies (Map p129; ☎ 216 7957; Grunewaldstrasse 16; mains €5-14; ⊗ dinner only) Bubbly and kitsch-free Greek taverna where you build your meal from a large selection of hot and cold appetisers.

TOP END

Storch (Map p129; ☎ 784 2059; Wartburgstrasse 54; mains €14-20; ⏰ dinner only) This is a classic neighbourhood charmer off the tourist circuit. Regulars are often greeted by owner Volker Hauptvogel himself, but the polite-to-a-fault staff make everyone feel welcome. The *Flammkuchen* (Alsatian 'pizza' topped with cream, onion and bacon) is superb, and robust Alsatian mains like stuffed goose or wild boar ragout also convince discerning diners.

Hakuin (Map p129; ☎ 218 2027; Martin-Luther-Strasse 1; mains €15-19; ⏰ closed Mon; ✗) Run by Buddhists, this all-vegetarian, nonsmoking restaurant pairs exotic spices and fresh herbs with an array of interesting ingredients – exotic mushrooms, algae and tofu included. Some dishes are suitable for vegans.

DRINKING

Berlin's bar and lounge scenes take on different personalities in each of the districts. Venues in Charlottenburg (especially around Savignyplatz and side streets) tend to be grown-up and upmarket, catering for a chic, professional crowd. In Kreuzberg, Oranienstrasse, eclipsed by Mitte and Prenzlauer Berg after reunification, is making a comeback with a new generation of scenesters sharing beers with graying exanarchists who never left the 'hood. The new young scene is now firmly entrenched in Friedrichshain, which has seen an explosion of places along Mühlenstrasse and around Boxhagener Platz. Mitte, meanwhile, though eschewed as too 'touristy' by many Berliners, presents a wonderfully diverse scene from pricey, precious haunts around Gendarmenmarkt to creative havens in the Scheunenviertel. Prenzlauer Berg still preserves a bit of an experimental edge, although less so around increasingly commercial Käthe-Kollwitz-Platz and its side streets. For more authenticity, head to the streets north of Danziger Strasse and the Helmholtzplatz area.

Mitte & Prenzlauer Berg

Seven Lounge (Map pp98-9; ☎ 2759 6979; Ackerstrasse 20) Soft lighting gives everybody a shot at looking good in this classy lounge where you can sprawl on taupe couches or even hop onto the big bed by the bar. Owner

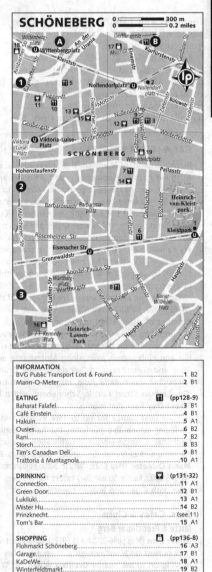

INFORMATION	
BVG Public Transport Lost & Found	1 B2
Mann-O-Meter	2 B1

EATING	🍴 (pp128-9)
Baharat Falafel	3 B1
Café Einstein	4 B1
Hakuin	5 A1
Ousies	6 B2
Rani	7 B2
Storch	8 B3
Tim's Canadian Deli	9 B1
Trattoria á Muntagnola	10 A1

DRINKING	🍸 (p131-32)
Connection	11 A1
Green Door	12 B1
Lukiluki	13 A1
Mister Hu	14 B2
Prinzknecht	(see 11)
Tom's Bar	15 A1

SHOPPING	🛍 (pp136-8)
Flohmarkt Schöneberg	16 A3
Garage	17 B1
KaDeWe	18 A1
Winterfeldtmarkt	19 B2

Mo Asumang, erstwhile host of an erotic TV show, is often around to greet guests. Happy hour from 6pm to 9pm.

La Bodeguita del Medio (Map p126; ☎ 442 9698; Lychener Strasse 6) Ernest Hemingway's favourite Havana hang-out was the inspiration for this high-energy watering hole, complete with Latin rhythms, tasty tapas and a wicked assortment of rum and tequila concoctions.

X-Bar (Map p126; ☎ 443 4904; Raumerstrasse 17) Check your liver at the door or risk serious damage when confronted with the global cocktail menu featuring over 300 entries – from classic martini to the house creation 'Gorilla Milk'. Protein from the sushi bar

might help keep up your stamina. Happy hour is 6pm to 8pm.

925 Lounge Bar (Map pp98-9; ☎ 2018 7177; Taubenstrasse 19) If you want to stand out in Mitte, you better think of a clever shtick. Here it is 70kg of real silver (hence the name – '925' is a quality designation for silver) wrought into the must-be-seen-to-be-believed bar. The rest of the décor is a

GAY & LESBIAN BERLIN

Berlin's legendary liberalism has spawned one of the world's biggest gay and lesbian scenes. Anything goes in 'Homopolis' – and we mean anything – from the high-brow to the hands-on, the bourgeois to the bizarre, the mainstream to the flamboyant.

Berlin's emergence as a gay mecca was kick-started by sexual scientist Magnus Hirschfeld who, in 1897, founded the Scientific Humanitarian Committee in the city, which paved the way for gay liberation. The 1920s were especially wild and wacky, a demimonde that drew and inspired writers like Christopher Isherwood until the Nazis put an end to the fun in 1933. Postwar recovery came slowly, but by the 1970s the scene was firmly re-established, at least in the western city. Since 2001, Berlin has been governed by an openly gay mayor, Klaus Wowereit, who outed himself by saying 'I'm gay, and that's a good thing', which has since become a popular slogan in the community.

Gay history, art and culture are the focus of the **Schwules Museum** (Map pp100-1; Gay Museum; ☎ 693 1172; Mehringdamm 61; adult/concession €5/3; ⏰ 2-6pm Wed-Fri & Sun, 2-7pm Sat), which puts together often excellent temporary shows and, as of late, also has a small permanent exhibit. Lectures, film screenings, readings and other events make the place a hub of the scene.

As befits Berlin's decentralised nature, there is no dedicated gay ghetto, although established bar and club scenes exist along Motzstrasse and Fuggerstrasse in Schöneberg, Schönhauser Allee and Gleimstrasse in Prenzlauer Berg, Oranienstrasse in Kreuzberg, and Mühlenstrasse in Friedrichshain. In early June, huge crowds turn out for the **Schwul-Lesbisches Strassenfest** (Gay-Lesbian Street Fair) in Schöneberg, which basically serves as a warm-up for **Christopher Street Day** later that month.

Your best source for up-to-date listings and news is the freebie *Siegessäule* (www.siegess aeule.de), which also publishes the handy English/German booklet *Out in Berlin* (www.out-in-berlin.de). German-language publications include *Sergej*, another magazine that caters strictly for men, and *Zitty* and *030*, which have listings. For advice and information, men should turn to **Mann-O-Meter** (Map p129; ☎ 216 8008; Bülowstrasse 106), while the **Lesbenberatung** (Map pp96-7; ☎ 215 2000; Kulmer Strasse 20a) caters for women. Unless mentioned otherwise, places listed here have both a gay and lesbian clientele.

Bars, Cafés & Clubs
Mitte & Prenzlauer Berg
Stiller Don (Map pp96-7; ☎ 445 5957; Erich-Weinert-Strasse 67) A leftover from the GDR era, this place gets busiest on Monday nights when a low-key crowd comes for beer and free peanuts before moving on to the nearby **Greifbar** (Map p126; ☎ 444 0828; Wichertstrasse 10), a cruising den with a busy darkroom. Men only.

Ackerkeller (Map pp98-99; ☎ 280 7216; Ackerstrasse 12; ⏰ Tue & Fri) An island of grunge in chic Mitte, Ackerkeller comes to life on Tuesday nights. Expect cheap drinks, a student-age crowd and lots of wacky pop music. It's in the second courtyard.

Kino International (Map pp96-7; ☎ 247 5600; Karl-Marx-Allee 33) Glitter curtains, slippery parquet floors and glitzy glass chandeliers – this GDR-era cinema is glam central. Monday goes 'MonGay' with homo-themed classics and imports. Also hosts Klub International and other parties on an off-and-on schedule. Look for flyers.

sexy red that gives everyone a healthy glow. Happy hour is from 5pm to 9pm, Monday to Friday.

Broker's Bier Börse (Map p98-9; ☎ 2647 4823; Schiffbauerdamm 8) This is a unique beer hall where, after 5pm, demand determines the drink prices, just like in a mini stock exchange. Sure, it's gimmicky and tourists love it, but the fun factor is undeniable.

Bar am Lützowplatz (Map pp96-7; ☎ 262 6807; Lützowplatz 7) Sip your Mai Tai as Mao looks on at this grown-up bar that has made lots of loyal fans with its classic mixed drinks. The champagne menu, currently with a selection of 126 different varieties, is a speciality. Happy hour is from 2pm to 9pm.

Kumpelnest 3000 (Map pp100-1; ☎ 261 6918; Lützowstrasse 23) The time to stumble into this

Flax (Map p126; ☎ 4404 6988; Chodowieckistrasse 41; ☾ nightly) Popular bar in Prenzlauer Berg that's busiest early in the evening.

Schall und Rauch (Map p126; ☎ 448 0770; Gleimstrasse 23; ☾ from 9am) A bistro by day, this place morphs into a chic cocktail bar when the moon gets high. It's great for breakfast any day, but the Sunday brunch has cult status.

Café Amsterdam (Map p126; ☎ 448 0792; Gleimstrasse 24; ☾ from 4pm Mon-Fri, from 10am Sat & Sun) Next door, this friendly café-bar is a good place to get the evening started with house and techno. The food's pretty good, especially the cakes. Young crowd.

Kreuzberg & Friedrichshain
Roses (Map pp100-1; ☎ 615 7570; Oranienstrasse 187; ☾ from 9pm) Kitschy yet pretty, Roses has been a Kreuzberg fixture for over 10 years and still draws patrons in party mode with its strong drinks and seductively plush setting.

Melitta Sundström (Map pp100-1; ☎ 692 4414; Mehringdamm 61; ☾ from 10am) A great place for breakfast or a coffee and chat while the sun's up, this place turns considerably more cruisy after dark, especially at weekends when drag queens and party lions invade to liquor up before moving on to the **SchwuZ** disco at the back.

Die Busche (Map pp100-1; ☎ 296 0800; Mühlenstrasse 11-12; ☾ Wed-Sat) The ghosts of communism have long been exorcised from what used to be East Berlin's only gay disco, but the place is still alive and kicking. Loud music, mirrored rooms and a young mixed clientele make up the ingredients for its raunchy dance parties.

SO36 (Map pp100-1; ☎ 6140 1306; Oranienstrasse 190; ☾ closed Tue) A former haunt of the alternative punk scene, the 'Esso' now has theme nights popular with lesbigays, including the Electric Ballroom (techno) on Monday, Hungry Hearts (house) on Wednesday and Café Fatal (German pop and ballroom dancing) on Sunday. Gayhane, on the fourth Saturday of the month, mixes Turkish and German house and pop, drag queens and belly dancing.

Schöneberg
Connection (Map p129; ☎ 218 1432; Fuggerstrasse 33) On Friday and Saturday nights, this Schöneberg dinosaur is a magnet for action-oriented men. The warren of underground darkrooms is legendary, while upstairs there are three floors of cruising action, a mirrored dance floor and blaring techno music. The attached **Prinzknecht** (Map p129; ☎ 218 1431; Fuggerstrasse 33) is a good place to get the evening going, with plenty of outdoor seating in summer. Both are men only.

Tom's Bar (Map p129; ☎ 213 4570; Motzstrasse 19) Tom's is another main stop on the party circuit. Its dark cavernous bar is a serious pick-up joint, and there's an active cellar as well. If you're OFB – out for business – don't get here before midnight. Men only.

Lukiluki (Map p129; ☎ 2362 2079; Motzstrasse 28; ☾ nightly) Bronzed and styled topless waiters, drag queens behind the bar and a respectable Asian-fusion menu bring a steady stream of customers of all sexual stripes to this fabulous restaurant-bar.

Begine (Map pp96-7; ☎ 215 4325; Potsdamer Strasse 139) This men-free zone is mostly a cosy café and culture centre with concerts, readings and films. Every fourth Saturday of the month it's party time as the place turns into a happening disco.

wonderful den of iniquity is just before dawn. A former bordello, it still looks the part with its dim lighting, kitschy lanterns and slightly offbeat crowd.

Kreuzberg & Friedrichshain

Würgeengel (Map pp100-1; ☎ 615 5560; Dresdner Strasse 122) The classiest bar in eastern Kreuzberg beckons with dramatic blood-red walls, chic chandeliers and plump sofas. The strange name, which means 'strangler angel', refers to a 1962 Luis Buñuel movie. Cocktails are killer.

Astro Bar (Map pp100-1; ☎ 2966 1615; Simon-Dach-Strasse 40) Not only sci-fi fans gravitate to this Friedrichshain hot spot with its spaceship décor and out-of-this-world robot collection. After 10pm, a changing roster of DJs showers the crowd with electronica.

Goldfisch (Map pp100-1; Grünberger Strasse 67) Sleek cream-coloured banquettes, tangerine wallpaper and frilly shell lamps – this bar is glamorous enough for Mitte! Thankfully, its Friedrichshain location keeps the drink prices and attitude refreshingly low.

Haifischbar (Map pp100-1; ☎ 691 1352; Arndtstrasse 25) This island of style just off Bergmannstrasse offers a nice change from the usual Kreuzberg grunge. A low-key and chatty clientele squeezes onto the red sofas or fortifies itself on sushi morsels served out the back.

Ankerklause (Map pp100-1; ☎ 693 5649; Kottbusser Damm 104) Low on aesthetics but high on energy is this gritty Kreuzberg favourite in an old harbour master's house above the Landwehrkanal. Breakfast on the terrace, coffee after shopping the Turkish Market (p137), drinks and talk at night – this place packs 'em in at all hours. Thursday is disco night.

Golgatha (Map pp100-1; ☎ 785 2453; Dudenstrasse 48-64; ☽ Apr-Sep) The pilgrimage up the hill to this comfortable beer garden smack bang in Kreuzberg's leafy Viktoriapark is a beloved summer ritual. Relax with cool drinks and grilled snacks, then make a night of it in the attached disco.

Konrad Tönz (Map pp100-1; ☎ 612 3252; Falckensteinstrasse 30) Konrad Tönz was the longtime correspondent for a popular reality TV crime-solving show (sort of a 'Germany's Most Wanted'). The campy '70s bar that bears his name takes the retro concept to new heights, with orange plastic chairs,

disco balls and DJs working a pair of mono turntables.

Dachkammer (Map pp100-1; ☎ 296 1673; Simon-Dach-Strasse 39) This split personality place pairs a casual downstairs café with an intimate upstairs living room lounge where the crowd gets younger but the décor older (think grandma's sofas, flowery wallpaper). Love birds can disappear onto the tiny leaf-covered balcony.

Charlottenburg & Schöneberg

Galerie Bremer (Map p102; ☎ 881 4908; Fasanenstrasse 37) A prestigious gallery serves as the gateway to this classy *boîte* with a bar designed by Philharmonie architect Hans Scharoun. Kick back with a cool drink, listen in on arty conversations and keep an eye out for celebs.

Gainsbourg (Map p102; ☎ 313 7464; Savignyplatz 5) This American bar honours French singer-songwriter Serge Gainsbourg, best known for 'Je t'aime', his steamy duet with Jane Birkin. Award-winning cocktails and a smooth setting make this a favourite of the creative postcollege set. Also snacks and a nicely secluded terrace. Happy hour is from 5pm to 8pm.

Green Door (Map p129; ☎ 215 2515; Winterfeldtstrasse 50) Only the door is green at this shoebox-sized bar with a big neighbourhood following. Inside, you'll sip mojitos and cosmopolitans surrounded by vanilla walls and chocolate leather sofas. Happy hour is from 6pm to 9pm.

Mister Hu (Map p129; ☎ 217 2111; Goltzstrasse 39) Schöneberg scenesters make up the bulk of the crowd at Husen Ciawi's grottolike establishment with its Flintstone-esque bar and aquarium-coloured illumination. A local fixture.

Other recommendations:

Bar de Paris Bar (Map p102; ☎ 3101 5094; Kantstrasse 152) New adjunct to legendary restaurant favoured by celluloid celebs.

Dicke Wirtin (Map p102; ☎ 312 4952; Carmerstrasse 9) Quintessential old-timey Berlin pub filled with everyone from students to grouchy seniors.

ENTERTAINMENT

Berlin's party scene is one of the most diverse, raw and alternative in Europe, constantly spawning new trends and providing platforms for infinite experimentation in music, fashion and design. The most utting-edge clubs tend to be improvised and in industrial venues – abandoned factories, warehouses, postal offices. Electronica still dominates, but the sound spectrum now ranges from drum 'n' bass, house and trance to punk, Latin and African.

Berlin also has plenty in store for fans of highbrow pursuits. Despite serious budget shortfalls, the city sustains not one, not two but three world-class opera houses. Mainstream, offbeat and fringe theatre are all thriving, as are cabaret and variety shows. And in a city that hosts its own international film festival, there are cinemas aplenty, from slick multiplexes to scruffy art houses.

Listings

Zitty (www.zitty.de) and *Tip* are bi-weekly German-language listings magazines that let you keep the finger on the pulse of what's happening in Berlin. Your best sources for one-off parties are flyers found at cafés, bars, boutiques and hostels, or *The Flyer*, a free weekly booklet. [030] is another rag with up-to-date listings and a kicking website (www.berlin030.de), although unfortunately in German only.

The young guides conducting the walking tours (p119) as well as the staff at hostels can also help you get plugged into the scene of your choice.

Tickets

Credit-card bookings by telephone or online through a venue's box office are still not commonplace in Berlin. Most will take reservations over the phone but make you show up in person to pay for and pick up your tickets. If this is too much hassle, an alternative is to buy tickets through an agency, although this will add a service charge of up to 15% to the ticket price.

Berlin Tourismus Marketing (☎ 250 025; www .berlin-tourist-information.de)

Hekticket (www.hekticket.de) Alexanderplatz (Map pp98-9; ☎ 2431 2431; below S-Bahn bridge, Karl-Liebknecht-Strasse 12; ☒ 2-5pm Fri, noon-8pm Sat); Bahnhof Zoo (Map p102; ☎ 2309 9333; foyer of Deutsche Bank, Hardenbergstrasse 29a; ☒ noon-7pm Mon-Fri, 10am-8pm Sat)

Hekticket Last Minute (☎ 230 9930) Discounted tickets after 4pm for select performances that night.

Theaterkasse Centrum (Map p102; ☎ 882 7611; Meineckestrasse 25)

Cabaret & Varieté

The light, lively and lavish variety shows of the Golden Twenties have been undergoing a sweeping revival in Berlin. Get ready for an evening of dancing and singing, jugglers, acrobats and other entertainers. These 'cabarets' should not be confused with 'Kabarett', which are political and satirical shows with monologues and short skits.

Bar jeder Vernunft (Map p102; ☎ 883 1582; www.bar-jeder-vernunft.de; Schaperstrasse 24) The elegant Art Nouveau tent makes a perfectly nostalgic setting for the sophisticated cabaret, comedy and chanson acts this place is famous for. There's a free piano bar after the main show and lovely beer garden in summer. Located at the end of the parking lot.

Chamäleon Varieté (Map pp98-9; ☎ 282 7118; www.chamaeleon-variete.de; Hackesche Höfe) This intimate club presents variety shows – comedy, juggling acts and singing – often in sassy and unconventional fashion.

Wintergarten-Das Varieté (Map pp96-7; ☎ 2500 8888; www.wintergarten-berlin.de; Potsdamer Strasse 96) Come here for vaudeville shows updated for the 21st century in a glitzy theatre with a starry-sky ceiling. The crowd's tourist-heavy, but many shows are still well worth seeing.

Friedrichstadtpalast (Map pp98-9; ☎ 2326 2326; Friedrichstrasse 107) Las Vegas–style dance extravaganzas with showgirls in scanty outfits and feather headdresses are the bread and butter of this historic venue.

THE AUTHOR'S CHOICE

Berlin's ultimate chill-out zone is not in a pounding nightclub but in the salt waters of a futuristic indoor pool called **Liquidrom** (Map pp100-1; ☎ 7473 7171; Möckernstrasse 10, Neues Tempodrom; 2hr admission €15, extra hr €4; ☒ 10am-10pm Sun-Thu, 10am-midnight Fri & Sat, 10-2am full moon nights). As you float on your back in the tepid fluid, your head semisubmerged, you'll be listening to 'liquid sounds' – whales to jazz to ambient to orchestral – piped in through underwater loudspeakers as soft psychedelic light effects are projected onto the walls and domed ceiling. A bar, sauna, steam room and Jacuzzi provide additional playgrounds. Soothing, sensual and just slightly surreal.

Cinemas

Movie tickets in Berlin can be costly, although you can usually save a few euros by seeing flicks early in the week, before 5pm and on *Kinotag* ('Film Day', usually Tuesday or Wednesday). There's no shortage of cinemas showing original versions (denoted 'OV' in listings) or movies shown in the original language but with English or German subtitles ('OmU' for *Original mit Untertiteln*). While multiplexes focus on Hollywood blockbusters, independent cinemas present more experimental and eclectic programming. Watching movies al fresco in a *Freiluftkino* (outdoor cinema) is a venerable summer tradition. Venues listed below all show English-language films, but check the listings magazines for additional options.

Acud (Map pp98-9; ☎ 4435 9498; Veteranenstrasse 21)

Arsenal (Map pp98-9; ☎ 2695 5100; Filmhaus, Potsdamer Strasse 2, Sony Center)

Babylon (Map pp100-1; ☎ 6160 9693; Dresdner Strasse 126)

CinemaX Potsdamer Platz (Map pp98-9; ☎ 01805-246362; Potsdamer Platz)

Eiszeit (Map pp100-1; ☎ 611 6016; Zeughofstrasse 20)

Hackesche Höfe (Map pp98-9; ☎ 283 4603; Rosenthaler Strasse 40/41, Hackesche Höfe)

Clubs

Maria am Ufer (Map pp100-1; ☎ 2123 8190; Stralauer Strasse 34/35, An der Schillingbrücke; ☯ concerts from 9pm, 11pm Fri & Sat) The legendary Maria, Berlin's most progressive club, has moved again, hopefully to a more permanent riverside location. It's still the place to hear experimental electronica and the sounds of tomorrow. It's concerts during the week, DJs at the weekend.

Sage Club (Map pp98-9; ☎ 278 9830; Köpenicker Strasse 76; ☯ Thu-Sun) Inside the Heinrich-Heine-Strasse U-Bahn station, this club has a loyal following among dedicated house fans. Two dance floors, outdoor area with pool and strict door policy.

Magnet Club (Map p126; ☎ 4285 1335; Greifswalder Strasse 212-213; ☯ Fri-Sun) A former fashion factory has been reborn as a night-time fun zone with most music styles represented – disco to house to '80s – along with up-and-coming bands. Two dance floors, friendly staff and down-to-earth crowd.

Casino (Map pp100-1; ☎ 2900 9799; Mühlenstrasse 26-30; ☯ from 11pm Fri & Sat) Right on the Mühlenstrasse party mile, Casino is one of the best places for full-powered electronic immersion. A relaxed door policy, young crowd and painlessly priced drinks.

90° Grad (Map pp100-1; ☎ 2300 5954; Dennewitzstrasse 37; ☯ Thu-Sat) In this chic party den where hot young things keep the champagne flowing, nothing recalls its 1989 underground roots. DJs spin an eclectic mix heavy on house and black music from a giant chancel situated above the dance floor. Alas, the elite door policy is a major turn-off.

Sternradio (Map pp98-9; ☎ 2472 4982; Alexanderplatz 5; ☯ from 11pm Fri & Sat, special nights earlier) Lucky GDR citizens once came to the Haus der Reisen (House of Travel) to pick up their travel documents. Now it houses a mega-cool dance temple with classic house and low-key techno sounds.

Far Out (Map p102; ☎ 3200 0717; Kurfürstendamm 156; ☯ Tue-Sun) One of oldest party venues in the western city, Far Out is anything but and definitely lacks the edge of eastern clubs. It is, however, a comfortable place to swing a leg. If you're over 30, entry is free on Wednesday. There's an after-work party on Tuesday.

Other recommendations:

Sophienklub (Map pp98-9; ☎ 282 4552; Sophienstrasse 6) A GDR remnant – unpretentious, comfortable, party-hearty to a full menu of sounds.

Kalkscheune (Map pp98-9; ☎ 2839 0065; Johannisstrasse 2) Varied party schedule, including Schöne Party for the over-30 set and Gaymeboy for young gays.

KitKat Club (☎ 7871 8963; Bessemerstrasse 4) Be brave, be bold, be naked. Decadence made in Berlin at this sex-and-dance club. Watching only not allowed.

Culture Centres

Neues Tempodrom (Map pp100-1; ☎ 263 9980; www.tempodrom.de; Möckernstrasse 10) No longer the experimental tent venue of the '80s and '90s, the Tempodrom of the new millennium is all grown up and, most notably, permanent. Performing acts run the gamut from concerts to theatre to parties to festivals, including the popular Heimatklänge world music festival in summer.

Waldbühne (☎ 2308 8230; Am Glockenturm) From May until September, this outdoor amphitheatre hosts rock, pop and classical concerts as well as popular film nights. Take the U2 to Olympia-Stadion Ost, then a free shuttle or bus No 18.

Cafe Podewil (Map pp98-9; ☎ 247 496; www.podewil.de; Klosterstrasse 68-70) Podewil offers a mixed bag of contemporary arts, including film, theatre and live music, as well as a café, in a 1704 building. In fine weather, the beer garden is open to 9.30pm.

Tacheles (Map pp98-9; ☎ 282 6185; www.tacheles.de; Oranienburger Strasse 54-56) Behind the post-atomic shell is an active offbeat venue with dance, jazz, movies, cabaret, readings, workshops, artist studios and galleries, and a cinema.

UFA-Fabrik (☎ 755 030; Viktoriastrasse 10-18) In the former UFA film studios, located in the south of the city, this venue presents music, theatre, dance, cabaret and circus shows year round (outdoors in summer). There's also music and other workshops and a children's circus school. Take the U6 to Ullsteinstrasse.

Kulturbrauerei (Map p126; ☎ 443 150; www.kulturbrauerei.de; Knaackstrasse 97, cnr Danziger Strasse) The original red-brick buildings of this 19th-century brewery have been turned into a happening nightlife complex with a motley mix of live concerts, dance club, theatre, restaurants, cinemas and more.

Live Music
CLASSICAL & OPERA
Berliner Philharmonie (Map pp100-1; ☎ 254 880; www.berlin-philharmonic.com; Herbert-Von-Karajan-Strasse 1) Try to hear a concert at this justly famous hall with its supreme acoustics. All seats are excellent, so if money matters, even the cheapest ticket will do.

Konzerthaus Berlin (Map pp98-9; ☎ 203 092 101; www.konzerthaus.de; Gendarmenmarkt) This lavish Schinkel-designed concert hall is another of Berlin's top venues. The 'house band' is the Berliner Symphonie Orchester, and there are also organ concerts and children's events.

Staatsoper Unter den Linden (Map pp98-9; ☎ 203 540; www.staatsoper-berlin.org; Unter den Linden 7) Berlin's oldest and most gorgeous opera house presents opera from four centuries along with classical and modern ballet, including high-calibre visiting troupes.

Deutsche Oper Berlin (Map p102; ☎ 343 8401; www.deutscheoperberlin.de; Bismarckstrasse 35) This 1960s opera house presents classical and modern operas, along with ballet, operettas and concerts.

Komische Oper (Map pp98-9; ☎ 4799 7400; www.komische-oper-berlin.de; Behrenstrasse 55-57, box office Unter den Linden 41) Musical theatre, light opera, operetta and dance are the mainstays at this historic venue with its plush interior.

JAZZ
A-Trane (Map p102; ☎ 313 2550; www.a-trane.de; Bleibtreustrasse 1, cnr Pestalozzistrasse) There's not a bad seat in this intimate place with round cocktail tables and a small stage with acts by both emerging and established performers. Styles run the gamut from modern jazz to funk to vocal.

Quasimodo (Map p102; ☎ 312 8086; www.quasimodo.de; Kantstrasse 12a) Besides jazz, this well-established smoky basement club also brings in blues, funk, soul and folk bands to pad the schedule. Nice café upstairs.

B-flat (Map pp98-9; ☎ 283 3123; www.b-flat-berlin.de; Rosenthaler Strasse 13) This modern jazz club juxtaposes high-quality performances, mostly by local and regional artists, with spicy tango and salsa nights when the crowd gets younger, hipper and more energy-driven. Cool cocktails too.

Junction Bar (Map pp100-1; ☎ 694 6602; www.junction-bar.de; Gneisenaustrasse 18) Check your lungs at the door when entering this groovy, smoke-filled cellar where you'll be showered by everything from traditional jazz to jazz-rap, along with blues, soul and funk. After the show, DJs keep the sounds coming and the crowd hopping. The upstairs bar serves snacks.

Sport
Hertha BSC (☎ 01805-189 200 or www.herthabsc.de for tickets; Olympic Stadium) Berlin's football (soccer) club plays at the Bundesliga level and has put in a fairly respectable performance in recent years. The season runs from early September to May/June with a winter break in December and January.

Alba Berlin (☎ 308 785 685 or www.albaberlin.de for tickets) The city's pro men's basketball team, has dominated the German league, winning the championship trophy every year between 1997 and 2003. Games take place at the **Max-Schmeling-Halle** (Map p126; Am Falkplatz).

LTCC Rot-Weiss (☎ 895 7550; Gottfried-von-Kramm-Weg 47-55, Grunewald) In May, the German Open women's tennis tournament is held at this tennis club and usually attracts a fair share of high-ranking players. Take the S3 or S7 to Grunewald.

The Berlin Marathon is held in late September, the same month as the ISTAF, an international track and field meet.

Berlin has three horse racing courses:

Galopprennbahn Hoppegarten (☎ 03342-389 30; Goetheallee 1, Dahlwitz-Hoppegarten) Situated northeast of the city; S5 to Hoppegarten.

Trabrennbahn Karlshorst (☎ 500 170; Treskowallee 129, Lichtenberg) S3 to Karlshorst.

Trabrennbahn Mariendorf (☎ 740 1212; Mariendorfer Damm 222, Mariendorf) U6 to Mariendorf, then bus No 176 or 179.

Theatre

Berlin has 150 theatres, many of which cluster in two areas. Stages along the Ku'damm in Charlottenburg have crowd-pleasing, light fare, while theatres in Mitte generally take a more heady, experimental approach. Berlin's not stuffy, so come dressed as casual or as fancy as you like. Many theatres are dark on Monday and from mid-July to late August.

Deutsches Theater (Map pp98-9; ☎ 2844 1225; Schumannstrasse 13a) This historic theatre achieved its greatest acclaim under Max Reinhardt who directed it from 1905 to 1933. Classic plays to experimental works by contemporary authors make for a stimulating repertory.

Berliner Ensemble (Map pp98-9; ☎ 2840 8155; Bertolt-Brecht-Platz 1) Brecht's former theatre has a lavish interior and presents works by him and other European 20th-century playwrights, with the occasional Shakespeare thrown into the mix.

Volksbühne am Rosa-Luxemburg-Platz (Map pp98-9; ☎ 240 6772; Linienstrasse 227) Nonconformist and radical, cutting-edge and provocative are the maxims of the shows here. Performances are not for tender souls.

Friends of Italian Opera (Map pp100-1; ☎ 691 1211; Fidicinstrasse 40) Despite the name, this is actually Berlin's most established English-language theatre. Visiting troupes from the US, UK, Canada and other countries supplement the in-house productions.

Hackesches Hof-Theater (Map pp98-9; ☎ 283 2587; Rosenthaler Strasse 40/41) A centre for Yiddish theatre and music right in the Hackesche Höfe.

SHOPPING

Berlin's decentralised character means that there isn't a single, clearly defined shopping strip like London's Oxford Street or New York's Fifth Avenue. Which is not to say that there isn't some good shopping to be done in this city. Prices tend to be competitive compared with other world capitals and are lowest during end-of-season sales. Big splashy one-off sales with deep discounts across the store are still relatively rare in Germany.

Ku'damm and Tauentzienstrasse in Charlottenburg are great for mainstream clothing, as is the Potsdamer Arkaden mall at Potsdamer Platz. For international designer labels, head to Fasanenstrasse and other Ku'damm side streets or to the architecturally stunning **Friedrichstadtpassagen** near Gendarmenmarkt. Young designers cluster in Mitte and Prenzlauer Berg, especially along Kastanienallee, the Hackesche Höfe, Alte Schönhauser Strasse and Schönhauser Allee. Multicultural Kreuzberg is great for browsing for second-hand and bric-a-brac treasures, particularly along Mehringdamm and Bergmannstrasse, although Maassenstrasse and Goltzstrasse in Schöneberg also have some candidates.

Berlin Designers

Thatchers (Map p126; ☎ 2462 7751; Kastanienallee 21 & Hof IV, Hackesche Höfe) Ralf Hensellek and Thomas Mrozek like their women's clothing to be rather minimalist, sleek and body-hugging. Some outfits can be rather daring.

Eisdieler (Map p126; ☎ 2790 8683; Kastanienallee 1. Not just flavour of the month – the urban streetwear designed by this five-person coop and sold in a former ice-cream parlour has firmly established itself in the Berlin design world.

Lisa D (Map pp98-9; ☎ 282 9061; Hackesche Höfe) Those not shy about flaunting flamboyant designs should be well taken care of by Lisa D's theatrical collections.

Nix (Map pp98-9; ☎ 281 8044; Auguststrasse 86) The name stands for New Individual X-tras, a line of unusual but wearable and fairly affordable fashions for hip women, men and children designed by Barbara Gebhardt.

Department Stores & Malls

KaDeWe (Kaufhaus des Westens; Map p129; ☎ 212 10; Tauentzienstrasse 21) Shopaholics will get their

Sculpture-framed Kaiser-Wilhelm-Gedächtniskirche (p114), Berlin

Brandenburg Gate, Berlin (p103)

Sun decoration, Sanssouci Park
(p145), Potsdam

Jüdisches Museum (Jewish Museum; p111), Berlin

JOHN BORTHWICK

Karl Marx sculpture (p189), Leipzig

ANDREA SCHUI

Gildehaus, Fischmarkt (p208), Erfurt

Meissen (p180), Central Saxony

fix at this amazing, seven-floor department store, which sells just about anything from yarn to washing machines. If pushed for time, make a beeline to the gourmet food hall on the 6th floor – it's legendary.

Wertheim bei Hertie (Map p102; ☎ 880 030; Kurfürstendamm 231) Almost as huge as KaDeWe, but considerably more down-to-earth and with lower prices, this is where Berliners shop.

Dussmann (Map pp98-9; ☎ 2025 2440; Friedrichstrasse 90; ☽ 10am-10pm) It's easy to lose track of time as you browse through the several floors of CDs (ask about the free portable CD players for test-listening), books and videos. The café, Internet terminals and readings provide additional temptations to linger.

Galeries Lafayette (Map pp98-9; ☎ 3020 9480; Friedrichstrasse 76) This beautiful Berlin branch of the exquisite French chain is worth a visit if only to admire its dramatic central light cone shimmering in a rainbow of colours. Designer wear upstairs and a great food court in the basement.

Potsdamer Platz Arkaden (☎ 255 9270; Alte Potsdamer Strasse, Potsdamer Platz) This pleasant multi-level, American-style indoor mall brims with chains like H&M, Mango, Esprit (all clothing), Hugendubel (books) and Saturn (electronics and music). There's several food options too.

Schönhauser Allee Arcaden (Map p126; ☎ 4471 1711; Schönhauser Allee 79-80) This is a lively allpurpose mall that gets mostly local traffic. Post office to supermarket to shoe store, it's all here.

Farmers' Markets

Every Berlin neighbourhood has its own farmers' market where you can stock up on fresh produce along with breads, cheeses, meats, candles, gift items, flowers, delicatessen and lots more. The best mainstream market is the **Winterfeldtmarkt** (Map p129; Winterfeldtplatz; ☽ 8am-2pm Wed & Sat) in Schöneberg, where you should plan on capping off your shopping spree with coffee or breakfast at an area café.

For more exotic flavours, head to the **Turkish Market** (Map pp100-1; Maybachufer; ☽ noon-6.30pm Tue & Fri) along the Landwehr canal in Kreuzberg to put together a great picnic with fruits, loaves of Turkish bread, olives, creamy fetta spreads and other delectable

goodies. Grab your loot and head a bit west along the canal to carve out your spot on the more scenic Fraenkelufer.

Flea Markets

Flea markets are great places to engage in some urban archaeology. You never know what kind of treasure you'll dig up among the trash 'n' treasures. Bargaining is encouraged. Here are some of the best markets:

Flohmarkt am Tiergarten (Map p102; Strasse des 17 Juni; ☽ 10am-5pm Sat & Sun) West of the Tiergarten S-Bahn station, this market is a tourist favourite and has good Berlin memorabilia; it's expensive but fun to browse.

Flohmarkt am Arkonaplatz (Map pp96-7; Arkonaplatz; ☽ 10am-4pm Sun) This flea market feeds the current retro frenzy with lots of groovy furniture, accessories, clothing, vinyl and books.

Hallentrödelmarkt Treptow (Map pp100-1; Eichenstrasse 4, Treptow; ☽ 10am-4pm Sat & Sun) This indoor market has piles of funky and trashy stuff requiring patience and a solid 'shit-detector'. Good for vintage furniture.

Flohmarkt Schöneberg (Map p129; Rathaus Schöneberg; ☽ 9am-4pm Sat & Sun) Pros and non-pros mix it up at this neighbourhood market, which often has good deals on used clothing and books.

Flohmarkt am Moritzplatz (Map pp100-1; Moritzplatz; ☽ 8am-4pm Sat & Sun) This one is pretty junky, but the rock bottom prices are hard to resist. Keep an eye out for that perfect Berlin memento.

Galleries

Berlin has about 300 private galleries holding forth in courtyards, stately patrician villas, old warehouses or factories, or in spacious, elegant collections of rooms on major boulevards. You'll find concentrations of them along Ku'damm and Fasanenstrasse in Charlottenburg, as well as on Auguststrasse and in and around the Hackesche Höfe and Sophienhöfe in Mitte.

For a comprehensive and up-to-date overview, pick up a copy of *Berlin Artery – Der Kunstführer* (in both German and English) available at newsstands, bookshops and some museums.

Second-hand & Vintage Clothing

Colours Kleidermarkt (Map pp100-1; ☎ 694 3348; 1st fl, Bergmannstrasse 102) This huge loft has great vintage goodies suitable for the office or your next costume party. Most items are in great condition and supercheap. Good range of accessories too. It's in the back courtyard, upstairs on the right.

Garage (Map p129; ☎ 211 2760; Ahornstrasse 2) At this basement warehouse you buy your clothing by weight, with 1kg costing €14, but you really have to pick your way through the racks for untattered and unsoiled items.

Sterling Gold (Map pp98-9; ☎ 2809 6500; Heckmannhöfe) Connect with your inner princess when slipping into one of the superb gowns and cocktails dresses from the '50s to the '80s available here.

Buttenheim Levi's Store (Map pp98-9; ☎ 2759 4460; Neue Schönhauser Strasse 15) Named after the German birthplace of the jeans inventor, Buttenheim has a solid assortment of vintage Levi's and accessories.

GETTING THERE & AWAY
Air
Berlin has three airports; the general information number for all is ☎ 0180-500 0186 (www.berlin-airport.de). Tegel (TXL) is about 8km northwest of Bahnhof Zoo and primarily serves destinations within Germany and Western Europe. Schönefeld (SXF), some 22km from Bahnhof Zoo, handles flights to/from Eastern Europe, the Americas, Asia and Africa. Central but small, Tempelhof (THF), 6km southeast of Bahnhof Zoo, is a hub for quick city hops within Germany and central Europe.

AIRLINE OFFICES
Airlines serving Berlin include:
Air France (☎ 01805-830 830)
AirBerlin (☎ 01801-737 800) Low-cost flights from London-Stansted, Milan, Rome, Barcelona, Madrid and other European cities.
British Airways/Deutsche BA (☎ 01805-266 522)
Cirrus Airlines (☎ 0180-444 4888) Flies to Saarbrücken and the islands of Sylt and Usedom from Tempelhof.
Delta Air Lines (☎ 0180-333 7880)
Eurowings (☎ 0231-924 5333)
KLM-Northwest Airlines (☎ 01805-214 201)
Lufthansa (☎ 01803-803 803)
MALEV-Hungarian Airlines (☎ 264 9545)
RyanAir (☎ 0190-170 100, €0.62 per minute) Budget flights from London-Stansted to Schönefeld.
Swiss (☎ 01803-000 334)

Bus
Berlin's central bus station, ZOB (Map pp96-7; Masurenallee 4-6), is about 4km west of Bahnhof Zoo, right by the Funkturm radio tower in western Charlottenburg. The closest U-Bahn stop is Kaiserdamm (U2, U12). Tickets are available from the **ZOB Reisebüro** (☎ 301 8028 for information, ☎ 301 0380 for reservations; 6.30am-9pm), although many in-town travel agencies and ride-share agencies also sell them. The main operator is **BerlinLinienBus** (☎ 0180-154 6436 outside Berlin, ☎ 860 960 within Berlin) with departures for destinations throughout Germany and Europe. **Gulliver's** (☎ 311 0211; www.gullivers.de) also has an extensive route system. Both companies offer discounts to students and people under 26 and over 60.

Bus About (www.busabout.com) serves Berlin from Amsterdam with onward service to Dresden and Prague; pick-up is from the A&O Hostel am Zoo next to Bahnhof Zoo (p122).

Car & Motorcycle
The A10 ring road around the city links Berlin with other German and foreign cities, including the A11 to Szczecin (Stettin) in Poland; the A12 to Frankfurt an der Oder; the A13 to Dresden; the A9 to Leipzig, Nuremberg and Munich; the A2 to Hanover and the Ruhrgebiet cities; and the A24 to Hamburg.

RIDE SERVICES
Berlin has several *Mitfahrzentralen*, which typically charge €17 for shared rides to Hamburg, €31 to Cologne and €32 to Munich. The people answering the phone in these offices usually speak English well.
CityNetz Mitfahrzentrale (Map p102; ☎ 194 44; Joachimstaler Strasse 17)
Mitfahr2000 (☎ 194 2000; www.mitfahr2000.de; 8am-8pm) Bahnhof Zoo (Map p102; Joachimstaler Strasse 1); Kreuzberg (Map pp100-1; Yorckstrasse 52); Prenzlauer Berg (Map p126; ☎ 440 9392; Oderbergerstrasse 45)

Train
Bahnhof Zoo (Map p102) and Ostbahnhof (Map pp100-1) are Berlin's two major train stations for national and international long-distance services, with most trains stopping at both stations. Superfast ICE trains make regular departures to such cities as

Hamburg, Hanover, Dortmund, Leipzig, Weimar, Frankfurt, Wittenberg, Nuremberg and Munich. The IC train destinations include Spreewald towns, Dresden, Warsaw, Prague, Budapest and Vienna. Trains bound for Stralsund and Rügen Island leave from Ostbahnhof only.

At both stations you'll find good infrastructures, with left-luggage services, coin lockers, car-hire agencies and currency exchange. Bahnhof Zoo is still the bigger of the two. Here you'll find the helpful EurAide office (p103), a McClean station where you can take a shower (€6), and the BVG public transportation information kiosk right outside the main entrance.

Deutsche Bahn (DB) train tickets to/from Berlin are valid for all train stations on the city S-Bahn, which means that on arrival you can use the S-Bahn network (but not the U-Bahn) to connect or get to your final destination. Conversely, you can use the S-Bahn to go to the station from where your train leaves for another city, if you have a booked ticket. Rail passes are also valid on the S-Bahn. For information on timetables, fares, reservations etc, call ☎ 01805-996 633 any time or log on to www.bahn.de.

GETTING AROUND
To/From the Airport
SCHÖNEFELD

Schönefeld airport is served several times daily by the SFX Express Shuttle (€3, 50 minutes), operated by BVG, with departures from the KaDeWe department store (Map p129), Potsdamer Platz and Rudow U-Bahn station. Buses stop right at the terminal.

Alternatives include taking either the S9 (€2.20, 50 minutes) or an RE train (€2.20, 35 minutes), which depart frequently throughout the day and stop at the Schönefeld train station, located about 300m from the terminal; they're linked by a free shuttle bus every 10 minutes. Bus No 171 links the terminal directly with the U-Bahn station Rudow (U7) with connections to central Berlin. A taxi between Schönefeld and central Berlin costs between €25 and €35.

TEGEL

Tegel is connected to Mitte by the JetExpressBus TXL (€4.10, 30 minutes), which drops off and picks up at such strategic stops as Unter den Linden and Alexanderplatz. If you're headed for the western city centre around Bahnhof Zoo, your best bet is to hop aboard bus Nos X9 or 109 (€2.20, 30 minutes).

The closest U-Bahn station to the airport is Jakob-Kaiser-Platz (U7), which is on the route of bus No 109. Alternatively, you could take bus No 128 from the airport to the Kurt-Schumacher-Platz station with onward service on the U6.

A taxi between Tegel and either Bahnhof Zoo or Mitte costs about €20.

TEMPELHOF

Tempelhof airport is easily reached on the U6 (get off at Platz der Luftbrücke) or by bus No 119 from Kurfürstendamm via Kreuzberg (€2.20, 30 minutes).

A taxi to Bahnhof Zoo or Mitte costs about €15.

Car & Motorcycle

Berlin is less congested than other major cities and drivers are fairly disciplined, making getting around by car comparatively easy.

Parking in garages is expensive (about €1 to €2 per hour), but often it'll be your only choice. Parking meters are rare but the 'pay and display' system is quite widespread. Free street parking, while difficult to find in central areas, is usually available in the outer districts. Watch out for signs indicating parking restrictions or you risk a ticket or even being towed.

CAR HIRE

You'll find all the major international car-rental chains represented in Berlin with branches at the airports, major train stations and throughout town, including several conveniently clustered near Bahnhof Zoo (listed below). For other branches, check under *Autovermietung* in the Yellow Pages. Prices vary greatly and depend on demand, so it pays to shop around.

Avis (Map p102; ☎ 230 9370; Budapester Strasse 41)

Europcar (Map p102; ☎ 235 0640; Kurfürstenstrasse 101)

Hertz (Map p102; ☎ 261 1053; Budapester Strasse 39)

Robben & Wientjes Kreuzberg (Map pp100–1; ☎ 616 770; Prinzenstrasse 90–91); Prenzlauer Berg (Map pp100–1; ☎ 421 036; Prenzlauer Allee 96) Local agency with fair prices.

Sixt Budget (Map p102; ☎ 219 9090; Kurfürstenstrasse 101)

MOTORCYCLE HIRE

Numerous outfits in Berlin hire out motor-cycles, which are fun for excursions to the countryside. Prices range from €50 to €130 per day, depending on the model.

Classic Bike Harley-Davidson (Map pp100-1; ☎ 616 7930; Skalitzer Strasse 127/8)

V2-Moto (Map pp100-1; ☎ 6128 0490; Skalitzer Strasse 69)

Public Transport

Berlin's public transport system is composed of services provided by the **Berliner Verkehrsbetriebe** (BVG; information ☎ 194 49; ⏱ 24hr) and **Deutsche Bahn** (DB; ☎ 01805-996 633). The BVG operates the U-Bahn, buses, trams and ferries, while DB is in charge of the S-Bahn, Regionalbahn (RB) and Regionalexpress (RE). One type of ticket is valid on all forms of transport (with the few exceptions noted below).

The **BVG Information Kiosk** (Map p102; Hardenbergplatz; ⏱ 6am-10pm), outside Bahnhof Zoo, sells tickets and also has free route network maps and general information on buses, U-Bahns, trams and ferries.

For information on S-Bahn, RE and RB connections, visit the Reisezentrum office inside the station.

BUYING & USING TICKETS

Bus drivers sell single tickets and day passes, but tickets for U/S-Bahn trains and other multiple, weekly or monthly tickets must be purchased before boarding. These are available from the orange vending machines (with instructions in English) in U/S-Bahn stations, as well as from the ticket window at station entrances and the BVG information kiosk outside Bahnhof Zoo (Map p102).

Tickets must be stamped (validated) in a red machine *(Entwerter)* at the platform entrances to S-Bahn and U-Bahn stations or at bus stops before boarding. If you're caught by an inspector without a ticket (or even an unvalidated one), there's a €40 fine.

FARES & TICKETS

Berlin's metropolitan area is divided into three tariff zones – A, B and C. Tickets are valid in at least two zones (AB or BC) or in all three zones (ABC). Unless you're venturing to Potsdam or the very outer suburbs, you'll only need the AB ticket. Single tickets are valid for unlimited travel for

two hours. The Group Day Pass is valid for up to five people travelling together. Kids under age six travel free. Children aged six to 14 qualify for reduced *(ermässigt)* rates.

Ticket type	AB	BC	ABC
single	€2.20	€2.25	€2.60
day pass	€5.60	€5.70	€6
group day pass (up to 5 people)	€14	€14.30	€15
7-day pass	€23.40	€24	€29

REGIONAL TRAINS

The S-Bahn network is supplemented by the RB (Regionalbahn) and RE (Regional-Express) trains, whose routes are also marked on the BVG network map. You'll need an ABC or DB rail ticket (including rail passes) to use these trains.

ALL ABOARD!
BERLIN FROM BUS NOS 100 & 200

One of the best bargains in Berlin is a city tour aboard a public double-decker bus. Both bus No 100 and 200 follow routes that hit nearly every major sight in the central city for the modest price of €2.20, the standard single BVG ticket. You can even get off as often as you wish within the two hours of its validity. If you plan on exploring all day, the *Tageskarte* (Day Pass) for €5.60 is your best bet.

Bus No 100 travels from Bahnhof Zoo to Prenzlauer Berg passing by such landmarks as the Gedächtniskirche, Tiergarten with the Victory Column, the Reichstag, the Brandenburg Gate, Unter den Linden and Alexanderplatz, where most people disembark.

Bus No 200 also starts at Bahnhof Zoo but takes a more southerly route past the Kulturforum and Potsdamer Platz before travelling on to the Brandenburg Gate and Unter den Linden as well.

If you don't interrupt your trip, the entire one-way journey on either route takes about 45 minutes (more during heavy traffic). There's no commentary (unless you're lucky to have a chatty bus driver), so pick up a map and information leaflet from the BVG information kiosk outside Bahnhof Zoo (Map p102).

TRAMS & BUSES

Berlin's buses are rather slow, but being ensconced on the upper level of a double-decker is a mighty fine (and inexpensive) way to do some relaxed sightseeing – see the boxed text All Aboard! Berlin from Bus No 100 & 200 (p140).

Bus stops are marked with a large 'H' (for Haltestelle) and the name of the stop. Drivers sell tickets and can give change. The next stop is usually announced via a loudspeaker or displayed on a digital board. Push the button on the handrails if you want to get off.

From Sunday to Thursday, nightbus lines take over from the U/S-Bahn between 1am and 4am, running roughly at 30-minute intervals. Normal fares apply.

The trams only operate in the eastern districts.

U-BAHN & S-BAHN

The most efficient way to travel around Berlin is by U-Bahn, which operates from 4am until just after midnight, except at weekends when services continue through the night on all lines except the U1, U4 and U12.

S-Bahn trains make fewer stops than U-Bahns and are therefore handy for longer distance, but they don't run as frequently. They, too, operate from around 4am to 12.30am and throughout the night on Friday, Saturday and holiday nights. The S-Bahn is free for rail pass holders.

The next station is announced on most U-Bahn (but not S-Bahn) trains and is also displayed at the end of carriages on some newer trains. It's best, though, to know the name of the station before you get to the one you need. To help you do this, large route maps are plastered on the ceilings above the doors in most U-Bahn cars. Large versions of the same maps are on station platforms.

Taxi

Taxi stands with 'call columns' *(Rufsäule)* are beside all main train stations and throughout the city. Flag fall is €2.50, then it's €1.50 per kilometre up to 7km and €1 for each additional kilometre. A fifth passenger costs €1.25 extra and bulky luggage is €1 per piece. You can order a taxi by calling ☎ 194 10, ☎ 210 101 or ☎ 210 202.

For short trips, there's a €3 flat rate which entitles you to ride for 2km, but it's only available if you flag down a moving taxi and request the €3 rate before getting in.

Velotaxis

A nonpolluting alternative for short hops is a **Velotaxi** (www.velotaxis.com), comfortable pedicabs aided by an electric engine, which seat two people. They operate from April to September along four routes: Kurfürstendamm, Unter den Linden, Friedrichstrasse and Tiergarten. Simply flag one down or call ☎ 0151-122 8000 or ☎ 443 1940. The cost is €2.50 per person for the first kilometre, then €1 for each additional kilometre. Half-hour tours are €7.50 per person.

Brandenburg

CONTENTS

Getting There & Around	144
Potsdam & Havelland	**144**
Potsdam	144
Brandenburg an der Havel	151
Spreewald	**153**
Lübben	153
Lübbenau	154
Cottbus	155
Märkische Schweiz &	
Oderbruch	**155**
Buckow	156
Frankfurt an der Oder	157
Northern Brandenburg	**158**
Sachsenhausen	
Concentration Camp	158
Rheinsberg	159
Lower Oder Valley	
National Park	161
Chorin	162
Niederfinow	162

Despite its proximity to the ever-popular Berlin, Brandenburg has suffered from a poor reputation since reunification. Many western Germans still think of Brandenburgers as archetypal *Ossis* (East German), ambivalent about the demise of the GDR and perhaps even a touch xenophobic. Declining population figures, economic depression and high unemployment have also contributed to social problems in urban areas. However, the situation is nowhere near as bad as some would have you believe – in fact, most travellers are pleasantly surprised at the wealth of attractions and the friendliness of the locals in this much-maligned state, and the pride people take in their home towns here can be amazingly infectious.

The uncontested high point of any trip here is a visit to the stunning town of Potsdam, the 'German Versailles', with its wealth of parks, museums, stately palaces and the famous UFA film studios at Babelsberg. However, it's also worth taking the time to explore further afield and discover some fascinating and distinctly undervisited corners of eastern Germany. The largely flat countryside is thoroughly waterlogged and remains a firm favourite with local day-trippers and holiday-makers, with the Havelland, Spreewald and Lower Oder Valley regions providing some of the country's richest wetlands and myriad options for hikers, bikers and boaters of all persuasions.

The legacy of the powerful margraves of Brandenburg can be seen in the many palaces and fortifications they left behind in towns such as Brandenburg an der Havel, Rheinsberg and Lübben; the darker history of the recent past is also represented and commemorated in the former Sachsenhausen Concentration Camp. Those more interested in living traditions should head south towards the border with Saxony to encounter the Sorbs, Germany's only indigenous minority group.

HIGHLIGHTS

- **Parks & Palaces**
  Tackle all Potsdam's treasures – don't miss the beautiful Chinesisches Haus (Chinese Teahouse; p147)

- **History**
  Visit the sombre Sachsenhausen Concentration Camp Memorial & Museum at Oranienburg (p158)

- **Waterways**
  Strike out into the Spreewald Biosphere Reserve from the charming punt town of Lübben (p153)

- **Castles**
  Explore the inner workings of Friedrich Wilhelm I's magnificent Schloss (Palace) in Rheinsberg (p159)

- **Music**
  Attend a summer concert in the atmospheric 13th-century Chorin monastery (p162)

- **Drinking**
  Take in an Oktoberfest at the newly renovated Marienberg in Brandenburg (p152)

★ Rheinsberg
Chorin ★
★ Oranienburg
Brandenburg ★   ★ Potsdam
★ Lübben

- POPULATION: 2.6 MILLION
- AREA: 24,479 SQ KM

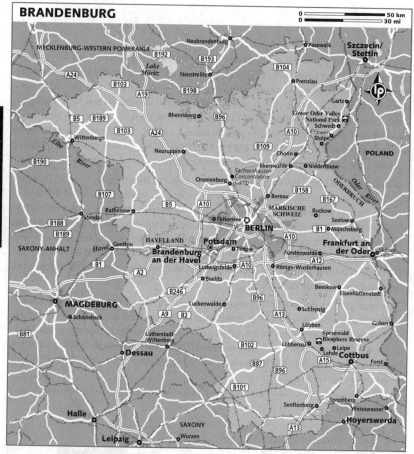

GETTING THERE & AROUND

The Berlin airports are the main points of entry to Brandenburg, which also benefits from the excellent local transport system, with S-Bahn and train lines radiating from the capital like tentacles (see p140). The **DB Brandenburg-Ticket** (€23; valid 9-3am Mon-Fri) gives five people one day's unlimited travel on any regional lines and on public transport in major towns, including Berlin.

POTSDAM & HAVELLAND

The prime attraction of Brandenburg state and the most popular day trip from Berlin, Potsdam is a mere 24km southwest of Berlin's city centre and easily accessible by S-Bahn. If time allows, try to make it another 36km west to the historic city of Brandenburg an der Havel, the centre of the watery Havelland region; picturesque and less tourist-saturated than Potsdam, it's a perfect introduction to the state for which it's named.

POTSDAM

☎ 0331 / pop 131,000

Potsdam, on the Havel River just beyond the southwestern tip of Greater Berlin, is the capital of Brandenburg state. In the 17th century, Elector Friedrich Wilhelm of Brandenburg made it his second residence. With the creation of the Kingdom of Prussia, Potsdam became a royal seat and garrison town; in the mid-18th century, Friedrich II (Frederick the Great) built many of the marvellous palaces which visitors flock to today.

In April 1945, RAF bombers devastated the historic centre of Potsdam, including the City Palace on Alter Markt, but fortunately most other palaces escaped undamaged. To emphasise their victory over the German military machine, the Allies chose Schloss Cecilienhof for the Potsdam Conference of August 1945, which set the stage for the division of Berlin and Germany into occupation zones.

The Potsdam suburb of Babelsberg is the site of a historic – and now once again functioning – film studio (with less historic theme park). In 2001, Potsdam hosted the *Bundesgartenschau* (National Garden Show), for which this already lovely metropolis was further spruced up; whatever your tastes, a visit here is essential if you're spending any time in the area at all.

Orientation

Potsdam Hauptbahnhof (central train station) is just southeast of the city centre, across the Havel River. Heading west, the next two stops are Charlottenhof and Sanssouci, which are closer to Sanssouci Park and the palaces; however, these are served only by RegionalBahn (RB) trains, not the Regional Express (RE) or S-Bahn, which most people use to get here from Berlin. It's about 2km to Charlottenhof.

Information
BOOKSHOPS
Buchhandlung Alexander von Humboldt (☎ 200 460; www.avh-buch.de; Friedrich-Ebert-Strasse) Large shop in the Stadtbibliothek building.
Das Internationale Buch (☎ 291 496; Friedrich-Ebert-Strasse) Stocks maps and some English-language publications.

EMERGENCY
Emergency medical service (☎ 713 300)
Police (☎ 56860; Kaiser-Friedrich-Strasse 143)

INTERNET ACCESS
Cyberspace (Bahnhofspassage; €1.50 per hr)
Hell Net (☎ 280 0555; www.hellnet.com; Schlossstrasse 13; €1.50 per hr)
Staudenhof (☎ 280 0554; Am Alten Markt 10; €1.50 per hr; 🕑 from 9am)

MEDICAL SERVICES
Gesundheitszentrum Potsdam (☎ 232 80; Hebbelstrasse 1A) Private clinic.

MONEY
Commerzbank (☎ 281 90; cnr Charlottenstrasse & Lindenstrasse)
Dresdner Bank (☎ 287 8200; Yorckstrasse 28)
Eurochange (☎ 280 4033; Brandenburger Strasse 29)

POST
Main post office (Am Kanal)

TOURIST INFORMATION
Potsdam Information (☎ 275 580; www.potsdam tourismus.de; Neuer Markt 1; 🕑 9am-7pm Mon-Fri, 10am-6pm Sat & Sun Apr-Oct, 10am-6pm Mon-Fri, 10am-2pm Sat & Sun Nov-Mar)
Sanssouci Besucherzentrum (☎ 969 4202; www .spsg.de; An der Historischen Windmühle; 🕑 8.30am-5pm Mar-Oct, 9am-4pm Nov-Feb)

Sights
SANSSOUCI PARK
This large park west of the city centre is open from dawn till dusk year-round; the palaces and outbuildings all have different hours and admission prices, and many only open on weekends and holidays outside the main season. A two-day pass including all sights in the park costs €15 for adults, and other combi-tickets are available.

The park itself is a sprawling beast, with crisscrossing trails strewn throughout; take along the free map provided by the tourist office or you'll find yourself up the wrong path at almost every turn. The palaces are fairly well spaced – for example, it's 2km between the Neues Palais (New Palace) and Schloss Sanssouci, and about 15km to complete the entire circuit. Sadly, cycling in the park is strictly *verboten* (forbidden).

Schloss Sanssouci & Around
Begin your park tour with Georg Wenzeslaus von Knobelsdorff's **Schloss Sanssouci** (1747), the celebrated rococo palace with glorious interiors (☎ 969 4190; mandatory tour adult/concession €8/5; 🕑 Tue-Sun 9am-5pm Apr-Oct, 9am-4pm Nov-Mar). Only 2000 visitors a day are allowed entry (a rule laid down by Unesco), so tickets are usually sold out by 2.30pm, even in the quiet seasons – arrive early and avoid weekends and holidays. Tours run by the tourist office (see Tours p149) guarantee entry.

BRANDENBURG

POTSDAM

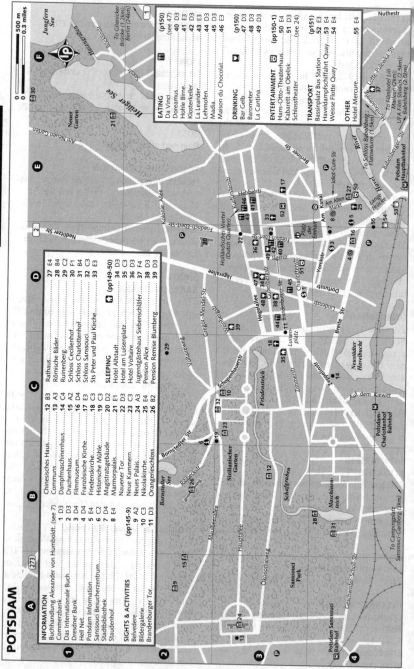

INFORMATION
Buchhandlung Alexander von Humboldt..(see 7)
Commerzbank..1 D3
Das Internationale Buch..........................2 D3
Dresdner Bank.......................................3 D4
Hell Net...4 D4
Potsdam Information................................5 E4
Sanssouci Besucherzentrum.......................6 C2
Stadtbibliothek......................................7 D4
Staudenhof...8 E4

SIGHTS & ACTIVITIES (pp145-9)
Belvedere...9 A2
Bildergalerie...10 C3
Brandenburger Tor..................................11 D3

Chinesisches Haus...................................12 B3
Communs...13 A3
Dampfmaschinenhaus..............................14 C4
Filmmuseum..15 D4
Französische Kirche.................................16 D4
Friedenskirche.......................................17 B4
Historische Mühle...................................18 C3
Magistratsgebäude.................................19 C3
Marmorpalais..20 D2
Nauener Tor..21 E1
Neue Kammern......................................22 D3
Neues Palais...23 A3
Nikolaikirche...24 C3
Orangerieschloss....................................25 E4

Rathaus...26 B2
Römische Bäder.....................................27 E4
Ruinenberg..28 B4
Schloss Cecilienhof.................................29 C2
Schloss Charlottenhof..............................30 F1
Schloss Sanssouci...................................31 B4
Sts Peter und Paul Kirche..........................32 C3

SLEEPING (pp149-50)
Hotel Altstadt..33 E3
Hotel am Luisenplatz...............................34 D3
Hotel Voltaire..35 C3
Jugendgästehaus Siebenschläfer..................36 D3
Pension Alice...37 F4
Pension Remise Blumberg..........................38 D3
                                                   39 D3

EATING (p150)
Da Vinci..40 D3
Doreamus...41 E3
Hohle Birne..42 D3
Klosterkeller...43 E3
La Leander...44 D3
Lehmofen...45 D3
Madia..46 E3
Maison du Chocolat.................................(see 47)

DRINKING (p150)
Bar Gelb..47 D3
Barometer..48 D3
La Cantina..49 D3

ENTERTAINMENT (pp150-1)
Hans-Otto-Theaterhaus.............................50 E4
Kabarett am Obelisk.................................51 D3
Schlosstheater.......................................(see 24)

TRANSPORT (p151)
Bassinplatz Bus Station..............................52 E3
Haveldampfschifffahrt Quay........................53 E4
Weisse Flotte Quay..................................54 E4

OTHER
Hotel Mercure.......................................55 E4

Our favourite rooms include the frilly rococo **Konzertsaal** (Concert Hall) and the bed chambers of the **Damenflügel** (Ladies' Wing; adult/concession €2/1.50; ☉ 10am-5pm Tue-Sun mid-May–mid-Oct), including a 'Voltaire slept here' one (don't ask what he was doing in the ladies' wing). From the northern terrace of the palace you can see the **Ruinenberg**, a group of classical 'ruins' that actually make up a folly built by Frederick the Great in 1754.

Just opposite the palace is the **Historische Mühle** (Historic Windmill; ☎ 969 4284; adult/concession €2/1; ☉ 10am-6pm April-Oct) designed, like the Queen's Hamlet at Versailles, to give the palace grounds a rustic, rural air. The palace is flanked by the twin **Neue Kammern** (New Chambers; ☎ 969 4206; adult/concession €2.50/1.50; ☉ 10am-5pm Tue-Sun mid-May–mid-Oct), which served as a guesthouse and orangery. It includes the large Ovidsaal, with its gilded reliefs and green and white marble floor, and Meissen porcelain figurines in the last room to the west.

Next door, the **Bildergalerie** (Picture Gallery; ☎ 969 4181; adult/concession €2.50/1.50; ☉ 10am-5pm Tue-Sun mid-May–mid-Oct) was completed in 1764 as Germany's first purpose-built art museum. It contains a rich collection of 17th-century paintings by Rubens, Caravaggio and others.

Just west of the Neue Kammern is the **Sizilianischer Garten** (Sicilian Garden) of subtropical plants, which was laid out in the mid-19th century.

Orangerieschloss & Around

The Renaissance-style **Orangerieschloss** (Orangery Palace; ☎ 969 4280; mandatory tour adult/concession €3/2.50; ☉ 10am-5pm Tue-Sun mid-May–mid-Oct), built in 1864 as a guesthouse for foreign royalty, is the largest of the Sanssouci palaces but hardly the most interesting. The six sumptuous rooms on display include the **Raphaelsaal**, with 19th-century copies of the Italian Renaissance painter's work, and a tower that can be climbed (€1) for great views over the Neues Palais and the park. Part of the west wing is still used to keep more sensitive plants alive in the cold north German winter.

Two interesting buildings west of the Orangery are the pagodalike **Drachenhaus** (Dragon House, 1770), which houses a café-restaurant (closed Monday), and the rococo **Belvedere** (☉ daily Apr-Oct), the only building in the park to suffer serious damage during WWII (it was fully restored in 1999).

Neues Palais

Built in 1769 as the summer residence of the royal family, the late-baroque **Neues Palais** (New Palace; ☎ 969 4255; adult/concession €5/4; ☉ 10am-5pm Sat-Thu), is one of the most imposing buildings in the park and the one to see if your time is limited. The tour (€6/5 including admission) takes in about a dozen of the palace's 200 rooms, including the **Grottensaal** (Grotto Hall), a rococo delight of shells, fossils and baubles set into the walls and ceilings; the **Marmorsaal**, a large banquet hall of Carrara marble with a wonderful ceiling fresco; the **Jagdkammer** (Hunting Chamber) with lots of dead furry things and fine gold tracery on the walls; and several chambers fitted out from floor to ceiling in rich red damask. Note the *Fahrstuhl*, an electric 'stair lift' from 1899 that transported ageing royals from the ground to the 1st floor.

The **Schlosstheater** in the south wing has classical music concerts on the weekend (see Entertainment p150). Opposite the New Palace is the **Communs**, which originally housed the palace servants and kitchens but is now part of Potsdam University.

Schloss Charlottenhof

Karl Friedrich Schinkel's main contribution (1826) to the park, **Schloss Charlottenhof** (☎ 969 4228; mandatory tour adult/concession €4/3; ☉ 10am-5pm Tue-Sun mid-May–mid-Oct) is considered one of his finest works, but don't wait around if the entry queues are too long. In truth, the exterior (modelled after a Roman villa) is more interesting than the interior, especially the Doric portico and the bronze fountain to the east.

A short distance to the northeast, on the edge of the Maschinenteich (Machine Pond), the **Römische Bäder** (Roman Baths; adult/concession €2/1.50; ☉ 10am-5pm Tue-Sun mid-May–mid-Oct) were built in 1836 by a pupil of Schinkel but were never used. The floor mosaics and caryatids inspired by the baths at Herculaneum are impressive, and we also like the flounder spitting into a clamshell near the entrance.

Follow the path north along the west bank of the Schafgraben to Ökonomieweg, then head east, and you'll come to what many consider to be the pearl of the park: the **Chinesisches Haus** (Chinese Teahouse; ☎ 969 4222;

admission €1; ⏲ 10am-5pm Tue-Sun mid-May–mid-Oct), a circular pavilion of gilded columns, palm trees and figures of Chinese musicians and animals, built in 1757. One of the monkeys is said to have the features of Voltaire!

ALTSTADT

The baroque **Brandenburger Tor** (Brandenburg Gate), on Luisenplatz at the western end of the old town, is hardly on the scale of its namesake in Berlin but is actually older (1770) and considerably cleaner. From this square, the pedestrianised Brandenburger Strasse runs due east to the **Sts Peter und Paul Kirche** (Church of Sts Peter and Paul, 1868). Just to the southeast on Charlottenstrasse, and once the seat of the town's Huguenots, is the **Französische Kirche** (French Church, 1753).

Northwest of the churches, bounded by Friedrich-Ebert-Strasse, Hebbelstrasse, Kurfürstenstrasse and Gutenbergstrasse, the **Holländisches Viertel** (Dutch Quarter) has some 134 gabled red-brick houses built for Dutch workers who came to Potsdam in the 1730s at the invitation of Friedrich Wilhelm I (they didn't stay long). The homes have been prettily restored and now house galleries, cafés and restaurants. Further up Friedrich-Ebert-Strasse is the **Nauener Tor** (Nauen Gate, 1755), another monumental arch.

Southeast of central Platz der Einheit, on Alter Markt, is the great neoclassical dome of Schinkel's **Nikolaikirche** (⏲ 2-5pm Mon, 10am-5pm Tue-Sat, noon-5pm Sun) built in 1850. On the eastern side of the square is Potsdam's old **Rathaus** (Town hall; ⏲ 2-7pm Tue-Sun), dating from 1753, which now contains several art galleries upstairs.

West of the Alter Markt on Breite Strasse and housed in the **Marstall** (1746), the former royal stables designed by Knobelsdorff, is the smallish **Filmmuseum** (☎ 271 8112; www.filmmuseum-potsdam.de; Breite Strasse; adult/concession €2/1, films €4.50/3.50; ⏲ 10am-6pm). It contains exhibits on the history of the UFA and DEFA studios in Babelsberg, Marlene Dietrich costumes, and footage of Nazi-era and GDR films.

A short distance beyond the 'bay' of the Havel is the wonderful **Dampfmaschinenhaus** (Pump House; ☎ 969 4248; cnr Breite Strasse & Zeppelinstrasse; adult/concession €2/1.50 including tour; ⏲ 10am-5pm Sat & Sun mid-May–mid-Oct), a Moorish-style structure often called the *Moschee* (mosque),

METROPOLIS

Potsdam isn't readily associated with class warfare, but it was here, at the UFA studios, that Fritz Lang shot much of his allegorical melodrama *Metropolis* (1927), which deals with exactly that. The film depicts a society literally split in two, with the Thinkers living in idle luxury above ground and the Workers toiling in subterranean caverns to serve the terrible Moloch machine; threatened by nonviolent protest advocated by the saintly Maria, the Thinkers dispatch a robot clone of her to provoke riots. The sheer scale of the film was unprecedented (Lang hired 10,000 extras), and its relevance has endured, not just in its message of class cooperation but also in its themes of revolution, technology and voyeurism. Some elements were even ahead of their time – the robot Futura is a clear predecessor of the Terminator!

which was built in 1842 to house the palace waterworks.

NEUER GARTEN (NEW GARDEN)

This winding lakeside park on the west bank of the Heiliger See is a fine place to relax after all the baroque-rococo and high art of Sanssouci Park. Right on the lake, the **Marmorpalais** (Marble Palace; ☎ 969 4246; adult/concession €2.50/1.50; ⏲ 10am-5pm Tue-Sun Apr-Oct, 10am-4pm Sat & Sun Nov-Mar), built in 1792 by Carl Gotthard Langhans, has recently been carefully restored. Note the gilded angels dancing around the cupola.

Further north is **Schloss Cecilienhof**, a rustic English-style country manor contrasting with the extravagant rococo palaces and pavilions of Sanssouci. Cecilienhof was the site of the 1945 Potsdam Conference, and large photos of the participants – Stalin, Truman and Churchill – are displayed inside. Note the star of red roses in the courtyard, planted especially for the gathering. The conference room can be visited on a **guided tour** (☎ 969 4244; adult/concession €4/3; ⏲ 9am-5pm Tue-Sun).

To get to Schloss Cecilienhof, take bus No 116 from Wannsee to Glienicker Brücke and walk from there, or tram to Reiterweg/Alleestrasse from Potsdam Hauptbahnhof, then take bus No 692 to Am Neuen Garten.

BABELSBERG

The **Filmpark Babelsberg** (☎ 721 2755; www.filmpark.de; Grossbeerenstrasse; adult/concession/child €15/14/9; 🕑 10am-6pm mid-Mar–Oct), Germany's one-time response to Hollywood, are east of the city centre. Shooting began in 1912 but the studio had its heyday in the 1920s, when such silent-movie epics as Fritz Lang's *Metropolis* (see opposite) were made, along with some early Greta Garbo films.

Nowadays the place resembles a mini version of Universal Studios in America, with haunted house, volcano, live shows with audience participation, an impressive stunt show and a few poky rides. During the studio tour, staff whisk you around the back lot for a peek at the film sets and production, as well as into the props and costumes room.

To reach the film park, take the S7 to Babelsberg station (one stop from Potsdam Hauptbahnhof) and then bus No 694 to the Ahornstrasse stop. You can also get off at Griebnitzsee station and take bus No 696 to the Drewitz stop.

Schinkel's neo-Gothic **Schloss Babelsberg** (☎ 969 4250; adult/concession €5/4; 🕑 10am-5pm Tue-Fri Apr-Oct, 10am-4pm Sat & Sun Nov-Mar) is near the lakes. You can also stroll in the pleasant park past Schinkel's **Flatowturm** (☎ 969 4249; adult/concession €2/1.50; 🕑 10am-5pm Sat & Sun Apr–mid-Oct). A €3 combination ticket will get you into both the palace and the tower.

Tours

Potsdam Information (☎ 275 580; www.potsdamtourismus.de; Neuer Markt 1) runs a wide range of tours, from basic city tours (€8) to 3½-hour combined boat-and-walking tours (€32). There's also a full **Sanssouci Park tour** (€26; 🕑 11am Tue-Sun Apr-Oct, Fri-Sun Nov-Mar), which includes the Schloss.

Weisse Flotte (☎ 275 9210; www.schiffahrt-in-potsdam.de; Lange Brücke 6; 🕑 8.45am-4.15pm Apr-Oct) operates boats on the Havel and the lakes around Potsdam, departing regularly from the dock just below the Hotel Mercure near Lange Brücke. There are frequent boats to Wannsee (€7), Werder (€6.50) and Spandau (€15 return). Its sister company **Haveldampfschifffahrt** (☎ 275 9233; tours from €9.50) has steamboat tours of the same areas, leaving from the southern end of Lange Brücke (bridge; opposite the Weisse Flotte quay).

Festivals & Events

Potsdam's biggest annual events include the **Tulip Festival** in the Dutch quarter in mid-April, the **Musikfestspiele Potsdam Sanssouci** (☎ 293 859) during the second and third weeks of June, the **Filmfestival Potsdam** in mid-June, and the **Bachtage** (☎ 0700-1685 1750; www.bachtage-potsdam.de) in August/September (see the boxed text Bach-ing Mad below). The **Potsdamer Schlössernacht** (☎ 0180-523 7454) is an August weekend with music and fireworks in Sanssouci Park.

Sleeping

While most people visit Potsdam as a day trip from Berlin, accommodation can still be pretty scarce in the high season so it's worth booking ahead. Conversely, low-season prices can be great bargains. The tourist office arranges private rooms from €15 per person (bookings ☎ 275 5820).

Jugendgästehaus Siebenschläfer (☎ 741 125; jghpotsdam@aol.com; Lotte-Pulewka-Strasse 43; dm €18.50) This is great value for money and convenient for the Hauptbahnhof – bus No 695 stops almost in front of the door.

Campingplatz Sanssouci-Gaisberg (☎ 951 0988; info@recra.de; An der Pirschheide 41; sites €1.25-5 & adult/

BACH-ING MAD

The state of Brandenburg has links with many influential German composers, but few can compete with Johann Sebastian Bach – even the most blinkered techno-head has probably heard of the *Brandenburg Concertos*! These six *concerti grossi* were composed in 1721 for Margrave Christian Ludwig of Brandenburg, who was then based (a tad ironically) at Köthen in Saxony-Anhalt.

Some years later, in 1747, Frederick the Great managed to lure Bach to Potsdam, where the great composer wrote *The Musical Offering* on a theme proposed by the king himself. Since then Bach's place in Brandenburg history has been assured, but it's only in recent times that his legacy has been fully celebrated: in 2000 the first Potsdamer Bachtage (Bach Days) were introduced, comprising a two-week festival of concerts, workshops and readings dedicated to making the master's work accessible to modern audiences.

child €4.75/1.95; ☐) About 3km southwest of the centre on the Templiner See lakeshore, this is the closest camp site. Take the train or bus No 631 from Luisenplatz to Bahnhof Pirschheide.

Pension Alice (☎ 292 304; Lindenstrasse 16; s/d €25/50) Potsdam's most central budget option, with a few quirky rooms above a busy café.

Filmhotel Lili Marleen (☎ 743 200; www.filmhotel .potsdam.de; Grossbeerenstrasse 75; s €49-65, d €65-90; P) You're near Babelsberg here, although the posters on the walls treacherously salute Hollywood more than German cinema.

Pension Remise Blumberg (☎ 280 3231; www .pension-blumberg.de; Weinbergstrasse 26; s/d €55/68; P ✕) Well placed for Sanssouci, the large apartment-style rooms here are ideal for families or self-caterers (breakfast isn't included). Bike hire is available, and the garden café sports an almost cheery mural of Caspar David Friedrich's *Isle of the Dead*.

Hotel Altstadt (☎ 284 990; www.hotel-altstadt -potsdam.de; Dortusstrasse 9/10; s €60-72, d €80-90; P ✕) A good range of rooms and plenty of extra services make this place a decent bet.

Hotel Voltaire (☎ 231 70; nhvoltaire@nh-hotels .com; Friedrich-Ebert-Strasse 88; s €79-158, d €92-181; P ✕ ✕) The modern, quiet Voltaire has a posh address opposite the Dutch quarter and is nicely renovated, with two restaurants, roof terrace and the customary 'wellness area'.

Hotel am Luisenplatz (☎ 971 900; www.hotel -luisenplatz.de; Luisenplatz 5; s €79-109, d €119-139; ✕) This cosy, private, four-star establishment is a perfect central choice, with big rooms and some balconies overlooking the Brandenburger Tor. The house restaurant is a local favourite.

Eating

Madia (Lindenstrasse 53; food from €3.50; ☒ noon-7pm) A fair-trade haven for veggies, hippies and eco-warriors, tucked away in a nice courtyard behind a record store and a dubious 'headshop'.

Doreamus (☎ 201 5860; Brandenburger Strasse 30/31; mains €7.80-13.50) An unobtrusive doorway leads upstairs to some of the finest views you'll get over the Altstadt, with decent food to boot.

Da Vinci (☎ 280 5189; Dortusstrasse 4; pasta €6.50-11, mains €13-19) Classy and popular Italian with impressive chandeliers and a gallery overlooking the main floor, often inhabited by live musicians as well as diners.

Klosterkeller (☎ 291 218; Friedrich-Ebert-Strasse 94; mains €9.45-12.75) The Klosterkeller has a restaurant, wine bar, beer garden and cocktail bar and serves traditional regional dishes. It's a bit touristy, with multilingual menus and frequent costumed events, but still good fun.

Lehmofen (☎ 280 1712; Hermann-Elflein-Strasse 10; mains €10-17) This smart Turkish place may do kebabs, but it's a world away from your average doner shop, serving up tasty and authentic dishes from its eponymous clay oven.

The Dutch quarter is particularly good for eating options. Favourites include:

La Leander (☎ 270 6576; Benkertstrasse 1; light meals €3.50-4.75) This café on the northern edge of the quarter has a discreet gay following (the rainbow flag is a bit of a giveaway).

Hohle Birne (☎ 280 0715; Mittelstrasse 19; mains €6-13) There's earthy but tasty German cuisine here, plus a huge beer and wine menu. The name (literally 'hollow pear') is a local insult!

Maison du Chocolat (☎ 237 0730; Benkertstrasse 20; mains €14.50-17.50) As the name suggests, this is a fantastic spot for cakes and confectionery, but also has a varying menu of interesting savoury meals.

Drinking

The area around Dortusstrasse, Gutenbergstrasse and Lindenstrasse is a hotspot for nightspots.

Bar Gelb (Dortusstrasse 6) Popular with a young crowd, this lively place has an untranslatable pun in its name – *gelb* means yellow, which it is indeed, while *Bargeld* means cash, which is also clearly essential.

Barometer (☎ 270 2880; Gutenbergstrasse 103) More one for the grown-ups, who can pay serious money for serious cocktails in the classy red surrounds. Drinks prices go up to €17.90!

La Cantina (☎ 270 4969; Gutenbergstrasse 30) This Spanish *enoteca* is perfect for a liquid lunch, with a vast selection of wines and some good light meals to soak up the booze.

Entertainment

Hans-Otto-Theaterhaus (☎ 981 18; Alter Markt) The box office here has tickets for performances on site and for concerts in the **Schlosstheater** (☎ 969 4202; Neues Palais).

Kabarett am Obelisk (☎ 291 069; Charlottenstrasse 31; tickets €5-12.50) Come here for satirical programmes with contemporary themes and a nightly cabaret pub from Tuesday to Sunday.

Getting There & Away
BUS
Potsdam's bus station, just south of the Hauptbahnhof, is accessible from the Rathaus Spandau in Berlin on bus No 638 (hourly 5am to 9pm) and from Schönefeld on bus No 602.

TRAIN
S-Bahn line S7 links central Berlin with Potsdam Hauptbahnhof about every 10 minutes. Some regional (RB/RE) trains from Berlin-Zoo stop at all three stations in Potsdam, and RB22 trains connect to Berlin-Schönefeld airport. Berlin transit passes must cover Zones A, B and C (€2.60) to be valid for the trip to Potsdam by either S-Bahn or BVG bus.

Many trains between Hanover and Berlin-Zoo also stop at Potsdam Hauptbahnhof. Train connections south are poor; most require a change in Magdeburg or Berlin.

Getting Around
Potsdam is part of Berlin's S-Bahn network but has its own local trams and buses; these converge on Lange Brücke near the Hauptbahnhof. A two-zone ticket costs €1.40 and a day pass €3.

For a taxi, ring ☎ 292 929 or ☎ 707 070.

Bike hire is available from many hotels for around €7.50 per day.

BRANDENBURG AN DER HAVEL
☎ 03381 / pop 75,400
Brandenburg is the oldest town in the March of Brandenburg, with a history going back to at least the 6th century, when Slavs settled near today's cathedral. It was an important bishopric from the early Middle Ages and the seat of the Brandenburg margraves until they moved to Berlin in the 15th century. Severe damage suffered during WWII and GDR neglect is gradually being restored, and the baroque churches and waterside setting make for a refreshing day trip or overnight stay.

Orientation
Brandenburg is split into three sections by the Havel River, the Beetzsee and their canals. The Neustadt occupies an island in the centre; the Dominsel is to the north and the Altstadt, on the mainland, to the west. There are worthwhile sights in all three areas, which are connected by six bridges. The train station is on Am Hauptbahnhof, about 1km south of the central Neustädtischer Markt.

Information
Dresdner Bank (☎ 2670; Neustädtischer Markt 10)
Post office (St Annenstrasse 30-36)
Tourist Information (☎ 585 858; www.stadt-brandenburg.de; Steinstrasse 66/67; ☺ 8.30am-7pm Mon-Fri, 10am-3pm Sat & Sun May-Oct, 10am-6pm Mon-Fri, 10am-2pm Sat Nov-Apr)
Vobis (☎ 224 161; Kurstrasse 13; €1.80 per hr) Internet access.

Walking Tour
Begin a stroll through Brandenburg at the Romanesque **Dom St Peter und Paul** (Cathedral of Sts Peter & Paul; ☎ 211 2221; Burghof 9; ☺ 10am-4pm Mon-Fri, 10am-5pm Sat, 11am-5pm Sun, 10am-noon Wed Jun-Sep only) on the northern edge of Dominsel. Begun in 1165 by Premonstratensian monks and completed in 1240, it contains the wonderfully decorated **Bunte Kapelle** (Coloured Chapel), with a vaulted and painted ceiling; the carved 14th-century **Böhmischer Altar** (Bohemian Altar) in the south transept; a fantastic baroque organ (1723), restored in 1999; and the **Dommuseum** (☎ 200 325; adult/concession €3/2). Much of the cathedral is being rebuilt, probably until 2010, so some items may be moved around – or out.

From the cathedral, walk south on St Petri to Mühlendamm. Just before you cross the Havel to the Neustadt, look left and you'll see the **Hauptpegel**, the 'city water gauge' erected to measure the river's height. On the other side is the **Mühlentorturm** (Mill Gate Tower), which marked the border between Dominsel and Neustadt in the days when they were separate towns.

Molkenmarkt, the continuation of Mühlendamm, runs parallel to Neustädtischer Markt and leads to the **Pfarrkirche St Katharinen** (Parish Church of St Catherine; ☺ 10am-4pm Mon-Sat, 1-4pm Sun). This Gothic brick church was originally two chapels, the first dating from

1395. See if you can spot your favourite New Testament characters on the 'Meadow of Heaven' painted ceiling.

To reach the Altstadt, walk up the pedestrianised Hauptstrasse and then west over the Jahrtausendbrücke (Millennium Bridge). Passing the **Glockenspiel** (Ritterstrasse 64; rung hourly 9am-7pm), you reach the **Stadtmuseum im Frey-Haus** (☎ 522 048; Ritterstrasse 96; adult/concession €3/1.50; ☀ 9am-5pm Tue-Fri, 10am-5pm Sat & Sun). It's a local history museum with much emphasis on the EP Lehmann factory, which produced cute mechanical toys and pottery.

Just a short distance northeast is the redbrick Gothic **Altstädtische Rathaus**, a gembox with a signature statue of Roland (1474) in front symbolising the town's judicial independence.

Tours
CRUISES
Several boat companies run cruises around the Havel lakes, leaving from Am Salzhof in the Altstadt. Companies include **Nordstern** (☎ 455 019; www.nordstern-reederei.de) and **Reederei Röding** (☎ 522 331; www.fgs-havelfee.de; €6 per 2hr), which offers tours on the 1940s MS *Havelfee*.

Festivals & Events
Brandenburg has numerous music and cultural events year-round but the big draw is the Havelfest Brandenburg, a free folk festival held throughout the Altstadt in mid-June. Rapidly gaining popularity is the new local Oktoberfest, held as tradition dictates at the end of September. The tourist office has all the relevant information on these and other events.

Sleeping
The tourist office can arrange **private rooms** (from €13 per person).

Pension Blaudruck (☎ 225 734; Steinstrasse 21; s/d €22/44) Blaudruck means indigo dyeing, a style which decorates some of the rooms of this quirky central establishment above a popular café. Showers and toilets are shared.

Pension Zum Birnbaum (☎ 527 500; Mittelstrasse 1; s €34-41, d €48-62; ☒) Well placed for the station and the Neustadt, the assortment of varying rooms here provides good value and decent facilities.

Pension La Rose (☎ 566 110; Mühlentorstrasse 17; s/d €38/58) This place is loaded with country charm, though some rooms face a busy intersection and the Altstadt location is a touch out of the way.

Campingplatz Malge (☎ 628 50; www.malge.de Malge 3, Breitlingsee; tent €4-8, caravan €7-11) This well-equipped, family-friendly camp site is right on the Breitlingsee, about 5km west of town.

Sorat Hotel Brandenburg (☎ 5970; brandenburg@ sorat-hotels.com; Altstädtischer Markt 1; s €94-120, d €110 136; ☒ ☒ ☒) Across from the Rathaus, the modern Sorat is Brandenburg's main top end choice and the only place in town with wheelchair access. Champagne breakfast and sauna use are included; weekend rates are significantly cheaper.

Eating
Kartoffelkäfer (☎ 224 118; Steinstrasse 56; mains €4 13) One of several options on Steinstrasse with tubers galore dominating a surprisingly varied menu.

Marienberg (☎ 794 960; Am Marienberg 1; mains €6.50-12.50; ☀ 11am-10pm Tue-Fri, 10am-10pm Sat & Sun Apr-Sep; 5-10pm Wed-Fri, 10am-10pm Sat & Sun Oct-Mar) This huge beer garden and restaurant in the Stadtpark northwest of the Altstadt was massively popular in the 1920s and has recently been restored to its former glory It hosts Brandenburg's newly inaugurated Oktoberfest.

Bismarck Terrassen (☎ 300 939; Bergstrasse 20 mains from €5.80, set menus from €7.50) See if you don't feel Prussian while dining on some of the city's most elegant French-German food amid a festival of Bismarck memorabilia.

Kultur-Café (☎ 6660; Ritterstrasse 69; mains €6-11 ☀ from 3pm) Part of the busy Kulturlabor cultural centre, this arty spot attracts a clued-up crowd and boasts a great balcony overlooking the Havel and the Jahrtausend brücke.

Getting There & Around
Frequent regional trains link Brandenburg with Berlin-Zoo station (€5.70, one hour and Potsdam (€4.50, 30 minutes). There are also twice-hourly services to Frankfurt an der Oder (€12.80, two hours).

Tram Nos 6 and 9 run from Brandenburg Hauptbahnhof to Hauptstrasse via Steinstrasse. A single ride is €1.15 and a day ticket is €2.50.

SPREEWALD

Renowned throughout Germany for its gherkins, the rivers, canals and streams of the 'Spree Forest' (287 sq km), 80km southeast of Berlin, are the closest thing the capital has to a back garden. Day-trippers and weekend warriors come here in droves to punt on more than 400km of waterways, hike countless nature trails and fish in this region, which was declared a Biosphere Reserve by Unesco in 1990. The focal points of much of this activity are the twin towns of Lübben and Lübbenau. The Spreewald is also home to most of Germany's Sorbian minority (see the boxed text The Sorbs), who call the region the Blota.

LÜBBEN

☎ 03546 / pop 15,000

There's an ongoing debate among Berliners over Lübben (Lubin in Sorbian) and its neighbour Lübbenau (Lubnjow), 13km away: which is the more historic and picturesque 'Spreewald capital'? For our money, Lübben, a tidy and attractive town at the centre of the drier Unterspreewald, feels more like a 'real' town and just pips Lübbenau with a history going back at least two centuries further. That said, you'll find a visit to either town has its merits.

Lübben's train station is southwest of the centre. To reach the Markt (square) walk northeast along Friedensstrasse and then through the Hain, a large park.

Information

Dresdner Bank (☎ 277 16; Hauptstrasse 13)
Internet Imbiss (Hafen 4, Ernst-von-Houwald-Damm 15)
Sparkasse (Hauptstrasse 9-10) Bank.
Tourist Information (☎ 3090/182 661; www.luebben .de; Hafen 1, Ernst-von-Houwald-Damm 15; ⏰ 10am-6pm, shorter hours in winter)

Sights & Activities

It's worth seeing the compact **Schloss** (☎ 187 478; Ernst-von-Houwald-Damm 14; adult/concession €4/2; ⏰ 10am-6pm Tue-Sun May-Sep, 10am-4pm Wed-Fri, 1-5pm Sat & Sun Oct-Apr), but the real highlight is a (free) wander through the gardens of the **Schlossinsel**, an artificial archipelago with gardens concealing cafés, jetties and all kinds of play areas.

The Spreewald has hiking and walking trails to suit everyone – the tourist office sells a good range of useful maps. From Lübben an easy trail follows the Spree south to Lübbenau (13.2km) and north to Schlepzig (12.3km).

You can board punts and other boats at various harbour points along the Spree by the tourist office. Of the many companies jostling for business, **Fährmannsverein Lustige Gurken** (☎ 7122; www.lustige-gurke.de; adult/child tours from €7/4) is a major player for punts, while **Bootsverleih Gebauer** (☎ 7194; www.spreewald-boots verleih.de) offers kayaks and canoes from €7 an hour.

BRANDENBURG

THE SORBS

The ancestors of the Sorbs, Germany's only indigenous minority (pop 60,000), were the Slavic Wends, who settled between the Elbe and Oder Rivers in the 5th century in an area called Lusatia (Luzia in Sorbian).

Lusatia was conquered by the Germans in the 10th century, subjected to brutal Germanisation throughout the Middle Ages and partitioned in 1815. Lower Sorbia, centred on the Spreewald and Cottbus (Chóśebuz), went to Prussia while Upper Sorbia, around Bautzen (Budyšin), went to Saxony. Upper Sorbian, closely related to Czech, enjoyed a certain prestige in Saxony, but the Kingdom of Prussia tried to suppress Lower Sorbian, which is similar to Polish. The Nazis, of course, tried to eradicate both.

The Sorbs were protected under the GDR, but their proud folk traditions didn't suit the bland 'proletarian' regime. Since reunification, interest in the culture has been revived through media broadcasts and theatre in the language. The more colourful Sorbian festivals include the *Vogelhochzeit* (Birds' Wedding) on January 25, a horseback procession at Easter and a symbolic 'witch-burning' on April 30, a local variant of Walpurgisnacht (see p281 for more about this).

For further details, check out www .sorben-wenden.de or contact the **Sorbian Institute** (☎ 03591-497 20; www.serbski -institut.de; Bahnhofstrasse 6, Bautzen) or the **Institute of Sorbian Studies** (☎ 0341-973 7650; www.uni-leipzig.de/~sorb; Beethovenstrasse 15, Leipzig).

Festivals & Events

The highlight of the Spreewald Summer festival of cultural events is the Tage der Sorbischen Kultur/Dny serbskeje kultury (Days of Sorbian Culture) in the Markt in Lübben during the first week in June. The less highbrow Spreewälder Gurkentag (Gherkin Day) follows in July, while the Spreewaldfest, with its colourful *Kahnkorso* (punt competition), is held in late September.

Sleeping

In summer a daily list of available accommodation is posted outside the tourist office, which books rooms for a €3 fee. Both Lübben and Lübbenau have dozens of private rooms and holiday flats available, with prices starting around €12.50 per person. Rates quoted are for summer and can be significantly cheaper in the off season.

DJH hostel (☎ 3046; www.jh-luebben.de; Zum Wendenfürsten 8; dm €11.50-14.10; P X) Lübben's DJH hostel is about 2.5km south of the town centre.

Spreewald-Camping (☎ 7053; www.spreewald -camping-luebben.de; Am Burglehn; tent/car/adult/child €3.50/2/5.50/3.50) This well-equipped camp site is nestled among the trees just across the Spree from the tourist office.

Pension Am Markt (☎ 3272; fernseh-heinrich@ t-online.de; Hauptstrasse 5; €25-28 per person; X 💻) Cosy and well equipped, this is a slightly idiosyncratic place with its own beauty salon above an electronics shop.

Hotel Spreeufer (☎ 27260; www.spreewaldhotel.de; Hinter der Mauer 4; €30-45 per person) The smart, friendly Hotel Spreeufer is near the bridge just south of Hauptstrasse.

Eating

Bubak (☎ 186 144; Ernst-von-Houwald-Damm 9; mains €6.50-15) Named from a local bogeyman story, this cosy roadside restaurant has plenty of character, including a singing proprietor (CD out soon!).

Goldener Löwe (☎ 7309; Hauptstrasse 15; mains €7-11.50) Tourists favour the well-kept Golden Lion, which has a lovely beer garden, complete with old boat.

Dodge City Saloon (☎ 4051; Bergstrasse 1; mains €6.50-20) Possibly the least likely location for a Wild West–themed restaurant ever, but Dodge City seems infallibly popular with locals and serves up specialities you won't often find elsewhere: buffalo, kudu, reindeer...

Getting There & Around

Daily regional trains serve Lübben every one to two hours from Berlin-Ostbahnhof (€12.80, one hour) en route to Cottbus (€3.90, 25 minutes). There are frequent buses to Lübbenau on weekdays, but it's much quicker to catch a train.

LÜBBENAU

☎ 03542 / pop 15,700

Lübbenau, in the Oberspreewald (Upper Spreewald), is just as picturesque as Lübben but has more of a model-village air about it, despite being considerably bigger. The secluded Altstadt is almost invariably crammed with tourists trying to get onto the canals on *Kähne* (punt boats), once the only way to get around in these parts. The train and bus stations are on Poststrasse, about 600m south of the Altstadt.

Information

Haus für Mensch und Natur (☎ 892 10; br-spreewald@lngs.brandenburg.de; Schulstrasse 9; ☯ 10am-5pm Mon-Fri, also Sat & Sun Apr-Nov) Information about the Spreewald Biosphere Reserve.
Sparkasse (☎ 875 60; Topfmarkt 8)
Tourist Information (☎ 3668; www.spreewald -online.de; Ehm-Welk-Strasse 15; ☯ 9am-6pm Mon-Fri, 9am-1pm Sat)

Activities

There are several 'harbours' in the Altstadt: the biggest are the **Kleiner Hafen** (☎ 403 710; www.spreewald-web.de; Spreestrasse 10a), about 100m northeast of the tourist office, and the more workmanlike **Grosser Hafen** (☎ 2225; www.grosser -spreewaldhafen.de; Dammstrasse 77a), 300m southeast. Boats can be hired from €3.50 per hour – a canal tour takes about two hours. There are dozens of boat companies vying for business; try **Bootsverleih Francke** (☎ 2722; Dammstrasse 72).

Walkers can follow a **nature trail** (30 minutes) west to Lehde, the 'Venice of the Spreewald', with its wonderful **Freiland-museum** (☎ 2472; adult/concession €3/2; ☯ 10am-6pm Apr-Sep, 10am-5pm Sep-Oct) of traditional Sorbian thatched houses and farm buildings. The **Leiper Weg**, which starts near the Grosser Hafen, is part of the E10 European Walking Trail from the Baltic to the Adriatic and leads southwest to Leipe, accessible only by boat since 1936.

Sleeping

Pension Am Alten Bauernhafen (☎ 2930; familie .kusche@t-online.de; Stottoff 5; per person €19-22.50; P) Charming apartment-style rooms and a fantastic riverside location make this big family-run house a bit of a bargain.

Naturcamping Am Schlosspark (☎ 3533; www .spreewaldcamping.de; Schlossbezirk; adult/child/car €4.50/ 2/4) This four-star camp site, a short distance east of the Schloss, has just about all the amenities you could think of.

Ebusch (☎ 3670; www.pension-ebusch.de; Topfmarkt 4; s €36-41, d €40-60; P) A friendly guesthouse just west of the Altstadt, with decent rooms and a traditional restaurant.

Hotel Schloss Lübbenau (☎ 8730; www.schloss -luebbenau.de; Schlossbezirk 6; s €62-82, d €104-134; P ⊠) Check into your local castle for a surprisingly reasonable splurge, with all the class you can handle and lovely park surroundings.

Eating

Zum Rudelhaus (☎ 831 45; Dammstrasse 77a; mains from €5) The Grosser Hafen's resident eatery is a bright place with a varied menu and fewer oars around the place than you might expect. Fridays are barbecue nights in summer.

Strubel's (☎ 2798; Dammstrasse 3; mains €6.50-14) Try Strubel's for fresh Spree eel, pike and perch (Aal, Hecht, Zander) or a wide assortment of local meat and game dishes. Enter from Apothekengasse.

Pension Spreewald-Idyll (☎ 2251; Spreestrasse 13; mains €6-14) This restaurant/beer garden serves good local and sea fish.

Getting There & Around

Lübbenau is on the same train line as Lübben; the DB office in the station is closed on Wednesdays and weekends. For bike hire, try **Fahrradverleih Enrico Arndt** (☎ 872 910; Dammstrasse 10-12).

COTTBUS

☎ 0355 / pop 104,000

Cottbus (Chośebuz), the unofficial capital of the Sorbian Blota region, is a pretty town with some wonderful architecture and a decent number of cultural offerings for visitors. Local students and graffiti artists

apparently have less to occupy them – the town is often nicknamed 'Cotzbus', a pun on the German word for 'puke'!

The **tourist office** (☎ 754 20; cottbus-service@ cmt-cottbus.de; Berliner Platz 6; 🕙 9am-6pm Mon-Fri, 9am-1pm Sat) is in the glass-fronted Stadthalle, behind the Spree Galerie shopping centre.

The Sorbian cultural centre **Lodka** (☎ 4857 6468; stiftung-lodka@sorben.com; August-Bebel-Strasse 82; 🕙 10am-4.30pm Mon-Fri) has a wide range of information and literature. Its café, Gosćéne Lubina, also serves excellent (and authentic) Sorbian specialities (which may include beef with horseradish and poppyseed cake).

Those interested in the Sorbs should also check the **Wendisches Museum/Serbski muzej** (☎ 794 930; Mühlenstrasse 12; adult/concession €2.50/ 1.50; 🕙 8.30am-5pm Tue-Fri, 2-6pm Sat & Sun), which thoroughly examines this Slavic people's history, language and culture.

Other places worth a visit include the 15th-century **Oberkirche** on Oberkirchplatz, west of the central Altmarkt; the Jugendstil **Staatstheater** on Schillerplatz to the southwest; and **Branitzer Park** to the southeast, which contains a lovely 18th-century baroque Schloss, the Fürst-Pückler-Museum and the *Seepyramide*, a curious grass-covered pyramid 'floating' in a little lake.

Regional trains link Cottbus to Berlin Ostbahnhof (€16.50, 1¾ hours) roughly hourly, and also serve the Spreewald twin towns (€3.90, 22-29 minutes) and Frankfurt an der Oder (€9.20, 80 minutes).

MÄRKISCHE SCHWEIZ & ODERBRUCH

As the highest 'peak' in this region reaches a mere 129m (Krugberg, north of Buckow), you might think 'Switzerland of the March of Brandenburg' is a rather grandiose misnomer. But it is a lung for Berlin – a land of clear streams, lakes and beautiful, low-lying hills. Buckow, the 'pearl of the Märkische Schweiz', has long been a popular place for rest and recreation for Berliners. The Oderbruch region to the south couldn't be more different: it is flat, marshy, prone to flooding and has as its anchor the unfavoured city of Frankfurt an der Oder.

BRANDENBURG

BUCKOW

☎ 033433 / pop 1800

In 1854 Friedrich Wilhelm IV's physician advised His Majesty to visit this village, where 'the lungs go as on velvet', and Fontane praised its 'friendly landscape' in *Das Oderland* (1863), the second book in his four-volume travelogue (see Brandenburg's Fontane of Knowledge p160). However, Buckow only really made it onto the map in the 1950s, when Bertolt Brecht and Helene Weigel spent their summers here, away from the hot and humid capital of the new GDR. It's now morphing into a popular spa town.

Orientation & Information

Buckow, in the centre of the 205 sq km Märkische Schweiz Nature Park, is surrounded by five lakes; the largest is the Schermützelsee (146 hectares in area, 45m deep). Berliner Strasse, the main street, runs parallel to the lake before becoming Wriezener Strasse, where you'll find the **tourist office** (☎ 575 00; buckow-tourist@t-online.de; Wriezener Strasse 1a; ☼ 9am-noon & 1-5pm Mon-Fri, 10am-5pm Sat & Sun Apr-Oct, 10am-2pm Sat & Sun Nov-Mar), and then Hauptstrasse.

There's also a new **Besucherzentrum** (Visitors centre; ☎ 158 41; Lindenstrasse 33; ☼ 10am-4pm Mon-Fri, 10am-6pm Sat & Sun) on the edge of the national park, with displays in German.

For money and postal services go to **Sparkasse** (Wriezener Strasse 2) and the **post office** (Hauptstrasse 84) respectively.

Sights

The **Brecht-Weigel-Haus** (☎ 467; Bertolt-Brecht-Strasse 29; adult/concession €2/1; ☼ 1-5pm Wed-Fri, 1-6pm Sat & Sun Apr-Oct, 10am-noon & 1-4pm Wed-Fri, 11am-4pm Sat & Sun Nov-Mar) is where the GDR's 'first couple of the arts' spent their summers from 1952 to 1955. The easiest way to reach it is west along Werderstrasse, but it's more fun strolling along Ringstrasse and Bertolt-Brecht-Strasse admiring the posh prewar villas. Brecht's house is relatively simple, with an overhanging roof, geometric patterns outside and a relief of Europa riding a bull over the front door. Among the photographs, documents and original furnishings inside is Mother Courage's covered wagon; outside in the fine gardens are copper tablets engraved with Brecht's words.

The **Eisenbahnmuseum** (Railroad Museum; adult/child €2/1.50; ☼ 10am-4pm Sat & Sun May-Oct) is at the Hauptbahnhof. The Buchower Kleinbahn is the little forest train that has been running for 100 years between here and Müncheberg to the south.

Activities

Buckow is a paradise for hikers and walkers. You can follow the Panoramaweg from north of Buckow clear around the Schermützelsee (7.5km), the Drachenkehle north to Krugberg (5km), the Grosser Tornowsee to Pritzhagener Mühle (9km), or the Alter Schulsteig to Dreieichen (10km). The tourist office sells some useful maps with marked walks.

In summer you can hire rowing boats or go on a cruise with **Seetours** (☎ 232; seetours ms@kurstdat-buckow.de; tours adult/concession €6/3; ☼ 10am-5.30pm Tue-Sun) from the dock at the north tip of the Schermützelsee. A trip to Hotel Buchenfried and the Fischerkehle restaurant at the southwestern end costs adult/concession €4/2.

Sleeping & Eating

The tourist office can organise private rooms from €15 per person. A *Kurtaxe* of €1 per person/night is added to most hotel bills.

DJH hostel (☎ 286; jh-buckow@jugendherberge.de; Berliner Strasse 36; juniors/seniors €10.50/18; ☒) The Jugendherberge Buckow has bungalows, dorms and regular grill nights.

Besucherzentrum Drei Eichen (☎ 201; www.dr eichen.de; Königstrasse 62; dm €6, r €10.50, camping per person €4; P ☒) For something completely different, try this environmental centre about 3km out of town; it's popular with school groups (so don't expect total tranquillity, especially in summer) and offers all kinds of eco-related activities.

Pension Grahl (☎ 572 83; Hauptstrasse 9; s/d €22/30; P) This pension has the narrowest driveway in the civilised world but has great budget rooms and a nice lakeside location.

Hotel Buchenfried (☎ 287; buchenfried@kurstadt -buckow.de; Am Fischerberg 9; s/d €38/58; ☒) Though it enjoys an enviable position on the southwestern shore of the Schermützelsee, the Buchenfried is a bit far away from whatever action there is in Buckow; three restaurants and instant lake access largely make up for it.

Bergschlösschen (☎ 573 12; www.bergschloesschen .com; Königstrasse 38; s €45-55, d €75-85; P ☒) It ay resemble the house from *Psycho*, but you'd be mad (ha ha) to complain about the upstairs views from this excellent hillside hotel.

Stobbermühle (☎ 668 33; www.stobbermuehle.de; riezener Strasse 2; s €54, d €78-88, ste €84-180; meals €7-6; ✗) Fancier than Louis XIV's undies, this apartment hotel' has a superb and inventive restaurant, with fabulous duck and a separate lobster menu (€28 to €42). Rooms are plush and fantastically over-equipped, boasting fax machine, VCR and the odd Jacuzzi.

Fischerkehle (☎ 374; Am Fischerberg 7; mains 10.50-18) Near the Buchenfried, this popular historic restaurant (1911) is on the southwest shore of the lake, and serves fish and local specialities.

Getting There & Away

Buckow is no longer served by normal train services – don't get confused and go to the 'other' Buckow, an even smaller village near Beeskow! To get to the right place, take the RB26 from Berlin-Lichtenberg to Müncheberg, where you can catch either the No 928 bus or the Buckower Kleinbahn. A slower but cheaper alternative is to take the S5 to Strausberg and board the bus there.

FRANKFURT AN DER ODER
☎ 0335 / pop 68,000

Germany's second Frankfurt, 90km east of Berlin, has had its share of troubles despite a successful start. Commanding a strategic crossing on the Oder, the town prospered as a trade centre from the early 13th century, and within 150 years had become a member of the Hanseatic League. For centuries it was known for its three annual fairs, and 750 of its medieval houses survived into the 20th century.

During WWII the town was evacuated, but in the last few days before Germany's surrender, Nazi guerrillas engaged in hand-to-hand combat with Polish soldiers here; Frankfurt was burned to the ground, leaving only five of the old houses standing. In the summer of 1997, the area was struck by the 'flood of the century', causing millions of Deutschmarks' worth of damage.

Frankfurt is trying to overcome its miserable reputation by promoting some interesting architecture, a new convention centre and the rebuilt Hauptbahnhof, all in connection with the town's 750th anniversary celebrations in 2003. Easy access to Poland is another selling point; with visitor numbers on the rise, things may be looking up for this oft-neglected area.

Orientation

The Hauptbahnhof is a few minutes' walk from Karl-Marx-Strasse, the main road through the centre of town. The 24-storey GDR **Oderturm** (Oder Tower, 1976), overlooking Brunnenplatz, is the main landmark here. The new **Kleistforum** convention centre (2001) is about a kilometre across town.

Rosa-Luxemburg-Strasse heads east-west to the Polish border and is almost invariably crammed with traffic. Słubice, just over the Stadtbrücke, seems to exist only to supply Frankfurters with cut-rate tobacco and booze; what impact Poland's membership of the EU will have on this dubious sub-economy remains to be seen.

Information

California (☎ 685 1316; Rosa-Luxemburg-Strasse 10; €2 per hr) Internet access.

Fix-Copy & T-Shirt Center (☎ 387 0083; C-Ph-Emmanuel-Bach-Strasse 22; €1 per hr) Internet access.

Frankfurt Information (☎ 325 216; www.frankfurt-oder-tourist.de; Karl-Marx-Strasse 8a; ☻ 10am-6pm Mon-Fri, 10am-12.30pm Sat)

Sights

Take a look inside the unusual **St Gertraud-kirche** (☎ 500 4736; Gertraudenplatz 6; ☻ 10am-noon & 2-5pm Tue-Sat). Its overblown treasures were all brought here from the huge but derelict Gothic **Marienkirche** (St Mary's Church; Grosse Scharrnstrasse), currently undergoing renovation as a 'ruin under a roof'.

The striking 14th-century **Rathaus**, on Marktplatz just north of Bischofstrasse, has a peculiar fountain outside and a golden herring hanging from the lovely south gable. Inside the tower is the **Galerie Junge Kunst** (☎ 552 4150; www.museum-junge-kunst .de; adult/child €1.50/1.05; ☻ 11am-5pm Tue-Sun), displaying GDR art.

Near the river is the **Kleist-Museum** (☎ 531 155; www.kleist-museum.de; Faberstrasse 7; adult/concession €2.50/2; ☻ 11am-5pm Tue-Sun), with displays on the life and works of Heinrich von Kleist, the Frankfurt-born dramatist.

Konzerthalle CPE Bach (☎ 664 8877; Collegien-strasse 8; admission €1.50; ☻ 11am-5pm) is an old

Gothic monastery church (1270), now converted into the town's main concert hall. It houses an exhibit on the life of quirky composer Carl Philipp Emmanuel Bach, son of the great Johann Sebastian.

Sleeping & Eating

Pension Am Kleistpark (☎ 238 90; Humboldtstrasse 14; s/d €33/56; ✗) A short walk from the centre, you'll find these large, light budget rooms opposite the park.

Eurocamp Helenesee (☎ 556660; info@helenesee-og .de; Helenesee; adult/child €1.60/1.10, car €1.60, tent €4-7) There are plenty of activities at this new camp site. Take the B87 south from town and turn left at Helenesee.

City Park Hotel (☎ 553 20; hotel-citypark@blue band.de; Lindenstrasse 12; s €61-81, d €83-108; ℗ ✗) It's a bit of an eyesore, but the location opposite the Gertraudkirche is perfect and the tower rooms are especially good. Prices fluctuate throughout the year.

Turm 24 (☎ 504 517; Logenstrasse 8; mains €7.80-15.90) With panoramic views from the top floor of the Oderturm, this smart, contemporary place serves an international menu at lunch and dinner.

Getting There & Around

Frankfurt is served hourly by regional trains from Berlin-Ostbahnhof (€8.10, 70 minutes) and Cottbus (€9.20, 80 minutes). There are also good connections to Eberswalde via Niederfinow and international trains to Poland and Russia.

To reach the centre of town from the Hauptbahnhof, walk north on Bahnhofstrasse and east on Heilbronner Strasse, or jump on tram No 1 or 3 and get off at Schmalzgasse. Single tickets cost €1.10.

NORTHERN BRANDENBURG

SACHSENHAUSEN CONCENTRATION CAMP

In 1936 the Nazis opened a 'model' *Konzentrationslager* (concentration camp) for men in a disused brewery in Sachsenhausen, near the town of Oranienburg (pop 30,000), about 35km north of Berlin. Inmates such as political undesirables, gays, Jews, Roma (gypsies) – the usual Nazi targets – were forced to make bricks, hand grenade weapons, counterfeit dollar and poun banknotes (to flood Allied countries an wreak economic havoc) and even to test ou boot leather for days on end on a specia track. By 1945 about 220,000 men from 2 countries had passed through the gates labelled, as at Auschwitz in southwester Poland, *Arbeit Macht Frei* (Work Sets Yo Free). About 100,000 were murdered here their remains consumed by the fires of th horribly efficient ovens.

After the war, the Soviets and the com munist leaders of the new GDR set up Speziallager No 7 (Special Camp No 7) fo political prisoners, ex-Nazis, monarchist and anyone else who didn't happen to fi into their mould. An estimated 60,000 peo ple were interned at the camp between 1945 and 1950, and up to 12,000 are believed to have died here. There's a mass grave of vic tims at the camp and another one 1.5km to the north.

Orientation & Information

The walled camp (31 hectares) is an easy, signposted 20-minute walk northeast of Oranienburg train station. Follow Stralsunder Strasse north and turn east (right) onto Bernauer Strasse, left at Strasse der Einheit and then right on Strasse der Nationen, which leads to the main entrance. You can also catch bus No 804 or 805 as far as the corner of Bernauer Strasse and Strasse der Einheit. For the Oranienburg **tourist office** (☎ 03301-704 833; www.oranienburg.de; Bernauer Strasse 52; 🕑 9am-6pm Mon-Fri, 9am-2pm Sat, 9am-1pm Sun May-Sep, 9am-5pm Mon-Fri only Oct-Apr) turn left from Stralsunder Strasse.

The camp bookshop sells maps, brochures and books from €0.25; you can borrow an excellent, chilling audio-guide (€2.50) in English or German at the gate.

The visit is best done as a day trip from Berlin.

Gedenkstätte und Museum Sachsenhausen

Before you enter here, at the intersection of Strasse der Einheit and Strasse der Nationen, you'll see a **memorial** to the 6000 prisoners who died on the *Todesmarsch* (Death March) of April 1945, when the Nazis tried to drive the camp's 33,000 inmates to the Baltic in advance of the Red Army.

The **Gedenkstätte und Museum Sachsenhausen** (☎ 03301-200 200; ⏱ 8.30am-6pm Tue-Sun Apr-Sep, 8.30am-4.30pm Oct-Mar) consists of several parts. About 100m inside the camp on your left is a mass grave of 300 prisoners who died in the infirmary after liberation on 22 and 23 April 1945. Further, on the right, you'll find the camp commandant's house and the so-called Green Monster, where SS troops were trained in the finer arts of concentration-camp maintenance. At the end of the road is the **Neues Museum** (New Museum), with excellent exhibits including a history of anti-Semitism and audiovisual material.

East of the New Museum are **Barracks 38 & 39**, reconstructions of two typical huts housing most of the 6000 Jewish prisoners brought to Sachsenhausen after Kristall-nacht (9-10 November 1938). Number 38 was rebuilt after being torched by neo-Nazis in September 1992, just days after a visit by the late Israeli Prime Minister Yitzhak Rabin.

Just north of here is the **prison**, where particularly brutal punishment was meted out to prisoners confined in stifling blackened cells. Inside the prison yard is a **memorial** to the homosexuals who died here, one of the few monuments you'll see anywhere to these 'forgotten victims' (there's another one at the Nollendorfplatz U-Bahn station in Berlin).

To get to the **Lagermuseum** (Camp Museum), with its moth-eaten, dusty exhibits that focus on both the Nazi concentration camp and Special Camp No 7, walk north along the parade ground, past the site of the gallows. The museum is housed in the building on the right, once the camp kitchen. In the former laundry room opposite, a particularly gruesome film of the camp after liberation is shown throughout the day. Steel yourself before entering.

Left of the tall, ugly monument (1961) erected by the GDR in memory of political prisoners interned here is the **crematorium** and **Station Z extermination site**, a pit for shooting prisoners in the neck with a wooden 'catch' where bullets could be retrieved and reused. A memorial hall on the site of the **gas chamber** is a fitting visual metaphor for the 'glorious' Third Reich and the 'workers' paradise' of the GDR. Subsiding slowly, its paving stones are cracked and the roof is toppling over an area contain-

ing, we're told, 'considerable remains from corpses incinerated in the crematorium'.

To the northeast, beyond the wall, are **stone barracks** built in 1941 to house Allied POWs. From 1945 German officers and others sentenced by the Soviet military tribunal were imprisoned here. To the north is a mass grave from the latter period.

Getting There & Away

The easiest way to get to Sachsenhausen from Berlin is to take the frequent S1 to Oranienburg (€6.45, 50 minutes). There are also RB trains from Berlin-Lichtenberg (€6, 30 minutes).

RHEINSBERG

☎ 033931 / pop 5300

Rheinsberg, a delightful town hugging the shore of the Grienericksee about 50km northwest of Berlin, has much to offer visitors: a charming Renaissance palace, walks in the lovely Schlosspark, plenty of boating and some top-notch restaurants. The central Markt lies about 1km northwest of the train station.

Information

Infoladen (☎ 395 10; rts@rheinsberg.de; Rhinpassage, Rhinstrasse 19; ⏱ 10am-6pm Mon-Sat, 10am-4pm Sun) Private tourist office with Internet access (€2 per hr).

Main post office (☎ 01802-3333; Paulshorster Strasse 18b)

Media Meeting Point (☎ 438 07; Schlossstrasse 17; €1.50 per hr; ⏱ noon-8pm Mon-Fri) Internet access.

Sparkasse (☎ 7200; Berliner Strasse 16) Bank.

Tourist Information (☎ 2059; www.rheinsberg.de; Kavalierhaus, Markt; ⏱ 10am-5pm Mon-Sat, 10am-4pm Sun)

Volksbank (☎ 01801-888 800; Rhinstrasse 10)

Schloss Rheinsberg

The first moated castle here was built in the early Middle Ages to protect the March of Brandenburg's northern border from the marauders of Mecklenburg. However, the present **Schloss Rheinsberg** (☎ 7260; adult/concession €4/3, tour €5/4; ⏱ Tue-Sun 9.30am-5pm Apr-Oct, 10am-5pm Nov-Mar) only began to take shape in 1566, when its owner, Achim von Bredow, had it reconstructed in the Renaissance style.

Friedrich Wilhelm I purchased the castle in 1734 for his 22-year-old son, Crown Prince Friedrich (the future Frederick the Great), and spent a fair wedge expanding the palace and cleaning up the town. The prince, who spent four years here studying and preparing for the throne, later said this period was the happiest of his life; he personally oversaw much of the remodelling of the palace, and some say this was his 'test', on a minor scale, for the much grander Sanssouci (1747) in Potsdam (see p145).

During WWII, art treasures from Potsdam were stored here; sadly the palace was looted in 1945, and was subsequently used as a sanatorium by the communists. Today the place is a mere shadow of its former self, but it is being renovated at a furious pace.

A tour of the palace takes in about two dozen, mostly empty, rooms on the 1st floor, including the oldest ones: the **Hall of Mirrors**, where young Friedrich held flute contests; the **Tower Chamber**, which he re-created in the Berlin Schloss in 1745; and the **Bacchus Room**, with a ceiling painting of a worn-looking Ganymede. Among our favourites are the **Lacquer Room**, with its chinoiserie, **Prince Heinrich's bedchamber**, which sports an exquisite trompe-l'oeil ceiling, and the rococo **Shell Room**.

The ground floor of the north wing contains a small **Gedenkstätte** (museum; adult/concession €2/1) dedicated to the life and work of writer Kurt Tucholsky (1890–1935). He wrote a popular novel called *Rheinsberg – ein Tagebuch für Verliebte* (Rheinsberg – A Lovers' Diary) in which young swain Wolfgang traipses through the Schloss with his beloved Claire in tow, putting the palace and Rheinsberg itself firmly on the literary map.

Activities

Reederei Halbeck (☎ 38619; reederei-halbeck@t-online .de; Markt 11; tours from €5.50), next to the tourist office, offers a range of lake and river cruises and hires out canoes, kayaks and pedaloes. **Rheinsberger Adventure Tours** (☎ 392 47; www.rhintour.de, German only; Schlossstrasse 42) also hires out canoes, boats and bikes, and can arrange all kinds of excursions in the area.

Festivals & Events

The **Rheinsberger Musiktage** (Rheinsberg Music Days; ☎ 7210) is a three-day festival of music round the clock – from jazz and chamber music to children's cabaret. It takes place around Whitsun/Pentecost in May/June. The **Kammeroper Schloss Rheinsberg** (Chamber Opera; ☎ 7250; www.kammeroper-schloss-rheinsberg.de) is a major in-ternational opera festival promoting young talent, held from July to August.

Sleeping

Private rooms (from €13 per person) are plentiful in Rheinsberg – just look for the 'Zimmer Frei' signs.

Zum Jungen Fritz (☎ 4090; www.junger-fritz.de; Schlossstrasse 8; s €45-55, d €65-80; P) Near the Kirche St Laurentius is this sweet little guesthouse with a decent restaurant.

Haus Rheinsberg (☎ 3440; www.hausrheinsberg .de; Donnersmarckweg 1; s €45-65, d €85-105; P X) This large, modern lakefront place is one of the few hotels in Germany (or indeed the world) specially designed for disabled guests, with wheelchair access throughout, in-house care and lots of sports facilities.

Pension Holländermühle (☎ 2332; Schwanow Strasse; d €50-55; P X) It's a bit of a walk from town but the setting of this windmill urned-pension is nice and quiet and there's a good restaurant.

Pension Am Rheinsberger Schlosspark (☎ 392 71; pension-rhbger-schlosspark@t-online.de; Fontaneplatz 2; €50-55, d €70-75; P ⊠) This is a sprawling but comfy pension located south of the Schloss, with its own bowling alley.

Seehof (☎ 4030; www.seehof-rheinsberg.com; Seestrasse 18; s €65-85, d €75-120) This central and very smart hotel is the place to splash out, not just for the bright modern rooms but for the superb food on offer in the restaurant, beer garden, conservatory and cellar (mains €8 to €18).

Eating

Cafe Tucholsky (☎ 343 70; Kurt-Tucholsky-Strasse 30a; mains €5-10.50) Opposite the yacht club, this smart café serves up a varied menu with live music and entertainment most weekends in summer.

Zum Alten Fritz (☎ 2086; Schlossstrasse 11; mains €6-13.90) This is an excellent place for north German specialities and fish dishes, and does a beautifully presented apple strudel.

Zum Fischerhof (☎ 2625; Uferpromenade; mains €6-14.50; ☺ Wed-Mon Apr-Oct) An authentic local *Raucherei* (smokehouse), serving up fish straight off the boat as well as its own smoked specials.

Entertainment

Musikakademie Rheinsberg (☎ 7210; Kavalierhaus, Markt) Performs opera and classical music in venues around town from late-June to mid-August. Tickets are available from the tourist office or from ticket agencies in Berlin.

Autokino (☎ 033923-704 26; www.autokino-zempow .com; Dorfstrasse; €1 per car, €4-5 per person) When was the last time you went to a drive-in? Visit the Autokino in Zempow, 15km northwest of Rheinsberg. Obviously you'll need a car.

Shopping

Rheinsberg is a traditional centre of faïence and ceramics; local firms **Rheinsbergische Keramik Manufaktur** (RKM; ☎ 723 75; www.rkm -rheinsberg.de) and **Carstens Keramik** (☎ 2003) both have factory outlets in the Rhinpassage (Rhinstrasse 19).

Getting There & Around

Rheinsberg is no longer served by direct trains from central Berlin; you'll have to change at Herzberg, where you can get trains to Berlin-Spandau (€8.10) or Löwenberg (for Oranienburg and RE5 services north).

Two buses a day make the trip between Rheinsberg and Oranienburg, stopping at Mühlenstrasse, southeast of the Markt.

You can hire bikes from **Fahrradhaus Thäns** (☎ 2622; Schlossstrasse 16; €6-8 per day).

LOWER ODER VALLEY NATIONAL PARK

The Lower Oder Valley (Unteres Odertal) is one of the last relatively unspoiled delta regions in Europe. Established in 1995, the 105-sq-km cross-border reserve (another 60 sq km lie in Poland) has an enormous range of flora and fauna, and acts as a breeding ground for over 120 kinds of birds, including sea eagles, black storks and other endangered species. Meadows, marshland and deciduous forest make up a large part of the grounds, which are 60km long but just 2km to 3km wide in most spots. One-tenth has been designated a 'total reserve' (ie no human interference); by 2010, this proportion will rise to half. In October, the sky darkens with up to 13,000 migratory cranes, which stop off in the park on their way south.

Orientation & Information

Gartz is the northernmost town on the German side of the Oder, just across from the Polish city of Stettin (Szczecin). Stolpe is the largest settlement to the south, situated just off a part of park delta. Halfway in between lies the village of Crewin, where the new **Besucherzentrum** (☎ 03332-267 7244; adult/child €1/0.50) makes a good place to launch your trip. Run by the Nationalparkverwaltung (National Park Authority), it's a one-stop shop for all your hiking and biking needs.

The park's main **tourist office** (☎ 03332-255 90; www.unteres-odertal.de; Berliner Strasse 47; ☺ 9am-6pm Mon-Fri, 9am-1pm Sat May-Sep, 9am-5pm Mon-Fri Oct-Apr) is in Schwedt.

Activities

Boats and bikes can be hired from **Fahrrad- und Bootverleihring Butzke** (☎ 03332-839 500; rad-kanu@swschwedt.de; Kietz 11, Schwedt; bikes €4.50-6/ day, canoes €25-35) with – get this – delivery and pick-up services available (a per kilometre charge applies). Most hotels also have bikes for guest use, and a number of places along the river hire out canoes and kayaks.

Sleeping

Campingplatz Mescherin (☎ 033332-807 07; Dorfstrasse 6; adult/child €4/2, car €2, tent €3.50-7) This small leafy site is the only camp site in the park, set on the bank of the Oder near the northern end of Mescherin.

Getting There & Away

Take the RE or IC train from Berlin to Angermünde (€15.40, one hour) and then take the bus toward Schwedt, which stops in Crewin. Alternatively, catch a train to Schwedt and take the bus toward Angermünde; RE and RB trains go to Schwedt from Eberswalde (€6.40, one hour), Chorin (€5.20, 45 minutes) and Berlin (€15, 1¾ hours).

For drivers, the park is 30km to 50km due east of the north–south Berlin-Stettin autobahn A11.

CHORIN

☎ 033366 / pop 520

In this little town, 60km northeast of Berlin, is the **Kloster Chorin** (Chorin Monastery; ☎ 703 77; Amt Chorin 11a; adult/child €2.50/1.50, parking €2.50; ☑ 9am-6pm Apr-Oct, 9am-4pm Nov-Mar), considered to be one of the finest red-brick Gothic structures in northern Germany.

There's no tourist office, but the reception desk at the **Hotel Haus Chorin** (☎ 500; Neue Klosterallee 10) across the lake acts as a sort of de facto information centre.

Chorin was founded by Cistercian monks in 1273, and 500 of them laboured over six decades to erect their monastery and church of red brick on a granite base (a practice copied by the Franciscans at the Nikolaikirche and Marienkirche in Berlin). The monastery was secularised in 1542 and fell into disrepair after the Thirty Years' War; renovation has gone on in a somewhat haphazard fashion since the early 19th century.

The entrance to the monastery is through the ornate western façade and leads to the central cloister and ambulatory. To the north is the early-Gothic **Klosterkirche**, with its wonderful carved portals and long lancet windows. Have a look along the walls at floor level to see the layer of granite supporting the porous handmade bricks.

Expect to hear some top talent at the celebrated **Choriner Musiksommer** (☎ 03334-657 310; Schickelstrasse 5, Eberswalde Finow), which takes place in the monastery cloister on Saturdays and Sundays from June to August. At 4pm some Sundays from late May to August there are chamber music concerts in the church, said to have near-perfect acoustics.

Getting There & Away

Chorin is served by regional trains from Berlin-Ostbahnhof (€6.90, 50 minutes) about every two hours. The train station is a 3km drive northwest of the monastery, but you can reach it via a pretty, marked trail through the woods in less than half an hour. If you're stopping off here en route to somewhere else, note that there is no left luggage (or indeed anything else) in the station.

Buses link Chorin with Eberswalde Hauptbahnhof, which is served by train from Berlin (40 minutes) as well as from Frankfurt an der Oder (two hours). They stop close to the monastery entrance along the B2.

NIEDERFINOW

☎ 033362 / pop 700

The **Schiffshebewerk** (Ship lift; ☎ 033369-461; Hebewerkstrasse; adult/child €1/0.50; ☑ 9am-6pm May-Sep, 9am-6pm Oct-Apr) at Niederfinow, southeast of Chorin, is one of the most remarkable feats of engineering from the early 20th century (1934). It's also fun, especially for kids. Ships sail in to a sort of giant bathtub, which is then raised or lowered 36m vertically, water and all, between the Oder River and the Oder-Havel Canal. This being Germany, technical data about the structure is posted everywhere, but it's enough just to watch 1200-tonne Polish barges laden with coal on the hoist.

The lift can be viewed from the street (free), but it's much more fun climbing to the upper platform to view the 20-minute operation from above. The neighbouring car park is full of snack stalls catering for drive-by tourists, with some maps and brochures for sale.

Oder-Havel Schifffahrt (☎ 633; adult/concession €5/4; ☑ Apr-Oct) has 1½-hour boat trips along the Oder-Havel Canal and down onto the Oder River via the Schiffshebewerk. The embarkation point is along the canal about 3km west of the lift.

Niederfinow is reachable by regional train from Berlin-Lichtenberg (€8.70, 70 minutes) with a change at Eberswalde, or direct from Frankfurt an der Oder (€9.20, 1¼ hours). The Schiffshebewerk is about 2km north of the station; turn left and follow the road.

Saxony

CONTENTS

Central Saxony	**165**
Dresden	165
Around Dresden	177
Saxon Switzerland	178
Meissen	180
Western Saxony	**181**
Chemnitz	181
Augustusburg	183
Leipzig	184
Around Leipzig	194
Zwickau	194
Eastern Saxony	**196**
Bautzen	196
Görlitz	198
Zittau	200

SAXONY

Saxony is densely populated, highly industrialised and, along with Bavaria, somehow the most German of the German states, taking great pride in its unique identity. Known as the birthplace of the German language, the impenetrable local dialect is a treasured artefact, and rich veins of history in all its forms run through the region – the current borders with Poland and the Czech Republic, for example, were only fixed after WWII, having shifted back and forth between warring families, kings and states almost since the first boundaries were marked out. Luckily the centuries of Slav-bashing are a thing of the past, and Saxony is now a convenient (and amicable) gateway to Eastern Europe.

The two main cities here are Leipzig and Dresden, relatively insignificant statistically but known throughout the country for the sheer scope of history, culture, architecture, art and nightlife they represent; with increasingly busy airports, major developments ongoing in both cities and Leipzig bidding for the 2012 Olympic Games, this national reputation should soon extend worldwide. If you're going to spend any time in Saxony, these thrilling but contrasting towns are absolutely the best places to start.

However, it's the smaller towns that really establish the Saxon character, with dozens of distinctive, well-preserved settlements dating back centuries scattered around the wildly variable landscape. The dramatic Elbe valley runs right through the state and offers amazing hiking opportunities, as do the Erzgebirge mountains in the south; elsewhere you'll find palaces, steam trains, car factories and the rural folk traditions of the indigenous Sorb people, not to mention the odd relic of the Wild West. It's well worth taking the time to explore everything this fascinating up-and-coming state has to offer.

HIGHLIGHTS

- **Architecture**
  Tour the Zwinger, the Semperoper and the Albertinum – the top classics in Dresden (p165)
- **Nightlife**
  Take in the atmosphere (and the beverages) in Leipzig, the city of the Peaceful Revolution (p184)
- **Fine Dining**
  Eat off classic local china and relish the views over hilly Meissen (p180)
- **Views**
  Stand atop the Bastei for stunning panoramas over Saxon Switzerland and the Elbe (p178)
- **Trains**
  Chug into the Zittau mountains with the narrow-gauge Bimmelbahn (p201)
- **Castles**
  Catch codpieces and carnival spirit at Schloss Weesenstein's annual Mittelalterfest (p177)

★ Leipzig
★ Meissen
★ Dresden   Zittau
Weesenstein ★ ★ Bastei   ★

- POPULATION: 4.38 MILLION
- AREA: 18,413 SQ KM

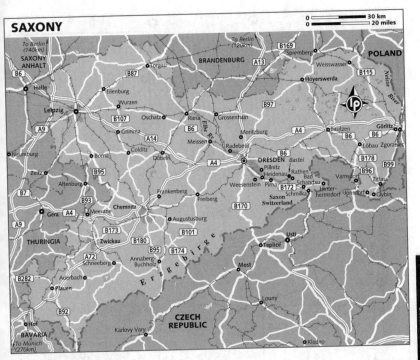

CENTRAL SAXONY

The Saxon heartland is very much central to the state, with the Elbe River flowing north–south and the state capital Dresden squarely in the middle. This region was hit hard by the *Jahrhundertflut* flood in August 2002, when the Elbe reached its highest level for 100 years (up to 9.5m in places), causing millions of euros of damage; Meissen and Dresden, which straddle the river, were among the worst sufferers. However, a costly clean-up operation was completed admirably quickly, and you can now see plaques in many affected towns commemorating this (hopefully) once-in-a-lifetime event. Ironically, the river hit almost record low levels during the scorching summer of 2003, causing the cancellation of many boat services.

DRESDEN

☎ 0351 / pop 479,000

In the 18th century the Saxon capital was famous throughout Europe as the 'Florence of the north', a centre of artistic activity presided over by Augustus the Strong and his son Augustus III. Since February 1945, however, Dresden has been synonymous with the Allied bombing campaign that devastated the city, killing 35,000 people (many of whom were refugees from other cities) in attacks that had scant strategic justification. The resurrection and restoration of Dresden as a cultural bastion is founded to some degree on this historical resonance, giving the city's great baroque buildings a gravitas all their own.

Reminders of Dresden's golden age are also a big attraction: Canaletto's many depictions of the era's rich architecture now hang in Dresden's Old Masters Gallery (see Zwinger p172) alongside countless masterpieces purchased for Augustus III with income from the Saxony's silver mines. Outside the historic Altstadt (old town), however, modern life has firmly asserted itself – the (only slightly newer) Neustadt has one of the densest concentrations of nightlife anywhere in Germany, and Dresden's many students are never short of ideas for entertainment.

SAXONY

DRESDEN

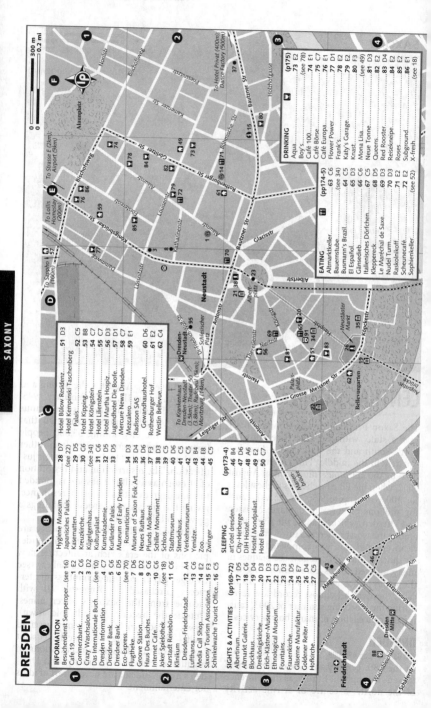

INFORMATION
Besucherdienst Semperoper......(see 16)
Café 19......................................1 E2
Commerzbank..............................2 C6
Crazy Waschsalon.........................3 D2
Das Internationale Buch..........(see 10)
Dresden Information......................4 C7
Dresdner Bank.............................5 C6
Dresdner Bank.............................6 D5
Eco-Express...........................(see 70)
Flugthek......................................7 D6
Groove Station..............................8 D2
Haus Des Buches...........................9 C6
Internet Spielothek.......................10 C6
Joker Reisebüro......................(see 18)
Karstadt Reisebüro.......................11 C6
Klinikum
    Dresden-Friedrichstadt..............12 A4
Lufthansa...................................13 C6
Media Call Shop..........................14 E2
Saxony Tourism Association...........15 F3
Schinkelwache Tourist Office.........16 C5

SIGHTS & ACTIVITIES   (pp169-72)
Albertinum................................17 D5
Altmarkt Galerie..........................18 C6
Blockhaus..................................19 D4
Dreikönigskirche.........................20 D3
Erich-Kästner-Museum..................21 D3
Ethnological Museum....................22 C3
Fountains...................................23 D5
Frauenkirche..............................24 D5
Gläserne Manufaktur....................25 E7
Goldener Reiter...........................26 D4
Hofkirche...................................27 C5

Hygiene Museum..........................28 D7
Japanisches Palais...................(see 22)
Käsematten................................29 D5
Kreuzkirche................................30 C6
Kügelgenhaus.............................31 D2
Kulturpalast...........................(see 34)
Kunstakademie............................32 D5
Kurländer Palais..........................33 D5
Museum of Early Dresden
    Romanticism......................(see 70)
Museum of Saxon Folk Art.............34 D3
Neues Rathaus............................35 D4
Pfunds Molkerei..........................36 D6
Schiller Monument........................37 F3
Schloss......................................38 D3
Stadtmuseum..............................39 C5
Stendehaus................................40 D6
Verkehrsmuseum.........................41 C5
Yenidze.....................................42 C5
Zoo...43 B4
Zwinger.....................................44 E8
....45 C5

SLEEPING   (pp173-4)
art'otel dresden..........................46 B4
City-Herberge.............................47 D6
DJH Hostel.................................48 A6
Hostel Mondpalast.......................49 E2
Hotel Bastei...............................50 C7

Hotel Bülow Residenz...................51 D3
Hotel Kempinski Taschenberg
    Palais...................................52 C5
Hotel Kipping..............................53 B8
Hotel Königstein.........................54 C7
Hotel Lilienstein..........................55 C7
Hotel Martha Hospiz.....................56 D3
Jugendhotel Die Boofe..................57 D1
Mercure Newa Dresden..................58 C7
Metzaleo...................................59 E1
Radisson SAS
    Gewandhaushotel.....................60 D6
Rothenburger Hof........................61 E2
Westin Bellevue..........................62 C4

EATING   (pp174-5)
Altmarktkeller.............................63 C6
Bauernstube..........................(see 34)
Busmann's Brazil.........................64 C5
El Español..................................65 D3
Gänsedieb..................................66 C6
Italienisches Dörfchen...................67 C5
Klepperbeck...............................68 D5
Le Maréchal de Saxe.....................69 D3
Nudel Turm................................70 D3
Raskolnikoff...............................71 E2
Scheunecafé..........................(see 52)
Sophienkeller..............................72 E2

DRINKING   (p175)
Aqua..73 E2
Boy's...................................(see 78)
Café 100....................................74 E1
Café Börse.................................75 C7
Café Europa................................76 E1
Flower Power...............................77 D1
Frank's......................................78 E2
Katy's Garage.............................79 E2
Knast..80 F3
Mona Lisa..................................81 D3
Neue Tonne................................82 C5
Queens.....................................83 D4
Red Rooster...............................84 E2
Reisekneipe...............................85 E1
Roses.......................................86 E1
Subground.............................(see 52)
X-fresh.................................(see 18)

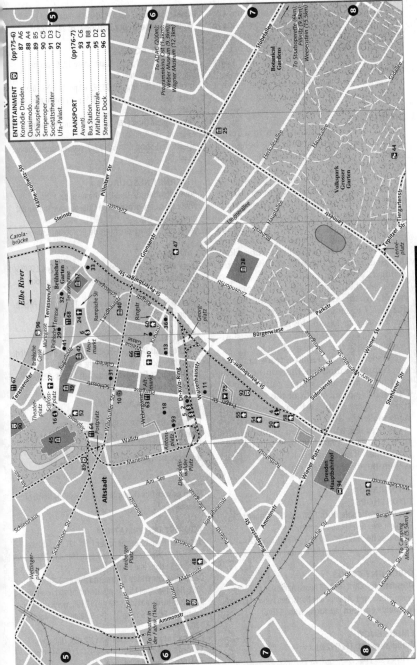

SAXONY

ENTERTAINMENT (pp175-6)
Komödie Dresden.........87 A6
Quasimodo..................88 A4
Schauspielhaus............89 B5
Semperoper................90 C5
Societätstheater............91 D3
Ufa-Palast..................92 C7

TRANSPORT (pp176-7)
Avanti.......................93 C6
Bus Station.................94 B8
Mitfahrzentrale.............95 D2
Steamer Dock...............96 D5

This sprawling city invariably wins the affection of visitors; with major restoration work going on for its 800th anniversary in 2006 and a bid for European Capital of Culture 2010 in the offing, the next few years should see Dresden garner even more fans. Take a few days and make the most of what this monumental city has to offer.

Orientation

The Elbe River splits the town in a rough V-shape, with the Neustadt, the bohemian pub district, to the north and the Altstadt to the south.

From the Hauptbahnhof (central train station), the pedestrianised Prager Strasse leads north into the Altstadt. Major redevelopment is under way around the Hauptbahnhof and Prager Strasse, which should result in yet more interesting architecture. The lovely Brühlsche Terrasse runs along the Elbe between the Albertinum and the Zwinger, with boat docks below.

In Neustadt, the main attractions for visitors are the Albertplatz and Anton Stadt quarters. On many of its sidestreets, it also has a cosier feel than the Altstadt. Hauptstrasse is pedestrianised and connects Albertplatz with the Augustusbrücke.

Dresden has two main train stations: the Hauptbahnhof, on the southern side of town, and the more contemporary Dresden-Neustadt north of the river. Most trains stop at both, and tram and S-Bahn lines make the 10-minute run between the two. Dresden-Mitte station is little more than a forlorn platform between the two main ones. The Dresden-Klotzsche airport is 9km north of the city centre.

Information

BOOKSHOPS

Das Internationale Buch (☎ 656 460; Altmarkt 24) Excellent selection of English books.
Haus Des Buches (☎ 402 060; Dr-Külz-Ring 12; 🖳) Lots of Lonely Planet titles, plus Internet access.

DISCOUNT CARDS

Dresden City-Card (€18; 48 hours) Admission to 12 museums, discounted city tours and boats, free public transport.
Museums day card (adult/concession €10/6)

EMERGENCY

Ambulance (☎ 112/19222)
Police (☎ 110)

Red Cross Clinic (☎ 648 010; Hauptbahnhof)
Women's emergency hotline (☎ 281 7788)

INTERNET ACCESS

Café 19 (☎ 804 3068; Alaunstrasse 19; €3 per hr) Hairdressers & internet café.
Internet Café (Altmarkt 25; €2.80 per hr; 🕙 10am-10pm Mon-Fri, 10am-6pm Sat & Sun) In the Authohaus Globisch car showroom.
Joker Spielothek (☎ 288 0034; Altmarkt Galerie; €3 per hr; 🕙 9am-2am)
Media Call Shop (☎ 656 7277; Rothenburger Strasse; €3 per hr)

INTERNET RESOURCES

www.dresden.de Dresden's home page.
www.dresden-dresden.de Offbeat guide to unusual corners of the city.
www.restaurant-dresden.de Restaurant listings.

LAUNDRY

Crazy Waschsalon (Louisenstrasse 6; wash/dry €2.50/0.50)
Eco-Express (cnr Bautzener Strasse & Königsbrücker Strasse; wash/dry €1.90/0.50)
Groove Station (Katharinenstrasse 11-13; 🖳) Popular multipurpose lounge, with pool tables and music.

MEDICAL SERVICES

Krankenhaus Dresden-Friedrichstadt (www.khdf.de; Friedrichstrasse 41) Northwest of the Altstadt.
Krankenhaus Dresden-Neustadt (☎ 8560; www.khdn.de; Industriestrasse 40)

MONEY

Commerzbank (☎ 86380; Prager Strasse)
Dresdner Bank (☎ 4890; Prager Strasse) Also has a branch in Neumarkt.
Reisebank (☎ 471 2177; Hauptbahnhof)

POST

Main post office (Königsbrücker Strasse 21) North of Albertplatz.

TOURIST INFORMATION

Besucherdienst Semperoper (☎ 491 10; Schinkelwache, Theaterplatz 2; 🕙 10am-6pm Mon-Fri, 10am-1pm Sat) Opera tickets and tours.
Deutscher Zentraler Zimmernachweis (☎ 830 9061; Hauptbahnhof) Books private rooms and hotel rooms.
Dresden Information (☎ 4919 2100; www.dresden-tourist.de; Prager Strasse 21; 🕙 9.30am-6pm Mon-Fri, 9.30am-4pm Sat)
Saxony Tourism Association (☎ 491 700; www.sachsen-tour.de; Bautzner Strasse 45/47) Books accommodation throughout the state.

Stained-glass window, Rathaus (town hall; p277), Quedlinburg

DAVID PEEVERS

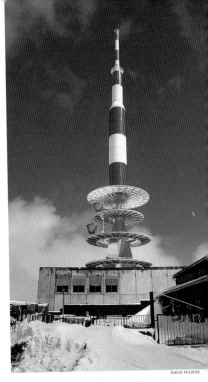

DAVID PEEVERS

Brockenhaus (p277), Brocken Mountain

Alter Schwede (p302), Wismar

DAVID PEEVERS

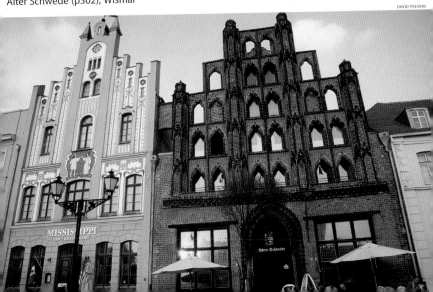

Beer tent, Oktoberfest (p341), Munich

ANDREA SCHULTE-PEEVERS

Walhalla (p416), Bavaria

Schloss Neuschwanstein (p375), Füssen

THOMAS WINZ

Road approaching the Bavarian Alps
(p378)

SAXON SPEAK

The Saxons speak a dialect as incomprehensible to non-Saxons as Bavarian is to outsiders. Many visitors find themselves saying 'Huh?' more often than usual. It's as if the Saxons learned German from the Scots, with their very soft pronunciation of consonants. For example, when a Saxon says '*lahip*-tsch', he means Leipzig. And the 'ü' sound is pronounced like an English short 'i' – '*bit*-nershtrazze' for Büttnerstrasse.

But Saxon-speak is far from an odd offshoot of German; on the contrary, it was from Saxony that the German language developed. Martin Luther's translation of the Bible into the Saxon language laid the foundation for a standard German language, and Saxons could also hark back to a 1717 Dutch reference to the Saxon dialect as 'the purest, most comprehensible, charming and delightful to the ear of all German dialects'.

In general, though, no outside praise is needed to reinforce Saxon pride in their dialect; '*sächseln*' is the norm, and the worst thing a native can do here is '*berlinern*' – start talking with a Berlin accent!

chinkelwache Tourist Office (☎ 491 1705; heaterplatz 2; ◷ 10am-6pm Mon-Fri, 10am-4pm at & Sun)

TRAVEL AGENCIES

Flugtheke (☎ 496 0248; Kreuzstrasse 3)
Karstadt Reisebüro (☎ 861 2510; Karstadt, Prager trasse 12)
Lufthansa (☎ 499 8822; Pfarrgasse 1)

Sights

YENIDZE

West of the Altstadt, you can't miss what looks like a gaudy mosque, bearing the word Yenidze on its stained-glass onion dome. The building actually started life as a tobacco factory in 1907, manufacturing an unsuccessful pseudo-exotic cigarette named Salaam Alakhem. The place has been in financial turmoil since an expensive postunification facelift, but there's a great **restaurant** (☎ 490 5990) in the dome and events inside feature performers from around the globe.

NEUSTADT

Despite its name, Neustadt is an old part of Dresden largely untouched by the wartime bombings. After reunification, Neustadt became the centre of the city's alternative scene, but as entire street blocks are renovated it's losing some of its bohemian feel. Königstrasse, which runs roughly parallel and to the west of Hauptstrasse, is developing into a swish shopping district.

The **Goldener Reiter** statue (1736) of Augustus the Strong stands at the northern end of the Augustusbrücke. This leads to the pleasant pedestrian mall of Hauptstrasse. Here in the Kügelgenhaus, an impressive baroque structure, is the **Museum of Early Dresden Romanticism** (☎ 804 4760; Hauptstrasse 13; adult/concession €1.53/0.77; ◷ 10am-6pm Wed-Sun).

Moving north you'll come to the newly renovated **Dreikönigskirche** (☎ 812 4102; tower adult/concession €1.50/1; ◷ 10am-6pm Mon-Sat, 11.30am-6pm Sun Mar-Oct, 10am-4.30pm Mon-Sat, 11.30am-4.30pm Sun Nov-Feb), the parish church designed by Pöppelmann. It houses some lovely Renaissance artworks, including the Dance of Death frieze that once hung in the Schloss (Palace).

On **Albertplatz** two lovely fountains flank the walkway down the centre, representing turbulent and still waters. North of the circle is an evocative marble **Schiller monument** and a fountain sourced from an artesian well, where Dresdeners still get water for their coffee.

Museums in the Neustadt area include the **Erich-Kästner-Museum** (☎ 804 5086; www.erich-kaestner-museum.de; Antonstrasse 1; adult/concession €2/1; ◷ 10am-6pm Sun-Tue, 10am-8pm Wed) an interesting biographical exhibition dedicated to the much-loved satirical author, and the **Museum of Saxon Folk Art** (☎ 803 0817; Köpckestrasse 1; adult/concession €3/2; ◷ 10am-6pm Tue-Sun) a large and varied collection of traditional artefacts housed in the 1568 Jägerhof. Inside the not-very-Japanese Japanisches Palais (1737) is Dresden's famous **Ethnological Museum** (☎ 814 450; Palaisplatz 11; adult/concession €4/2; ◷ 10am-6pm Tue-Sun), which boasts well over 70,000 anthropological items from far-flung corners of the world.

PFUNDS MOLKEREI

It's billed as 'the world's most beautiful dairy shop', and with good reason: the interior of

SAXONY

Pfunds Molkerei (☎ 816 20; Bautzner Strasse 79) is a riot of hand-painted tiles and enamelled sculpture (it's all Villeroy & Boch and worth a packet, so don't break anything). Founded by the Pfund brothers in 1880, the dairy claims to have invented condensed milk. It was nationalised by the GDR in 1972 and fell into disrepair before restoration in 1995. The shop sells replica tiles, wines, cheeses and of course milk, and there's a café-restaurant upstairs with a strong lactose theme.

GREAT GARDEN
Southeast of the Altstadt is the Grosser Garten, enchanting in summer and home to the excellent **Zoo** (☎ 478 060; www.zoo-dresden .de; Tiergartenstrasse 1; adult/concession €6/4; 8.30am-6.30pm Apr-Oct, 8.30am-4.30pm Nov-Mar). There are 2600 animals representing more than 400 species and a famous ape breeding programme. Last entry is 45 minutes before closing time. At the garden's northwestern corner are the **Botanical Gardens** (admission free). The hothouse is especially lovely during a freezing Dresden winter.

Also on the edge of the park is the striking Volkswagen **Gläserne Manufaktur** (Transparent Factory; ☎ 0180-589 6268; www.glaeserne manufaktur.de; cnr Grunaerstrasse & Lennéstrasse; adult/ concession €5/4; 8am-8pm), opened in 2001. As the name suggests, this is a working factory producing VW's prestige Phaeton range, with much of the process visible through the great glass panels. Essentially a huge exercise in brand marketing, the building made such an impact that it even hosted operas while the Semperoper was closed in 2002!

OTHER MUSEUMS
In a park west of the Great Garden, just off Blüher Strasse, is the unique **Hygiene Museum** (☎ 484 60; www.dhmd.de; Lingnerplatz 1; adult/concession €4/2; 9am-5pm Tue-Fri, 10am-6pm Sat & Sun). Established by Odol-mouthwash mogul Karl August Lingner, it'll appeal to anyone with a healthy interest in the human body, and contains cutaway models, the transparent man and other health-related exhibits, including a good one on STDs and AIDS. Entry is free after 1pm on Fridays.

In the southeastern suburb of Pillnitz is the interesting **Carl Maria von Weber Museum** (☎ 261 8234; Dresdner Strasse 44; adult/concession €1.53/ 0.77; 1-6pm Wed-Sun). This was the summer home of the composer and conductor, who lived and worked here for several years before his death in England in 1826 at age 39. The staff are very keen, and there are regular concerts here as well. Take bus No 83 to Van-Gogh-Strasse.

Further southeast, in a truly serene setting, is the impressive **Richard Wagner Museum** (☎ 03501-548 229; Richard-Wagner- Strasse 6, Graupa; adult/concession €2.50/1.25; 10am-noon & 1-4pm Tue-Sun). Dedicated staff talk you unsparingly through each and every detail of the stormy composer's life (the maestro's favourite breakfast food? We won't give it away), but there are some very nice exhibits, and the grounds are lovely. Take bus No 83.

Historic Centre Walking Tour
Our 3.5km circuit begins at Altmarkt and makes an arc northwest along the Elbe taking in the main churches, the Albertinum, the Semperoper and the Zwinger palace. It's a 1½-hour stroll, but with stops at several places it could easily stretch the tour to a day.

The **Altmarkt** area is the historic centre of Dresden, but it still hasn't fully recovered from the bombings. For a long time, this meant lots of stark granite and an impractically wide area (which sometimes contained a market). But as the city grows wealthier the Altmarkt is improving both economically and aesthetically. Many restaurants have set up street-side cafés, and when the markets aren't operating it's nice to

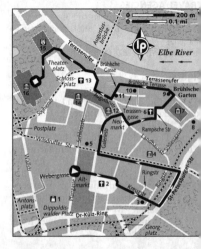

it outside and gaze across the square. The spanking new **Altmarkt Galerie (1)** shopping centre is also excellent.

From the square, proceed east to the rebuilt **Kreuzkirche (2**; Mon-Sat 10am-6pm Apr-Oct, 10am-4pm Nov-Mar; Sun from 11am). Originally the Nikolaikirche (1792), the church was renamed for a cross (Kreuz) found floating in the Elbe River by fishermen. The church is famous for its 400-strong boys' choir, the **Kreuzchor** (performances 6pm Sat).

Behind the Kreuzkirche stands the neo-Renaissance **Neues Rathaus** (New Town Hall; **3**; 1905–10), topped by a shining golden statue of Hercules. Today it's the offices of the city administration, and while you can enter and gawk at the lobby, there are no scheduled tours of the building.

ALTMARKT TO ALBERTINUM

Cross the wide Wilsdruffer Strasse to the **Stadtmuseum (4**; 6564 8612; stadtmuseum.dresden .de; Wildsruffer Strasse 2), housed in a building erected in 1775. Currently being renovated, it's due to reopen fully in autumn 2005, but its **Galerie Dresdener Kunst** (Dresden Art Gallery) should be open from the summer of 2004. Due west of here, opposite the Altmarkt, is a centre of the city's cultural life, the obnoxiously squat **Kulturpalast (5**; 486 60; www.kulturpalast-dresden.de; Schlossstrasse 2), which hosts a huge range of concerts and performances year-round.

Pass through Galeriestrasse to the right of the Kulturpalast and you'll reach the grassy **Neumarkt** – no longer a market these days – with the **Frauenkirche (6**; Church of Our Lady; 439 3934; www.frauenkirche-dresden.org) wrapped in scaffolding at its eastern end.

The Frauenkirche (1726–43), built under the direction of baroque architect George Bähr, is one of Dresden's most beloved symbols. Until the end of WWII it was Germany's greatest Protestant church, its enormous dome known as the 'stone bell'. The bombing raids of 13 February 1945 flattened it, and the communists decided to leave the rubble as a war memorial. After reunification, the grass-roots movement to rebuild the church prompted reconstruction and a huge archaeological dig began in 1992. Reassembly is scheduled for completion in 2006 (Dresden's 800th anniversary), but funding has been so generous that it's likely to finish early! You can take a one-hour guided tour (hourly 10am to 4pm) of the site – it's free, but donations are greatly encouraged, especially from British and American visitors, who are made to feel more than a little guilty for blowing it up in the first place.

From the Frauenkirche, turn east up Rampiche Strasse and veer northeast through the path which leads to the Brühlscher Garten, the lovely green park east of the main terrace.

In front is the **Albertinum (7**; 491 4619; combined museum ticket adult/child €6/3.50; 10am-6pm Fri-Wed). It houses many of Dresden's art treasures, including the **New Masters Gallery**, with 19th- and 20th-century paintings from leading French and German Impressionists, and the **Skulpturensammlung**, which includes classical and Egyptian works. Here, too, is one of the world's finest collections of jewel-studded precious objects, the **Grünes Gewölbe** (Green Vault). Treasures include the world's biggest green diamond (all 41 carats worth), tiny sculptures fashioned from odd-shaped pearls, and a stunning group of 137 gem-studded figures entitled Court of Delhi on the Birthday of the Great Mogul, fashioned by Johann Melchior Dinglinger, court jeweller of Augustus the Strong. The collection will eventually be relocated to its original site in the Schloss.

Opposite the east end of the Albertinum is JC Knöffels' **Kurländer Palais (8)**, which was destroyed in 1945 and is being restored for 2006.

BRÜHLSCHE TERRASSE TO AUGUSTUSSTRASSE

From the Albertinum, do an about-face and go west, passing the gilded **Kunstakademie (9**; Academy of Arts) on your way to the **Brühlsche Terrasse**, a spectacular promenade that's been called the balcony of Europe, with a pavement nearly 15m above the southern embankment of the Elbe. In summer it's a must for strolling, with expansive views of the river and, on the opposite bank, the **Japanisches Palais** (Japanese Palace) and the baroque **Blockhaus**, a guardhouse designed by the French architect Zacharias Longuelune.

Beneath the promenade is the Renaissance brick bastion known as the **Kasematten (10**; 491 4786; adult/child €3.10/2; 10am-5pm), which has a museum. For an extra €1 you can get an audio tour in English (or six other languages).

SAXONY

Take the double-sided staircase down to Brühler Gasse, which leads back to the Neumarkt. From here, turn right onto the fabulous Augustusstrasse, with its 102m-long Procession of Princes mural depicted on the outer wall of the former **Stendehaus** (11; Royal Stables). The scene, a long row of royalty on horses, was first painted in 1876 by Wullhelm Walther and then transferred to some 24,000 Meissen porcelain tiles, which make up the mural. Join the crowds standing across the street and squinting.

Here you'll also find a fascinating collection including penny-farthings, trams, dirigibles and carriages at the **Verkehrsmuseum** (12; Transport Museum; ☎ 864 40; www.verkehrsmus eum.sachsen.de; Augustusstrasse 1; adult/concession €2/1; ☺ 10am-5pm Tue-Sun). Included in the admission is a great 40-minute film with original black-and-white footage of Dresden of the 1930s and German commentary.

SCHLOSSPLATZ

Augustusstrasse leads directly to Schlossplatz and the baroque Catholic **Hofkirche** (13; ☎ 484 4712; Schlossplatz; ☺ 9am-5pm Mon-Thu, 1-5pm Fri, 10.30am-4pm Sat, noon-4pm Sun May-Oct; 10.30am-5pm Sat Nov-Apr). Completed in 1755, its crypt contains the heart of Augustus the Strong. Restoration work is still going on here, despite being slated to finish in 2001!

Just south of the church is the neo-Renaissance **Schloss (14)**, which is being reconstructed as a museum. Restoration of the palace is scheduled, a bit optimistically, to finish in 2006, although the **Hausmannsturm** (Servant's tower; adult/concession €4/2.50; ☺ 10am-6pm Tue-Sun Apr-Oct) is now open to the public.

THEATERPLATZ

On the western side of the Hofkirche is Theaterplatz, with Dresden's dramatic and long-suffering **Semperoper (15**; ☎ 491 1496; tours adult/concession €5/3). The original opera house on the site opened in 1841 but burned down less than three decades later. Rebuilt in 1878, it was pummelled in WWII and reopened only in 1985, after the communists invested millions in restoring this neo-Renaissance jewel; the 2002 floods closed it down yet again, albeit only briefly, and repairs were ongoing at time of research. Thanks to a recent beer commercial, the Semperoper is probably one of the best-known buildings in Germany.

The Dresden opera has a tradition going back 350 years – many works by Richard Strauss, Carl Maria von Weber and Richard Wagner premiered here, and the Dresden State Orchestra also performs here.

ZWINGER

From the opera house, proceed south a few metres to reach the sprawling baroque **Zwinger (16**; Theaterplatz 1; ☺ 10am-6pm Tue-Sun) Its lovely, fountain-studded courtyard is framed by an open-air gallery and several charming portals (one is reachable via a long footbridge over a moat). The Zwinger (1728) was badly damaged during the war but has been mostly rebuilt, although work is ongoing. Conceived by star architect Mattaeus Pöppelmann for royal tournaments and festivals, the exterior has some fine examples of baroque sculpture (which are endlessly photographed), and the courtyard is a popular summer venue. Atop the western pavilion stands a tense-looking Atlas with the world on his shoulders; opposite him is a cutesy carillon of 40 Meissen porcelain bells, which chime on the hour.

The Zwinger houses six museums. The most important are the **Old Masters Gallery** (☎ 491 4619), which features masterpieces including Raphael's Sistine Madonna, and the **Rüstkammer** (Armory; ☎ 491 4619), with its superb collection of ceremonial weapons. A combined ticket costs €6/3.50 adult/concession.

The dazzling **Porcelain Collection** (☎ 491 4622; adult/concession €5.50/3.50) is another highlight, with plenty of Meissen classics. Old instruments, globes and timepieces are displayed in the **Mathematics and Physics Salon** (☎ 491 4622; adult/concession €2/1.50). The **Naturhistorische Sammlungen** (Natural History Museum; ☎ 892 6326; adult/concession €2.05/1.02) and the **Museum of Minerology and Geology** (☎ 495 2503; adult/concession €3/1.50) are found in the Unterm Kronentor part of the fortress.

Tours

The tourist office on Prager Strasse books tours with a number of organisations. Unusual options include:

Barokkokko (☎ 479 8184; www.erlebnisrundgang .de; adult/concession €15/9) Elaborate 2½-hour 'experience' tours with costumed staff and an entertaining dash of pretension. Good German skills are required.

Hamburger Hummelbahn (☎ 494 0404; www.sta trundfahrt-dresden.de; adult €13-19, concession €12-17) This company runs double-decker buses, 'choo-choo' trains and other touristy ve- icles around the city, stopping at all the major sights. Tours (in German) leave from Postplatz daily from April to October, and go for 1½ hours.

Igeltour (☎ 804 4557; www.igeltour-dresden.de; adult/concession €6/5) You can get off the beaten track with all kinds of thematic tours from this highly professional outfit.

Sächsische Dampfschiffahrt (☎ 866 090; www saechsische-dampfschiffahrt.de; adult/child €10/5) River tours are run on rebuilt steam ships; the company prides itself on having the world's oldest fleet of paddle-wheel steamers. Ninety-minute tours leave from the Ter- rassenufer dock at 11am, 1pm, 3pm and 5pm daily. See also Elbe River Excursions p178.

Trabi Safari (☎ 899 0060; post@high-live.de; from €17.90 per person) Get behind the wheel of the ultimate GDR-mobile for this 1½-hour guided drive.

Festivals & Events

Dresden's annual events include the **Parade of the Sächsische Dampfschiffahrt fleet** on 1 May, a unique, smoke-puffing sight; the **International Dixieland Festival** in early May, with around 250 concerts held at 60 ven- ues; the **Dresden Music Festival** in June/July, with classical concerts in the palaces, theatres and churches; and the **Dresden City Festival** in late August, with something for everyone.

Sleeping

The **tourist offices** (☎ 4919 2222) can find **pri- vate rooms** (from around €17.50 per person).

BUDGET

Accommodation in Dresden can be horren- dously expensive, with hotel rates among the highest in Germany. Luckily, several new budget places have emerged in or near the centre; the Neustadt is a particularly good area for interesting, youth-oriented hostels. Breakfast is not included unless otherwise stated.

Jugendhotel Die Boofe (☎ 801 3361; www.boofe .com; Hechtstrasse 10; s €29, d €44-48; ✖) Well known locally, rooms here are nicer than your aver- age hostel and the bar is a popular hangout.

DJH hostel (☎ 492 620; jghdresden@djh-sachsen.de; Maternistrasse 22; s/d €25/42; ✖ 🖳) The DJH Ju- gendgästehaus Dresden is a tower block that was once a Communist Party training cen- tre, but now it's a fantastic hostel, with small dorms and a bistro (breakfast included), plus wheelchair access and lift. Take tram No 7 or 10 to the corner of Ammonstrasse and Freiberger Strasse.

Camping Mockritz (☎ 471 5250; www.camping -dresden.de; Boderitzerstrasse 30; adult/child €4.50/2, car €1, tent €1.50-3) Next to a nature reserve, this popular camp site is 5km out of town, served by the No 76 bus.

Mezcalero (☎ 810 770; www.mezcalero.de; Königs- brücker Strasse 64; dm €15-23, s €30-45, d €50-60; 🅿) Definitely one for the 'oddities' basket: how often do you get to stay in a Mexican/Aztec B&B, complete with sombreros, red-yellow colour scheme, tiles and tequila bar? Very random, very cool.

Hostel Mondpalast (☎ 804 6061; www.mondpalast .de; Louisenstrasse 77; dm €13.50, s €29-39, d €37-50; ✖) Looking even better after a quick move and a TV appearance, the Moon Palace has bedrooms décorated by theme (Australia, Greece, space travel) and a great bar/café.

Lollis Homestay (☎ 810 8458; www.lollishome.de; Seitenstrasse 2a; dm €13, s/d €25/34; ✖ 🖳) We've had some very good feedback about this small, friendly place north of the Neustadt. As the name suggests, you're essentially a house guest.

City-Herberge (☎ 485 9900; www.city-herberge.de; Lingnerallee 3; s/d €36.50/63; 🅿) Large and in a central location, this basic tourist hotel is a good bet if you arrive at a busy time. Breakfast is included in the price.

MID-RANGE

Hotel Kipping (☎ 478 500; www.hotel-kipping.de; Winck- elmannstrasse 6; s €70-95, d €85-115; 🅿 ✖) Just south of the Hauptbahnhof, this is a great family- run, family-friendly hotel which comes with fervent reader recommendations.

Hotel Martha Hospiz (☎ 817 60; marthahospiz .dresden@t-online.de; Nieritzstrasse 11; s €54-84, d €102- 118; 🅿) Quiet reigns in this ample yet lovely inn with country furnishings, once owned by a church.

Hotel Privat (☎ 811770; www.das-nichtraucher-hotel .de; Forststrasse 22; s €46-61, d €62-82; 🅿 ✖) East of the Neustadt is Germany's only entirely nonsmoking hotel, with three-star facilities, conservatory and wine cellar.

SAXONY

Rothenburger Hof (☎ 812 60; www.rothenburger-hof.de; Rothenburger Strasse 15-17; s/d €95/130; P ✗ ⛌) In the middle of Neustadt you'll find this place with a clean, bright atmosphere and lots of beauty treatments, including steam room and sauna.

Mercure Newa Dresden (☎ 481 4109; 1577@accor-hotels.com; St-Petersburger-Strasse 34; s €98-110, d €106-126; P ✗ ⛌) Almost entirely rebuilt after flood damage, the Mercure has sneakily hiked prices up by 20% to match the new facilities; thanks to its commanding location, it can just about get away with it.

Hotel Bastei (☎ 4856 6661; s €60-66, d €72-78; ✗ ⛌); **Hotel Königstein** (☎ 4856 6662; s €56-62, d €68-74; ✗ ⛌); **Hotel Lilienstein** (☎ 4856 6663; s €56-62, d €68-74; ✗ ⛌) The three Ibis Hotels lining Prager Strasse are identical 1960s properties: tall, drab and central. The Bastei has slightly better facilities (Internet connections etc). Breakfast costs an extra €9.

TOP END

Now we're talking – if you've got the cash to flash, Dresden is a fantastic place to live it up. Wheelchair access comes as standard, and all these places offer 'Arrangements', combining several nights' stay and other attractions such as hard-to-come-by Semperoper tickets.

Hotel Bülow Residenz (☎ 800 30; www.buelow-residenz.de; Rähnitzstrasse 19; s/d €170/210, ste €260-380; P ✗ ⛌) A real gem, tucked away on a quiet street near Palaisplatz. Breakfast is extra but the minibar is included (priorities!), and the house restaurant is rated one of the best in Saxony, run by award-winning young chef Stefan Hermann.

Radisson SAS Gewandhaushotel (☎ 494 90; info.dresden@radissonsas.com; Ringstrasse 1; r €135-200, ste €450-900; P ✗ ⛌ ⛌) Another top choice for class and personal service. Housed in a former fabric warehouse, the public areas are stunning and almost all the rooms have whirlpool baths in their marble-fitted bathrooms.

art'otel dresden (☎ 492 20; aodrinfo@artotels.de; Ostra-Allee 33; s/d €160/175; P ✗ ⛌) Decked out with works by local boy AR Penck, this fanciful modern hotel has nice rooms full of quirky touches.

Hotel Kempinski Taschenberg Palais (☎ 491 20; www.kempinski-dresden.de; Taschenberg 3; s €255-340, d €285-370, ste €450-1400; P ✗ ⛌ ⛌) This restored 18th-century mansion is Dresden's

heavyweight, with views over the Zwinger, incredibly quiet corridors and Bulgari toiletries. Even the occasional cow-print pouffe can't dent the sophisticated veneer.

Westin Bellevue (☎ 8050; hotelinfo@westin-bellevu.de; Grosse Meissner Strasse 15; s/d from €133/150; P ✗ ⛌ ⛌) The squat, block-like Westin has fully-featured American-style rooms but the real highlight is the unparalleled views of the Brühlsche Terrasse and the city on the other side of the Elbe.

Eating

ALTSTADT

Italienisches Dörfchen (☎ 498 160; www.italienische-doerfchen.de; Theaterplatz 3; mains €5-20) This collection of four restaurants offers stylish surroundings and varied cuisine, from bargain barbecue on the terrace to swanky Italian and Saxon dishes inside.

Sophienkeller (☎ 497 260; www.sophienkeller-dresden.de; Taschenberg 3; mains €9-16.50) Don't be put off by the tourist-oriented 1730s theme: it's a bit overdone but the costumed wenches do actually serve up good local specialities and wines. Try the famous Dresden *Trichter* (drinking funnel).

Busmann's Brazil (☎ 862 1200; Kleine Brüdergasse 5; mains €9.60-21.20) For a taste of Brazilian culture beyond the usual caipirinha, try this huge, swish place, which boasts such strange delicacies as frogfish and, dauntingly, rattlesnake (€40.90).

Altmarktkeller (☎ 481 8130; www.altmarktkeller-dresden.de; Altmarkt 4; mains €7.80-11.50) Hearty but creative Saxon and Bohemian dishes in what must be one of Dresden's longest cellars.

Weisse Gasse, near the Kreuzkirche, and Münzgasse/Terrassengasse, between Brühlsche Terrasse and the Frauenkirche, are crammed with restaurants representing all kinds of local and international cuisine. Good options include:

Gänsedieb (☎ 485 0905; Weisse Gasse 1; mains €6.50-10.80) Goose dishes are the pick of the menu in this inventive café-restaurant; the full range of Bavarian Paulaner beers is also on offer.

Kleppereck (☎ 496 5123; www.kleppereck.de; Münzgasse 10; mains €9.20-18.90) You get good Saxon cooking and great views of the Brühlsche Terrasse steps here.

NEUSTADT

Raskolnikoff (☎ 804 5706; www.raskolnikoff.de; Böhmische Strasse 34; mains €5.20-7) This place couldn't be more bohemian if it tried – it's even on Bohemian Street! The menu sorts its good-value light meals by compass direction, and includes Eastern European dishes such as *borscht* (beetroot soup) and *pelmeni* (Russian ravioli). There's a gallery and **pension** (r €30-45) upstairs.

Scheunecafé (☎ 802 6619; Alaunstrasse 36-40; mains €6.40-10.10) Indian food in an alternative rock venue? Way better than it sounds – just watch the crowds gather in the beer garden.

Bauernstube (☎ 527 91; Kügelgenhaus, Hauptstrasse 13; mains €6.40-10.50) For something special, dine here, below the Museum of Early Romanticism. It has a good range of local Saxon dishes, and there's a beer cellar beneath the restaurant.

Le Maréchal de Saxe (☎ 810 5880; Königstrasse 5; mains €8.70-14) One of several upmarket restaurants in this smart area offering proper 18th-century Saxon court cuisine. The local FDP like to meet here for earnest discussions.

El Español (☎ 804 8670; www.elespanol.de; An der Dreikönigskirche 7; menus €6.20-15.10) Readers have written to us recommending this cosy Spanish tapas restaurant; there's a paella buffet here on Mondays.

Nudel Turm (☎ 804 3094; www.wok.de; Bautzner Strasse 1; mains €4.80-12.90) A lifesaver for families, this varied, imaginative pasta place has cartoony menus and great views.

Drinking

The finest all-round listings guide to Dresden is *SAX* (€1.50), available at newsstands around the city. The guide has listings for local clubs, restaurants, schools, cafés, travel agencies, cheap tickets and a whole lot more. The twice-yearly *Spot!* and its English equivalent *Maxity* have ad-style listings for museums and shops as well as restaurants and bars; regular freebies include *Blitz*, *Fritz*, *Fresh* and the *Kneipensurfer* and *Nachtfalter* maps.

Note that Dresden is one of the few places in Germany where beer gardens and outdoor cafés are allowed to stay open as long as they like – a real bonus in summer.

ALTSTADT
X-fresh (☎ 484 2791; Altmarkt Galerie; mains €6.50-14.90) Billed as a 'Wellness-bistro', the food here is refreshingly healthy, with a good range of salads and shakes and a prosecco-tinged Sunday breakfast buffet (€7.80, 9am

to 2pm). On Thursdays there's an after-shopping disco from 6pm.

Café Börse (☎ 490 6411; Prager Strasse 8a; meals €6.80-9.80) Drinks, crêpes (€6.40-7.50) and people-watching are the thing in this contemporary glass lounge above busy Prager Strasse.

NEUSTADT
This area has Dresden's finest selection of late-night café-bars, with most concentrated in the area around Alaunstrasse and Louisenstrasse.

Café Europa (☎ 389 923; Königsbrücker Strasse 68; 💻) Newspapers, intimate lighting and free Internet feature at this smart, relaxed café.

Reisekneipe (☎ 889 4111; www.reisekneipe.de; Görlitzer Strasse 15) Experience Africa, Asia, Arabia, Russia and Europe just by wandering through this exotic and massively popular bar. Hardened globetrotters give talks (with slides, of course) every Wednesday.

Aqua (☎ 810 6116; www.aqualounge.de; Louisenstrasse 56) Relaxed, very cool lounge bar with weekend DJs and many cocktails.

Café 100 (☎ 801 7729; Alaunstrasse 100) This candle-lit pub has an underground vibe and more than 300 types of wine.

Frank's (☎ 802 6727; Alaunstrasse 80) Famed for its huge cocktail menu, this is a long-running Neustadt stalwart.

Flower Power (☎ 804 9814; www.nubeatz.de/fpd; Eschenstrasse 11) Another staple of the Dresden student scene, with DJs every night.

Red Rooster (☎ 829 6645; www.redrooster-pub.de; Rähnitzstrasse 10) Dresden's oldest pub is in a quieter area but can still pack 'em in.

Knast (☎ 801 4667; Bautzner Strasse 30) If you've ever wondered what an East German prison was like, check the décor here.

Entertainment
CINEMA
Undubbed English films are shown at **Programmkino Ost** (☎ 310 3782; Schandauer Strasse 73), south of the Altstadt, **Quasimodo** (☎ 866 0211; Adlergasse 14) and **Ufa-Palast** (☎ 482 50; Prager Strasse), which incorporates the modern glass Kristallpalast and the round Rundkino (recently restored). Check www.kinokalender.com for monthly listings.

CLASSICAL MUSIC
Dresden is synonymous with opera, and performances at the spectacular **Semperoper**,

SAXONY

opposite the Zwinger, are brilliant. Tickets for the Semperoper cost from €15, but they're usually booked out well in advance. In fact, the Schinkelwache office suggests that for major performances you should reserve as far as a year in advance. Some performances by the renowned Philharmonic are held there, but most are in the Kulturpalast (☎ 486 60).

GAY & LESBIAN VENUES

Dresden's gay scene is concentrated in the Neustadt. *Gegenpol* magazine has listings.

Sappho (☎ 404 5136; Hechtstrasse 23) This new women's café is an excellent addition to Dresden's thriving gay map.

Mona Lisa (☎ 803 3151; www.monalisa-dresden.de; Louisenstrasse 77) This is a quasi-Caribbean cocktail bar with a mixed following.

Queens (☎ 803 1650; www.queens-dresden.de; Görlitzer Strasse 3) A young crowd hangs out at this bar/lounge/disco.

Boy's (☎ 796 8824; www.boysdresden.de; Alaunstrasse 30) Lively bar/club with events most nights.

NIGHTCLUBS

Strasse E (www.strasse-e.de; Werner-Hartmann-Strasse 2) With 6000 sq m of 'cultural centre' comprising no fewer than eight different club spaces, this complex north of town offers a wide range of nights, from disco to drum'n'bass. Take tram No 7 to Industriegelände.

Subground (Bischofsweg 14; admission €2.50) Not quite as underground as the name suggests, but still one of the city's best venues for all things hip-hop.

Dance Factory (☎ 502 2451; www.factory-discothek .de; Bautzner Strasse 118; ☽ Thu-Sat) This very popular spot, east of the Neustadt, has the usual mix of R&B, cheese and trance/techno in four rooms. The bouncers can be choosy.

U-Boot (Bautzner Strasse 75) Anything from reggae to nu-punk, catering for the skater crowd.

ROCK, JAZZ & OTHER MUSIC

A huge variety of concerts are held in the Kulturpalast (☎ 486 60), which changes its programmes daily.

Katy's Garage (cnr Alaunstrasse & Louisenstrasse) Key venue for indie gigs and club nights throughout the week.

Neue Tonne (☎ 802 6017; www.jazzclub-tonne.de; Königstrasse 15; admission free-€15) Dresden's best jazz club, now in a new, more central location.

Sächsische Dampfschiffahrt (see Tour p172) runs fun **Dixieland cruises** (☎ 866 090 adult/child €16/8; ☽ 7-10pm Fri & Sat), swinging up the Elbe with music, food and drinks.

THEATRE

There's an active theatre scene in Dresden. Many small companies perform throughout the city; the best bet is to check in *SAX*. Theatre tickets can be bought at the tourist offices or the theatre box office an hour before performance. Many theatres close from mid-July to the end of August.

Schauspielhaus (☎ 491 350; Theaterstrasse 2) The renowned Staatsschauspiel theatre plays here, near the Zwinger.

Staatsoperette (☎ 207 990; Pirnaer Landstrasse 131) This theatre is in Leuben in the far east of the city.

Theater in der Fabrik (☎ 421 4505; Tharandter Strasse 33) This alternative theatre is near the Jugendgästehaus Dresden, west of the Aldstadt.

Theater 50 (☎ 859 0995; Fechnerstrasse 2A) This former GDR business centre, northwest of Neustadt, is another alternative theatre.

Komödie Dresden (☎ 866 410; World Trade Centre, Freibergerstrasse 39) One of Dresden's favourite comic theatres.

Societätstheater (☎ 803 6810; www.societaetsthea ter.de; An der Dreikönigskirche 1a) A good venue for modern and experimental theatre.

Getting There & Away

Dresden-Klotzsche airport (☎ 881 3031; www.flug hafen-dresden.de) is served by Lufthansa, KLM and other major airlines.

Dresden is two hours south of Berlin-Ostbahnhof (€30.20). The Leipzig–Riesa–Dresden service (€16.80, 70 minutes) runs hourly. The S-Bahn runs half-hourly to Meissen (€4.80, 45 minutes). There are connections to Frankfurt (€66.80, 4½ hours) and Munich (€97.60, 6¾ hours) and direct international services to Vienna (7¾ hours) and Prague (three hours).

Dresden's **bus station** is next to the Hauptbahnhof; regional buses depart for more remote Saxon destinations.

To drive to or from Leipzig, take the A14/A4. From Berlin, take the A113 to the A13 south. To the Czech Republic, take the B170 south. From Munich, take the A9 the A72 and on to the A4. Information r drivers is available at **ADAC** (☎ 44330; riesener Strasse 37).

A ride-share service operates from the **itfahrzentrale** (☎ 194 40; www.mitfahren-online e; Dr-Friedrich-Wolf-Strasse 2).

etting Around

he airport is served by S-Bahn No 2 €1.50, 30 minutes). The Airport City Liner us serves Dresden-Neustadt (€3) and the auptbahnhof (€4), with stops at key points n town including some hotels. A taxi to the auptbahnhof is about €10.

Dresden's transport network charges 1.50 for a single ticket; daytickets cost €4. he family day ticket, for two adults and up o four kids, is a good deal at €5.

All major car-rental firms have offices t the airport. Driving in town is a cinch; igns are good and parking is easy. Note hat there are parking ticket machines in he centre.

Starting rate for taxis is €2.10. Taxis line p at the Hauptbahnhof and Neustadt staion; you can also ring ☎ 211 211. Bicycle ire is available at the Hauptbahnhof and Neustadt station; you could also try **Avanti** Wallstrasse 20).

AROUND DRESDEN

Weesenstein

ust 16km southeast of Dresden, **Schloss Weesenstein** (☎ 035027-6260; www.schloss-weesenstein.de; adult/concession/child €3.50/2.50/2; 9am-6pm pr-Oct, 10am-5pm Nov-Mar) is one of the most unervisited and untouched extant medieval astles in Germany. Built by the margraves f Dohna, who owned land stretching into Bohemia, the castle was begun in the 13th entury as a fortification along busy trade outes.

In 1385, a feud began when a son of the margrave's family danced too closely to the vife of Jeschka, a knight from Colbitz. Over he next 20 years the feud escalated into ull-scale battle between the families, and he margrave of Meissen was called in to be n impartial judge in the conflict. He imartially awarded the castle to himself and gave it to his cronies in the Bühnau family, who lived here for the next 360 years. The astle was later the home of King Johann who, from 1860 on, ran the Saxon court rom here rather than Pillnitz.

Today, the castle is a mixture of Gothic, Renaissance and baroque architectural styles. Exhibits are designed to let you see how royalty and servants really lived – right down to the toilets. The **Schlossbrauerei**, where they have brewed Weesenstein beer since the 16th century, is now a restaurant, and the lovely **chapel** hosts regular concerts. Manuscripts of music by the Bühnau family's court composers have just been rediscovered in state archives, and a CD of recordings of the music is available (€16.50) from the cashier.

Behind the castle are the **baroque gardens**; unfortunately these were almost totally destroyed by floods in August 2002, and are being painstakingly reconstructed.

During Pfingsten (Pentecost or Whitsun), the town holds its **Mittelalterfest** (medieval festival; adult/concession €7/5), which features jousting, medieval crafts, local speciality foods and freshly brewed beer. If the weather's fine, it's some of the most fun you can have in Germany and not at all on the tourist track.

Königliche Schlossküche (☎ 035027-624 18; weesenstein@q-linar.com; Am Schlossberg 1; mains €10-18) Dresdeners drive here for nice dinners out, and so should you. It has excellent Saxon specialities with local produce and nice touches like flower petals in the *Lauchsuppe* (leek soup). Out of season it only opens four or five days a week.

GETTING THERE & AWAY

Trains from Dresden via Pirna or Schöna serve Weesenstein's train station (€4.50, 35 minutes), about 500m south of the castle – follow the road up the hill. By car, head east out of Dresden along the B172 to Altenberg, turn right just past the overpass (signed to Dohna), and follow the signs to the Schloss (about 7km).

Pillnitz Palace

From 1765 to 1918, this exotic palace on the Elbe, about 10km southeast of Dresden, was the summer residence of the kings and queens of Saxony. The most romantic way to get there is on one of Dresden's old steamers, which depart six times a day from the Sächsische Dampfschiffahrt dock in Dresden (€8.50, 1¾ hours). See also Elbe River Excursions (p178).

Otherwise, take tram No 14 from Wilsdruffer Strasse or tram No 9 from in front

SAXONY

of the Dresden Hauptbahnhof east to the end of the line, then walk down to the riverside and cross the Elbe on the small ferry, which operates year-round. Bus No 83 also goes almost all the way to the palace. There's a **museum** (☎ 261 30; ⊗ 10am-6pm Tue-Sun May-Oct), but the **gardens** stay open till 8pm and the **palace exterior**, with its Oriental motifs, is far more interesting than anything inside.

Schloss Moritzburg

Rising impressively from a lake 14km northwest of Dresden is the **Schloss Moritzburg** (☎ 035207-8730; www.schloss-moritzburg.de; adult/concession €6/4; ⊗ 10am-5.30pm daily Apr-Oct, Tue-Sun Nov-Mar). Erected as a hunting lodge for the Duke of Saxony in 1546, Moritzburg was completely remodelled in baroque style in 1730, and it has an impressive interior. Guided tours in German (€1.50) are conducted hourly. The palace also has lovely parkland ideal for strolling, and hosts an international **chamber music festival** (☎ 0351-810 5495; www.moritzburgfestival .de) in August. Bus 457 runs to Moritzburg from behind Dresden's Neustadt train station.

Radebeul

One of this area's strangest attractions is the **Karl-May-Museum** (☎ 0351-837 300; www.karl-may -museum.de; Karl-May-Strasse 5; adult/concession/child €5/ 4/2; ⊗ Tue-Sun 9am-6pm Mar-Oct, 10am-4pm Nov-Feb), a tribute to Germany's greatest adventure writer. May (1842–1912) still ranks as one of the country's most widely read authors, and his rousing tales of the Wild West and the exotic Orient have sold over 100 million copies worldwide.

May's stories made him a celebrity in the 1880s; he would pose for photos in cowboy duds and sign autographs as Old Shatterhand. **Villa Shatterhand** contains his personal collection of weapons, hunting trophies and other incongruous items from America and the Near East, while **Villa Bärenfett** has a highly rated exhibition on the Native Americans. In May Radebeul hosts a huge **Karl-May-Fest**, a mecca for hard-drinking Germans in feather headdresses and chaps.

From Dresden, take the S1 north to Radebeul-Ost or tram No 4 to Schildenstrasse (€3, 20 minutes).

Elbe River Excursions

At Schmilka the Elbe River has cut a deep valley through the sandstone, producing abrupt pinnacles and other striking rock formations.

Sächsische Dampfschiffahrt (☎ 0351-866 09) From May to November there are frequent services upriver from Dresden via Pirna (€9.50) and Bad Schandau (€17) to Schmilka (€17).

Local trains return to Dresden from Schmilka-Hirschmühle (opposite Schmilka) about every half-hour until late in the evening (€6, 54 minutes). Boats also run downriver as far as Meissen (€10.50).

SAXON SWITZERLAND

The Sächsische Schweiz (Saxon Switzerland) is a 275-sq-km national park 50km south of Dresden, near the Czech border. Its wonderfully wild, craggy country dotted with castles and tiny towns along the mighty Elbe. The landscape varies unexpectedly and radically: its forests can look deceptively tropical, while the worn cliffs and plateaus recall the parched expanses of New Mexico or central Spain (generally without the searing heat).

The region is a favourite with hikers and climbers, and here you'll see archetypal German nature lovers in their element, complete with walking sticks, day-packs and knee stockings. Highlights include the Bastei lookout and the border resort of Bad Schandau; you can get information from the Dresden tourist offices.

Bastei

The open fields and rolling hills surrounding the Bastei, on the Elbe some 28km southeast of Dresden, give little clue as to the drama within. One of the most breathtaking spots in the whole of Germany, it features towering outcrops 305m high and unparalleled views of the surrounding forests, cliffs and mountains, not to mention a magnificent sightline right along the river itself. Look out for the wooden figure perched on top of the Monk's Peak.

The crags are linked by a series of footbridges that encompass the **Neue Felsenburg** (☎ 03501-581 00; adult/concession €1.50/0.50; ⊗ 9am-6pm), the 13th-century remains of a Saxon outpost. Centred on the **Basteibrücke**, that fortress was the site of a medieval catapult

replica stone-thrower and artefacts from
the period are displayed in the terrain. You
can pay into a can after 6pm and still gain
access.

During sieges, the bridges could be
released quickly, sending the attackers
plummeting to their deaths. The modern
visitor walkways are more fixed but pretty
transparent, so it's definitely not for those
afraid of heights.

There's a marked path leading down to
the riverside resort of Rathen (25 minutes),
with the lovely **Felsenbühne** (open-air theatre;
☎ 035024-7770) halfway up.

SLEEPING & EATING
There's only one hotel option inside the
park.

Berghotel Bastei (☎ 035024-7790; www.bastei
berghotel.de; s €41-44, d €33-56; **P** ☎) The GDR-
era Berghotel has comfy rooms and a decent
restaurant with superb views, plus extras
like bowling and sauna.

Otherwise, you can find rooms from
about €13 per person in **Lohmen** (Tourist office ☎ 03501-581 024; Schloss Lomen 1), a couple
of kilometres due northeast, or in **Rathen**
(☎ 035024-704 22; Füllhölzelweg 1).

GETTING THERE & AWAY
The nearest train station is Rathen, from
where it's a steep 25-minute walk to the top.
By bus, take the frequent No 236/23T from
Pirna train station (€1.50). There's also an
open-topped double-decker bus, the **Bastei-
Kraxler**, serving Königstein, Hohnstein and
Bad Schandau. In summer there's a shuttle
service between the inner and outer Bastei
parking lots (€0.50); otherwise it's a half-
hour walk from the main road.

If driving, follow the many brown signs
from Pirna, 12km southeast of Dresden, to
the turn-off.

Bad Schandau
☎ 035022 / pop 3300
Bad Schandau, a poky little spa town on the
Elbe just 5km north of the Czech border, is
a superb base for hikes. The private **tourist
office** (☎ 900 30; www.bad-schandau.de; Markt 12;
☼ 9am-7pm Mon-Fri, 9am-4pm Sat & Sun Easter-Oct,
9am-6pm Mon-Fri Nov-Easter) and the **Nationalparkhaus** (☎ 502 30; www.lanu.org; Dresdner Strasse
2B) are in the centre of town; there's also
an **office** (☎ 412 47; www.touristinfo-badschandau.de;

☼ 8am-6pm Apr-Oct, 9am-4pm Nov-Mar) in the
station.

At the southern end of town you'll find
the **Personenaufzug** (passenger lift; adult/concession
€2.50/1.50; ☼ 9am-7pm), which will whisk you
up a 50m-high tower for a commanding
view. The structure is linked via a 35m
footbridge to a pretty forest path that runs
partially along the ridge. You can also
save your euros and climb the hundreds
of steps up the hill, close to the tourist
office.

The **Kirnitzschtalbahn** is a museum-piece
tram that runs 7km northeast along the Kirnitzsch River to the **Lichtenhainer Wasserfall**,
a good spot to begin a hike along the sandstone cliffs so typical of the region. The line
was closed for repairs at time of research,
replaced by rather less fun buses (€1.50);
on reopening it should run at least hourly
in summer.

A favourite day trip for locals is to the
tiny community of **Hinterhermsdorf**, in a
remote cul-de-sac about 14km east of Bad
Schandau. Here you can hire flat-bottomed
boats on the Kirnitzsch River, which is lined
on either side by steep rock faces – you can't
feel much more secluded than this. Bus No
241 leaves from Bad Schandau every three
hours (€1.50, 45 minutes).

SLEEPING & EATING
Staff at the tourist offices will book **private
rooms** (from around €13 per person).

DJH hostel (☎ 424 08; Dorfstrasse 14, Ostrau; juniors/
seniors €16.40/19.10) Reachable by ferry, the DJH
Jugendherberge Bad Schandau is in the
nearby village of Ostrau.

Ostrauer Mühle (☎ 427 42; www.ostrauer-muehle
.de; adult/child €4.25/2.75, car/tent €1.75/2.75-3.75) This
camp site is on the Kirnitzsch River east of
town.

Lindenhof (☎ 4890; www.lindenhof-bad-schandau
.de; Rudolf-Sendig-Strasse 11; s €44-50, d €58-84; **P**)
This smart townhouse hotel has a good
traditional restaurant.

GETTING THERE & AWAY
There are trains to Dresden (€4.50, 50 minutes), Meissen (€6, 1¾ hours) and Prague
(two hours). The north–south B172 runs
right through town. Sächsische Dampfschiffahrt boats run twice daily between
Dresden and Bad Schandau (€14.50, 6½
hours).

MEISSEN

☎ 03521 / pop 29,000

Some 27km northwest of Dresden, Meissen is a compact, perfectly preserved old town and the centre of a rich wine-growing region, with red-tiled roofs reminiscent of coastal Croatia. Its medieval fortress, the Albrechtsburg, crowns a ridge high above the Elbe River and contains the former ducal palace and Meissen Cathedral, a magnificent Gothic structure. Augustus the Strong of Saxony created Europe's first porcelain factory here in 1710.

Like Dresden, the city was struck by record flood levels in 2002, with water pushing quite a distance into the Altstadt. Look out for plaques marking the highest points.

Meissen celebrates its 1075th anniversary in 2004, with a busy programme of events from April to December.

Orientation

Meissen straddles the Elbe, with the old town on the western bank and the train station on the eastern. The bridge behind the station is the quickest way across and presents you with a picture-postcard view of the river and the Altstadt.

From the bridge, continue up Obergasse, then bear right through Hahnemannsplatz and Rossplatz to the Markt, the town's central square.

Sächsische Dampfschiffahrt boats arrive and depart from the landing on the west side of the Elbe, about 300m east of the Markt.

Information

Commerzbank (☎ 410 90; Hauptbahnhof)
Internet café (☎ 407 852; Burgstrasse 9; €4 per hr)
Sparkasse (☎ 752 9776; cnr Dresdner Strasse & Bahnhofstrasse)
Tourist information (☎ 419 40; www.touristinfo-meissen.de; Markt 3; ☒ 10am-6pm Mon-Fri, 10am-4pm Sat & Sun Apr-Oct, 9am-5pm Mon-Fri, 10am-3pm Sat Nov-Mar)

Sights & Activities

On the Markt (square) are the **Rathaus** (1472) and the 15th-century **Frauenkirche** (☎ 453 832; tower entry adult/concession €1/0.50; ☒ 10am-noon & 1-5pm May-Oct). The church's tower (1549) has a porcelain carillon which chimes every quarter-hour, contrasting strangely with

the church's traditional bells. Climb the tower for fine views of Meissen's Altstadt; pick up the key in the church or from the adjacent *Pfarrbüro* (parish office).

Steep stepped lanes lead up to the **Albrechtsburg**, with its towering medieval **Dom** (Cathedral; ☎ 452 490; Domplatz 7; adult/concession €2/1.50; ☒ 10am-6pm Mar-Oct, 10am-4pm Nov-Feb) containing an altarpiece by Lucas Cranach the Elder. Beside the Dom is the remarkable 15th-century **palace** (☎ 470 70; Domplatz 1; adult/concession €3.50/2.50; ☒ 10am-6pm Mar-Oct, 10am-5pm Nov-Feb, closed Jan 10-31), widely seen as the birthplace of Schloss architecture, with its ingenious system of internal arches. A combined ticket for both buildings costs €5/2.50.

Meissen has long been renowned for its chinaware, with its trademark insignia of blue crossed swords. The Albrechtsburg palace was originally the manufacturing site, but the **Porzellan Manufaktur** (Porcelain Factory; ☎ 468 700; Talstrasse 9; collection adult/concession €4.50/4, workshop €3; ☒ 9am-6pm May-Oct, 9am-5pm Nov-Apr) is now 1km southwest of the Altstadt in an appropriately beautiful building dating from 1916. There are often long queues for the workshop demonstrations, but you can view the porcelain collection upstairs at your leisure. A highlight here is the 3.6m-high 'table-top temple' on the 2nd floor, built for Prince Elector Augustus II in 1749.

Tours

From April to October the **tourist office** runs daily 1½-hour guided tours (adult/concession €4/2) at 1pm and evening walks with costumed staff every Wednesday (adult/concession €5/4). The local **transport authority** (☎ 741 60; www.vg-meissen.de) also offers CityBus tours (adult/concession €3.60/2.50).

Sleeping

Budget accommodation is fairly scarce, but Meissen-Information can often find **private rooms** (from around €15 per person).

Jugendgästehaus (☎ 453 065; Wilsdrufferstrasse 28; dm €12) This non-DJH place is about 20 minutes' walk south of the Markt. Call first – if the place is full they say so on their answering machine.

Pension Schweizerhaus (☎ 457 162; www.schweizerhaus-meissen.de; Rauhentalstrasse 1; r €28-57; P) Near the porcelain factory, this yellow half-

mbered house does have a certain Swiss
ir about it.

Mercure Grand Hotel Meissen (☎ 722 50; h1699@
:corhotels.com; Hafenstrasse 27-31; s/d €52/66, ste €120;
P **⊠**) It comes as something of a shock to
ind out that this palatial building on the
ast bank is actually a Mercure chain hotel.
'or once you can't complain about any lack
f individuality!

Hotel Burgkeller (☎ 414 00; burgkeller@meis
en-hotel.com; Domplatz 11; s/d €69/115; **P**) This
uxury hill-top option has everything you
ould want – commanding views, glori-
us beer garden and cathedral-adjacent
ocation.

Hotel Am Markt Residenz (☎ 415 10; residenz@
neissen-hotel.com; An der Frauenkirche 1; s €60, d €95-125;
P) This smart, stately hotel, along with its
sister Am Markt 6, offers classic rooms with
multiple shades of green and all kinds of art
around the place. The rock-hewn wine cellar here is particularly atmospheric.

Eating

Gaststätte Winkelkrug (☎ 453 711; Schlossberg
13; mains €4-7.50; ⏱ evenings only, Wed-Sun) This
quaint wine house is near the Albrechtsburg, in a lovely old building with a flourishing garden section.

Grüner Humpen (☎ 453 382; Burgstrasse 15; mains
€4.70-9.40) On your way up the hill, you can
stop here for home-style German cooking.

Domkeller (☎ 457 676; Domplatz 9; mains €6.60-
12.40) Meissen's oldest restaurant offers
breathtaking terrace views over town and
good local dishes; the menu's even 'translated' into Saxon.

Pfeffersack (☎ 404 819; Webergasse; mains €7.70-
13.80) This typical touristy medieval theme
joint is worth a look, if only to try the

FUMMEL VISION

While you're in Meissen it's virtually compulsory to try the peculiar local patisserie
known as the *Meissner Fummel*. Resembling an ostrich egg made of very delicate
pastry, legend has it the Fummel was invented in 1710 as a test to stop the royal
courier from drinking between deliveries –
great care is required if you want to get it
home in one piece! Test your skills at the
150-year-old **Café Zieger** (Burgstrasse), by
the foot of the Rote Stufen.

---

charmingly named *Arschleder* (beef with
beetroot and pickle).

Weinschänke Vincenz Richter (☎ 453 285; An
der Frauenkirche 12; mains €6.80-17; ⊠) A classy
Romantik-Restaurant, with veranda, full
cheese menu and torture chamber making
for atmosphere a-plenty.

Getting There & Away

Half-hourly S-Bahn trains run from Dresden's Hauptbahnhof and Neustadt train
stations (€4.80, 45 minutes). To visit the
porcelain factory, get off at Meissen-
Triebischtal (one stop after Meissen).

A more interesting way to get here is by
steamer (between May and September).
Boats leave from the Sächsische Dampfschiffahrt dock in Dresden at 9.15am and
head back at 3pm (€15 return, two hours).

WESTERN SAXONY

CHEMNITZ

☎ 0371 / pop 250,000

Chemnitz (pronounced *kem*-nits), in the
northern Erzgebirge 80km southwest of
Dresden, is used to being called names.
Its smokestack industries prompted the
nickname of 'Saxon Manchester' in the
19th century, and the GDR dubbed it
'Karl-Marx-Stadt' in 1953, although the
great communist theorist had little in
common with the place. The city still bears
the heavy stamp of Stalinist planning, but
some interesting new architecture and a few
Renaissance gems have helped to restore
its humanity, and there's some exciting
new development going on in the central
'Mittelstandsmeile', due for completion by
the end of 2004.

Orientation

The River Chemnitz flows south to north
along the western side of the Altstadt. The
Markt and the Rathaus lie 1km southwest
of the train station along Strasse der Nationen, while the bus station is just down
Georgstrasse, on the western side.

Information

INTERNET ACCESS

Surf Inn (☎ 666 3340; Galeria Kaufhof, Am Rathaus 1;
€3 per hr)

Vobis (☎ 533 6515; Roter Turm Galerie; €1.80 per hr)

INTERNET RESOURCES
Chemnitz home page (www.chemnitz.de)

LAUNDRY
SB Waschsalon (Hartmannstrasse; €3.50)

MONEY
SpardaBank (☎ 030-4208 0420; Hauptbahnhof)
Sparkasse (Am Markt 5)

POST
Main post office (cnr Posthof & Strasse der Nationen)

TOURIST INFORMATION
Chemnitz Service (☎ 690 680; www.chemnitz
-tourismus.de; Markt 1; ☖ 9.30am-5.30pm Mon-Fri)

TRAVEL AGENCIES
Reisecenter Alltours (☎ 242 880; Rathauspassage)
Multipurpose centre with travel library, multimedia area
and cocktail bar.

Sights
THEATERPLATZ
Head south on Strasse der Nationen and
you'll reach Theaterplatz, home to the
gentle opera house and the hulking König
Albert Museum, containing the Museum für
Naturkunde (Natural History Museum; ☎ 488 4551;
naturkundemuseum@stadt-chemnitz.de; Theaterplatz 1;
adult/concession €5/2.50; ☖ 9am-noon & 2-5pm Tue, Thu
& Fri, 9am-noon & 2-7.30pm Wed, 11am-5pm Sat & Sun).
The Versteinerter Wald (Petrified Forest)
display is outside its east wing; some of the
stony trunks are 250 million years old.

The same building houses the Kunstsammlungen (Chemnitz Art Gallery; ☎ 488 4424; kunst
sammlungen@stadt-chemnitz.de; adult/concession €3/2;
☖ noon-7pm Tue-Sun). Exhibits include graphic
art and works by local artist Karl Schmidt-
Rottluff, a noted expressionist painter
and founding member of the Die Brücke
group.

AM ROTEN TURM
Further down Strasse der Nationen, turn
right onto Brückenstrasse and you'll see a
two-storey bronze head of Karl Marx (1971) by
Soviet artist Lew Kerbel. Behind it there's
an oppressive GDR office building with
a giant frieze exhorting 'Workers of all
countries, unite!'.

Turn around and look across the square,
past the Stadthalle/Hotel Mercure complex,
to one of the city's oldest defence towers, the
handsome 12th-century Roter Turm (☖ 11a
5pm Sat & Sun). Directly behind it is the ne
Galerie Roter Turm shopping mall, which re
injects contemporary Deco levity into th
bleak surroundings.

MARKT
Head left around the Galerie to the bustlin
Markt in the shadow of the Altes Rathaus, a
imposing white 15th-century building wit
a Renaissance portal. Musical chimes pla
several times a day (at some length), whil
revolving figures come and go in the win
dow above the door.

Next door are the Hoher Turm and th
Neues Rathaus, with some lovely Art Deco
features in the foyer. Enter the east side and
you'll see a marble fountain – turn around
and look up at the painted gallery, with its
vaults of ochre and grey leaves. The adjacent Jakobikirche is a Gothic church topped
by a neat roof turret and updated with an
Art Deco façade.

MARKTHALLE
This riverside district on the western edge
of the Altstadt features a renovated warehouse (now an informal shopping mall)
and former docks that are a testament to
creative uses of old buildings.

SCHLOSS AREA
Across the river, the Schlossteich is a large
park-ringed pond, with a music pavilion for
summer concerts. Towering over it is the
Schlosskirche (☖ 10am-5pm Tue-Sat, 2.30-5.30pm
Sun), a 12th-century Benedictine monastery
later recast into a weighty Gothic hall
church. Its treasures include Hans Witten's
intriguing sculpture Christ at the Column
(1515). Just south of the church stands the
reconstructed Schloss itself, which houses
the Schlossbergmuseum (☎ 488 4501; Schlossberg
12; adult/concession €3/1.80; ☖ 11am-5pm Tue-Fri,
11am-6pm Sat & Sun Apr-Sep, 11am-4pm Tue-Fri, 11am-
5pm Sat & Sun Oct-Mar). The vaulted interior is
actually better than the displays.

Sleeping
All hotels have cheaper weekend rates –
just ask.

Pension am Zöllnerplatz (☎ 425 986; www.pension
-zoellnerplatz.de; Mühlenstrasse 108; s/d €35/50) This
3rd-floor pension is in a nice location north
of the centre.

Hotel Sächsischer Hof (☎ 461 480; www.saech scher-hof.de; Brühl 26; s/d €55/75; **P**) A decent mid-ange option a couple of blocks down from the bus station.

Hotel Chemnitzer Hof (☎ 6840; chemnitzer.hof@ ennewig.de; Strasse der Nationen 56; s €82-92, d 08-126; **P** ⊠) Like its cheaper sister the uropa down the road, this excellent four-ar establishment looks a bit stolid from the outside but has some great views over heaterplatz. Bauhaus-style interiors and n open terrace make this a top choice.

ating & Drinking

uszta Csárda (☎ 240 4505; Hartmannstrasse 7c; mains 5.90-9.50) A good simple Hungarian restau-ant catering for a discerning local crowd.

Schalom (☎ 695 7769; www.schalom-chemnitz.de; arolastrasse 7; mains €6.25-16.50; ⊗ closed Fri) You on't see many kosher restaurants in Ger-nany, but this one is well worth seeking ut, with a varied menu including *blinz*, ouscous and some interesting desserts.

Ausspanne (☎ 330 0225; Schlossberg 4; mains 7.40-17.90) One of a cluster of smart options t the foot of the castle hill, this lovely half-imbered house has a good fish menu and ine Saxon dishes.

Ratskeller (☎ 694 9875; Markt 1; mains €7.80-19.50) This atmospheric place is wildly popular for uge portions of local cuisine, and has over 20 dishes on the menu! You can choose etween rustic and sophisticated sections, nd the painted, vaulted ceilings are so gor-eous you may want to eat them too.

Buschfunk (☎ 631 366; www.buschfunk-online.de; schopauer Strasse 48) With 22m of bar, 350 cock-ails and 77 nonalcoholic mixed drinks, this s an essential stop on any pub crawl.

Getting There & Around

Chemnitz is on the Nuremberg–Dresden ine, with IC and regional trains to Dres-len (€10.70, 1½ hours), Leipzig (€12.40, ½ hours), Prague (€50-60, 4¾ hours via Dresden), Nuremberg (€42.80, four hours) nd Berlin (€28.40, 3½ hours). The auto-ahn A4 (Bad Hersfeld–Dresden) runs outh of town, where the A72 (Munich) riginates.

On public transport, single tickets cost 1.40, and a day ticket costs just €3. The egular City Bus (No 77) circles the city rom the Hauptbahnhof, stopping at the Rathaus and several other main sights.

AUGUSTUSBURG
☎ 037291 / pop 5345

If you need a break from all that Stalinist architecture, take an afternoon – or maybe a few days – to cool your heels at Augustus-burg, 13km east of Chemnitz. Its medieval palace, on a steep mountain overlooking forests and rapeseed meadows, is one of those relatively undiscovered gems people rave about, with friendly locals to boot.

Orientation & Information

All the sights and the old town are on the mountain. The **Drahtseilbahn** (Funicular; ☎ 202 65) station from Erdmannsdorf is located just southwest of the Schloss.

The **tourist office** (☎ 395 50; www.augustusburg .de; Marienberger Strasse 24; ⊗ 9am-noon & 1-5pm Mon-Fri) sells the useful Wanderwege (hiking) map of routes – easy and strenuous – in Augustusburg and environs (€3.75). Slip into your walking gear and enjoy a look around this stunning unspoiled area.

Sights & Activities

The town's big draw is the oversized **Schloss** (☎ 380 18; augustusburg-schloss@t-online.de; combined museum ticket adult/concession €6.15/4.65; ⊗ 9am-6pm Apr-Oct, 10am-5pm Nov-Mar). The summer resi-dence of the Elector August (1526–86), the great-great-great grandfather of Saxon ruler Augustus the Strong, this sprawling com-plex was built in just four years by Leipzig mayor and architect Hieronymus Lotter.

You'll also find the **Motorradmuseum** here, which houses Germany's largest collection of motorcycles, 170 in all, including clas-sic Horch, NSU and BMW roadsters and some very rare models. In the outer court-yard is the former castle stables, now the **Kutschenmuseum**, with some of the snootiest horse-drawn coaches you'll ever see. In the upper floors of the Schloss you'll find the **Hasenhaus**, with displays of hunting and game shown in dioramas and antler-filled rooms.

The **Schlosskirche**, which boasts an altar-piece by Lucas Cranach the Younger, can only be visited on a **castle tour** (€2.60/1.90). You also have to pay separately to climb the **Aussichtsturm** (€1), for views clear across the region.

Outside the north entrance is the **Adler-und Falkenhof** (Falconry; demonstrations adult/concession €5/4.50; ⊗ 11am & 3pm Tue-Sun Mar-Oct), with owls,

SAXONY

buzzards, eagles, and other trained hunting birds. You can sneak a peek at the feathered beauties on their perches from the moat bridge.

If it's all just too stately, you may get some relief at the **Sommerrodelbahn** (☎ 124 50; 1/5/10 trips €1.80/7.50/13), a 577m metal luge track with some demon curves. In winter it's a slalom course. Enter by the Drahtseilbahn station.

Sleeping & Eating

DJH hostel (☎ 202 56; jhaugustusburg@djh-sachsen .de; Schloss Augustusburg; juniors/seniors €14.90/17.60) Right in the Schloss, the recently renovated DJH Jugendherberge Augustusburg is a delight which has dorms once slept in by knights.

Hotel Waldfrieden (☎ 203 79; www.hotel-waldfrie den-augustusburg.de; Schlossweg 2; s/d €40/57; **P**) The friendly Siefert family welcomes you, halfway between the Drahtseilbahn and the Schloss. The restaurant is also fine, with a nice seafood menu.

Hotel Waldhaus (☎ 203 17; www.hotel-waldhaus .de; Am Kurplatz 7; s €44-52, d €62-72; **P**) This is professionally run Schloss-like hotel is in a lovely wooded setting at the edge of town.

Bäckerei Fischer (Untere Schlossstrasse 4) A tiny overhanging terrace cobbled on to this small local bakery provides some of the best views you'll get across the surrounding countryside.

Zur alten Post (☎ 606 37; Hohe Strasse 7; mains €4.95-13; ⊙ Wed-Mon) On Mondays, when everything else closes, this neighbourhood place has good cheap local specialities and pizza, as well as another great rear terrace.

Gasthof Landsknecht (☎ 685 77; Markt 1; mains €6.50-9) A rustic, vault-ceilinged restaurant stressing game dishes and *Rauchemad*, a weird dessert made of potatoes, sugar, cinnamon and apple sauce.

Augustuskeller (☎ 207 40; mains €7.90-12.30) Situated in the Schloss courtyard, this is the medieval option, with lots of tasty game, traditional Saxon fare and, um, pasta.

Getting There & Away

Trains run from Chemnitz to Erdmannsdorf (€2.30, 20 minutes), from where you take the Drahtseilbahn to Augustusburg (€2.10, eight minutes). Motorists should take the B180, which skirts Chemnitz and goes right past the castle.

LEIPZIG

☎ 0341 / pop 493,000

In Goethe's *Faust* a character named Frosc calls Leipzig 'a little Paris'. He was wrong Leipzig is more fun and infinitely less self important than the Gallic capital. It's a important business and transport centre a trade-fair mecca, and arguably the mos dynamic city in eastern Germany.

Leipzig became known as the *Stadt de Helden*, City of Heroes, for its leadin, role in the 1989 democratic revolution Its residents organised protests against th communist regime in May of that year; b October, hundreds of thousands were tak ing to the streets, placing candles on th steps of Stasi headquarters and attendin, peace services at St Nicholas Church.

By the time the secret police got roun to pulping their files, Leipzigers were party ing in the streets, and they still haven' stopped – from late winter street-side cafés open their terraces, and countless bars and nightclubs keep the beat going through the night.

Leipzig also has some of the finest classical music and opera in the country, and its art and literary scenes are flourishing. It was once home to Bach, Wagner and Mendelssohn, and to Goethe, who set a key scene of *Faust* in the cellar of his favourite watering hole. And the university still attracts students from all over the world. It's the kind of city you just can't help liking.

The big news for Leipzig, however, is its strong Olympic bid for 2012, which is gleefully backed by chancellor Gerhard Schröder and looks set to rocket the city to international stardom alongside Berlin, Munich and Frankfurt, as well as boosting the Saxon economy by millions of euros. Big things are expected here in the next few years, and we can only recommend that you get a piece of the action.

Orientation

Leipzig's city centre lies within a ring road that outlines the town's medieval fortifications. To reach the city centre from the Hauptbahnhof, cross Willy-Brandt-Platz and continue south along Nikolaistrasse for five minutes; the central Markt is a couple of blocks southwest.

The impressive 26-platform Hauptbahnhof (1915, renovated 1998) isn't just the largest passenger terminus in Europe, but it also houses a fabulous three-storey shopping mall with more than 150 shops (many open on Sunday). It's probably the only station on the planet where it's genuinely fun to shop, despite the hideously expensive toilets (€1.10!). Outside the southern entrance is the central tram terminus.

The vast Augustusplatz, three blocks east of the Markt, is ex-socialist Leipzig, dominated by the boxy designs of the university (due for reconstruction), Neues Gewandhaus concert hall and opera house.

Leipzig's dazzling Neue Messe (trade fairgrounds) are 5km north of the Hauptbahnhof (take tram No 16).

The Leipzig-Halle airport is 20km to the north of the city (see Getting Around p193).

Information
BOOKSHOPS
Hugendubel (☎ 226 240; Petersstrasse 12-14) Three floors of books, including foreign-language novels.

CULTURAL CENTRES
Amerika Haus (☎ 2133 8420; Wilhelm-Seyfferth-Strasse 4)
British Council (☎ 564 6712; Lumumbastrasse 11-13)

DISCOUNT CARDS
Leipzig Card (1/3 days €5.90/11.50) Free or discounted admission to attractions, plus free travel on public transport.

EMERGENCY
Police station (☎ 9660; Dimitroff Strasse 5)

INTERNET ACCESS
Copytel.de (☎ 993 8999; Grimmaischer Strasse 23; €2.50 per hr)
Highway-Five (☎ 225 2840; Nürnberger Strasse 5; €1.25 per 30 min)
Le Bit Café (☎ 998 2020; Kohlgartenstrasse 2; €2.50 per hr) Drinks, lounge chairs and sand on the floor!
Surf Inn (☎ 224 5195; Galeria Kaufhof, Neumarkt 1; €3 per hr)
Webcafé (☎ 0700-1999 3000; www.netladen.com; Reichsstrasse 18; €2.60 per hr)

LAUNDRY
Maga Pon (☎ 993 8798; Gottschedstrasse 11; wash/dry €3.50/0.50) Combination laundry and hip café.
Schnell und Sauber (Dresdner Strasse 19; €3)

LIBRARIES
Deutsche Bücherei (☎ 227 10; Deutscher Platz 1; 📖) One of the two largest German-language libraries in the world.
University library (☎ 973 0577; Beethovenstrasse 6; 📖) Good for periodicals and foreign-language books.

MEDICAL SERVICES
Doctor (☎ 192 92; 🕑 7pm-7am)
Krankenhaus St Georg (☎ 909 00; Delitzscher Strasse 141) Take tram No 16 to this hospital.
Löwenapotheke (☎ 960 5027; Grimmaischer Strasse 19)
University clinic (☎ 971 08; Liebigstrasse 21) Hospital and clinic.

MONEY
Reisebank (☎ 980 4588; Lower Level, south hall, Hauptbahnhof)

POST
Main post office (Augustusplatz 1)
Station branch (Hauptbahnhof)

TOURIST INFORMATION
ADAC (☎ 211 0551; Augustusplatz 5-6)
Leipzig Tourist Service (☎ 710 4260; www.leipzig.de; Richard-Wagner-Strasse 1; 🕑 9am-7pm Mon-Fri, 9am-4pm Sat, 9am-2pm Sun) Information, accommodation and tours (€6 to €8).

TRAVEL AGENCIES
Atlas Reisen (☎ 251 8959; Hauptbahnhof)
Campus Travel (☎ 211 1901; www.campustravel.de; Universitätsstrasse 20)
Reisebüro Arcadia (☎ 211 0777; service@arcadia-travel.de; Dittrichring 1)
Thomas Cook (☎ 211 5032; leipzig@thomascook.de; Nikolaistrasse 42)

Dangers & Annoyances
Don't leave any valuables in your car, as there is plenty of smash-and-grab theft.

Sights
BACH MUSEUM
Opposite the St Thomas Church, in a baroque house, is the **Bach Museum** (☎ 964 110; Thomaskirchhof 16; adult/concession €3/2; 🕑 10am-5pm), which focuses on the composer's life in Leipzig: the Matthäus Passion, Johannes Passion, Weihnachts Oratorium and the h-Moll Messe, among others, were written here. There are portraits, manuscripts and other Bach memorabilia. Guided tours are given in German (11am and 3pm, €4.50).

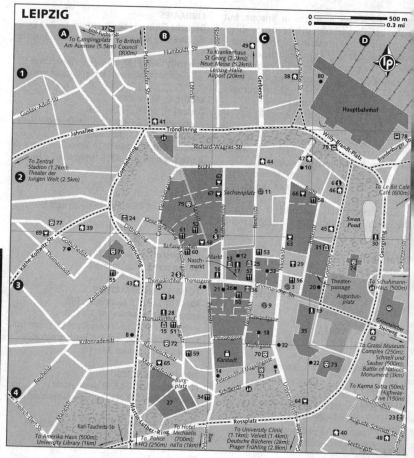

MENDELSSOHN-HAUS & SCHUMANN-HAUS

Two other important composers have museums dedicated to them in Leipzig: Felix Mendelssohn Bartholdy, who lived (and died) in the **Mendelssohn-Haus** (☎ 127 0294; www.mendelssohn-stiftung.de; Goldschmidtstrasse 12; ☼ 10am-6pm); and Robert Schumann, who spent the first four years of his marriage to Leipzig pianist Clara Wieck in the **Schumann-Haus** (☎ 393 9620; www.schumann-verein.de; Inselstrasse 18; ☼ 2-5pm Wed-Sat).

MUSEUM DER BILDENDEN KÜNSTE

Housed temporarily in the Handelshof is the **Museum de Bildenden Künste** (☎ 216 990; Grimmaische Strasse 1-7; adult/concession €2.50/1;

☼ 10am-6pm Tue & Thu-Sun, 1-8pm Wed), with an excellent fine arts collection of old masters. A grand new site is being built on Sachsenplatz; it was originally scheduled for completion in March 2003, but at the current rate of progress it may just about be finished by the time you read this.

ZEITGESCHICHTLICHES FORUM

Opened in 1999, the haunting and uplifting **Zeitgeschichtliches Forum** (Forum of Contemporary History; ☎ 222 20; Grimmaische Strasse 6; ☼ 9am-6pm Tue-Fri, 10am-6pm Sat & Sun) depicts the history of the GDR from division and dictatorship to resistance and demise. You can see legendary harsh GDR cleaning products and video clips of families stifling tears as the Berlin Wall was

INFORMATION
ADAC..(see 42)
Campus Travel..................................**1** C4
Commerzbank....................................**2** B3
Copytel.de.......................................**3** C2
Deutsche Bank.................................(see 54)
Hugendubel.....................................**4** B3
HypoVereinsbank..............................**5** C3
Leipzig Tourist Service.....................**6** D2
Löwenapotheke................................(see 3)
Maga Pon...**7** A3
Reisebüro Arcadia............................**8** B3
Surf Inn...**9** C3
Thomas Cook..................................**10** C2
Webcafe...**11** C2

SIGHTS & ACTIVITIES   (pp185–90)
Alte Börse.......................................**12** C3
Altes Rathaus..................................**13** C3
arko (Café Richter)...........................**14** C4
Bach Museum..................................**15** B3
Egyptian Museum...........................(see 59)
GDR Diorama..................................**16** C3
Goethe Statue.................................**17** C3
Handelshof....................................(see 25)
Innenhof Passage...........................**18** C3
Karl Marx Diorama..........................**19** D3
Kroch Haus.....................................**20** D3
Königshaus Passage........................**21** C3
MDR Tower.....................................**22** D4
Mendelssohn-Haus...........................**23** D4
Ministerium für Staatssicherheit or Stasi.**24** B2
Museum der Bildenden Künste.........**25** C3
Mädlerpassage................................**26** C3
Neues Rathaus.................................**27** B4
New Bach Memorial.........................**28** B3
Nikolaikirche...................................**29** C3
Richard Wagner Statue.....................**30** D2
Royal Palace....................................**31** D2
Schinkelturm...................................**32** C4
Specks Hof......................................**33** C3
Thomaskirche..................................**34** B3
Universität Leipzig............................**35** C3
Zeitgeschichtliches Forum (GDR
  Museum)......................................**36** C3
Zoo...**37** A1

SLEEPING   (pp190–1)
Holiday Inn Garden Court.................**38** C1
Hostel Sleepy Lion............................**39** A2
Hotel Adagio...................................**40** D4
Hotel Fürstenhof..............................**41** B1
Hotel Mercure.................................**42** D3
Kosmos-Hotel..................................**43** B3
Marriott Leipzig...............................**44** C2
Mitwohnzentrale & Mitfahrzentrale...**45** D2
Novotel..**46** D2
Seaside Park Hotel...........................**47** D2
Weisses Ross...................................**48** D4
Westin Leipzig.................................**49** C1

EATING   (p191)
Auerbachs Keller..............................**50** C3
Bachstübl & Café Concerto...............**51** B3
Barthel's Hof...................................**52** B2
Café Riquet.....................................**53** C3
Escados Steakhouse & Bar................**54** C4
Koslik...**55** B3
Medici..**56** C3
Mövenpick......................................**57** C3
Ratskeller.....................................(see 27)
Retschenka......................................**58** D2
Thüringer Hof.................................**59** B4
Zill's Tunnel....................................**60** B3
Zum Arabischen Coffe Baum............**61** B3

DRINKING   (pp191–2)
Blaue Trude.....................................**62** C3
Bounce 87.......................................**63** C3
Cocktail Bars..................................(see 7)
Mephisto Bar.................................(see 50)
Milchbar......................................(see 43)
Moritz-Bastei...................................**64** C4
Nachtcafe.......................................**65** B4
New Orleans....................................**66** C2
Rosa Linde....................................(see 58)
Sixtina..**67** C2
Spizz..**68** B3
Vodkaria...**69** A3

ENTERTAINMENT   (pp192–3)
Academixer.....................................**70** C4
Krystallpalast..................................**71** C4
Leipziger Pfeffermühle.....................**72** B4
Neues Gewandhaus..........................**73** D4
Opernhaus......................................**74** D3
Passage Kinos.................................**75** B2
SanftWut.....................................(see 26)
Schauspielhaus...............................**76** B3
Theater Neue Szene.........................**77** A2

TRANSPORT   (pp193–4)
Bus Station.....................................**78** D2
Tram Stop.......................................**79** D2
Zweirad Eckhardt............................**80** D1

OTHER
Galeria Kaufhof.............................(see 9)

built between them, and it's hard not to feel moved by the Gentle Revolution that started right here in Leipzig. An English-language pamphlet translates the main captions.

STASI MUSEUM
Even more chilling is the former headquarters of the East German secret police, the **Ministerium für Staatssicherheit** (Stasi; ☎ 961 2443; Dittrichring 24; ⏱ 10am-6pm). It's in the building known as the Runde Ecke (Round Corner) and is now a museum.

At the front are photographs of demonstrations in October and November 1989, and of Lieutenant General Manfred Hummitsch, the former Stasi head in Leipzig. Inside are exhibits on propaganda, preposterous disguises, surveillance photos and mounds of papier-mâché created when officers shredded and soaked secret documents before the fall of the GDR. Bus tours to the Stasi **bunker** outside town are available.

EGYPTIAN MUSEUM
Recently moved to an interim location, the university's **Egyptian Museum** (☎ 973 7010; www.uni-leipzig.de/~egypt; Burgstrasse 21; adult/concession €2/1; ⏱ 1-5pm Tue-Sat, 10am-1pm Sun) has more than 9000 Egyptian antiquities, making it one of the most important collections of its type in Europe. Displays include stone vessels from the first half of the third millennium BC, Nubian decorative arts and sarcophagi.

GRASSI MUSEUM COMPLEX
This large university complex on Täubchenweg, just east of Augustusplatz, is currently being renovated, and should reopen around the beginning of 2005. When completed, the new Grassi will reunite the **Museum für Völkerkunde** (Ethnological Museum; ☎ 268 9568; www.mvl-grassimuseum.de; Mädlerpassage, Grimmaische Strasse 2-4; adult/concession €2/1; ⏱ 10am-6pm Tue-Fri, 10am-5pm Sat & Sun), the **Musikinstrumenten-Museum** (☎ 687 0790; www.musikmuseum.org; Thomaskirchhof 20; adult/concession €3/1.50; ⏱ 11am-5pm Tue-Sun) and the **Museum für Kunsthandwerk** (Craft Museum; ☎ 213 3719; Neumarkt 20; adult/concession €4/3; ⏱ 10am-6pm Tue, Thu & Sun, 10am-8pm Wed). For updates click onto www.grassimuseum.de.

ZOO
Northwest of the Hauptbahnhof is Leipzig's **zoo** (☎ 593 3500; www.zoo-leipzig.de; Pfaffendorfer Strasse 29; adult/concession €9/5; ⏱ 9am-7pm May-Sep, 9am-6pm Apr & Oct, 9am-5pm Nov-Feb), renowned for its breeding of lions and tigers.

BATTLE OF NATIONS MONUMENT
Southeast of the centre is Leipzig's monolithic 1913 **Völkerschlachtdenkmal** (www.voelkerschlachtdenkmal-leipzig.org; adult/concession €2.50/1.25;

⊕ 10am-6pm Apr-Oct, 10am-4pm Nov-Mar). This 91m-high monument commemorates the decisive victory here by the combined Prussian, Austrian and Russian forces over Napoleon's army 100 years earlier; its 90th birthday in 2003 was celebrated with a series of events around the city.

GALERIE EIGEN+ART

Founded in Leipzig in 1983, the private **Galerie Eigen+Art** (☎ 960 7886; www.eigen-art.com; Ferdinand-Rhode-Strasse 14; ⊕ 11am-6pm Tue-Sat) has an international reputation for championing work by contemporary artists. There is a sister gallery in Berlin, and temporary exhibitions have been held everywhere from Weimar to Tokyo.

Historic Centre Walking Tour

This 4km circuit starts at the Markt and moves clockwise to Augustusplatz before exploring the attractive south of the old quarter. It's a 1½-hour walk, but will take the best part of a day if you make all the stops.

On the Markt, the Renaissance **Altes Rathaus** (**1**; 1556), one of Germany's most stunning town halls, houses the **City History Museum** (☎ 965 130; Markt 1; adult/child €2.50/2; ⊕ 10am-6pm Tue-Sun).

At the southern end of the square is a bronze **GDR diorama (2)** depicting the march of history, from oppressed medieval workers on the left to emancipated socialist man and woman, the apex of civilisation, on the right.

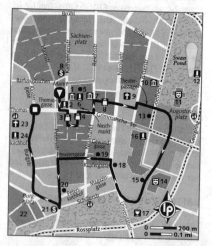

KÖNIGSHAUS & MÄDLER PASSAGES

Move south across the street and you'll enter the orange baroque **Apelshaus (3**; 1606–07) with its lovely bay windows. It's now a contemporary shopping mall known as the Königshaus Passage, but in its heyday overnight guests included Peter the Great and Napoleon.

Königshaus Passage leads directly into the **Mädlerpassage (4)**, which must be one of the world's most beautiful shopping centres. A mix of neo-Renaissance and Art Nouveau, it opened as a trade hall in 1914 and was renovated at great expense in the early 1990s. Today it's home to shops, restaurants, cafés and, most notably, Auerbachs Keller (see Eating p191). There are statues of Faust, Mephistopheles and some students at the northern exit; according to tradition you should touch Faust's foot for good luck.

NASCHMARKT

Turn north out of the Mädler Passage and you'll reach the **Naschmarkt** or snack market, which is dominated by the **Alte Börse (5**; ☎ 961 0368; ⊕ Mon-Fri by appointment), an ornate former trading house (1687). In front is a **statue of Goethe (6**; 1903), who studied law at Leipzig University. Today the Alte Börse is a cultural centre, with concerts, plays and readings throughout the year, and the courtyard is a wonderful place for a drink on sunny afternoons. On your right is the **Handelshof (7)**, the old trade hall, which temporarily houses the **Museum der Bildenden Künste (6**; Museum of Fine Arts; see p186).

From the Naschmarkt, continue east along Grimmaische Strasse and turn left down a corridor toward **Specks Hof (8)**, another shopping arcade. You'll pass a water basin that functions as an upside-down bell; ring it by wetting your hands with the water and running them back and forth over two pommels. If you hit it right, the water starts to fizz. **Specks Hof** itself contains a beautiful series of tile and stained glass reliefs by Halle artist Moritz Götze.

NIKOLAIKIRCHE

At the eastern portal of Specks Hof you'll see the 1165 **Nikolaikirche (9**; St Nicholas Church; ☎ 960 5270; ⊕ 10am-6pm). Begun in Romanesque style, it was enlarged and converted to late Gothic, with an amazing classical interior. More recently, the church was the chief meeting point for peaceful demonstrators from May 1989, shortly before the GDR imploded. A pamphlet tells the story of 600 party members who were sent to the church to break up the services, but ended up listening to the sermon and joining the protesters. The church still runs 'Swords to Ploughshares' services on Monday at 5pm.

AUGUSTUSPLATZ

Carry on east through the Theaterpassage to reach **Augustusplatz**, Leipzig's cultural nerve centre. The glass structures (lifts to the underground car park) glow at night, lending the concrete slabs some much-needed warmth. Pivot left to see the neoclassical **Royal Palace (10)**, now a university building.

To the north is the functional **Opernhaus (11;** opera house; 1956–60), with a **statue of Richard Wagner (12)** out the back. To the west, the 11-storey **Kroch Haus (13)** was Leipzig's first 'skyscraper' and now houses part of the university's art collection. Topped by a clock and two muscular bronze sentries who bash the bell at regular intervals, the Latin motto reads 'Work conquers all'. At the southern end of the square are the modern, heroic **Neues Gewandhaus (14;** 1981), home to the city's classical and jazz concerts, and the **MDR tower (15;** lift €1.50), built in 1970 and occupied by the Mitteldeutscher Rundfunk broadcasting company. A new concert hall is currently under construction at its base.

Stop a moment to admire, on the west side of the square at the Leipzig University entrance, another revolting bronze **diorama (16)**, this one depicting Karl Marx. The red steel A-frame around the diorama is a **monument** to St Paul's Church (Paulinerkirche), which stood on this site. Leipzigers have never quite forgiven the church's destruction during WWII.

Moving south between the Gewandhaus and the MDR tower, you'll arrive at the **Moritz-Bastei (17)**, the stone fortress cellar that is surely Europe's largest student club (see Clubs p192). Swinging around to the right, up Universitätsstrasse, is the **Schinkeltor (18)**, a mid-19th-century gate that is one of the few bits of the original university to survive WWII and the GDR.

INNENHOF PASSAGE

Just west of the Schinkeltor is the **Innenhof Passage (19)**, in the spectacularly renovated Städtisches Kaufhaus. Pass the Kaiser Maximilian restaurant and you'll come upon a courtyard, formerly a cloth exchange (Gewandhaus) and site of the city's first concert hall. Composer Felix Mendelssohn once led a music school here; there are free concerts in summer.

Exiting Innenhof Passage, a left and a quick right takes you west down Preussergasse toward Petersstrasse, one of the city's main shopping boulevards. Turn left on Petersstrasse and you'll come to **arko (20;** ex-Café Richter; ☎ 960 5235; Petersstrasse 43), the oldest coffee retailer in town (since 1879). This fabulous eclectic building, with its golden iron spiral staircase, is worth a gander; the luscious beans are wonderful too.

Wander south to the end of Petersstrasse for a glimpse of monetary history. In 1991, when the German government offered a 1:1 exchange rate for Ostmarks, tonnes of cash was shipped to the east. Leipzig held a lot of it in its safes, particularly in the **Deutsche Bank (21;** cnr Schillerstrasse & Petersstrasse). Looking at its Italian Renaissance headquarters today, you might suspect they held back a little: gilt ceiling mouldings, marble pillars, etched glass and a skylight so large it illuminates the entire teller area.

NEUES RATHAUS

A few steps on from Deutsche Bank, you confront the impressive 108m-high tower of the baroque **New Town Hall (22;** ☎ 1230; ⏱ 6.45am-4.30pm Mon-Fri). Although the building's origins date back to the 16th century, its current manifestation was completed in 1905. Recently renovated, the interior makes it one of the finest municipal buildings in Germany, with a grand staircase straight out of a Donald Trump dream. In the lobby are rotating art exhibitions, mostly on historical themes.

THOMASKIRCHE

From Burgplatz, turn north and walk up Burgstrasse to the **Thomaskirche (23;** St Thomas Church; ☎ 212 4676; www.thomaskirche.org; ⏱ 9am-6pm), which contains the tomb of composer Johann Sebastian Bach. Built in 1212, the church was extended and converted to the Gothic style in 1496, and was the site of the baptisms of Richard Wagner, Karl Liebknecht and all of Bach's offspring.

Bach worked here as a cantor from 1723 until his death in 1750. Outside the church is the **New Bach Memorial** (24; 1908) showing the composer standing against an organ, with his left-hand jacket pocket turned inside-out (with 20 children from two marriages, the great composer always claimed to be broke).

The St Thomas Choir, once led by Bach, is still going strong and now includes 80 boys aged eight to 18 (see Classical Music p192). Church services are held at 9.30am on Sunday.

The walking tour ends here.

Festivals & Events

Leipzig's annual events calendar includes the **Book Fair** in late March, which includes lots of readings and book-related events, and is the second biggest in the country after Frankfurt. The **Honky Tonk Pub Festival** in late May and early November is the largest of its kind in Europe, with a shuttle bus between drinking holes. The city also hosts an annual 10-day **Bach Festival**, usually around Ascension Day; information is available on ☎ 964 4182 or at www.bach -leipzig.de.

Sleeping

Leipzig Tourist Service runs a free **accommodation service** (☎ 710 4255), with singles/doubles from around €22.50/40.

Mitwohnzentrale (☎ 194 30; Goethestrasse 7-10; ⏲ 9am-8pm) arranges flat rental (€17.50 to €30 per person per day).

BUDGET

Kosmos-Hotel (☎ 233 4422; www.kosmos-hotel.de; Gottschedstrasse 1; s/d €35/60) Ever fancied waking up next to Marilyn Monroe? You can in this fantastically different hotel, which seems to have taken inspiration from the theatre next door in decorating its highly individual rooms. Baroque, Arabian, jungle, cow print – take your pick...

Hostel Sleepy Lion (☎ 993 9480; www.hostel -leipzig.de; Käthe-Kollwitz-Strasse 3; dm €14-15, s/d €24/36; ✗ 💻) Opened in 2000, this playful hostel is a great deal in a nicer location than its new sister Globetrotter. Breakfast costs an extra €3.

Weisses Ross (☎ 960 5951; Auguste-Schmidt-Strasse 20; s €26-35, d €41-55) The neighbourhood's nothing special but this is a good, simple

cheap option within easy walking distance of Augustusplatz.

Campingplatz Am Auensee (☎ 465 1600; Gustav-Esche-Strasse 5; adult/child €4/3, car €3, tent €3-5, cabins €20-35) This camp site is in a pleasant wooded spot on the city's northwestern outskirts (take tram No 10 or 28 to Wahren). The cabins are A-frame bungalows.

MID-RANGE

Mid-range accommodation in the centre is the preserve of the big chains (particularly the many Accor brands); for something a little more individual you'll have to look a bit further afield.

Hotel Michaelis (☎ 267 80; www.hotel-michaelis .de; Paul-Gruner-Strasse 44; s €70-95, d €85-125; ⓟ ✗) Just south of the ring road, this is a superior three-star townhouse with well-equipped rooms.

Hotel Adagio (☎ 216 699; www.hotel-adagio.de; Seeburgstrasse 96; s/d €67/79; ⓟ) Small, stylish private hotel in a quiet area; rooms are smartly decked out with a black/white theme.

Seaside Park Hotel (☎ 985 20; info@parkhotelleip zig.de; Richard-Wagner-Strasse 7; s €105-125, d €126-140; ⓟ 🖫) The Seaside occupies a nice Art Nouveau house in the town centre; there's also a commendable restaurant. Weekend rates are substantially cheaper.

Hotel Mercure (☎ 214 60; www.hotel-mercure -leipzig.de; Augustusplatz 5-6; s €61-88, d €71-105; ⓟ ✗ 💻) Despite its joyless façade, the location is tip-top and the rooms are comfortable. If you don't mind trams going by, rooms facing Augustusplatz have nice views.

Holiday Inn Garden Court (☎ 125 10; reservation@ hi-leipzig.com; Kurt-Schuhmacher-Strasse 3; s €72-134, d €82-144; ⓟ ✗ 🖫) This is a plush option with much cheaper weekend rates.

Novotel (☎ 995 80; h1784@accor-hotels.com; Goethe-strasse 11; s €88-125, d €103-140; 🖫) Located opposite the train station, this smart block has specialised facilities for disabled guests.

TOP END

Hotel Fürstenhof (☎ 1400; Tröndlinring 8; s €125-270, d €151-300; ⓟ ✗ 🖳) Ultra-luxurious Grand Hotel with a 200-year tradition and more mod cons than you can pay someone to shake a stick at.

Westin Leipzig (☎ 9880; info@westin-leipzig.com; Gerberstrasse 15; s €162-219, d €177-234; ⓟ ✗ 💻 🖳)

This vast 27-storey establishment caters for an international clientele; views from the top-floor restaurant make up for the monotonous exterior.

Marriott Leipzig (☎ 965 30; leipzig.marriott@ marriott.com; Am Hallischen Tor 1; s/d €149/160; P ⊠ ☒ ☐ ☒) This all-American complex is virtually self-contained, with restaurants, bars, health club, ballroom and a sizeable shopping centre.

Eating
GERMAN
Auerbachs Keller (☎ 216 100; www.auerbachs-keller -leipzig.de; Mädlerpassage; mains €10.50-20.60) Founded in 1525, Auerbachs Keller is one of Germany's classic restaurants. Goethe's *Faust – Part I* includes a scene here, in which Mephistopheles and Faust carouse with some students before they ride off on a barrel. The historic section of the restaurant includes the Goethe room (where the great writer came for 'inspiration') and the Fasskeller; note the carved tree-trunk in the latter, depicting the whole barrel-riding shenanigans. Group tours, including both dinner and drink, are available.

Thüringer Hof (☎ 994 4999; Burgstrasse 19; mains €7.90-13.15) Luther's favourite pub was completely destroyed in WWII and what you see today is entirely new. There's a traditional vaulted-ceiling restaurant in front, a glass-roofed atrium in the back, and a good range of options for vegetarians and seniors.

Ratskeller (☎ 123 6202; Neues Rathaus; mains €7.20-13.80) Enjoy cream goulash with red cabbage and dumplings alongside trompe-l'oeil diners in this fabulously renovated space.

Zill's Tunnel (☎ 960 2078; Barfussgässchen 9; mains €8.60-13.40) This place offers outstanding Saxon specialities and some fine seasonal dishes, with outside seating on the street and in the covered 'tunnel' courtyard.

Barthel's Hof (☎ 141 310; Hainstrasse 1; mains €8-14) This is a sprawling, historic place with some fantastic buffets (€8.30 to €11.99) and quirky Saxon dishes such as *Heubraten* (marinated lamb roasted on hay).

INTERNATIONAL
Medici (☎ 211 3878; Nikolaikirchhof 5; mains €19.50-23) It may resemble a suspension bridge inside, but this impossibly classy Italian is widely tipped as one of the best restaurants

in Leipzig. For a real treat, try the three- to five-course set menus (€38 to €59).

Mövenpick (☎ 211 7722; Am Naschmarkt 1-3; mains €7.50-15, buffets €4.60-13.70) This restaurant in the Handelshof offers outstanding value, with a self-service cafeteria and nightly buffets full of imaginative salads, casseroles and desserts.

Koslik (☎ 998 5993; cnr Gottschedstrasse & Zentralstrasse; mains €7.80-13, pizza/pasta €5.60-8.90) A stylish wood interior complements excellent mixed cuisine here, with great breakfasts and meals from Italian standards to duck *à l'orange*. There's jazz on Sunday and DJs on Wednesday night.

Retschenka (☎ 149 2235; Steibs Hof, Brühl 64/66; mains €6.80-12.50) This is an engaging traditional Russian restaurant with folk music evenings and even Russian pop to accompany your meal.

Escados Steakhouse & Bar (☎ 960 7127; www .escados.de; Martin-Luther-Ring 2; mains €8.50-18.40) In the vault section of Deutsche Bank, the suave Escados is tropical-meets-classical, with palm trees and rattan amid the columns and lots of Argentine beef.

Karma Sutra (☎ 124 8570; Nürnberger Strasse; mains €7.90-13.90) An upscale Indian bar-restaurant offering plenty of choice and a welcome abundance of veggie options.

CAFÉS
Zum Arabischen Coffe Baum (☎ 965 13 21; Kleine Fleischergasse 4; mains €7.50-15) Leipzig's oldest coffee bar has a restaurant and café offering excellent meals over three floors, plus a coffee museum on top (free). Composer Robert Schumann met friends here, and if you ask nicely you can sit at his regular table.

Café Riquet (☎ 961 0000; Schuhmachergässchen 1) This upmarket café is in a superb Art Nouveau building (note the bronze elephant heads above the entrance).

Two cafés worth a visit are the **Bachstübl** (☎ 960 2382) and **Café Concerto** (☎ 960 4779), on Thomaskirchhof.

Drinking
Kreuzer (€1.50) is the best magazine for what's on in Leipzig, with great listings, the best events calendar and a good travel section.

Of the free monthly listings magazines, *Fritz*, *Blitz* and *ZeitPunkt* are the most common; *Leipzig Im* and *Nachts in Deutschland* also have excellent coverage. Check also the *Leipzig Jazz Kalender*, printed monthly and available at Leipzig Tourist Service.

Barfussgässchen and Kleine Fliescher-gasse, west of the Markt, form one of Leipzig's two 'pub miles', packed with outdoor tables that fill up the second the weather turns warm. The other is on Gottsched-strasse, a wider cocktail strip just west of the Altstadt. As you trawl the bars, look out for scene regular JPS, aka the 'Girl in the Hat' – her picture graces the walls of the Maga Pon laundry-café.

Mephisto (☎ 216 1022; Mädlerpassage) Above Auerbachs Keller, this bar continues the Faust theme with a mirror that laughs devilishly and, if the barman's in the mood, shows Satan himself. In 2002 it was declared one of the 200 best bars in Germany by *Playboy* magazine, no less.

Vodkaria (☎ 442 8868; Gottschedstrasse 15; meals €6.60-12.60) Need a break from beer? This stylish new place pours some 120 types of vodka, with occasional live music.

Spizz (☎ 960 8043; Markt 9) This very slick place is one of the coolest bars in town, with excellent live jazz and a disco downstairs. It has three levels, a good range of wines and beers and slow service due to sheer weight of numbers.

Milchbar (☎ 980 9594; Gottschedstrasse 1) Part of a complex including the Kosmopolitan theatre and bar and the Ground Zero nightclub, the Milk Bar is a popular preclub bar with what seem to be huge molecules on the ceiling.

Sixtina (☎ 0177-476 4855; Katharinenstrasse 11) At some point in the last few years the word 'absinthe' has ceased to mean 'bad idea', and the result is places like Sixtina, wholly dedicated to the deadly green fairy. We blame the parents.

Chillum (☎ 390 105; Karl-Liebknecht-Strasse 76) Named after a tribal hash pipe, with cocktails, chill-out music and food served till 7am on weekends. You could be forgiven for thinking this was a stoner bar, though if it is they're amazingly subtle about it.

Entertainment
BALLET & OPERA
The Leipzig Ballet performs at the Opernhaus, featuring classics, the modern and just about everything in between. Tickets cost €6 to €17.50.

Composer Udo Zimmermann, the director of the Opernhaus, favours operas from Wagner and Albert Lortzing for their Leipzig connections. But he also likes modern opera, especially by Stockhausen, as well a electronic music and Jörg Herchet. Tickets range from €6 to €32.50.

CINEMA
Passage Kinos (☎ 217 3860; Hainstrasse 19a) In the Jägerhof centre, the Passage screens films with German subtitles, and is also hosting the 'Grassi in Exile' until the complex is completed in 2005.

Prager Frühling (☎ 306 5333; www.kinobar-leipzig .de; Bernhard-Göring-Strasse 152) 'Prague Spring' might sound a bit militant, but this is actually an excellent arthouse cinema showing offbeat foreign films in the original.

CLASSICAL MUSIC
Neues Gewandhaus (☎ 127 0280; Augustusplatz 8; €10-30) This hall is home to Europe's longest-established orchestra, with a tradition dating back to 1743 – Mendelssohn was one of its conductors. Today it covers the entire spectrum of classical music, with guest appearances by soloists, conductors and orchestras from around the world.

Regular concerts are held at the **Bach Museum** (see p185; adult/concession €10/7.50). Organ concerts take place at 5pm every Saturday in the **Nikolaikirche**, and the **Thomaskirche** has performances by the Boys Choir on Saturdays over the summer.

Special concerts take place throughout holiday times, and during the Bach Festival there are plenty of free concerts on the Markt.

CLUBS
Velvet (☎ 590 2570; www.clubvelvet.de; Körnerstrasse 68) South of the city centre, Leipzig's premier club attracts plenty of beautiful people for healthy servings of house, trance, electro and techno, with 'name' DJs from all over Germany.

Moritz-Bastei (☎ 702 590; Universitätsstrasse 9) One of the best student clubs in Germany, located in a spacious cellar below the old city walls. It has live bands or DJs most nights, runs films outside in summer and serves a great Sunday brunch.

Bounce 87 (☎ 149 6687; Nikolaistrasse 12-14) Upfront hip-hop flava with a lively, fun crowd.

Nachtcafé (☎ 211 4000; Markgrafenstrasse 10) A regular student favourite, this 2-level club has a large plastic swimming pool outside, which can be great fun (in summer, anyway).

GAY & LESBIAN VENUES
GegenPol magazine and several free papers keep track of the ever-changing gay scene.

Rosa Linde (☎ 484 1511; www.rosalinde.de; Steibs Hof, Brühl 64/66) Nice, intimate bar, café and information centre for men and women.

Blaue Trude (☎ 212 6679; Katharinenstrasse 17) This popular courtyard bar has videos and a downstairs area for dancing and other activities.

New Orleans (☎ 960 7989; Brühl 56; 🖳) A low-key mixed place with some Cajun flavour.

ROCK & JAZZ
naTo (☎ 303 9133; Karl-Liebknecht-Strasse 46) This is a great jazz venue. It's a cultural house, meeting spot and generally cool hang-out.

There's also jazz at the **Neues Gewandhaus** (☎ 127 0280; Augustusplatz 8) and at the Opernhaus. Large rock concerts are held at the **Neue Messe** (☎ 6780; tram No 16), north of the city, and at the Zentral Stadion, 10 minutes west from the city centre near Jahnallee.

THEATRE & CABARET
Schauspielhaus (☎ 126 8168; Bosestrasse 1) Leipzig's largest theatre is a few blocks west of the Markt. It typically presents classics infused with modern elements.

Theater Neue Szene (☎ 126 8168; www.schauspiel -leipzig.de; Gottschedstrasse 16) Modern performances are held here.

Theater der Jungen Welt (☎ 486 600; Lindenauer Markt 21) This theatre specialises in plays with themes that appeal to younger audiences (late teens to early 20s), but also has puppet shows.

Krystallpalast (☎ 140660; www.krystallpalastvariete .de; Magazingasse 4) This company puts on the finest variety shows in town, with snake women, flamenco, trapeze acts and more.

There are three well-known cabaret theatres in Leipzig:

Leipziger Pfeffermühle (☎ 960 3253; www.kabarett -leipziger-pfeffermuehle.de; Thomaskirchhof 16) One of Leipzig's most famous cabarets, the Pfeffermühle even has an active touring company.

Academixer (☎ 2178 7878; Kupfergasse 3) This place is just south of the university.

SanftWut (☎ 961 2346; Mädlerpassage) Sanft-Wut has a small stage where just a few performers carry the evening.

Getting There & Away
AIR
The enormous and increasingly popular Leipzig-Halle airport is served by domestic and international flights from several companies, including **Lufthansa** and its subsidiary **Eurowings** (☎ 224 1600), **Delta** (☎ 0180-333 7880) and **Cirrus** (☎ 224 2176). Most airlines have their offices in Terminal B.

CAR & MOTORCYCLE
Leipzig lies just south of the A14 Halle–Dresden autobahn and 15km east of the A9, which links Berlin to Nuremberg. It's best to leave your vehicle in one of the well-marked parking lots that ring the Altstadt.

RIDE SERVICES
The **Mitfahrzentrale** (☎ 194 30; Goethestrasse 7-10; 🕙 9am-8pm) can organise shared rides.

TRAIN
Leipzig is an important link between eastern and western Germany, with connections to all major cities. There are frequent services to Frankfurt (€56.40, 3¼ hours), Munich (€65.20, five hours), Dresden (€16.80, 70 minutes), Berlin (€33.20, 1½ hours), Hanover (€38.40, three hours) and Hamburg (€65.80, 4¼ hours).

Getting Around
TO/FROM THE AIRPORT
Leipzig-Halle airport, roughly equidistant from both cities, is served by RE and IC trains three times hourly (€3.20, 15 minutes); a new ICE terminal was completed in June 2003, connecting the airport to the national long-distance network. Zubringerbusse Leipzig runs shuttles to the Hauptbahnhof (adult/child €6.50/4) approximately every half-hour.

BICYCLE
Zweirad Eckhardt (☎ 585 1240; Güterstrasse) hires out bikes, as do many hotels.

PUBLIC TRANSPORT
Trams are the main option, with most lines running via Willy-Brandt-Platz, in front of the Hauptbahnhof. The S-Bahn circles the

SAXONY

city's outer suburbs. A single ticket costs €1.50 and a day card €4.40; four-journey strips cost €5.40.

TAXI
Funktaxi (☎ 4884) and **Löwen Taxi** (☎ 982 222) are the main local firms. Rates are €1.80 hire charge and €1 per kilometre. From 10pm to 7am, any bus or tram driver will arrange for a taxi to meet you at your stop.

AROUND LEIPZIG
Colditz Escape Museum
In the secluded Zwickauer Mulde valley, some 46km southeast of Leipzig, lies the sleepy town of Colditz and its impressive (though run-down) fortress. The Renaissance structure was used by Augustus the Strong as a hunting lodge in the 17th century and, after the dawn of German psychiatry in the 1800s, it became a mental hospital. Built on a crag high above town, it seemed the ideal site for a high-security prison in WWII, and the Nazis dubbed the place Oflag IVc (Officer's Camp IVc).

Its inmates, mostly cunning Allied officers who had already escaped elsewhere, proved this was a mistake. Between 1939 and 1945 there were over 300 escape attempts, earning Colditz the reputation of a 'bad boys' camp. Some 31 men managed to flee, aided by ingenious self-made gadgetry, including a glider made of wood and bedsheets and a homemade sewing machine for making German uniforms. Most astounding, perhaps, is a 44m-long tunnel (under the chapel) that French officers dug in 1941–42 before the Germans caught them.

A number of prisoners turned writer after the war, and their tales have spawned more than 70 books, several films and at least one BBC TV series. However, all this Allied escapism embarrassed the GDR, which suppressed the story in the east after WWII.

Today the fortress houses a small but fascinating **Escape Museum** (☎ 034381-449 87; adult/concession €3/2; ⊙ 10am-5pm), run by the Städtisches Museum (Tiergartenstrasse 1).

GETTING THERE & AWAY
Bus Nos 931 and 690 run to Colditz from Leipzig; you can also take a train to Bad Lausick and catch bus 613 from there. The town is at the junction of the B107 and B176 roads between Leipzig and Chemnitz.

ZWICKAU
☎ 0375 / pop 102,000
Once a major centre of GDR industry, Zwickau, one hour south of Leipzig, is perhaps best known as the place from where the mighty Trabants rolled, very slowly, off their assembly lines.

First mentioned in 1118, Zwickau began life as a trading and silver-mining town, but it's been a seat of the German auto industry since 1904, when the Horch factory churned out roadsters here. Herr Horch later split off to found Audi. Horch was nationalised by the GDR, and when it had sufficiently devolved, Trabant production began.

Since reunification, Volkswagen seems to have taken over the city (exit signs on the Autobahn read 'VW Werk'), and the former, unusable, Trabi factory now houses an auto museum and office park.

Zwickau was also the birthplace of the composer Robert Alexander Schumann (1810–56), and his house is now open as a museum. This, plus a lovely city centre and an impressive cathedral, make Zwickau worth a stop.

Orientation
The Altstadt is surrounded by the circular Dr-Friedrichs-Ring. The Hauptbahnhof (central train station) is west of the Altstadt, and is connected to it by Bahnhofstrasse and Schumannstrasse. Leipzigerstrasse is the main road jutting north from Dr-Friedrichs-Ring; it becomes the B175/B93, which splits off north of the city.

Just south of the Markt and Rathaus, there's a new terminus equipped to take InterCity trains servicing the Dresden-Nuremberg line. They now roll right into the Altstadt, on rails parallel to the city trams. The Hauptbahnhof remains 1km west of the centre.

Information
Central post office (Hauptbahnhof)
Deutsche Bank/Dresdner Bank (⊙ 27190; cnr Innere Plauensche Strasse & Dr-Friedrichs-Ring)
Kultour Z (☎ 194 33; www.kultour-z.de; Hauptstrasse 6; ⊙ 9am-6.30pm Mon-Fri, 10am-4pm Sat) Tourist information.

Multimedia-Treff (☎ 273 6663; www.mmzz.de;
Bahnhofstrasse 1; ⊙ 9am-9pm) Register for free internet
access (max 1hr).
Schnell und Sauber (Leipzigstrasse 27) Laundry.
Tourismusverband WestSachsen (☎ 293 711;
www.tourismus-westsachsen.de; Herschelstrasse 5) Tourist
information.

Sights
CITY CENTRE
At Hauptmarkt, the southern end of Hauptstrasse, sits the **Rathaus**, looking for all the
world like a theatre; next door is the **city
theatre**, looking like a city administration
building.

Here too is the prominent **Schumann monument** (1901), which was shuffled around
town several times before returning to its
original site in 1993.

Behind the theatre is the **Kleine Bühne
Puppet Theatre** and **Theater in der Mühle** (see
Entertainment p196).

Behind Hauptmarkt is the **Schumann-Haus**
(☎ 215 269; Hauptmarkt 5; adult/concession €2.50/1.50;
⊙ 10am-5pm Tue-Sat). It features exhibits on
the composer and his wife, Clara, herself
a noted pianist.

The city's **Marienkirche** (1219), where
Schumann was baptised, is justifiably a
place of pride. It was converted to the late-
Gothic style from 1453 to 1565, and the
steeple was added in the late-17th century.
Inside, the church has an impressive stone
font (1538), and a wonderful high altar
shrine. Next to the photo boards showing
the Dom (Cathedral) restoration, there's a
particularly gruesome rendition of Christ –
wearing a real wig up on the cross.

Just south of Marienkirche is the **Kornmarkt**, which had a monopoly on Zwickau
grain sales until 1832. On one side stands
the eccentric **Schiffchen**, a 15th-century house
built in the form of a ship's prow and originally owned by a family of ropemakers.

On Dr-Friedrichs-Ring, on the corner of
Schillerstrasse and just in front of the West-
sächsische Hochschule, is the **Solar-Anlage**,
an enormous solar-powered sculpture that
shows the date, time and temperature.

CAR MUSEUM
An ugly, out-of-the-way building houses
Zwickau's **Automobilmuseum** (☎ 332 3854; www
.automobilmuseum-zwickau.de; Walter-Rathenau-Strasse
51; adult/concession €3/2; ⊙ 9am-noon & 2-5pm Tue-Thu,

10am-5pm Sat & Sun). But what do you expect?
It was a factory.

Originally built by August Horch, founder of the long-defunct car company bearing his name and later Audi ('Horch' is the
root for 'to hear' in German, as 'Audi' is
in Latin), this factory first produced Audis
and later Trabants. After reunification, VW
employed many former Trabant workers,
and its subsidiary Audi coughed up DM12
million for structural renovations to the
antiquated factory.

Some 50 cars are on display, from classic Horst limousines to the various Trabant
models and prototypes; sadly there's rather
more technical than historical information
on the exhibits.

The museum is housed in a temporary
building round the corner at Crimmitscher
Strasse 36g until renovations on the original
site finish sometime in 2004.

JOHANNISBAD
North of the Altstadt, on the Zwickauer Mulde River, **Johannisbad** (☎ 272 560;
www.johannisbad.de; Johannisstrasse 16; adult/concession
1hr €2.50/2, 2hr €4/3; ⊙ 10am-10pm Mon & Wed, 8am-
10pm Tue & Thu, 10am-11pm Fri, 9am-11pm Sat, 9am-9pm
Sun) is a beautiful old Art Deco swimming

CHARIOTS ON FIRE

The Trabant (1949–90) was intended to
be the GDR's answer to Volkswagen –
an economical, convenient car for the
masses. Sadly, the car matched VW only
in its ubiquity. Despite production times
from hell (the *average* owner waited nine
years to get this lemon), the 'Trabi', as it's
affectionately called, can still be seen on
the road all over eastern Germany.

Each Trabi took so long to build
because its plastic parts (that is, most of the
vehicle) were made individually by workers
running hand-operated moulding systems.
Powered by a two-stroke engine similar
to that of a large lawnmower, this rolling
environmental disaster pumped out five
times the amount of fumes as the average
Western vehicle. Berlin residents still talk
of waking up the day the Wall opened to
see a vast queue of Trabants stretching
down the road, with a dull brown cloud
gathering overhead...

pool complex. Even if you don't swim, the ornate interior, renovated in 2000, is worth a look. Walk up Max-Pechstein-Strasse and take a right at Osterweihstrasse.

Sleeping

The tourist office books private rooms at no extra cost.

Zum Uhu (☎ 295 044; www.zum-uhu.de; Bahnhofstrasse 51; s/d €33/66) A decent little pension with its own restaurant, convenient for the Hauptbahnhof and the centre.

Hotel Park Eckersbach (☎ 475 572; parkeckersbach@t-online.de; Trillerplatz 1; s €43.50-49, d €64-70; P) This attractive old villa is situated in a wooded neighbourhood outside of the centre.

Achat Hotel (☎ 8720; zwickau@achat-hotel.de; Leipzigerstrasse 180; s €64-84, d €74-94; P ✕ ☐) North of the Altstadt is this spotless, modern place with comfortable rooms on the main drag. Its **Bistro Basilikum** restaurant is considered one of the city's best, with an international menu (mains €4.50 to €16).

Eating

Grünheimer Kapelle (☎ 204 8255; www.gruenhainer -kapelle.de; Peter-Breuer-Strasse 3; mains €6.75-11.75) This place is in an old chapel with fabulous carved furniture, uneven art exhibits and friendly service. Speciality of the house is 'besoffne Wildsau' – drunken wild boar!

Allinone (☎ 273 7721; Bahnhofstrasse 19; mains €7-13) Excellent bistro and piano bar offering French-German cuisine, an intelligent drinks selection and a big conservatory area.

Ringkaffee (☎ 212 596; www.ringkaffee.com; Dr-Friedrichs-Ring 21; mains €6.50-15.30) Big windows overlooking the busy streets complement hearty regional cooking at this smart first-floor coffee-house and restaurant. The Ringkeller bar in the basement is good too.

Drei Schwäne (☎ 204 7670; www.drei-schwaene.de; Gartenstrasse 1; mains €18-22) Outside the city centre, this is the place to splurge on tip-top French and Mediterranean cuisine in a romantic Tuscan atmosphere.

Drinking

Roter Oktober (☎ 294 493; Kolpingstrasse 54) This place, on the corner of Leipzigstrasse, is a scream: a tiny bar dedicated to all things GDR, with posters of communist luminaries, propaganda, flags and drink specials like Intershop Weissbier and Castro Libre.

Nachtcafé (☎ 390 9359; www.nachtcafé-zwickau.de; Oskar-Arnold-Strasse 14) By the river east of the centre, this is probably Zwickau's trendiest club, with an emphasis on house and black music at weekends.

1470 (☎ 282 728; Mareinstrasse 50) A wonderful wooded pub over two floors, 1470 also serves decent food.

egghead (☎ 303 3386; Peter-Breuer-Strasse 10) This is a chic but fun modern cocktail bar with all kinds of shakes and mixed drinks.

Scheune (☎ 298 966; Bahnhofstrasse 18) This rustic pub near the station also does better-than-average food, including a huge grill platter (€11.20).

Entertainment

There's lots of theatre, dance, concerts and puppet shows at the **Theater Zwickau** (☎ 834 647), **Kleine Bühne Puppentheater** (☎ 215 875) and **Theater in der Mühle** (☎ 216 009), all on or just behind Hauptmarkt.

Kommunales Kino (☎ 215 875; Hauptmarkt) At the Kleine Bühne, the Kommunales shows some English-language films.

Getting There & Around

There are direct trains to Zwickau every two hours, or hourly with one change, from Leipzig's Hauptbahnhof (€12.40, 1¼ hours). By car, it's about a 1½-hour drive from Leipzig on the B93. Signage is poor in the city, so it's easiest to park at the new Arkaden shopping area in the centre and walk from there.

Trams and buses (single €1) service outlying areas.

EASTERN SAXONY

BAUTZEN

☎ 03591 / pop 42,700

The deep valley of the Spree River and the medieval towers that rise from cliffs above it create a fine metaphor for the dual nature of Bautzen, which celebrated its 1000th anniversary in 2002. This town in Upper Lusatia is undeniably German, but its heritage is also influenced by the Sorbs, Germany's sole indigenous minority, whose Slav forebears settled in present-day Saxony and Brandenburg in the 7th century (see the boxed text The Sorbs p153). Many Sorb cultural institutions are based ere, and signs on streets and public buildings are bilingual (though you'll be lucky to hear the language spoken).

The joint Catholic–Protestant cathedral – the only one of its kind in eastern Germany – is another fitting emblem, holding services for each denomination a couple of hours apart. The town's sunny disposition stands in contrast to the high-security GDR prison that was once synonymous with the city.

Though badly damaged many times over its history, the layout of the Altstadt has hardly changed for centuries, and a large number of historic buildings remain, including no fewer than 17 towers and ramparts. Many other buildings have been spruced up, and the old quarter is evolving into a smart tourist centre.

Orientation

The Spree River forms a cradle around Bautzen's egg-shaped old quarter, centred on the Hauptmarkt, site of the towering Rathaus. The Dom is a few metres to the north, on the adjacent Fleischmarkt, while the medieval Ortenburg complex lies at the eastern end. The Hauptbahnhof is a 15-minute walk southeast of the Altstadt, reached via Bahnhofstrasse and Karl-Marx-Strasse.

Information

HypoVereinsbank (☎ 351 360; Kornstrasse 2-4)
Main post office (Postplatz)
Sparkasse (Kornmarkt)
Touristinformation (☎ 420 16; touristinfo@bautzen .de; Hauptmarkt 1; ☺ 9am-6pm Mon-Fri, 10am-4pm Sat & Sun Mar-Oct, 9am-5pm Mon-Fri, 10am-2pm Sat & Sun Nov-Feb)
www.bautzen.de Bautzen home page
www.biergeiger.de Online version of this nifty pub guide.

Sights

REICHENTURM

As you come from the Hauptbahnhof you're likely to pass the **Reichenturm** (adult/child €0.50/ 0.25; ☺ Apr-Oct), looking a bit naked with its blanched medieval base and baroque cupola (the gate below was torn down in 1837). Also called the Leaning Tower, the 55m-high Reichenturm deviates 1.4m from the centre. Although it's no Pisa, this makes it one of the steepest leaning towers north of the Alps, though you'll scarcely notice from the viewing platform.

HAUPTMARKT

The Reichenstrasse – Street of the Rich – leads west from the tower past some wealthy-looking baroque houses to the **Hauptmarkt**, site of thrice-weekly markets. The square is dominated by the impressive **Rathaus**, with an 18th-century baroque exterior that masks a Gothic façade. The intriguing **sundial** on the yellow tower not only measures time but also the lengths of the days and nights for the respective date.

Opposite is the **Gewandhaus**, site of the first bazaar in Upper Lusatia.

DOM ST PETRI

Just north of the Rathaus is **Fleischmarkt**, the old meat market. Here you'll find **St Peter's Cathedral**, with an 85m-high tower that contains an apartment halfway up that's still occupied. You notice something odd as you enter the sanctuary – this is a so-called *Simultankirche* serving Catholics and Protestants. When the Reformation reached Bautzen in 1524, both congregations agreed to share the church, with the Protestants taking the nave and the Catholics the choir. There's a waist-high iron grating separating the two (it was 4m high until 1952!). Both sections are equipped very differently, with a bombastic high altar in the Catholic area and a simple flat one for the Protestants.

Just behind the Dom is the **Domstift** (Cathedral Chapter), housed in a courtyard palace with a richly décorated portal (1755). Loads of objects gleam inside the ecclesiastical **treasury** (☺ 10am-noon & 1-4pm Mon-Fri). In the courtyard you'll see a chimney on the west wing with the stone head of a man peeking out; this peculiarity dates from 1619, when a Catholic–Protestant feud led to a storming of the cathedral deanery. Legend has it that the dean crawled up the chimney to signal for help.

SCHLOSS ORTENBURG

On the western edge of town stands the **Ortenburg**, probably erected in 958 by Otto I to keep the Milzener (forebears of the Sorbs) at bay. The cliff-top location made strategic good sense but didn't stop it from burning down several times. The place came under Hungarian rule in the 15th century, and then-king Matthias Corvinus took a great interest in the creation of his

SAXONY

own likeness. An ornate version took its place at the **Matthiasturm** above the main gate of the fortress.

The Ortenburg courtyard is home to the **Sorbian Museum** (☎ 421 05; adult/concession €1.50/1; ☼ 10am-5pm Mon-Fri, 10am-6pm Sat & Sun Apr-Oct, 10am-4pm Mon-Fri, 10am-5pm Sat & Sun Nov-Mar), which displays folk art, musical instruments, costumes and other items in the old salt store.

A few paces south, along the old town wall, is the **Alte Wasserkunst** (Old Waterworks), which for centuries was Bautzen's most important building.

Gedenkstätte Bautzen

Just outside the city walls is Bautzen II, the old **prison** (☎ 404 74; www.gedenkstaette-bautzen.de; Weigangstrasse 8a; ☼ 10am-4pm Tue-Sun), built in 1904 and used for political prisoners by both the Nazis and the GDR regime. Bautzen I, on the other side of town, is still in use as a correctional facility.

Sleeping

The tourist office can book **private rooms** (from about €15 per person).

DJH hostel (☎ 403 47; jhbautzen@djh-sachsen.de; Am Zwinger 1; juniors/seniors €14.90/17.10; ✗) The DJH Jugendherberge Bautzen is staffed by friendly folk, in the old fortifications next to the Nicolaikirche.

Spree-Pension (☎ 489 60; www.spree-pension.de; Fischergasse 6; s/d €36/50; P ✗) Friendly little pension in a lovely house down by the river, with easy access to the station, the centre and the castle.

Pension Dom-Eck (☎ 501 330; www.sorbisches-hotel-dom-eck.de; Breitengasse 2; s €46-51, d €62-66; P) Right by the Dom, this Sorbian family pension has surprisingly modern rooms and a bright greenhouse for a breakfast area.

Schloss-Schänke (☎ 309990; www.schloss-schaenke.net; Burgplatz 5; s €47-59, d €66-84; meals €9.90-16.90; P) This was once a Franciscan residence, but the renovated rooms are rather less sparse Spartan these days. The restaurant is a great place for a treat, with set menus from €20.

Hotel Goldener Adler (☎ 486 60; www.goldener adler.de; Hauptmarkt 4; s/d €67/87; P ✗) A historic (1540) building bang in the centre houses Bautzen's flagship hotel, with all the usual four-star perks and a gourmet restaurant.

Eating & Drinking

Zur Apotheke (☎ 480 035; www.crepes-boulangerie.de Schlossstrasse 21; mains €6.80-11.90) Probably the best selection of vegetarian dishes in Bautzen, with great salads (eg with sorrel, nettle or dandelion), pasta and wholemeal dishes Of course meat-eaters don't come up short either.

Wjelbik (☎ 420 60; Kornstrasse 7; mains €7.50-12.50) Run by the same family as the Dom-Eck, this is a great place to try specialities such as the Sorbian Wedding (braised beef with horseradish sauce) under wonderful beamed ceilings, with informal Sorbian tuition on the side.

Mönchshof (☎ 490 141; www.moenchshof.de; Burglehn 1; mains €6-14.95) It goes a bit overboard on the monk theme, but the medieval-style food here is worth the drama.

Zum Haseneck (☎ 479 13; Kurt-Pchalek-Strasse 1; mains €7-13) East of the Reichenturm is this rabbit-lovers' heaven; cartoon bunnies on the menu may discourage the squeamish. Bizarrely, it's actually named after the owner.

Tatort (☎ 372 606; Burglehn 2) Just opposite, this irreverent bar stays open later than anywhere else in town; at time of research its 'Leck mich am Arsch' (better left untranslated) discount nights were a local institution.

Getting There & Away

Regional trains service Bautzen from Görlitz (€6.60, 35 minutes) and Dresden (€8.10, one hour). The A4 Dresden-Görlitz autobahn runs just south of town. You can park cheaply at Parkplatz Am Theater on Aussere Launenstrasse.

GÖRLITZ

☎ 03581 / pop 76,600

Some 100km east of Dresden on the Neisse River, Görlitz emerged from WWII with its beautiful old town virtually unscathed, though the town was split in two under the Potsdam Treaty, which took the Neisse as the boundary between Germany and Poland.

A major trading city and cultural bridge between east and west and north and south, Görlitz's wealth is obvious from its buildings, which have survived wars but not, unfortunately, three great fires over the years. Sections destroyed in successive fires were ebuilt in the style of the day, and today he city's Renaissance, Gothic and baroque rchitecture is better preserved than that of ny city its size in Saxony. Special federal unding has been allocated to restore its enire Altstadt and many of its 3500 historic uildings.

The town is a surprisingly cosmopolitan place, with plenty of ambition – it's even bidding for European Capital of Culture 2010, acing heavy local competition from Dresden. With an increasing focus on visitors, Görlitz makes an excellent overnight stop.

Orientation

The Altstadt spreads to the north of the Hauptbahnhof; Berliner Strasse and Jacobstrasse connect the two. There are several linked squares: Postplatz, at the northern end of Jacobstrasse, contains the main post office. Further north are Demianiplatz/Marienplatz, home to Karstadt and the town's main bus and tram stops, and Elisabethstrasse, where a lively market takes place. Still further up is Obermarkt, for all intents and purposes the main town square.

East of Obermarkt is Untermarkt, which leads to Neissestrasse and finally to the Neisse River. The Polish town of Zgorzelec (zgo-zhe-lets), part of Görlitz before 1945, is on the eastern side of the river. West of the city towers is the Landeskrone, a dormant volcano topped by a viewing tower.

The city sits on 15° longitude, the dividing line for Central and Eastern European time. Cross into Poland and you lose an hour.

Information

Deutsche Bank (☎ 483 30; Demianiplatz)
Dresdner Bank (Postplatz)
Görlitz-Information (☎ 475 70; www.g-tm.de; Obermarkt 29; ☉ 9am-6.30pm Mon-Fri, 10am-4pm Sat, 10am-1pm Sun)
I-Point (☎ 649 892; ipointgoerlitz@t-online.de; Fischmarktstrasse 1; €0.04 per min; ☉ 2-11pm Mon-Fri, 2pm-midnight Sat & Sun) Internet access.
I-Vent (☎ 421 362; www.i-vent-online.de; Obermarkt 33) Tourist information.
www.goerlitz.de Görlitz home page

Sights

OBERMARKT & SOUTHERN ALTSTADT

At the eastern end of Obermarkt (formerly Leninplatz) is the 16th-century **Dreifaltigkeitskirche**, a former cloister and guard-

house. Opposite, even the **tourist office** can boast a bit of history: Napoleon addressed his troops from the balcony above the entrance in 1813.

At the western end of Obermarkt are the remains of town fortifications – two structures that are now open as museums. The seven floors of the **Reichenbacherturm** (☎ 671 355; adult/concession €1.50/1; ☉ 10am-5pm Tue-Sun) were used until 1904 by 'tower families' entrusted to keep a watchful eye out for fires in the town. Dating from 1490, and now home to temporary art exhibitions, is the **Kaisertrutz** (☎ 671 355; kaisertrutz@goerlitz.de; adult/concession €1.50/1; ☉ 10am-5pm Tue-Sun).

Behind the Kaisertrutz is the **city theatre** and the **Blumenuhr**, a flower clock handy as a meeting point.

South of Postplatz is the newly restored **Strassburg Passage**, connecting Berliner Strasse and Jacobstrasse. It's at least as impressive as the Art Nouveau **Karstadt** department store, once a hotel. Walk into the centre and gawk at its amazing skylight.

At the northern end of Demianiplatz/Marienplatz is the **Dicker Turm**, also known as the Frauenturm or Steinturm, and almost 6m thick in some places.

UNTERMARKT

Perhaps the most beautiful section of town, Untermarkt is built around a **fountain** of Neptune and contains the **Rathaus**, begun in 1537 and built in three sections and three styles. The oldest is at the southwestern corner of the square, with a tower featuring a spectacular astrological clock and gold-plated lion (which roars for guided tours). Heading east on Neissestrasse takes you past the town's only purely baroque house, the **Barockhaus** (☎ 671355; www.museum-goerlitz.de; Neissestrasse 30; adult/concession €1.50/1), the **Biblisches Haus** next door, with a façade adorned with biblical scenes, and down to the riverscape.

North from Untermarkt, walk along Petersstrasse to the Gothic **Peterskirche** (☉ 10.30am-4pm), built in 1497 and containing a fascinating 'sun organ' built by Silesian-Italian Eugenio Casparini and his son, with tiny pipes shooting off like rays.

Tours

Görlitz-Information (☉ 2pm Mon-Sat, 10.30am Sun Mar-Oct, 2pm Wed, Fri & Sat Nov-Feb; €2.50) runs walking tours of the Altstadt.

SAXONY

Sleeping

DJH hostel (☎ 406 510; Goethestrasse 17; juniors/seniors €13.40/16.10; ✗) Exit the Hauptbahnhof via the Südlichen Ausgang, turn left and walk for 15 minutes (or take tram No 1 to Goethestrasse). It's sober but well equipped.

Piccobello Pension (☎ 420 830; www.picobello -pension.de; Uferstrasse 32; r €22-35; P) Near the river, these bargain apartments are surprisingly good considering the state of some of the surrounding buildings.

Pension Kästner (☎ 407 131; Weberstrasse 21; s/d €30/50) Just off Untermarkt, this very friendly guesthouse has nice rooms and apartments, although the internal courtyard can get a bit noisy.

Sorat Hotel Görlitz (☎ 406 6577; goerlitz@sorat -hotels.com; Struvestrasse 1; s €79-109, d €99-129; P ✗) Görlitz's most central hotel is on Marienplatz, with tasteful, modern rooms (some with wheelchair access) and champagne breakfast. Weekend rates are great value.

Hotel Tuchmacher (☎ 473 10; www.tuchmacher.de; Petersstrasse 8; s €84-99, d €109-125; P ✗) The town's most tasteful option, this very posh private RomantikHotel is just by the Peterskirche.

Mercure Parkhotel (☎ 6620; h1945@accor-hotels .com; Uferstrasse 17f; s €92-117, d €115-145; P) This huge high-end place is in a green section of town overlooking the river.

Eating

Zum Nachtschmied (☎ 411 657; Obermarkt 18; mains €6.50-10.50) This is an earthy inn with an open hearth and baroque dining hall.

Vierradenmühle (☎ 406 661; www.vierradenmue hle.de; Hotherstrasse 20; mains €5-11.90) Service is slow but the food is excellent at this place, which sticks out into the river on the site of one of the bridges that spanned the Neisse before WWII. There's also a water filtration station here.

Gasthaus Zum Flyns (☎ 400 697; www.flyns.de; Langenstrasse 1; mains €6.90-14.50; ✆ closed Wed) With vaulted ceilings and romantic nooks, this restaurant has nice wines and unusual dishes like 'Flyns Steak' (pork cutlet with banana and curry sauce).

Destille (☎ 405 302; www.destille-goerlitz.de; Nicolais -trasse 6; mains €7.50-11.50) This is a top-notch but affordable place, serving local speciality Silesian Heaven (pork fillet and smoked ham with baked fruit and dumplings). You can view the Jewish bath in the cellar for €1.

Acanthus (☎ 661 810; Neissstrasse 20; mains €7.70 12.20) Among the many eating options on Neissstrasse is this superb, versatile restau rant with a varied menu, secluded riverside beer garden, and a confusing but atmos pheric network of internal passages.

Getting There & Away

Frequent trains run between Görlitz, Dres den (€14.80, 1½ hours) and Berlin (€15 three hours); buses and LausitzBahn train also serve Zittau (€5).

Görlitz is an important border cross ing. Daily Frankfurt–Warsaw and Berlin Kraków trains stop here before heading into Poland via the historic Neisseviaduk bridge (1847), a 475m-long, 35m-high spa with 35 arches. Trains also run to Wrocla three times daily, with one continuing to Warsaw.

Görlitz is just south of the A4 autobah from Dresden – turn off after the König shainer Berge tunnel (Germany's longest) The B6, B99 and B115 converge just nortl of town.

ZITTAU

☎ 03583 / pop 27,000
About 35km south of Görlitz, Zittau is Sax ony's most intriguing outpost. Situated o the *Dreiländereck*, a knoblet of German with Poland and the Czech Republic on ei ther side, the place has an unexpected Italia feel, with its town hall palazzo, warm hue and fountain-studded squares. A burgeonin trade in textiles and machinery made Zitta wealthy during the 17th and 18th centurie aided by its proximity to vital passes throug the Zittauer Gebirge (Zittau Mountains).

Orientation & Information

The Altstadt is a 10-minute walk south o the Hauptbahnhof via Bahnhofstrasse an Bautzener Strasse. The **tourist office** (☎ 75. 137; www.zittau.de; Markt 1; ✆ 8am-6pm Mon-Fri, 9am 1pm Sat, 1-4pm Sun May-Sep only), in the Rathaus finds rooms and also runs **city tours** (adult/chil €2.50/1.50; 2pm Tue).

The **post office** (Haberkornplatz 1), is just inside the ring road; there's a Sparkasse on the corner of Neustadt and Frauenstrasse.

Sights & Activities

Karl Friedrich Schinkel was instrumental in shaping Zittau's distinctive look, particu arly the square, turreted **Rathaus** (tours €1.50; pm & 3pm Wed), designed in Italian Renaissance style (1845) to complement the lovely patrician houses on the Markt. Behind it is he spacious **Neustadt** square, with several fountains and at one end, the weighty **Marstall** (stables) with its shiny red mansard roof. Originally a 16th-century salt store, it now houses shops and restaurants.

Just to the north of the Markt stands the **Johanniskirche** (tower entry adult/concession €1.50/1; noon-3pm), a neoclassical church rebuilt to Schinkel's design in 1833. Unusual features include wooden Greek columns and an enormous crucifix in the shallow nave. For a view of the mountains, climb the 50m **tower**.

Exit the north portal to come to the **Kreuzkirche** (☎ 500 8920; adult/concession €2/1.50; 10am-5pm Tue-Sun), a fancy red Bohemian Gothic church that has been converted into a museum to house the **Grosses Zittauer Fastentuch** (Lenten embroidery; 1472). This huge tapestry shows a complete illustrated Bible with 90-odd scenes.

Just down Klosterstrasse is the **Klosterhof**, a former Franciscan monastery containing the **Städtische Museum** (City Museum; ☎ 554 790; Klosterstrasse 3; adult/concession €1.50/1; 10am-noon & 1-5pm Tue-Sun), with a cellar display of rather unmonastic torture instruments and a working well.

Zittau Mountains

The most romantic way into the Zittau Mountains is by the narrow-gauge Bimmelbahn, which puffs its way to the sleepy resort villages of Oybin and Jonsdorf. Originally laid for brown-coal mining, the line snakes up into the mountains through thick forests and past tree-topped crags, splitting at Bernsdorf. The service to Oybin (€5.70, 45 minutes, four daily) stops at **Teufelsmühle** (Devil's Mill), built for silver miners in the 17th century; here you can glimpse the **Töpfer** peak (582m) to the east.

Alternatively, you can hike to Oybin on a clearly marked trail, taking you south along the Neisse River before veering off into the hills (11km). Oybin and Jonsdorf both make good bases for extended hikes, though Oybin is more picturesque.

Berg Oybin (adult/concession €2/1.50; 9am-6pm May-Aug, 9am-4pm Sep-Apr), a former fortress and monastery on a hill just north of the town, was built by Bohemian king Charles IV. The dramatic ruins are an ideal setting for summer concerts, or just for poking around on your own.

Sleeping & Eating

Hotel Dreiländereck (☎ 5550; www.hotel-dle.de; Bautzener Strasse 9; s €60-65, d €75-85; P ⊠) The only hotel within the Altstadt, this is an excellent, smart place with brasserie, cocktail bar and a green-and-gold theme. The only downside is the proximity of the Johanniskirche bells!

Hotel Schwarzer Bär (☎ 5510; www.hotel-schwarzer-baer.de; Ottokarplatz 12; s/d €41/54; P) Just outside the ring road, this traditional guesthouse is conveniently situated for the border with Poland.

Pension Dany (☎ 512 143; Heydenreichstrasse 12; s/d €17/26; P) Though removed from the centre and equipped with some odd plumbing options, Dany has decent no-nonsense rooms and a terrace to relax on. Breakfast is extra.

Savi (☎ 708 297; Bautzener Strasse 10; food €1.80-5.30;) This is a pleasant café-bar-gallery with a decent menu, including pasta, local dishes and tasty milkshake concoctions.

Filmriss (☎ 794 751; Markt 8; mains €2.50-6) A 100-year-old building houses this movie-themed café serving schnitzels, soups and snacks.

Dornspachhaus (☎ 795 883; Bautzener Strasse 2; mains €5.20-11.80) Situated in a 16th-century house next to the Johanniskirche, the Dornspachhaus has vaulted ceilings and a lovely courtyard. It's named after the mayor who commissioned it.

Getting There & Away

There are frequent trains to Bautzen (€8.10, 1½ hours), Dresden (€14.50, two hours) and Prague. The private LausitzBahn runs all the way to Binz (€37, 7½ hours), on Rügen island, via Görlitz (€5, 50 minutes) and Berlin (€ 17, four hours).

The B96 (to Bautzen), B178 (to Löbau) and B99 (to Görlitz) all converge in the town centre.

Thuringia

CONTENTS

Getting There & Away	204
Getting Around	204
Central Thuringia	**204**
Erfurt	204
Weimar	212
Around Weimar	219
Gotha	219
Northern Thuringia	**221**
Mühlhausen	221
The Kyffhäuser	222
Thuringian Forest	**223**
Eisenach	223
Rennsteig	226
Friedrichroda	227
Ilmenau	228
Schmalkalden	228
Meiningen	230
The Saale Valley	**231**
Jena	231
Around Jena	234
Rudolstadt	234
Saalfeld	234

Visitors often have to remind themselves that Thuringia (Thüringen) was once part of the GDR: this scenic state, aptly known as the 'green heart' of Germany, has an excellent tourist infrastructure and is packed with charming small towns that show little sign of socialist interference, architecturally or otherwise. In fact, many of Thuringia's best-loved places have stayed relatively untouched for centuries, and the rich history of towns such as Erfurt, Weimar and Eisenach is a big part of the state's appeal, providing the raw materials for the countless museums, galleries and monuments that cater for the region's many visitors.

History does, however, bring its own problems – after the WWII Thuringia had a dubious reputation for having received the National Socialist regime particularly warmly, and the grim memorial of the former Buchenwald concentration camp, occupying a vast tract of land scant kilometres from the humanist haven of Weimar, brings home the atrocities of both the Nazis and their socialist successors.

The state has largely escaped the shadows of its recent past, but still suffers from many of the same problems as the other former East German states, with rising unemployment and decreasing population figures; so far, however, it has remained comparatively well off, thanks largely to its central position and consistent tourism income.

Today Thuringia is a huge favourite with travellers from all over the world, revelling in the cultural traditions that inspired Goethe, Schiller, Thomas Mann and so many other great figures. Away from the towns, too, the countless forest trails are well trodden in summer and the lush countryside, despite a relatively high population density, allows visitors the rare luxury of an escape from the urban *Hektik*.

THURINGIA

HIGHLIGHTS

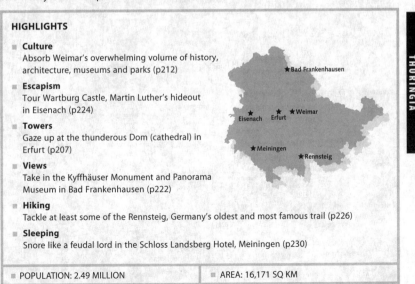

- **Culture**
  Absorb Weimar's overwhelming volume of history, architecture, museums and parks (p212)

- **Escapism**
  Tour Wartburg Castle, Martin Luther's hideout in Eisenach (p224)

- **Towers**
  Gaze up at the thunderous Dom (cathedral) in Erfurt (p207)

- **Views**
  Take in the Kyffhäuser Monument and Panorama Museum in Bad Frankenhausen (p222)

- **Hiking**
  Tackle at least some of the Rennsteig, Germany's oldest and most famous trail (p226)

- **Sleeping**
  Snore like a feudal lord in the Schloss Landsberg Hotel, Meiningen (p230)

★ Bad Frankenhausen
★ Weimar
★ Erfurt
★ Eisenach
★ Meiningen
★ Rennsteig

- POPULATION: 2.49 MILLION
- AREA: 16,171 SQ KM

GETTING THERE & AWAY

Thuringia's main cities, Erfurt and Weimar, are serviced by daily trains from Berlin, Frankfurt, Dresden and Hanover; contact **Deutsche Bahn** (☎ 118 61 for reservations, ☎ 0800-150 7090 for automated timetable information; www.bahn .de) for full details.

If you're driving, the area's main arteries are the east–west A4, which runs just south of Erfurt and Weimar (linking Frankfurt and Dresden), and the north–south B4, which skirts Erfurt before heading into the heart of the Thuringian Forest on its way south to Munich. The Berlin–Munich A9 cuts through the eastern part of Thuringia.

GETTING AROUND

Train services are supplemented by comprehensive local bus networks and an efficient road system – the A4 highway bisects the state and gives easy access to the major cities. There are two good-value DB discount tickets available in Thuringia. The Thüringen-Ticket (€21) gives up to five people or one family unlimited travel on regional trains for one day; the Hopper-Ticket (€4) is valid for a day return to any town within 50km of your starting point, and also covers Saxony-Anhalt.

The new RegioMobil Tageskarte (regional daycard, €8) is a steal. It's good for all public transportation in and between Jena, Weimar and Erfurt, including DB trains.

CENTRAL THURINGIA

ERFURT

☎ 0361 / pop 202,000

Thuringia's charming capital was founded by St Boniface as a bishopric in 742. In the Middle Ages the city catapulted to prominence and prosperity through its position on an important trade route and for producing a precious blue pigment from the woad plant. The many well-preserved buildings of the Altstadt (Old Town) attest to that period's wealth; however, none are from before the 15th century due to a major fire that raged through the city in 1472.

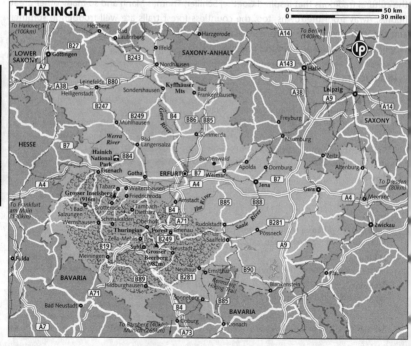

THURINGIA

Erfurt's university was founded in 1392 by rich merchants who allowed students to study common law, not just church law. It became a stronghold of progressive thinking and humanist ideas that questioned traditional religious dogma, an ethos that certainly rubbed off on alumnus Martin Luther. Ironically, Erfurt was also known as the 'Thuringian Rome' – some 90 churches stood within its walls, and at one time it was governed by the bishop of Mainz!

During WWII, damage was extensive, and the GDR regime did little to restore the city's former glories. Over the past decade, however, Erfurt has become an extremely attractive, lively town that deserves a day or two of exploration and makes a good central base for exploring the rest of the state.

Orientation

Most of the car traffic is routed around the Altstadt via two ring roads, making it a pleasure to walk between the main sights (watch out for fast-moving trams, though). The Hauptbahnhof (central train station) and bus stations are just beyond the southeastern edge of the town centre, and were undergoing a massive reconstruction at the time of writing. It's a five-minute walk north along Bahnhofstrasse to Anger, the main shopping and business artery. The little Gera River bisects the Altstadt, spilling off into numerous creeks.

Bus No 99 runs frequently to Erfurt's small airport (€1, 16 minutes). A taxi should cost around €10.

Information

DISCOUNT CARDS

ErfurtCard (24/72hr €7/14) Admission to museums, public transport, guided city tour and entertainment discounts.

Erfurt Family Card (72hr €33) Two adults and all children; includes additional benefits.

EMERGENCY

Ambulance (☎ 112)

Police (☎ 110; Andreasstrasse 38)

INTERNET ACCESS

FAM (☎ 601 2733; Fischmarkt 18-20) Wireless internet points for laptops.

Joker Spielothek (Forum 1, Augustmauer; €3 per hr)

Lokal-Global (☎ 262 3834; Ratskellerpassage, Fischmarkt 5; €1.30 per hr; ☯ 1-8pm Mon-Sat)

MEDICAL SERVICES

Emergency Clinic (☎ 224 990; Puschkinstrasse 23)

MONEY

Reisebank (☎ 643 8361; Hauptbahnhof; ☯ 8am-7pm Tue-Fri, 8am-4pm Sat & Mon)

POST

Main post office (Anger)

TOURIST INFORMATION

Erfurt Tourismus (☎ 664 00; www.erfurt-tourist -info.de; Benediktsplatz 1; ☯ 10am-7pm Mon-Fri, 10am-4pm Sat & Sun)

Sights

MUSEUMS

At the eastern end of the Altstadt, the intricately carved late-Renaissance **Haus zum Stockfisch** was once the home of a woad merchant, but is now occupied by the **Stadtmuseum** (☎ 562 4888; Johannesstrasse 169; adult/concession €1.50/0.75; ☯ 10am-6pm Tue-Sun). Highlights here include a medieval bone-carver's workshop and an exhibit on Erfurt in the 20th century, including the GDR era.

For an insight into Thuringian folk art, visit the **Museum für Thüringer Volkskunde** (☎ 655 5601; Juri-Gagarin-Ring 140a; adult/concession €1.50/0.75; ☯ 10am-6pm Tue-Sun) where you can see the reassembled workshops of a glassblower, toy carver, mask maker and other craftspeople as well as their products, including pottery, carvings, painted furniture and traditional garments.

West of the city centre is the **ega** (Erfurter Gartenausstellung; ☎ 223 220; adult/concession €3.60/2.60; ☯ 8am-8pm), a huge garden show centred on **Cyriaksburg castle** (Gothaer Strasse 38). Take tram No 2 from Anger.

GALLERIES

In addition to the Kunsthalle, Erfurt has many galleries that are treasure-troves of contemporary art and sculpture. **Galerie Haus Dacheröden** (☎ 562 4182; Anger 37-38; ☯ 10am-6pm Tue-Sun) is inside a historic building that is the seat of various international associations. Another good gallery is **Galerie Waidspeicher** (☎ 561 2080; Michaelisstrasse 10), inside the Kulturhof Krönbacken cultural centre (see Entertainment p211).

THURINGIA

Walking Tour

Most sights are conveniently grouped together in the Altstadt. This walking tour begins at the Hauptbahnhof and ends at Fischmarkt in the heart of the city. It takes you to all the major attractions and will last anything from two hours to a full day, depending on how many places you visit.

From the Hauptbahnhof head north on Bahnhofstrasse. Just after crossing Juri-Gagarin-Ring, you'll come upon the 14th-century **Reglerkirche (1)** on the eastern side of the street. The portal and the southern tower of the former monastery church are Romanesque, and the large carved altar dates back to 1460.

Bahnhofstrasse intersects with Anger, which is lined with houses from seemingly different historical periods (most of them are actually only 100 years old). To your right you'll see the enormous new shopping complex **Anger 1 (2)**, while immediately to your left the yellow, stuccoed **Angermuseum (3; ☎ 562 3311; Anger 18; adult/concession €1.50/0.75; ☯ 10am-6pm Tue-Sun)** is original baroque (1712) and houses extensive collections of medieval

art and crafts, 19th- and 20th-century landscape paintings and 18th-century Thuringian *faïence* (glazed earthenware).

As you head west on Anger, pay attention to the opulent façades at No 23 and No 37-38. You'll also pass the **Bartholomäusturm (4)**, a tower with a 60-bell *Glockenspiel* (live concerts 11am Saturday; automatic melodies several times daily).

When you get to the majestic **Angerbrunnen (5)** fountain, keep to the right and follow Regierungsstrasse past the **Wigbertikirche (6)** to the part-Renaissance, part-baroque **Stadthalterpalais (7)**, now the office of Thuringia's chancellor. Turn north on Meister-Eckehart-Strasse, then right on Barfüsserstrasse, where the haunting **Barfüsserkirche (8; ☎ 646 4010; adult/concession €1/0.50 ☯ 10am-1pm & 2-6pm Apr-Oct)** awaits. A ruined medieval gem left as a memorial after WWII bombing, its restored choir now houses a small museum of medieval art.

Backtrack to Meister-Eckehart-Strasse and turn right to get to the 13th-century **Predigerkirche (9; ☎ 5504 8484; Predigerstrasse 4 ☯ 10am-5pm Tue-Sat, noon-4pm Sun)**, a basilica with

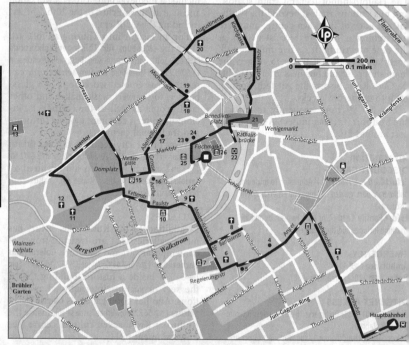

a reconstructed baroque organ. From here head west on Paulstrasse and Kettenstrasse, past the GDR-themed **Thüringer Produkte Museum** (10; ☎ 561 6080; Paulstrasse 26; ☒ 10am-6pm Wed & Thu, 1-6pm Sat-Mon) to the giant Domplatz, presided over by the stunning Severikirche and the imposing cathedral itself, joined by a flight of 70 stone steps.

DOM ST MARIEN

Planned as a simple chapel in 752, **Dom St Marien** (St Mary's Cathedral; **11**; ☎ 646 1265; Domplatz; ☒ 9-11.30am & 12.30-5pm Mon-Fri, 9-11.30am & 12.30-4pm Sat, 2-4pm Sun) wasn't completed until the 14th century. The hillside occupied by the earlier church had to be artificially raised, creating the enormous substructure on which the cathedral now perches. This also required construction of the stone staircase, which you must climb to enter the church via the richly ornamented triangular portal. In July, the stairs are the site of the **Dom-stufenfestspiele**, where operas are performed against the dramatic background.

Highlights inside include the superb **stained-glass windows** (1370–1420) with Biblical scenes; the **Wolfram** (1160), a bronze candelabrum in the shape of a man; the **Gloriosa bell** (1497); a Romanesque stucco **Madonna**; and the 14th-century **choir stalls**.

AROUND THE DOM

Adjacent to the cathedral is the **Severikirche** (**12**; ☎ 576 960; Domplatz; ☒ 9am-12.30pm & 1.30-5pm Mon-Fri), a five-aisled hall church (1280) boasting a stone **Madonna** (1345) and a 15m-high baptismal **font** (1467), as well as the sarcophagus of **St Severus**, whose remains were brought to Erfurt in 836.

North of the Dom complex, on another hill, is the **Citadelle Petersberg** (**13**; ☎ 211 5270; ☒ 10am-6pm Tue-Sun). Many of the city's churches were demolished to erect this fortress – the reason Erfurt has so many towers without churches attached – and today there is a fascinating series of subterranean tunnels within the walls, which can only be seen on a **guided tour** (adult/concession €4.50/2.50; ☒ 2pm Tue-Sun) from the tourist office. The tour is also the only way to view the remains of the Romanesque **Peterskirche (14)**.

Back on the Domplatz, take a look at the ornate façades of the houses on its eastern side, then duck into the tiny Mettengasse. Immediately to your right is the

Waidspeicher (15), now a puppet theatre and cabaret but formerly a storage house for *Waid* (woad) crops. A few metres further is the **Haus zum Sonneborn** (**16**; 1536), with its spectacular portal; it's now the city's wedding office.

ANDREAS QUARTER

At the end of Mettengasse, turn north into Grosse Arche, cross Marktstrasse and head northeast on Allerheiligenstrasse to the former university quarter, which is still being restored. At Allerheiligenstrasse 20, is the **Haus zur Engelsburg (17)**, where a group of humanists met between 1510 and 1515 to compose at least two of the contentious *Dunkelmännerbriefe* (Obscurantists' Letters), satirical letters mocking contemporary theology, science and teaching practices.

Further along you'll find the Gothic **Michaeliskirche** (**18**; ☎ 642 2090; cnr Michaelisstrasse & Allerheiligenstrasse; ☒ 10am-6pm), where Martin Luther preached in 1522. It boasts a magnificent 1652 **organ** by Erfurt master Ludwig Compenius.

Diagonally across the street is the **Collegium Majus (19)**, the site of the main building of Erfurt's venerable university. A WWII ruin until 1998, the Collegium was being reconstructed at the time of writing. The arched portal is the only section from the original structure. The university itself – founded in 1392, closed in 1816 and refounded after the *Wende* (fall of communism) – was so influential that even Luther called it 'my mother to which I owe everything'.

Turn right onto Augustinerstrasse and you'll see the **Augustinerkloster** (**20**; ☎ 576 600; adult/concession/child €3.50/2.50/1.50; ☒ tours hourly 10am-noon & 2-5pm Tue-Sat, 11am Sun), where Luther was a monk from 1505 to 1511 and read his first mass after being ordained as a priest. The church has ethereal stained-glass windows, and the cloister exudes an otherworldly serenity. Also on view are an exhibit on the Reformation and Luther's cell. The grounds and church are free of charge throughout the day; enter from Kirchgasse or Comthurgasse. An order of Protestant nuns – the *Communität Casteller Ring*, formed in 1950 – has resided at the monastery since 1996. Their prayer services are held four times daily, and are open to the public.

From the monastery, Gotthardtstrasse leads south to the medieval **Krämerbrücke**

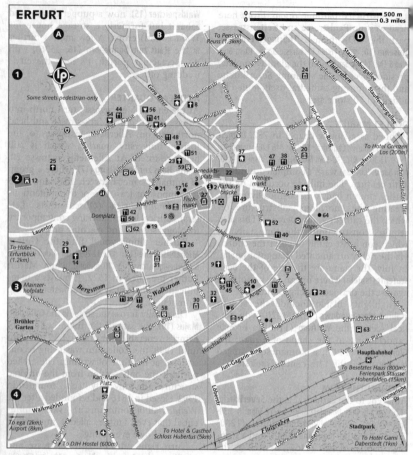

ERFURT

0 ———— 500 m
0 ———— 0.3 miles

(**21**; merchant bridge), an 18m-wide, 120m-long curiosity spanning the Gera River; it's lined by two rows of houses and buttressed by six arches.

A short detour takes you to the **Begegnungsstätte Kleine Synagoge** (**22**; ☎ 655 1660; An der Stadtmünze 4/5; ☒ 11am-6pm Tue-Sun) a cultural and educational facility with an emphasis on Jewish tradition and history. It occupies a classical building that was Erfurt's synagogue from 1840 until 1884. In the basement is an exhibit on Jews in Erfurt, as well as a small **mikve** (bath for ritual purification).

FISCHMARKT

Head back to the western end of Krämerbrücke and walk down Marktstrasse to Fisch-

markt, the medieval market square with a gilded statue of a Roman warrior at its centre. It is flanked by several noteworthy buildings, including the **Haus zum Breiten Herd** (**23**; 1584), with a rich Renaissance façade and frieze depicting the five human senses, which continues with the four virtues on the adjacent **Gildehaus** (**24**; 1892). Also note the **Haus zum Roten Ochsen** (**25**; 1562), another Renaissance gem that now houses the art museum **Kunsthalle Erfurt** (☎ 642 2188; Fischmarkt 7; adult/concession €2.50/1.50; ☒ 11am-6pm Tue, Wed & Fri-Sun, 11am-10pm Thu). Opposite is the neo-Gothic **Rathaus** (Town hall; **26**; ☒ 8am-6pm, to 4pm Wed, to 2pm Fri, 10am-5pm Sat & Sun), built from 1870–75 and containing a series of interior murals depicting scenes

INFORMATION		
Emergency Clinic..................................	1	A4
Erfurt Tourismus................................	2	C2
FAM...	3	B2
Joker Spielothek...............................	4	C3
Lokal-Global (Ratskellerpassage)......	5	B2

SIGHTS & ACTIVITIES	(pp205-9)	
Angerbrunnen...................................	6	C3
Angermuseum..................................	7	C3
Augustinerkloster............................	8	B1
Barfüsserkirche................................	9	C3
Bartholomäusturm..........................	10	C3
Begegnungsstätte Kleine Synagoge....	11	C2
Citadelle Petersberg........................	12	A2
Collegium Majus..............................	13	B2
Dom St Marien.................................	14	A3
Galerie Haus Dacheröden.................	15	C3
Galerie Waidspeicher.......................	(see 59)	
Gildehaus..	16	B2
Haus zum Breiten Herd....................	17	B2
Haus zum Roten Ochsen..................	18	B2
Haus zum Sonneborn......................	19	B2
Haus zum Stockfisch........................	20	C2
Haus zur Engelsburg........................	21	B2
Krämerbrücke..................................	22	C2
Kunsthalle Erfurt.............................	(see 18)	
Michaeliskirche...............................	23	B2
Museum für Thüringer Volkskunde....	24	C1
Peterskirche....................................	25	A2

Predigerkirche.................................	26	B3
Rathaus..	27	B2
Reglerkirche....................................	28	D3
Severikirche....................................	29	A3
Stadthalterpalais..............................	30	B3
Stadtmuseum...................................	(see 20)	
Thüringer Produkte Museum............	31	B3
Wigbertikirche.................................	32	C3

SLEEPING	🏠	(pp209-10)
Augustinerkloster............................	(see 8)	
Dorint Hotel....................................	33	C2
Hotel & Gasthof Nikolai...................	34	B1
Hotel Ibis.......................................	35	C3
Hotel Zumnorde..............................	36	C3
Sorat Hotel.....................................	37	C2

EATING	🍴	(pp210-11)
Alboth's Restaurant.........................	38	C2
Altstadt Café...................................	39	B3
Anger Maier....................................	40	C3
Café am Augustinerkloster................	(see 8)	
Don Camillo....................................	41	B1
Eiscafé San Remo............................	42	B2
Erfurter Brauhaus............................	43	C3
Haus Zur Pfauen.............................	44	B1
Henner...	45	C3
Il Mulino..	46	B3
Louisiana..	47	C2
Moses..	48	B2

Silberschale....................................	49	C2
Vamos..	50	B2
Wirtshaus Christoffel........................	51	B2
Zum Alten Schwan..........................	(see 37)	

DRINKING	🍷	(p211)
Bar-Café Flair..................................	52	C2
Centrum...	53	D3
Double B...	54	B1
Franxx..	55	B1
Hemingway.....................................	56	B1
Presseklub......................................	57	A4
Studentenzentrum		
Engelsburg.................................	(see 21)	

ENTERTAINMENT	🎭	(p211)
DasDie..	58	B3
Die Arche Cabaret...........................	(see 62)	
Jazzkeller..	(see 16)	
Kulturhof Krönbacken......................	59	B2
P33..	60	B2
Schauspielhaus................................	61	B3
Theater Waidspeicher.......................	62	B2

TRANSPORT		(pp211-12)
Central Bus Station..........................	63	D3

OTHER		
Anger 1 Shopping Centre..................	64	D2
Forum 1..	(see 4)	

from the life of Luther, as well as the Tannhäuser and Faust legends. On the 3rd floor is an extravagant festival hall. The walking tour ends here.

Tours

The tourist office offers two-hour **walking tours** (adult/concession €4.50/2.50; 1pm, also 11am Sat & Sun) of the Altstadt and various other themed tours.

Sleeping

BUDGET

The tourist office can book **private rooms** (☎ 664 0110) from as little as €10 per person; there's lots of choice and some surprisingly central options.

DJH hostel (☎ 562 6705; jh-erfurt@djh-thueringen .de; Hochheimer Strasse 12; juniors/seniors €17/20; P ⊠ 🖥) Erfurt's nicely renovated DJH Jugendherberge is about 2km south of the city centre (take tram No 5 to Steigerstrasse).

Pension Reuss (☎ 731 0344; www.pension-reuss.de; Spittelgartenstrasse 15; s €26, d €42-46; P) North of the city centre, the pine-heavy rooms here are a great bargain.

Hotel Garni Daberstedt (☎ 373 1516; garnidaber stedt@aol.com; Buddestrasse 2; s €35-43, d €51-56; P) A good budget option in the suburb of Daberstedt, southeast of the Altstadt. Rooms even have a small minibar.

Ferienpark Stausee Hohenfelden (☎ 036450-420 81; www.hohenfelden.de; Hohenfelden; adult/child €4.50/2.50, car/tent €2/2.50) This sprawling camp site is one of Thuringia's largest and most modern facilities, about 15km south of Erfurt by a lake in the scenic Ilmtal. Take bus No 155 to Hohenfelden Stausee (€2.50).

MID-RANGE

Augustinerkloster (☎ 576 600; www.augustinerkloster .de; Augustinerstrasse 10; s/d €45/76; P ⊠) Stay in a room where Martin Luther might have slept, in this very popular lodging next to the old monastery. The Great Reformer probably didn't have private bathroom or TV, but you can.

Hotel Grenzenlos (☎ 6013 2600; www.behinder tenverband-erfurt.de; s €35-45, d €50-70; P ⊠) This excellent little place just outside the ring road is aimed particularly at physically disabled guests, with easy wheelchair access and other facilities.

Hotel & Gasthof Nikolai (☎ 598 170; www.hotel -nikolai-erfurt.com; Augustinerstrasse 30; s €65-75, d €84-90; P ⊠) Some of the singles are tiny, but with most rooms overlooking the river the yellow Nikolai is a lovely, quiet central choice.

Hotel Erfurtblick (☎ 220 660; www.hotel-erfurt blick.de; Nibelungenweg 20; s/d €60/70; P ⊠) West of the Altstadt, this is a family-run hotel with 11 intimate rooms.

Hotel & Gasthof Schloss Hubertus (☎ 664 110; Arnstädter Chaussee 9; s/d €51/62; P) If you've got a car you could do a lot worse than check out this charming traditional guesthouse and its rustic, gabled building.

THURINGIA

Hotel Ibis (☎ 664 10; Barfüsserstrasse 9; r €72; P ⊠) There are no surprises in this functional business hotel, but the location opposite the Barfüsserkirche is unbeatable for this price. On slow weekends, rates may drop considerably.

TOP END

Hotel Zumnorde (☎ 568 00; www.hotel-zumnorde.de; Anger 50/51; s €100-120, d €120-150; P ⊠ ⊠) One of Erfurt's finest hotels, filled with character and amenities, the Zumnorde has a lovely courtyard, conservatory and roof garden. Enter from Weitergasse.

Sorat Hotel (☎ 674 00; erfurt@sorat-hotels.com; Gotthardtstrasse 27; s €99-192, d €119-212; P ⊠ ⊠) Built onto the historic Zum Alten Schwan restaurant (see Eating), the Sorat offers contemporary designer flair and a dream location right by a willow-fringed arm of the Gera and the romantic Krämerbrücke. Breakfast is a killer champagne-infused buffet.

Dorint Hotel (☎ 594 90; info.erferf@dorint.com; Meienbergstrasse 26-28; s €110-174, d €145-198; P ⊠ ⊠) The Dorint has all the comforts of a state-of-the-art business hotel, and can even afford to play real music in the lifts.

Eating
TRADITIONAL

Zum Alten Schwan (☎ 674 00; Gotthardtstrasse 27; mains €12-15) Now part of the Sorat Hotel, this restaurant dates back to the Middle Ages and has an excellent reputation for superior regional food with French touches. There are regular seasonal offers and a cheap express lunch deal.

Anger Maier (☎ 566 1058; www.angermaier.de; Schlössersstrasse 8; mains €3.30-9.80) This tunnel-like restaurant is an Erfurt institution, with cheap, quality eats – prices have apparently risen by just 1.1% since 2001. It's always busy, often smoky, and you may get on TV just by being here.

Moses (☎ 642 2850; Michaelisstrasse 35; mains €7-9) One of several varied options on this winding thoroughfare, the stick-to-the-ribs fare here is popular with students, and there are some great special buffet deals. Noncarnivores can find budget-priced salads and casseroles.

Erfurter Brauhaus (☎ 566 9835; Anger 21; mains €5.90-12.90) This big brewery restaurant serves up good hearty local fare, plus various kinds of house-brewed beers from the big coppe[r] tanks.

Haus Zur Pfauen (☎ 211 5209; Marbacher Gasse 12-13; mains €7-10) Multi-roomed and atmospheric, this is another micro-brewery restaurant with a large beer garden, a well-upholstered clubroom and a pension upstairs.

Wirtshaus Christoffel (☎ 262 6943; Michaelisstrasse 41; mains €7.50-9) You might feel transported back to Crusader times here, with heavy décor and Middle-Age-meets-New-Age music.

INTERNATIONAL

Il Mulino (☎ 561 7069; Lange Brücke 37A; mains €4-13.75) When the weather's warm, this trattoria across town positively bustles thanks to its lovely riverside garden setting.

Alboth's Restaurant (☎ 568 8207; Futterstrasse 15-16; set menus €33-67; ⊠ from 6pm Tue-Sat) Very highly rated gourmet restaurant with a French emphasis, dealing mainly in superbly balanced four-course menus. Downstairs is the rather less highbrow Lutherkeller, a medieval theme restaurant.

Silberschale (☎ 654 7723; Kürschnergasse 3; mains €8-9.50) Patrons of all ages and budgets enjoy this friendly restaurant-pub, with German and international bistro fare. Seating is spread over three levels, including a conservatory and a wooden terrace overhanging the Gera River.

Louisiana (☎ 568 8209; Futterstrasse 14; mains €10-12) There's a touch of the bayou at this Cajun place, breezy and agreeable with a big patio area and specials such as alligator steak.

Vamos (☎ 654 6765; Domstrasse 15; tapas €2.50-4.80) Facing out onto Domplatz, this cosy tiled tapas bar is a nice option in a busy area.

Don Camillo (☎ 260 1145; Michaelisstrasse 29; pizza & pasta €5.10-9.20) Tasty pizza and pasta made by real Italians is the highlight at this attractive restaurant, cocktail bar and pension.

CAFÉS

Café am Augustinerkloster (☎ 576 6020; Augustinerstrasse 10) The resident nuns offer a warm, quiet place to sit, as well as coffee, tea and homemade cake at prices so low they're almost godly.

Altstadt Café (☎ 225 5540; www.erfurt-altstadt café.de; Fischersand 6; mains €3.50-6) In summer, try to grab a terrace table above the little canal here, just west of Lange Brücke.

THURINGIA

Henner (☎ 654 6691; Weitergasse 8; sandwiches ɔm €1.90) This hyper-modern sandwich bar nd bistro offers all the classics plus some ɪventive and interesting fillings (turkey ɪango curry, anyone?).

Eiscafé San Remo (☎ 643 0449; Marktstrasse 21; ɪecials €3-8) Near the Dom, San Remo makes ɔme of the city's most beautiful ice-cream ɪreations.

▪rinking

ɪrfurt's former university quarter, the An-ɪreasviertel, is a hub of nightlife, pubs, bars ɪc. There is a slight political bent running ɪɪrough the scene here: it's the home of ɪ unique anti-fascist campaign known as ɪet Drunk Against the Right' (www.saufen ɪegen-rechts.de)!

Double B (☎ 642 1671; Marbacher Gasse 10) This ɔsy scene pub recently celebrated its 10th ɪear of dishing up all-day breakfasts to ɪe student hordes – with over two dozen ɪarieties, you'll never look at a hotel buffet ɪgain.

Hemingway (☎ 211 5678; Michaelisstrasse 26) This ɪlace has a faint Caribbean ambience and ɪan get really rowdy during festivals.

Bar-Café Flair (☎ 602 7610; Pilse 27) If it's char-ɪcter you want, this peculiar little cocktail ɪar has it in spades. There's a sauna and ɔlarium upstairs.

▪ntertainment

ɪree magazines such as *Erfurt magazin*, ɪakt, *Partysan* and the local editions of ɪlitz and *Fritz* provide nightlife and event ɪstings for Erfurt and other major towns.

▪LUBS & LIVE MUSIC

ɪtudentenzentrum Engelsburg (☎ 244 770; www ▪burg.de; Allerheiligenstrasse 20-21) This student ɪaunt in historic digs has bands, DJs and ɪl kinds of performances most nights.

Presseklub (☎ 262 3369; www.presseklub.net; ɪalbersweg 1) This stylish new place in a glori-ɪus building dominates Karl-Marx-Platz ɪnd has live music on weekends.

Centrum (☎ 789 7388; www.centrum-club.de; Anger ▪) Back in town, Centrum has an eclectic ▪rogramme of movies, DJs and bands. ɪnter through the alleyway across from ɪe post office.

Franxx (☎ 211 4686; Michaelisstrasse 31) Some of ɪe best hip-hop nights in town take place ɪt this bar/club.

Besetztes Haus (www.topf.squat.net; Rudolstädter-strasse 1) East of the Altstadt, this long-term squat and alternative cultural centre has strong politics and a variety of concerts, films and talks on the bill.

JAZZ
Jazzkeller (☎ 561 2535; Gildehaus, Fischmarkt 13/16) Quality jazz is performed here Thursday to Sunday. Enter through the alley next to the Meissen porcelain store and follow the signs.

Kulturhof Krönbacken (☎ 655 1960; Michaelis-strasse 10) In summer, you might catch a jazz concert among the many events in this courtyard with an ancient chestnut tree, surrounded by former woad warehouses.

THEATRE & CLASSICAL MUSIC
Schauspielhaus (☎ 223 30; Klostergang; tickets ☎ 223 3155; Dalbergsweg 2) The town's Schauspielhaus, south of the Domplatz, has two stages and presents classical theatre, musicals and ballet.

Theater Waidspeicher (☎ 598 2924; Domplatz 18) On the ground floor of a woad warehouse (reached via Mettengasse), this puppet theatre is popular with all ages. Above is the Die Arche cabaret.

P33 (☎ 210 8714; Pergamentergasse 33) This is a warehouse-sized pub-theatre with beamed ceilings that presents a mixed bag of variété, cabaret and music at weekends.

DasDie (☎ 551 166; www.dasdielive.de; Marstall-strasse 12) Two venues offering entertain-ment from live bands to hypnotists and everything in between.

From the end of May throughout sum-mer, classical concerts take place beneath linden trees in the romantic courtyard of Michaeliskirche (Friday). Organ concerts are at the Predigerkirche and Michaeliskirche (Wednesday) and at the Dom (Saturday).

Getting There & Away
Erfurt's Hauptbahnhof has direct IR and ICE links to Berlin-Zoo (€41.20, 3¼ hours), Dresden (€39, 2¼ hours) and Frankfurt-am-Main (€41.80, 2¼ hours). There are also services to Meiningen (€24, 1¾ hours) and Mühlhausen (€9, 45 minutes). Trains to Wei-mar (€4, 15 minutes) and Eisenach (€8.10, 50 minutes) run several times hourly.

Erfurt is just north of the A4 and crossed by the B4 (Hamburg to Bamberg) and the

B7 (Kassel to Gera). The new A71 autobahn runs south to Ilmenau. Most major car rental agencies have offices at the airport.

Getting Around
Erfurt's tram and bus system is divided into three zones, but you're likely to travel only within the city centre (yellow zone). Tickets are €1.20 and €3 for a day pass. For information, call ☎ 194 49. The Regio-Mobil Tageskarte (see p204) also covers Erfurt's public transport. To order a taxi, ring ☎ 511 11 or ☎ 666 666.

WEIMAR
☎ 03643 / pop 62,000
Neither a monumental town nor a medieval one, Weimar appeals to cultural and intellectual tastes and is something of a pilgrimage site for Germans. Its position as the epicentre of this country's Enlightenment, and the birthplace of much that is considered great in German thought and deed, is unrivalled. However, these traditions are not always apparent to visitors in a hurry; the parks and small museums need to be savoured, not downed in one gulp.

The pantheon of intellectual and creative giants who lived and worked here amounts to a virtual Germanic hall of fame: Cranach the Elder, Johann Sebastian Bach, Wieland, Schiller, Herder, Goethe, Liszt, Nietzsche, Gropius, Feininger, Kandinsky, Klee...the list goes on (and on, and on). Look out for quotes from famous Weimar names

painted on the side of buildings all over town.

Abroad, the town is best known as the place where Germany's first republican constitution was drafted after WWI (see How the Weimar Republic Got Its Name, below) though there are few reminders of this historical moment here. The ghostly ruins of the Buchenwald concentration camp, on the other hand, still provide haunting evidence of the terrors of the Nazi regime.

Because of its historical significance Weimar has received particularly large hand-outs for the restoration of its many fine buildings, and in 1999 was the European Capital of Culture. While the city can sometimes feel like a giant museum teeming with tourists, it is one of Germany's most fascinating places and belongs on any itinerary.

Orientation
The town centre is a 20-minute walk south of the Hauptbahnhof (central train station). Several buses serve Goetheplatz, on the northwestern edge of the Altstadt.

Information
Museums and sights administered by the Stiftung Weimarer Klassik are open 9am to 6pm April to October and 9am to 10am to 4pm November to March. These hours apply to the Goethe Haus, Goethe Nationalmuseum, Schiller Haus, Fürstengruft, Wittumspalais, Liszt Haus, Goethe

HOW THE WEIMAR REPUBLIC GOT ITS NAME
Despite its name, the Weimar Republic (1919–33), Germany's first dalliance with democracy, was never actually governed from Weimar. The town on the Ilm was merely the place where, in 1919, the National Assembly drafted and passed the country's first constitution.

Assembly delegates felt that the volatile and explosive political climate rocking post-WWI Berlin would threaten the democratic process if it took place there, and looked for an alternative location. Weimar had several factors in its favour: a central location, a suitable venue (the Deutsches Nationaltheater), and a humanist tradition entirely antithetical to the militaristic Prussian spirit that had led to war.

The resulting constitution certainly lived up to these traditions, even including a radical clause allowing the electorate to propose bills in the Reichstag by petition (not something you'd find in modern politics!). This was balanced by giving the president considerable executive power, including the authority to intervene if the republic was threatened – ironically, this was the measure later exploited by the Nazis to gain control.

Weimar's spot in the democratic limelight lasted only briefly: with the situation in Berlin calming down, the delegates returned to the capital just one week after passing the constitution on 31 July.

GOETHE

As you might gather from seeing his name everywhere, Johann Wolfgang von Goethe bestrides German history like a bookish colossus. Even calling him the 'German Shakespeare' is understating the case – if Shakespeare had lived to be 82, written novels, fairy tales, essays, literary criticism, philosophical treatises, scientific articles and travelogues as well as plays and poetry; dabbled in politics, town planning, architecture, landscaping and social reform; and collaborated with, say, Christopher Marlowe, he might just be in the same ballpark as his Teutonic counterpart.

Born in Frankfurt am Main and trained as a lawyer, Goethe quickly overcame the disadvantages of a wealthy background and a happy childhood to become the driving force of the Gothic-influenced 1770s *Sturm und Drang* (Storm and Stress) literary movement. In his work with Friedrich Schiller, Goethe fostered another of Germany's best-loved talents, developing the theatrical style known as Weimar classicism. Never one to be pigeon-holed, however, he continued to experiment with different styles, forms and genres throughout his long and incredibly prolific career; the Weimar Edition of his complete works numbers 133 *volumes*! Goethe himself once described his work as 'fragments of a great confession', and *Die Leiden des jungen Werthers* (The Sufferings of Young Werther, 1774) is an early example of the characteristic blend of personal emotion, intellectualism and reflection that colour much of Goethe's greatest fiction.

To describe the rest of Goethe's career in a few sentences is well-nigh impossible. He was essentially the last great European Renaissance man, excelling at everything he turned his hand to; his Weimar period is a perfect illustration of his versatility, providing him with the opportunity to contribute to society on every level in his post as minister to the court. Even during his lifetime he was such a revered figure that Napoleon invited him to France to be the Imperial Laureate, and was probably the first author ever to have a celebrity stalker – the talented but tormented JMR Lenz (1751–92), part of the Sturm und Drang circle, was so obsessed with his mentor that he imitated his writing, followed him around and even slept with his old lovers!

The real defining work of this extraordinary figure, however, is his astounding *Faust*, a lyrical but highly charged retelling of the classic legend of a man selling his soul for knowledge. It took Goethe almost his entire life to complete it to his own satisfaction, and is still probably the most-performed piece of theatre in Germany today; a fitting legacy for a genuine giant.

Gartenhaus, Römisches Haus, and Tiefurt Schloss (Tiefurt Palace) and Park. A combined ticket for all except the Goethe Haus and the Rokokosaal costs adult/concession €20/15.

BOOKSHOPS
Thalia (☎ 828 10; Schillerstrasse 5a)

DISCOUNT CARDS
WeimarCard (72 hrs, €10) Admission or discounts for museums, travel on city buses and other benefits.

INTERNET ACCESS
Die Eule (☎ 850 388; www.die-eule-buchhandlung.de; Frauentorstrasse 9; €0.50 per 5 min)
Vobis (☎ 90 29 95; Graben; €1.80 per hr)

EMERGENCY
Police station (☎ 850 729; Markt 15)

MONEY
Sparkasse (Graben 4)

POST
Main post office (☎ 2310; Goetheplatz 7-8) Public fax-phone and photocopier.

TOURIST INFORMATION
Buchenwald Information (☎ 430 200; Markt 6; ⊙ 10am-12.30pm & 1-5pm Mon-Fri, 10am-3pm Sat, 10am-2pm Sun)
DJH Service Centre (☎ 850 000; www.djh-thueringen .de; Carl-August-Allee 13; ⊙ 1-4pm Mon, 9am-noon & 1-5pm Tue & Thu, 9am-noon Fri) Reservations and information for DJH hostels.
Stiftung Weimarer Klassik (Weimar Classics Foundation; ☎ 545 401; www.swkk.de; Frauentorstrasse 4; ⊙ 8.30am-4.45pm) Museum tickets and literature.
Tourist Information (☎ 240 00; www.weimar.de; Markt 10; ⊙ 9.30am-6pm Mon-Fri, 9.30am-3pm Sat & Sun)

Sights
GOETHE HAUS
No other individual is as closely associated with Weimar as Johann Wolfgang von

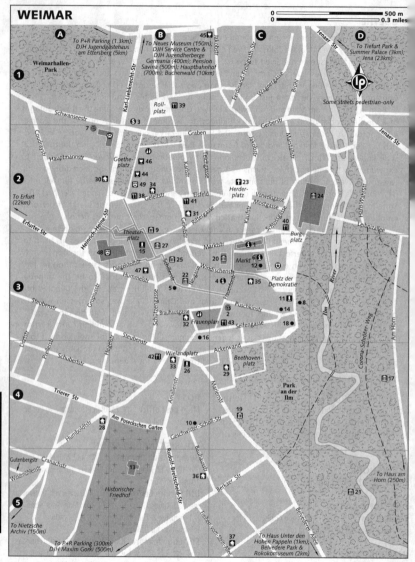

WEIMAR

0   500 m
0   0.3 miles

Some streets pedestrian-only

Weimarhallen-Park

To P+R Parking (1.3km);
DJH Jugendgästehaus
am Ettersberg (5km)

To Neues Museum (150m);
DJH Service Centre &
DJH Jugendherberge
Germania (400m); Pension
Savina (500m); Hauptbahnhof
(700m); Buchenwald (10km)

To Tiefurt Park &
Summer Palace (3km);
Jena (23km)

Roll-platz

Graben

Goethe-platz

Herder-platz

To Erfurt
(22km)

Eisfeld

Theater-platz

Markt

Burg-platz

Platz der
Demokratie

Frauenplan

Wielandplatz

Beethoven-platz

Park
an der
Ilm

Brauhausgasse

Historischer
Friedhof

To Nietzsche
Archiv (150m)

To P+R Parking (300m);
DJH Maxim Gorki (500m)

To Haus am
Horn (250m)

To Haus Unter den
Hohen Pappeln (1km);
Belvedere Park &
Rokokomuseum (2km)

THURINGIA

Goethe, who lived here from 1775 until his death in 1832. In 1792 his sponsor and employer, Duke Carl August, gave him a house as a gift. Known today as **Goethe Haus** (☎ 545 401; Frauenplan 1; adult/concession €6/4.50; ⏱ closed Mon), it was here that he worked, studied, researched and wrote such immortal works as *Faust*.

Goethe's original 1st-floor living quarters are reached via an expansive Italian Renaissance staircase decorated with sculpture and paintings brought back from his travels to Italy. Each of the rooms is painted in a different shade, according to Goethe's own theories about the correlation of mood and colour. You'll see his dining

INFORMATION			Kunstsammlungen zu Weimar	(see 24)	Hotel Elephant	35 C3
Buchenwald Information	1 C3		Liszt Haus	19 C4	Villa Hentzel	36 B5
Die Eule	2 C3		Rathaus	20 C3	Wolff's Art Hotel	37 C5
Sparkasse	3 B1		Römisches Haus	21 D5		
Stiftung Weimarer Klassik	4 C3		Schiller Haus	22 B3	EATING	(pp218-19)
Thalia	5 B3		Schlossmuseum	(see 24)	Anno 1900	38 B2
Tourist Information	6 C3		Stadthaus	(see 6)	Der Kaukasische Kreidekreis	39 B1
Vobis	7 A2		Stadtkirche St Peter & Paul		Residenz-Café	40 C2
			(Herderkirche)	23 C2	Scharfe Ecke	41 B3
SIGHTS & ACTIVITIES	(pp213-17)		Stadtschloss	24 D2	Sommer's	42 B4
Anna Amalia Library	8 C3		Stadtsclites	25 B3	Zum Weissen Schwan	43 C3
Bauhaus Museum	9 B2		Weimar Haus	25 B3		
Bauhaus Universität	10 B4		Wieland Statue	26 B4	DRINKING	(p219)
Carl August Statue	11 C3		Wittumspalais	27 B3	Mon Ami	44 B2
Cranachhaus	12 C3				Planbar	45 B1
Fürstengruft	13 B5		SLEEPING	(pp217-18)	Studentenclub Kasseturm	46 B2
Fürstenhaus	14 C3		DJH am Poseckschen Garten	28 A4	Studentenclub Schützengasse	47 B3
Goethe & Schiller Statue	15 B3		Dorint Hotel	29 C4		
Goethe Haus	16 B3		Grand Hotel Russischer Hof	30 A2	ENTERTAINMENT	(p219)
Goethe Nationalmuseum	(see 16)		Hababusch	31 B3	Deutsches Nationaltheater	48 A3
Goethes Gartenhaus	17 D4		Hotel Am Frauenplan	32 B3	Kommunales Kino	49 B2
Haus der Frau von Stein	18 C3		Hotel Amalienhof	33 B4	Theater im Gewölbe	(see 12)
			Hotel Anna Amalia	34 B2		

room, study and the bedroom with his deathbed.

Because demand often exceeds capacity, you'll be given a time slot to enter. Once inside, you can stay as long as you want.

GOETHE NATIONALMUSEUM

Those who come here expecting to learn all about the great man of letters will probably be disappointed. Rather than focusing on Goethe himself, the **Goethe Nationalmuseum** (☎ 545 401; Frauenplan 1; adult/concession €2.50/2; ⓧ closed Mon) offers a survey of the late 17th- and early 18th-century period, referred to as German Classicism. Goethe's fellow thinkers are given as much exposure as his ducal patrons (Anna Amalia and Carl August), his muses (Charlotte von Stein) and various other bit-players.

Paintings, books, manuscripts, sculptures, letters and objets d'art are presented in a nonchronological, loose fashion on two main floors, connected by both a cascading wood-panel staircase and a dramatically spiralling one.

Be sure to take a look inside the **Faustina café** (actually part of the Dorint hotel), with its controversial Christoph Hodgson mural depicting Weimar's glorious Who's Who; lurking among the famous faces is one Adolf Hitler.

SCHILLER HAUS

The dramatist Friedrich von Schiller lived in Weimar from 1799 until his early death in 1805 but, unlike Goethe, he had to buy his own house, **Schiller Haus** (☎ 545 401; Schillerstrasse 12; adult/concession €3.50/2.50; ⓧ closed Tue). The study at the end of the 2nd floor contains

his deathbed, as well as the desk where he penned Wilhelm Tell and other works. His wife's quarters are on the 1st floor and the servants lived on the ground floor. Enter via Neugasse.

Both Goethe and Schiller were interred at the **Historischer Friedhof** (Historic Cemetery) in the neoclassical **Fürstengruft** (adult/concession €2/1.50; ⓧ closed Tue), along with Duke Carl August.

PARK AN DER ILM

The sprawling Ilm Park, the eastern flank of the Altstadt, is an inspiring and romantic Unesco-protected spot named after the little river that runs through it. Its most famous feature is **Goethes Gartenhaus** (☎ 545 401; adult/concession €3/2; ⓧ closed Tue). This simple cottage was an early present (1776) from Duke Carl August and was intended to induce Goethe to stay in Weimar. It worked: he lived in this building until 1782 and also helped landscape the park. Admission is limited. In 1999 an exact replica of the house was built to protect the original from the tourist invasions.

Within view of the Gartenhaus is the **Römisches Haus** (☎ 545 401; adult/concession €2/1.50; ⓧ closed Mon), Carl August's summer retreat, built between 1792 and 1797 under Goethe's supervision. The first neoclassical house in Weimar, it perches atop an artificial bluff. It now contains restored period rooms and an exhibit on the Ilm Park.

On the western edge of the park stands the **Liszt Haus** (☎ 545 401; Marienstrasse 17; adult/concession €2/1.50; ⓧ closed Mon). The composer and pianist Franz Liszt resided in Weimar in 1848 and again from 1869 to 1886, when

THURINGIA

he wrote *Hungarian Rhapsody* and *Faust Symphony*.

ART NOUVEAU IN WEIMAR

Architecture fans may want to see the home of Belgian Art Nouveau architect, designer and painter Henry van de Velde, **Haus Unter den Hohen Pappeln**. Visible only from the outside, it looks a bit like a ship on its side and features natural stone, stylised chimneys, loggias and oversized windows. To reach it, take bus No 1 or 12 to Papiergraben.

Van de Velde also designed the entrance of the **Nietzsche Archiv** (☎ 545 401; Humboldt-strasse 36; adult/concession €2/1.50; ☼ Tue-Sun 1-6pm Apr-Oct, 1-4pm Nov-Mar), where the philosopher spent his final years, and the building now housing the **Bauhaus Universität** (Geschwister-Scholl-Strasse).

More splendidly restored Art Nouveau buildings cluster on Cranachstrasse, Gutenbergstrasse and Humboldtstrasse, just west of the Historischer Friedhof.

BAUHAUS IN WEIMAR

The Bauhaus School and movement was founded in Weimar in 1919 by Walter Gropius, who managed to draw top artists including Kandinsky, Klee, Feininger and Schlemmer as teachers. In 1925 the Bauhaus moved to Dessau and from there to Berlin, in 1932, where it was dissolved by the Nazis. The **Bauhaus Museum** (☎ 545 401; Theaterplatz; adult/concession €4/3; ☼ 10am-6pm Tue-Sun) chronicles the evolution of the group, explains their innovations in design and architecture, and spotlights the main players.

Despite its later influence on modern architecture, only one Bauhaus building was ever constructed in Weimar. Called the **Haus am Horn** (☎ 904 054; Am Horn 61; admission €1.50; ☼ 11am-6pm Wed, Sat & Sun Apr-Oct, 11am-5pm Wed, Sat & Sun Nov-Mar), it opened to the public in 1999.

For more on the movement, see Modern Design (p57), as well as the Berlin chapter (p87) and Dessau (p243).

NEUES MUSEUM

A recent addition to Weimar's list of attractions, **Neues Museum** (☎ 5460; Carl-August-Allee; adult/concession €3/2; ☼ 10am-6pm Tue-Sun Apr-Oct, 10am-4.30pm Tue-Sun Nov-Mar), north of the Altstadt, displays top-drawer contemporary art. The complex was built in 1863 as museum, but was used as a *Halle der Volksgemeinschaft* (literally 'people's solidarity hall') by the Nazis and renamed Karl-Marx-Platz under the GDR.

BELVEDERE & TIEFURT PARKS

Outside Weimar, the lovely **Belvedere Park** harbours Carl August's former hunting palace, with the **Rokokomuseum** (☎ 545 401; adult/concession €3.50/2.50; ☼ 10am-6pm Tue-Sun Apr-Sep, 10am-4.30pm Tue-Sun Oct) displaying glass, porcelain, faïence and weapons from the late 17th and 18th centuries. Also here is the **Collection of Historical Coaches** (admission €1). Bus No 12 runs hourly from Goetheplatz.

A few kilometres east of the Hauptbahnhof, **Tiefurt Park** is an English-style garden that envelops Anna Amalia's summer palace (☎ 545 401; Hauptstrasse 14, Weimar-Teifurt; adult/concession €3.50/2.50; ☼ closed Mon), her own 'temple of the muses'. It was here that she held her round-table gatherings, which often included Goethe. The palace is furnished and may be visited; bus No 3 will get you to the park.

WEIMAR HAUS

Around the bend from Schiller House, the **Weimar Haus** (☎ 901 890; www.weimarhaus.de; Schillerstrasse 16-18; adult/concession €6.50/5.50; ☼ 10am-8pm Apr-Oct, 10am-6pm Nov-Mar) offers a half-hour Disneyland-style multimedia history of Weimar from prehistory to classicism, with an animatronic Goethe as your guide. Sophisticates may roll their eyes, but it's a decent, basic introduction and available in English.

Walking Tour

Our tour begins on Herderplatz, dominated by the **Stadtkirche St Peter und Paul** (1; ☎ 851 518; Herderplatz; ☼ 10am-noon & 2-4pm Mon-Sat, 11am-noon & 2-3pm Sun). Built in 1500, it is popularly known as the Herderkirche after Johann Gottfried Herder, whom Goethe brought to Weimar as court preacher in 1776. His statue stands on the church square, and he's buried inside. The church itself has a famous altarpiece (1555), begun by Lucas Cranach the Elder and completed by his son. In the left aisle is an interesting triptych showing Martin Luther as a knight, professor and monk.

Walk east on Vorwerksgasse to Burgplatz, anchored by the **Stadtschloss (2)**, former resi-

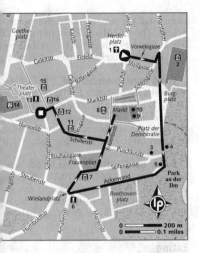

Shakespeare's works into German. Then turn north onto Frauenplan, where you'll find the **Goethe Haus** and **Goethe National-museum** (**7**; see p213).

A short walk further north leads to the Markt, with its neo-Gothic **Rathaus** (**8**; 1841) facing two Renaissance jewels: the **Cranach-haus** (**9**), where painter Lucas Cranach the Elder lived for two years before his death in 1553, and the **Stadthaus** (**10**), which now houses the tourist office.

Backtrack a few steps, then turn right onto the pedestrianised Schillerstrasse, which leads past the **Schiller Haus** (**11**; see p215) and the new **Weimar Haus** (**12**; see opposite) to Theaterplatz. Here, the famous statue of **Goethe and Schiller** (**13**; 1857) fronts the **Deutsches Nationaltheater** (**14**; German National Theatre), best known as the place where the national assembly drafted the constitution of the Weimar Republic in 1919. The theatre has several artistic claims to fame: Goethe was director here from 1791 to 1817, and Liszt and Strauss were its music directors in the late 19th century.

Across from here is the **Bauhaus Museum** (**15**; see opposite), adjacent to the baroque **Wittumspalais** (**16**; ☎ 545 401; adult/concession €3.50/2.50; ☒ closed Mon), once a residence of Anna Amalia, the premier patron of the arts in late-18th-century Weimar. The walking tour ends here.

Sleeping

BUDGET

Although Weimar's hotel capacity has increased enormously in recent years, demand occasionally exceeds supply. The tourist office arranges private rooms for a €2.55 fee, starting from €12.50 per person. Unless noted, all prices include breakfast and rooms with shower and toilet (except hostels).

Pension Savina (☎ 866 90; Meyerstrasse 60 & Rembrandtweg 13; s/d €35/55; ☒) On quiet side streets near the Hauptbahnhof, this pension and its annexe offer excellent value, with sauna, solarium and even a shuttle service.

Hababusch (☎ 850 737; Geleitstrasse 4; dm €10) This central hostel manages to be even cheaper than the DJH, but don't expect too much from the rooms.

At last count Weimar had four DJH hostels. The **DJH Service Centre** (☎ 850 000; Carl-August-Allee 13) books rooms:

lence of the ducal family of Saxe-Weimar. nside is the **Schlossmuseum** (☎ 5460; Burgplatz; dult/concession €4.50/3.50; ☒ 10am-6pm Tue-Sun pr-Oct, 10am-4.30pm Tue-Sun Nov-Mar), with arts nd craft objects, sculptures, and paintings. Highlights include the Cranach Gallery, everal portraits by Albrecht Dürer, and ollections of Dutch masters and German omanticists. Several restored palace resi-lence rooms can also be seen.

South of here, on Platz der Demokratie, s the **Fürstenhaus (3)**, a former palace that is now home of a renowned music academy ounded by Franz Liszt in 1872. The statue n front represents Duke Carl August. On he eastern side of the square is the **Anna Amalia Library (4)**, once managed by Goethe and still home to 900,000 books. Access o the library and its famous **Rokokosaal** Rococo Room; ☎ 545 401; Platz der Demokratie 1; dult/concession €2.50/2; ☒ 11am-12.30pm Mon-Sat pr-Oct) is strictly limited while the building s being restored.

The pink building behind the Fürsten-haus is the **Haus der Frau von Stein (5)**. She was a married woman who was Goethe's long-time muse and, if author Ettore Ghibellino s to be believed, acted as his lover to cover up the great author's socially unacceptable affair with Duchess Anna Amalia. The house is now home to the Goethe Institut, a language school and culture centre.

Head west on Ackerwand to Wieland-platz, with the **Wieland statue (6)**. It was Wieland (1733–1813) who first translated

THURINGIA

Am Poseckschen Garten (☎ 850 792; www
.jh-posgarten.de; Humboldtstrasse 17; juniors/seniors
€17/20; ✗ ➡) Near the Historischer Friedhof.

Jugendherberge Germania (☎ 850 490; jh-germ
ania@djh-thueringen.de; Carl-August-Allee 13; juniors/
seniors €17/20; ✗) Central.

Jugendgästehaus Maxim Gorki (☎ 850 750; Zum
Wilden Graben 12; juniors/seniors €18/21; Ⓟ ✗ ➡)
On the hilly southern side of town.

Jugendgästehaus am Ettersberg (☎ 421 111;
Ettersbergsiedlung; juniors/seniors €18/21; Ⓟ ✗
➡ ➡) In a nature reserve north of town.

MID-RANGE

Wolff's Art Hotel (☎ 540 60; call@wolffs-art-hotel.de;
Freiherr-vom-Stein-Allee 3a/b; s €69-85, d €99-110; Ⓟ ✗)
Quiet, classy and very contemporary, Wolff's
has a fully equipped spa/fitness area (with
treatments), and is also known for its gourmet restaurant.

Hotel Anna Amalia (☎ 495 60; www.hotel-anna
-amalia.de; Geleitstrasse 8-12; s €60-65, d €85-100; Ⓟ
✗) Just off Goetheplatz, this is a smart and
very central hotel with unfussy, comfortable rooms and a nice rear terrace.

Villa Hentzel (☎ 865 80; hotel-villa-hentzel@t-online
.de; Bauhausstrasse 12; s €54-67, d €77-98; Ⓟ) This
friendly, contemporary place is an excellent
bet, offering large, individually designed
rooms in a residential neighbourhood near
the Ilmpark.

Hotel Am Frauenplan (☎ 494 40; www.hotel-am
-frauenplan.de; Brauhausgasse 10; s/d €51/77; Ⓟ) Set
in its own courtyard, this is a decent new
guesthouse and pub-restaurant just opposite the Goethe Haus.

Hotel Fürstenhof (☎ 833 231; www.fuerstenhof
-weimar.de; Rudolf-Breitscheid-Strasse 2; s €52-72, d €80-
100; ➡) A nice modern alternative to the
ubiquitous 'period' décor elsewhere, with
abstract prints scattered around and an
almost startlingly yellow breakfast room.

Hotel Amalienhof (☎ 5490; amalienhofweimar@
t-online.de; Amalienstrasse 2; s €60-80, d €80-100; Ⓟ)
This lovely church-affiliated hotel is the
other end of the scale: a neoclassical villa
boasting a matching interior and historical
pamphlets in the rooms.

TOP END

Hotel Elephant (☎ 8020; elephant.weimar@arabella
sheraton.com; Markt 19; s €179-219, d €205-245, ste
€286-455; Ⓟ ➡) A true classic, the marble
Bauhaus-Deco splendour of the Elephant
has seen most of Weimar's great and good

come and go; just to make the point,
golden Thomas Mann looks out over th
Markt (square) from a balcony at the fron
The Elephantenkeller restaurant is also
local institution.

Grand Hotel Russischer Hof (☎ 7740; ww
.russischerhof.com; Goetheplatz 2; s €135-228, d €155-26
Ⓟ ✗ ✗) This huge, bombastic neoclassi
cal hotel has been around almost as long a
the Elephant, and offers a choice of moder
or historical rooms. The lobby area is qui
spectacular.

Dorint Hotel (☎ 8720; info.erfwei@dorint.cor
Beethovenplatz 1-2; s €100-152, d €118-185; Ⓟ ✗ ✗
Decked out in prison stripes, this five-sta
establishment has two floors of Italiana
spa designed by Munich artist Christop
Hodgson.

Eating

Apparently Weimar's humanist ethos ex
tends to animals as well – vegetarians wi
find far more choice here than in most othe
cities in Germany.

Residenz-Café (☎ 594 08; www.residenz-café.d
Grüner Markt 4; mains €5-15) Known as the 'Res
by regulars, this is one of Weimar's mos
popular haunts and has been for mor
than 160 years. Food comes in super-size
portions, with a top-notch Sekt/champagn
brunch for two (€45.50).

Zum Weissen Schwan (☎ 202 521; Frauentorstras
23; mains €8-16; ☽ Wed-Sun) You can dine her
like Goethe, Schiller and Liszt did. The gou
met menu includes Thuringian cuisine an
exotica like venison, and the kitchen als
caters for the renowned Elephantenkeller.

Anno 1900 (☎ 903 571; www.anno1900-weimar.d
Geleitstrasse 12a; mains €8.50-12.20) In an Art Nou
veau–style conservatory, this grand caf
serves international favourites, includin
almost a dozen vegetarian dishes and som
evil desserts.

Der Kaukasische Kreidekreis (Rollplatz 12; mair
€6-10) As you'd expect from anything name
after a Brecht play, intelligence and imagi
nation are manifest in this modern Geor
gian restaurant, which must be the best c
the many Russian and Eastern Europea
places in town.

Sommer's (☎ 400 691; www.wein-sommer.com; Hun
boldtstrasse 2; mains €4.50-10.90) Choose from fou
cosy rooms in this traditional restaurant
with a huge wine list and a fine menu, that'
probably the easiest choice you'll have!

THURINGIA

Scharfe Ecke (☎ 202 430; www.gasthaus-scharfe ecke.de; Eisfeld 2; mains €8.70-11) Head here for an immersion in Thuringian cuisine and generous DIY steak plates from €11.

Drinking

Weimar has never been renowned for throbbing nightlife, but there are a few good places catering for the student population.

Planbar (☎ 502 785; Jakobsplan 6) Young people gather at this big, trendy pub opposite a block of student flats.

Studentenclub Kasseturm (☎ 851 670; www kasseturm.de; Goetheplatz 10) A Weimar classic, Kasseturm is a historic round tower with three floors of live music, DJs, cabaret or just games nights.

Mon Ami (☎ 847 711; Goetheplatz 11) An alternative cultural centre with regular live gigs, club nights and other events.

Studentenclub Schützengasse (☎ 778 996; www schuetzengasse.de; Schützengasse 2) Similar to the Kasseturm, this large club has 20 different beers (from €1).

Entertainment

Deutsches Nationaltheater (German National Theatre; ☎ 755 334; www.nationaltheater-weimar.de; Theaterplatz; closed Jul-Aug). Expect a grab-bag of classic and contemporary plays, plus ballet, opera and classical concerts.

Theater im Gewölbe (☎ 777 377; Markt 11/12) In the Cranachhaus, this small theatre stages anything from Goethe to cult barfly Charles Bukowski.

Kommunales Kino (☎ 847 745; Goetheplatz 11; adult/concession €5/4) Film fans looking for undubbed arthouse fare will find it here.

Getting There & Away

Weimar is on the ICE route from Frankfurt (€44.20, 2½ hours) to Leipzig (€22.40, 50 minutes) and Dresden (€36.40, two hours), and an IR stop en route to Berlin-Zoo (€39.20, three hours). All leave at two-hour intervals. Erfurt (€4, 15 minutes) and Eisenach (€10.70, one hour) are served several times hourly, plus there's frequent services to Jena West (€4, 15 minutes).

Getting Around

Walking is the only way of getting around central Weimar. For trips outside the centre, there's a good bus system (single €1.40, day pass €3.50). For a taxi, call ☎ 903 600. The RegioMobil Tageskarte (see p204) covers Weimar's public transport.

Unless staying in an Altstadt hotel, drivers must leave their car in one of the paid parking lots outside the centre. Look for the signs saying 'P+R'.

AROUND WEIMAR

Buchenwald

The Buchenwald concentration camp **museum and memorial** (☎ 03643-4300; Ettersberg Hill; www.buchenwald.de; admission free; 9.45am-6pm, May-Sep; 8.45am-5pm, Oct-Apr) are 10km northwest of Weimar. You first pass the memorial erected atop the mass graves of some of the 56,500 victims from 18 nations, including German antifascists, Jews, and Soviet and Polish prisoners of war. The concentration camp and museum are 1km beyond the memorial. Many prominent German communists and social democrats, Ernst Thälmann and Rudolf Breitscheid among them, were murdered here. After 1943, prisoners were exploited in the production of weapons. Many died during medical experimentation. Shortly before the end of the war, some 28,000 prisoners were sent on death marches. Between 1937 and 1945, more than one-fifth of the 250,000 incarcerated here died. On 11 April 1945, as US troops approached and the SS guards fled, the prisoners rebelled (at 3.15pm – the clock tower above the entrance still shows that time), overwhelmed the remaining guards and liberated themselves.

After the war, the Soviet victors turned the tables by establishing Special Camp No 2, in which 7000 so-called anticommunists and ex-Nazis were literally worked to death. Their bodies were found after the Wende in mass graves north of the camp and near the Hauptbahnhof.

Pamphlets and books in English are sold at the bookshop. Last admission is three-quarters of an hour before closing.

To get here take bus No 6 from Weimer; by car, head north on Ettersburger Strasse from Weimar station and turn left onto Blutstrasse.

GOTHA

☎ **03621 / pop 49,000**

Gotha was first mentioned in 775 in a document signed by Charlemagne, and rose to prominence when Duke Ernst I made it his residence and built the enormous yet gracious Schloss Friedenstein. The descendants of this founder of the House of Saxe-Coburg-Gotha now occupy the British royal throne, having changed their name to Windsor after WWI. In the 18th century, an extended stay by the French philosopher Voltaire turned the court into a centre of the Enlightenment in Germany. Even today, the Schloss, which contains several top-rated museums and a resplendent baroque theatre, remains Gotha's cultural centre and its star attraction.

A pleasant provincial town, Gotha is also a gateway to the Thuringian Forest and the terminus of the Thüringerwaldbahn, a historic tram that shuttles through the forest several times daily (see Getting There & Away opposite). Environmental issues are taken very seriously here – look out for the solar-powered parking meters!

Orientation

Schloss Friedenstein and its gardens, sitting on the Schlossberg mound, take up about half of Gotha's city centre, with the Altstadt to the north and the Hauptbahnhof (central train station) to the south. It's a brisk 15-minute walk from the Hauptbahnhof to the central squares – the long Hauptmarkt and the busier Neumarkt. The central bus station is on Mühlgrabenweg, northeast of the centre.

Information

CM System (☎ 510 20; Friemarer Strasse 38) Internet access.

Gotha-Information (☎ 222 138; www.gotha.de; Hauptmarkt 2; ☒ 9am-6pm Mon-Fri, 10am-3pm Sat, Sun Apr-Oct only 10am-3pm) Tourist information.

Main post office (Ekhofplatz 1) Public fax-phone, currency exchange.

Tourist information (☎ 363 111; Margarethenstrasse 2-4; ☒ 11am-6pm Tue-Fri, 10am-1pm Sat)

Sights

SCHLOSS FRIEDENSTEIN

Built between 1643 and 1654, this horseshoe-shaped palace is the largest surviving early baroque palace in Germany; it was never bombed, supposedly because of the link with the British royal family, and survived WWII thanks to one Josef Ritter von Gadolla, who surrendered the town to the Allies in 1945 and was executed by his own side. The exterior remains largely

unchanged, with two distinctive towers one round and the other square. Amon the museums it contains, the **Schlossmuseu** (☎ 823 414; adult/concession €4/2; ☒ 10am-5pm Tu Fri) deserves top billing. In fact, it's wort visiting Gotha just to tour its lavish baroqu and neoclassical royal apartments and th eclectic collections they hold. Expect t spend at least two hours here.

A main attraction of the medieval co lection is the ethereal painting *Gotha Liebespaar* (artist unknown). This depic tion of two lovers is considered the firs double portrait in German painting. Als noteworthy are several artworks by Luca Cranach the Elder, including the hauntin *Verdammnis und Erlösung* (Damnation an Deliverance; 1529).

On the 2nd floor you'll find the **Festsaa** an exuberant hall of stuccoed ceilings, wal and doors. The less flashy neoclassica wing contains a collection of sculpture of which the Renaissance work by Conra Meit called *Adam und Eva* deserves speci mention. The **Kunstkammer** is jammed wit miniature curiosities and treasures, includ ing exotica like engraved ostrich eggs an a cherry pit sporting a carved portrait c Ernst the Pious; the palace also houses on of Europe's oldest Egyptian collections.

In the west tower is the **Museum fü Regionalgeschichte und Volkskunde** (☎ 823 45 museum.regionalgeschichte@gmx.de; adult/concession €4/ ☒ 10am-5pm Tue-Sun), one of the most impo tant museums of regional history in Thu ingia. A real gem, though, is the refurbishe **Ekhof-Theater**, one of the oldest baroqu theatres in Europe. The stage tradition a Schloss Friedenstein goes back to 1683 an a still-functional mechanised set-changin device survives from that period. Perform ances take place during the summer festiva in July and August, and there's also an ex hibit on its history.

The **Schlosskirche** occupies the northeast ern corner, while the east wing contains **research library** with more than half a mi lion books from 12 centuries. You can als take a tour of the atmospheric **Kasematte** (underground passages; €3.50; ☒ 11am, 1pm, 3pm 4pm Tue-Sun).

HAUPTMARKT

The **Rathaus**, with its gorgeously restore Renaissance façade and 40m-tall towe commands the rectangular, sloping Haupt-markt, the focal point of the Altstadt. Built as a department store in 1567, the structure was later inhabited by Duke Ernst I until Schloss Friedenstein was completed, and was finally turned into the town hall in 1665. At the top of the slope, towards the palace, is the **Wasserkunst**, a cascading fountain. Noteworthy houses flanking the square include No 42, where Martin Luther stayed in 1537, and No 17, which was the birthplace of Lucas Cranach's wife. Of modest importance is the **Augustinerkirche**, one block west, where Luther preached four times and which has an unusual pulpit balancing on a slender wood pillar.

Sleeping

Gotha has a reasonable range of accommodation to choose from; weekend rates are generally significantly cheaper. The tourist office makes free reservations, including **private rooms** (around €17 per person).

Pension am Schloss (☎ 853 206; Bergallee 3; s/d €21.50/48; P) Not far away, this lovely 1920s home near the foot of the palace has friendly owners and a flowery garden. Some rooms have antiques and private bathroom.

Café Suzette (☎ 856 755; www.café-suzette.com; Rebelstrasse 8; s €31.50-36, d €54; P) Tiny but well-equipped pension with basic rooms above a cake shop, five minutes from the Hauptbahnhof. Bike hire is available here.

Pension Regina (☎ 408 020; www.pension-regina.de; Schwabhäuser Strasse 4; s/d €36/59; P) Centrally located yet quiet, this family-friendly pension has rooms with private shower/toilet.

Toscana (☎ 295 93; www.toscana-gotha.de; Pfortenwallstrasse 1; s/d €45/65; P) An excellent Italian-flavoured hotel and restaurant on the ring road north of the Altstadt, with good rooms, tasty pasta and a cocktail menu organised by taste and strength.

Hotel Am Schlosspark (☎ 4420; www.hotel-am-schlosspark.de; Lindenauallee 20; s €90-110, d €115-136; P X R) The only top-end choice in town, this modern place is also the best option for wheelchair users. Unusually, not all rooms have TVs – the large spa/fitness centre should provide enough entertainment though.

Eating

Old-world coffee-house culture reigns in Gotha's Altstadt, with most eating options

centred on the area around the Hauptmarkt and Neumarkt.

Café Loesche (☎ 240 25; Buttermarkt 6; cakes €0.80-1.50) Expansive windows give you a great view of people heading to the Hauptmarkt as you enjoy the gorgeous cakes in a classic grand café environment.

Zum Goldenen Schelle (☎ 891 950; Hauptmarkt 40; mains €4-6; ⊙ Mon-Fri) At the foot of Hauptmarkt, this restaurant is atmospheric and historic.

Maharadscha Palace (☎ 892 400; Hauptmarkt 20; mains €6-13) Curry and pasta is an unusual combination, but these guys seem to make it work. What's really bizarre is that this is by no means the only Indo-Italian restaurant in Germany, or even in this area!

Pavarotti (☎ 709 115; Waltershäuserstrasse 9; mains €6-14) The menu here certainly wouldn't do much for the great tenor's diet plan, with huge portions of Italian classics and takes on German staples like schnitzel.

Weinschänke (☎ 301 009; Gartenstrasse 28; mains €10-17) For dining in historical surrounds with a large game menu including elk and kangaroo, try this big traditional wine house by the ring road.

Getting There & Away

Gotha is easily reached by train from Eisenach (€4, 25 minutes), Erfurt (€4, 20 minutes) and Weimar (€6.60, 35 minutes). It's also an IR train stop (every two hours) to Berlin-Zoo (€44.60, 3¾ hours) and Frankfurt (€35.20, 2¼ hours). Gotha is just north of the A4 and is crossed by the B247 and B7.

For access to the Thuringian Forest, take the **Thüringerwaldbahn** (☎ 4310; www.waldbahn-gotha.de; tram No 4), which makes the trip to Friedrichroda (€2.40, 50 minutes) and Tabarz (€2.80, one hour) several times hourly.

NORTHERN THURINGIA

MÜHLHAUSEN

☎ 03601 / pop 39,000

About 40km north of Gotha, in the picturesque Unstrut River valley, lies Mühlhausen, which experienced its greatest glory as a 'free imperial city' in the Middle Ages. Its historical core, crisscrossed by cobbled alleyways, reflects 800 years of changing architectural styles. There's a good collection of half-timbered houses with gorgeous carved and painted doors.

Information

Ambulance (☎ 3323)
Deutsche Bank (☎ 88 120; Untermarkt 27)
Police (☎ 500; Karl-Marx-Strasse 4)
Post office (Bahnhofsplatz 1)
Tourist information (☎ 452 321; www.muehlhausen .de; Ratsstrasse 20; ☉ 9am-5pm Mon-Fri, 10am-2pm Sat)

Sights

Mühlhausen's historic core is encircled by its 12th-century **town wall** (adult/concession €3/2), just under 3km long, with two gates and three towers still standing. It's partly accessible between Frauentor and Rabenturm.

Mühlhausen's skyline is characterised by the steeples and spires of 13 churches, of which the **Marienkirche** at Am Obermarkt, with its neo-Gothic steeple, is the most notable. The five-nave construction makes it the second-largest church in Thuringia, after the Dom in Erfurt. In 1525, priest and reformer Thomas Müntzer preached here to his rebel following before the disastrous final battle of the Peasants' War on the Schlachtberg, and there is a **memorial** (☎ 870 023; adult/concession €3/2) to him here.

A museum dedicated to the history of the Peasants' War is nearby in the **Kornmarktkirche** (☎ 816 904; Ratsstrasse; adult/concession €3/2).

At the **Divi-Blasii Kirche** (Divi-Blasii church), just south of the Altstadt on Felchtaer Strasse, Johann Sebastian Bach – followed by his cousin and then by his fourth son – worked as organist, inaugurating a new organ in 1709. Also worth a look is the **Rathaus** (☎ 4520; Ratsstrasse 19; adult/concession €2/1), a sprawling cluster of buildings from several centuries built around a Gothic core.

Sleeping & Eating

DJH hostel (☎ 813 318; jh-muehlhausen@gmx.de; Auf dem Tonberg; juniors/seniors €12.50/15.50; ✗ 🖳) This hostel is about 2km from the city centre (bus No 5 or 6 to Blobach).

Hotel An der Stadtmauer (☎ 465 00; Britenstrasse 15; s €49-55, d €75; 🅿 ✗) This friendly hotel near the city wall and the new Burg Galerie shopping centre has nicely fitted rooms, some opening onto a courtyard, plus a small fitness room and solarium.

Brauhaus zum Löwen (☎ 4710; Kornmarkt 3; www .brauhaus-zum-loewen.de; s/d €60/90; 🅿) A traditional brewery restaurant (try the extra long Bratwurst) with a good hotel attached right in the centre of town.

Postkeller (☎ 440 091; Steinweg 6; mains €7-17) Healthy portions of local food are served in a lovely room with Art Nouveau tiles and a pub/club upstairs; for anyone doubting the German sense of humour, there's a chalk sign boasting that Goethe *didn't* live here!

Zum Nachbarn (☎ 447 10; Steinweg 65; mains €10-13.50) Thuringian fare is on the menu in this old red house with beamed ceilings and many windows. Special deals are available for kids and seniors.

Getting There & Away

There are hourly trains from Erfurt (€9, 45 minutes); coming from Eisenach (€9, 1¼ hours) requires a change in Gotha. Mühlhausen is at the crossroads of the B249 from Sondershausen and the B247 from Gotha.

THE KYFFHÄUSER

The Kyffhäuser is a low forested mountain range wedged between the Harz Mountains to the north and the Thuringian Forest to the south. Besides being good hiking and cycling territory, it harbours several unique and intriguing sights. A good base from which to explore the area is Bad Frankenhausen, a quiet spa town at the forest's southern edge. The **Tourismusverband Kyffhäuser** (☎ 034671-717 16; www .kyffhaeuser-tourismus.de; Anger 14; ☉ 9.30am-6pm Mon-Fri, 9.30am-12.30pm Sat) sells the **Kyffhäuser Card** (adult/child €13/6) for admission to the main attractions here.

Kyffhäuser Monument

Above the dense forests and steep ravines of the 457m-high Kyffhäuser mountain looms the bombastic **Kyffhäuser Monument** (☎ 034651-2780; adult/concession €4/2.50; ☉ 9am-7pm) to Emperor Wilhelm I, built in 1896. A statue showing Wilhelm on horseback stands below a 60m-high tower and above the stone throne of Emperor Friedrich I (1125–90), better known as Barbarossa, whom he considered his spiritual predecessor.

The monument stands on the foundations of the Oberburg (Upper Castle) of the medieval Burg Kyffhausen, Germany's largest castle complex (608m long, 60m

·ide) before its destruction in 1118. Today, ·e only ruins remaining are those of the ·nterburg (Lower Castle), as well as a gate ·nd a 172m-deep well.

The remote monument is best reached by ·ar, but there's also a sporadic bus service ·om Bad Frankenhausen.

·anorama Museum

·n the Schlachtberg, 3km north of Bad ·rankenhausen's centre, stands a giant ·oncrete cylinder that harbours a truly epic ·ainting – of proportions and content. **Früh·ürgerliche Revolution in Deutschland** (Early Civil ·evolution in Germany; ☎ 034671-6190; www.panorama-·useum.de; adult/concession/child €5/4/1; ☒ 10am-6pm ·ue-Sun year-round, 1-6pm Mon Jul-Aug) is an oil ·ainting measuring 14m by 123m (!) and ·epresenting a style called 'fantastical real·ism', reminiscent of such classical artists as Bruegel and Hieronymus Bosch. More than 3000 figures, assembled in numerous scenes, metaphorically depict the tumultuous tran·sition from the Middle Ages to the modern ·era in 15th- and 16th-century Europe.

It took artist Werner Tübke and his five ·assistants five years to complete this com·plex allegorical work, which opened in 1989 as one of the last official acts of the GDR government. The work's artistic merit and political context have been questioned, but its sheer size and ambitious themes do not fail to impress.

Barbarossahöhle

Some 5km from Bad Frankenhausen, this impressive series of plaster caves at **Barbaros·sahöhle** (☎ 034671-5450; www.hoehle.de; Mühlen 6, Rottleben; adult/child €6/4; ☒ 10am-5pm, tours hourly) can be visited on a guided tour. Among the highlights are the slabs described by legend as Barbarossa's table and chair.

Sleeping & Eating

All of the following also have restaurants.

Alte Hämmelei (☎ 034671-5120; www.alte-haem melei.de; Bornstrasse 33; dm €24, s/d €35/60; ℗) A very traditional hostel and pension with nice pine-filled rooms and tons of character.

Hotel Grabenmühle (☎ 034671-798 82; Am Wall graben 1; s/d €32/54; ℗) This central hotel is similar in style but a bit more modern.

Hotel Residenz (☎ 034671-750; www.residenz-frank enhausen.de; Am Schlachtberg 3; s/d €69/99; ℗ ☒ ☒) At the top of the hotel food chain, this big

white place near the Panorama Museum has a huge spa section.

Getting There & Around

Getting to Bad Frankenhausen by train usually requires a change in Bretleben or Sömmerda. From Erfurt, connections cost €8.10 to €10.70 and take around 1½ hours. By car or motorcycle, take the B4, B86 and then the B85.

To reach the outlying sights, it's best to be under your own steam. For bike rental, try the **FAU Radwanderzentrum** (☎ 777 71; Hauptbahnhof).

THURINGIAN FOREST

The Thuringian Forest, a mountainous area roughly bordered by the Werra River in the west and the Saale River in the east, sprawls out south of the A4. It incorporates the 76-sq-km **Hainich National Park** (☎ 3603-390728; www.nationalpark-hainich.de; administration office Bei der Marktkirche 9, 99947 Bad Langensalza). Not all of the forest is pristine; many of the trees are suffering the effects of acid rain from decades of air pollution, and several beau·tifully situated towns, like Suhl, have been ravaged by industry or blighted by high-rise GDR apartment blocks.

Despite these drawbacks, the climate, dense woodlands, unhurried lifestyle and relative lack of commercialism still make the Thuringian Forest a wonderful place to explore. The tallest peaks are just under 1000m and provide good opportunities for winter sports. The Rennsteig, one of Ger·many's most popular trails, runs along the mountain ridges for 168km.

EISENACH

☎ 03691 / pop 44,000

Eisenach, a small, pretty city on the edge of the Thuringian Forest, is the birthplace of Johann Sebastian Bach and an important venue in the life of the reformer Martin Luther, but the town's big-ticket attraction is the Wartburg, the only German castle to be named a Unesco World Heritage Site. The historical associations of the place must rival just about any other single building in Thuringia.

The castle aside, Eisenach itself still has plenty to offer visitors and boasts plenty of cultural options. The town's modest size and charming atmosphere make it a very pleasant alternative to the larger, more popular destinations of Weimar and Erfurt.

Orientation

The Markt is a 15-minute walk from the Hauptbahnhof (central train station); and except for the Wartburg, which is 2km southwest of town, most sights are concentrated on this area. Local buses stop right outside the Hauptbahnhof; overland buses on Müllerstrasse one block northwest.

Information

Copy Inn (☎ 784 565; Sophienstrasse; €1 per 15 min) Internet access.

Eisenach Classic Card (€12, 72hr) Public transport and free or reduced admission to important sights.
Main post office (Markt 6)
Tourist information (☎ 792 30; www.eisenach.de; Markt 9; ⏰ 10am-6pm Mon, 9am-6pm Tue-Fri, 10am-2pm Sat & Sun)
Volksbank (☎ 887 826; Schillerstrasse 16)
Wartburg Information (☎ 2500; Schlossberg; ⏰ 9am-12.30pm & 1-5pm Tue-Fri)

Sights

WARTBURG

A superb medieval castle perched on hill high above the town, **Wartburg** (☎ 250 www.wartburg-eisenach.de; tour adult/concession €6/ museum & Luther room only €3.50/2; ⏰ tours 8.30am 5pm) is said to go back to Count Ludwig de

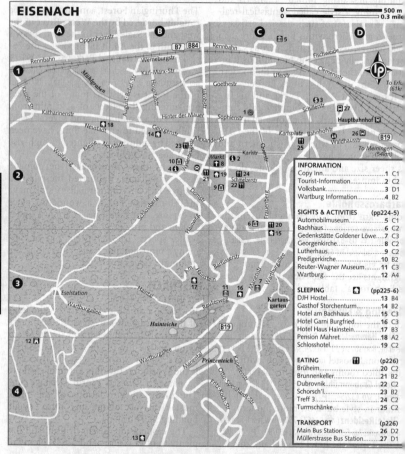

INFORMATION
Copy Inn.....................1 C1
Tourist-Information.....................2 C2
Volksbank.....................3 D1
Wartburg Information.....................4 B2

SIGHTS & ACTIVITIES (pp224-5)
Automobilmuseum.....................5 C1
Bachhaus.....................6 C2
Gedenkstätte Goldener Löwe.....7 C2
Georgenkirche.....................8 C2
Lutherhaus.....................9 C2
Predigerkirche.....................10 B2
Reuter-Wagner Museum.....................11 C3
Wartburg.....................12 A4

SLEEPING (pp225-6)
DJH Hostel.....................13 B4
Gasthof Storchenturm.....................14 B2
Hotel am Bachhaus.....................15 C3
Hotel Garni Burgfried.....................16 C3
Hotel Haus Hainstein.....................17 B3
Pension Mahret.....................18 A2
Schlosshotel.....................19 B2

EATING (p226)
Brüheim.....................20 C2
Brunnenkeller.....................21 B2
Dubrovnik.....................22 C2
Schorsch'l.....................23 B2
Treff 3.....................24 C2
Turmschänke.....................25 C2

TRANSPORT (p226)
Main Bus Station.....................26 D2
Müllerstrasse Bus Station.....................27 D1

springer (the Jumper); you'll hear the story of how the castle got its name many times, but listen out for how Ludwig got his peculiar moniker as well.

Richard Wagner based his opera *Tannhäuser* on a famous minstrels' contest that took place at the castle between 1206 and 1207. It was also notably the residence of the much-revered Elisabeth, wife of the landgrave of Thuringia. She was canonised shortly after her death in 1235 for abandoning a pompous court lifestyle in favour of helping the poor.

From 1521 to 1522 Martin Luther went into hiding here under the assumed name of Junker Jörg after being excommunicated and put under papal ban; during this time he translated the entire New Testament from Greek into German, contributing enormously to the development of the written German language. His modest, wood-panelled **study** is part of the guided tour (available in English), which is the only way to view the interior; most of the rooms you'll see are extravagant 19th-century impressions of medieval life rather than original fittings. The Romanesque **Great Hall** is amazing.

The **museum** houses the famous Cranach paintings of Luther and important Christian artefacts from all over Germany, and also offers another rarity: excellent English signage.

Between Easter and October, crowds can be horrendous; arrive before 11am.

To get to the Wartburg from the Markt, walk one block west to Wydenbrugkstrasse, then head up Schlossberg through the forest via Eselstation (40 minutes, parts are rather steep). A more scenic return route is via the Haintal (50 minutes). From April to October, buses No 10 and 13 run roughly hourly to the Eselstation, just below the castle (€1.10).

CITY CENTRE

The Markt is dominated by the galleried **Georgenkirche** (10am-noon & 2-4pm), where members of the Bach family, including Johann Sebastian himself, served as organists between 1665 and 1797. Its collection of ancient tombstones includes that of Wartburg founder Ludwig der Springer.

A few steps south is the half-timbered **Lutherhaus** (298 30; www.lutherhaus-eisenach.de;

Lutherplatz 8; adult/concession €2.50/2; 9am-5pm) where Martin Luther lived as a schoolboy between 1498 and 1501. The exhibit traces important stages in the reformer's life through paintings, manuscripts and illustrated works, as well as through a series of interactive multimedia terminals (German and English).

South of here stands the **Bachhaus** (793 40; www.bachhaus.de; Frauenplan 21; adult/concession €4/3; 10am-6pm), a memorial exhibit on the composer, who was born in 1685 in a now-demolished house nearby. The visit concludes with a 25-minute concert played on antique instruments, reminding you just why Bach is so adored.

Fans of the more controversial composer Richard Wagner should check out the exhibition on his life and works at the **Reuter-Wagner Museum** (743 293; Reuterweg 2; adult/concession €3/1.50; 10am-5pm Tue-Sun) in writer Fritz Reuter's former villa.

The first nationwide proletarian movement, the Social Democratic Workers Party, was founded in Eisenach by August Bebel and Wilhelm Liebknecht in 1869. The **Gedenkstätte Goldener Löwe** (Golden Lion Memorial; 754 34; Marienstrasse 57; 9am-4pm Mon-Fri) has an interesting exhibit covering the 19th-century workers' movement in Germany.

In the **Predigerkirche** (784 678; Predigerplatz 2; adult/concession €2.60/1.60; 9am-5pm Tue-Sun) you'll find an exhibit on medieval art in Thuringia.

Eisenach's long car-manufacturing tradition is celebrated in the **Automobilmuseum** (772 12; Friedrich-Naumann-Strasse 10; adult/concession €2.10/1.10; 10am-5pm Tue-Sun), where you can admire 100 years of cars, including the Dixi and the Wartburg 1.3.

Sleeping

The tourist office has a free room-finding service – private rooms start at €15/25 a single/double. All hotel prices here include breakfast and private bathroom.

DJH hostel (743 259; jh-eisenach@djh-thueringen.de; Mariental 24; juniors/seniors €15/18; P X) Eisenach's DJH Jugendherberge Artur Becker has been recently renovated.

Gasthof & Wanderpension Storchenturm (07 00-4040 4050; Georgenstrasse 43; dm €18, r €35) For cheap stays in the centre of town, try this hostel-like place with guest rooms and monastic dorms, plus a fun restaurant in a former barn.

Pension Mahret (☎ 742 744; www.puppenstuben hotel.de; Neustadt 30; r per person €22.50-44) East of the centre, on the edge of the Wartburg woods, this is a self-styled 'dolls-house hotel' offering apartment-style rooms of varying sizes.

Hotel am Bachhaus (☎ 204 70; www.hotel-am -bachhaus.de; Marienstrasse 7; s €45, d €65-75) This new hotel offers comfortable modern rooms and a central location, as well as a traditional hand-painted restaurant.

Hotel Haus Hainstein (☎ 2420; www.hainstein.de; Am Hainstein 16; s €45-50, d €70-80; Ⓟ Ⓧ) One of a cluster of handsome Art Nouveau villas in the hilly south of town, this fantastic church-affiliated mansion has a park-like setting, great views of the Wartburg, light, stylish rooms and a nice restaurant.

Hotel Garni Burgfried (☎ 732 619; Marienstrasse 60; s €49-60, d €75-87, ste €113; Ⓟ) A turn-of-the-century villa at the foot of the Wartburg access road, with large, mostly modern rooms and a smart atmosphere.

Schlosshotel (☎ 214 260; www.schlosshotel-eisen ach.de; Marktplatz 10; s €74, d €97-108; Ⓟ) Most rooms here face the interior courtyard in this big shiny complex, a quiet haven in the centre of town. The wine cellar restaurant offers Luther-era theme nights.

Eating

Brüheim (☎ 203 509; Marienstrasse 1; cakes €0.50-1.50) To top off your day, Eisenach's best cakes are here, near the Bachhaus.

Treff 3 (☎ 213 108; Schmelzerstrasse 3; ☾ 2-6pm) An admirable church-run 'integration café' designed to bring disabled residents, travellers and anyone else open-minded together in a friendly environment.

Schorsch'l (☎ 213 049; Georgenstrasse 19; snacks around €4) This happening bistro-pub has light meals and (often) live music.

Brunnenkeller (☎ 212 358; Markt 10; mains €7-9) For good hearty Thuringian dishes in an authentic Weinkeller setting, try the old monastery cellars on the south side of the Georgenkirche.

Dubrovnik (☎ 210 400; Schmelzerstrasse; mains €8-11) Grilled meat in vast quantities forms the basis of an extensive menu at this commendable Croatian restaurant. Children and seniors get to choose from the same slightly patronising budget menu.

Turmschänke (☎ 213 533; Wartburgallee 2; mains €22-25) For an upmarket dining experience your best bet is this classy and thoroughly atmospheric wine restaurant, part of the Hotel Kaiserhof.

Getting There & Away

Frequent direct trains run to Erfurt (€8.10, 50 minutes), Gotha (€4, 25 minutes) and Weimar (€10.70, one hour). ICE trains to Frankfurt-am-Main (€35.80, 1¾ hours) and IC trains to Berlin-Zoo (€47.40, 3¾ hours) also stop here. Bus services are sporadic at best; useful connections include No 280b to Friedrichroda and No 30 to Mühlhausen.

If you're driving, Eisenach is right on the A4 (exits Eisenach Ost or Eisenach West) and crossed by the B7, B19 and B84.

RENNSTEIG

Eisenach is the western gateway to the Rennsteig, one of Germany's most popular long-distance walks. From the suburb of Hörschel, the trail wends 168km southeast along mountain ridges through largely uninterrupted forest to Blankenstein on the Saale River, offering beautiful views of dreamy valleys, snug villages and medieval hill-top castles. It's well maintained and signposted with markers bearing the letter 'R'. The best hiking time is May/June and September/October, though mid-summer is tolerable too because most of the walking is done at elevations above 700m. You should be moderately fit, but no serious hiking experience or equipment is required.

Hiking the entire distance can be done in five days, though day hikes – especially between Hörschel and Oberhof – are a pleasant way to sample the region. Although there's little in the way of accommodation directly on the trail, there are plenty of pensions and hotels in the villages below.

Before setting out, pick up maps (Kompass Wanderkarte No 118 is a good one) and information at the **Rennsteigwanderhaus** (☎ 036928-911 94; Rennsteigstrasse 9, Hörschel; ☾ 7.30am-noon & 1-4pm Mon-Fri, 7.30-10.30am & 3-5pm Sat & Sun).

According to local tradition, you must dip your walking stick into the Werra and pick up a pebble from its waters before starting out. Upon leaving the Rennsteig, the pebble must be given back to the forest.

To get to the trailhead, take bus No 93 direction: Oberellen) from the Müllertrasse bus station in Eisenach. If you hike he entire distance to Blankenstein, you an then catch a train to Saalfeld, Jena and •eyond.

RIEDRICHRODA

☎ 03623 / pop 5500

'riedrichroda is scenically located in the orest about 20km south of Gotha. During jDR days, it was the country's second-ousiest resort, with more than one million >vernight stays a year. Numbers dropped lramatically after the Wende, but Friedichroda is once again gaining in popularity, specially after improvements to infrastrucure and a reorientation towards health nd spa tourism. In 1998 a state-of-the-art herapeutic bath centre opened here; it's lso a popular site for winter sports.

)rientation & Information

'riedrichroda has two train stations: Bahnof Friedrichroda in the east and Bahnhof Reinhardsbrunn north of the centre, which s the stop for the Thüringerwaldbahn. Che **tourist office** (☎ 332 00; www.friedrichroda.de; Marktstrasse 13-15; ⊗ 9am-5pm Mon-Thu, 9am-6pm Fri, am-noon Sat) is in the centre of town.

Sights & Activities

'riedrichroda's prime attraction is the Marienglashöhle (☎ 304 953; tour adult/concession .4/3.50; ⊗ tours 9am-5pm), a large gypsum cave eaturing an underwater lake and a crystal ;rotto. You enter the latter in the dark, hen – just to give you that otherworldly eel – the theme from *Close Encounters of he Third Kind* plays in the background ts the light gradually brightens, unveiling ι sparkling universe. Most of the crystalised gypsum here has been harvested and ised to decorate statues of the Virgin Mary ιnd altars in the region and beyond.

The cave is about a 40-minute walk hrough the woods from the city centre and s also a stop on the Thüringerwaldbahn see Getting There & Away p228).

In the northern part of town, in the midst)f a lavish English park with ancient trees, tands the neo-Gothic **Schloss Reinhardsbrunn** 1828), built on the foundations of a medival Benedictine monastery founded by Vartburg builder Ludwig the Springer.

Queen Victoria of England first met her cousin, Duke Albert of Saxe-Coburg-Gotha, here; they married in 1840. The palace, which is being restored, can only be viewed from the outside. A hotel on the premises was also being renovated at the time of writing.

Just south of the Schloss is the lovely landscaped **Kurpark**, home to the Ludowinger spring, which bubbles up excellent mineral water from a depth of 58m. Much of it is bottled, but you can also go to one of the glass pavilions in the park and fill up from the taps.

For an easy day excursion into the forest, you can take the Thüringer Wald-Express (€3.50) to the **Heuberghaus** on the mountain ridge, hike along the ridge to the **Inselsberg** peak (90 minutes), then take the Inselsberg Express (€3.50) down to Tabarz and catch the Thüringerwaldbahn back to Friedrichroda (€0.80).

Also popular is the **Heimatstube** (folk museum; ☎ 200 557; Reinhardsbrunner Strasse 6; adult/child €1.30/0.75, ⊗ 9am-noon Tue, 10am-noon & 3-5pm Wed & Thu, 10am-noon Sat), with exhibits on Thuringian history, local grottoes and the history of curative baths.

Sleeping & Eating

Friedrichroda is absolutely crammed with pensions, hotels and **private rooms** (from €12.50), and you'll seldom have trouble finding somewhere to stay. A *Kurtaxe* of €1.20 is added to all accommodation bills.

Pension Feierabend (☎ 304 386; Büchig 1; s/d €21/36; (P)) Near Bahnhof Reinhardsbrunn and opposite the Kurpark, this lovely three-storey timbered house is great value for money.

Pension Villa Phönix (☎ 200 880; www.villa -phoenix.de; Tabarzer Strasse 3; s €36, d €46-56) In town you'll find this rustic but comfortable hotel, with cosy rooms and a restaurant whose menu includes vegetarian dishes. Some rooms have balconies.

Berghotel (☎ 354 4440; reservierung.berghotel@ t-online.de; Bergstrasse 1; s €32.75-45, d €45-65; (P) (⚑)) This 983-bed GDR block is an absolute beast; the rooms are a bit basic but the hilltop location is great and you can't beat the views from the terrace restaurant (mains €8 to €11.50).

Brauhaus (☎ 304 259; Bachstrasse 14; mains around €10) A brewery restaurant possibly dating back as far as 800 years, the constant pop radio detracts a bit from the ambience here but traditional surrounds and an inventive menu compensate nicely.

Getting There & Away

The Thüringerwaldbahn (tram No 4), a historic tram, serves Gotha and Tabarz several times hourly (Gotha/Tabarz €2.40/ 0.80). The most scenic stretch begins right after Friedrichroda, through the forest to Tabarz. Bus 451 runs to Schmalkalden twice on weekdays.

If you're driving, take the Waltershausen/ Friedrichroda exit off the A4. The town is also on the B88 to Ilmenau.

ILMENAU

☎ 03677 / pop 27,000

Ilmenau is a sleepy little town enlivened by several handsome historic buildings and a small student population. In the Middle Ages it derived its wealth from silver and copper mining, but when that was exhausted the town plunged into deep depression. It fell upon Johann Wolfgang von Goethe (who else?), in his capacity as minister to the court of Saxe-Weimar, to revive the mining industry, but even he had little success.

Goethe is still the main reason people make the pilgrimage to Ilmenau, which is the gateway to the famous Goethewanderweg hiking trail (see opposite). Look out for the statue of the great man reposing on a bench at the Markt.

The **tourist office** (☎ 202 358; www.ilmenau.de; Lindenstrasse 12; 🕘 9am-6pm Mon-Fri, 9am-1pm Sat) makes reservations for hotels and private rooms from €12.50.

The modernised **DJH hostel** (☎ 884 681; jh -ilmenau@djh-thueringen.de; Am Stollen 49; juniors/seniors €15/18; 🍴 💻) is near the municipal swimming pool.

The modern **Hotel Tanne** (☎ 6590; www.hotel -tanne-thueringen.de; Lindenstrasse 38; s €55-60, d €75-85, ste €100), near the edge of town makes a comfortable Ilmenau 'base camp', with a nice breakfast, spa and bike rental station.

Direct trains to Erfurt leave about once an hour (€8.10, 1¼ hours); change in Neudietendorf for Eisenach (€12.40, 1¾ hours). Ilmenau is easily reached via the B88 from Eisenach, the B4 from Erfurt and the B87 from Weimar.

SCHMALKALDEN

☎ 03683 / pop 19,000

Hugging the southwestern slopes of the Thuringian Forest about 17km south of Friedrichroda, Schmalkalden is a beautiful little town that has preserved its medieval feel. Historically, the town will forever be tied to the Reformation because it was here, in 1530, that the Protestant princes formed the Schmalkaldic League to counter the central powers of Catholic Emperor Charles V, paving the way for the Peace of Augsburg and freedom of religion for the German states in 1546.

Schmalkalden today offers few reminders of those tumultuous and eventful times. Narrow streets are lined with carefully restored half-timbered houses (said to make up 90% of the Altstadt's buildings), and there's a handsome hill-top castle, Schloss Wilhelmsburg. In 2004 the town celebrates its 1130th anniversary.

Orientation & Information

It's about a 10-minute walk from the train and bus stations to the Altmarkt, the town's central square, and another seven minutes to Schloss Wilhelmsburg. There's a Sparkasse bank on Weidebrunner Gasse; the post office is at the southern end of the Altmarkt.

The **tourist office** (☎ 403 182; www.schmalkalden .de; Mohrengasse 1a; 🕘 9am-6pm Mon-Fri, 10am-3pm Sat) is just off the Altmarkt.

Sights & Activities

Towering above the city centre is the well-preserved, late-Renaissance–style **Schloss Wilhelmsburg** (☎ 403 186; Schlossberg 9; adult/concession €3/2; 🕘 9am-5pm Tue-Sun). It was built between 1585 and 1590 by Landgrave Wilhelm IV of Hessen as a hunting lodge and summer residence. The paintwork's looking a bit tatty outside, but lavish murals and stucco decorate most rooms, of which the **Riesensaal**, with its coffered and painted ceiling, is the most impressive. Notable, too, is the playful **Schlosskirche**, the palace chapel, whose ornate white and gilded decorations reflect secular rather than religious themes. The rare wood organ still works.

Other highlights include an exhibit on the Reformation and Renaissance, the restored castle **kitchens**, and a copy of a 13th-century **mural** depicting scenes from the Iwein le-end, a variation on the King Arthur myth by 12th-century poet Hartmann von Aue. The original, in the Hessenhof in town, is not open to the public.

The **Rathaus** (1419) on Altmarkt functioned as the meeting place of the Schmalkaldic League; nearby the incongruous unmatching towers of the late-Gothic **St Georgenkirche**, where Luther once preached, also look out over the square.

Schmalkalden is the western terminus of the **Martin-Luther-Weg**, a 17km easy-to-moderate hiking trail that ends at Tambach-Dietharz, from where there's bus service

GOETHEWANDERWEG

This lovely, at times challenging, 18.5km day hike follows in the footsteps of Johann Wolfgang von Goethe, who spent much time around Ilmenau in the employ of Carl August, Duke of Saxe-Weimar. The hike encompasses level forest terrain, steep climbs and everything in between; it's marked with the letter 'G' in Goethe's own handwriting. An excellent 1:30,000 hiking map by Grünes Herz is available at the tourist office (€4).

The starting point is the Amtshaus, a subdued baroque structure on the Markt that was Goethe's Ilmenau home. Five rooms have been turned into a **memorial exhibit** (☎ 202 667; adult/concession €1/0.50; 9am-noon, 1-4.30pm).

From here the trail heads west to the village of Manebach, where the steep climb up the **Kickelhahn** (861m) begins. Near the top, you'll pass the replica of the little forest cabin, **Goethehäuschen**, where Goethe wrote the famous poem *Wayfarer's Night Song*. At the top is a restaurant, **Berggasthaus Kickelhahn** (☎ 202 034; Kickelhahn 1) and **lookout tower**, with views over the great green blanket of the Thuringian Forest.

The trail descends to **Jagdhaus Gabelbach** (☎ 202 626; adult/concession €2/1.50; 9am-5pm Wed-Sun), a hunting lodge and former guesthouse of Duke Carl August who also liked to throw lavish parties here, often with Goethe in attendance. Today it contains an exhibit on the latter's scientific research. From here, the trail meanders south to the village of Stützerbach, where the **Goethehaus** (☎ 036784-502 77) features the originally furnished rooms where Goethe used to stay and work, plus an exhibit on the local glass industry. Hours and prices are the same as the Jagdhaus; check with the tourist office about the No 300 bus service back to Ilmenau.

If you don't have much time or simply want to do a shorter hike, you can walk directly to the Kickelhahn from Ilmenau, bypassing Manebach, in about 1½ hours. Or you can drive up Waldstrasse to the parking lot at Herzogröder Wiesen, from where it's a 25-minute uphill walk to the Kickelhahn peak.

back to town (weekdays only; check times with the tourist office).

Around 6km north of town is the 'technological monument' **Neue Hütte** (☎ 403 018; Gothaer Strasse; adult/concession €2/1; ◷ 10am-5pm Wed-Sun Apr-Oct only), one of the last surviving 19th-century smelting plants in central Europe. Techie types will love the machines, tools and turbines on display.

Sleeping & Eating
Hotel Grünes Tor (☎ 6630; www.hotel-gruenes-tor.de; Weidebrunner Gasse 12; s/d €42/62; ⓟ ✗) The big, light rooms in this galleried converted barn are furnished with imagination and taste, and offer some good views of town and castle, as well as occasional live bands in the bar/restaurant.

Teichhotel (☎ 402 661; Teichstrasse 21; s/d €42/70; ⓟ ✗) Another good choice just outside the Altstadt.

Maykel's (☎ 608 970; Lutherplatz 1; mains €5.20-10.50) Central and popular brasserie offering cocktails and international dishes.

Getting There & Away
Trains to Erfurt (€19.40, 1¾ hours) require changes in Wernshausen and Eisenach. Schmalkalden is about 5km east of the B19, which connects Eisenach and Meiningen.

MEININGEN
☎ 03693 / pop 22,000
Idyllic, stately and cultural, Meiningen lies about 30km south of Schmalkalden, tucked between the Thuringian Forest and the Rhön mountain range. This town on the Werra River was once the residence of the dukes of Saxe-Meiningen and owes its continuing reputation as a regional cultural centre to the vision of Duke Georg II (1826–1914). In 1866 he founded a resident theatre troupe, which toured its lavish productions as far as Moscow and London, and is said to be the forerunner of the Royal Shakespeare Company. All in all, they gave 2591 performances in 38 cities. Georg also catapulted the court orchestra – the Meininger Hofkapelle – to international fame by appointing pianist-conductor Hans von Bülow as musical director; the baton later passed to Richard Strauss and Max Reger. The annual theatre festival in spring enjoys an excellent reputation throughout German-speaking countries.

Orientation & Information
Two large parks, the Schlosspark to the west and the English Garden to the north fringe Meiningen's town centre. The train and bus stations are on the eastern side of the English Garden, which also contains the Meiningen Theatre. It's about a 10-minute walk to the Markt from here. The main post office is at Eleonorenstrasse 1-3.

The **tourist office** (☎ 446 50; www.meiningen.de; Markt 14; ◷ 10am-6pm Mon-Fri, 10am-3pm Sat) is behind the Stadtkirche.

Sights
The handsome baroque **Schloss Elisabethenburg** (☎ 503 641; www.meiningermuseen.de; adult/concession €3/2; ◷ 10am-6pm Tue-Sun), located at the northwestern edge of the centre, was built immediately after the founding of the duchy of Saxe-Meiningen in 1680 and served as ducal residence until 1918. It now contains several permanent exhibits, including a medieval and Renaissance **art collection**; the **Music Museum**, a series of rooms dedicated to the musical directors of the Meininger Hofkapelle; and, just down the road, the **Baumbachhaus** (☎ 502 848; Burggasse 2), a small literature museum.

Another building on the grounds houses the **Theatermuseum** (☎ 471 290; tour adult/concession €2.50/1.50; ◷ 10am, noon, 4pm Tue-Sun Oct-Apr), displaying some of the 275 original stage backdrops from the early days of the Meininger Theater, sketches of set designs and costumes drawn by Georg II, and historic photographs of well-known actors.

A combined ticket for both museums costs €5/3 (€5.50 on weekends).

Sleeping & Eating
Gasthof Schlundhaus (☎ 813 838; www.meininger-hotels-mit-flair.de; Schlundgasse 4; s €50-55, d €70-80; ⓟ) This historic hotel has an intricately carved façade, charming rooms and an atmospheric restaurant (mains €6 to €13) supposedly the place where Thuringian potato dumplings were invented. The same people run the stunning **Schloss Landsberg** (☎ 440 90; Landsberger Strasse 150; s €70-105, d €90-130; ⓟ), a genuine castle converted into fabulous luxury hotel on the northern edge of town.

Sächsischer Hof (☎ 4570; saechsischer-hof@romantikhotels.com; Georgstrasse 1; s €76-98, d €105-135; ⓟ ✗) This 200-year-old full-service inn is a destination

ination in itself, with palatial rooms and a renowned restaurant.

Zum Bratwurstglöckle (☎ 476 528; Untere Kaplaneistrasse 8; s/d €26/52; **P**) An unusual combination of pension, butcher's and cafeteria, with probably the best cheap grub in town (meals €1 to €10).

Turmcafé (☎ 881 036; Schloss Elisabethenburg; food €2-5) Atop the museum, this refined baroque café is a great place for afternoon coffee and cake, or soup and salad.

Knasthaus Zur Fronveste (☎ 478 641; An der Oberen Mauer; mains €6.40-12.90; ☖ from 6pm) Enjoy the comforts of prison life in an entertainingly different theme restaurant. Even the menu warns you against the authentic 'water soup'!

Getting There & Away

Direct trains travel to Erfurt every two hours (€13.50, 1¾ hours). Buses link Meiningen with Schmalkalden, Zella-Mehlis and other towns in the Thuringian Forest. Meiningen is on the B19 from Eisenach to Schweinfurt in Bavaria, and is also on the B89 to Sonneberg in southern Thuringia.

THE SAALE VALLEY

JENA

☎ 03641 / pop 101,000

The university town of Jena, about 23km east of Weimar, has hosted a galaxy of German luminaries, though it lacks much of its neighbours' charm and museum-like character. However, even industrialisation and GDR architectural sins can't keep a good college town down, and as Jena rebuilds, its friendly, funky spirit is coming back. The Kulturarena Jena, a world music festival covering most of July and August, is a major event in the Thuringian calendar.

Science buffs know Jena in connection with the development of optical precision technology and names like Carl Zeiss, Ernst Abbe and Otto Schott. It's a tradition that continues to this day, with corporations like Carl Zeiss Jena, Schott Jenaer Glaswerk, JENOPTIK and Jenapharm still based in the city.

Orientation

Jena's main attractions are all within walking distance of each other. There are two main train stations: Jena West, in the southwest, and Jena Paradies, next to the Saale near the centre and the main bus station. The Saalbahnhof station north of town is rarely used.

Information

Ambulance (☎ 112, ☎ 44 44 44)
C-Net (☎ 357 352; www.cafe-c.net; Teutonengasse 2; €1 per 15 min; ☖ 1pm-midnight Mon-Fri, 11-1am Sat & Sun) Internet access. Entrance on Grietgasse.
Dresdner Bank (☎ 4010; Holzmarkt 9)
JeNah Service Centre (☎ 414 330; www.jenah.de; Dornburger Strasse 17) Transport and local information.
Main post office (Engelplatz 8)
Police (☎ 810; Anger 30)
Tourist information (☎ 806 400; www.jena.de; Johannisstrasse 23; ☖ 9am-6pm Mon-Fri, 9am-2pm Sat)
Vobis (☎ 443 241; Goethe Galerie; €1.80 per hr) Internet access.

Sights
AROUND THE MARKT

The **Markt** is one of the few places in Jena that still reflects some of the city's medieval heritage. At its southern end stands the **Rathaus** (1380), with an astronomical clock in its baroque tower. Every hour, on the hour, a little door opens and a devil/fool called Schnapphans appears, trying to catch a golden ball (representing the human soul) dangling in front of him.

The square is anchored by a **statue** of Prince-Elector Johann Friedrich I, founder of Jena's university and popularly known as 'Hanfried'. The handsome building with the half-timbered upper section at the western end contains the **Stadtmuseum Göhre** (☎ 359 80; pr@stadtmuseum.jetzweb.de; adult/concession €3/1.50; ☖ 10am-5pm, to 6pm Wed, closed Mon) which has an interesting regional history collection on themes as diverse as wine-making, the Reformation and student fraternities.

A walkway beneath the museum leads to the Gothic **Stadtkirche St Michael**, which contains the original engraved tombstone of Martin Luther. There's a passageway right under the altar which cannot be seen from inside.

Nearby, the town's most obvious landmark is the 120m-tall cylindrical **Intershop tower** (€3; ☖ 11am-midnight), jokingly called *phallus Jenensis*. In the early 1970s, the medieval Eichplatz was razed to make room for this concrete behemoth, built as a Zeiss

THURINGIA

research facility. When it turned out to be unsuitable for that purpose, it languished for years, but at the time of writing it was getting a welcome facelift.

UNIVERSITÄT JENA
Jena's university was founded as Collegium Jenense in 1558 in a former monastery in Kollegiengasse. Still part of the campus today, it features a nice courtyard festooned with the coat of arms of Johann Friedrich I. North of here, in an excellent example of urban re-engineering, is the former **Zeiss optics factory**, now part of the university. Several buildings wrap around Ernst Abbe Platz, dotted with abstract sculptures by Frank Stella; the copies of antique sculptures in the lobby of the main building are a little more aesthetically pleasing. The campus borders the **Goethe Galerie**, a high-tech, split-level glass shopping mall.

The university **headquarters** (Füstengraben 1) are in a century-old complex on the north-eastern edge of the Altstadt. Inside are a Minerva bust by Rodin and a wall-sized painting showing Jena students going off to fight against Napoleon.

GOETHE & SCHILLER
As minister for the elector of Saxe-Weimar, Goethe spent five years in Jena. When not busy regulating the flow of the Saale, building streets, designing the botanical garden or cataloguing the university library, he crafted *Faust* and *Wilhelm Meister*. He also discovered an obscure jawbone in the **Anatomieturm** (cnr Teichgraben & Leutragraben), a former fortification tower. Most of the time he lived in what is now the **Goethe Gedenkstätte** (☎ 949 009; Fürstengraben 26; adult/concession €1/0.50; ☺ 11am-3pm Wed-Sun Apr-Oct), which focuses on his accomplishments as a natural scientist, poet and politician. Goethe himself planted the ginkgo tree just east of here, which is part of the **Botanical Garden** (☎ 949 274; adult/concession €2/1; ☺ 9am-6pm).

Goethe is also credited with bringing Schiller to Jena University; a plaque near the headquarters marks where Schiller gave his inaugural lecture. He liked Jena and stayed for 10 years – more than anywhere else – mostly in the **Gartenhaus** (☎ 931 188; Schillergässchen 2; adult/concession €2/1; ☺ 11am-3pm Tue-Sun). Schiller wrote *Wallenstein* in the little wooden shack in the garden, where

he also liked to wax philosophical with Goethe.

CARL ZEISS & ERNST ABBE
These scientists are two more notables responsible for putting Jena on the map. Zeiss opened his mechanical workshop here in 1846 and began building primitive microscopes. After enlisting Abbe's help in 1866, he developed the first scientific microscope. In cooperation with Otto Schott, the founder of Jenaer Glasswerke, they pioneered the production of optical precision instruments that propelled Jena to global prominence in the early 20th century.

Their life stories and the evolution of optical technology are the themes of the **Optisches Museum** (☎ 443 165; Carl-Zeiss-Platz 12; adult/concession €5/2.50; ☺ 10am-4.30pm Tue-Fri, 11am-5pm Sat). As well as microscopes, cameras, binoculars and other instruments, there's a collection of spectacles through the ages, plus an interactive room with various simplified eye tests. An English-language pamphlet describes the exhibits, and there are tours of the reconstructed Zeiss workshop (1866) next door. The octagonal **pavilion** outside the museum, designed by Belgian Art Nouveau artist Henry van de Velde, dates from 1911 and contains a marble bust of Abbe.

The **Zeiss Planetarium** (☎ 885 488; www.planet arium-jena.de; Am Planetarium 5; adult/concession €5/4; ☺ Tue-Sun) located in the northern city centre, houses the world's oldest public planetarium (1926). Today it boasts a huge state-of-the-art telescope. A combined ticket for the Optical Museum and the planetarium is €8/6.

Opened late 2000, the **Schott GlasMuseum** (☎ 681 765; Otto-Schott-Strasse 13; ☺ 1-6pm Tue-Fri) is on the grounds of the Schott glass factory. Audioguides and exhibits, available in English, offer a thorough and often engaging history of glass, although the Otto-worship can get a bit heavy at times, particularly in the biographical exhibitions in the Schott Villa, his former home. You can also shop at the outlet store.

Sleeping
The tourist office makes free reservations for hotels and **private rooms** (from €17.50), which can be excellent value. All prices here include private bathroom and breakfast; weekend rates are generally cheaper.

IB Jugendgästehaus (☎ 687 230; jugendgaestehaus -jena@internationaler-bund.de; Am Herrenberge 9; s/d €25/ 37; **P**) This hostel is in a rather ugly GDR-era building outside the centre. Take bus No 10, 11, 33 or 40 to Mühlenstrasse.

Campingplatz Unter dem Jenzig (☎ 666 688; www.jenacamping.de; Am Erlkönig 3; adult/child €4/2, car €3, tent €2-3) This nice camp site is conveniently close to town.

Gästehaus Lara (☎ 463 90; gaestehaus-lara@web .de; Lutherstrasse 47; s/d €36/52; **P** **X**) Just a short walk from the centre of town, with spotless if generic rooms, a holiday apartment (with kitchen) and nice staff.

Motel Jembo Park (☎ 6850; www.jembo.de; Rudol-städter Strasse 93, Göschwitz; s/d €54/72; **P** **X**) Families with cars should take a look at this park complex off the A4, which has all kinds of extras (including bowling and petting zoo) to keep the young 'uns entertained.

Gasthof Zur Schweiz (☎ 520 50; Quergasse 15; s/d €50/70; **P** **X**) Here you'll find attractive, rustic rooms near the main restaurant area, with its own kitchen serving up good local specials.

Hotel Papiermühle (☎ 459 80; www.jenaer-bier .de; Erfurter Strasse 102; s/d €50/75; **P**) A couple of kilometres from the centre, walkers could try this historic red-brick house with brewery attached.

Hotel Schwarzer Bär (☎ 4060; www.schwarzer -baer-jena.de; Lutherplatz 2; s €40-70, d €75-90; **P**) Martin Luther was the first famous face to grace this historic inn, and it hasn't been short of custom since then, offering 500 years of tradition, 66 rooms, seven restaurants and ample parking day or night.

Steigenberger Hotel Esplanade (☎ 8000; www .jena.steigenberger.de; Carl-Zeiss-Platz 4; s €115, d €155-195; **P** **X** **X**) Central, quiet, fully wheelchair-accessible and boasting a dramatic atrium design, the Esplanade is Jena's top of the line. The wood-and-chrome theme works well, but we're not so sure about the carpets.

Eating

Literaten-Café (☎ 443 154; Unterm Markt 3; cakes from €1.20) For keen readers rather than budding scribes, the first-floor seating here is perfect to watch the world go by or peruse one of the second-hand books on offer.

Quergasse No 1 (☎ 447 411; Quergasse 1; meals €2.80-6.90) In the heart of the main drinking district, No 1 provides a good selection of light meals and pasta in a candlelit, pub-like atmosphere.

Roter Hirsch (☎ 443 221; info@jembo.de; Holzmarkt 10; mains €3.55-13.05) Another historic inn, affiliated with the Jembo Park motel and a pension in Hungary, this very traditional place specialises in Thuringian food, with a good choice of beer and German wines. Try to get a seat upstairs.

Rotonda (☎ 8000; Goethe Galerie; mains €7-12) The huge, casually stylish Rotonda, part of the Hotel Esplanade, has a great salad bar, international dishes and bizarre specials like a 'horoscope menu'. There's a jazz brunch every first Sunday of the month.

Zur Noll (☎ 441 566; Oberlauengasse 19; mains €7.70-15.50) For a grown-up atmosphere and some of the best German food in town (including a suckling-pig buffet), head to this historic restaurant-pub that is decorated with original artwork.

Drinking

Jena's 'pub mile' is along Wagnergasse, on the northwestern edge of the city centre. Several nightclubs can also be found in this area.

Café Stilbruch (☎ 827 171; Wagnergasse 2) This intimate but hugely popular café-restaurant serves coffee, beer and bistro fare.

Café Bohème (☎ 824 677; Johannisplatz 15) This hang-out on the corner is the gateway to the nightlife district.

Rosenkeller (☎ 931 190; Johannisstrasse 13) Steps away, this historic student club with a network of cellars offers live concerts and party nights.

F-Haus (☎ 558 10; www.f-haus.de; Johannisplatz 14) Linked to the university, serious student clubbers get a full programme of events (and bowling) here. Enter from Krautgasse.

Getting There & Away

ICE trains to Berlin-Ostbahnhof (€42.20, 2¾ hours) and Hamburg-Altona (€74.80, 5¼ hours), plus hourly regional services to Rudolstadt (€5.50, 45 minutes) and Saalfeld (€6.60, 50 minutes), depart from either Westbahnhof or Paradiesbahnhof. To get to Weimar (€4, 15 minutes) and Erfurt (€6.60, 30 minutes), you must go to Westbahnhof.

Jena is just north of the A4 from Dresden to Frankfurt and just west of the A9 from Berlin to Munich. It's also crossed by the B7 (east–west) and B88 (north–south).

THURINGIA

Getting Around

The RegioMobil Tageskarte (see p204) covers Jena's public transport.

Day passes for buses and trams within Jena are €3, and there are also 24-hour group passes for up to five people (€5.50, weekends only). For a taxi, call ☎ 458 888.

AROUND JENA
Dornburger Schlösser

This magnificent trio of palaces from different eras, romantically resting atop a steep hillside about 15km north of Jena, makes for a pleasant excursion.

The southernmost is the **Renaissance Palace** (☎ 036427-222 91; adult/concession €2/1.50; ☉ 9am-6pm Tue-Sun), where Goethe sought solitude after the death of his patron, Duke Carl August. The rooms he stayed in have been restored more or less to their 1828 state.

The **Rococo Palace** blends beautifully with the garden, although it is scheduled to be closed for renovation until late 2004. The uppermost structure, known as the **Altes Schloss**, is a mix of Romanesque, late-Gothic, Renaissance and baroque elements, and can only be viewed from the outside. The **gardens** (☉ 8am-dusk) are open year-round.

Trains go hourly from Jena Paradies to Dornburg (€2.40, 15 minutes), from where it's a steep 20- to 30-minute climb uphill. Bus No 407 leaves every two hours on weekdays (less frequently on weekends) from Jena's central bus station.

RUDOLSTADT
☎ 03672 / pop 28,000

The main residence of the princes of Schwarzburg-Rudolstadt until 1918, Rudolstadt experienced a heyday in the Age of Enlightenment in the late-18th century. It was here that the first meeting between Goethe and Schiller took place in 1788; later Liszt, Wagner and Paganini all worked at the theatre, founded in 1793 and still in operation today. The manufacture of decorative porcelain (mostly kitsch but artfully painted figurines) has also been an important local industry since then, concentrated on Breitscheidstrasse.

Environmental concerns are a source of much contention here due to proposed road construction projects; you'll see banners around town ominously reminding people 'what happened to Cologne'. Read www.rettet-rudolstadt.de for full details.

Rudolstadt's **tourist office** (☎ 424543; Markt strasse 57; ☉ 9am-6pm Mon-Fri, 9am-1pm Sat) is just west of the Markt.

The town's landmark is the local rulers' former digs, the baroque **Schloss Heidecksburg** (☎ 429 00; www.heidecksburg.de; adult/concession €4.50/2.50; ☉ 10am-6pm Tue-Sun), a hulking edifice on a lofty bluff. Besides lavishly decorated and furnished rooms, the complex also harbours regional history exhibits and collections of paintings, weapons and minerals. Perhaps the palace's best features, though, are free: a terrific view over the valley, the porcelain in the ticket office hall and, especially, the fantastic wooden sleighs by the entrance. It's a 10-minute uphill walk from the central Markt.

Other sights include the **Stadtkirche St Andreas** on Kirchgasse, a Gothic hall-church rich in treasure, and the **Handwerkerhof** (☎ 400 377; Mangelgasse 18), a former convent for noblewomen that has been converted into an assembly of galleries, shops and cafés around a flower-festooned inner courtyard. South of the station in the Heinrich-Heine-Park is the **Museum Thüringer Bauernhäusern** (Kleiner Damm; ☉ 10am-noon & 1-5pm Wed-Sun Mar-Nov), which displays a collection of restored traditional farmhouses.

A unique play area for adults and kids is **Spielhaus Richtersche Villa** (☎ 411 451; Schwarzburger Chaussee 74; adult/concession €2.50/1.50; ☉ 1-6pm Mon-Fri), where you can fashion miniature buildings in turn-of-the-last century style using stone bricks called *Anker* ('Anchor'), a classic German plaything.

There's an hourly train service to Jena (€5.50, 45 minutes). Long-distance trains require a change in Saalfeld, which is served twice hourly (€1.60, eight minutes). Rudolstadt is on the B88 between Ilmenau and Jena and the B85 to Weimar.

SAALFELD
☎ 03671 / pop 30,000

About 15km south of Rudolstadt, Saalfeld is over 1100 years old and has an attractive centre brimming with historical buildings. It's also home to one of Thuringia's most heavily visited natural attractions, the **Feen-grotten** (Fairy Grottoes).

The Hauptbahnhof lies east of the Saale River, about a 10-minute walk from the

Markt and the **tourist office** (☎ 522 181; www
.saalfeld-info.de; Markt 6; ⏱ 9am-6pm Mon-Fri, 10am-
2pm Sat).

Walking Tour

From the Hauptbahnhof, head west on
Bahnhofstrasse to the **Saaltor**, one of the
four surviving town gates. It's worth
climbing to the top for a peek at the town
layout. Continue west via Saalstrasse to the
Markt. On its south side looms the striking
Renaissance **Rathaus**, a symphony of spiky
turrets, ornate gables, frilly oriels and other
design elements. Opposite is the partly Romanesque **Marktapotheke**, the former town
hall and a pharmacy since 1681.

Behind the Markt, the twin towers of
the Gothic **Johanniskirche** (☎ 2784; Kirchplatz 2;
⏱ 11am-4pm Mon-Fri, 1-3pm Sat & Sun) come
into view. One of Thuringia's largest hall
churches, it is richly decorated and features
dramatic cross and net vaulting, plus a life-
size carved figure of John the Baptist.

Brudergasse, west of the Markt, leads
uphill to the former Franciscan monastery,
now home to the **Stadtmuseum** (☎ 598 471;
www.museumimkloster.de; Münzplatz 5; adult/concession
€2/1.50; ⏱ 10am-5pm Tue-Sun). Its major allure is
the celestial building itself and the collection
of local, late-Gothic carved altarpieces.

Feengrotten

Saalfeld's main magnet are these underground **grottoes** (☎ 550 40; www.feengrotten.de;
tour adult/concession €4/3.50; ⏱ 9am-5pm Mar-Oct,
10am-3.30pm Dec-Feb, Nov 10am-3.30pm Sat & Sun only),
about 1.5km outside town (take bus B, half-
hourly weekdays, hourly weekends). These
former alum slate mines were actively
mined from 1530 to 1850, and opened
for tours in 1914. In 1993 they entered the
Guinness Book of Records as the world's
most colourful grottoes, but don't expect
a kaleidoscopic spectacle – 'colour' here
refers mostly to different shades of brown,
ochre and sienna, with an occasional sprinkling of green and blue. Small stalactite and
stalagmite formations add to a bizarre and
subtly impressive series of grottoes with
names like Butter Cellar and Blue-Green
Grotto. The highlight is the **Fairytale Cathedral** and its 'Holy Grail Castle' – it allegedly
inspired Richard Wagner's son Siegfried's
Tannhäuser set design in the 1920s.

Sleeping & Eating

Accommodation is comparatively inexpensive here, and the **tourist office** (☎ 339 50) can
book rooms of all kinds.

Jugendwanderheim (☎ 511 395; Am Schieferhof
4; dm €12; pn) The town's restored hostel is
operated by the German Red Cross. Guests
without reservations should report between
6pm and 8pm.

Hotel Anker (☎ 5990; www.hotel-anker-saalfeld.de;
Am Markt 25/26; s €47-60, d €74-90; ℗) Dating back
to 1486, this gracious hotel situated in the
centre of town is a real classic. Its friendly,
elegant restaurant is one of the oldest in
Germany.

Café Goebel (☎ 530 808; Blankenburger Strasse 19)
A lovely little café with an Art Deco vibe,
hand-painted throughout in styles from
different centuries.

Zum Pappenheimer (☎ 330 89; www.zum-pappen
heimer.de; Fleischgasse 5; mains €6.80-11) This cosy,
artistic pub occasionally has jazz evenings.

Getting There & Away

Regional trains run twice hourly to Rudolstadt (€1.60, eight minutes) and hourly
to Jena (€6.60, 50 minutes). There's also
an ICE connection to Berlin-Ostbahnhof
(€47.40, three hours). Saalfeld lies at the
intersection of routes B281 and B85 from
Weimar or Jena.

THURINGIA

Saxony-Anhalt

CONTENTS

Magdeburg	238
The Altmark	**242**
Stendal	242
Around Stendal	243
Eastern Saxony-Anhalt	**243**
Dessau	243
Around Dessau	247
Lutherstadt Wittenberg	248
Southern Saxony-Anhalt	**253**
Halle	253
Eisleben	256
Saale-Unstrut Region	**257**
Naumburg	257
Freyburg	259
Schulpforte	260
Bad Kösen	260

Once the GDR's industrial powerhouse – its answer to the Ruhr district – Saxony-Anhalt (Sachsen-Anhalt) has found German unification something of a double-edged sword. On the one hand, the area's bleak, polluted landscape seems transformed since the former East German districts of Magdeburg and Halle were made the state of Saxony-Anhalt again in 1990. Environmentally friendly wind turbines now dot the countryside and the cities have been spruced up. On the other hand, much of the cleanup has come about because the industries that once pumped thick, caustic smoke into the atmosphere have closed. As even official unemployment figures have risen above 20% in some areas, Saxony-Anhalt has been declared Germany's most economically troubled region, and population figures are in freefall as people move west.

Still, the state has plenty of appeal reaching further back into its history. The fact that 16th-century reformer Martin Luther carried out most of his life's work in and around Lutherstadt Wittenberg attracts religious pilgrims, while Dessau's association with the seminal Bauhaus school of design pulls in the architecture groupies. Germans have themselves recently rediscovered Saxony-Anhalt as an extension of the popular cycling trail along the Elbe River. However, foreigners are likely to be equally intrigued by reminders of the GDR or find the southeastern wine region of the Saale Valley an indulgent retreat.

None of this is to ignore the Harz Mountains, the most visited part of the state. However, as the mountains also cross over into Lower Saxony (Niedersachsen), they are dealt with in a separate chapter (see p262).

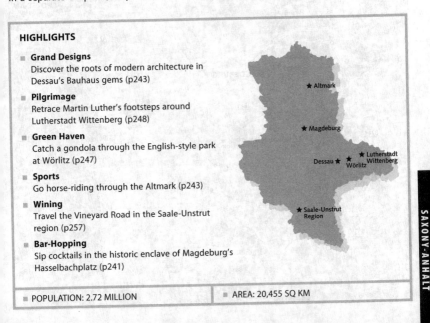

HIGHLIGHTS

- **Grand Designs**
  Discover the roots of modern architecture in Dessau's Bauhaus gems (p243)

- **Pilgrimage**
  Retrace Martin Luther's footsteps around Lutherstadt Wittenberg (p248)

- **Green Haven**
  Catch a gondola through the English-style park at Wörlitz (p247)

- **Sports**
  Go horse-riding through the Altmark (p243)

- **Wining**
  Travel the Vineyard Road in the Saale-Unstrut region (p257)

- **Bar-Hopping**
  Sip cocktails in the historic enclave of Magdeburg's Hasselbachplatz (p241)

★ Altmark

★ Magdeburg

Dessau ★ ★ ★ Lutherstadt
         Wörlitz Wittenberg

★ Saale-Unstrut
  Region

SAXONY-ANHALT

- POPULATION: 2.72 MILLION
- AREA: 20,455 SQ KM

MAGDEBURG

☎ 0391 / pop 228,000

Sometimes in Magdeburg just turning the corner can transport you into another century – metaphorically, at least. Saxony-Anhalt's capital is largely a city of wide boulevards and huge concrete *Plattenbauten* apartment complexes, built after WWII and given a cheery lick of paint in recent years. However, step onto tree-lined Hegelstrasse and you find yourself on pristine cobbled footpaths, surrounded by immaculately restored terraced buildings from the early 1900s. Looking north, you see Magdeburg's famous medieval cathedral. Continue south to Hasselbachplatz and you remain in an enclave of pretty-as-a-picture historic streets.

It feels like a film set plonked down in the middle of GDR-town, as the patrons in the cluster of trendy bars and cafés here would probably agree.

The city's other beauty spots are its parks, from the Stadtpark Rotehorn on the Elbe River to the Elbauenpark with its huge wooden tower housing a science museum. A journey to leafy Herrenkrug Park on the outskirts is another local tip.

History

You have to wonder about a city whose greatest claim to international fame is as the birthplace of vacuum technology. (Will there be anything there?) Yet, the invention of the air pump by physicist and Magde-

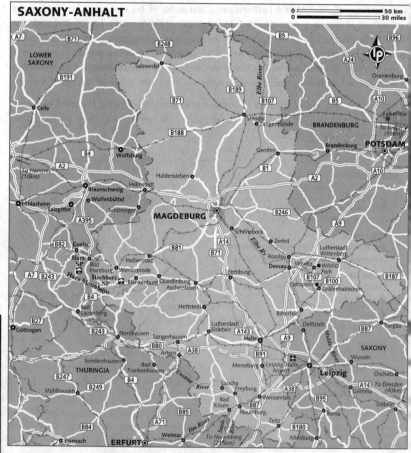

burg mayor Otto von Guericke (1602–86), and his experiments in creating vacuums from the 1650s onwards, is probably what the city is best known for abroad.

Fortunately, the reputation of Magdeburg within Germany is more rounded. Founded as a strategic trading post by Charlemagne in 805, it gained importance after King Otto I established it as an archbishopric in 968.

Apart from the cathedral where Otto is buried, most of what you see today in Magdeburg was rebuilt after 1945, when bombs destroyed 90% of the centre. But locals still feel a sense of continuity and are planning huge celebrations for the city's 1200th birthday in 2005.

Orientation
To reach the town centre from the Hauptbahnhof (central train station), turn left (north) out of the main Kölner Platz exit, cross the square and turn right (east) into Ernst-Reuter-Allee. The tourist office is just after Ernst-Reuter-Allee meets the major north–south artery, Breiter Weg. From here, you can walk a block north to the Alter Markt (old market square) or carry on east across the Neue Strombrücke bridge and the Elbe River to the Stadthalle (city hall).

Northwards, Breiter Weg leads to Universitätsplatz; heading south it takes you to the Dom (cathedral) and Hasselbachplatz.

Information
Anne's Waschparadies (☎ 541 2593; Walther-Rathenau-Strasse 60) Weekday service laundry, just west of Universitätsplatz.
B@gels (☎ 734 6350; Olvenstedter Strasse 45a; €5 per hr) Internet access.
Commerzbank (☎ 592 30; Breiter Weg 200)
Krankenhaus Altstadt (☎ 591 90; Max-Otten-Strasse 11-15) Hospital.
Orbit (☎ 620 9835; Keplerstrasse 7; €5 per hr) Internet access.
Post office (Breiter Weg 203-206; ☒ 9am-7pm Mon-Fri, 9am-noon Sat) South of Commerzbank.
Reisebank (Hauptbahnhof)
Stadtbibliothek (☎ 540 4821; Breiter Weg 109) Library.
TIM Tourist Information Magdeburg (☎ 5404 9000; www.magdeburg-tourist.de; Ernst-Reuter-Allee 12; ☒ 10am-6pm Mon-Fri, 10am-1pm Sat) Offers German-language tours (€2.50) at 11am daily and historical walking tour brochures in English.

Sights & Activities
DOM
Apparently the first of its kind on German soil when built (1209–1363), Magdeburg's Gothic **Dom** (cathedral; ☎ 543 2414; ☒ 10am-4pm Mon-Sat, 11.30am-4pm Sun) features an impressive, high-ceilinged interior. Here, you'll find the **tomb of Otto I** and art spanning eight centuries. This includes a pensive **WWI memorial** by Ernst Barlach and, through the doors beside it, the sculpture of the **Magdeburger Virgins** (dating from the 13th century and due for a much-needed refurbishment). There are German-language **tours** (☒ 2pm daily, 11.30am Sunday, adult/concession €3/1.50) and English tours by arrangement.

KLOSTER UNSER LIEBEN FRAUEN
South of Ernst-Reuter-Allee, near the river, stands Magdeburg's oldest building, the 12th-century Romanesque **cloister** (☎ 565 020; admission free; ☒ 10am-5pm Tue-Sun), which also houses a **museum** (adult/concession €2/1). There's not much in the cloister apart from the courtyard and pleasant café, but the museum has religious relics and rotating exhibits. The front door, designed by popular local artist Heinrich Apel (b. 1935), is fun; you knock with the woman's necklace and push down on the man's hat to enter.

JAHRTAUSENDTURM & ELBAUENPARK
With its recreation of Roman streets, model of the solar system and all manner of wacky scientific contraptions, the interior of the conical, wooden **Jahrtausendturm** (Millennial Tower; ☎ 01805-251 999; www.elbauenpark.de; Tessenowstrasse 5a; adult/child/family including park admission €2.60/2/6; ☒ 10am-6pm Tue-Sun Apr-Oct) makes a memorable sight. And German-speakers will be even more thrilled by the museum of science history to which these exhibits belong, as staff demonstrate experiments first performed by the likes of Galileo and Otto von Guericke. It's an amateur scientist's dream. The surrounding park has rose, sculpture and other gardens. Take tram No 6 from Ernst-Reuter-Allee in front of the tourist office to Messegelände/Elbauenpark.

OTHER PARKS
Just to the east of the Hubbrücke is the **Stadtpark Rotehorn**, with playgrounds, picnic areas, the Stadthalle concert hall and

SAXONY-ANHALT

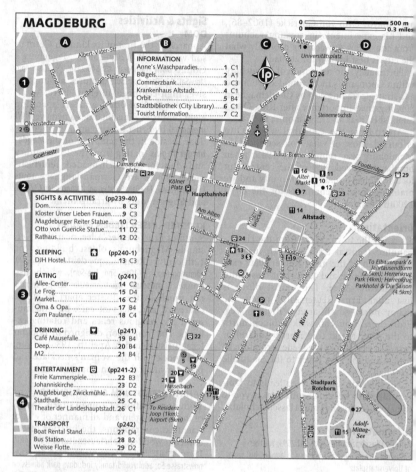

MAGDEBURG

0 — 500 m
0 — 0.3 miles

INFORMATION
Anne's Waschparadies.................1 C1
B@gels..2 A1
Commerzbank..............................3 C3
Krankenhaus Altstadt..................4 C1
Orbit..5 B4
Stadtbibliothek (City Library).....6 C1
Tourist Information.....................7 C2

SIGHTS & ACTIVITIES   (pp239-40)
Dom..8 C3
Kloster Unser Lieben Frauen......9 C3
Magdeburger Reiter Statue......10 C2
Otto von Guericke Statue.........11 D2
Rathaus..12 D2

SLEEPING   🏠   (pp240-1)
DJH Hostel...................................13 C3

EATING   🍴   (p241)
Allee-Center................................14 C2
Le Frog...15 D4
Market..16 C2
Oma & Opa..................................17 B4
Zum Paulaner..............................18 C4

DRINKING   🍷   (p241)
Café Mausefalle..........................19 B4
Deep..20 B4
M2...21 B4

ENTERTAINMENT   🎭   (pp241-2)
Freie Kammerspiele....................22 B3
Johanniskirche............................23 D2
Magdeburger Zwickmühle.........24 C2
Stadthalle.....................................25 C4
Theater der Landeshauptstadt.26 C1

TRANSPORT   (p242)
Boat Rental Stand.......................27 D4
Bus Station...................................28 B2
Weisse Flotte...............................29 D2

Adolf-Mittag-See (Adolf-Mittag Lake), where you can hire rowboats. Tram No 6 stops about 300m north of the lake. Staying on Tram No 6 until it reaches its terminus will take you to **Herrenkrug Park**, a popular spot to stroll and cycle.

OTHER ATTRACTIONS

At the southeastern end of the so-called old market, or Alter Markt (mostly rebuilt after WWII), is a gold-plated copy of the iconic **Magdeburger Reiter** (1240), said variously to be city champion King Otto and his two wives, or the king of Hungary and companions, or perhaps just any old king.

The bronze door to the **Rathaus** (town hall; 1698), depicting the city's history to

1969, is by Heinrich Apel. Above the door is an image of the **Magdeburger Jungfrau** (Magdeburg Maiden), the city symbol. North of the Alter Markt, the **Otto von Guericke statue** commemorates the father of the vacuum (1602–86).

Tours

Scenic boat trips on the Elbe lasting 1½ hours are run by **Weisse Flotte** (☎ 532 8891; adult/child €8/4). The mooring point is north of the Neue Steinbrücke.

Sleeping

Magdeburg has a great hostel, two nationally renowned luxury hotels and little worthwhile in between. The tourist office an, however, book private rooms and here's camping 8km north of town.

DJH hostel (☎ 532 101; jh-magdeburg@djh-sachsen anhalt.de; Leiterstrasse 10; juniors/seniors €18/20.70; **P**) Its combination of modern premises and a central, but quiet, location make Magdeburg's Jugendherberge possibly the best hostel in Saxony-Anhalt. There are private bathrooms, friendly staff and late closing hours.

Hotel Stadtfeld (☎ 506 660; www.hotelstadtfeld.de; Maxim-Gorki-Strasse 31/37; s/d €55/70; **P**) This pleasant three-star hotel feels a little bit like a aristocratic Englishmen's club. That's partly because of the no-nonsense, masculine furnishings, but the location atop an apartment building and the top-floor reception also create a sense of chummy privacy. Parking is €5.50.

Residenz Joop (☎ 626 60; www.residenzjoop.de; Jean Burgerstrasse 16; s €84-124, d €102-124; **P**) In a residential neighbourhood near trendy Hasselbachplatz, Residenz Joop is one of those small luxury hotels offering a home away from home – but with a degree of elegance and pampering that most of us only dream of *chez nous*. Traditional yet chic, it has weekend rates from €64/80. Parking is €6.

Herrenkrug Parkhotel (☎ 850 80; www.herrenkrug .de; Herrenkrug 3; s €120-155, d €155-195; **P** **X** **Q**) The Herrenkrug's rooms aren't much different from other four-star hotels. What sets it apart is its parkland setting, giving it the atmosphere of a country retreat, and its spa and jaw-dropping Art Deco restaurant (see the following Eating section). Weekend rates are available.

Eating
RESTAURANTS & CAFES
Oma & Opa (☎ 543 9419; cnr Einsteinstrasse & Leibnizstrasse; mains €4.50-13) Grandma and Grandpa's cosy little place is festooned with odd bric-a-brac (a stuffed fox, for example) and has a straightforward menu of dishes like spaghetti and Wurst (sausage). Like true grandparents, too, the proprietors send you home well fed.

Le Frog (☎ 531 3556; Heinrich-Heine-Platz 10; mains €5.50-14) Its lakeside setting and fancy French cuisine, interspersed with some more generic international dishes, have made Le Frog a Magdeburg institution.

Zum Paulaner (☎ 543 8813; Einsteinstrasse 13b; mains €6-17) On the corner of Einsteinstrasse

and historic Hegelstrasse, this restaurant is a good place to sit out in summer, soaking up the atmosphere and partaking of Bavarian and other German fare.

Die Saison (☎ 850 80; Herrenkrug 3; mains €17-28) With its high ceiling and ornately detailed dark-green walls, the Art Deco dining room of the Herrenkrug Parkhotel is immensely appealing, but the seasonal menus sound just as good. German with a modern international twist, they might include mango-glazed chicken breast or fish with a peppery berry sauce.

QUICK EATS & SELF-CATERING
Head for the Allee-Center shopping complex or try the Hauptbahnhof. Off the Alter Markt, there's a covered **market** (☯ 9am-6pm Mon-Fri, 9am-noon Sat), with fruits, vegetables and meats.

Drinking
There's a bar every few steps around Hasselbachplatz. Listings guide *DATEs* has further details.

Deep (☎ 544 2791; Breiter Weg 231) This dimly lit basement bar is hip but extremely friendly. DJs spin discs on weekends, and eye-catching upright log seats are placed on the pavement in summer. Despite the official address, the door is on Einsteinstrasse, west of Breiter Weg.

Café Mausefalle (☎ 543 0135; Breiter Weg 224) Crowds spilling out of here on a weekend prove that Mausefalle's relaxed mix of drinks, music and the occasional bit of communal TV hits the spot in Magdeburg.

M2 (☎ 555 6837; Otto-von-Guericke-Strasse 56) The brasserie-style M2 is the place for a relaxed 20- to 30-something crowd. Drinks range from beer to fancy cocktails, but steer clear of the bar food, which can be pretty ordinary.

Entertainment
ROCK & JAZZ
Stadthalle (☎ 593 4529; Stadtpark Rotehorn) From Mozart to Motorhead – as Magdeburg's premier venue, this 2000-seat venue in the leafy central park has pretty well heard it all.

THEATRE & CLASSICAL MUSIC
Johanniskirche (St John's Church; ☎ 540 2146; Jacobstrasse) A deservedly popular venue for

classical music concerts, the atmospheric Johanniskirche dates back, in parts, to 1131, although much of it has been newly renovated.

Theater der Landeshauptstadt (☎ 540 6444, Universitätsplatz 9) The Magdeburg Philharmonic plays here, and it's also a venue for opera, ballet and theatre performances.

German-speakers should check out the acclaimed cabaret **Magdeburger Zwickmühle** (☎ 541 4426; www.magdeburger-zwickmuehle.com; Leiterstrasse 2a) or, for innovative theatre, **Freie Kammerspiele** (☎ 540 6345; www.freiekammerspiele.de; Otto-von-Guericke-Strasse 64).

Getting There & Away

Regional trains to/from Berlin-Zoo take about 1½ hours (€20.20). Magdeburg is on the main route from Rostock (€33.60, four hours) to Leipzig (€17.20, two hours) or Erfurt (€30.20, 2½ hours).

The city is just south of the A2 Berlin-Hanover autobahn, and the A14 runs to Leipzig.

Flugplatz Magdeburg (☎ 622 7877) is a regional airport with limited scheduled and charter services.

Getting Around

Single bus and tram tickets cost adult/concession €1.40/1.15, and day tickets (valid 9am to midnight) are €3. Four-trip tickets cost €4.90.

Free street parking is more plentiful north and south of the centre. Parking near the Hauptbahnhof and bus station is by permit only.

Taxis wait outside the Hauptbahnhof (Kölner Platz exit). Call **Taxi Ruf** (☎ 737 373) or **Taxi Zentrale** (☎ 544 444).

THE ALTMARK

STENDAL

☎ 03931 / pop 39,000

Stendal is the largest town of the sparsely populated Altmark region. This former Hanseatic trading centre flourished until the 17th century, when it was devastated by fires, the plague and finally, the Thirty Years' War (1618–48). However, many splendid medieval buildings survived and have been renovated since German unification, making it a pleasant stopover.

Orientation

The town is compact and easily seen o foot. The Altstadt (old town) is a five minute walk northeast of the Hauptbahn hof along Bahnhofstrasse.

Information

Post office (Breite Strasse 75)

Stendal tourist office (☎ 651 190; stendal@t-online .de; Markt 1; ⏰ 9am-5pm Mon-Fri, 10am-1pm Sat Nov-Mar, plus 10am-1pm Sun Apr-Oct)

Sights

TOWN GATES

At the extreme south and northwest of th Altstadt you'll find two handsome tow gates, the **Tangermünder Torturm** and the **Uen linger Tor** (adult/concession €1/0.50; ⏰ 10am-noo 3-5pm). Built more for prestige than defenc these fancy brick portals look a bit lonel now that most of the town wall has gone, b they do afford great views of the Altstadt.

KORNMARKT

The old market square is dominated by th late-Renaissance **Rathaus** and an 8m-hig statue of the legendary knight Rolan clutching a 4m-long sword. Upstairs in th Rathaus is a 1462 wood carving of biblic and local heroes. Ask for the key at th tourist office.

Behind the Rathaus is the **Marienkirch** (Church of St Mary; ☎ 212 877; ⏰ 10am-5pm Mon-F 10am-4pm Sat & Sun), with a dazzling 16t century **astronomical clock** set under th organ gallery.

OTHER ATTRACTIONS

The economical Gothic brick style of th **Dom St Nicolaus** (☎ 212 136; Am Dom; ⏰ 10a noon & 3-5pm; 1-2pm Mon-Fri in winter), southwe of the centre, only emphasises its colou ful **stained-glass windows**. If the cathedral locked, get the key from the church offic at Halbstrasse 28.

At the north end of Breite Strasse stand **Jakobikirche**, with some more stained gla and a colourful **pulpit**. Just northeast of th church is a strikingly broad avenue wi a village green called **Altes Dorf**, the olde part of town.

Sleeping & Eating

The tourist office can book **private roor** (from €17.50 per person).

HORSING AROUND

The Altmark is one of Germany's great horse-breeding areas, and there's no shortage of horse shows, parades or markets. With its abundance of unspoilt pastures and riverside paths, it's a charming spot to go riding, and you can hire a steed from €8 per hour.

The **Fremdenverkehrsverband Altmark** (Altmark Tourist Association; ☎ 039322-432 32; Marktstrasse 13, 39590 Tangermünde) will send you a list of Reiterhöfe, which offer spartan lodgings for you and a stable for your hired horse, averaging a total €25 to €30 per night. Many Reiterhöfe offer riding lessons and have enjoyable leisure facilities for a great summer holiday.

Pension Ramme (☎ 210 623; fax 715 809; Moltkestrasse 31c; s/d €20/40; P) This tiny pension in a historic house doesn't serve breakfast, but its rooms were renovated at the start of the 1990s and have private bathrooms.

Hotel am Uenglinger Tor (☎ 684 80; fax 643 130; Moltkestrasse 17; s/d €45/55; P) Just minutes from Uenlinger Tor, this hotel has friendly staff and clean, modern rooms.

Zur Kulisse (☎ 715 502; Karlstrasse 1; mains €6.25-14.50; evenings only) This French bistro and beer garden near the Theater Der Altmark attracts a broad mix of customers, including some thespians.

Getting There & Around

Stendal is an important rail junction connecting north–south lines to east–west lines. There's IC services to Berlin-Zoo (€20.40, 45 minutes) and Leipzig (€29, 2½ hours), as well as cheaper regional trains. Regional services also run to Magdeburg (€8.10, 50 minutes). The B188 and B189 intersect in the south of town.

You can hire bicycles from the tourist office for €5 per day, plus €25 deposit.

AROUND STENDAL

Tangermünde

☎ 039322 / pop 10,000

Picture-book pretty, Tangermünde was the second home of Charles IV, king of Bohemia in the 14th century. Its ostentatious towers, gates and castle sit at the confluence of the Elbe and Tanger Rivers.

The Altstadt is a five-minute walk south of the Hauptbahnhof, along Albrechtstrasse. The **tourist office** (☎ 3710; tangermuende-info@t-online.de; Marktstrasse 13; 10am-5pm Mon-Fri, 11am-4pm Sat & Sun) will book rooms for free.

Built in 1300, the **Stadtmauer** (city walls) counts as one of Germany's most complete municipal defences, crowned at the western end by the angular medieval **Neustädter Tor**, which looks like its cousins in Stendal. The **Rathaus** was being restored at the time of writing, but its façade might be visible again by the time you visit. Moving east through the cobblestone lanes takes you past lovely half-timbered houses to **St Stephanskirche**, housing a 17th-century organ that's reputedly one of the most valuable in Europe.

The **Schloss** (castle), which overlooks a crook in the Elbe, was sacked in 1640 by the Swedes and quietly crumbled until the early 20th century, when it was made into a public park. Its only surviving building is the ruined **Kanzlei**, originally a dance hall. Bring a picnic – this is one of the most charming spots on the Elbe.

SLEEPING & EATING

Ringhotel Schloss Tangermünde (☎ 7373; Amt 1; s €65-85, d €80-130) You can pick the level of luxury you want inside this hillside castle (not the Schloss destroyed by the Swedes). Whichever you choose, the overall environment ensures you will feel like royalty.

Exempel (☎ 448 99; Kirchstrasse 40; mains €4-12) This charming café inside a creaky former schoolhouse serves local specialities and great cakes, coffee and drinks.

GETTING THERE & AWAY

Trains run hourly to Stendal (€1.50, 17 minutes) some 10km northwest. The **Reederei Kaiser** (☎ 0171-421 8162) runs two-hour scenic trips up the Elbe (€7.50), and also sails to Magdeburg (€14/22.50 one way/return).

EASTERN SAXONY-ANHALT

DESSAU

☎ 0340 / pop 79,500

Dessau will forever be linked to the 20th century's most influential school of architecture and art, the Bauhaus. The seven years (1925–32) the eponymous institute of design was based here proved to be its heyday, and before Nazis drove its leading exponents to Berlin and then into US exile the block-faced logo 'Bauhaus Dessau' had won a place in history.

But the town has even more to offer than some of the earliest buildings by Walter Gropius & Co. Although much of its centre was reconstructed after WWII and is typically Eastern Bloc uninspiring, Dessau is also surrounded by a thick green belt – more a girdle really – of 18th-century, English-style landscaped parks. As a tourist destination, it's crying out for the headline 'Bauhaus and Garden'.

Orientation

The town is south of the confluence of the Elbe and Mulde Rivers. The leading Bauhaus sights are west of the Hauptbahnhof, within easy walking distance. The town centre lies east, reachable on foot or by tram.

Information

Commerzbank (☎ 252 10; Kavalierstrasse 39)
Post office (Kavalierstrasse 30-32)
Tourist office (☎ 204 2242; www.dessau.de; Rathaus, Zerbster Strasse 4; ☾ 9am-6pm Mon-Fri, 9am-1pm Sat, April-Oct, 9am-5pm Mon-Fri, 10am-1pm Sat Nov-Mar) Sells the three-day Dessau Card (€8), allowing unlimited travel on buses and trams and free or discounted museum entry. Also offers tours (☾ 10am Sat Apr-Oct) in German.
Worldnet computer (☎ 220 2381; Ferdinand von Schiller Strasse 28a; €3 per hour)

Sights

BAUHAUSGEBÄUDE

The first port of call for most design fan are the hallowed halls of the **Bauhaus Gebäud** (Bauhaus Building; ☎ 650 8251; Gropiusallee 38; tou adult/concession €5/4, combination ticket with Meiste häuser €8/6; ☾ 10am-6pm Tue-Sun). Not only a example of Walter Gropius' handiwork an a forerunner of untold modernist building worldwide, this was the very Hochschul für Gestaltung (Institute for Design) whe the architect and his colleagues taught.

Today, it houses a small, postgradua **Bauhaus Kolleg** (☎ 650 8403; www.bauhaus-dess .de), but the three-sectioned ensemble glass, steel and concrete (built in 1925–2 remains open to the public. One-hour tou (in German) start at 11am and 2pm dai (and 4pm Saturday, Sunday and holidays on weekdays you can wander inside b yourself. At the time of writing, howeve renovations meant certain areas were of limits.

Design-related exhibitions are held i the workshop wing, while there's a grea gift shop selling books, posters, postcar and trinkets, from toys and egg cookers, t ashtrays, wine glasses, crockery and lamp

The complex is a five-minute walk we of the Hauptbahnhof via Schwabestrass and Bauhausstrasse.

MEISTERHÄUSER

Since a leading Bauhaus aim was to pro vide housing appropriate for a moder

---

BAUHAUS COMES TO TOWN

Dessau's inextricable association with Bauhaus is supremely ironic, given that many of the school's teachers had to be dragged kicking and screaming to this industrial city – the home of Junker aircraft. Many locations were considered when the Bauhaus Hochschule für Gestaltung (Institute of Design) was expelled from Weimar in 1925 (see the boxed text Design for Life on p246), and Dessau wasn't top of the list. According to Elaine S Hochman in Bauhaus: Crucible of the Modern (1999), director Walter Gropius cabled back 'Dessau impossible' from a business trip when the option was mooted. Painter Wassily Kandinsky's first impression of the place was 'not too hot'.

What convinced these nay-sayers was a promise by Dessau's mayor Fritz Hesse to award Bauhaus disciples firm building contracts, which is why the city now owns Walter Gropius' first purpose-built school, elegant duplexes, experimental steel buildings and the world's first housing estate.

Several of these were damaged during WWII and others fell into disrepair during the GDR period. Only in the mid- to late 1990s did Dessau start to reclaim its Bauhaus legacy with major restoration work. The original school building (the Bauhausgebäude) and the Meisterhäuser for senior staff were granted Unesco protection in 1996.

ndustrial lifestyle, the white, concrete **Meisterhäuser** (master craftsmen's houses; Ebertallee 63-71; admission to all three houses adult/concession €5/4, combined Bauhaus tour & Meisterhäuser tickets adult/concession €8/6; 10am-5pm Tue-Sun, 10am-6pm mid-Feb–Oct) are in a sense more illuminating than the Bauhausgebäude, even if they're the second stop on most itineraries. The houses were built by Gropius for senior institute staff, and while parts of their interiors are given over to administrative or museum purposes and the rest is largely unfurnished, photos help recall what it must have been like, say, at home with the Kandinskys, where furniture was donated by Marcel Breuer, and Paul Klee or László Moholy-Nagy might drop in for tea.

The clean, elegant lines of the renovated houses show modernism's best side. Originally there was a stand-alone home for the Bauhaus director, plus three duplexes, each half of which provided a living/working space for a senior staff member and family. Sadly, the director's home was destroyed in WWII, along with one half of the neighbouring duplex (originally the Moholy-Nagy/Feiningerhaus).

The remaining **Feiningerhaus**, where artist Lyonel Feininger once lived, now pays homage to another German icon with the **Kurt-Weill-Zentrum** (619 595). There's a room devoted to Dessau-born Weill, who became writer Bertolt Brecht's musical collaborator in Berlin and composer of The Threepenny Opera and its hit 'Mack the Knife'.

The **Muche/Schlemmer Haus** is the most evocative, with its partial recreation of an all-black bedroom that Marcel Breuer foisted on Georg Muche (painting it while Muche was out of town). According to the information provided at the Muche/Schlemmer Haus, on getting out of bed on the morning of his return, Muche recoiled to see his shadow surrealistically reflected and spookily distorted in the uneven surface of the glossy black walls. 'After this demonstration, I never again set foot in that bedroom,' Muche wrote. 'It became a storeroom for suitcases and unwanted household items. For that, white [walls] would have sufficed.' Oskar Schlemmer inhabited the duplex's other side.

Finally comes the **Kandinsky/Klee Haus** (661 0934), most notable for the varying pastel shades in which Wassily Kandinsky and Paul Klee painted their walls (recreated today). There's also biographical information about the two artists and special exhibitions of their work.

To reach the Meisterhäuser, turn right (north) onto Gropiusallee from the Bauhausgebäude and continue a few minutes before turning left (west) into Ebertallee. Alternatively, bus No 10 or 11 from the train station will drop you close by (stop: Gropiusallee).

A further 20-minute walk north on Elballee, on the Elbe, stands the **Kornhaus**, a beer-and-dance hall designed by Carl Flieger, a Gropius assistant. It is now a terraced restaurant with river views (see p247). From the Hauptbahnhof, take bus No 10 or 11 to Kornhausstrasse and then walk.

TÖRTEN

If the term 'housing estate' conjures up an image of grim concrete tower blocks, rubbish-blown courtyards and shutters flapping on the abandoned communal shop, leafy Törten, in Dessau's south, will prompt a rethink. Built in the 1920s, it is *the* prototype of the modern working-class estate. However, it's refreshingly low-rise, and you can see what the architects were trying to achieve. Although many of the 300-plus homes have been altered in ways that would have outraged their purist creator Walter Gropius (rustic German doors added to a minimalist façade?), others retain their initial, pleasing symmetry.

The **Stahlhaus** (Steel House; 858 1420; Südstrasse 5; admission free; 10am-5pm Tue-Sun, 10am-6pm Feb-Oct) is home to a Bauhaus information centre and the starting point for German-language **tours** (adult/concession €4/3; 2pm Tue-Fri, 3pm Sat & Sun) of the Törten estate. These look inside one of the red-brick, balcony-access apartments by the second Bauhaus director, Hannes Meyer.

Other highlights include the **Konsumgebäude** (co-op building, still the site of a communal shop) and the **Moses Mendelssohn Zentrum** (850 1199; Mittelring 38; adult/child €2/1; 10am-7pm Mar-Oct, 1-4pm Sat & Sun Jan-Feb). Here you can learn about Dessau-born humanist philosopher Moses Mendelssohn, who was the grandfather of composer Felix Mendelssohn-Bartholdy. It's also the only

DESIGN FOR LIFE

'Less is more,' asserted the third and final Bauhaus director, Ludwig Mies van der Rohe. Given that a school that survived fewer than 15 years exerted more influence on 20th-century design than any other, one has to bow to his logic. As Frank Whitford put it in *Bauhaus: World of Art* (1984): 'Everyone sitting on a chair with a tubular steel frame, using an adjustable reading lamp or living in a house partly or entirely constructed from prefabricated elements is benefiting from a revolution…largely brought about by the Bauhaus.'

Founded in Weimar in 1919 by Berlin architect Walter Gropius, this multidisciplinary school aimed to abolish the distinction between 'fine' and 'applied' arts and unite the artistic with the everyday. Gropius decreed that form follows function and exhorted his students to craft items with an eye to mass production. Consequently, Bauhaus products stripped away decoration and ornamentation and returned to the fundamentals of design, with strong, clean lines.

Already in Weimar the movement attracted a roll call of the era's greatest talents, including Lyonel Feininger, Wassily Kandinsky, Paul Klee, László Moholy-Nagy, Piet Mondrian and Oskar Schlemmer, plus now legendary product designers Marianne Brandt, Marcel Breuer (the father of the tubular steel frame chair) and Wilhelm Wagenfeld. After conservative politicians closed the Weimar school in 1925, these artists all moved to Dessau.

Right-wing political pressure continued, however, against what was seen as the Bauhaus' undermining of traditional values, and Gropius resigned as director in 1928. He was succeeded by Swiss-born Hannes Meyer, whose Marxist sympathies meant that he, in turn, was soon replaced by Ludwig Mies van der Rohe. The latter was at the helm when the school moved to Berlin in 1932 to escape Nazi oppression.

Mies ran the school as a private institution until it was dissolved by the Third Reich in 1933 and the Bauhaus' leading lights fled the country. But the movement never quite died. After WWII, Gropius took over as director of Harvard's architecture school, while Mies van der Rohe (the architect of New York's Seagram Building) held the same post at the Illinois Institute of Technology in Chicago. Both men found long-lasting global fame as purveyors of Bauhaus' successor, the so-called International Style.

Walter Gropius building on the estate where you can look inside.

To reach Törten, take tram No 1 towards Dessau Süd. Alight at Damaschkestrasse, where there are signposts to the 'Bauhaus Architektur'.

GEORGIUM

While the region's famous parkland is mostly outside the city centre (see Around Dessau, opposite), certain sections lie close in. That's particularly true of the **Georgium**, a sprawling 18th-century park northwest of the Hauptbahnhof. At its heart stands the neoclassical **Schloss Georgium**, housing the **Anhalt Art Gallery** (☎ 613 874; Puschkinallee 100; adult/concession €2.60/1.60; ۝ 10am-5pm Tue-Sun), with paintings by the old masters, including Rubens and Cranach the Elder. The leafy grounds are also dotted with ponds and fake ruins. At the Georgium's eastern edge is the **Lehrpark**, an educational garden and zoo with the huge domed **mausoleum** you can see from the train station.

CITY CENTRE

Its centre is a mere footnote to Dessau's other attractions. The **Rathaus**, rebuilt in simplified form after the war, has a Bauhaus-style clock; the carillon plays the Dessau March at noon daily. Nearby is the late-Gothic **Marienkirche** (rebuilt 1989–94).

The **Anhaltisches Theater** (☎ 251 110; www.anhaltisches-theater.de; Friedensplatz 1a) is a pompous neo-Roman structure commissioned by the Nazis that is at odds with most of the town's other architecture, be it Bauhaus or GDR. It hosts a variety of dramas, musical theatre ballet and concerts.

Festivals & Special Events

Although more closely associated with Berlin and, later, New York, the composer Kurt Weill was born in Dessau. Every March in his honour, the city hosts a **Kurt Weill Festival** (www.kurt-weill.de; German only), reprising and updating his collaborations with Bertolt Brecht such as *The Threepenny Opera*. Performances take place in Dessau and surrounds.

Sleeping

DJH hostel (☎ 619 452; JH-Dessau@djh-sachsen-anhalt
.de; Waldkaterweg 11; juniors/seniors €15.50/17.20; P)
Because the DJH Jugendherberge Dessau
is pretty basic, closes its doors early and
is slightly tricky to reach without a car, it's
probably more convenient for most budget
travellers to book a room at the Bauhaus
Gästehaus (see following).

Bauhaus Gästehaus (☎ 650 8318; oede@bauhaus
-dessau.de; Heidestrasse 33; dm €15) Sadly, while
renovation of the Bauhaus building is underway the apartments there are closed, but
the Bauhaus Stiftung (Bauhaus administration) has its own 1970s *Plattenbau* apartment complex, with great views.

An den 7 Säulen (☎ 619 620; www.pension7saeulen
.de; Ebertallee 66; s €50-55, d €65-75; P) Not the
most luxurious, but certainly the most
memorable, option in town, this pleasant
pension has a garden and glass-fronted
breakfast room overlooking the Meisterhäuser across the leafy street. Popular with
cyclists and families, it has a relaxed feel.

NH Hotel (☎ 251 40 or 0800 0115 0116; nhdessau@
nh-hotels.com; Zerbster Strasse 29; r €65-105; 🖳 P)
Despite its neutral room furnishings in
white and grey, this chain hotel manages
through good service to feel more stylish
than clinical. Set in one of the pedestrianised areas leading to the Rathaus and tourist office, it's also reasonably well located.

Hotel Fürst Leopold (☎ 251 50; fax 251 5177;
Friedensplatz; s €100, d €130; 🖳 P) Dessau's top
option has it all. It's a minute's walk from
the Hauptbahnhof, offers great service and
has Bauhaus design touches. There's also a
spa and a good restaurant. Weekend rates
are available.

Eating

For other restaurants, stroll along the
pedestrianised Zerber Strasse, between
the Rathaus and the NH Hotel. They're
all much of a muchness, so pick whatever
takes your fancy.

Bauhaus Klub (☎ 650 8444; Gropiusallee 38; mains
€4.50-6.50) Tuna melts, salads, omelettes and
other low-key fare make this café in the
Bauhaus basement a reliable staple in a
town generally lacking remarkable places
to eat. Although several Bauhaus staff
prefer to live in Berlin and commute daily,
some students and hangers-on congregate
here for evening drinks.

Kornhaus (☎ 640 4141; Kornhausstrasse 146; mains
€7-13) You can kill several birds with one
stone at Kornhaus: see the remarkable
Bauhaus dining room, enjoy the view over
the sandy Elbe banks and acquaint yourself with local specialities from the hands
of an acclaimed chef. Try 'heaven and
earth' (slices of Anhalt potatoes and pears,
with crispy smoked pork) or the Elbe
potpourri.

Getting There & Around

RE trains serve Dessau from Berlin-Zoo
(€16.80, 1¾ hours). Regional trains come
from Lutherstadt Wittenberg (€5.80, 40
minutes). Dessau is almost equidistant from
Leipzig, Halle and Magdeburg (all €8.10,
one hour). The Berlin–Munich autobahn
A9 runs east of town.

Single bus and tram tickets cost €1 (valid
60 minutes). **Fahrradverleih Dieter Becker**
(☎ 216 0113; Coswiger Strasse 47; €5-7.50 per day) hires
out bicycles.

AROUND DESSAU
Wörlitz Park & Schloss

With peacocks feeding on the lawn before
a Gothic house, a tree-lined stream flowing
towards a Grecian-style temple and a gap
in a hedge framing a distant villa, the 112-
hectare English-style **Wörlitz Park** (admission
free) is a surprising find in eastern Germany. It owes its existence to anglophile
Prince Leopold III (Friedrich Franz von
Anhalt-Dessau), who oversaw its creation
between 1764 and 1800 in a quest to enrich
the local cultural heritage.

Under Unesco protection today, the park
is as enticing as ever, with paths winding
past hedges, sculptures and architectural
follies. Between May and early November,
hand-cranked **ferries** (adult/concession €0.60/0.30)
cross the Wörlitzer See, which lies between
garden sections. During these months, 45-
minute **gondola tours** (adult/concession €6/4) ply
the lake, departing when eight people or
more gather at the dock. Weekend concerts
are another summer highlight.

On the edge of the park nearest the town
lies Prince Leopold's former country house,
Schloss Wörlitz (☎ 034905-409 20; adult/concession
€4.50/2.50; 🕑 tours only, 10am-4pm Tue-Sun, 11am-5pm
May-Sep), which displays neoclassical English
touches. Like the garden, it could almost be
in England.

Wörlitz-Information (☎/fax 034905-202 16; Am Neuen Wall 103; ☺ 9am-6pm Mar-Oct, 9am-4pm Mon-Fri Nov-Feb) can provide more details, plus a free map of the garden.

GETTING THERE & AWAY

The train from Dessau to Wörlitz only operates Wednesday, Saturday and Sunday, from March to November, and then only makes five return trips a day, so check the train station timetable carefully. Bus No 333 operates every two hours daily from around 9am to 4pm (€3.50, 30 mins). By road from Dessau, take the B185 east to the B107 north, which brings you right into town.

Wörlitz is only 23km from Lutherstadt Wittenberg; by car take the B187 west and head south on the B107.

The large lakeside car park charges €3/1 for cars/motorbikes for the day; two other car parks in town charge €0.50 per hour.

Other Palaces

There are three palaces besides Schloss Georgium (see p246) and Schloss Wörlitz around Dessau. Recently reopened are both the baroque Dutch **Schloss Oranienbaum** (☎ 034904-202 59; admission €3.50; ☺ 10am-5.30pm Tues-Sun May-Oct, noon-4pm Mar & Apr, closed Nov-Feb) and the rococo **Schloss Mosigkau** (☎ 0340-521 139; Knobelsdorfallee 3, Dessau; admission €4.50; ☺ 10am-5.30pm May-Sept, 10am-4.30pm Oct-Apr), which is still being refurbished. For Oranienbaum, take bus Nos 333 and 331; for Mosigkau, which is southwest of central Dessau, take bus No 16 or 17. **Schloss Luisium** (☎ 0340-218 3711; Dessau; admission €4.50; 10am-6pm Tues-Sun May-Sept, 10am-5pm Apr & Oct, 10am-4pm Wed-Sun Nov-Mar), a combination of neo-Gothic and classical styles, is also open for tours. To get here take bus No 13 to Vogelherd.

You can even stay overnight in an elegant pavilion in the grounds of the **Landschaftsgarten Grosskühnau** (☎ 0340-521 139; Dessau; admission free; ☺ year-round). To get here take bus No 10 or 11 to Burgreinaer Strasse.

Ferropolis

Some 15km south of Wörlitz, Ferropolis answers that nagging question: 'What do you do with an abandoned open-pit GDR coal mine and leftover mining equipment that look like they were dispatched from some postapocalyptic nightmare?'

In 1991, some Bauhaus-inspired designers came up with a solution – a 25,000-seat concert venue and museum (of course!). An amphitheatre was built, the mine pit was filled with water diverted from the Mulde River and the monstrous machines (with charming names like Mad Max, Big Wheel and Medusa) were placed just so.

The **museum** (☎ 034953-351 20; adult/concession €3.50/2; ☺ 10am-5pm Mon-Fri, 10am-7pm Sat & Sun in summer, 10am-dusk in winter) is an interesting monument to mining, and the changes wrought by industrial society. Most people go to Ferropolis, however, to attend the concerts and raves held there. Ask at the Dessau, Lutherstadt Wittenberg and Wörlitz tourist offices for information about forthcoming gigs.

GETTING THERE & AWAY

There's a bus link from Dessau (direction: Gräfenhainichen) to the Ferropolis gate (€2.50/3.75 one way/return, 30 minutes). From there, it's a dusty 2km walk into the grounds, although plans for a shuttle bus in summer are underway. By car, take the B185 east to the B107 and turn south towards Gräfenhainichen (20 minutes in all). The entrance to Ferropolis is on your left, just past Jüdenberg.

From Lutherstadt Wittenberg, you can take a train to Gräfenhainichen (20 minutes) and a bus to the gate. Driving from Lutherstadt Wittenberg, take the B100 to its junction with the B107 and turn north; the entrance is on the right.

LUTHERSTADT WITTENBERG
☎ 03491 / pop 53,000

As the crucible of the Reformation, where Protestants first split from the Roman Catholic Church, Lutherstadt Wittenberg (also known as Wittenberg) is among Saxony-Anhalt's most popular destinations. Religious pilgrims, scholars, fans of the Joseph Fiennes film *Luther* and the merely curious all swarm here to retrace the footsteps of Martin Luther, whose campaigning zeal changed the face of Europe and the course of history.

It isn't just that long-term resident Luther wrote his 95 theses – challenging what he regarded as the church's corruption – in Wittenberg in 1517, or that Protestantism was born here. Rather, 16th-century Wit-

LUTHER LORE

'When the legend becomes fact, print the legend,' a journalist famously tells Jimmy Stewart in the classic Western movie *The Man Who Shot Liberty Valance,* and that is exactly what has happened with Martin Luther and his 95 theses. It's been so often repeated that Luther nailed a copy of his revolutionary theses to the door of Wittenberg's Schlosskirche on 31 October 1517 that only serious scholars continue to argue to the contrary.

Certainly, Luther did write 95 theses challenging some of the Catholic practices of the time, especially the selling of 'indulgences' to forgive sins and reduce the buyer's time in purgatory. However, it's another question entirely as to whether he publicised them in the way popular legend suggests.

Believers point to the fact that the Schlosskirche's door was used as a bulletin board of sorts by the university; that the alleged posting took place the day before the affluent congregation poured into the church on All Saints' Day (1 November); and the fact that at Luther's funeral, his influential friend Philipp Melanchthon said he witnessed Luther's deed.

But Melanchthon didn't arrive in town until 1518 – the year *after* the supposed event. It's also odd that Luther's writings never once mentioned such a highly radical act.

While it's known that he sent his theses to the local archbishop to provoke discussion, some locals think it would have been out of character for a devout monk, interested mainly in an honest debate, to challenge the system so publicly and flagrantly without first exhausting all his options.

In any event, nailed to the church door or not, the net effect of Luther's theses was the same. They prompted the onset of the Reformation and Protestantism, altering the way that large sections of the world's Christian population worshipped and continue to worship today.

tenberg was a hotbed of progressive ideas, where priests got married and delivered services in German, not Latin, where educators like Philipp Melanchthon argued for schools to teach in German and to accept female pupils, and where famous Renaissance painter Lucas Cranach the Elder captured the action in fine detail.

Quaint and picturesque, Wittenberg can be seen in a day from Berlin, but it is worth a longer look. The town is busiest in June, during **Luther's Wedding festival** (Luthers Hochzeit), and on October 31, the publication date of the 95 theses.

Orientation

Hauptbahnhof Lutherstadt-Wittenberg is the stop for trains to/from outlying regions, but smaller stations, such as Wittenberg-Markt and Wittenberg-Elbtor exist for local trains. Bus No 304 (€1.10, every 15 minutes) goes from the Hauptbahnhof to the city centre; otherwise it's a signposted 15- to 20-minute walk.

Most major sights can be found within the Altstadt ring. The main street, Collegienstrasse, runs east–west through the Markt and becomes Schlossstrasse at its western end.

Information

Commerzbank (☎ 495 20; Markt 25)

Paul-Gerhardt-Stiftung (☎ 500; Paul-Gerhardt-Strasse 42) Hospital.

Post office (Wilhelm-Weber-Strasse 1)

Sisters (☎ 433 694; Fleischerstrasse 6; €3 per hr) Internet access.

Wittenberg-Information (☎ 498 610 for information, ☎ 414 848 for room reservations; www.wittenberg.de; Schlossplatz 2; ☼ 9am-6pm Mon-Fri, 10am-3pm Sat, 11am-4pm Sun) Offers a portable audio-guide to the town in several languages (€6 plus passport as collateral), two-hour city tours (€7; ☼ 2pm May-Oct) in German, night tours, English tours and more.

Sights & Activities

LUTHERHAUS

If you only visit one of the several museums in Germany devoted to the father of the Reformation, make it the **Lutherhaus** (☎ 420 30; www.martinluther.de; Collegienstrasse 54; adult/concession €5/3; ☼ 9am-6pm Apr-Oct, 10am-5pm Tue-Sun Nov-Mar). The exhibition here, in Luther's one-time home, was revamped in 2003 to the tune of €17.5 million and it shows. Even those with no previous interest in the subject will be drawn in by its combination of accessible narrative (in German and English), personal artefacts (ie

SAXONY-ANHALT

LUTHERSTADT WITTENBERG

To Hundertwasser Schule (1km); Potsdam (70km)

INFORMATION
Commerzbank	1 B3
Paul-Gerhardt-Stiftung	2 D2
Sisters	3 C3
Tourist Information	4 A2

SIGHTS & ACTIVITIES (pp249-51)
Galerie im Cranachhaus	5 B3
Haus der Geschichte	6 B3
Luthereiche (Luther's Oak)	7 D3
Lutherhaus	8 C3
Melanchthon Haus	9 C3
Rathaus	10 B2
Schlosskirche	11 A3
Schlossturm	12 A3
Stadtkirche St Marien	13 B3
Wittenberg English Ministry	(see 4)

SLEEPING (pp251-2)
Art Hotel	14 A1
Best Western Stadtpalais	15 C3
Brauhaus Wittenberg	16 B3
DJH Hostel	17 A3
Goldener Adler	18 B3
Pension am Schwanenteich	19 B2
Stadthotel Wittenberg Schwarzer Baer	20 B3

EATING (p252)
Café Hundertwasserschule	21 B2
Tante Emmas	22 B3
Zum Schwarzen Baer	(see 20)
Zur Schlossfreiheit	23 B2

DRINKING (p252)
Barrik	24 B3
Brauhaus Wittenberg	(see 16)
Independent	25 C3
Irish Harp Pub	26 C3

ENTERTAINMENT (pp252-3)
Brettl-Keller	27 A3

SHOPPING (p253)
Historische Druckerstube	(see 5)

TRANSPORT (p253)
Bus Station	28 C2

Bibles, cloak), oil paintings by Cranach the Elder and interactive multimedia displays. There's also an original room furnished by Luther in 1535, decorated with a bit of royal graffiti from Russian tsar Peter the Great in 1702.

The **Luthereiche** (Luther's oak), the spot where the preacher burned the 1520 papal bull threatening his excommunication, is on the corner of Lutherstrasse and Am Bahnhof, though the oak tree itself was planted around 1830.

SCHLOSSKIRCHE

Legend has it that it was the door of the **Castle Church** (admission free; 10am-5pm Mon-Sat, 11.30am-5pm Sun) where Luther nailed his 95 theses on 31 October 1517 (see the boxed text Luther Lore, p249). There's no hard evidence that this happened, especially as the door in question was destroyed by fire in 1760. In its place, however, stands an impressive bronze memorial (1858) inscribed with the theses in Latin.

Inside is Luther's tombstone; it lies below the pulpit, opposite that of his friend

and fellow reformer Philipp Melanchthon. Information sheets are available in several languages.

Next door, you can climb the city's landmark **Schlossturm** (castle tower; adult/concession € 0.50; noon-4pm Mon-Fri, 10am-4pm Sat & Sun), but be warned that the view is expansive rather than breathtaking.

STADTKIRCHE ST MARIEN

If the Schlosskirche was the billboard used to advertise the forthcoming Reformation, its sister **Stadtkirche St Marien** (City Church of Marien; 9am-5pm Mon-Sat, 11.30am-5pm Sun) was where the ecumenical revolution began, with the world's first Protestant worship services in 1521. It was also here that Luther preached his famous Lectern sermons in 1522 and three years later married ex-nun Katharina von Bora.

The centrepiece is the large altar, designed jointly by Lucas Cranach the Elder and his son. The side facing the nave shows Luther, Melanchthon and other Reformation figures, as well as Cranach himself, in biblical contexts. Unusually, though, the

ltar is painted on its reverse side. Behind
, on the lower rung, you'll see a seemingly
efaced painting of heaven and hell. Medival students etched their initials into the
ainting's divine half if they passed their
inal exams – and into purgatory if they
ailed.

CHURCH SERVICES

From April to October, the **Wittenberg Eng-
ish Ministry** (☎ 498 610; www.wittenberg-english
ministry.com; Schlossplatz 2) holds Saturday
evening services in English from 6.30pm
to 7.30pm in either the Schlosskirche or
Stadtkirche. Watch for notices around
town, or ask at the tourist office. Services
in English are also held at 4pm Wednesday and 11.30am Friday in the tiny Fron-
leichnamskapelle (Corpus Christi Chapel)
attached to the Stadtkirche.

HAUS DER GESCHICHTE

Another side to Luther-obsessed Wittenberg is shown at the ambiguously named
Haus der Geschichte (House of History; ☎ 409 004;
Schlossstrasse 6; adult/senior & student/family €3/2/6;
🕑 10am-5pm Tue-Fri, 11am-6pm Sat & Sun), which
turns out to be a heart-warming museum
of everyday life in the GDR. The ground
floor is devoted to temporary exhibitions,
while living rooms, kitchens, bedrooms
and bathrooms on the next two levels have
been reconstructed in various styles from
the 1940s to 1980s. Even if the brand names
mean nothing to you personally, there's
something comforting about the homely
lounge suites, clunky early consumer items,
and the tins and jars that would have been
gold dust for the son recreating the good ole
East in the hit movie *Good Bye, Lenin!*

TRABI RENTAL

To savour more of the same *Ostalgie* (nostalgia for the old East Germany) pedalled
by the Haus der Geschichte, hire a Trabant
East German car from **Event & Touring** (☎ 660
195; Dessauer Strasse 38). The cost is €22/51/80
per hour/five hours/10 hours, or ask about
Trabi Safaris for groups.

HUNDERTWASSERSCHULE

Wittenberg's Martin-Luther-Gymnasium
is usually called the **Hundertwasserschule**
(Hundertwasser School; ☎ 881 131; Strasse der Völker-
freundschaft 130; tours €1; 🕑 1.30-5pm Tue-Fri, to 4pm

Nov-Mar, 10am-4pm Sat & Sun), because the famous
Viennese artist and architect Friedensreich
Hundertwasser designed its current look.
Shortly before his death in 2000, he helped
remodel a series of East German concrete
blocks into one of his signature buildings,
with organic curves, brightly coloured elements, touches of gold, mosque-like cupo-
las and rooftop vegetation.

The school is a 20-minute walk northeast of the centre. From the Markt, follow
Judenstrasse, turn left into Neustrasse and
continue into Geschwister-Scholl-Strasse.
Turn left into Sternstrasse, right into
Schillerstrasse, and the school is at the next
intersection on the left. Of course, it's possible to view the exterior anytime, but tours
of the interior wait for at least four participants before they start. Ring ahead for
tours in English. Unbelievably, at the time
of writing this fantastically well-equipped,
modern high school was threatened with
closure, so if there's no response, it could
mean that has transpired.

OTHER ATTRACTIONS

Alongside the Lutherhaus, the former
homes of two other Reformation stalwarts
are now museums. The **Galerie im Cranach-
haus** (☎ 420 1911; Schlossstrasse 1; adult/concession
€3/2; 🕑 10am-5pm Mon-Sat, 1-5pm Sun) is devoted
to artist Lucas Cranach the Elder; while the
rather text-heavy **Melanchthon Haus** (☎ 403
279; Collegienstrasse 60; adult/concession €2.50/1.50;
🕑 9am-6pm Tue-Sun Apr-Oct, to 5pm Nov-Mar) dis-
cusses the life of university lecturer and
humanist Philipp Melanchthon. An expert
in ancient languages, Melanchthon helped
Luther translate the Bible into German
from Greek and Hebrew, becoming the
preacher's friend and his most eloquent
advocate.

The 16th-century **Rathaus** (☎ 421 720; Markt
26; adult/concession €1.50/1; 🕑 10am-5pm Tue-Sun)
houses a collection of 2nd-century religious
art. Ask about combination tickets to these
museums.

Sleeping
BUDGET

Private rooms can be booked through
Wittenberg-Information (p249).

Pension am Schwanenteich (☎/fax 402 807;
Töpferstrasse 1; s/d €32/60; 🅿) This small pension
has much nicer rooms than you'd expect for

the price, plus a convenient location. That and the charming owners make this Wittenberg's best budget option (despite their inability to accept payment by credit card).

DJH hostel (☎ /fax 403 255; jugendherberge@witten berg.de; Schloss; juniors/seniors €16.80/19.50; **P** **☐**) It's novel having a hostel in a castle building, but the dim lighting, wood-laminate walls, and kindergarten-style furniture means this is nothing special, really. And there are plenty of stairs to climb.

Marina-Camp Elbe (☎ 4540; www.marina-camp -elbe.de; Brückenkopf 1) On the banks of the Elbe near the Wittenberg-Elbtor train station, this is a very comfortable modern camp site.

MID-RANGE

Stadthotel Wittenberg Schwarzer Baer (☎ 420 4344; www.stadthotel-wittenberg.de; Schlossstrasse 2; s/d €55/70; **P**) In the heart of the old town, this hotel has clean, modern rooms. At the same time, there's just enough olde-worlde charm in the public areas to keep it atmospheric and interesting.

Brauhaus Wittenberg (☎ 433 130; www.brauhaus -wittenberg.de; Im Beyerhof, Markt 6; s/d €50/70; **P**) For a room with a brew, try this central, busy hotel/restaurant. The accommodation is spacious and clean, although the tiled floors can't really dampen the noise from the pub below.

Goldener Adler (☎ 505 660; fasbender.haiser@t-on line.de; Markt 7) At the time of writing, this central hotel was temporarily closed for renovations until 2004, but the plan was to keep it furnished in the same, slightly upmarket, traditional German style.

Art Hotel (☎ 467 310; www.art-hotel.com; Puschkin strasse 15b; s/d €60/85; **✂** **P**) Despite trying to differentiate itself by showing modern art in its public rooms, this hotel doesn't quite manage to avoid a generic feel. However, it's a comfy, convenient place to stay and has a sauna and solarium.

TOP END

Best Western Stadtpalais (☎ 4250; info@stadtpalais .bestwestern.de; Collegienstrasse 56/57; s €90-100, d €110-120; **P** **✗** **✂**) 'Best Western in Germany is not like Best Western in America,' one tourism official informed us sniffily, and it's true the hotels have more character – this one with slightly Asian touches. The standard of accommodation, however, is just as high. Parking costs €6.

Eating

Try some Lutherbrot, a gingerbread-lik concoction with chocolate and sugar icin

Café Hundertwasserschule (☎ 410 685; Markt mains €4-14) There's a health-conscious strea at this modern café, from the no-smokir policy to the vegetarian options and fres juices, but you're still free to indulge you self with lamb, venison, home-made cak or beer should you choose. Hundertwass touches pepper the room.

Zur Schlossfreiheit (☎ 402 980; Coswigerstrasse mains €6.50-10.50; ☾ closed Sun) Cosy, dark-woo surrounds and slightly different fare, inclu ing historical theme dishes such as Luthe schmaus (scrumptious duck in peppe sultana sauce), make this place a real trea Weekday lunch specials cost €5.25.

Tante Emmas Bier-und Caféhaus (☎ 419 75 Markt 9; mains €8.50-14) From the dried-fru wreath over its portal to the pink-on-whi embroidered wall hangings and other bri a-brac, Tante Emma's is German countr kitchen–style through and through. Th traditional cuisine matches perfectly.

Zum Schwarzen Baer (☎ 411 200; Schlossstrasse mains €3.50-12) This faux-rustic Kartoffelha (potato house) is geared to the passing tou ist trade, so expect a filling feed rather tha a gourmet experience. Dishes range fro jacket potatoes and potato pizza to lam cutlets, chicken schnitzels and steak.

Drinking

Brauhaus Wittenberg (☎ 433 130; Im Beyerhof, Mar 6) The cobbled courtyard and indoor brew ery, with its shiny copper vats, thrum wit the noise of people having a good time, o both summer and winter evenings.

Barrik (☎ 403 260; Collegienstrasse 81) This wir bar really does feel like an upscale Ne York club, so it's surprising to learn that was built more than 500 years ago, durin Luther's lifetime.

Other pubs to try include the **Irish Ha Pub** (☎ 410 150; Collegienstrasse 71), where you find Guinness and live music, or **Indepen ent** (☎ 413 257; Collegienstrasse 44), which has a 'international table' (usually with Englis speakers) on Monday evenings. See the list ings magazine *Ingo* for further details.

Entertainment

Ask at the tourist office about the frequen musical performances in summer. Th

Stadtkirche has organ concerts at 6pm Friday from May to October, while the Schlosskirche has choir and organ music at 2.30pm every Tuesday during the same period.

German-speakers will find **Brettl-Keller** (☎ 402 085; Schlossplatz) carrying on the fine national tradition of political and satirical cabaret.

Shopping

Historische Druckerstube (☎ 432 817; Cranach-Hof, Schlossstrasse 1) This basement gallery sells ancient-looking black-and-white sketches of Martin Luther, typeset and printed by hand.

Getting There & Away

Wittenberg is on the main train line to Halle and Leipzig (€9, one hour), and Berlin-Ostbahnhof (€16.20, 1½ hours). All the Berlin-bound trains stop at Schönefeld airport. Be sure to board for 'Lutherstadt-Wittenberg', as there's also a Wittenberge west of Berlin.

Getting Around

The main bus station is along Mauerstrasse just west of Neustrasse; single tickets are €1.10/0.55 for adults/children.

Parking enforcement is quite stringent, so use the car parks on the fringes of the Altstadt (eg near Elbtour and along Fleischerstrasse).

SOUTHERN SAXONY-ANHALT

HALLE

☎ 0345 / pop 239,500

Best known as the birthplace of composer Georg Friedrich Händel, Halle presents a rather discordant mix. It's a blend of grimy medieval towers, lovely restored houses and dilapidated, graffiti-covered buildings that attest to Halle's previous role as centre of the GDR's chemical industry. However, hang around to explore this university town's cafés, culture and people and you'll come to like it at least a little.

In the Middle Ages, Halle was a powerful religious centre as well as a nexus of the salt trade ('Halle' derives from the word for 'salt'

used by the prehistoric Celts who settled the area). Even as recently as last century, it was the capital of Saxony-Anhalt and then of the GDR's Halle district. But its communist links backfired after unification, when Magdeburg usurped its crown.

Perhaps that loss of status is why Halle isn't content just to host the **Händel Festival** every June and has ambitiously decided to leap for the big one. It's riding piggyback on Leipzig's bid for the 2012 Olympics – first-round football matches would be held here – hence the cranes on the horizon and jackhammers digging up the streets.

Orientation

The Altstadt – the centre of town – is circled by a road known as the Stadt Ring, and lies northwest of the Hauptbahnhof. To walk to the centre from the Bahnhof takes about 15 to 20 minutes; head left from the main entrance and turn left into the underpass known as Der Tunnel. Continue along pedestrianised Leipziger Strasse to the Markt, Halle's central square. Take care when entering the Markt, as trams (streetcars) career through here at speed.

Information

Post office (Grosse Steinstrasse 72)

Halle Tourist Information (☎ 472 330; www.halle-tourist.de; Stadtcenter Rolltreppe, Grosse Ulrichstrasse 60; ☀ 10am-6pm Mon-Fri, 10am-2pm Sat) The website is in German only. Guided 1½-hour tours (adult/concession €5/3.50) leave from here 2pm Monday to Friday, 2pm and 1.30pm Saturday, and 4pm Sunday.

Dangers & Annoyances

Undesirables hang around the Hauptbahnhof at all hours. Use common sense in and around Der Tunnel, which runs between the station and the eastern end of Leipziger Strasse.

Sights

BEATLES MUSEUM

Imagine! The Continent's only full-time **Beatles Museum** (☎ 290 3900, www.beatlesmuseum.halle.de; Alter Markt 12; adult/concession €2.50/1.50; ☀ 10am-6pm Wed-Sun, closed Sep) is in the unlikely location of Halle. All the same, it's a pleasant surprise. Owner Rainer Moers began collecting in 1964 and moved his memorabilia here when rents in Cologne became prohibitive. Even in this roomy, three-storey building only a fraction of his 10,000 items are displayed – from legendary photos, record covers and film posters to merchandise like wigs, jigsaws and even talcum powder. The gift shop sells many Beatles souvenirs.

HÄNDELHAUS

In marked contrast to the Beatles Museum, **Händelhaus** (☎ 500 900; www.haendelhaus.de; Grosse Nikolai Strasse 5-6; adult/concession €2.60/1.60; ⏱ 9.30am-5.30pm Fri-Wed, 9.30am-7.30pm Thu) presents a musical legacy readily associated with Halle. It's the house in which Händel was born in 1685 and charts the composer's life through his moves to Hamburg, Hanover, Italy and eventually London, where he achieved great fame before dying in 1759. The exhibition boards are in German, but call ahead and the museum will arrange a tour in your own language for no extra charge. Much of the space is taken up, anyway, with a collection of antique musical instruments, including a charming 'glass harmonica' which was designed by the father of hypnosis, Franz Anton Mesmer.

SCHLOSS MORITZBURG

In one tower of the atmospheric 15th-century **Schloss Moritzburg** (Moritzburg Castle; ☎ 212 590; www.moritzburg.halle.de; Friedemann-Bach-Platz 5; adult/concession €5/3, free Tue; ⏱ 11am-8.30pm Tue, 10am-6pm Wed-Sun) you'll find a small but well-presented collection of German Expressionism and other contemporary art. Works include several by Franz Marc, Ernst Ludwig Kirchner, Erich Heckel and influential Bauhaus devotee Lyonel Feininger, who painted many scenes of Halle. There are also single pieces by Edvard Munch and Emil Nolde, while temporary exhibitions occupy other halls.

MARKTKIRCHE

The four tall towers of the 500-year-old **Marktkirche** (⏱ 9am-noon & 2-5pm Mon-Sat, 11am-5pm Sun) look rather timeworn, but the interior is more impressive. The late-Gothic hall has a folding altar painted at the workshop of Lucas Cranach the Elder. There's a Romanesque bronze baptismal font, and two spectacular organs (Händel first doodled his Messiah on the smaller one).

The chief treasure is the death mask of Martin Luther, cast when Luther's body was placed here for the night on its way back to Wittenberg for burial. It's locked behind the altar (ask to see it during a city tour).

Organ concerts are held at 4pm on Tuesday and Thursday, and services at 10am on Sunday.

OTHER ATTRACTIONS

Any visitor walking into town from the Hauptbahnhof won't fail to notice the psychedelic graffiti covering every inch of the pedestrian underpass known as **Der Tunnel**. In a fit of common sense, the local authorities decided that if you can't beat 'em, join 'em, and legalised street art here.

Sleeping

Contact the tourist office about private rooms or camping, north of town.

DJH hostel (☎ 202 4716; August-Bebel-Strasse 48a; juniors/seniors €17.50/21.20; 🖳) The high point of this hostel – in a converted old house – is the dining room, where you can make believe you've been returned to the 1930s. The hostel's a 15-minute walk north of the centre but is closer to the nightlife of Kleine Ulrichstrasse.

Zum Kleinen Sandberg (☎ 682 5913; fax 682 5914; Kleiner Sandberg 3; s/d €40/80) In a quiet location minutes from the main pedestrian thoroughfare of Leipziger Strasse, this half-timbered house has a rustic restaurant and spotless, if fairly basic, modern rooms.

Dorint Hotel Charlottenhof (☎ 292 30; www.dorint.com\halle; Dorotheenstrasse 12; s €120-150, d €130-170; 🅿 ⊠ 🐾) The staff are so proud that this hotel has repeatedly been named the best Dorint in Germany, they're extra careful to ensure standards of service don't slip. The rooms are lovely, too, decorated in an understated blend of Art Deco and contemporary styles.

Most of Halle's nicer mid-range options are a bit removed from the centre, including **City Hotel am Wasserturm** (☎ 298 20; www.cityhotel-halle.de; Lessingstrasse 8; s/d €60/80; 🅿), a renovated older hotel; and the newer, flashier **Hotel Magistralen Carré** (☎ 693 10; www.hotel-magistralen-carre.de; Neustädter Passage 5; s €70 d €85; 🅿).

Eating

Ackerbürgerhof (☎ 2798 0432; Grosse Klausstrasse 15; mains €4-11) Once stables, before being converted into a house in the 13th century, this six-room restaurant claims that both

Goethe and Händel have partaken of its traditional German cuisine.

Gasthof zum Mohr (☎ 520 0033; Burgstrasse 2; mains €6-11; ☺ closed Mon Jan-Apr) Extending its traditional German menu to cater to vegetarians, this 500-year-old restaurant near Giebichstein castle serves mushroom schnitzels and soya steaks, alongside meatier fare. The leafy beer garden is a summer hit with families.

Drei Kaiser (☎ 203 1868; Bergstrasse 1; mains €8-15) The Drei Kaiser's attempt at rustic style is a bit fake, but its food is mighty fine. Fish dishes, veggie casseroles and healthy salads are offset by cholesterol-packed specialities like *Ofenfrischer Brotlaib* – smoked pork, white wine and crème fraîche baked in a hollow loaf.

Lesecafé nt (☎ 205 0222/0223; Grosse Ulrichstrasse 51; ☺ closed Mon evening) This café is not just a good place before an evening at the edgy Neues Theater (think Ibsen, Brecht and contemporary playwrights). Behind its eye-catching glass, imprinted with the names of literary greats, and its window display of teacups and sets, you can fuel up on breakfast, lunch and, most evenings, dinner.

Drinking

Sternstrasse is one nightlife hub, where **Don Camillo** (☎ 304 1741; Sternstrasse 3) is one of the most interesting bars. However, a newer, trendier quarter has sprung up along Kleine Ulrichstrasse. **Lujah** (☎ 478 9900; Kleine Ulrichstrasse 36) is young, hip and happening; **Emilie** (☎ 202 5333; Kleine Ulrichstrasse 36) is more relaxed; while the elegant Art Nouveau(-ish) **Café Bar Noir** (☎ 582 2707; Kleine Ulrichstrasse 30) offers a relaxed, often jazz-filled evening for a slightly older crowd. For further listings, consult the free magazines *Fritz* or *Blitz*.

Entertainment
CINEMA

Zazie (☎ 209 7826; Grosse Ulrichstrasse 27) As well as being a designer bar and restaurant, Zazie also has a cinema showing English-language films, subtitled rather than dubbed into German.

DISCOS & CLUBS

The popular eastern German disco franchise **Flower Power** (Moritzburgring 1) has moved into Halle, giving **Easy Schorre** (☎ 212 240; Philipp-Müller-Strasse 77-78) some competition. **Objekt 5**

(☎ 522 0016; Seebener Strasse 5) and **Turm** (☎ 202 5190; Kleine Ulrichstrasse 24a) are where to head for music events including jazz and tango.

THEATRE & CLASSICAL MUSIC

Händel-Halle (☎ 292 90; Salzgrafenplatz 1) This modern 1900-seat venue hosts a wide range of artists, from, say, classical *enfant terrible* Nigel Kennedy to comeback rock queen Nena and even, ahem, the Chippendales male strip show. There are also music festivals and dance contests.

Getting There & Away
AIR

Leipzig-Halle airport lies between both cities, which are about 25km apart. It's a major link with Frankfurt, Munich, and other major German and European cities. ICE trains head from the new airport train station to Leipzig and Dresden in one direction and Halle, Magdeburg and Hanover in the other.

CAR & MOTORCYCLE

From Leipzig, take the A14 west to the B100. A new extension of the A14 connects Halle and Magdeburg in about one hour. The B91 runs south from Halle and links up with the A9 autobahn, which connects Munich and Berlin.

TRAIN

Leipzig and Halle are linked by frequent trains (€5.20, 35 minutes). Halle is also on the fast train route from Magdeburg (€12.40, 1½ hours), Erfurt (€15, 1¼ hours) and Berlin-Zoo (€28.40, two hours). Local trains serve Eisleben (€5.50, 40 minutes) and Wittenberg (€9, one hour).

Getting Around

Bus No 300 runs every 30 minutes during the day and less frequently at night between the airport and the Hauptbahnhof. The fare is €5. Taxis cost about €25.

For drivers, the one-way street system in Halle is fiendishly complex, and the streets busy. Your best bet is to park near the Hauptbahnhof or at one of the municipal garages and walk.

Bus and tram tickets cost €0.90 for rides of up to four stops and €1.40 for others. A book of four tickets costs €4.35, while the HalleCard is €3.50/9.50 per day/week.

EISLEBEN
☎ 03475 / pop 24,500

It seems odd for a well-travelled man whose ideas revolutionised Europe to have died in the town where he was born. However, as native son Martin Luther himself put it before expiring here, 'Mein Vaterland war Eisleben' (Eisleben was my fatherland). Whereas Lutherstadt Wittenberg has other distractions, this former mining town focuses these days on the devout follower. Every way you turn, it's Luther, Luther, Luther, in this town also known as Lutherstadt Eisleben.

Orientation

Most sights are knotted together around the Markt, just southwest of Hallesche Strasse-Freistrasse (B80), the main thoroughfare. From the train station (turn left out of the main exit), it's a 10-minute walk north along Bahnhofsring and Bahnhofstrasse.

Information

Fremdverkehrsein Lutherstadt Eisleben (☎ 60 2124; www.eisleben-tourist.de; Bahnhofstrasse 36; ☘ 10am-5pm Mon-Fri, 10am-6pm Tue, 9am-noon Sat) Tourist information; website is in German only.

Kreisinformationzentrum Mansfelder Land (☎ 66 7790; www.mansfelderland.de; Markt 58; ☘ 9am-5.30pm Mon-Fri) Tourist information. Has a tendency to put a price on brochures.

Post office (Schlossplatz 7)

Sights

LUTHER MUSEUMS

Perhaps it's the annexe out back that's the most interesting at **Luthers Geburtshaus** (Luther's birth house; ☎ 602 775; Seminarstrasse 16; adult/concession €2/1; ☘ 10am-6pm Apr-Oct, 10am-5pm Tue-Sun Nov-Mar). It's chock-full of Luther souvenirs throughout the ages, which rather overshadow the sparse artefacts in the main house, where the reformer was born. A combined ticket that includes entry to Luthers Sterbehaus costs €3.

In the centre of town, just past the Markt, lies **Luthers Sterbehaus** (Luther's death house; ☎ 602 285; Andreaskirchplatz; adult/concession €2/1), the house where he died on 18 February 1546. It's an altogether more sombre affair than the Geburtshaus, with lots of information (in German) about the Reformation downstairs and Luther's reconstructed living quarters and death chamber upstairs,

including copies of his death mask and last testimony. Luther returned to Eisleben to help settle a legal dispute over the family copperworks, but was already ill and died a day after finalising an agreement.

MARKT & CHURCHES

See where Luther delivered his last sermon in 1546! That's the **St Andreaskirche** (☘ 10am noon & 2-4pm Mon-Sat, 11am-1pm & 2-4pm Sun May-Oct), a late-Gothic hall church on the hill behind the central Markt. See where Luther stayed while district vicar! That would be the apartments of the **St Annenkirche** (☘ 1-3pm Mon-Fri May-Oct) 10 minutes west of the Markt. This church also features a stunning Steinbilder-Bibel (stone-picture Bible; 1585), the only one of its kind in Europe, and a wittily decorated pulpit. Finally, see where Luther was baptised – the **St Petri Pauli Kirche** (Church of Sts Peter & Paul; ☘ 1-3pm Mon-Fri May-Oct) near the Fremdverkehrsein.

By now, we think you get the picture of what Eisleben is about. The historic cloister has recently been refurbished and is home to a community of nuns; this **Kloster Helfta** (☎ 711 500; Lindenstrasse 34) does group tours by arrangement or organises religious workshops.

Sleeping & Eating

Parkhotel (☎ 540; fax 253 19; Bahnhofstrasse 12; s €40, d €50) There's no postmodern irony about the '70s decor here – it's simply vaguely old-fashioned. In its favour, though, this pleasant enough family-run hotel has a quiet and pretty hilltop setting, across from a leafy park.

Hotel an der Klosterpforte (☎ 714 40; klosterpforte.eisleben@vch.de; Lindenstrasse 34; s/d €50/70; P ⊠) If staying at this modern hotel in the grounds of the cloister and having the chance to participate in the daily prayer services doesn't appeal, you can always just drop in for a meal and a home-brewed beer.

Mansfelder Hof (☎ 6690; hotel@mansfelderhof.de; Hallesche Strasse 33; s/d €50/80; P) Behind its vine-covered, faded green stucco façade, the Mansfelder Hof turns out to have modern but entirely forgettable rooms. The real draw is the restaurant (mains €7 to €12) serving local specialities, often with Luther-related names.

Graf von Mansfeld (☎ /fax 250 722; Markt 56; s/d €50/80; ⊠) This hotel's light and airy rooms, with just a hint of rococo, are really appealing. The modern menu (mains €7 to €17) also sounds good, but unfortunately the food doesn't quite match the standard of the accommodation.

Getting There & Away
There are trains to Halle (€5.50, 35 minutes), Leipzig (€10.70, 70 minutes), Erfurt (€13.50, 1¾ hours) and Weimar (€15.80, two hours).

Eisleben is a half-hour drive west of Halle on the B80.

SAALE-UNSTRUT REGION

It will never rival the likes of Bordeaux as a connoisseur's paradise, but the wine-growing region along the Saale and Unstrut (pronounced 'zah-leh' and 'oon-shtroot') Rivers nevertheless provides a wonderfully rural summer retreat. Bicycle and hiking paths meander through rolling, castle-topped hills and past small family-owned vineyards, where you can stop to sip the local produce. Naumburg provides the perfect base for exploring the region, but local tourist offices will happily help with accommodation in smaller towns.

NAUMBURG
☎ 03445 / pop 31,500
Somebody obviously thought the ornate medieval buildings lining the central Markt here were so beautiful they deserved their own architectural name: the Rathaus, the Portal von 1680 at the eastern end and even the tourist office building are all examples of what's called 'Naumburg Renaissance' style. Despite this, charming Naumberg is best known for its huge cathedral and the fact that philosopher Friedrich Nietzsche spent some of his final years here.

Orientation
The Hauptbahnhof is 1.5km northwest of the old town, which is encircled by a ring road. You can take bus No 2 from the Hauptbahnhof to the Markt (€1.10) or walk along Rossbacher Strasse (keep bearing left and uphill). Doing the latter takes you past the cathedral en route. The Zentral Omnibus Busbahnhof (ZOB; bus station), is at the northeastern edge of town on Hallesische Strasse, should you want to

catch a bus rather than a train into the Saale-Unstrut region.

Information
Main post office (Heinrich von Stephan Platz 6) Just north of Marientor.
State (☎ 208 881; Marienplatz 12) Free internet access on two terminals when you buy snacks or drinks.
Tourist- und Tagungservice Naumberg
(☎ 201 614; www.naumburg-tourismus.de; Markt 6; 9am-6pm Mon-Fri, 10am-4pm Sat)

Sights
DOM
In the western quarter of town, on a road in from the train station, stands the enormous medieval **Cathedral of Sts Peter & Paul** (☎ 201 675; Domplatz 16-17; adult/concession/child €4/3/2). Its

FOLLOW THE VINEYARD ROAD

Saale Unstrut is the ideal location for a **Weinstrasse** (Vineyard Road), as devised by the **Weinbauverband Saale-Unstrut** (☎ 034464-261 10; www.natuerlich-saale-unstrut .de), with more than 750 vineyards. As Europe's most northerly wine region, it produces crisp white wines and fairly sharp reds, and if you follow the Vineyard Road, you can sample these for free. Or, for a fee of between €2.50 and €7.50, you can drink up to six large glasses accompanied by bread and cheese and a vineyard history.

Local tourist offices sell copies of *Weinstrasse – Land der Burgen* (€5), a regional map showing the Vineyard Road as well as bicycle paths. At the Naumburg tourist office, you can also collect the free *Wein- & Winzerangebote Saale-Unstrut*, a vineyard guide with tour and tasting prices.

There's something magical about riding a bike and stopping for wine-tasting; you can hire bikes in Naumburg or Freyburg. If you plan to do some serious tasting, a ferry runs from the Blütengrund camp site to Freyburg (see Freyburg, p260). The Saale-Unstrut region is also locally famous for its apples, which hang heaviest on the trees in autumn. For honey, apples, potatoes or other vegetables and fruit juices, try the **Agrar-und Absatzgenossenschaft Naumburg** (☎ 702 976), at the northern end of Naumburg on the road out to Henne.

size is impressive enough, but the cathedral is also possibly unique in having two choirs. The western choir, built in 1250–60 in late Romanesque style is the more interesting. Considered the magnum opus of the anonymous Master of Naumburg, it not only contains some of Germany's oldest and most valuable stained-glass windows, but also houses the celebrated 13th-century **statues of Uta and Ekkehard**, who were among the dome's many benefactors. Uta of Naumberg is a German icon and her serene face decorates souvenirs all over town.

The elevated eastern choir was built around 1330 in Gothic style. The staircase up to it is interesting, too, although it's a contemporary touch. Magdeburg artist Heinrich Apel has decorated the banisters with all sorts of farmyard animals, hobgoblins and fairy-tale characters.

An informative tour (in German) is included in the admission price, but you can pick up a leaflet, or buy a brochure in English (€5), and walk around on your own.

NIETZSCHE HAUS

The home of Friedrich Nietzsche's mother, who brought the philosopher here to nurse him when he was dying from syphilis, requires a lot of concentration, just like the man's work itself. That's to say there's not much to the **Nietzsche Haus** (☎ 201 638; Weingarten 18; adult/concession €1.50/1; ⏰ 2-5pm Tue-Fri, 10am-4pm Sat-Sun) apart from photos and reams of biographical text (all in German). Even if the exhibition pointedly stays *stumm* (mum) on the controversy surrounding the man who wrote *Also Sprach Zarathustra* and became a Nazi favourite, many interested amateur philosophers make a beeline for this place.

STADTKIRCHE ST WENZEL

The baroque Hildebrand organ is the highlight of the **Stadtkirche St Wenzel** (St Wenceslas Church; ☎ 208 401; Topfmarkt; admission free; ⏰ 10am-noon & 2-5pm Mon-Sat, 10am-5pm Sun), but it also features a bronze Gothic baptismal font and two paintings by Cranach the Elder. The 76m-high tower (adult/concession €1.50/0.75; ⏰ 10am-5pm) can be climbed for pleasant views.

OTHER ATTRACTIONS

There's a town museum in the late 15th-century **Hohe Lilie** (☎ 200 648; Markt 18; adult/child

€2/free), while nooks and crannies worth exploring include the renovated **Marientor** - part of the city's medieval defences.

Festivals & Special Events
KIRSCH FEST

The town goes wild on the last weekend in June with the **Kirsch Fest** (Cherry Festival) held at the Vogelwiese field at the southeastern end of town. It celebrates the unlikely medieval tale of the lifting of a blockade by Czech soldiers, when their leader, Prokop, gave in to requests by the town's children (dressed in their Sunday finest) to please leave and let the townsfolk eat again.

Tent stalls offer regional food, wine and beer, and there is live music, too. An enormous fireworks display and a parade, with actors dressed as Uta and Ekkehard, are held on the Sunday.

Sleeping
BUDGET

If you're after a **private room** (€16-25 per person), get in touch with Tourist- und Tagungsservice Naumberg (p257).

DJH hostel (☎ 703 422; JH-Naumburg@djh-sachsen -anhalt.de; Am Tennisplatz 9; juniors/seniors €13.50/16.20) Naumburg's large and well-equipped hostel is 1.5km south of the town centre.

Camping Blütengrund (☎ 202 711; www.camping naumburg.de; Blütengrund Park; camp sites/car €4/2, tent €3-4) This camp site, 1.5km northeast of Naumburg at the confluence of the Saale and Unstrut Rivers, is popular with German families.

MID-RANGE

Hotel Garni St Marien (☎ 235 40; fax 235 422; Marienstrasse 47; s/d €45/85; P) A few homy touches, like the magazine rack and the honour bar, plus this hotel's small size, offset the fairly impersonal (but comfortable) modern rooms. Set back from the street, it ensures a good night's rest.

Auspanne Zum Alten Krug (☎ /fax 200 406; Lindenring 44; s/d €45/60) Because it's in an old building, this pension offers a slightly higgledy-piggledy assortment of differently shaped rooms. There's a certain rough-hewn quality to them, but they're comfortable enough and have atmosphere.

Hotel Stadt Aachen (☎ 2470; www.hotel-stadt -aachen.de; Markt 11; s €50-70, d €80-100) With its country-style floral curtains, its patterned duvet covers and its heavy wooden wardrobes, the Stadt Aachen is the place for those looking for rustic German charm. The vine-covered façade is located right on the Markt, in the heart of town.

Zur Alten Schmiede (☎ 243 60; www.hotel-zur-alten-schmiede.de; Lindenring 36-37; s/d €60/85) Combining the friendly (very) smiley service of a family-run business with effortless, unstuffy elegance, this is the most chic place to stay in Naumburg. It's on the ring road circling the town centre.

Hotel Stadt Naumburg (☎ 7390; www.hotel-stadt-naumburg.de; Friedensstrasse 6; s €49-55, d €80-95 P) With their blond wood and touches of pine green, the rooms in this modern business hotel, just south of the Nietzsche Haus, have a pleasant Scandinavian feel.

Eating

Alt Naumburg (☎ 205 294; Marienplatz 13; mains from €3.60) Although many come here just for the local wines or fine beer (see Drinking, following), Alt Naumburg also serves a range of casual fare, from jacket potatoes and salads to fish and schnitzels. The outside tables on the cobblestones are packed in summer.

Carolus Magnus (☎ 205 577; Markt 11; mains €9-18; ☺ closed Sun) Local specialities, coupled with Italian dishes, are on offer in this charming, comfortable restaurant in the Hotel Stadt Aachen.

Zur Alten Schmiede (☎ 243 60; Lindenring 36-37; mains €9-17) Come here for top-notch Argentine steaks and sophisticated regional dishes like a hulking casserole of pork medallions and mushrooms atop Späetzle (noodles).

Drinking

Alt Naumburg (☎ 205 294; Marienplatz 13) This place remains the most popular meeting point of an evening.

Kö Pi (☎ 201 617; Engelgasse 5) A great little Irish pub just behind the Rathaus, Kö Pi has live music on weekends and attracts a young crowd.

Other options include:

Blue Moon Café (☎ 710 748; Marienplatz 5) Relaxed café/bar across the square from Alt Naumburg.

Kanzlei (☎ 200 522; Markt) Slightly yuppie bar.

Getting There & Around

There are fast trains to Naumburg from Halle (€6.60, 40 minutes), Leipzig (€8.10,

1½ hours), Jena (€5.50, 35 minutes) and Weimar (€6.60, 30 minutes). A local line runs to Freyburg (€1.60, eight minutes) and Bad Kösen (€1.60, five minutes).

ICE trains serve Frankfurt (€52, 3½ hours), Berlin (€39, 2½ hours) and Munich (€70.50, 4½ hours).

By road from Halle or Leipzig, take the A9 to either the B87 or the B180 and head west; the B87 is less direct and more scenic, though it's the first exit from the A9.

You can hire bicycles at the **Radhaus** (☎ 203 119; Herrenstrasse 4; €10 a day, €14 for the weekend).

FREYBURG
☎ 034464 / pop 5000

With its cobbled streets and medieval castle above vine-covered slopes, sleepy, wine-growing Freyburg has a vaguely French atmosphere. It's the sort of village that puts the 'r' in rustic – or would if it could stay awake to do so. It only really comes alive for its **wine festival** in the second week of September.

Orientation

To reach the town centre from the train station, turn right at the Fiedelak shop, left into the park and cross the bridge over the river. For the castle, take the second road to the right (Schlossstrasse). Keep bearing left for the Markt and tourist office.

Information

The **Freyburg tourist office** (☎ 272 60; www.freyburg-info.de; Markt 2; ☺ 7am-5pm Mon-Fri, 7am-1pm Sat) can organise city tours in German for €2.50 per person, including the Rotkäppchen sparkling wine factory and the castle. The website is in German only.

Sights

Established in 1856, and one of the best known sparkling wine producers in the former GDR, the **Rotkäppchen sparkling wine factory** (☎ 340; www.rotkaeppchen.de – German only; Sektkellereistrasse 5; tours €3.50; ☺ tours 2pm daily & 11am Sat & Sun) has enjoyed something of a (slightly Ostalgie-fuelled) comeback in the united Germany. Its Sekt (sparkling wine) is perhaps a little sweet for some tastes, but the name (meaning 'Little Red Riding Hood') gives the brand extra cachet.

One-hour tours of the factory include the two-storey 120,000L Sekt barrel (no

SAXONY-ANHALT

longer in use) decorated with ornate carvings; a tasting; and the Lichthof, a glorious, gymnasium-sized hall with 100-year-old skylights, where concerts are held year round. Telephone for details.

If a tour bus has just pulled up and you're overwhelmed by the size of the queue for a tour, you can taste and buy a whole range of Sekt at the shop out front between 10am and 5pm.

The large medieval **Schloss Neuenburg** (☎ 355 30; www.schloss-neuenberg.de – in German; Schloss 25; adult/concession €2.50/1.50; ⏱ 10am-5pm Tue-Sun Nov-Mar, to 6pm Apr-Oct) on the hill above town houses an excellent museum. It features an unusual, two-storey or 'double' chapel, plus fascinating explanations of medieval life. The free-standing tower behind the castle, the **Dicker Wilhelm** (adult/concession €1.20/0.60; ⏱ 10am-5pm Tue-Sun Nov-Dec, to 6pm Apr-Oct, closed Jan-Mar), offers further historical exhibitions and splendid views. For a pleasant 20-minute walk back down, take the path from the castle through the Herzoglichen Weinberg (ducal vineyard).

Getting There & Around

Trains run every hour (€1.60, eight minutes), as do buses (€1, 15 minutes), between Naumburg's Hauptbahnhof/ZOB and Freyburg's Markt; the services are drastically curtailed on weekends. The well-marked bicycle route (Radwandern) between the two cities makes for a wonderful ride. Bikes can be hired from **Fiedelak** (☎ 7080; Bahnhofstrasse 4; €7 per day).

Perhaps the most scenic way to get to Freyburg is by boat from Blütengrund, at the confluence of the Saale and Unstrut Rivers, just outside Naumburg. **The MS Fröhliche Dörte** (☎ 03445-202 830) tootles its way up the Unstrut at 11am, 1.30pm and 4pm daily between May and September. The 70-minute journey costs €6/3.80 per adult/child one way, and €8/5 return. It runs back from Freyburg at 12.15pm, 2.45pm and 5.15pm.

SCHULPFORTE

Between Naumburg and Bad Kösen lies Schulpforte, a quiet little village that's home to the famous **Landesschule Pforta** (State School Pforta), Friedrich Nietzsche's *alma mater* (from 1858 to 1864) and for centuries one of the finest high schools in Germany. Founded by Cistercian monks in 1137, it's still going strong and visitors are allowed to roam the romantic grounds.

Facing the main road is a very pleasant little wine bar and shop, the **tasting room** (☎ 034463-261 21; Schulpforte; ⏱ 10am-6pm) of the state-owned winery Landesweingut Kloster Pforta. Across the Saale is the main **Kloster Pforta winery** (☎ 03446-30 00; Saalhäuser, Bad Kösen), with its 1000-year-old Pfortenser Küppelburg vineyard and spectacular **Fasskeller**, a wine cellar where you can taste and buy.

Buses between Naumburg and Bad Kösen stop in Schulpforte.

BAD KÖSEN

☎ 034463 / pop 5200

There are spa towns and there are spa towns, and while Bad Kösen attracts as many elderly visitors as most, it distinguishes itself by having the largest therapeutic saltworks of its kind still operating in Europe. The town's skyline is dominated by a huge *Gradierwerk* – a 20m-high and 320m-long construction of wood and blackthorn twigs, over which saline water is piped. It's an historical curiosity that will put 'healthy' salt air into your lungs and a smile on your face.

Orientation

The town straddles the Saale River, 7km upstream from Naumburg. Its main sights are on the eastern side; turn left (north) out of the train station and follow Bahnhofstrasse, before bearing right (east) over the bridge for these and the tourist office. The Himmelreich lookout lies southwest of the train station; follow the signposts to Himmelreich and Jugendherberge.

Information

For tourist information go to **Bad Kösen Tourist Information** (☎ 282 89; fax 282 80; Ritterbad Carré shopping centre, Naumberger Strasse 13; ⏱ 10am-6pm Mon-Fri, 9am-5pm Sat).

Sights & Activities

The **Gradierwerk** (literally, graduation works) is the high point of the town's therapeutic salt works, designed to further purify the mountain air and cure respiratory diseases. The **Wasserrad** (water wheel) on the river drives a long pair of drills via an elaborate **system of wooden levers**, pushing water uphill, firstly to the **Solschacht** (brine well). The salty olution is then pumped further upwards and poured over the more than 200,000 bunches of blackthorn twigs in the Gradierwerk. The twigs catch impurities and insoluble crystals, supposedly leaving the air with the correct degree of salinity. You can walk around the Gradierwerk platform, but you'll be encouraged to first hire a white hooded gown (€2.50) to protect your clothes from the salty water. And all these people in white hoods sniffing the air make for a memorable, and rather comical, sight. At night, the Gradierwerk is beautifully lit.

The **Romanisches Haus** (☎ 276 68; Loreley Promenade; adult/concession €2/1.50; ☉ 10am-noon & 1-5pm Tue-Fri, 10am-5pm Sat & Sun) was built in 1037 and is the oldest secular building in central Germany. Today it's a museum of local history and of dolls, the latter highlighting the famous stuffed toys that are produced at the nearby Kösen factory. The factory is closed to the public, but you can pick up souvenirs at **Spielzeug Bad Kösen factory outlet** (☎ 613 63; Ritterbad Carré shopping centre, Naumberger Strasse 13).

If you have your own transport, head southwest to the lookout at **Himmelreich**. It peers down on a wonderful scene of fairytale castle ruins at **Saaleck** and **Rudelsburg**.

Getting There & Away

Trains run to and from Naumburg hourly (€1.60, eight minutes). Bus services between the two towns (€1.10) finish by midafternoon and are skeletal on weekends.

Harz Mountains

CONTENTS

Information	264
Activities	264
Getting There & Away	265
Getting Around	265
Western Harz	**265**
Goslar	265
Around Goslar	268
Hahnenklee	268
Bad Harzburg	269
Braunlage	270
St Andreasberg	271
Clausthal-Zellerfeld	272
Eastern Harz	**273**
Wernigerode	273
Rübeland Caves	275
Schierke	275
Mittelbau Dora	276
Brocken & Torfhaus	277
Quedlinburg	277
Gernrode	280
Thale	281

The Harz Mountains rise picturesquely from the North German Plain, covering an area 100km long and 30km wide at the junction of Saxony-Anhalt, Thuringia and Lower Saxony. Although the scenery here is a far cry from the dramatic peaks and valleys of the Alps, the Harz region is a great year-round sports getaway, with plenty of opportunities for hiking, cycling and skiing, of both the downhill and cross-country variety. It's also one of the few remaining areas in western Europe where the rare lynx can still be seen in the wild – with a bit of patience and local advice even casual wildlife-spotters have a good chance of a sighting.

The regular influx of visitors in all seasons is testament to the enduring appeal of the Harz; historically, too, its status as a prime national holiday destination has never been questioned. From 1952 until reunification, the region was divided between West and East Germany, effectively becoming an uneasy political holiday camp straddling the Iron Curtain.

The Brocken (1142m) is the focal point of the Harz, and has had more than its fair share of illustrious visitors: the great Goethe himself was frequently seen striding the local trails and set 'Walpurgisnacht', an early chapter of his play *Faust*, on the mountain, while satirical poet Heinrich Heine spent a well-oiled night here, described in his *Harzreise* (Harz Journey) in 1824. Elsewhere the charming medieval towns of Wernigerode and Quedlinburg pull in the crowds, while equally venerable steam trains pull them along between the many little mountain villages, spas and sports resorts that litter the region. Get out your knee socks or your ski mask and treat yourself to a taste of the active life.

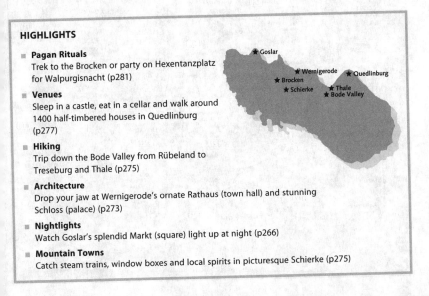

HIGHLIGHTS

- **Pagan Rituals**
  Trek to the Brocken or party on Hexentanzplatz for Walpurgisnacht (p281)

- **Venues**
  Sleep in a castle, eat in a cellar and walk around 1400 half-timbered houses in Quedlinburg (p277)

- **Hiking**
  Trip down the Bode Valley from Rübeland to Treseburg and Thale (p275)

- **Architecture**
  Drop your jaw at Wernigerode's ornate Rathaus (town hall) and stunning Schloss (palace) (p273)

- **Nightlights**
  Watch Goslar's splendid Markt (square) light up at night (p266)

- **Mountain Towns**
  Catch steam trains, window boxes and local spirits in picturesque Schierke (p275)

INFORMATION

The main information centre for the Harz Mountains is the **Harzer Verkehrsverband** (☎ 05321-340 40) in Goslar, but information on the eastern Harz is best picked up in towns there, particularly in Wernigerode.

For information on camping, ask any tourist office for the free *Der Harz Camping* brochure (in German), which lists major camp sites and facilities open all year.

The *Freizeit im Harz* map (€6.50) provides the best general overview of sights and trails for the entire Harz.

Discount offers include the HarzTour-Card (three days, €14.50), which gives free travel and discounted admission to attractions, and the HarzMobilCard (one month, €13), which entitles the user to concession-priced tickets on all public transport.

ACTIVITIES
Cycling

Anyone seeking a challenge will enjoy cycling or mountain biking in the Harz, especially in quieter eastern areas. Buses will transport your bike when space allows.

Hiking

The main attraction in summer is hiking the area incorporates two national parks the Harz and Hochharz National Parks Every town has its own short trails, often linking up to long-distance ones, and there are usually traditional restaurants along the way. Trail symbols are colour-coded in red, green, blue and yellow on a square or triangular plate. Maps put out by the **Harzklub** (www.harzklub.de) hiking association also show trail numbers; the 1:50,000 editions are the best for hikers. Harzklub offices in mountain towns are also good sources of information, including hiking tips, itineraries and the availability of partners and guides. Tourist offices also stock the club's leaflets. Most trails are well marked, but it doesn't hurt to ask the way occasionally. Weather conditions can change quickly throughout the year; be prepared.

Skiing

The main centres for downhill skiing are Braunlage, Hahnenklee and St Andreasberg, with many other smaller runs dotted

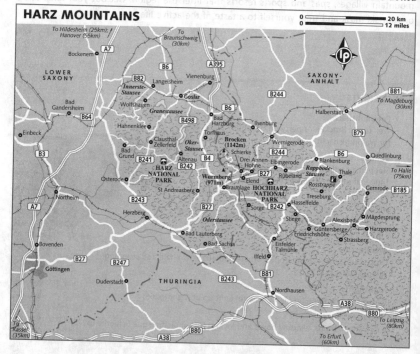

throughout the mountains. The quality of the slopes might disappoint real enthusiasts; conditions for cross-country skiing, however, can be excellent, with lots of well-marked trails and equipment-hire shops. For weather reports and snow conditions, ring the **Harzer Verkehrsverband** (☎ 05321-340 40). There's also a German-language **information service** (☎ 05321-200 24).

Spas
Often mocked by young Germans as a pensioners' paradise, the Harz is sprinkled with thermal spas and baths where the weary and/or infirm can take a cure. Most spa towns have a *Kurzentrum* (spa centre) or *Kurverwaltung* (spa administration), which often doubles as a tourist office.

GETTING THERE & AWAY
The area's main towns of Goslar, Wernigerode and Quedlinburg are serviced by daily trains, with Hanover the nearest major hub for onward travel; contact **Deutsche Bahn** (☎ 118 61 for reservations, ☎ 0800-150 7090 for automated timetable information; www.bahn.de).

BerlinLinienBus (www.berlinlinienbus.de) runs to Goslar from Berlin (€34), and there are plenty of regional bus services to take you further into the mountains.

If you're driving, the area's main arteries are the east–west B6 and the north–south B4, which are accessed via the A7 (which skirts the western edge of the Harz on its way south from Hanover) and the A2 (which runs north of the Harz between Hanover and Berlin).

GETTING AROUND
The Harz is one part of Germany where you'll rely on buses as much as trains, and the various local networks are quite reliable, although weekend services are still pretty sparse. Narrow-gauge steam trains run to the Brocken and link major towns in the eastern Harz.

WESTERN HARZ

GOSLAR
☎ 05321 / pop 46,000
Goslar, the hub of tourism in the western Harz, has one of Germany's best-preserved medieval town centres, with plenty of elaborately carved half-timbered buildings.

Founded by Heinrich I in 922, Goslar's early importance centred on silver and the Kaiserpfalz, the seat of the Saxon kings from 1005 to 1219. Largely due to its mines, Goslar enjoyed a second period of prosperity in the 14th and 15th centuries, after which it fell into decline, reflecting the fortunes of the Harz as a whole. The town temporarily lost its mine to Braunschweig in 1552 and its soul to Prussia in 1802. It then changed hands several times before being incorporated into the state of Lower Saxony.

In 1992 the town and nearby Rammelsberg mine were included on Unesco's World Heritage List, and Goslar's Kaiserpfalz is one of Germany's best restored Romanesque palaces. It can get crowded on summer weekends, when it's advisable to make reservations in advance.

Goslar is a lively town with regular influxes of visitors and plenty of modern touches complementing its medieval charm. The annual *Schützenfest* (shooting festival) at the end of June is one of the biggest in the region, and is a great (if busy) time to be in town.

Orientation
Goslar has a medieval circular layout, the heart of which is the Markt and the Kaiserpassage, a large pedestrian mall. Rosentorstrasse leads to the Markt, a 10-minute walk from the train and bus stations. The small Gose River flows through the centre south of the Markt. Streets in the old town are numbered up one side and down the other.

Information
Ambulance (☎ 1303)
City-Textilpflege (Petersilienstrasse 9) Laundry.
Harz Kliniken (☎ 440; Kösliner Strasse 12) Medical services, about 6km north of town.
Harzer Verkehrsverband (☎ 340 40; www.harzinfo.de; Bäckergildehaus, Marktstrasse 45; ⏱ 8am-5pm Mon-Fri) Tourist information.
Main post office (Klubgartenstrasse 10) Just northwest of the town centre.
MuseumSpass (adult/child €9/4.50) This card allows admission to five of Goslar's major attractions.
Police (☎ 791; Heinrich-Pieper-Strasse 1) About 1.5km north of the city centre.
Spielzentrum (☎ 427 89; Breite Strasse; €2 per hr) Internet access.
Tourist-Information (☎ 780 60; www.goslarinfo.de; Markt 7; ⏱ 9.15am-6pm Mon-Fri, 9.30am-4pm Sat, 9.30am-2pm Sun)

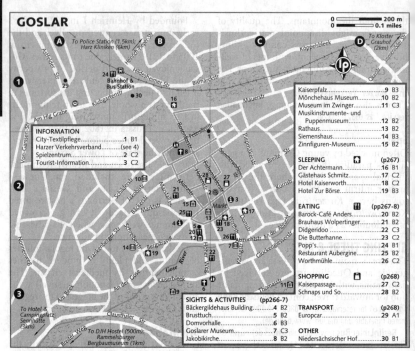

GOSLAR

0 — 200 m
0 — 0.1 miles

To Police Station (1.5km);
Harz Kliniken (6km)

To Kloster
Grauhof
(2km)

Köppelsbleek

Bahnhof &
Bus Station

INFORMATION
City-Textilpflege.....................1 B1
Harzer Verkehrsverband............(see 4)
Spielzentrum...........................2 C2
Tourist-Information...................3 C2

Markt

To Hotel &
Campingplatz
Sennhütte
(3km)

To DJH Hostel (500m);
Rammelsburger
Bergbaumuseum (1km)

Kaiserpfalz.............................9 B3
Mönchehaus Museum...............10 B2
Museum im Zwinger..................11 C3
Musikinstrumente- und
Puppenmuseum....................12 B2
Rathaus.................................13 B2
Siemenshaus...........................14 B3
Zinnfiguren-Museum.................15 B2

SLEEPING 🛏 (p267)
Der Achtermann......................16 B1
Gästehaus Schmitz...................17 C2
Hotel Kaiserworth....................18 C2
Hotel Zur Börse.......................19 B3

EATING 🍴 (pp267-8)
Barock-Café Anders..................20 B2
Brauhaus Wolpertinger..............21 B2
Didgeridoo.............................22 C3
Die Butterhanne.......................23 C2
Popp's...................................24 B1
Restaurant Aubergine................25 B2
Worthmühle............................26 C2

SHOPPING 🛍 (p268)
Kaiserpassage.........................27 C2
Schnaps and So.......................28 B2

SIGHTS & ACTIVITIES (pp266-7)
Bäckergildehaus Building...........4 B2
Brusttuch...............................5 B2
Domvorhalle............................6 B3
Goslarer Museum......................7 C3
Jakobikirche............................8 B2

TRANSPORT (p268)
Europcar................................29 A1

OTHER
Niedersächsischer Hof...............30 B1

Sights

AROUND THE MARKT

There are some fine half-timbered houses on or near the Markt. The **Hotel Kaiserworth** (see Sleeping p266) was erected in 1494 to house the textile guild, and sports almost life-size figures on its orange façade. The impressive late-Gothic **Rathaus** comes into its own at night, when light coming through its stained glass windows illuminates the town square. The highlight is a beautiful cycle of 16th-century religious paintings in the **Huldigungssaal** (Hall of Homage; adult/child €2/1; ⏰ 11am-4pm).

The **market fountain**, crowned by an eagle symbolising Goslar's status as a free imperial city, dates from the 13th century, but the eagle itself is a copy of the (slightly chickenlike) original. Opposite the Rathaus is the **Glockenspiel**, a chiming clock depicting four scenes of mining in the area. It plays at 9am, noon, 3pm and 6pm.

The baroque **Siemenshaus** (☎ 238 37; Schreiberstrasse 12; ⏰ 9am-noon Tue & Thu) is the ancestral home of the Siemens industrial family. The **Brusttuch**, at Hoher Weg 1, and the **Bäckergil-**

dehaus, on the corner of Marktstrasse and Bergstrasse, are two fine early 16th-century houses.

KAISERPFALZ

A reconstructed 11th-century Romanesque palace, **Kaiserpfalz** (☎ 311 9693; Kaiserbleek 6; adult/concession €4.50/2.50; ⏰ 10am-5pm) is Goslar's pride and joy. The interior frescoes of idealised historical scenes date from the 19th century. On the southern side is **St Ulrich Chapel**, housing a sarcophagus containing the heart of Heinrich III. Below the Kaiserpfalz is the recently restored **Domvorhalle**, displaying the 11th-century Kaiserstuhl, the throne used by Salian and Hohenstaufen emperors. In the pleasant gardens behind the palace is an excellent sculpture by Henry Moore, the *Goslarer Krieger* (Goslar Warrior).

RAMMELSBERGER BERGBAU MUSEUM

About 1km south of the town centre, visitors can descend into the shafts of this 1000-year-old **mine** (☎ 7500; www.rammelsberg .de; Bergtal 19; tour adult/concession €8.50/5.50; ⏰ 9am-

6pm, last admission 4.30pm), now a museum. Admission to the mine includes a German-language tour and a pamphlet with English explanations of the 18th- and 19th-century Roeder Shafts, the mine railway and the ore processing section. Bus No 808 stops here.

OTHER MUSEUMS

The five-floor private **Musikinstrumenten- und Puppenmuseum** (☎ 269 45; Hoher Weg 5; adult/child €3/1.50; ☺ 11am-5pm) will delight both kids and fans of musical instruments and/or dolls. The owner began collecting instruments more than 40 years ago; the doll collection is his daughter's addition.

The **Zinnfiguren-Museum** (☎ 258 89; Münzstrasse 11; adult/concession €3.50/1.50; ☺ 10am-5pm) exhibits a colourful collection of painted pewter figures in a courtyard.

For a good overview of the natural and cultural history of Goslar and the Harz, visit the **Goslarer Museum** (☎ 433 94; Königstrasse 1; admission €3/1.50; ☺ 10am-5pm Tue-Sun). One room contains the treasures from the former Goslar Dom (cathedral), and there's also a cabinet with coins dating from the 10th century.

The **Mönchehaus Museum** (☎ 295 70; Mönchestrasse 3; adult/children €3/1.50; ☺ 10am-5pm Tue-Sat, 10am-1pm Sun), in a 16th-century half-timbered house, exhibits works of modern art, including changing exhibitions and some interesting sculptures in the peaceful garden.

For a real 'scream', take a look inside the **Museum im Zwinger** (☎ 431 40; www.zwinger.de; Thomasstrasse 2; adult/child/youth €2/1.20/1.30; ☺ 10am-5pm, closed mid-Nov–Feb), a 16th-century tower that was once part of the ramparts, which has a collection of such late-medieval delights as torture implements, coats of armour and weapons used during the Peasant Wars.

Sleeping

DJH hostel (☎ 222 40; jh-goslar@djh-hannover.de; Rammelsberger Strasse 25; juniors/seniors €14/16.70) The pretty DJH hostel is south of the Kaiserpfalz. Bus 808 to Theresienhof.

Hotel & Campingplatz Sennhütte (☎ 225 02; Clausthaler Strasse 28; s €19-21, d €37-42, adult/child €2.50/1.50, car/tent €2/3) Bus No 830 to Sennhütte. This place is 3km south of Goslar via the B241. The rooms are simple but clean; it's advisable to reserve through the tourist office before setting out.

Gästehaus Schmitz (☎ 234 45; Kornstrasse 1; s/d €30/40) Just east of the Markt, this friendly, slightly eccentric guesthouse offers spotless, spacious rooms in a friendly atmosphere, plus comfortable apartments in excellent condition. Book ahead.

Kloster Grauhof (☎ 8816; www.klostergrauhof.de; Gut 2; apartments €29-72; P ✕) About 2km outside town, this former monastery has been converted into an apartment complex aimed at families, with extensive park grounds, communal areas and plenty of activities.

Hotel Zur Börse (☎ 345 10; Bergstrasse 53; s €25-65, d €50-85; P ✕) Lagging slightly behind the top-end places with a mere 400 years of history, this is a great option in a beautiful, well-restored corner of the Altstadt (old town).

Hotel Kaiserworth (☎ 7090; www.kaiserworth.de; Markt 3; s €58-95, d €101-171; P ✕) The magnificent 500-year-old building is a bit of a giveaway: this is a good old-fashioned hotel with a deep sense of tradition. Look out for weekend and package deals.

Der Achtermann (☎ 700 00; www.der-achtermann.de; Rosentorstrasse 20; s €99-119, d €145-165; P 🚊) Another historic luxury hotel, the Achtermann is losing custom to the much smarter Niedersächsischer Hof nearby, but still has the edge on facilities if not service.

Eating

Barock-Café Anders (☎ 238 14; Hoher Weg 4; mains €2.40-12.60) The terrace out the back looks a bit basic, but inside is anything but at this very posh coffee house and restaurant.

Worthmühle (☎ 434 02; Worthstrasse 4; mains €6-15) Downstream from a working 16th-century waterwheel, this is the only place you'll find the medieval speciality Gose-Bier on tap. The traditional food and décor also go down well.

Popp's (☎ 303 603; Bahnhof; mains €5.10-12.80) Popular with a younger crowd, this American-style bar-diner serves up the usual Tex-Mex with a few more interesting options, and has regular house music nights with DJs.

Didgeridoo (☎ 468 37; Hoher Weg 13; mains €4-12.50) Come for Australian 'cuisine' like kangaroo burgers, crocodile steak and shark, plus a good selection of Australian wines till late.

Brauhaus Wolpertinger (☎ 221 55; Marstallstrasse 1; mains €7.40-14.90) Part of the small Brauhof-Plaza restaurant and bar complex, this brewery courtyard pulls in the crowds in any weather.

Die Butterhanne (☎ 228 86; Marktkirchhof 3; mains €5-14) With an atmospheric interior and an outdoor terrace, this traditional place turns out scrumptious pastries and average German dishes. The name refers to a famous local frieze showing a milkmaid churning butter while clutching her buttock to insult her employer!

Restaurant Aubergine (☎ 421 36; Marktstrasse 4; mains €11-19.50, pasta €6.50-9.50) Upmarket and quite convincingly Mediterranean, you can get some fine Turkish cooking here alongside the classy French and Italian dishes.

Shopping

Hoher Weg is packed with shops selling souvenirs. Local crafts such as ceramics, puppets and marionettes, many of them portraying witches, are available at a few shops; the better ones go for about €100. Try the Harzer Roller, a slightly bland local sour-milk cheese. **Schnaps und So** (☎ 396 636; Hokenstrasse 3) is a great local booze store, but approach the Harz fruit wines and herbal schnapps with caution – some of them may leave you the worse for wear.

Getting There & Away

BUS

The office of **Regionalbus Braunschweig** (RBB; ☎ 194 49; www.rbb-bus.de; Bahnhof), from where buses depart, has free timetables for services throughout the Harz region. Bus Nos 808 and 61/432 run between Goslar and Altenau, to the south. Bus No 61/432 continues on to St Andreasberg (one hour). Bus No 830 runs to Clausthal-Zellerfeld via Hahnenklee. For Bad Harzburg, where you can change buses for Torfhaus, take bus No 810. The BEX BerlinLinienBus runs daily to Berlin (€34) via Magdeburg. For timetables and bookings, refer to **DER-Reisebüro** (☎ 757 90; Bahnhof).

CAR & MOTORCYCLE

The B6 runs north to Hildesheim and east to Bad Harzburg, Wernigerode and Quedlinburg. The north–south A7 is reached via the B82. For Hahnenklee, take the B241. Car rental is available at **Europcar** (☎ 251 38; Lindenplan 3).

TRAIN

Bad Harzburg–Hanover trains stop here often, as do trains on the Braunschweig–

Göttingen line. There are direct trains to Wernigerode (€6.60, 50 minutes); for more frequent services change at Vienenburg.

Getting Around

Local bus tickets cost €1.70. To book a taxi, ring ☎ 1313.

AROUND GOSLAR
Oker Valley

The Oker Valley, which begins at Oker, a small industrial town now part of Goslar, is one of the prettiest in the western Harz. An 11km hike (marked with a red triangle) follows the course of the Oker River and leads to a 47 million cu metre **dam**, constructed in the 1950s to regulate water levels and generate power. Along the way you'll pass the 60m-high **Römkerhalle** waterfall, created in 1863. The B498 leads to the dam. If travelling by bus, take bus No 805, 806 or 810 to the Okertalsperre stop. **Okersee-Schiffahrt** (☎ 05329-290; www.okersee.de) runs boat trips and tours on the Oker lake.

HAHNENKLEE
☎ 05325 / pop 2200

This small, neat thermal spa 15km southwest of Goslar is one of the more tasteful ski resorts in the Harz Mountains and makes a good base for summer hikes in the western Harz.

The **tourist office** (☎ 510 40; www.hahnenklee.de; Kurhausweg 7; 9am-1pm & 2-6pm Mon-Fri, 10am-noon Sat & Sun) is in the Kurverwaltung building off Rathausstrasse.

Sights & Activities

Hahnenklee is proud of its **Gustav-Adolf-Kirche** (Gustav-Adolf Church; 1907), a Norwegian-style wooden stave church with an attractive interior of Byzantine and Scandinavian features. In the centre of town is the **Paul-Lincke-Platz**, a small square dedicated to the noted operetta composer; a ring bearing his name is awarded to a suitably deserving German musician every two years (Udo Lindenberg received the honour in 2003).

In winter, most visitors come for the downhill and cross-country skiing on the Bocksberg. Day tickets for the cable car and lifts cost €17. The **Skikeller in der Seilbahnstation** (☎ 2186; Rathausstrasse 6) hires out downhill ski equipment and cross-country ski gear; **Wehrsuhn** (☎ 2235; Rathausstrasse 19) and he **Berghotel** (☎ 2505; An der Buchwiese 1) are ther options. **Snow-Fun** (☎ 2172; Hindenburg-trasse 4) has snowboards and skis for hire. Ice kates can be hired at all these places when he Kranicher Teich (a large pond) freezes over. The **Hahnenkleer Skischule** (☎ 2186; Rathaus-trasse 19) runs various ski courses.

Hahnenklee is also popular for its hiking, with trails leading to the Bocksberg from the car park near the stave church and longer trails to Goslar (trail 2G, blue dot, 11km) via Windsattel and Glockenberg. Remember to take the Harzclub 1:50,000 walking map and be prepared for changing weather conditions.

Sleeping & Eating

Hahnenklee levies a nightly *Kurtaxe* (resort tax) of €1.75 per person – keep your resort card for discounts. A reduced tax is charged on hostel and camping accommodation. The tourist office has a free reservation service and can book apartments for longer stays.

DJH hostel (☎ 2256; jh-hahnenklee@djh-hannover .de; Hahnenklee Strasse 13; juniors/seniors €13.80/16.50) Everything is clean and correct in the sprawling house of this DJH Jugendherberge.

Hotel Hahnenkleer Hof (☎ 511 10; www.hahnen kleerhof.de; Parkstrasse 24a; s/d €57/114; P 🗙 🖥 🖳) An engaging mix of modern complex and Swiss chalet, this big hotel has an interesting display on local landscape artist Wilhelm Ripe, known as the 'Merian of the Harz', whose works are dotted around the building.

Restaurant-Café Zum Kachelofen (☎ 2535; Kurhausweg 4; mains €7-14; 🕑 closed Wed) The biggest menu in town, with more than 20 different options for seniors alone. It's all good value, too.

Getting There & Away

Hahnenklee is just west of the B241, between Goslar and Clausthal-Zellerfeld. Bus No 830 serves Hahnenklee from Goslar on the way to Clausthal-Zellerfeld. The BEX BerlinLinienBus stops here daily.

BAD HARZBURG

☎ 05322 / pop 258,000

Just 9km from Goslar, Bad Harzburg is a pretty spa town with a long pedestrian zone and a large, leafy *Kurpark*. However, unless you're one of the many cure-seekers, the main attraction is not the town but the nearby Harz National Park and trails, which offer excellent access to some typically gorgeous Harz landscapes.

Information

Haus der Natur (☎ 784 337; Berliner Platz; adult/concession €2/1; 🕑 10am-6pm) Harz National Park information centre.

Stadtbücherei (☎ 901 515; Kurzentrum, Herzog-Wilhelm-Strasse 86) Internet access.

Tourist-Information (☎ 753 30; www.bad-harz burg.de; Kurzentrum, Herzog-Wilhelm-Strasse 86; 🕑 8am-8pm Mon-Fri, 9am-4pm Sat, 10am-1pm Sun)

Verkehrsverein (☎ 2927; Am Bahnhof; 🕑 9am-1pm & 3-5.30pm Mon-Fri, 10am-1pm Sat) Transport and tourist information.

Activities

It's worth hiking or riding up to **Grosser Burgberg**, a hill above Bad Harzburg with the ruins of an 11th-century fortress built by Heinrich IV. There's a 481m-long **cable car** (☎ 753 80; adult/child return €3/1.60; 🕑 9am-6pm) to the fortress, reached by walking up Bummelallee to the Kurpark.

Marked hiking trails lead into the national park from Berliner Platz and Grosser Burgberg, the latter just over 3km from Berliner Platz on foot. Among the many walks are those from Berliner Platz to Sennhütte (1.3km), Molkenhaus (3km) and to scenic Rabenklippe (7km), overlooking the Ecker Valley. All destinations have restaurants; a blackboard near the cable-car station indicates which ones are open.

From Grosser Burgberg you can take the Kaiserweg trail, which leads to Torfhaus and connects to the Brocken. A marked trail also leads to the 23m-high **Radau Waterfall**, some 7km from Grosser Burgberg. If snow conditions are good, it's possible to ski cross-country to/from Torfhaus, which has equipment-hire facilities (see Brocken & Torfhaus p277).

Anyone with kids should appreciate the **Märchenwald** (☎ 3590; www.maerchenwald-harz.de; Nordhäuser Strasse 1a; adult/child €3/2; 🕑 10am-6pm), a fairy-tale park with model trains, cars and tableaux from everyone's favourite bedtime stories.

Festivals & Events

Bad Harzburg has plenty of concerts, though most are fairly staid affairs. Nevertheless, it pays to check the tourist office's events calendar. An annual music festival is held in June, and the historic **Gallopp-Rennwoche** horse races, a notable bright spot for punters, are held just outside town in July.

Sleeping & Eating

A nightly *Kurtaxe* of €2 is charged on all hotel stays. There are several good hotels west of the tourist office on Am Stadtpark. Bad Harzburg is also an excellent place to rent a holiday apartment, with over 200 to choose from!

Hotel-Penson Marxmeier (☎ 911 090; Am Stadtpark 41; s/d €38.50/67; P 🐕) Rooms can be a bit crowded at this good-value pension, but it's central and packs in a lot for the price.

Ringhotel Braunschweiger Hof (☎ 7880; www .hotel-braunschweiger-hof.de; Herzog-Wilhelm-Strasse 54; s €82-102, d €128-138; P ✗ 🐕) One of Bad Harzburg's top hotels, with the full complement of health and beauty facilities.

Hexenklause (☎ 2982; Berliner Platz 3; mains €8.50-17.70) In the Kurpark near the cable car, this witch-themed restaurant serves up a full range of traditional German dishes.

Getting There & Around

The Hauptbahnhof and bus station are on the northern side of town, a 10-minute walk from the pedestrian mall. Bus No 810 leaves regularly for Goslar, and bus No 877 heads for Wernigerode (€3, 45 minutes). Bus No 820 shuttles almost hourly to Braunlage (€3.50, 40 minutes) via Radau Waterfall and Torfhaus. Frequent train services link Bad Harzburg with Goslar, Hanover, Braunschweig and Wernigerode.

Bad Harzburg is on the A395 to Braunschweig; the B4 and B6 lead to Torfhaus and Wernigerode, respectively.

BRAUNLAGE

☎ 05520 / pop 6000

Braunlage is the largest winter sports centre in the Harz, and is popular with hikers in summer. The skiing here is the best in the region, although it can get crowded on the slopes when the snow is good.

Orientation

Braunlage's heart is the junction of Elbingeröder Strasse and the main thoroughfare, Herzog-Wilhelm-Strasse. The latter changes names several times.

Information

Post office (Marktstrasse 16)

Stadtbücherei (☎ 1209; Elbingeröder Strasse 11; €1.3 per 20 min; 🕒 10am-noon Mon-Fri, 3-6pm Mon-Wed, 3-7pm Thu) Internet access.

Tourist-Info (☎ 930 70; www.braunlage.de; Kurverwaltung, Elbingeröder Strasse 7; 🕒 9am-12.30pm & 2-5pm Mon-Fri, 9.30am-noon Sat)

Volksbank (☎ 8030; Herzog-Wilhelm-Strasse 19)

Activities

HIKING

The tourist office has two good free leaflets: *Wandervorschläge Rund Um Braunlage* (Hiking Suggestions Around Braunlage) covering trails in the area and restaurant stops; and *Wanderwege Braunlage* (Braunlage Hiking Trails). If you are heading east, a trail follows the B27 to Elend (red triangle, 7km), where you can pick up the narrow-gauge railway to Wernigerode.

SKIING

A cable car will take you up the 971m **Wurmberg**, from where you can ski down or use the three lifts on the mountain itself. Return tickets cost €10. Downhill ski equipment can be rented at **Café-Restaurant Zur Seilbahn** (☎ 600) from €20 a day, or at one of the many ski shops dotted around town. Braunlage has several smaller pistes, groomed cross-country trails, and a ski jump where high fliers can land on the former East German border. Plenty of places in town offer cross-country skis for hire.

Sleeping & Eating

A *Kurtaxe* of €1.60 is charged nightly on hotel stays (less for camp sites and hostels).

DJH hostel (☎ 2238; jh-braunlage@djh-hannover.de; Von-Langen-Strasse 28; juniors/seniors €14/16.70) On the northern edge of town, this is a typically efficiently run DJH Jugendherberge.

Pension Parkblick (☎ 1237; Elbingeröder Strasse 13; per person €20-25; P) This nice-looking, friendly pension has simple, comfortable rooms backing onto the Kurpark.

Romantik Hotel Zur Tanne (☎ 931 20; zur-tanne@ romantik.de; Herzog-Wilhelm-Strasse 8; s €52-100, d €80-150; P ✗) One of the finest accommodation options in the Harz, rooms here are smart but cosy, and the densely furnished suites are practically holiday cottages in themselves.

Omas Kaffeestube und Weinstube (☎ 2390; Elbingeröder Strasse 2; food €1.35-3.45) This café serves coffee, cakes and some light meals throughout the day in a very olde-worlde atmosphere.

Getting There & Away
Bus No 850 runs to St Andreasberg (€1.70, 30 minutes) from the Von-Langen-Strasse stop. For Torfhaus and Bad Harzburg, take bus No 820 from the bus station, which is south of the town centre at Buchholzplatz, off Bahnhofstrasse. The B4 runs north to Torfhaus and Bad Harzburg. The B27 leads southwest to the St Andreasberg turn-off and northeast to the eastern Harz.

ST ANDREASBERG
☎ 05582 / pop 2500
Known for its mining museums, clean air and hiking and skiing options, this hill-top resort sits on a broad ridge surrounded by mountains, 10km southwest of Braunlage. St Andreasberg is a pleasant town that offers a quiet base for trips into the national park; it's wonderful to visit during a warm snowless spring or a 'golden October'.

The **tourist office** (☎ 803 36; www.sankt-andreas berg.de; Am Kurpark 9; ✆ 9am-12.30pm & 2-5pm Mon, Tue, Thu & Fri, 9am-12.30pm Wed, 10am-noon Sat, 11am-noon Sun) is in the split-level Kurverwaltung building, which won an award for its wheelchair-friendly design.

Most shops close for several hours around noon.

Sights & Activities
German-language tours of the interesting **Grube Samson Mining Museum** (☎ 1249; tours €4; ✆ 8.30am-4.30pm, tours 11am & 2.30pm) take you 20m down to view early forms of mine transportation. Follow the signs from Dr-Willi-Bergmann-Strasse. The nearby Catharina Neufang **tunnel** (admission €2; ✆ 10am & 1.45pm Mon-Sat) includes a mining demonstration, and the **Harzer Roller Kanarien-Museum** (Canary Museum; admission free; ✆ 8.30am-4pm Mon-Sat, 10am-4pm Sun) illustrates the local history of the 'miner's best friend'.

Skiing in St Andreasberg can be excellent. The closest piste is on **Mathias-Schmidt-Berg** (☎ 265); day passes are €15 or it's €1.60 per ride. You'll also find pistes with lifts out of town on **Sonnenberg** (☎ 265) and **Jordanshöhe** (☎ 260), but they're difficult to reach by public transport. **Sport Pläschke** (☎ 260; www.plaeschke-online.de; Dr-Willi-Bergmann-Strasse 10)

> ### GALLOWS HUMOUR
> If you wander down Arme-Sünder-Gasse (Poor Sinner Alley), on the southwestern edge of town, you might notice the little carving depicting a chained prisoner with his spike-helmeted police escort, just above the street sign. This isn't just an oblique German joke – the road is in fact the start of the trail up to the Galgenberg, where for many years criminals were taken to be hung. These days visitors don't need to be dragged up the hill, but spare a thought for the poor sinners who never came back down…

rents out ski and snowboard equipment and has some good three-day deals.

Cross-country skiers should pick up the *Wintersportkarte* map (€1) from the tourist office, which shows groomed and ungroomed trails and some good ski hikes.

The Rehberger Grabenweg is a unique hiking trail that leads into the Harz National Park and to the **Rehberger Grabenhaus** (☎ 789; ✆ closed Mon), a forest café 3km from St Andreasberg and only accessible on foot. In the evening from late December to early March you can sit in the darkened café and watch wild deer feeding outside. To avoid disturbing the animals, visitors have to arrive by 5pm and aren't let out until 7pm.

There are exhibits on the area's cultural history, plus park information and a multimedia show in the new **Nationalparkhaus** (☎ 923 074; www.nationalpark-harz.de; Erzwäsche 1; ✆ 9am-5pm).

Sleeping & Eating
A small *Kurtaxe* is charged in the town of St Andreasberg.

DJH hostel (☎ 809 948; Am Gesehr 37; juniors/seniors €24/26.50) Popular with school groups, prices at this hostel include full board.

Pension Haus am Kurpark (☎ 1010; www.haus .am.kurpark.harz.de; Am Kurpark 1; s €20-28, d €27.80-51) This quiet, friendly place just outside the park offers a choice of shared and private bathrooms.

Hotel Tannhäuser (☎ 918 80; Am Gesehr 1a; s/d €40/60; Ⓟ ✗) Farmhouse-style rooms, sledge hire and traditional fare from €10.

HARZ MOUNTAINS

Getting There & Away

Bus No 850 runs between St Andreasberg and Braunlage. Bus No 832 offers direct services several times daily to Goslar and Bad Lauterberg. The frequent bus No 845 runs to Clausthal-Zellerfeld (€2.35, one hour).

St Andreasberg can be reached by the B27, which winds along the scenic Oder Valley from Bad Lauterberg to Braunlage. The L519 (Sonnenberg) leads north to the B242 and Clausthal-Zellerfeld, to the B4 and Bad Harzburg, and to Goslar (B241 or the B498 along the Oker Valley).

CLAUSTHAL-ZELLERFELD

☎ 05323 / pop 15,300

Actually two settlements that were united in 1924, this small university town was once the region's most important mining centre. Its main attractions are mineral and spiritual: an excellent mining museum and a spectacular wooden church. Outdoor enthusiasts will feel at home here too, with 66 lakes and ponds, mostly created for the mines, in the immediate area.

Orientation & Information

As in many similar linear towns in the Harz, Clausthal-Zellerfeld's main street changes names several times, with Kronenplatz as the hub. Clausthal lies to the south, while Zellerfeld begins just beyond Bahnhofstrasse, roughly 1km to the north.

The **tourist office** (☎ 810 24; www.harztourismus.com; Bahnhofstrasse 5a; ☼ 9am-1pm & 2-5pm Mon-Fri, 10am-noon Sat) and **Harzklub HQ** (☎ 817 58; www.harzklub.de; ☼ 9am-noon Mon-Fri) are in the former train station, just a 10-minute walk north of Kronenplatz.

Sights

The **Oberharzer Bergwerksmuseum** (☎ 989 50; www.oberharzerbergwerksmuseum.de; Bornhardtstrasse 16; adult/concession €4/2; ☼ 9am-5pm) has an interesting open-air exhibition of mine buildings and mining methods, including a model of a horse-driven carousel used to convey minerals. There are lots of mineral exhibits and artefacts in the museum building, and tours in German (translators are available) take you down into the depths. On weekends and holidays old **trains** (€4.50/2.25; ☼ 11am & 2.30pm May-Oct) run to the Ottiliae-Schacht shaft in Clausthal.

Also of interest is the **Geosammlung** (☎ 722 737; Adolph-Roemer-Strasse 2a; adult/concession €1.50/1; ☼ 9.30am-12.30pm & 2-5pm Tue-Fri, 2-5pm Sat, 10am-1pm Sun), south of Kronenplatz, which has Germany's largest collection of mineral samples.

Consecrated in 1642, the impressive baroque **Marktkirche Zum Heiligen Geist** (☎ 7005; Hindenburgplatz 1; ☼ 10am-12.30pm & 2-5pm Mon-Sat, 1-5pm Sun) can seat more than 2000 people, which makes it the country's largest wooden church. Its onion-shaped domes are a welcome change from the more stolid structures found in the Harz region. The church is situated just off Adolph-Roemer-Strasse, opposite the imposing yellow Oberbergamt.

Sleeping & Eating

A nightly *Kurtaxe* of €0.75 is charged by hotels.

Pension Am Hexenturm (☎ 1330; hexenturm@harz.de; Teichdamm 9; s €31, d €46-50; P) Decked out in pine, the rooms at this family house are small but great value, and the service is thoroughly personable.

Friese Hotel (☎ 938 10; hotel.friese@harzpreiswert.de; Burgstätter Strasse 2; s/d €48/68; P) The brown-toned reception at this inn behind the Marktkirche isn't overly welcoming, but the rooms are good and the hotel has two restaurants.

Goldene Krone (☎ 9300; www.goldenekrone-harz.de; Am Kronenplatz 3; s €50-65, d €70-110; P) This place is centrally located and has tasteful, modern rooms. The attached Italian restaurant is also recommended (pasta €6.65).

Restaurant Glück Auf (☎ 1616; Hindenburgplatz 7; Rollstrasse; mains €7.10-13.10) Established in 1720, this is an outstanding traditional restaurant with lots of game specials, a popular seniors' *Stammtisch* (regulars' table), and a huge historic banquet room with seating for 200 people.

Getting There & Around

Regular bus services leave 'Bahnhof', the former train station, and Kronenplatz for Goslar and Bad Grund. Catch bus No 845 for St Andreasberg and bus No 831 for Altenau. The B241 leads north to Goslar and south to Osterode, the B242 goes east to Braunlage and St Andreasberg. To reach the A7, take the B242 west.

EASTERN HARZ

WERNIGERODE
☎ 03943 / pop 35,000

Flanked by the foothills of the Harz Mountains, Wernigerode is a busy tourist centre attracting thousands of German holidaymakers in summer visiting the Hochharz National Park. A romantic ducal castle rises above the Altstadt, which counts some 1000 half-timbered houses spanning five centuries. The town is the northern terminus of the steam-powered narrow-gauge Harzquerbahn (see Narrow-Gauge Railways p275), which has chugged the breadth of the Harz for almost a century; the trail to the summit of the Brocken (1142m), the highest mountain in northern Germany, also starts here.

Wernigerode celebrates its 775th anniversary in 2004, with major restoration works and lots of events.

Orientation
The bus and train stations are on the northern side of town. From Bahnhofplatz, Rudolf-Breitscheid-Strasse leads southeast to Breite Strasse, which runs southwest to the Markt.

Burgberg, Nussallee and Schlosschaussee all lead to the fairy-tale castle on the Agnesberg hill to the southeast.

Information
Harz-Klinikum Wernigerode (☎ 610; Ilsenburger Strasse 15) Medical services.
Police (☎ 65 30; Nicolaiplatz 4)
Post office (cnr Marktstrasse & Kanzleistrasse)
SB-Waschsalon (Burgstrasse; wash/dry €3.50/3) Laundry.
Wernigerode Tourismus (☎ 633 035; www .wernigerode.de; Nicolaiplatz 1; 9am-7pm Mon-Fri, 10am-4pm Sat, 10am-3pm Sun) Tourist information.
Zimmervermittlung (☎ 606 000; Krummelsches Haus, Breite Strasse 72; 10am-7pm) Tourist information.

Sights
ALTSTADT
On the Markt, the spectacular towered **Rathaus** began life as a theatre around 1277, but what you see today is mostly late-Gothic from the 16th century. Legend tells us that the artisan who carved the town hall's 33

wooden figures fell out with authorities and added a few mocking touches. The neo-Gothic **fountain** (1848) was dedicated to charitable nobles, whose names and coats of arms are immortalised on it.

In Oberpfarrkirchhof, which surrounds the **Sylvestrikirche**, you'll find **Gadenstedtsches Haus** (1582), with its Renaissance oriel. The **Harz Museum** (☎ 654 454; Klint 10; adult/concession €1.50/1; 10am-5pm Tue-Sun May-Sept, Mon-Sat Oct-Apr), a short walk away, focuses on local and natural history.

Crossing the Markt to Breite Strasse, the pretty **Café Wien** building (1583) at No 4 is a worthwhile stopover for both architectural and gastronomical reasons. The carved façade of the **Krummelsches Haus** depicts various countries symbolically; America is portrayed, reasonably enough, as a naked woman riding an armadillo.

You can also visit the **Krell'sche Schmiede** (☎ 601 772; www.schmiedemuseum-wernigerode.de; Breite Strasse 95; adult/concession €2/1; 10am-2pm Sat), a historic smithy built in 1678 in the south German baroque style.

Just off Breite Strasse you'll find the **Feuerwehrmuseum** (Fire Brigade Museum; ☎ 633 402; Steingrube 3; 2.30-4.30pm Tue, 2.30-5pm Sat), a collection of fire-fighting machines from 1890 onwards staffed by volunteers of almost the same vintage!

SCHLOSS
First built in the 12th century, **Wernigerode Schloss** (☎ 553 030; schlosswr@t-online.de; adult/concession/child €4.50/4/2.50; 10am-6pm, closed Mon Nov-Apr) has been restored and enlarged over the centuries, and is now one of the most-visited museums in Germany. Its fairy-tale façade came courtesy of Count Otto of Stolberg-Wernigerode in the 19th century. The museum includes portraits of Kaisers, beautiful panelled rooms with original furnishings and the opulent **Festsaal**.

The stunning **Schlosskirche** (1880) has an altar and pulpit made of French marble. You can climb the castle **tower**, but the views from the castle or restaurant terrace (best appreciated late in the day) are free and just as spectacular.

You can walk (1.5km) or take a Bimmelbahn or Schlossbahn wagon ride (€4/1 return) from stops at Marktstrasse or Breite Strasse. In summer, horse-drawn carts make the trek from the Markt.

Activities

The beautiful deciduous **forest** behind the castle is crisscrossed with lovely trails and *Forstwege* (forestry tracks). Wernigerode is also a good starting point for hikes and bike rides into the Hochharz National Park.

Festivals & Events

The **Harz-Gebirgslauf** (☎ 632 832; harz.gebirgslauf@ t-online.de) is an annual charity hiking event held on the second Saturday in October, including a Brocken marathon. An annual festival of music and theatre is held in the castle from early July to mid-August.

Sleeping

A *Kurtaxe* of €1.40 is added to most hotel bills.

Jugendgästehaus (☎ 632 061; Friedrichstrasse 53; dm juniors/seniors €19.80/16, s €16; **P**) Better located than its DJH counterpart, this city hostel has a few quirks: junior price is for under-18s, and includes full board.

Hotel und Restaurant zur Post (☎ 690 40; Marktstrasse 17; s/d €31/72; **P**) This half-timbered house has economical but comfortable rooms with tiled floors.

Pension Schweizer Hof (☎ 632 098; Salzbergstrasse 13; s €35-40, d €50-70; **P**) This Harzklub branch on the southwestern edge of town should be the first choice for those keen on hiking.

Hotel zur Tanne (☎ 632 554; Breite Strasse 57-59; s €41, d €49-75; **P**) The rooms are modern, there's a restaurant downstairs where the boss still cooks personally, and if you're so inclined you can try an infrared sauna.

Hotel am Anger (☎ 923 20; www.hotel-am-anger .de; Breite Strasse 92; s €40, d €72-80; **P** **X**) This hotel offers bright, pleasant rooms and holiday flats with plenty of pine furniture and some views towards the castle.

Altwernigeroder Aparthotel (☎ 949 260; www .appart-hotel.de; Marktstrasse 14; s/d €51/75; **P** **X**) This large central building has stylish apartment rooms of varying sizes, plus extended sauna area and a popular potato-based restaurant out front.

Hotel Gothisches Haus (☎ 6750; gothisches-haus@ tc-hotels.de; Am Markt 1; s €103, d €150-176; **P** **X**) This historic house, named from the 19th-century habit of calling anything old 'Gothic', is a great luxury option; the adjoining Nonnenhof is no less historic and has a traditional restaurant with Harz

specialities. Off-season prices and package deals are good value.

Eating

Lion King (☎ 626 292; Gustav-Petri-Strasse 2-4; mains €6-12.50) You suspect whoever chose the name hasn't ne seen the film – this is actually Chinese restaurant, with good-value lunch deals and not an Elton John song in sight.

Ins kleine Paradies (☎ 632 050; Unterengengasse 6-8; mains €6.15-14.60) Just off the Markt, this very traditional place serves up excellent authentic Harz specialities.

Krummelsches Haus (☎ 602 626; Breite Strasse 7; mains €8-12) The house with the great façade also has a good restaurant, with breakfasts, sandwiches and bistro meals.

Konditorei und Café am Markt (☎ 604 030; Marktplatz 6-8; mains €6.90-14.90) This café near Breite Strasse has a chic interior, tall windows and a good range of international meals and snacks.

Eselskrug (☎ 632 788; An der Malzmühle 1b; mains €6.70-19.50) One for carnivores: amid all the pork, game, hot-stone steaks and fondue, this traditional pub by the Brockenbahn manages to avoid offering a single vegetarian option.

Drinking

Ars Vivendi (☎ 626 606; Bahnhofstrasse 33; ☺ from 8pm Wed-Sat) Wernigerode's contribution to cocktail culture is a smart modern joint near the station, with some Art Deco touches and a good drinks menu.

Humphrey's (☎ 905 445; Grosse Bergstrasse 2; mains €6.20-12.50) We think Humphrey must be Bogart, but it's not entirely obvious what he has to do with the New Orleans décor and Cajun/Tex-Mex menu in this offbeat brasserie and dance bar.

Filmkneipe Capitol (☎ 606 712; Burgstrasse mains €5-13) This is a glitzy bar and restaurant with movie-theme décor (more Bogart) and standard food.

Getting There & Away

There are frequent trains to Goslar (€6.60, 5 minutes) and Halle (€16, 1¼ hours). Change at Halberstadt for Quedlinburg (€6.60, 5 minutes) and Thale (€8.10, one hour).

Direct buses run to most major towns in the region; the timetable (€1.75) available from the **WVB bus office** (☎ 564 134; Hauptbahnhof) includes a train schedule. Bus No 25

uns to Blankenburg and Thale, bus No 257
erves Drei Annen Hohne and Schierke.

Getting Around

Bus Nos 1 and 2 run from the bus station to
he Rendezvous bus stop just north of the
Markt, connecting with bus No 3. Tickets
ost €0.80. For a taxi, call ☎ 633 053.

RÜBELAND CAVES

Rübeland, a small, rather claustrophobic
own just 13km south of Wernigerode,
has two of Germany's more beautiful **caves**
(☎ 039454-491 32; www.ruebeland.com; adult/child €5/
3; ☺ 9am-6pm). Admission gets you a guided
our, in German, of either cave.

Baumannshöhle was formed about 500,000
years ago, and the first tourists visited in
1646, just over a century after its 'rediscov-
ery'. Human presence in the caves dates
back 40,000 years. The Goethesaal, which
has a pond, is sometimes used for concerts
and plays.

Hermannshöhle was formed 350,000 years
ago and was rediscovered in the 19th century.
Its stalactites and stalagmites are spectacular,
especially in the transparent Kristallkammer.
Salamanders, introduced from southern
Europe by researchers, inhabit one pond.

WVB bus No 265 leaves Wernigerode
for Rübeland hourly (€2.50, 30 minutes).

You can join the magnificent Bodetal trail
(blue triangle, 16km) to Thale at Rübeland,
crossing the Rappbodetalsperre, a 106m-
high dam wall across the Harz's largest
reservoir, on foot. Look out for lynxes – a
small captive-bred population was recently
reintroduced here.

If driving from Wernigerode, take the
B244 south to Elbingerode, then the B27
east.

SCHIERKE

☎ 039455 / pop 1000
Schierke, a gorgeous little mountain village
16km southwest of Wernigerode, is the last
stop for the Brockenbahn before it climbs
to the summit. It's also a popular starting
point for exploring the Hochharz National
Park and the home of the ubiquitous 'Sch-
ierker Feuerstein' digestif.

Information

DAV Basislager Brocken (☎ 515 46; Mühlenweg)
Local HQ of the German Alpine Club.
Kurverwaltung & Nationalpark Info (☎ 310; Brockenstrasse 10; ☺ 9am-noon & 1-4pm Mon-Fri, 10am-noon
& 2-4pm Sat, 10am-noon Sun) Tourist information.

Activities

Schierke is a popular place for climbing,
offering all levels of difficulty on nearby

NARROW-GAUGE RAILWAYS

Fans of old-time trains or unusual journeys will be in their element on any of the three narrow-
gauge railways crossing the Harz. This 132km integrated network – the largest in Europe – is
served by 25 steam and 10 diesel locomotives, which tackle gradients of up to 1:25 (40%) and
curves as tight as 60m in radius. Most locomotives date from the 1950s, but eight historical
models, some from as early as 1897, are proudly rolled out for special occasions.

The network, a legacy of the GDR, consists of three lines. The *Harzquerbahn* runs 60km on
a north–south route between Wernigerode and Nordhausen. The serpentine 14km between
Wernigerode and Drei Annen Hohne includes 72 bends; you'll get dropped off on the edge of
Hochharz National Park.

From the junction at Drei Annen Hohne, the *Brockenbahn* begins the steep climb to Schierke
and the Brocken. Direct services to the Brocken can also be picked up from Wernigerode and
Nordhausen, or at stations en route; tickets cost €14/22 single/return from all stations.

The third service is the *Selketalbahn*, which begins in Gernrode and runs to Eisfelder Talmühle
or Hasselfelde. At Eisfelder Tal, you can change trains for other lines. The picturesque Selketalbahn initially follows Wellbach, a creek with a couple of good swimming holes, through deciduous forest to Mädgesprung, before joining the Selke Valley and climbing past Alexisbad to high
plains around Friedrichshöhe, Stiege and beyond.

Passes for three/five/seven days cost €35/40/50 for adults (children half-price). Timetables and
information can be picked up from **Harzer Schmalspurbahnen** (☎ 03943-5580; www.hsb-wr.de;
Friedrichstrasse 151, Wernigerode).

cliffs. The **Aktiv-Center-Schierke** (☎ 868 12; Brockenstrasse 10) hires out climbing gear, mountain bikes and skiing equipment for the 70km of groomed trails. Courses are also offered, and there's a climbing wall.

You can hike to the Brocken via the bitumen Brockenstrasse (12km), closed to private cars and motorcycles. More interesting is the 7km hike via Eckerloch. Pick up the free *Wanderführer 2* hiking guide from Nationalpark Info. Marked trails also lead to the rugged rock formations of Feuersteinklippen (30 minutes from the tourist office) and Schnarcherklippen (1½ hours).

Horse-drawn wagons travel from Schierke to the Brocken and cost adults/child €20/10 return. **Dirk Klaus** (☎ 512 12) also operates horse-drawn sleigh services in winter.

On the night of 30 April, Walpurgisnacht, Schierke attracts about 25,000 visitors, most of whom set off on walking tracks to the Brocken.

Sleeping & Eating

There is plenty of accommodation in town, particularly along Borckenstrasse, but you may need to book ahead. The local *Kurtaxe* is €1.20.

Hotel König (☎ 383; www.harz-hotel-koenig.de; Kirchberg 15; s €32.50-49.50, d €44-72) This hotel has a beautiful foyer and some nice rooms, with a choice of private or shared bathrooms. The restaurant is also good.

Waldschlösschen (☎ 8670; www.waldschloesschen -schierke.de; Hermann-Löns-Weg 1; s €57, d €77-88; P ⊠) A modern hotel tacked onto a Jugendstil villa, this excellent place has lots of facilities, including an Italian-style panorama restaurant. Rooms in the Jugendstil wing are nicest.

Getting There & Around

WVB bus No 876 runs six times daily to Braunlage via Elend. Bus No 257 to Wernigerode is also quite frequent and connects with the No 876. Narrow-gauge railway services between Wernigerode and Schierke cost €4/8 single/return. If driving from the west, take the B27 from Braunlage and turn off at Elend. From Wernigerode, take Friedrichstrasse.

MITTELBAU DORA

From late in 1943, thousands of slave labourers – mostly Russian, French and Polish prisoners of war – toiled under horrific conditions digging tunnels in the cha[..] hills north of Nordhausen. From a 20k[..] labyrinth of tunnels, they produced the V[..] and V2 rockets that rained destruction o[..] London, Antwerp and other cities durin[..] the final stages of WWII.

The camp, called Mittelbau Dora, wa[..] created as a satellite of the Buchenwal[..] concentration camp after British bomber[..] destroyed the missile plants in Peenemünd[..] in far northeastern Germany. During th[..] last two years of the war, at least 20,00[..] prisoners died at Dora, many having sur[..] vived Auschwitz only to be worked to deat[..] here.

The US army reached the gates in Apr[..] 1945, cared for survivors and removed a[..] missile equipment before turning the are[..] over to the Russians two months late[..] Much of the technology was later employec[..] in the US space programme.

During the period of the GDR, Dora[..] mouldered away, marked only by a coupl[..] of small memorials. The horrible truth o[..] the place belies any need for extensive[..] facilities, and a visit to the camp may be[..] among the most unforgettable experiences[..] you have in Germany.

Orientation & Information

Mittelbau Dora is 5km north of Nordhausen, a dull modern town of interest only as regards changing trains.

The grounds, including the crematorium and a **museum** (☎ 03631-495 80; www.buchenwald.de; ☉ Tue-Sun 10am-6pm Apr-Sept, 10am-4pm Oct-Mar), are open daily. The tunnels, which are the diameter of an aircraft hangar, are only accessible by guided tour. Within the dank walls you can see partially assembled rockets that have lain untouched for over 50 years.

Free tours run at 11am and 2pm Tuesday to Friday, and at 11am, 1pm and 3pm weekends (also 4pm April to September).

Getting There & Away

The Harzquerbahn links Nordhausen with Wernigerode (€4, three hours). The nearest stop to Dora is Nordhausen-Krimderode, served by almost hourly trains from Nordhausen-Nord (11 minutes), next to the main station.

From the Krimderode stop, cross the tracks and walk south along Goetheweg, which curves and becomes Kohnsteinweg. Follow this for 1km towards the unassuming hill and you are at the camp.

Trains run to Halle (€13.50, 1¾ hours) and to Göttingen (€13.50, 1½ hours) from Nordhausen.

BROCKEN & TORFHAUS
There are prettier landscapes and hikes in the Harz, but the 1142m Brocken is what draws the crowds: about 50,000 on a summer's day. When he wasn't exploring mines, Goethe also scaled the mountain – in stockings.

Goetheweg from Torfhaus
The 8km Goetheweg trail to the Brocken from the western Harz starts at Torfhaus. Easier than other approaches, it initially takes you through bog, follows a historic aqueduct once used to regulate water levels for the mines, then crosses the Kaiserweg, a sweaty 11km trail from Bad Harzburg. Unfortunately, your next stop will be a dead forest, though the trail becomes steep and more interesting as you walk along the former border – from 1945 to 1990 the Harz region was a frontline in the Cold War, and the Brocken was used by the Soviets as a military base. Hike along the train line above soggy moorland to reach the open, windy summit, where you can enjoy the view, eat pea soup and *Bockwurst*, and think of Goethe and Heine.

On top is the **Brockenhaus** (☎ 039455-500 05; www.brockenhaus.de; adult €4, concession €3-3.50, child €2; ☻ 9.30am-5pm), with interactive displays and a viewing platform, plus an **alpine garden** and a 2.5km trail following what was once a wall around the summit.

Torfhaus itself is little more than a collection of cafés and souvenir shops, but is a good starting point for cross-country skiing or winter ski treks, with plenty of equipment for hire. Downhill skiing is limited to 1200m (two pistes); one recommended route is the Kaiserweg. Make sure you pack a good map and take all precautions. The **Nationalparkhaus** (☎ 05320-263; www.torfhaus.info; Torfhaus 21; ☻ 9am-5pm Apr-Oct, 10am-4pm Nov-Mar) has information on the parks.

Getting There & Away
Bus No 820 stops at Torfhaus on the well-served Bad Harzburg–Braunlage route.

QUEDLINBURG
☎ 03946 / pop 23,600
Unspoiled Quedlinburg is a popular year-round destination, especially since being added to Unesco's World Heritage List in 1994. Almost all the buildings in the historic town centre are half-timbered – street after cobbled street of them – and they are slowly being restored.

The history of Quedlinburg is closely associated with the *Frauenstift*, a medieval foundation for widows and daughters of the nobility that enjoyed the direct protection of the Kaiser. The Reich itself was briefly ruled by two women from here, Theophano and Adelheid, successive guardians of the 10th-century child-king Otto III.

Today the town is a pleasure for visitors of all genders, with plenty of cultural offerings to complement the atmospheric Altstadt.

Orientation
The circular medieval centre of the old town is a 10-minute walk from the Hauptbahnhof (central train station) along Bahnhofstrasse. To reach the Markt, turn left onto Heiligegeiststrasse after the post office. Hohe Strasse, off the Markt, leads south to the castle. The Bode River flows northeastwards through the town.

Information
CR Electronics (☎ 901 550; Steinweg 21; ☻ 10am-7pm Mon-Fri, 10am-1pm Sat) Internet access.
Dorothea Christiane Erxleben Clinic (☎ 9090; Ditfurter Weg 24) Medical services.
Police (☎ 9770; Schillerstrasse 3)
Post office (Bahnhofstrasse)
Quedlinburg-Tourismus (☎ 905 625; www.quedlinburg.de; Markt 2; ☻ 9am-7pm Mon-Fri, 10am-4pm Sat & Sun Apr-Oct, 9.30am-5 .30pm Mon-Fri, 9.30am-2pm Sat Nov-Mar) Tourist information.

Sights
AROUND THE MARKT
The **Rathaus**, built in 1320, has been expanded over the years. It received its Renaissance façade in 1616. Quedel, the small hound above the entrance, is the city's mascot and is said to protect those who enter. Inside, the beautiful Festsaal is decorated with a cycle of frescoes focusing on Quedlinburg's colourful history. The **Roland statue** (1426) in front of the Rathaus dates

QUEDLINBURG

INFORMATION	
CR Electronics	1 C2
Quedlinburg-Tourismus	2 B2

SIGHTS & ACTIVITIES	(pp277-9)
Alter Klopstock	3 B2
Fachwerkmuseum Ständebau	4 B3
Klopstockhaus	5 A3
Lyonel-Feininger-Galerie	6 A3
Marktkirche St Benedikti	7 B2
Rathaus	8 B2
Schloss	9 A3
Stiftskirche St Servatius	10 A3
Zur Börse	11 C2

SLEEPING	(p279)
DJH Hostel	12 B1
Familie Klindt	13 A3
Hotel am Dippeplatz	14 B2
Hotel zur Goldenen Sonne	15 C2
Romantik Hotel Theophano	16 B2
Schlosshotel Zum Markgrafen	17 A3
Zum Alten Fritz	18 C2

EATING	(pp279-80)
Brauhaus Lüdde	19 A3
Hössler	20 B3
Kartoffelhaus No 1	21 B2
Keramik & Kaffee im Fachwerk	22 B2
Wispel Bierpub	(see 15)
Zum Roland	23 B2

ENTERTAINMENT	(p280)
Gildehaus zur Rose	24 B2

TRANSPORT	(p280)
Rad Pavillon	25 C3

---

from the year Quedlinburg joined the Hanseatic League.

The late-Gothic **Marktkirche St Benedikti** is behind the Rathaus. On the tower you'll see a small house used by town watchmen until 1901. The **mausoleum** nearby survived the relocation of the church graveyard during the 19th century.

There are some fine half-timbered buildings near Marktkirche, arguably the most spectacular is the **Gildehaus zur Rose** (1612) at Breite Strasse 39. The richly carved and panelled interior makes it the town's best night-time haunt (see p280 for details).

Return to the Markt and walk through Schuhhof, a shoemakers' courtyard on the east side, with shutters and stablelike 'gossip doors'. **Alter Klopstock** (1580) at Stieg 28 has scrolled beams typical of Quedlinburg's 16th-century half-timbered houses.

Zwischen den Städten, an old bridge, connects the old town and **Neustadt**, which developed alongside the town wall around 1200 when peasants fled a feudal power struggle on the land. Many of the houses here have high archways, and courtyards are dotted with pigeon towers. Of special note are the **Hotel zur Goldenen Sonne** building (1671) at Steinweg 11 and **Zur Börse** (1683) at No 23.

MUSEUMS
Fachwerkmuseum Ständebau

One of Germany's oldest half-timbered houses (1310) houses the **Fachwerkmuseum Ständebau** (☎ 3828; Wordgasse 3; adult/concession €2/1.50; ☉ 11am-5pm Fri-Wed), with perpendicular struts supporting the roof. Inside, visitors can learn about the history and construction of half-timbered buildings and view models of local styles.

Klopstockhaus

The early classicist poet Friedrich Gottlieb Klopstock (1724–1803) is one of Quedlinburg's most celebrated sons. He was born in this 16th-century house, which now houses a **museum** (☎ 2610; Schlossberg 12; adult/concession €2.50/1.50; ☉ 10am-5pm Tue-Sun) containing some interesting exhibits on Klopstock himself and Dorothea Erxleben (1715–62), Germany's first female doctor.

LYONEL-FEININGER-GALERIE
The work of influential Bauhaus artist Lyonel Feininger (1871–1956) is stored in the **Lyonel-Feininger-Galerie** (☎ 2238; Finkenherd 5a; adult/concession €3/1.25; ☒ 10am-6pm Tue-Sun). Feininger was born in Germany and became an American citizen. The original graphics, drawings, watercolours and sketches on display are from the years 1906 to 1936 and were hidden from the Nazis by a Quedlinburg citizen. One highlight is the much-reproduced *Selbstbildnis mit Tonpfeife* (Self-Portrait with Clay Pipe).

SCHLOSSBERG
The castle district, perched above Quedlinburg on a 25m-high plateau, was established during the reign of Heinrich I, from 919 to 936. The present-day Renaissance **Schloss** (☒ 6am-10pm), partly built upon earlier foundations, dates from the 16th century and offers good views over the town. The Residenzbau in the north wing houses the **Schlossmuseum** (☎ 2730; adult/concession €2.50/1.50; ☒ 10am-6pm), which has some mildly interesting exhibits on local natural and social history. The centrepiece, however, is the restored baroque **Blauer Saal** (Blue Hall).

The 12th-century **Stiftskirche St Servatius** (☎ 709 900; adult/concession €3/2; ☒ 10am-6pm Tue-Fri, 10am-4pm Sat, noon-6pm Sun) is one of Germany's most significant of the Romanesque period. Its treasury contains valuable reliquaries and early Bibles. The crypt has some early religious frescoes and contains the graves of Heinrich and his widow, Mathilde, along with those of the abbesses.

Forty-five-minute rides through the Altstadt and Neustadt on the **Bimmelbahn** (☎ 918 888; €4; ☒ 10am-4pm Apr-Oct) leave hourly from Carl-Ritter-Strasse, near Schlossberg.

MÜNZENBERG & WIPERTIKIRCHE
Across Wipertistrasse, on the hill west of the castle, are the ruins of **Münzenberg**, a Romanesque convent. It was plundered during the Peasant Wars in 1525, and small houses were later built among the ruins. The settlement then became home to wandering minstrels, knife grinders and other itinerant tradespeople.

The **Wipertikirche** crypt was built around 1000, and the church itself was used as a barn from 1812 until its restoration in the 1950s. The only way to see the church is by

taking a **tour** (adult/child €3/2; ☒ May-Oct) from the tourist office.

Festivals & Events
A programme of classical music is held in the Stiftskirche every year from June to September. For tickets and information, contact the tourist office.

Sleeping
DJH hostel (☎ 811 703; jh-quedlinburg@djh-sachsen-anhalt.de; Neuendorf 28; juniors/seniors €13.50/16.20; ☒) This cheery DJH Jugendherberge is on a quiet street near the town centre.

Familie Klindt (☎ 702 911; Hohe Strasse 19; s/d €20/32; P) This three-room private family establishment is rather basic but it's central and pretty decent for the price.

Zum Alten Fritz (☎ 704 880; alter-fritz@quedlinburg.de; Pölkenstrasse 18; s/d €45/55; P) Less traditional than the competition, this hotel is still a pleasant place, and offers newly renovated deluxe 'Romantik' rooms for €95/125.

Hotel am Dippeplatz (☎ 771 40; hotel@amdippeplatz.de; Breite Strasse 16; s €45, d €60-75; P) Nice big rooms here, which are generally bright and clean but sometimes a bit smoky.

Hotel zur Goldenen Sonne (☎ 962 50; www.hotelzurgoldenensonne.de; Steinweg 11; s €46-51, d €67-82; P ☒ ☐) Another historic place, the building is at a bit of a strange angle but the interiors are fine, with spacious and suitably wooden fittings.

Romantik Hotel Theophano (☎ 963 00; www.hoteltheophano.de; Markt 13-14; s €62, d €93-113; P ☒ ☐) This historic building is highly recommended for a night of rustic luxury; individually decorated rooms have four-poster beds, the vaulted cellar restaurant/bar is excellent and the staff are very friendly. One drawback: there are lots of steep stairs and no lift.

Schlosshotel Zum Markgrafen (☎ 811 40; www.schlosshotel-zum-markgrafen.de; Weingarten 30; s €95, d €140-165; P ☒) For a real splurge, though, this sturdy castle hotel is absolutely the last word, offering 12 fantastic double rooms (some with Jacuzzi), terrace café, restaurant, cocktail bar, sauna/fitness area and the highest tower in Quedlinburg, all set in its own park grounds behind the city wall.

Eating
Keramik & Kaffee Im Fachwerk (☎ 915 422; www.keramik-café.de) Tucked away in yet another

half-timbered house, this tiny café provides coffee and tea specialities, ice cream and local ceramics.

Wispel Bierpub (☎ 702 254; Steinweg 9; mains €1.20-4) Missing the '80s? Relive the music, the mullets and the rock-bottom prices at this old-school Kneipe.

Hössler (☎ 915 255; Steinbrücke 21; meals €2.50-8) This excellent budget fish cafeteria serves good main dishes and filling fish rolls.

Kartoffelhaus No 1 (☎ 708 334; Breite Strasse 37; mains €1.50-11.60) This popular chain is the place to come for diverse and interesting potato dishes. Enter from Klink.

Brauhaus Lüdde (☎ 705 206; Blasiistrasse 14; s/d €80/130; mains €8.50-13; P) This is a lively microbrewery, which serves up hearty lunches and dinners, and also houses a lot of coach parties. Try the Lüdde-Alt dark beer or the low-alcohol Pubarschknall.

Zum Roland (☎ 4532; Breite Strasse 2-6; mains €6-15) Spread over seven different houses, this quirky but charming café-restaurant can seat up to 736 people for traditional meals, pasta and international dishes.

Entertainment
After-dark options in Quedlinburg are extremely limited. **Gildehaus zur Rose** (☎ 2694; Breite Strasse 39) is the most popular nightspot in town; the interior alone justifies a visit. It also serves light meals.

Getting There & Away
For trains to Wernigerode (€6.60, 50 minutes), change at Halberstadt. A branch line runs to Gernrode (€1.60, 13 minutes); other frequent trains go to Thale (€1.60, nine minutes). The station hall closes at 6pm; you can buy tickets on the train, but check before using the luggage lockers, as there's no access after closing.

The **QBus** office (☎ 2236; www.qbus-ballenstedt .de; Hauptbahnhof) has timetables and information on its frequent regional services.

The **Strasse der Romanik** (Romanesque Road; not to be confused with the Romantic Road in Bavaria) leads south to Gernrode. This theme road connects towns that have significant Romanesque architecture. The B6 runs west to Wernigerode, Goslar, and A395 (for Braunschweig) and the A7 between Kassel and Hanover. For Halle take the B6 east, and for Halberstadt the B79 north.

Getting Around
Cars can be hired from **National Car Rental** (☎ 770 70; Gernröder Weg 5b). There's a **taxi service** (☎ 707 070) in town. **Rad Pavillon** (☎ 709 507; Bahnhofstrasse 16) hires out bicycles.

GERNRODE
☎ 039485 / pop 4000
Only 8km south of Quedlinburg, Gernrode makes an ideal day trip. Its Stiftskirche St Cyriakus is one of Germany's finest churches, while hikers, picnickers and steam-train enthusiasts will also enjoy this pretty town, which boasts the largest thermometer and *Skat* (a card game) table in the world.

The **tourist office** (☎ 354; www.gernrode.de; Suderode Strasse 250; ✆ 10am-3.30pm Mon-Fri) is a 10-minute walk from the Hauptbahnhof and another 10 minutes from the town centre.

Sights & Activities
Stiftskirche St Cyriakus (☎ 275; ✆ 9am-5pm Mon-Sat, 11.45am-5pm Sun Apr-Oct) is one of the purest examples of Romanesque architecture from the Ottonian period. Construction of the basilica, which is based on the form of a cross, was begun in 959. Especially noteworthy is the early use of alternating columns and pillars, later a common Romanesque feature. The octagonal **Taufstein** (Christening stone), whose religious motifs culminate in the Ascension, dates from 1150. In the south aisle you will find **Das Heilige Grab**, an 11th-century replica of Christ's tomb in Jerusalem. The 19th-century **organ** is both visually and aurally impressive. The tourist office has information on summer concerts and tours.

The **narrow-gauge railway** (€2.50, 30 minutes) from Gernrode to Mägdesprung (see Getting There & Around, p281) is especially picturesque; you can break the trip at Sternhaus Ramberg, where a short trail leads through the forest to **Bremer Teich**, a pretty swimming hole with a camp site and hostel. You can also walk to Mägdesprung and beyond from Gernrode along paths beside the train track.

From the corner of Bahnhofstrasse and Marktstrasse, marked hiking trails lead east to Burg Falkenstein (11km), the historic castle in the Selke valley, and west to Thale (about 13km).

etting There & Around

egular QBus services for Thale and Qued-
nburg stop at the Hauptbahnhof and
i front of the tourist office. Three night
uses also stop here, including the Nacht3
e Thale. Small trains chug almost hourly
cross from Quedlinburg. Gernrode is the
ailhead for the Selketalbahn (see Narrow-
auge Railways p275); buy tickets at the
Hauptbahnhof (☎ 9400).

HALE

☎ 03947 / pop 15,000

ituated below the northern slopes of the
Harz Mountains, Thale's mainstay was
once its steelworks, the Eisen-und Hütten-
verk Thale, which in GDR times employed
ome 8000 workers. That number has now
dropped to 500 and part of the factory is a
nuseum, but Thale has kept its identity as
a workers' town.

The main focus for visitors, however, is
he sensational landscape of rugged cliffs
and a lush river valley that makes for ideal
niking. On the two cliffs at the head of the
valley are Hexentanzplatz and Rosstrappe,
both magnets for postmodern pagans, who
gather in grand style and numbers each year
on 30 April to celebrate Walpurgisnacht.

Orientation & Information

Thale's two main streets are Poststrasse,
which runs diagonally off Bahnhofstrasse
(left from the Hauptbahnhof), and Karl-
Marx-Strasse, which runs northeast to the
Bode River.

The **tourist office** (☎ 2597; www.thale.de; Rathausstrasse 1; ⏱ 9am-5pm Mon-Fri, 10am-3pm Sat & Sun) is
opposite the Hauptbahnhof. Pick up the
English-language brochure *Thale Fabulous*
or book a themed tour with a witch or devil
(€3.40 to €3.90).

There's a Sparkasse bank at the top of
Karl-Marx-Strasse; the post office is in the
Kaufhaus department store at No 16.

Sights

Hexentanzplatz and **Rosstrappe** are two rugged outcrops flanking the Bode Valley, that
once had Celtic fortresses and were used
by Germanic tribes for occult rituals and
sacrifices (see Witches & Warlocks below).
The landscape also inspired the myth of
Brunhilde, who escaped a loveless marriage to Bohemian prince Bodo by leaping
the gorge on horseback; her pursuing fiancé
couldn't make the jump and plunged into
the valley that now bears his name, turning into a dragon on the way. The impact

WITCHES & WARLOCKS

The Bodetal once contained Celtic fortresses built to fend off northern tribes; by 500 BC Germanic tribes had driven out the Celts and appropriated the sites for meetings and ritual sacrifices. These played an important role in the 8th-century Saxon Wars, when Charlemagne embarked upon campaigns to subjugate and Christianise the local population. Harz mythology blends these pagan and Christian elements.

One popular – but misleading – explanation for the Walpurgisnacht festival is that it was an invention of the tribes who, pursued by Christian missionaries, held secret gatherings to carry out their rituals. They are said to have darkened their faces one night and, armed with broomsticks and pitchforks, scared off Charlemagne's guards, who mistook them for witches and devils. In fact the name 'Walpurgisnacht' itself probably derives from St Walpurga, but the festival tradition may also refer to the wedding of the gods Wodan and Freya.

According to local mythology, witches and warlocks gather on Walpurgisnacht at locations throughout the Harz before flying off to the Brocken on broomsticks or goats. There they re-count the year's evil deeds and top off the stories with a bacchanalian frenzy, said to represent copulation with the devil. Frightened peasants used to hang crosses and herbs on stable doors to protect their livestock; ringing church bells or cracking whips was another way to prevent stray witches from dropping by.

One of the best places to celebrate Walpurgisnacht is Thale, where not-so-pagan hordes of 35,000 or more arrive for colourful variety events and the Walpurgishalle tells you all you need to know about sacrifices, rituals and local myths. Schierke, also popular, is a starting point for Walpurgisnacht treks to the Brocken. Wherever you are, expect to see the dawn in with some very strange characters!

of Brunhilde's landing supposedly left the famous hoof imprint in the stone on Rosstrappe. It is worth a climb or ride up for the magnificent views alone.

A modern **cable car** (€4.50 return; ⏰ 9.30am-6pm May-Sep, 9.30am-4.30pm Oct-Apr) runs to Hexentanzplatz, or you can take a **chairlift** (€3 to Rosstrappe; ⏰ 9.30am-6pm May-Oct, weekends & holidays Nov-Apr). Go early or late in the day to avoid crowds. Signs direct you from the Hauptbahnhof.

The wooden museum **Walpurgishalle** (Hexentanzplatz; adult/child €1.50/0.50; ⏰ 9am-5pm) has exhibitions and paintings on matters heathen (German only), including the *Opferstein*, a stone once used in Germanic sacrificial rituals. Nearby is a 10-hectare **Tierpark** (☎ 2880; adult/concession €3/2; ⏰ 8am-dusk) with lynxes, wild cats and other animals. The Hexentanzplatz itself is now basically a coach park full of souvenir shops.

Activities

HIKING

The brochures *Wanderführer* and *Führer durch das Bodetal* (€1.50 each) are excellent if your German is up to it. Highly recommended is the Bode Valley walk between Thale and Treseburg (blue triangle, 10km). If you take QBus No 18 from Thale to Treseburg, you can walk downstream and enjoy the most spectacular scenery at the end. Another 10km trail (red dot) goes from Hexentanzplatz to Treseburg; combine with the valley walk to make a round trip.

Festivals & Events

The open-air **Harzer Bergtheater** (☎ 2324; www.harzer-bergtheater.de; Hexentanzplatz) celebrated 100 years of thespianism in 2003; it has a summer programme of music and plays, plus a performance on Walpurgisnacht. Tickets are sold at the venue and the tourist office.

Sleeping & Eating

Book extremely early for Walpurgisnacht. The number of cheap private rooms is

limited, but the tourist office can help, especially in finding holiday flats.

DJH hostel (☎ 2881; jh-thale@djh-sachsen-anhalt.de; Bodetal-Waldkater; juniors/seniors €13.50/16.20; ☐) This DJH Jugendherberge is nestled in lush valley surroundings just five minutes from the Hauptbahnhof; go south along Hubertusstrasse from the top of Friedenspark. The Bode Valley trail begins at the door.

Kleiner Waldkater (☎ 2826; www.kleiner-waldkater.de; Bodetal-Waldkater; s/d €33/52; ☐) The rustic Kleiner Waldkater, in the valley alongside the hostel, is also good value. The location alone makes its restaurant a good place to drop in.

Hotel Haus Sonneneck (☎ 496 10; www.haus-sonneneck.de; Heimburgstrasse 1a; s/d €35/52; ☐ ☒) Square and very neat, the Sonneneck is on the way to the lifts from the station. Families, seniors and pets are all welcome.

Hoffmann's Gästehaus (☎ 410 40; www.hoffmanns-gaestehaus.de; Musesteig 4; r €44-62, ste €82; ☐) South of the river, near the eastern end of Karl-Marx-Strasse, this lovely villa was fully renovated in 1999 but still retains some of its original 19th century fittings.

Various restaurants and hotels can be found on Hexentanzplatz and Rosstrappe. For a change from German standards, the **Punjabi** (☎ 772 088; Karlstrasse 1; mains €8-14.50), surprisingly good Indian restaurant north of the river in town.

Getting There & Around

Frequent trains travel to Halberstadt (€35 minutes), Quedlinburg (€1.60, 10 minutes), Wernigerode (€8.10, one hour) and Magdeburg (€12.40, 1½ hours). Karl-Marx-Strasse leads to the main junction for road to Quedlinburg and Wernigerode.

The bus station is on Bahnhofstrasse, just past the tourist office. For Wernigerode take WVB 253; for Treseburg, take QBus 18. WVB 264 goes to Treseburg and Blankenburg via Rosstrappe. Night buses N3 and N4 go to Harzgerode and Quedlinburg respectively, via Hexentanzplatz.

Mecklenburg-
Western Pomerania

CONTENTS

Accommodation	285
Food	285
Getting There & Around	285
Mecklenburger Seenplatte	**286**
Schwerin	286
Around Schwerin	290
Güstrow	290
Neubrandenburg	291
Around Neubrandenburg	293
Müritz National Park	294
Coastal Mecklenburg-	
Western Pomerania	**294**
Rostock	294
Around Rostock	300
Wismar	301
Poel Island	304
Vorpommersche	
Boddenlandschaft	
National Park	304
Western Pomerania	**305**
Stralsund	305
Greifswald	308
Around Greifswald	310
Rügen Island	**311**
Information	311
Getting There & Away	312
Getting Around	312
Deutsche Alleenstrasse	313
Mönchgut Peninsula	313
Binz	314
Prora	315
Jasmund National Park	315
Wittow	315
Hiddensee Island	316

MECKLENBURG-WESTERN POMERANIA

Sparsely populated and refreshingly unurbanised, Mecklenburg-Western Pomerania (Mecklenburg-Vorpommern) doesn't enjoy a particularly high profile internationally, but anyone in Germany will fill you in with glee – the state is Germany's finest domestic holiday spot, much like Blackpool in the UK but with more sun, better beaches and fewer piers. In summer thousands of visitors descend on the resort islands of Rügen and Usedom to enjoy the sparkling sand, brisk sea air and all-too-brief swimming season, as well as touring pretty coastal towns like Wismar and Warnemünde.

Unlike Blackpool, however, the region has a lot more to offer than a bit of quality sun-lounger time. Towns such as Stralsund and Greifswald boast some of the best-preserved examples of red-brick Gothic architecture anywhere in Germany, all displaying the turreted gable style typical of the north. The state capital, Schwerin, has an incredible castle at its heart and is among the most stunning little cities in the country; the historical centres of Stralsund and Wismar were Unesco-listed in 2002; even Rostock, once a gritty shipbuilding town, has become a major tourist centre by hosting the annual International Garden Exhibition in 2003, and is rapidly building a reputation as a party city. Elsewhere, you can get off the beaten track into the area's delightfully wild national parks or sail into the sunset with any number of fishing, diving, cruise and ferry companies.

The state does have its problems – the second-highest unemployment figures in Germany for one. But thanks to Mecklenburg's long tradition of hospitality it's generally easy to get around. There's also a solid tourist infrastructure to sort you out, particularly around the well-frequented coastal towns and resorts. Trust the southerners' judgement and spend some quality holiday time in a corner of Germany that is only going to get more popular.

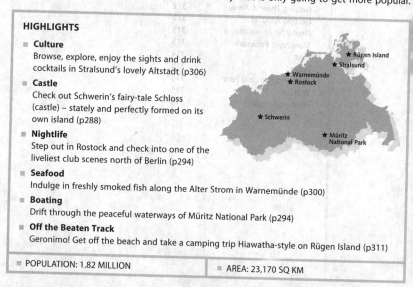

HIGHLIGHTS

- **Culture**
  Browse, explore, enjoy the sights and drink cocktails in Stralsund's lovely Altstadt (p306)
- **Castle**
  Check out Schwerin's fairy-tale Schloss (castle) – stately and perfectly formed on its own island (p288)
- **Nightlife**
  Step out in Rostock and check into one of the liveliest club scenes north of Berlin (p294)
- **Seafood**
  Indulge in freshly smoked fish along the Alter Strom in Warnemünde (p300)
- **Boating**
  Drift through the peaceful waterways of Müritz National Park (p294)
- **Off the Beaten Track**
  Geronimo! Get off the beach and take a camping trip Hiawatha-style on Rügen Island (p311)

- POPULATION: 1.82 MILLION
- AREA: 23,170 SQ KM

ACCOMMODATION

In addition to the usual options, dozens of the state's 2000 castles are open as hotels (Schlösser und Herrenhäuser). Some are used as spas, others as resorts and executive retreats. Prices start around €50 per person per night. For a comprehensive list of castle hotels, contact **Tourismusverband Mecklenburg-Vorpommern** (☎ 0381-403 0600; www.auf-nach-mv.de; Platz der Freundschaft 1, Rostock). You can also book hotels throughout the state via its reservation service (☎ 0180-500 0223).

Note that hotel rates are often substantially discounted on weekends and in the low season. In high season (July to September), conversely, you'll need to book well in advance for anywhere on the coast, particularly around the first weekend of August.

FOOD

Much of the truly regional cooking is traditional German with a sweet-and-sour twist. Prime examples are *Rippenbraten* (rolled roast pork stuffed with lemon, apple and plums) and *Eintopf* (potato stew served with vinegar and sugar on the side). Fresh fish, cooked in every conceivable way, is very popular, as is *Heringe in Sahnestipp* (herring in cream sauce). In Wismar, try *Wismarer Spickaal* (young eel smoked in a way unique to the area).

GETTING THERE & AROUND

Deutsche Bahn offers the Mecklenburg-Vorpommern Ticket, which gives the usual day's unlimited regional travel for €21. In summer the Ostsee-Ticket gives 40% off the standard price of a return journey from Berlin and Brandenburg to the major coastal cities (not Schwerin). Unusually, this includes IC and EC as well as regional lines.

Cyclists also get a good deal in Mecklenburg: the Mehrtages-Fahrradkarte (€13) allows you to bring your bike on any train journey for five separate days within a four-month period.

Wheelchair users might like to check out www.spezialreisen.com, which has tips (in German) for the Mecklenburg-Western Pomerania region and some special deals.

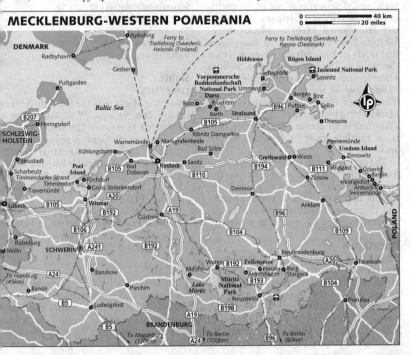

MECKLENBURGER SEENPLATTE

At the doorstep of the state capital, Schwerin, the Mecklenburg Lake Plains is one of the area's prettiest regions. A wilderness spreading across the centre of the state, the area may well become one of the most popular outdoor and sport destinations for visitors looking for peace, quiet and reasonably pristine wilderness.

The plains are crisscrossed by roads and highways that make getting around very easy if you're travelling under your own steam. The roads (often canopied by trees planted by medieval fish merchants to shield wagons from the heat of the summer sun) meander through charming little villages and hamlets – many of them untouched by changes in government either after WWII or the *Wende* (reunification).

SCHWERIN

☎ 0385 / pop 100,000

State capital Schwerin is one of the prettiest cities in northern Germany. The oldest city (established 1160) in Mecklenburg-Western Pomerania, it has so many lakes that locals and officials can't even agree on the number. The town gets its name from a Slavic castle known as *Zuarin* (Animal Pasture) on the site of the present Schloss. This former seat of the Grand Duchy of Mecklenburg is an interesting mix of 16th-, 17th- and 19th-century architecture, and is an absolute must for travellers in this area.

The centre is small enough to explore on foot, but if you have a bit of time you can take two or three days just to get to know the city and its environs. Schwerin's beauty and charm are infectious, and few people regret spending a bit of extra time here.

Orientation

The Altstadt is a 10-minute walk south from the Hauptbahnhof (central train station) along Wismarsche Strasse. Wismarsche Strasse ends at the Marienplatz shopping district with the Schlosspark-Center mall. A couple of blocks east of the Hauptbahnhof is the rectangular Pfaffenteich, a pretty, artificial pond marked (or marred, depending

on your tastes) on its southwestern corner by the orange, fairy-tale–style Arsenal.

Heading east on Schlossstrasse from Marienplatz, turning left on the small street after Mecklenburgstrasse will take you to the Markt (square). Schlossstrasse continues towards Burg Island on the Schweriner See, topped with its lovely Schloss. Along the way you'll pass the Alter Garten (Old Garden) and can view the Marstall (stables). Burg Island connects to two gardens, the Schlossgarten and the lesser-known Grüngarten.

Information

Buchhaus Weiland (☎ 594 950; Marienplatz 3) Bookshop.
HypoVereinsbank (☎ 530 30; Mecklenburger Strasse)
In-Ca (☎ 500 7883; Wismarsche Strasse 123; €2.50 per hr; ☼ 1pm-midnight) Internet access.
Main post office (Mecklenburgstrasse)
Marktbuchhandlung (☎ 565 976; Am Markt 13) Bookshop.
Netz-Games (☎ 593 6960; Ritterstrasse 1; €3 per hr; ☼ noon-midnight) Internet access.
Reisebank (☎ Hauptbahnhof)
Schwerin-Information (☎ 592 5212; www.schwerin.de; Markt 10; ☼ 9am-7pm Mon-Fri, 10am-6pm Sat & Sun)
Stadtklinikum (☎ 5200; 397 Wismarsche Strasse) Medical services.

Sights
CHURCHES

Above the Markt rises the tall 14th-century Gothic **Dom** (cathedral; ☎ 565 014; Am Dom 4; ☼ 10am-5pm Mon-Fri, noon-5pm Sun), a superb example of north German red-brick architecture. Locals hotly point out that its 19th-century cathedral tower (118m) is a whole 50cm taller than Rostock's Petrikirche (church). You can climb up to the viewing platform (€1).

Another example of this type of architecture is the **Paulskirche** (☎ 557 660; Am Packhof 9; ☼ 10am-noon & 2-5pm Tue-Thu, 10am-noon Fri), south of the Hauptbahnhof.

ALTSTADT

The Markt is a bustling place, home to the **Rathaus** and the neoclassical **Neues Gebäude** (1780–83), which houses the classy Café Röntgen and is fronted by a lion monument honouring the town's founder, Heinrich der Löwe. Take a good look at the

SCHWERIN

0 — 300 m
0 — 0.2 miles

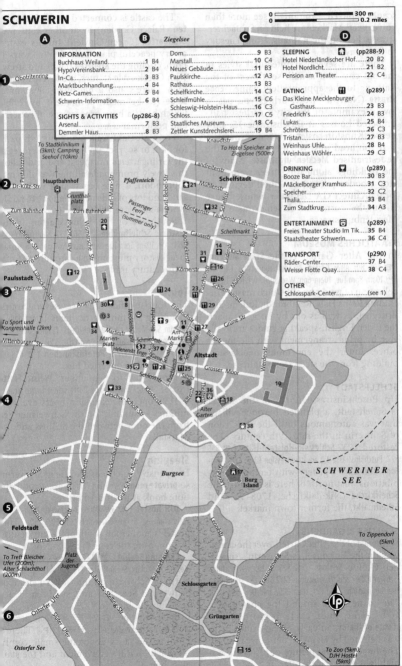

INFORMATION
Buchhaus Weiland..................1 B4
HypoVereinsbank..................2 B4
In-Ca....................................3 B3
Marktbuchhandlung..............4 B4
Netz-Games...........................5 B4
Schwerin-Information............6 B4

SIGHTS & ACTIVITIES (pp286-8)
Arsenal.................................7 B3
Demmler Haus......................8 B3
Dom....................................9 B3
Marstall................................10 C4
Neues Gebäude....................11 B3
Paulskirche...........................12 A3
Rathaus................................13 B3
Schelfkirche..........................14 C3
Schleifmühle.........................15 C6
Schleswig-Holstein-Haus.......16 C3
Schloss.................................17 C5
Staatliches Museum..............18 C4
Zettler Kunstdrechslerei.........19 B4

SLEEPING (pp288-9)
Hotel Niederländischer Hof.....20 B2
Hotel Nordlicht.....................21 B2
Pension am Theater...............22 C4

EATING (p289)
Das Kleine Mecklenburger
  Gasthaus............................23 B3
Friedrich's.............................24 B3
Lukas...................................25 B4
Schröters..............................26 C3
Tristan..................................27 B3
Weinhaus Uhle......................28 B4
Weinhaus Wöhler..................29 C3

DRINKING (p289)
Booze Bar.............................30 B3
Mäckelborger Kramhus..........31 C3
Speicher...............................32 C2
Thalia..................................33 B4
Zum Stadtkrug......................34 A3

ENTERTAINMENT (p289)
Freies Theater Studio Im Tik....35 B4
Staatstheater Schwerin...........36 C4

TRANSPORT (p290)
Räder-Center.........................37 B4
Weisse Flotte Quay................38 C4

OTHER
Schlosspark-Center................(see 1)

MECKLENBURG-WESTERN POMERANIA

scenes depicted – you might see more than you expect! Markets are held on Schlachterstrasse, behind the Rathaus, from Tuesday to Saturday.

There are several architectural styles in the old city, and a walk southwest of the Rathaus to the appropriately named **Enge Strasse** (Narrow Street) brings you past a lovely example of the city's earliest half-timbered houses at Buschstrasse 15, now Zettler Kunstdrechslerei (wood-turners).

If you head west you'll emerge onto the pedestrianised **Mecklenburgstrasse**. Many of the buildings along this street were built atop wooden pilings, a method devised by local architect GA Demmler, whose house is on the corner of Arsenalstrasse and Mecklenburgstrasse.

STAATLICHES MUSEUM
In the Alter Garten is the **State Museum** (☎ 595 80; Alter Garten 3; adult/concession €4/2.50; ☼ 10am-8pm Tue, 10am-6pm Wed-Sun), which has a collection of works by old Dutch masters including Frans Hals, Rembrandt, Rubens and Brueghel, as well as oils by Lucas Cranach the Elder. English-speaking guides are available by prior arrangement with the tourist office. Enter the enormous neoclassical building from the steep stone staircase.

SCHELFSTADT
Up Puschkinstrasse north of the Markt is Schelfstadt, a planned baroque village that was autonomous until the expansion of Schwerin in the mid-19th century. The restored 1737 **Schleswig-Holstein-Haus** (☎ 555 527; Puschkinstrasse 12; adult/concession €3/2; ☼ 10am-6pm) contains a gallery with temporary exhibitions. Just north of here is the baroque **Schelfkirche** (Nikolaikirche; 1708–13) and **Schelfmarkt**, the former town market.

SCHLOSS & GARDENS
Southeast of the Alter Garten, over the causeway on the Burginsel, is Schwerin's superb neo-Gothic **Schloss** (☎ 525 2920; www.schloss-schwerin.de; adult/concession €4/2.50; ☼ 10am-6pm Tue-Sun mid-Apr–mid-Oct; 10am-5pm mid-Oct–mid-Apr). The castle, built around the chapel of a 16th-century ducal castle, is guarded by a **statue of Niklot**, an early Slavic prince, who was defeated by Heinrich der Löwe in 1160. The huge, graphic picture of his death is a highlight of the castle interior.

The castle is connected to the **Schlossgarten** (Palace Garden) by another causeway **Grüngarten** (Green Garden), further east, is a very peaceful place indeed. Walkways in both, circling the **Kreuzsee** (lake) and strewn with Greek-style statues, are lovely in summer. There's also a big open-air summer **stage** (to be made permanent by 2009), which hosts a busy programme of concerts and performances.

For a pleasant walk along smooth paths for 5km or so, pick up the Franzosenweg at the Grüngarten's northeast end and follow this lovely promenade all the way down to Zippendorf, a nice beach area with white sand and lots of kids near the **zoo** (☎ 395 510; www.zoo-schwerin.de; Waldschulweg 1).

Southeast of the Schlossgarten is the historic **Schleifmühle** (☎ 562 751; adult/concession €2/1; ☼ 10am-5pm Tue-Sun Easter-Nov only), a small local history museum in a carefully restored 19th-century mill.

Tours
The tourist office organises several tours, including 90-minute **city tours** (11am daily & 1.30pm Sat-Mon), **castle viewings** (11am Sat & Sun) and **evening walks** (8.30pm Fri). You can also tour the city in a **Petermännchen** (☎ 658 00; €6-9; ☼ Apr-Oct) converted bus.

From May to September, **Weisse Flotte** (☎ 557 7770; www.weisse-flotte-schwerin.de; cruises €8-11.50) operates excursion boats every 30 minutes in summer on the Schweriner See from the quay between the Schloss and the Marstall.

Sleeping
Inexpensive hotel beds are rare in Schwerin, so **private rooms** (s/d from €18/32) are a good option; book at the tourist office.

DJH hostel (☎ 326 0006; jh-schwerin@djh-mv.de; Waldschulweg 3; juniors/seniors €14.50/17.50) This hostel is about 4km south of the city centre, just opposite the zoo. Take bus No 14.

Camping Seehof (☎ 512 540; www.seehof-camping.de; Zum Zeltplatz, Seehof; sites €10-15) About 10km north of Schwerin on the western shore of Schweriner See, this camp site is easily accessible with bus No 8.

Hotel Nordlicht (☎ 558 150; www.hotel-nordlicht.m-vp.de; Apothekerstrasse 2; s/d €46/64; P) There's nothing too fancy about the small, comfy Nordlicht, but it's convenient and the staff give their all.

Pension am Theater (☎ 593 680; www.pensionam
heater.m-vp.de; Theaterstrasse 1-2; r €50-82; P) In
the shadow of the huge theatre building
and (just) within sight of the castle, you
get a friendly welcome and big, comfortable
rooms here, although you may miss little
things like soap in the bathrooms.

Hotel Niederländischer Hof (☎ 591 100; www
.niederlaendischer-hof.de; Karl-Marx-Strasse 12-13; s/d from
€90/118; P) You can't beat the Pfaffenteich
location or the swanky rooms and marble
bathrooms at this exceedingly classy hotel.
There's even a library with an open fire.

Hotel Speicher am Ziegelsee (☎ 500 30; www
.speicher-hotel.de; Speicherstrasse 11; s €80-100, d €100-120;
P ✗) Waterfront location, sauna, solarium,
gym, bar, restaurants: this family-friendly,
disabled-friendly, pet-friendly former warehouse is about the best-equipped hotel in
town.

Eating
Tristan (☎ 572 7587; Burgstrasse 1; mains €7.50-11.50;
☽ dinner Tue-Sat, lunch Sun) More designer cooking, this time ultra-modern *Neue Deutsche
Küche*, in a historic cellar setting.

Lukas (☎ 565 935; Grosser Moor 5; mains €7-17)
Fish-lovers should head straight to this top
conservatory restaurant, with a great range
of dishes and some extravagant prawn and
lobster options. See if you can look at the
aquarium without feeling guilty.

Alter Schlachthof (☎ 593 8668; Bleicherufer 3;
mains €9-13) This big modern restaurant,
tapas bar and cocktail lounge is part of the
Treff Bleicher Ufer complex southwest of
the centre, which also includes a multiplex
cinema, Aldi supermarket and the Crowne
Plaza hotel.

Weinhaus Wöhler (☎ 555 830; Puschkinstrasse 26;
mains €8-16) Providing the main competition
to the Uhle, this sprawling courtyard house
also incorporates a tapas/cocktail bar and
six luxury double rooms (€75 to €120).

Friedrich's (☎ 555 473; Friedrichstrasse 2; mains
€8-15.50) Overlooking the Pfaffenteich, this
Parisian-style café dates back to 1886. On
offer is a selection of salads, grills and vegetarian options.

Schröters (☎ 550 7698; www.schroeters-restaurant
.de; Schliemannstrasse 2; set menus €30-135) Run by
Erik Schröter, Mecklenburg's no 1 chef,
this place is way out of everything else's
league, offering incredible regional cooking with a French twist. Menus start at

three courses and go right the way up to a
10-course banquet!

The longstanding traditional family
wine merchant, **Weinhaus Uhle** (☎ 562 956;
www.weinhaus-uhle.de; Schusterstrasse 13-15; mains €9-16)
has vaulted ceilings in the downstairs restaurant and a lovely Weinstube upstairs, as
well as running the more modern **Das Kleine
Mecklenburger Gasthaus** (☎ 555 9666; Puschkinstrasse
37; mains €7.50-10.90). The food is excellent and
the wine list is practically encyclopaedic.

Drinking
Schwerin is not exactly overburdened with
nightlife, but the bar scene is thriving; *Piste,
Schwerin Magazin* and *Wohin in Schwerin*
provide free listings. *Homo Scout* is a calendar with listings of gay and lesbian venues
throughout the state.

Booze Bar (☎ 562 576; Arsenalstrasse 16) Connected to the somewhat cheesy Moon Club,
this is *the* place to come for cocktails, with
an extensive and inventive menu including
the staff's own creations.

Speicher (☎ 512 105; Röntgenstrasse 20/22) The
very popular Speicher cultural centre has
live music, DJ nights and a cinema with some
arthouse fare. Enter from Schelfstrasse.

Mäckelborger Kramhus (☎ 581 3105; Puschkinstrasse 15) Art gallery, café, bar, jazz club...you'll
find it all here.

Zum Stadtkrug (☎ 593 6693; Wismarsche Strasse
126) A central, traditional micro-brewery
pub, the homebrew here was declared
among the best in Germany by *Stern* magazine, no less.

Thalia (☎ 550 9901; Geschwister-Scholl-Strasse 2)
This busy dance club hosts Schwerin's biggest gay and lesbian night, up to four times
monthly.

Entertainment
Sport und Kongresshalle (☎ 761 900; www.stadt
hallen-schwerin.de; Wittenburger Strasse 118) Large
pop and rock concerts are held here, 2km
west of the centre (bus No 5, 10 or 11).

Staatstheater Schwerin (☎ 530 00; Alter Garten)
The state theatre offers an impressive
range of concerts as well as varied theatrical performances.

Freies Theater Studio Im Tik (☎ 562 401;
Mecklenburgstrasse 28) There's theatre, comedy,
music and cabaret in this temporary location while the permanent stage (Mecklenburgstrasse 2) is being renovated.

Getting There & Away

Trains arrive regularly from Rostock (€12.40, one hour), Magdeburg (€25.20, 3½ hours) and Stralsund (€21.60, two hours). Direct trains run to/from Wismar (€5.50, 30 minutes) throughout the day. Trains from Berlin (€27.20, 2¾ hours) go via Wittenberge.

Regional buses depart for Wismar and Lübeck from Grunthalplatz, outside the Hauptbahnhof.

By road from Rostock, head southwest on the B105 (E22), then follow the signs in Wismar. There's perpetual construction on this road and it's busy as well, so count on a travel time of about 1½ hours.

Getting Around

City buses and trams cost €1.20/3 single/day pass. In summer a ferry circumnavigates the Pfaffenteich (€0.50). You can hire bikes from the **Räder-Center** (☎ 500 7630; Schusterstrasse 3 & Hauptbahnhof).

AROUND SCHWERIN
Ludwigslust
☎ 03874 / pop 12,500

While it can't compete with Schwerin's Schloss, the sturdy **ducal residence** (☎ 571 90; www.schloss-ludwigslust.de; adult/child €3/2; ☽ 10am-6pm Tue-Sun) at Ludwigslust, 36km south, is one of the most popular day trips from the capital. The expansive English-style park gardens and the baroque planned town surrounding them are well worth a visit.

Such was the charm of this place that when the ducal seat moved to Schwerin in 1837, members of the family continued to live here until 1945. In 1986 the palace came under the control of the Schwerin State Museum, and rooms have been renovated one by one since reunification; the stately, gilt-columned, high-ceilinged **Golden Hall** is the unrivalled high point.

In the gardens, the **Café im Schloss** (☎ 219 86; mains €7.10-11.50) overlooks a quiet meadow and offers a good light menu, as well as ice cream and cakes.

Trains run from Schwerin every two hours (€5.50, 30 minutes). To get to the castle from Ludwigslust station, walk south on Bahnhofstrasse to Platz des Friedens, cross the canal to Kanalstrasse and turn right on Schlossstrasse.

GÜSTROW
☎ 03843 / pop 32,000

Some 50km south of Rostock and about 60km from Schwerin is the charming city of Güstrow, which reached the grand old age of 775 in 2003. The city's small but stately Renaissance Schloss, former residence of Herzog Ulrich III and sculptor Ernst Barlach (see boxed text below), still dominates the city. It's definitely worth at least a day trip to view the castle and the Barlach museum.

The city's Markt is at the centre of the Altstadt; the Schloss is southeast, the Dom southwest and the Barlach museum northwest.

Güstrow Information (☎ 681 023; www.guestrow .de; ☽ 9am-6pm Mon-Fri, 9.30am-1pm Sat & Sun, closed Sun Oct-Apr) is at Domstrasse 9.

Sights & Activities

There has been a castle of some sort at Franz-Parr-Platz since 1556; the current **Schloss** (☎ 7520; www.schloss-guestrow.de; adult/ concession €3/2; ☽ 10am-6pm Tue-Sun) was completed in 1599. Today it's a museum with a cultural centre, art exhibitions and occasional concerts. The **Städtisches Museum** also recently relocated to No 10 and should open sometime in 2004.

The Gothic **Dom** (☎ 682 433; www.dom-guest row.de; Philipp-Brandin-Strasse 5), begun around

---

ERNST BARLACH

It's hard to avoid the traces of Güstrow's most famous son, the expressionist sculptor and playwright Ernst Barlach (1870–1938) who spent 28 years here, the majority of his prolific working life. Influenced by the time he spent in Russia, Barlach's strength lay in his deeply empathic portrayals of human suffering, best seen in the blank, blind eyes of his massive, simple sculptures.

Unsurprisingly, this profoundly humanist approach did not sit well with Nazi aesthetics, and 381 of Barlach's works were destroyed during artistic 'purges'. Much of what survived can be seen in Güstrow and in the Ernst Barlach House in Hamburg; sadly the artist himself died at the peak of the ideological frenzy, making the heartfelt message of his legacy all the more poignant.

1225, was eventually completed in the 1860s. It contains one of two copies of Barlach's *Hovering Angel*, made secretly from the original mould after the Nazis destroyed the original; the other now hangs in Cologne. On the Markt, the Renaissance **Rathaus** competes with the towering **Pfarrkirche** for prominence.

Bronze and wood carvings by Ernst Barlach are housed along with a biographical exhibition at his former studio, the **Atelierhaus** (☎ 822 99; www.ernst-barlach-stiftung.de; Heidberg 15; adult/concession €3.50/2.50; ☟ Tue-Sun 10am-5pm Apr-Oct, 11am-4pm Nov-Mar), 4km south of the city at Inselsee (take bus No 204). In town, the memorial in the **Gertrudenkapelle** (☎ 683 001; Gertrudenplatz 1; adult/concession €3/2; ☟ Tue-Sun 10am-5pm Apr-Oct, 11am-4pm Nov-Mar) displays many of his original works.

Getting There & Around
Trains leave for Güstrow once or twice an hour from Rostock's Hauptbahnhof (€4.30, 25 minutes) and hourly from Schwerin (€9.70, one hour). Buses leave for Rostock three times daily.

NEUBRANDENBURG
☎ 0395 / pop 72,000
At the eastern end of the Mecklenburger Seenplatte lies the charming walled city of Neubrandenburg, hugging the Tollensesee some 95km south of Stralsund. Although it's surrounded by modern urban sprawl, the Altstadt dates back to the 13th century and is highly amenable, despite some harsh GDR architecture.

Writer and satirist Fritz Reuter (1810–74) lived for two years in a house (now a café) at Stargarder Strasse 35.

Orientation
The Hauptbahnhof is at the northern end of the Altstadt, and the bus station is 100m west of it. The Altstadt's wall effectively creates the largest roundabout outside Britain; it's circled by Friedrich-Engels-Ring. The best way to see the Altstadt is to walk around the interior wall – while the outside is also nice, the traffic on the ring road can be hellish.

Inside the walls is a grid of north–south and east–west streets with the Marktplatz at its centre. The main shopping street is Turmstrasse, pedestrianised between Stargarder Strasse (the main north–south thoroughfare) and the eastern wall.

Information
Ärztehaus (☎ 544 2266; An der Konzertkirche) Medical services.
Chat Up (☎ 421 2222; Ravensburgerstrasse 3; ☟ daily) Internet access.
Deutsche Bank (☎ 558 80; cnr Treptowerstrasse & Stargarder Strasse)
Main post office (☎ 01802-3333; Marktplatz Center, Markt)
Stadt Info (☎ 194 33; www.neubrandenburg.de; Stargarder Strasse 17; ☟ 10am-7pm Mon-Fri, 10am-6pm Sat) Tourist information.
Vobis (☎ 422 6619; cnr Stargarder Strasse & Neutorstrasse; €1.80 per hr; ☟ 9am-8pm Mon-Fri) Internet access.

Sights
CITY GATES
The city was founded in 1248 by Herbord von Raven, a Mecklenburg knight granted the land by Brandenburg Margrave Johann I, and building progressed in the usual order: defence system, church, town hall, pub. The security system was the enormous stone wall that survives today, with four city gates set into it.

The **Friedländer Tor**, begun in 1300 and completed in 1450, was first. **Treptower Tor**, at the western end of the Altstadt, is the largest, and contains what's billed as the **Regional History Museum** (☎ 555 1271; adult/concession €1/0.50; ☟ 10am-5pm) but is really more of an archaeological collection.

At the southern end of the city is the gaudy **Stargarder Tor**; the simple brick **Neues Tor** fronts the east side of the Altstadt and houses a small exhibition on Fritz Reuter.

CHURCHES
Neubrandenburg's centrepiece was the once-enormous Gothic **Marienkirche** (1270; www.konzertkirche-nb.de; viewing €1), which was seriously damaged in WWII. Since then major portions have been rebuilt, notably the steeple, which crowns a 90m tower. The interior is now a concert hall known as the **Konzertkirche**, and is often open to casual visitors, though it's far more interesting to catch a performance.

Also worth a look is the late-Gothic **Johanniskirche** (begun 1260), with its adjacent **cloister**.

MECKLENBURG-WESTERN POMERANIA

WIEKHÄUSER

The city wall had 56 sentry posts built into its circumference. When firearms rendered such defences obsolete in the 16th century, the guardhouses were converted into *Wiekhäuser*, homes for the poor, people with disabilities and elderly. Some 25 of these remain today, rebuilt with half-timber fronts; most are craft shops, galleries, cafés and the like, while Nos 28 and 49 have been converted into holiday apartments.

FANGELTURM

West of Johanniskirche is the **Fangelturm**, once the city dungeon. Inside you can climb the 74 steps of the very steep and narrow staircase to the top, or just peer down through the grating to see the dungeon. You can get the (free) key from Wiekhaus 11 or the Regional History Museum; at the top, kick the door to break the bird-crap seal and you will get a unique view of a side of the Johanniskirche.

GROSSE WOLLWEBERSTRASSE

The only row of houses to survive WWII lines Grosse Wollweberstrasse in the southwestern section of the city. The must-see house on the street is the very blue one at **No 25**, owned by graphic artist Gerd Frick. When he's home he may give curious visitors a tour.

Further down at No 24 is the new city **Kunstsammlung** (art gallery; ☎ 555 1290; www.kunst sammlung-neubrandenburg.de; adult/concession €3/1.50; ❤ 10am-5pm Tue-Sun), displaying a high-class 20th-century collection.

HAUS DER KULTUR UND BILDUNG

The saving grace of the city's obnoxious GDR-era **Haus der Kultur und Bildung** (House of Culture & Education; ☎ 582 2933; Marktplatz 1; lift €1; ❤ 10am-8pm) is the viewing platform on the roof of the ugly 56m tower, which offers great views of the region on clear days. The top two floors also house a bar and a café.

Neubrandenburg's last **statue of Karl Marx** is in the beer garden adjacent to the building's north side; kids now put ice-cream cones (and sometimes condoms) in the statue's hand.

Activities

If cycling is your thing, the tourist office publishes the *Radwandern* pamphlet, which

details 60 (!) tours around the state. For bike-hire outlets, see Getting Around (p293). Several moderate and clearly marked bicycle routes are near the town; there are cheap overnight accommodation options on routes south of the city.

Walkers can pick up trail maps (€1) and a detailed free pamphlet called *Auf Wanderschaft durch das Neubrandenburger Tollensebecken* at the tourist office.

TOLLENSESEE

In the summer months, people flock to this large lake southwest of the centre for swimming, boating, camping and sunbathing.

The best swimming places are both fun and free: Strandbad Broda at the northwest tip of the lake and Augustabad on the northeastern side. You can hire all kinds of boats from the **Freizeittreff am Kulturpark** (☎ 566 5352; www.freizeittreff-behn.de; Parkstrasse 15; €4.50-20 per hr) at the northern end of the lake.

Sleeping

The **tourist office** (☎ 566 7660) books **private rooms** (d from €25), mostly just outside the Altstadt.

Camping Gatsch-Eck (☎ 566 5152; www.camping -gatsch-eck.de; adult/child €4.50/2.50, car €2, tent €3.50-4.50) Down the western side of the lake, on the edge of Brodaer Wood, this is a simple place with basic facilities.

Hotel Horizont (☎ 569 8428; www.hotelhorizont.de; Otto-von-Guericke-Strasse 7; s/d €46/61; P) Hotel Horizont is in a quiet spot on the edge of town, with well-equipped rooms, pool table and a children's playground.

Hotel St Georg (☎ 544 3788; www.hotel-sankt -georg.de; Sankt Georg 6; s/d/ste €51/62/75; P) Next to the chapel of the same name, this red-brick establishment just west of the city walls is great value, even if the daytime staff aren't over-keen.

Hotel Am Ring (☎ 5560; www.hotel-am-ring.de; Grosse Krauthöferstrasse 1; s/d €70/85; P X) How can you resist a place with a 'panorama sauna'? This multicoloured, multistorey hotel on the ring road isn't exactly easy on the eyes, but the views and facilities make up for it.

Radisson SAS (☎ 558 60; Treptower Strasse 1; s €77-89, d €92-104; P X X) On the Markt, this top-end place makes the best of its GDR shell, even adding a touch of colour to the square. Wheelchair access and some not-

-patronising-as-they-sound 'Lady Rooms'
re available.

ating

or Café (☎ 584 1132; Friedländer Tor; food €3-7) The
or has a very comfortable atmosphere,
ub food and friendly staff.

Café im Reuterhaus (☎ 582 3245; Stargarder
rasse 35; mains €7.70-11.80) In the daytime, come
ere for light meals, snacks and soups; when
closes, the smoky but cosy *bierstube* next
oor swings into action.

Le Coq (☎ 544 1218; Turmstrasse 14; mains €6.60-
3.10) One of a bundle of options on Turm-
trasse, this bar-restaurant is not even
aguely French, but the varied bistro dishes
re good anyway.

Fürstenkeller (☎ 569 1991; Stargarder Strasse 37;
mains €7.90-13.50) This lovely old place has
aulted ceilings and good regional dishes,
ncluding vegetarian options.

Wiekhaus 45 (☎ 566 7762; 4th Ringstrasse 44; mains
€6.20-15.80; ☒ 11.30am-2pm, 5-9.30pm) This is a
ovely example of a renovated guardhouse,
with tasty food and athletic servers who zip
up and down narrow staircases.

Drinking

Piste, the local edition of *Fritz*, has a cultural
calendar and club and pub listings. *lespress*
is a good local magazine for lesbians.

Kelly's Irish Pub (☎ 582 6005; Turmstrasse 28)
Less cod-Irish than some, Kelly's is good for
live music and proper toasted sandwiches.

Konsulat (☎ 544 2579; Jahnstrasse 12) Bands
at this well-hidden basement venue play
mostly jazz, blues and rock.

Alter Schlachthof (☎ 582 2391; Rostocker Strasse
33) A great crowd of all ages congregates at
this club in a former abattoir, with several
dance floors and a couple of restaurants.

Colosseum (☎ 778 2105; www.colosseum-disco.de;
Hochstrasse 4; ☒ Tue, Fri & Sat) The Colosseum attracts a young, practically teenage crowd.

Initiative Rosa-Lila (☎ 194 46; Friedländer Strasse
14; ☐) This gay and lesbian centre has all
the info on where to go.

Entertainment

Latücht (☎ 544 2570; www.latuecht.de; Grosse Krauthöferstrasse 16) For an alternative to the multiplex
diet at the local CineStar, try this offbeat art
house screen in a former church hall.

Schauspielhaus (☎ 569 9832; Pfaffenstrasse) You
can catch varied performances on the lively

stage or just take a break in the conservatory
café at this place, founded in 1770.

Getting There & Away

Trains leave every two hours for Berlin-Zoo
(€20.80, two hours) via Neustrelitz. There
are hourly services to/from Rostock (€17,
2¼ hours, via Güstrow) and Stralsund
(€12.40, 1¼ hours).

By road from Berlin take the A10 northwest to Neuruppin, then head east towards
Löwenberg, where you catch the B96 north;
follow the signs for Stralsund. From Stralsund or Greifswald, head south on the
B96. From Rostock, take the A19 south to
Güstrow then follow the B104 east all the
way. Parking is tricky in Neubrandenburg's
Altstadt.

Getting Around

Bike-hire outlets include **Fahrradhaus Lef-
fin** (☎ 581 660; Friedrich-Engels-Ring 22) and the
Freizeittreff am Kulturpark (☎ 566 5352; www.freiz
eittreff-behn.de; Parkstrasse 15).

AROUND NEUBRANDENBURG

South and west of the city lies a wonderful
region of wilderness that's great for day
trips, hikes or biking. Most people stay in
Neubrandenburg, although there's camping in Müritz National Park and small
guesthouses here and there.

Penzlin

☎ 03962 / pop 2600

The main attractions at Penzlin, 15km
southwest of Neubrandenburg, are its witch
museum and generally weird atmosphere.
Parts of the city feel as if you've just walked
into a black-and-white WWII movie. Penzlin's sights can easily be seen in an hour.

The **Hexenkeller** (☎ 210 494; Alte Burg; adult/
concession €3/2; ☒ 9am-5pm Tue-Fri, 10am-5pm Sat &
Sun May-Oct, 10am-1pm Tue & Wed, 1pm-4pm Sat & Sun
Nov-Apr) has displays on the Penzliner witch-
hunts of the late-17th century, and is worth
a look. The museum is in the old **Burg**, a
castle three minutes' walk from the town's
main Markt.

Bus No 012 from Neubrandenburg to
Waren stops in Penzlin.

By car, take the B104 west out of Neubrandenburg and turn south on the B192,
which leads into the Markt. There's parking
at the Alte Burg.

Ankershagen

☎ 039921 / pop 400

Ancient-history buffs should visit this tiny town's **Heinrich-Schliemann-Museum** (☎ 3252; www.schliemann-museum.de; Lindenallee 1; ⊙ 10am-5pm Tue-Sun), dedicated to the brilliant but controversial archaeologist who discovered the legendary ruins of Troy and Mycenae. As well as the biographical stuff, there's a 6m-high Trojan horse in the grounds.

Ankershagen is a few kilometres south of the Penzlin–Waren Rd (B192); the turn-off is about 12km west of Penzlin. Ankershagen is served by bus No 019 from Penzlin and No 039 from Waren.

MÜRITZ NATIONAL PARK

The two main sections of lovely Müritz National Park sprawl over 300 sq km to the east and (mainly) west of the lakeside town of Neustrelitz, about 20km south of Penzlin. Declared a protected area in 1990, the park consists of bog and wetlands, and is home to a wide range of waterfowl, including ospreys, white-tailed eagles and cranes. It has more than 100 lakes and countless other ponds, streams and rivers; dedicated boaters can make it all the way from here to Hamburg! Working with a good set of maps from the park rangers, you can do a paddle-and-camp trip between Neustrelitz and Waren, a busy museum town on Lake Müritz at the park's western end.

Orientation & Information

The park's waterway begins on the Zierker See, west of Neustrelitz. The main information centre is the **Nationalparkamt** (National Park Office; ☎ 039824-2520; www.nationalpark-mueritz .de; Schlossplatz 3, Hohenzieritz).

Tourist offices, hostels and camp sites in the area have trail and park maps, and also sell day passes giving you unlimited bus travel in the park, including bicycle transport (adult/concession €6.50/3) or a combination bus/boat pass (€13/6).

Activities

The national park office arranges regular tours and excursions throughout the park, some led by rangers. Hiking is permitted on marked trails.

Haveltourist (☎ 03981-247 90; www.haveltourist .de) operates camp sites throughout the park (see Sleeping, following), and also hires out

kayaks from €5/15 per hour/day. Rowi boats (€3/25), and sail and motorbo (from €11/50) are available from **Santa Yachting** (☎ 03981-205 896) at the eastern e of the Zierker See.

Sleeping

You must use designated camp sites, which there are over a dozen within t park, including two FKK (naturist) sit Rates at Haveltourist sites start at €3.6 2.30 per tent plus €4.40/2.40 per person high/low season.

COASTAL MECKLENBURG-WESTERN POMERANIA

ROSTOCK

☎ 0381 / pop 199,000

Rostock, the largest city in sparsely pop lated northeastern Germany, is a maj Baltic port and shipbuilding centre. Fi mentioned in 1161 as a Danish settleme the city began taking shape as a Germ fishing village around 1200. In the 14 and 15th centuries, Rostock was an impo tant Hanseatic trading city; parts of the c centre, especially along Kröpeliner Stras retain the flavour of this period.

As a major shipbuilding and shippi centre, the city was devastated in WW and later pummelled by socialist archite tural 'ideas'; the old city is surrounded I eyesores thrown up to house dock wor ers along the Warnow River. Howeve Rostock's uncompetitive shipyards a being replaced by industries like biotec fostered by the city's venerable universit and the whole character of the city remai upbeat.

Rostock hosted the *Internationale Ga tenausstellung* (IGA; International Gard Show) in 2003, giving the local touri industry a massive boost and raising t international profile of a city often ju thought of as a port. Many of the centr pretty gabled structures have been spruc up, the general infrastructure is excelle and the nightlife is the busiest in the state it's definitely worth spending some tin here.

rientation

he city begins at the Südstadt (southern ity), south of the Hauptbahnhof, and xtends north as far as the Warnemünde istrict on the Baltic Sea. Much of the ity is on the western side of the Warnow iver, which creates a long shipping chan-el from the Altstadt practically due north o the sea.

The Altstadt is an oval area approximately .5km north of the recently revamped Hauptbahnhof. Rosa-Luxemburg-Strasse uns north from the station to Steintor, which unofficially marks the southern oundary of the Altstadt; the northern side f the Altstadt slopes handsomely down to-vards the Warnow inlet, while the western oundary is Kröpeliner Tor.

The airport, Flughafen Rostock-Laage, is bout 30km south of town.

nformation

OOKSHOPS
niversitätsbuchhandlung Thalia (☎ 492 2603; reite Strasse 15-17; 🖳)

ISCOUNT CARDS
ombined museums ticket (€8)
ostock Card (48 hours €8) Unlimited bus/tram trans-ort, discounts for many sights.

NTERNET ACCESS
as Netz (☎ 490 0270; das-netz@q-dial.de; rubenstrasse 49; €2 per hr; 🕑 2-8pm Tue-Thu & Sun, om-midnight Fri & Sat)
iek Ut (Am Hauptbahnhof; €2.50 per hr)
urf Inn (☎ 375 6216; Galeria Kaufhof, Lange Strasse; 1 per 15 min)
reffpunkt Café (☎ 643 8062; www.e-treffpunkt.de; m Vögenteich 23; 🕑 9am-8pm Mon-Fri) 20 minutes free ith any order.

IBRARIES
tadtbibliothek (☎ 381 2840; Kröpeliner Strasse 82)

MEDICAL SERVICES
rztehaus (☎ 456 1622; Paulstrasse 48)
linikum Süd (☎ 440 10; Südring)

MONEY
itibank (☎ 459 0081; Kröpeliner Strasse)
ostbank (Neuer Markt 3-8) In the main post office.

OST
ain post office (Neuer Markt 3-8)

TOURIST INFORMATION
Tourist-Information (☎ 381 2222; www.rostock.de; Neuer Markt 3; 🕑 10am-7pm Mon-Fri, 10am-4pm Sat & Sun)

TRAVEL AGENCIES
Atlas Reisewelt (☎ 3800; www.atlasreisen.de; Lange Strasse 38)
Zimmerbörse (☎ 454 444; www.zimmerboerse.de; Reisecenter Delphini, Lange Strasse 19) Books rooms and package tours.

Sights
MARIENKIRCHE
Rostock's pride and joy is the 13th-century **Marienkirche** (☎ 453 325; Am Ziegenmarkt; admission €1; 🕑 10am-5pm Mon-Sat, 11.15am-noon Sun), built in 1290, which was the only one of Rostock's four main churches to survive WWII unscathed. The long north–south transept was added after the ceiling collapsed in 1398.

The 12m-high **astrological clock** (1470–72), hand-wound every morning, is behind the main altar. At the very top are a series of doors; at noon and midnight the innermost right door opens and six of the 12 apostles march out to parade around Jesus (note that Judas is locked out). The lower section has a disc that tells the day, the date and the exact day on which Easter falls in any given year. The discs are replaceable and accurate for 130 years; the current one expires in 2017, and the university already has a new one ready.

Other highlights include the Gothic bronze **baptismal font** (1290), the **baroque organ** (1770) and, on the northern side of the main altar, some fascinating tombstones in the floor. Ascend the 207 steps of the 50m-high church tower for the view.

Just behind the Marienkirche is the ornate Renaissance doorway of the former **city mint**, now a bank branch.

KRÖPELINER STRASSE & UNIVERSITÄTSPLATZ
Kröpeliner Strasse, a broad, lively, cobblestone pedestrian mall lined with 15th- and 16th-century burghers' houses, runs from Neuer Markt west to Kröpeliner Tor.

At the centre of the mall is **Universitätsplatz**, positively swarming with people year-round, and its centrepiece, the crazy rococo **Brunnen der Lebensfreude** (Fountain

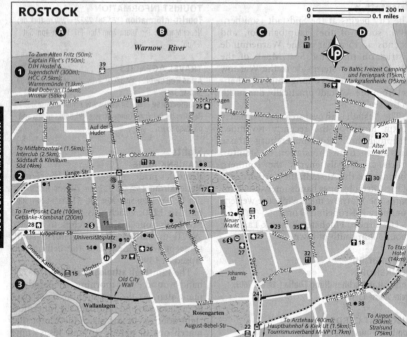

ROSTOCK

of Happiness). True to its name, the square is lined with university buildings, including the handsome terracotta **Hauptgebäude** (1866–70), which replaced the famous 'White College'. The university itself is the oldest on the Baltic (founded 1419), and currently has about 11,000 students.

At the south side of the square stands an impressive bronze **statue** of Field Marshal Blücher of Wahlstatt, Rostock's most beloved military hero, who helped defeat Napoleon at Waterloo. On the statue's rear is a poem by Goethe, and on the other side a relief depicting the battle at Waterloo.

At the northern side of Universitätsplatz are the **Five-Gables Houses**, modern interpretations of the residences that lined the square before WWII.

At the southwestern end of Universitätsplatz is the **Kloster Zum Heiligen Kreuz**, a convent established in 1270 by Queen Margrethe of Denmark. Today it houses the **Cultural History Museum** (☎ 203 590; Klosterhof 18; adult/concession €3/1.50; ☉ 9am-6pm Tue-Sun), with an excellent collection including Victorian furniture and sculptures by Ernst Barlach.

A combined ticket with the Kröpeliner To costs €4.50.

CITY WALLS & GATES
Today only two gates (at one time ther were 32) and a small brick section remain of the old city wall. The **Steintor**, at th southern end of the Altstadt, is surrounde by tram tracks. Its Latin inscription mean 'Within these walls, let unity and genera prosperity prevail'.

West of Steintor is **Wallstrasse**, which lead to the biggest surviving part of the *Wallan lagen* (city walls). From here, you can stro west through the pleasant park south of the wall to reach the 55m-high **Kröpeliner To** containing the city's **Regional History Museum** (☎ 454 177; adult/concession €3/1.50; ☉ 10am-6pm Wed Sun). The top floor is dedicated to the GDI days, and includes a leather jacket given t GDR supremo Erich Honecker in 1980 b West German rocker Udo Lindenberg.

NEUER MARKT
The splendid and rather pink 13th-centur **Rathaus** is at the eastern side of this ope

INFORMATION
Atlas Reisewelt...............................1 A2
Citibank...2 A2
Das Netz..3 C2
Stadtbibliothek...............................4 B2
Surf Inn..5 B2
Tourist-Information..........................6 C3
Universitätsbuchhandlung Thalia.........7 B2
Zimmerbörse..................................8 B2

SIGHTS & ACTIVITIES   (pp295-7)
Blücher Statue.................................9 A3
Brunnen der Lebensfreude................10 B3
Five-Gables Houses.........................11 A2
Fountain.......................................12 C2
Gabled Houses...............................13 C2
Hauptgebäude................................14 A3
Kloster Zum Heiligen Kreuz & Cultural History Museum...15 A3
Kröpeliner Tor & Regional History Museum...16 A3
Marienkirche.................................17 B2
Nikolaikirche.................................18 D3
Old Mint......................................19 B2
Petrikirche....................................20 D2
Rathaus & Ratskeller.......................21 C2
Schiffahrtsmuseum..........................22 C3
Slüter..(see 20)
State Archives................................23 C2
Steintor.......................................24 C3

SLEEPING   (pp297-8)
City-Pension..................................25 B1
Courtyard by Marriott......................26 B3
Hotel Kleine Sonne..........................27 C3
Radisson SAS................................28 A2
Steigenberger Hotel Sonne................29 C3

EATING   (p298)
Albert & Emile...............................30 C1
Hanse Center................................31 C1
Krahnstöver Likörfabrik....................32 C3
Tre Kronor...................................33 B2
Zur Kogge....................................34 B1

DRINKING   (pp298-9)
Farelli's......................................35 C2
Hemingway..................................36 D1
Studentenkeller..............................37 B3

TRANSPORT   (pp299-300)
Joyride.......................................38 D3
Rostocker Personenschiffahrt Quay......39 A1

OTHER
Galeria Kaufhof.............................(see 5)
Rostocker Hof...............................40 B3

square, which is just north of the Steintor. The baroque façade was added in 1727 after the original brick Gothic structure collapsed. Hermann Henselmann, the architect of the building's northern annexe, was a GDR favourite; his works grace other eastern German cities with equal delicacy. Just behind the Rathaus is the intricate Gothic building housing the state archives.

Opposite the Rathaus is a lovely series of restored gabled houses and a stylised sea-themed fountain (2001) by artist Waldemar Otto. The explanatory plaque says the four figures around it are Neptune and his sons, although locals seem to think they represent the four elements. The northern end of the square leads to the Marienkirche.

SCHIFFFAHRTSMUSEUM
Rostock's good **Maritime Museum** (☎ 252 060; August-Bebel-Strasse 1; adult/concession €3/1.50; ✆ 10am-6pm Tue-Sun), on the corner of Richard-Wagner-Strasse near the Steintor, has displays on the history of Baltic navigation.

PETRIKIRCHE & AROUND
The Gothic **Petrikirche** (☎ 211 01; Alter Markt; tower entry €2; ✆ 10am-5pm) has a 117m-high steeple – a mariner's landmark for centuries – that was restored in 1994, having been missing since WWII. You can climb the steps or take the lift up to the viewing platform.

Next door, the **Slüter monument** honours Joachim Slüter, a reformer who preached in the *Niederdeutsch* (Low German) dialect outside the church. Three blocks south is the **Nikolaikirche**, Rostock's oldest church.

Tours
The tourist office runs 90-minute guided tours (€4) at 2pm daily in summer (11am Sunday). English-language tours can be arranged for groups. You can also cruise round the harbour on a boat from **Rostocker Personenschiffahrt** (☎ 686 3172, 0172-405 3861; rostockerpersonenschiffahrt@t-online.de), or float over the surrounding countryside with **Ostsee-Ballooning** (☎ 458 3858; www.ostsee-ballooning.de) or **Happy Air** (☎ 038201-202; www.happyair.de).

Festivals & Events
Annually, from June to September, the **Festspiele Mecklenburg-Vorpommern** (☎ 0385-591 8585; www.festspiele-mv.de), a classical music festival, is held at various venues in town and throughout the region.

The second weekend in August, **Hanse Sail Rostock** (☎ 208 5233; www.hansesail.com) is the biggest of the city's many regattas, bringing countless sailing ships to the city and Warnemünde harbours.

Sleeping
Rostock's accommodation capacity has not entirely caught up with the demand surrounding the garden show, the IGA; book in advance for summer, particularly at weekends. The tourist office can book good-value **private rooms** (from €15). Head down to the city harbour for two of Germany's more interesting offerings, the DJH hostel and Jugendschiff.

DJH hostel (☎ 670 0320; ms-georg-buechner@t-online.de; Am Stadthafen 72-3; dm juniors/seniors €17/20, s/d €27.50/50) This is on board the 1950s Belgian cargo ship MS *Georg Büchner*, the hostel offers hostel-style dorms as well as spacious standard rooms and an amazing wood-panelled dining room.

Jugendschiff (☎ 495 8107; r €52-62) In the next berth to the DJH hostel, the Jugendschiff is a much smaller boat with some nice doubles.

baltic-Freizeit Camping- und Ferienpark (☎ 04 544-800 313; www.baltic-freizeit.de; Dünenweg 27, Markgrafenheide; sites €9-28) On the east side of the Warnow River, this is an enormous city-run affair with 1200 pitches. Take tram No 4 to Dierkower Kreuz, then bus No 18 (45 minutes).

Etap Hotel (☎ 038204-122 22; Am Handelspark 5, Broderstorf; s/d €37/44; P ✗ ✗) About 8km east of the Altstadt, this is a great budget option if you have a car.

City-Pension (☎ 252 260; Krönkenhagen 3; s €44-55, d €66-88; P) A small family pension occupying a lovely quiet street near the harbour, in the heart of the old-fashioned northern Altstadt.

Hotel Kleine Sonne (☎ 497 3153; www.die-kleine-sonne.de; Steinstrasse 7; s/d €79/99; P ▢) The 'budget' offshoot of the fancier Hotel Sonne across the street, this is actually an excellent place in its own right, with a very modern style and art by Nils Ausländer dotted around.

Courtyard by Marriott (☎ 497 00; courtyard-hotel-rostock@t-online.de; Schwaansche Strasse 6; s €109-140, d €121-152; P ✗ ✗) Connecting to the Rostocker Hof shopping centre on Kröpeliner Strasse, the Courtyard has great service, a historic building and plenty of frills.

Steigenberger Hotel Sonne (☎ 497 30; info@hotel-sonne-rostock.de; Neuer Markt 2; s €110-129, d €132-159; P ✗ ▢) The Kleine Sonne's daddy is an elegant hotel with contemporary gabled façade, posh, modern rooms and a prestigious location, not to mention a clutch of classy restaurants.

Radisson SAS (Kröpeliner Strasse) This new top-end Altstadt option was somewhat optimistically due to open in May 2004.

Eating

Krahnstöver Likörfabrik (☎ 4377 7654; Grubenstrasse 1; mains €5-8) Rostock's oldest family-run wine merchants owns this multifaceted bistro/bar/café, next to an artificial stream near the city wall and the Nikolaikirche. They also have a brasserie in the Hotel Sonne.

Zur Kogge (☎ 493 4493; Wokrenterstrasse 27; mains €8-14.50) Like most fishy restaurants here this very good seafood place comes with plenty of boat-related ephemera, but the life preservers on the walls certainly outdo the competition.

Captain Flint's (☎ 252 4763; Warnowufer 64a; mains €9-16) The swashbuckling theme at the Captain's is so over the top you're almost embarrassed for the staff, but it's fun to look at and the tiered waterfront terraces are great.

Tre Kronor (Hansepassage, Lange Strasse; mains €7.50-16) Set in a strange split-level glass-fronted pillar box at the back of a shopping centre, the Three Crowns serves up good interesting Swedish dishes, including the classic elk steak.

Zum Alten Fritz (☎ 208 780; Warnowufer 65; mains €8-17) One of four establishments in an expanding local brewery chain, this is a big pub-restaurant down on the docks with a good range of standards, plus organic meats and specials like turkey in beer.

Albert & Emile (☎ 493 4373; Altschmiedestrasse 28; mains €12.50-17) Up the road from the Petrikirche, an ivy-covered façade conceals this very posh French restaurant, which offers some of Rostock's finest haute cuisine.

The quayside Hanse Center has a couple of international restaurants and is the best place in town to catch sunset over the harbour.

Drinking

The city puts out a free quarterly pamphlet *Die Stadt erleben*, listing everything from car repairs to concerts and events. *Szene* and *Piste* are the main free monthlies, geared predominantly towards music. The gay and lesbian organisation **Rat+Tat** (☎ 453 156; www.schwules-rostock.de) is very active; check www.hansegay.de or the *Homo Scout* calendar for general listings.

Getränke-Kombinat (☎ 200 3745; Doberaner Strasse 6) Intimate bar with a quiet rear garden and a huge range of absinthe, hosting stand-up and barbecues as well as DJs.

Hemingway (☎ 492 2424; Faule Strasse 13) A touch of Caribbean flavour just off the ring road.

Farelli's (☎ 490 7111; Grubenstrasse 6) One for the beautiful people, it's cocktails and whisky all the way in this club lounge.

Studentenkeller (☎ 455 928; Universitätsplatz 5; ☺ Tue-Sat) This cellar and garden joint has been rocking Rostock's learned youth for years.

HCC/Halle 600 (☎ 207 6340; Industriestrasse 10, Evershagen) The Holiday City Centre is a huge leisure complex north of the centre, with big club nights on weekends.

Interclub (☎ 377 8737; Erich-Schlesinger-Strasse 19a, Südstadt) Serious dance music of various shades and flavours.

Getting There & Away

AIR
Rostock-Laage (☎ 038454-313 39; www.rostock-airport .de) is served by an increasing number of national and international airlines, with regular services to Nuremberg, Munich, Hamburg, Düsseldorf and Palma de Mallorca.

BOAT
Several ferry companies operate out of Rostock, chiefly **Scandlines** (☎ 673 1217; www.scand lines.de) and **TT-Line** (☎ 670 790; www.tt-line.de) to Denmark and Sweden. Boats depart from the seaport on the east side of the Warnow; take tram No 4 to Dierkower Kreuz, then change for bus No 19 or 20.

Scandlines runs at least seven daily ferries to Gedser, Denmark (car €62 to €84, walk-on passengers €5 to €8, two hours) and three to Trelleborg in Sweden (car €95 to €135, walk-on €15 to €20, cabins €31 to €90, 5¾ hours). Prices depend on time, day and season.

TT-Line also sails to/from Trelleborg four times daily, completing the crossing in as little as 5½ hours. The complicated tariffs vary according to the number of people and the date of travel; a tourist car with up to five people costs between €98 and €189, while walk-ons pay €18 to €30.

A third company, **Silja Line** (☎ 350 4350; www .silja.com), sails to/from Helsinki via Tallinn three times a week from June to early September (car from €100, adult seat €67 to 87, cabins from €328; 24 hours).

BUS
Buses run to most major (and minor) destinations in the region, but as elsewhere they're seldom a better option than the trains.

CAR & MOTORCYCLE
To reach Rostock from Berlin, head north or south out of the city to the A10. Follow it

northwest to the A24, which leads straight into the A19 running directly north to Rostock (2½ hours). From Neubrandenburg, take the B104 west to the A19 and turn north (1½ hours).

You can hire cars from local chain **Joyride** (☎ 776 210; www.joyride.de; Bleicherstrasse). For a lift, get in touch with the **Mitfahrzentrale** (☎ 194 40; Goethestrasse 8).

TRAIN
There are frequent direct trains to Rostock from Berlin (€29.60, three hours) and hourly services to Stralsund (€10.70, 70 minutes), Wismar (€8.10, 1¼ hours) and Schwerin (€12.40, one hour).

Getting Around

TO/FROM THE AIRPORT
Bus Nos 116 and 127 run to Flughafen Rostock-Laage (€4), about 30km south of town. A taxi should cost around €36.

BICYCLE
Cycling isn't much fun in the centre because of heavy traffic, but things quickly improve outside the city. You can hire bicycles from the **RadStation** (☎ 252 3990), outside the Hauptbahnhof. In Warnemünde, try **Reinhard Bergmann** (☎ 519 1955; Am Leuchtturm 16).

CAR & MOTORCYCLE
With complicated one-way systems, confusing street layouts and dedicated parking-ticket police, Rostock is not a driver-friendly city. There are several convenient parking lots off Lange Strasse.

PUBLIC TRANSPORT
Journeys within Rostock city, including Warnemünde, cost €1.40/2.80 for a single/day pass, valid on the Warnow ferries as well as land transport. The surrounding area is zoned; a single/day pass costs €1.20/2.40 for one zone or €4.30/8.60 for all zones.

Tram Nos 2, 11 and 12 travel from the Hauptbahnhof up Steinstrasse, around Marienkirche and down Lange Strasse. Take tram No 11 or 12 to get from the Hauptbahnhof to the university.

TAXI
Basic hire is €2, plus a varying per kilometre rate; prices actually go down at night! From Warnemünde to the Hauptbahnhof

will set you back about €13.50. Ring **Hanse-Taxi** (☎ 685 858).

AROUND ROSTOCK
Warnemünde
☎ 0381 / pop 6600

Warnemünde, at the mouth of the War-now River on the Baltic Sea just north of Rostock, is among eastern Germany's most popular beach resorts. It's hard to see it as a small fishing village these days, but the boats still bring in their catches and some charming streets and buildings persist amid the tourist clutter.

ORIENTATION & INFORMATION

The train station is at the eastern end of town, east of the Alter Strom, the main canal on which all the fishing and tour boats moor. To the east of the train station is the Neuer Strom, across which is the Hohe Düne and the camp site at Markgrafenheide.

The main action takes place on the promenade along Seestrasse, which fronts dunes and a wide, surprisingly white beach. The town's main drags are Am Strom (the walkway along the Alter Strom) and Kirchenstrasse, which leads west from the bridge over the Strom to Kirchenplatz and finally on to Mühlenstrasse, which is lined with cafés, shops and cheap bistros.

The **tourist office** (☎ 548 000; www.warnemuende .de; Am Strom 59; ⊗ 10am-7pm Mon-Fri, 10am-4pm Sat & Sun) is in the historic Vogtei building.

There's a Reisebank by the station, an **SB-Waschsalon** (☎ 510 7170; Heinrich-Heine-Strasse 13) with café and play area in the centre, and an **Internet café** (Am Bahnhof) in the Baltic Point building.

SIGHTS

Am Strom is a picturesque street lined with quaint fishers' cottages. Just south of Kirchenstrasse, the church and the main square is the **Heimatmuseum** (Local History Museum; ☎ 526 67; Alexandrinenstrasse 31; adult/concession €3/1; ⊗ 10am-6pm Tue-Sun) in a converted fishers' cottage.

Restaurants (some quite touristy) and shops line the inlet on the west side, while boats moored at the quay sell fish and rolls or offer cruises (around €6, weather permitting).

The crowded **seafront promenade** to the north is where the tourists congregate. Warnemünde's broad, sandy beach stretches west from the **lighthouse** (1898) and the Tee-pott exhibition centre, and is chock-a-block with bathers on hot summer days.

SLEEPING

For private rooms, contact the tourist office or **Warnemünde Zimmervermittlung & Reisedienst** (☎ 0700-9276 3683; www.zimmervermittlung -wde.m-vp.de; Am Bahnhof 1; d €26-70). Some insist on a two- or three-night minimum stay in summer.

DJH hostel (☎ 548 170; jh-warnemuende@djh-mv .de; Parkstrasse 47; juniors/seniors €20/24; ℗ 🖳) This shiny new hostel opened in 2001 on the far western side of town, near Diedrichshagen.

Antik-Pension Birnbom (☎ 548 160; www.birn bom.de; Alexandrinenstrasse 30; s €35-50, d €60-80; 🗙) Lovers of antiques and gourmet home cooking should check straight into this lovely family guesthouse, which also offers painting courses, fishing and bike hire.

Hotel am Alten Strom (☎ 548 230; www.hotel -am-alten-strom.de; Am Strom 60; s €55-60, d €72-85; ℗ 🗙 🖳) Privately owned but ambitious, this big, well-equipped place right opposite the station is a serious mid-range spa contender.

Strand-Hotel Hübner (☎ 543 40; www.hotel-hueb ner.de; Seestrasse 12; s €115-160, d €140-185; ℗ 🗙) A stylish modern hotel with a library Kamin stube (open hearth room), two restaurants and lots of natural light. First-floor rooms have the best balconies.

Hotel Neptun (☎ 777 7777; www.hotel-neptun.de; Seestrasse 19; s €91-148, d €150-206; ℗ 🗙 🖳) Ugly but unrivalled for amenities, every single room here has a great view of the beach.

EATING

Smoked-fish fans will be in heaven here, as many of the boats lining the Alter Strom smoke their catches on site and sell them cheaply.

Café Twee Linden (☎ 516 77; Am Strom 185; main €8.20-14.50) This is a cosy but sophisticated harbourside place.

Salsarico (☎ 519 3565; Am Leuchtturm 15; main €7.90-15.90) This lively Mexican is also popular as a scene cocktail bar in the evenings and has sister branches in Rostock and Stralsund.

Fischerklause (☎ 525 16; Am Strom 123; main €9-15.10) Hungry? Try the DIY Steuerrad ('steering wheel', €21.50) at this well-respected restaurant: a whopping 300g of freshly smoked fish with bread, fried potatoes and a local *digestif*.

GETTING THERE & AWAY
The double-decker S-Bahn has frequent services to Rostock (€1.40); some continue to Güstrow (€4.30) or Berlin (€30.80).

Bad Doberan
☎ 038203 / pop 11,600
About 15km west of Rostock lies the former summer ducal residence of Bad Doberan, once the site of a powerful Cistercian monastery. It has an impressive Münster (church), horse races in July and August and is the starting point for the Molli Schmalspurbahn, a popular narrow-gauge steam train.

The town's racecourse is also the unlikely venue for the **Zappanale** (☎ 598 207; www.arf -society.de), Germany's only Frank Zappa festival, which has been held here every July since 1989 and now attracts audiences of up to 3000, as well as several of the great man's former bandmates. In 2002 a Zappa **memorial** was erected in the centre of town amid much psychedelic rejoicing.

The **tourist office** (☎ 915 30; www.bad-doberan .de; Alexandrinenplatz 2) is five minutes' walk from the train station.

MÜNSTER
On the eastern side of town is the **Münster** (☎ 627 16; Klosterstrasse 2; adult/concession €1.50/1; tour adult €2.50-4, concession €2-3; ☺ 9am-6pm Mon-Sat, 11.30am-6pm Sun, closed Mon Nov-Feb), a stunning brick Gothic hall church typical of northern Germany. Its chief treasures include a lovely high altar and an ornate pulpit. The rest of the monastery complex and grounds, parts of which held IGA 2003 garden and art exhibitions, is currently being renovated and should soon fill up with craft shops, galleries, cafés and the like.

MOLLI SCHMALSPURBAHN
'Molli', as she's affectionately known, began huffing and puffing her way to fashionable Heiligendamm in 1886 for the likes of Duke Friedrich Franz I. Today it's operated by Mecklenburger Bäderbahn (☎ 4150) and also services **Kühlungsborn**, a Baltic resort full of lovely Art Deco buildings.

Trains depart from Bad Doberan's Hauptbahnhof up to 10 times a day; there's

a bar car on some journeys and the scenery is lovely. The journey takes 10 minutes to Heiligendamm (single/return €3/5) and 40 minutes to Kühlungsborn (€5/9). Concessions and family fares are also available.

GETTING THERE & AWAY
Trains serve Rostock Hauptbahnhof (€2.40, 25 minutes) and Wismar (€5.50, 45 minutes) roughly hourly. By car, take the B105 towards Wismar.

WISMAR
☎ 03841 / pop 46,500
Wismar, about halfway between Rostock and Lübeck, joined the powerful Hanseatic trading league in the 13th century – the first town east of Lübeck to do so. For centuries the town was in and out of Swedish control, and traces of that rule can still be seen, particularly in the colourful 'Swedish heads' once used to indicate navigable channels into the harbour and now copied all over town. Quieter than Rostock or Stralsund, Wismar can still fill up with visitors pretty quickly in high season; it's definitely worth an overnight stay, and is also the gateway to Poel Island, a lovely little piece of green to the north.

Orientation
The Altstadt is the city centre, built up around the Markt, which is said to be the largest medieval town square in northern Germany. The Bahnhof is at the northeastern corner of the Altstadt and the Alter Hafen port is at the northwestern corner; a canal runs from Alter Hafen almost due east across the northern half of the Altstadt. The streets around the Markt are pedestrianised and the main night-time entertainment area is around Alter Hafen.

Information
Klinikum Friedenshof (☎ 330; Friedrich-Wolf-Strasse) Medical services.
Main post office (Mecklenburger Strasse)
Tourist-Information (☎ 251 3025; www.wismar.de; Am Markt 11; ☺ 9am-6pm)

Sights
MARKT
Wismar's **gabled houses** on the Markt have been lovingly restored; the interiors are near original. The **Rathaus** (1817–19) is at

the square's northern end. Its basement houses an excellent **Historical Exhibition** (adult/concession €1/0.50; ☺ 10am-6pm), with displays including an original 15th-century *Wandmalerei* (mural) recently uncovered by archaeologists, maps and models of the city, and a glass-covered medieval well – stand over it if you dare.

Alter Schwede, at the southeastern side of the Markt, has a characteristic brick Gothic façade and is now home to one of the city's most popular restaurants. In front is the **Wasserkunst** (waterworks), an ornate, 12-sided well completed in 1602, which supplied the town's drinking water until 1897.

Busy **markets** (☺ 8am-6pm Tue-Thu, 8am-1pm Sat) are held on the Markt. On Saturday, a lively fish market takes place at Alter Hafen.

CHURCHES

Wismar was a target for Anglo-American bombers just a few weeks before the end of WWII. Of the three great red-brick churches that once rose above the rooftops, only the **St-Nikolai-Kirche** (1381-1487; €1; ☺ 8am-8pm May-Sep, 10am-6pm Apr & Oct, 11am-4pm Nov-Mar), containing a font from its older sister church, the St-Marien-Kirche, was left intact.

The massive red shell of **St-Georgen-Kirche** is being restored for use as a church, concert hall and exhibition space, and was partially opened in 2002 (completion by 2010). In 1945 a freezing populace was driven to burn what was left of the church's beautiful wooden statue of St George and the dragon.

Cars now park where the 13th-century **St-Marien-Kirche** once stood, although its great brick steeple (1339), now partly restored, still towers above the city. Its base houses occasional art exhibits.

The 14th-century Gothic **Heiligen-Geist-Kirche**, in the courtyard west of the Markt, is a concert venue in summer (enter from Neustadt). The courtyard also houses the city **Music School**.

KITTCHEN & FÜRSTENHOF

Just west of the Marienkirche is the city's juvenile detention centre, also called the *Kittchen*, or 'clink'. Across the street from it is the prison restaurant and pool hall, decorated with cartoon prisoners laugh-

---

BLOOD AND WATER

Wismar is not exactly Hollywood, but it does have some resonance for German filmmakers: the town notably provided a backdrop for the award-winning 1987 TV adaptation of Alfred Andersch's novel *Sansibar oder der letzte Grund*, the story of a group of people in a small Baltic village in 1939 dreaming of fleeing to the African island of Zanzibar to escape the Nazi regime. Themed tours from the tourist office take you round some of the Wismar locations used.

The tradition started, however, with FW Murnau's classic expressionist vampire film *Nosferatu* (1922) – while the story is set in the port town of Bremen, much of it was actually filmed in Wismar, as the medieval Altstadt had a more authentic period look. Recognisable places appearing include the Nikolaikirche in the establishing town shots, and the Hafen area, which features heavily in several sequences. Keen geographers might also spot parts of Lübeck and Rostock; the one thing you won't find is a single frame of Bremen!

---

ing and pointing at the real ones across the street.

Around a little corner from the prison is the Italian Renaissance **Fürstenhof** (1512–13), now the city courthouse, which is undergoing a sweeping renovation. The façades are slathered in terracotta reliefs depicting town history and, under the arch in the courtyard, biblical scenes.

HISTORICAL MUSEUM

The town's historical museum is in the Renaissance **Schabbellhaus** (☎ 282 350; www.schabbellhaus.de; Schweinsbrücke 8; adult/concession €2/1; ☺ 10am-8pm Tue-Sun May-Oct, 10am-5pm Nov-Apr) in a former brewery (1571), just south of the Nikolaikirche across the canal. The museum's pride and joy is the large tapestry *Die Königin von Saba vor König Salomon* (The Queen of Sheba before King Solomon; 1560–75); admission is free on Fridays.

Regional artist Christian Wetzel's four charming **pig statuettes** grace the nearby **Schweinsbrücke**. The storybook telling how this quirky bridge got its name and other Wismar lore, is sold in local cafés (€2.95).

SCHEUERSTRASSE
About 400m northwest of the Markt is Scheuerstrasse, a street lined with charming gabled houses; look for **No 15**, with its towering façade, and **No 15a**, with the cargo crane.

Activities
Clermont Reederei (☎ 224 646; www.reederei-clermont.de) operates hour-long harbour cruises five times daily from May to September, leaving from Alter Hafen (adult/concession €6/3). Boats also go to Poel Island once a day (€10/5 return). Various other companies run tours on historic ships during the summer; contact the **harbour** (☎ 389 082; www.alterhafenwismar.de) for details. **Fritz Reuter** (☎ 05254-808 500; www.ms-fritz-reuter.de) also organises wreck dives all along the Baltic coast.

The huge indoor water park **Wonnemar** (☎ 327 623; www.wonnemar.de; Bürgermeister-Haupt-Strasse 38; day ticket adult/concession/child €15/13/11.50) has several pools, tennis, bowling, badminton, massage, sauna, steam baths and six (count 'em!) water slides.

Hanse-Sektkellerei (☎ 636 282; www.altes-gewoelbe-wismar.de; Turnerweg 4b), the champagne factory south of the city centre, produces several varieties – from dry (Hanse Tradition) to extra dry (Hanse Selection). Tours are offered to groups of at least 15 (€7.50 per person) on Wednesdays and Saturdays by appointment; three-hour pirate-themed dinner tours are also available (€34). On your own? Try the tourist office.

Tours
In summer there are 1½-hour walking tours of the city, in German, leaving the tourist office at 10.30am (adult/concession €4/3; also 2pm Saturday, Sunday and holidays). English-language tours can be arranged at a day's notice and cost €45 to €55 for up to 20 people.

Festivals & Events
Annual events include the **Hafenfest** (Harbour Festival) in mid-June, featuring old and new sailing ships and steamers, music and food, and a free street theatre festival in July/August. Wismar also holds a **Schwedenfest** in the third weekend of August, commemorating the end of Swedish rule in 1903.

Sleeping
Wismar is incredibly popular in the peak summer season, and just about every single hotel, pension and holiday apartment gets booked up. Reserve well in advance for this period. **Private rooms** start at €15 through the tourist office.

DJH hostel (☎ 326 80; jh-wismar@djh-mv.de; Juri-Gagarin-Ring 30a; juniors/seniors €16/19; P ✗) The city's DJH Jugendherberge Am Schwedenstein has a spanking new interior in a pretty old brick building west of town, not far from the water park.

Pension Chez Fasan (☎ 213 425; www.pension-chez-fasan.de; Bademutterstrasse 20a; s/d €25/50; P) The best budget deal in town, with en suite rooms, TVs and a great central location.

Hotel Altes Brauhaus (☎ 211 416; hotel-willert@t-online.de; Lübsche Strasse 37; s €48-58, d €73-85; P) You'll find comfortable, nicely furnished rooms here, near the Heiligen Geist church.

Hotel Stadt Hamburg (☎ 2390; www.wismar.steigenberger.de; Am Markt 24; s/d from €85/108; P ✗ 💻) This is a very flash place with sauna facilities in a beautifully renovated building on the Markt.

Another good upmarket option is the **Hotel Alter Speicher** (☎ 211 746; www.hotel-alter-speicher.de; Bohrstrasse 12; s €66-105, d €90-140; P ✗ 🐾), the 'Old Warehouse' is a striking red building with lots of wood fittings and the budget **Wismaria guesthouse** (s/d €21/31) next door.

Eating
Fischerklause (☎ 252 850; Fischerreihe 4; mains €7-10.90) A tiny but characterful fish restaurant with a mainly local crowd, just off the Altstadt ring road near the Alter Hafen.

Zum Weinberg (☎ 283 550; Hinter dem Rathaus 3; mains €6.80-16.10) This lovely Renaissance house serves gargantuan portions of fruity Mecklenburg specialities, including a corking duck, and throws in some nice wines too.

Wismar's picturesque 'restaurant row' is along the pedestrianised Am Lohberg, near the Alter Hafen. Some favourites include:

To'n Zägenkrog (☎ 282 716; Ziegenmarkt 10; mains €7.20-12.75) This popular pub, crammed with maritime mementoes and boasting harbour views, serves excellent fish dishes.

Brauhaus am Lohberg (☎ 250 238; Kleine Hohe Strasse 15; mains €7-17.50) This building was once home to the town's first brewery; restored in 1995, it's now brewing again, taking up three floors and offering a good seafood menu. Look out for the painted penguins.

New Orleans (☎ 268 60; Runde Grube 3; www.hotel -new-orleans.de; mains €6-18.50) Locals can't get enough of this Cajun-style hang-out with swamp jazz, gumbo and po' boys.

Getting There & Away
Trains travel every hour to/from Rostock (€8.10, 70 minutes) and Schwerin (€5.50, 30 minutes). There is limited direct service to/ from Berlin-Zoo (€30.40, 2½ hours). Trains from Hamburg (€21.60, two hours) travel via Lübeck (€10.70, 85 minutes) or Schwerin.

Bicycles can be hired at the station (☎ 224 670) and the youth hostel.

POEL ISLAND
☎ 038425 / pop 2900
Poel Island, in Mecklenburg Bay inlet north of Wismar, is popular with day-trippers but remains relatively underexplored, and feels like the countryside. It's a good spot for cycling, windsurfing, fishing, sport boating, sailing and horse riding; in high summer its beaches accommodate all comers.

The remains of a trading ship from 1354 were discovered recently at Timmendorf, on the west coast of the island; the vessel is being comprehensively restored, and can be seen in Wismar's Alter Hafen until the end of 2004.

Orientation & Information
The island's main road access is found just northwest of the village of Gross Strömkendorf. Most of the action takes place in Kirchdorf, in the centre of the island and home to Poel's main fishing port and marina. Many of the outdoor activities take place in the village of Timmendorf on the island's western side.

Poel's **tourist office** (☎ 203 47; www.insel-poel .de; Wismarsche Strasse 2, Kirchdorf; ⏱ 8am-noon & 2-5pm Mon-Fri) hands out excellent street plans and cycling and hiking maps of the island.

There's a Sparkasse in the small Gemeindezentrum in Kirchdorf and a Volksbank next to the tourist office. The post office is inside the Mahlbuch newsagent.

Activities
The island is flat and perfect for cycling. Get maps and hire bicycles for €4 to €6 per day at the tourist office. Horse riding is available in Neuhof, west of Kirchdorf, and at **Reiterhof Plath** (☎ 207 60; Timmendorf).

Sleeping & Eating
The tourist office operates a free accommodation service, as does the privately run **Ferienhausverwaltung und Zimmervermittlung Hanni Evers** (☎ 209 94; Krabbenweg 5, Kirchdorf; private rooms per person €10-20), where rates include breakfast.

Campingplatz Leuchtturm (☎ 202 24; Timmendorf Strand; adult/child €5/2, car €2.50, tent €4.50-5.50; ⏱ Apr-Oct) Tempting as it may be, camping wild is prohibited, but you can stay here near the beach and the lighthouse.

Poeler Forellenhof (☎ 4200; www.poeler-forellen hof.de; Wismarsche Strasse 13, Niendorf; apartments & cottages €45-135) Private cottages surround a popular restaurant with its own smokehouse and water views, a stone's throw from Kirchdorf.

There are restaurants at most of the pensions and hotels, serving mainly seafood and Mecklenburg specialities.

Getting There & Away
From the bus station in Wismar, take the hourly bus No 430 (€2, 30 minutes) directly to the island. It stops at each village. You can also take the ferry.

By road from Wismar, take Poeler Strasse due north and follow the yellow signs to 'Insel Poel' through Gross Strömkendorf (20 minutes).

VORPOMMERSCHE BODDENLANDSCHAFT NATIONAL PARK
Covering 805 sq km between Rostock and Stralsund, the Western Pomeranian Boddenlandschaft National Park takes in the Baltic coast to Stralsund, the islands of Weder, Bock and Hiddensee, the Darss/ Zingst Peninsula and Rügen's west coast. Created in 1990, its main features are mud flats, dunes, pine forests, meadows and heath; only one-eighth of its area consists of solid land. It's the biggest resting ground in central Europe for migratory cranes – some 60,000 rest here every spring and autumn.

In summer there are regular guided tours on Zingst, Hiddensee and other areas, both on foot and by bicycle. Contact the national parks authority, **Nationalparkamt Vorpommersche Boddenlandschaft** (☎ 038234-5020; poststelle@nlp-vbl.de; Im Forst 5, Born, Darss), for further information. You can also hire horses from any number of places, including **Reiterhof Gränert** (☎ 038231-829 10; Im Felde 2, Pruchten).

WESTERN POMERANIA

STRALSUND
☎ 03831 / pop 60,000

About 70km east of Rostock on the Baltic coast, Stralsund was the second-most powerful member of the medieval Hanseatic League, after Lübeck. In 1648 Stralsund, Rügen and Pomerania came under the control of Sweden, which had helped in their defence. The city remained Swedish until it was incorporated into Prussia in 1815.

The town's importance grew with the completion of the Rügendamm, the causeway to Rügen Island across the Strelasund channel, in 1936. After WWII, Stralsund became the third-largest port in the GDR, and today it's the biggest town in Western Pomerania; the harbour attracts everything from cargo ships and passenger ferries to Grand Prix motorboats.

Stralsund is an attractive, accessible town of imposing churches and elegant townhouses, boasting more examples of classic red-brick Gothic gabled architecture than almost anywhere else in northern Germany. While it lacks the bijou Schloss of Schwerin and the all-in nightlife of Rostock, it's worth at least as much time as either of them.

MECKLENBURG-WESTERN POMERANIA

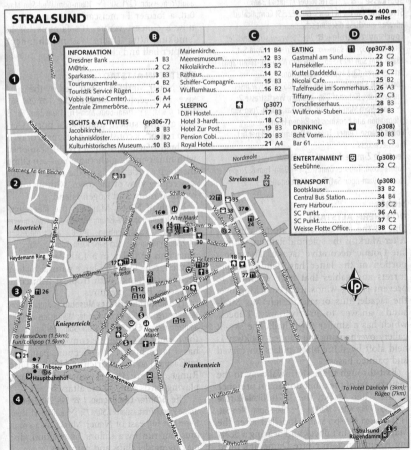

STRALSUND

INFORMATION		EATING	(pp307-8)
Dresdner Bank	1 B3	Gastmahl am Sund	22 C2
M@trix	2 C2	Hansekeller	23 B3
Sparkasse	3 B3	Kuttel Daddeldu	24 C2
Tourismuszentrale	4 B2	Nicolai Cafe	25 B2
Touristik Service Rügen	5 D4	Tafelfreude im Sommerhaus	26 A3
Vobis (Hanse-Center)	6 A4	Tiffany	27 C3
Zentrale Zimmerbörse	7 A4	Torschliesserhaus	28 B3
		Wulfcrona-Stuben	29 B3
SIGHTS & ACTIVITIES	(pp306-7)		
Jacobikirche	8 B3	DRINKING	(p308)
Johanniskloster	9 B2	8cht Vorne	30 B3
Kulturhistorisches Museum	10 B3	Bar 61	31 C3

		ENTERTAINMENT	(p308)
Marienkirche	11 B4	Seebühne	32 C2
Meeresmuseum	12 B3		
Nikolaikirche	13 B2	TRANSPORT	(p308)
Rathaus	14 B2	Bootsklause	33 B2
Schiffer-Compagnie	15 B3	Central Bus Station	34 B4
Wulflamhaus	16 B2	Ferry Harbour	35 C2
		SC Punkt	36 A4
SLEEPING	(p307)	SC Punkt	37 C2
DJH Hostel	17 B3	Weisse Flotte Office	38 C2
Hotel 3-hardt	18 C3		
Hotel Zur Post	19 B3		
Pension Cobi	20 B3		
Royal Hotel	21 A4		

Orientation

The Altstadt is effectively on its own island, surrounded by lakes and the sea. Its main hubs are Alter Markt in the north and Neuer Markt in the south; a few blocks south of the latter is the central bus station. The Hauptbahnhof (central train station) is across the Tribseer Damm causeway, west of the Neuer Markt. The harbour is on the Altstadt's eastern side.

Information

Dresdner Bank (☎ 611 00; Tribseer Strasse 20)
Main post office (Neuer Markt 4)
M@trix (☎ 278 80; Wasserstrasse 8-9; €4 per hr; ☻ 2pm-midnight) Internet access.
Police (☎ 289 00; Böttcherstrasse 19)
Sparkasse (☎ 221 516; Neuer Markt 7) Bank.
Stralsund Card (48 hours; card €2.35) Complicated advance-purchase discount scheme.
Tourismuszentrale (☎ 246 90; www.stralsund.de; Alter Markt 9; ☻ 9am-7pm Mon-Fri, 9am-2pm Sat, 10am-2pm Sun May-Sep, 9am-5pm Mon-Fri, 10am-2pm Sat Oct-Apr; ⌨) Tourist information.
Touristik Service Rügen (☎ 285 70; www.insel -ruegen.com; Bahnhof Rügendamm, Werftstrasse 2; ☻ 8am-9pm Mon-Fri, 9am-8pm Sat, 10am-7pm Sun) Information and bookings for Rügen Island.
Vobis (Hanse-Center, Tribseer Damm; €1.80 per hr) Internet access.
Zentrale Zimmerbörse (☎ 293 894; reiseladen@ hotmail.com; Tribseer Damm 2; ☻ 9am-1pm & 2-6pm Mon-Fri, 9am-noon Sat) Tourist information.

Sights

NORTHERN ALTSTADT

One of the two structures dominating the Alter Markt is the splendid **Rathaus**, with its late-Gothic decorative façade. The upper portion of the latter has slender copper turrets and gables that have openings to prevent strong winds from knocking over the façade; this ornate design was Stralsund's answer to its rival city, Lübeck, which has a similar town hall. The sky-lit gallery overhanging the vaulted walkway is held aloft by shiny black pillars on carved and painted bases.

Exit through the eastern walkway to the main portal of the other dominant presence in the Alter Markt, the 1270 **Nikolaikirche** (☎ 299 799; Alter Markt; ☻ 10am-5pm Mon-Sat, 11.15am-noon & 2-4pm Sun). Modelled after the Marienkirche in Lübeck and bearing a fleeting resemblance to Notre Dame, it's filled

with art treasures: the **main altar** (1708), designed by the baroque master Andreas Schlüter, shows the eye of God flanked by cherubs, capped with a depiction of the Last Supper. Also worth a closer look is the **high altar** (1470), 6.7m wide and 4.2m tall, showing Jesus' entire life. Behind the altar is the **astronomical clock** (1394), allegedly the oldest in the world – sadly it's never worked very well.

Opposite the Rathaus you'll find the **Wulflamhaus** (Alter Markt 5), a beautiful 15th-century townhouse named after an old mayor. Its turreted step gable mirrors the Rathaus façade.

On Schillstrasse, reached via Külpstrasse, is the **Johanniskloster** (☎ 666 488; Schillstrasse 26; adult/concession €2/1.50; ☻ 10am-6pm Wed-Sun May-Oct), a former Franciscan monastery that's now a concert venue. It's famous for its 'smoking attic' (there was no chimney), chapter hall and cloister.

SOUTHERN ALTSTADT

The Neuer Markt is dominated by the massive 14th-century **Marienkirche** (☎ 298 965; Neuer Markt; ☻ 10am-6pm Mon-Fri, 10am-5pm Sat & Sun), another superb example of north German red-brick construction. Its main draw is the huge **F Stellwagen organ** (1659), festooned with music-making cherubs. You can climb the steep wooden steps up the tower (€1) for a sweeping view of the town, with its lovely red-tiled roofs, and Rügen Island.

North of Neuer Markt is the **Meeresmuseum** (Oceanographic Museum; ☎ 265 010; www.meeres museum.de; Katharinenberg 14-20; adult/concession €4/2.50; ☻ 9am-6pm Jun-Sep, 10am-5pm Oct-May), an aquarium complex in a 13th-century convent church. There's a large natural history section and tanks with tropical fish, coral and scary Baltic creatures.

The **Kulturhistorisches Museum** (Cultural History Museum; ☎ 287 90; khm@gmx.de; Mönchstrasse 25/27; adult/concession €3/1.50; ☻ 10am-5pm Tue-Sun) is in the former St Catherine convent nearby. It has a large historical collection, paintings by Caspar David Friedrich and Philipp Otto Runge, faïence (tin-glazed earthenware), playing cards and Gothic altars.

The **Schiffer-Compagnie** (☎ 298 510; Frankenstrasse 9; adult/concession €1.50/0.75; ☻ 9.30am-11.30pm, 1-4pm Mon-Fri), east of Neuer Markt, is a small museum run by a sailors' association, displaying model ships and paintings.

Activities

Weisse Flotte (☎ 268 138; www.weisse-flotte.com; Fährstrasse 16; passenger €2.30, bikes €1.50; ☽ May-Oct) operates ferries seven times daily to the scenic fishing village of Altefähr on Rügen. One-hour **harbour cruises** depart four times daily (€6). The ferry harbour is on the northeastern edge of the Altstadt.

Bootsklause (☎ 383 045; €2 per hr plus adult/child €1/0.50; ☽ 10am-11pm Mon-Fri, 9am-11pm Sat & Sun) hires out boats on the Kneiperteich.

Between May and September, the **Hanse-Bahn** (☎ 0177-324 6022; ☽ Mon-Sat), a miniature motorised train tours the town's sights at irregular intervals. The 40-minute tour starts after 11am (on Saturday afternoon) and costs €5/3 per adult/child. Stops usually include the Neuer Markt, the Alter Markt and the ferry terminal; the route can change, but you can hop on almost anywhere it turns up.

The massive **HanseDom** (☎ 373 30; www.hansedom.de; Grünhufer Bogen 18-20; ☽ 8am-midnight), west of Tribseer Damm, has just about every kind of pool, bath, sauna and sports facility imaginable (see the boxed text below), including an Inca Temple and a James Bond Rock (??), plus the four-star Dorint Hotel.

Sleeping

The tourist office and Zimmerbörse book **private rooms** (from €15), mostly outside the Altstadt, for a €3 fee.

DJH hostel (☎ 292 160; Am Kütertor 1; juniors/seniors s/d €14.50/17.50; ☒) This hostel is inside a 17th-century town gate.

Pension Cobi (☎ 278 288; www.pension-cobi.de; Jakobiturmstrasse 15; s €32-42, d €46-62; ℗) In the shadow of the Jakobikirche, this is a great location for exploring the Altstadt, and also offers bike hire. Rooms are smart, clean and some have balconies.

Hotel Dänholm (☎ 297 090; Am Alten Marinehafen 16; s/d €45/66; ℗ ☒) This unfancy but very quiet hotel on Dänholm Island, off the Rügendamm causeway, is a good place to try at peak times or if you just fancy a bit of space.

Hotel 3-hardt (☎ 285 658; Heilgeiststrasse 50; s/d €45/70; ☒) A stone's throw from both the docks and the centre, the 3-hardt is a friendly, cosy operation with a nice restaurant and an Irish cellar pub.

Royal Hotel (☎ 295 268; www.royal-hotel.de; Tribseer Damm 4; s/d €65/80, ste from €90; ℗) A regal Art Nouveau building near the train station houses this excellent-value option; 12m buffet meals and lovely big affordable suites easily make up for a bit of street noise. Mind the doors.

Hotel zur Post (☎ 200 500; www.hotel-zur-post-stralsund.de; Tribseer Strasse 22; s €84, d €115-125; ℗ ☒) You can't beat the Neuer Markt location, and rooms are modern and immaculate. The Hemingway bar is a popular haunt for well-heeled drinkers and cigar-puffers.

Eating

Nicolai Cafe (☎ 290 765; Alter Markt 12; meals €1.20-5.40) Stop for lunch in this tiny arty café, run by the Nikolaikirche.

'BAD' COMPANY

The HanseDom, like Wonnemar in Wismar (p303), is just one example of a German social phenomenon, the man-made *Bad*. Even in Mecklenburg-Western Pomerania, one of the most 'wateriest' places in Germany, there are dozens of these artificial spas and swimming places scattered around; pick up the free brochure *Der Weg zur Gesundheit* (The Road to Health) for an idea of just how many.

Like Japan, another waterlogged place, Germany has long been obsessed with the curative properties of warm waters and hot steam. But unlike in Japan, or even Europe's mountain regions, there's no thermal spring water bubbling up from the ground in this German state. To cope with this dilemma, communities throughout northern Germany have built water parks with multiple pools, water slides, steam rooms, fitness centres and restaurants, so people can get the benefits of a spa whatever the weather.

These complexes also feed the national obsession with *Wellness*, a concept that combines everything from workouts and massage to beauty treatments, solaria and indoor beaches. So next time you see that unseasonal tan and sixpack abs, you'll know exactly where they've been...

Tiffany (☎ 3090 088; Am Langenwall; buffet €5)
This loosely themed breakfast bar is simply
fantastic, darling. Try the Audrey Hepburn
drink-all-you-can champagne buffet (€28,
incuding fruit bowl).

Wulfcrona-Stuben (☎ 666 062; Heilgeiststrasse 30;
mains €3.50-12.60) Near Alter Markt, you get
a nice mix of traditional (wooden beams)
and contemporary (um, fairy lights) in this
upscale bistro, which also claims to have
Stralsund's finest beer garden.

Hansekeller (☎ 703 840; Mönchstrasse 48; mains
€7.50-13) In an old guardhouse, the Hansekeller serves up hearty regional dishes at moderate prices in its vaulted brick cellar.

Torschliesserhaus (☎ 293 032; Am Kütertor 1;
mains €7.48-14.90) Next to the hostel, this 1281
building in the city wall provides a modern
menu of steaks, fish and lots of snacks in an
atmospheric setting.

Tafelfreude im Sommerhaus (☎ 299 260; klatte
.mueller@t-online.de; Jungfernstieg 5a; mains €12.50-
18.50) An unassuming yellow building on
the west side of the Knieperteich houses
one of Stralsund's finest gourmet dinner
spots, with theme weeks and a surprise set
menu for €23.50.

Guess what – there are plenty of fish (and
tourist) restaurants around the harbour.
Try **Gastmahl am Sund** (☎ 306 209; Seestrasse 2),
with its 40-odd dishes, or the eccentric **Kut-
tel Daddeldu** (☎ 299 526; Hafenstrasse), which has
little lighthouses on every table.

Drinking & Entertainment

Bar 61 (☎ 291 761; Wasserstrasse 61) For our
money the best cocktails in Stralsund,
served up in appealing Art Deco surrounds.
Worthy competition for Schwerin's great
Booze Bar.

8cht Vorne (☎ 281 888; Badenstrasse 45) A scene
stalwart, furnishing Stralsund's student
population with drink, DJs and dancing
every night.

Fun/Lollipop (☎ 399 039; Grünhufer Bogen 11-14)
Out by the HanseDom, this is the biggest
mainstream club in town.

Between May and September organ
recitals take place at 8pm on Wednesday,
alternating between Marienkirche (adult/
concession; €4.50/3) and the Nikolaikirche
(€4/2). The floating Seebühne, which is run
by the **Theater Vorpommern** (☎ 264 6124), hosts
a variety of summer performances in the
harbour.

Getting There & Away
BOAT

Reederei Hiddensee (☎ 0180-321 2150; www.reederei
-hiddensee.de) ferries leave Stralsund up to
three times daily for Hiddensee Island.
One-way/return tickets to Neuendorf cost
€8.50/15.50; to Vitte and Kloster it's €10/16.
Bikes are an extra €7.

See p312 for details of services between
the Stralsund region and Rügen Island.

CAR & MOTORCYCLE

If coming from the west – Lübeck, Wismar
or Rostock – avoid travelling on the B105,
a torturously slow, jammed and speed-
trapped country road. Instead get on the
A20, or take the B110 from Rostock to the
B194 (via Bad Sülze) and head north. From
points east, you'll use the B96.

TRAIN

Regional trains travel to/from Rostock
(€10.70, 1¼ hours), Berlin-Ostbahnhof
(€30.80, 3½ hours) and Hamburg (€33, 4
hours) at least every two hours. There are
lots of trains to Sassnitz (€8.10, 50 minutes)
and Binz (€8.10, 50 minutes), on Rügen
Island.

International trains between Berlin and
either Stockholm or Oslo use the car-ferry
connecting Sassnitz Fährhafen on Rügen
with Trelleborg in Sweden.

Getting Around

Your feet will do just fine in the Altstadt,
but for the outlying areas there's a reasonable bus system. You can also hire a bicy-
cle from **SC Punkt** train station (☎ 306 158); harbour
(☎ 280 155).

GREIFSWALD
☎ 03834 / pop 53,500

About 35km southeast of Stralsund lies
the old university town of Greifswald, on
the Ryck River. Greifswald went through
a rapid evolution from Cistercian monastery in 1199 to Hanseatic city only a century
later. It's justly famous for its university, the
second oldest in northern Germany, and
survived WWII largely unscathed thanks
to a courageous German colonel who surrendered to Soviet troops, a move usually
punishable by execution.

Despite being the fourth-largest city in
the state, Greifswald is known mainly as a

ourist town, with its handsome Altstadt
and pretty harbour pulling in the crowds
n summer. It's also a convenient gateway
or the equally popular island of Usedom.

Orientation & Information
The Altstadt is northeast of the train station,
on the bank of the Ryck. It's partly encircled by a road, partly by railway tracks. The
mostly pedestrianised Lange Strasse bisects
the Altstadt from east to west and is quickly
reached via Karl-Marx-Platz. Around 4km
east is the gull- and mast-filled harbour
neighbourhood of Wieck, complete with
drawbridge.

Greifswald Information (☎ 521 380; www.greifs
wald.de; Markt; ⏰ 9am-6pm Mon-Fri, 9am-noon Sat) is
in the Rathaus; you'll also find banks and
the post office near it on the Markt. Internet
access is available at Spielbörse 1 (☎ 77 661;
Mühlestrasse 27-28; €3 per hr).

Sights
MARIENKIRCHE
This 12th-century red-brick hall church
(☎ 2263; Brüggstrasse; ⏰ 10am-5pm Mon-Fri, 10am-
noon Sat & Sun), a square three-nave tower
rimmed with dainty turrets, is teasingly
called 'Fat Mary' for its generous dimensions. The interior is modest except for
one jewel: the awesome Renaissance pulpit
(1587), constructed with 60 types of wood
by Rostock carver Joachim Melekenborg.

MARKT & AROUND
The many historical buildings on the Markt
hint at Greifswald's stature in the Middle Ages. The Rathaus, at the western end,
started life as a 14th-century department
store with characteristic arcaded walkways.
The red-brick gabled houses on the eastern
side are worthy of inspection; No 11 is a good
example of a combined living and storage
house owned by Hanseatic merchants.

Walk one block east on Mühlenstrasse
to the Pommersches Landesmuseum (Pomeranian
tate Museum; ☎ 831 20; Theodor-Pyl-Strasse 1-2; adult/
concession €2.50/1.50; ⏰ 10am-6pm Tue-Sun). Once a
Franciscan monastery, it now has a major
gallery of paintings as well as history and
natural history exhibits.

DOM ST NIKOLAI & UNIVERSITY AREA
West of the Markt, the spires of Greifswald's
Dom St Nikolai (☎ 2627; Domstrasse; ⏰ 10am-4pm

Mon-Sat, 11.30am-12.30pm Sun) rise above a row of
historic façades. Dubbed 'Long Nicholas' for
its 100m onion-domed tower, the cathedral
has an austere, light-flooded, completely
whitewashed interior with a large and solitary golden cross. The *Greifswalder Bach-
wochen*, a series of Bach concerts, has
been taking place in the Dom since 1946.
You can climb the tower (adult/concession
€1.50/1) and, yes, there is a great view from
the top.

Single-storey, half-timbered buildings
in a sea of red brick make up the former
St Spiritus Hospital (☎ 3463; www.kulturzentrum
.greifswald.de; Lange Strasse 49), clustered around a
small courtyard. It's now an alternative cultural centre, with a beer garden and a small
stage for concerts in summer. For maximum
visual effect, enter via Rubenowplatz.

Rubenowplatz, to the west, is the heart
of the university area, with a monument to
Heinrich Rubenow, the university's founder,
in the middle of the little park. The university's main building flanks the square's
south side. Only the former library, used
as the assembly hall since 1881, is worth a
closer look.

Sleeping
The tourist office books private rooms (from
€15). Like everywhere on the coast, places fill
up quickly in summer.

ALTSTADT
Hotel Alter Speicher (☎ 777 00; www.alter-speicher
.de; Rossmühlenstrasse 25; s/d €62/77; Ⓟ ⊠) The
Alter Speicher occupies a renovated warehouse overlooking the river just outside
the centre, with lovely quarters and a good
regional restaurant.

Hotel Galerie (☎ 773 7830; www.hotelgalerie.de;
Mühlenstrasse 10; s/d €75/95; Ⓟ ⊠) Rooms in
this sparkling modern hotel across from the
state museum are filled with a changing collection of work by contemporary artists.

WIECK
Schipp In (☎ 840 026; Am Hafen 3; r €36-62) This
tiny pension acts as a branch of the tourist
office and has a public coin laundry and
sauna. Breakfast is not included.

This brand-new (2003) complex of Mari-
times Jugenddorf Wieck (☎ 830 2950; www.maju
wi.de; Yachtweg 3; dm €16-25; Ⓟ ⊠ 🖳) is a superior alternative to the DJH hostel (☎ 516 90;

jh-greifswald@djh-mv.de; Pestalozzistrasse 11/12), with a vast range of activities on offer.

Eating & Drinking

Domburg (☎ 700 37; Domstrasse 2; mains €4.50-10) In the shadow of the Dom, this cosy traditional place has a wide-ranging menu with plenty of bistro and pasta dishes.

Brasserie (☎ 790 100; Lange Strasse 22; mains €11-17.40) You can get breakfast, lunch and dinner at this establishment in the smart Hotel Kronprinz, with an emphasis on bistro fare.

Zur Brücke (☎ 836 160; Am Hafen) and **Zur Fähre** (☎ 840 049; Fährweg 2) are among the handsome fish restaurants on the harbour at Wieck. Expect to pay €7.40 to €17.50 for main courses.

Zur Falle (☎ 578 737; Mühlentor 1) This legendary student pub is located in a cellar at the edge of the Altstadt, near the active university Mensa.

Getting There & Away

There are regular train services to Rostock (€14, 1½ hours), Stralsund (€5.50, 25 minutes) and Berlin-Lichtenberg (€30, 2½ to three hours).

Greifswald is well connected by bus to other communities in Mecklenburg-Western Pomerania, though service is either restricted or suspended on weekends. The B105 and B96 roads from Rostock and Stralsund are notoriously slow; the B96 also continues to Berlin.

Getting Around

It's easy to get around Greifswald's centre on foot, but to reach outlying areas you may want to make use of the bus system. Single/day tickets cost €1.30/3.10. You reach Wieck via a 4km foot/bike path, or bus No 6 ends here. If you're driving, head east towards Wolgast; the turn-off is on your left.

AROUND GREIFSWALD
Usedom Island

Usedom lies in the delta of the Oder River about 30km east of Greifswald, and is separated from the Pomeranian mainland by the wide Peene River. The greatest assets of this island, which Germany shares with Poland, are the 42km stretch of beautiful beach and the average 1906 annual hours of sunshine, which make it the sunniest place in Germany. It earned the nickname *Badewanne Berlins* (Berlin's Bathtub) in the prewar period and was a sought-after holiday spot in GDR days.

Since the *Wende*, Usedom has been somewhat overshadowed by neighbouring Rügen, but as sprucing-up continues it's coming into its own. Elegant 1920s villas with wrought-iron balconies grace many traditional resorts, including Zinnowitz and Ückeritz in the western half and Bansin, Heringsdorf and Ahlbeck further east.

Usedom Tourismus (☎ 038375-234 10; www.usedom.de; Bäderstrasse 5, Ückeritz; ⏰ 8am-7pm Mon-Fri) books accommodation all over the island; holiday apartments are common here.

PEENEMÜNDE

Usedom's only attraction of historical importance is Peenemünde, on the island's western tip. It was here that Wernher von Braun developed the V2 rocket, first launched in October 1942. It flew 90km high and a distance of 200km before plunging into the Baltic and marked the first time in history that a flying object had exited the earth's atmosphere. The research and testing complex was destroyed by the Allies in July 1944, but the Nazis continued their research in Nordhausen in the southern Harz (see Mittelbau Dora p276).

Peenemünde is immodestly billed as 'the birthplace of space travel' at the **Historisch-Technisches Informationszentrum** (Historical & Technological Information Centre; ☎ 038371-5050; www.peenemuende.de; adult/concession €5/4; ⏰ 9am-6pm Apr-Oct, 10am-4pm Nov-Mar, closed Mon Oct-May).

Nearby, **Phänomenta** (☎ 038371-260 66; Museumstrasse 12; adult/child €5/4; ⏰ 10am-6pm, last entry 5.15pm) is a hands-on science museum with 253 interactive experiments. Combined tickets for both places cost €9/7.

The **harbour** is another popular spot for visitors, with plenty of boats and the battered **U461 submarine** (☎ 285 66; www.alpha-group.de; admission €5; ⏰ 9am-9pm).

GETTING THERE & AWAY

Züssow is the gateway to Usedom, reached by train from Stralsund (€6.60, 45 minutes) and Greifswald (€7.10, 30 minutes); Usedomer Bäderbahn trains continue to Zinnowitz, Peenemünde and other resorts (day card €10). Buses also connect Wolgast, one stop from Züssow, with the island.

MECKLENBURG-WESTERN POMERANIA

RÜGEN ISLAND

Germany's largest island, Rügen has 574km of coast and a tourist tradition reflecting Germany's recent past and the people who played a role in it.

In the 19th century, luminaries such as Einstein, Bismarck and Thomas Mann came to unwind in the fashionable coastal resorts here, as did the wives and children of Germany's wealthy, leaving their husbands at work in the cities. Later, Hitler picked one of the most beautiful beaches to build a monstrous holiday resort for his loyal troops; the GDR, too, made Rügen the holiday choice for dedicated comrades,

not to mention top apparatchik Erich Honecker.

Much of Rügen and its surrounding waters are national park or protected nature reserve. The Jasmunder Bodden inlet area is a bird refuge, popular with bird-watchers. The main resort area is around the settlements of Binz, Sellin and Göhren on the east coast. Today, the island is rapidly becoming one of the most popular destinations in the Baltic, and accommodation is often completely booked out during the peak summer period.

INFORMATION

The **RügenCard** (www.ruegencard.de; 3/7/14 days €9/19/35) gives free bus transport, entry to

RÜGEN & HIDDENSEE ISLANDS

museums and galleries, and various discounts around the island.

For emergency medical services, ring ☎ 03838-802 30.

Tourismus Rügen (☎ 03838-807 70; www.ruegen.de; Am Markt 4, Bergen) is the island's main information office, but does not book rooms. The **Verbund Rügener Zimmervemittlungen** (☎ 01805-334 433; www.insel-ruegen.org) has an island-wide reservation line.

Dozens of private agencies also handle accommodation, including: **Rügen-Besucher-Service** (☎ 038301-605 13; August-Bebel-Strasse 1, Putbus), **Touristik Service Rügen** (☎ 038306-6160; Hauptstrasse 18, Altefähr) and **Touristinformation Binz** (☎ 038393-337 89; Proraer Chaussee 2, Binz; 🖳). Note that breakfast, taxes and cleaning fees (for holiday flats) are not always included.

GETTING THERE & AWAY
Boat
Rügen is a stop for domestic ferries (with links to the mainland and Hiddensee Island) and international ferries (Denmark and Sweden).

THE MAINLAND
A small passenger ferry shuttles between Stralsund and Altefähr on Rügen's southwestern shore every 30 minutes in high season (€1.50, bikes €1). Car ferries run by **Weisse Flotte** (☎ 0170-347 2418) leave Stahlbrode, 15km southeast of Stralsund, for Glewitz every 20 minutes, April to November only (car/passenger €3.80/1.10). Bikes cost €1.10.

HIDDENSEE ISLAND
Reederei Hiddensee (☎ 0180-321 2150) runs ferry services between Schaprode, on Rügen's western shore, and points on Hiddensee several times daily between April and mid-September. Return fares to Neuendorf are €12.10, to Kloster and Vitte €14.20; bikes cost €6. See p308 for details of routes between Hiddensee Island and the mainland.

SWEDEN
Five **Scandlines** (☎ 01805-7226 3546 37) ferries run daily from Sassnitz Mukran, several kilometres south of Sassnitz, to Trelleborg (adult/child €15/7.50 June to August, €10/5 September to May; 3¾ hours). Cars are €90 to €100 in summer, including passengers (low season €85); motorcycles are €45/30

and bicycles €20/14, high/low season including driver. Ask about special round-trip packages.

DENMARK
Scandlines also runs ferries between Sassnitz and Rønne on Bornholm Island from April to November (Thursday, Saturday and Sunday April to June and September to November; daily June to September). The trip takes 3¾ hours and costs €17/8.50 per adult/child high season. Cars costs €100/150 for midweek/weekend travel from mid-June to August and €65 at other times.

Bus
BerlinLinienBus (☎ 0130-719 107) offers a weekly service between Berlin and Binz, Sellin, Baabe and Göhren (€30, 4¾ hours). Reservations are essential.

Car & Motorcycle
The most obvious way to get to Rügen is via the Rügendamm, the causeway across the Strelasund channel. During rush hour and the peak season, however, it can become a complete bottleneck, especially as it opens five times daily to let ships through. The alternative is the Stahlbrode–Glewitz car ferry (see The Mainland this page).

Train
A new IC train connects Binz to Hamburg (€44.20, four hours), Cologne (€82.60, 8½ hours) and Frankfurt (€89.80, nine to 10 hours). Local trains run hourly from Stralsund to Sassnitz (€8.10, 50 minutes) and also to Binz (€8.10, 1¼ hours). To get to Putbus, change in Bergen; for Sellin, Baabe and Göhren, you can catch the historic Rasender Roland train in Putbus or Binz (see Train p313).

GETTING AROUND
Bicycle
Sharing roads with cars cannot always be avoided. Ask for the *Fahrrad & Nahverkehrskarte* at tourist offices: besides being a map, it includes route recommendations and a list of hire and repair shops.

Bus
Rügen has a comprehensive bus system, with links to practically all communities. In summer, there are half-hourly services

...om Binz to Göhren and Sassnitz, but serv-
...e to other towns is sporadic; sometimes
...here are just a few daily departures. A day
...ard for the whole network costs €7.50.
...ocal tourist offices have timetables and
...aps, or call ☎ 03838-194 49.

...ar & Motorcycle

...f you don't have much time, a car is the
...est mode of transport on Rügen Island.
...he main artery is the B96. Parking meters
...bound, so carry plenty of change.

...rain

The Rasender Roland steam train is an
integral part of Rügen's public transport
system. It shuttles between Putbus and
Göhren between 5.30am and 9pm daily,
stopping in Binz, Jagdschloss Granitz, Sellin and Baabe. The route is divided into five
zones, each costing €1.60 (Putbus–Binz is
two zones; Putbus–Göhren five zones).
Bikes cost €2.10.

DEUTSCHE ALLEENSTRASSE

After crossing the Rügendamm, if you turn
east towards Putbus you'll soon be driving
beneath a lush canopy of chestnut, oak, elm
and poplar trees that lines the two-lane
road for the next 60km to the coastal resort
of Sellin. This stretch is the first segment
of the Deutsche Alleenstrasse, an ambitious
project aiming to construct a route of leafy
boulevards through Germany from here all
the way south to Lake Constance, on the
Swiss border. On Rügen, it leads through
the island's largely agricultural, thinly
populated south where, in spring, brilliant
yellow fields of rape alternate with potato
fields and meadows.

Putbus

☎ 038301 / pop 5000

Having passed through the modest farming villages that surround it, Putbus will
seem like a mirage. Some 16 large, white
neoclassical buildings surround the **Circus**,
a gigantic circular plaza resembling a roulette wheel. Its 75-hectare **English park** – filled
with ginkgoes, cypresses, Japanese spruces
and other exotic trees – lets you take a botanical journey around the world.

Putbus is an oddity, conceived and
realised in the 19th century by an overly
ambitious local prince, Wilhelm Malte I

of Putbus (1783–1854). It stands as the
last European town to be purpose-built as
a royal seat. Today, it prides itself on being
Rügen's cultural centre and has the island's
only theatre.

Putbus is the western terminus of the
Rasender Roland (see Train this page),
which used to plough on for another 40km
west to Altefähr; this stretch is now covered
by a wonderful bike trail including sections
leading right through the forest.

Putbus Info (☎ 431; www.putbus.de; Markt 8;
9am-6pm Mon-Fri) keeps limited summer
weekend hours.

MÖNCHGUT PENINSULA

The Mönchgut Peninsula in Rügen's southeast has a wildly irregular coastline, deep
bays, sandy beaches, softly rising hillsides
and stretches of forest; it was first settled by
monks in the 14th century, hence the name.
As the monks prevented the people who settled with them from mixing with the other
islanders – who were pagan Slavs – the people developed their own traditions over the
centuries. Some of these, such as costumes
and dances, have survived to this day.

Göhren

☎ 038308 / pop 1400

Göhren is a pleasant, laid-back resort town
squatting on the Nordperd, a spit of land
jutting into the sea on the peninsula's east
side. The beach is split into the quieter
Südstrand and the livelier, more developed
Nordstrand, with a pier, park and a promenade that leads to the neighbouring village
of Baabe. Göhren is also the eastern terminus of the Rasender Roland steam train.

The **tourist office** (☎ 259 40; www.goehren-ruegen
.de; Berliner Strasse 8; 7am-6pm Mon-Fri, 4-6pm Sat &
Sun) is on the main central street, up the hill
from the station.

A cultural highlight here is the **Monchgüter
Museen** (☎ 2175; www.moenchguter-museen-ruegen.de;
combined ticket €8), a collection of four historic
sites: the **Heimatmuseum**, the **Museumshof**
farm, the **Rookhus** (an unusual chimney-less
house) and the museum ship **Luise**.

SLEEPING & EATING

There are **private rooms** (from €10 per person)
available in Göhren. There are also plenty
of camp sites in the area; contact the tourist
office for further information.

Zum Fischer Franz (☎ 2340; Thiessower Strasse 23; s/d €26/42; P) The accommodation isn't fancy, but it's a nice thatched house with a good fish menu, and you're about 250m from the south beach.

Hotel Seestern (☎ 665 44; Poststrasse10; s/d €45/80) It's a bit tatty in the corridors but the rooms are light and perfectly comfortable in this large central choice.

Waldhotel (☎ 505 00; www.waldhotelgoehren.de; Waldstrasse 7; s €59-80, d €67-96; P ☻) At the top of the steps leading up from the beach, you get all the trimmings and then some at this top-end villa.

Hotel Hanseatic Rügen (☎ 515; www.hotel-hanseatic.de; Nordperdstrasse 2; s €58-112, d €86-138; P ☒ ☻) Another of Rügen's superior four-star establishments, you'll find palatial rooms and a fancy restaurant here.

BINZ
☎ 038393 / pop 5500

Binz is Rügen's largest and most celebrated seaside resort. It lies along one of the island's best beaches, fringed by dunes and forest with glorious views of Prorer Wiek bay and its white chalk cliffs. Thanks to heavy restoration, Binz has once again blossomed into a fully fledged, charming beach town, looking much as it did a century ago.

The **tourist office** (☎ 2782; www.ostseebad-binz .de; Paulstrasse 2; ☙ 9am-7pm Mon-Fri, 10am-6pm Sat, 10am-2pm Sun) and the **Kurverwaltung** (☎ 148 148; Heinrich-Heine-Strasse 7; ☙ 9am-6pm Mon-Fri, 10am-6pm Sat & Sun) provide information and accommodation, as does the private **Tourismusgesellschaft Binz** (☎ 134 60; info@binz.de; Hauptstrasse 1), which has English-speaking staff.

Sights & Activities

Binz is known for its collection of late-19th-century houses built in the Romantic style called *Bäderarchitektur* (spa architecture). Typical of this style are the large covered balconies decorated with white filigree latticework fashioned from wood and wrought iron. Most of these elegant villas have been renovated recently, including the superb quartet at Schillerstrasse and Margaretenstrasse.

Art oddities are on view at the **Fälscher-museum** (Museum of Art Forgeries; ☎ 131 48; Margaretenstrasse 20; adult/concession €3.25/2.25; ☙ 10am-6pm Tue-Sun), amusingly translated as the 'Interna-tional Imaginary Museum'. A €6 combination card also buys entry to the **Binz-Museum** (☎ 502 22; Zeppelinstrasse 8; adult/concession €3.25/2.2 ☙ 10am-6pm Tue-Sat, 2-5pm Sun Apr-Oct only).

Binz has a 4km-long beach promenade its focal points are the long pier and th palatial Kurhaus. At the northern end i the IFA holiday park and its state-of-the art **Vitamar pool** (☎ 911 02; Strandpromenade 74 adult 1/3 hrs €2/4, child €1.50/2.50; ☙ to 8pm), wit slides, whirlpool, saunas and waterfalls.

Jagdschloss Granitz (☎ 2263; adult/concessio €2.50/2; ☙ 9am-6pm May-Sep, 10am-4pm Tue-Sun Oct Mar), a hunting palace built in 1723 on top of the 107m Tempelberg, was significantly enlarged and altered by Wilhelm Malte I. whose flights of fancy also gave Rügen the grandiose Putbus. Malte added the palace's main attraction, a 38m-high tower.

From Binz, you can walk to the Schloss in an hour or catch the motorised Jagdschloss-Express minitrain (adult/child €7/3 return). If you're driving, you must leave your vehicle in a parking lot before heading to the palace.

Sleeping

Private rooms (from €13 per person) are available in Binz. There's a spa tax of €2.10; all prices come down a lot in low season.

DJH hostel (☎ 325 97; jh-binz@djh-mv.de; Strand-promenade 35; juniors/seniors €18.50/22.50) A beach-side location means the hostel is always popular – book ahead.

Pension Haus Colmsee (☎ 325 56; www.haus colmsee.de; Strandpromenade 8; d €73; P ☒) A big, pleasant villa by the beach at the eastern edge of town, with some of the best high-season prices around.

Villa Neander (☎ 5290; glasner@binz.de; Hauptstrasse 16; d €85-95; P) In the centre of town, the up-market Neander has lovely, large rooms with nice bathrooms, plus charming staff.

Hotel Kurhaus (☎ 6650; kurhaus-binz@tc-hotels.de; Strandpromenade 46; s/d from €126/161; P ☒ ☻) This vast place has a commanding position at the focal point of the promenade, oppo-site the pier. General luxury, including the many restaurants.

Eating

Strandcafé (☎ 323 87; Strandpromenade 29; mains €5-18) One of the many smart options along the beach, this is good for coffee and cakes as well as square meals.

Lütt Lut (☎ 348 640; Strandpromenade 42; mains 7.60-18.40) Eccentric cellar-restaurant with very traditional grandma-style cooking and plastic gulls mobbing the ceiling.

Orangerie (☎ 503 33; Zeppelinstrasse 8; mains 9-23) This excellent regional restaurant is part of the plush Hotel Vier Jahreszeiten, next to the Binz-Museum. The daily buffets (€20) are top class; reservations are recommended.

Drinking

For nightlife, Binz is pretty much your only option on Rügen; most of the top-end hotels have bars and/or nightclubs (high season only).

PRORA
☎ 038393

Prora lies just north of Binz, along almost 5km of uninterrupted, fine white-sand beach. However, running parallel to this beautiful stretch of coast is a wall of six hideous six-storey buildings, each 500m long. This eyesore, begun in 1936, was the Nazis' idea of a holiday resort for 20,000 people. The outbreak of WWII stopped its completion; after the war, Soviet troops tried to blow up the existing structures, but failed.

What to do with the buildings is an ongoing debate, but for the time being a portion of these stark surroundings house the **Museumsmeile** (Museum Row), with a half-dozen museums. Among them, the **Museum Prora** (☎ 326 40; www.museum-prora.de; Objektstrasse 3-5; ☼ 10am-6pm Apr-Sep, 10am-4pm Oct-Mar) is a complex comprising: the **Historisches Prora-Museum**, which chronicles Prora's various stages as having 'period rooms' from the Nazi and GDR eras; the **Museum zum Anfassen** (Hands-On Museum), which aims to make science concepts accessible; and **Wasserwelt** (Water World), which gives the sea the same treatment. Entry to each of these costs adult/child €3.50/2.50; it's €6/3.50 for any two, or €7.50/4.50 for all three.

JASMUND NATIONAL PARK

The rugged beauty of Jasmund National Park in Rügen's northeast has inspired a long line of artists, led by the Romantic painter Caspar David Friedrich. His favourite spot was the **Stubbenkammer**, an area at the northern edge of the park, where jagged white-chalk cliffs plunge into the jade-coloured sea.

The most famous of these cliffs is the **Königstuhl** (King's Chair; admission €1) – at 117m it's Rügen's highest point. Sadly, enjoyment of the scenery is often marred by everyone else trying to see it too; on busy weekends, up to 10,000 people drive through the deer-filled countryside to visit the Königstuhl. Fortunately, few people make the trek a few hundred metres east to the **Victoria-Sicht** (Victoria View), which provides the best view of the Königstuhl itself.

Bus No 408 and special summer services go to the Stubbenkammer from Sassnitz. If you're driving, leave your vehicle in the (paid) parking lot in Hagen, then either catch the 419a shuttle bus or walk 2.5km past the legendary Herthasee through the forest. After 6pm you can drive all the way to the Königstuhl. The nicest way to approach the area, though, is by making the 10km trek from Sassnitz along the coast through the ancient forest of Stubnitz. The trail also takes you past the gorgeous **Wissower Klinken** chalk cliffs, another famous vista painted by Friedrich.

A new visitor centre has been built by the Königstuhl in the former Hotel Stubbenkammer, and should open by summer 2004.

Most people now only go to Sassnitz to board one of the ferries headed for Denmark or Sweden; however, the town has been redeveloping its Altstadt and has a nice fishing harbour. Its **tourist office** (☎ 038392-5160; Seestrasse 1; ☼ 8am-7pm Mon-Fri, 3-7pm Sat & Sun) has information on the national park.

The **Panorama-Hotel Lohme** (☎ 038302-9221; www.lohme.com; Dorfstrasse 35, Lohme; s €60, d €80-106; P), west of the Stubbenkammer, has what may be the island's most romantic restaurant, particularly when the sun sets over Kap Arkona on summer nights. The *Eintopf* (stew) is wonderful.

WITTOW

Wittow, the northernmost area on Rügen, began life as an island of its own. It later became connected to the main island, after enough sand had washed up between the islands to form the Schaabe. It's a thinly populated, windswept stretch of land used mostly for agriculture.

MECKLENBURG-WESTERN POMERANIA

Schaabe

This narrow strip of land, connecting the Jasmund Peninsula with Wittow, has arguably the nicest beach on the island. It's a 10km-long crescent of fine, white sand bordered by fragrant pine forest. The fact that it's practically devoid of infrastructure (no lifeguards, snack bars etc) only adds to its untamed charm.

Kap Arkona

Rügen ends at the rugged cliffs of Cape Arkona, with its famous pair of lighthouses. The older Schinkel-Leuchtturm (☎ 038391-121 15; adult/concession €3/2.50), designed by the legendary Karl Friedrich Schinkel, was completed in 1827. It's square, squat and 19.3m high. Inside are exhibits by Rügen artists; from the viewing platform there's a wonderful view over a colourful quilt of rape fields, meadows and white beaches, all set off against the dark-blue Baltic Sea. The views are better still from the adjacent 36m-high Neuer Leuchtturm (adult/concession €3/2.50), which has been in business since 1902.

A few metres east of the lighthouses is the Burgwall, a complex that harbours the remains of the Tempelburg, a Slavic temple and fortress built for the four-headed god Svantevit. The castle was taken over by the Danes in 1168, paving the way for the Christianisation of Rügen.

VITT

If you follow the coast for about 1.5km in a southeasterly direction, you will reach the charming fishing village of Vitt. The toy-sized village has 13 thatched cottages and a few restaurants and snack bars. The whitewashed octagonal chapel at the village entrance is open daily and contains a copy of an altar painting by Philipp Otto Runge (the original is in Hamburg).

GETTING THERE & AWAY

The gateway to Kap Arkona is the village of Putgarten, served infrequently by bus No 403 from Altenkirchen in central Wittow. If you're staying in the northern half of Rügen

and not driving, it's probably best to travel here by bicycle.

If you are driving, leave the vehicle in Putgarten, about 1.5km south of the lighthouses. It's a nice walk through the village to the cape, though you can also cover the distance aboard a motorised minitrain. A second train serves Vitt.

For a slightly different approach to this area, get in touch with Rügen Safari (☎ 0173 610 6514; www.ruegen-safari.de), which runs unusual adventure tours here and in Jasmund National Park. You can try a jeep safari, mountain biking or an Indian canoe tour with real tepees!

HIDDENSEE ISLAND

☎ 038300 / pop 1280

Hiddensee is a narrow island off Rügen's western coast, 17km long and 1.8km at its widest point. It's a quiet and peaceful place with no cars and little infrastructure. Locals refer to their island as 'Dat söte Länneken', which translates as 'the sweet little land'. In the 19th and early 20th centuries, Hiddensee bewitched artists like Thomas Mann, Asta Nielsen, Max Reinhardt, Bertolt Brecht and Gerhart Hauptmann (who is buried here).

There's little mass tourism on Hiddensee, and its three villages – Kloster, Neuendorf and Vitte – have preserved an innocent charm rarely found these days. Hiddensee is best explored by bike, and there are hire places everywhere.

The tourist office (☎ 642 26; fax 642 25; Norderende 162; ⏱ 8am-5pm Mon-Fri, Jul-Sep 10am-noon Sat & Sun) is in Vitte.

There are no camp sites on Hiddensee. Private rooms (from €10 per person, high season) are available in all three villages, but they tend to be shabby.

The Hotel Hitthim (☎ 6660; Hafenweg, Kloster; r €40-65; P) may have a funny name, but this appealing timbered building is one of Hiddensee's best accommodation options.

Hiddensee is served by ferries from Schaprode on Rügen (see Boat p312) and from Stralsund (see Boat p308).

Bavaria

CONTENTS

Munich	**319**
History	319
Orientation	321
Information	322
Dangers & Annoyances	331
Sights	331
Activities	339
Munich for Children	339
Quirky Munich	339
Tours	340
Festivals & Events	340
Sleeping	340
Eating	344
Drinking	347
Entertainment	349
Shopping	352
Getting There & Away	352
Getting Around	353
Around Munich	**354**
Dachau Concentration	
Camp Memorial	354
Chiemsee	354
Starnberg	356
Schleissheim	357
Bad Tölz	358
The Romantic Road	**359**
Orientation & Information	359
Getting There & Away	359
Getting Around	359
Würzburg	360
Around Würzburg	365
Rothenburg ob der Tauber	365
Dinkelsbühl	369
Nördlingen	370
Augsburg	371
Füssen & Schwangau	375
Around Füssen	378
Bavarian Alps	**378**
Getting Around	378
Garmisch-Partenkirchen	378
Around Garmisch-Partenkirchen	380
Oberstdorf	382
Berchtesgaden &	
Berchtesgadener Land	383
Franconia	**385**
Nuremberg	386
Erlangen	394
Bamberg	396

Bayreuth	399
Coburg	402
Around Coburg	403
Altmühltal Nature Park	404
Eichstätt	405
Ingolstadt	406
Eastern Bavaria	**409**
Regensburg	409
Around Regensburg	416
Straubing	416
Passau	417
Bavarian Forest	420

BAVARIA

Bavaria

If you only have time to visit one part of Germany, this is it. Bavaria (Bayern) is, in man ways, a microcosm of the whole country. All the old stereotypes of lederhosen, beer hall oompah bands and romantic castles are here, right alongside the hightech power centre of BMW and Siemens. Modern Bavaria is a land of contrast and diversity, deeply tradition but also staunchly independent. Bavarians see themselves as a people apart and are justl proud of their high-tech enterprises and, at the same time, their spectacular folk music an carnivals, epic arts events and exquisite architecture.

The most popular route through the region is the Romantic Road, a stretch of incredibl medieval towns of cobbled lanes and ancient watchtowers culminating at the world's mos famous castle, the sugary Neuschwanstein in the Bavarian Alps. Castles and cowbells aside the mountains have top-class resorts for hiking and skiing, incredible scenery and a wealth of beautiful frescoed villages. To the east you'll find the rugged wilderness of the vast Bavar ian Forest, while further north are some of Europe's hidden jewels, the fabulous cities o Nuremberg, Regensburg and Bamberg. However, it is Munich, the 'Paris of Germany', that is Bavaria's heart and soul. This chic, cosmopolitan city is a centre of culture and a relaxed place full of *Gemütlichkeit* – the German *joie de vivre*.

Wherever you go in Bavaria be prepared for the legendary hospitality and with it copious quantities of meat and oceans of glorious Bavarian beer.

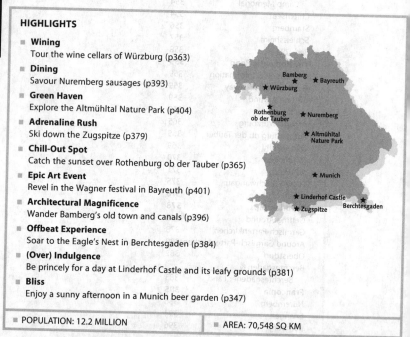

HIGHLIGHTS

- **Wining**
  Tour the wine cellars of Würzburg (p363)
- **Dining**
  Savour Nuremberg sausages (p393)
- **Green Haven**
  Explore the Altmühltal Nature Park (p404)
- **Adrenaline Rush**
  Ski down the Zugspitze (p379)
- **Chill-Out Spot**
  Catch the sunset over Rothenburg ob der Tauber (p365)
- **Epic Art Event**
  Revel in the Wagner festival in Bayreuth (p401)
- **Architectural Magnificence**
  Wander Bamberg's old town and canals (p396)
- **Offbeat Experience**
  Soar to the Eagle's Nest in Berchtesgaden (p384)
- **(Over) Indulgence**
  Be princely for a day at Linderhof Castle and its leafy grounds (p381)
- **Bliss**
  Enjoy a sunny afternoon in a Munich beer garden (p347)

Bamberg ★ ★ *Bayreuth*
★ *Würzburg*
Rothenburg ★ ★ *Nuremberg*
ob der Tauber
★ *Altmühltal*
  Nature Park

★ *Munich*

★ *Linderhof Castle* ★
★ *Zugspitze* *Berchtesgaden*

- POPULATION: 12.2 MILLION
- AREA: 70,548 SQ KM

History

...varia was ruled for centuries as a duchy in ...e Holy Roman Empire. In the 19th century, ...apoleon's conquest of the territories and his ...jigging of the German royal hierarchy ele-...ted Bavaria to the rank of kingdom and ...publed its size. The fledgling nation became ...e object of power struggles between Prussia ...nd Austria and, in 1871, was brought into ...e German Reich by Bismarck.

Bavaria was the only German state that ...efused to ratify the Basic Law (Germany's ...ear-constitution) following WWII. In-...tead, Bavaria's leaders opted to return to ...s prewar status as a 'free state', and drafted ...heir own constitution. Almost ever since, ...he *Land* (state) has been ruled by the arch-...onservative CSU.

Getting There & Around

...Munich is Bavaria's main transport hub ...vith international flight and rail connec-...ions. There are also rail connections to all ...najor German cities and bus connections ...o Berlin via Ingolstadt, Nuremberg, Bay-...reuth and Leipzig. For more information ...on travel to and from Munich see p352.

Although a car will allow more flexibility ...n your travel plans, the Bavarian rail net-...work is extensive and easy to use. In remote ...regions you may have to rely on buses, how-...ever, and trips along the Romantic Road are ...easiest by tour bus. For detailed information ...on travel to and from specific towns see their ...separate entries later in the chapter.

If you're travelling in a group, or can ...assemble one, you can make enormous ...savings with the Bayern ticket. It costs just ...€21 and allows up to five adults unlimited ...travel on one weekday from 9am to 3am. ...It's good for 2nd-class rail travel across ...Bavaria as well as all public transport in ...greater Munich and Nuremberg.

Accommodation

Most Bavarian hostels only accept guests ...aged under 26, but some will take in people ...over the official age limit for a slightly higher ...price. Unfortunately, hostels can't advertise ...this as they would risk their membership, ...but it won't hurt to ask. Hostel prices gener-...ally include bed linen and breakfast.

Bavaria's parks, as well as certain popular ...rafting routes, are generally open to free ...camping. In some parks, such as the Alt-

mühltal Nature Park, camping is restricted to designated areas and a small fee is charged. Be sure to follow the local code of ethics and common decency and pack up everything you brought along – litter, bottles, cans – and bury human waste before you leave.

Bavaria for Children

Kinderland Bavaria is a new system of classification for family-friendly sights, hotels, leisure facilities, museums and camp sites. For more information, go to www.kinderland.by.

MUNICH

☎ 089 / pop 1.2 million

Munich (München) is the Bavarian mother lode. It's home to world-class museums, a lively cultural scene, splendid architecture, boisterous nightlife and some spectacular festivals. It's also one of Germany's most prosperous cities, fuelled by high-powered industry, bourgeois boutiques, and a re-nowned academy of art and music.

Despite this cultural sophistication, a charming touch of provincialism pervades the city. Conservative traditions remain and the people's attitudes are relaxed and carefree – Müncheners will be the first to admit that their 'metropolis' is little more than a *Weltdorf*, a world village.

Whether you see it during the tourist-packed summer, the madness of Oktoberfest or the cold stillness of a February afternoon, you can't help but be impressed by the city.

HISTORY

In the 7th and 8th centuries monks settled in what is now Munich, and the city derives its name from the medieval German *'Ze den Munichen'* ('with the monks'). However, the city's official birth date is 1158 when the Imperial Diet in Augsburg sanctioned the rule of Heinrich der Löwe.

In 1240, the city passed to the House of Wittelsbach, which would run Munich (as well as Bavaria) until the 20th century. Mu-nich prospered as a centre for salt trade but was hit hard by the plague in 1349. It was 150 years before the epidemic began to subside and the *Schäffler* (coopers) began a ritualistic dance, which they vowed to perform every seven years while the city was spared further

BAVARIA

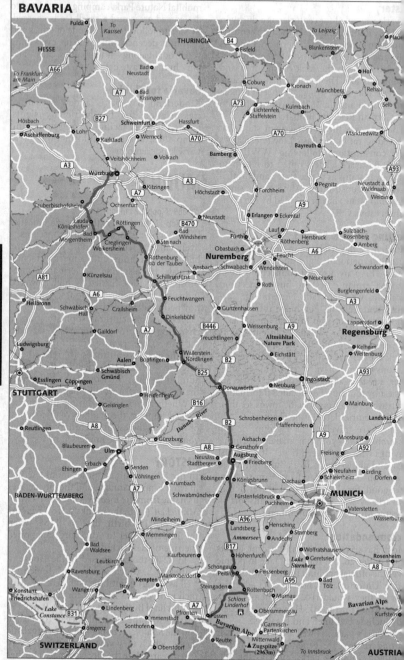

outbreaks. The *Schäfflertanz* is re-enacted daily by the little figures on the city's *Glockenspiel* (carillon) on Marienplatz.

The 18th and early 19th centuries saw an explosion of spectacular baroque and Italianate architecture as successive kings worked on turning the city into a cultural and artistic centre. By the time Ludwig II held the throne, from 1864, his grandiose construction projects (such as Neuschwanstein Palace) bankrupted the royal house and threatened the government. Ironically, they are the biggest money-spinners for the Bavarian tourism industry today.

Munich has seen many turbulent times, but last century was particularly rough. WWI practically starved the city to death, and WWII brought bombing and more than 200,000 deaths. Reconstruction was largely finished when the city was awarded the 1972 Olympic Games, a celebration that ended in tragedy when 17 people were killed in a terrorist hostage-taking incident.

Today Munich has a rich, self-assured reputation and is recognised for having the highest quality of life of any German city.

ORIENTATION

The Hauptbahnhof (central train station) is less than 1km west of Marienplatz, the heart of the historic **Altstadt** (old town). To get there, walk east on Bayerstrasse to Karlsplatz, then take Neuhauser Strasse – Munich's main shopping street – to Marienplatz.

North of Marienplatz is the **Residenz** (the former royal palace), packed with museums and theatres, and **Odeonsplatz** with the landmark Theatinerkirche St Kajetan. To the east of Marienplatz is the **Platzl** quarter with its traditional pubs and restaurants such as the Hofbräuhaus. Hipper bars and venues are south of the square in the Gärtnerplatzviertel quarter which, along with the Glockenbachviertel west of here, is the centre of Munich's gay and lesbian scene. The Isar River flows through the eastern part of the city from south to north.

Munich is divided into various districts, each with their own distinct character. Schwabing, north of the Altstadt, is home to Munich's university and a host of cafés and restaurants. East of Schwabing is the **Englischer Garten** (English Garden), one of Europe's largest city parks. North of Schwabing, the main attraction is the **Olympiapark**, site of the 1972 Olympic Games, and further north again the BMW Museum.

East of the Altstadt is the district of Haidhausen, a trendy neighbourhood packed with pubs. South and west of the Altstadt and near the Hauptbahnhof is Ludwigsvorstadt, a half-seedy, half-lively area packed with shops, restaurants, cafés and cheap hotels. The Westend, further west, was once a slum area, but now bristles with renovated houses, hip cafés and wine bars. It's just west of the Theresienwiese, where the Oktoberfest is held.

North of here is cosmopolitan Neuhausen, a more residential area that's home to the city's most popular hostel. **Schloss Nymphenburg** (Nymphenburg Palace) and its lovely gardens are a little further northwest. Munich's airport is almost 30km northeast of the city.

INFORMATION
Bookshops
Anglia English Bookshop (Map p329; ☎ 283 642; Schellingstrasse 3) Wacky but well stocked.

Geobuch (Map pp326-7; ☎ 265 030; Rosental 6) Best travel bookshop in town.

Hugendubel (Map pp326-7; ☎ 01803-484 484; Marienplatz; Karlsplatz) National chain with tons of English-language books.

Max&Milian (Map pp326-7; ☎ 260 3320; Ickstattstrasse 2) Best gay bookshop.

Words' Worth Books (Map p329; ☎ 280 9141; Schellingstrasse 21a) Good selection of English-language books.

Cultural Centres
Amerika Haus (Map p330; ☎ 552 5370; Karolinenplatz 3)

British Council Info Point (Map pp326-7; ☎ 2060 3310; Goethestrasse 20)

Goethe-Institut (Map pp326-7; ☎ 551 9030; Sonnenstrasse 25)

Institut Français (Map p329; ☎ 286 6280; Kaulbachstrasse 13)

Discount Cards
Munich Welcome Card (€6.50/15.50 for one/three days; €22.50 for three-day card for up to five adults) Unlimited public transport and up to 50% discount on 30 museums and attractions.

Emergency
Ambulance (☎ 192 22)

Fire (☎ 112)

Police (☎ 110) Police station on Arnulfstrasse right beside the Hauptbahnhof.

Internet Access
Cyberice-C@fe (Map p329; ☎ 3407 6955; Feilitzschstrasse 15; €3/5 per 30/60min; ☒ 10am-1pm)

easyEverything (Map pp326-7; Bahnhofplatz 1; price depends on demand; ☒ 7.30am-11.45pm)

Internet (Map pp326-7; ☎ 544 910; Dachauerstrasse 25; €2.50 per hr; ☒ 8am-1am)

Internet Café Altstadt (Map pp326-7; ☎ 260 7815; Altheimer Eck 12; €3 per 30min; ☒ 11am-1am); Neuhausen (Map p330; ☎ 129 1120; Nymphenburger Strasse 145; ☒ 11am-4pm) Offers free Internet access with a main course purchase.

Internet Point (Map pp326-7; ☎ 2070 2737; Marienplatz 20; €2 per 30min; ☒ 24hr)

Times Square Online Bistro (Map pp326-7; ☎ 550 8800; Bayerstrasse 10a; €2.50 per 15min; ☒ 6.30am-1am)

Internet Resources
www.muenchen-tourist.de Munich's official website.

www.munichfound.de Munich's expat magazine.

Laundry
Laundries can be difficult to find around the city. Typical costs are about €2.50 to €4 per load, plus about €0.50 for 10 or 15 minutes dryer time.

24-hour Waschsalon (Map p330; Landshuter Strasse 77; ☒ 24hr)

City-SB Waschcenter (Map pp326-7; Paul-Heyse Strasse 21; ☒ 7am-11pm)

Der Wunderbare Waschsalon (Map p330; Theresienstrasse 134; ☒ 6am-midnight) The best laundry close to the centre.

Schnell + Sauber (Map pp326-7; Klenzestrasse 18; ☒ 7am-11pm)

Left Luggage
Gepäckaufbewahrung (Staffed storage room; ☎ 1308 3468; main hall, Hauptbahnhof; €2.05 per piece; ☒ 8am-8pm Mon-Sat, 8am-6pm Sun)

Lockers (Hauptbahnhof main hall & opposite tracks 16, 24 & 28-36; €1-2 per 24hr; ☒ 4am-12.30am)

Libraries
Bavarian State Library (Map p329; ☎ 286 380; Ludwigstrasse 16)

Stadtbücherei Haidhausen (City library; Map p328; ☎ 4809 8316; Rosenheimer Strasse 5); Schwabing (Map p329; ☎ 336 013; Hohenzollernstrasse 16); Westend (Map p329; ☎ 507 109; Schrenkstrasse 8)

Universitätsbibliothek (Map p329; ☎ 2180 2428; Geschwister-Scholl-Platz 1)

(Continued on page 331)

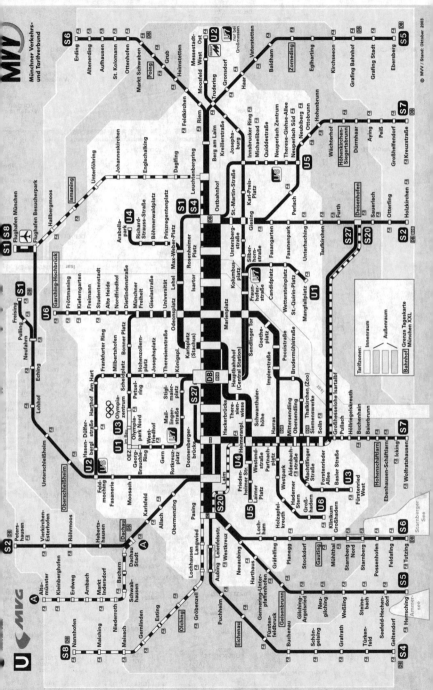

See Nymphenburg, Neuhausen & Olympiapark Map (p330)

0 — 2 km
0 — 1 mile

MOCHINGER

OF · Ⓤ Harthof

ENAU · Ⓤ Am Hart

KIEFERN-
GARTEN

FROTTMANINGER
HEIDE · Ⓤ Kieferngarten

GROSSLAPPEN

Heidemannstr

A9

A99

Feringasee

Gr Elbach · Fahrbach · Brunnbach

Seebach

MILBERTSHOFEN

tshofen

Ⓤ Frankfurter
Ring

Ⓤ Milbertshofen

FREIMANN · Ⓤ Freimann

UNTERFÖHRING

🚉 Unterföhring

Frankfurter Ring

RIESENFELD

Domagkstr

Föhringer Ring

Münchner Str

Kieststr

JOHANNESKIRCHEN

pia-
um
uerling Str

GEORGEN-
SCHWAIGE

Ⓤ Luitpold-
park
Scheidplatz

Ⓤ Studentenstadt

STUDENTENSTADT

Alte
Heide · Nordfriedhof

Hirscham

SANKT EMMERAM

See Schwabing Map (p329)

Nordfriedhof

Johanneskirchner Str

Fleischhütten

OBERFÖHRING

Karl-Theodor-Str · Ⓤ Rheinstr

BIEDERSTEIN

Ⓤ Dietlindenstr

FIDELIOPK

ENGLSCHALKING

Börner
Platz

Herzogstr

Ⓤ Hohenzollernplatz

SCHWABING

Hohenzollernstr

Ⓤ Münchener
Freiheit

Klein-
hesseloher
See KLEIN-
HESSELOHE

HIRSCHAU

HERZOG-
PARK

Effnerstr

PRIEL

COSIMAPARK

Cosimastr

Arabella-
park · Englschalkinger Str

🚉 Englschal-
king

Ostpreussenstr

Josephs-
platz

Ⓤ Giselastr

ARABELLPARK

DAGLFING

Ⓤ Theresienstr

Englischer
Garten

Ⓤ Universität

Ⓤ Richard-
Strauss-Str
Bürgerpark

Richard-Strauss-Str

Welfenstr

DENNING

RIEM

gimaierplatz

Ⓤ Königsplatz

BOGENHAUSEN

Von-der-...

Bölmerwald-
platz · Ⓤ

PARKSTADT

ZAMDORF

A94

Riemer Str
Toginger Str

To Passau (155km);
New Fairgrounds;
Flohmarkt Riem

Ⓤ Odeonsplatz

Prinzregentenstr

Ⓤ Prinzregentenplatz

Toginger Str

Karlsplatz

Ⓤ Lehel

STEINHAUSER

Berg Am
Laim · Truderinger Str

AM MOOSFELD

hof

PLATZL
QUARTER

Ⓤ Max-
Weber-
Platz

Neumarkter...

Schatzbogen

Am Mittelfeld

Ⓤ Marienplatz
Sendlinger
Tor

Ⓤ Isartor

HAIDHAUSEN

BAUMKIRCHEN

KIRCHTRUDERING

bethe-
latz · Ⓤ Fraunhoferstr

🚉 Ostbahnhof

BERG AM
LAIM

See Central
Munich Map (pp326-7)

🚉 Rosenheimer
Platz

See Haidhausen Map (p328)

JOSEPHSBURG

STRASSTRUDERING

Wassenburger Landstr

Ⓤ Kolumbus-
platz

Welfenstr

Innsbrucker
Ring

Schachener Str

Ⓤ Michaelibad

MICHAELIBURG

TRUDERING

NEUTRUDERING

Silberhornstr · Ⓤ

Wertherstr

Martinstr
Karl-Preis-
Platz

Wilramstr

Hechtseestr

Wieflindstr

Ostpark

GARTENSTADT
TRUDERING

Candidstr

Ⓤ Untersbergstr

GIESING

Ⓤ Giesing

Chiemgaustr

Balanstr

RAMERSDORF

Quiddestr

NEUPERLACH

Ⓤ Neuperlach
Zentrum

Karl-Marx-Ring

TRUDERINGER
GRENZKOLONIE

IRCHEN

Stadelheimer Str

Ottobrunner Str

Ständlerstr

Therese-
Giehse-
Allee

Fritz-Erler-Str

NEUPERLACH

SIEBENBRUNN

NEUPERLACH

ACHING

A995

Münchner-Kind-Weg

A8

Ⓤ Neuperlach
Süd

Perlacher Forst

NTERSCHWAIGE

WALDPERLACH

NEUBIBERG · 🚉 Neubiberg

UNTERHACHING

To Salzburg
(125km)

INFORMATION
American Express......1 E1
American Express......2 D2
Atlas Reisen......(see 95)
Bahnhof-Apotheke......3 C2
British Council......4 D2
City-SB Waschcenter......5 C1
easyeverything......6 C1
EurAide......7 C1
Geobuch......8 A2
Goethe-Institut......9 D2
Hugendubel......10 D2
Hugendubel......11 A1
Hypovereinsbank......12 A1
Internet Café......13 E2
Internet Point......14 B1
Internet......15 C1
Jugendinformationszentrum......16 C2
Ludwigs-Apotheke......17 E2
Max&Milian......18 E3
Postbank......19 C2
Reisebank......20 C1
Schnell + Sauber Laundrette......21 E3
Sparkasse......22 B2
Times Square Online Bistro......23 C2
Tourist Office – Hauptbahnhof......24 C1
Tourist Office......25 E3

SIGHTS & ACTIVITIES (pp331-9)
Altes Rathaus......26 B1
Altes Residenztheater (Cuvilliés Theater)......27 F1
Asamkirche......28 E2
Bavaria Statue & Ruhmeshalle......29 A3
Damenstiftskirche......30 D2
Departure point for Mike's Bike Tours......(see 26)
Deutscher Alpenverein......31 F2
Discover Bavaria......32 F2
Feldherrnhalle......33 F1
Fischbrunnen......34 B1
Frauenkirche......35 E2
Fünf Höfe......(see 41)
Glockenspiel......36 A1
Heiliggeistkirche......37 B2
Herle......38 C1
Jüdisches Museum München......39 E3
Karlstor......40 D2
Kunsthalle der Hypo-Kulturstiftung......41 E1
Lion Statues......42 F1
Mariensäule......43 A1
Michaelskirche......44 D2
Münzhof......45 F2
Nationaltheater......46 F2
Neues Rathaus......47 B1
Residenz......48 C1
Residenzmuseum......49 F1
Schatzkammer der Residenz......50 F1
Sendlinger Tor......51 F1
Spielzeugmuseum......52 D3
St Peterskirche......53 B2
Staatliches Museum Ägyptischer Kunst......54 F1
Stadtmuseum......55 A2
Theatinerkirche St Kajetan......56 E1
Verkehrszentrum......57 A3
Viktualienmarkt......58 A2
Zentrum für Aussergewöhnliche Museen (ZAM)......59 F2

SLEEPING (pp340-4)
4 you münchen......60 C1
Andi München City Center......61 C1
Bayerischer Hof......62 E1
City Wohnzentrale......63 C1
Cortiina......64 F2
Creatif Hotel Elephant......65 C1
Deutsche Eiche......66 E3
Deutscher Kaiser......67 C1
Easy Palace......68 C3
Euro Youth Hotel......69 C2
Hotel Advokat......70 F3
Hotel Alcron......71 F2
Hotel Bristol......72 D3
Hotel Brunnenhof......73 C1
Hotel Helvetia......74 C2
Hotel Mirabell......75 C2
Hotel Monaco......76 C1
Hotel Schlicker......77 B2
Hotel Schweiz......78 C2
Hotel Seibel......79 B2
Hotel Uhland......80 C3
Hotel-Pension Mariandl......81 C3
IN VIA Marienherberge......82 C2
Jaegers......(see 69)
Kempinski Vier Jahreszeiten München......83 F2
Pension Am Gärtnerplatztheater......84 E3
Pension Eulenspiegel......85 D3

EATING (pp344-7)
Alois Dallmayr......86 B1
Andechser am Dom......87 A1
Buxs......88 F3
Café am Beethovenplatz......(see 81)
Dukatz im Literaturhaus......89 E1
Fraunhofer......90 E3
Grillpfanne......(see 98)
Hundskugel......91 E2
Interview......92 E3
Joe Peña's......93 F3
Kandil......94 D2
Kaufhof......95 A1
La Fiorentina......96 C3
Mensa......97 C2
Müller Bakery......98 D2
Münchner Suppenküche......99 E2
Nordsee......(see 98)
Prinz Myschkin......100 E2
Ratskeller......101 A1
Ristorante Ca' doro......102 C2
Shida......103 E3
Sho-ya......104 F2
Stadtcafé......(see 55)
Vinzenzmurr......105 D2
Vinzenzmurr......106 D2
Woerners......107 A1

DRINKING (pp347-9)
Augustiner-Grossgaststätte......108 D2
Baader Café......109 F4
Braunauer Hof......110 F3
Hofbräuhaus......111 F2
Pacific Times......112 F3

ENTERTAINMENT (pp349-52)
Atelier......113 D2
Atlantis......114 D2
Bei Carla......115 F3
Brunnenhof der Residenz......116 F1
Deutsches Theater......117 D2
Filmmuseum......(see 55)
Fortuna Musikbar......118 E1
Iwan......119 D2
Kartenvorverkauf......120 A1
LeTra/Lesbentelefon......121 E3
Mister B's......122 C4
Moritz......123 E3
München Ticket......124 A1
München Ticket......(see 47)
Münchener Kammerspiele......125 F2
Münchner Marionettentheater......126 E3
New York......127 D2
Nil......128 E3
Old Mrs Henderson......129 F3
Residenztheater......130 F1
Schwules Kommunikations und Kulturzentrum......131 D3
Soul City......132 E1
Staatstheater am Gärtnerplatz......133 E3
The Stud......134 D3
Theater im Marstall......135 F1

SHOPPING (p352)
Foto-Video Sauter......136 D3
Loden-Frey......137 E2
Ludwig Beck......138 B1

TRANSPORT (pp352-4)
ADAC......139 D3
ADM-Mitfahrzentrale......(see 63)
Deutsche Touring......140 C1
Lufthansa......141 D1

OTHER
Panorama Tours......142 C1

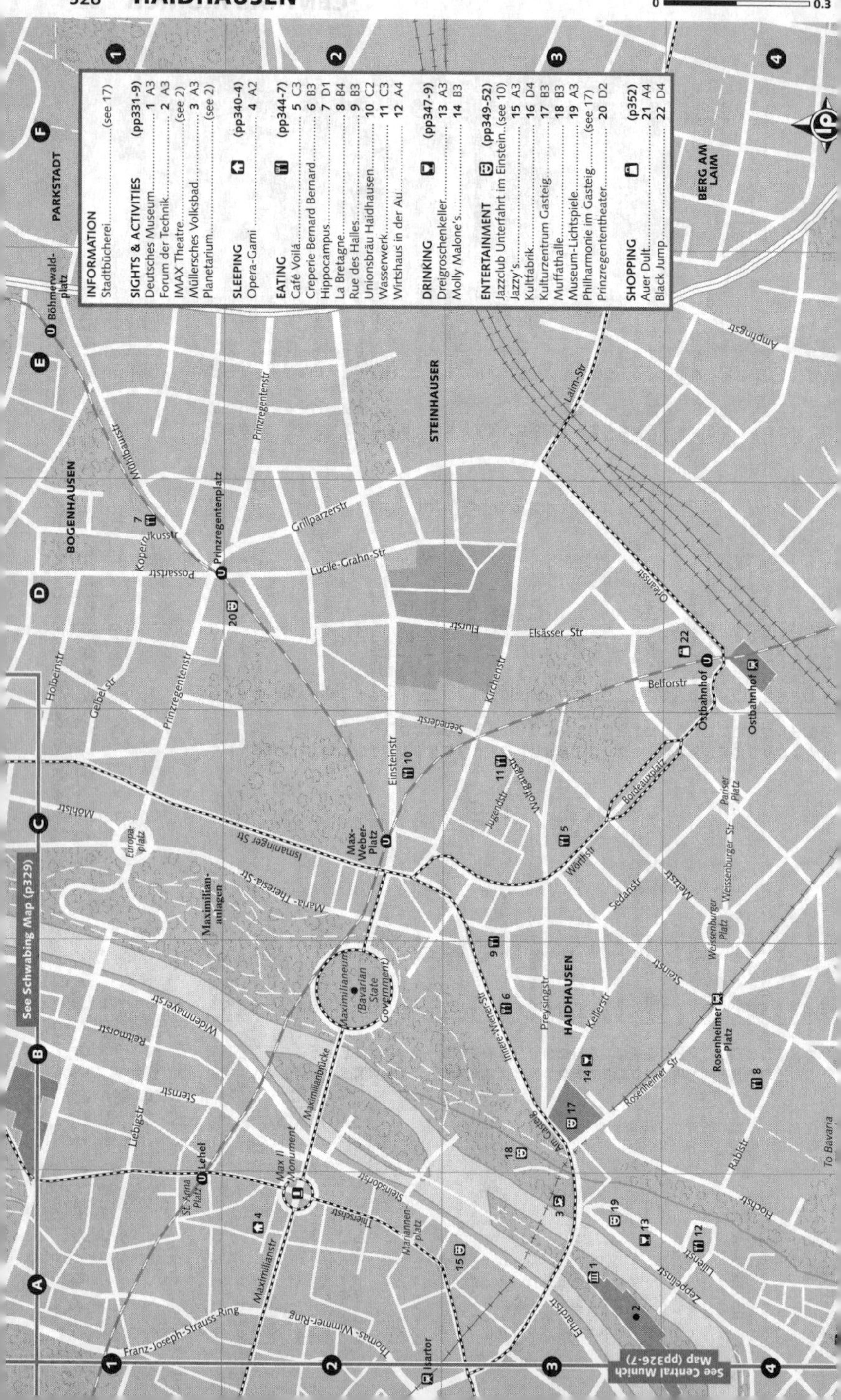

0 — 500
0 — 0.3

INFORMATION
Stadtbücherei...........................(see 17)

SIGHTS & ACTIVITIES   (pp331-9)
Deutsches Museum...................1 A3
Forum der Technik...................2 A3
IMAX Theatre.........................(see 2)
Müllersches Volksbad................3 A3
Planetarium..........................(see 2)

SLEEPING   (pp340-4)
Opera-Garni..........................4 A2

EATING   (pp344-7)
Café Voilà...........................5 C3
Creperie Bernard Bernard............6 B3
Hippocampus.........................7 D1
La Bretagne..........................8 B4
Rue des Halles......................9 B3
Unionsbräu Haidhausen..............10 C2
Wasserwerk.........................11 C3
Wirtshaus in der Au................12 A4

DRINKING   (pp347-9)
Dreigroschenkeller.................13 A3
Molly Malone's.....................14 B3

ENTERTAINMENT   (pp349-52)
Jazzclub Unterfahrt im Einstein...(see 10)
Jazzy's............................15 A3
Kultfabrik.........................16 D4
Kulturzentrum Gasteig..............17 B3
Muffathalle........................18 B3
Museum-Lichtspiele.................19 A3
Philharmonie im Gasteig............(see 17)
Prinzregententheater...............20 D2

SHOPPING   (p352)
Auer Dult..........................21 A4
Black Jump.........................22 D4

PARKSTADT

BERG AM LAIM

Böhmerwald-platz

BOGENHAUSEN

Prinzregentenplatz

STEINHAUSER

See Schwabing Map (p329)

Maximilian-anlagen

Europa-platz

Maximilianeum (Bavarian State Government)

Max-Weber-Platz

Einsteinstr

Elsässer Str

Ostbahnhof

Belforstr

HAIDHAUSEN

Rosenheimer Platz

Wörthstr

Wiener Platz

See Central Munich Map (pp326-7)

To Bavaria

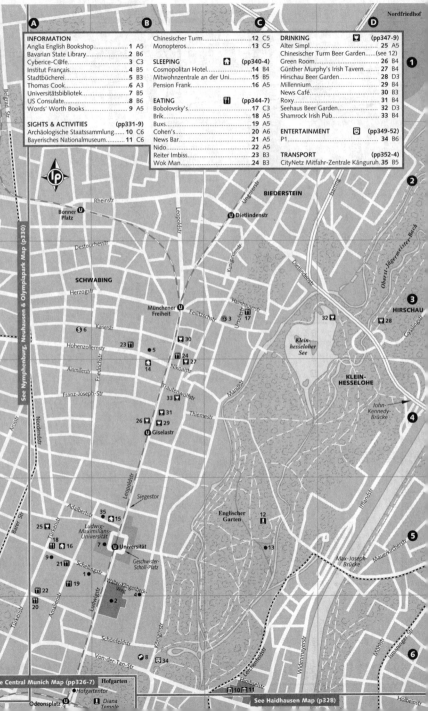

Nordfriedhof

INFORMATION
Anglia English Bookshop	**1**	A5
Bavarian State Library	**2**	B6
Cyberice-C@fe	**3**	C3
Institut Français	**4**	B5
Stadtbücherei	**5**	B3
Thomas Cook	**6**	A3
Universitätsbibliotek	**7**	B5
US Consulate	**8**	B6
Words' Worth Books	**9**	A5

SIGHTS & ACTIVITIES (pp331-9)
Archäologische Staatssammlung	**10**	C6
Bayerisches Nationalmuseum	**11**	C6
Chinesischer Turm	**12**	C5
Monopteros	**13**	C5

SLEEPING (pp340-4)
Cosmopolitan Hotel	**14**	B4
Mitwohnzentrale an der Uni	**15**	B5
Pension Frank	**16**	A5

EATING (pp344-7)
Bobolovsky's	**17**	C3
Brik	**18**	A5
Buxs	**19**	A5
Cohen's	**20**	A6
News Bar	**21**	A5
Nido	**22**	A5
Reiter Imbiss	**23**	B3
Wok Man	**24**	B3

DRINKING (pp347-9)
Alter Simpl	**25**	A5
Chinesischer Turm Beer Garden	(see 12)	
Green Room	**26**	B4
Günther Murphy's Irish Tavern	**27**	B4
Hirschau Beer Garden	**28**	D3
Millennium	**29**	B4
News Café	**30**	B3
Roxy	**31**	B4
Seehaus Beer Garden	**32**	D3
Shamrock Irish Pub	**33**	B4

ENTERTAINMENT (pp349-52)
P1	**34**	B6

TRANSPORT (pp352-4)
CityNetz Mitfahr-Zentrale Känguruh	**35**	B5

BIEDERSTEIN

HIRSCHAU

KLEIN-HESSELOHE

Englischer Garten

Ludwig-Maximilians-Universität

SCHWABING

Klein-hesseloher See

John-Kennedy-Brücke

See Central Munich Map (pp326-7) Hofgarten

See Haidhausen Map (p328)

0 ————— 500
0 ————— 0.3 r

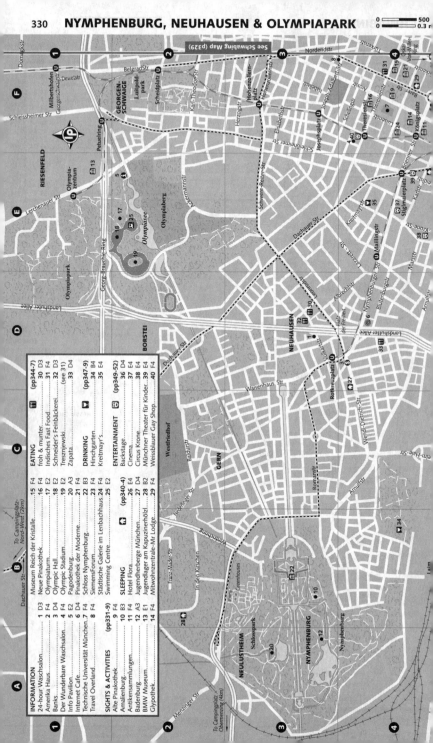

To Campingplatz
Nord-West (2km)

Dachauer Str

See Schwabing Map (p329)

Nordendstr

BelgradStr

GEORGEN-
SCHWAIGE

Luitpold-
park

Scheidplatz

Petuelring

RIESENFELD

Olympia-
zentrum

Lerchenauer Str

Olympiapark

Olympiasee

Olympiaberg

Georg-Brauchle-Ring

Landshuter Allee

BORSTEI

Waisenhaus Str

Westfriedhof

GERN

NEUHAUSEN

Rotkreuzplatz

Landshuter Allee

Dachauer Str

NEULUSTHEIM

Schlosspark

Greenhouses

NYMPHENBURG

Nymphenburg

To Campingplatz
Obermenzing (4km)

Menzinger Str

In den Kirschen

Romanstr

Arnulfstr

INFORMATION
24-hour Waschsalon.................15 F4
Amerika Haus...........................16 F4
Banks.......................................17 F4
Der Wunderbare Waschsalon....18 E2
Info Pavilion.............................19 E2
Internet Cafe............................20 A3
Technische Universität München..7 F4
Travel Overland.........................8 F4

SIGHTS & ACTIVITIES   (pp331-9)
Alte Pinakothek..........................9 F4
Amalienburg.............................10 B3
Antikensammlungen..................11 F4
Badenburg................................12 A3
BMW Museum............................13 E1
Glypothek................................14 F4

Museum Reich der Kristalle.......15 F4
Neue Pinakothek.....................16 F4
Olympiaturm.............................17 E2
Olympic Hall.............................18 E2
Olympic Stadium......................19 E2
Pagodenburg............................20 A3
Pinakothek der Moderne...........21 F4
Schloss Nymphenburg..............22 B3
SiemensForum..........................23 F4
Städtische Galerie im Lenbachhaus..24 F4
Swimming Centre.....................25 E2

SLEEPING   (pp340-4)
Hotel Flora..............................26 F4
Jugendherberge München.........27 D4
Jugendlager am Kapuzinerhölzl..28 B2
Mitwohnzentrale-Mr Lodge.......29 F4

EATING   (pp344-7)
froh & munter...........................30 D3
Indisches Fast Food..................31 F4
Schneider's Feinbäckerei...........32 D3
Treszniewski...........................(see 31)
Zapata....................................33 D4

DRINKING   (pp347-9)
Hirschgarten...........................34 B4
Kreitmayr's.............................35 E4

ENTERTAINMENT   (pp349-52)
Backstage................................36 D4
Cinema...................................37 E4
Circus Krone............................38 E4
Münchner Theater für Kinder....39 E4
Weissblauer Gay Shop.............40 F4

(Continued from page 322)

Medical Services

The US and UK consulates can provide lists of English-speaking doctors on request (see p744). Most pharmacies have some employees speaking passable English, but there are several designated 'international' ones with English-speaking staff.

Airport pharmacy (☎ 9759 2950)
Ambulance (☎ 192 22)
Bahnhof-Apotheke (Map pp326-7; ☎ 551 771; Bahnhofplatz 2) Pharmacy.
Emergency dentist (☎ 723 3093)
Emergency pharmacy (☎ 594 475)
Kassenärztlicher Notfalldienst (☎ 551 771) For medical help.
Ludwigs-Apotheke (Map pp326-7; ☎ 260 3021; Neuhauser Strasse 11) Pharmacy.

Money

American Express north (Map pp326-7; ☎ 2280 1465; Promenadeplatz 6); centre (☎ 2289 1387; Neuhauser Strasse 47)
Citibank (Rotkreuzplatz)
Deutsche Bank (Rotkreuzplatz)
Hypovereinsbank (Map pp326-7; Marienplatz)
Postbank (Map pp326-7; Bahnhofplatz 1)
Reisebank (Map pp326-7; Hauptbahnhof) EurAide's newsletter the *Inside Track* gets you a 50% reduction on commissions at this branch.
Sparkasse (Map pp326-7; Sparkassenstrasse 2)
Thomas Cook (Map p329; ☎ 383 8830; Kaiserstrasse 45)

Post

Main post office (Bahnhofplatz 1; ☻ 7am-8pm Mon-Fri, 8am-4pm Sat, 9am-3pm Sun)
Poste Restante (Postlagernd, Bahnhofplatz 1, 80074 Munich)

Telephone

There are public phones all over the city; most are card operated.

Tourist Information

EurAide (Map pp326-7; ☎ 593 889; www.euraide.de; Room 3, Track 11, Hauptbahnhof; ☻ 7.45am-noon & 1-6pm Jun-Oct; 7.45am-12.45pm & 2-6pm Jun-Oct; 8am-noon & 1-4pm Mon-Fri Nov-May) The office makes reservations, sells tickets for DB trains and a variety of tours and finds rooms (€3 per booking). EurAide's free newsletter, the *Inside Track*, is packed with practical info about the city and surroundings, and gives discounts on money changing (see Money above).

Jugendinformationszentrum (Youth Information Centre; Map pp326-7; ☎ 5141 0660; Paul-Heyse-Strasse 22; ☻ noon-6pm Mon-Fri, to 8pm Thu) A wide range of information for young visitors.
Tourist Office Hauptbahnhof (Map pp326-7; ☎ 2333 0257/58; Bahnhofsplatz 2; ☻ 9am-8pm Mon-Sat, 10am-6pm Sun); Marienplatz (Map pp326-7; ☎ 2332 8242 or ☎ 222 324; Neues Rathaus; ☻ 10am-8pm Mon-Fri, 10am-4pm Sat) The room-finding service is free or you can book in person by calling ☎ 2333 0236/37.

Travel Agencies

EurAide (see Tourist Information) is the best place to go with complicated rail pass inquiries or to book train travel in Germany or elsewhere in Europe.

Atlas Reisen (Map pp326-7; ☎ 269 072; Kaufinger-strasse 1-5) Also other outlets in Kaufhof department stores.
Travel Overland (Map p330; ☎ 2727 6100; Barer Strasse 73)

Universities

Munich is home to about 100,000 students.
Ludwig-Maximilians-Universität München (Map p329; ☎ 218 00; Geschwister-Scholl-Platz 1)
Technische Universität München (Map p330; ☎ 289 01; Arcisstrasse 21)

DANGERS & ANNOYANCES

During Oktoberfest crime and staggering drunks are major problems, especially at the southern end of the Hauptbahnhof. It's no joke: drunk people in a crowd trying to get home can get violent, and there are about 100 cases of assault every year. Leave early or stay very cautious, if not sober, yourself.

The *Föhn* (pronounced 'foon') is a weather-related annoyance peculiar to southern Germany. Static-charged wind from the south brings exquisite views clear to the Alps – and an area of dense pressure that sits on the city. Asthmatics, rheumatics and hypochondriacs complain of headaches; other Müncheners claim that it simply makes them cranky.

SIGHTS

Munich's major sights are clustered around the Altstadt, with the main museum district near the Residenz. However, it will take another day or two to discover the delights of Bohemian Schwabing, the sprawling **Englischer Garten**, and trendy Haidhausen

THE WHITE ROSE

Public demonstrations against the Nazis were rare during the Third Reich; after 1933, intimidation and the instant 'justice' of the Gestapo and SS served as powerful disincentives. One of the few groups to rebel were the ill-fated Weisse Rose (White Rose), led by Munich University students Hans and Sophie Scholl.

Hans joined the Hitler Youth, and his older sister, Inge, became a group leader of its female counterpart, the Bund Deutscher Mädel. Hans soon became disillusioned with the Nazis and attempted to build his own, liberal group within the Hitler Youth. This triggered a Gestapo raid on the Scholl home in Ulm in 1937, and from then on the family were marked as enemies of the state.

In 1942 Hans and Sophie met a group of like-minded medical students and formed the Weisse Rose, which aimed to encourage Germans to resist Hitler. At first its members acted cautiously, creeping through the streets of Munich at night and smearing slogans such as 'Freedom!' or 'Down with Hitler!' on walls. Growing bolder, they printed and distributed anti-Nazi leaflets, leaving them in telephone boxes and sending them to other German cities. The leaflets reported on the mass extermination of the Jews and other Nazi atrocities. One read: 'We shall not be silent – we are your guilty conscience. The White Rose will not leave you in peace.'

In February 1943 Hans and Sophie took a suitcase of leaflets to university and placed stacks outside each lecture hall. Then, from a top landing, Sophie dumped the remaining brochures into an inner courtyard. A janitor saw her, and she and Hans were both were arrested and charged with treason along with their best friend, Christoph Probst. After a four-hour trial, the three were condemned to death and beheaded the same afternoon. Sophie had hoped that thousands would be stirred to action by their self-sacrifice, but there was to be no more resistance at Munich University – in fact, some fellow students applauded the executions.

After WWII, Inge set up an adult education centre in Ulm to help ensure that the Nazi horrors would never happen again. In Munich, there's a memorial exhibit to the Weisse Rose, called DenkStätte, at the **Ludwig-Maximilian-Universität** (Map p329; ☎ 2180 3053; Geschwister-Scholl-Platz 1; admission free; ⏱ 10am-4pm Mon-Fri, 10am-9pm Thu).

to the east. Northwest of the Altstadt you'll find cosmopolitan **Neuhausen**, the **Olympiapark**, and one of Munich's jewels – **Schloss Nymphenburg**.

Altstadt Walking Tour

Attractions described in the sections from Marienplatz to Viktualienmarkt are linked as a walking tour; you can also treat each entry as a separate sight, picking what you would like to visit (see also Map pp326-7).

This circuit takes in the main sights within the bounds of Munich's historic centre and covers about 6km. Include visits to all the museums and churches and you've got (at least) a two-day itinerary on your hands.

MARIENPLATZ

The walking tour begins in Marienplatz, the heart and soul of the Altstadt. At the centre of the square is the **Mariensäule** (1; Mary Column), erected in 1638 to celebrate the removal of Swedish forces. At the top

is the golden figure of the Virgin Mary, carved in 1590 and originally located in the Frauenkirche.

NEUES RATHAUS

The blackened façade of the neo-Gothic Neues Rathaus (2; New Town Hall; 1867–1908) is festooned with gargoyles and statues, including, on the corner, a wonderful dragon climbing the turrets. Inside, six stately courtyards are used for festivals and events throughout the year. For a good view of the city you can also go to the top of the 85m **tower** (admission €2/1; ⏱ 9am-7pm Mon-Fri, 10am-5pm Sat & Sun).

The highlight of the building is the **Glockenspiel** (carillon), which has three levels: two portray the **Schäfflertanz** (see History p319) and the other the **Ritterturnier**, a knights' tournament held in 1568 to celebrate a royal marriage. The characters spring into action at 11am and noon (also 5pm November to April). The night scene featuring the Münchener Kindl (Munich children) and Nachtwächter (night watchman) characters runs at 9pm.

ST PETERSKIRCHE
Opposite the Neues Rathaus, on the southern end of Marienplatz, is **St Peterskirche** (3; Church of St Peter), Gothic in its core but with a flamboyant baroque interior. The magnificent high altar (1517) is by Erasmus Grasser and the eye-catching statues of the four church fathers (1732) by Egid Quirin Asam. For spectacular views of the city, you can climb the rectangular 92m **tower** (adult/concession €1.50/1; ☺ 9am-6pm Mon-Sat, 10.15am-7pm Sun) – also known as 'Alter Peter' – via 297 steps.

FISCHBRUNNEN
Local legend suggests that dipping an empty purse into the **Fischbrunnen (4)** on Ash Wednesday guarantees that it will always be full. The Fish Fountain was used to keep river fish alive during medieval markets, and later as the ceremonial dunking spot for butchers' apprentices.

ALTES RATHAUS
The Gothic Altes Rathaus (5; 1474) was destroyed by lightning and bombs, and then rebuilt in a plainer style after WWII. In its south tower is the city's **Spielzeugmuseum** (Toy Museum; ☎ 294 001; Alter Rathausturm; adult/concession €3/1; ☺ 10am-5.30pm) with its huge collection of European and American toys. Look out for the wind-powered sculpture by the

entrance that releases pent-up energy by clanging and banging.

Behind the Altes Rathaus, the **Heiliggeistkirche** (6; Church of the Holy Spirit; Tal 77), built in 1392, first appears almost economical in design until you look up to see the frescoes by Cosmas Damian Asam, completed during the interior revamp in 1727–30.

MARIENPLATZ TO MAX-JOSEPH-PLATZ
Head east on Im Tal from the Heiliggeistkirche, then north on Maderbräustrasse to Orlandostrasse and the celebrated, if infamous, **Hofbräuhaus (7)**. The ballroom upstairs was the site of the first large meeting of the National Socialist Party on 20 February 1920, but downstairs is Munich's most famous beer hall, crawling with tourists throughout the year.

From the Hofbräuhaus, head west on Münzstrasse, turn left into Sparkassenstrasse, then duck into the Ledererstrasse alleyway which leads to Burgstrasse. Turn right (north) here to get to the central courtyard of the **Alter Hof (8)**, the Wittelsbach residence until they outgrew it and built the Residenz you'll see later on this tour.

Exit the courtyard at its northern end and continue north on Hofgraben, past the former **Münzhof (9**; mint).

MAX-JOSEPH-PLATZ
Just past the old mint is **Maximilianstrasse**, Munich's most glamorous shopping street. Turning left, you'll reach **Max-Joseph-Platz**,

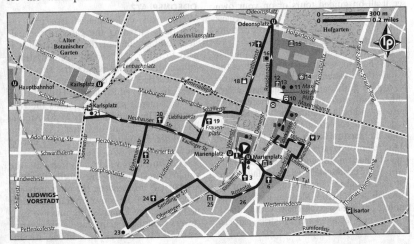

home to some of Munich's most beloved buildings. Among them is the five-tiered **Nationaltheater (10)**, home to the Bavarian State Opera and the granddaddy of them all – the Residenz. The square's anchor is a statue of **Bavarian king Max I Joseph**, who proclaimed Germany's first constitution in 1818.

At the southern end of the square is the **old central post office** with a frescoed Italianate arcade.

RESIDENZ

On the north side of Max-Joseph-Platz looms the oldest section (1571) of the **Residenz (11)**, the huge palace that housed Bavarian rulers from 1385 to 1918. Northern wings were added to create several interior courtyards, including the Emperor, the Apothecary and the Fountain courtyards and two smaller ones, Chapel and King's Tract. There are separate entrances to the various attractions inside the Residenz; to continue the walking tour, head north on Residenzstrasse.

Residenzmuseum

The treasures of the Wittelsbach dynasty are displayed in a maze of roughly 130 rooms in the **Residenzmuseum** (12; ☎ 290 671; enter from Max-Josephs-Platz 3; adult/concession/under 18 with parents €5/4/free; ☼ 9am-6pm Apr–mid-Oct, 9am-8pm Thu, 10am-4pm mid-Oct–Mar). The museum is so large that it's divided into two sections, one open in the morning, one in the afternoon. You can see it all on guided tours or on your own with a copy of the excellent English-language guide (€4), which has room-by-room tours with photographs and explanations.

The enclosed Grotto Court, one of the first places you'll see when you enter, features the wonderful **Perseusbrunnen** (Perseus Fountain). Next door is the famous **Antiquarium**, a lavishly ornamented barrel vault, smothered in frescoes and built to house the Wittelsbach's huge antique collection. Other highlights include the **Ancestral Gallery**, with 121 portraits of the rulers of Bavaria (note the larger paintings of Charlemagne and Ludwig the Bavarian); the **Schlachtensäle** (Battle Halls); the **Porcelain Chambers**, containing 19th-century porcelain from Berlin, Meissen and Nymphenburg; and the **Asian Collections**, with Chinese and Japanese lacquerware, tapestries, carpets, furniture and jewellery.

Schatzkammer der Residenz

The Residenzmuseum entrance also leads to the **Schatzkammer der Residenz** (Residence Treasury; **13**; ☎ 290 671; enter from Max-Joseph-Platz 3; adult/concession/under 18 with parents €4/2/free; ☼ 9am-6pm, 9am-8pm Thu). It exhibits an Aladdin's cave-worth of jewels, ornate gold work and other precious objects. Included among the mind-boggling treasures are portable altars, the ruby jewellery of Queen Therese, amazing pocket watches, and 'exotic handicrafts', including applied art from Turkey, Iran, Mexico and India. It's well worth the entry price. The English-language guide to the collection is another €3.50.

Altes Residenztheater

The Residenz also harbours one of Europe's finest rococo theatres, the **Altes Residenztheater** (Old Residence Theatre; **14**; Cuvilliés Theatre; ☎ 290 671, enter from Residenzstrasse 1; adult/concession/under 18 with parents €2/1.50/free; ☼ 9am-6pm, 9am-8pm Thu). It has a stunning interior designed by Belgian architect François Cuvilliés.

Staatliches Museum Ägyptischer Kunst

An excellent collection of Egyptian antiquities, artwork, monuments and statues is on display at the **Staatliches Museum Ägyptischer Kunst** (Egyptian Art Museum; **15**; ☎ 298 546, enter from Hofgartenstrasse 1; adult/concession €2/1.50; ☼ 9am-5pm Wed-Fri, 9am-5pm & 7-9pm Tue, 10am-5pm Sat & Sun) where exhibits date from the Old, Middle and New Kingdoms (2670–1075 BC).

ODEONSPLATZ

Walk north on Residenzstrasse, past the two lions guarding the gates to the palace. Rubbing one of the lions' shields is said to bring you wealth. Residenzstrasse culminates in Odeonsplatz, the site of the so-called Beer Hall Putsch (revolt) by the Nazis in 1923, which landed Hitler in jail. At the square's south end looms the **Feldherrnhalle (16**; Field Marshals' Hall). Among its statues is the one of General Tilly, who surrendered Munich to the Swedes during the Thirty Years' War (1618–48).

The mustard-yellow church at the square's west side is the **Theatinerkirche St Kajetan (17**; Theatinerstrasse 22), built between 1663 and 1690 to commemorate the birth of Prince Max Emanuel. Its massive twin towers flanking a giant cupola are a landmark of Munich's skyline. Inside, the intensely ornate high dome stands above the **Fürstengruft** (royal crypt), containing the remains of Wittelsbach family members.

At the east side of Odeonsplatz, a neo-classical gate leads the way to the former **Hofgarten** (Royal Gardens).

ODEONSPLATZ TO KARLSPLATZ

Heading south on Theatinerstrasse will soon get you to the eastern entrance of the **Fünf Höfe (18)**, an exclusive shopping centre built around five courtyards. A perfect example of minimalist architecture (plenty of metal and glass), it's a maze of passageways lined by top-notch retailers. Also part of the complex is the **Kunsthalle der Hypo-Kulturstiftung** (☎ 224 412; adult/child €6/3, half-price Mon evenings; Theatinerstrasse 8; ⊙ 10am-8pm), which has excellent rotating exhibitions.

Continue south on Theatinerstrasse, then turn right on Schäfflerstrasse which leads to Frauenplatz, dominated by the twin copper onion domes of the late Gothic **Frauenkirche (19**; Church of Our Lady, 1468–88). In contrast to the heavy red-brick exterior, the interior is a soaring passage of light with the tomb of Ludwig the Bavarian, guarded by knights and noblemen, in the choir. There are good views of the city from the 98m south **tower** (adult/concession €2.50/1.50; ⊙ 10am-5pm Mon-Sat Apr-Oct).

Walk south on Liebfrauenstrasse to Kaufingerstrasse, the main shopping drag, then turn right and continue 200m along what becomes Neuhauser Strasse to the **Michaelskirche (20**; St Michael's Church) at No 52. Architecturally a transition from Renaissance to baroque, its most distinctive feature is the 20m-wide barrel-vaulted ceiling – without supporting pillars. The main façade, with its rich figural ornamentation, depicts three eras of history, from the dark ages to the 16th century, with St Michael playing a central role. The church crypt contains the tombs of some members of the Wittelsbach family, including the humble final resting place of 'Mad King' Ludwig II.

Neuhauser Strasse culminates in Karlsplatz, punctuated by the medieval **Karlstor (21)**, the western gate and perimeter of the Altstadt, and an enormous **modern fountain**, a favourite meeting point. It's also a major tram, bus, U-Bahn and S-Bahn connection point.

KARLSPLATZ TO SENDLINGER STRASSE

From Karlsplatz, double back and turn right onto Eisenmannstrasse, where you'll see the ornate **Damenstiftskirche (22)** to your left, then continue south to **Sendlinger Tor (23)**, the 14th-century southern gate. From there, head northeast onto Sendlinger Strasse; at No 62 is the small St Johann Nepomuk church, better known as the **Asamkirche (24**; 1733–46), designed and built by the Asam brothers. The brothers lived next door and this was originally their private chapel. The jaw-dropping interior shows a harmonious unity of architecture, painting and sculpture, with scarcely a single unembellished surface. As you enter note the golden skeleton of Death trying to cut the string of Life.

Carry on along Sendlinger Strasse, then turn right on Rosental, which runs into the **Stadtmuseum** (City Museum; **25**; ☎ 2332 5586; St-Jakobs-Platz; adult/concession €2.50/1.50; ⊙ 10am-6pm, closed Mon). The outstanding exhibits cover brewing, fashion, musical instruments, photography and puppets. Films are shown nightly here as well; see p349.

VIKTUALIENMARKT

Carry on east down Rosental to emerge at the bustling **Viktualienmarkt (26)**, one of Europe's great food markets. In summer the entire place is transformed into one of the finest and most expensive beer gardens around, while in winter people huddle for warmth and schnapps in the small pubs around the square. The merchandise and food are of the finest quality, but there aren't many bargains.

Shooting up from the centre of the square is the **Maypole**, bearing artisans' symbols and the traditional blue-and-white Bavarian stripes. On the south side of the square you'll see a statue of famous comedian Karl Valentin. Marienplatz is just to the northwest.

Königsplatz & Around   Map p330

Northwest of the Altstadt is Königsplatz (take the U2 or tram No 27), a Greek Revivalist square created under Ludwig I. It is anchored by the Doric-columned **Propyläen** gateway and orbited by three museums. A short walk north of Königsplatz is the Technical University and Munich's three major art museums – a day ticket for all

BAVARIA

three Pinakothek museums costs adult/concession €12/7.

ALTE PINAKOTHEK

A treasure-trove of the works of old European masters awaits visitors to the newly renovated **Alte Pinakothek** (Map p330; ☎ 2380 5216; Barer Strasse 27; adult/concession €5/3.50; ⏲ 10am-5pm, 10am-10pm Tue & Thu, closed Mon). Enter the gallery from Theresienstrasse. Highlights include Dürer's Christ-like *Self-Portrait* and his *Four Apostles*, Rogier van der Weyden's *Adoration of the Magi*, and Botticelli's *Pietà*.

NEUE PINAKOTHEK

Just north of the Alte Pinakothek is the **Neue Pinakothek** (Map p330; ☎ 2380 5195; Barer Strasse 29; adult/concession €5/3.50; ⏲ 10am-5pm, 10am-10pm Wed & Thu, closed Tue), which is also entered from Theresienstrasse. It contains an extensive collection of 18th- and 19th-century paintings and sculpture, from rococo to *Jugendstil* (Art Nouveau). Don't miss Walter Crane's *The Seeds of Neptune* or Goya's chilling kitchen still-life *Plucked Turkey*.

PINAKOTHEK DER MODERNE

Germany's biggest museum of modern art is the newly opened **Pinakothek der Moderne** (Map p330; ☎ 2380 5360; Barer Strasse 40; adult/concession €9/5; ⏲ 10am-5pm, 10am-8pm Thu & Fri, closed Mon). The stunning glass-and-concrete building (entered from Theresienstrasse) presents a thorough survey of 20th-century and contemporary art, design, sculpture, photography and video. In addition to works by such modern masters as Dali, Picasso, Warhol and Matisse, there are special sections dedicated to architecture and industrial and graphic design.

SIEMENSFORUM

About 350m southeast of the Pinakothek der Moderne is the **SiemensForum** (Map p330; ☎ 6363 2660; Oskar-von-Miller-Ring 20; admission free; ⏲ 9am-5pm, closed Sat). It's a fun, hands-on kind of place with five floors of promotional exhibits on electronics and microelectronics from the telegraph to the multimedia personal computer.

LENBACHHAUS

Franz von Lenbach (1836–1904), a leading late 19th-century painter, used his consid-

erable fortune to construct a residence in Munich between 1883 and 1889. His widow sold it to the city in 1924 and threw in a bunch of his works as part of the deal. Today this fabulous residence is the **Städtische Galerie im Lenbachhaus** (Map p330; ☎ 2333 2000; Luisenstrasse 33; adult/concession €6/3; ⏲ 10am-6pm, closed Mon). It features a staggering range of 19th-century masterpieces by Munich and other German masters, and holds exhibitions of international modern art.

OTHER MUSEUMS

Munich's oldest museum is the **Glyptothek** (☎ 286 100; Königsplatz 3; adult/concession €3/2, free Sun, combined with Antikensammlungen €5/3; ⏲ 10am-5pm, 10am-8pm Tue & Thu). It presents a comprehensive collection of Greek and Roman sculpture, classical marbles and portraits of Roman kings and Greek philosophers and leaders.

One of Germany's best antiquities collections is housed in the **Antikensammlungen** (☎ 598 359; Königsplatz 1; adult/concession €3/2, free Sun; ⏲ 10am-5pm, 10am-8pm Tue & Thu). It features vases, gold and silver jewellery and ornaments, bronze work, and Greek and Roman sculptures and statues.

The **Museum Reich der Kristalle** (☎ 2394 4312; Theresienstrasse 41; adult/concession €2.50/1.50; ⏲ 1-5pm Tue-Fri, 1-6pm Sat & Sun), entered from Barer Strasse, has a truly dazzling collection of crystals. Exhibits demystify the formation of crystals and their underlying molecular structures. A large Russian emerald and numerous diamonds are among the museum's most prized possessions.

Englischer Garten & Around

The Englischer Garten is nestled between the Altstadt, Schwabing and the Isar River. One of the largest city parks in Europe, it's a great place for strolling, drinking, sunbathing, paddle-boating and even surfing (see Activities p339). In hot weather it's not unusual for hundreds of naked sunbathers to be in the park on a normal working day, with their jackets, ties and dresses stacked neatly beside them.

The **Chinesischer Turm** (Chinese Tower), now in the centre of the city's best-known beer garden, dates back to 1789. Just south of here is the heavily photographed **Monopteros** (1838) monument.

Don't even think about spending the night in the park. Police patrol frequently, and muggers, junkies, proselytisers and other colourful characters are everywhere.

BAYERISCHES NATIONALMUSEUM
Off the southeastern corner of the Englischer Garten is a highlight of Munich's museum scene, the **Bayerisches Nationalmuseum** (Bavarian National Museum; ☎ 211 2401; Prinzregentenstrasse 3; adult/concession €3/2, Sun free; ☻ 10am-5pm Tue-Sun, 10am-8pm Thu). It's chock-full of exhibits illustrating the art, folklore and cultural history of southern Germany and Bavaria in particular.

The ground floor has paintings, sculpture, tapestries, furniture and weapons from the early Middle Ages to the rococo period, including carved sculptures by Erasmus Grasser and Tilman Riemenschneider, two of the greatest of the era. Upstairs, the eastern wing concentrates on the 19th century. Highlights include Nymphenburg porcelain, precious glass and an exquisite collection of *Jugendstil* items. The west wing has specialised collections of musical instruments, games and silverware. In the basement is a celebrated collection of cots from the 17th to the 19th centuries. To get there take the U-Bahn to Lehel, tram No 17 or bus No 53.

ARCHÄOLOGISCHE STAATSSAMMLUNG
You can trace the settlement of Bavaria from the Stone Age to the early Middle Ages at the **Archäologische Staatssammlung** (☎ 211 2402; Lerchenfeldstrasse 2; adult/concession €4.50/2.50, Sun free; ☻ 9am-4.30pm, closed Mon), which is behind the Nationalmuseum. The exhibit features objects from Celtic, Roman and Germanic civilisations, including the well-preserved body of a ritually sacrificed young girl.

Olympiapark & Around   Map p330
More than 30 years after the Olympic Games for which it was built, Olympic Park is still an integral part of life in the city. The centre-pieces are the 290m Olympiaturm (Olympic Tower) and the massive undulating 'tented' roof covering the west side of the Olympic Stadium, hall and swimming centre.

Today the complex is open as a collection of public facilities, and the grounds are the site of celebrations, concerts, firework displays and professional sporting events throughout the year. Both the swimming

hall and ice-skating rink are open to the public. There's an **Info Pavilion** (☎ 3067 2414) at the Olympia-Eissportzentrum (ice-skating rink).

Wandering around the grounds is free but you'll have to pay to see inside the **Olympia-Stadion** (adult/children €4/3; ☻ 9am-4.30pm Oct–mid-Apr, 8.30am-6pm mid-Apr–Sep, closed event days). From April to October you can take a **Soccer Tour** (adult/concession €5/3.50; 1hr), which visits the Olympic Stadium, VIP area and locker rooms, or an **Adventure Tour** (€7/5; 90min) that covers the entire Olympiapark both on foot and in a little train. When the weather's good you can enjoy stunning views of the city from the top of the **Olympiaturm** (adult/concession €3/2; ☻ 9am-midnight, last trip 11.30pm) or have a meal at its revolving **restaurant** (☎ 3066 8585).

BMW MUSEUM
Off the northeast corner of Olympiapark is the popular **BMW Museum** (☎ 3822 3307; Petuelring 130; adult/concession €3/2; ☻ 9am-5pm, last entry 4pm), a haven for car enthusiasts. Just look for the striking silver cylinders – an architectural attraction in their own right – that also house the BMW (Bayerische Motoren Werke) headquarters.

Museum exhibits include BMW cars, motorcycles, planes, concept cars and, near the top, simulators and interactive displays. Free tours of the factory line (in German and English) are run at the **BMW factory** (☎ 3822 3306), adjacent to the headquarters and museum.

South of the Altstadt
DEUTSCHES MUSEUM
You can spend days wandering through the **Deutsches Museum** (Map p328; ☎ 217 91; Museumsinsel 1; adult/concession/family €7.50/5/15, children under 6 years free; ☻ 9am-5pm), said to be the world's largest science and technology museum. This vast museum is on an island southeast of Isartor (Isar Gate) and features just about anything ever invented. There are loads of interactive displays (including glass blowing and paper making), model coal and salt mines, an electric power hall that produces lightning and wonderful sections on musical instruments, caves, geodesy, microelectronics and astronomy.

In the northeast corner of the island, near Rosenheimer Strasse, is the Deutsches

Museum-affiliated **Forum der Technik** (Forum of Technology; Map p328; ☎ 2112 5183; Museumsinsel 1). It comprises two attractions: an **IMAX Theatre** (2D/3D films €7/8.50) boasting a changing roster of big-screen movies, and a state-of-the-art **planetarium** (normal show/laser show €6/7.50) with educational programming.

To get to Museumsinsel take the S-Bahn to Isartor or tram No 18 from Karlsplatz.

JÜDISCHES MUSEUM MÜNCHEN

An under-visited exhibition on the history of Jewish people in Munich and Bavaria can be seen at the **Jüdisches Museum München** (Munich Jewish Museum; Map p326-7; ☎ 2000 9693; Reichenbachstrasse 27; admission free; ☺ 2-6pm Tue, 10am-noon & 2-6pm Wed, 2-8pm Thu). The hours are limited due to budgetary constraints, so donations are welcomed.

Theresienwiese

The Theresienwiese (Theresa Meadow), better known as 'Wiesn', just southwest of the Altstadt, is the site of the annual Oktoberfest (see p340). At the western end of the meadow is the **Ruhmeshalle** (Hall of Fame) containing statues of Bavarian leaders as well as the **Bavaria statue** (Map pp326-7; adult/concession/under 18 with parents €2.50/1.50/free; ☺ 10am-noon & 2-4pm Tue-Sun). The statue has a cunning design that makes it seem as if it's solid, but you actually climb up to the head to get a so-so view of the city or a great view of the Oktoberfest.

VERKEHRSZENTRUM

To celebrate the Deutsches Museum's 100th anniversary in 2003, a new annexe dedicated entirely to transport research and inventions was opened. The **Verkehrszentrum** (Transport & Mobility Centre; Map p326-7; ☎ 217 9529; Thersienhöhe 14a; adult/child €2.50/1.50; ☺ 9am-5pm, 9am-8pm Thu) shows fascinating exhibits on famous and pioneering research and inventions, cars, boats and trains and the history of car racing, with lots of hands-on experiments and demonstrations making it fun for all the family.

Schloss Nymphenburg   Map p330

If the Residenz hasn't satisfied your passion for palaces, visit the amazing **Schloss Nymphenburg** (Map p330; ☎ 179 080; combined ticket to everything except Marstallmuseum adult/concession €7.50/6) about 5km northwest of the Altstadt.

Begun in 1664 as a villa for Electress Adelaide of Savoy, the palace and gardens were continually expanded and built upon over the next century to create the royal family's summer residence. To get there take tram No 17 or 41 from Karlsplatz.

SCHLOSS

The main palace building (adult/concession €3.50/2.50; ☺ 9am-6pm, 9am-8pm Thu) consists of a main villa and two wings. The rooms are all sumptuous, but one of the most majestic is the **Schönheitengalerie** (Gallery of Beauties), in the southern wing, formerly the apartments of Queen Caroline. It's now the home of 38 portraits of women whom Ludwig I considered beautiful; most famous of these is Schöne Münchnerin, the portrait of Helene Sedlmayr, daughter of a shoemaker.

Also in the south wing are the coaches and riding gear of the royal families, suitably displayed in the **Marstallmuseum** (adult/concession €2.50/2; ☺ 9am-6pm, 9am-8pm Thu). On the 1st floor is a collection of porcelain made by the Nymphenburger Manufaktur.

The north wing is occupied by the **Museum Mensch und Natur** (Museum of Humankind & Nature; adult/concession/under 15 with parents €2/1/free; ☺ 9am-5pm Tue-Sun). This is a fun place to bring children for the interactive, if aged, displays in German and the upstairs exhibits on animals and the earth.

GARDENS & OUTBUILDINGS

The royal gardens are a magnificently sculpted English-style park and contain a number of intriguing buildings, including the **Amalienburg** (adult/concession €1.50/1; ☺ 9am-6pm, 9am-8pm Thu), a small hunting lodge with a large domed central room; the **Pagodenburg** Chinese teahouse; and the **Badenburg** (adult/concession €1.50/1; ☺ 9am-6pm, 9am-8pm Thu) sauna and bathing house.

Other Attractions

MÜNCHENER TIERPARK HELLABRUNN

About 5000 animals are housed in Munich's 'geo-zoo' (one with distinct sections dividing animals by continents). The **Münchener Tierpark Hellabrunn** (Map pp324-5; ☎ 625 080; Tierparkstrasse 30; adult/concession €7/4; ☺ 8am-6pm Apr-Sep, 9am-5pm Oct-Mar) was one of the first of its kind and has some 460 species, including rhinos, elephants, deer and gazelles. It's absolutely worth the admission if only to gain access to the petting zoo, which is full of sheep, deer and lambs that you can feed. To get there take the U-Bahn to Thalkirchen or bus No 52 from Marienplatz.

ALLIANZ ARENA
Sporting and architecture fans alike should take a side trip to the northern Munich suburb of Fröttmaning to see Munich's sparkling new football stadium. Due for completion in summer 2005, the €280 million Allianz Arena has walls made of inflatable cushions and has already been nicknamed the 'life belt' and the 'rubber boat'. The state-of the-art stadium will seat 66,000 spectators and will host the opening game of the 2006 World Cup. To get there take U-Bahn 6 to Fröttmaning.

BAVARIA FILMSTADT
An often-missed treasure is the **Bavaria Filmstadt** (☎ 6499 2304; Bavariafilmplatz 7; adult/concession €10/7; tours 9am-5pm) in the southern suburb of Geiselgasteig. You'll see sets of *Enemy Mine*, *Das Boot*, *Cabaret* and *The Never-Ending Story*, all of which were filmed here. Stunt shows (€7) take place at 11.30am, 1pm and 2.30pm. To get there take the U-Bahn to Silberhornstrasse, then tram No 25 to Bavariafilmplatz.

ACTIVITIES
Munich makes a perfect base for outdoor activities. For information about hiking and climbing, contact the Munich chapter of the **Deutscher Alpenverein** (German Alpine Club; Map pp326-7; ☎ 551 7000; Bayerstrasse 21) near the Hauptbahnhof.

Boating
The most popular spot in town to take a leisurely boat trip is at the Kleinhesseloher See (Kleinhesseloher Lake) in the Englischer Garten (see p336), where rowing/pedal boats cost around €7 per half-hour for up to four people. You can also hire boats at the Olympiapark (see p337).

Cycling
Munich is an excellent place for cycling.
Radius Tours & Bikes (Map pp326-7; ☎ 596 113; www.radiusmunich.com; at the end of tracks 31-33 in the Hauptbahnhof; ☯ 10am to 6pm May–mid-Oct) hires out bikes for €3/14 per hour/day, with a €50 deposit. Staff speak English and are

happy to provide tips and advice on touring around Munich.

Mike's Bike Tours (☎ 25543987/88; www.mikesbike tours.com; standard/extended tour €22/33; ☯ Apr–mid-Nov) offers guided bike tours of the city. The company doesn't have an office in town – their representative is **Discover Bavaria** (Map pp326-7; cnr Brauhausstrasse & Hochbrückenstrasse). The standard tour covers about 6.5km in four hours (with a 45-minute beer garden break); the extended tour goes for seven hours and covers 16km. Tours leave from the archway of the Altes Rathaus on Marienplatz (in front of the Toy Museum). You don't have to be in shape as the guide stops about every 400m to explain a point of interest.

Surfing
At the southern tip of the Englischer Garten is an artificially created wave in the Isar River where surfers practise their moves.

Swimming
Bathing in the Isar River isn't advisable because of pollution. The two best public swimming pool options are the **Olympia-Schwimmhalle** (Map p330; ☎ 3067 2290; Olympiapark; adult/child €3/250; ☯ 7am-11pm), and the spectacular Art Nouveau **Müllersches Volksbad** (Map p328; ☎ 2361 3434; Rosenheimer Strasse 1; adult/child €2.90/2.30; ☯ 7.30am-11pm) in Haidhausen. To get there take tram No 18 from Karlsplatz.

MUNICH FOR CHILDREN
Munich is a great city for children, as many of the museums have hands-on exhibits to play with, the zoo is stunning and there are lots of parks and plenty of children's theatre events. The Munich tourist office has an excellent publication, **Familianspass in München** (Family Fun in Munich), which lists sights, activities, sports, playgrounds and events suitable for families.

QUIRKY MUNICH
ZENTRUM FÜR AUSSERGEWÖHNLICHE MUSEEN (ZAM)
Munich's most bizarre sight is just a short walk east of Viktualienmarkt. The **Zentrum für Aussergewöhnliche Museen** (Centre for Unusual Museums; Map pp326-7; ☎ 290 4121; Westenriederstrasse 41; adult/concession €4/3; ☯ 10am-6pm) houses the most peculiar collection of

chamber pots, perfume bottles, Easter bunnies and locks. There's also a collection of items associated with 'Sisi' (that's Empress Elisabeth of Austria to you). We could make lots of jokes about this place, but to paraphrase Groucho Marx, it doesn't need our help.

TOURS

Munich Walks (☎ 0171-274 0204; www.munichwalk tours.de) offers a variety of different walks, all starting at the entrance to the Neues Rathaus. The **City Walk** (adults/under 26/under 14 €10/9/free; ⏱ 10.45am & 3pm May-Aug; 2hr) takes you through the heart of the city and provides good historical background and architectural information. The **Third Reich Tour** (adults/under 26/under 14 €10/9/free; ⏱ 10am Apr-Oct, Mon, Wed, Sun Mar & Nov; 2½ hr) visits all major sites associated with the growth of the Nazi movement.

Panorama Tours (Map pp326-7; ☎ 5502 8995; Arnulfstrasse 8; adult/child €11/6; 10 tours daily, 1hr) Runs bus tours around Munich leaving from the Hertie department store opposite the Hauptbahnhof. Longer themed tours are offered on a regular schedule as well (around €23), as are day trips to the surrounding countryside (around €41). They're all right but the commentary is given in two languages, which can get tedious.

Taxi Sightseeing Tours (☎ 0175-481 2848; www .taxi-guide-muenchen.de; €68 for 4 people, 1hr) Taxi tours are available in a variety of languages and you get to decide the route with your driver.

FESTIVALS & EVENTS

Munich always seems to have something to celebrate. The list below gives just a few of the highlights; for more information check www.muenchen-tourist.de.

JANUARY/FEBRUARY

Fasching Six-week carnival beginning on 7 January with all kinds of merriment, including costume parades and fancy-dress balls.

APRIL

Frülingsfest Theresienwiese fills with beer tents and amusements for the Spring Festival.

MAY

Maidult Traditional fair on Mariahilfplatz with crafts, antiques and a fairground.

JUNE/JULY

International Film Festival (www.filmfest-muenchen .de) World premieres of international and independent films.
Jakobidult Traditional fair on Mariahilfplatz with crafts, antiques and a fairground.
Opera Festival (☎ 2185 1021; www.bayerische.staats oper.de) Month-long festival of opera concluding on 31 July with Wagner's 'Die Meistersinger von Nürnberg'.
Tollwood Festival (☎ 383 8500; www.tollwood.de) World culture festival with nightly world-music concerts at the Olympiapark.

OCTOBER

Oktoberfest (see the boxed text, p341) Legendary beer-swilling party running from mid-September to the first Sunday in October.

NOVEMBER/DECEMBER

Christkindlmarkt Traditional Christmas market on Marienplatz.

SLEEPING

Room rates in Munich tend to be high and can rise 10% to 15% in summer, and skyrocket during Oktoberfest; at any time you'd be well advised to book ahead.

The hostels are the cheapest option – the most popular ones are northwest of the centre in cosmopolitan Neuhausen. There are also lots of budget pensions and hotels, of varying standards, clustered around the Hauptbahnhof. This area is swamped with places to stay and also has plenty of more upmarket options. The Altstadt has the largest number of top-end hotels.

Around the Hauptbahnhof
BUDGET

4 you münchen (Map pp326-7; ☎ 552 1660; www .the4you.de; Hirtenstrasse 18; dm/s/d €16.50/43.50/68.50; ✗ ; wheelchair access) This popular place bills itself as an ecologically correct hostel. Rooms are basic but spotless and the more expensive ones have private bathrooms. Childcare, lockers, luggage storage and laundry facilities are all available. Guests over 26 pay 16% more.

Hotel Jedermann (☎ 543 240; www.hotel-jeder mann.de; Bayerstrasse 95; s €34-99, d €49-149; P ✗ ✗ 💻) This recently renovated hotel is excellent value with small but comfortable rooms with dataports. Family rooms have connecting doors. There's also free Internet access downstairs, but you may have to queue. The friendly staff speak English.

OKTOBERFEST

In October 1810 Bavarian Crown Prince Ludwig I married the Saxon-Hildburghausen Princess Therese and an enormous party was held in front of the city gates. That was the beginning of what is now the largest beer festival in the world, Oktoberfest. A 15-day extravaganza that attracts over seven million people a year, it is Munich's largest and most economically important tourist attraction.

During the event, the Theresienwiese fairgrounds are transformed into a city of beer tents, amusements, rides – just what beer drinkers need after several frothy ones – and kiosks selling snacks and sweets. The action kicks off with the Brewer's Parade at 11am on the first day of the festival. The parade begins at Sonnenstrasse and winds its way to the fairgrounds via Schwanthalerstrasse. At noon, the lord mayor stands before the thirsty crowds at Theresienwiese and with due pomp, slams a wooden tap into a cask of beer. As the beer gushes out, the mayor exclaims, *Ozapft ist's!* (It's tapped!).

The following morning a young girl on a horse leads 7000 performers (wearing pretzel bras and other traditional drunkenwear) from all over Europe through the streets of the city centre.

The action runs from about 10.30am to 11.30pm daily. Midday to mid-afternoon is the least busy time, and it's best to leave the fair by about 9pm or 10pm, as crowds can get a bit touchy when the beer and schnapps supplies are turned off. Thursday is Children's Day, when all children's rides and attractions are half-price. On the first Sunday of the festival there's a big gay meeting at the Bräurosl tent, with legions of butch-looking guys in leather gear.

No admission is charged, but most of the fun costs something. One way to cut your bill is by eating before you arrive, as the reluctance to part with €11 and up for a beer and a chicken leg tends to fade after a litre or two of amber liquid. The Turkish shops and snack bars at the western end of Schwanthalerstrasse make inexpensive doner kebabs, pizzas and filled pastries.

Hotels book out very quickly and prices skyrocket during the fair, so reserve accommodation as early as you can (like a year in advance). If you show up during Oktoberfest, expect to find only extremely pricey rooms – if any at all – in Munich. Otherwise, consider staying in the suburbs or nearby cities – Augsburg, Garmisch-Partenkirchen or Bad Tölz are all under an hour's train ride away.

The festival is held at the Theresienwiese, a 15-minute walk southwest of the Hauptbahnhof, and is served by its own U-Bahn station. If you're asking directions, say '*d'wies'n*' (dee-veezen), the diminutive nickname for the grounds. Trams and buses heading that way have signs reading 'Zur Festwiese' (literally 'to the Festival Meadow').

Hotel Helvetia (Map pp326-7; ☎ 590 6850; www.hotel-helvetia.de; Schillerstrasse 6; s €30-50, d €40-95; ✗ ☐) Another very popular choice is this simple hotel with modern rooms with IKEA-type furniture. Rooms have phones and soundproofed windows, a laundry service (€6) is available and there's free Internet access.

Hotel Monaco (Map pp326-7; ☎ 545 9940; www.hotel-monaco.de; Schillerstrasse 9; s €55-155, d €66-165; ✗ ☐) On the 5th floor of this inauspicious building you'll find an exercise in floral elegance. Artful paper roses adorn the halls, layers of swag and net curtains line the windows and there's a good variety of rooms. It's a cosy effect if that's what you like.

Side by side on Senefelderstrasse you'll find the popular **Euro Youth Hotel** (Map pp326-7; ☎ 5990 8811; www.euro-youth-hotel.de; Senefelderstrasse 5; dm/s/d €17.50/38/48; ✗) and **Jaegers** (Map pp326-7; ☎ 555 281; www.jaegershotel.de; Senefelderstrasse 3; dm/s/d from €17.50/45/68). Both offer a choice of clean, bright dorms or simple private rooms. There's little to choose between them.

Other recommendations are:

IN VIA Marienherberge (Map pp326-7; ☎ 555 805; INVIA.Muenchen.Marienherberge@t-online.de; Goethestrasse 9; dm/s/d €17/25/40; ✗) Women-only (under 25) Catholic hostel with a midnight curfew.

Hotel Flora (Map p330; ☎ 597 067; www.hotel-flora.de; Karlstrasse 49; s €35-70, d €50-95) Quiet, simple hotel with good-value rooms.

MID-RANGE

Hotel Mirabell (Map pp326-7; ☎ 549 1740; www.hotelmirabell.de; Landwehrstrasse 42; s €71-133, d €87-164; P ✗ ☐) Behind the garish purple façade, the friendly Mirabell has attractive rooms of a high standard, with soundproofed windows, light wood panelling and pleasant wall prints. There are also three apartments for family stays.

Creatif Hotel Elephant (Map pp326-7; ☎ 555 785; creatif-hotel-elephant@munich-hotel.net; Lämmwestrasse 6; s €49-149, d €69-189; P ✗) This sparkling new hotel offers a range of simple rooms with modern décor and good facilities. It is family run and the service is extremely friendly with a big welcome for children.

Hotel Brunnenhof (Map pp326-7; ☎ 545 100; www.brunnenhof.de; Schillerstrasse 36; s €60-170, d €80-195; P 🖳 ; wheelchair access) Bright, airy rooms, a central yet quiet location and reasonable rates make this modern hotel worth a look. The spacious rooms are centred round a small interior courtyard but don't have many facilities.

Hotel Schweitz (Map pp326-7; ☎ 543 6960; www .hotel-schweitz.de; Goethestrasse 26; s €70-87, d €90-160; P ✗ 🖳) Recently renovated and upgraded, this modern hotel has bright but cosy rooms with maple-wood furniture. The sixth floor has a modest wellness area with infrared sauna and an open-air terrace.

Andi München City Center (Map pp326-7; ☎ 552 5560; fax 5525 5666; Landwehrstrasse 33; s €60-105, d €77-145; P 🖳) South of the Hauptbahnhof, this hotel has simple but quiet rooms that are tastefully furnished and well equipped. Service is very friendly but the cheaper rooms don't have private bathrooms.

Hotel Bristol (Map pp326-7; ☎ 5951 5154; www .bristol-muc.com; Pettenkofer Strasse 2; s €62-125, d €83-150; P ✗ 🖳) This modern hotel looks humble enough from the street but has comfortable, well-furnished rooms, all with dataports. Service is friendly and the breakfast will keep you going all day.

TOP END

Deutscher Kaiser (Map pp326-7; ☎ 545 30; nhdeutsch erkaiser@nh-hotels.com; Arnulfstrasse 2; s €99, d €134; ✗ 🖳) This Spanish-influenced hotel is bathed in light, and the spacious rooms and bathrooms are decorated in a stylish modern mix of plush leather, dark wood and stainless steel. Most command fantastic views over the city.

Altstadt & Around   Map pp326-7
MID-RANGE

Hotel Schlicker (☎ 242 8870; www.hotel-schlicker.de; Im Tal 8; s/d €105/200; P 🖳) The charming

400-year-old Schlicker is ideally located near Viktualienmarkt and is a pretty good deal for its spacious, modern rooms. Prices don't go up in summer or at Oktoberfest, but the place is very popular and reservations are advisable.

Pension am Gärtnerplatztheater (☎ 202 5170; pensiongaertnerplatztheater@t-online.de; Klenzestrasse 45; s/d €50/80) Escape the tourist rabble – check in at this fine establishment with antique-filled rooms in the cool Gärtnerplatz quarter. The décor is a little over the top for anyone with a modernist streak, but you can't argue with the very reasonable prices and quality ambience.

Hotel Alcron (☎ 228 3511; Ledererstrasse 13; www .hotel-alcron.de; s €60-70, d €80-90; ✗ 🖳) This quaint hotel is ideally located just stumbling distance from the Hofbräuhaus. A wonderful spiral wooden staircase leads up to the small, simple rooms with traditional furnishings and comfortable beds to sleep off any excesses.

TOP END

Hotel Advokat (☎ 216 310; www.hotel-advokat.de; Baaderstrasse 1; s €130-170, d €150-190; ✗ 🖳) Munich's first boutique hotel has deceptively simple but extremely sleek and stylish rooms. A wonderful breakfast is served on the roof terrace where you can overlook the fashionable Gärtnerplatz district and spy on fashion victims below. A must for any self-respecting modernist.

Bayerischer Hof (☎ 212 00; www.bayerischerhof.de; Promenadeplatz 2-6; s €170-228, d €276-406; P ✗ ✗ 🖳 🍽 ; wheelchair access) One of the *grandes dames* of the Munich hotel trade is the lovely Bayerischer Hof. The historic hotel boasts a super-central location, a pool and a jazz club. Marble, antiques and oil paintings predominate and you can dine till you drop at any one of the three fabulous restaurants. Children are welcome.

Kempinski Vier Jahreszeiten München (☎ 212 50; www.kempinski-vierjahreszeiten.de; Maximilianstrasse 17; s €275-475, d €395-545; P ✗ ✗ 🖳 🍽) This illustrious hotel has a grand façade featuring statues of the managers, the four seasons, and four continents. The individually decorated rooms don't have as many amenities as you'd think, but the suites are palatial and children and adults alike will enjoy a swim in the elegant rooftop pool.

SOMETHING SPECIAL

Two fabulous, but totally different hotels in this district just cry out to be visited.

Cortiina (Map pp326-7; ☎ 242 2490; www .cortiina.com; Ledererstrasse 8; s €144-214, d €164-234; P ☒ ☒ ☐) This stunning modern hotel is a great place for anyone looking for stylish elegance without the antiques. The design is chic and minimalist without losing with comfort. Dark wood and low lighting run throughout the hotel, while the bedrooms are lined with oak panelling, have parquet floors and individual furnishings, as well as glass-encased bathrooms lined with Jura stone.

Opera-Garni (Map p328; ☎ 5210 4940; www.hotel-opera.de; Annastrasse 10; r €165-295, ste €265-295; ☒ ☐) Step inside the Opera and you'll step back in time. This charming hotel is pure old-world elegance and refinement. Breakfast is served in the garden between graceful statues and the sumptuous rooms are stunningly decorated with individual combinations of rich colours and fabrics, antiques, chandeliers and Persian carpets.

Schwabing
BUDGET
Map p329

Pension Frank (☎ 281 451; www.pension-frank.de; Schellingstrasse 24; s €40-45, d €50-60) Large rooms and a convivial atmosphere make this small pension a popular choice with young backpackers and school groups. Rooms (all with shared bathroom) have lovely wrought-iron beds; there is a small collection of English novels and a communal kitchen.

MID-RANGE
Cosmopolitan Hotel (☎ 383 810; www.cosmopolitan -hotel.de; Hohenzollern Strasse 5; s/d €100/130; P ☒) The Cosmopolitan is a good-value modern hotel with comfortable, tastefully furnished rooms with plenty of dark wood and subtle lighting. Ideally located for access to Schwabing's nightlife, it's a good place for party animals to get their beauty sleep.

Neuhausen, Nymphenburg & Around
BUDGET
Map p330

DJH hostel (☎ 141 4300; www.the-tent.com; In den Kirschen 30; sleeping pad/bunk bed €9/11; ☒ Jun–Aug)

Nicknamed 'The Tent', Munich's summer budget favourite is the Jugendlager am Kapuzinerhölzl, a mass camp north of Schloss Nymphenburg. There's no curfew but a 26-year age limit applies (with priority given to people under 23). To get there take tram No 17 from Hauptbahnhof to Botanischer Garten (Botanical Garden), from where it's a two-minute walk.

DJH hostel (☎ 131 156; jhmuenchen@djh-bayern.de; Wendl-Dietrich-Strasse 20; dm €20.80; ☒ closed Dec; ☒) The Jugendherberge München is the most central DJH hostel and is northwest of the Altstadt. Although it's relatively loud and very busy, it's also popular and friendly. There's no curfew or daytime closing, and there's a restaurant, garden and bikes for hire. Take the U-Bahn to Rotkreuzplatz.

Other recommendations are:

Campingplatz Nord-West (☎ 150 6936; www .campingplatz-nord-west.de; Auf den Schrederwiesen 3; tent €3.10-6.20 car/person €2.60/3.90) Pleasant camp site about 2km from Olympiapark and within walking distance of three swimming lakes.

Campingplatz Obermenzing (☎ 811 2235; fax 814 4807; Lochhausener Strasse 59; tent/car/person €4/3.50/4.50; ☒ mid-Mar–Oct) Parklike camp site in western Munich with coin laundry and small store.

Westend & Ludwigsvorstadt
BUDGET
Map pp326-7

Easy Palace (☎ 558 7970; www.easypalace.de; Mozartstrasse 4; dm/s/d €16.90/29/50; P ☐) This new hostel has a good range of facilities, from pool tables to bike hire and luggage storage. The rooms are fairly simple but comfortable and the management is friendly.

MID-RANGE
Hotel-Pension Mariandl (☎ 534 108; www.hotel .mariandl.com; Goethestrasse 51; s €60, d €80-145) There's old-world charm and huge rooms with high ceilings and giant windows at this neo-Gothic mansion overlooking Beethovenplatz. The downstairs restaurant has live jazz or classical music nightly at 8pm (see Eating, p345 and Entertainment, p351). Children are welcome.

Hotel Uhland (☎ 543 350; www.hotel-uhland.de; Uhlandstrasse 1; s €66-120, d €80-165; P ☐) Just east of the Theresienwiese you'll find this lovely Art Nouveau villa with a relaxed atmosphere and English-speaking staff. The large, comfy rooms (some with a tiny balcony), quaint garden and good service make it an enduring favourite with visitors. There's also an Internet terminal for guests.

Hotel Petri (☎ 581 099; www.hotel-petri.de; Aindorferstrasse 82; s €55-98, d €100-120; P ⊠ 🖳 🐾) This is perhaps the best deal in the Westend. Rooms have distinctive antique furniture and a TV, and there's also a garden and small indoor swimming pool. Take the U-Bahn to Laimer Platz.

Hotel Seibel (☎ 540 1420; www.seibel-hotels-munich .de; Theresienhöhe 9; s €59-149, d €80-189; ⊠) This hotel has a pleasant atmosphere, very friendly staff, Bavarian-style rooms with lovely wrought-iron beds and hardwood furniture. Rooms at the back are quieter, away from the busy thoroughfare at the front.

Southwest of the City
BUDGET

DJH hostel (☎ 723 6550/60; jghmuenchen@djh-bayern .de; Miesingstrasse 4; dm €20.80; P ⊠) Still fairly accessible to the centre, and a good deal, the modern Jugendgästehaus München is southwest of the Altstadt in the suburb of Thalkirchen. There's no curfew. Take the U-Bahn to Thalkirchen and then follow the signs.

DJH hostel (☎ 793 0643/44; info@jugendherberge -burgschwaeck.de; Burgweg 4-6; dm €14.60; 🕑 closed mid-Dec–mid-Jan; P) The Jugendherberge Burg Schwaneck is in a grand old castle in the southern suburbs. All rooms have shower and toilet and it's a good deal but inconveniently located. Take the S-Bahn to Pullach, and then it's a 10-minute walk.

Campingplatz Thalkirchen (☎ 7243 0808; fax 724 31 77; Zentralländstrasse 49; tent €2.50-4 car/person €4.50/4.80; 🕑 mid-Mar–Oct) This is the closest camp site to the city centre but can get very crowded. It's scenically located on the Isar River 5km southwest of the city centre. Take the U3 to Thalkirchen, then bus No 57 or it's a 15-minute walk.

Gay & Lesbian Accommodation
For more listings than the following, try www.munich-cruising.de.

Deutsche Eiche (☎ 231 1660; www.deutsche-eiche .com; Reichenbachstrasse 13; s €66-76, d €92-102; P) This 150-year-old Munich institution was once saved from the wrecker's ball by German film director Rainer Fassbinder. Its modern rooms are fully equipped and there's a big sauna and roof terrace.

Pension Eulenspiegel (Map pp326-7; ☎ /fax 26? 678; Müllerstrasse 43a; s €40-50, d €65-71) This is a small and cosy guesthouse in a quiet back courtyard in Munich's gay district. Rooms are simple but comfortable and all have shared bathroom. The gate is locked at midnight.

Long-Term Rentals
If you're planning to stay in Munich for a month or longer, you might consider renting through a *Mitwohnzentrale* (flat-sharing agency). Accommodation can be anything from rooms in shared student flats to furnished apartments.

Generally speaking, a room in a flat costs about €330 to €450 per month, while a one-bedroom apartment ranges from €430 to €700. Commission (up to one month's rent) and VAT (16%) must be added to the rental rate.

Agencies to try include:

City Mitwohnzentrale (Map pp326-7; ☎ 194 30; www.mwz-muenchen.de; Lämmerstrasse 4)

Mitwohnzentrale an der Uni (Map p329; ☎ 286 6060; www.mwz-munich.de; Adalbertstrasse 6)

Mitwohnzentrale – Mr. Lodge (Map p330; ☎ 340 8230; www.mrlodge.de; Barer Strasse 32)

EATING
Cafés & Bistros
ALTSTADT & AROUND　　　　　　Map pp326-7

Dukatz im Literaturhaus (☎ 291 9600; Salvatorplatz 1; mains €5-22) A stomping ground for the chic and the intellectual, the Dukatz serves up designer sandwiches and latte macchiato in its café section and stratospherically priced but impressive mains in its restaurant.

Stadtcafé (☎ 266 949; Stadtmuseum, St-Jakobs-Platz 1; mains €5.50-12.50) This culture haunt inside the city museum has panoramic windows with a view of the square and attracts a chatty crowd of students, creative types and museum-goers. The lovely courtyard is a treat in summer.

Interview (☎ 202 1649; Gärtnerplatz 1; mains €4.50-14) This is a pleasant street-side café with popular front-row views of the Theater am Gärtnerplatz. Specialities include grilled fish and creative pasta using seasonal ingredients. Breakfast is served till 5pm.

Woerners (☎ 265 231; Marienplatz 1; dishes €3-15) Two cafés merge into one here: the outdoor Café am Dom on the ground floor, giving some of the best seating on the square, and

MAIDHAUSEN   **Map p328**

Café Voilà (☎ 489 1654; Wörthstrasse 5; mains €4.50-) High stucco ceilings, giant mirrors and large windows make this café a great place for watching the world go by. It's buzzing for breakfast and later in the day for fairly priced baguettes, burgers and interesting vegetarian dishes.

Creperie Bernard Bernard (☎ 480 1173; Innere-Viener-Strasse 32; mains €5-8; ☺ closed Sun) The best crepes in town can be found at this small place that serves up delicious savouries oozing goat's cheese or shrimp and lavish desserts dripping with the finest French chocolate.

Wasserwerk (☎ 4890 0020; Wolfgangstrasse 19; mains €7-15; ☺ dinner only) This quirky bistro strewn with ducts, pipes and wheels reflecting the waterworks theme is a fun place to eat and serves up a delicious range of quality international cuisine.

LUDWIGSVORSTADT

Café am Beethovenplatz (Map pp326-7; ☎ 5440 4348; Goethestrasse 51; mains €4.50-10) This relaxed café with a musical theme has high ceilings, chandeliers and a winning atmosphere. The breakfast selections are named after famous composers and the divine evening meals are accompanied by live jazz or classical music.

SCHWABING

Tresznjewski (Map p330; ☎ 282 349; www.tresznjewski .de; Theresienstrasse 72; mains €8-12) This classy brasserie with daring artworks and waiters in full-length aprons appeals to the trendy set. It serves up a varied menu of delicious international cuisine from interesting pastas and sandwiches to burgers and bratwurst.

Brik (Map p329; ☎ 2899 6630; Schellingstrasse 24; sushi €5-10) This slick Japanese-style café, bar and lounge is a temple of minimalism and draws a hip crowd as much for the drinks as the delicious sushi snacks.

News Bar (Map p329; ☎ 281 787; Amalienstrasse 55; mains €5-10). This trendy café has a great selection of magazines and newspapers, including English ones, for sale. It's an ideal spot for brunch or a lazy morning poring over a paper.

Bobolovsky's (Map p329; ☎ 297 363; Ursulastrasse 10; mains €7-10) The varied menu at this bustling bistro includes all the old favourites such as fajitas, *quesadillas* and chilli. Portions are very generous and on weekdays this place takes the Happy Hour concept to new lengths, with incredibly cheap deals on breakfast, lunch and cocktails.

Nido (Map p329; ☎ 2880 6103; Theresienstrasse 40; mains €6) This popular place is a trendy spot with lots of brushed aluminium and great big windows. They serve a small menu of simple, Italian-influenced dishes and a large dose of unpretentious cool.

NEUHAUSEN

froh & munter (Map p330; ☎ 187 997; Artilleriestrasse 5; dishes €3.50-8) Near Rotkreuzplatz, this is a welcoming and totally untouristed place to munch on snacks, soups and great Spanish-style tapas washed down with organic Unertl beer. The menu changes nightly.

Quick Eats & Student Cafeterias

In Munich alone 100,000 *Weisswurst* (white veal sausages) are eaten every day and can usually only be ordered in odd numbers.

Throughout the city, branches of Vinzenzmurr have hot buffets and prepared meals; a very good lunch – such as *Schweinebraten mit Knödel* (roast pork with dumplings) and gravy – can be as low as €4, and hamburgers cost about €2.50. Some branches even have salad bars.

For quick snacks, any Müller bakery Stehcafé offers coffee (around €1.30) and pretzels or bread rolls covered with melted cheese (about €1.70) or with bacon or ham (€1.70 to €2.50).

Student-card holders can fill up for around €3 in any of the university *Mensas* (food service 11am to 2pm). The best one is on Schillerstrasse just north of Pettenkoferstrasse, and there are others at Leopoldstrasse 13a, Arcisstrasse 17 and Lothstrasse 13d.

AROUND THE HAUPTBAHNHOF

Doner and pizza rule the fast-food scene in Munich. South of the Hauptbahnhof on Bayerstrasse are lots of tourist traps, but you can grab a quick, cheap bite at the street window of **Ristorante Ca' doro** (Map pp326-7; pizza €4.80-6.50, slice €2.50). Another good bet is **Kandil** (Map pp326-7; Landwehrstrasse 8; mains

€2-8), which offers a varied selection of full cafeteria-style eats and also does breakfast.

ALTSTADT & AROUND

Cheap eating is also available in various department stores in the centre. Right opposite Karlsplatz, on the ground floor of the Kaufhof department store, are three good options: a Müller bakery, Nordsee seafood and Grillpfanne for sausages (Map pp326-7).

Another good spot, just north of the Frauenkirche, is **Münchner Suppenküche** (Map pp326-7; Schäfflerstrasse 7; dishes €3-6; ☼ closed Sun), a self-service soupery serving chicken casseroles, chilli con carne and other filling snacks.

SCHWABING

Schwabing has lots of cheap places to eat, including **Reiter Imbiss** (Map p329; Hohenzollernstrasse 24; meals around €3.50), a good source for budget-priced dishes heaped with meaty stuff and salad. Back on the main drag **Wok Man** (Map p329; Leopoldstrasse 68; mains €4.50-6) dishes up a good selection of decent Chinese food.

For cheap Indian food try **Indisches Fast Food** (Map p330; Barer Strasse 46; mains €6-8) near the Neue Pinakothek, where fragrant Basmati rice accompanies the tasty Indian standards.

Restaurants
ASIAN

Sho-ya (Map pp326-7; ☎ 523 6249; Gabelsbergerstrasse 85; sushi €10-15) It may look nondescript on the outside, but this place is proudly hailed as one of the best sushi joints in town. It's ideally located and serves giant *ebi* and superb *maguro*. The basement boasts a lively karaoke bar.

Shida (Map pp326-7; ☎ 269 336; Klenzestrasse 32; mains €11-16) Shida's excellent Thai food and intimate atmosphere are justly famous and perennially popular. It's only the size of a shoe box but packs a mean punch in the food stakes. Reservations are essential.

BAVARIAN & GERMAN

Ratskeller (Map pp326-7; ☎ 219 9890; Marienplatz 8; mains €10-18) No animal is safe from the menu of this vast, cavernous restaurant underneath the historic Rathaus. The quality is dependably high, service is efficient, and the surroundings couldn't get much more atmospheric.

Hundskugel (Map pp326-7; ☎ 264 272; Hotte strasse 18; mains €10-18) Munich's oldest re taurant, founded in 1440, feels a bit lik an old-fashioned doll's house it's so tin It's famous for its honest Bavarian hom cooking but you'll have to squeeze in a best you can.

Fraunhofer (Map pp326-7; ☎ 266 460; Fraunhofe strasse 9; mains €5.50-12) This bustling restaurar is a homely place where the olde-world atmosphere (featuring mounted anima heads and a portrait of Ludwig II) contras with the menu, which offers fresh takes o classical fare, and the hip, intergenerationa crowd.

Unionsbräu Haidhausen (Map p328; ☎ 477 67 Einsteinstrasse 42; mains €6-14) Dried hops dan gle from the ceiling of this sophisticate brew-pub that caters to business types a lunchtime and a more rollicking crew afte dark. There's a jazz club in the basemen (see p351).

Other recommendations include:

Andechser am Dom (Map pp326-7; ☎ 298 481; Weinstrasse 7a; mains €5-14.50) A traditional restaurant frequented by a bourgeois crowd. Great views from the rooftop terrace.

Wirtshaus in der Au (Map p328; ☎ 448 1400; Lilienstrasse 51; mains €8-16) Creative Bavarian cuisine in an unpretentious setting.

FRENCH

Rue des Halles (Map p328; ☎ 485 675; Steinstrasse 18, mains €19-28) Excellent but expensive French cuisine attracts a Rolls-Royce crowd to this bright modern restaurant near the Kulturzentrum Gasteig Count on about €80 for a three-course meal, including a glass of wine.

La Bretagne (Map p328; ☎ 487 220; Rablstrasse 37; mains €17-20; ☼ dinner only) This intimate Breton restaurant has a loyal following for its seafood specialities and traditional French fare. Self-control is needed if you want to leave room to try the divine deserts. Bookings are recommended.

ITALIAN

La Fiorentina (Map pp326-7; ☎ 534 185; Goethestrasse 41; mains €7.50-12) This small local hangout has a cosy atmosphere that attracts a young, unpretentious crowd. It serves up good-value Tuscan country cooking, mouth-watering pizzas and lovingly prepared daily specials.

Hippocampus (Map p328; ☎ 475 855; Mühlbaur-strasse 5; mains €15-28) One of Munich's top restaurants, this trendy, upmarket Italian place right near the Prinzregententheater serves a great range of Italian specials. It has a stylish interior, romantic ambience and celebrity clientele.

JEWISH

Cohen's (Map p329; ☎ 280 9545; Theresienstrasse 31; mains €9-14) Tucked away in a courtyard, this rightly lit, modern place serves up big portions of German/Eastern European dishes that change with the seasons. Specials include *Königsberger Klopse* (veal dumplings in caper sauce) and gefilte fish.

LATIN AMERICAN

Joe Peña's (Map p326-7; ☎ 226 463; Buttelmelcher-strasse 17; mains €11-17) This festive cantina-style restaurant is regarded as Munich's best Tex-Mex place and can get very crowded especially during Happy Hour (5pm to 8pm). The food's tasty but calibrated to Germanic tastes.

Zapata (Map p330; ☎ 166 5822; Schulstrasse 44; mains €6-16; dinner only) Munich's revolutionary diner is packed with sombreros, saddles, cacti, good food and some refined pina colada drinkers. The menu includes all the usual suspects served up in decent portions and at reasonable prices.

VEGETARIAN

Buxs Altstadt (Map pp326-7; ☎ 291 9550; Frauenstrasse 9; dishes €2 per 100g; closed Sat eve & Sun); Schwabing (Map p329; ☎ 2802 9940; Amalienstrasse 38) Freedom of choice reigns at these bright, modern self-service places serving some 45 different kinds of soups, salads and antipasti, not to mention the glorious smoothies and desserts. 'Weigh' your appetite carefully, as the final bill adds up quickly.

Prinz Myschkin (Map pp326-7; ☎ 265 596; www.prinzmyshkin.com; Hackenstrasse 2; mains €8-16.50; closed Sun) Considered by many Munich's best vegetarian restaurant, this spacious, trendy haunt has an impressive Italian- and Asian-influenced menu, including some macrobiotic choices. If you just want a light snack, half-portions are available.

Das Gollier (☎ 501 673; Gollierstrasse 83; mains €7.50-12) This wonderful place serves up generous portions of tasty fare direct from a brick oven. All menu items, including the

beers and sugar-free soft drinks, are made with organic ingredients. Take U4 or U5 to Schwanthalerhöhe and walk 500m.

Self-Catering

There are bakeries all over town but one of the best is **Schneider's Feinbäckerei** (Map p330; Volkartstrasse 48), close to the hostel in Neuhausen.

Supermarkets large and small can be found throughout the city. Norma and Aldi are the cheapest places to buy staples, but for a last-minute stock-up before your train leaves, hit **Tengelmann** (Bayerstrasse 5), just opposite the Hauptbahnhof. The supermarket in the basement of the Kaufhof department store opposite Karlsplatz has a far more upmarket selection, plus goodies like fresh mozzarella, superb sliced meats and cheeses, and a good bakery.

At Viktualienmarkt, south of Marienplatz, deep-pocketed travellers can put together a gourmet picnic of breads, cheeses and salad to take off to a beer garden or the Englischer Garten. Prices are high, so choose carefully. Make sure you figure out the price before buying, and don't be afraid to move on to another stall.

More prosperous picnickers might prefer the legendary **Alois Dallmayr** (Map pp326-7; Dienerstrasse 14), one of the world's greatest (and priciest) delicatessens, with an amazing range of exotic foods imported from every corner of the earth.

DRINKING

Not surprisingly, beer drinking is an integral part of Munich's nightlife. Germans in general each drink an average of 127l of the amber liquid per year, but Bavarians average some 170l!

Beer Halls & Gardens

One of the finer ways to sample Bavaria's best brews is in the beer halls and beer gardens. People come here primarily to drink, and although food may be served it is generally of low quality. (For food options at beer halls, see the boxed text on p348.) A few places still allow you to bring along a picnic lunch and just buy the beer; in most cases, though, outside food is now forbidden.

Most places listed here are either gardens or gardens-cum-restaurants: almost all open from 10am to at least 10pm. Even in the touristy places, be careful not to sit at the *Stammtisch*, a table reserved for regulars (there will be a brass plaque).

You sometimes have to pay a *Pfand* (deposit) for the glasses (usually €2.50). Beer costs €5 to €6.50 per litre.

ALTSTADT
Map pp326-7

Hofbräuhaus (☎ 221 676; Am Platzl 9) This is certainly the best-known and most celebrated beer hall in Bavaria but it is generally so packed with tipsy tourists that it loses all sense of authenticity. A live band plays Bavarian folk music most of the day.

Augustiner-Grossgaststätte (☎ 5519 9257; Neuhauser Strasse 27) This sprawling place has a less raucous atmosphere and better food. Altogether it's a much more authentic example of an old-style Munich beer hall, complete with hidden courtyards and hunting trophies on the walls.

Braunauer Hof (☎ 223 613; Frauenstrasse 42) Near the Isartor, this pleasingly warped beer garden is centred on a snug courtyard. There's a hedge maze, a fresco with a bizarre bunch of historical figures and a golden bull that's illuminated at night.

ENGLISCHER GARTEN

There are three beer gardens in the park (Map p329).

Chinesischer Turm (☎ 383 8730; Englischer Garten 3) A very mixed crowd of businessfolk, tourists and junkies clump around this classic Chinese pagoda, entertained by what has to be the world's drunkest oompah band (in the tower above the crowd, fenced in like the Blues Brothers).

Less crowded are **Hirschau** (☎ 369 942; Gysslingstrasse 15) and **Seehaus** (☎ 381 6130, Kleinhesselohe 3) on the lakeshores.

NEUHAUSEN

Augustiner Keller (☎ 594 393; Arnulfstrasse 52) This enormous place, about 500m west of the Hauptbahnhof, is a giant leafy beer garden buzzing with life and good cheer. It's a beautiful spot with a laid-back atmosphere ideal for leisurely drinking.

Hirschgarten (Map p330; ☎ 172 591; Hirschgartenallee 1) Locals and some savvy tourists flock to the Hirschgarten, just south of Schloss Nymphenburg. The shady garden is enormous with deer wandering just the other

---

AND THERE'S FOOD, TOO

In beer gardens, tables laid with a cloth and utensils are reserved for people ordering food. If you're only planning a serious drinking session, or have brought along a picnic, don't sit there.

If you do decide to order food, you'll find very similar menus at all beer gardens. Typical dishes include roast chicken (about €9 for a half), spare ribs (about €11.50, and probably not worth it), huge pretzels (about €3) and Bavarian specialities such as *Schweinebraten* and schnitzel (€9 to €12).

Radi is a huge, mild radish that's eaten with beer; you can buy prepared radish for about €4.50 or buy a radish at the market and a *Radimesser* at any department store; stick it down in the centre and twist the handle round and round, creating a radish spiral. If you do it yourself, smother the cut end of the radish with salt until it weeps to reduce the bitterness (and increase your thirst!).

Obatzda (oh-batsdah) is Bavarian for 'mixed up' – this cream-cheese-like speciality is made of butter, ripe Camembert, onion and caraway (about €4 to €6). Spread it on *Brez'n* (a pretzel) or bread.

Another speciality is *Leberkäs* (liver cheese), which is nothing to do with liver or cheese but is instead a type of meatloaf that gets its name from its shape. It's usually eaten with sweet mustard and soft pretzels.

---

side of the fence. To get there take the S Bahn to Laim.

Pubs & Bars

Alter Simpl (Map p329; ☎ 272 3083; Türkenstrasse 57) This watering hole has good jazz, a reasonable menu (€5 to €13) and an arthouse vibe. Thomas Mann and Hermann Hesse were among the writers and artists that used to meet here in the early 20th century.

Dreigroschenkeller (Map p328; ☎ 489 0290; Lilienstrasse 2) Cosy and labyrinthine, this cellar pub has rooms based upon Bertolt Brecht's *Die Dreigroschenoper* (The Threepenny Opera), ranging from a prison cell to a red satiny salon. There's great beer and wine, and an extensive menu (mostly hearty German stuff).

Kreitmayr's (Map p330; 448 9140; Kreitmayrstrasse) ..st east of Erzgiessereistrasse, Kreitmayr's is real bar-crawler's bar, with bar food, good ..rinks, a pool table, darts and pinball, and ..ve music on Thursday (from Irish folk to ..zz). It also has a beer garden in summer.

Other recommendations are:

..aader Café (Map pp326-7; 201 0638; Baader-..asse 47) A literary think-and-drink place with a high ..lebrity quotient and possibly the best Sunday brunch ..town.

..acific Times (Map pp326-7; 2023 9470; Baader-..asse 28) Trendy joint decked out in dark wood and ..icker chairs to attract the beautiful people.

..CHWABING   Map p329
..f you want a variety of hip bars within spit-..ing distance of each other, then Leopold-..trasse is for you.

The **Green Room** (3304 0724; Leopoldstrasse 13) ..his funky alternative bar is on the verge of ..eing discovered and invaded by the trendy ..et. For the moment though, it's a serious ..drinking establishment with a vast cocktail ..nenu and a bit of an edge.

Roxy (349 292; Leopoldstrasse 48) *The* place to ..alent spot and people watch, this slick bar ..attracts a designer crowd keen to hang out, ..ook good and sip cocktails. By day it offers ..surprisingly good food at decent prices.

Millennium (3839 8430; Leopoldstrasse 42) An-..other spot to see and be seen is this funky ..orange place with a strangely sloping ceil-..ing and quirky seating. Mingle with the ..cocktail crew by night and come back in the ..morning for the great breakfast.

News Café (3838 0600; Leopoldstrasse 74) Plush ..leather seating, rows of glowing red lamps ..and African-inspired art make this hip joint ..a great place to hang out. It serves light food ..and a multitude of cocktails.

Irish Pubs
Munich has a huge Irish expat population; if you're out looking for friendly, English-speaking people, you're in luck. Most of the pubs have live music at least once a week and seem to cluster in Schwabing.

Günther Murphy's Irish Tavern (Map p329; 398 911; Nikolaistrasse 9a) One of the most popular Irish pubs in Munich, this cellar bar is usu-ally packed to the gills with a good mix of locals, expats and tourists.

Shamrock (Map p329; 331 081; Trautenwolfstrasse 6) Shamrock is fun, loud, boisterous and

crowded every night. Arrive early if you want a table and be prepared to squeeze your way to the bar if you stay on late. Live sports are shown on a big screen.

Molly Malone's (Map p328; 688 7510; Keller-strasse 21) This award-winning Irish pub is a better bet if you'd like a quiet drink or a decent conversation. It's famous for its authentic fish and chips and has over 100 types of whisky on hand.

ENTERTAINMENT
Munich's entertainment scene will keep you busy. Apart from discos, pubs and beer halls, try not to miss the city's excellent clas-sical, jazz and opera venues.

Listings
Go Muenchen (www.gomuenchen.com; €3) What's-on guide to the city including exhibitions, concerts etc.

In München (www.in-muenchen.de; free) The best source of information; available free at bars, restaurants and ticket outlets.

München im... (€1.85) Excellent A-to-Z listing of almost everything the city has to offer.

Münchner Stadtmagazin (€2.50) Complete guide to the city's bars, discos, clubs, concerts and nightlife in general.

Munich Found (www.munichfound.de; €2.50) English-language city magazine with somewhat useful listings.

Munich in your Pocket (€3) Excellent English-language guide to just about anything you need to know about Munich.

Tickets
Tickets to entertainment venues and sports events are available at official ticket outlets (*Kartenvorverkauf*).

Kartenvorverkauf Karlsplatz (Map pp326-7; 5450 6060); Marienplatz (Map pp326-7; 264 640) Branches all over the city and kiosks in these U-Bahn stations.

München Ticket (Map pp326-7; www.muenchenticket .de; Neues Rathaus; 5481 8181)

Cinemas
For show information check any of the list-ings publications. Admission usually ranges from €6.50 to €8.50, though one day, usu-ally Monday or Tuesday, is 'Kinotag', with reduced prices. Non-German films in main-stream cinemas are almost always dubbed. Films showing in the original language with subtitles are denoted 'OmU' (Original mit Untertiteln); those without subtitles are denoted 'OV' or 'OF' (Originalversion or

BAVARIA

Originalfassung). **Amerika Haus** shows un-dubbed films, as do the following movie theatres:

Atelier (Map pp326-7; ☎ 591 918; Sonnenstrasse 12)

Atlantis (Map pp326-7; ☎ 555 152; Schwanthaler-strasse 2)

Cinema (Map p330; ☎ 555 255; Nymphenburger Strasse 31).

Filmmuseum (Map pp326-7; ☎ 2332 4150; St-Jakobs-Platz 1) In the Stadtmuseum.

Museum-Lichtspiele (Map p328; ☎ 482 403; Lilienstrasse 2)

Clubs

Munich has a thriving club scene with something to suit most tastes. Bouncers are notoriously rude and 'discerning', so dress to kill (or look, as locals say, *schiki-micki*) and keep your cool. The cover prices for discos vary but average between €4 and €10.

Kultfabrik (Map p328; www.kultfabrik.info; Grafinger-strasse 6) Munich's largest complex of pubs, bars and clubs is a party animal's mecca where you can roam from '80s disco to hip hop, trance and heavy metal. If you're an aficionado of Russian pop try **Kalinka**, a trendy place decked out with lots of red velvet, dancing girls and a giant bust of Lenin. Other options include **Black Raven**, a loud, head-banging metal hang-out where a black uniform and body piercings are *de rigueur*; **Raphael**, a more mainstream choice cater-ing to disco divas; and **Living4**, which plays a good mix of hip hop, Latin and house. To get there take U5 to the Ostbahnhof.

P1 (Map p329; ☎ 294 252; Prinzregentenstrasse 1) P1 is a bit of a Munich institution and is still the see-and-be-seen place for the city's wannabes, with extremely choosy and ef-fective bouncers, snooty staff and the oc-casional celebrity.

Muffathalle (Map p328; ☎ 4587 5075; Zellstrasse 4) This is another big complex that holds large concerts and, in summer, an open-air disco on Friday with drum 'n' bass, acid jazz and hip hop (it's always crowded, so expect long queues).

Backstage (Map p330; ☎ 183 330; Helmholzstrasse 18) Less pretentious, this concert venue and disco offers crossover, psychedelic, hip hop, trash and various other alternative sounds.

Gay & Lesbian Munich

Munich has a strong gay and lesbian com-munity and the best listings can be found in

the German-language **Rosa Seiten** (Pink Page €3.50) or **Our Munich** (free), a monthly guid to gay and lesbian life in the city. You ca pick up both at the **Weissblauer Gay Shop** (Ma p330; ☎ 522 352; Theresienstrasse 130) or **Black Jum** (Map p328; ☎ 4800 4332; Orleansstrasse 51). Anothe good bet for information is the websit www.munich-cruising.de.

Information and support for gay men an lesbians is available through **Schwules Komm•nikations und Kulturzentrum**, dubbed 'the Sub (Map pp326-7; ☎ 260 3056; counselling ☎ 194 4• Müllerstrasse 43; ✆ 7-11pm, counselling 7-10pm Mon-Fr and **LeTra/Lesbentelefon** (Map pp326-7; ☎ 725 427. Angertorstrasse 3; ✆ 2.30-5pm Mon & Wed, 10.30am-1pr Tue, 7-9pm Thu).

BARS & CAFÉS

Nightlife is centred in the so-called 'Ber muda Triangle' formed by Sendlinger Tor Gärtnerplatz and the Isartor.

Morizz (Map pp326-7; ☎ 201 6776; Klenzestrass 43) *The* spot to hang out in town, Moriz; resembles an Art Deco Paris bar with rec leather armchairs and plenty of mirrors The service is impeccable, the food's good and the wine and whisky list will keep every-one happy. It's quiet early in the evening but livens up as the night wears on.

Deutsche Eiche (Map pp326-7; ☎ 231 1660; Reichen-bachstrasse 13) A Munich institution, this was once film maker Rainer Werner Fassbind-er's favourite hang-out. It's still a popular spot and packs in a mixed crowd for its comfort food and fast service.

Soul City (Map pp326-7; ☎ 5231 0242; Maximilians-platz 5) The two-level Soul City features a bar and café on the 1st level, while the 2nd level has a disco and dance floor that attracts a young and extremely mixed crowd. It's mostly men on Friday and Saturday.

Iwan (Map pp326-7; ☎ 554 933; Josephspitalstrasse 15) Iwan was once an ultra-chic and ex-tremely exclusive place that's broadened its clientele. The two floors host a very mixed crowd that spills out into the leafy courtyard in summer.

Nil (Map pp326-7; ☎ 265 545; Hans-Sach-Strasse 2) This place attracts a young fun-loving crowd and a handful of faded German stars to its octagon bar. The atmosphere is pretty chilled though and it's a good place to see and be seen.

Bei Carla (Map pp326-7; ☎ 227 901; Baaderstrasse 16) Behind a fairly humble exterior is this

ne, exclusively lesbian, bar. It's a popular
pot with a good mixed-age crowd, lots of
gulars and snack foods if you're feeling
eckish.

The Stud (Map pp326-7; ☎ 260 8403; Thalkirchner
rasse 2; ⊙ Thu-Sun) This is a Levis-and-
ather place with a dark, coal-mine-like
iterior and lots of butch guys with no
air. The clientele is gay and lesbian but
ey're always looking for more lesbians.
's men-only on Sundays.

Other recommendations include:

rtuna Musikbar (Map pp326-7; ☎ 554 070; Maxi-
liansplatz 5) Popular lesbian bar and disco.

ew York (Map pp326-7; ☎ 591 056; Sonnenstrasse 25)
sing, preening and cruising club with nonstop high-
ergy dance music.

d Mrs Henderson (Map pp326-7; ☎ 263 469; Rum-
rdstr 2) The best transvestite cabaret in town.

Iusic

LASSICAL MUSIC

hilharmonie im Gasteig (Map p328; ☎ 480 980;
ntrale@gasteig.de; Rosenheimer Strasse 5) As home
the city's Philharmonic Orchestra, Mu-
ich's premier high-brow cultural venue
as a packed schedule. The Symphonie-
rchestra des Bayerischen Rundfunks is
lso based here, and performs on Sundays
roughout the year.

Nationaltheater (Map pp326-7; box office ☎ 2185
20; tickets@st-oper.bayern.de; Max-Joseph-Platz 2)
he Bayerische Staatsoper (Bavarian State
pera) performs here. It is also the site
f many cultural events, particularly dur-
g the opera festival in July. You can buy
ckets at regular outlets or at the box office
pen 10am to 6pm weekdays, 10am to 1pm
aturday).

Staatstheater am Gärtnerplatz (Map pp326-7;
box office 2185 1960; tickets@st-gaertner.bayern.de;
irtnerplatz 3) This venue has occasional classi-
al concerts, but opera, operetta, jazz, ballet
nd musicals also feature on the entertain-
ent menu.

AZZ

Iunich has a very hot jazz scene with
lenty of possibilities.

Jazzclub Unterfahrt im Einstein (Map p328;
448 2794; Einsteinstrasse 42) This is perhaps the
est-known place in town, with live music
om 9pm and regular international acts.
here's a small art gallery in one corner and
pen jam sessions on Sunday nights.

Mister B's (Map pp326-7; ☎ 534 901; Herzog-
Heinrich-Strasse 38) Just west of Goetheplatz
you'll find Munich's smallest jazz club,
which also features rhythm and blues. It
serves great cocktails, attracts an older,
mellow crowd and has live music from
Thursday to Saturday.

Jazzy's (Map p328; ☎ 2166 8447; Steinsdorfstrasse
21) This classy jazz club on the banks of
the Isar dishes up a combination of killer
cocktails and live jazz every night from
8pm. It's also popular with the trendy set
for its enormous Sunday brunch.

Café am Beethovenplatz (Map pp326-7; ☎ 5440
4348; Goethestrasse 51) Dine on fine foods while
you sit back and enjoy the nightly concerts
in this atmospheric café. Weekdays generally feature live jazz or classical music and
the jazz accompaniment to Sunday lunch is
absolute heaven.

ROCK

Large rock concerts are staged at the Olympiapark. Most other rock venues are listed
under Clubs earlier.

Brunnenhof der Residenz (Map pp326-7; ☎ 936
093; Residenzstrasse 1) Try this place for something a little different. It hosts open-air
performances ranging from rock, jazz and
swing to classical and opera in stunning
surroundings.

Theatre

Munich has a lively theatre scene. The
two biggest companies are the Bayerisches
Staatschauspiel and the Münchener Kammerspiele. The **Bayerisches Staatschauspiel**
(☎ tickets 2185 1940) performs at the **Residenztheater** (Map pp326-7; Max-Joseph-Platz 1), at the
intimate rococo Cuvilliés Theater (also
within the Residenz) and at the **Theater
im Marstall** (Marstallplatz), which is located
behind the Nationaltheater (see Classical
Music opposite).

Münchener Kammerspiele (Map pp326-7; ☎ 2333
7000; Maximilianstrasse 26-28) This theatre stages
large productions of serious drama by German playwrights or by foreign playwrights
whose works have been translated into
German.

Deutsches Theater (Map pp326-7; ☎ 5523 4444;
Schwanthalerstrasse 13) This is Munich's answer
to London's West End: touring road shows
(usually popular musicals like *Beauty and
the Beast*) perform here.

Kulturzentrum Gasteig (Map p328; ☎ 480 980; Rosenheimer Strasse 5) This is a major cultural centre with theatre, classical music and other special events in its several halls.

Other venues include the **Prinzregententheater** (Map p328; ☎ 2185 2959; Prinzregentenplatz 12) and the **Kleine Komödie am Max II** (☎ 221 859; Maximilianstrasse 47), which shows light-weight comedy.

Children's theatres include:

Münchner Theater für Kinder (Map p330; ☎ 593 858; Dachauer Strasse 46) Children's performances year-round.

Münchner Marionettentheater (Map pp326-7; ☎ 265 712; Blumenstrasse 32) Munich's main puppet theatre.

Circus Krone (Map p330; ☎ 545 8000; Zirkus-Krone-Strasse 1-6; ⏰ Dec-Apr) A big hit with children.

SHOPPING

Fashionistas with a flexible credit card should head for Maximilianstrasse, Theatinerstrasse, Residenzstrasse and Brienner Strasse. For high street shops and department stores try the pedestrian area around Marienplatz, Neuhausser Strasse and Kaufingerstrasse. For trendier street clothes Gärtnerplatz, Glockenplatz, Schwabing and Haidhausen all have smaller alternative boutiques. Beer steins and *Mass* (1l tankard) glasses are available at all the department stores, as well as from the beer halls.

Ludwig Beck (Map pp326-7; ☎ 2423 1575; Marienplatz 11) Munich's most venerable department store has some chic but reasonably priced clothes, a large CD shop, a coffee bar and restaurant. It also has a branch of Heinemann's, which makes some of Germany's finest filled chocolates.

Foto-Video Sauter (Map pp326-7; ☎ 551 5040; Sonnenstrasse 26) A good stock of all the top names fills the shelves at this photo emporium. Good deals can be had on Leica cameras and binoculars.

Loden-Frey (Map pp326-7; ☎ 210 390; Maffeistrasse 5-7) Bavarian dress is the most distinctive of traditional German clothing and can be bought in specialist shops and most larger department stores. Loden-Frey stocks a wide range of Bavarian wear. Expect to pay at least €200 for a good leather jacket, lederhosen or a women's dirndl dress.

The **Christkindlmarkt** (Christmas market; Mariahilfplatz) in December is large and well stocked but predictably expensive. The **Auer Dult** (Map p328; Mariahilfplatz), a huge flea market in Au

has great buys and takes place during t last weeks of April, July and October.

GETTING THERE & AWAY

Air

Munich's Franz-Josef Strauss airport second in importance only to Frankfurt international and domestic flights. Ther direct service to/from many destinatio including London, Paris, Rome, Athens, J hannesburg, New York and Sydney as w as all major German cities.

AIRLINE OFFICES

Air France (☎ 01805-830 830)
BMI Baby (☎ 01805-0264 2229) No-frills fares from Cardiff and East Midlands in the UK.
British Airways/Deutsche BA (☎ 01805-266 522)
Delta Air Lines (☎ 0180-333 7880)
Easy Jet (01803-654 321) Cheap fares from Stansted in the UK.
El Al (☎ 210 6920)
Finnair (☎ 01803-346 624)
Lufthansa (Map pp326-7; ☎ 552 5500/545 599; Lenbachplatz 1)
Scandinavian Airlines (SAS; ☎ 0622-141 50)

Bus

Munich is a stop for **Busabout** (www.busab .com), with links to Croatia and Italy, Par the Rhine Valley, Amsterdam and other c ies (also see p759).

Europabus (see p764) links Munich to t Romantic Road. For details of fares a timetables inquire at **EurAide** (see Tour Information, p331) or **Deutsche Touring** (M pp326-7; ☎ 8898 9513; www.deutsche-touring.cc ⏰ 8.30am-6pm Mon-Fri 8.30am-noon Sat) near pl form No 26 off Arnulfstrasse on the nor side of the Hauptbahnhof.

BEX BerlinLinienBus (☎ 0180-154 6436; w .berlinlinienbus.de) runs daily buses betwe Berlin and Munich (one way/return €6 79, nine hours), via Ingolstadt, Nurember Bayreuth and Leipzig. They pick up fro the Hauptbahnhof, Arnulfstrasse 5. The are significant reductions on one-way far for passengers aged under 26 or over 60. S Getting There & Away under individual c ies and towns for other fares and service

Car & Motorcycle

Munich has autobahns radiating on sides. Take the A9 to Nuremberg, the A9 A3 to Passau, the A8 to Salzburg, the A o Garmisch-Partenkirchen and the A8 to Ulm or Stuttgart.

For information, try **ADAC** (the German Auto Association; Map pp326-7; ☎ 5491 7234; Sendlinger-Tor-Platz).

All major car-hire companies have offices at the airport. Sixt (Budget), Hertz, Avis and Europcar have counters on the 2nd level of the Hauptbahnhof. An independent car hire company with good rates is **Allround** (☎ 723 8383; www.allroundrent.de; Boschetsriederstrasse 12) whose smallest car costs €35 per day, including 300km, 16% VAT and insurance. It is located near the DJH Jugendgästehaus in southern Munich.

For shared rides, contact the **ADM-Mitfahrzentrale** (Map pp326-7; ☎ 194 40; www.mitfahrzentralen.de; Lämmerstrasse 4; ☽ 8am-8pm Mon-Sat), near the Hauptbahnhof. Sample fares (including commission) are: Vienna €25, Berlin €32, Amsterdam €43, Paris €46, Prague €26 and Florence €35.

The **CityNetz Mitfahr-Zentrale Känguruh** (Map p329; ☎ 194 44; www.citynetz-mitfahrzentrale.de; Adalbertstrasse 10-12) in Schwabing arranges lifts for women with female drivers. Sample fares include: Berlin €29, Barcelona €64, Paris €39 and Rome €53.

Train

Train services to/from Munich are excellent. There are rapid connections at least every two hours to all major cities in Germany, as well as frequent but usually nondirect services to European cities such as Vienna (5½ hours), Prague (seven hours) and Zürich (six hours).

There are direct connections to Berlin (€110, 6½ hours) and Hamburg (€107, six hours). Going to Frankfurt requires a change in Fulda, Würzburg or Mannheim (€59, 3½ hours).

Prague extensions are sold at the rail-pass counters in the Reisezentrum at the Hauptbahnhof, or through EurAide (see p331).

GETTING AROUND

Central Munich is compact enough for exploring on foot. In order to get to the outlying suburbs, make use of the efficient public transport system.

To/From the Airport

Munich's Flughafen Franz-Josef Strauss (www.munich-airport.de) is connected by

the S1 and S8 to the Hauptbahnhof – €8 with a single ticket or €7.60 if using eight strips of a Streifenkarte (see Public Transport following). The trip takes about 40 minutes and runs every 20 minutes from 3.30am until around 12.30am.

The Lufthansa Airport Bus travels at 20-minute intervals from Arnulfstrasse near the Hauptbahnhof (one way/return €9/14.50, 45 minutes) between 5.10am and 9.45pm. A taxi from the airport to the Altstadt costs about €45 to €50.

Car & Motorcycle

It's not worth driving in the city centre; many streets are pedestrian-only, ticket enforcement is Orwellian and parking is a nightmare. The tourist office map shows city car parks, which generally cost about €1.50 to €2 per hour.

Public Transport

Getting around is easy on Munich's excellent public transport network (MVV). The system is zone-based, and most places of interest to visitors (except Dachau and the airport) are within the 'blue' inner-zone (Innenraum).

Tickets are valid for the S-Bahn, U-Bahn, trams and buses but must be time-stamped in the machines at station entrances and aboard buses and trams before use. Failure to validate a ticket puts you at the mercy of ticket inspectors (usually plain clothes) who speak perfect English, have seen and heard all possible excuses and possess admirable efficiency when it comes to handing out fines (around €35) for unauthorised travel.

Short rides (four bus or tram stops; two U-Bahn or S-Bahn stops) cost €1, while longer trips cost €2. It's cheaper to buy a strip-card of 10 tickets called a *Streifenkarte* for €9, and stamp one strip per adult on rides of two or less tram or U-Bahn stops, two strips for longer journeys.

Some of the other deals on offer are:

Bayern-Ticket (€21) Entitles up to five people unlimited travel on all local DB, BOB, RGB and VGB trains as well as the underground, tram and bus from 9am to 3pm the following day. Monday to Friday only.

Day passes One day (individual/up to 5 people €4.50/7.50); Three day (€11/17.50) Only valid for the inner zone.

Isarcard (€13.00) Weekly pass covering all four zones but valid Monday to Sunday only – if you buy on Wednesday, it's still only good until Sunday.

Partner Tageskarte (€7.50) Good for unlimited travel on bus, tram, S-Bahn and U-Bahn in all 4 zones for up to five people.

Rail passes are also valid on S-Bahn trains. Bicycle transport costs €2.25 per trip or €2.50 for a day pass, but is forbidden during rush hour (6am to 9am and 4pm to 6pm Monday to Friday).

The U-Bahn ceases operation around 12.30am on weekdays and 1.30am at weekends, but a network of night buses (Nachtbusse) still operates. Pick up the latest route and time schedule from any tourist office.

Taxi

Taxis are expensive and not much more convenient than public transport. For a radio-dispatched taxi, ring ☎ 216 10 or ☎ 194 10. Taxi ranks are indicated on the city's tourist map.

AROUND MUNICH

DACHAU CONCENTRATION CAMP MEMORIAL

> The way to freedom is to follow one's orders; exhibit honesty, orderliness, cleanliness, sobriety, truthfulness, the ability to sacrifice and love of the Fatherland.
>
> *Inscription from the roof of the concentration camp at Dachau*

Dachau (☎ 08131-1741; Alte-Roemer-Strasse 75; admission free; ☷ 9am-5pm Tue-Sun) was the very first Nazi concentration camp, built by Heinrich Himmler in March 1933. It 'processed' more than 200,000 prisoners, and 31,531 were reported killed here. In 1933 Munich had 10,000 Jews. Only 200 survived the war.

The camp is now one of the most popular day trips from Munich, though the experience may be too disturbing for children.

On arrival make your way to the main exhibition hall. Outside the hall a monument, inscribed in English, French, Yiddish, German and Russian, reads 'Never Again'. Nearby are large stakes onto which prisoners were hanged, sometimes for days, with their hands shackled behind their backs.

Inside the main hall you'll find photographs and models of the camp, its officers and prisoners, and of the horrifying 'scientific experiments' carried out by the Nazi doctors. There's also a whipping block a chart showing the system for prisoner identification by category (Jews, homosexuals, Jehovah's Witnesses, Poles, Romas and other 'asocial' types) and exhibits on the rise of the Nazi party and the establishment of the camp system. An English-language documentary is shown at 11.30am and 3.30pm.

Also on the grounds are reconstructed bunkers, the crematorium and a gas chamber (never used) disguised as showers. Outside the gas chamber building is a statue to 'honour the dead and warn the living'. Several religious shrines are also nearby.

Expect to spend two to three hours here.

Tours

To appreciate the site fully a guided tour is highly recommended.

Radius Tours & Bikes (☎ 986 015; €18; ☷ 9.20am & 1pm Tue-Sun Apr-Oct, plus 11.20am May-Aug, noon Nov-Mar; 4-5hr) Tours leave from opposite tracks 31-33 at the Hauptbahnhof.

Into Munich Tours (☎ 225 592; adult/concession €9/7; ☷ 9.30am, 11.45am, 3.45pm Mon-Sat May-Oct, 11.45am Mon-Sat Nov-Apr) Meet outside the tourist office at the Rathaus.

Dachauer Forum & Action Reconciliation (free; ☷ 12.30pm Tue-Sun Jun-Aug, Sat & Sun only Sep-May; 2hr) Meet at the main hall.

Getting There & Away

The S2 (direction: Laim) leaves Munich Hauptbahnhof every 20 minutes and makes the journey to Dachau Hauptbahnhof in 22 minutes. You'll need a two-zone ticket (€5, or four strips of a *Streifenkarte*), including the bus connection. From here change to local bus No 724 or 726 and show your stamped ticket to the driver. By car, follow Dachauer Strasse straight out to Dachau and follow the KZ-Gedenkstätte signs. Parking is €1.75.

CHIEMSEE
☎ 08051

The Bavarian Sea, as Chiemsee is affectionately known, is a haven for water rats, stressed-out city dwellers and anyone on the grand palace tour. Most visitors come to see King Ludwig II's homage to Versailles – Schloss Herrenchiemsee – built on one of the islands, but the lake's natural beauty and the many possibilities for water sports make it worthy of a night or two.

The towns of Prien am Chiemsee and, about 5km south, Bernau am Chiemsee, both on the Munich-Salzburg rail line, are good bases for exploring the lake. Of the two, Prien is the larger and more commercial.

The **Chiemsee Info-Center** (☎ 965 550; www .chiemsee.de; 🕑 9am-7pm Mon-Fri, 10am-4pm Sat & Sun) is on the southern lakeshore, just off the Bernau-Felden autobahn exit. The centre covers information for the whole area. Separate tourist offices are also located in **Prien** (☎ 690 50; www.tourismus.prien.de; Alte Rathausstrasse 11) and **Bernau** (☎ 986 80; www .bernau-am-chiemsee.de; Aschauer Strasse 10).

Schloss Herrenchiemsee

The island Herreninsel in the Chiemsee is home to another fantastic palace spawned by the warped imagination of Ludwig II: **Schloss Herrenchiemsee** (☎ 688 70; adult/concession/under 18 €6.50/5.50/free; 🕑 tours continuously 9am-5.15pm Apr-Sep, 10am-4.40pm Oct-Mar). Begun in 1878, it was never intended as a residence but as a homage to absolutist monarchy, as epitomised by Ludwig's hero, the French Sun King, Louis XIV. Ludwig spent only 10 days here and even then was rarely seen, preferring to read at night and sleep all day.

The palace is both a knock-off and an attempted one-up of Versailles, with larger and more lavishly decorated rooms. Ludwig managed to spend more money on this palace than on Neuschwanstein and Linderhof combined. When cash ran out in 1885, one year before his death, 50 rooms remained unfinished.

The rooms that were completed outdo each other in opulence. The vast **Ambassador Staircase**, a double staircase leading to a frescoed gallery and topped by a glass roof, is the first visual knock-out on the guided tour but fades in comparison to the stunning **Great Hall of Mirrors**. This tunnel of light runs the length of the garden (98m; 10m longer than that in Versailles!) and sports 52 candelabra and 33 great glass chandeliers with 7000 candles, which used to take 70 servants half an hour to light. In late July it becomes a superb venue for classical concerts.

The **Paradeschlafzimmer** resembles a chapel, with the canopied bed perching altarlike on a pedestal behind a golden balustrade. This was the heart of the palace, where morning and evening audiences were held. However, it is the king's bedroom, the **Kleines Blaues Schlafzimmer**, that tops the bill. The decoration is sickly sweet, encrusted with gilded stucco and wildly extravagant carvings. The room is bathed in a soft blue light emanating from a glass globe at the foot of the bed. It supposedly took 18 months for a technician to perfect the lamp to the king's satisfaction.

Admission to the palace also entitles you to a spin around the **König-Ludwig II-Museum**, where you can see the king's christening and coronation robes, blueprints for even more phantasmagorical architectural projects and his death mask.

To get to the palace take the ferry from Prien-Stock (€5.70 return, 15 to 20 minutes) or from Bernau-Felden (€6.20, 25 minutes, May to October). From the boat landing on Herreninsel, it's about a 20-minute walk through lovely gardens to the palace. The palace tour, offered in German or English, takes 30 minutes.

Fraueninsel

This island is home to the **Frauenwörth Abbey**, founded in the late 8th century and one of the oldest nunneries in Bavaria. The 10th-century abbey church, whose freestanding campanile sports a distinctive onion-dome top (11th century), is worth a visit. Opposite the church is the AD 860 **Carolingian Torhalle** (☎ 08054-72 56; admission €1.50; 🕑 11am-6pm May-Oct). It houses medieval *objets d'art*, sculpture and changing exhibits of regional paintings from the 18th to the 20th centuries.

Return ferry fare, including a stop at Herreninsel, is €6.80 from Prien-Stock and €7.30 from Bernau-Felden.

Swimming & Boat Hire

The most easily accessed swimming beaches are at Chieming and Gstadt (both free) on the lake's eastern and northern shores, respectively. Boats, for hire at many beaches, range from €5 to €20 per hour, depending on the type. In Prien, **Bootsverleih Stöffl** (☎ 2000; Seestrasse 64) has two-seater paddleboats for €5 per hour and electric boats for €9 to €19.

The futuristic-looking glass roof by the harbour in Prien-Stock shelters **Prienavera**

BAVARIA

(☎ 609 570; Seestrasse 120; 4hr pass adult/concession €7/3.50, day pass €10/5; ☒ seasonal, usually 10am-9pm). It's an enormous pool complex with sauna, steam baths, slides, Jacuzzi and fitness area. The name is a weak pun on the Italian *primavera*, meaning 'spring'.

Sleeping

The tourist offices can set up **private rooms** (from €18 per person) in town and in farmhouses.

Panorama Camping Harras (☎ 904 60; www .camping-harras.de; person/tent/car €6/3/4.90) This camp site is scenically located on a peninsula with its own private beach. It offers catamaran and surfboard hire and has a restaurant with a lakeview terrace. Prices are 15% higher for stays under four days.

DJH hostel (☎ 687 70; jhprien@djh-bayern.de; Carl-Braun-Strasse 66; dm €15.70; ☒ closed Dec–mid-Jan) Prien's hostel is a 15-minute walk from the Hauptbahnhof and can sleep 130 people in 23 rooms. The hostel has lots of games and activities and a green conscience. There's also an environmental study centre for young people here.

Landgasthaus Kartoffel (☎ 9670; www.kartoffel -bernau.de; Aschauer Strasse 22, Bernau; s €23-37, d €46-74; ℗ ☐) Simple, modern rooms at this super-central, yet quiet, guesthouse are good value by any standard. It's a friendly place with a progressive flair (Internet access, PC hire) and a small restaurant that specialises in potato dishes, meats and salads (€5 to €12.50).

Hotel Garni Möwe (☎ 5004; www.hotel-garni -moewe.de; Seepromenade 111, Prien; s €49, d €64-98; ℗) This traditional Bavarian hotel sits right on the lakefront and is excellent value. It has its own bike and boat hire as well as a sauna and fitness centre, and the large garden is a bonus for anyone travelling with children.

Hotel Bonnschlössl (☎ 890 11; www.alter-wirt -bernau.de; Kirchplatz 9, Bernau; s €44-72, d €72-104; ℗) For something special yet affordable, head over to this charming hotel in a fully restored palace built in 1477. Rooms are stylish and packed with amenities and there's a wonderful rambling garden.

Eating

Badehaus (☎ 970 300; Rasthausstrasse 11, Bernau; mains €6-15) Near the Chiemsee Info-Center and the lakeshore, this contemporary beer hall and garden has quirky décor and gour-met fare enjoyed by a mix of locals and visitors. A special attraction is the so-called 'beer bath', a glass tub filled (sometimes) with a mix of beer and water.

Der Alte Wirt (☎ 890 11; Kirchplatz 9, Bernau; mains €8.50-13; ☒ closed Mon) For great Bavarian cuisine with swift service, drop by this massive half-timbered inn where the Leberkäs is clearly the star of the menu. The waitresses dart round the dining halls as if on roller blades.

Hacienda (☎ 4448; Seestrasse 94, Prien; tapas €2-3, mains €7-14; ☒ dinner only, closed Sun) For something a little more hip, slick Hacienda serves up some delicious tapas and traditional Spanish food including *jamon serrano* (cured ham) and a mean paella. The crowd is young and lively and heads straight for the cocktails.

Getting There & Around

Prien and Bernau are served by hourly trains from Munich (€12.40, one hour). Hourly bus No 9505 connects the two lake towns.

Local buses run from Prien Bahnhof to the harbour in Stock. You can also take the historic Chiemseebahn (1887), the world's oldest **narrow-gauge steam train** (€1.80/3 one way/return; ☒ May-Sep).

Ferries operated by **Chiemsee Schifffahrt** (☎ 6090; Seestrasse 108) ply the lake every hour with stops at Herreninsel, Fraueninsel, Seebruck and Chieming on a schedule that changes seasonally. You can circumnavigate the entire lake and make all these stops (getting off and catching the next ferry that comes your way) for €9.90. Children aged six to 15 get a 50% discount.

Radsport Reischenböck (☎ 4631; Bahnhofsplatz 6, Prien) hires out city/mountain bikes for €7/10 per day.

STARNBERG
☎ 08151 / pop 22,000

Once a royal retreat and still popular with politicians, celebrities and the merely moneyed, Starnberger See is a fast and easy option to get out onto the water and away from the urban bustle of Munich.

The town of Starnberg, at the northern end of the lake, is the heart of the Fünf-Seen-Land (Five-Lakes-District). Besides Lake Starnberg the district comprises the Ammersee and the much smaller Pilsensee, Wörthsee and Wesslinger See. Swimming, achting and windsurfing are popular activities on all lakes.

The district **tourist office** (☎ 08151-906 00; www.sta5.de; Wittelsbacherstrasse 2c; ☑ 8am-6pm Mon-ri & 9am-1pm Sat May–mid-Oct) is in Starnberg.

Lake Starnberg is best known as the place where King Ludwig II died (see the boxed ext Ludwig II, the Fairy-Tale King, p376). The spot where his body was found, near he Votivkapelle in exclusive Berg on the eastern shore, is now marked with a cross erected in the water (bus No 961 from Starnberg).

From Easter Sunday to mid-October, **Bayerische-Seen-Schifffahrt** (☎ 120 23) offers scheduled boat service from Starnberg to the other lake towns, as well as 60/90/180-minute tours (€7.20/9.20/13.80) from its docks behind the S-Bahn station. Boats pass by five palaces as well as the Ludwig II cross.

You can also take the ferry south to the **Buchheim Museum** (☎ 259 393; Bernried; adult/child €7.80/3.50; combined boat & museum ticket €16; ☑ 10am-6pm Mon-Fri, 10am-8pm Sat & Sun Apr-Oct; 10am-5pm Tue-Fri, 10am-6pm Sat & Sun Nov-Mar). The museum has a fascinating collection of expressionist art and German modern art as well as folklore and ethnological exhibits from around the world.

If you'd rather get around the lake yourself, you can hire bikes at **Bike It** (☎ 746 430; Maximilianstrasse 4; city bike/full suspension bike €15/20 per day) and rowing/pedal/electric-powered boats (€5/12/20 per hour) from the boat-hire booths just west of the Hauptbahnhof.

Starnberg is just 30 minutes by S-Bahn (S6) from Munich (two zones or four strips of a *Streifenkarte*).

Andechs

One of the district's main tourist attractions is the Benedictine monastery of **Andechs** (☎ 08152-3760; admission free; ☑ 8am-7pm Apr-Sep, 8am-5pm Oct-Mar), rebuilt in 1675 after a disastrous fire. The lovely hill-top rococo structure has long been a place of pilgrimage and you can see some of Germany's oldest votive candles inside. The church has been under restoration for years but is due to be completed in 2004.

Most visitors come to the 'Holy Hill', as Andechs is known, really come to worship at the **Braustüberl**, the monastery's beer hall and garden. The resident monks have been brewing beer for over 500 years. Six varieties are on offer, from the rich and velvety Doppelbock Dunkel to the fresh, unfiltered Weissbier. The place is often so overrun by tourists, it's easy to forget that you're in a religious institution, pious as your love for the brew may be. Summer weekends are especially busy and queues in the canteen can be up to an hour long.

Andechs is served three times daily (twice on Sunday) by bus from the S-Bahn station in Starnberg (S6; 35 minutes) and the one in Herrsching (S5; 10 minutes). The last bus from Andechs to Herrsching leaves at 6.40pm, to Starnberg at 4.43pm.

SCHLEISSHEIM

The northern Munich suburb of Schleissheim is worth a visit for its three palaces and aviation museum.

The crown jewel of the palatial trio is the **Neues Schloss Schleissheim** (☎ 315 8720; Max-Emanuel-Platz 1; adult/concession/under 15 €2/1.50/free; ☑ 9am-6pm Apr-Sep, 10am-4pm Oct-Mar, closed Mon). This pompous palace, modelled after Versailles, was dreamed up by prince-elector Max Emanuel in 1701. Inside, you'll be treated to stylish period furniture and a vaulted ceiling smothered in frescoes by the prolific Cosmas Damian Asam. The palace is surrounded by an impressive park that's ideal for picnics.

Nearby, the **Renaissance Altes Schloss Schleis-sheim** (☎ 315 5272; Maximilianshof 1; adult/concession €3/2; ☑ 9am-6pm Apr-Sep, 10am-4pm Oct-Mar, closed Mon) is only a shadow of its former self and houses exhibits on religious festivals and on Prussia.

On a little island at the eastern end of the Schlosspark stands **Schloss Lustheim** (☎ 315 8720). Closed for renovation at the time of writing, it normally houses a famous collection of Meissen porcelain.

Near the palaces, on what is Germany's oldest airfield (1912), is **Flugwerft Schleissheim** (☎ 315 7140; Effnerstrasse 18; adult/concession €3.50/2.50; ☑ 9am-5pm), the aviation branch of the Deutsches Museum (p337). Displays are housed in three historical buildings – the command, tower and construction hall – as well as a new hall, and include about 60 planes and helicopters, as well as hang-gliders, engines and flight simulators.

To get to Schleissheim take the S1 (direction: Freising) to Oberschleissheim. It's

BAVARIA

about a 15-minute walk from the station along Mittenheimer Strasse towards the palaces. By car, take Leopoldstrasse north until it becomes Ingolstadter Strasse. Then take the A99 to the Neuherberg exit, at the south end of the airfield.

BAD TÖLZ
☎ 08041 / pop 17,000

Bad Tölz is a beautiful spa town with a sloping main street that winds its way among frescoed houses and a host of quaint shops, bars and cafés. The town is a favourite day trip for Munich residents because of the good swimming at Alpamare, the alpine slide at Blomberg Mountain, and rafting down the Isar River. It's also the gateway to the Tölzer Land, an outdoor playground around two beautiful lakes, the Walchensee and the Kochelsee.

On 6 November each year, the town celebrates the patron saint of horses, Leonhard, with the famous **Leonhardifahrt**, a pilgrimage up to the Leonhardi chapel on Kalvarienberg. It features townsfolk dressed in traditional lederhosen and fancy dirndls, brass bands and up to 80 flower-festooned horse-drawn carts.

Bad Tölz's **tourist office** (☎ 786 70; www .bad-toelz.de; Max-Höfler-Platz 1; ☺ 9am-6pm Mon-Fri, 9am-2pm Sat, 10am-noon Sun) can book accommodation and organise tours.

Altstadt
Cobbled and car-free, Bad Tölz' main drag, the **Marktstrasse**, gently slopes through the town flanked by statuesque townhouses with painted façades and overhanging eaves. It is also home to the **Heimatmuseum** (☎ 504 688; Marktstrasse 48; adult/concession €2/1; ☺ 10am-noon & 2-4pm, closed Mon). The sprawling exhibit touches on practically all aspects of local culture and history and has interesting collections of painted armoires (the so-called Tölzer Kisten), beer steins, folkloric garments and some pretty odd religious items.

In a side alley a few steps south of Marktstrasse, through Kirchgasse, is the **Pfarrkirche Maria Himmelfahrt** (☎ 761 260; Frauenfreithof), a late Gothic three-nave hall church with some brilliantly painted glass windows and an expressive floating Madonna. Wandering down Marktstrasse, you'll soon spot the baroque **Franziskanerkirche** (☎ 769 60; Franziskanergasse 1) across the Isar. Flanked by lovely

gardens, its stark whitewashed interior is enlivened by several beautiful altars.

Above the town on Kalvarienberg, loom Bad Tölz' landmark, the twin-towered **Kalvarienbergkirche** (☺ 761 260; Auf dem Kalvarienberg ☺ 8am-7pm Apr-Sep, 8am-5pm Oct-Mar; admission free), an enormous baroque church, with a large central staircase. Beside it is the **Leonhardikapelle** (1718), a tiny chapel that is the destination of the Leonhardi pilgrimage.

Alpamare
In the spa section of town, west of the Isar River, you'll find the fantastic water complex **Alpamare** (☎ 509 991; Ludwigstrasse 14; 4h adult/child pass €23/17, day pass €30/20; ☺ 9am-9pm Mon-Thu, 9am-10pm Fri-Sun). The huge centre has heated indoor and outdoor mineral pools, a wave and surfing pool, a series of wicked waterslides (including Germany's longest, the 330m-long Alpabob-Wildwasser), saunas, solariums and its own hotel.

There's a bus stop on Wilhelmstrasse nearby, served almost hourly from the Hauptbahnhof, which is 3km away. Parking is free.

Blomberg
Southwest of Bad Tölz towers the Blomberg (1248m), a family-friendly mountain with a natural toboggan track in winter and fairly easy hiking and a fun alpine slide in summer.

Unless you're walking, getting up the hill involves a chairlift ride aboard the **Blombergbahn** (☎ 3726; top station return adult/child €7/4, midway one way €2; ☺ 9am-6pm May-Oct, 9am-4pm Nov-Apr weather permitting). The **alpine slide** is a 1226m-long fibreglass track that snakes down the mountain from the middle station. You ride down through the 17 hairpin bends on little wheeled bobsleds that have a joystick to control braking (push forward to go, and pull back to brake). You can achieve speeds of about 40km/h to 50km/h, but chances are if you do, you're going to either ram a rider ahead of you or fly off the track. If you do try for speed, wear a long-sleeved shirt and jeans.

Riding up to the midway station and sliding down costs €4/3 (adult/concession), with discounts for multiple trips. In winter, day passes good for skiing or the toboggan track are €15/13; sleds can be hired for €3 per day.

Getting There & Away

Bad Tölz has hourly train connections with Munich (€8.10; one hour) on the private **Bayerische Oberlandbahn** (BOB; ☏ 08024-997 171; www.bayerischeoberlandbahn.de). The trains depart from the Munich Hauptbahnhof. Alternatively, take the S2 from central Munich to Holzkirchen, then change to the BOB.

THE ROMANTIC ROAD

The Romantic Road (Romantische Strasse) links some of the most picturesque towns and cities in Bavaria (and a few in Baden-Württemberg). Two million people ply the road every year, making it by far the most popular of Germany's holiday routes. That means lots of signs in English and Japanese, tourist coaches and kitsch galore.

Despite the hordes of visitors, it's worth falling for the sales pitch – you won't be alone, but you certainly won't be disappointed. For the best trip pick and choose your destinations or risk an overdose of the incredible medieval architecture.

ORIENTATION & INFORMATION

The Romantic Road runs north–south through western Bavaria, from Würzburg to Füssen near the Austrian border, passing through more than two dozen cities and towns, including Rothenburg ob der Tauber, Dinkelsbühl and Augsburg.

Each town en route has its own local tourist office, in addition to the central **Romantic Road tourist office** (☏ 09851-902 71; www .romantischestrasse.de; Marktplatz) in Dinkelsbühl.

GETTING THERE & AWAY

Though Frankfurt is the most popular gateway for the Romantic Road, Munich is a good choice as well, especially if you decide to take the bus (see p352).

Bicycle

With its ever-changing scenery and gentle gradients, the Romantic Road makes an ideal bike trip. Bikes can be hired from most large Hauptbahnhof, and tourist offices keep lists of bicycle-friendly hotels that permit storage. Also ask for a copy of *Radwandern*, a German-language publication that contains maps and route suggestions.

Bus

Half a dozen daily buses connect Füssen and Garmisch-Partenkirchen (€8.10, all via Neuschwanstein and most via Schloss Linderhof). There are also several connections between Füssen and Oberstdorf (via Pfronten or the Tirolean town of Reutte).

Train

To start at the southern end, take the hourly train link from Munich to Füssen (€18.20, two hours). Rothenburg is linked by train to Würzburg and Munich via Steinach, and Nördlingen to Augsburg via Donauwörth (€10.70).

BerlinLinienBus (☏ 0130-831144; www.berlinlinien bus.de) runs buses between Berlin and Rothenburg (€53/71, seven hours).

Deutsche Touring's Europabus (☏ 069-790 350; www.deutsche-touring.com) operates a daily Castle Road coach service between Heidelberg and Rothenburg (€40/56 one way/return, 4½ hours).

OVF has a daily morning bus (No 8805) from Nuremberg Hauptbahnhof to Rothenburg (€17; two hours), which returns late in the afternoon.

GETTING AROUND

Bus

It is possible to do this route using train connections or local buses but it's complicated, tedious and slow. For flexibility, the ideal way to travel is by car, though many foreign travellers prefer to take the Europabus, which can get incredibly crowded in summer. From April to October Europabus runs one coach daily in each direction between Frankfurt and Füssen (for Neuschwanstein); the entire journey takes about 12 hours. There's no charge for breaking the journey and continuing the next day.

RESERVATIONS & FARES

Tickets are available for short segments of the trip, and reservations are only necessary at peak-season weekends. Reservations can be made through **Deutsche Touring** (☏ 069-790 350; www.deutsche-touring.com), **EurAide** (☏ 089-59 38 89; www.euraide.de) in Munich or from many travel agents and Deutsche Bahn Reisezentrum offices in Hauptbahnhof.

The most heavily travelled circuits along with the one way/return fares from Frankfurt are listed following:

BAVARIA

Destination	Cost (one way/return)
Augsburg	€59/83
Füssen	€82/115
Munich	€70/98
Nördlingen	€49/69
Rothenburg ob der Tauber	€37/52
Würzburg	€21/29

Fares from Munich are:

Destination	Cost (one way/return)
Augsburg	€11/15
Nördlingen	€21/29
Rothenburg ob der Tauber	€33/46
Würzburg	€49/69

Luggage (€2 piece) and bicycles (€9/15 up to/over 12 stops) cost extra. Students, children, pensioners and rail-pass holders qualify for discounts of between 10% and 60%.

WÜRZBURG
☎ 0931 / pop 131,000

Official gateway to the Romantic Road, Würzburg (*vurts*-boorg) is a charming city renowned for its art, architecture and delicate wines.

Würzburg was a Franconia duchy when, in 686, three Irish missionaries tried to persuade Duke Gosbert to convert to Christianity and – oh yes – ditch his wife, his brother's widow. Apparently Gosbert was mulling it over when his wife had the three bumped off in 689. When the murders were discovered decades later, the martyrs became saints and Würzburg became a pilgrimage city and, in 742, a bishopric.

For centuries the resident prince-bishops wielded enormous power and wealth and the city grew in opulence under their rule. A beautiful collection of historic buildings survives in the city core, most painstakingly reconstructed after the near total destruction of WWII. Their crowning glory is the Residenz, one of the finest baroque structures in Germany and a Unesco World Heritage Site.

Orientation

Würzburg's centre is compact and easy to navigate. The Hauptbahnhof and bus station are at the northern end of the Altstadt. Kaiserstrasse, the main shopping street, goes south from here into the town centre. The Main River forms the western boundary o the Altstadt; the fortress and hostel are on th west bank, other sights are on the east. Th Residenz is on the Altstadt's eastern edge.

Information
BOOKSHOPS
Hugendubel (☎ 354 040; Schmalzmarkt 12)

DISCOUNT CARDS
Welcome Card (€2) Reduced admission to all the main sights and on tours. Valid for seven days.

EMERGENCY
Ambulance (☎ 192 22)
Ärztliche Notfallpraxis (Medical Emergency Practice; ☎ 322 833; Domerschulstrasse 1, Theresienklinik bldg)

INTERNET ACCESS
Log Inn (☎ 205 6923; Juliuspromenade 64, 1st fl; €3.50 per hr; ⊙ 10am-midnight)
Stadtbücherei (City Library; ☎ 373 294; Falkenhaus am Markt; €0.75 per 15 min; ⊙ 10am-6pm Mon-Fri, 10am-2pm Sat) In the same building as the tourist office.

INTERNET RESOURCES
www.wuerzburg.de The town's website

LAUNDRY
SB Waschsalon (☎ 416 773; Frankfurter Strasse 13a; €4 per load)

MONEY
Deutsche Bank (Juliuspromenade 66)
Postbank (Bahnhofplatz 2)
Sparkasse (Barbarossaplatz)

POST
Post office (Bahnhofsplatz 2 & Paradeplatz)

TOURIST INFORMATION
Tourist office Marktplatz (☎ 372 398; Falkenhaus; ⊙ 10am-6pm Mon-Sat, 10am-2pm Sun Apr-Dec, 10am-4pm Mon-Fri, 10am-1pm Sat Jan-Mar); Am Congress Centrum (☎ 372 335; Am Congress Centrum; ⊙ 8am-5pm Mon-Thu, 8am-1pm Fri)

TRAVEL AGENCIES
STA Travel (☎ 521 76; Zwinger 6)

Sights
RESIDENZ
A symbol of wealth and prestige for the Würzburg bishops, Neumann's baroque masterpiece, the **Residenz** (☎ 355 170;

WÜRZBURG

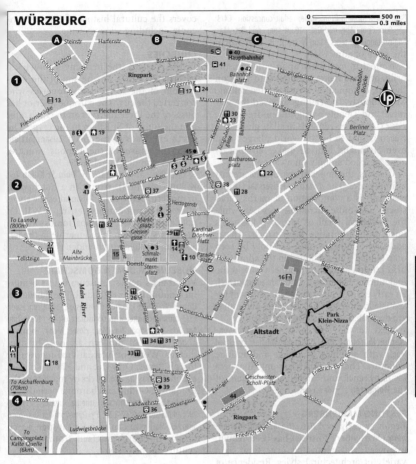

INFORMATION
Ärztliche Notfallpraxis	**1** B3
Deutsche Bank	**2** B2
Hugendubel	**3** B3
Log Inn	**4** B2
Post Office	**5** C1
Postbank	(see 5)
Sparkasse	**6** B2
STA Travel	**7** B4
Stadtbücherei	(see 9)
Theresienklinik	(see 1)
Tourist Office Am Congress Centrum	**8** A2
Tourist Office Falkenhaus	**9** B2

SIGHTS & ACTIVITIES (pp360-3)
Dom St Kilian	**10** B3
Festung Marienberg	**11** A4
Fürstenbaumuseum	(see 11)
Hofkirche	(see 16)
Lusamgärtlein	(see 14)
Mainfränkisches Museum	(see 11)
Martin-von-Wagner-Museum	(see 16)
Museum am Dom	**12** B3

Museum im Kulturspeicher	**13** A1
Neumünster	**14** B3
Rathaus	**15** B3
Residenz	**16** C3
Röntgen Museum	**17** B1

SLEEPING (p363)
DJH Hostel	**18** A4
Hotel am Congress Centrum	**19** A2
Hotel Rebstock	**20** B3
Hotel Strauss	**21** B2
Hotel-Gasthof Zur Stadt Mainz	**22** C2
Pension Siegel	**23** C1
Pension Spehnkuch	**24** B1
Würzburger Hof	**25** B2

EATING (pp363-4)
Backöfele	**26** B3
Brückenbäck	**27** A3
Bürgerspital Weinstuben	**28** C2
Café-Bar-Bistro	**29** B3
Erich Zeiss	(see 30)
Kiliansbäck	**30** C1

Le Clochard Bistro	**31** B3
Mosquito Cantina	**32** A2
Natur-Feinkostladen	**33** B4
Uni-Café	**34** B3

ENTERTAINMENT (p364)
Café Reu	**35** B4
Kult	**36** B4
Meyers Piano Bar	**37** B2
Omnibus	**38** C2

TRANSPORT (p364)
Fahrrad Service Erthal-Sozialwerk	**39** B4
Fahrradstation	**40** C1
Main Bus Station	**41** C1
Mitfahrzentrale	**42** C1
Schiffstouristik Kurth & Schiebe	(see 43)

OTHER
Bürgerspital Weingut	(see 28)
Haus des Frankenweins	**43** A2
Main University Building	**44** C4
Weingut Juliusspital	**45** B2

BAVARIA

Balthasar-Neumann-Promenade; adult/concession €4/3; ☺ 9am-6pm Apr–mid-Oct, 10am-4pm mid-Oct–Mar; English-language tours 11am & 3pm), is well worth the price of admission.

Almost immediately upon entering, the brilliant **grand staircase** comes into view on the left, canopied by a vast vaulted ceiling. Miraculously, the ceiling survived the war intact and Tiepolo's magnificent fresco *The Four Continents* remains in all its glory. The fresco is said to be the world's largest and even Neumann himself makes an appearance, perched smugly on a cannon.

Upstairs, the imperial apartments are just as impressive. The dazzling **Kaisersaal** (Imperial Hall) is a combination of marble, gold stucco and more incredible frescoes, while the **Spiegelsaal** (Hall of Mirrors), has walls lined with decorative glass panels. These, and several other rooms, can only be seen on a guided tour (included in the admission price). In the building's southern wing is the magnificent **Hofkirche** (Court Church; admission free), an early example of Neumann's penchant for spatial illusionism. The side wings of the altar are decorated with paintings by Tiepolo.

Next to the church is the **Martin-von-Wagner Museum** (☎ 312 288; admission free; ☺ closed Mon), with graphics, paintings and antique sculpture. The museum backs onto the spectacular French and English-style gardens of the **Hofgarten** (☺ dawn-dusk).

FESTUNG MARIENBERG

Begun as early as 1201, the **Festung Marienberg** (Marienberg fortress) has been rebuilt, expanded and renovated over time in a variety of architectural styles. Residence of the prince-bishops until 1719, today it is the symbol of the city, visible from almost everywhere. It's a lovely 20-minute walk up the vine-covered hill from the river. Alternatively take bus No 9 from the central bus station.

In the eastern wing is the **Fürstenbaumuseum** (☎ 438 38; adult/concession €2.50/2; ☺ 9am-6pm Tue-Sun Apr–mid-Oct; 10am-4pm Tue-Sun mid-Oct–Mar). It contains the reconstructed apartments of the prince-bishops as well as the city history museum. The baroque Zeughaus (armoury) houses the **Mainfränkisches Museum** (☎ 205 940; adult/concession €3/2, combined ticket for both museums €4/2.50; ☺ 9am-6pm Tue-Sun Apr–mid-Oct; 10am-4pm Tue-Sun mid-Oct–Mar). It has the largest collection of works by master sculptor Tilman Riemenschneider and also

covers the cultural history of Lower Franconia, including wine growing.

CHURCHES

In the Altstadt, the perfectly symmetrical **Neumünster** stands on the site of the martyrdom of the ill-fated missionaries who converted the city. The baroque interior has busts of the three martyrs on the high altar and the tomb of St Kilian in the crypt. The north exit leads to the lovely **Lusamgärtlein** with the grave of the famous minstrel Walther von der Vogelweide.

On the same square is **Dom St Kilian** (St Kilian Cathedral), rebuilt in a hotchpotch of modern, baroque and Romanesque styles after significant damage during WWII. Of note are the prince-bishops' tombstones on the pillars; the two in red marble in the left aisle are by Riemenschneider.

MUSEUM AM DOM & DOMSCHATZ

Würzburg's newest museum is in a beautiful building by the cathedral. The **Museum am Dom** (☎ 386 261; Domerschulstrasse 2; adult/concession €3/2 combined ticket with Domschatz €4; ☺ 10am-7pm Apr-Oct; 10am-5pm Nov-Mar, closed Mon) houses a collection of modern art on Christian themes. Works of international renown by Joseph Beuys, Otto Dix and Käthe Kollwitz are on display as are works by masters of the Romantic, Gothic and baroque periods.

At the **Domschatz** (Cathedral Treasury; ☎ 386 290; adults/students €2/1.50; ☺ 2pm-7pm Apr-Oct, 2pm-5pm Nov-Mar) you can wander through a rich display of church artefacts from the 11th century to the present.

MUSEUM IM KULTURSPEICHER

In a cleverly converted historic granary right on the Main River you'll find the **Museum im Kulturspeicher** (☎ 322 250; Veitshöchheimer Strasse 5; adult/concession €3/2; ☺ 11am-6pm Tue-Sun). This fascinating museum collection includes representational art from the 19th to the 21st centuries, with an emphasis on German impressionism, neorealism and contemporary art. It also houses the post-1945 constructivist art of the Peter C Ruppert Collection, which includes computer art, sculpture, paintings and photographs.

RÖNTGEN GEDÄCHTNISSTTÄTTE

Würzburg's most famous modern scion is Wilhelm Conrad Röntgen, discoverer of the

X-ray. The **Röntgen Gedächtnisstätte** (Röntgen Museum; ☎ 351 1103; Röntgenring 8; admission free; ⏰ 9am-4pm Mon-Thu, 9am-3pm Fri) is a tribute to his life and work.

Tours
Schiffstouristik Kurth & Schiebe (☎ 585 73; Alter Kranen; €8, 40min) offers river cruises.

The tourist office offers **tours** Morning Tour (adult/concession €8/6, including admission to the Residenz; ⏰ 11am, May-Oct; 2hr); Evening Tour (€5; ⏰ 6.30pm, Jun-Oct; 2hr) departing from Falkenhaus. You can also borrow a cassette with a recorded tour (€5.50) of all the major sights.

Würzburg is the centre of the Franconian wine industry and you can sample some of the area's finest vintages on a tour of the historic wine cellars. Reservations are advised.

Bürgerspital Weingut (☎ 350 3403; Theaterstrasse 19; tours €5; ⏰ tours 2pm Sat Mar-Oct)
Haus des Frankenweins (☎ 390 1111; Kranenkai 1) Wine sampling and sales.
Weingut Juliusspital (☎ 393 1400; Juliuspromenade 19; tours €5; ⏰ tours 3pm Fri mid-Apr–Oct; German only)

Festivals & Events
In 2004 Würzburg celebrates its 1300th year with a series of special events, activities and concerts. For full details check www.wuerzburg.de.

Africa-Festival (tickets from the tourist office) Europe's largest festival of Black music; late May/early June.
Mozart Festival (☎ 373 336 to reserve tickets) The Residenz is the ultimate backdrop for this series of classical concerts; late May/early June.

Sleeping
The toll-free 24-hour room reservation hotline is ☎ 0800-194 1408.

BUDGET
DJH hostel (☎ 425 90; jhwuerzburg@djh-bayern.de; Burkarder Strasse 44; dm €16.90; wheelchair access) The well-equipped Jugendgästehaus, below the fortress, has room for 254 in three- to eight-bed dorms. There is also a youth centre and café on site. Take tram No 3 or 5 to Ludwigsbrücke, then it's a five-minute walk north along the river.

Campingplatz Kalte Quelle (☎ 655 98; camping .kalte-quelle@web.de; Winterhäuser Strasse 160; person €3.50, tent €2.50-4) The nearest camp site is about 6km from town on the west bank of the Main. It has a restaurant and small shop on site.

There are plenty of cheap pensions in town but they have no frills and little charm. Two convenient options include **Pension Spehnkuch** (☎ 547 52; fax 547 60; Röntgenring 7; s/d €29/55) and **Pension Siegel** (☎ 529 41; fax 529 67; Reisgrubengasse 7; s/d €29/52).

MID-RANGE
Hotel-Gasthof Zur Stadt Mainz (☎ 531 55; www .hotel-stadtmainz.de; Semmelstrasse 39; s/d €60/110; P) This charming inn with an ornate façade dates back to the 15th century. The rooms are traditional in style but all have modern facilities, and the excellent hotel restaurant serves authentic Franconian food.

Würzburger Hof (☎ 553 814; www.hotel-wuerz burgerhof.de; Barbarossaplatz 2; s €70-97, d €110-165) Right in the heart of the city, this hotel is ideally located for rambling along the shopping streets. The rooms are bright and airy but decorated with heavy furniture and lots of floral patterns.

Hotel am Congress Centrum (☎ 502 44; www.hotel -am-congress-centrum.de; Pleichertorstrasse 26; s €79-90, d €100-120; P X) This hotel near the congress centre is another bastion of tradition with stylish but frilly décor. The service is friendly and the bright, spacious rooms are comfortably furnished and have modern facilities.

Hotel Strauss (☎ 305 70; www.hotel-strauss.de; Juliuspromenade 5; s/d €65/88; P) A family-run business for over 100 years, this conveniently located hotel, with pink stucco façade, has simple, modern rooms featuring light wood, comfortable furniture and modern facilities. You can also hire bicycles.

TOP END
Hotel Rebstock (☎ 309 30; www.rebstock.com; Neubaustrasse 7; s €96-135, d €158-212; P) Class, hospitality and a touch of nostalgia are the characteristics of this family-run hotel in a meticulously restored rococo mansion. Rooms are superb, lack no amenities and are decorated with exquisite furnishings.

Eating
For a town of this size, Würzburg has a bewildering array of enticing pubs, beer gardens, cafés and restaurants, with plenty of student hang-outs among them.

CAFÉS
Café-Bar-Bistro (☎ 460 6014; Martinstrasse 2; mains €3-5; ⏰ 9am-7pm Mon-Fri, 9am-4pm Sat) This trendy

BAVARIA

Italian bistro is conveniently tucked into a quiet street just off Marktplatz and is ideal for a quick snack. The warm orange walls and stylish furniture complement the tasty pastas, soups and snacks.

Brückenbäck (☎ 414 545; Zellerstrasse 2; dishes €4-9) Bask on the terrace in fine weather and enjoy great views of the river and the Altstadt while you sip some exquisite tea, quaff wine or sample a light meal.

Uni-Café (☎ 156 72; Neubaustrasse 2; snacks €3-7) This is a hugely popular student hang-out on the lively Neubaustrasse strip. It has two floors of chilled-out clientele who come for the cheap snacks, cool music and most of all, some fun.

QUICK EATS

For wholesome snacks **Natur-Feinkostladen** (Sanderstrasse 2a; dishes from €2.80) sells healthy fare like grain burgers and runs a specialist grocery store next door. South of the Hauptbahnhof the **Kiliansbäck** (Kaiserstrasse 22) bakery is a good bet for cheap snack specials and tasty goodies. Next door, the butcher shop **Erich Zeiss** offers sausages, chicken and roast pork sandwiches for €2 to €4.50.

RESTAURANTS

Bürgerspital Weinstuben (☎ 352 880; Theaterstrasse 19; mains €7-10; ⏲ closed Aug) The cosy nooks of this labyrinthine medieval place are among Würzburg's most popular eating and drinking spots. Choose from a broad selection of Franconian wines and wonderful regional dishes at decent prices.

Backöfele (☎ 590 59; Ursulinergasse 2; mains €6-18) This rustic restaurant set around a pretty courtyard has romantic atmosphere galore. The menu features both traditional and innovative game and fish dishes, and serves giant meaty slabs grilled over the wood oven.

Mosquito Cantina (☎ 510 22; Karmelitenstrasse 31; mains €8-12.50; ⏲ dinner only) This popular Mexican restaurant serves all the old favourites as well as some interesting vegetarian options. It's a relaxed place for a meal in the early evening and a lively place to hang out later on.

Le Clochard Bistro (☎ 129 07; Neubaustrasse 20; dishes €3.50-9) This trendy hang-out for bright young things has a French-influenced menu and a host of divine sweet and savoury crepes to choose from. The daily three-course special for €9 is great value.

Entertainment

Fritz is the town's monthly listing magazine in German language.

Omnibus (☎ 561 21; Theaterstrasse 10; cover charge €8-12) This suitably faded venue is the city's oldest jazz cellar and has been bringing some of the best live rock, jazz, blues, soul, salsa and folk to town for decades. Acts change nightly.

Meyers Piano Bar (☎ 173 00; Bronnbacher Gasse 43) Live piano music sets a moody tone in this stylish but mellow bar. It's a great place for some serious chilling out and people watching and also serves some good international food (€4 to €8).

Café Reu (☎ 134 17; Sanderstrasse 21) This café has a vast cocktail menu and just a few simple things to nibble on. The distressed metal furnishings lure a young, trendy, energetic crowd intent on having a good time.

Kult (☎ 53143; Landwehrstrasse 10) This is an alternative venue for students and locals. It has a relaxed atmosphere but gets busy at night when the music is cranked up and the crowds stumble in.

Getting There & Away

Regional trains run every two hours to Frankfurt (€19.20, 1¾ hours) and Nuremberg (€14.40, 1¼ hours), but faster and pricier ones run more frequently.

The Romantic Road Europabus stops at the main bus station but the trip to Rothenburg ob der Tauber (one way/return €16/22, three hours) is cheaper by train (€9, 1½ hour).

BerlinLinienBus (☎ 0180-154 6436) makes the journey to/from Berlin three times a week (€47/65 one way/return, six hours). The **Mitfahrzentrale** (☎ 194 48 or ☎ 140 85) is on Bahnhofsplatz.

Getting Around

Würzburg is best seen on foot, but you can also take a bus or tram for €1.50/2 for short/regular journeys. The cheaper ticket will do for trips in town. Day passes are €4.10. Day passes bought on a Saturday can also be used on the Sunday. For a taxi call ☎ 194 10.

Bicycle-hire shops include the **Fahrradstation** (☎ 574 45; Hauptbahnhof; city/mountain bikes €8/10; ⏲ closed Sun & Mon) and the nonprofit **Fahrrad Service Erthal-Sozialwerk** (☎ 359 9739; Sanderstrasse 27; €5.50/8).

AROUND WÜRZBURG
Aschaffenburg
☎ 06021 / pop 69,000
Known as the Bavarian Nice, this charming town of cobbled lanes and half-timbered houses makes a good day trip from Würzburg (or Frankfurt).

The **tourist office** (☎ 395 800; www.info-aschaffenburg.de; Schlossplatz 1; ☒ 9am-5pm Mon-Fri, 10am-1pm Sat) runs 90-minute guided walks (€3) on Saturdays at 2pm from April to October.

Aschaffenburg's most spectacular draw is the magnificent Renaissance **Schloss Johannisburg**, the summer residence of the Mainz archbishops. Today it is home to the **Schlossmuseum** (☎ 386 570; Schlossplatz 4; adult/concession €3/2.50, combined ticket with Pompejanum €4.50/3.50; ☒ 9am-6pm Tue-Sun Apr-Sep, 10am-4pm Tue-Sun Nov-Mar). The modest interior has the usual lot of oil paintings and period furniture, but the true highlight is the stunning collection of architectural cork models depicting landmarks from ancient Rome.

Behind the beautiful palace garden is the **Pompejanum** (☎ 386 570; adult/concession/free €3/2.50/under 15; ☒ 9am-6pm Tue-Sun Apr-Sep). Built for King Ludwig I, this replica of a Pompeian villa comes complete with frescoes, mosaics and Roman antiquities.

From there, follow Schlossgasse into the Altstadt. On Stiftsplatz you'll come upon the **Stiftskirche**, with origins in the 10th century but now an oddly skewed, but impressive mix of Romanesque, Gothic and baroque styles. The attached **Stiftsmuseum** (☎ 330 463; adult/concession €2.50/1.50; ☒ 10am-1pm & 2-5pm Wed-Mon) is home to some intriguing relics and paintings.

Three kilometres west of town lies the **Park Schönbusch**, a shady 18th-century expanse dotted with ornamental ponds and follies, and the **Schlösschen** (☎ 386 570; Kleine Schönbuschallee 1; tours adult/concession €2.50/2; ☒ 9am-6pm Tue-Sun Apr-Sep) a country retreat of the archbishops. The hourly tours are in German.

Hearty Franconian fare can be found at the tiny **Schlossgass' 16** (☎ 123 13; Schlossgasse 16; mains €8-13) wine tavern, and **Wirtshaus Zum Fegerer** (☎ 156 46; Schlossgasse 14; mains €8-15), a charming traditional inn.

Trains to/from Würzburg (€12.40, one hour) and Frankfurt (€6.60, 40 minutes) operate at least hourly. The A3 autobahn runs right past town.

ROTHENBURG OB DER TAUBER
☎ 09861 / pop 12,000
Perched on a hill with magnificent views, Rothenburg is a medieval gem, crowded with tourists but still exceptionally beautiful. Conservation orders here are the strictest in Germany and the Altstadt is a patchwork of winding cobbled lanes lined with incredibly picturesque old houses interspersed with trickling fountains. Rothenburg is the main tourist destination along the Romantic Road and can get painfully crowded in summer and at Christmas, but see it in the soft evening light after the last tour buses have left and you can't help but be impressed.

Orientation
The Hauptbahnhof is a 10-minute walk east of the Altstadt along Ansbacher Strasse. The main shopping drag is Schmiedgasse; at its southern end is the Plönlein (little place), a scenic fork in the road anchored by a half-timbered cottage and fountain that's Rothenburg's unofficial emblem.

Information
Dresdner Bank (Galgengasse 23)
Post office Altstadt (Milchmarkt 5); Bahnhof (Zentro mall, Bahnhofstrasse 15)
Rothenburger Reisebüro (☎ 4611; Hauptbahnhof) Travel agency.
Tourist office (☎ 404 92; www.rothenburg.de; Marktplatz 2; ☒ 9am-noon & 1-6pm Mon-Fri, 10am-3pm Sat May-Oct; 9am-noon & 1-5pm Mon-Fri, 10am-1pm Sat Nov-Mar; ☐)
Volksbank (Marktplatz) To the right of the tourist office.
Wäscherei Then (☎ 2775; Johannitergasse 9; €3.50 per load) Laundry.
www.rothenburg.de The town's excellent website.

Sights
RATHAUS
The town hall on the Markt was begun in Gothic style in the 14th century and completed during the Renaissance. Majestic views over the town and the Tauber Valley can be seen from the 220-step viewing platform of the **Rathausturm** (€1/0.50; ☒ 9.30am-12.30pm & 1.30-5pm Apr-Oct, noon-3pm Dec). In the **Historiengewölbe** (Historical Vaults; adult/concession €2/1.50; ☒ 9.30am-5.30pm Apr-Oct) you can visit the incredibly creepy subterranean prison and torture room and see some hokey depictions of life during the Thirty Years' War (1618–48).

BAVARIA

ROTHENBURG OB DER TAUBER

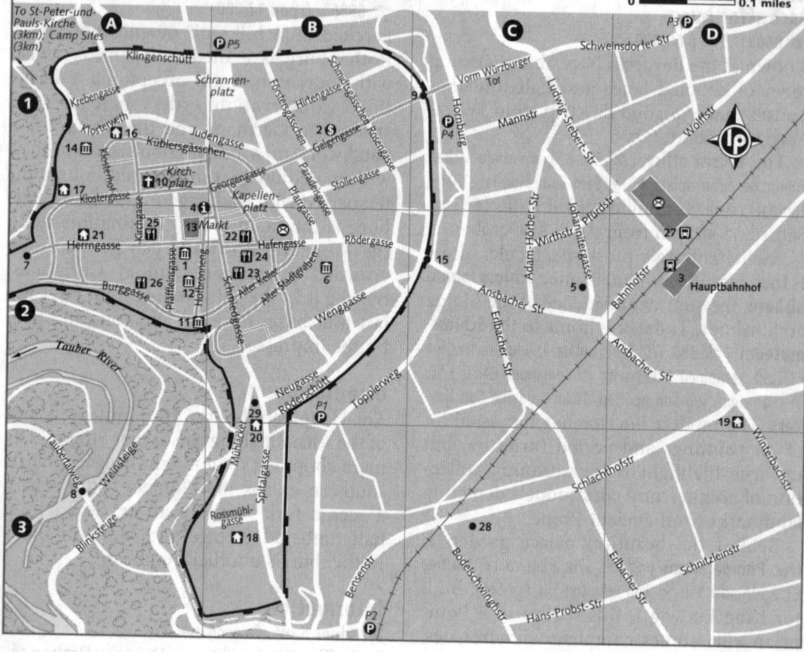

INFORMATION
- Deutsches Weihnachtsmuseum....1 A2
- Dresdner Bank....2 B1
- Rothenburger Reisebüro....3 D2
- Tourist Office....4 A2
- Volksbank....(see 4)
- Wäscherei Then (Laundry)....5 C2

SIGHTS & ACTIVITIES (pp356-7)
- Alt-Rothenburger Handwerkerhaus....6 B2
- Burgtor (Town Gate)....7 A2
- Doppelbrücke....8 A3
- Galgentor....9 C1
- Historiengewölbe....(see 13)
- Jakobskirche....10 A1
- Mittelalterliches Kriminalmuseum....11 A2
- Puppen- und Spielzeugmuseum....12 A2
- Rathaus....13 A2
- Rathausturm....(see 13)
- Reichsstadtmuseum....14 A1
- Röderturm....15 C2

SLEEPING (p368)
- Altfränkische Weinstube....16 A1
- Burg-Hotel....17 A1
- DJH Hostel....18 B3
- Gästehaus Eberlein....19 D2
- Hotel Garni Uhl....20 B3
- Hotel Meistertrunk....21 A2

EATING (p368)
- Albig's Quick Restaurant....22 B2
- Baumeisterhaus....23 B2
- Bosporos Doner....24 B2
- Pizzeria Italia....25 A2
- Zur Höll....26 A2

SHOPPING (p368)
- Käthe Wohlfahrt Weihnachtsdorf....(see 1)

TRANSPORT (pp368-9)
- Main Bus Park....27 D2
- Rad & Tat....28 C3

OTHER
- Plönlein....29 B2

JAKOBSKIRCHE

Rothenburg's major pilgrimage site is the glorious Gothic **Jakobskirche** (☎ 700 60; Klingengasse 1; adult/concession €1.50/0.50, free during services; 🕒 9am-5.30pm Apr-Oct, 10am-noon & 2-4pm Nov-Mar). The main attraction is the carved **Heilige Blut altar** (Holy Blood altar), said to contain a drop of Christ's blood. It depicts the Last Supper with Judas at the centre, taking bread from Christ.

MITTELALTERLICHES KRIMINALMUSEUM

Brutal implements of torture and punishment from medieval times are on display at the fascinating **Mittelalterliches Kriminalmuseum** (Medieval Crime Museum; ☎ 5359; Burggasse 3; adult/concession €3.20/2.10; 🕒 9.30am-6pm Apr-Oct, 2-4pm Nov & Jan-Mar, 10am-4pm Dec). Displays include chastity belts, masks of disgrace for gossips, a cage for errant bakers, a neck brace for quarrelsome women and a beer-barrel pen for drunks. All exhibits are explained in English.

TOWN WALLS & ST-PETER-UND-PAULS-KIRCHE

The intact city walls form a ring around the city. You can walk 2.5km of the wall and get good city views from the eastern tower, **Röderturm** (Rödergasse; adult/concession €1.50/1). For the most impressive views, though, go to the west side of town, where a sweeping view of the Tauber Valley includes the **Doppelbrücke**, a double-decker bridge. Also visible is the head of a trail that leads down the valley and over to the lovely Romanesque **St-Peter-und-Pauls-Kirche** (☎ 5524; Detwang; adult/child €1/0.50; ⏱ 8.30am-noon & 1.30-5pm Apr-Oct; 10am-noon & 2-4pm Nov-Mar, closed Mon) which contains another stunning Riemenschneider altar. There's a beer garden about halfway along the trail.

REICHSSTADTMUSEUM
The city's showcase of local art, culture and history is the **Reichsstadtmuseum** (Imperial City Museum; ☎ 939 043; Klosterhof 5; adult/concession €3/2; ⏱ 10am-5pm Apr-Oct, 1-4pm Nov-Mar), which is housed in a former convent. Highlights include the superb *Rothenburger Passion* (1494) by Martinus Schwarz and the convent rooms themselves, including a 14th-century kitchen. The **gardens** are ideal for a quiet stroll.

OTHER MUSEUMS
The **Alt-Rothenburger Handwerkerhaus** (☎ 942 80; Alter Stadtgraben 26; adult/concession €2.20/1.60; ⏱ 9am-6pm Apr-Oct, 2-4pm Mon-Fri, 10am-4pm Sat & Sun Nov-Dec) reconstructs the working and social life of Rothenburg's medieval citizens. For the nostalgic, the **Puppen-und Spielzeugmuseum** (Doll & Toy Museum; ☎ 7330; Hofbronnengasse 13; adult/concession €4/3.50; ⏱ 9.30am-6pm Mar-Dec, 11am-5pm Jan-Feb) has an amazing collection of doll's houses, teddy bears and toy carousels. Also worth a visit is the **Deutsches Weihnachtsmuseum** (German Christmas Museum; ☎ 409 365; Herrngasse 1; adult/concession €4/2; ⏱ 10am-5.30pm Apr-Dec, weekends only Jan-Mar), which depicts various Christmas customs as they developed through the ages.

Tours
The tourist office runs 90-minute English-language walking tours (€4) at 2pm daily from April to October. Every evening a lantern-toting Nachtwächter (night watchman) dressed in traditional costume leads an entertaining tour of the Altstadt. English tours (€4) meet at the Rathaus at 8pm, German tours (€3) head off at 9.30pm.

Festivals & Events
The **Historisches Festspiel 'Der Meistertrunk'** (see the boxed text below) takes place each year on Whitsuntide, with parades, dances and a medieval market. The highlight, though, is the re-enactment of the mythical Meistertrunk story.

The play itself is performed three more times: once during the **Reichsstadt-Festtage** in early September, when the entire town history is being re-enacted in city streets; and twice during the Rothenburger Herbst, an autumn celebration in October.

The **Historischer Schäfertanz** (Historical Shepherds' Dance), featuring colourfully dressed couples, takes places on Marktplatz several times between April and October.

DRINK & YE SHALL BE FREE

In 1631 the Thirty Years' War – pitching Catholics against Protestants – reached the gates of Rothenburg ob der Tauber. Catholic General Tilly and 60,000 of his troops besieged the Protestant market town and demanded its surrender. The town resisted but couldn't stave off the onslaught of marauding soldiers, and the mayor and other town dignitaries were captured and sentenced to death.

And that's pretty much where the story ends and the legend begins. As the tale goes, Rothenburg's town council tried to sate Tilly's bloodthirstiness by presenting him with a mug of wine fit for a giant. Tilly, after taking a sip or two, presented the men with an unusual challenge: 'If one of you has the courage to step forward and down this mug of wine in one gulp, then I shall spare the town and the lives of the councilmen!' Mayor Georg Nusch accepted – and succeeded! And that's why you can still wander though Rothenburg's wonderful medieval lanes today.

It's pretty much accepted that Tilly was really placated with hard cash. Nevertheless, local poet Adam Hörber couldn't resist turning the tale of the *Meistertrunk* into a play, which, since 1881, has been performed every Whitsuntide (Pentecost), the 7th Sunday after Easter. It's also re-enacted several times daily by the clock figures on the tourist office building.

The **Weihnacht-Reiterlersmarkt** (Christmas Market) in Rothenburg is one of the most romantic in Germany. It takes place each year from late November until 22 December.

Sleeping

Despite its popularity, Rothenburg has surprisingly good-value accommodation. The tourist office has an electronic room reservation board in the foyer. The 24-hour room referral hotline is ☎ 194 12.

DJH hostel (☎ 941 60; jhrothenburg@djh-bayern.de; Mühlacker 1; dm €16.60) Rothenburg's hostel is housed in two enormous renovated old buildings in the south of town. It's extremely well equipped and very popular so book in advance.

Gästehaus Eberlein (☎ 4672; hotel@eberlein.rothen burg.de; Winterbachstrasse 4; s €40, d €50-65; P ☐) A familial atmosphere reigns in this charming pension behind the Hauptbahnhof. Each of the 21 rooms is individually decorated, and guests also have access to the sauna, solarium and fitness room and bikes.

Hotel Meistertrunk (☎ 6077; meistertrunk@roman ticroad.com; Herrngasse 26; s €50-80, d €80-150; P) This old mansion has been converted into a charming family-friendly inn with a winning atmosphere. Rooms are bright and airy and tastefully decorated in a subtle traditional style.

Burg-Hotel (☎ 948 90; www.burghotel.rothenburg .de; Klostergasse 1-3; s €90-100, d €100-150; P ☐) The best views in town are from this charming hotel built right into the town fortifications. If you're looking for a romantic getaway and price is no object, this is it.

Other recommendations are:

Hotel Garni Uhl (☎ 4895; Plönlein 8; s/d from €30/50; P) A quiet, family-run hotel with spacious modern rooms.

Altfränkische Weinstube (☎ 6404; www.altfraen kische.de; Klosterhof 7; s €45, d €50-60) An enchanting inn with atmosphere-laden rooms filled with knick-knacks.

Campers should head for the suburb of Detwang, where you'll find **Campingplatz Tauber-Idyll** (☎ 3177; Camping-Tauber-Idyll@t-online.de; Detwang 28a) and **Campingplatz Tauber-Romantik** (☎ 6191; info@camping-tauberromantik.de; Detwang 39) which charge about €4 per person, €4.50 for a tent and open from Easter to late October.

Eating

Rothenburg's most obvious speciality is *Schneeballen*, balls of sweet dough dipped in cinnamon or sugar, and available all over town.

Altfränkische Weinstube (☎ 6404; Am Klosterhof 7; mains €5-13; ☒ dinner only) This is a cosy place with friendly staff, romantic lighting and a riot of flowers. Mains are incredibly good value – a favourite is *Schweinelendchen mit Preiselbeeren* (pork tenderloins with cranberries).

Zur Höll (☎ 4229; Burggasse 8; dishes €4.50-15) This medieval wine tavern with a lovely atmosphere is in the town's oldest original building. The menu of regional specialities is limited but refined, though it's the wine that people really come for.

Baumeisterhaus (☎ 947 00; Obere Schmiedgasse 3; mains €8-22) This traditional German inn is in an atmospheric old frescoed building set around a beautiful vine-clad courtyard. The menu changes daily and has a wealth of traditional fare.

Pizzeria Italia (☎ 2225; Herrngasse 8; mains €4-14) This is your better-than-average pizza joint run by friendly people. It's a great place to sit out on the street in summer and just people watch.

For quick snacks you could try **Bosporos Doner** (☎ 934 716; Hafengasse 2; dishes €3-6) for delicious kebabs and Middle Eastern goodies, including vegetarian selections, or just next door, **Albig's Quick Restaurant** (Hafengasse 3; dishes €1.50-7) for schnitzels, fries and burgers.

Shopping

Eternal Christmas reigns at **Käthe Wohlfahrt Weihnachtsdorf** (☎ 4090; Herrngasse 1), with its mind-boggling assortment of Christmas decorations and ornaments, as well as souvenirs. Many of the items are handcrafted with amazing skill and imagination and prices are accordingly high.

Getting There & Away

There's frequent train service from Würzburg (€9, 1½ hours) but travel to/from Munich (from €36.40, 3½ hours) may require two or three changes. The Europabus stops in the main bus park at the Hauptbahnhof. The A7 autobahn runs right past town.

Getting Around

The city has five car parks right outside the walls (€1/2 for five hours/all day), P5 is free and P3 is free for cars but not camper vans. The entire town centre is closed to nonresident vehicles from 11am to 4pm and 7pm to 5am weekdays and all day weekends; hotel guests are exempt.

Some hotels have bicycle hire, or try **Rad & Tat** (☎ 879 84; Bensenstrasse 17; €13 per day). Horse-drawn carriage rides of 25 to 30 minutes cost about €6 per person, but you can haggle for a better price. Call ☎ 4405 for taxis.

DINKELSBÜHL

☎ 09851 / pop 12,000

Dinkelsbühl, another colourful medieval town, has a far less contrived feel than its more famous neighbour Rothenburg, as well as fewer tourists and buses. The whole town is immaculately preserved; even the side streets are flawless, at times verging on the clinical. For a good overall impression of the town, walk along the fortified walls with their 16 towers and four gates.

Orientation & Information

The post office and police station are next to the bus station. The Altstadt is five minutes' walk west of here, via Wörnitzer Tor. The **tourist office** (☎ 902 40; www.dinkelsbuehl.de; Marktplatz; ⏰ 9am-6pm Mon-Fri, 9am-1pm & 2-4pm Sat, 9am-noon Sun, Apr-Oct, 9am-5pm Mon-Fri & 9am-noon Sat Nov-Mar) is opposite Münster St Georg. You'll find the central **Romantic Road tourist office** (☎ 902 71; ⏰ 9am-6pm Mon-Fri, 9am-1pm & 2-4pm Sun, 9am-noon Sun, Apr-Oct, 9am-5pm Mon-Fri & 9am-noon Sat Nov-Mar) here as well.

Sights

MÜNSTER ST GEORG & WEINMARKT

One of southern Germany's purest late Gothic hall churches, the massive **Münster St Georg** (Marktplatz; ⏰ 9am-noon & 2-6pm) may look humble enough from the outside but has a stunning interior with incredible fan vaulting. Take time to look at the bejewelled bones of the martyr St Aurelius before heading up the **tower** (€1.50; ⏰ weekends only May-Sep) for great views of town.

Opposite the church is an ensemble of magnificent half-timbered mansions on Weinmarkt, the town's main square. The Renaissance Gustav-Adolph and Deutsches Haus have the most elaborate façades.

MUSEUM OF THE 3RD DIMENSION

Dedicated to optical illusions and special effects, the **Museum of the 3rd Dimension** (☎ 6336; Nördlinger Tor; adult/concession €5.50/4.50; ⏰ 10am-6pm Apr-Oct, 11am-4pm Sat & Sun Nov-Mar) has three floors of entertainment well worth the price of admission. Displays include holographic images, stereoscopic mind-blowers and a 3-D film. You can easily spend an hour here; borrow an English-language guide and follow the numbers.

Tours

Altstadt walking tours (€2, one hour) start at Münster St Georg at 2.30pm and 8.30pm from April to October (2.30pm Saturday November to March). There's also a free night-watchman tour in German at 9pm daily April to October (Saturday only in winter).

Festivals & Events

In the third week of July, Dinkelsbühl celebrates the 10-day **Kinderzeche** (Children's Festival; www.kinderzeche.de), commemorating a legend from the Thirty Years' War that tells how the children of the town successfully begged the invading Swedish troops to leave Dinkelsbühl unharmed. The festivities include a pageant, re-enactments in the Stadt Festsaal, lots of music and other entertainment.

During **Dinkelsbühl's Jazz Festival** (admission €15 Fri/Sat, €20 for both Fri & Sat, free Sun) in late May, local and international groups perform throughout the Altstadt. Contact the tourist office for more details.

Sleeping

The tourist office can help find **private rooms** (from €25).

DJH hostel (☎ 9509; cballheimer@t-online.de; Koppengasse 10; dm €13.60; ⏰ closed Nov-Feb) Dinkelsbühl's hostel is in the western Altstadt in a beautifully restored 15th-century granary.

DCC-Campingplatz Romantische Strasse (☎ 7817; www.campingpark-dinkelsbuehl.de; Kobeltsmühle 2; tent/person €7.50/5.50) This camp site set on a swimmable lake is about 300m northeast of Wörnitzer Tor.

Gasthof Goldenes Lamm (☎ 2267; www.goldenes.de; s €35-48, d €59-70) This relaxed family-run inn has pleasant rooms at the top of a creaky staircase and a funky rooftop garden deck with plump sofas. The attached restaurant serves Franconian-Swabian specialities, including some vegetarian choices (€5.50 to €16).

Privat Hotel Dinkelsbühler Kunststuben (☎ 67 50; www.kunst-stuben.de; Segringer Strasse 52; s €50, d €55-70) No room is the same in this snug bohemian B&B where guests receive personal attention. The whole place drips with charm and character and the lovely inner courtyard is perfect for relaxing in warm weather.

Hotel Goldene Kanne (☎ 572 910; www.hotel-goldene-kanne.de; Segringer Strasse 8; s €49-73, d €68-102) This child-friendly hotel has a good range of comfortable, spacious rooms with dark wood and understated décor. The excellent restaurant (mains €10 to €19) serves a variety of local and international treats and some unusual specials.

Eating

For more places to eat see the hotels listed under Sleeping, several of which have excellent restaurants.

Weib's Brauhaus (☎ 579 490; Untere Schmiedgasse 13; dishes €2.50-12) A female brewmaster supervises the workings of the copper vats at this lively restaurant-pub. The menu is mainly traditional and many dishes feature the house brew, including the popular Weib's Töpfle (woman's pot).

Café Extrablatt (☎ 2297; Weinmarkt 10; dishes €4-12) This trendy bistro with a beautiful garden bustles morning to night and serves everything from big breakfasts to local fare and healthy salads. Hollywood posters and plenty of knick-knacks form the backdrop.

Bäckerei Stadtcafé (☎ 9473; Dr-Martin-Luther-Strasse 15; snacks €2.50-8) This friendly bakery is a good bet for casseroles, salads, meaty snacks and breakfast.

Getting There & Around

Dinkelsbühl is not served by trains. Regional buses to/from Rothenburg (€5.50, one hour) and to Nördlingen (€4.50, 40 minutes) stop at the Busbahnhof. The Europabus stops right in the Altstadt at Schweinemarkt.

The tourist office hires out bicycles for €3.60/€15 per day/week. The Altstadt is closed to vehicles from noon to 6pm on Sunday, Easter to October.

NÖRDLINGEN

☎ 09081 / pop 21,000

The charming medieval town of Nördlingen sees relatively few tourists and manages to retain a real air of authenticity. It's almost perfectly circular and still surrounded by its original 14th-century walls, and you can get a bird's-eye view from the tower of St Georgkirche.

Nördlingen lies within the Ries Basin, a huge crater created by a mega-meteorite more than 15 million years ago. The crater – some 25km in diameter – is one of the best preserved on earth, and was used by US astronauts to train for the first moon landing.

Orientation & Information

St Georgskirche is the heart of circular Nördlingen. From here five main roads radiate towards the town gates. The Eger River runs through the northern Altstadt. The Hauptbahnhof, which embraces the main post office, is outside the walls, just southeast of the centre. You can circumnavigate the entire town in about an hour by taking the sentry walk (free) on top of its covered old walls.

The **tourist office** (☎ 4380; www.noerdlingen.de; Marktplatz 2; ☉ 9am-6pm Mon-Thu, 9am-4.30pm Fri, 9.30am-1pm Sat, Easter-early Nov, Mon-Fri only mid-Nov–Easter) is right in the centre of town.

Sights

ST GEORGSKIRCHE

The massive late Gothic **St Georgskirche** is one of the largest in southern Germany. Its high altar and the intricate 1499 pulpit are worth a look, but the real draw is the 90m **Daniel Tower** (adult/concession €1.75/1; ☉ 9am-8pm Apr-Oct, 9am-5.30pm Nov-Mar). Scramble up the 350 steps to truly appreciate Nördlingen's shape and the gentle landscape of the Ries crater. The watchman who lives at the top sounds out the watch every half-hour from 10pm to midnight.

RIESKRATER MUSEUM

Situated in an ancient barn, the **Rieskrater Museum** (☎ 273 8220; Eugene-Shoemaker-Platz 1; adult/concession €3/1.80, combination ticket with Stadtmuseum €4.50/2.50; ☉ 10am-noon & 1.30-4.30pm Tue-Sun) explores the formation of meteorite craters and the consequences of such violent collisions with earth. Rocks, including a genuine moon rock (on permanent loan from NASA), fossils and other geological displays shed light on the mystery of meteors.

OTHER MUSEUMS

The **Stadtmuseum** (☎ 273 8230; Vordere Gerbergasse 1; adult/concession €3/1.50; ☉ 10.30am-4.30pm Tue-Sun Mar-early Nov) features costumes and displays

on local history. The **Stadtmauermuseum**
(☎ 9180; Löpsinger Torturm; admission €1; ☒ 10am-
4.30pm Apr-Oct) has an exhibition on the history
of the town walls and fortification system.

Tours
The tourist office runs hour-long German-
language walking tours (€2.50, under 12 free)
at 2pm from Easter to October and at 8.30pm
(€3) from mid-May to mid-September.

Festivals & Events
The largest annual celebration is the 10-
day **Nördlinger Pfingstmesse** at Whitsuntide.
It's an exhibition of regional traders, with a
huge market featuring beer tents, food stalls
and entertainment.

Sleeping & Eating
DJH hostel (☎ 271 816; Kaiserwiese 1) The hostel
is closed for renovations and will reopen
in 2005.

Braunes Ross (☎ 290 120; braunesross@t-online.de;
Marktplatz 12; s/d €26/50) Right beside St Georg,
this guesthouse has simple, good-value
rooms with private bathroom. There's a
nice garden to relax in and good international food at the restaurant (€4.50 to €12).
Children are very welcome.

Kaiserhof Hotel Sonne (☎ 5067; kaiserhof-hotel
-sonne@t-online.de; Marktplatz 3; s €50-60, d €80-95; ☒)
This is one of Nördlingen's top hotels and
dates back to 1405. Since then it has hosted
an entire parade of emperors and their
entourages, and rooms tastefully mix traditional charm with modern comforts. The
restaurant serves regional dishes (€5.50 to
€14.50).

Café Radlos (☎ 5040; Löpsinger Strasse 8; mains €5-10;
☒ closed Tue) This hip café serves a good
range of international cuisine, including
some vegetarian options. Slinky jazz sets a
mellow tone for surfing the net (€1.50 per
30 minutes) or just enjoying a drink in the
beer garden.

La Fontana (☎ 211 021; Bei den Kornschrannen 2;
mains €4.30-11.50; ☒ closed Mon) This stylish Italian eatery occupies a vast 1602 blood-red
barn house. The restaurant serves up tasty
pasta and pizza as well as some more expensive Mediterranean meat and fish dishes.

For quick snacks, try **Café Ihle** (☎ 257 993;
Rübenmarkt 3; snacks €2-4) for baked goods or
Kochlöffel (☎ 280 81; Marktplatz 9; dishes €2.50-3.50)
for decent fast food.

Getting There & Around
There are hourly trains to Munich (€25.80,
two hours) and regular services to Augsburg (€10.70, one hour) and Stuttgart
(€16.20, 2½ hours). The Europabus stops
at the Rathaus. The regional VGN bus (No
501/868) going to Dinkelsbühl and Feucht-
wangen also stops at the Rathaus (€3, 40
minutes).

There are free car parks at all five city
gates.

You can hire bicycles at **Radsport Böckle**
(☎ 801 040; Reimlinger Strasse 19) or **Zweirad Müller**
(☎ 5675; Gewerbestrasse 16) from €8 per day.
Call ☎ 1660 or ☎ 877 78 for a taxi.

AUGSBURG
☎ 0821 / pop 259,000
One of the oldest cities in Germany, Augsburg was originally founded by the step-
children of Roman emperor Augustus over
2000 years ago. During the Middle Ages it
became an economic powerhouse of trade
and was home to some of Europe's most
powerful merchant families: the Fuggers
and the Welsers.

Reminders of this golden era can be seen
in the Renaissance and baroque façades of
the palaces and patrician houses dotted
around what is now Bavaria's third-largest
city. Augsburg has a very relaxed attitude
and strolling the leafy streets is a real
pleasure. An easy day trip from Munich,
it's a good accommodation option during
Oktoberfest and an ideal base for exploring
the Romantic Road.

Orientation
The Hauptbahnhof is at the eastern end
of Bahnhofsplatz, which runs into Fuggerstrasse at Königsplatz, the city's main bus
transfer point. The heart of the Altstadt is
Rathausplatz, reached on foot from Königsplatz up Annastrasse.

Information
BOOKSHOPS
Buchhandlung Rieger & Kranzfelder (☎ 517 880;
Maximilianstrasse 36, Fugger Stadtpalast) Stocks lots of
English-language books.

INTERNET ACCESS
Surf Inn (☎ 5022 22168; Bürgermeister-Fischer-Strasse
9, inside Galeria Kaufhof; €1.50 per 30min; ☒ 9.30am-
8pm Mon-Sat)

BAVARIA

INTERNET RESOURCES
www.augsburg-tourismus.de The town's website.

LAUNDRY
Waschcenter HSB (☎ 419 451; Wolfgangstrasse 1;
€3.50 per load; ❧ 6am-11.30pm) Take tram No 2.

MEDICAL SERVICES
Ambulance (☎ 192 22)
Zentralklinikum (☎ 400 01; Stenglinstrasse 2)

MONEY
Citibank (Bahnhofstrasse 2)
Hypovereinsbank (Bahnhofstrasse 11)
Postbank (Hauptbahnhof)

POST
Main post office (Hauptbahnhof)

TOURIST INFORMATION
Tourist office Bahnhofstrasse (☎ 502 070; Bahnhofstrasse 7; ❧ 9am-6pm Mon-Fri Apr-Oct, to 5pm Nov-
Mar) Rathausplatz (☎ 502 0724; ❧ 9am-5pm Mon-Fri,
10am-4pm Sat, 10am-2pm Sun Apr-Oct, 9am-5pm Mon-Fri,
10am-1pm Sat Nov-Mar)

TRAVEL AGENCIES
Fernweh (☎ 155 035; Dominikanergasse 10) STA Travel
representative.
Travel Overland (☎ 314 157; Zeuggasse 5)

Sights
RATHAUSPLATZ
This is the heart of the city and is dominated by the twin onion-dome spires of
Augsburg's Renaissance **Rathaus** (1615–20).
Crowning the building is a 4m pine cone,
the city's emblem and an ancient fertility
symbol. Inside, the star attraction is the
meticulously restored **Goldener Saal** (☎ 3240;
Rathausplatz; adult/concession €2/0.50; ❧ 10am-6pm),
the city's main meeting hall. It is a dazzling
space canopied by a gilded and coffered
ceiling, interspersed with frescoes.

For a city panorama, climb the **Perlachturm**
(☎ 502 070; Rathausplatz; adult/concession €1/0.50;
❧ 10am-6pm Apr-Oct, 2-7pm Sat & Sun Dec) next door.

DOM
North of Rathausplatz you'll find **Dom
Maria Heimsuchung** (Hoher Weg; ❧ 10.15am-6pm
Mon-Sat) whose original structure dates back
to the 11th century. Over the years many
alterations have been made, including the
addition of the 14th-century bronze doors,

which present Old Testament scenes. The
cathedral's oldest section is the crypt underneath the west choir, which features a
Romanesque Madonna. Other treasures
include medieval frescoes, the *Weingartner
Altar* by Hans Holbein the Elder, and dating from the 12th century, the *Prophets'
Windows* (depicting Daniel, Jonah, Hosea
and Moses), some of the oldest stained-
glass windows in Germany.

ST ANNA KIRCHE
The rather plain-looking **St Anna Kirche** (Annastrasse; admission free; ❧ 10am-12.30pm & 3-6pm
Tue-Sat, noon-6pm Sun) contains a bevy of treasures as well as the sumptuous **Fuggerkapelle**,
where Jacob Fugger and his brothers lie
buried, and the lavishly frescoed **Gold-
schmiedekapelle** (Goldsmiths' Chapel; 1420).
The church played an important role during the Reformation. In 1518, Martin
Luther, in town to defend his beliefs before
the papal legate, stayed at what was then
a Carmelite monastery. His rooms have
been turned into the **Lutherstiege**, a small
museum on the Reformation.

FUGGEREI
Built to provide homes for poor Catholics,
the Fuggerei is one of the earliest welfare
settlements in the world. Jacob Fugger financed the project in the 16th century and
it is still home to several hundred people.
The 52 apartments have now been modernised, but the rent has remained stable over
the centuries at 1 Rhenish Gilder (about
€1) per year, plus utilities and three daily
prayers. Gates close from 10pm to 6am and
residents are fined for returning late!

To see how Fuggerei residents lived in
the past, visit the **Fuggereimuseum** (☎ 319 881;
Mittlere Gasse 13; adult/concession €1/0.50; ❧ 10am-6pm
Mar-Dec).

MAXIMILIANSTRASSE
This grand boulevard, where only the richest merchant families could afford to live,
is lined by many delightful cafés and proud
patrician mansions. The restored former
residence of Jakob Fugger, the **Fugger Stadtpalast** is at No 36–38. A few doors down is
the **Schaetzlerpalais** (☎ 324 4102; Maximilianstrasse
56; adult/concession €3/1.50; ❧ 10am-5pm Tue-Sun).
Built between 1765 and 1770, this rococo
palace today houses the German Baroque

Gallery and the Bavarian State Gallery. The *pièce de résistance*, though, is not a painting but the 23m-long ballroom, a riot of carved decorations, stucco and mirrors, all lorded over by a dashing ceiling fresco.

MAXIMILIAN MUSEUM
This restored patrician house dating from 1546 is home to the newly reopened **Maximilian Museum** (☎ 324 4125; Philippine-Welser Strasse 24; ⏰ 10am-7pm Tue-Sun), which traces the cultural and municipal history of Augsburg. It also has a large exhibition of gold and silver work from baroque and rococo masters. A second floor, opening autumn 2005, will display sculptures and architectural models.

GALERIE NOAH & KUNSTMUSEUM WALTER
Augsburg's newest museum is housed in what is known as the Glas Palace, an industrial monument made of iron, concrete and glass. It now houses two modern art museums: **Galerie Noah** (☎ 815 1163; www.galerienoah .com; Beim Glaspalast 1; admission free; ⏰ 10am-5pm Tue-Fri, 11am-2pm Sat & Sun); and **Kunstmuseum Walter** (☎ 815 1163; admission free; ⏰ 10am-5pm Tue-Fri, 11am-6pm Sat & Sun). Between them they showcase a fascinating collection of more than 6000 pieces of modern art.

BERTOLT-BRECHT-GEDENKSTÄTTE
A pilgrimage site for Brecht fans, the **Bertolt-Brecht-Gedenkstätte** (☎ 324 2779; Am Rain 7; adult/ concession €1.50/1; ⏰ 10am-5pm Tue-Sun) is the birthplace of the famous playwright and poet. Brecht's work was banned by the Nazis for his communist leanings and he was later shunned by West Germans for the same reason. For more on Brecht, see the boxed text on p107.

SYNAGOGUE
Right behind the tourist office on Bahnhofstrasse is **Synagoge Augsburg**, an Art Nouveau temple built between 1914 and 1917. Inside is the excellent **Jewish Cultural Museum** (☎ 513 658; Halderstrasse 8; adult/concession €2/1.50; ⏰ 9am-4pm Tue-Fri, 10am-5pm Sun), with exhibitions on Jewish life in the region, Germany and Central Europe.

MARIONETTE THEATRE
The celebrated **Augsburger Puppenkiste** (☎ 434 440; www.augsburger-puppenkiste.de; Spitalgasse 15; after-

noon shows €7.50-9.50, evening shows €13-18; ⏰ 3pm & 7.30pm Wed, Fri-Sun) holds performances of modern and classic fairy tales that are so endearing, and the sets and costumes so fantastically elaborate, that even non-German speakers will enjoy a show. Advance reservations are advised.

Tours
City walking tours (€3) leave from the Rathausplatz tourist office at 2pm from April to October (Saturday only November to March).

Sleeping
The tourist offices can help you find accommodation for a €2 fee.

DJH hostel (☎ 339 09; jugendherberge@kvaugsburg -stadt.brk.de; Beim Pfaffenkeller 3; dm €13.60) This is rather down-at-heel but central. Take tram No 2 to Mozarthaus, then walk east on Mittleres Pfaffengässchen for about 300m.

Campingplatz Augusta (☎ 707 575; www.camping platz-augusta.de; Mühlhauser Strasse 54b; tent/car/person €3.10/3.10/4.10) This camp site, which also has a few family rooms, is on a swimming lake, some 7km from the city centre. Take bus No 23 to the terminus, from where it's a 2km walk.

Jakoberhof (☎ 510030; www.jakoberhof.de; Jakoberstrasse 41; s/d €26/39; (P)) One of the best-value options is this simple place near the Fuggerei. Rooms have no frills but are bright and airy and the service is always friendly. Advance bookings are advised.

Georgsrast Hotel Garni (☎ 502 610; fax 502 6127; Georgenstrasse 31; s/d €35/60) This place, in the northern city centre, is a fairly quiet option within easy walking distance of the sights. It offers basic but full amenities in bright, comfortable modern rooms.

City Hotel Ost am Kö (☎ 502 040; www.ostamkoe .de; Fuggerstrasse 4-6; s/d €55/70; (P) (⊠) (♿); wheelchair access) Inside the 1960s concrete façade awaits an efficiently run hotel with extremely friendly staff and a warm welcome for children. Rooms feature updated yet traditional décor, and the breakfast buffet is sumptuous.

Altstadthotel Ulrich (☎ 346 10; www.hotel-ulrich .de; Kapuzinergasse 6; s/d €55/85; (P) (⊠)) This upmarket hotel is in an old patrician mansion on a quiet side street. Rooms are modern and well equipped and almost half are for nonsmokers. Children are welcome.

BAVARIA

Dom Hotel (☎ 343 930; www.domhotel-augsburg .de; Frauentorstrasse 8; s €64-80, d €73-134; P ☒ ☻) This charming hotel with spacious, tastefully decorated rooms is excellent value. The smaller attic rooms have beamed ceilings and great views. Guests have free use of the garden, pool and sauna, and children are welcome.

Steigenberger Drei Mohren Hotel (☎ 503 60; www.augsburg.steigenberger.de; Maximilianstrasse 40; s/d €115/150; P ☻ ☒) This landmark hotel is a stunning place where both Mozart and Goethe have stayed. Marble bathrooms, original art and a beautiful garden terrace are among the elegant touches, and despite the luxurious décor children are very welcome.

Eating

In the evening Maximilianstrasse is the place to hang out, with cafés overflowing onto the pavements and plenty of young things watching the world go by.

QUICK EATS

There are lots of cheap places to eat or buy snacks on Bahnhofstrasse. The local **Stadt- markt** (btwn Fuggerstrasse & Annastrasse; ⏱ 7am-6pm Mon-Fri, 7am-2pm Sat) is a snacker's fantasy. Besides fresh produce, bread and meat, you'll find dozens of stand-up eateries serving everything from Thai and Bavarian to Greek.

RESTAURANTS

Drei Königinnen (☎ 158 405; Meister-Veits-Gässchen 32; mains €9-15) Lighter cuisine, including lots of interesting salads and pastas, is served here alongside standard regional offerings. Readings and other cultural events take place occasionally, and there's a great beer garden.

Bistro 3M (☎ 503 60; Maximilianstrasse 40; mains €7-9) This stylish French bistro is a great place to while away the evening. Sample some of the Gallic delights from the kitchen or just chill over a drink.

Magnolia (☎ 319 9999; Beim Glaspalast 1; mains €8-16) This designer restaurant attracts a young, hip crowd with its slick minimal- ist lines and fusion foods. It has a lovely outdoor seating area and innovative dishes merging European and Asian influences.

Der Andechser (☎ 349 7990; Johannisgasse 4; mains €5-9) This beautiful secluded restaurant and

beer garden is a great place to sit and relax. The food is traditional but lighter than usual and goes down well with a glass of local brew.

Helsinki Bar (☎ 372 90; Barfüsserstrasse 4; dishes €3-6) A café by day and a bar by night, this place attracts the beautiful people, intent on hanging out in an alternative venue with cool Nordic fare and slick furnishings.

Courage (☎ 349 9430; Jakoberstrasse 7; dishes €4-10) This cosy restaurant-pub pays homage to Bertolt Brecht. Quotations from his plays decorate the slate ceiling, a life-size Brecht plaster statue overlooks the room and Brecht-themed postcards are for sale.

Other recommendations include:

Bauerntanz (☎ 153 644; Bauerntanzgässchen 1; mains €7-16) A local favourite serving big portions of creative Swabian and Bavarian food.

Fuggereistube (☎ 308 70; Jakoberstrasse 26; mains €10-20) Vintage 1970s hunting-lodge décor with Bavarian food and good service.

BEER GARDENS

Arguably Augsburg's coolest beer garden, **Thing** (☎ 395 05; Vorderer Lech 45) is a city in- stitution and often gets crowded in the evenings.

Alternatively, try the outrageous **Zeughaus** (☎ 511 685; Zeughausplatz 4), a 17th-century ar- moury that is now a trade school, cinema and a superb place for a brew. It also does good food and some tasty vegetarian dishes (€5 to €15).

Getting There & Away

Nonstop regional trains run hourly between Augsburg and Munich (€9, one hour) and every other hour to Nuremberg (€19.20, 1½ hours). ICE (InterCity Express) trains travel to Würzburg (€37.80, two hours) and Regensburg (€19.60, 2½ hours).

The Romantic Road bus stops at the Hauptbahnhof. Augsburg is just off the A8 autobahn northwest of Munich.

Getting Around

Most journeys within town on the bus and tram network cost €1.10; longer trips to the outlying suburbs are €2. A 24-hour ticket costs €5 and is good for up to three adults. The **Lufthansa Airport Bus** (☎ 502 2534) runs between Augsburg's Hauptbahnhof and Munich airport six times daily (€15/24 one way/return, 70 minutes).

For bicycle hire, **Zweirad Bäuml** (☎ 336 21; akoberstrasse 70; €5/30 per day/week) has a good ange of bikes.

ÜSSEN & SCHWANGAU
☎ 08362 / pop 14,000 Füssen; 3700 Schwangau

The last stop on the Romantic Road is Füssen, a small town nestled between towering Alpine peaks. Together with Schwangau, a village about 4km further east, it forms the **Königswinkel** (Royal Corner), home to Germany's biggest tourist attractions: Ludwig I's two palaces, Neuschwanstein and Hohenschwanstein. Never at a loss for visitors, the area's tourism industry was given yet another boost in 2000 with the opening of the melodramatic musical *Ludwig II* in a custom-built theatre on the Forggensee.

Orientation & Information
Füssen's Hauptbahnhof and central bus station are about a three-minute walk west of the **tourist office** (☎ 938 50; www.fuessen.de; aiser-Maximilian-Platz 1; 🕑 8.30am-6pm Mon-Sat May-Oct, 9am-5pm Mon-Sat Nov-Apr). There is a *Kurtaxe* (resort tax) of €1.60. Schwangau has its own **tourist office** (☎ 819 80; www.schwangau.de; Münchener Strasse 2). The *Kurtaxe* is €1.30.

Schloss Neuschwanstein
Appearing through the mountain-top mist like a surreal fantasy is the world's best-known castle, **Schloss Neuschwanstein** (☎ 930 830; adult/concession €8/7 or €15/13 in combination with Hohenschwanstein; 🕑 9am-6pm Apr-Sep, 10am-4pm Oct-Mar).

Ludwig planned this castle himself with the help of a stage designer rather than an architect, and it provides a fascinating glimpse into the king's state of mind. Built as a romantic medieval castle, it was started in 1869 and, like so many of Ludwig's grand schemes, was never finished. For all the money spent on it, the king spent just over 170 days in residence.

Neuschwanstein was conceived as a giant stage to recreate the world of Germanic mythology immortalised in the operatic works of Richard Wagner. Its centrepiece is the lavish **Sängersaal** (Minstrels' Hall), created so that Ludwig could feed his obsession with Wagner and medieval knights. Wall frescoes in the hall depict scenes from the opera *Tannhäuser*. Though the hall wasn't used during Ludwig's time, concerts are now held there every September.

Other completed sections include: **Ludwig's bedroom**, dominated by a huge Gothic-style bed crowned with intricately carved Gothic spires; a gaudy artificial grotto (another allusion to *Tannhäuser*); and the Byzantine **Thronsaal** (Throne Room) with a great mosaic floor and a chandelier shaped like a giant crown.

The wooded hills framing the castle make for some wonderful walks. For the postcard view of Neuschwanstein and the plains beyond, walk 10 minutes up to **Marienbrücke** (Mary's Bridge), which spans the spectacular Pöllat Gorge over a waterfall just above the castle.

Schloss Hohenschwangau
Ludwig spent his childhood at the sun-yellow **Schloss Hohenschwangau** (☎ 930 830; adult/concession €8/7 or €15/13 in combination with Neuschwanstein; 🕑 9am-6pm Apr-Sep, 10am-4pm Oct-Mar). Originally built by Schwangau knights during the 12th century, its current visage stems from the 1830s after Ludwig's father, Maximilian II, had the ruin reconstructed in neo-Gothic fashion. It's much less ostentatious than Neuschwanstein and has a distinct lived-in feeling. After his father died, Ludwig's main alteration was having stars, illuminated with hidden oil-lamps, painted on the ceiling of his bedroom.

It was here that Ludwig first met Wagner, and the **Hohenstaufensaal** features a square piano where the composer would entertain Ludwig with excerpts from his latest oeuvre. Some rooms feature frescoes from German history and legends (including the Wagner subject Lohengrin, the Swan Knight).

TICKETS & TOURS
Both castles must be seen on guided tours (in German or English), which last about 35 minutes. Tickets are available only from the **Ticket Centre** (☎ 930 830; www.ticket-center -hohenschwangau.de; Alpseestrasse 12) at the foot of the castles. In summer it's highly advisable to come as early as 8.30am to ensure you get a ticket.

It's a steep 30- to 40-minute walk between the castles, though you can shell out €5 for a horse-drawn carriage ride, which is only slightly faster.

If you're pressed for time, consider going on an organised tour. EurAide (see Information in the Munich section, p331) runs

BAVARIA

LUDWIG II, THE FAIRY-TALE KING

Every year on 13 June, a stirring ceremony takes place in Berg on the eastern shore of Lake Starnberg. A small boat quietly glides towards a cross just offshore and a plain wreath is fastened to its front. The sound of a single trumpet cuts the silence as the boat returns from this solemn ritual in honour of the most beloved king ever to rule Bavaria – Ludwig II.

The cross marks the spot where Ludwig died under mysterious circumstances in 1886. His early death capped the life of a man at odds with the harsh realities of a modern world no longer in need of a romantic and idealistic monarch.

Prinz Otto Ludwig Friedrich Wilhelm was a sensitive soul, fascinated by romantic epics, architecture and music, but his parents, Maximilian II and Marie, took little interest in his musings and he suffered a lonely and joyless childhood. In 1864, at 18 years old, the prince became king. He was briefly engaged to the sister of Elisabeth (Sisi), the Austrian empress, but as a rule he preferred the company of men. He also worshipped composer Richard Wagner, whose Bayreuth opera house was built with Ludwig's funds.

Ludwig was an enthusiastic leader initially, but Bavaria's days as a sovereign state were numbered, and he became a puppet king after the creation of the German Reich in 1871 (which had its advantages, as Bismarck gave Ludwig a hefty allowance). Ludwig now withdrew completely to drink, draw castle plans and view concerts and operas in private. His obsession with French culture and the Sun King, Louis XIV, inspired the fantastical palaces of Neuschwanstein, Linderhof and Herrenchiemsee – lavish projects that spelt his undoing.

Contrary to popular belief, though, it was only Ludwig's purse – and not the state treasury – that was being bankrupted. However, by 1886 his ever-growing mountain of debt and erratic behaviour was perceived as a threat to the natural order of things. The king, it seemed, needed to be 'managed'.

In January 1886, several ministers and relatives arranged a hasty psychiatric test that diagnosed Ludwig as mentally unfit to rule. That June he was removed to Schloss Berg on Lake Starnberg. One evening the dejected bachelor and his doctor took a lakeside walk and were found several hours later, drowned in just a few feet of water.

No-one knows with certainty what happened that night. There was no eyewitness or any proper criminal investigation. The circumstantial evidence was conflicting and incomplete. Reports and documents were tampered with, destroyed or lost. Conspiracy theories abound. That summer the authorities opened Neuschwanstein to the public to help pay off Ludwig's huge debts. King Ludwig II was dead, but the myth was just being born.

tours to Neuschwanstein and Linderhof with a brief stop in Oberammergau (€40 plus admission to the palaces). It operates daily from April to October and on a more limited schedule in other months.

Ludwig II Musical

Since April 2000, the tragic story of Ludwig II's life unfolds in music, sound and special effects on the western shore of the Forggensee. The musical, sentimentally subtitled **Longing for Paradise** (☎ 01805-583 944; zentrale@ludwigmusical.com; €43-117), is part fantasy, part history and all monumental spectacle. Sung in German with English supertitles, it takes place nightly and on weekend afternoons on the largest revolving stage in Germany. You can even take a **backstage tour** (€7/3.50; ☽ 3pm & 4pm Tue-Fri, 11am

& noon Sat & Sun; 1hr), which shows the secrets behind the staging of the spectacle.

Tours from Munich are offered by **Panorama Tours** (☎ 5490 7560; panoramatours@auto busoberbayern.de). Packages including tickets and bus transfer start at €75/85 weekday/ weekend.

Altstadt Füssen

Füssen's compact historical centre is a tangle of lanes lorded over by the **Hohe Schloss**, a late Gothic confection and former summer residence of the bishops of Augsburg. The inner courtyard is a masterpiece of illusionary architecture dating back to 1499; you'll do a double take before realising that the gables, oriels and windows are not quite as they seem. The north wing of the palace contains the **Staatsgalerie im Hohen** chloss (☎ 903 164; Magnusplatz 10; adult/concession 2.50/2, combined ticket with museum €3; 🕑 11am-4pm pr-Oct, 2-4pm Nov-Mar, closed Mon) with regional aintings and sculpture from the 15th and 6th centuries, while the floor below has n emphasis on 19th-century artists. The nost spectacular draw, however, is the **Rittersaal** (Knight's Hall) with its magnificent offered ceiling.

Below the Hohe Schloss, integrated into he former Abbey of St Mang, is the **Museum Füssen** (☎ 903 146; Lechhalde 3; adult/concession/under 4 €2.50/2/free; 🕑 11am-4pm Apr-Oct, 2-4pm Nov-Mar, losed Mon). It recalls Füssen's heyday as a violin-making centre in the 16th century, and provides access to the abbey's festive baroque rooms, the Romanesque cloister and the St Anna Kapelle (AD 830).

TEGELBERGBAHN

For fabulous views of the Alps and the Forggensee take the **Tegelbergbahn** (☎ 983 60; return tickets €14; 🕑 8.30am-5pm Jul-Oct, 9am-5pm Nov-Jun) to the top of the Tegelberg (1707m), also a prime launch point for hang-gliders and parasailers. From here it's a wonderful hike down to the castles (two to three hours; follow the signs to Königsschlösser). To get to the valley station, take RVA bus No 9713 from the Bahnhof in Füssen or from the Schwangau village centre.

Sleeping

Accommodation in the area is surprisingly good value and the tourist offices can find **private rooms** from €18 per person.

DJH hostel (☎ 7754; jhfuessen@djh-bayern.de; Mariahilferstrasse 5, Füssen; dm €14.60; 🕑 closed mid-Nov–Christmas) Füssen's hostel is by the train tracks, a five- to 10-minute walk west of the station. Reservations are strongly recommended.

Pension Kössler (☎ 7304; fax 399 52; Kemptener Strasse 42, Füssen; s/d €30/60; P) This small pension with a friendly atmosphere offers outstanding value. Rooms are simple but comfortable and have private bathroom, TV, phone and balcony – some overlook the attractive garden.

Hotel zum Hechten (☎ 916 00; www.hotel-hechten.com; Ritterstrasse 6, Füssen; s/d €39/78; P) This is one of Füssen's oldest hotels and is set around a quiet inner courtyard. Public areas are traditional in style but the bedrooms are bright and modern. Children are welcome.

Hotel Weinbauer (☎ 9860; www.ho... .de; Füssener Strasse 3, Schwangau; s/d €40/8... bright rooms decorated in contemp... styles and with a decent range of ame... ties make this friendly hotel a winner. Th... frescoed restaurant downstairs (mains €8 to €16) opens onto a pretty garden.

Hotel Garni Elisabeth (☎ 6275; Augustenstrasse 10, Füssen; s €30-46, d €60-94; P) This beautiful old house hotel is set in glorious gardens and has an attractive range of comfortable rooms, all tastefully decorated. Breakfast is a real feast and families are welcome.

Campers should head for the modern lakeside camp sites:

Campingplatz Bannwaldsee (☎ 930 00; www.camping-bannwaldsee.de; Münchner Strasse 151, Schwangau; site/person €6/7)

Campingplatz Brunnen am Forggensee (☎ 8273; www.camping-brunnen.de; Seestrasse 81, Schwangau; site/person €6/7)

Eating

Gasthaus zum Hechten (☎ 916 00; Ritterstrasse 6, Füssen; mains €6-11) This popular restaurant occupies the 1st floor of the hotel by the same name (see Sleeping, opposite). The kitchen produces stick-to-the-ribs Bavarian fare in small and large portions, but there's also a self-service buffet with salads.

Franziskaner Stüberl (☎ 371 24; Kemptener Strasse 1, Füssen; mains €7.50-13.50; 🕑 closed Thu) This quaint restaurant is a bastion of tradition and specialises in *Schweinshaxe* (pig's trotters) and schnitzel, prepared in infinite varieties. Or try the excellent *Kässpätzle* (cheese pasta) and other meatless dishes.

Pizzeria San Marco (☎ 813 39; Füssener Strasse 6, Schwangau; mains €5-9) This cosy place decorated in rustic Italian style serves up a good range of interesting pizzas and pastas as well as healthy salads and other Mediterranean fare.

Snack options include the local **Nordsee** (Reichenstrasse 40) and **Vinzenzmurr** (Reichenstrasse 35), both in Füssen.

Getting There & Away

If you want to 'do' the royal castles on a day trip from Munich (€18.20, two to 2½ hours) you'll need to start early. The first train leaves Munich at 5.45am, getting to Füssen at 7.54am. Later trains depart at roughly five minutes to the hour but always check schedules before you go.

to the castles from ...chwangau village ...pping also at the ...tion. Taxis to the

...... one side and the lake-
...... plains on the other, the area around
Füssen is a cyclist's paradise. You can hire
two-wheelers at the **Kurhotel Berger** (☎ 913 30;
Alatseestrasse 26, Füssen; €6 per day) or **Radsport Zacherl** (☎ 3292; Kemptener Strasse 119, Füssen; €7 per day).

AROUND FÜSSEN
Wieskirche

In 1743 a farmer in Steingaden, about 30km
northeast of Füssen, witnessed the miracle
of his Christ statue crying. Over the next
few years so many pilgrims poured into the
town that the local abbot commissioned a
new church to house the weepy work.

These days, as many as one million visitors a year – art lovers and spiritual pilgrims
alike – flock to what became known as the
Wieskirche (or Wies for short), a Unesco
World Cultural Heritage Site. The church is
a rococo jewel that rates as the most accomplished work by the brothers Dominikus
and Johann Baptist Zimmermann. Inside,
gleaming white pillars are topped by gold
capital stones and swirling decorations that
resonate against the pastel ceiling fresco
celebrating Christ's resurrection.

From Füssen or Schwangau take the
regional RVO bus No 9715 or 1084, which
makes the journey up to six times daily
(€4.40/5.80 one way/return, one hour). By
car, take the B17 northeast and turn right
(east) at Steingaden. The church is clearly
signposted.

BAVARIAN ALPS

Stretching west from Germany's remote
southeastern corner to the Allgäu region
near Lake Constance, the Bavarian Alps
(Bayerische Alpen) take in most of the
mountainous country fringing the Austrian border. While not as high as their
sister summits further south, they rise so
abruptly from the rolling hills that their appearance seems all the more dramatic.

The region is dotted with quaint frescoed villages, spas and health retreats and,

for those with the time, energy and money
year-round resorts for skiing, snowboarding, hiking, canoeing and paragliding. The
ski season lasts from about late December
until April, summer activities from late
May to November.

One of the largest resorts in the area is
Garmisch-Partenkirchen, one of Munich's
favourite getaway spots. Other noteworthy bases are Berchtesgaden, Füssen and
Oberstdorf.

Most of the resorts have plenty of reasonably priced accommodation, though some
places levy a surcharge (usually about €3) for
stays of less than two or three days in peak
seasons. Most resorts also charge a *Kurtaxe*
(less than €2) for overnight stays, but this
entitles you to certain perks, like free tours,
city bus service and entry to special events.

GETTING AROUND

Buses are the most efficient method of public transport in the alpine area; there are few
direct train routes between main centres. If
you're driving, sometimes a short-cut via
Austria works out to be quicker (such as
between Garmisch-Partenkirchen and Füssen or Oberstdorf).

Regional (RVO) passes giving unlimited
travel (with certain route restrictions) on the
upper-Bavarian bus network are excellent
value (adult/child day pass €7/€3.50, five
days of travel in one month €22.50/€11).
Buy them directly from the bus driver. One
of the most useful routes is bus No 1084,
which goes from Garmisch-Partenkirchen
to Oberstdorf via Oberammergau, the Wieskirche, Schwangau and Füssen.

GARMISCH-PARTENKIRCHEN
☎ 08821 / pop 27,000

The open-year-round resort of Garmisch-Partenkirchen is a favourite haunt for outdoor enthusiasts. The gateway to the best
skiing in Germany, it offers access to three
ski fields, including those on Germany's
highest mountain, the Zugspitze (2964m).
The towns of Garmisch and Partenkirchen
were merged on the occasion of the 1936
Winter Olympics and continue to host important international skiing events.

Garmisch-Partenkirchen also makes a
handy base for excursions to Ludwig II's
palaces, including nearby Schloss Linderhof
and the lesser-known Jagdschloss Schachen.

Orientation

The train tracks that divide the two towns culminate at the Hauptbahnhof. From here, turn west on St-Martin-Strasse to get to Garmisch and east on Bahnhofstrasse to reach Partenkirchen. From the Hauptbahnhof the centre of Garmisch is about 500m away, the centre of Partenkirchen about 1km.

Information

Commerzbank (Marienplatz 2a)
Computerhaus (☎ 949 033; Klammstrasse 2; €4 per hr) Internet access.
Post office (Bahnhofplatz)
Tourist office (☎ 180 700; www.garmisch-parten kirchen.de; Richard-Strauss-Platz 1, Garmisch; ☽ 8am-6pm Mon-Sat, 10am-noon Sun)

Sights & Activities

ZUGSPITZE

Views from the top of Germany are quite literally breathtaking, especially during *Föhn* weather when they extend into four countries. Skiing and hiking are the main activities here and to get to the top, you can walk (see Hiking), take a cogwheel train or a cable car.

The **Zugspitzbahn** (the cogwheel train) has its own station right behind the Hauptbahnhof. From here it chugs along the mountain base to the Eibsee, a forest lake, then winds its way through a mountain tunnel up to the Schneeferner Glacier (2600m). From here a cable car makes the final ascent to the summit.

Alternatively, the **Eibsee-Seilbahn**, a steep cable car, sways and swings its way straight up to the summit from the Eibsee lake in about 10 minutes (not for the faint-hearted!). Most people come up on the train and take the cable car back down, but it works just as well the other way around. The entire trip costs €34/21 adult/child in winter and €43/29.50 in summer. Winter rates include a day ski-pass.

Expect serious crowds at peak times in winter and through much of the summer. Skiers may find it easier, but slower, to schlep their gear up on the train, which offers exterior ski-holders.

SKIING

Garmisch has three ski fields: the Zugspitze plateau (2964m), the Classic Ski Area (Alpspitze, 2050m; Hausberg, 1340m; Kreuzeck,

1651m; day pass €28/18 adult/child) and the Eckbauer (1236m; day pass €16.50/11). A Happy Ski Card (three-day minimum, €80/48 adult/child) covers all three ski areas, plus three other ski areas around the Zugspitze, including Mittenwald. Local buses serve all the valley stations.

Cross-country ski trails run along the main valleys, including a long section from Garmisch to Mittenwald. Call ☎ 797 979 for a weather or snow report.

For ski hire and courses try:
Flori Wörndle (☎ 583 00; www.skischule-woerndle.de; Alpspitze & Hausberg)
Sport Total (☎ 1425; www.agentursporttotal.de; Marienplatz 18) They also organise paragliding, mountain biking, rafting and ballooning.

HIKING

Garmisch-Partenkirchen is prime hiking territory and mountain guides are at the tourist office on Monday and Thursday between 4pm and 6pm to give help and information to hikers. At other times brochures and maps with route suggestions for all levels are available.

Hiking to the **Zugspitze summit** is only possible in the summer months and not recommended for those without mountaineering experience. Another popular route is to King Ludwig II's hunting lodge, **Jagdschloss Schachen** (☎ 2996; admission €2.50, under 14 free; ☽ Jun-Oct), which can be reached via the Partnachklamm (see below) in about a four-hour hike. It is a plain wooden hut with some surprisingly magnificent rooms.

For guided hikes and courses contact:
Bergsteigerschule Zugspitze (☎ 589 99; Dreitorspitzstrasse 13)
Deutscher Alpenverein (☎ 2701; Hindenburgstrasse 38)

PARTNACHKLAMM

One of the area's main tourist attractions is the magnificent **Partnachklamm** (☎ 3167; adult/children €2/1), a narrow 700m-long gorge with walls rising up to 80m high. A circular walk hewn from the rock takes you through the gorge, which is really spectacular in winter when you can walk beneath curtains of icicles and frozen waterfalls.

Sleeping

There is an outdoor room-reservation board at the tourist office and a 24-hour reservation hotline (☎ 194 12). A *Kurtaxe* of €2 is charged for accommodation for people over 16 years.

DJH hostel (☎ 2980; jhgarmisch@djh-bayern.de; Jochstrasse 10) The hostel is undergoing a complete overhaul and will reopen in spring 2005.

Campingplatz Zugspitze (☎ 3180; fax 947 594; Griesener Strasse 4, Grainau; tent/person/vehicle €3.50/5.50/3.50) The camp site closest to Garmisch is along the B24 to Grainau. Take the blue-and-white bus outside the Hauptbahnhof in the direction of the Eibsee.

Hotel Schell (☎ 9575; www.hotel-schell.de; Partnachauenstrasse 3; s/d from €25/45; Ⓟ) This traditional Alpine home is a real winner for its friendly service and spotless, good-value rooms. It's close to the Hauptbahnhof but very quiet, and children and adults alike will enjoy the garden.

Zum Rassen (☎ 2089; www.gasthof-rassen.de; Ludwigstrasse 45; s €30-52, d €46-88; Ⓟ Ⓧ) Bright, modern rooms contrast with the traditional décor of the public areas of this beautifully frescoed 14th-century building. A former brewery, the massive event hall houses the oldest folk theatre in Bavaria.

Hotel Garmischer Hof (☎ 9110; www.garmischer-hof.de; Chamonixstrasse 10; s €52-75, d €84-124; Ⓟ Ⓐ) This top-notch establishment has modern rooms, some with views of the Zugspitze, and lots of amenities. Children are welcome and the downstairs restaurant, although a bit stuffy, comes recommended.

Other recommendations include:

Haus Reiter (☎ 2223; www.reiter-gap.com; Burgstrasse 55; s €22-32, d €44-64; Ⓟ Ⓧ) Chalet-style guesthouse with modern rooms and garden.

Gasthaus Pfeuffer (☎ 2238; fax 4617; Kreuzstrasse 9; d €46-56; Ⓟ) Central and simple guesthouse with cable TV.

Eating

Isi's Goldener Engel (☎ 948 757; Bankgasse 5; mains €9.50-15) This local favourite has wacky décor that blends frescoes, stags' heads and a gilded stucco ceiling. The huge menu selection ranges from simple schnitzel to game dishes, though the best deal is the generous lunch special.

Spago (☎ 966 555; Partnachstrasse 50; mains €6-8) This trendy café and restaurant just off the main drag makes a nice change from all the tradition. The slick design, outdoor seating area and international menu serve a local clientele rather than the tourist rabble.

Ristorante Da'enzo (☎ 722 26; Bankgasse 16; mains €5.50-17) Tables inside and out throng with

fresh-faced punters at this ever-popula local winner for fine Italian cooking. Th menu includes excellent pasta and pizza a well as delicious fish and meat dishes.

Bräustüberl (☎ 2312; Fürstenstrasse 23; mai €6-16) This place, a bit outside the centr is quintessential Bavarian, complete wit enormous enamel coal-burning stove an dirndl-clad waitresses. The dining room to the right, the beer hall to the left.

Other recommendations are:

Zirbel (☎ 7671; Promenadestrasse 2; meals €3.50-11) Relaxed, tunnel-shaped pub serving snacks and small meals

Gasthaus zur Schranne (☎ 1699; Griesstrasse 4; mains €8-14; Ⓨ closed Thu) Atmosphere-laden tavern featuring regional snacks and daily specials.

Getting There & Around

Garmisch is serviced by hourly trains fror Munich (€14, 1½ hours), and special pack ages combine the return trip with a Zug spitze day ski pass. RVO bus No 1084 trave to Oberstdorf with stops at the Wieskirche Neuschwanstein, Hohenschwanstein an Füssen. The A95 from Munich is the direc road route.

Bus tickets cost €1.20 for journeys i town (free with *Kurkarte*, see p735). Fo bike hire try **Fahrrad Ostler** (☎ 3362; Kreuzstrass 1; from €12/42 per day/week) or **Bike Verleih** (☎ 54 46; Alpspitzstrasse 16; €7/16/60 per hr/day/week).

AROUND GARMISCH-PARTENKIRCHEM

Oberammergau
☎ 08822 / pop 5400

Approximately 20km north of Garmisch Partenkirchen is Oberammergau, a stud in genuine piety as well as religious kitscl and commercialism. Sitting in a wide valle, surrounded by forest and mountains, thi undeniably beautiful village is packed witl souvenir shops and tourists.

For information visit the **tourist offic** (☎ 923 10; www.oberammergau.de; Eugen-Papst-Strass 9a; Ⓨ 8.30am-6pm Mon-Fri, 9am-5pm Sat, 1-5pm Su mid-Jun–mid-Oct, 8.30am-6pm Mon-Fri, 8.30am-noon Sa mid-Oct–mid-Jun).

Oberammergau is famous for its epic **Passion Play**, performed by the townspeo ple every decade (the next one is in 2010) since 1634 to give thanks for being spared from the plague. Tours of the **Passionstheater** (☎ 923 10; Passionswiese 1; tours adult/concession €2.50/ 1.50; Ⓨ tours 9.30am-5pm May-Oct, 10am-4pm Nov-Apr) include a history of the play and a peek at ıe costumes and sets. In the years between ıe Passion plays, spectacular opera events ⲥe held once a month between July and ⲉptember. Ask at the tourist office for ⲉtails.

The town's other claim to fame is the ⲩe-popping house façades painted in an ⲓlusionist style called **Lüftmalerei**, or trompe ⲟeil. Images usually have a religious fla-ⲟur, but some also show hilarious beer-ⲓall scenes or fairy-tale motifs, like *Hansel* ⲕ *Gretl* at Ettaler Strasse No 41, and *Little* *ⲅed Riding Hood* at Ettaler Strasse 48. The *ⲓèce de résistance*, however, is the **Pilatus-ⲓaus** (☎ 923 10; Ludwig-Thoma-Strasse 10; admission ⲅee; ⊙ 1-6pm Mon-Fri May-Oct), which also con-ⲁins a gallery and several workshops.

Oberammergau is also known for its ⲓntricate **woodcarvings**. Workshops abound around town, churning out everything from saints to corkscrews you wouldn't accept as a gift. Some of the most accomplished work can be seen in the little parish cemetery on ⲢPfarrplatz and in the **Oberammergau Museum** (Dorfstrasse 8), which will reopen after refur-bishment in May 2004.

You can stay at the **DJH hostel** (☎ 4114; jhober ammergau@djh-bayern.de; Malensteinweg 10; dm €13.60), which is about a 15-minute walk from the Hauptbahnhof or, for much more comfort, the **Hotel Alte Post** (☎ 9100; www.altepost.ogau.de; Dorfstrasse 19; s/d €43/71; Ⓟ ⊠) right in the centre of town. This traditional Bavarian hotel also has a popular restaurant (mains €8 to €16).

Hourly trains connect Munich with Oberammergau (change at Murnau, €13.50, 1¾ hours). RVO bus No 9606 operates to/from Garmisch-Partenkirchen and Füssen almost hourly.

Schloss Linderhof

King Ludwig II's smallest but most mag-nificent palace, **Schloss Linderhof** (☎ 08822-920 30; adult/concession €6/5 Apr–mid-Oct, €4/3 mid-Oct–Mar; parking €2; ⊙ 9am-6pm Apr–mid-Oct, 10am-4pm mid-Oct–Mar) is about 13km west of Oberam-mergau and 26km northwest of Garmisch-Partenkirchen. Built between 1869 and 1878, the Linderhof hugs a steep hillside and is surrounded by formal French gar-dens with whimsical fountains, pools and follies. Ludwig used the palace as a retreat and hardly ever received visitors here. Like Herrenchiemsee (see p355), Linderhof was

inspired by Versailles and dedicated to Louis XIV, Ludwig's idol.

Linderhof is chock-full of unbeliev-able treasures and frescoes of mythological scenes, evidence of the king's creativity as well as his ostentatious taste. The largest room is his **private bedroom**, heavily orna-mented and anchored by an enormous 108-candle crystal chandelier weighing 500kg. An artificial waterfall, built to cool the room in summer, cascades just outside the window. The **dining room** reflects the king's fetish for privacy and new inven-tion; its central fixture is a table that sinks through the floor to be laid in the kitchen below, allowing Ludwig to dine without seeing his servants.

The gardens and outbuildings (open April to October) are just as fascinating as the castle itself. The highlight is the oriental-style **Moorish Kiosk**, where Ludwig, often dressed in oriental costume, presided over evening entertainment from the elab-orate peacock throne. Also worth a visit is the **Venus Grotto**, an artificial stalactite cave inspired by a stage set for Wagner's *Tann-häuser*. Underwater lighting (a pioneering technical achievement for the time) illu-minates the room and the empty conch-shaped boat waiting by the shore.

Bus No 9622 makes the trip out to Linder-hof from Oberammergau twice daily on weekdays and four times at weekends, while RVO bus No 9606 comes from Garmisch-Partenkirchen (€6.50, 1½ hours).

Mittenwald

☎ 08823 / pop 8300

Stunningly picturesque Mittenwald, 20km southeast of Garmisch-Partenkirchen, was a famous violin-making centre long before the first tourists arrived. Nowadays the sleepy village, with its clear air and snow-capped peaks, is a favourite Alpine getaway for weary urban types. The narrow winding streets reveal alpine views at every corner and the ornate gables and beautifully fres-coed walls give it a charming, but authentic, feel.

For local information go to the **tourist office** (☎ 339 81; www.mittenwald.de; Dammkarstrasse 3; ⊙ 8am-5pm Mon-Fri, 9am-noon Sat, 10am-noon Sun May-Sep). There is a *Kurtaxe* of €1.60.

Mittenwald is an excellent place for hiking and cycling. Popular local hikes with cable-car access go to the Alpspitze (2628m), the Wank (1780m), Mt Karwendel (2384m) and the Wettersteinspitze (2297m). Return tickets to the Karwendel, which boasts Germany's second-highest cable-car route, cost €19/11 adult/child.

The Karwendel ski field has one of the longest runs (7km) in Germany. Combined day ski passes covering the Karwendel and nearby Kranzberg ski fields cost €25/18. For both equipment hire and ski/snowboard instruction, contact the *Erste Skischule Mittenwald* (☎ 3582; Bahnhofsplatz).

Other special events include **Fasnacht** (carnival) held in late February or early March where locals in traditional masks, handed down through families over centuries, mix old rituals with modern celebrations and attempt to drive out winter.

You can stay at the inconveniently located **DJH hostel** (☎ 1701; jhmittenwald@djh-bayern .de; Buckelwiesen 7; dm €13.60; ❤ closed mid-Nov–late-Dec), 4km north of town, or at the town gem, **Hotel-Gasthof Alpenrose** (☎ 927 00; www.alpenrose -mittenwald.de; Obermarkt 1; s €25-35, d €50-70; ℗), an ornate 18th-century inn with cosy rooms, old-style eating (mains €7.50 to €13.50) and live Bavarian music almost nightly. For local gourmet fare head to **Restaurant Arnspitze** (☎ 2425; Innsbrucker Strasse 68; mains €15.50-22; ❤ closed Tue), one of the top places in town.

Mittenwald is served by hourly trains from Munich (€16.60, two hours), Garmisch-Partenkirchen (€3.10, 25 minutes) and Innsbruck (€10, one hour).

RVO bus No 9608 connects Mittenwald with Garmisch-Partenkirchen (30 minutes) several times a day, though the timetable changes frequently.

OBERSTDORF
☎ 08322 / pop 11,000
Spectacularly situated in the western Bavarian Alps is the car-free resort of Oberstdorf. Both the main **tourist office** (☎ 7000; www.ober stdorf.de; Marktplatz 7; ❤ 8.30am-noon & 2-6pm Mon-Fri, 9.30am-noon Sat) and the **branch office** (☎ 700 217; Bahnhof; ❤ 9am-8pm Mon-Sat, 9am-6pm Sun May-Oct, 9am-noon & 2-6pm Nov-Apr) can help with finding accommodation. A *Kurtaxe* of €2.20 is charged here.

Like Garmisch, Oberstdorf is surrounded by towering peaks and offers superb hiking. For an exhilarating day walk, ride the Nebelhorn cable car to the upper station,

(adult/child €17.50/13.50) then hike down via the **Gaisalpseen**, two lovely alpine lakes (six hours).

In-the-know skiers value the resort for its friendliness, lower prices and less crowded pistes. The village is surrounded by 70km of groomed cross-country trails and three ski fields: the **Nebelhorn** (day/half-day passes €29/24), **Fellhorn/Kanzelwand** (day/half-day passes €30.50/24), and **Söllereck** (day/half-day passes €22.50/18). Ski passes good at all areas cost €53/75/145 for two/three/six days.

For ski hire and tuition, try **Neue Skischule** (☎ 2737; www.neue-skischule-oberstdorf.de; Oststrasse 39), with outlets at the valley stations of the Nebelhorn and Söllereck lifts.

The **Eislaufzentrum Oberstdorf** (☎ 915 130) behind the Nebelhorn cable-car station is the biggest ice-skating complex in Germany, with three separate rinks.

Sleeping & Eating
Oberstdorf is chock-full of private guesthouses but some owners may be reluctant to rent rooms for just one night, especially during high season.

DJH hostel (☎ 2225; jhoberstdorf@djh-bayern.de; Kornau 8; dm €14.60; ❤ closed mid-Nov–late Dec) This hostel is in the suburb of Kornau near the Söllereck chairlift. Take the Kleinwalsertal bus to the Reute stop.

Hotel Zum Paulanerbräu (☎ 967 60; fax 967 613; Kirchstrasse 1; s €24-35, d €48-90) Right in the Altstadt, this friendly place has comfortable, well-equipped rooms. Its restaurant (mains €6 to €10) serves such belly-filling selections as *Grillhaxen* (roast leg of pork) with potent dark Salvator beer.

Filser Kur-und Ferienhotel (☎ 7080; www.filser hotel.de; Freibergstrasse 15; s €76-99, d €130-180; ℗ ✗ ; wheelchair access) This is one of many luxurious, but good-value, health resorts in the area with sparkling new facilities, including fitness rooms, pool and sauna. Rooms are stylishly decorated with modern simplicity and some elegant traditional touches, and children are welcome.

Beim Dorfwirt (☎ 4648; Hauptstrasse 6; mains €9-14) This traditional restaurant at the Hotel zur Traube comes complete with waitresses dressed in lederhosen and a large beer garden. The menu is mostly meaty, but the salad bar provides some relief.

Vinzenzmurr (Hauptstrasse 1; snacks from €1.50) The friendly bakery and butcher shop is the est bet for a sandwich, sausage or selection om its salad bar.

etting There & Away

here are some direct trains from Munich (€23, 2½ hours) and more with a change a Immenstadt. RVO bus No 1084 shuttles everal times daily between Oberstdorf, üssen and Garmisch-Partenkirchen.

BERCHTESGADEN & BERCHTESGADENER LAND

☎ 08652 / pop 8200

Hugging the Austro-German border, Berchtesgadener Land is a self-contained universe of wooded hilltops and valleys framed by six formidable mountain ranges. It's an idyllic setting and Germany's secondhighest mountain, the Watzmann (2713m), towers above the crystalline lakes, rushing streams, elegant church steeples, and quiet alpine villages.

About half of the terrain is protected as the Berchtesgaden National Park, home to the pristine Königssee, Germany's highest lake. The park also offers wonderful hiking and other outdoor opportunities. In summer, the mountain-top Eagle's Nest, a lodge built by the Nazis, is a major drawcard, as is the Dokumentation Obersalzberg, a museum which chronicles the region's dark history as the party's southern headquarters.

Information

The tourist office (☎ 9670; www.berchtesgadener -land.de; Königsseer Strasse 2; ☺ 9am-6pm Mon-Sat, 10am-1pm & 2-6pm Sun May–mid-Oct, 9am-5pm Mon-Fri, 9am-noon Sat mid-Oct–Apr) has a free room-booking service and an electronic room reservation board outside. There is a *Kurtaxe* of €2. For hiking information try the Nationalpark office (☎ 643 43; www.nationalpark-berchtesgaden.de; Franz-iskanerplatz 7, Berchtesgaden; ☺ 9am-5pm Mon-Sat).

The Hauptbahnhof in Berchtesgaden also contains the post office and bus station. You can change money at the Hypovereinsbank (Weihnachtsschützenplatz 2½).

Sights

DOKUMENTATION OBERSALZBERG

From 1933 to 1945, Obersalzberg, a quiet mountain retreat 3km east of Berchtesgaden, was the southern headquarters of Hitler's Nazi government, a sinister period that's given the full historical treatment at the fascinating Dokumentation Obersalzberg (☎ 947 960; Salzbergstrasse 41; adult/concession €2.50/ 1.50; ☺ 9am-5pm Apr-Oct, 10am-3pm Tue-Sun Nov-Apr). This comprehensive exhibit chronicling the forced takeover of the area, the construction of the compound and the daily life of the Nazi elite should be your first stop on any tour of Berchtesgadener Land. The exhibits illuminate all facets of the Nazi terror regime, including Hitler's near-mythical appeal, his racial politics, the

---

HITLER'S MOUNTAIN RETREAT

Of all the German towns tainted with the pall of the Third Reich, Berchtesgaden has been cursed with a larger share than most. Hitler fell in love with nearby Obersalzberg in the 1920s and bought a small country home here, later enlarged into the imposing Berghof.

After becoming chancellor in 1933, he established part-time headquarters here and brought the party brass with him. They bought or confiscated over 12 sq miles of land, tore down ancient farmhouses, erected a seven-foot-high barbed-wire fence, built guardhouses along the three access roads, and eventually turned the Obersalzberg into the fortified, southern headquarters of the NSDAP (National Socialist German Workers' Party). In 1938, Hitler hosted British prime minister Neville Chamberlain here for the first of a series of negotiations (later continued in Munich with other European leaders), which led to the infamous promise of 'peace in our time' at the expense of the invasion of Czechoslovakia.

Little is left of Hitler's 'Alpine Fortress' today. In the final days of WWII, the Royal Air Force levelled much of the Obersalzberg, though the Eagle's Nest, Hitler's mountaintop eyrie, was left strangely unscathed.

The Dokumentation Obersalzberg, which opened in 2000, has been a wild success, far exceeding visitor projections. The trend looks set to continue with a controversial new luxury resort now under construction and planned to be complete by 2005. It seems that – for Berchtesgaden – there's just no escaping from Hitler's shadow.

resistance movement, foreign policy and the death camps. A small section of the underground bunker network is also open for touring. To get there take bus No 9538 from the Hauptbahnhof.

EAGLE'S NEST

Berchtesgaden's most sinister draw is on top of Mt Kehlstein, a sheer-sided peak at Obersalzberg where Martin Bormann, one of Hitler's right-hand men, engaged 3000 workers to build a diplomatic meeting-house for the Führer's 50th birthday. Perched at 1834m, the innocent-looking lodge (known as Kehlsteinhaus in German) occupies one of Germany's most breathtakingly scenic spots. Ironically, Hitler is said to have suffered from vertigo and rarely enjoyed the spectacular views himself.

From mid-May to October, the **Eagle's Nest** is open to visitors. To get there, drive, or take bus No 9549 (€3.50 return) from the Hauptbahnhof to the Kehlstein bus departure area. From here the road is closed to private traffic and you must take a special **bus** (adult/child €13/12; ⏱ 7.40am-4pm, 35 minutes) up the mountain. The final 124m stretch to the summit is in a luxurious, brass-clad lift (elevator). The Eagle's Nest now contains a restaurant (☎ 2969) that donates profits to charity.

SALZBERGWERK

Berchtesgaden was once a major salt-mining centre and a tour of the local **salt mines** (☎ 600 20; adult/concession €12/10; ⏱ 9am-5pm May-mid-Oct, 12.30-3.30pm Mon-Sat mid-Oct-Apr, 90 min) is well worth considering. It's more fun that it sounds with traditional protective miners' gear to be worn and a ride down a whooshing wooden slide into the depths of the mine. Down below, the highlights include mysteriously glowing salt grottoes and the crossing of a 100m-long subterranean salt lake on a wooden raft.

KÖNIGSSEE

At 603m the beautiful, emerald-green **Königssee** (parking €3) is the country's highest lake. Framed by steep mountain walls, the lake lies like a misplaced fjord 5km south of Berchtesgaden. Electric boat tours (€10.80, two hours) operate year-round to **St Bartholomä**, a quaint onion-domed chapel on the western shore. At some point, the boat will

stop and the guide will play a Flügelhorn towards the amazing **Echo Wall**. In the valley about an hour's hike from the dock at St Bartholomä is the **Eiskapelle**. As snow gathers in the corner of the rocks here, an ice dome emerges that reaches heights of over 200m. In summer as the ice melts, the water forms tunnels and creates a huge opening in the solid ice.

Activities

HIKING

The wilds of the 210-sq-km Berchtesgaden National Park offer some of the best hiking in Germany. A good introduction is a 2km path up from St Bartholomä beside the Königssee to the Watzmann-Ostwand. Beware: scores of mountaineers have died attempting to climb this massive 2000m-high rock face. Another popular hike goes from the southern end of the Königssee to the Obersee. For detailed hiking information visit the Nationalpark office (see p383). There are also offices in Schönau, Ramsau and on the Bartholomä Peninsula.

SKIING

The Jenner area (☎ 958 10; daily/weekly passes €20/84) at Königssee is the biggest of Berchtesgaden's five ski fields.

For equipment hire and courses try:
Outdoor Club (☎ 977 60; www.outdoorclub.de; Gmundberg 7) They also organise mountaineering, paragliding and rafting.
Skischule Treff-Aktiv (☎ 667 10 or ☎ 0171-726 4289; Jennerbahnstrasse 14)

WATZMANN THERME

This is Berchtesgaden's thermal wellness and fun pool **complex** (☎ 946 40; Bergwerkstrase 54; tickets €7.70/10.20 2/4hr, €14.50/all day; ⏱ 10am-10pm). It has several indoor and outdoor pools with various hydro-therapeutic treatment stations, a sauna and fabulous alpine views.

Tours

An excellent way to experience the creepy legacy of the Obersalzberg area, including the Eagle's Nest and the underground bunker system, is by taking a tour with **Eagle's Nest Tours** (☎ 649 71; www.eagles-nest-tours .com; adult/child €36/28; ⏱ 1.30pm mid-May-Oct, 4hr). Buses depart from the tourist office and reservations are advised, although a secnd service runs at 8.30am when there is sufficient demand.

Sleeping

JH hostel (☎ 943 70; jhberchtesgaden@djh-bayern.de; ebirgsjägerstrasse 52; dm €12.70, juniors only; ☒ closed Nov-late Dec) This 360-bed hostel is situated in the suburb of Strub and has great views of Mt Watzmann. It's a 25-minute walk from the Hauptbahnhof or a short journey on bus No 9539.

Berchtesgaden has plenty of **private rooms** from €25 per person. Check with the tourist office about availability.

Rupertiwinkel (☎ 4187; info@gaestehaus-ruperti winkel.de; Königsseer Strasse 29; s/d €25/45; ℗) This incredibly friendly and English-speaking pension is just past the tourist office and within walking distance of the station. The comfortable, modern rooms are great value and some have spacious balconies.

Hotel Watzmann (☎ 2055; fax 5174; Franziskan-erplatz 2; s €25-39, d €44-68; ☒ closed Nov–mid-Dec; ℗ ☒) There's a good range of rooms at this rambling time-warped place in the centre of town. The rooms are small but good value and ooze character with their quirky traditional décor and animal hides mounted on the walls.

Hotel Rosenbichl (☎ 944 00; www.hotel.rosenbichl de; Rosenhofweg 24; s €40, d €70-95; ℗ ☒) This traditional hotel in the middle of the pro-tected nature zone offers exceptional value. The rooms are spacious and modern and here's also a sauna, whirlpool, solarium and fitness programme.

Hotel Vier Jahreszeiten (☎ 9520; millers-hotel@ -online.de; Maximilianstrasse 20; s €40-69, d €72-120; ℗ ☒) A traditional Alpine lodge with modern touches such as a pool, sauna and solarium, this hotel has a range of rooms as well as panoramic views of the mountains and a good restaurant.

Of the five camp sites in Berchtesgadener Land, the nicest are near the Königssee in Schönau. **Campingplatz Mühlleiten** (☎ 4584; www.camping-muehlleiten.de; Königsseer Strasse 70; site/ person €5/4.70) and **Camping Grafenlehen** (☎ 4140; www.camping-grafenlehen.de; Königsseerfussweg 71; site/ person €6/4.50) are the best bets.

Eating

Hubertusstube (☎ 9520; Maximilianstrasse 20; mains €7-18) Part of the Hotel Vier Jahreszeiten, this restaurant offers rich pickings such

as venison and sirloin steak specialities as well as a good choice of vegetarian dishes. The dining areas all have good views of the mountains.

Gasthaus Neuhaus (☎ 2182; Marktplatz 1; mains €5-15) This huge place serves *Brotzeiten* (cold snacks) and more substantial old-style Bavarian fare, including seasonal spe-cials. The daily three-course menu is good value at €9, and there's a beer garden with live music on summer evenings.

Holzkäfer (☎ 621 07; Buchenhöhe 40; dishes €4-9; ☒ dinner only, closed Tue; wheelchair access) If you're driving, this funky log-cabin restaurant in the Obersalzberg hills is a great spot. Crammed with antlers, carvings and back-wood oddities, it's great for an evening drink or a light meal.

Other possibilities include:

Gasthaus Bier-Adam (☎ 2390; Markt 22; mains €5-18) Cheerful place with a good range of traditional fare.

Weekly market (Marktplatz; ☒ 8-11am Fri, Apr-Oct) An incredible array of fresh produce and meats.

Getting There & Away

For the quickest train connections to Berchtesgaden, it's usually best to take a Munich-Salzburg train and change at Frei-lassing (€23.60, three hours). There are di-rect trains from Salzburg (€6.60, one hour), although RVO bus No 9540 makes the trip in about 45 minutes and has more departures. Berchtesgaden is south of the Munich–Salzburg A8 autobahn.

Getting Around

The various communities of Berchtes-gadener Land are well connected by RVO bus (☎ 944 820). Pick up a detailed sched-ule at the tourist office (p383). To get to the Königssee, take bus No 9541 or 9542 from the Hauptbahnhof. Bus No 9538 goes up the Obersalzberg. For a taxi call ☎ 4041.

FRANCONIA

Franconia occupies the northern part of Bavaria, and its lovely rolling hills are home to a beautiful wine region, stunning parks and the unmissable cities of Nuremberg, Bamberg and Würzburg.

The Franconian wine region, in the north-west of the state, produces some exceptional wines, served in a distinctive flattened teardrop-shape bottle, the *Bocksbeutel*. For outdoor enthusiasts, Southern Franconia's Altmühltal Nature Park offers wonderful hiking, biking and canoeing. However, it is Franconia's incredible cities that attract and impress most tourists.

NUREMBERG

☎ 0911 / pop 493,000

Nuremberg (Nürnberg), Bavaria's second-largest city, is a vibrant place where the nightlife is intense and the beer as dark as coffee. The city is one of Bavaria's biggest draws and throngs with tourists during summer and the spectacular Christmas market.

For centuries Nuremberg, positioned at the intersection of medieval trade routes,

was the unofficial capital of the Holy Roman Empire and the preferred residence of German kings. It was also a centre for the arts and guardian to the crown jewels and many priceless artworks. Today, these legions of valuable masterpieces can be seen in the city's fabulous museums and churches.

In the 20th century the city became burdened by the legacy of the Nazis. It was here that the infamous party rallies were held, the boycott of Jewish businesses began and the infamous Nuremberg Laws revoking Jewish citizenship were enacted. On 2 January 1945 allied bombers reduced the city to rubble and 6000 people were killed.

After WWII, the city was chosen as the site of the War Crimes Tribunal, now known

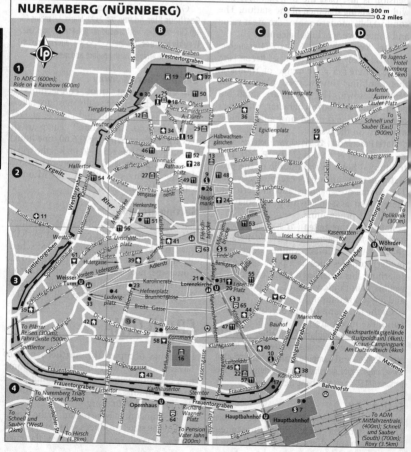

NUREMBERG (NÜRNBERG)

s the Nuremberg Trials. Later, the painstaking reconstruction – using the original stone – of almost all the city's main buildings, including the castle and the three old churches in the Altstadt, returned the city to some of its former glory.

Orientation

Most major sights are within the reconstructed city walls of the Altstadt. The Hauptbahnhof is just outside the walls at the Altstadt's southeast corner. From here pedestrian Königstrasse runs to the city centre, where the shallow Pegnitz River flows from east to west.

The biggest 'attractions' outside the Altstadt are the Reichsparteitagsgelände, the Nazi rally grounds about 4km southeast of the centre (also called Luitpoldhain); and the courthouse in which the Nuremberg Trials were held, just to the west of the Altstadt.

Information

BOOKSHOPS

Buchhandlung Edelmann (☎ 992 060; Kornmarkt 8) Travel section upstairs and some English-language novels downstairs.

Hugendubel (☎ 236 20; Ludwigplatz 1) Huge branch with lots of English-language books and a good travel section.

Schmitt & Hahn (Hauptbahnhof) Stocks English-language newspapers.

CULTURAL CENTRES

Amerika Haus (☎ 230 690; Gleissbühlstrasse 13) Impressive range of cultural and artistic programmes each month.

EMERGENCY

Ambulance (☎ 192 22)

INTERNET ACCESS

Internet Café Max (☎ 232 384; Färberstrasse 11, 3rd floor; €3.60 per hr; ☯ noon-11pm Mon-Sat, 3-11pm Sun)

INTERNET RESOURCES

www.nuernberg.de Nuremberg's comprehensive website in German and English.

LAUNDRY

Schnell und Sauber (☎ 180 9400; €4 per load; ☯ 6am-midnight) East (Sulzbacher Strasse 86; tram No 8 to Deichslerstrasse); South (Allersberger Strasse 89; tram Nos 4, 7 & 9 to Schweiggerstrasse); West (Schwabacher Strasse 86; U2 to St Leonhard)

LIBRARIES

Germanisches Nationalmuseum (German National Museum; ☎ 133 10; Kartäusergasse 1; ☯ 10am-6pm Tue-Sun, 10am-9pm Wed) Research library with 500,000 volumes and 1500 periodicals.

MEDICAL SERVICES

Poliklinik (☎ 192 92; Kesslerplatz 5)
Unfallklinik Dr Erler (☎ 272 80; Kontumazgarten 4-18)

MONEY

Commerzbank (Königstrasse 21)
Hypovereinsbank (Königstrasse 3)
Reisebank (Hauptbahnhof)

POST

Main post office (Bahnhofplatz 1)

INFORMATION	
Amerika Haus	1 D4
Buchhandlung Edelmann	2 B3
Commerzbank	3 C3
Hugendubel	4 B3
Hypovereinsbank	5 C3
Internet Café Max	6 B3
Reisebank	7 C4
Schmitt & Hahn	8 C4
Tourist Office - Hauptmarkt	9 B2
Tourist Office - Künstlerhaus	10 C4
Unfallklinik Dr Erler	11 A2

SIGHTS & ACTIVITIES	(pp388-91)
Albrecht-Dürer-Haus	12 B1
Altes Rathaus	13 C2
Der Hase (The Hare) Sculpture	14 B1
Dürer Monument	15 B2
Ehekarussell Brunnen	(see 33)
Felsengänge	(see 15)
Germanisches Nationalmuseum	16 B4
Handwerkerhof	17 C4
Historischer Kunstbunker	18 B1
Kaiserburg Museum	(see 19)
Kaiserburg	19 B1
Lochgefängnisse	(see 13)
Lorenzkirche	20 C3

Naussauer Haus	21 B3
Neues Museum	22 C4
Peter-Henlein-Brunnen	23 B3
Pfarrkirche Unsere Liebe Frau	24 C2
Pilatushaus	25 B1
Schöner Brunnen	26 B2
Spielzeugmuseum	27 B2
St Sebalduskirche	28 B2
Stadtmuseum Fembohaus	29 B2
Tiergärtnertor	30 B1
Tugendbrunnen	31 C3
Weinstadel	32 B2
Weisser Turm	33 A3

SLEEPING	(pp391-2)
Agneshof	34 B2
Am Jakobsmarkt	35 A3
Burg-Hotel Stammhaus	36 C1
DJH Hostel	37 B1
Grand Hotel	38 C4
Hotel Avenue	39 B3
Hotel Drei Raben	40 C4
Hotel Garni Keiml	(see 45)
Hotel Lucas	41 B3
Hotel Steichele	42 A3
Lette'm sleep	43 B4
Pension Sonne	44 C3
Probst-Garni Hotel	45 C4

EATING	🍴 (pp392-3)
Alte Küch'n	46 B2
Barfüsser Kleines Brauhaus	47 C3
Bratwurst-Röslein	48 C2
Bratwurstglöcklein	(see 17)
Bratwursthäusle	49 B2
Burgwächter	50 B1
Café am Trödelmarkt	51 B2
Goldenes Posthorn	52 B2
Heilig-Geist-Spital	53 C2
Kettensteg	54 A2
Lorenz	55 C3
Naturkostladen Lotus	56 B3
Proun	57 C3

DRINKING	🍷 (p393)
Cosmo	58 B4
Meisengeige	59 D2
O'Shea's	60 C3
Treibhaus	61 A3
Zwinger Bar	62 C3

ENTERTAINMENT	🎭 (pp393-4)
Dai Cinema	(see 1)
Mach 1	63 B3
Städtische Bühnen	64 B4
Viper Room	65 C3

BAVARIA

TOURIST INFORMATION

Nürnberg Card (€18) Two days unlimited public transport and admission to all museums and attractions in Nuremberg and Fürth. Available to overnight guests only.

Tourist office Künstlerhaus (☎ 233 6131/32; Königstrasse 93, opposite the Hauptbahnhof; ◷ 9am-7pm Mon-Sat); Hauptmarkt (☎ 233 6135; Hauptmarkt 18, Altstadt; ◷ 9am-6pm Mon-Fri, 10am-4pm Sun May-Sep, 9am-7pm Mon-Sat & 10am-7pm during Christkindlmarkt)

TRAVEL AGENCIES

Plärrer Reisen (☎ 929 760; Gostenhofer Hauptstrasse 27)

Altstadt Walking Tour

This circuit, which goes north to the castle and loops anticlockwise back to the market square, covers the main sights of the historic city centre over a leisurely 2.5km walk. With stops, though, it could take the best part of two days.

The tour starts on the bustling **Hauptmarkt**. At the square's eastern end is the ornate Gothic **Pfarrkirche Unsere Liebe Frau** (**1**; 1350–58), more simply known as the Frauenkirche. The figures beneath the clock, seven electoral princes, march clockwise three times around Charles IV every day at noon.

Near the tourist office stands the 19m **Schöner Brunnen** (**2**; Beautiful Fountain), rising from the square like a Gothic spire. A replica of the late 14th-century original, it is a stunning golden vision of 40 electors, prophets, Jewish and Christian heroes and other allegorical figures. On the market side

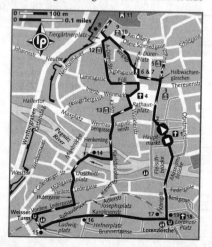

hangs a seamless **golden ring**, polished bright by millions of hands. A local superstition has it that if you turn it three times, you wish will come true.

ALTES RATHAUS & ST SEBALDUSKIRCHE

Walk north of Hauptmarkt to Rathausplatz and the Altes Rathaus (1616–22), a hulk of a building with lovely Renaissance-style interiors. It houses the gory **Lochgefängnisse** (**3**; medieval dungeons; ☎ 231 2690; Rathausplatz; tours adult/concession €2/1; ◷ 10am-4.30pm Tue-Sun Apr-Oct, 10am-4.30pm Tue-Fri Nov-Mar, daily during Christkindlesmarkt). These must be seen on a guided tour (held every half-hour) and might easily put you off lunch.

Opposite the Altes Rathaus is the 13th-century **Sebalduskirche** (**4**), Nuremberg's oldest church, whose exterior is smothered in religious sculptures and symbols. The **Bridal Doorway** to the north has ornate carvings of the Wise and Foolish Virgins. Inside, the highlight is the bronze shrine of **St Sebald**, a Gothic and Renaissance masterpiece that took its maker, Peter Vischer the Elder, and his two sons, more than 11 years to complete.

STADTMUSEUM FEMBOHAUS

Further north, Rathausplatz gives way to Burgstrasse, whose main visitor attraction is the **Fembo House Municipal Museum** (**5**; ☎ 231 2595; Burgstrasse 15; adult/concession €4/2 for Noricama/general exhibit, €6/3 for both; ◷ 10am-5pm Tue-Sun, 10am-8pm Thu Mar-Oct, 1-5pm Tue-Fri, 10am-5pm Sat & Sun Nov-Feb). The museum, in an ornate 16th-century merchant house, provides an entertaining overview of 950 years of city history. A flashy multimedia show, called Noricama, highlights facets of Nuremberg history using video, sound, slides and other technologies.

FELSENGÄNGE

By backtracking south on Burgstrasse, then turning right (west) on Halbwachsengässchen you'll get to Albrecht-Dürer-Platz, appropriately anchored by the **Albrecht Dürer Monument** (**6**). Directly beneath it is the four-storey subterranean warren of the **Felsengänge** (**7**; ☎ 227 066; adult/concession €4/3; tours 11am, 1pm, 3pm & 5pm, 3-person minimum). Burrowed into the sandstone in the 14th century to house a brewery and beer cellar, it also served as an air-raid shelter during

WWII. The tunnels, which can only be seen on a tour, can get pretty chilly so take a jacket. The tours depart from the Albrecht Dürer Monument.

TIERGÄRTNERPLATZ

Continue north on Bergstrasse to get to this square, framed by lovely half-timbered houses and lorded over by the **Tiergärtnertor (8)**, a square tower from the 16th century. On the square's eastern edge stands the beautiful late Gothic half-timbered **Pilatushaus (9)** fronted by Jürgen Goetz's 1984 bronze sculpture *Der Hase – Hommage à Dürer* (The Hare – A Tribute to Dürer). This nod to Dürer's watercolour original called *Junger Feldhase* (1502) shows the dire results of tampering with nature.

A few steps further east is the **Historischer Kunstbunker** (**10**; ☎ 227 066; Obere Schmiedgasse 52; tours adult/concession €4/3; ⌚ tours 3pm Apr-Oct & Dec, Sat & Sun only Jan-Mar & Nov), a moisture-proof bomb shelter used to protect key artworks during WWII.

KAISERBURG

Tiergärtnertor leads on to the humungous **Kaiserburg** (**11**; Imperial Castle; ☎ 225 726; Burg; adult/concession €5/4, including museum, €2/1.50 well & tower only; ⌚ 9am-6pm Apr-Sep, 10am-4pm Oct-Mar). The complex is roomier than the exterior lets on, embracing the Kaiser's living quarters, a Romanesque chapel, the Imperial and Knights' Halls and the **Sinwellturm** (Sinwell Tower; 113 steps). There's also the amazing **Tiefer Brunnen** (Deep Well; 48m), which still yields drinking water.

Also inside is the **Kaiserburg Museum** (☎ 200 9540; Burg; adult/concession €4.50/3.50; ⌚ 9am-5pm Apr-Sep, 9.30am-4pm Oct-Mar), which chronicles the history of the castle and sheds light on the evolution of defence techniques.

Behind the castle is a beautiful garden that's open seasonally. The grassy knoll in the southeast corner is **Am Ölberg**, a favourite spot to sit and gaze out over the city's rooftops.

TIERGÄRTNERPLATZ TO LUDWIGSPLATZ

Backtrack to Tiergärtnerplatz and around the corner to the **Albrecht-Dürer-Haus** (**12**; ☎ 231 2568; Albrecht-Dürer-Strasse 39; adult/concession €4/2; ⌚ 10am-5pm, 10am-8pm Thu). Dürer, Germany's famous Renaissance draughtsman, lived here from 1509 to 1528. As well as learning about his life, you can view several of the master's graphic works and see demonstrations in the recreated workshop.

Continue south along Albrecht-Dürer-Strasse, then turn left (east) on Füll and wind around the back of the Sebalduskirche to Karlsstrasse, where you'll come upon the **Spielzeugmuseum** (**13**; Toy Museum; ☎ 231 3164; Karlstrasse 13-15; adult/concession €4/2; ⌚ 10am-5pm Tue-Sun, 10am-9pm Wed) exhibiting playthings from many different periods.

From the Spielzeugmuseum carry on south, then cross Karlsbrücke to reach a tiny island surrounded by a particularly scenic stretch of the Pegnitz River. On the north side is the impressive half-timbered **Weinstadel (14)**, an old wine depot festooned with geraniums in summer. Also here is the covered wooden **Henkersteg** (Hangman's Bridge).

LUDWIGSPLATZ TO LORENZPLATZ

South of Henkersteg, continue along Hutergasse to Vordere Ledergasse, turn right (west), then south on Schlüsselstrasse to get to the fortified **Weisser Turm** (White Tower). At its foot stands the amazing **Ehekarussell Brunnen (15)**, a large metallic fountain with six interpretations of marriage (some of them quite harrowing) based on a verse by Hans Sachs, the medieval cobbler-poet. Head east on Ludwigsplatz to get to another modern fountain, the **Peter-Henlein-Brunnen (16)** on Hefnerplatz, dedicated to the 16th-century tinkerer credited with making the first pocket watch.

Continue east on Karolinenstrasse to reach the city's oldest house, **Nassauer Haus (17)** at No 2. Karolinenstrasse eventually culminates in Lorenzplatz.

LORENZKIRCHE

Lorenzplatz is dominated by the massive **Lorenzkirche** (**18**; Church of St Lawrence), which is crammed with artistic highlights. Spend some time studying the 15th-century tabernacle in the left aisle whose delicate carved strands wind up to the vaulted ceiling. The stained-glass windows (including a Rosetta window 9m in diameter) are remarkable, as is Veit Stoss' *Engelsgruss* (Annunciation), a wooden carving with life-size figures, suspended above the high altar.

On the north side of the church stands the **Tugendbrunnen (19)**, a fountain with seven

Virtues proudly spouting water from their breasts, in the shadow of a figure of Justice. Continuing north up Königstrasse will return you to the Hauptmarkt, where this tour started.

Other Sights
REICHSPARTEITAGSGELÄNDE
The infamous black-and-white images of ecstatic Nazi supporters thronging the streets to see goose-stepping troops salute their Führer were filmed in Nuremberg. This orchestrated propaganda campaign began as early as 1927, but in 1933 Hitler decided that a purpose-built venue would be a better backdrop and plans began for the **Reichsparteitagsgelände** (Nazi Party Rally Grounds).

Much of the ridiculously outsized Reichsparteitagsgelände was destroyed during the 1945 bombing raids, but enough is left to get a sense of the dimension and scale of this gigantic complex.

At the area's northwestern edge once stood the **Luitpoldarena**. Designed for mass SS and SA parades, it's now a park. South of here, the half-built **Kongresshalle** (Congress Hall), meant to outdo Rome's Colosseum in both scale and style, is the largest remaining monumental building from the Nazi era.

To put the grounds into a historical context and to create a place of learning and dialogue, a permanent **Dokumentationszentrum** (Documentation Centre; ☎ 231 5666; Bayernstrasse 110; adults/students €5/2.60; ☼ 9am-6pm Mon-Fri, 10am-6pm Sat, 10am-7pm Sun) was opened in the north wing of the Kongresshalle. A stunning walkway of glass cuts diagonally through the complex, ending in a terrace with a view of the interior of the congress hall. Inside, the exhibit *Fascination and Terror* chronicles the rise of the NSDAP, examines the cult around Hitler, the propaganda and reality of the party rallies and the Nuremberg Trials. Don't miss it.

East of the Kongresshalle, across the artificial Dutzendteich (Dozen Ponds), is the **Zeppelinfeld**, fronted by a 350m-long grandstand – the **Zeppelintribüne** – where most of the big Nazi parades, rallies and events took place.

The grounds are bisected by the incredible 60m-wide **Grosse Strasse** (Great Road), which culminates, 2km south, at the **Märzfeld** (March Field), planned as military exercise grounds. West of the Grosse Strasse was to have been the **Deutsches Stadion** with a seating capacity of 400,000. Its construction never progressed beyond the initial excavation; the hole later filled with groundwater and is today's Silbersee.

Discussion about an appropriate use of the grounds has been going on since 1945; nowadays the Zeppelintribüne hosts sporting events and rock concerts. To get to the grounds, take tram No 4 to Dutzendteich or tram No 9 to Luitpoldhain. Both trams pass the Hauptbahnhof.

NUREMBERG TRIALS COURTHOUSE
In 1945–46 captured Nazi war criminals were tried in **Schwurgerichtssaal 600** (Courtroom 600; ☎ 231 5421; Fürther Strasse 110; adult/concession €2/1; ☼ tours 1-4pm hourly Sat & Sun). The Allies chose Nuremberg for symbolic and practical reasons. In 1935, the so-called Nürnberger Gesetze (Nuremberg Laws), to justify the arrest and later extermination of Jews, were passed here. In addition, the building was easily accessible and one of few such complexes to survive the war intact.

The trials resulted in the conviction and sentencing of 22 Nazi leaders and 150 underlings, and the execution of dozens. Among those condemned to death were Joachim von Ribbentrop, Alfred Rosenberg, Wilhelm Frick and Julius Streicher, the notoriously sadistic Franconian party leader who was publisher of the anti-Semitic weekly *Der Stürmer*. Hermann Göring, the Reich's portly field marshall, cheated the hangman by taking a cyanide capsule in his cell hours before his scheduled execution. To get there take the U1 to Bärenschanze.

JÜDISCHES MUSEUM FRANKEN IN FÜRTH
A quick U-Bahn ride away in the neighbouring town of Fürth is the **Jüdisches Museum Franken in Fürth** (Frankish Jewish Museum; ☎ 770 577; Königstrasse 89; adult/concession €3/1.50; ☼ 10am-5pm Sun-Fri, 10am-8pm Tue). Fürth once had the largest Jewish congregation of any city in southern Germany, and the museum, housed in a handsomely restored building, chronicles the history of Jewish life in the region from the Middle Ages to today. The exhibits highlight religious and everyday aspects of life and include a historical room to celebrate the Feast of Tab-

ernacles, and a ritual bath in the basement. To get there take the U1 to Rathaus.

GERMANISCHES NATIONALMUSEUM
Spanning the period from prehistory to the early 20th century the **Germanisches National-museum** (☎ 133 10; Kartäusergasse 1; adult/concession €5/4; ☾ 10am-6pm Tue-Sun, 10am-9pm Wed) is one of the most important museums of German culture in the country. It features works by German painters and sculptors, an archaeological collection, arms and armour, musical and scientific instruments and toys.

Among its many highlights are Dürer's *Hercules Slaying the Stymphalian Birds*, confirming the artist's superb grasp of anatomical detail. Free guided tours in English take place at 2pm on the first and third Sunday of each month (normal admission is still charged).

In Kartäusergasse, at the museum's entrance is the **Way of Human Rights**, a symbolic row of 29 white concrete pillars (and one oak tree) bearing the 30 articles of the Universal Declaration of Human Rights. Each pillar is inscribed in German and, in succession, the language of a people whose rights have been violated. The oak represents the languages not explicitly mentioned.

NEUES MUSEUM
The most recent addition to Nuremberg's already impressive museum landscape is the **Neues Museum** (☎ 240 2010; Luitpoldstrasse 5; adult/concession €3.50/2.50; ☾ 10am-8pm Tue-Fri, 10am-6pm Sat & Sun). Housed in a spectacular building fronted entirely by glass, it's a stunning space with a very impressive collection. The upper floor is dedicated to contemporary art (mostly of the abstract variety), while the lower showcases design of all kinds since 1945. For a free peek at the exhibits, just stand in the courtyard outside.

HANDWERKERHOF
The Handwerkerhof, a re-creation of a crafts quarter of old Nuremberg, is a walled tourist trap by the Königstor. It's about as quaint as a hammer on your thumbnail, but if you're cashed up, you may find some decent merchandise.

Tours
The tourist office runs English-language walking tours (€7.50 plus admission to

Kaiserburg, under 14 free) at 1pm from May to October and in December. Tours leave from the Hauptmarkt branch and take 2½ hours.

Other organised tours include:
History for Everyone (☎ 332 735; adult/concession €5/3.50; ☾ 2pm Sat & Sun, Sun only Dec-Mar; 2hr) Interesting tours of the Nazi rally grounds by a nonprofit association. Meet at Luitpoldhain, the terminus of tram No 9.
Nachtwaechterin (☎ 997 207; admission €6; ☾ 9pm Mar-Sep, 7pm Oct-Dec) Night watchman tours; meets at Hauptmarkt.
Nürnberger Altstadtrundfahrten (tourist train; ☎ 421 919; adult/concession €4/2; ☾ 10.30am then every 45min Apr-Oct, Sat & Sun only Nov-Mar; 30min) Train tour through the Altstadt from outside the tourist office. Minimum of five people for English-language tours.

Festivals & Events
From late November to Christmas Eve, the Hauptmarkt is taken over by the most famous **Christkindlesmarkt** in Germany. Scores of colourful stalls selling mulled wine, spirits, roast sausages and trinkets litter the square as the smell of *Lebkuchen*, large, spicy soft biscuits wafts overhead.

Sleeping
Accommodation gets tight during the Christmas market as well as the toy fair (trade only) in late January to early February. At other times, cheap rooms can be found, especially if you book ahead. For online bookings try www.hotel.nuremberg.de.

BUDGET
Lette 'm sleep (☎ 992 8128; seeyou@backpackers.de; Frauentormauer 42; dm/s/d €17/28/44; 🖳) Open to people of all ages, this independent hostel is conveniently located five minutes from the Hauptbahnhof, just within the old town wall. It has a variety of dorms and doubles, a kitchen, TV lounge and bar.

DJH hostel (☎ 230 9360; jhnuernberg@djh-bayern .de; Burg 2; dm €18.60) This excellent Jugendgästehaus is in the historic Kaiserstallung (former stables) next to the castle, and is a little less than 1½km from the Hauptbahnhof.

Pension Vater Jahn (☎ 444 507; fax 431 5236; Jahnstrasse 13; s €25-30, d €35-50; 🅿) One of the city's best budget options is this simple and friendly pension, just southwest of the Hauptbahnhof. Rooms have no frills but are excellent value – some even have TV. Children are welcome.

Pension Sonne (☎ 227 166; Königstrasse 45; s/d €30/50) This is one of the city's prize budget places and often gets booked out so you'd be well advised to call ahead. Enter from Theatergasse. The rooms, all with shared bathroom, are simple but good value.

Two good central choices are right next to each other on Luitpoldstrasse: **Hotel Garni Keiml** (☎ 226 240; fax 241 760; Luitpoldstrasse 7; s €26-47, d €41-67) and **Probst-Garni Hotel** (☎ 203 433; fax 205 93 36; Luitpoldstrasse 9; s €29-40, d €43-67). Both have a range of good-quality rooms at reasonable prices.

Other recommendations are:
Jugend-Hotel Nürnberg (☎ 521 6092; jugend-hotel-nuernberg@t-online.de; Rathsbergstrasse 300; dm/s/d €18.50/26/41) Good option for those aged over 26. U2 to Herrnhütte, then bus No 21 north to Felsenkeller.
Knaus-Campingpark 'Am Dutzendteich' (☎ 981 2717; knaus.camp.nbg@freenet.de; Hans-Kalb-Strasse 56; tent/person €2/5) Camp site near the lakes in the Volkspark, southeast of the city centre. Take the U1 to Messezentrum, then walk about a kilometre.

MID-RANGE
Hotel Lucas (☎ 227 845; www.hotel-lucas.de; Kaiserstrasse 22; s €65-105, d €85-125; ✗ 💻) This trendy hotel in the heart of the city offers excellent value and service. The rooms are an oasis of restrained international design and comfort and all have fax and ISDN connections.

Am Jakobsmarkt (☎ 200 70; www.hotel-am-jakobsmarkt.de; Schottengasse 5; s €65-100, d €90-120; 🅿 ✗ 💻) Choose from contemporary or traditional rooms at this well-run place, reached via a tiny courtyard near the Spittlertor. Unexpected extras include a sauna, solarium and fitness room, and ISDN hubs in all rooms.

Hotel Drei Raben (☎ 274 380; hotel-drei-raben@t-online.de; Königstrasse 63; s €50-170, d €80-170; ✗) This design-conscious boutique hotel has a great variety of rooms with some at surprisingly good rates. The slick interior and minimalist décor give a cool, airy feel without losing any comforts.

Hotel Avenue (☎ 244 000; avenue-hotel@t-online.de; Josephsplatz 10; s/d €75/113; 🅿 ✗) South of the Pegnitz River, the Avenue's spacious modern rooms are first-rate and lack no facilities – a very good deal for the price. Special weekend deals make it an even better bargain.

Burg-Hotel Stammhaus (☎ 203 040; nuernberg@burghotel-stamm.de; Schildgasse 14-16; s €59-69, d €89-109; 💻 🐕) This friendly hotel near the Kaiser-burg offers good value in small but comfy rooms. Guests can enjoy the indoor pool and delightful breakfast room with great views of the old town.

Hotel Steichele (☎ 202280; hotelsteichele@steichele.de; Knorrstrasse 2-8; s €52-90, d €80-130; 🅿) Rustic public rooms and a charming traditional restaurant contrast with the simple, modern bedrooms at this atmospheric hotel in an old wine house. It's centrally located on a quiet street just inside the city walls.

TOP END
Agneshof (☎ 214 440; info@agneshof-nuernberg.de; Agnesgasse 10; s €90-145, d €115-190; 🅿 ✗ 💻; wheelchair access) The Agneshof is a real pleasure – an oasis of calm with an upbeat artsy air, top-notch facilities and elegant modern rooms – and, if you feel like some pampering, in-house health treatments are also available.

Grand Hotel (☎ 232 20; www.grand-hotel.de; Bahnhofstrasse 1-3; s €120-255, d €195-340; 🅿 ✗; wheelchair access) Crystal chandeliers and polished marble line the halls of what is Nuremberg's top hotel, host to aristocrats, celebrities and the well heeled. Recently renovated and refitted, the spacious rooms are well equipped if a little frilly.

Eating
QUICK EATS
Alte Küch'n (Albrecht-Dürer-Strasse 3; dishes €5-9) Blue-and-white tiles, lots of bric-a-brac and an open kitchen transport you back to a time long gone. The house speciality here is *Backers*, a kind of potato pancake with various side dishes.

Naturkostladen Lotus (Untere Kreuzgasse; dishes €2-8) Help unclog arteries with organic, wholesome fare from the small menu at this health-food shop. The fresh bread and cheese counter is worth a look for picnic supplies, although it's all rather pricey.

RESTAURANTS
Lorenz (☎ 205 9390; Lorenzer Platz 23; mains €7-12) One of the best new restaurants in town is this ultra chic and very popular place, where not only is it cool to be seen but the food is extremely good. The menu has a good mix of international dishes at very reasonable prices.

Barfüsser Kleines Brauhaus (☎ 204 242; Königstrasse 60; mains €5-11) Munch on hearty Franconian food or seasonal specials among the copper vats, framed old advertisements and bundles of knick-knacks of this atmospheric old grain warehouse. Carp is the house speciality in months with the letter 'r'.

Proun (☎ 237 3181; Klarissenplatz; mains €10-13.50) Right next to the Neues Museum, this trendy restaurant has absorbed the best of style and design from its neighbour. The food is appropriately light and beautifully prepared and pulls inspiration from around the globe.

Kettensteg (☎ 221 081; Maxplatz 35; mains €6.50-15) This leafy restaurant is Nuremberg's best open-air option away from the crowds. It offers a modern twist on Franconian fare, serving traditional dishes with a waistline-friendly approach.

Café am Trödelmarkt (☎ 208 877; Trödelmarkt; dishes €3.50-11) A lovely place on a sunny day, this café is an excellent choice for breakfast or lunch. It overlooks the covered Henkersteg bridge and the Weinstadel and offers continental breakfasts, filled baguettes and salads.

Goldenes Posthorn (☎ 225 153; Glöckleinsgasse 2; mains €9-22; closed Sun) Light seasonal cuisine is the hallmark at this regional gourmet emporium, in business since 1498 and filled with historic art and trinkets. The set menus are particularly good value.

Other recommendations are:

Heilig-Geist-Spital (☎ 221 761; Spitalgasse 12; mains €7.50-19) Classic Nuremberg restaurant with an extensive wine list.

Burgwächter (☎ 222 126; Am Ölberg 10; mains €5.50-12) Beer garden with good steaks and a wonderful view of the city.

NUREMBERG SAUSAGES

There's heated competition between Regensburg and Nuremberg over whose sausages are the best; the latter's are certainly more famous.

Bratwursthäusle (☎ 227 695; Rathausplatz 1; dishes €4.50-12; closed Sun) Cooked over a flaming grill, the little links at this popular rustic inn are served with huge portions of potato salad, sauerkraut or horseradish and are best washed down with a local Patrizier or Tucher brew.

Bratwurst-Röslein (☎ 214 860; Rathausplatz 6; dishes up to €6.66) This is one of the best, and cheapest, Altstadt restaurants. Choose to mix with the hoards in the massive din-

ing hall, or go for quieter dining in the individually decorated smaller rooms or the beer garden.

Bratwurstglöcklein im Handwerkerhof (☎ 227 625; Handwerkerhof; dishes €3-7) Despite its location in the kitsch Handwerkerhof (by the Königstor), the sausages here are just as good but you're less likely to meet any locals.

Drinking

Cosmo (☎ 244 7241; Kornmarkt 7; meals €4.50-8) This is one of the coolest haunts in town and serves excellent Vietnamese food to boot. It's a bustling café by day but really comes to life after dark when the rooftop terrace packs with a mix of students and designer types.

Zwinger Bar (☎ 220 48; Lorenzer Strasse 33) Grab a drink at the quieter front bar before moving to the back where things get busy with a mix of live bands and funky DJs playing anything from hip hop to drum 'n' bass.

O'Shea's (☎ 232 895; Wespennest 6-8) This is a huge peach of a place just south of Schütt Island, with cavernous vaulted rooms, Guinness and Kilkenny beers, and traditional Irish dishes such as shepherd's pie and trimmings (€8).

Other recommendations include:

Meisengeige (☎ 282 83; Am Laufer Schlagturm 3) Comfortable café-bar with an intellectual clientele.

Treibhaus (☎ 223 041; Karl-Grillenberger-Strasse 28) Bustling student café that serves till the wee hours.

Entertainment

The excellent **Plärrer** (www.plaerrer.de; €2), available at newsstands throughout the city, is the best source for events around town and also has information for both gays and lesbians. Otherwise try the free **Doppelpunkt** (www.doppelpunkt.de), a monthly listings magazine found in bars, restaurants and the tourist office. Both publications are in German.

NIGHTCLUBS

Mach 1 (☎ 203 030; Kaiserstrasse 1-9) This dance club with futuristic décor is party central with four different bars and music ranging from disco to hip hop. Fridays are special events nights, Saturdays it's house, and on the first Sunday of the month it's gay night. The door policy is pretty strict.

Viper Room (☎ 222 381; Königstrasse 39) This quirky little place, with its flowery wallpaper and black-and-white tiled floor, is one of *the* in spots in town. Thursday night is reggae,

BAVARIA

Fridays is 'cult party', and Saturdays alternate between house and gay nights.

Hirsch (☎ 429 414; Vogelweiherstrasse 66) A converted factory south of the centre, the Hirsch has live alternative music concerts almost daily, as well as theme nights and a good beer garden. Take the U1 to Frankenstrasse.

CINEMAS
Roxy (☎ 488 40; Julius-Lossmann-Strasse 116) This cinema shows English-language first-run films, but it's not central and is hard to get to by public transport.

DAI Cinema (☎ 230 690; Gleissbühlstrasse 13) The Deutsch-Amerikanisches Institut screens first-run and classic films regularly.

THEATRE & CLASSICAL MUSIC
Nuremberg's **Städtische Bühnen** (Municipal Theatres; www.theater.nuernberg.de) do theatre, opera and ballet on two stages – the **Schauspielhaus** and the **Kammerspiele** at Richard-Wagner-Platz 2–10, just west of the Hauptbahnhof. Tickets are available at the box offices or by calling ☎ 231 3908. The Nürnberger Philharmoniker also performs here.

Getting There & Away
Nuremberg airport (☎ 937 00), 7km north of the centre, is served by regional and international carriers, including **Lufthansa** (☎ 01803-803 803), **Air Berlin** (☎ 01801-737 800) and **Air France** (☎ 0180-583 0830).

Trains run hourly to/from Frankfurt (€35.60, 2½ hours) and Stuttgart (€31, 2¼ hours) and every other hour to Munich (€25.80, 2½ hours). There are direct connections several times daily to Berlin (€86, five hours) and Vienna (5½ hours), while a few also go to Prague (5½ hours).

BerlinLinien buses leave for Berlin daily at 12.10pm (standard one way/return €56/71, 2½ hours).

Several autobahns converge on Nuremberg, but only the north-south A73 joins B4, the ring road.

There's an **ADM Mitfahrzentrale** (☎ 194 40; www.mitfahrzentralen.de; Strauchstrasse 1; ⏰ 8am-8pm Mon-Sat) about 500m southeast of the Hauptbahnhof.

Getting Around
TO/FROM THE AIRPORT
U-Bahn No 2 runs every few minutes from Hauptbahnhof to the airport (€1.80, 12 minutes) between 5am and 12.30am. A taxi to/from the airport costs about €14.

BICYCLE
The tourist office sells the ADFC's *Fahrrad Stadtplan* (€5), a detailed map of the city and surrounding area. It also hands out a list of bicycle-friendly hotels in town that are willing to store bicycles for travellers.

For bike hire try:

Fahrradkiste (☎ 287 90 64; Knauerstrasse 9; children's/mountain/tandem bikes €5/8/16 per day)

Ride on a Rainbow (☎ 397 337; Adam-Kraft-Strasse 55; bikes €8 per day)

Allgemeiner Deutscher Fahrrad Club (ADFC; ☎ 396 132; Rohledererstrasse 13) Organises group rides throughout the year.

PUBLIC TRANSPORT
It's best to walk in and around the Altstadt. Tickets on the VGN bus, tram and U-Bahn/S-Bahn networks cost €1.40/1.80 per short/long ride. A day pass costs €3.60.

TAXI
Dial ☎ 194 10.

ERLANGEN
☎ 09131 / pop 103,000
About 20km north of Nuremberg is Erlangen, a charming university town with quaint streets, ivy-covered buildings and a lovely Schloss. The city languished in relative obscurity until Huguenots, expelled from France in 1683, settled here and established the town as an industrial and trading centre. Today it has a vibrant atmosphere and is a thriving centre for electrical engineering, with industrial giant Siemens employing thousands locally.

Orientation
The Hauptbahnhof is in the northwest of the city very near Schlossplatz. The main north–south artery is the largely pedestrianised Hauptstrasse, which leads south to Hugenottenplatz and then Rathausplatz.

Information
Dresdner Bank (Schlossplatz)

Hypovereinsbank (Hugenottenplatz)

Post office (Cnr Henkestrasse & Nürnberger Strasse)

Stadtbücherei (City Library; Palais Stutterheim, Marktplatz 1; €3 per hr) Internet access. Enter from Hauptstrasse.

Tourist office (☎ 895 10; www.ekm-erlangen.de; Rathausplatz 1; ⊗ 8am-6pm Mon, 8am-4.30pm Tue-Thu, 8am-12.30pm Fri) 1km south of the Hauptbahnhof.

Sights & Activities

Your first stop should be Erlangen's cultural heart, Theaterplatz, where you'll find the **Markgrafentheater**, the city's finest building. This part-baroque, part-rococo gem was built in the style of Italian opera houses and is still in regular use. Opposite is the **Redoutensaal**, built as a festival hall. Other cultural events take place at **Palais Stutterheim** on Marktplatz. This was formerly the Rathaus and is now a cultural centre with two galleries and a public library.

Erlangen's **Schloss** now houses the university administration. Behind it, the **Schlossgarten** is a fabulous and picnic-friendly park with an eye-catching fountain, the Hugenottenbrunnen. The park begins in formal French style with a horseshoe-shaped Orangerie to the north. Concerts occasionally take place here or in the adjacent **Botanischer Garten** (Botanical Garden; ☎ 852 2669; admission free; ⊗ 8am-6pm). The greenhouses have shorter opening hours.

The city also has several interesting churches, including the **Hugenottenkirche**, cleverly designed to give the illusion that the church interior is circular, and the **Universitätskirche**, which has rich stucco work. Both churches are on Hugenottenplatz, but unfortunately are usually closed outside services.

In the beautiful baroque **Altstädter Rathaus** in the northern part of the city centre, is the **Stadtmuseum Erlangen** (☎ 862 400; Martin-Luther-Platz 9; adult/concession €3/2; ⊗ 9am-1pm Tue-Fri, 2-5pm Tue-Wed, 11am-5pm Sat & Sun), which chronicles local history, starting with the Huguenot settlement.

Festivals & Events

The **Erlanger Bergkirchweih** is an immensely popular 12-day folk and beer festival that many visitors much prefer to the Munich Oktoberfest. Kick-off is at 5pm on the Thursday before Whitsuntide, and it all takes place on the Burgberg, against a panorama of the city.

Sleeping

DJH hostel (☎ 862 555; jugendherberge@stadt.erlangen .de; Südliche Stadtmauerstrasse 35; dm €13.60) The Jugendherberge Frankenhof is in the Freizeitzentrum Frankenhof, a leisure centre with a public pool and an inviting courtyard, and has been known to admit people over 26 if there's room.

Hotel Central (☎ 788 50; www.hotel-central-er langen.de; Westliche Stadtmauer 12; s/d €45/65) One of the best deals in town is this newly renovated hotel by the Hauptbahnhof with comfortable and pleasantly furnished rooms. Rooms at the back are pricier (and quieter). Children are welcome.

Art Hotel (☎ 714 00; www.art-hotel-erlangen.de; Aussere Brucker Strasse 90; s €60-80, d €80-100; Ⓟ ⊠ 🖵) Just south of the centre, this modern hotel offers good value for money and plenty of facilities. Rooms are bright and comfortable and all have ISDN connections. Other benefits include a sauna, fitness room and beautiful beer garden.

Luise (☎ 1220; www.hotel-luise.de; Sophienstrasse 10; s €79-104, d €95-124; Ⓟ ⊠ ; wheelchair access) This four-star hotel has a green conscience, sports furnishings and amenities good for body and rainforest. Choose a Feng-Shui room or an eco room for even more Brownie points. Service is warm and friendly and children are welcome.

Eating

Pleitegeier (☎ 207 324; Hauptstrasse 100; dishes €2-7) This popular pub has filling international fare for strained wallets, including sandwiches, pizza, Greek specialities like *gyros* and tzatziki, and vegetarian food. The beer garden is a great spot in fine weather.

Alter Simpl (☎ 256 26; Bohlenplatz 2; mains €6.50-13) This warren of a restaurant is decorated in a rustic style with a great outdoor seating area. The menu focuses on hearty meat dishes – try one of the specials grilled over beechwood.

Intermezzo (☎ 209 989; Martin-Luther-Platz 10; mains €7-12) This modern Italian bar and restaurant is a great place for a break from rib-sticking local fare. The menu has plenty of pizza and pastas but also a good selection of international dishes to tempt the taste buds.

There's a bakery, butcher and *Imbiss* (stand-up food stall) at Bahnhofplatz 5, right as you exit the Hauptbahnhof. A **farmers' market** (Schlossplatz) is held daily except Wednesday and Sunday. Student-oriented restaurant-pubs cluster in the Altstadt

BAVARIA

quarter north of Martin-Luther-Platz, about 500m north of Schlossplatz.

Getting There & Around

Regional trains to Nuremberg leave several times hourly (€3.60, 20 minutes). Erlangen is on the A73 autobahn, 24km north of Nuremberg and just north of the A3.

BAMBERG

☎ 0951 / pop 70,000

Bamberg is widely acknowledged as one of Germany's most beautiful cities. With a majestic historical centre, wonderful cathedral and superb palaces of the archbishop, it is magnificent, and duly recognised as a Unesco World Heritage Site.

Miraculously, Bamberg emerged from the WWII bombing raids with hardly a scratch, and most of the city's finest buildings are originals. Pristine examples of all major architectural styles from the Romanesque era onwards have survived, and a genuine charm and romance pervade the city. However, relatively few tourists make it here and you can wander the narrow, winding cobbled streets with ease.

Orientation

Two waterways bisect the city: the Main-Danube Canal, just south of the Hauptbahnhof, and the Regnitz River, which flows through the town centre. The city's bus hub, the Zentral-Omnibus Bahnhof

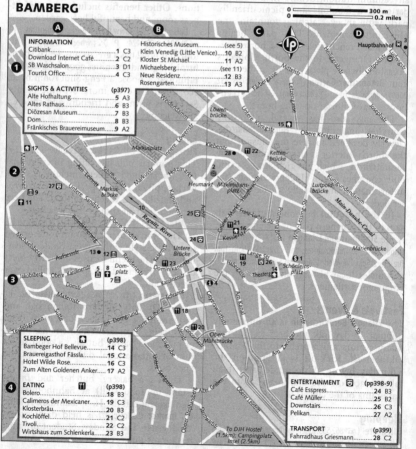

BAMBERG

0 ____ 300 m
0 ____ 0.2 miles

INFORMATION	
Citibank	1 C3
Download Internet Café	2 C2
SB Waschsalon	3 D1
Tourist Office	4 C3

SIGHTS & ACTIVITIES	(p397)
Alte Hofhaltung	5 A3
Altes Rathaus	6 B3
Diözesan Museum	7 B3
Dom	8 B3
Fränkisches Brauereimuseum	9 A2

Historisches Museum	(see 5)
Klein Venedig (Little Venice)	10 B2
Kloster St Michael	11 A2
Michaelsberg	(see 11)
Neue Residenz	12 B3
Rosengarten	13 A3

SLEEPING	(p398)
Bamberger Hof Bellevue	14 C3
Brauereigasthof Fässla	15 C2
Hotel Wilde Rose	16 C3
Zum Alten Goldenen Anker	17 A2

EATING	(p398)
Bolero	18 B3
Calimeros der Mexicaner	19 C3
Klosterbräu	20 B3
Kochlöffel	21 C2
Tivoli	22 C2
Wirtshaus zum Schlenkerla	23 B3

ENTERTAINMENT	(pp398-9)
Café Esspress	24 B3
Café Müller	25 B2
Downstairs	26 C3
Pelikan	27 A2

TRANSPORT	(p399)
Fahrradhaus Griesmann	28 B3

Hauptbahnhof

To DJH Hostel
(1.5km); Campingplatz
Insel (2.5km)

(ZOB) is on Promenadestrasse, just off Schönleinsplatz. Bus Nos 2 and 11 connect the Hauptbahnhof with the centre.

Information

Bamberg Card (€7.50/14.50 for 1/2 people) 48 hours of admission to city attractions, use of city buses and a walking tour.

Citibank (Schönleinsplatz)

Download Internet Café (☎ 201 494; Frauenstrasse 5; €5 per hr; ☼ 11-1am) Internet access.

Post office (Ludwigstrasse 25)

SB Waschsalon (☎ 204 940; Atrium mall) Laundry next to the Hauptbahnhof.

Tourist office (☎ 871 161; www.bamberg.info; Geyerswörthstrasse 3; ☼ 9.30am-6pm Mon-Fri, 9.30am-2.30pm Sat, 9.30am-2.30pm Sun Apr-Dec)

Sights

ALTSTADT

Bamberg's main appeal lies in its sheer number of fine historic buildings, their jumble of styles and the paucity of modern eyesores. Most attractions are sprinkled along the Regnitz River, but the town's incredibly statuesque **Altes Rathaus** is actually on it, perched on twin bridges like a ship in dry dock. (Note the cherub's leg sticking out from the fresco on the east side.) To the northwest are the charming half-timbered homes of **Klein Venedig** (Little Venice), complete with punts, canals and river docks.

DOM

The princely and ecclesiastical roots of Bamberg are primarily in evidence around the Domplatz on the southern bank of the Regnitz. The dominant structure is, of course, the soaring **cathedral**, which is the outcome of a Romanesque-Gothic duel fought by church architects after the original edifice burnt down (twice) in the 12th century. Politics, rather than passing styles, dictated the final floor plan, which was altered each winter during 20 years of building.

Inside, the pillars have the original light hues of Franconian sandstone, while traces of the bright 13th-century reliefs can still be seen in the choir. Look out for the **Lächelnde Engel** (Smiling Angel) in the north aisle, who smirkingly hands the martyr's crown to the headless St Denis. The star turn, however, and Bamberg's greatest and most enduring mystery, is the statue of the chivalric king-knight, the **Bamberger Reiter**. Nobody knows for sure who the fetching young king on the steed is. One leading theory points towards Konrad III, the Hohenstaufen king buried in the cathedral, another towards St Stephen, the king of Hungary and Henry II's brother-in-law.

Outside, an intriguing feature is the **Prince's Portal**, which shows Christ in an ornate sculpture of the Last Judgment. The work broke with convention and portrays the devil as being much larger than Mary or John, and the king, pope and rich man among the doomed.

On the south side of the Dom, in a separate building off the cloisters, is the **Diözesan Museum** (☎ 502 325; Domplatz 5; adult/concession €2/1; ☼ 10am-5pm Tue-Sun). Top ranking among its ecclesiastical treasures goes to Heinrich II's Blue Coat of Stars.

AROUND DOMPLATZ

Northwest of the Dom is the **Alte Hofhaltung** (old court hall), which contains the **Historisches Museum** (☎ 871 142; In der Alten Hofhaltung; adult/concession €2.10/1.50; ☼ 9am-5pm Tue-Sun May-Oct). It focuses on the history of the region and of 19th-century Bamberg.

Across the square, you'll spot the stately **Neue Residenz** (☎ 519 390; Domplatz 8; adult/concession €3/2; ☼ 9am-6pm Apr-Sep, 9am-4pm Oct-Mar), a huge episcopal palace. Showpieces are the elaborately decorated Kaisersaal (Imperial Hall), the Chinese cabinet, and paintings from the Bavarian State Gallery. The **Rosengarten** (Rose Garden) behind the palace has fabulous views of the city.

MICHAELSBERG

Above Domplatz, at the top of Michaelsberg, is the Benedictine **Kloster St Michael**, a former monastery and now an old people's home. The monastery church is a must-see, both for its baroque art and the meticulous depictions of nearly 600 medicinal plants and flowers on the vaulted ceiling. The manicured garden terrace boasts a splendid city panorama.

Also up here is the **Fränkisches Brauereimuseum** (Franconian Brewery Museum; ☎ 530 16; Michaelsberg 10f; adult/concession €2/1.50; ☼ 1-5pm Wed-Sun Apr-Oct). It shows plaster(ed) dummies of monks brewing their robust Benediktiner Dunkel beer, as well as exhibits from malt production to the final product.

Tours

German-language guided **walking tours** (adult/child €5.50/4; 10.30am & 2pm Mon-Sat, 11am Sun Apr-Oct, 2pm Mon-Sat, 11am Sun Nov-Mar) depart from the tourist office. If you'd rather not join a tour you can borrow an audio guide (€5) from the tourist office.

Sleeping

To book a room through the room reservations hotline, call ☎ 871 154.

DJH hostel (☎ 560 02; jh-bamberg@stadt.bamberg.de; Oberer Leinritt 70; dm €13.60; closed mid-Dec–Jan) The juniors-only Jugendherberge Wolfsschlucht is on the west bank of the Regnitz, closer to town than the camp site. Take bus No 18 to Rodelbahn.

Campingplatz Insel (☎ 563 20; www.campinginsel.de; Am Campingplatz 1; tent €3.40-6.70, adult/car €3.90/3.40) Camping options are limited to this well-equipped place, in a calm spot right on the river. Take bus No 18 to Campingplatz.

Brauereigasthof Fässla (☎ 265 16; www.faessla.de; Obere Königstrasse 19-21; s/d €34/52; P) Those interested in serious research of the local beer offerings should consider staying right here where snug but modern rooms are a mere staircase up from a pub with some of the city's strongest beers.

Zum Alten Goldenen Anker (☎ 665 05; fax 665 95; Untere Sandstrasse 73; s/d €40/75; P) This small, old-world inn north of Michaelsberg has pleasant, traditionally furnished rooms and a beautiful hidden inner courtyard. The attached vaulted restaurant is a popular spot in the evening.

Hotel Wilde Rose (☎ 981820; www.hotel-wilde-rose.de; Kesslerstrasse 7; s/d €60/90; P ✗) This traditional family-run hotel in the heart of the city has bright, comfortable rooms with modern furnishings and friendly service. Children are made very welcome and you can hire bikes.

Bamberger Hof Bellevue (☎ 985 50; www.bambergerhof.de; Schönleinsplatz 4; s/d €90/145; P) Style, tradition and period charm make this one of Bamberg's top hotels. The elegant rooms are spacious and service is excellent. More expensive rooms have sitting areas and four-poster beds.

Eating

Bamberg is famous for its beer, and over 200 varieties are produced locally. The town and the hills surrounding it are dotted with wonderful beer gardens, and the city's brewery-restaurants should be the first stop for local dishes such as stuffed Bamberger onion with beef in smoked beer sauce. A popular local brew is Rauchbier, a dark-red ale with a smooth, smoky flavour and an aftertaste of bacon (much better than it sounds).

Klosterbräu (☎ 522 65; Obere Mühlbrücke 3; mains €5-11; closed Mon) In a picturesque riverside location, this beautiful half-timbered brewery serves a youthful clientele who wash down the filling slabs of meat and other solid standard fare with its excellent beers.

Wirtshaus zum Schlenkerla (☎ 560 60; Dominikanerstrasse 6; dishes €3.50-9.50; closed Tue) This rustic 16th-century restaurant with long wooden tables is a justly famous place, with tasty Franconian specialities and its own superb Rauchbier. It gets busy in the evening so plan to arrive early.

Tivoli (☎ 234 63; Kleberstrasse 14; mains €6.50-12.80) For some light Italian food you couldn't do better than this beautiful place tucked in off the main drag. Choose from tasty pastas and pizzas or the grilled fish specialties.

Bolero (☎ 509 0290; Judenstrasse 7-9; tapas €2.75, mains €6.40-12.80; dinner only) Tapas are the main draw at this sprawling but atmospheric place where customers lounge around wooden tables illuminated by candlelight. It's a popular spot and often full of happy diners.

Calimeros der Mexicaner (☎ 201 172; Lange Strasse 8; mains €4.50-10) Another excellent choice is this Tex-Mex place with heaped plates of jambalaya with shrimp, massive steaks and some interesting salads. Things liven up in the evening when the tequila breaks out.

Grüner Markt, Bamberg's main shopping drag, has a number of fast-food options, including a Kochlöffel at No 18.

Entertainment

Consult the free listings (German-language) magazine *Fränkische Nacht*, usually laid out in pubs, for the latest 'in' spots and special events. For chilled-out entertainment the best place to head for is Austrasse, where the hip hang out by day and night. A very good option in this area is **Café Müller** (☎ 202 943; Austrasse 63), a hugely popular Parisian-style lounge, and just up the street **Café Esspress** (☎ 519 0431; Austrasse 33), a student-oriented place that changes seamlessly from coffee house to cocktail bar.

Other possible options include **Pelikan** (☎ 603 410; Untere Sandstrasse 45), a candle-lit pub with occasional live music, and **Downstairs** (☎ 208 3786; Generalsgasse 3), a cool alternative dance club with an underground vibe.

Getting There & Around

There are at least hourly RE and RB trains from Nuremberg (€9, 45/60 minutes) or from Würzburg (€14, 1¼ hours), as well as ICE trains every two hours to/from Munich (€43.40, 2½ hours) and Berlin (€83.60, 6½ hours). The A73 runs direct to Nuremberg.

Walking is the best option in town, but you can also hire bicycles at **Fahrradhaus Griesmann** (☎ 229 67; Kleberstrasse 25; €5.50 per day). The tourist office has a huge selection of bicycle-path maps. Cars are a pain in town, so park on the outskirts and walk or take a bus (€1.10, or €6.20 for a Tourist Ticket good for 48 hours of unlimited travel). For a taxi, call ☎ 150 15.

BAYREUTH
☎ 0921 / pop 74,000

Lined with magnificent baroque and rococo buildings and boasting one of the world's great music events, Bayreuth is a true capital of culture. It was the seat of margraves from 1603, but it was Wilhelmine, sister of King Frederick the Great of Prussia, who transformed the city. Forced to marry Margrave Friedrich rather than English royalty, Wilhelmine's loss became Bayreuth's gain as she invited the finest artists, poets, composers and architects in Europe to come to court here. By the time she finished, the city was home to some of the most spectacular architecture in Europe.

Later, Richard Wagner (1813–83), lured by the offer of a purpose-built stage for his epic compositions, came to live here and began the Bayreuth Wagner Festival. It continues today as a pilgrimage for die-hard fans, with over 600,000 people vying for fewer than 60,000 seats.

Orientation

The Hauptbahnhof is just north of the historic centre, reached by walking south on Bahnhofstrasse to Luitpoldplatz and on to the pedestrianised Maximilianstrasse, the main drag.

Information

Bayreuth Card (€9) Good for unlimited trips on city buses, entrance to the town's museums and a two-hour guided city walk (in German).
Café am Sternplatz (☎ 761 610; Ludwigstrasse 1; €3 per 30min) Internet access.
Commerzbank (Luitpoldplatz 8)
Post office (Kanzleistrasse 3)
Theaterkasse (☎ 690 01; ticketservice@bayreuth -tourismus.de) Sells tickets to concerts and other events.
Tourist office (☎ 885 88; www.bayreuth-tourismus.de; Luitpoldplatz 9; 9am-6pm Mon-Fri, 9.30am-4pm Sat, 10am-1pm Sun)

Sights

Except during the Wagner Festival in July/August, the streets can be very quiet as Bayreuth slips into a kind of provincial slumber. This is really the best time to see the sights without queues, and the town's strong musical traditions ensure there are good dramatic and orchestral performances year-round.

MARKGRÄFLICHES OPERNHAUS

Designed by Giuseppe Galli Bibiena, a famous 18th-century architect from Bologna, the **Markgräfliches Opernhaus** (Margravial Opera House; ☎ 759 6922; Opernstrasse; tours adult/concession/ under 18 €4/3/free; tours 9am-6pm, 9am-8pm Thu, Apr-Sep, 10am-4pm Oct-Mar) is a favourite musical venue. It's a stunning baroque masterpiece, with a lavish interior smothered in carved, gilded and marbled wood and sumptuous decoration. Richard Wagner deemed the place too quaint for his serious work, and conducted here just once. German speakers especially will enjoy the 45-minute sound-and-light multimedia show, with projected images of the royals and lurid lighting. In May/June the house hosts a festival of opera and ballet, the Fränkische Festwoche.

NEUES SCHLOSS & HOFGARTEN

It took just two years to build Wilhelmine's **Neues Schloss** (New Palace; ☎ 759 6921; Ludwigstrasse; adult/concession €3/2.50, combination ticket with opera house €6/5; 9am-6pm Apr-Sep, 10am-4pm Oct-Mar), which gives way to the vast **Hofgarten** (admission free; 24hr). The palace façade is pretty sober but the interior is a celebration of rococo exuberance. The annual VIP opening celebrations of the Wagner Festival are held in the Cedar Room and on the ground floor

BAVARIA

you'll find a collection of porcelain made in Bayreuth in the 18th century. Also worth a look is the **Spiegelscherbenkabinett** (broken mirror cabinet), which is lined with irregular shards of broken mirror – supposedly Wilhelmina's response to the vanity and false glamour of her era.

RICHARD WAGNER MUSEUM & FESTSPIELHAUS

To learn more about the man behind the myth, visit Haus Wahnfried, the composer's former home, which now contains the **Richard Wagner Museum** (☎ 757 2816; Richard-Wagner-Strasse 48; adult/concession €4/3; ⏰ 9am-5pm, 9am-8pm Tue & Thu Apr-Oct). Wagner had this lovely home built with cash sent by King Ludwig II. Inside is an undynamic, if thorough, chronological exhibit on Wagner's life, with glass cases crammed with documents, photographs, clothing and private effects. Unless you're a Wagner aficionado or at least a German speaker, it's hard to fully appreciate.

The rather Spartan **Festspielhaus** (☎ 787 80; Festspielhügel 1-2; adult/concession €2.50/2; ⏰ tours 10am, 10.45am, 2.15pm & 3pm, closed Nov & festival afternoons), constructed in 1872, also had Ludwig's financial backing. The huge stage was specially designed to accommodate Wagner's massive works and the acoustics are truly amazing. (See the boxed text below.)

EREMITAGE

Just northeast of the centre is the large and lusciously landscaped park, the **Eremitage**, home to the **Altes Schloss** (☎ 759 6937; Eremitage; adult/concession €2.50/2; ⏰ tours half-hourly 9am-6pm mid-Apr-Sep, 10am-3pm Oct, closed mid-Oct-Mar). It was a gift to Wilhelmine from her husband in 1735 and became the couple's summer residence. Its rooms are a mix of rococo indulgence and sparse monastic cells. One of the most beautiful is the Japanischer Saal (Japanese Room) filled with elegant furniture and Asian treasures.

The park also contains the horseshoe-shaped **Neues Schloss**, anchored by a Sun Temple topped by a gilded Apollo sculpture. Around both palaces you'll find grottoes whose hundreds of fountains start gushing hourly from May to mid-October.

To get there take bus No 2 from Markt (€1.50, 20 minutes).

MAISEL'S BRAUEREI-UND-BÜTTNEREI-MUSEUM

Listed in the Guinness Book of World Records as the world's most comprehensive beer museum, the enormous **Maisel's Brauerei-und-Büttnerei-Museum** (Maisel's Brewery and Coopers Museum; ☎ 401 234; Kulmbacher Strasse 40; tours €3.60; ⏰ tours 10am Mon-Sat) is next door to the eponymous brewery. A fascinating 90-minute guided tour (in German) takes you into the sweet-smelling bowels of a

RICHARD WAGNER

Richard Wagner (1813–83) was born in Leipzig but moved to Bayreuth in 1872. With the financial backing of Ludwig II, his biggest patron and protector, Wagner built his spectacular home, Haus Wahnfried.

Wagner's operas, including *Götterdämmerung*, *Parsifal*, *Tannhäuser* and *Tristan and Isolde*, are powerful pieces supporting his grandiose belief that listening to opera should be work (his *The Ring of the Nibelungen* is literally four days long), not a social affair, and that music carries messages about life that are too important to ignore.

Wagner designed his own festival hall in Bayreuth. The acoustic architecture in the hall is as bizarre as his works are popular. The orchestra performs beneath the stage, and reflecting boards and surfaces send the sound up and onto the stage, where it bounces from the wall behind the singers and, mixed with the singers' voices, finally makes its way to the house. The design also took the body density of a packed house into account and the results are remarkable.

Wagner is also well known for his reprehensible personal qualities: he was a notorious womaniser, an infamous anti-Semite and a hardliner towards 'non-Europeans'. So extreme were these views that even fun-loving Friedrich Nietzsche called Wagner's works 'inherently reactionary, and inhumane'. Wagner's works – and by extension he himself – were embraced as a symbol of Aryan might by the Nazis, and even today there is great debate among music lovers about the 'correctness' of supporting Wagnerian music and the Wagner Festival in Bayreuth.

9th-century plant, covering all aspects of the business. Arguably, the best part is the foaming glass of Weissbier served at the end in the bottling room, now a private saloon with old-fashioned slot machines.

Tours

Walking tours (adult/child €4.50/2.50) of the Altstadt leave from the tourist office at 10.30am from May to October and on Saturday only from November to April.

Festivals & Events

The **Wagner Festival** has been held every summer for over 120 years. The event lasts 30 days, with each performance attended by an audience of 1900. Demand is insane, and it takes an average of seven years to score tickets (although word has it that applicants from abroad needn't wait as long). To apply, send a letter (no phone, fax or email) to the Bayreuther Festspiele, Kartenbüro, Postfach 10 02 62, 95402 Bayreuth, before September of the year before you want to attend. You must write in every year until you 'win'. The lucky concert-goers face another endurance test – the seats are hard wood, ventilation is poor and there's no air-conditioning.

Sleeping

DJH hostel (☎ 764 380; jhbayreuth@djh-bayern.de; Universitätsstrasse 28; dm €13.60; ☻ closed mid-Dec–Jan) The 150-bed hostel near the university has lovely rooms, and in peak season the city council operates a simple **camp site** (☎ 511 239; tent/person €2/3; ☻ Jul-Aug) behind the building. It's about a 15-minute walk south of the centre or you can take bus No 6 to Kreuzsteinbad.

Pension zum Edlen Hirschen (☎ 764 430; fax 764 4328; Richard-Wagner-Strasse 75; s €31-46, d €46-67; P) Located near the Wagner villa, this is one of the best budget options close to the sights. Most of the comfy rooms in this family guesthouse have private bathroom and children are welcome.

Hotel Lohmühle (☎ 530 60; www.hotel-lohmuehle .de; Badstrasse 37; s €56-77, d €89-102; P X; wheelchair access) Set in a beautiful half-timbered house by a stream, this central hotel offers rustic country-style rooms with exposed beams and traditional furniture and, in a new annexe, bright, modern rooms with an uncluttered style. Children are very welcome.

Hotel Goldener Anker (☎ 650 51; www.anker-bay reuth.de; Opernstrasse 6; s €65-105, d €95-155; P X) The refined elegance of this hotel, just a few metres from the opera house, has been popular with composers, singers and musicians over the years. The rooms are individually decorated in a heavy traditional style with swag curtains and dark wood.

Eating

Foodwise you'll be spoilt for choice in Bayreuth.

Oskar (☎ 516 0553; Maximilianstrasse 33; dishes €3.50-10; wheelchair access) This updated version of a Bavarian beer hall bustles from morning to night, with patrons often spilling into the street. The menu includes salads and baked potato dishes, but the speciality is anything involving dumplings.

Sinnopoli (☎ 620 17; Badstrasse 13; mains €4-8) Eccentric lamps and artwork set the scene in this contemporary café which serves up creative pastas, baguettes, vegetarian dishes and at the weekends an all-you-can-eat breakfast buffet (€11). There's a lovely garden and terrace area and children are welcome.

Braunbierhaus (☎ 696 77; Kanzleistrasse 15; mains €6.50-17; ☻ closed Mon) Enormous portions of down-to-earth local dishes, including some vegetarian options, are wheeled out to the masses at this pub in the town's oldest surviving building. Try the home-made bread or the Holzfäller steak.

Richters (☎ 507 5880; Riedricstrasse 10; mains €9-17; ☻ 10am-1am) This trendy restaurant on a quiet street has slick, minimalist décor but a very classical feel. The menu features modern international dishes with innovative combinations of flavours and a good wine list.

For quick bites try **Santora** (Sophienstrasse 3; dishes under €5), a hole-in-the-wall Italian joint dishing up delicious pasta and pizza, or the **Wundertüte Café** (Richard Wagner Strasse 33; mains €5.80; ☻ closed Sun) for healthy soups, pastas and salads. For something more refined, you might want to try tea at the elegant **Café an der Oper** (Opernstrasse 16), where dainty cakes on bone china are served on the beautiful terrace.

Other restaurant recommendations are: **Miamiam Glouglou** (☎ 656 66; Von-Römer-Strasse 28; mains €6.20-11.50) Delightful Parisian-style restaurant with respectable prices.

BAVARIA

Hua Hin (☎ 644 97; Ludwigstrasse 30; mains €8-16; ☻ 11.30am-2.30pm & 5.30-11.30pm) A temple of tasty Thai food.

Getting There & Away

Bayreuth is well served by rail connections from Nuremberg (€13.50, one hour). Trains from Munich (€46.40, three hours) and Regensburg (€25.40, 2½ hours) require a change in Nuremberg.

COBURG

☎ 09561 / pop 43,000

A small town that packs a royal punch, Coburg is a little-known gem with an intriguing history and some beautiful buildings. Over four centuries, the princes and princesses of the house of Saxe-Coburg intrigued, romanced and ultimately wed themselves into the dynasties of Belgium, Bulgaria, Denmark, Portugal, Russia, Sweden and, most prominently, Great Britain. The crowning achievement came in 1857, when Albert of Saxe-Coburg-Gotha took vows with his first cousin, Queen Victoria, founding the present British royal family.

During the Cold War, Coburg languished in the shadow of the Iron Curtain, but since reunification the town has undergone a revival, rekindling visitors' interest in its proud Veste, one of Germany's finest medieval fortresses.

In mid-July, the streets explode in a feast for the senses during the annual **Samba Festival**, which draws around 50 bands and as many as 2000 dancers, not to mention hundreds of thousands of visitors.

Orientation

Markt is the old town's central square. The Hauptbahnhof lies to the northwest, Veste Coburg to the northeast.

Information

Postbank (Hindenburgstrasse 6)
Stadtbücherei Coburg (☎ 891 421; Herengasse 17; €1.50 per 30min; ☻ noon-6pm Mon-Tue & Thu, 9am-1pm Wed, 11am-5pm Fri, 9am-noon Sat) Internet access.
Tourist office (☎ 741 80; www.coburg-tourist.de; Herrngasse 4; ☻ 9am-6.30pm Mon-Fri, 9am-1pm Sat Apr-Oct, 9am-5.30pm Mon-Fri Nov-Mar) Just off Markt.

Sights & Activities

Markt, the town's most magnificent square is awash with colour and oozes aristocratic

charm. The fabulous Renaissance façade and ornate oriels of the **Stadthaus** (Town House) and the **Rathaus** compete for attention and lord over the imposing statue of Prince Albert.

Nearby is lavish **Schloss Ehrenburg** (☎ 808 832; Schlossplatz; tours in German adult/concession/under 18 €3/2.50/free; ☻ tours hourly, 9am-5pm Tue-Sun Apr-Sep, 10am-3pm Tue-Sun Oct-Mar), once the town residence of the Coburg dukes. This sumptuous tapestry-lined, antique-crammed palace dates from the 16th century and only got its neo-Gothic mantle later on. Albert spent his childhood here and Queen Victoria stayed in a room with Germany's first flushing toilet (1860). The most splendid room is the huge **Hall of Giants**, whose baroque ceiling is supported by 28 statues of Atlas.

Towering above the town is the storybook medieval fortress, the **Veste Coburg**. With its triple ring of fortified walls it is one of the largest and most impressive fortresses in Germany. Most of the existing building dates from the 16th and 17th centuries and it houses the vast collection of the **Kunstsammlungen** (☎ 8790; adult/concession €3/1.50; ☻ 10am-5pm Tue-Sun Apr-Oct, 1-4pm Tue-Sun Nov-Mar). As well as works by famous names such as Rembrandt, Dürer and Cranach the Elder, the collection includes 350,000 copper etchings, an impressive display of glass, ceremonial carriages and the elaborately carved Jagdintarsien-Zimmer (Hunting Marquetry Room) a masterpiece in woodwork. The quarters occupied by Protestant reformer Martin Luther in 1530, the year he was tried for heresy, are a historical highlight.

To get to the fortress take bus No 8 (€1.25 each way) from Herngasse near the Markt. From April to October, a tourist train plies the route every 30 minutes for €3 return. Otherwise it's a steep 3km climb up the path by foot.

Sleeping

There are few cheap hotels in the old town centre and it may be worth considering a longer walk to find a better deal.

DJH hostel (☎ 153 30; fax 286 53; Parkstrasse 2; dm from €14.60) Housed in a mock red-brick castle, this spick-and-span youth hostel is just 2km from town and accessible by bus No 1 from Markt (€1.25).

Gasthof Fink (☎ 249 40; www.gasthof-fink.de; Lützelbucher Strasse 22; s/d €28/46) This smart tradiional inn outside town has well-equipped rooms and a popular traditional restaurant. ust opposite is their modern addition, **Landhaus Fink** (☎ 249 43; s/d €40/61; P ✕ ; wheelchair ccess) with excellent-value, simple, modern rooms with patio or balcony. It's a quiet, friendly place and well worth the extra effort to get there. Take bus No 4, (€1.25, 10 min) from the Hauptbahnhof.

Hotel Pension Bärenturm (☎ 794 90; www.baerenturm-hotelpension.de; Untere Anlage 2; s €70, d €90-110; P ✕) This small family-run hotel is set in a beautiful historical building with loads of atmosphere. The rooms are individually decorated in a comfortable contemporary style and the service is extra friendly.

Coburger Tor (☎ 250 74; fax 288 74; Ketschendorfer Strasse 22; s €59-80, d €80-130; P ✕) A refined ambience, impeccable service, nicely equipped rooms with thoughtful décor and one of the best restaurants in town (mains €18-26) make this place a winner. It's about a 15-minute walk from the centre.

Eating
Many of the hotels in the town centre have excellent restaurants while the hills around Coburg are chock-a-block with enchanting beer gardens (see the Around Coburg section). While in the region you should try to sample the local specialities, such as the *Coburger* (a sharp-tasting long sausage grilled over pine cones), *Schmätzen* (gingerbread) and *Elizenkuchen* (almond cake).

Ratskeller (☎ 924 00; Markt 1; mains €5-15) Regional dishes from Thuringia and Franconia are the speciality at this rambling place in atmospheric surroundings. It's mostly hearty meat and fish dishes so work up a good appetite before you arrive.

Restaurant Rio Brasil (☎ 511 277; Theatergasse 1; mains €8-16; ✆ dinner only) This fun and funky Brazilian restaurant is a change from Coburg's more staid establishments and is popular with a young crowd. It goes on serving excellent Latin American food into the small hours.

Naturkost (☎ 334 48; www.naturkost-restaurant.de; Leopoldstrasse 14; mains €8-14; ✆ from 5pm Tue-Sun) Heavenly food made with fresh organic ingredients features on the menu at this bright vegetarian restaurant. Dishes range from vegetarian classics to Asian inspirations, with the odd fish or meat dish for the unconverted.

Getting There & Away
Direct trains to Bamberg (€8.10, 45 minutes) and Nuremberg (€16.20, 1½ hours) leave every other hour. The trip to Bayreuth (€12.40, two hours) requires a change in Lichtenfels. Berlin Linien Bus (www.berlinlinienbus.de) goes to Berlin on Friday and Sunday (€50 one way, 5½ hours).

AROUND COBURG
About 25km south of Coburg, near the town of Staffelstein, is the dignified 18th-century pilgrimage church and rococo masterpiece, **Basilica Vierzehnheiligen** (☎ 09571-950 80; admission free; ✆ 6.30am-7pm Apr-Oct, from 7.30am to dusk Nov-Mar). The church is built on the spot where a local shepherd is said to have had recurring visions of the Christ child flanked by the 14 saints of Intercession. Statues of the saints line the central altar, the focal point of the sumptuously decorated interior. The church is one of the greatest works of Balthasar Neumann, and the curving lines, intersecting oval rotundas, play of light and trompe l'oeil ceiling are a showcase of his spatial illusions, making the interior appear much larger than it is and creating a sense of constant motion.

On its perch across the valley is **Kloster Banz**, a former Benedictine monastery that is now a conference and training centre. There's a lovely view from the Franz Josef Strauss memorial, which is dedicated to the former party leader of the CSU (Christian Social Union).

Alte Klosterbrauerei (☎ 09571-3488; snacks €3.50-5; ✆ 10am-8pm) is a wonderful brewery attached to the adjacent convent at the back of Vierzehnheiligen, up past the wooden stands peddling kitsch. The sprawling beer garden has stunning views and plenty of the bracing *Nothelfertrunk* (Auxiliary Saint's Drink) on tap. Snacks include hearty bread-and-sausage platters, but you can also bring your own. Stay long enough and you may glimpse the nun in habit who brings in cases for refill.

Getting There & Away
Both churches are about 4km south of Lichtenfels, just off the B173, about a 30-minute drive from Coburg. Regional trains connect Coburg with Lichtenfels (€4, 20 minutes) from where there are two buses a day (€1.50, 10 minutes) to Vierzehnheiligen.

Regular buses between Lictenfels and Staffelstein pass within walking distance of the basilica. A taxi is about €6.

ALTMÜHLTAL NATURE PARK

In southern Franconia, the Altmühl River gently meanders through a region of little valleys and hills before joining the Rhine-Main Canal and eventually emptying into the Danube. The 2900-sq-km Altmühltal Nature Park is one of Germany's largest nature parks and covers some of Bavaria's loveliest lands. Despite this, it sees only a trickle of foreign tourists. You can explore the park on your own via well-marked hiking and biking trails, or canoe for an hour or several days. There's basic camping (€4) in designated spots along the river, and plenty of accommodation in the local area.

The park's main information centre is in the city of Eichstätt (p405), a charming town at the southern end of the park that makes an excellent base for exploring.

For information on the park and help with planning an itinerary, contact the **Informationszentrum Naturpark Altmühltal** (☎ 987 60; www.naturpark-altmuehltal.de; Kloster Notre Dame, Kardinal-Preysing-Platz, Eichstätt; ⊙ 9am-5pm Mon-Sat, 10am-5pm Sun Apr-Oct, 9am-noon & 2-4pm Mon-Thu, 9am-noon Fri Nov-Mar). It's also a font of knowledge on accommodation options and bike, boat and car hire in the area.

Upstairs in the information centre is a museum of the park's wildlife and habitats, complete with a re-creation of landscapes in its garden.

Orientation

The park takes in the area just southwest of Regensburg, south of Nuremberg, east of Treuchtlingen and north of Eichstätt. The eastern boundaries of the park include the town of Kelheim.

There are bus and train connections between Eichstätt and all the major milestones along the river, including Gunzenhausen, Treuchtlingen and Pappenheim (from west to east). North of the river, activities focus around the towns of Kipfenberg, Beilngries and Riedenburg.

Activities

CANOEING & KAYAKING

The most beautiful section of the river is from Treuchtlingen or Pappenheim to Eichstätt or Kipfenberg, about a 60km stretch that you can do lazily in a kayak or canoe in two to three days. There are lots of little dams along the way, as well as some small rapids about 10km northwest of Dollnstein. Signs warn of impending doom but locals say that if you heed the warnings to stay to the right, you'll be pretty safe.

San-Aktiv Tours (☎ 09831-4936; www.san-activ-tours.de; Bühringer Strasse 8, 91710 Gunzenhausen) and **Natour** (☎ 09141-922 929; www.natour.de; Gänswirtshaus 34, 91781 Weissenburg) are the largest and best-organised canoe-hire companies in the park, with a network of vehicles to shuttle canoes, bicycles and people around the area.

Canoe trips through the park run from April to October and cost about €23 for a half-day trip and €150 for a three-day tour. You can canoe alone or join a group. Packages generally include the canoe, swim vests, maps, instructions, transfer back to the embarkation point and, for overnight tours, luggage transfer and accommodation. Most trips start in Dietfurt near Treuchtlingen.

You can hire canoes and kayaks in just about every town along the river. Expect to pay about €14/€28 per day for one/two-person boats, more for bigger ones. Staff will haul you and the boats to or from your embarkation point for an additional fee (sample fee: Eichstätt-Dollnstein is €24 for the first boat, and then €3.50 for each additional boat).

You can get a full list of boat-hire outlets from the Informationszentrum Naturpark Altmühltal (see earlier). Some recommendations include:

Bootsverleih Otto Rehm (☎ 08422-987654; Dollnstein)

Fahrradgarage (☎ 08421-21 10; Eichstätt)

Franken-Boot (☎ 09142-46 45; Treuchtlingen)

Lemming Tours (☎ 09145-235; Solnhofen)

San-Aktiv Tours (☎ 09831-4936; www.san-activ-tours.de; Bühringer Strasse 8, 91710 Gunzenhausen)

CYCLING & HIKING

Around 800km of bicycle trails and 3000km of hiking trails crisscross the nature park; the most popular route is the Altmühltal Radweg which runs parallel to the river for 160km. Trails are clearly labelled and have long, rectangular brown signs bearing a bike symbol. Hiking-trail markers are yellow.

You can hire bikes in almost every town within the park, and prices are more or less uniform. Most bike-hire agencies will also store bicycles. Ask for a list of bike-hire outlets at the Informationszentrum Naturpark Altmühltal (p404).

In Eichstätt Fahrradgarage (see Canoeing & Kayaking, p404) hires out bicycles for €7 per day. Staff will bring the bikes to you or take you and the bikes to anywhere in the park for an extra fee.

Getting There & Away

BUS

From mid-April to October the FreizeitBus Altmühltal-Donautal takes passengers and their bikes around the park. Route FzB1 runs from Regensburg and Kelheim to Riedenburg on weekends and holidays only. Route FzB2 travels between Dollnstein, Eichstätt, Beilngries, Dietfurt and Riedenburg with all-day service on weekends and holidays and restricted service on weekdays.

All-day tickets cost €8.50/€5.50 for passengers with/without bicycles, or €19.50/€14 per family with/without bikes.

TRAIN

Trains run between Eichstätt Bahnhof and Treuchtlingen hourly or better (€4, 25 minutes), and between Treuchtlingen and Gunzenhausen at least hourly (€5.60, 15 minutes). RE trains from Munich that run through Eichstätt Bahnhof also stop in Dollnstein, Solnhofen and Pappenheim. Some require a change in Ingolstadt.

EICHSTÄTT

☎ 08421 / pop 14,000

The wide, cobbled streets of Eichstätt meander past elegant buildings and leafy squares and give this sleepy town a general sense of refinement and Mediterranean flair. Italian architects, notably Gabriel de Gabrieli and Maurizio Pedetti, rebuilt the town after Swedes razed the place during the Thirty Years' War (1618–48) and it has remained undamaged ever since. In 1980 it became home to the only Catholic university in Germany, where 4000 students now study.

Orientation

Eichstätt has two train stations. Mainline trains stop at the Bahnhof, 5km from the centre, from where diesel trains shuttle to

the Stadtbahnhof. From here walk north across the Spitalbrücke and you'll end up in Domplatz, the heart of town. Willibaldsburg castle is about 1km southwest of the Stadtbahnhof. Everything is well signposted.

Information

Informationszentrum Naturpark Altmühltal
(☎ 987 60; www.naturpark-altmuehltal.de; Kloster Notre Dame, Kardinal-Preysing-Platz, Eichstätt; ♥ 9am-5pm Mon-Sat, 9am-10am Sun Apr-Oct, 9am-noon & 2-4pm Mon-Thu, 9am-noon Fri Nov-Mar)

Kreiskrankenhaus (☎ 6010; Ostenstrasse 31) Hospital.

Post office (Domplatz 7)

Raiffeisen Bank (Domplatz 5)

Tourist office (☎ 988 00; www.eichstaett.de; Domplatz 8; ♥ 9am-6pm Mon-Sat & 10am-1pm Sun Apr-Oct; 10am-noon & 2-4pm Mon-Thu, 10am-noon Fri, Nov-Mar)

Sights

TOWN CENTRE

Eichstätt's centre is dominated by the **Dom** (Domschatz & Diözesanmuseum; ☎ 507 42; Residenzplatz 7; adult/children €2/1; ♥ 10.30am-5pm Wed-Fri & 10am-5pm Sat & Sun Apr-Nov), which is filled, not surprisingly, with riches. Features worth noting include an enormous stained-glass window by Hans Holbein the Elder, and the **Pappenheimer Altar** (1489–97), carved from sandstone and depicting a pilgrimage from Pappenheim to Jerusalem. The seated statue of St Willibald, the town's first bishop, is also worth a gape. The museum displays the cathedral's treasures, including the robes of St Willibald and baroque Gobelin tapestries.

Walking out of the Dom you'll find yourself in the magnificent **Residenzplatz**, a sweeping open area lined with baroque and rococo palaces. At its centre is the Mariensäule, a 19m-high column crowned with a golden statue of Mary.

One of the square's most notable buildings is the **Residenz** (Residenzplatz; €1; ♥ tours 11am & 3pm Mon-Thu, 11am Fri, 10.15am & 3.30pm Sat), a Gabrieli building and former princebishops' palace built between 1725 and 1736. It has a stunning main staircase and a Spiegelsaal, with mirrors and a fresco from Greek mythology.

North of the Dom is another baroque square, the **Markt**. This is the heart of Eichstätt's commercial district and markets are held here on Wednesday and Saturday mornings. About 300m northwest of here,

BAVARIA

on Westenstrasse, is the **Kloster St Walburga**, the burial site of St Willibald's sister and a pilgrimage site thanks to a 'mysterious' occurrence – every year between mid-October and late February, water oozes from Walburga's relics and drips down into a catchment. The nuns bottle diluted versions of the so-called *Walburgaöl* (Walburga oil) and give it away to the faithful. The walls in the upper chapel are covered with beautiful *ex voto* tablets as thank yous to the saint.

WILLIBALDSBURG
The hill-top castle of Willibaldsburg (1355) houses two museums. The **Jura-Museum** (☎ 4730; Burgstrasse 19; adult/concession/under 18 €3/2/free; ☺ 9am-6pm Apr-Sep, 10am-4pm Nov-Mar, closed Mon) is great even if fossils usually don't quicken your pulse; highlights are a locally found archaeopteryx (the oldest-known fossil bird) and the aquariums with living specimens of fossilised animals.

Also in the castle is the **Museum of Pre-History & Early History** (☎ 894 50; Burgstrasse 19; adult/concession/under 18 €3/2/free; ☺ 9am-6pm Apr-Sep, 10am-4pm Nov-Mar, closed Mon). The star attraction here is the 6000-year-old mammoth skeleton. Also look for the 76.5m-deep well – toss in a coin and listen for about 10 seconds for the ting or the plop. The gardens near the car park have fantastic views of Eichstätt.

Looking across the valley, you can make out the **limestone quarry** and **information centre** (€1; ☺ 9am-5pm) at the **Museum Berger** (☎ 4663; Harthof; adult/child €2/0.50; ☺ 1.30-5pm Mon-Sat, 10am-noon Sun Apr-Oct, otherwise on request). It's at the base of the quarry and displays a lot of geological samples.

Tours
The tourist office runs walking tours of the town centre (€3; 1½ hours) at 1.30pm on Saturday from April to October (also Wednesday at 1.30pm in July and August).

Sleeping & Eating
DJH hostel (☎ 980 410; jheichstaett@djh-bayern.de; Reichenaustrasse 15; dm €15.70; ☺ closed Dec–mid-Jan) This is a comfortable modern place overlooking the Altstadt, but it's frequently booked up with school groups.

Camping Daum (☎ 5455; fax 807 63; Westenstrasse 47; site €5.50; ☺ Apr-Oct) This camp site is on the

northern bank of the Altmühl River, about 1km east of the town centre.

Hotel Schiesstätte (☎ 982 00; xhillner@aol.com Schiesstättberg 8; s €43-68, d €68-82; P ☒) This newly renovated hotel offers great value in a wonderfully quiet location close to the centre of town. The bright, spacious rooms are tastefully furnished in a contemporary style and children are very welcome.

Hotel Adler (☎ 6767; adler.stigler@t-online.de, Markplatz 22; s €59-67, d €82-102; P ☒; wheelchair access) A superb ambience reigns at this ornate 300-year-old building right on Markt. Rooms are bright, airy and modern and it offers all the trappings, including bike and boat hire and a generous breakfast buffet.

Café im Paradeis (☎ 3313; Markt 9; mains €6.50-14.50) Good either for a snack or a full meal, this café has a great selection of dishes, including some vegetarian options. Sit on the terrace and soak up the atmosphere or dine inside in classical surroundings laden with antiques.

Restaurant Zum Kavalier (☎ 908 045; Residenzplatz 17; mains €6-15) Located in an atmospheric old theatre building with a great interior as well as plenty of outdoor eating areas, this Italian restaurant dishes up an enticing selection of pastas and pizzas.

For fast food try Metzgerei Schneider on the Markt.

Getting There & Away
Trains run hourly or better between Ingolstadt and Eichstätt (€4, 25 minutes). For more connections, see p405.

INGOLSTADT
☎ 0841 / pop 118,000
Ingolstadt is a charming medieval city with beautiful streets and buildings, a museum church with the largest flat fresco ever made and a fascinating military museum. Although it administratively belongs to Upper Bavaria, geographically and logistically, it makes a good gateway to the Altmühltal Nature Park.

Walking the prosperous streets of the old city centre, it's easy to forget that this is actually an industrial city that owes much of its wealth to oil refineries and, above all, to Audi. The car manufacturer has its headquarters here and employs 29,000 people locally.

Orientation

The Hauptbahnhof is 2.5km southeast of the Altstadt; bus Nos 10, 11, 15 and 16 run between them every few minutes (€1.60). The Danube is south of the Altstadt; the Audi factory is about 2km north of the centre.

Information

All the main banks are on Rathausplatz.

Café Fronte (☎ 975 159; Münchener Strasse 119; €5 per hr; ☺ 10am-11pm) Internet access.

Post office (Hauptbahnhof, Am Stein)

Stadtbücherei (☎ 305 1831; Hallstrasse 2-4; free) Internet access.

Tourist office (☎ 305 3030; www.ingolstadt.de /tourismus; Rathausplatz 2; ☺ 8am-5.30pm Mon-Fri, 9am-2pm Sat, 10am-3pm Sun)

Sights

ASAMKIRCHE MARIA DE VICTORIA

The crown jewel among Ingolstadt's sights is the **Asamkirche** (☎ 175 18; Neubaustrasse 11/2; adult/concession €1.50/1; ☺ 9am-noon & 1-5pm Tue-Sun Mar-Oct; 10am-noon & 1-4pm Nov-Mar), a baroque masterpiece designed by brothers Cosmas Damian and Egid Quirin Asam between 1732 and 1736.

Its shining glory is the trompe l'oeil ceiling (painted in just six weeks in 1735); the world's largest fresco on a flat surface. It is a mesmerising piece of work full of stunning visual illusions. Stand on the little circle in the diamond tile near the door and look over your left shoulder at the archer with the flaming red turban. Wherever you walk in the room the arrow points right at you. Focus on anything – the Horn of Plenty, Moses' staff, the treasure chest – and it will appear to alter dramatically when you move around the room. Asam took the secret methods he used in the painting to his grave.

Before leaving ask the caretaker to let you into the side chamber to see the Lepanto Monstrance, a gold and silver depiction of the Battle of Lepanto (1571).

DEUTSCHES MEDIZINHISTORISCHES MUSEUM

Located in the stately Alte Anatomie (Old Anatomy) building at the city's university, the **Deutsches Medizinhistorisches Museum** (German Museum of Medical History; ☎ 305 1860; Anatomiestrasse 18/20; adult/concession €2.50/1.25; ☺ 10am-noon & 2-5pm Tue-Sun) chronicles the evolution of medical science as well as the many instruments and techniques used.

The ground floor eases you into the exhibition with birthing chairs, enema syringes and lancets for blood-letting. Upstairs things get closer to the bone in displays of human

FRANKENSTEIN'S BABY

Mary Shelley's *Frankenstein*, published in 1818, is one of the most enduring monster tales ever written. The story is well known: young scientist Viktor Frankenstein travels to Ingolstadt to study medicine. Here, he becomes madly obsessed with the idea of creating a human being from grisly spare parts robbed from local graves. Unfortunately his creature turns out to be a bit of a problem child and promptly sets out to destroy its maker.

So why in the world did Shelley pick Ingolstadt as her novel's setting? For centuries, Ingolstadt, along with Prague and Vienna, was home to one of the most prominent universities in central Europe. In the 18th century, a cutting-edge laboratory for scientists and medical doctors was housed in a beautiful baroque building, the Alte Anatomie (now the German Museum of Medical History). In the operating theatre on the 1st floor, professors and students performed experiments on corpses and dead tissue. And so it was only fitting that Ingolstadt became the imaginary birthplace of Frankenstein's monster.

Shelley originally became aware of Ingolstadt because it was the founding place of a secret society called the Illuminati. Its list of illustrious members included Goethe and Herder as well as Mary Shelley's husband, Percy Bysshe Shelley.

Ingolstadt has largely refrained from exploiting the Frankenstein myth, but German speakers might consider joining **Dr Frankenstein's Murder & Mystery Tour** (☎ 326 243; www.frankenstein.at; adult/concession €7/6; ☺ 10pm; check with the tourist office for dates), a spooky, 70 minute night-time walk led by a character dressed as the good old doctor. The evening concludes with a visit to 'Frankenstein's Kabinett', a re-created laboratory-cum-Frankenstein-memorabilia room upstairs at Zum Daniel (see Eating p409).

skeletons with preserved musculature and organs, foetuses of conjoined twins, a pregnant uterus and a cyclops.

Although presented in a completely scientific, almost clinical, fashion, there's an undeniable ghoulishness to this museum. After your visit, you can recover in the bucolic medicinal plant garden, which includes a garden of smells and touch designed for the blind.

NEUES SCHLOSS & BAYERISCHES ARMEE MUSEUM

The ostentatious New Palace was built for Duke Ludwig the Bearded in 1418. Fresh from a trip to wealth-laden France, Ludwig borrowed heavily from Gallic design and created an ostentatious new home with 3m-thick walls, Gothic net vaulting and individually carved doorways. Today the building houses the **Bayerishces Armee Museum** (Bavarian Military Museum; ☎ 937 70; Paradeplatz 4; adult/concession €3/2.50, €1 on Sunday, combined ticket with Reduit Tilly €4/3.50; ❧ 8.45am-4.30pm Tue-Sun). The exhibits include armaments from the 14th century to WWII and a collection of 17,000 tin soldiers.

Part two of the museum is in the **Reduit Tilly** (adult/concession €3/2.50, €1 on Sunday, combined ticket with military museum €4/3.50; ❧ 8.45am-4.30pm Tue-Sun) across the river. Named after the general of the Thirty Years' War, it features exhibits covering the history of WWI and post-WWI Germany.

MUSEUM MOBILE

This high-tech museum is part of the **Audi Forum** (☎ 283 4444; Ettinger Strasse 40; admission adult/ concession €1.60/1.50, tours €3.50/2.80; ❧ 10am-8pm). Exhibits on three floors chronicle the company's history, from humble beginnings in 1899 to the latest successes. Some 50 cars and 20 motorbikes are on view, including 14 prototypes that perpetually glide past visitors on an open lift (elevator). One-hour tours (some in English) run twice hourly. Take bus No 11 to the terminus from the Hauptbahnhof or Paradeplatz.

You can also take a two-hour tour of the **Audi factory** (☎ 0800-282 4444; tours free; ❧ 9am-2pm production days only).

LIEBFRAUENMÜNSTER

The city's minster was founded by Duke Ludwig the Bearded in 1425 and built up over the next 100 years. Ostensibly a classic Gothic hall church, its most distinctive exterior feature is the pair of oblique square towers that flank the main entrance. Inside, subtle colours and a nave flooded with light intensify the magnificence of the soaring ceiling vaults, where strands of delicate stonework sensuously intertwine into geometric filigree patterns that somehow seem completely organic.

Also worth a closer look are the brilliant stained-glass windows and the high altar by Hans Mielich (1560).

KREUZTOR

The red-brick Gothic **Kreuztor** (1385), with a fairy-tale outline, was one of the four main gates into the city until the 19th century and is now the emblem of the city. This and the main gate within the Neues Schloss are all that remain of the city gates, but the former **fortifications**, now flats, still encircle the city.

OTHER ATTRACTIONS

Modern-art buffs will love the **Museum für Konkrete Kunst** (Museum of Concrete Art; ☎ 305 1871; Tränktorstrasse 6-8; adult/concession €2/1; ❧ 11am-6pm Tue-Sun), which has a beautiful sculpture garden and displays that have nothing to do with leftover building materials but feature modern abstracts and fascinating three-dimensional works.

The **Stadtmuseum** (City Museum; ☎ 305 1885; Auf der Schanz 45; adult/concession €2.50/1.25; ❧ 9am-5pm Tue-Fri, 10am-5pm Sat & Sun) houses oodles of ancient artefacts as well as the **Spielzeugmuseum** (Toy Museum), with playthings and mechanical toys from the 18th to 20th centuries.

Sleeping

DJH hostel (☎ 341 77; jugendherberge.ingolstadt@Web .de; Friedhofstrasse 41/2; dm €13.60; ❧ closed mid-Dec–Jan; wheelchair access) This beautiful hostel is in a renovated city fortress (1828), about 150m west of the Kreuztor. It's a well-equipped place near the swimming pool and skating rink.

Azur Campingplatz Auwaldsee (☎ 961 1616; ingolstadt@azur-camping.de; tent/person/car €2.10/6/4.60) This huge forested camp site at Auwaldsee, a lake about 3km southeast of the city centre, has a shop and restaurant and you can hire rowing and sailing boats. An infrequent

us No 60 goes this way; a taxi from the cen-
re will cost about €9.

Hotel Anker (☎ 300 05; hotel-anker@t-online.de;
ränktorstrasse 1; s/d €50/75) Bright, modern
ooms, reasonable rates and friendly service
nake this family-run hotel a good central
hoice. Rooms have direct-dial phone and
able TV, and the typical German restau-
ant (mains €4.10 to €12.60) attracts a loyal
ocal following.

Hotel Rappensberger (☎ 3140; www.rappensber
er.de; Harderstrasse 3; r €95-175; P) This small,
tylish hotel has well-designed modern
ooms in a very convenient location close
o the centre of town. It's attached to a
ively traditional pub that gets busy in the
evenings.

Kult Hotel (☎ 951 00; www.kult-hotel.de; Theodor-
Heussstrasse 25; s €120-180, d €135-195; P X ☐)
This stunning designer hotel is all clean
lines and attention to detail, with chrome
features and natural fabrics in muted colours adorning the wonderful rooms. Look
out for special offers that reduce the rack
rates considerably.

Eating
Local drinkers are especially proud that the
world's oldest health-and-safety regulation,
Germany's Beer Purity Law of 1516, was issued in Ingolstadt. To find out why, try a
mug of smooth Herrnbräu, Nordbräu or
Ingobräu.

Dollstrasse and Thieresenstrasse are
packed with places to eat and drink and
are a good bet on any night.

Zum Daniel (☎ 352 72; Roseneckstrasse 1; mains
€5.50-9; closed Monday) This is the oldest pub
in town and just drips with character and
tradition. The Daniel has a Frankenstein
exhibit upstairs and, according to some
locals, the town's best pork roast.

Café Reitschule (☎ 931 2870; Mauthstrasse 8;
dishes €5-13) Dominated by a huge bar and
some incongruous palm trees, this lively
café is popular with a young crowd and
serves up everything from soup, salads and
schnitzel to hearty rump steaks.

Restaurant Lemon (☎ 171 00; Tränktorstrasse 2;
mains €9.50-17.50) This stylish modern restaurant specialises in gourmet food inspired
by Mediterranean flair. Both meat lovers
and vegetarians will be duly impressed by
the colourful fresh ingredients and elegant
presentation.

Tapas Bar Bodega del Medico (☎ 379 5625;
Schnalzingergasse 15; tapas €1.80-2.50; 6pm-2am,
closed Sun) For tasty food and a wild night out
try this spirited Spanish bar. The excellent
tapas are cheap enough that you can try a
whole selection and still afford a cocktail.

The university **Mensa** (☎ 331 91; Konviktstrasse
1; mains €3.70-4; 11am-2.30pm) has an inexpensive salad buffet, plus hot and cold dishes.
It's one block from the Maria de Victoria
museum church.

Getting There & Around
Trains to Regensburg (€10.70, one hour)
and Munich (€12.40, one hour) leave
hourly. BEX BerlinLinien buses leave for
Berlin daily at 10.55am (one way/return
€42/78, five hours).

Single journeys on local buses cost €1.75.

EASTERN BAVARIA

Romantic ancient cities, vast tracts of forest
and lush, undulating farmland make up the
little-explored area of Eastern Bavaria. This
low-key destination is one of the region's
best-kept secrets and is dotted with picturesque villages full of the understated charm
of small-town Germany. The pace of life is
unhurried, the locals are genuinely glad to
see you and by German standards it's very
good value.

A prime destination is Regensburg, one
of Germany's loveliest and liveliest cities.
From here the Danube gently winds its
way to Passau (about 120km away) where
several long-distance cycling routes converge. East of here is the Bavarian Forest,
a region known for its rugged wilderness
and fabulous glass.

REGENSBURG
☎ 0941 / pop 128,000
A treasure-trove of architecture, Regensburg is one of the best-preserved medieval
towns in Europe with 1500 listed landmarks
in the centre alone. The city has relics from
all periods, yet integrates them into an unpretentious, very livable whole. A former
Roman settlement, Regensburg became the
capital of Bavaria's first duchy in the 11th
century, and was one of Germany's most
prosperous trading hubs during the Middle Ages. Little has changed in the Altstadt

since then and the patrician tower-houses are as arresting as the populace is friendly and unspoiled.

Oskar Schindler lived in Regensburg for years, and now one of his houses bears a plaque to his achievements commemorated in the Spielberg epic *Schindler's List*.

Orientation

The city is divided by the east-flowing Danube, which separates the Altstadt from the northern banks. Islands in the middle of the river, mainly Oberer and Unterer Wöhrd, are populated as well.

The Hauptbahnhof is at the southern end of the Altstadt. Maximilianstrasse leads north from there to Kornmarkt, the centre of the historic district. The university is at the southern end of the city.

Information
BOOKSHOPS
Hugendubel (☎ 585 320; Wahlenstrasse 17) Good collection of English-language and travel books.
Internationale Presse Stand (Hauptbahnhof) Stocks English books and magazines.

DISCOUNT CARDS
Verbundkarte (adult/concession/family €5.60/2.50/11) Good for entry to four of the city's main museums.

EMERGENCY
Ambulance (☎ 192 22)
Police (☎ 506 2121; Minoritenweg 1)

INTERNET ACCESS
C@fe Netzblick (☎ 599 9700; Am Römling 9; €3/5 per 30/60min; ☺ 7pm-1am Tue-Sun)

INTERNET RESOURCES
www.regensburg.de Regensburg's useful website.

LAUNDRY
Münz Wasch Center (Winklergasse 14; €3 per 6kg load; ☺ 6am-10pm Mon-Sat)
Schnell & Sauber (Hermann-Geib-Strasse 5; €3.50 per load; ☺ 7.30am-9pm)

LIBRARIES
Stadtbücherei (☎ 507 1477; Haidplatz 8, Thon Dittmer Palais)

MEDICAL SERVICES
Evangelisches Krankenhaus (☎ 504 00; Emmeramsplatz)

MONEY
More banks are located along Maximilianstrasse.
Postbank (next to the Hauptbahnhof)
Sparkasse City Center (Neupfarrplatz)

POST
Post office (Hauptbahnhof & Domplatz)

TOURIST INFORMATION
Tourist office (☎ 507 4410; Altes Rathaus; ☺ 9.15am-6pm Mon-Fri, 9.15am-4pm Sat, 9.30am-4pm Sun)

Sights
DOM ST PETER
Considered one of Bavaria's most important Gothic cathedrals, the **Dom St Peter** (☎ 597 1002; Domplatz; admission free, tours in German adult/concession €2.50/1.50; ☺ tours 10am, 11am & 2pm Mon-Sat, 1pm Sun May-Oct, 11am Mon-Sat & 1pm Sun Nov-Apr) dates from the late 13th century, but the distinctive filigree spires weren't added until the 19th. The extravagantly detailed western façade is festooned with sculptures, while inside the cathedral is dark and cavernous. Its most prized possessions are the kaleidoscopic 13th- and 14th-century **stained-glass windows** above the choir and in the south transept. Another highlight is a pair of charming **sculptures** (1280), attached to pillars just west of the altar. One shows the Angel of the Annunciation, his smiling mug beaming at the Virgin on the opposite pillar as he delivers the news that she's pregnant. The Regensburger Domspatzen boys' choir sings at the 9am Sunday service.

The **Domschatzmuseum** (Cathedral Treasury; ☎ 576 45; adult/concession €1.50/0.80; ☺ 10am-5pm Tue-Sat, noon-5pm Sun Apr-Nov) has the usual assortment of vestments, monstrances, tapestries and other church treasures. Opening hours are shorter in winter.

SCHLOSS THURN UND TAXIS & MUSEUMS
In the 15th century, Franz von Taxis (1459–1517) established the European postal system; the family retained a monopoly in Bavaria until the dissolution of the Holy Roman Empire some 250 years later. To compensate for the loss, the family was given a new palace, the former Benedictine monastery in Regensburg.

The **Schloss Thurn und Taxis** (☎ 504 8133; Emmeramsplatz 6; combined ticket adult/concession €10/8.50; ☺ 11am-5pm Mon-Fri, 10am-5pm Sat & Sun) was soon

odated to become one of the largest aristocratic homes in Europe and featured such luxuries as flush toilets and electricity. You can see the lavish state rooms on a tour of the **palace** (adult/concession €8/7; cloister only €4/3.50) which also includes a look at the cloister of St Emmeram (see Churches for details, p412), the palace chapel. Also here is the

Marstallmuseum (tours only, adult/concession €4.50/4), which includes the opulent festival rooms as well as historic carriages and sleighs. The fascinating **Thurn und Taxis-Museum** (adult/concession €4/3.50) displays a collection of jewellery, porcelain, glass and furniture that, for many years, belonged to the wealthiest family in Germany.

REGENSBURG

Map scale: 0 — 200 m / 0 — 0.1 miles

INFORMATION	
C@fe Netzblick	1 B2
Evangelisches Krankenhaus	2 B4
Hugendubel	3 C3
Internationale Presse	4 D5
Münz Wasch Center	5 A2
Sparkasse City Center	6 C3
St Ulrich Kirche	7 D3
Stadtbücherei	(see 47)
Tourist Office	8 B2

SIGHTS & ACTIVITIES	(pp410-12)
Alte Kapelle	9 D3
Altes Rathaus	10 C2
Basilika St Emmeram	11 B4
Brückturm-Museum	12 C2
Diözesanmuseum	(see 7)
Document Neupfarrplatz	13 C3
Dom St Peter	14 C3
Domschatzmuseum	(see 14)
Historisches Museum	15 D3

Kepler-Gedächtnishaus	16 B2
Marstallmuseum	(see 19)
Oskar Schindler Haus	17 D2
Porta Praetoria	18 D2
Reichstagsmuseum	(see 8)
Schloss Thurn und Taxis	19 B4
Schottenkirche St Jakob	20 A3
Steinerne Brücke	21 C2
Thurn and Taxis-Museum	(see 19)
Torture Chambers	(see 10)
Uhrenmuseum	22 B2

SLEEPING	(pp413-14)
Bischofshof am Dom	23 C2
Hotel Am Peterstor	24 C4
Hotel D'Orphée	25 C2
Hotel Roter Hahn	26 B3
Kasierhof am Dom	27 C2
Künstlerhaus	28 D3

EATING	(p414)
Asia Paradise	29 C3
Café Orphée	30 C3
Dampfnudel Uli	31 C2
Dicker Mann	32 B3
Hinterhaus	33 B3
Historische Wurstküche	34 C2
Leerer Beutel	35 D3
Raan Thai Imbiss	36 C2
Rive Droite	37 B2
Spaghetteria	38 B2
Sushihaus	39 A2
Würstl Toni	40 D3

DRINKING	(pp414-15)
Augustiner	41 C3
Hemingway's	42 C3
Neue Film Bühne	43 A3
Wunderbar	44 B2

ENTERTAINMENT	(p415)
Film Galerie	(see 35)
Garbo-Filmtheater	45 B2
Jazzclub im Leeren Beutel	(see 35)
Statt Theater	46 A2
Theater am Haidplatz	47 B2
Theater Regensburg	48 A3
Theaterkasse am Bismarckplatz	(see 48)
Thon Dittmer Palais	(see 47)
Velodrom	49 A2

TRANSPORT	(p415)
ADAC	50 D4
Albertstrasse Bus Transfer Point	51 D5
Boat Cruises	52 C2
Mitfahrzentrale	53 C2

BAVARIA

JEWISH MEMORIALS

Regensburg had a thriving medieval Jewish community centred around Neupfarrplatz, but when the city fell on hard economic times in the early 16th century the townspeople expelled all Jews and burned their quarter to the ground.

The subterranean **Document Neupfarrplatz** (☎ 507 1452; tours adult/concession €2.50/1.25; ☼ Thu-Sat 2.30pm) is a multimedia exhibition beginning in antiquity and explaining events on the square right up until the formation of the Nazi resistance movement in 1942–43. Remains and reconstructed buildings include a Roman legionary fortress, Jewish houses and both Gothic and Romanesque synagogues.

There's a memorial plaque to Regensburg's Jews in the pavement west of the Neupfarrkirche as well as a memorial to the concentration-camp victims on the north side of the Steinerne Brücke.

ALTES RATHAUS & REICHSTAGSMUSEUM

The seat of the Reichstag for almost 150 years, the **Altes Rathaus** is now home to Regensburg's three mayors and the **Reichstagsmuseum** (Imperial Diet Museum; ☎ 507 4411; Altes Rathaus; adult/concession €2.80/1.40; ☼ tours 9.30am, 11.30am, 2-4pm Mon-Sat, 10am-noon Sun; tours in English 3.15pm Mon-Sat). You can see the Imperial Chambers and the **original torture chambers** in the basement. Walk into the old holding cell and look down to the dungeon before entering the interrogation room, which bristles with tools such as the rack, the Spanish Donkey (a tall wooden wedge on which naked men were made to sit) and spiked chairs.

STEINERNE BRÜCKE

An incredible feat of engineering for its day, Regensburg's **Steinerne Brücke** (Stone Bridge) was at one time the only fortified crossing of the Danube. The 850-year-old bridge used to support vehicular traffic, but private vehicles were banned in a bid to conserve it.

Ensconced in the southern tower of the Steinerne Brücke is the **Brückturm-Museum** (☎ 567 6015; Weisse-Lamm-Gasse 1; adult/concession €2/1.50; ☼ 10am-5pm Apr-Oct), featuring a small historical exhibit about the bridge. Most people come for the bird's-eye view of the town.

CHURCHES

The humble exterior of the graceful **Alte Kapelle** (Alter Kornmarkt 8) belies the stunning interior with its rich and harmonious rococo decorations. The core of the church, however, is Romanesque, while the Gothic vaulted ceilings were added in the Middle Ages. It's only open during services but you can always take a peek through the wrought-iron gate.

Near the Schloss is a masterpiece by the Asam brothers, the **Basilika St Emmeram** (☎ 510 30; Emmeramsplatz 3; ☼ closed Fri & Sun morning). It is an elaborate work supporting two giant ceiling frescoes and, sheltered in its crypt, the remains of Sts Emmeram, Wolfgang and Ramwold.

The 12th-century main portal of the **Schottenkirche St Jakob** (Jakobstrasse 3) is considered one of the major examples of Romanesque architecture in Germany. It's festooned with numerous reliefs and sculptures, the meaning of some of which continues to baffle even the experts.

OTHER SIGHTS

The most tangible reminder of the ancient Castra Regina (Roman fortress), the origin of the name 'Regensburg', is the remaining **Roman wall**, which follows Unter den Schwibbögen onto Dr-Martin-Luther-Strasse. The seriously impressive **Porta Praetoria** arch dates from AD 179.

The **Historisches Museum** (☎ 507 2448; Dachauplatz 2-4; adult/concession €2.20/1.10; ☼ 10am-4pm Tue-Sun) houses exhibits ranging from the Stone Age to the Middle Ages, a large collection of Bavarian folklore, and 14th- and 15th-century artworks.

For religious art the **Diözesanmuseum** (☎ 516 68; Domplatz 2; adult/concession €1.50/0.80, €3.50 including cathedral treasury; ☼ 10am-5pm Tue-Sun Apr-Oct) is the place to go. It's housed in the painted medieval St Ulrich Kirche.

Other interesting visits include the house of astronomer and mathematician Johannes Kepler, now the **Kepler-Gedächtnishaus** (Kepler Memorial House; ☎ 507 3442; Keplerstrasse 5; tours adult/concession €2.20/1.10; ☼ tours 10am, 11am, 2pm, 3pm Tue-Sun Apr-Oct, no tours Sun afternoon Nov-Mar) and the small **Uhrenmuseum** (☎ 502 7970; Ludwigstrasse 1; adult/concession €5/4; ☼ 2-5pm, closed Tue) with its collection of valuable and notable watches.

Tours

Guided English-language walking tours (adult/children €6/3, 1½ hours) start at the tourist office at 1.30pm Wednesday and saturday from May to September. German-language tours depart year round at 2.45pm Monday to Saturday and at 10.45am and 2pm on Sunday.

The **Schifffahrtsunternehmen Klinger** (☎ 521 34; www.schifffahrtklinger.de; €6.50; ⊙ tours hourly 10am-4pm, late-Mar–Oct) operates 50-minute Danube cruises from the landing just east of the Steinerne Brücke.

Festivals & Events

For three days in late June the city celebrates the **Regensburger Bürgfest**, when the streets of the Altstadt are overrun with thousands of revellers gathered for the daily concerts, special events, music and food stalls that fill the streets.

In winter the biggest event is the **Weihnachtsmarkt** (admission adult/child €3/1), which runs from late November until Christmas at the Schloss Thurn und Taxis.

Sleeping

Regensburg is blessed with a range of good and interesting hotels. The tourist office also has a list of **private rooms** (from €20 per person).

BUDGET

DJH hostel (☎ 574 02; jhregensburg@djh-bayern.de; Wöhrdstrasse 60; dm €15.80, juniors only) Regensburg's modernised hostel is in a beautiful old building on Unterer Wöhrd island about a 10-minute walk north of the Altstadt. Take bus No 3 from Albertstrasse to Eisstadion.

Gasthof Spitalgarten (☎ 847 74; www.spitalgarten .de; St-Katharinen-Platz 1; s/d €23/46; P) North of the Steinerne Brücke in a 13th-century hospice, this brewery-inn provides basic but comfortable rooms at excellent prices. It's attached to a beautiful beer garden overlooking the Danube.

Hotel Am Peterstor (☎ 545 45; fax 545 42; Fröhliche-Türken-Strasse 12; s/d €40/50; P) A convenient location, bright modern rooms and affordable rates make this hotel a good choice. It's a no-frills place with simple taste but the rooms are more than adequate.

Campers should head for **Azur-Campingplatz** (☎ 270 025; info@azur-camping.de; Weinweg 40; person/car/tent €4.50-6/2.80/2.10) about 2km from the Altstadt on the southern bank of the Danube. Bus No 6 from the Hauptbahnhof goes right to the entrance.

MID-RANGE

Künstlerhaus (☎ 571 34; kuenstlerhaus-regensburg@ t-online.de; Alter Kornmarkt 3; s €60-75, d €75-105) Let your fantasies go wild in any of the five themed rooms in what is the Altstadt's narrowest house. Choices include the Space Room (calling all Trekkies), the Asian-style Wind & Water Room and the mysterious Oriental Room.

Hotel Roter Hahn (☎ 595 090; www.roter-hahn .com; Rote-Hahnen-Gasse 10; s €75-105, d €87-130; P) Old on the outside but modern within, this swish family-run hotel is a winner for its quirky rooms – some with trompe l'oeil murals, others very modern – and good restaurant.

Kaiserhof am Dom (☎ 585 350; www.kaiserhof-am -dom.de; Krangasse 10-12; s €55-70, d €89-118; ▣) This historic city mansion has comfortable modern rooms with hidden little extras like underfloor heating. Some rooms also have beautiful views of the cathedral. Breakfast is served in a 14th-century chapel to the accompaniment of classical music.

TOP END

Bischofshof am Dom (☎ 584 60; www.hotel-bischof shof.de; Krauterermarkt 3; s €67-97, d €149-175; P; wheelchair access) The warrenlike residence of the former bishops is now a romantic upmarket hotel with stylish rooms set

---

SOMETHING SPECIAL

Hotel D'Orphée (☎ 596 020; www.hotel -orphee.de; Wahlenstrasse 1; s €69-98, d €79-115) Behind a humble door right in the heart of the city lies a world of genuine charm, unexpected extras and real attention to detail. Hotel D'Orphée just oozes character and is a pleasure to recommend. The striped floors, wrought-iron beds, original sinks, and common rooms with soft cushions and well-read books give the whole place the feel of a home lovingly attended rather than a hotel. Each room is unique: No 7 is stunningly romantic, while No 5 has a bathroom accessed through a hidden door. For single travellers on a budget there's one attic room (€31) that allows a taste of luxury at an affordable rate. A mouth-watering breakfast is served around the corner at the Café Orphée (see Eating, p414).

BAVARIA

around a beautiful leafy courtyard. If you can't afford to stay, pop in to the sprawling beer garden, a popular spot on summer evenings.

Eating

Regensburg specialities include Regensburger *Bratwurstl* and *Händlmaier's Süsser Hausmachersenf* (a distinctive sweet mustard) – a delicious combination best washed down with a locally made Kneitinger Pils.

QUICK EATS

There is a daily fresh produce market, **Viktualienmarkt**, at Neupfarrplatz.

Historische Wurstküche (Thundorfer Strasse 3; dishes €2.70-7.60; wheelchair access) Tourists and locals alike love the little sausages grilled over beechwood and served with *Kraut* (cabbage) and mustard. On request, they'll also make a *Bratwurstsemmel* – sausage and *Kraut* in a bun – for €1.80. Inside look out for the flood levels marked on the walls. If the Wurstküche is closed, your next best bet is **Würstl Toni** (Am Kornmarkt), a simple stand with cult status among night owls.

For another Regensburg speciality try the steamed doughnuts with custard (€4) at quirky **Dampfnudel Uli** (☎ 532 97; Watmarkt 4; dishes under €5; ☾ closed Sun & Mon). **Raan Thai Imbiss** (Untere Bachgasse 1; meals under €5) or **Asia Paradise** (Domplatz 5; dishes €3-8) both serve up a tasty collection of stir-fries, curries and spring rolls.

RESTAURANTS

Rosenpalais (☎ 599 7579; Minoritenweg 20; bistro mains €11-18, restaurant mains €22.50-29; ☾ closed Sun) This two-tone establishment caters for a well-heeled clientele at the graceful silver-service restaurant upstairs, and for gourmets on a more restrictive budget downstairs. Either way the food is superb. For the best possible deal try the weekday two-course lunch special (€9.50).

Spaghetteria (☎ 0130-785 700; Am Römling 12; dishes €5.50-8.50) For heavenly pastas and a spirited crowd, step into this former 17th-century chapel. You can pick fresh noodles, sauces and side dishes from the buffet and get out the door, with a glass of house wine, for under €11.

Café Orphée (☎ 529 77; Untere Bachgasse 8; mains €10.50-16.50) This delightful brasserie decked out in red velvet, dark wood and plenty of

mirrors is straight off a Parisian street. It' perfect for a leisurely coffee, a light lunch o some delectable French cuisine.

Dicker Mann (☎ 573 70; Krebsgasse 6; mains €8.50 13) One of the oldest restaurants in town this classically stylish place has dependabl Bavarian food, swift service and a beautifu little beer garden. The schnitzel special (€5 Tuesday and Wednesday) is a great deal.

Sushihaus (☎ 567 6480; Wollwirkergasse 2; sush €7.60-12.60) Japanese food fans should head straight for this delightful little place tucked into a side street. The simple design and minimalist approach concentrate you mind on the excellent sushi and impressive lunch specials (€8.90).

Leerer Beutel (☎ 589 97; Bertoldstrasse 9; mains €8-16) This stylish restaurant in the cultural centre serves creative light cuisine, including lots of salads. Black-and-white photographs of jazz greats form the backdrop. For the best deal try the two-course weekday lunch menu (€5.80).

Other recommendations include:

Rive Droite (☎ 520 21; Drei-Mohren Gasse 3-5; mains €5.40-8) Trendy but unpretentious restaurant good for a quick baguette or light pastas.

Hinterhaus (☎ 599 8134; Rote-Hahnen-Gasse 2; mains €4-9) Atmospheric place with good choice of vegetarian dishes and jazzy beats.

Drinking
BEER GARDENS

Augustiner (☎ 584 0455; Neufarrplatz 15; meals €3.90-17.50) This popular beer garden and restaurant is ideally located in the heart of the city. The sprawling garden and cavernous interior swell with happy locals enjoying the good food and local brews.

Alte Linde (☎ 880 80; Müllerstrasse 1; meals €5.50-11) A lovely place at any time of year but especially worth a visit on summer evenings, the Alte Linde is a large and leafy beer garden with a panoramic view of the Altstadt.

PUBS & BARS

Hemingway's (☎ 561 506; Obere Bachgasse 5) Black wood, big mirrors and lots of photos of Papa himself add to the cool atmosphere of this Art Deco–style bar. It fills up with the trendy set in the late evening.

Wunderbar (☎ 531 30; Keplerstrasse 11; cocktails €7-10; ☾ 10pm-3am Sun-Thu) This hip hang-out, with a diverse taste in music, is one of the only late-night venues in town. Crowds

ome for the killer cocktails, especially the
hampagne specials.

Neue Film Bühne (☎ 570 37; Bismarckplatz 9)
Theatrical decor and the odd disco ball
characterise this funky café-bar frequented
by an eclectic crowd of students, yuppies and
young families. In summer, the terrace overlooking Bismarckplatz is great for lounging.

Entertainment

Ask for a free copy of *Logo*, the local listings
magazine, or the free city-published *Regensburger Kulturkalendar* events guide at the
tourist office; both are in German only. **RESI**
Regensburger Schwulen-und-Lesben-Initiative; ☎ 514 41;
Blaue-Lilien-Gasse 1) is a gay and lesbian contact
group.

CINEMAS
Film Galerie (☎ 560 901; Bertoldstrasse 9) Part of
the Leerer Beutel cultural centre, this cinema concentrates on arthouse films, often
shown in the original language, including English. Look for the acronym OmU
(Original mit Untertiteln).

Garbo-Filmtheater (☎ 575 86; Weissgerbergraben)
This theatre shows classic Hollywood and
modern filmic fare in English.

JAZZ
Jazzclub im Leeren Beutel (☎ 563 375; Bertoldstrasse
9) This moody jazz club in the arts centre
has concerts two to three times weekly and
attracts a mixed crowd. The centre also has
an art gallery, cinema and stylish restaurant
(see Eating, p414).

THEATRE
Regensburg's municipal theatre operates
three venues. Tickets for all are available
at the tourist office or at **Theaterkasse am
Bismarckplatz** (☎ 507 2424; kartenservice@theater
regensburg.de).

The main theatre is the newly renovated
Theater Regensburg (Bismarckplatz), which runs
a packed and varied programme. **Theater am
Haidplatz** (Haidplatz 8) runs its own programme
and also has open-air performances in summer in the courtyard of the **Thon Dittmer Palais** (Haidplatz 8). The third venue is the **Velodrom**
(☎ 507 2424; Arnulfsplatz 4b), a converted bicycle
rink now home to opera, theatre, musicals
and ballet.

The **Statt Theater** (☎ 533 02; Winklergasse 16;
✆ closed Mon-Tue & July) is a privately owned

venue that stages alternative dramas, plays
and cabaret.

Getting There & Away
Mainline trains from Frankfurt go through
Regensburg on their way to Passau and Vienna. Several Munich-Leipzig and Munich-
Dresden services also pass through. Sample
ticket prices are Frankfurt (€45.80, 3¼
hours), Munich (€19.20, 1½ hours), Nuremberg (€14, 1½ hours) and Passau (€16.60,
one hour).

The A3 autobahn runs northwest to Nuremberg and southeast to Passau, while the
A9 runs south to Munich.

For general information, head to **ADAC**
(☎ 551 665; Luitpoldstrasse 2). For a lift, call the city
Mitfahrzentrale (☎ 194 40; Weisse Hahnengasse 1).

Regensburg is a key destination on the
Danube Bike Trail (see Central Black Forest, p463, for details); all approaches to the
city are well signposted along bike paths.
There are bike lockers at the Hauptbahnhof
on platform 1 (€0.50 per day).

Getting Around
BICYCLE
Rent-a-Bike (☎ 599 8193; Hauptbahnhof; adult/child
bikes €9/6; ✆ 9am-2pm & 3-7pm Mon-Sat) also
has bike storage, and staff can help plan
bike trips along the Danube and in other
regions.

BUS
The main point for city bus transfers is
one block north of the Hauptbahnhof, on
Albertstrasse. Other points include Arnulfsplatz, Domplatz and Neupfarrplatz. Bus
tickets cost €1.50/2.10 for short/long journeys in the centre; strip tickets cost €5.10
for five rides (two strips per ride in town).
An all-day ticket (€3.30 at the tourist office
or €4.40 on the bus) is a better deal. On
weekdays, the Altstadtbus runs between
the Hauptbahnhof and the Altstadt every
six minutes for just €0.50.

CAR & MOTORCYCLE
The Steinerne Brücke and much of the
Altstadt is closed to private vehicles. Car
parks in the centre charge from €1.20 per
hour and are well signposted.

TAXI
For a taxi, call ☎ 194 10 or ☎ 520 52.

AROUND REGENSBURG
Klosterchenke Weltenburg
When you're this close to the world's oldest monastic brewery, there's just no excuse to miss out. **Klosterschenke Weltenburg** (☎ 09441-3682; www.klosterschenke-weltenburg.de; Asamstrasse 32; ☉ 8am-7pm mid-Mar–mid-Nov, closed Mon-Tue Mar & Nov) has been brewing its delicious dark beer since 1050. Now a state-of-the-art brewery, it is a favourite excursion spot for locals and tourists, and the beautiful beer garden can get uncomfortably crowded on warm weekends and around holidays.

Not everyone comes for the brew alone, though, for the complex is also home to the most magnificent church, **Klosterkirche Sts Georg und Martin**, designed by Cosmas Damian and Egid Quirin Asam. Its most eye-popping feature is the high altar, which shows St George triumphant on horseback, with the dead dragon and rescued princess at his feet. Also worth noting is the oval ceiling fresco, with a stucco sculpture of CD Asam leaning over the railing.

The nicest approach to Weltenburg is by boat from Kelheim via the **Danube Gorge**, a particularly dramatic stretch of the river as it carves through craggy cliffs and past bizarre rock formations. From mid-March to October, several boat operators offer trips up the gorge for €4.50/7 one way/return; bicycles are an extra €1.50/3.

Walhalla
Modelled on the Parthenon in Athens, **Walhalla** (adult/children €4.50/3; ☉ 9am-6pm Apr-Sep, 10am-noon & 1-4pm Oct-Mar) is a breathtaking Ludwig I monument. Over 350 marble steps lead up from the banks of the Danube to this stunning marble hall dedicated to great and famous Germans. Inside you'll find busts of 125 of the country's heroes.

To get there take the Danube Valley country road (unnumbered) 10km east from Regensburg to the village of Donaustauf, then follow the signs. Alternatively, you can take a boat cruise with **Schifffahrtsunternehmen Klinger** (☎ 521 04; €6.50/9.50 one way/return; ☉ 10.30am & 2pm Apr–mid-Oct; 2hr), which includes a one-hour stop at Walhalla.

Befreiungshalle
Perching above Kelheim and the Danube is this pale yellow cylinder known as the **Befreiungshalle** (Hall of Liberation; ☎ 09441-15 84; Befreiungshallestrasse 3; adult/concession €3/2; ☉ 9am-6pm; 9am-4pm Oct-Mar). Built in 1863, it's monumental piece of architecture commissioned by King Ludwig I to commemorate the victorious battles against Napoleon between 1813 and 1815. Inside it's a veritable shrine lorded over by a ring of larger-than-life winged white marble sculptures of the Roman goddess Victoria.

STRAUBING
☎ 09421 / pop 44,000
Straubing, some 30km southeast of Regensburg, is an attractive town that enjoyed a brief heyday as part of an unusual alliance that formed the Duchy of Straubing-Holland. The historical centre is chock-a-block with attractive buildings and well worth a visit. The town is, however, most famous for the 10-day **Gäubodenfest**, one of Bavaria's biggest collective drink-ups. Begun in 1812 as a social gathering for grain farmers, the fair lubricates more than a million visitors in August when the town centre becomes an enormous beer garden with 23,000 seats.

Orientation & Information
The historical centre, compact and easily walkable, is sandwiched between the Danube to the north and the Hauptbahnhof to the south. The central square is shaped more like a street and consists of Theresienplatz and Ludwigsplatz. The **tourist office** (☎ 944 307; tourismus@straubing.de; Theresienplatz 20; ☉ 9am-5pm Mon-Fri, 9am-noon Sat) makes free room referrals.

Sights & Activities
Lined with pastel-coloured houses from a variety of periods, the pedestrianised central area is lorded over by the **Stadtturm** (1316), a proud, Gothic watch tower that separates Theresienplatz from Ludwigsplatz and doubles as the town's symbol.

Next to the tower is the **Rathaus**, which originally consisted of two 14th-century merchants' homes but was repackaged in neo-Gothic style in the 19th century. Just east of the tower is the gleaming golden **Dreifaltigkeitssäule** (Trinity Column), erected in 1709 as a nod to Catholic upheavals during the Spanish War of Succession.

Straubing has about half a dozen historic churches. Among the most impressive is

St Jakobskirche (Pfarrplatz) a few steps north of the tourist office. This late Gothic hall church has preserved its original stained-glass windows but received a partial baroque makeover in the 18th century, courtesy of the Asam brothers. The two also designed the exuberant interior of the **Ursulinenkirche** on Burggasse, their final collaboration. Its ceiling fresco depicts the martyrdom of St Ursula surrounded by allegorical representations of the four known continents. Also worth a look is the nearby baroque **Karmelitenkirche** on Hofstatt.

North of here is the former ducal residence **Herzogsschloss** (Schlossplatz), which overlooks the river. It's an austere 14th-century building that now serves as a government tax office and is home to the **Sammlung Ridolf Kriss** (☎ 211 14; admission €2.50; ⊙ 10am-4pm Tue-Sun Apr-Dec), which houses a collection of religious folk art.

One of Germany's most important collections of Roman treasures is in the small but exquisite **Gäubodenmuseum** (☎ 974 10; Frauenhoferstrasse 23; adult/concession €2.50/1.50; ⊙ 10am-4pm Tue-Sun). Displays include imposing armour and masks for both soldiers and horses.

For some liquid refreshment you might want to try **AQUA-therm** (☎ 864 444; Wittelsbacherhöhe 50-52; adult/concession €3/1.80; ⊙ usually 9am-9pm), Straubing's enormous swimming pool complex with indoor and outdoor pools and several massage parlours. Take bus No 2 from Ludwigsplatz.

Getting There & Away
Straubing is on a regional train line from Regensburg (€6.60, 30 minutes) and Passau (€10.70, one hour). Trains to/from Munich (€19, two hours) require a change, usually in Plattling. The town is well placed at the junction of the B8 and B20 highways, just south of the Nuremberg-Passau autobahn A3.

PASSAU
☎ 0851 / pop 51,000
Ideally located at the confluence of the Danube, Inn and Ilz Rivers, Passau has long been an important trading point. Originally a Roman camp, the city later evolved into the Holy Roman Empire's largest bishopric. The beautiful historical centre consists of winding medieval lanes, tunnels and archways, fantastic baroque architecture and the

lovely monastic district, the Dreiflüsseeck, where the rivers meet.

Passau is also the hub of long-distance cycling routes, eight of which converge here, and a good jumping off point for explorations into upper Austria.

Orientation
The Altstadt is a narrow peninsula with the confluence of the three rivers at its eastern point. The little Ilz approaches from the north, the Danube from the west and the Inn from the south. The Hauptbahnhof is about a 10-minute walk west of the heart of the Altstadt. The Veste Oberhaus and the hostel are on the north side of the Danube.

Information
Commerzbank (Ludwigstrasse 13)
CompUse (Neuburger Strasse 19; €3 per hr; ⊙ 1-10pm) Internet access.
Post office (Bahnhofstrasse) Just east of the Hauptbahnhof.
Rent-Wash (Neuburger Strasse 19; €3.50 per load) Laundry.
Sparkasse (Residenzplatz 9) Bank.
Tourist office Altstadt (☎ 955 980; Rathausplatz 3; ⊙ 8.30am-6pm Mon-Fri, 9.30am-3pm Sat & Sun, closed lunchtime & weekends mid-Oct–Easter) Hauptbahnhof (☎ 955 980; Bahnhofstrasse 36; ⊙ 9am-5pm Mon-Thu, 9am-4pm Fri year-round, 9am-1pm Sat & Sun Easter–mid-October)
www.passau.de The town's informative website.

Sights
VESTE OBERHAUS
This 13th-century fortress, built by prince-bishops for defence purposes (and later taken over by Napoleonic troops), towers over the city with patriarchal pomp. Views are superb, either from the castle tower (€1) or from the **Battalion Linde**, a lookout that gives the only bird's-eye view of the confluence of all three rivers.

Inside the bastion is the **Oberhausmuseum** (☎ 493 350; Oberhaus 125; adult/concession usually €4/2.50; ⊙ 9am-5pm Mon-Fri, 10am-6pm Sat & Sun, closed Jan–late-Mar). It presents local history as well as special exhibits of international importance. The admission price varies depending on the exhibition.

DOM ST STEPHAN
The characteristic green onion domes of Passau's cathedral float serenely above the

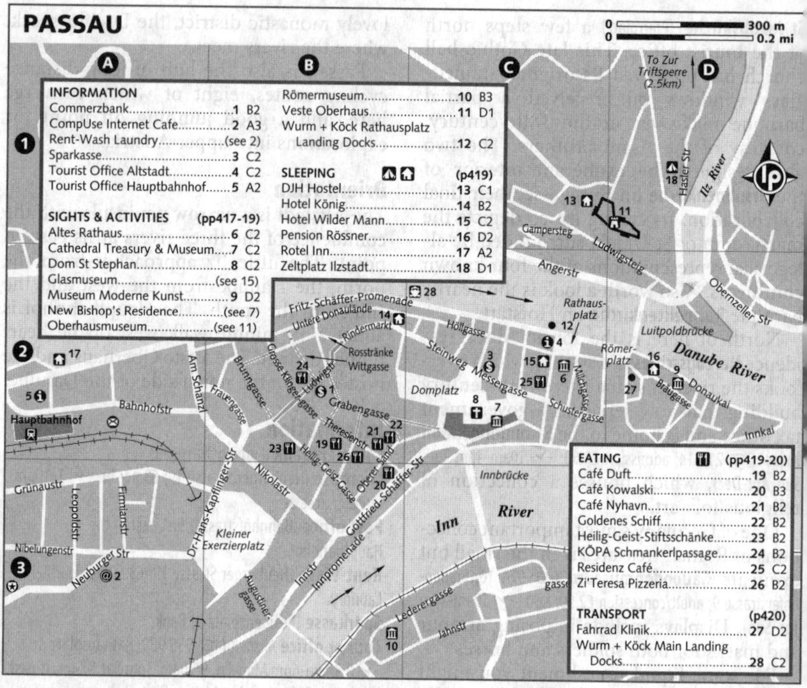
PASSAU
0 300 m
0 0.2 mi
A
B
C
D
1
2
3
To Zur Triftsperre (2.5km)
INFORMATION
Commerzbank....1 B2
CompUse Internet Cafe....2 A3
Rent-Wash Laundry....(see 2)
Sparkasse....3 C2
Tourist Office Altstadt....4 C2
Tourist Office Hauptbahnhof....5 A2
SIGHTS & ACTIVITIES (pp417-19)
Altes Rathaus....6 C2
Cathedral Treasury & Museum....7 C2
Dom St Stephan....8 C2
Glasmuseum....(see 15)
Museum Moderne Kunst....9 D2
New Bishop's Residence....(see 7)
Oberhausmuseum....(see 11)
Römermuseum....10 B3
Veste Oberhaus....11 D1
Wurm + Köck Rathausplatz Landing Docks....12 C2
SLEEPING (p419)
DJH Hostel....13 C1
Hotel König....14 B2
Hotel Wilder Mann....15 C2
Pension Rössner....16 D2
Rotel Inn....17 A2
Zeltplatz Ilzstadt....18 D1
EATING (pp419-20)
Café Duft....19 B2
Café Kowalski....20 B3
Café Nyhavn....21 B2
Goldenes Schiff....22 B2
Heilig-Geist-Stiftsschänke....23 B2
KÖPA Schmankerlpassage....24 B2
Residenz Café....25 C2
Zi'Teresa Pizzeria....26 B2
TRANSPORT (p420)
Fahrrad Klinik....27 D2
Wurm + Köck Main Landing Docks....28 C2
Danube River
Inn River
Ilz River
Hauptbahnhof
Bahnhofstr
Grünaustr
Leopoldstr
Firmianstr
Nibelungenstr
Neuburger Str
Am Schanzl
Dr-Hans-Kapfinger-Str
Kleiner Exerzierplatz
Fritz-Schäffer-Promenade
Untere Donaulände
Rindermarkt
Rosstränke
Wittgasse
Höllgasse
Steinweg
Messergasse
Domplatz
Schustergasse
Milchgasse
Rathausplatz
Römerplatz
Bräugasse
Donaukai
Innkai
Luitpoldbrücke
Obernzeller Str
Angerstr
Ludwigsteig
Gampersteg
Hasler Str
Brunngasse
Frauengasse
Grosse Klingergasse
Ludwigstr
Grabengasse
Theresienstr
Heilig-Geist-Gasse
Oberer Sand
Nikolastr
Gottfried-Schäffer-Str
Innbrücke
Innpromenade
Innstr
Augustinergasse
Lederergasse
Jahnstr

town silhouette. The **Dom** has 14th-century Gothic origins, but got its current baroque look after a devastating fire in 1662. The interior was designed by a collaboration of Italian artists, notably architect Carlo Lurago and stucco master Giovanni Carlone. The frescoes show fascinating scenes of heaven, but the true masterpiece is the church organ; it's the world's largest and has 17,774 pipes. Acoustically stunning organ recitals are held on weekdays at noon, and on Thursday at 7.30pm from May to October (€3/1 lunchtime; €5/3 evening).

From the right (south) aisle, a spiralling staircase leads to the New Bishop's Residence, which contains the **Cathedral Treasury & Museum** (adult/concession €1.50/0.50; 🕑 10am-4pm Mon-Sat May-Oct). It showcases a wealth of ecclesiastical finery in a setting that includes a lovely rococo staircase.

ALTES RATHAUS

The carillon in the colourful Rathaus (1399; tower 1891) chimes several times daily (hours are listed on the wall, which also shows historical flood levels). Inside, the **Grosser Rathaus Saal** (Great Assembly Room; adult/concession €1.50/1; 🕑 10am-4pm Apr-Oct) has wonderful murals by local artist and crackpot Ferdinand Wagner. If it's not used for a wedding, also sneak into the adjacent **Small Assembly Room** for a peek at the ceiling fresco showing buxom beauties and a fierce-looking man as allegories of the three rivers.

Wagner, who used to live in the huge building on the north bank of the Danube, just to the right of where the Luitpoldbrücke suspension bridge is today, threatened to move out of town if the bridge was built. It was, he did, and after viewing the paintings, you wonder whether the city made the right choice.

GLASMUSEUM

A splendid collection of over 30,000 examples of Bohemian glasswork and crystal from over 250 years is on view at the **Glasmuseum** (Passau Museum of Glass; ☎ 350 71; Hotel Wilder Mann, Am Rathausplatz; adult/concession €5/3; 🕑 1-5pm). Even if you charge through the place, you'll need an hour to view the 36 rooms filled with baroque, classical, Art Nouveau and Art Deco pieces.

OTHER MUSEUMS

The **Museum Moderne Kunst** (Modern Art Museum; ☎ 383 8790; Bräugasse 17; normal admission €5/3; ⊗ 10am-6pm Tue-Sun) shows an ambitious cycle of temporary exhibits, often of international merit, in a fascinating jumble of buildings. Across the Fünferlsteg Inn footbridge, in the Kastell Boiotro is the **Römermuseum** (☎ 347 69; Kastell Boiotro; adult/concession €2/1; ⊗ 10am-noon & 2-4pm Tue-Sun Mar-May & Sep-Nov, 10am-noon, 1-4pm Jun-Aug) depicts Passau's original settlement.

Activities

From March to November, **Wurm + Köck** (☎ 929 292; www.donauschiffahrt.de; Höllgasse 26; adult/child €6.50/3.50, 45 min; €9.50/6.50, 2hr) runs cruises to the confluence of the three rivers from the docks near Rathausplatz.

It's a pleasant, easy hike across the isthmus and through the tunnel to **Zur Triftsperre** (☎ 511 62; Triftparre Strasse 15) a wonderful beer garden and restaurant along a peaceful section of the Ilz. Ask at the tourist office for hiking maps.

Sleeping

DJH hostel (☎ 493 780; jhpassau@djh-bayern.de; Veste Oberhaus 125; dm €15.70) The beautifully renovated hostel is right in the fortress. To get there, see Getting Around, p420.

Zeltplatz Ilzstadt (☎ 414 57; Halser Strasse 34; adult/child €5/4) This camp site is for tents only and located beyond the Ilz River bridge. Take bus No 1, 2, 3 or 4 to Exerzierplatz-Ilzbrücke from the Hauptbahnhof.

Rotel Inn (☎ 951 60; www.rotel-inn.de; Donaulände am Hauptbahnhof; s/d €20/40; ⊗ May-Sep; Ⓟ) This quirky place caters primarily to bicycle tourists but anyone is welcome. Built in the profile of a reclining man, it is incredibly cheap, has tiny yet efficient rooms and pop art decoration.

Pension Rössner (☎ 931350; www.pension-roessner .de; Bräugasse 19; s €35, d €45-60; Ⓟ) You'll get more for your money at this immaculate pension in a restored mansion on the eastern tip of the Altstadt. Rooms have private bathroom and many also have fortress views.

Hotel König (☎ 3850; www.hotel-koenig.de; Untere Donaulände 1; s €50-70, d €75-125; Ⓟ ☒ ; wheelchair access) Spacious modern rooms, great views

over the river and a good central location make the König an excellent mid-range option. The hotel also has a good restaurant (mains €7.50 to €10.50) with a beautiful outdoor seating area.

Hotel Wilder Mann (☎ 350 71; www.wilder-mann .de; Am Rathausplatz; s €49, d €78-138; Ⓟ) Royalty and celebrities, from Empress Elizabeth of Austria to Neil Armstrong, have stayed at this historical hotel. Rooms seek to recapture a lost grandeur, but some of the singles are very small. The best rooms overlook the garden at the back.

Eating

Heilig-Geist-Stiftsschänke (☎ 2607; Heilig-Geist-Gasse 4; mains €7.90-11.90) Traditional food is prepared with panache, and served either in the classy, walnut-panelled tangle of dining rooms or the leafy beer garden where hedges create separate dining areas. The three-course set menu (€15.90) is excellent value.

Goldenes Schiff (☎ 344 07; Unterer Sand; mains €4.50-9.50) This is one of the most promising places for vegetarians, though the menu also features German and Austrian classics. In summer try snaring a table in the small garden at the back.

Residenz Café (☎ 363 50; Schrottgasse 12; meals €3.10-11.50) For a touch of elegance visit this stylish café where you can dine beneath crystal chandeliers for surprisingly good prices. In good weather the outdoor tables offer better people-watching as you relax over coffee and cake.

Theresienstrasse and its side streets are lined with cafés and restaurants and are popular places to just hang out.

Zi'Teresa Pizzeria (☎ 2138; Theresienstrasse 26; meals €4.80-12.50) Perennially popular, this lively Italian restaurant is kept busy with people of all ages who come here for the delicious pizzas and pastas as well as the good appetisers and salads.

Café Kowalski (☎ 2487; Oberer Sand 1; dishes €3.50-10) This place is popular with students thanks to its excellent-value changing lunch specials (€4.50) and enormous schnitzels. It's a kicking joint by night with a lively crowd and cheap drinks.

For cheap eats, **KÖPA Schmankerlpassage** (Ludwigstrasse 6) has fruit stalls, meat and fish counters. The restaurant upstairs serves breakfast and lunch for under €6.

BAVARIA

Other recommendations include:

Café Duft (☎ 346 66; Theresienstrasse 22; mains €3.40-8.20) A vaulted chamber with low lights, dark wood and a good range of dishes.

Café Nyhavn (☎ 375 57; Theriesenstrasse 31; €3-8.80) Modern, funky café dishing up good-value baguettes, salads and hot snacks.

Getting There & Away

TRAIN

Passau is on the main train line linking Cologne, Frankfurt, Nuremberg (€34.60, 2½ hours), Regensburg (€19.20, 1½ hours) and Vienna (€37.50, 3½ hours). There are also direct trains to Munich (€25.20, 2½ hours) and Linz (€19.20, 1½ hours). The trip to Zwiesel (€15.40, 1¾ hours) and other Bavarian Forest towns requires a change in Plattling.

Regional buses to and from Zwiesel (€9.50), Grafenau and Bayerisch Eisenstein stop at the Hauptbahnhof concourse outside the main post office.

The A3 runs from Passau to Linz and Vienna in Austria, or back to Regensburg. The A92 from Munich connects with the A3.

From mid-April to early October, **Wurm + Köck** (☎ 929 292; www.donauschiffahrt.de; Höllgasse 26) has a daily (except Monday) boat service to Linz (Austria), leaving Passau at 9am and 1.10pm (€21/24 one way/return, €25 return by bus or train). Boats leave from the main landing docks near Untere Donaulände.

Getting Around

Passau is compact, so most sights are reachable on foot. The City Bus regularly connects the Bahnhof with the Altstadt (€0.50). Longer trips within Passau cost €1.50; a day pass or four-trip ticket costs €3.50 (€4 for a family).

The walk up the hill to the Veste or the hostel, via Luitpoldbrücke and Ludwigsteig path, takes about 30 minutes. From April to October, a shuttle bus operates from Rathausplatz (€1.50/2 one way/return). A taxi will cost about €7.

The **Fahrrad-Klinik** (☎ 334 11; Bräugasse 10) hires out bikes from €11 per day.

BAVARIAN FOREST

Together with the Bohemian Forest on the other side of the Czech border, the Bavarian Forest (Bayerischer Wald) forms the largest continuous woodland area in Europe. It's a lovely landscape of rolling hills and tree-covered mountains interspersed with small, little-disturbed valleys. A large area is protected as the surprisingly wild and rugged Nationalpark Bayerischer Wald.

Despite being incredibly good value, the region sees very few international tourists and remains quite traditional. A centuries-old glass-blowing industry is still active in many of the towns along the **Glasstrasse** (Glass Road), a 250km holiday route connecting Neustadt a.d. Waldnaab with Passau. You can visit the studios, factories and shops and stock up on the magnificent designs.

Orientation

The ranges of the Bavarian Forest stretch northwest to southeast along the German-Czech border, and its wild frontier nature is still the region's chief attribute. One of the bigger towns, and an ideal base for its good train and bus connections, is Zwiesel.

Information

The **Zwiesel tourist office** (☎ 09922-840 523; www.zwiesel-tourismus.de; Stadtplatz 27) has lots of information and brochures on the area. If you're driving there's a **branch office** (☒ 10am-1pm & 2-5pm Mon-Fri, 1-3pm Sat) with English-speaking staff just outside town on the main road towards Regan. The **Grafenau tourist office** (☎ 08552-962 343; www.grafenau.de; Rathausgasse 1; ☒ 9am-noon & 2-6pm Mon-Thu, 9am-4pm Fri, 10-11.30am Sat) is another good place for information.

Sights & Activities

Forest, local customs and glass making are the main themes of exhibits at Zwiesel's **Waldmuseum** (Forest Museum; ☎ 09922-608 88; Stadtplatz 28; adult/concession €2/1.50; ☒ 9am-5pm Mon-Fri, 10am-noon & 2-4pm Sat & Sun mid-May–mid-Oct, reduced hours in winter). Also in Zwiesel is the **Dampfbier-Brauerei** (☎ 09922-846 60; Regener Strasse 9; Zwiesel; tours €7; ☒ tours 10am Wed) where you can join a brewery tour and sample its peppery ales.

The Frauenau **Glasmuseum** (☎ 09926-940 035) is closed until summer 2004 when a brand new building will open to house it and a new tourist office. The museum traces 2500 years of glass-making and explains the technology behind it.

On the southern edge of the Bavarian Forest, in Tittling, there's the **Museumsdorf** ayerischer Wald (☎ 08504-8482; Herrenstrasse 11; dult/concession €2.50/1.50; ☺ 9am-5pm Apr-Oct). This ?0-hectare open-air museum features 150 ypical Bavarian Forest buildings from the 16th to the 19th centuries. Also on display s clothing, furniture, pottery, farming im-plements and tools. Take RBO bus No 8771 o Tittling from Passau Hauptbahnhof.

NATIONALPARK BAYERISCHER WALD

A paradise for outdoor enthusiasts, the Bavarian Forest National Park stretches for about 24,250 hectares along the Czech border from Bayerisch Eisenstein in the north to Finsterau in the south. Its thick forest, most of it mountain spruce, is crisscrossed by hundreds of kilometres of hiking, cycling and cross-country skiing trails. The three main mountains – Rachel, Lusen and Grosser Falkenstein – rise up to between 1300m and 1450m and are home to deer, wild boar, fox, otter and countless bird species.

The park's superb visitor centre is housed in the **Hans-Eisenmann-Haus** (☎ 08558-96150; fax 2618; Böhmstrasse 35, Neuschönau; ☺ 9am-5pm). You can pick up maps and leaflets (some in Eng-lish) and see exhibits on the park's flora, fauna and environmental issues; there's also a children's discovery room and a li-brary. See p422 for details about transport in the park.

HIKING & SKIING

Two long-distance routes cut through the Bavarian Forest: the European Distance Trails E6 (Baltic Sea to the Adriatic) and E8 (North Sea to Carpathia). There are mountains huts all along the way. Other popular hiking trails include the Gläserne Steig (Glass Trail) from Lam to Grafenau. Detailed maps and hiking suggestions are available at the local tourist offices and at the Hans-Eisenmann-Haus.

The Bavarian Forest has seven ski areas, but downhill skiing is low-key, even though the area's highest mountain, the Grosser Arber (1456m) occasionally hosts European and World Cup ski races. The best resorts are in the north, such as Bischofsmais near the Geisskopf (1097m), Bodenmais near the Grosser Arber and Neukirchen near the Hoher Bogen (1079m). The major draw here is cross-country skiing, with 2000km of prepared routes through the ranges.

Sleeping

Accommodation in this area is a real bargain; Zwiesel and Grafenau have the best choices.

HOSTELS & CAMPING

All hostels close for at least a month around November and December.

DJH Zwiesel (☎ 09922-1061; jhzwiesel@djh-bayern.de; Hindenburgstrasse 26; dm €13.60 juniors only) This 53-bed hostel is about 2km south of the Hauptbahnhof.

DJH Frauenau (☎ /fax 09926-735; Hauptstrasse 29a; dm €11.30 juniors only) Church-run and rather old-fashioned.

DJH Neuschönau-Waldhäuser (☎ 08553-6000; jhwaldhaeuser@djh- bayern.de; Herbergsweg 2; dm €14.80 juniors only) Right in the national park and an ideal base for hikers.

Azur-Ferienpark Bayerischer Wald (☎ 09922-802 595; zwiesel@azur-camping.de; Waldesruhweg 34, Zwiesel; person €4.50-6.50, tent €4-5) 500m north of the Hauptbahnhof, near public pools and sports facilities.

PENSIONS & HOTELS

Pension Herta (☎ 09922-2135; Ahornweg 22, Zwiesel; s/d €18/36; P) In a quiet location right next to the forest, is this lovely little pension with comfortable rooms with private bathroom. They also hire out bikes and can pick you up from the Hauptbahnhof.

Hotel-Gasthaus Zum Kellermann (☎ 08552-967 10; www.hotel-zum-kellermann.de; Stadtplatz 8, Grafenau; s/d €23/46; ☺ closed Wed; P) Bright, modern rooms at very reasonable rates make this simple guesthouse in Grafenau a good bet. There's a pretty terrace area outside and the restaurant (mains €6 to €12) serves up tasty traditional dishes.

Hotel Zur Waldbahn (☎ 09922-3001; www.zurwald bahn.de; Bahnhofplatz 2, Zwiesel; s €45, d €70-92; P 🐾) Tradition and modern comforts blend seamlessly at this friendly inn, conveniently located opposite the Hauptbahnhof. The warm, wood-panelled rooms are tastefully furnished and the restaurant is top-notch (mains €7 to €16).

Hotel Hubertus (☎ 08552-96490; www.hubertus -grafenau.de; Grüb 20, Grafenau; s €36-49, d €72-98; P 🐾) This modern hotel in Grafenau of-fers incredible value for the weary traveller. The stylish rooms are spacious and most have balconies. Guests are treated to a pool and sauna, and delicious buffet meals.

Eating

Many of the hotels mentioned in Sleeping, p421, also have good restaurants.

Restaurant Nepomuk (☎ 09922-605 30; Stadtplatz 30, Zwiesel; mains €5.50-13) This place opposite the tourist office is popular with locals and has a good range of traditional dishes as well as some lighter choices and a few vegetarian options.

Salto (☎ 09922-5225; Spitalstrasse 2, Grafenau; mains €7-14) This atmospheric old house is now a stylish restaurant with an excellent menu featuring a combination of light traditional dishes, interesting pizzas and pastas and special salads. In the evening the garden area is lit with flares and the barbecue is fired up for slabs of steak.

Getting There & Around

From Munich, Regensburg or Passau, Zwiesel is reached by rail via Plattling; most trains continue to Bayerisch Eisenstein on the Czech border, with connections to Prague. The Waldbahn shuttles directly between Zwiesel and Bodenmais and Zwiesel and Grafenau.

There's also a tight network of regional buses, though service can be infrequent. The Igel-Bus navigates around the national park on four routes. A useful one is the Lusen-Bus (one-/three-day ticket €3.30/8.20), which leaves from Grafenau Hauptbahnhof and travels to the Hans-Eisenmann-Haus, the Neuschönau hostel and the Lusen hiking area.

From mid-May to October, the best value is usually the Bayerwald-Ticket (€5), a day pass good for unlimited travel on bus and train throughout the forest area.

Baden-Württemberg

CONTENTS

History	425
Stuttgart	425
Around Stuttgart	434
Schwäbisch Hall	435
Around Schwäbisch Hall	437
Tübingen	437
Burg Hohenzollern	439
Heidelberg	440
Around Heidelberg	448
Mannheim	449
Ulm	450
Northern Black Forest	**454**
Karlsruhe	454
Baden-Baden	457
Schwarzwald-Hochstrasse	461
Freudenstadt	461
Central Black Forest	**463**
Kinzig Valley	463
Triberg	464
Danube Bike Trail	465
Southern Black Forest	**466**
Villingen-Schwenningen	466
Freiburg	467
Around Freiburg	471
Feldberg	473
Titisee-Neustadt	474
Schluchsee	475
St Blasien	476
Wutachschlucht	477
Lake Constance	**478**
Konstanz	479
Around Konstanz	482
Meersburg	483
Around Meersburg	485
Friedrichshafen	486
Ravensburg	487
Lindau	488

Baden-Württemberg is one of Germany's main holiday regions, rivalled only by Bavaria in its breadth of sights and landscapes. The prosperous state was created in only 1951 out of three smaller regions: Baden, Württemberg and Hohenzollern. Most of it is covered by the Black Forest (Schwarzwald), a vast nature playground whose lakes and peaks are irresistible to boaters, bikers and hikers. Fairy-tale castles shrouded in mist dot the countryside while students still gather in the crusty old beer halls of medieval Heidelberg. Baden-Baden dominates the hedonistic scene with spas that have been steam-cleaning the stressed since the Roman era. Vibrant Freiburg, nestled in a valley near the Swiss border, makes an ideal base to discover the Black Forest.

Lake Constance (Bodensee), which embraces sections of Germany, Switzerland and Austria, is justifiably one of Baden-Württemberg's biggest drawcards, especially in the summer. But don't miss the less-travelled regions, including the gentle hills of the Schwäbische Alb and the medieval gem of Schwäbisch Hall. The student town of Tübingen, with its narrow lanes and hill-top fortress, positively oozes charm.

Nearly in the centre of it all presides Stuttgart, home of Mercedes-Benz, Porsche, and a wealth of urban pleasures – museums, fine dining, nightlife and parks. Residents eschew brew for one of the many local wines available for tasting and sale in the city. To the north and west are two big wine-growing regions (Baden and Württemberg), famous mainly for whites but also producing some very drinkable reds. The rolling vineyards are yet another aspect of Baden-Württemberg's scenic treasures.

HIGHLIGHTS

- **Wining**
  Go *Besenwirtschaft*-hopping around Stuttgart
  (p432)

- **Dining**
  Prepare a picnic from the outstanding produce
  at the Markthalle in Stuttgart (p431)

- **Green Haven**
  Hike through the dramatic Wutachschlucht
  (Wutach Gorge) in the Southern Black Forest
  (p477)

- **Adrenaline Rush**
  Explore the Höllental near Freiburg in the
  Southern Black Forest (p473)

- **Indulgence**
  Relax with a soak in one of Baden-Baden's famous
  spas (p457)

★ Baden-Baden   ★ Stuttgart

★ Freiburg
★ Southern Black Forest

■ POPULATION: 10.6 MILLION   ■ AREA: 35,751 SQ KM

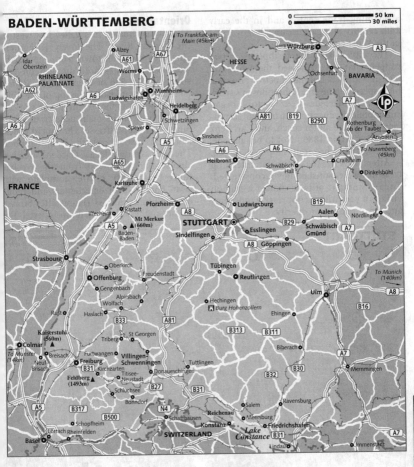

BADEN-WÜRTTEMBERG

HISTORY

Baden was the first area of today's Baden Württemberg to be unified. It was made a grand duchy by Napoleon, who also promoted Württemberg to the rank of kingdom in 1806. Both areas, in conjunction with Bavaria and 16 other states, formed the Confederation of the Rhine under French protection – part of Napoleon's plan to undermine Prussia. In 1866 Baden and Württemberg sided with Austria against Prussia, but the states were ultimately drafted into the German Empire in 1871. The Baden-Württemberg of today was created from the three smaller regions (Baden, Württemberg and Hohenzollern) in 1951.

STUTTGART

☎ 0711 / pop 587,000

Stuttgart is best known as the home of Mercedes-Benz (even the train station sports the familiar three-pointed star), and most travellers imagine it as an industrial city. Nothing could be further from the truth. Swathed in a belt of parks and thick hillside forests, Stuttgart could be the greenest city in Europe. Over half its surrounding area is covered with orchards, vineyards, meadows and forest; while over 500 vineyards produce some excellent wines, many cellared and consumed locally.

The city began as a stud farm (*Stuotgarten*, whence the name comes) on the Nesenbach Stream around AD 950. By 1160 it was a booming trade centre, and in the early 14th century Stuttgart became the royal seat of the Württemberg family.

The city is also the birthplace of two gadgets that have changed the world we live in: Gottlieb Daimler's petrol-powered, high-speed engine and Robert Bosch's spark plug. The Mercedes-Benz factory began automobile production here in 1926. (Daimler patented the motor coach, and Carl Benz the motor car, in 1886.) Not to be outdone, Ferdinand Porsche set up shop here as well.

After WWII, the city's architectural treasures were painstakingly reconstructed. Today, Stuttgart attracts almost a million visitors a year with its impressive museums and air of relaxed prosperity.

Orientation

The city is situated in a valley just west of the Neckar River. The lovely Kriegsberg vineyards overlook town from the northwest. Steep grades are common on city streets – over 500 of them end in *Stäffele* (staircases) that lead to the top of the hills.

The Hauptbahnhof (central train station) is just north of the main pedestrian shopping street, Königstrasse. The tourist office, i-Punkt, is just opposite the Hauptbahnhof. The Schlossgarten (Palace Garden) stretches almost 4km southwest from the Neckar River to the city centre, complete with swan ponds, street entertainers and modern sculptures. Across Hauptstätter Strasse to the southeast lies the Bohnenviertel, the

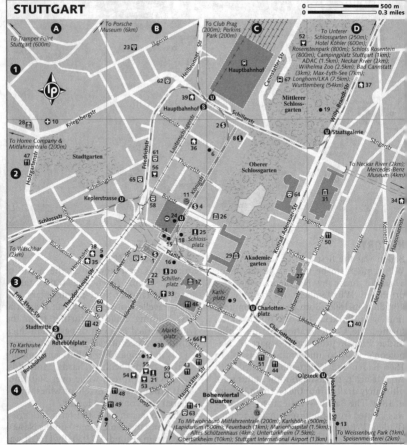

old labourers' quarter today filled with pubs, restaurants and galleries.

The ubiquitous Mercedes star could almost be taken as Stuttgart's emblem, adorning the tower at the Hauptbahnhof. The **Mercedes platform** (admission free; ☺ 10am-9pm Tue-Sun summer, 10am-7pm winter) is open to the public and can be reached via the south entrance to the Hauptbahnhof, offering a wonderful panorama of the surrounding hillsides. The Mercedes-Benz museum is east of the Neckar River, about 15 minutes by tram from the city centre; the company's factory is in the suburb of Sindelfingen, southwest of the city centre. Bad Cannstatt, site of Germany's second-largest beer festival, is east of the city's zoo and botanical gardens at Wilhelma.

Information
BOOKSHOPS
Lindemann Books (☎ 248 9990; Nadlerstrasse 4-10) South of the Rathaus. Stocks English-language books and has a very good travel section.
Wittwer (☎ 250 70; Königstrasse 30) Great foreign-language and travel sections (with some Lonely Planet titles).

CULTURAL CENTRES
Deutsch-Amerikanisches Zentrum (German-American Centre; ☎ 228 180; Charlottenplatz 17) Situated in the Institute for Foreign Affairs. Offers lots of resource material in English.

DISCOUNT CARDS
The Stuttcard is a three-day ticket providing free entry to all public museums, as well as discounts for cultural events and leisure activities. It's a bargain at €8.50. The three-day Stuttgart Card Plus (€14) affords unlimited bus and train travel within city boundaries (including the airport), as well as the advantages of the Stuttcard.

If you're under 26, you'll be eligible for the 'Young and Fun' deal (€42). This includes one overnight-hotel stay with breakfast, a non-alcoholic drink in the hotel, a Stuttcard, a city guide and a city magazine.

For transport within the city limits, a hotel reservation entitles you to a three-day ticket for €8 that covers an adult and two children. There is also a €11 ticket good for travel throughout the entire metropolitan area.

All passes are available from the i-Punkt tourist office tourist.

INTERNET ACCESS
Das Bistro (☎ 470 4948; Olgastrasse 70a; per 30min/1hr €2/3.50)
Level One (☎ 120 4665; Königstrasse 22; per 15min/1hr €2/4.50)

INTERNET RESOURCES
www.stuttgart-tourist.de This is an excellent website with English translations.

LAUNDRY
Tramper Point Stuttgart (☎ 817 7476; Wiener Strasse 317) This hostel also has a washing machine.
WaschBar (☎ 636 3700; Bebelstrasse 49)
Waschsalon (☎ 241 275; Hohenheimer Strasse 33; ☺ Mon-Fri)

INFORMATION		
American Express	1	B3
American Express	2	C2
Das Bistro	3	C4
Deutsch-Amerikanisches Zentrum	(see 9)	
Dresdner Bank	4	B2
Explorer	5	A3
First Reisebüro	6	C2
Flugbörse	7	A4
i-Punkt Tourist Office	8	C2
Institute for Foreign Affairs	9	C3
Katharinen Hospital	10	A2
Level One	11	B2
Lindemann Books	12	B4
Waschsalon	13	D4
Wittwer	14	B3

SIGHTS & ACTIVITIES	(pp482-9)	
Alexander Calder's Mobile	15	B3
Alte Kanzlei	16	B3
Altes Schloss	17	B3
Börse (Stock Exchange)	18	B3
Carl Zeiss Planetarium	19	D1
Freidrich Schiller Statue	20	B3
Hans im Glück Statue	21	B4
Instrumenten Museum	22	B3
Kriegsberg Vineyards	23	B1
Königsbau	24	B2
König Wilhelm Jubilee Column	25	B3

Kunstverein (Municipal Art Gallery)	26	C2
Landesbibliothek (State Library) & Archives	27	C3
Linden Museum	28	A2
Neues Schloss	29	C3
Rathaus	30	B4
Staatsgalerie	31	D2
Stadtbücherei (City Library)	32	C3
Stiftskirche	33	B3
Württemberg State Museum	(see 17)	

SLEEPING	(pp430-1)	
DJH Hostel	34	D2
Gasthof Alte Mira	35	A3
Hotel Unger	36	B2
Inter-Continental	37	D1
Museumstube	38	A3
Steigenberger Graf Zeppelin	39	B1
Wirt am Berg	40	D3

EATING	(pp431-2)	
Amadeus	(see 9)	
Brunnenwirt	41	B4
Calwer-Eck-Bräu	42	A3
Cortijo	43	B4
Der Zauberlehrling	44	C4
Iden	45	B3
Markthalle	46	B3

Mensa	47	A2
Nirvan	48	B4
Schark	49	B4
Urbanstuben	50	D3
Weinhaus Stetter	51	C4

DRINKING	(p432)	
Beer Garden	52	C1
Deli	53	B4
Hans im Glück	54	B4
Max and Moritz	55	B4
Palast der Republik	56	B2

ENTERTAINMENT	(pp432-3)	
Atelier	57	B4
Climax	58	B2
Club Zap	59	B4
King's Club	60	A3
Kommunales Kino	61	B2
Lupe	62	B1
Roger's Kiste	63	B4
Staatstheater	64	C2
Varieté im Friedrichsbau	65	B2

SHOPPING	(p433)	
Breuninger Shopping Centre	66	B4

TRANSPORT	(pp433-4)	
Bus Station	67	C1

LIBRARIES

Landesbibliothek (☎ 2120; Konrad-Adenauer-Strasse 8) This library has a huge state collection.

Staatsarchiv (☎ 212 4335; Konrad-Adenauer-Strasse 4) Stores the original Bannandrohungsbulle, the papal bull that threatened Martin Luther with excommunication for heresy.

Stadtbücherei (☎ 216 570; Konrad-Adenauer-Strasse 2) This is the city library.

MEDICAL SERVICES

For a doctor call (☎ 262 8012) or (☎ 280 211). The following are the city's largest hospitals:

Katharinen Hospital (☎ 2780; Kriegsbergstrasse 60)

Marienhospital (☎ 648 90; Böheimstrasse 37).

MONEY

American Express office (☎ 162 4920; Schillerplatz 4) Across the street I-Punkt tourist office.

Dresdner Bank (Königstrasse 9)

Reisebank This branch is at the Hauptbahnhof.

POST

Main post office (Lautenschlagerstrasse 17) There's also a branch at the Hauptbahnhof.

TOURIST INFORMATION

i-Punkt Tourist Office (☎ 222 8259, 222 8240; www .stuttgart-tourist.de; Königstrasse 1a; ☺ 9.30am-8.30pm Mon-Fri, 9.30am-6pm Sat, 10.30am-6pm Sun) This office has multilingual staff who book rooms and sell tickets to just about everything in town. Ask about special accommodation deals during Stuttgart's festivals and the 'Young and Fun' deal. For more information, see Discount Cards (p427).

TRAVEL AGENCIES

Explorer (☎ 162 5211; Theodor-Heuss-Strasse) Offers some very cheap flight deals and great service.

First Reisebüro (☎ 794 2055; Kronenstrasse 7) A last-minute ticketing service.

Flugbörse (☎ 964 3344; Tübinger Strasse 25) A good bucket shop.

Dangers & Annoyances

Stuttgart is generally a safe city, but some rather sleazy characters gather after dark in the Klett Passage below the Hauptbahnhof. Avoid the Palace Garden after sunset, too.

Sights

SCHLOSSPLATZ

This square provides a crash course in architecture. Stand in the middle, beneath the **König Wilhelm Jubilee column,** flanked by fountains representing the eight rivers of Baden-Württemberg, then spin clockwise. The classical **Königsbau** is a focal point on warm evenings, when crowds gather to watch buskers perform amid its columns. Downstairs are shops, upstairs, the city's **Börse stock exchange**.

To the right is a fine example of 1950s architecture in the **Olgabau**, home to **Dresdner Bank**. Further right is the **Art Nouveau Kunstverein**, which contains the municipal art gallery and the Württemberg Art Society. The late-baroque/neoclassical front section of the **Neues Schloss**, once the residence of kings Friedrich I and Wilhelm I, now houses the state finance and culture ministries. At **Karlsplatz**, you'll find a statue of Wilhelm looking noble and serious on a bronze steed.

At the western end of Schlossplatz is **Alexander Calder's Mobile**, a modern sculpture the city bought in 1981 for around €500,000. Stuttgarters (known for what other Germans might call 'miserliness' but which they themselves call 'thrift') initially went ballistic over the cost, but are now happy since the work has tripled in value.

SCHILLERPLATZ

Opposite Schlossplatz is Schillerplatz – named after the poet-dramatist Friedrich Schiller – whose statue stands in the centre. In its southwestern corner, in the **Stiftsfruchtkasten**, a former wine depot topped by a Bacchus statue, is the **Instrumenten Museum** musical collection. Next to it stands the reconstructed **Stiftskirche** (church), with its twin 61m-high late-Gothic towers (by law, no Stuttgart building can be built taller). On the opposite side of the courtyard is the Renaissance **Alte Kanzlei** (Old Chancellory).

Through the tunnel to the east is **Altes Schloss**, with a large statue of Eberhard, Württemberg's first duke and founder of Tübingen University. The old palace now holds the **Württemberg State Museum** (☎ 279 3400; Schillerplatz 6; adult/concession €2.60/1.50, includes Instrumenten Museum; ☺ 10am-1pm Tue, 10am-5pm Wed-Sun), with exhibitions on the Württemberg crown jewels. The elk above the clock on the tower ram their horns on the hour.

MUSEUMS

The **Staatsgalerie** (State Gallery; ☎ 212 4050; Konrad-Adenauer-Strasse 30-32; adult/concession €9/6; ☺ 10am-

5pm Tue-Sun, 10am-9pm Thu, 10am-12am 1st Sat of every month) contains Stuttgart's best art.

The impressive **Mercedes-Benz Museum** (☎ 172 2578; Mercedesstrasse 137/1; admission free; ☾ 9am-5pm Tue-Sun), 2km east of the Neckar River, tells the story of the partnership of Gottlieb Daimler and Karl Benz via recorded commentary amid numerous gleaming vehicles. To get there take the S1 line on S-Bahn to Gottlieb-Daimler-Station.

The **Porsche Museum** (☎ 911 5685; Porschestrasse 42; admission free; ☾ 9am-4pm Mon-Fri, 9am-5pm Sat & Sun) has its own share of very sexy cars (take the S6 line on the S-Bahn to Neuwirtshaus).

The state ethnological **Linden Museum** (☎ 202 2456; Hegelplatz 1; adult/concession €3/2; ☾ 10am-5pm Tue-Sun, 10am-8pm Wed) has a large display focusing on South America, Asia and Africa.

PARKS & ZOO
Royal Gardens
The parts of the Schlossgarten (Palace Garden) – Unterer, Mittlerer and Oberer (Lower, Middle and Upper) – are all exceptional. They're filled with meandering walkways, fountains and sunbathing folk watching the world – and the inline skaters – go by. There's a very good beer garden in the Unterer Schlossgarten, about seven minutes' walk northeast of the Hauptbahnhof.

At the north end of the Unterer Schlossgarten you probably won't even realise that you've crossed into the **Rosensteinpark**, which jigs west through glorious copses to the corner of Nordbahnhofstrasse and Pragstrasse, through the **Löwentor** (Lion's Gate).

Within Rosensteinpark is the amazing **Schloss Rosenstein** (☎ 893 60; Rosenstein 1; adult/concession €2/1; ☾ 9am-5pm Tue-Fri, 10am-6pm Sat & Sun), now the city's Natural History Museum. The whole history of evolution is imaginatively displayed with natural habitats lovingly reconstructed. The highlight is a 13m-long whale.

Wilhelma Zoo
Animals from around the world feature at the enormously popular **Wilhelma Zoo** (☎ 540 20; Rosensteinpark; adult/concession €9.40/6.40; ☾ 8.15am-nightfall). It's in an amazing botanical garden in the grounds of Schloss Rosenstein, at the northern edge of Rosensteinpark.

Lapidarium
Hardly known to tourists and many locals, the **Lapidarium** (admission free; ☾ 2-5pm Wed, Thu, Sat & Sun Apr–mid-Sept) is an enchanting little park on a hillside near Marienplatz, south of the city centre. Nestled amid its lush greenery are fragments of buildings destroyed in WWII: doorways, portals, façade ornamentation, statues, gargoyles and parts of fountains. There's also a collection of about 200 Roman artefacts.

When it's closed, you can peep through the fence; just walk up the Willy-Reichert-Stäffel (steps) to Mörikestrasse 24/1 at the top of Karlshöhe park.

Karlshöhe
The hillcrest just northeast of the Lapidarium is Karlshöhe, another great park with sweeping views of the city and lovely hillside vineyards. You can reach it via the Willy-Reichert-Staffel (steps) or through Humboldtstrasse.

That yeasty smell is coming from the nearby **Dinkel Acker Brewery** (☎ 648 10; Tübinger Strasse 46). Call ahead and you may be able to take a free tour (German language), though you'll have to join a group.

Weissenburg Park
Weissenburg is another lovely hillside park offering great views of the city (take the U5, U6 or 7U7 to Bopser then walk south). At the top of the hill is the spectacular **Teehaus** (teahouse).

PLANETARIUM
In the southeast of the Mittlerer Schlossgarten is the pyramid-shaped **Carl Zeiss Planetarium** (☎ 162 9215; Willy-Brandt-Strasse 25; adult/concession €5/2.50), housing one of the best planetariums in the country. A higher admission price is charged for special shows that run at 10am and 3pm Tuesday to Friday, 8pm Wednesday and Friday, as well as 2pm, 4pm and 6pm on weekends. You can catch most U-Bahn lines going to Staatsgalerie.

Tours
BOAT
From March to October, **Neckar-Personen-Schiffahrt** (☎ 5499 7060) operates a variety of boat tours on the Neckar River (from €6.50) departing from its dock opposite Wilhelma in Bad Cannstatt.

BUS

The city runs 2½-hour bus tours in English and German at 2pm and 4.30pm daily April to October (weekends only the rest of the year). The €17/13.50 charge includes admission to the TV Tower. The i-Punkt office can arrange a great variety of walking tours as well.

TAXI

If you're willing to invest €100 for four people (€130 on weekends and holidays), we highly recommend a 2½-hour taxi tour (in English, French, Spanish or German) with official city guide, **Anselm Vogt-Moykopf** (☎ 0172-740 1138). Herr Vogt-Moykopf is both a knowledgeable and easy-going fellow who really loves the city, its architecture, his job and taking people to out-of-the-way, beautiful regions nearby.

Festivals & Events

The city organises a number of notable annual events, including the **Sommerfest** in August, an open-air festival with live music and food at Schlossplatz. Later in the same month, at Schlossplatz and the Upper Palace Garden, is the **Weindorf**, where the year's vintages are sold from hundreds of booths.

The **Cannstatter Volkfest** (locals call it the 'Wasen' after the river nearby) is Stuttgart's version of Oktoberfest. It's held in late September and early October, with better-behaved crowds and beer stands throughout town.

The **Christmas market** is held on Markt and Schillerplatz from late November.

Sleeping
BUDGET

For private rooms and long-term rentals, Stuttgart has two *Mitwohnzentralen* (accommodation-finding services): **AMB-Mitwohnbüro** (☎ 194 22; Hauptstätter Strasse 154) and the **Home Company** (☎ 221 392; Frank-Korn-Lerchenstrasse 72).

Tramper Point Stuttgart (☎ 817 7476; camp stuttgart@t-online.de; Wiener Strasse 317; dm €8, maximum stay 3 nights; ⊗ late-Jul–early-Sep) If you're between 16 and 27 years, this spartan wooden hostel is the best deal in town. There are kitchen facilities and a washing machine. Check-in is from 5pm to 11pm. It's northwest of the city centre. To get there, take U6 line on the U-Bahn to Sportpark Feuerbach.

DJH hostel (☎ 241 583; www.jugendherberge -stuttgart.de; Haussmannstrasse 27; juniors/seniors €17.30/ 20) This hostel is a signposted 15-minute walk east of the Hauptbahnhof (take the U15 line on U-Bahn to Eugenplatz). Curfew is at midnight.

Jugendgästehaus (☎ 241 132; fax 2366 1110; Richard-Wagner-Strasse 2; s/d €23.50/42) This non-DJH hostel is southeast of the city centre (take the U15 line on the U-Bahn to Bubenbad).

Museumstube (☎ 296 810; Hospitalstrasse 9; s/d with shared bathroom €30/45, d with private bathroom €65) These super-clean, spiffy rooms with new rugs and beds are an excellent deal. Breakfast is €5 extra per person but there are several cafés nearby if you opt out.

Gasthof Alte Mira (☎ 222 9502; fax 222 950 329; Büchsenstrasse 24; s/d with shared bathroom from €31/55, with private bathroom from €41/65) Well located, but the slightly shabby rooms and unwelcoming vibe make it a distinct second choice to the Museumstube.

Campingplatz Stuttgart (☎ 556 696; www.camp ingplatz-stuttgart.de; Mercedesstrasse 40; tent/person €6.50/5; ⊗ year-round) You can pitch your tent 500m from the Bad Cannstatt S-Bahn station on the Wasen River.

MID-RANGE
Wirt am Berg (☎ 241 865; fax 236 1348; Gaisburgstrasse 12a; s/d from €45/85; ℗ ⊗) This quiet backstreet hotel provides excellent value for money. The rooms are nicely furnished, and contain telephones and satellite TV. The small staff is friendly and helpful; however, reception is closed at night, so make sure to call ahead if you're arriving late.

Hotel Unger (☎ 209 90; www.hotel-unger.de; Kronenstrasse 17; s/d from €92/128; ℗ ⊗) Hotel Unger is very central, with a quiet location southwest of the i-Punkt office. It has pleasant rooms, and is also the outlet for bicycle hire; see Getting Around (p433).

Hotel Köhler (☎ 166 660; fax 166 633; Neckarstrasse 209; s/d with shared bathroom €35/57, s/d with private bathroom €50/70) This isn't a bad choice, although the only parking available is on the street. Rooms have TV and telephone. To get there, take either line U1, U11 or U14 on the U-Bahn to Metzstrasse.

TOP END
Steigenberger Graf Zeppelin (☎ 204 80; www.stut tgart.steigenberger.de; Arnulf-Klett-Platz 7; s/d €195/220;

P **⊠**) Looming over the Hauptbahnhof is this super-luxurious hotel. In an original touch, you can choose among three distinct styles: classical, elegant or avant-garde. There's a Zen-style spa, restaurant, bistro, bar and cigar lounge.

Inter-Continental (☎ 20200; www.stuttgart.interco ntinental.com; Willy-Brandt-Strasse 30; r from €250; **P** **⊠** **⊠** **⊠** **⊠**) A business-travellers' favourite, the curvy Inter-Continental has the usual hyper-comfortable rooms (all with bay windows overlooking the Unterer Schlossgarten).

Eating
BEER GARDENS
The best are in the Unterer Schlossgarten, Karlshöhe, southwest of the city centre, and the Teehaus in Weissenburg park, also to the southeast.

Amadeus (☎ 292 678; Charlottenplatz 17; mains €5-9.50, salads under €5.50) The popular Amadeus is in the courtyard of the Institute for Foreign Affairs. It sells Dinkel Acker beer and other labels, along with great Swabian-style food.

Altes Schützenhaus (☎ 649 8157; Burgstallstrasse 99; mains from €5.50; ⏱ 7pm-1am Mon-Thu, 7.30pm-3am Fri & Sat, 5pm-1am Sun) This place at Südheimer Platz is typically packed with students who sit outside this old castle-like building. There's a salsa party on Sunday and a wide range of musical styles on other nights.

QUICK EATS
The superb Markthalle, an Art Nouveau–style market, is a destination worth seeing, even if you don't wish to avail yourself of the excellent produce to prepare a memorable picnic. There are also Italian, Spanish and Swabian restaurants. It's on Dorotheenstrasse, and is open 7am to 6pm Monday to Friday and 7am to 4pm on Saturday.

Mensa (Holzgartenstrasse 11; lunches around €3) The upstairs university dining hall is reserved for students, but the ground-floor cafeteria and the small **Mensa Stüble** in the basement are open to all.

Brunnenwirt (☎ 569 475; Brunnenstrasse 15) This is a quirky little sausage stand in the Bohnenviertel. Half-grungy, half-chic, this local institution draws an eclectic crowd – from passing vagrants to Mercedes coupé drivers.

RESTAURANTS
The dining centres of Stuttgart lie south of Charlottenstrasse, principally along Eberhardstrasse and the narrow streets between Charlottenstrasse and Pfarrstrasse. Trendy Italian bistros, ethnic hideaways and relaxed cafés abound here, and many have tables outdoors when the weather is mild.

Iden (☎ 235 989; Eberhardstrasse 1; meals around €5.75; ⏱ closed Sat dinner & Sun) This is a cafeteria-type hideaway with an amazing spread of cheap wholefood eats.

Weinhaus Stetter (☎ 240 163; Rosenstrasse 32; dishes from €5; ⏱ 3-11pm Mon-Fri, 11am-3pm Sat) This place has simple regional specialities like *Linsen und Saiten* (lentils with sausage) and a great wine selection.

Nirvan (☎ 240 561; Eberhardstrasse 73; meals from €6.75) Just off Eberhard-Passage, Nirvan has great Persian dishes (lamb, fish and vegetarian), and a special lunch menu for €5. Its sister deli inside the passage serves stand-up lunches.

Cortijo (☎ 243 221; Eberhardstrasse 10; mains from €6.50) Gazpacho, tapas and tasty grilled sardines bring a touch of Iberia to the city centre. Catch a live flamenco performance on weekend nights.

Calwer-Eck-Bräu (☎ 2224 9440; Calwer Strasse 31; meals from around €7.10) This is a comfortable brewery/pub with excellent Swabian-Bavarian fare, including the Stuttgartian speciality *Maultaschensuppe* (€3.50). Save your appetite for Sunday when there's an all-you-can-eat menu for €7.77.

Schark (☎ 649 9637; Tübinger Strasse 17/B; mains from €7.10) The stunning Oriental décor is reason enough to come here. The delights of Turkish, Egyptian and Tunisian kitchens are prepared with panache, and vegetarians won't be disappointed. Live bands play the sinuous sounds of Oriental music on weekends, and there's an Oriental brunch every Sunday (€13.90).

Urbanstuben (☎ 245 108; Eugensstrasse 12; meals from €12) This cosy restaurant, on the corner of Urbanstrasse, has Swabian and international dishes, and some excellent local wines.

Der Zauberlehrling (☎ 237 7770; Rosenstrasse 38; mains €12.50-16; ⏱ closed lunch Sat & Sun) This is a fine restaurant in the Bohnenviertel featuring Swabian dishes infused with American, French and other influences. The preparation is sophisticated and the emphasis is on the best possible ingredients.

Speisemeisterei (☎ 456 0037; Am Schloss Hohenheim; fixed-price menus €48-110; ❧ dinner only Wed-Sat, closed Sun-Tue) Rated two Michelin stars, this is Stuttgart's best restaurant. Housed in a castle southeast of the city, the lavish dining chambers drip baroque furnishings. It's haute cuisine in haute style.

Drinking

Tiny Geissstrasse, just a block from Eberhardstrasse, has several little café-pubs that spill out onto what's unofficially called Hans-im-Glück Platz – a little square with a fountain depicting the caged German fairy-tale character 'Lucky Hans'.

Palast der Republik (☎ 226 4887; Friedrichstrasse 27) This grandly named bar is a tiny kiosk with streetside tables that's become an institution. You won't find the name (there isn't room), but look for 'Schwaben Bräu' on the front.

Max and Moritz (☎ 239 9239; Geissstrasse 3) This is a very friendly place serving great pasta and pizza.

Deli (☎ 236 0200; Geissstrasse 7) This is a chic local favourite.

Hans im Glück (☎ 245 859; Geissstrasse 8) This is probably the best-known pub, restaurant and cocktail bar in Stuttgart. Its house drink is a gimlet that's heavy on the gin.

Entertainment

Lift Stuttgart is an easy-to-use city magazine in German available throughout the city. *Prinz* is another listings magazine that does about the same thing, but not as well. *Uni-Tip* is a magazine published by Lift that is especially geared to students.

CINEMAS

The following cinemas screen Englishlanguage films. Check *Lift Stuttgart* and *Prinz* for programmes.

Atelier (☎ 294 995; Kronprinzstrasse 6) **Kommunales Kino** (☎ 221 320; Friedrichstrasse 23a) Located in the old Amerika Haus building.

Lupe (☎ 226 1496; Kriegsbergstrasse 11)

DISCOS & CLUBS

Climax (☎ 294 849; Friedrichstrasse 31) Edgy 20-somethings in leather head here for House.

Club Prag (☎ 817 602; Heilbronnerstrasse 261) The trendy Club Prag launched the careers of those hip-hop superheroes Die Fantastischen Ver. For more information, see Contemporary Music (p60).

Perkins Park (☎ 256 0062; Stresemannstrasse 39) This is a massive place with two dance floors, a restaurant, a pool table and a very mixed crowd. There's techno, Brazilian, rock and roll, soul…you name it.

Club Zap (☎ 235 227; Hauptstätterstrasse 40) In the Schwabenzentrum (Swabian Centre), this is an eclectic place where the crowd sways to jazz, soul and hip-hop.

GAY & LESBIAN

King's Club (☎ 226 4558; Calwer Strasse 21) This place is predominantly gay but some lesbians come as well. It's techno all the way.

BESENWIRTSCHAFT

From October to March, wine growers throughout the region attach brooms to the front of their homes to indicate that they're a *Besenwirtschaft*, a small restaurant that allows people to come in and taste the new vintage (around €2.50 for 0.25l). They open from 11am, and also serve lunch and dinner featuring typical Swabian dishes like *Kartoffelsuppe*, *Gaisburger Marsch* (a stew of sliced potatoes, noodles and beef) and the evil-sounding *Schlachtplatte* (sauerkraut with pork belly, liver, lard, sausage and smoked meat, with peas and other vegetables).

Some Besenwirtschaft open every year, but most don't. Check in *Lift Stuttgart* or *S-Trip*, published in the *Stuttgarter Zeitung* on the last Wednesday of the month during vintage times.

Besenwirtschaft that operate every year include the home of **Jürgen Krug** (☎ 859 081, Wildensteinstrasse 24), which is in the suburb of Feuerbach, which holds free art shows and performances by artists – singers, cabaret performers, speciality acts etc (take tram No 6 to Feuerbacher Krankenhaus). The **Family Ruoff** (☎ 321 224; Uhlbacher Strasse 31, Obertürkheim), is in a fabulous house built in 1550 (take the S1 to Obertürkheim). In Untertürkheim, **Helmut Zaiss** (☎ 331 149; Strümpfelbacher Strasse 40) has a romantic vaulted wine cellar. Bus Nos 60 and 61 (going towards Rotenberg/Fellbach) stop right at the front.

ROCK & JAZZ
Longhorn/LKA (☎ 409 8290; Heiligenwiesen 6) Live rock is a regular fixture here.

Roger's Kiste (☎ 233 148; Hauptstätter Strasse 35) This hole in the wall is the city's leading jazz venue.

Theaterhaus (☎ 402 070; Ulmer Strasse 241) Regular jazz and rock is played at Theaterhaus. To get here, take line U4 or U9 on the U-Bahn to Im Degen.

THEATRE & CLASSICAL MUSIC
The Stuttgart area has 40 theatres and dozens of music venues.

Staatstheater (☎ 202 090; www.staatstheater-stuttgart.de; Oberer Schlossgarten) The Staatstheater holds regular orchestral, ballet and opera performances. Tickets cost from €8, and are heavily subsidised. The Stuttgart Ballet is renowned as one of the best companies in Europe, producing the star choreographer John Cranko.

Variété im Friedrichhaus (☎ 225 7070; www.friedrichsbau.de; Friedrichstrasse 24) This place is locally famous for its excellent variety shows and cabaret productions.

Theaterhaus (☎ 402 070; Ulmer Strasse 241) The Theaterhaus stages anything from serious theatre to jazz concerts and cabaret. It's east of the city centre in Wangen (take line U4 or U9 on the U-Bahn to Im Degen).

Shopping
Of the many weekly markets, the biggest are the food markets on the Markt and the flower markets on Schillerplatz. They both take place from 7am to 12.30pm on Tuesday, Thursday and Saturday. There's a large flea market every Saturday at Karlsplatz.

Many varieties of wine are produced in the region; most are whites, but locals also go for Trollinger, a full-bodied red made from a variety of grape originally from South Tirol in Austria. Stuttgarters account for twice the national average consumption of wine, so while Trollinger is readily available here, they're not really exporting a lot. There's no shortage of wine shops in the city, and the i-Punkt tourist office has lists of vineyards open for tastings.

Stuttgart isn't renowned for bargain shopping, but a neat place to browse is the Breuninger shopping centre, a huge and expensive department store south of the Markt.

Getting There & Away
AIR
Stuttgart international airport (☎ 9480), 13km south of the city, is served by domestic and international airlines. There are four terminals, all within walking distance of each other.

CAR & MOTORCYCLE
The A8 from Munich to Karlsruhe passes Stuttgart, as does the A81 from Würzburg south to Lake Constance.

At the **ADAC** (☎ 280 00; Am Neckartor 2), north of the Hauptbahnhof, staff can help motorists plan their car trips.

For ride services contact **ADM Mitfahrzentrale** (☎ 636 8036; Lerchenstrasse 65).

TRAIN
There are frequent departures for all major German and many international cities, including IC and ICE trains to Frankfurt (€44.60, 1½ to two hours), Berlin (€103, 5½ to 9½ hours) and Munich (€42.80, 2½ hours).

There are frequent regional services to Tübingen (€9, one hour), Schwäbisch Hall (€12.40, 1½ hours), Ravensburg (€35.60, two hours) and Ulm (€13, one hour).

Getting Around
TO/FROM THE AIRPORT
S2 and S3 trains run frequently between the airport and the Hauptbahnhof, taking about 30 minutes. A taxi to the city centre will cost around €25.

BICYCLE
You can hire bicycles at **Rent a Bike** (☎ 209 90; Hotel Unger, Kronenstrasse 17; €9.50/13 per half-day/day) or at the **i-Punkt tourist office** (☎ 222 8259).

Bike transport on the commuter trains is restricted. The S-Bahn allows bikes from 8.30am to 4pm and 6.30pm onwards Monday to Friday, and all day on Saturday, Sunday and holidays.

The U-Bahn allows bikes only after 7.30pm Monday to Friday, from 2pm on Saturday, and all day Sunday and holidays. Roving police will fine you at other times.

The **ADFC** (☎ 636 8637; Breitscheidstrasse 82) provides maps and information for drivers and on organised rides, but opening hours are limited.

CAR & MOTORCYCLE

Underground parking throughout the city centre costs about €2 for the first hour and €1.50 per subsequent hour.

Avis, Sixt and Europcar all have car-hire offices at Terminal One at the airport and at the Hauptbahnhof.

PUBLIC TRANSPORT

On Stuttgart's public transport network, single fares cost €1.60 within the central zone. A four-ride strip ticket costs €6. A day pass is better value at €4.80/7.80 for one/five person(s).

TAXI

Flagfall is €2.50, plus €1.50 per kilometre for the first 4km and €1.40 per subsequent kilometre. There is also a €1 charge for booking a **taxi** (☎ 194 10, 566 061).

AROUND STUTTGART

The region around Stuttgart is worth exploring and it's easy to get there on bus, tram, S-Bahn, U-Bahn or, better still, by bicycle. All of the following places are within 20 minutes of the city centre by S-Bahn or U-Bahn.

Especially worth visiting are the spectacular vineyards and lovely paths along the Neckar River, or the castles at Ludwigsburg.

Uhlbach

The best way to get into the spirit of the region is to head for the **Weinbaumuseum Uhlbach** (☎ 216 2857; Ulbacher Platz 4; admission free,

tastings €2; ⓨ 10am-noon, 2-6pm Fri & Sun, 2-6pm Sat Apr-Oct), in an old pressing house; look for the statue of the very happy-looking fellow outside. There are exhibits on the history of wine making, but the tasting room is the big draw, with up to 16 wines available for tasting at any given time. You can learn an awful lot about the region's wines here.

Opposite the museum is the late-Gothic/Renaissance **Andreaskirche**, with its distinctive steeple and, next to it, a WWII monument to locals who died.

Take tram No 4 or the S1 to Obertürkheim, then catch bus No 62 to the museum.

Württemberg

When Conrad von Württemberg established the Württemberg family dynasty, he sensibly built the family castle on this absolutely breathtaking hill southeast of Stuttgart. The hill is covered with vines and the castle has sweeping views down into a gorgeous valley.

Katherina Pavlovna, daughter of a Russian tsar and wife of Wilhelm I of Württemberg (1781–1864), reputedly told her husband that she'd never seen such a beautiful place and hoped to be buried here. When she died, Wilhelm tore down the Württemberg family castle and in its place built a Russian **Orthodox chapel** (admission free; ⓨ 10am-noon Wed, 10am-noon & 1-5pm Fri-Sun & holidays, Mar-Oct). The crypt is amazingly ornate. The tombs of Wilhelm and Katherina lie to the east; their daughter, Marie, is to the south.

PEDAL TO THE METAL

When Herman the German eases behind the wheel of his jet-black Mercedes, he's revving up for a pleasure as Teutonic as beer and bratwurst – fast driving. In a society famous for its adherence to rules and regulations, and for its passionate environmentalism, the autobahn is one of the few realms where Germans throw all caution to the wind. Where else can you travel at more than 200km (125 miles) per hour with no threat of a fine?

Germans argue vehemently to uphold their command of the autobahn. The magazine *Firmen Auto* has claimed that 'the danger of being overtaken drops sharply at 200km per hour, allowing the driver to concentrate fully on the traffic in front of the vehicle'. The AvD car club argues that 95% of all auto accidents in Germany involve drivers travelling less than 100km per hour.

Ironically, all but one-quarter of Germany's 11,000km of autobahns – the second-biggest network after the USA – have restrictions of 130km per hour or less due to endless construction work, noise pollution regulations for built-up areas and traffic jams. But long stretches remain, where the only limits are warp drive and a motorist's own nerve. Here, too, unwitting foreigners are given a rough lesson in autobahn etiquette by a BMW, Porsche or Mercedes that appears out of nowhere in the rear-view mirror, angrily flashing its lights at the vehicle ahead to MOVE OVER.

The grounds outside afford lovely views of the countryside and are a perfect place for a picnic. To get there, take bus No 61 from Obertürkheim S-Bahn station.

Max-Eyth-See & River Ride

Bring a bicycle on this little excursion along the most beautiful stretches of the Neckar River, northeast of Stuttgart. On warm summer days, young Stuttgarters head for the lake recreation areas at the Max-Eyth-See, a pleasant place for picnics – though the water in the lake isn't too pristine. Ride or take the U-Bahn (U14) one stop north to Seeblickweg, then bicycle down to the river bank.

There's a large, well-maintained bike path along this spectacular stretch of river bank. The steep hills still have some older terraced-style vineyards, and many of the little **Wengerter Häuschen** (tool sheds), which dot the hillside, are over 200 years old and are protected landmarks. You can follow the river all the way back into town.

Ludwigsburg

☎ 07141 / pop 83,000

Ludwigsburg is named for Duke Eberhard Ludwig, who built the Residenzschloss in this lovely baroque city, the childhood home of dramatist Friedrich Schiller. It's a 20-minute train ride north of Stuttgart.

ORIENTATION & INFORMATION

The S-Bahn station is at the southwestern end of town. Follow Myliusstrasse northeast to Arsenalstrasse and wend your way through the pedestrian centre to the Markt.

Ludwigsburg's **tourist office** (☎ 9102252; www .ludwigsburg.de; Wilhelmstrasse 10; ☼ 9am-6pm Mon-Fri, 9am-2pm Sat) is one block south of the Markt.

The main sights – the Residenzschloss and grounds, and Jagd-und Lustschloss Favorite (a hunting palace) – are at the eastern end of town.

SIGHTS & ACTIVITIES

Inspired by Versailles, the 18 buildings and 450-odd rooms comprising the baroque **Residenzschloss** (☎ 186 440; tours adult/concession €4/2) create a magnificent symphony of baroque, rococo and empire decoration. Some 75 rooms of the castle only (!) are open for visits, enough to reveal the ambition and imagination of Duke Eberhard Ludwig of

Württemberg, who began construction in 1704. Among the highlights are the *Jagdpavillon*, with its collection of Chinese laquerware, the *Spiegelkabinett* and its precious jewels, and the painted ceiling over the *Spielpavillon*. The castle can only be viewed on guided tours. Most tours are in German (contact the tourist office for times), except for those in English at 1.30pm Monday to Saturday, and at 11am, 1.30pm and 3.15pm Sunday March to October.

Duke Karl Eugen, a businessman and bon vivant, established a porcelain factory in the castle in 1758. You can see samples from its heyday as well as the stuff it makes today in the **Porzellan-Manufaktur**.

The amazing **Blühendes Barock** (baroque in bloom) floral festival is held in the castle gardens from May to early November (adult/concession €6.50/3; ☼ 7.30am-8.30pm). The grounds are yet another fabulous picnic area.

There are two more palaces of the former Württemberg rulers in the city. Just north of the Residenzschloss, in a cosy little nature reserve, is the **Jagd-und Lustschloss Favorite** (☎ 180 440; adult/concession €2.50/1.20; ☼ 10am-12.30pm & 1.30-5pm Mar-Oct, 10am-12.30pm & 1.30-4pm Nov-Feb), the scene of Duke Eugen's glittering parties.

The other palace, east of the city, is the **Seeschloss Monrepos** (☎ 225 50 for programme details), a former lakeside hunting lodge owned by the Württemberg family. There are concerts in summer, and you can hire boats on the lake.

The **Städtisches Museum** (☎ 9102 290; Wilhelm-strasse 9/1; admission free; ☼ 10am-noon & 1-5pm Wed-Sun) has exhibits on the town's history, industry and regional life. It's especially agreeable here during the Weihnachtsmarkt (Christmas fair).

GETTING THERE & AWAY

S4 and S5 go directly to Ludwigsburg Bahnhof. Alternatively, take a two-hour ferry ride (€13) from Bad Cannstatt to Ludwigsburg Hoheneck aboard a **Neckar-Personen-Schiffahrt** (☎ 0711-54 997 060) boat.

SCHWÄBISCH HALL

☎ 0791 / pop 35,800

Home of the Schwäbisch Hall banking and insurance company, this city is celebrated for its open-air theatre and its ancient buildings along the Kocher River. But the best reason to come here is to see a German town that really does look like the ones portrayed on chocolate boxes – a settlement of colourful half-timbered houses surrounded by rolling hills and covered bridges.

Because of its good hostel and camp sites, it's also a cheap way to explore Schwäbisch Alb – a series of plateau-like hills criss-crossed with hiking and biking trails.

Orientation & Information

There are two train stations: trains from Stuttgart arrive at the Hessental train station; those from Heilbronn go to the Hauptbahnhof at Schwäbisch Hall. Trains and buses run regularly between the two stations. The Hauptbahnhof is southwest of the Altstadt (Old Town); cross the bridge, walk down the stairs and follow the path, which will lead you across Roter Steg bridge and finally to the Markt.

The Kocher River runs south through the city separating the Altstadt (on the east) from the Neustadt (New Town). The central bus station is on the east side of the Kocher, north of Neue Strasse, the main shopping drag.

The **tourist information office** (☎ 751 246; www.schwaebischhall.de; Am Markt 9; ◷ 9am-6pm Mon-Fri, 10am-3pm Sat & Sun May-Oct, 9am-5pm Mon-Fri Oct-Apr) will help find accommodation free of charge, and provide maps and information about hikes in the region. The main post office is just west of the Markt.

Touristikgemeinschaft Neckar-Hohenlohe-Schwäbisch Wald (☎ 0791-751 385) offers information on cycling opportunities in the region and for a guide to bike trails.

Sights
MARKT

The centrepiece of the Markt isn't the **Rathaus** (town hall), reconstructed in baroque style after a town fire in 1728 and again after WWII bombing. Rather it is the **Stadtkirche St Michael**, begun in 1156 but mainly constructed during the 15th and 16th century in late-Gothic style. Note the classical net vaulting on the ceiling of the choir.

Outside, the staircase has been used every summer since 1925 for **Freilichtspiele** (open-air theatre).

Next to the tourist information office is the **Gotischer Fischbrunnen** (1509), a large tub used for storing river fish before sale. There

are still markets here every Wednesday an Saturday morning.

Just south of the Markt, at the end (Pfarrgasse, is the massive **Neubausaal**, us as an arsenal and granary, now used as theatre; walk up the stone staircase on i south side for a wonderful view of the cit Looking down to the river you can see th former **city fortifications** and, over the rive the covered **Roter Steg** bridge and the **Han man's Bridge** connecting Neue Strasse to th west side of the Kocher.

HÄLLISCH-FRANKISCHES MUSEUM

Housed in several buildings in the old cit the **Hällisch-Frankisches Museum** (☎ 751 36 Im Keckenhof 6; admission €2; ◷ 10am-5pm Tue-Su 10am-8pm Wed) covers the history of Swabi and Franconia. Exhibits include the house themselves, as well as artwork and craf from the 17th century.

One of the museum's more intriguin acquisitions is an original **synagogue** (1738 from the town of Steinbach, near where th camp site is today. It was torn down piece b piece by the Nazis and placed into storag a local man rediscovered the bricks whil renovating his house. The reconstructe synagogue will house an exhibit of Jewis life in the region.

Sleeping

DJH hostel (☎ 41050; info@jugendherberge-schwaebisc -hall.de; Langenfelder Weg 5; juniors/seniors €17.30/2(This pristine hostel, set in an attractiv former retirement home, is located jus 10 minutes on foot from the Markt. It' antiseptically clean, but service is warm and friendly.

Campingplatz Steinbacher See (☎ /fax 2984 Steinbacher See; tent/adult €5.10/4.60) This is a idyllic camp site with a good restaurant plus a washer/dryer and communal kitchen Take bus No 4 to Steinbach Mitte.

Hotel Garni Sölch (☎ 518 07; www.hotel-soelch.de Hauffstrasse 14; s/d €40/60; ✕ ℗) This hotel, o the edge of town, is modern with a pleasan rustic interior.

Hotel Garni Scholl (☎ 975 50; fax 975 58(Klosterstrasse 2-4; s/d from €64/95; ✕) Just behin St Michael, this hotel has very clean anc nicely furnished rooms.

Hotel Hohenlohe (☎ 758 70; www.hotel-hohenloh .de; Am Weilertor 14; s/d from €89/108; ✕ ▯ ℗ ✕ This is a smartly renovated, half-timbere nn and the town's chief blow-out option. You can spoil yourself with a sauna at the Wellness Centre or enjoy a relaxing massage.

Eating
Cafe Ilge (☎ 716 84; Im Weiler 2; snacks from €3.50) This 1st-floor artsy café boasts one of the best views in town from its two outdoor terraces overlooking the Kocher at the 'Hangman's Bridge'.

Hespelt (☎ 930 220; Am Spitalbach 17; lunches around €5.50) This is a big butcher-deli that puts together great hot lunches.

Da Cesare (☎ 857 626; cnr Blockgasse & Hallstrasse; meals €5-8) Da Cesare has enormous, scrumptious, New York-style pizza slices for around €2. There's a takeaway window, a sit-down restaurant serving full Italian meals, an ice-cream parlour and an outdoor café.

Weinstube Würth (☎ 6636; Im Weiler 8; meals around €8; ☻ closed Mon) Across the river, this restaurant offers some delicious Swabian specialities and has a lovely beer garden.

Getting There & Around
There's a train service at least hourly to Stuttgart (€11, 1½ hours), and every two hours to Heilbronn (€8, 40 minutes). The best way to go to Ulm is via Crailsheim; trains run at least hourly (€12.50, one hour). From Crailsheim, catch the regular service back to Schwäbisch Hall-Hessental and a connecting service to Schwäbisch Hall Hauptstadt.

Outfits hiring out bikes starting at around €5 a day include **2-Rad Zügel** (☎ 971 400; Johanniterstrasse 55) and **MHW-Radsport** (☎ 484 10; Schmollerstrasse 43).

AROUND SCHWÄBISCH HALL
Comburg
This former Benedictine monastery just 5km south of Schwäbisch Hall was established in a baron's castle in 1078. Today it's a teacher's college, but its **Stiftskirche St Nikolaus** (☎ 938 185; adult/concession €2.30/1.20; ☻ 10am-noon & 2-5pm Tue-Fri, 2-5pm Sat & Sun Apr-Oct) is a functioning Catholic church (services are on Sunday morning). The interior is impressive – note the huge Roman chandelier, lit only on special occasions. The views from the hill top are terrific. Take bus No 4 from Schwäbisch Hall.

Hohenloher Freilandmuseum
If you've any romantic illusions about farm life, a visit to the open-air **Hohenloher Freilandmuseum** (Farming Museum; ☎ 971 010; adult/concession €5/3; ☻ 10am-5pm Tue-Sat Sep-May, Tue-Sun 10am-5pm Jun-Aug) in Wackershofen, 6km west of Schwäbisch Hall, will surely cure them. The ancient farmhouses reconstructed here show just how bucolic (read: backbreaking) agriculture was before the 20th century. There are demonstrations of farming methods and equipment – we nearly got blisters just watching. To get here, take bus No 7 from Schwäbisch Hall.

TÜBINGEN
☎ 07071 / pop 82,400
Just 40km south of Stuttgart, the graceful university town of Tübingen can rival the most picturesque of German medieval castles. With its cobbled alleys, hill-top fortress and a stunning array of half-timbered houses, Tübingen is popular but lacks the summer crush of places like Heidelberg.

With 25,000 students (triple the local population), an ivy-league atmosphere seems to permeate everything. The town was a favoured haunt of Goethe, who published his first works here, and today it's a lovely place to relax for a few days, hit some pubs and paddle your way down the Neckar River.

Orientation
The Neckar flows from east to west in a boomerang arc through town; the Altstadt and all key sights are to the north. The 1m-wide Ammer River, a tributary, flows through town north of the Neckar. The Hauptbahnhof is on the south side, a five-minute walk from the Neckarbrücke, which links the city with an exit onto Platanenallee, a long, thin island in the middle of the Neckar extending to the west of the bridge.

Information
British Corner Haaggasse 1 (☎ 255 326) Wilhelmstr 44 (☎ 688 007) Stocks cheap second-hand English books.

Buchhandlung Heckenhauer Antiquariat (☎ 230 18; Holzmarkt 5) A national landmark; Hermann Hesse worked at this bookshop from 1895–99.

Commerzbank (Karlstrasse 4) Near the Hauptbahnhof.

Frauenbuchladen Thalestris (☎ 265 90; Bursagasse 2) Stocks enormous assortment of women's books (also in English). It's a women's information centre, too, and men aren't allowed inside.

Kopierzentrum (☎ 269 06; Mühlstrasse 12; €0.50 per 10 mins) Internet access, near the tourist office.

Main post office (cnr Hafengasse & Neue Strasse) Located in the Altstadt.

Postbank (Europlatz 2) Opposite the Hauptbahnhof, with an ATM.

Steinlach-Waschsalon (☎ 720 67; Albrechtstrasse 21) Laundry.

Tourist office (☎ 913 60; www.tuebingen.de; An der Neckarbrücke; ☉ 9am-7pm Mon-Fri, 9am-5pm Sat year-round, 2-5pm Sun May-Sep) Beside the bridge, this office has a hotel reservation board outside for booking at any time.

Waschsalon (Mühlstrasse 18) Laundry.

Dangers & Annoyances

The Platanenallee in the Neckar River attracts some particularly seedy characters and is often closed at night.

Sights

SCHLOSS

From the heights of the Renaissance Schloss Hohentübingen (now part of the university), there are fine views over the steep, red-tiled rooftops of the Altstadt. The Schloss now houses an **Egyptology & Archaeology Museum** (☎ 297 7384; Burgsteige 11; adult/concession €3/2; ☉ 10am-6pm Wed-Sun May-Sep, 10am-5pm Oct-Apr). Walk through the tunnel at the west side of the courtyard, past 'lovers' lane' and follow the path down through the narrow winding streets of the Altstadt and eventually onto Haaggasse.

MARKT

On the Markt in the centre of town (which overflows with geraniums in summer) is the **Rathaus** (1433), with a riotous 19th-century baroque façade. At the top is a glorious clock, moon-phase indicator and astronomical clock (1511). The four women of the **Neptune Fountain** represent the seasons, and the city council members who approved finance for the fountain modestly placed themselves in the decorative ironwork.

At the northern side of the Markt stands the **Lamm**, an erstwhile watering hole for many of Tübingen's leading figures; today it's owned by the Protestant church. Walk through the little passageway to see the beer garden.

STIFTSKIRCHE

The late-Gothic **Stiftskirche** (1470; Am Holzmarkt; ☉ 9am-5pm Feb-Oct, 9am-4pm Nov-Jan) was the site

of lectures before the main university buildings were erected. The church houses tombs of the Württemberg dukes and has excellent original medieval stained-glass windows (some dating to the early 15th century).

COTTA HAUS & GOETHE PLAQUE

Opposite the western side of the Stiftskirche is the home of Johann Friedrich Cotta, who first published the work of both Schiller and Goethe. Goethe, who was known to glean inspiration from local pubs, stayed here for a week in September 1797. One night he apparently staggered back, missed the front door and wrote a technicolour poem on the wall next door. If you look up at the 1st-floor window of that house, now a student dorm, you'll see a little sign: 'Hier Kotzte Goethe' (Goethe Puked Here).

OTHER SIGHTS

The **Platanenallee**, the long sliver of an island in the middle of the Neckar, is especially pleasant in late June when the fraternities hold their wildly popular punt races, which draw thousands of spectators.

Misbehaving students (as young as 14) were given the choice of losing their wine ration or being sent to the city's **Karzer**, the student jail on Münzgasse.

Shows at the **Kunsthalle** take place every couple of years, attracting droves of visitors; check with the tourist office for what's on.

Sleeping

DJH hostel (☎ 230 02; info@jugendherberge-tuebingen .de; Gartenstrasse 22/2; juniors/seniors €19/21.70) This hostel has a very pretty location on the north bank of the Neckar, 1km east of the tourist office.

Neckar Camping Tübingen (☎ /fax 431 45; Rappen-berghalde 61; tent/adult €5.30/3.80) This is a convenient camp site not far from the Altstadt.

Viktor-Renner-Haus (☎ 454 09; fax 440 003; Frondsbergstrasse 55; s/d €36/47) Just north of the Altstadt, this place is an excellent deal for clean, basic rooms.

Gästehaus An der Steinlach (☎ 937 40; fax 937 499; Johannesweg 14; s/d with private bathroom €38/64) This is a pleasant family-run guesthouse just a 10-minute walk southeast of the Hauptbahnhof.

Hotel am Schloss (☎ 929 40; www.hotelamschloss .de; Burgsteig 18; s/d from €51/92; P 🖳) Situated in the shadow of the castle, this hotel has ooms that are very reasonable for the central location. Ask for room No 26, which as views in all four directions. There's also a great restaurant here (see Eating, below).

Hotel Hospiz Tübingen (☎ 9240; www.hotel hospiz.de; Neckarhalde 2; s from €30, s/d with bathroom €62/92; P ✕) Very close to the Markt, this is a solid choice.

Hotel Krone Tübingen (☎ 133 10; www.krone-tue bingen.de; Uhlandstrasse 1; s/d from €85/123; P ✕) This is a very swish place near the Altstadt portals (and one of the few hotels in town with air-con). The rooms' cream-coloured décor is very Art Deco in style.

Eating

Markthalle Kelter, on the corner of Kelternstrasse and Schmiedtorstrasse, is a food hall with cheap takeaway outlets and restaurants, many selling organic products. Most snacks cost under €3.

Hanseatica (☎ 269 84; Hafengasse 2; coffee €1) For super coffee, Hanseatica can't be beaten; follow your nose.

X (☎ 249 02; Kornhausstrasse 6; snacks under €3) The best chips/French fries to be found in Baden-Württemberg are here, along with bratwurst and burgers.

The following are some places to eat inside the shopping mall at the Nonnenhaus, at the northern end of Neue Strasse.

Hotel am Schloss (☎ 929 40; Burgsteig 18; meals €6-10.50) The restaurant here literally wrote the book on the local speciality, a ravioli-like stuffed pasta called Maultaschen. The owner, Herbert Rösch, published the *Schwäbisches Maultaschen Buch*, which is available around town. The restaurant serves 28 types of Maultaschen, as well as salad plates and light meals. Sit on the back terrace for great views. Service is excellent.

Collegium (☎ 252 223; cnr Lange Gasse & Collegiums-gasse; dishes from €9; ☾ Mon-Sat) Collegium has good-sized Swabian and vegetarian dishes that you can wash down with reasonably priced beer and wine in a relaxed, informal space.

Entertainment

Neckarmüller (☎ 278 48; Gartenstrasse 4) Quite convenient to the DJH hostel, on the north side of the Neckarbrücke, this is a brewery/pub with a beer garden.

Tangente Jour (☎ 245 72; Münzgasse 17) This is the local Szene bar with lots of eats under

€8 – and not to be confused with Tangente Night.

Tangente Night (☎ 230 07; Pfleghofstrasse 10) This is a big disco and nightclub.

Club Voltaire (☎ 512 14; Haaggasse 26b) At the end of a little alley, Club Voltaire has gay and lesbian discos and cabaret.

JazzKeller (☎ 550 906; Haaggasse 15/2) This club has live jazz and 'funky soul' with a cover charge.

Shopping

Vinum (☎ 520 52; Lange Gasse 6) This shop has over 400 wines from around the region and all over the world, and samples are free. It also sells fine sherries and spirits, and a wonderful selection of olive oil.

British Corner Haaggasse 1 (☎ 255 326) Wilhelmstr 44 (☎ 688 007) These shops are about as well stocked as the average (small) supermarket. They stock (Aussie) Vegemite, and also buy and sell used English books.

Getting There & Away

Tübingen can be easily visited on a day trip from Stuttgart. Direct trains link the cities twice hourly (€16.73 return, one hour).

Staff at the **ADAC** (☎ 208 610; Wilhelmstrasse 3) can help plan your car trips.

Getting Around

You can book a taxi on ☎ 243 01. Bicycles are available for hire from **Radlager** (☎ 551 651; Lazarettgasse 19-21), and rowing boats/pedal-boats/canoes from **Bootsvermietung Märkle Tübingen** (☎ 315 29; Eberhardsbrücke 1), just east of the bridge, behind the tourist office down the little stairs.

A more stylish way of cruising the river is aboard one of the university fraternities' *Stocherkähne* (punts) for €52 per hour for up to 16 people. They're on the north bank of the river, west of the bridge, between May and October.

BURG HOHENZOLLERN

The Hohenzollern family were also the first and last monarchical rulers of the short-lived second German Reich (1871–1918) and their main stronghold was Burg Hohenzollern, about 25km south of Tübingen in the rolling Schwäbische Alb (Swabian Jura). The original 13th-century castle was destroyed during the Peasants' War in 1423 but the Hohenzollerns quickly rebuilt. The neo-Gothic version you see now (1850–67) is impressive from a distance, rising dramatically from an exposed crag, its vast medieval battlements often veiled in mist. Up close it looks more contrived, in line with the 19th-century fad of building romantic castles with little real defensive function.

The interior is definitely worth a look: its artworks, stained glass and fabulous **Schatzkammer** (treasury) justify the entry price, though the guided tour is in German only. You can view the grounds at your leisure (€2), and on clear days you can even see the Swiss Alps from here. The **castle** (☎ 07471-2428) is a few kilometres south of the town of Hechingen. Tours cost €5/3.50 (adult/concession), and take place from 9am to 5.30pm (9am to 4.30pm in winter).

There's one bus on Sunday from Hechingen train station at 11.20am, returning at 2.20pm (free if you've got a train ticket). Otherwise, return trips by taxi cost around €12 per person. Frequent trains to Hechingen from Tübingen take 20 to 30 minutes (€3.90).

HEIDELBERG
☎ 06221 / pop 141,000

Heidelberg, 130km northwest of Stuttgart, is a major tourist draw and for good reason. As befits Germany's oldest university city, the orderly red-roofed buildings stretched alongside the Neckar River manage to exude both the playfulness and rigour of student life.

The remarkable architectural unity here is due to the fact that most of the city was built all at once. Devastated in 1622 during the Thirty Years' War and then all but destroyed by invading French troops under Louis XIV, the city was entirely re-constructed in the 18th century. Its baroque style and evocative half-ruined castle looming over the town made it a haunt of 19th-century romantics, most notably the poet Goethe.

Although less-starry eyed, the American novelist and humorist Mark Twain began his European travels here in 1878 and recounted his comical observations in *A Tramp Abroad*. Britain's William Turner also loved Heidelberg, which inspired him to paint some of his greatest landscapes.

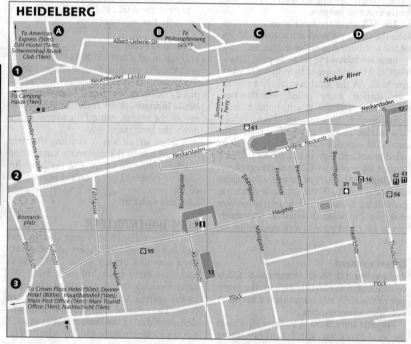

HEIDELBERG

Heidelberg is now loved nearly to death by some three million visitors a year. Even though it may seem like they're all there at once, Heidelberg remains remarkably authentic. With a student population of 32,000, it is the place for a serious pub crawl. There are dozens of earthy, enjoyable bars and pubs with good beer, friendly locals and heaps of tradition.

Orientation

The modern and less interesting western side of the city starts near the Hauptbahnhof. To find out what this place is really

INFORMATION			Studentenkarzer	23 E2	Zum Güldenen Schaf	43 D2
Deutsch-Amerikanisches Institut	1 A3		University Library	24 E3	Zur Herrenmühle	44 H1
H+G Bank	2 G2					
Private Tourist Office	3 G3		SLEEPING 🏠	(pp445-6)	DRINKING 🍺	(p447)
Private Tourist Office	4 G1		Hotel Am Kornmarkt	25 G2	Gasthaus Zum Mohren	45 E2
STA Travel	5 E2		Hotel Goldener Hecht	26 F1	Goldener Reichsapfel	46 F2
Waschsalon Wojtala	6 F2		Hotel Vier Jahreszeiten	27 F1	i Punkt	47 F2
			Hotel Zum Pfalzgrafen	28 F2	Kulturbrauerei	48 G1
SIGHTS & ACTIVITIES	(pp442-4)		Pension Jeske	29 F2	Mata Hari	49 G2
Alte Universität	7 E2		Romantik Hotel Zum Ritter St Georg	30 F2	Palmbräu Gasse	50 F2
Bootsverleih Simon			Sean Óg	31 D2	Schnookeloch	51 F1
(Boat Rental)	8 A1				Zum Roten Ochsen	52 G1
Bunsen Statue	9 B2		EATING 🍴	(p446)	Zum Sepp'l	53 G1
Ethnology Museum	10 H1		Bistro Backhaus	(see 22)		
Heiliggeistkirche	11 F2		Cafe Burkardt	32 F2	ENTERTAINMENT 🎭	(p447)
Hercules Fountain	12 F2		Café Journal	33 F2	Cave54	54 F2
Institue of Natural Sciences	13 C3		Cafe Knösel	34 F2	Gloria und Glorietta	55 B3
Jesuit Church	14 E2		MaxBar	35 F2	Harmonie	56 D2
Karl-Theodor Statue	15 F1		Mensa	36 E3	Napper Tandy's Irish Pub	57 F1
Kurpfälzisches Museum	16 D2		Mensa	(see 17)	Tangente	58 F3
Marstall	17 D1		Raja Rani	37 F2	Zimmertheater	59 E2
Monkey Statue	18 F1		Simplicissimus	38 F2	Zwinger3	60 F2
Neue Universität	19 E3		Starfish	39 F2		
Palais Boissereé	20 G2		Sudpfanne	40 H1	TRANSPORT	(pp447-8)
Rathaus	21 G2		Vetter im Schöneck	41 F1	Rhein-Neckar	
Schloss	22 H2		Viva Italia/Viva Mexico	42 D2	Fahrgastschifffahrt	61 C2

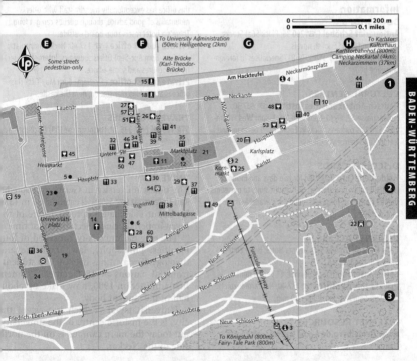

all about, head down Kurfürstenanlage to Bismarckplatz, where the romantic old Heidelberg begins to reveal itself. The Neckar River runs east–west just north of the Altstadt. Hauptstrasse is the pedestrian thoroughfare, leading 1600m – the so-called Royal Mile – eastwards through the heart of the old city from Bismarckplatz via the Markt to Karlstor.

Two main bridges cross the Neckar from the Altstadt: at the western end, north of Bismarckplatz, is Theodor-Heuss-Brücke; north of the Markt is the Alte Brücke (also known as Karl-Theodor-Brücke). On the north side of the Neckar is Heiligenberg (Holy Hill); halfway up is Philosophenweg (Philosopher's Walk).

The Schloss is at the southeastern end of the city up the hill. The DJH hostel is north of the Neckar, west of Theodor-Heuss-Brücke.

The US military communities of Mark Twain Village and Patrick Henry Village, with about 15,000 residents, are southwest of the Altstadt.

Information
BOOKSHOPS
Antiquariat Schöbel (☎ 260 36; Plöck 56a) Stocks some second-hand English novels.
Wetzlar (☎ 241 65; Plöck 79-81) Specialises in foreign-language books.

CULTURAL CENTRES
Deutsch-Amerikanisches Institut (☎ 607 30; Sofienstrasse 12; 1-6pm Mon-Fri, 1-8pm Wed, 10am-2pm Sat) Has concerts, films in English and German, and lectures and frequent exhibits.

DISCOUNT CARDS
Heidelberg Card (€2) Valid for two days and includes use of all public transport, as well as discounts to museums, theatres and even some restaurants. It's available from tourist offices.

INTERNET ACCESS
Café Gekco (☎ 604 510; Denner Hotel, Bergheimer Strasse 8; per 30min €2.10)
Coffee Internet (Hauptbahnhof; €1 per 10 min)
Private tourist office (☎ 137 40; Neckarmünzplatz; 9am-6pm Apr-Sep; €3 per 10 min)

INTERNET RESOURCES
www.heidelberg.de A good website, with English translations.

LAUNDRY
SB Waschsalon (Poststrasse 50)
Waschsalon Wojtala (Kettengasse 17; closed Sun) This is the more expensive option.

MEDICAL SERVICES
American hospital (☎ 571 600; Römerstrasse) Near Mark Twain Village.
Ärztlicher Notdienst (☎ 192 92; Alte Eppenheimer Strasse) In an emergency, contact this medical service, located near the Hauptbahnhof.

MONEY
American Express (☎ 450 50; Brückenkopfstrasse 1-2)
H+G Bank (Kornmarkt)
Reisebank (Hauptbahnhof)

POST
Main post office (Hugo-Stotz-Strasse 14) Located in the huge white building just to the right as you leave the Hauptbahnhof.

TOURIST INFORMATION
Main tourist office (☎ 194 33; www.cvb-heidelberg.de; 9am-7pm Mon-Sat, 10am-6pm Sun Mar-Oct, 9am-6pm Mon-Sat Nov-Feb) Outside the Hauptbahnhof, this office has exceptionally friendly staff who offer mountains of good advice, though queues can get long. There's a hotel reservation board outside.
Private tourist office (☎ 137 40; Neckarmünzplatz; 9am-6pm Apr-Sep) Offers souvenirs, Internet connection, brochures and some advice.
Private tourist office (9am-6pm May-Oct) This office is at the funicular station, near the castle.

TRAVEL AGENCIES
STA Travel (☎ 235 28; Hauptstrasse 139) Discount travel for students.

Sights
UNIVERSITY
The oldest university in Germany, **Ruprecht-Karl-Universität** (☎ 540) was established in 1386 by Count Palatinate Ruprecht I, one of the seven imperial prince-electors at that time.

The original university consisted of four faculties: philosophy, law, medicine and theology. Today it has over 30,000 students from 80 nations in 18 faculties. Women, first admitted in 1900, now make up about half of the student body.

Universitätsplatz, which is west of the city, is the historic centre of the university, but today the main campus is on the north side of the Neckar.

SCHLOSS

The city's chief drawcard is Heidelberg's large ruined **Schloss** (☎ 538 431; castle courtyard, rosses Fass & German Pharmaceutical Museum adult/concession €2.50/1.20, admission free to grounds; ⏰ 8am-5.30pm), one of Germany's finest examples of a Gothic-Renaissance fortress. Begun in the 13th century, its oldest remaining structures date from 1400. The castle housed a branch of the Wittelsbachs, the Bavarian royal family. Over the years, family and court intrigues led to many changes in ownership; the place was first sacked in 1622 by forces of the Catholic Wittelsbachs against Protestants within the castle. At the end of the Thirty Years' War, the castle was rebuilt but destroyed again in 1693, along with most other buildings in the city.

The castle's dilapidation actually enhances its romantic appeal. Seen from anywhere in the Altstadt, this striking red sandstone pile dominates the hillside. The Renaissance **castle courtyard** is amazing. Outside, just east of the entry, is the **Pulver Turm** (Gunpowder Tower), destroyed by French forces in 1693. The wall remains and chimney behind it are worth a look. There are several places to eat up here, too. As you enter the gates, look left at the tiny door with the iron ring, which is cracked. Legend has it that Ludwig V was prepared to give the castle to anyone who could bite through the ring; a witch supposedly gave it a shot.

The **terrace** provides huge views over the town and the Neckar. Look for the footprint in the stone, said to have been left by a knight leaping from the 3rd-storey window when the prince returned early to his wife's bedroom.

Don't miss seeing **Grosses Fass** (Great Vat), an enormous 18th-century keg, said to be capable of holding more than 220,000l. The contrast to the **Kleines Fass**, itself not exactly tiny, also earns a gasp from many visitors.

The **Deutsches Apothekenmuseum** (German Pharmaceutical Museum; ⏰ 10am-5.30pm) recalls the chemistry and alchemy of earlier times. Downstairs on the left-hand side is a memorial to Robert Bunsen, inventor of that Bunsen burner we all used in science class and of the colour-spectrum analyser. Other Bunsen-abilia in Heidelberg includes a plaque at the university and a statue on Hauptstrasse near Bismarckplatz.

You can also sign up for the rather dull guided tour of the interior (€3.50/1.70 adult/concession), which doesn't include the castle courtyard, Grosses Fass and pharmaceutical museum. For €3.50 you can buy an English-language audio guide, better than the tour.

To get to the castle either take the funicular railway from the lower Kornmarkt station (€1.75/1 one way adult/concession; €3.50/2.50 return adult/concession), or make the 10-minute walk through steep cobbled lanes. On foot, it's nice to start from the less-touristed path at the east side of Karlplatz, which brings you past the Goethe statue near the fountain.

KÖNIGSTUHL & FAIRY-TALE PARK

The funicular continues up to the Königstuhl, where there's a TV tower. The return fare from Kornmarkt, with a stop at the castle, is €6/4 (adult/concession).

Also at the top of the hill is the **Fairy-Tale Park** (☎ 234 16; adult/child €3/2; ⏰ 10am-6pm Mon-Fri Mar-Jun & Sep-Oct, 10am-7pm Jul-Aug), a wonderful playground with fairy-tale characters, hobby horses and other kiddies' stuff.

ALTE BRÜCKE

To get the most out of a town walk, begin at the Alte Brücke. The **Karl-Theodor-Statue** refers to the local legend that the prince fathered almost 200 illegitimate children. At the base of the bridge is a statue of a **brass monkey** holding a mirror and surrounded by mice: touch the mirror for wealth, the outstretched fingers to ensure you return to Heidelberg and the mice to ensure you have many children. The bridge foundation bears some pretty hairy high-water marks.

Opposite the bridge, note the plaque on the **Hotel Goldener Hecht**, which reads 'Goethe almost slept here'. Apparently, a clerk turned down the author who, to the enormous consternation of the owner, took rooms elsewhere.

MARKT

Located on the Markt (old town square), is the **Heiliggeistkirche** (1398–1441), an amazing Gothic cathedral with a baroque roof. There was, for a long time, a wall between the part used by Protestants and that used by Catholics, but it was torn down in 1936. Today, it's a Protestant place of worship.

BADEN-WÜRTTEMBERG

You can climb the 204 steps to the top of the **church spire** (admission €0.50; � 11am-5pm Mon-Sat, 1.30-5pm Sun).

The **market stalls** surrounding the church are a Heidelberg tradition. Across the street, on the south side of the Markt, the lavishly decorated former royal **pharmacy** has been reborn as a McDonald's.

In the centre of the Markt is a **Hercules fountain**; in medieval times petty criminals were chained to it and left to face the locals.

PALAIS BOISSEREÉ
A former palace located east of the Markt, **Palais Boissereé** (Hauptstrasse 235) is said to be the cradle of the Romantic movement. It once housed a collection of medieval altars and artworks that attracted poets, writers and artists (including Goethe and the Brothers Grimm, among many others).

JESUITENVIERTEL
East of Universitätsplatz is the Jesuit Quarter, a little square containing the city's former **Jesuit church** (1712–50), fronted by statues including St Ignatius Loyola, St Francis Xavier, Christ, at the façade's top centre, and Faith on the rooftop. The church is still Catholic but not Jesuit.

UNIVERSITY BUILDINGS
Dominating Universitätsplatz are the 18th-century **Alte Universität** and the **Neue Universität**, the old and new university buildings. Head south on Grabengasse to the **University Library** and then down Plöck to Akademiestrasse and the old **Institute of Natural Sciences**, where Robert Bunsen taught for more than 40 years. About 200m to the north of the square is the **Marstall**, the former stables and municipal armoury that now houses an ageing university cafeteria *(Mensa)*.

STUDENTENKARZER
From 1778 to 1914, university students were tossed into the **Studentenkarzer** (Student Jail; ☏ 54 2163; Augustinergasse 2; adult/concession €2.50/2; ☏ 10am-4pm Mon-Sat Apr-Oct, 10am-4pm Tue-Fri Nov-Mar) if convicted of misdeeds (eg singing, womanising, drinking or just plain goofing around). Sentences were generally a minimum of three days, and they were fed only bread and water; during longer sentences, the recalcitrants could interrupt their stay for critical reasons (say, to take exams).

A stint in the Karzer was considered de rigueur to prove one's manhood. Women who were admitted to the university from 1900 onwards, were never imprisoned here. Detainees passed their time by carving inscriptions and drawing graffiti, which still cover the walls.

KURPFÄLZISCHES MUSEUM
Tucked in behind a courtyard, the **Kurpfälzisches Museum** (Palatinate Museum; ☏ 583 40 Hauptstrasse 97; adult/concession €2.50/1.50; ☏ 10am-5p Tue & Thu-Sun, 10am-9pm Wed) contains regional artefacts and works of art, plus a copy of the jawbone of the 600,000-year-old Heidelberg Man. The original skeleton is kept across the river at the palaeontology centre, which is closed to the public.

PHILOSOPHENWEG
A stroll along the Philosophenweg, north of the Neckar River, provides a welcome respite from the tourist hordes. Leading through steep vineyards and orchards, the path offers those great views of the Altstadt and the castle that were such an inspiration to the German philosopher Hegel. It a well-known lovers' haunt, and many young local is said to have lost their head (and virginity) along the walkway. A little closer to the river bank is a meadow where people gather to watch the tri annual fireworks displays; see Festivals & Events (p445). There are also many other hiking possibilities in the surrounding hills.

Tours
The main tourist office arranges several tours of the city each week. There are guided tours (€6/4.50 adult/concession) in German at 10.30am daily year-round, and in English at 10.30am Thursday to Sunday from April to October; they depart from the Lion Fountain in Universitätsplatz.

Rhein-Neckar Fahrgastschifffahrt (☏ 201 8 has three-hour cruises that depart from the docks on the south bank of the Neckar A return trip costs €9.50/5.50 (adult/child and boats leave at 9.30am, 11am, 2pm an 2.40pm daily. Extra trips are sometime arranged, and the company offers a huge range of tours and trips throughout the Neckar Valley. It's a nice day trip uprive to Neckarsteinach and its four castles, buil by four brothers between 1100 and 1250 a a result of a family feud. Two of the castles are still residences of family members. Boats (adult/child €9.50/5.50, three hours return) leave from Heidelberg up to six times daily from April to October. Other day trips to castles include **Hirschhorn Castle** (adult/child €12.50/8) outside Neckarzimmern.

Rowboats and paddleboats can be hired at **Bootsverleih Simon** (☎ 411925), on the north shore of the Neckar by the Theodor-Heuss-Brücke.

Festivals & Events

Heidelberg has many annual festivals. The most popular are **Heidelberger Herbst**, the huge autumn festival during which the entire pedestrian zone is closed off for a wild party on the last Saturday in September, and the **fireworks festivals**, held three times a year (on the first Saturday in June and September, and the second Saturday in July).

During these festivities the castle is specially lit and the whole town, plus members of the US military communities, show up to watch the magic. Best viewing sites are from the northern bank of the Neckar and from Philosophenweg.

The **Christmas market**, held at the Markt in December, is also a treat.

Sleeping

BUDGET

Bargains are thin on the ground in Heidelberg, and in the high season finding a place to stay can be difficult. Arrive early in the day or book ahead – especially for the hostel. The tourist office can book a limited number of **private flats** (d from €35-70) in the city, but they book out very quickly and well in advance. Staff can advise you on options in the surrounding region.

DJH hostel (☎ 412 066; jh-heidelberg@tl-online.de; Tiergartenstrasse 5; juniors/seniors €14.90/17.60) This hostel is a rather long walk across the river from the Hauptbahnhof. It's a lively, noisy establishment, with a cafeteria, pub and a small disco; downstairs there's also a token-operated laundry. From the Hauptbahnhof or Bismarckplatz, take bus No 33 towards the zoo, stopping at Jugendherberge.

Pension Jeske (☎ 23733; www.pension-jeske-heidelberg.de; Mittelbadgasse 2; d per person €25) Large, colourful and decorated with flair, the rooms in this 250-year-old house are a resounding 'Nein' to cookie-cutter hotel rooms. There

are a handful of doubles, a triple and one five-bed dormitory room, which costs €20 a bed. The quiet street is central enough to make foraging for breakfast no problem.

Camping Neckartal (☎ 802 506; www.camping-heidelberg.de; Schlierbacher Landstrasse 151; tent/person €6/5.50; ⏰ Apr-Oct) This camp site is about 4.5km east of town by the river. Most helpful for budget travellers without camping equipment is the site's 'rent-a-van' programme, which provides bed and breakfast in a caravan for €12. Take bus No 35 from Bismarckplatz to Im Grund.

Camping Haide (☎ 2111; www.camping-haide.de; Ziegelhäuser Landstrasse, Haide; tent/person €4/4.60) This camp site is across the river and about 1km back towards the city centre. You can also rent a place in the dormitory lofts – like bunk barns – for €6.50 per person, or in more private log huts for one/two/four people for €10.50/17/30. Take bus No 35 from Bismarckplatz to the Orthopädische Klinik stop, from where the site is only a five-minute walk.

MID-RANGE

Hotel Am Kornmarkt (☎ 243 25; Kornmarkt 7; s/d with shared bathroom €49/79) Discreet and understated, this Altstadt favourite also has more expensive rooms with private bathroom and TV. Whatever the category, rooms are spacious and in mint condition.

Hotel Vier Jahreszeiten (☎ 241 64; www.4-jahreszeiten.de; Haspelgasse 2; s/d/t €70/99/119; P) Location, location, location. Right near the Alte Brücke you could hardly get more central, but nobody broke the bank on decorative flourishes for the beige-y rooms. It's claimed that Goethe himself once creased the sheets here. Of course, they've been changed since then.

Hotel Goldener Hecht (☎ 536 80; www.hotel-goldener-hecht.de; Steingasse 2; s/d €66.50/91) Goethe almost slept here: the hotel would have kept the famous author but the clerk at the time had not been quite so uppity. See Alte Brücke (p443).

Hotel Zum Pfalzgrafen (☎ 204 89; fax 536 141; Kettengasse 21; s/d from €69/89; P) Polished pine floors are a nice touch in these well-appointed rooms – private bathrooms have hair dryers. There's also an elevator, and parking is an additional €8.

Kohler (☎ 970 097; hotel-kohler@t-online.de; Goethestrasse 2; s/d with private bathroom €63/78, with shared bathroom €42/52; ⊠) Within walking distance east of the Hauptbahnhof, there's nothing particularly special about Kohler's tidy rooms. The bonus is the excellent location.

Sean Og (☎ 138 000; www.seanog.com; Hauptstrasse 93; s/d from €60/80; ⊠ Ⓟ) This cosy hotel is in the heart of Heidelberg's nightlife district, with an Irish pub of the same name downstairs.

TOP END

Romantik Hotel Zum Ritter St Georg (☎ 1350; www .ritter-heidelberg.de; Hauptstrasse 178; s/d from €125; ⌨ Ⓟ) This ornate 16th-century hotel on the Markt is one of the few town buildings that survived the French attacks of 1693. Rooms vary in size, but generally you'll find high ceilings, plush furniture and elegantly tall windows.

Denner Hotel (☎ 604 510; www.denner-hotel.de; Bergheimer Strasse 8; d from €95; ⊠ ⌨) This is a sleek place with rooms decked out in Southeast Asian furniture and modern décor by local artists. There are special weekend rates, and there's a pleasant Internet café downstairs. For details, see Internet access (p442).

Eating

You might expect a student town to have plenty of cheap eating options, but free-spending tourists seem to outweigh frugal scholars in Heidelberg. Hauptstrasse is crammed with restaurants offering specialities from around the world.

RESTAURANTS

Zum Güldenen Schaf (☎ 208 79; Hauptstrasse 115; mains from €11) This is a huge old tavern with an extensive menu, vegetarian fare and local specialities. The décor is eye-catching, but it can be a real tourist trap in summer.

Sudpfanne (☎ 163 636; Hauptstrasse 223; mains from €10; ☽ dinner only, closed Sun) Behind the barrel-shaped entrance, Sudpfanne serves vegetarian cuisine and local dishes, and is touristy mainly because of the rustic décor.

Starfish (☎ 602 587; Steingasse 16a; mains from around €9.50; ☽ Mon-Sat) Starfish serves quality 'natural food', like vegetable-and-nut tofu with chipped potatoes. Note, the place is small, so it fills up quickly.

Zur Herrenmühle (☎ 602 909; Hauptstrasse 237-39; mains €24-30) This is a slow but super-deluxe place serving small portions of outstand-ing nouvelle cuisine (don't blink or you'll miss it). You'll need loads of time and lots of dosh.

Simplicissimus (☎ 183 336; Ingrimstrasse 16; mains €17-23.50; ☽ dinner only, closed Tue) This is a white-linen kind of place as befits a fine French dining experience. There's a pretty inner courtyard; book ahead.

CAFÉS

Bistro Backhaus (☎ 979 70; Im Schlosshof; meals around €6) Inside the Schloss, this is a truly good deal offering local specialities – don't miss the Maultaschen and, if it's going, the turkey bratwurst with cabbage cooked in wine.

Prices for the following cafés range from €2 to €3.

MaxBar (☎ 244 19; Marktplatz 5) This is a big favourite, and it's a bit more varied than some of the posey 'intellectual' cafés.

Cafe Burkardt (☎ 166 620; Untere Strasse 27) When Hauptstrasse is crawling with tourists, locals come here for a little peace and quiet along with their coffee and pastries.

Café Journal (☎ 161 712; Hauptstrasse 162) You can linger in this local favourite for hours over coffee, or sample the varied menu of salads, fish or cold cut plates. The Sunday brunches are particularly popular.

Café Knösel (☎ 223 45; Haspelgasse 20) On the corner of Untere Strasse, Café Knösel sells 'student kisses' (chocolate-covered wafers) and other tasty morsels, along with very good coffee and cocoa.

QUICK EATS

Mensa (Universitätsplatz; ☽ 11.30am-2pm) Students pay only about €2.50 for a full meal here. There's another, less comfortable *Mensa* in the Marstall, a two-minute walk north of the university on Marstallstrasse.

Viva Italia/Viva Mexico (☎ 273 19; Hauptstrasse 113a; meals from €4) This place serves excellent pizza and some of the best Mexican food in Germany. It also offers doner kebab.

Raja Rani (☎ 244 84; Mittelbadgasse 5; meals around €4) Raja Rani serves decent Indian and Pakistani takeaway meals with a welcome assortment of vegetarian dishes.

Vetter im Schöneck (☎ 165 850; Steingasse 9; meals under €5.50) This restaurant serves good soups, salads and light dishes, along with its own microbrewed beer. See also the Drinking section (p447).

Drinking

Vetter im Schöneck (☎ 165 850; Steingasse 9; meals under €6.50) We went seriously overboard with the microbrewed beer here. It has a comfy atmosphere, lovely service and shiny beer vats. See also its entry under Eating (p446).

Kulturbrauerei (☎ 502 980; Leyergasse 6) With glossy plank floors, chandeliers and high ceilings, this relatively new microbrewery is an upscale version of a homey beer hall.

Palmbräu Gasse (☎ 285 36; Hauptstrasse 185) In the passage between Untere Strasse and Hauptstrasse, this amazing place has a medieval feel with its stonework and wooden benches. It also offers good service and gets a great crowd.

i Punkt (☎ 124 41; Untere Strasse 30) This is a modern place popular with 20-somethings.

Gasthaus Zum Mohren (☎ 212 35; Untere Strasse 5-7) This is another nook for scholars to knock back a few.

Schnookeloch (☎ 138 080; Haspelgasse 8) Schnookeloch first opened its doors in 1407. Some nights you'll catch fraternity members singing.

Goldener Reichsapfel (☎ 485 542; Untere Strasse 35) This original student hang-out hasn't quite gone the way of the other drinking holes. There's noisy chat, even louder music and nowhere to sit just about every night.

Mata Hari (☎ 181 808; Oberbadgasse 10) On the corner of Zwingerstrasse, this is a popular gay bar.

A self-respecting university town, Heidelberg naturally has oodles of backstreet pubs and cafés. The two most historical 'student' bars are **Zum Sepp'l** (☎ 230 85; Hauptstrasse 213) and **Zum Roten Ochsen** (☎ 209 77; Hauptstrasse 217), but nowadays students tend to avoid them in favour of less-touristy joints.

Entertainment

Meier is the monthly publication featuring information on clubs, pubs, restaurants, and gay and lesbian venues.

CINEMAS

Gloria und Glorietta (☎ 253 19; Hauptstrasse 146) This cinema screens English-language films regularly.

Harmonie (☎ 203 40; cnr Hauptstrasse & Theaterstrasse) English-language films are shown here occasionally.

DISCOS & CLUBS

Nachtschicht (☎ 164 404; Bergheimerstrasse 95) Near the Hauptbahnhof, Nachtschicht has Top-40 canned music on weekends, live music Monday to Friday and, on Thursday, soul and hip-hop.

Schwimmbad Musik Club (☎ 470 201; Tiergartenstrasse 13) Near the DJH hostel, this club plays lots of live music, and the programme changes constantly – 1980s and 1990s music, heavy metal and sometimes techno.

Tangente (☎ 169 444; Kettengasse 23) One of the town's most popular discos.

LIVE MUSIC

Schwimmbad Musik Club (☎ 470 201; Tiergartenstrasse 13) Live music is performed here.

Cave54 (☎ 221 58; Krämergasse 2) Opened in 1954, this is said to be the oldest jazz club in Germany, and Louis Armstrong once played here. It also has jam sessions.

Napper Tandy's Irish Pub (☎ 259 79; Haspelgasse 4) The only folk music performed regularly is Irish.

THEATRE & CLASSICAL MUSIC

A few times every summer, concerts are held in the Schloss and at the Thingstätte amphitheatre on Heiligenberg, which is signposted along Philosophenweg. Schedules for both venues are available from the main tourist office. Organ concerts are held every Saturday at 6.15pm and sometimes during the week at the Heiliggeistkirche on the Markt.

Zimmertheater (☎ 210 69; Hauptstrasse 118) Come here for mainstream comedies, dramas and the odd avant-garde production.

Theater der Stadt Heidelberg (☎ 583 523; Theaterstrasse 4) Besides Zimmertheater, this is Heidelberg's other best-known theatre.

Zwinger3 (☎ 583 546; Zwingerstrasse 3) A series of plays for children and young adults are performed here.

Kulturhaus Karlstorbahnhof (☎ 978 911; Am Karlstor 1) The 19th-century Bahnhof at Karlstor, east of the city centre, has been converted to an 'alternative' cultural centre featuring theatre, cinema, music, art shows and other events.

Getting There & Away
TO/FROM THE AIRPORT
Lufthansa runs its Airport Express service to/from Frankfurt airport several times a

day (€19, one hour) from the Crown Plaza Hotel. The timetable often changes; ring ☎ 069-69 694 433 for details.

CAR & MOTORCYCLE

The north–south A5 links Heidelberg with both Frankfurt and Karlsruhe. The **ADAC** (☎ 720 981; Carl-Diem-Strasse 2-4) provides help for motorists.

TRAIN

There are frequent train connections to/ from Frankfurt (€12.40, one hour), Stuttgart (€16, 1½ hours), Baden-Baden (€12.40, one hour), Munich (€47.20, three hours) and Nuremberg (€32.20 to €38.20, four hours).

Getting Around

BICYCLE

You can hire bicycles from **Per Bike** (☎ 161 148; Bergheimer Strasse 125; €10 per day).

CAR & MOTORCYCLE

There are well-marked underground car parks throughout the city, charging around €1.50 per hour. On weekends you can 'park and ride' for free, and take the frequent shuttle buses (also free) to the Altstadt; look for the 'P&R' signs.

PUBLIC TRANSPORT

Bismarckplatz is the main transport hub. The bus and tram system in and around Heidelberg is extensive and efficient. Single tickets cost €1.90 and a 24-hour pass costs €5. From 9am to 4pm Monday to Friday and all day Saturday and Sunday there's a 24-Plus pass that allows five people to travel for €8. Bus Nos 11, 21, 33, 34, 41 and 42, as well as tram No 1, run between Bismarckplatz and the Hauptbahnhof. Bus Nos 11 and 33 go directly from the Hauptbahnhof to Neckarmuntzplatz.

TAXI

Flag fall is €2.30 plus €1.30 per kilometre. **Taxis** (☎ 739 090) line up outside the Hauptbahnhof, or you can book one by phone. It costs about €7 to €8 from the Hauptbahnhof to the Alte Brücke.

AROUND HEIDELBERG

Excursions to the Neckar Valley offer a good introduction to the surrounding countryside. **Rhein-Neckar Fahrgastschifffahrt** (☎ 06221-201 81), on the south bank of th Neckar in Heidelberg, offers the most sce nic tours and some of the cheapest ways t get around the Neckar Valley, with boat to the main destinations (eg the castles a Neckarsteinach and Hirschhorn).

Schloss Schwetzingen

The apex of German rococo landscaping i marked by the magnificent **Schloss Schwetz ingen** (☎ 06202-814 81; adult/concession €6.50/3.2 Apr-Oct, €5/2.50 Nov; ☼ palace 10am-4pm Tue-Fr 11am-5pm Sat & Sun Apr-Oct, 11am-2pm Fri, 11am-3pr Sat & Sun Nov-Mar; garden 8am-8pm Apr-Sept, 9am-6pr Oct-Mar) and its gardens. When Prince-Elec tor Carl Theodor inherited the Palatinat region in the mid-18th century he mad Schwetzingen his summer residence an set about a full-scale redesign of the ancien palace and gardens. The palace reconstruc tion remained an unfinished project, bu his gardens are a jewel. His idea was t commission a whimsical garden in keepin with the era's love of follies. The garden' secluded charm (and sheer lack of obviou use) make it a great place to lose yoursel for a few hours.

The grounds, which took three decade for French architect Nicolas de Pigage t lay out and complete, radiate from a forma French garden with delicate statues, flora beds and wide gravelled promenades. O the outer edges are theme-park-like sprink lings of architectural genres, from Rome t China, linked to each other by shady path and a lacy waterway circuit.

The chief follies include **Temple Apollos** an auditorium built in the Greek-columne style of a shrine to the gods, perched self importantly on an artificial knoll. The silli ness of the genre continues in the **Römische Wasserweg**, a fake fortress and aqueduc conceived as an ivy-covered ruin, and th **Moschee** (Mosque), which sports an Orien tal dome above a rather Germanic baroqu entrance.

One of the main routes back crosses th incongruous **Chinesische Brücke**, an arche Chinese bridge.

The main **Jagdschloss** (Hunting Palace) i almost staid by comparison, its interior a toned-down version of rococo stucco an curlicued wallpaper. The highlight withi is the **Rokokotheater** (1752), another Pigag masterpiece with a deep-set stage tha draws on light and a tunnel illusion to enhance the dimensions. Ask the gatekeeper about the **clock** on the façade, completed in 1700; the big and little hands were reversed so that horsemen could read time more easily from a distance.

Prices include a guided tour of the palace and gardens. A visit to the gardens alone costs €4/2 (adult/child).

GETTING THERE & AWAY

Schloss Schwetzingen is 10km west of Heidelberg, just off the A6 autobahn 8km south of Mannheim. From Bismarckplatz in Heidelberg, take tram No 2 to Eppelheim, Kirchheimer Strasse, and switch to Bus No 20 to Schwetzingen (€3.10, 25 minutes). From Mannheim, take the train to Schwetzingen Bahnhof (€3.10, 25 minutes), where the VRN bus No 7007 (and others) depart for the Schloss (€0.60, eight minutes).

MANNHEIM

☎ 0621 / pop 308, 300

You won't find Mannheim on any Top 10 (or likely even Top 100) listing of German tourist destinations. It's hard to imagine that this sprawling industrial centre, 78km southwest of Frankfurt, was once a tiny fishing village, rising to prominence only in the early 18th century when Elector Carl Philipp moved the Palatinate court here from Heidelberg.

Like Karlsruhe to the south, Mannheim's old town was flattened in 1945 and replaced, by and large, with unsightly steel and concrete blocks. However, it (sort of) compensates with its big-city sense of fun, lively cultural scene and good shopping. Its streets also have a particularly quirky layout – a giant chessboard.

Orientation & Information

What's left of the old centre is north and northwest of the Hauptbahnhof, on a peninsula formed by the Rhine and Neckar Rivers.

The chessboard layout is a trip when you first arrive, with addresses such as 'Q3,16' or 'L14,5' sounding a bit like galactic sectors. But this grid system is practical once you get used to it. The centre is bisected by two largely pedestrianised shopping streets, the north–south Kurpfalzstrasse and the east–west Planken/Heidelberger Strasse.

The **tourist office** (☎ 0190-770 020; www.tourist -mannheim.de; Willy-Brandt-Platz 3; ☺ 9am-7pm Mon-Fri 9am-noon Sat) can help you find accommodation. It's opposite the Hauptbahnhof.

The main post office is situated in O2 in the city centre; the Reisebank is in the Hauptbahnhof. You can wash your smalls at **Waschsalon Stolz** (☎ 333 299; Mittelstrasse 20).

Internet access is available at the high-tech **Chat-Corner Internet cafe** (☎ 156 1512; L14, 16-17; ☺ 10am-3am; €3 per hr), near the tourist office. It also serves good pizzas and snacks.

Sights & Activities

Coming by train from the north you'll pass the **Residenzschloss** (☎ 292 2890; adult/concession €3/2; ☺ 10am-5pm Tue-Sun Apr-Oct, 10am-5pm Sat & Sun Nov-Mar), an imposing baroque palace. Soon after its completion, Elector Carl Theodor moved his court to Munich in 1777, rendering the Schloss a bit pointless. Today it's part of the university, and you can take a guided tour of the sumptuous interior. The flowery **Schlosskirche** in the western wing holds the remains of Carl Philipp's third wife, Violante Thurn und Taxis of the famous brewing dynasty.

Due north of the Hauptbahnhof, on the loud and busy Kaiserring, is the elegant **Wasserturm** (Water Tower) in the middle of pretty Friedrichplatz, flanked by a huge Art Deco fountain landscape. One of Mannheim's few oases of calm, the gardens are dotted with lazing students, ice-cream vendors and buskers in the warmer months.

On its south side is the highly acclaimed **Kunsthalle** (☎ 293 6430; adult/concession €2.50/1.50; ☺ 10am-5pm Tue-Sun, noon-5pm Thu), a museum of 19th- and 20th-century art, which houses, among other great works, Cezanne's *Pipe-smoker*, Manet's *Execution of Emperor Maximilian of Mexico* and sculptures by Ernst Barlach.

A few minutes northeast of the city centre, on Renzstrasse, is the lovely **Luisenpark** (admission €3; ☺ 9am-dusk), a sprawling green belt with hothouses, gardens and an aquarium.

Sleeping

Mannheim is primarily a business town and the hotel prices reflect this.

DJH hostel (☎ 822 718; Rheinpromenade 21; www .jugendherberg-mannheim.de; juniors/seniors €16.30/19;

(P)) This hostel is a 15-minute walk south of the Hauptbahnhof towards the Rhine.

Arabella Pension Garni (☎ 230 50; fax 156 4527; M2 12; s/d from €28/45) This is a rare exception (because it's cheap) in the city centre. Just north of the Schloss, it has basic rooms; breakfast costs an extra €5.

Central Hotel (☎ 123 00; www.centralhotelmannhe im.de; Kaiserring 26-28; s/d from €76/96; (P) ⊠) This modern hotel is perfectly situated near the Hauptbahnhof for an early getaway. The comfy rooms have soundproofed windows. Rates are less on weekends.

Maritim Parkhotel (☎ 158 80; fax 158 8800; Friedrichsplatz 2; s/d from around €129/160; (P) ⊠ ⓩ) Parkhotel offers traditional 1st-class creature comforts, plus pools, fitness gadgets and more.

Eating

The area around the central Planken offers a number of fast-food places. *Mensa*, which serves filling meals for €4 or less, is situated in the southwest corner behind the Schloss.

Gasthaus Zentrale (☎ 202 43; snacks from around €3.50) This pub/restaurant is a favourite student hang-out; however, it's packed in the evenings. It also sports a nice beer garden in the summer.

Eichbaum Brauhaus (☎ 353 85; Käfertaler Strasse 168; dishes around €9) Mannheim's largest brewery sits north of the Neckar River and serves hearty German fare, along with its signature beers.

Getting There & Away

The frequent Lufthansa bus takes about one hour make the journey to or from Frankfurt airport; the departure point is on the corner of L14 and Kaiserring (one way/return €19/35).

Mannheim is a major junction for trains on the Hamburg to Basel line, with ICE trains from Frankfurt (€22.40, 35 minutes), Basel (€44.20, 2½ hours) and Freiburg (€30 to €80, 1½ hours).

Mannheim is extremely well connected for driving, situated as it is at the junction of the A656 autobahn east to Heidelberg, the A650 west to Ludwighafen and the north–south A6/A67.

If you want to hitch a ride, contact the **City-Netz service** (☎ 194 44), in the tourist office.

Getting Around

Mannheim is huge, and the bus/tram network is well developed. Single short/regular journeys cost €1/1.80; a triple-zone 24-TicketPlus 24-hour pass costs €5.40.

If driving, it's best to park just east of the city centre along the Augustaanlage and walk in (note that Parkschein machines are in use). There's also a huge car park directly underneath the Hauptbahnhof.

ULM

☎ 0731 / pop 169,000

On the Danube River at the border between the states of Baden-Württemberg and Bavaria, Ulm is one of the region's most adventurous and free-thinking cities. Not every city would have dared to erect a startling piece of modern architecture (the Stadthaus) next to its most famous medieval landmark (the Münster tower). Small wonder that the founder of modern physics, Albert Einstein, was born in Ulm.

Before Einstein there was Albrecht Berblinger, a tailor who invented the hang-glider in 1802. A highly sceptical public watched as Berblinger attempted to fly across the river after leaping (some say he was kicked) from the city wall. The 'Tailor of Ulm', as the locals call him, made a splash landing, but his design worked and became the prototype of the modern hang-glider.

Orientation

Perhaps Ulm's inventive spirit comes from its idiosyncratic geography. Greater Ulm is actually split between two *Länder* (states), a curiosity that dates back to Napoleon, who decreed that the river would divide Baden-Württemberg and Bavaria. On the south side of the Danube, the Bavarian city of Neu-Ulm, with a population of 51,000, is a rather bland, ugly and modern city that was formerly home to the US Army's Wiley Barracks, now used as low-income housing and a cultural and entertainment complex.

On the north side of the river is Ulm, which counts 118,000 people and contains the main attractions. All the major sights are within the oval between Olgastrasse, a main thoroughfare, and the Danube to the south. The Hauptbahnhof is at the western end of the city, the university to the northwest and the hostel to the southwest.

ULM

0 ____ 300 m
0 ____ 0.2 miles

INFORMATION	
Contrum	1 B3
Deutsche Bank	2 B3
Herwig	3 B3
Hypovereinsbank	4 A2
Intercall	5 B3
Lanladen	6 C2
Schwörhaus	7 B3
Tourist Office	8 B3

SIGHTS & ACTIVITIES	(pp451-3)
Einstein Fountain	9 C2
Einstein Monument	10 A2
Metzgerturm	11 B3

Münster	12 B3
Museum der Brotkultur	13 B2
Rathaus	14 B3
Stadthaus	(see 8)
Ulmer Museum	15 B3

SLEEPING	(p453)
Garni Rose	16 D3
Hotel am Rathaus	17 B3
Hotel Bäume	18 B2
Hotel Reblaus	(see 17)
Hotel Schiefes Haus	19 B3
Hotel zum Anker/Spanische Weinstube	20 B2
Münster Hotel	21 B2

EATING	(pp453-4)
Allgäuer Hof	22 B3
Café Kässmeyer	23 B3
Drei Kannen	24 B2
Pflugmerzler	25 B2
Zunfthaus der Schiffleute	26 B3
Zur Forelle	27 B2

ENTERTAINMENT	(p454)
Barfüsser	28 B3
Enchilada	29 C3
Tagblatt	30 C3
Weinkrüger	31 B3

TRANSPORT	(p454)
Riverboat Docks	32 B3

The two cities share transport systems and important municipal facilities.

Information
BOOKSHOPS
Contrum (☎ 144 90; Hirschstrasse 12) Get your daily English-language news fix from the international stand here.
Herwig (☎ 962 170; Münsterplatz 18) A travel bookshop, with a few Lonely Planet titles and lots of other travel literature and maps.

INTERNET ACCESS
Intercall (☎ 398 8870; Neue Strasse 101; per 15 min/1hr €1/2.50)
Lanladen (☎ 176 1088; Bockgasse 21; per 15min/1hr €1/4)

LAUNDRY
Waschsalon Kaiser (Memminger Strasse 72/235) Located at the former Wiley Barracks; take bus No 6 to Marlene Dietrich stop or Memminger Strasse.

MEDICAL SERVICES
Deutsches Rotes Kreuz (☎ 192 22, 144 40; Frauenstrasse 125) For a doctor or an ambulance in an emergency, contact this centre.
Rape crisis centre hotline (☎ 698 84)

MONEY
Deutsche Bank (Münsterplatz)
Hypovereinsbank (Opposite Hauptbahnhof)

POST
Main post office (Hauptbahnhof, Bahnhofplatz 2)

TOURIST INFORMATION
Tourist office (☎ 161 2830; www.tourismus.ulm.de; Stadthaus bldg, Münsterplatz 50; 9am-6pm Mon-Fri, 9am-4pm Sat, 10.30am-2.30pm Sun May-Oct, 9am-6pm Mon-Fri, 9am-1pm Sat Nov-Apr) Sells the Ulm Card for €6/10, which offers one/two days of free and discounted sightseeing and transport. It also publishes a free monthly listings leaflet, Wohin in Ulm/Neu Ulm.

Sights
MÜNSTER
The main reason for coming to Ulm is to see the huge **Münster** (Cathedral; Münsterplatz; admission free; 9am-4.45pm Nov-Feb, 9am-5.45pm Mar, Sep & Oct, 9am-6.45pm Apr, 8am-6.45pm May-Aug), celebrated for its 161.6m-high steeple – the tallest on the planet. Though the first stone was laid in 1377, it took over 500 years for the entire structure to be completed. Note

the **hallmarks** on each stone, inscribed by cutters who were paid by the block.

Only by climbing to the viewing platform at 143m, via the 768 spiral steps, do you fully appreciate the tower's dizzying height: there are unparalleled views of the Black Forest and the Swabian Jura mountains, and on clear days you can even see the Alps. The last entry to the tower is one hour before closing. Allow 30 minutes for the ascent.

As you enter the church, note the **Israelfenster**, a stained-glass window above the west door that serves as a memorial to Jews killed during the Holocaust. The carved **pulpit canopy**, as detailed as fine lace, eliminates echoes during sermons; to one side is a tiny spiral staircase leading to a mini-pulpit for the Holy Spirit.

In the original 15th-century oak **choir stalls**, the top row depicts figures from the Old Testament, the middle from the New Testament. The bottom and sides show historical characters, such as Roman playwright Lucius Seneca, Nero's tutor (who committed suicide by slashing his wrists), and Pythagoras, who strums a lute.

The impressive **stained-glass windows** in the choir, dating from the 14th and 15th centuries, were removed for the duration of WWII. The oldest to the right of centre (1385) shows the Münster as it was in the 15th century. Organ concerts are held regularly, usually on weekends; sometimes there's a charge of around €2.50.

STADTHAUS
The other highlight of Münsterplatz is the **Stadthaus** (1993), designed by American architect Richard Meier. He caused an uproar for erecting a postmodern building next to the city's Gothic gem, but the result is both gorgeous and functional. It stages exhibitions and special events, and also houses the tourist office, the state's travel agency and an expensive café.

RATHAUS
The Rathaus nearby was a commercial building until 1419. The eastern side has a Renaissance façade with ornamental figures and an amazing **astrological clock** (1520). There's a standard clock with Arabic numbers above it. Not accurate enough? Check the **sundial** above that or listen for the bells,

which count off every quarter-hour. Inside the Rathaus you can see a replica of **Berblinger's flying machine**.

In the Marktplatz to the south is the **Fischkastenbrunnen**, a tank where fishmongers kept their river fish alive on market days.

CITY WALL & TOWERS
On the north bank of the Danube you can walk along the **Stadtmauer**, the former city wall. Its height was reduced in the early 19th century after Napoleon decided that a heavily fortified Ulm was against his best interests. Note the **Metzgerturm**, leaning 2m off-centre to the north.

East of the Herdbrucker is a monument at the spot where Albrecht Berblinger attempted his flight.

FISCHERVIERTEL
Every first Monday in July, the mayor swears allegiance to the town's 1397 constitution at the **Schwörhaus** (Oath House). From here, stroll between the buildings whose roofs almost touch in **Kussgasse** (Kissing Alley) and cross **Lügner-Brücke** (Liar's Bridge) into the charming **Fischerviertel** (Fisherman's Quarter), the old city's fishing and shipbuilding quarter, built along the tiny and sparkling clear Blau River, which flows into the Danube.

EINSTEIN FOUNTAIN & MONUMENT
About 750m northeast of the Münster, stands a fiendishly funny fountain dedicated to Albert Einstein, who was born in Ulm but left when he was one year old. Before WWII he was granted 'honorary citizenship', but the Nazis revoked it.

After the war, when Ulm asked the great man if he wanted this honour reinstated, he declined. The nearby health administration building, at Zeughaus 14, bears a single stone attached to the wall entitled Ein Stein (One Stone).

Over on Bahnhofstrasse is Max Bill's monument (1979) to the great physicist, a stack of staggered granite pillars on the spot where Einstein's home once stood.

MUSEUMS
The tourist office sells a museum pass for €5 that allows free entrance to eight museums.

The **Ulmer Museum** (☎ 161 4330; Marktplatz 9; adult/concession €3/2, free Fri; 🕙 11am-5pm Tue-Sun,

11am-8pm Thu) houses a collection of ancient
and modern art, including icons, religious
paintings, and sculptures. A highlight is the
20th-century **Kurt Fried Collection**, with works
from artists including Klee, Kandinsky, Picasso, Lichtenstein and Macke.

The **Museum der Brotkultur** (Bread Museum;
☎ 699 55; Salzstadelgasse 10; adult/concession €2.50/2;
10am-5pm Thu-Tue, 10am-8.30pm Wed), north of
Münsterplatz, celebrates bread as the staff
of life in the Western world. It also works
with universities to develop new strains of
wheat and other grain for use in developing countries.

Tours
In addition to walking tours in German
regularly conducted by the tourist office,
you can also book the popular **Sportiv Touren**
(☎ 970 9298), two- to three-hour canoe tours
(€20/13 adult/child under 14) from various
points on the Danube and Iller Rivers.

There are also cruises (€6.50/4 adult/
child) up the Danube at 2pm, 3pm and
4pm Monday to Saturday, and hourly
between 1pm and 5pm on Sunday. The
docks are on the Ulm side, just south of the
Metzgerturm.

Sleeping
DJH hostel (☎ 384 455; info@jugendherberge-ulm
.de; Grimmelfinger Weg 45; juniors/seniors €17.30/20)
From the Hauptbahnhof, take the S1 to
Ehinger Tor, then take bus No 4 or 8
to Schulzentrum, from where it's a five-
minute walk.

Gasthof Rose (☎ 778 03; u.hilpert@t-online.de; Kas-
ernstrasse 42a; s/d €20/40) Across the river in Neu
Ulm, the Rose has perfectly decent rooms.

Münster Hotel (☎/fax 641 62; Münsterplatz 14;
s/d with shared bathroom from €28/49; P) Friendly
and well located, this hotel offers excellent value for money, with neat, well-
maintained rooms that include TV. More
expensive rooms with private bathroom
are available.

Hotel zum Anker/Spanische Weinstube (☎/fax
632 97; Rabengasse 2; s/d from €30/48; P) Right beside the Münster, this place also has comfortable rooms. It has a good restaurant,
which is a very popular stop for cyclists
doing the Danube.

Hotel Bäumle (☎ 622 87; baeumle.ulm@t-online
.de; Kohlgasse 6; s/d with shared bathroom €30/45, with
private bathroom €40/55; P) This is a snug little

place with great views of the Münster – ask
for a room at the back. The restaurant is
also very good. See Eating (below) for more
details.

Hotel am Rathaus & Hotel Reblaus (☎ 968 490;
www.rathausulm.de; Kronengasse 10; s/d €45/65; P)
Right behind the Rathaus, these family-
run twin hotels offer comfortable upmarket
options.

Hotel Schiefes Haus (☎ 967 930; www.hotelschief
eshausulm.de; Schwörhausgasse 6; r €103-134) One
of Baden-Württemberg's sweetest hotels,
this romantic half-timbered house (1443)
claims a *Guinness Book of Records* listing
as the 'most crooked hotel in the world'
(the building, that is). Beds have specially-
made height adjusters and spirit levels, so
you won't roll out at night.

Eating
RESTAURANTS
Allgäuer Hof (☎ 674 08; Fischergasse 12; pancakes
from €8) Pancakes and more pancakes roll
out of the kitchen here. There are 42 varieties, from sweet to spicy, and the portions
are large.

Zunfthaus der Schiffleute (☎ 644 11; Fischergasse
31; meals €8-13) In a scenic location on the river,
this typical Swabian place serves enormous
portions of food and has a good vegetarian
menu. It's also a fun beer house.

Pflugmerzler (☎ 680 61; Pfluggasse 6; mains from
€10; ☯ lunch only Sat, closed Sun) Pflugmerzler is
the place to feast on home-style Swabian
dishes in the town's most romantic setting.
Try the luscious ravioli-like Fischmaul-
tasche, stuffed with spinach and ricotta.

Drei Kannen (☎ 677 17; Hafenbad 31; mains around
€10.50) North of Münsterplatz, Drei Kannen
has an Italian loggia and courtyard next to
a former patrician's beautiful home. The
fare is typically Swabian and the prices
reasonable.

Hotel Bäumle (☎ 622 87; Kohlgasse 6; meals from
€10; ☯ from 4pm, closed Sat & Sun) This is a rustic
inn with loads of wood panelling, ceramic
tiles, good wines and creative regional fare
(ask for the tasty spinach-filled Fröschle).
You can crawl upstairs after dinner. See its
entry under Sleeping.

Zur Forelle (☎ 639 24; Fischergasse 25; meals
€12-14) This is widely regarded as the best
seafood restaurant in town, with daily specials. (Note the cannonball lodged in the
wall outside.)

QUICK EATS
Café Kässmeyer (Münsterplatz) A top-rate bakery that is open daily.

Entertainment
Roxy (☎ 968 620; Schillerstrasse 1) This is a huge, multivenue centre with a concert hall, cinema, disco, bar and special-event forum.

Wiley Club (☎ 867 04; Memminger Strasse 72/234) On the former military base, this club hosts live jazz, rock and disco.

Arts & Crafts (☎ 980 7664; Memminger Strasse 72/235) Also on the former military base, in the former US Army gym, Arts & Crafts is now a concert hall, with performances of everything from Brahms to head-banging.

Barfüsser (☎ 602 1110; Lautenberg 1) This is another local favourite, mainly for its home-brewed beer and its Tuesday karaoke. There's also a branch across the river in Neu Ulm.

Tagblatt (Insel) The seasonal Tagblatt is known for its salads and impressive views over the Danube. Weekend breakfasts begin at 5am, perfect after a club crawl.

Weinkrüger (☎ 649 76; Weinhofberg 7) This is a quirky wine tavern in an old bathhouse on the Blau River.

Enchilada (☎ 608 59; Schelergasse 6) Yes, there is Mexicanish food, but everybody comes at Happy Hour (6pm to 8pm) for the tall, fruity cocktails discounted 50%.

Hades (Ehinger Strasse 19) House, club sound and star DJs make Hades hotter than you-know-where and probably with more sinners.

Getting There & Away
Ulm is on the main Stuttgart–Munich railway line – trains cost €13.50/20.40 Stuttgart/Munich and take one to 1½ hours.

For motorists, the B311 runs from Tuttlingen to Ulm, and the B16 from Ulm to Regensburg. The **ADAC** (☎ 962 1010; Neue Strasse 40) offers help for motorists.

Getting Around
Buses leave from the **central bus station** (☎ 166 21) at the Hauptbahnhof, and the Rathaus is a major transfer point. Bus tickets cost €1.50 for a single ride, and €5 for a day pass valid for up to four adults from 9am Monday to Friday.

Hire bikes from **Radstation** (☎ 150 0231) at the Hauptbahnhof.

NORTHERN BLACK FOREST

Passes
Most tourist offices in the Black Forest sell the three-day Schwarzwald Card, which provides free admission to over 100 attractions in the Black Forest, including the Triberg Waterfalls and Europa Park Rust. For adults the price is €40/35 with/without Europa Park Rust, and for two adults and three children the price is €147/110 with/without Europa Park Rust. For a complete list of attractions and points of sale, see www.schwarzwald-tourist-info.de.

KARLSRUHE
☎ 0721 / pop 279,500
Karlsruhe (literally 'Carl's Rest') was dreamed up in 1715 by Margrave Karl Wilhelm of Baden-Durlach as a residential retreat. The town is laid out like an Oriental fan: at its axis is the Schloss, nestled in the semicircular Schlosspark. From this inner circle 32 *tines* (straight streets) emanate, most feeding into a ring road.

Imaginative as this is, were it not for the Schloss and some stellar museums, there would be little reason to visit Karlsruhe, much less stay overnight. Most of Karlsruhe's neoclassical buildings were pummelled in WWII and, by and large, reconstruction has not flattered the place.

Orientation & Information
The Hauptbahnhof is on the southern edge of the town centre, with the Schloss 2km due north (take tram No 2 or 3 to Markt). The Bundesverfassungsgericht (federal court)

RESORT TAX
If you're spending more than one night almost anywhere in the Black Forest, you will be subject to a *Kurtaxe*, a resort or visitors' tax of usually around €1.50 to €3 per day. But unlike other places in Germany that also levy such a tax, here you'll be given a *Gästekarte* (Resort Card) that gives you discounts to museums, boat trips, cultural events and attractions throughout the region.

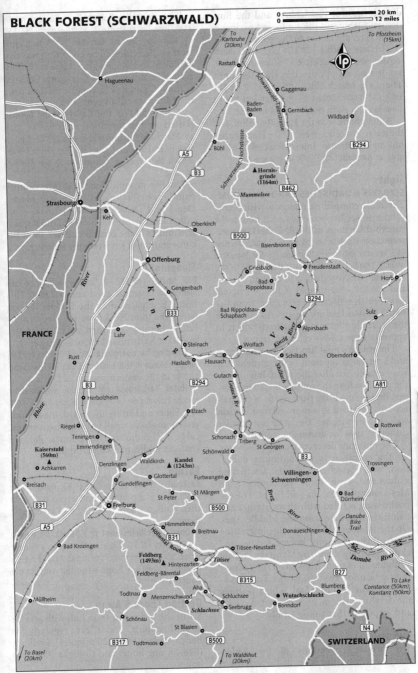

BLACK FOREST (SCHWARZWALD)

0   20 km
0   12 miles

To Karlsruhe (20km)

To Pforzheim (15km)

Rastatt

Hagueenau

Gaggenau

Baden-Baden

Gernsbach

Wildbad

B294

A5

Bühl

Schwarzwald-Hochstrasse

▲ Hornis-grinde (1164m)

B462

Mummelsee

Strasbourg

Kehl

Oberkirch

B500

Baiersbronn

Freudenstadt

Horb

Offenburg

Gengenbach

Griesbach

Bad Rippoldsau

B294

K i n z i g

B33

Bad Rippoldsau-Schapbach

V a l l e y

Sulz

Lahr

FRANCE

Rust

Steinach

Wolfach

Kinzig River

Alpirsbach

Haslach

Hausach

Schiltach

Oberndorf

River

B3

Gutach

Gutach Rv

Schiltach Rv

A81

Herbolzheim

B294

Elzach

Riegel

Schonach

Triberg

St Georgen

Rottweil

Teningen

Emmendingen

Schönwald

B3

Kaiserstuhl (560m)

Waldkirch

Kandel ▲ (1243m)

Villingen-Schwenningen

Trossingen

Achkarren

Denzlingen

Glottertal

Furtwangen

Breisach

Gundelfingen

St Peter

St Märgen

Brea

Bad Dürrheim

B31

Freiburg

B500

River

A5

Himmelreich

Breitnau

Donaueschingen

Danube Bike Trail

Höllental Route

B31

Bad Krozingen

Titisee-Neustadt

Titisee

Danube River

Feldberg (1493m) ▲

Hinterzarten

B27

Blumberg

To Lake Constance (50km); Konstanz (50km)

Feldberg-Bärental

Aha

B315

Müllheim

Todtnau

Menzenschwand

Schluchsee

● **Wutachschlucht**

Schluchsee

Seebrugg

Bonndorf

N4

Schönau

St Blasien

SWITZERLAND

B317

Todtmoos

B500

To Basel (20km)

To Waldshut (20km)

BADEN-WÜRTTEMBERG

directly west of the Schloss, and the Bundesgerichtshof, on the southwest perimeter of the ring, are closed to the public.

The **tourist office** (☎ 3720 5383; www.karlsruhe .de/tourismus; Bahnhofplatz 6; ⌚ 9am-6pm Mon-Fri, 9am-1pm Sat) is opposite the Hauptbahnhof. There's a **branch office** (☎ 3720 5376; fax 3720 5389; Karl-Friedrich-Strasse 9, ⌚ 9.30am-6pm Mon-Fri, 10am-3pm Sat). Both book rooms for free.

A Reisebank is in the Hauptbahnhof, and the main post office is east of the Hauptbahnhof on Poststrasse. Internet access is available at **Karstadt** (☎ 170 49; Kaiserstrasse 92).

Sights

SCHLOSS & BADISCHES LANDESMUSEUM

The most compelling reason to visit Karlsruhe is to see the Schloss, which houses the superb collections of the **Badisches Landesmuseum** (Baden State Museum; ☎ 926 6520; adult/concession €4/3, free after 3pm Fri; ⌚ 10am-5pm Tue-Thu, 10am-6pm Fri-Sun). The Schloss itself was destroyed in the war, but city custodians had enough sense – and money – to rebuild it in the original style, which reflects the transition from baroque to neoclassical. Be sure to climb the tower, really the only point from which to appreciate the town's eccentric layout.

The palace's dual function as a residence and a retreat is apparent in the gardens that were established after the rebuilding. While the public side to the south adhered to a formal design, the huge park north of the palace was designed in a more relaxed English style. In fine weather, the latter is a popular gathering spot for university students.

The museum deserves a couple of hours. At the entrance is the antiquity collection, with jewellery, objects, fascinating statues,and even some mummies from Mesopotamia, Anatolia and Egypt. The opposite wing is filled with altars, statues and paintings that date from the Middle Ages. On the 1st floor you'll find some interesting booty, including guns, knives, saddles and clothing, brought back by Margrave Ludwig Wilhelm of Baden from his 17th-century military campaigns against the Turks. Adjacent is the **Zähringer Saal**, which features the dazzling diadem, gem-encrusted crown and sceptre of that ruling family.

KUNSTHALLE

The private collections of the Baden margraves form the basis of the extensive collection at the **Kunsthalle** (Art Gallery; ☎ 926 3370; Hans-Thoma-Strasse 2; adult/concession €4/2.50; ⌚ 10am-5pm Tue-Fri, 10am-6pm Sat & Sun), just west of the Schloss. The collection was first exhibited in 1846, making it one of the oldest public museums in Germany. On view is the full range of European masters from the 14th to the 20th centuries.

A highlight is the **Gallery of Old German Masters** on the top floor, with works such as Matthias Grünewald's masterful *Crucifixion* and Lucas Cranach the Elder's *Frederick the Wise in Adoration of the Mother of God*.

On the ground floor are 19th-century paintings by French artists such as Manet, Degas and Delacroix, and Germans Corinth, Liebermann and Slevogt. The impressive murals in the central stairwell show the consecration of the Freiburg Münster.

Sleeping

DJH hostel (☎ 282 48; info@jugendherberge-karlsruhe.de; Moltkestrasse 24; juniors/seniors €17.30/20) This hostel is situated near the Schloss. To get here, take tram No 3 from the Hauptbahnhof to Europaplatz, then walk 10 minutes north on Karlstrasse to Moltkestrasse.

Camping Turmbergblick (☎ 497 236; fax 497 237; Tiengerer Strasse 40; tent/adult from €7.50/6) This camp site is in the eastern suburb of Durlach.

Hotel Barbarossa (☎ 372 50; www.hotel-barbarossa-karlsruhe.de; Luisenstrasse 38; s/d from €56/81; Ⓟ) Sober and straightforward, these modern rooms have small but sleek bathrooms, cable TV, radio and telephones. Parking costs an additional €8 per night.

Eating

Krokodil (☎ 273 31; Waldstrasse 63; mains around €7.50) This is a popular, boisterous hall with tiled walls, a wooden ceiling and an eclectic menu.

Oberländer Weinstube (☎ 250 66; Akademiestrasse 7; dishes from €12.50) This is the town's oldest wine locale, serving regional and French dishes. There's a huge wine list and lovely courtyard dining.

Getting There & Away

Karlsruhe is a major train hub with service in all directions. Trains leave regularly for Baden-Baden (€9.40, 20 minutes), Freiburg (€28.40, one hour) and Cologne (€64, two hours).

TOP FIVE SCENIC DRIVES IN THE BLACK FOREST

Whether self-propelled or on wheels, you'll find a wealth of scenic routes through the Black Forest.

More than just pretty drives, many of these roads follow themes: Franco-German friendship; wines; clock-making; or spas. Brochures on each of these drives are available from local tourist offices or from the **Schwarzwald Tourismusverband** (☎ 0761-296 2260; www.schwarzwald-tourist -info.de; Ludwigstrasse 23, 79098 Freiburg im Breisgau).

- Schwarzwald-Bäder-Strasse (Black Forest Spa Road) is a loop connecting all of the region's spa towns, including, of course, Baden-Baden and Freudenstadt.
- Badische Weinstrasse (Baden Wine Road) is an oenologists delight. From Baden-Baden south to Lörrach, the 160km route winds through the red-wine–producing Ortenau, the Burgundies of Kaiserstuhl and Tuniberg, and the white wines of Markgräflerland.
- Deutsche Uhrenstrasse (German Clock Road) is a 320km loop starting in Villingen-Schwenningen that centres on the story of clock-making in the Central Black Forest with stops at Triberg and Furtwangen.
- Grüne Strasse (Green Road) links the Black Forest with the Rhine valley and the Vosges Mountains in France, and was developed to emphasise the cultural links between the two countries. Popular with hikers and cyclists, this 160km route takes you through Kirchzarten, Freiburg, Breisach, Neuf-Brisach, Colmar and Munster.
- Schwarzwald-Hochstrasse (Black Forest Hwy) is the oldest tourist road in the Black Forest, connecting Baden-Baden with Freudenstadt 60km to the south. Originally used to transport lumber, the road takes you past the lovely Mummelsee.

Karlsruhe is on the A5 (Frankfurt–Basel) autobahn and the A8 to Munich, and is also reached by both the B3 and the B36. The **Mitfahrzentrale** (☎ 194 40) at Athystrasse, on the corner of Karlstrasse, offers ride services.

Getting Around

One-/two-zone rides on Karlsruhe's KVV transport network (buses, S-Bahns and trams) cost €1.35/1.85; four-block tickets are €4/5.40. The best deal is the 24-hour Citykarte, which costs €4.80 and covers a family of two adults and their children within the city limits. The more extensive Regiokarte costs €9 and covers three zones (going as far as, say, Baden-Baden).

There's a taxi service in front of the main Hauptbahnhof entrance.

BADEN-BADEN

☎ 07221 / pop 53,000

When Roman legionnaires came to Baden-Baden over 2000 years ago, they must have felt right at home. Just like Rome, this idyllic enclave at the foot of the Black Forest is built on a group of hills, yielding curative mineral waters that, since the 19th century,

have made the town the playground of the privileged classes. From Queen Victoria to the Vanderbilts, from Bismarck to Brahms and Berlioz, they all came – the royal, the rich and the renowned – to take the waters, or to lose their fortunes in the casinos.

Today, Baden-Baden is the grande dame among German spas, ageing but still elegant. It offers a townscape of palatial villas, stately hotels, tree-lined avenues and groomed parks. Greenery climbs up walls, spills from window sills and tumbles out of streetside pots. Whether indulging in an invigorating stroll up the steep streets, or bathing like a Roman in one of the famous spas, Baden-Baden offers many salubrious activities in a sophisticated yet relaxed atmosphere that doesn't necessarily require deep pockets to enjoy, unless, of course, your pleasure lies in the high-rolling Casino.

Orientation

The Hauptbahnhof is in the suburb of Oos, about 4km northwest of the town centre, with the central bus station immediately at the front. Bus Nos 201, 205 and 216 all make frequent runs to Leopoldsplatz,

BADEN-WÜRTTEMBERG

the heart of Baden-Baden. Most sights are within easy walking distance of Leopoldstrasse and the streets are extremely well marked, with signs pointing you to hotels, restaurants and car parks.

If you're driving on the autobahn, there's a convenient tourist office branch on the way into town.

Information

All overnight guests have to pay the *Kurtaxe* of €2.80 (just €1.10 in the suburbs). This entitles you to the *Kurkarte*, which is good for discounts on some concerts and events. Some useful facilities.

Commerzbank (Augustaplatz 4)

Library (☎ 932 251; Langestrasse 43) Offers the only internet access available.

Main post office (Lange Strasse 44) Inside the Kaufhaus Wagener. Not to be confused with Mode Wagener, a fashion store also on Lange Strasse.

Main tourist office (☎ 275 200; www.Baden -Baden.com; Kaiserallee 3; ☻ 9am-6pm Mon-Sat, 9am-1pm Sun) In the Trinkhalle.

Tourist office branch (Schwarzwaldstrasse 52; ☻ 10am-6pm Mon-Sat, 9am-1pm Sun)

SB-Waschcenter Melcher (☎ 248 19; Scheibenstrasse 14) This laundry is a steep climb uphill.

Sights
KURHAUS & CASINO

In the heart of Baden-Baden, just west of the Oos River, looms the palatial **Kurhaus**, the town's cultural centre, set in an impeccably designed and groomed garden. Two colonnades of shops, flanked by chestnut trees, separate the complex from the Kaiserallee. Corinthian columns and a frieze of mythical griffins grace the relatively modest exterior of this structure, designed by Friedrich Weinbrenner in 1824.

Modest, however, does not describe the Kurhaus interior. Besides a series of lavish festival halls – used for balls, conventions and concerts – it contains the **casino** (☎ 210 60; Kaiserallee 1; admission €3; ☻ 2pm-2am Sun-Thu, 2pm-3am Fri-Sat, baccarat tables ☻ 2pm-6am), an undeniably opulent affair. Its décor, which seeks to emulate the splendour of French palaces, led Marlene Dietrich to call it 'the most beautiful casino in the world'. After observing the action here, Dostoevsky was inspired to write *The Gambler*.

The rich and famous have passed through its doors since it opened in 1838 as Germany's first casino. Rooms include the **Wintergarten**, decked out in a golden colour scheme and crowned by a glass cupola interlaced with delicate wrought-iron ornamentation.

Precious Chinese vases line the walls. Adjacent is the **Rote Saal** (Red Hall), draped in damask and modelled after a room in the Versailles palace. The **Florentiner Saal**, with its fleet of chandeliers, is also known as the 'hall of the thousand candles'.

Games include French and American roulette, blackjack and poker. You need your passport to enter. During the week, minimum bets are €5. You do not have to gamble, but men must wear a jacket and tie (these may be rented for around €8 each), and women a suit or dress (trousers and blazer are acceptable).

A more casual alternative is to take a guided tour (English or German), offered every half-hour from 9.30am until noon daily (€4). The first tour is at 10am between October and March.

LICHTENTALER ALLEE

This elegant park promenade, comprising vegetation from around the world, follows the flow of the sprightly Oosbach from Goetheplatz, adjacent to the Kurhaus, to Kloster Lichtenthal about 3km south. Even today, it's not hard to imagine the movers and shakers of 19th-century Europe – aristocrats, diplomats and artists – taking leisurely strolls along this fragrant avenue.

The gateway to Lichtentaler Allee is formed by the **Baden-Baden Theater**, a white and red sandstone neo-baroque confection whose frilly interior looks like a miniature version of the Opéra-Garnier in Paris.

Nearby stands the **Staatliche Kunsthalle** (State Art Gallery; ☎ 300 763; Lichtenthaler Allee 8a; adult/concession €5/4; ☻ 11am-6pm Tue-Sun, 11am-8pm Wed), featuring rotating international exhibits, mostly of contemporary art.

A bit further on is **Brenner's Park Hotel**, one of the world's poshest. It oozes the old-world charm, glamour and perfection that have largely become extinct, and is the type of place where the concierge would remember your poodle's favourite food from your last visit.

About 1km south of here is the **Gönneranlage**, a rose garden ablaze with more than 300 varieties. For a quick detour, check the

Russische Kirche (Russian Church; 1882; Maria-Victoria-Strasse; admission €0.50; ☺ 10am-6pm Feb-Nov), just east of here. Built in the Byzantine style, it is topped with a shiny golden onion dome.

Lichtentaler Allee concludes at the **Kloster Lichtenthal**, a Cistercian abbey founded in 1245. Generations of the margraves of Baden lie buried in its chapel, and there's also a **Kloster Lichtenthal Museum** (adult/concession €2/0.50; ☺ Tue-Sun).

ALTSTADT

For wonderful views over Baden-Baden, climb to the terrace of the **Renaissance Neues Schloss** in Schlossstrasse. Until recently the palace was one of the residences of the margravial family of Baden-Baden, but acute cash flow problems forced them to auction off the furnishings and artworks. The palace is no longer open to the public, but you can wander around the courtyard and terrace.

Another panoramic vista of Baden-Baden is offered by the newly reopened **Rosenneuheitengarten** (Rose Novelty Garden) at Moltkestrasse on the Beutig hill top. Open 24 hours daily June to September, this beautifully landscaped rose garden is lit at night and, the view notwithstanding, makes a wonderful getaway.

On your way up to the Neues Schloss, you'll pass the **Stiftskirche** on the Markt, the foundations of which incorporate the ruins of the former Roman baths. Elsewhere, it's a hotchpotch of Romanesque, Gothic and baroque styles. Inside, look for the crucifix by Nicolaus Gerhaert, with a heart-wrenchingly realistic depiction of the suffering Christ.

Nearby is the **Stadtmuseum** (City Museum; ☎ 932 272; Küferstrasse 3; adult/concession €1/0.50; ☺ 10am-12.30pm & 2-5pm Tue-Sun), where highlights include historic roulette wheels and other gambling paraphernalia, as well as furnishings, photos and paintings from Baden-Baden's belle époque.

In the leafy park just north of the Kurhaus stands the **Trinkhalle** (Pump Room; Kaiserallee 3), which houses the tourist office. Here you can amble beneath a 90m-long portico decorated with 19th-century frescoes of local legends and myths. You can still get a free glass of curative mineral water from a tap inside the building linked to the springs below. The Trinkhalle also houses a wonderful café that shouldn't be missed.

Activities

SPAS

The **Roman bath ruins** (Römische Badruinen; Römerplatz; admission €2; ☺ 11am-5pm) have recently been reopened after an extensive renovation and are well worth visiting. Even more fun, though, is taking the waters yourself at the two extraordinary spas that are among Baden-Baden's main attractions. Built on either side of Römerplatz are the Friedrichsbad and the Caracalla-Therme.

The 19th-century **Friedrichsbad** (☎ 275 920; Römerplatz 1; admission €21; ☺ 9am-10pm Mon-Sat, noon-8pm Sun) looks more like a neo-Renaissance palace than a bathhouse. Most stunning is the circular pool ringed by columned arcades that blend into a graceful cupola embellished with ornaments and sculptures. Two bathing options are offered: the Roman-Irish (€24) and the Roman-Irish 'Creme Service' (€28). Your three or more hours of humid bliss consist of a timed series of hot and cold showers, saunas, steam rooms and baths that leave you feeling scrubbed, lubed and loose as a goose.

No clothing is allowed inside, and several of the bathing sections are mixed from 4pm on Tuesday, Wednesday, Friday and Saturday – so leave your modesty at the reception desk.

The **Caracalla-Therme** (☎ 275 940; Römerplatz 11; admission €11 for 2hr; ☺ 8am-10pm, last admission 8pm), opened in 1985, has more than 900 sq metres of outdoor and indoor pools, hot and cold water grottoes, various whirlpools, therapeutic water massages, a surge channel and a range of saunas. Bathing suits must be worn everywhere except the upstairs sauna, but neither suits nor towels are available for hire.

HIKING

The hills around Baden-Baden are good for hiking. The tourist office has put together a collection of maps and pamphlets for under €10 with suggested hikes from the easy variety to some more serious climbs. Popular destinations are the Geroldsauer waterfalls, the Yburg castle ruin in the surrounding wine country, the Altes Schloss above the town and Mt Merkur. A cable car runs daily every 15 minutes from 10am to 10pm (€4 return) up to the 660m-high summit of Mt Merkur. (Take bus No 204 or 205 from Leopoldsplatz to the cable-car station).

BADEN-WÜRTTEMBERG

Sleeping

As one might expect, hotels in Baden-Baden generally aren't cheap but a few bargains are available. The **tourist office** (☎ 275 200) has a free room-reservation service.

DJH hostel (☎ 522 23; info@jugendherberge-baden-baden.de; Hardbergstrasse 34; juniors/seniors €17.30/20) The local hostel is 3km northwest of the town centre. From the Hauptbahnhof, take bus No 201 to Grosse Dollenstrasse, then walk for 10 minutes.

Campingplatz Adam (☎ 07223-231 94; Campingplatzstrasse 1, Bühl-Oberbruch; tent/person €6.50/7.50) This is the closest camp site, about 12km southwest of town at Bühl-Oberbruch (no direct bus service to Baden-Baden, change in Bühl-Oberbruch).

Altes Schloss (☎ 269 48; fax 391 775; Alter Schlossweg 10; d with shared bathroom €33, 4-bed apt per person €38; P) This little pension, atop a hill, can only be reached by car or foot. It has a few simple rooms and apartments, so book ahead.

Pension Löhr (☎ 313 70; bcs@brandau-catering.de; Adlerstrasse 2; s €22-40, d €50-55) This centrally located guesthouse is one of the cheapest options in town. Rooms are small but neat.

Hotel am Markt (☎ 270 40; www.hotel-am-markt-baden.de; Marktplatz 18; s/d with shared bathroom €30/58, s/d with private bathroom €47/80; P) This family-run hotel is up by the Stiftskirche. Rooms have a white-on-white Spartan look, but are comfortable enough. Parking is included in the price.

Hotel Römerhof (☎ 234 15; fax 391 707; Sophienstrasse 25; s/d from €46/92; P) This hotel is classy, with bright clean rooms furnished in a traditional style.

Am Friedrichsbad (☎ 396 340; www.hotel-am-friedrichsbad.de; Gernsbacher Strasse 31; s/d from €79/109; P) This is a comfortable place in a classic building.

Hotel Deutscher Kaiser (☎ 2700; www.deutscher-kaiser-Baden-Baden.de; Merkurstrasse 9; s/d from €82/113; P) A traditional hotel, offering snug but quiet rooms.

Steigenberger Badischer Hof (☎ 9340; www.Badischer-hof.steigenberger.de; Lange Strasse 47; s/d from €112/172; P X) This is a place for splashing out, with plush, spacious quarters. It has an elegant inner courtyard, attentive staff and droves of bathrobed guests shuffling to and from the house's thermal baths. Parking costs an extra €11.50 per day.

Eating

Leo's (☎ 380 81; Luisenstrasse 10; dishes from €6) Near Leopoldsplatz, Leo's is a trendy movie-theme bistro that offers large salads and creative pasta dishes.

Rathausglöckl (☎ 906 10; Steinstrasse 7; dishes from €9.90; Wed-Sun) This small, rustic restaurant is one of the oldest in town and a good place to sample local Baden cuisine.

La Provence (☎ 216 50; Schlossstrasse 20; vegetarian dishes from €8, other meals around €12) Vaulted ceilings, Art Nouveau mirrors and hanging baskets of dried flowers feature at La Provence, where everyone from techno fiends to portly burghers dig into mouthwatering Franco-German dishes. Book ahead.

Namaskaar (☎ 246 81; Kreuzstrasse 1; mains €12; Wed-Mon) If you fancy something exotic, head to this Indian restaurant with imaginative meat, fish and vegetarian meals.

Rotisserie Bar and Restaurant (☎ 938 114; Sophienstrasse 27; mains €7.90-15.90) Giving globalisation a good name, this restaurant (belonging to the Hotel Quellenhof) interprets everything from gazpacho and miso soup to penne with rabbit. The weekday lunch menu is an outstanding bargain at €7.50.

Entertainment

Festspielhaus (☎ 301 30; Beim Alten Bahnhof 2, Robert-Schumann-Platz) The town's new theatre is in the historic old train station. Top-notch orchestras, soloists and ensembles regularly perform here (including the Filarmonica della Scala, Cecilia Bartoli, and the Vienna Philharmonic) from September to June, with a smattering of events in the summer.

Theater (Goetheplatz) This offers a repertory of classical and modern drama and musical theatre, with most tickets priced from €15 to €50. Afternoon performances are slightly cheaper. The Baden-Badener Philharmonie performs in two concert halls in the Kurhaus and charges about the same prices (but students get a 50% discount).

Tickets for these venues are available at the box office inside the **Kurhaus** (☎ 932 700) or from the **ticket hotline** (☎ 3013 301).

Getting There & Away

AIR

Baden-Baden's modern airport, 15km west of town, is big enough to handle Boeing 747s, but is mostly used for hops within Germany and Europe and charter flights.

BUS

Buses to many Black Forest towns depart from Baden-Baden. Bus No 212 makes hourly trips to Rastatt, while bus No 218 goes to Iffezheim, known for its prestigious annual horse race held in May and August. Bus No 245 goes twice daily to Mummelsee. For more details, see Schwarzwald-Hochstrasse (below).

CAR & MOTORCYCLE

Baden-Baden is close to the A5 Frankfurt–Basel autobahn and is on the B3 and the B500, the scenic Schwarzwald-Hochstrasse (Black Forest Hwy).

TRAIN

Baden-Baden is on the main north–south rail corridor. Trains leave every two hours for Basel (€26, 1½ hours) and Frankfurt (€35, 1½ hours). There are also services several times an hour to Karlsruhe (€9, 20 minutes) and Offenburg (€6.50, 30 minutes).

Getting Around

BUS

The **Stadtwerke Baden-Baden** (☎ 2771) operates a decent bus system. Single tickets cost €1.90 and four-block tickets are €5.80. The best deal, though, is the 24-hour pass (€4.80), which entitles two adults and two children under 16 to unlimited travel in three zones (including Karlsruhe €9).

BICYCLE

Baden-Baden is very hilly. If you choose to cycle, you can hire from any of the car parks at the Kurhaus, Vincenti or the Alter Bahnhof for €1/5 per two/10 hours from 8am to 6pm (no locks provided). The VeloBus will transport you and your bike to Sand and the Mummelsee lake for €10.

CAR & MOTORCYCLE

To cut traffic in the centre, the main road goes underground near Verfassungsplatz in the north and emerges just south of the town centre. Note that much of the centre is either pedestrianised or blocked off from traffic. It's best to park and walk.

SCHWARZWALD-HOCHSTRASSE

The scenically beautiful Schwarzwald-Hochstrasse (Black Forest Hwy), officially the mundanely named B500, wends its way from Baden-Baden to Freudenstadt, about 60km to the south. Large segments go right through the forest and along the ridge, with expansive views of the Upper Rhine Valley and, further west, the Vosges Mountains in Alsace, which form the border between Alsace and Lorraine in France. The road also skirts a number of lakes, of which **Mummelsee** is the best known. There are plenty of hotels along the road and a **DJH hostel** (☎ 07804-611; fax 1323; Schwarzwald-Hochstrasse, Zuflucht; juniors/seniors €17.30/20) in Zuflucht, about 17km north of Freudenstadt and easily reachable by bus.

FREUDENSTADT

☎ 07441 / pop 23,600

This spa town on the eastern border of the Black Forest was the brainchild of Duke Friedrich I of Württemberg who, in 1599, decided to build one of the first planned residences north of the Alps. Together with his own architect, Heinrich Schickardt, he scoured Bologna and Rome for inspiration and came back with the idea for a town laid out like a spider web.

At Freudenstadt's centre is a gigantic market square – Germany's largest – with each side measuring 220m. Friedrich hoped to adorn the square with a palace, but this grandiose design was never realised; partly as a result, Freudenstadt fell into obscurity after the duke's death in 1610. It did not rise again until the mid-19th century, when a rail link brought in the first waves of tourists. The French wrecked the town in WWII, but thanks to restoration, Freudenstadt retains some of its unique, quasi-urban charm.

Orientation & Information

Freudenstadt has two train stations, the Stadtbahnhof, centrally located about five minutes' walk north of the Markt, and the Hauptbahnhof, about 2km southeast on Dietersweilerstrasse, on the corner of Bahnhofstrasse. Some trains link the two, as does the No B bus. The central bus station is right outside the Stadtbahnhof.

The **tourist office** (☎ 864 733; www.freudenstadt.de; Marktplatz 64; 9am-6pm Mon-Fri, 10am-2pm Sat & Sun May-Oct; 10am-5pm Mon-Fri, 10am-1pm Sat, 11am-1pm Sun Nov-Apr) makes hotel reservations. There are a number of banks on the Markt with ATMs and currency-exchange facilities. The main post office (also on the Markt) has a late counter open until 7pm Monday to Friday. You can access the Internet in the **library** (☎ 890 279; Marktplatz 65; ⏰ 3-6pm Mon & Fri, 9-11am & 3-6pm Tue-Wed, 9-11am & 3-7.30pm Thu).

Sights & Activities

From the Stadtbahnhof and bus station take a short walk south along Martin-Luther-Strasse to the Markt. It's too huge to truly feel like a square, especially since it's bisected by a major thoroughfare. It's entirely lined by Italianate arched arcades providing weatherproof access to dozens of shops.

On the southwestern corner, the Markt is anchored by the **Stadtkirche** (1608), with its two naves built at a right angle, another unusual design by the geometrically minded duke. It's a bit of a mixture of styles, with Gothic windows, Renaissance portals and baroque towers. Of note inside are a **baptismal font** from the early 12th century with intricate animal ornamentations, a crucifix from around 1500 and a wooden lectern from 1140 carried on the shoulders of the four Evangelists.

In its early days, the church also provided a safe place of worship for the many Protestants who settled in Freudenstadt after having been banished from their Austrian homeland.

The Markt is also the site of a lively fountain display several times a day during the summer.

Located at elevations from 750m to 1000m, Freudenstadt is a place for moderately good winter sports, especially **cross-country skiing**, with eight groomed tracks between 4km and 12km long. There are also two ski lifts. For snow conditions, call ☎ 07442-6922.

Sleeping & Eating

Go to the tourist office if you need help finding a **private room** (from around €15 per person with private bathroom), they don't charge a booking fee. There's also no shortage of central and reasonably priced hotels. There's also a free telephone room-reservation service outside the tourist office with a complete list of hotels.

DJH hostel (☎ 7720; fax 857 88; Eugen-Nägele-Strasse 69; juniors/seniors €17.30/20) Freudenstadt's hostel is located about 500m from the Stadtbahnhof and 2.5km from the Hauptbahnhof.

You can hire bicycles and cross-country ski equipment here.

Camping Langenwald (☎ 2862; www.camping-langenwald.de; Strasburger Strasse 167; tent/person €7/5; ⏰ Easter-Oct) If you want to camp in the area, head to this excellent camp site about 3km west of town along the B28 (or take bus No 12 to Kniebis). It even has a heated outdoor swimming pool.

Hotel Adler (☎ 915 20; www.adler-fds.de; Forststrasse 15-17; s/d with shared bathroom from €35/56, s/d with private bathroom €42/76; 🖳 🅿) Located between Stadtbahnhof and Markt, this hotel has a no-nonsense appeal, and the 2nd-floor terrace is a nice place to relax and intermingle. A buffet breakfast costs an extra €8.50, and parking costs €3.50 per day. The hotel restaurant is more than a cut above average.

Hotel Schwanen (☎ 915 50; www.schwanen-freudenstadt.de; Forststrasse 6; s/d €44/80) Family run and friendly, the rooms here are tidily furnished in a contemporary style.

Turmbräu (☎ 905 121; Marktplatz 64; mains around €7.50) This microbrewery next to the tourist office is probably the most happening place at the centre of town, and it has a broad selection of hot and cold dinners to boot. Try the locally smoked ham and sausages, or just stop in for a drink.

Getting There & Away

The *Kinzigtalbahn* train leaves at two-hour intervals from the Stadtbahnhof. If you're north-bound, there's the hourly *Murgtalbahn* to/from Rastatt (€7.70, 1½ hours), which stops at both the Stadtbahnhof and the Hauptbahnhof.

Bus No 7628 makes a few trips on Monday to Friday to/from Tübingen. Bus No 7161 travels daily along the Kinzig Valley, with stops in Alpirsbach, Schiltach, Wolfach and Hausach.

Freudenstadt marks the southern end of the Schwarzwald-Hochstrasse (B500), which meanders northward some 60km to Baden-Baden. It's also on the B462, the Schwarzwald-Tälerstrasse (Black Forest Valley road), which runs from Rastatt to Alpirsbach.

Getting Around

Freudenstadt's **bus network** (☎ 8950, 1555) has four routes running at regular intervals, and each trip costs €1.40. There's a **bike-rental station** (☎ 864 732) in the Kurhaus charging €8.50 per day.

BADEN-WÜRTTEMBERG

CENTRAL BLACK FOREST

KINZIG VALLEY

The horseshoe-shaped Kinzig Valley begins south of Freudenstadt and follows the little Kinzig River south to Schiltach, then west to Haslach and north to Offenburg. Near Strasbourg, after 95km, the Kinzig is eventually swallowed up by the mighty Rhine. A 2000-year-old trade route through the valley links Strasbourg with Rottweil. The valley's inhabitants survived for centuries on mining and shipping goods by raft, and to this day you'll see plenty of felled trees awaiting shipping.

Getting There & Away

BUS

The Kinzig Valley has direct connections with Freiburg by bus No 1066, with four departures daily (two on weekends). Bus No 7160 traverses the valley on its route between Offenburg and Triberg. Bus No 7161 shuttles between Freudenstadt and Hausach.

CAR & MOTORCYCLE

The B294 follows the Kinzig from Freudenstadt to Haslach, from where the B33 leads back north to Offenburg. If you're going south, you can pick up the B33 to Triberg and beyond in Hausach.

TRAIN

From Freudenstadt's Stadtbahnhof, the *Kinzigtalbahn* train departs every two hours with stops in Alpirsbach, Schiltach, Wolfach and Hausach.

At the latter, it hooks up with the Schwarzwaldbahn, with hourly links north to Haslach, Gengenbach and Offenburg, and south to Triberg, Villingen, Donaueschingen and Konstanz.

Alpirsbach

☎ 07444 / pop 7000

The main attraction of this village, 18km or so south of Freudenstadt, is the 11th-century **Klosterkirche St Benedict**, formerly part of a monastery and now a Protestant parish church. An almost unadulterated Romanesque basilica, its austere, red sand-stone façade matches the streamlined interior with its flat ceiling and row of columned arcades.

The entire building is based on symmetrical proportions: the central nave with its choir is twice as long as the transept, which is itself only half as wide as the aisles. Guided tours cost €2.50/2 (adult/concession), and run at 10am, 11am, 2pm, 3pm and 4pm daily, except Sunday morning.

The **tourist office** (☎ 951 6281; www.alpirsbach .de; Hauptstrasse 20) is located inside the Haus des Gastes.

DJH hostel (☎ 2477; info@jugendherberge-alpirs bach.de; Reinerzauer Steige 80; juniors/seniors €17.30/20) This hostel is above the town, about 2km from the train station.

Schiltach

☎ 07836 / pop 4100

If you like half-timbered houses, you should not miss this timeless jewel of a town about 18km south of Alpirsbach at the confluence of the Kinzig and Schiltach Rivers. The wealth acquired by Schiltach in former times translated into a picture-perfect village that is at its most scenic around the triangular **Markt**, built against a steep hill. Take a closer look at the step-gabled **Rathaus**, with murals that provide a pictorial record of the town's history.

At Hauptstrasse 5, you'll find Schiltach's **tourist office** (☎ 5850; www.schiltach.de)

There's no hostel here, but private rooms (from €15 per person) are available, though some require a three-day minimum stay.

Campingplatz Schiltach (☎ 7289; Bahnhofstrasse 6; tent €2.50-5.50, per person €3.50; ☺ Easter–early Oct) This camp site isn't far from the tourist office.

Gutach

☎ 07685 / pop 2200

Technically not in the Kinzig Valley, but only a 4km detour south along the B33, which parallels the Gutach River, is one of the Black Forest's biggest tourist draws, the **Schwarzwald Freilicht Museum** (Black Forest Open-Air Museum; ☎ 07831-935 60; adult/concession €4.50/2; ☺ 9am-6pm, last admission 5pm Apr-Oct). It's worth braving the hordes of bus tourists for a first-hand look at the full range of historical farmhouses, brought here – and reassembled – from the entire region.

The museum centres around the **Vogt-bauernhof**, a traditional farming village that has stood in the valley since 1570 and was saved from demolition in 1962 by Hermann

Schilli, a former professor at the University of Freiburg and the museum's creator.

The other farmhouses – along with a bakery, sawmill, chapel and granary – have been moved here from their original locations. It's not entirely kitsch-free, but the houses are authentically furnished and craftspeople inside seem to know what they're doing.

Haslach
☎ 07832 / pop 6800
Back in the Kinzig Valley, the next town worth a brief stop is Haslach. During the Middle Ages it prospered from the nearby silver mines, but when these shut down it became a simple market town. Even today it still is something of a shopping hub for the immediate region, with some 30 clothing shops alone.

Haslach has a pretty Altstadt with some half-timbered houses, but the most interesting building is the former Capuchin monastery, which now contains the **Trachtenmuseum** (Museum of Folkloric Garments; ☎ 8080; Im Alten Kapuzinerkloster; admission €2; 🕑 9am-5pm Tue-Sat, 10am-5pm Sun Apr–mid-Oct, 9am-noon & 1-5pm Tue-Fri mid-Oct–Dec & Feb-Mar). This exhibit includes two types of traditional women's headdresses. The Bollenhut is a chalked straw bonnet festooned with woollen pompoms – red for the unmarried women, black for married. Originally, it hails from the village of Gutach, but is now a symbol of the entire Black Forest. The Schäppel is a fragile-looking crown made from hundreds of beads that can weigh as much as 5kg. These headdresses, along with their appropriate costumes, are still worn on important holidays, during processions and, occasionally, at wedding ceremonies. The outfits in this remote forest region have stayed pretty much the same over the centuries.

For information on Haslach and its surrounds stop by the **tourist office** (☎ 706 170; info@haslach.de; 🕑 9am-5pm Mon-Sat, 10am-5pm Sun Apr-Oct, 9am-noon & 1-5pm Mon-Fri Nov-Mar). It's housed in the same building as the museum. Staff can help with finding private rooms and hotel accommodation.

Gengenbach
☎ 07803 / pop 11,000
This romantic village, about 11km south of Offenburg, is often compared to Bavaria's Rothenburg ob der Tauber but has remained relatively unspoiled by mass tourism. You can stroll through its narrow lanes, past imposing patrician townhouses with crimson geraniums spilling out of flower boxes, and wander down to the Stadtkirche with its lovely baroque tower.

On the Markt you'll find a fountain with a statue of a knight, a symbol of the village's medieval status as a 'free imperial city'. Masks and costumes worn during Fasend (a local version of Carnival) can be admired on the seven floors of the **Narrenmuseum** (☎ 5749; Niggelturm, Hauptstrasse; admission €1; 🕑 2-5pm Sat & Sun, 10am-noon Sun Apr-Oct). The **tourist office** (☎ 930 143; www.stadt-gegenbach.de) is in the Winzerhof building.

TRIBERG
☎ 07722 / pop 5500
Wedged into a narrow valley and framed by three mountains (hence the name) about 17km south of Hausach, Triberg is the undisputed capital of cuckoo-clock country. Countless shops, decorated with flags from around the world, simply crawl with bus tourists thinking they're buying 'typical' German trinkets, when the label on that cute doll is more likely to say 'Made in Taiwan'. This is not to say that you can't find some authentic, locally made items, including clocks, though usually at a high price.

Triberg also boasts not just one, but two of the 'world's largest cuckoo clocks'. The local 'War of the Cuckoos' centres on Triberg and Schonach, which are pretty much the same village, except perhaps to those who live there. As you enter Triberg on the B33 from the Gutach Valley, signs direct you to 'The World's Biggest Cuckoo Clock', a small house in which the Schwarzenegger of all cuckoos nests.

Problem is, as you exit Triberg in the direction of Schonach, you'll find the *other* 'World's Biggest Cuckoo Clock', also a legitimate contender.

Fortunately, there are also some attractions unrelated to cuckoo clocks, including Germany's largest waterfall, some fine local museums and a historic Black Forest farmhouse where the inhabitants still smoke their own hams.

Orientation & Information
Triberg's only thoroughfare is the B500, which bisects the valley and is called Haupt-

strasse in town. The Hauptbahnhof is at its northern end, where the B500 meets the B33. It's a little over 1km to walk from the Hauptbahnhof to the Markt, and there's also a bus service. The Markt is the hub for regional buses.

Triberg's **tourist office** (☎ 953 230; www.triberg .de; Luisenstrasse 10; ☼ 9am-5pm Mon-Fri year-round, 10am-noon Sat May-Sep) is inside the Kurhaus, just east of the waterfalls. Staff have maps and suggestions about the many hikes available in the region. There's a **post office** (Markt 55) next to the Rathaus. The Sparkasse and the Volks-bank on Hauptstrasse exchange money.

Sights

Niagara they ain't, but Germany's tallest **waterfalls** do exude their own wild romanti-cism. Fed by the Gutach River, they plunge 163m in seven cascades bordered by mossy rocks. Energy has been generated from the falls since 1884, when it was first used to fuel the town's electric street lamps. You have to pay €1.50/1.20 (adult/concession) to even access the wooded **gorge** (☼ Apr-Oct weather permitting), but it's worth hiking the 20 to 30 minutes to the top of the falls.

For an imaginative overview of Triberg's history and social life in the region, head for the **Schwarzwaldmuseum** (☎ 4434; Wallfahrtstrasse 4; adult/concession €3.50/2; ☼ 10am-5pm Nov-Apr, Sat & Sun only mid-Nov–mid-Dec) for its displays of local crafts. One of Triberg's 'biggest' cuckoo clocks can be found 1km or so further on, inside a snug little **house** (☎ 4689; Untertalstrasse 28; admission €1, ☼ 9am-noon & 1-6pm). Its rival is integrated into a large **shop** (admission €1.50; ☼ 9am-6pm Mon-Sat, 10am-6pm Sun Easter-Oct) on the B33 in Triberg-Schonachbach.

Sleeping & Eating

Private accommodation will cost €12 to €20 per person. The tourist office finds ac-commodation for a fee of €1. Some places, including hotels, may charge slightly higher rates for one-night stays.

DJH hostel (☎ 4110; info@jugendherberge-triberg .de; Rohrbacher Strasse 3; juniors/seniors €17.30/20) Triberg's hostel is on a scenic ridge on the southern edge of town. It's a 45-minute walk from the Hauptbahnhof, but you can take any bus to the Markt, from where it's 1200m uphill.

Hotel Central (☎ /fax 4360; Markt; s/d from €36/ 52; **P**) Right at the centre of town, this

aptly named hotel has small rooms with all the amenities tightly packed in. It also has an elevator. Parking costs an additional €6 a day.

Romantik Parkhotel Wehrle (☎ 860 20; www.park hotel-wehrle.de; Gartenstrasse 7; s/d from €85/150; **P** 🖳 🖭) Here is a haven of style in Triberg's sea of kitsch. Even the well-travelled Ernest Hemingway, in Triberg to check the local trout streams, enjoyed his stay here, pos-sibly gazing out from one of the rooms with balconies. In the kitchen, the chef works his magic with creativity and panache; expect to pay €18 and up for a main course. Park-ing costs an extra €3 a day, and internet access costs €5 per 30 minutes.

All aforementioned hotels also have res-taurants serving regional cuisine at average prices.

Tresor (☎ 215 60; Hauptstrasse 63; dishes from €6) A bit touristy to be sure, but the steaks and regional dishes are decent.

Getting There & Away

Triberg is well connected to other Black For-est towns. The Schwarzwaldbahn railway line goes to Konstanz (€17.60, 1¾ hours) and Of-fenburg (€8.10, 45 minutes), with a service in either direction about once an hour.

The three main bus lines are No 7160, which travels north through the Gutach and Kinzig valleys to Offenburg; No 7265, which heads south to Villingen via St Geor-gen (one hour); and No 7270, which makes the trip to Furtwangen in 35 minutes.

Getting Around

There's a local bus service between the Hauptbahnhof and the Markt and on to the nearby town of Schonach.

DANUBE BIKE TRAIL

Donaueschingen, a small town about 50km east of Freiburg, marks the official begin-ning of one of Europe's greatest rivers, the Danube. The town itself isn't any great shakes, but offers a good launching point to the Donauradwanderweg (Danube Bike Trail), which ends 583km further east in Passau on the Austrian border.

Donaueschingen's **tourist office** (☎ 0771-857 221; www.donaueschingen.de; Karlstrasse 58; ☼ 9am-6pm Mon-Fri, 10am-noon Sat) provides plenty of maps and documentation about activities and accommodation along the Danube.

BADEN-WÜRTTEMBERG

SOUTHERN BLACK FOREST

Getting Around

Special bus tickets that are good value and valid on all routes in the South Baden area are available from **SüdbadenBus** (☎ 0761-361 72). The region encompasses locales like Freiburg, St Peter, Titisee, Donaueschingen, Villingen-Schwenningen, Bonndorf, Feldberg and Schiltach, and reaches all the way east to Konstanz on Lake Constance.

The SBG-Freizeit-Ticket costs €4.10 for one adult or €6.15 for a family of two adults with children under 13, and is valid for unlimited travel on one weekend day or holiday. Those spending more time in the Black Forest can get the 7-Tage-Südbaden-Bus-Pass, which costs €19.45 for one person, €28.10 for two people and €34.75 for a family. Tickets are available from bus drivers.

VILLINGEN-SCHWENNINGEN

☎ 07721 (Villingen), 07720 (Schwenningen) / pop 81, 700

When Villingen and Schwenningen were joined in 1972, the union couldn't have been more unlikely. Villingen is a spa town with a medieval layout; Schwenningen is a clock-making centre less than a century old. What's worse, Villingen used to belong to the Grand Duchy of Baden, while Schwenningen was part of the duchy of Württemberg, conflicting allegiances that apparently can't be reconciled. As one local was heard to say, 'They decided to merge before they understood. Now they understand and can no longer decide.'

From the tourist's point of view, Villingen has more to offer, though Schwenningen has a couple of museums devoted to clock-making.

Orientation & Information

Villingen's Altstadt is entirely contained within the ring road that follows the old fortifications. The Hauptbahnhof is just east of the ring on Bahnhofstrasse; regional buses depart from here also. Most of the sights are in the northern half of the Altstadt. Bus No 20 connects Villingen with Schwenningen every 20 minutes during the day.

The Villingen **tourist office** (☎ 822 340; www .villingen-schwenningen.de; Rietstrasse 8; ☉ 8.30am-7pm Mon-Fri, 8.30am-4pm Sat, 1-4pm Sun) is helpful. There's also an information office inside the Schwenningen Bahnhof.

The Sparkasse on the Markt in Villingen exchanges money, and the main post office is at Bahnhofstrasse 6. Schwenningen's post office is at Friedrich-Ebert-Strasse 22.

Sights

A few sights are clustered in Villingen's Altstadt, which wraps around two main streets laid out in the shape of a cross. Sections of the town wall and three towers still stand. The focal point is the vast high Gothic **Münster**, with its striking pair of disparate spires, one completely overlaid with coloured tiles.

Head west of here to Schulgasse, then south for a couple of blocks until you get to the **Franziskaner Museum** (☎ 822 351; Rietgasse 2; adult/concession €3/2; ☉ 10am-noon & 2-5pm Tue-Sat, 1-5pm Sun & holidays), housed in a former Franciscan monastery. It has a moderately interesting collection illuminating all aspects of the town's art and culture through the centuries; another department presents a wide range of folkloric and craft items.

Sleeping & Eating

The tourist office has a free room booking service.

DJH hostel (☎ 541 49; info@jugendherberge-villingen .de; St Georgener Strasse 36; juniors/seniors €16.30/19) This hostel is at the northwestern edge of town. Take bus No 3 or 4 to Triberger Strasse.

Gasthof Schlachthof (☎ 225 84; gasthaus-zur -schlachthof@t-online.de; Schlachthausstrasse 11; s/d €37/64) This is perhaps the cheapest option in Villingen.

Hotel Bären (☎ 555 41; baerenhotel@t-online.de; Bärengasse 2; s/d from €51/76) This central hotel in Villingen provides modern and spacious rooms.

Ratskeller (☎ 404 794; Obere Tor, Obere Strasse 37; meals from €6.50) This place in Villingen has a cosy bar area and a good vegetarian menu.

Getting There & Away

The town is on the scenic Schwarzwaldbahn railway line from Konstanz to Offenburg, and there's also direct services to Donaueschingen and Rottweil. To get to Freiburg you have to change in Donaueschingen

The IR trains between Kassel and Kontanz stop every two hours at Villingen-Schwenningen.

From Villingen, bus No 7265 makes regular trips north to Triberg via St Georgen. Bus No 7281 goes to Rottweil and No 7282 to Donaueschingen. To get to Furtwangen, take bus No 70. Villingen-Schwenningen is just west of the A81 (Stuttgart-Singen) and is also crossed by the B33 to Triberg and the B27 to Rottweil.

Getting Around

There's a bike-hire office at the Hauptbahnhof in Schwenningen. The tourist office in Villingen sells a 1:75,000 bike map called *Freizeitkarte Schwarzwald-Baar-Kreis,*

which highlights cycling, hiking and ski routes in the area.

FREIBURG

☎ 0761 / pop 208,300

As the gateway to the Southern Black Forest, Freiburg has the happy-go-lucky attitude of a thriving university community. Though badly disfigured by WWII, the city recovered through quick and tasteful restoration. It's framed by the velvety hills of the Black Forest and endowed with a wealth of historical attractions, led by the awe-inspiring Münster.

Add to this a lively cultural scene and an excellent range of restaurants, bars and clubs, and it's easy to understand why

FREIBURG

INFORMATION	
Alexis	1 C3
Alte Universität	2 C3
Alte Universitätsbibliothek	3 B4
Deutsche Bank	4 B3
Galeria Kaufhof	(see 8)
Herder	5 C3
Kollegiengebäude I	6 B4
Rombach	7 C4
Surf Inn	8 C4
Tourist Office	9 C3
Universität	10 B4
Volksbank	11 B3

SIGHTS & ACTIVITIES	(pp468-70)
Altes Rathaus	(see 23)
Augustinermuseum	12 D4
Bertoldsbrunnen	13 C4
Colombischlössle	14 B3
Gerichtslaube	15 C3
Haus zum Walfisch	16 C3

Historisches Kaufhaus	17 D4
Martinskirche	18 C3
Martinstor	19 C4
Museum für Neue Kunst	20 D4
Museum für Stadtgeschichte	21 D4
Museum für Ur-und	
Frühgeschichte	(see 14)
Münster	22 D3
Neues Rathaus	23 C3
Schwabentor	24 D4
Universitätskirche	25 C3
Wentzingerhaus	(see 21)

SLEEPING	(p470)
City-Hotel	26 C3
Hotel Minerva	27 B3
Hotel zum Roten Bären	28 D4
Oberkirch's Hotel & Weinstuben	29 D4
Stadthotel Kolping	30 D3

EATING	(pp470-1)
Engler's Weinkrügle	31 D4
Hausbrauerei Feierling	32 D4
Kolben-Kaffee-Akademie	33 C4
Markthalle	34 C4
Mensa	35 B4
Salatstuben	36 C4
Schlappen	37 C4
Sichelschmiede	38 D4

ENTERTAINMENT	(p471)
Jazzhaus	39 A4
Konzerthaus	40 A3
Sound	41 D3

TRANSPORT	(p471)
Central Bus Station	42 A3
Citynetz Mitfahr-Service	43 A4
Stadtbahnbrüke	44 A3

BADEN-WÜRTTEMBERG

Freiburg makes for such a terrific city to visit and to base yourself for exploring the Schwarzwald.

Orientation

The Hauptbahnhof and central bus station are on Bismarckallee, about 10 minutes west of the Altstadt. Follow either Eisenbahnstrasse or Bertoldstrasse east until you hit Kaiser-Joseph-Strasse, the centre's main artery. The Münster is on Münsterplatz, another block east. All sights are within walking distance of here.

Information

BOOKSHOPS

Herder (☎ 282 820; Kaiser-Joseph-Strasse 180) Stocks a good assortment of foreign-language books, periodicals and maps.

Rombach (☎ 4500 2400; Bertoldstrasse 10) A quality bookshop.

EMERGENCY

Ambulance (☎ 192 22)

Police station (Rotteckring)

INTERNET ACCESS

Alexis (☎ 217 2641; Merianstrasse 10; €2.40 per hr) A comfortable café.

Surf Inn (Kaiser-Joseph-Strasse 195; €1.50 per 30 mins) in the basement of the Galeria Kaufhof department store at Bertoldsbrunnen.

INTERNET RESOURCES

www.freiburg-online.com Freiburg's best website; features full English sections.

LAUNDRY

Wasch & Fun Laundry (☎ 287 294; Egonstrasse 25; ☻ 9am-10pm Mon-Sat)

MEDICAL SERVICES

Medical care (☎ 809 9800) For 24-hour emergency treatment.

MONEY

Deutsche Bank (Rotteckring 3) Opposite the tourist office.

Volksbank (Opposite the Hauptbahnhof) This bank has an automatic change machine.

POST

Main post office (Eisenbahnstrasse 58-62) This office has a public fax-phone. There's another inside the Hauptbahnhof.

TOURIST INFORMATION

The **Tourist office** (☎ 388 1880; www.freiburg.de Rotteckring 14; ☻ 9.30am-8pm Mon-Fri, 9.30am-5pm Sat, 10am-noon Sun May-Oct; 9.30am-6pm Mon-Fri 9.30am-2pm Sat, 10am-noon Sun Nov-Apr) is friendly and well stocked, with information about the region. It also has a hotel-room reservation board outside with telephone access The booklet *Freiburg – Official Guide* in English is a worthwhile investment. Also ask about the guided 'Kultour' walking tour held in English (adult/child €6/5) on Wednesday to Monday between April and October (Saturday only in winter) for groups of at least six people.

Münster

Freiburg's townscape is dominated by its magnificent Münster on the bustling market square. Begun as the burial church for the dukes of Zähringen, the cost of construction was shouldered by the local citizenry after the ruling family died out in 1218. A mere parish church until 1827, it was granted minster status when Freiburg became the seat of the Upper Rhenish bishopric, previously in Konstanz.

The Münster has been called 'the most beautiful in Christendom'. Its **square tower** is adorned at ground level with rich sculptural ornamentation depicting scenes from the Old and New Testaments in a rather helter-skelter fashion. Look for allegorical figures such as Voluptuousness (the one with snakes on her back and Satan himself) on the west wall. The sturdy tower base gives way to an octagon, crowned by a filigree 116m-high spire. An **ascent of the tower** provides an excellent view of the church's intricate interior; from up top you can see as far as the Kaiserstuhl and, on a clear day, the Vosges Mountains in France. At the time of writing, however, the tower was closed for renovation.

Inside the Münster, the kaleidoscopic **stained-glass windows** are truly dazzling. The **high altar** features a masterpiece triptych of the coronation of the Virgin Mary by Hans Baldung, which is best viewed on a guided tour (€1) of the ambulatory with its ring of richly outfitted side chapels.

South of Münsterplatz

Immediately south of the Münster on Münsterplatz stands the arcaded, reddish-brown

Historisches Kaufhaus (1530), a merchants' hall used as the central trade administration in the Middle Ages. The coats of arms in the oriels, as well as the four figures above the balcony, represent members of the House of Habsburg and indicate Freiburg's allegiance to these rulers.

The sculptor Christian Wentzinger built himself the **baroque townhouse** east of the Kaufhaus in 1761. Inside is a wonderful staircase with a wrought-iron railing that guides the eye to the elaborate ceiling fresco. Nowadays, the building is occupied by the **Museum für Stadtgeschichte** (Town History Museum; ☎ 201 2515; Münsterplatz 30; adult/concession €2.20/1; ☺ 10am-5pm Tue-Sun), where you can learn all about Freiburg's past up to the 18th century.

Admission to this museum also covers entrance (and vice versa) to the **Augustinermuseum** (☎ 201 2531; Salzstrasse 32; adult/concession €2.20/1). Housed in a former monastery, its extensive collection of medieval art includes paintings by Baldung, Matthias Grünewald and Cranach, while its assembly of stained glass from the Middle Ages to the present ranks as one of the most important in Germany.

The **Museum für Neue Kunst** (Museum of Modern Art; ☎ 201 2581; Marienstrasse 10; admission free; ☺ 10am-5pm Tue-Sun), about 200m further south in a *fin de siècle* former school building, makes an artistic leap into the 20th century with its collection of expressionist and abstract art.

Also in this neighbourhood, on Salzstrasse, there's the muralled 13th-century **Schwabentor** (Swabian Gate). Following the little canal west through the **Fischerau**, the former fishing quarter, will soon get you to the **Martinstor**, the only other surviving town gate. It's on Freiburg's main artery, Kaiser-Joseph-Strasse.

Western Altstadt

An eclectic mix of old and new buildings constitutes the **university quarter** extending just west of the Martinstor. The **Kollegiengebäude I** is an Art Nouveau concoction, while the **Alte Universitätsbibliothek** (Old University Library) is neo-Gothic. Heading north from the Martinstor along Kaiser-Joseph-Strasse leads you to the **Bertoldsbrunnen**, a fountain marking the spot where the central roads have crossed since the city's founding.

Northwest of here is the chestnut tree–studded **Rathausplatz** with another fountain that's a popular gathering place. Several interesting buildings surround the square. To the west rises the **Neues Rathaus**, a symmetrical structure in which two Renaissance town houses flank a newer, central arcaded section. The petite tower contains a carillon (played at noon daily). Part of the same structure as the Neues Rathaus is the **Altes Rathaus** (1559), also the result of merging several smaller buildings and a good example of successful postwar reconstruction. Freiburg's oldest town hall, the **Gerichtslaube** from the 13th century, is on Turmstrasse immediately west of the square.

The northeastern side of Rathausplatz is taken up by the medieval **Martinskirche**, which formerly belonged to the Franciscan monastery. Though severely damaged in WWII, it was rebuilt in the ascetic style typical of churches of this mendicant order. The antithesis to the Martinskirche is the extravagant, reddish-brown **Haus zum Walfisch** (House of the Whale), with its gilded late-Gothic oriel garnished with gargoyles. Located behind the church on Franziskanergasse, the building was the temporary refuge of the philosopher Erasmus von Rotterdam after his expulsion from Basel in 1529.

Further west, in a little park opposite the tourist office, is the neo-Gothic **Colombischlössle**, a villa housing the **Museum für Ur- und Frühgeschichte** (Museum of Pre- and Early History; ☎ 201 2571; Rotteckring 5; adult/concession €2/1 donation requested; ☺ 10am-5pm Tue-Sun). Via the cast-iron staircase, you'll reach an eclectic bunch of archaeological exhibits spanning prehistory and the Middle Ages.

Freiburg Beneath Your Feet

As you stroll through the town, be sure to look down at the pavement for the cheerful **mosaics** usually found in front of shopfronts. A diamond marks a jewellery shop, a cow is for a butcher, a pretzel for a baker and so on. Also be careful not to step into the **Bächle**, the permanently flowing, Lilliputian-like rivulets that run parallel to many footpaths. Originally an elaborate delivery system for nonpotable water, these literal 'tourist traps' now provide welcome relief for hot feet on sweltering summer days. And, since you've got your eyes to the ground, try to

BADEN-WÜRTTEMBERG

spot the decorative canalisation lids bearing Freiburg's coat of arms.

Schauinsland

A ride on the **cable car** (adult/concession €11.30/6.70 return) to the 1286m Schauinsland peak is a popular trip to the Black Forest highlands and a welcome escape from summer heat. Numerous easy, well-marked trails make the Schauinsland area ideal for walks. From Freiburg's Hauptbahnhof (or from Bertoldsbrunnen), take tram No 4 south to Günterstal and then bus No 21 to Talstation. The cable car operates daily year-round, except during maintenance periods in early spring and late autumn. Ring ☎ 0180-5019 703 to check weather conditions.

Sleeping

The tourist office has a room-reservation service (€2.55 booking fee, which is discounted from your hotel price). Finding a reasonably priced room anywhere near the town centre can be difficult. The tourist office may be able to find a private room for you, but don't count on it. For long-term rentals, contact **Home Company Mitwohnzentrale** (☎ 194 45; Brombergstrasse 17c).

DJH hostel (☎ 676 56; info@jugendherberge-freiburg .de; Kartäuserstrasse 151; juniors/seniors €19/21.70) Freiburg's huge hostel, east of town, is often brimming with German students, so phone ahead for reservations. Take tram No 1 from Stadtbahnbrücke to Römerhof and follow the signs down Fritz-Geiges-Strasse (about a 10-minute walk).

Camping Hirzberg (☎ 350 54; fax 289 212; Kartäuserstrasse 99; tent/person €5/5; 🖳) This is the most convenient camp site. Take tram No 1 from Stadtbahnbrücke to Stadthalle (towards Littenweiler). It's a short walk left through the park to the river. Cross the footbridge to Kartäuserstrasse and the entrance is on the left. The site is open year-round.

Hotel Schemmer (☎ 207 490; www.hotel-schemmer .de; Eschholzstrasse 63; s/d €39/59) Behind the Hauptbahnhof is this good budget option, which also offers cheaper rooms with shared bathroom.

Gasthaus Deutscher Kaiser (☎ 749 10; fax 709 822; Günterstalstrasse 38; s/d from €49/67; P) This creaky hotel, a 10-minute walk south of the Altstadt, has basic but spacious rooms. Cheaper rooms with shared bathroom are also available.

Hotel Minerva (☎ 386 490; info@minerva-hotel.de; Poststrasse 8; s/d from €69/85; P ✗) The comfortable Hotel Minerva is run by friendly young staff. It has a great Art Deco elevator, and offers an OK deal with the Bahnhof car park (€8 per 24 hours). You even have access to a sauna and solarium.

City-Hotel (☎ 388 070; www.cityhotelfreiburg.de; Weberstrasse 3; s/d from €76/98; P) This sleek and glossy place makes you appreciate modernity. Rooms are large and have plenty of closet space, plus such extras as towel heaters and hair dryers.

Stadthotel Kolping (☎ 319 30; www.stadthotel -kolping.de; Karlstrasse 7; s/d €77/97; P ✗ 🖳) This hotel, just north of the Altstadt, has comfortable rooms furnished in a business-like style and you won't be disappointed in the service. Rooms have Internet access, and the hotel even welcomes pets!

Oberkirch's Hotel & Weinstuben (☎ 202 6868; info@hotel-oberkirch.de; Münsterplatz 22; s/d from €86/ 132; P) If you deserve a splurge, come here. There are two restaurants in the hotel, one casual and one more formal, and the rooms are delightful. Parking costs an extra €6 a day.

Hotel zum Roten Bären (☎ 387 870; www.roter -baeren.de; Oberlinden 12; s/d from €103/133; P 🖳) One of the more expensive options, this classy but traditional place near Schwabentor claims to be the oldest guesthouse (established 1311) in Germany. Each room is lovingly furnished in a distinctive style and is flush with modern conveniences, such as satellite TV, Internet access and minibar. A copious buffet breakfast is included in the price.

Eating

As a university town, Freiburg virtually guarantees cheap eating. All in all, there are around 700 restaurants to choose from.

If you can produce student ID, the university *Mensa* branches at Rempartstrasse 18 and Hebelstrasse 9a have salad buffets and lots of filling fodder.

You'll find a good number of eating houses around the Martinstor.

Salatstuben (☎ 359 11; Löwenstrasse 1; meals under €4.75; ⏱ 10.30am-8pm Mon-Fri, 10am-4pm Sat) This place has a wide choice of wholesome salads and filling daily specials.

Schlappen (☎ 334 94; Löwenstrasse 2; meals from €5.50) With its jazz-themed décor, series of casual, convivial dining rooms and reasonably priced pizza, pasta, salads and local dishes, this is one of Freiburg's most popular and relaxed pubs. You can even try a version of evil absinthe.

Upstairs in the Markthalle, at Martinsgasse 235, you'll be hit with a wonderful confusion of smells from Mexican, Italian, Indian, French and other self-service counters, which offer fast, delicious and cheap lunches.

Pubs and restaurants also cluster along Konviktstrasse.

Kolben-Kaffee-Akademie (☎ 387 0013; Kaiser-Joseph-Strasse 233; large coffee €1.50; ☺ 8am-6.30pm Mon-Fri, 8am-5pm Sat & Sun) This is an old-fashioned stand-up coffeehouse.

Hausbrauerei Feierling (☎ 266 78; Gerberau 46; meals from €8.50) In a renovated old brewery, this is a haunt of the in-crowd, with a good vegetarian menu and absolutely enormous schnitzels with salad and *Brägele* (chipped potatoes).

Sichelschmiede (☎ 350 37; Insel 1; mains around €12) This is a snug wine bar decked out in wood and wrought iron.

Englers Weinkrügle (☎ 383 115; Konviktstrasse 12; 4-course meals from €13; ☺ closed Mon) This place serves affordable Badener food and wine.

Entertainment

The free cultural events listing *Freiburg Aktuell* is published monthly and available at hotels and the tourist office. Also look for *Freizeit & Kultur*, a tad edgier and packed with up-to-date insider tips.

Jazzhaus (☎ 349 73; Schnewlinstrasse 1) This is one of Germany's hottest music venues, with live jazz nearly every night, including appearances by internationally acclaimed artists.

Sound (☎ 354 34; Nussmannstrasse 9) Plays hip-hop, rock, pop and oldies.

Konzerthaus (☎ 348 74; Konrad-Adenauer-Platz 1) Located between the Hauptbahnhof and the Altstadt, fine orchestras perform in this hulking modern concert hall, which also doubles as a centre for other cultural events and conventions.

Getting There & Away
BUS

Freiburg is a major hub for buses to rural Black Forest communities. Bus No 1066 travels to Hausach in the Kinzig Valley, with some departures continuing on to Wolfach and Schiltach. Bus No 7200 goes to the Europa Park Rust; bus Nos 7205, 7209 and 7216 go to St Peter; and bus No 7272 goes to Furtwangen.

CAR & MOTORCYCLE

The A5, which links Frankfurt and Basel, also passes through Freiburg. The usually clogged but very scenic B31 leads east into the Höllental (Hell's Valley) route and on to Lake Constance. The B294 leaves the town northwards and travels into the Central Black Forest. Car-hire agencies include **Europcar** (☎ 515 100; Löracherstrasse 10) and **Avis** (☎ 197 19; St-Georgener-Strasse 7). For ride services call **Citynetz Mitfahr-Service** (☎ 194 44; Belfortstrasse 55).

TRAIN

Freiburg lies in the north–south train corridor, so it's highly accessible. There are frequent departures for destinations such as Basel (€9, 40 minutes) and Baden-Baden (€14.40, 45 minutes). Freiburg is the western terminus of the Höllentalbahn to Donaueschingen via Titisee-Neustadt. There's also a local connection to Breisach (€4.40, 26 minutes).

Getting Around

Freiburg has an efficient public transport system that is part of a regional network called Regio, extending to all communities within a radius of approximately 30km. It's divided into three zones, with tickets costing €1.80/3/4.40 for one/two/three zones. The Regio 24-hour ticket is available either for one zone (€4.60 one person, €6.50 two people) or all zones (€9.20 one person, €13 two people); up to four children under the age of 15 travel for free on this ticket. Buy tickets from vending machines or the driver, and be sure to validate upon boarding.

AROUND FREIBURG
Breisach
☎ 07667 / pop 13,300

About 25km west of Freiburg, separated from France by the Rhine, Breisach is an ancient town that has often been caught in the crossfire of conflict. The Romans first built a fortress atop the volcanic Breisachberg. After becoming an imperial city under Rudolf von Habsburg in 1275, Breisach became involved in a power struggle between Staufian and Habsburg rulers, the French and the Austrians. In 1793 the French demolished the town, and in 1815 it fell to the Grand Duchy of Baden.

Not to be missed on any visit to Breisach is the huge **Münster St Stephan**. It is reached after a short walk from the Hauptbahnhof: cross Bahnhofstrasse to Poststrasse, then keep going straight to the Gutgesellentor and up the Münsterberg. The Münster was built between the 12th and the 15th centuries, and rebuilt after being badly damaged during WWII. Of note inside is the fairly faded fresco cycle (1491) of *The Last Judgment* by Martin Schongauer in the west end and the sweeping rood loft from around the same period. There's also a nice Renaissance pulpit (1597) and a silver shrine containing the relics of the town's patron saints. Top billing, though, goes to the magnificent high **altar triptych** (1526), with figures carved entirely of linden wood by an artist simply known as Master HL. From the Münster terrace, there's a great view across the Rhine into France and the Vosges Mountains.

The **tourist office** (☎ 940 155; www.breisach.de; Marktplatz 16) can help with accommodation for a fee of €1.

DJH hostel (☎ 7665; info@jugendherberge-breisach .de; Rheinuferstrasse 12; juniors/seniors €18.40/21.10) This hostel is about a 15-minute walk south of the Hauptbahnhof.

There's an hourly train service between Freiburg and Breisach (26 minutes).

Kaiserstuhl

Northeast of Breisach is the Kaiserstuhl, a 560m-high mountain that's actually an extinct volcano. Its terraced slopes constitute one of Germany's finest wine-growing areas, noted especially for its late Burgundies. The wines owe their quality to an ideal microclimate, the result of plenty of sunshine and the fertile loess (clay and silt) soil that retains the heat during the night.

Another popular grape variety here is the Grauburgunder (Pinot Gris). On weekends between April and October, at least one wine estate opens for cellar tours and tastings on a rotating basis. For details, see the tourist office in Breisach.

The *Kaiserstuhlbahn* train from Breisach to Riegel is a good way to get to the area, though it's best explored by foot, for example, by hiking the 15km Winzerweg (Wine Growers' Trail) from Riegel to Achkarren. By bicycle, you could pedal along Kaiserstuhl Radwanderweg, a 64km loop trail starting in Breisach. Bikes may be hired at the Hauptbahnhof in Breisach or at **Zweirad-Sütterlin** (☎ 6399; Im Gelbstein 19; €11 per day).

St Peter

☎ 07660 / pop 2300

St Peter, on the southern slopes of Mt Kandel (1243m), is one of those supernaturally bucolic Black Forest villages that appears to be caught in a time warp. The fresh-faced folk of St Peter are deeply committed to their ancient traditions and customs. One third of the community still lives in neat farmhouses often owned by the same family for centuries. At local events you can see the villagers – from young boys and girls to grey-haired matriarchs and patriarchs – proudly sporting their colourful Trachten (folkloric costumes), handmade locally by skilled craftspeople.

The most outstanding feature of St Peter is the former **Benedictine Abbey** (1727), a baroque, rococo jewel designed by the masterful Peter Thumb of Vorarlberg. Its predecessor was founded in 1093 by Duke Berthold II of Zähringen as a private monastery, as well as a burial place for his family. Many of the period's top artists collaborated on the sumptuous interior decoration, including Joseph Anton Feuchtmayer, who carved the statues of the various Zähringer dukes affixed to the pillars. You can take a guided tour (€3) of the monastery complex but times vary, so check first with the **tourist office** (☎ 910 224; www.st -peter-schwarzwald.de; Klosterhof 11; 9am-noon & 2-5pm Fri, 11am-1pm Sat Jun-Oct).

From Freiburg's central bus station you can take bus No 7205 to St Peter (one hour). Bus Nos 7209 and 7216 take only about 40 minutes, but operate less frequently.

If you're driving, take the B3 north, then turn east in the direction of Glottertal. This will put you right onto the **Schwarzwald Panorama Strasse** (Black Forest Panorama road), a scenic route across a plateau with dreamy views of the Feldberg (1493m) and other mountains.

Europa Park Rust

So you don't have time to go to Paris, London, Amsterdam and Venice during your rip to Europe? Don't despair. The people of the **Europa Park** (☎ 01805-776 688; www.europa ark.de; adult/child aged 4-11 €25/22.50; ☼ 9am-6pm, pen later in peak season weather permitting, late Mar–arly Nov & Dec–early Jan) have brought the conti-nent's best sights together right here at their heme park in Rust, about 30km north of reiburg. Sure, it's not the real thing, but where else can you meander effortlessly rom a Swiss chalet to a Greek village and be back in time for lunch at the Rock-Café – without even taking your passport? And f you need to brush up on German archi-ectural styles, just take a walk down 'Main street Germany', where you'll find it all – Gothic red brick and cute half-timber to urvy baroque, and a Christmas market in December. There's even have a big mouse walking around. Sound familiar?

From Freiburg's bus station, bus No 7200 makes daily trips directly to the park. By ar, you should take the A5 north to the Herbolzheim exit.

Höllental

When in Freiburg, you shouldn't miss a ride through 'hell', the wildly romantic Höllen-al (Hell's Valley to be precise), stretching ast of the city en route to Titisee. It's easily seen by car along the B31 or by rail on the Höllentalbahn from Freiburg to Donaue-chingen, although to truly experience its natural splendour, you should walk.

In a wonderful twist of names, the western gateway to 'hell' is the village of Himmelreich (Kingdom of Heaven), after which you're plunged into the narrow, craggy stone canal that in parts is so steep hat the sunlight doesn't reach the bottom until mid-morning. Near-vertical jagged ock faces, alternating with tree-covered hillsides, dwarf everything beneath them.

A famous landmark is the **Hirschsprung** (Stag's Leap), the narrowest point of the valley between Himmelreich and Posthalde, nd allegedly the spot where a male deer being pursued by hunters rescued itself by leaping across the crevice.

The valley was virtually impassable until he construction of its railway at the turn of he 20th century. This was another amazing eat of engineering accomplished by Robert Gerwig, who also built the Schwarzwald-bahn. On its way, the train passes through nine tunnels and travels along the 222m-

long viaduct over the Ravenna Gorge before coming out of the valley at Hinterzarten.

FELDBERG
☎ 07655 / pop 1800
At 1493m the Feldberg is the highest moun-tain in the Black Forest and the region's premier downhill skiing area, with a dense network of runs and ski lifts. On clear days, the view of the chain of Alps in the south is stunning. The actual mountain top is treeless and not particularly attractive, looking very much like a monk's tonsured skull. This lack of trees is not because of an unusually low tree line, as some tourist brochures would have you believe, but the result of heavy log-ging by the area's early settlers.

Feldberg is also the name given to a clus-ter of five resort villages, of which **Altglashüt-ten** is the administrative centre. It's the site of the **tourist office** (☎ 8019; www.feldberg-schwarz wald.de; Kirchgasse 1; ☼ 8am-5.30pm or 6pm Mon-Fri year-round; 9am-noon Sat, 10am-noon Sun Jun-Oct, Dec-Mar), which helps find accommodation, and has a wealth of information about hiking and skiing in the area.

The post office is about 100m north of here on Bärentaler Strasse, with a bank im-mediately adjacent.

Together with **Neuglasshütten**, Altglashüt-ten used to be a centre for glass-blowing, a tradition kept alive by just a single work-shop today.

Just north of these twin communities is **Bärental**, where traditional Black Forest farmhouses snuggle against the hillsides. Germany's highest train station (967m) is here. East of Bärental is **Falkau** in the Haslach Valley, a family-friendly resort with a cute waterfall for a nearby attraction. Also not far away is the idyllic **Windgfällweiher**, a good lake for swimming or rowing.

About 7km west of these four villages, there's **Feldberg-Ort** (area code ☎ 07676) right in the heart of the 42-sq-km nature preserve that covers much of the mountain. All the ski lifts are here, as is the popular chairlift to the Bismarck monument for wonderful panoramic views.

Activities
HIKING
In summer, the Feldberg area is a great place for hiking, with some rather challeng-ing trails. The most strenuous hike takes

you to the top of the Feldberg (1493m), while the scenic hike through the Höllental is only of moderate difficulty. Since much of the region is part of a nature preserve, you're quite likely to encounter some rare wildflowers or animal species such as mountain hens and chamois. The Westweg trail (Pforzheim to Basel) also crosses the Feldberg.

The tourist office can offer suggestions for hiking trails and an assortment of maps, including the *Wanderkarte Feldberg* (1:30,000).

SKIING

The Liftverbund Feldberg comprises a network of 26 ski lifts, and you'll only need one ticket to use them all. There are 36 runs totalling 50km in length. Day ski-lift tickets are €22, from 11am €21, from noon €19 and from 1pm €15.50. Discounts on multiday tickets are available. If you prefer cross-country skiing, you can choose from among four groomed trails ranging from 2.5km to 20km in length.

The snow season usually lasts from November until the end of February. For the latest snow conditions, ring ☎ 07676-1214. Four ski schools offer a variety of packages. If you want to hire downhill or cross-country skis, look for signs which read 'Skiverleih'. **Skiverleih Schubnell** (☎ 560) in Altglashütten and **Skischule Weyler** (☎ 423) in Feldberg-Ort are good options.

Schwarzwaldkaufhaus Faller (☎ 07676-223) hires out snowboards. There's a free shuttle service from all Feldberg communities to the ski lifts if you have a ski-lift ticket or your *Gästekarte*.

Sleeping

DJH Turnerheim Altglashütten (☎ 900 10; 900 199; Am Sommerberg 26; juniors/seniors €14.50/17.50) Altglashütten's renovated hostel is about a 15-minute walk south of that village's train station.

DJH hostel (☎ 07676-221; info@jugendherberge -feldberg.de; Passhöhe 14; juniors/seniors €17.30/20) The DJH Hebelhof is perched at 1234m in Feldberg-Ort (take bus No 7300 from the Bärental train station to Hebelhof). The hostel offers paragliding courses year-round and snowboard training in winter.

Berggasthof Wasmer (☎ 07676-230; fax 430; An der Wiesenquelle 1; s/d €27.50/59; **P**) A more com-

fortable yet still affordable option is right next to the ski-lift area. Cheaper rooms are available with shared bathroom.

Getting There & Away

Bärental and Altglashütten are stops on the *Dreiseenbahn* train from Titisee to Seebrug, on the Schluchsee. From the train station in Bärental, bus No 7300 makes direct trips every 30 minutes to Feldberg-Ort.

If you're driving, take the B31 (Freiburg Donaueschingen) to Titisee, then the B317 to Feldberg-Ort via Bärental. To get to Altglashütten, get on the B500 in Bärental.

TITISEE-NEUSTADT
☎ 07651 / pop 12,000

Titisee, named for the glacial lake on which it is located, is an extraordinarily popular summer holiday resort with too much infrastructure for its own good. The village hugging the lake's northeastern end is on giant beehive of activity filled with souvenir shops, kiosks, cafés and restaurants and swarming mostly with families and elderly tourists taking advantage of the healthy air of the Black Forest's oldest spa.

The lake itself – 2km long and 750m wide – is reasonably scenic and best appreciated from the relative isolation of a rowing or pedal boat. Windsurfing and sailing are popular activities here, and equipment for both sports can be hired. The scenic trails around the lake provide more escape routes from the crowds.

Titisee's train station is at Parkstrasse, only a short walk from the lake shore. The train station in Neustadt is also centrally located on Bahnhofstrasse. Post office and banks are in the immediate vicinity of both train stations. The **tourist office** (☎ 980 40; www.titisee-neustadt.de; Strandbadstrasse 4; 🕙 8am-noon & 1.30-5.30pm Mon-Fri, 10am-1pm Sat & Sun) is helpful.

Sleeping & Eating

The tourist office has a free room-finding service for **private rooms** (from €12.50 per person). There's often a small surcharge for stays of one or two nights. As for hotels and pensions, Titisee-Neustadt is flooded with options. There is also a good selection of camp sites.

DJH hostel (☎ 238; info@jugendherberge-titisee-ve tishof.de; Bruderhalde 27; juniors/seniors €17.30/20) This

bulous hostel is on the northern lake
hore. To get there take bus No 7300
om the train station to Feuerwehrheim/
ugendherberge or it's 30 minutes on foot.

DJH hostel (☎ 7360; info@jugendherberge-titisee
udenberg.de; Rudenberg 6; juniors/seniors €17.30/20)
'here's a second DJH hostel in Neustadt,
ituated on the eastern edge of town. It's
bout 20 minutes' walk from Neustadt train
tation).

Terrassencamping Sandbank (☎ 8243; www.camp
g-sandbank.com; Seerundweg; tent/person €5/4.40;
Apr–mid-Oct). This top-rate camp site is
ight on the lake shore. It doesn't take res-
rvations and is usually full by noon in the
igh season.

Campingplatz Bühlhof (☎ 07652-1606; fax 1827;
ühlhofweg 13; tent/person from €6/6) On the other
ide of the lake, a little way off the lakeside,
'itisee's second camp site is a 15-minute
valk from the centre of town.

Treschers Schwarzwaldhotel Am See (☎ 8050;
ww.schwarzwaldhotel-trescher.de; Seestrasse 10; s/d
91/128; P ⚑) High style and magnificent
iews over the lake make this the hotel of
hoice, and the restaurant is one of the
est in the region. Mains start at €17.50,
ut the grilled Black Forest trout make it
vorth a splurge.

Getting There & Away
BUS
itisee-Neustadt is a transport hub for the
outhern Black Forest. Bus No 7257 makes
ourly trips to Schluchsee.

From Titisee train station, bus No 7300
oes to Feldberg and continues to Basel in
witzerland. From Neustadt's train station,
here are hourly links to Bonndorf with
us No 7258 and to St Märgen with bus
No 7261.

CAR & MOTORCYCLE
itisee-Neustadt is at the junction of the
331 and the B500.

TRAIN
The *Höllentalbahn* train from Freiburg to
Donaueschingen stops at both Titisee and
Neustadt train stations.

The *Dreiseenbahn* train to both Feldberg
and Schluchsee leaves from Titisee train
tation. Neustadt is linked approximately
very two hours with Donaueschingen and
Jlm on the *Donautalbahn* train.

Getting Around
Bus No 7257 connects Titisee with Neustadt every hour. There's a free shuttle to the
Feldberg ski area if you hold a ski-lift ticket.
In Titisee bikes may be hired from **Ski-Hirt**
(☎ 922 80; Wilhelm-Stahl-Strasse) and **Bootsvermietung Drubba** (☎ 981 200, Seestrasse 37).

SCHLUCHSEE
☎ 07656 / pop 2600
Schluchsee, the name of both a lake and
town, is about 10km south of Titisee. Less
commercial than its bigger neighbour, it's
also a popular summer holiday-resort area
and a centre for outdoor activities of all
kinds, especially swimming, windsurfing,
sailing and scuba diving. Thanks to its location at the foot of the Feldberg, the forests
around Schluchsee offer some wonderful
hiking on about 160km of trails.

Orientation & Information
The railway tracks and road run parallel to
Schluchsee's eastern shore. The community
of Aha caps the north end of the lake, the
town of Schluchsee is about two-thirds
down and Seebrugg is at the southern end.
The western shore is accessible only by
bike or on foot. The lake's circumference
is 18.5km.

The **tourist office** (☎ 7733; www.schluchsee.de;
Haus des Gastes, Fischbacher Strasse 7; 🕐 8am-noon &
2-6pm Mon-Fri Oct-Apr; 8am-6pm Mon-Fri, 10am-noon
Sat & Sun May-Sep) helps find accommodation.
The **post office** (Lindenstrasse) is a short walk
northwest of the tourist office.

Sleeping & Eating
As you'd expect, the whole gamut of accommodation from top resorts to simple **private
rooms** (from €14 per person) is available along the
Schluchsee. At no charge, the tourist office
can help you wade through the bewildering
number of choices.

DJH hostel (☎ 329; info@jugendherberge-schluchsee
-wolfsgrund.de; Im Wolfgrund 28; juniors/seniors €17.30/
20) This hostel is nicely located on the
peninsula jutting into the lake, about a
10-minute walk north of Schluchsee train
station.

DJH hostel (☎ 494; info@jugendherberge-schluch
see-seebrugg.de; Haus Nr 9; juniors/seniors €17.30/20)
There's a second hostel in Seebrugg, about
a five-minute walk from Seebrugg train
station.

BADEN-WÜRTTEMBERG

Campingplatz Wolfsgrund (☎ 573; tent/person €5.50/4.50; ⊙ year-round) This is a modern facility situated on the eastern lake shore, just north of the Schluchsee town centre.

Haus Pfrommer (☎ 867; hauspfrommer@freenet.de; Hinterer Giersbühlweg 4; r €20 per person; P) This welcoming place has a charming enclosed terrace and the rooms contain nicely painted furniture.

Pension Simone (☎ 420; www.sbo.de/simone; Dresselbacher Strasse 17; r €31 per person; P) A bit more upmarket, all rooms are cheery and have a balcony dripping with red flowers.

Pension am See (☎ 513; www.pension-am-schluchsee.de Im Wolfsgrund 1; r €37 per person; P) Among the less expensive options, this pension has tastefully decorated rooms.

Hotel Sternen (☎ 251; Dresselbacher Strasse 1; mains from €8.50) This restaurant offers solid regional fare, and its Rumpelfass bar is recommended for good beer and cheer.

Hotel Schiff (☎ 975 70; Kirchplatz 7; meals from €11) It's worth paying more at this restaurant for a table on the terrace overlooking the lake.

Getting There & Away

Bus No 7257 makes regular trips to/from Titisee-Neustadt, though it's probably more convenient to take the *Dreiseenbahn* train, with hourly service between Titisee and Seebrugg. From the south, Seebrugg is also served by bus No 7319 to/from St Blasien. To get to the Wutachschlucht (Wutach Gorge), take bus No 7343 to Bonndorf.

Schluchsee is on the B500, which hooks up with the B31 in Titisee.

Getting Around

Bicycles are available for hire at **Hotel Schiff** (☎ 975 70; Kirchplatz 7). The tourist office sells a map outlining bike trails.

In season, **G Isele** (☎ 449) offers boat service around the Schluchsee, departing up to eight times daily with stops in Aha, at the dam (Staumauer), in Seebrugg and in Schluchsee town. You can get on and off as you please; the whole round trip takes one hour and costs €5.50 (less for single stops).

ST BLASIEN

☎ 07672 / pop 4200

St Blasien is a health resort at the southern foot of the Feldberg, about 8km south of Schluchsee town. Despite its dwarfish size, St Blasien has been a political and cultural giant in this region throughout its 1000-year history. This is reflected in its almost urban appearance and flair that's hardly typical of the Black Forest.

St Blasien's power was anchored in its Benedictine monastery, founded in the 9th century. The monastery's influence reached its zenith in the 18th century under the prince-abbot Martin Gerbert. He was responsible for St Blasien's outstanding landmark, the magnificent Dom. After secularisation in 1806, the monastery did time as an ammunition, then weaving, factory before being turned into a boarding school by the Jesuits in 1933. Today, it ranks as one of Germany's top private schools.

Thanks to its healthy, fogless climate, St Blasien has also been a popular spa resort since the late 19th century. In winter, it offers a small range of cross-country skiing tracks and ski lifts. The communities of Menzenschwand, about 8km to the north-west, and Albtal, about 3km to the south, are now a part of St Blasien.

Orientation & Information

The Dom and former monastery complex dominate St Blasien's small centre. Bus No 7321 shuttles between here and Menzenschwand. The **main tourist office** (☎ 414 30; www.st-blasien.de; Am Kurgarten 1-3; ⊙ 10am-noon, 3-5pm Mon-Fri, 10am-noon Sat) has a Menzenschwand **office branch** (☎ 07675-930 90; fax 1709; Hinterdorfstrasse 15), which is open the same hours.

There's a **Sparkasse** (Bernau-Menzenschwander Strasse 1), with the post office on the same road at No 5.

Dom St Blasien

crowned by an enormous copper cupola, the massive **Dom St Blasien** (⊙ 8am-6.30pm May-Sep, 8am-5.30pm Oct-Apr), seems oddly out of place in this remote town. It's an early masterpiece by French architect Pierre-Michel d'Ixnard, who paved the way from the baroque period to neoclassicism. The former monastery complex surrounding the Dom is of equally generous proportions, measuring 105m by 195m. The cupola has a diameter of 33.5m, making it the third largest in Europe after the Pantheon in Rome and the Église du Dôme, containing Napoleon's tomb, in Paris.

Having entered the Dom through a columned portico, you'll find yourself in a light-flooded rotunda of overwhelming symmetry and harmony. Twenty Corinthian columns support the cupola, whose massiveness is mitigated by 18 windows. The rectangular choir has the same length as the cupola's diameter. It's all bathed in white light.

Throughout the summer, the Dom is used as a venue for a series of free classical concerts.

Sleeping & Eating

The tourist office can help find **private rooms** (from €14 per person).

DJH hostel (☎ 07675-326; info@jugendherberge -menzenschwand.de; Vorderdorfstrasse 10; juniors/seniors €17.30/20). This hostel is situated in Menzenschwand in a gorgeous Black Forest farmhouse.

Gasthof Birkenhof (☎ 1079; Hinterdorfstrasse 25; r from €16 per person) This typical Black Forest guesthouse is not far from the ski lifts in Menzenschwand. Some rooms have good views over the surrounding hills.

Hotel Klostermeisterhaus (☎ 848; www.kloster meisterhaus.de; Im Süssen Winkel 2; s/d €40/75; ✗) This roomy hotel has modern rooms and a restaurant that serves regional specialities.

Gasthaus Alter Hirschen (☎ 503; Hauptstrasse 39; mains around €8; ✋ closed Fri) In St Blasien, you might also try this place.

Hotel Sonnenhof (☎ 905 60; www.schwarzwald hotel-sonnenhof.de; Vorderdorfstrasse 58; snacks from €5) This three-star hotel serves regional and standard German food, well-priced daily specials and an inexpensive *Vesper* (supper) menu.

Getting There & Away

Train tracks into the Southern Black Forest terminate at Seebrugg, about 6km northeast of St Blasien. Seebrugg is reached on the *Dreiseenbahn* train from Titisee (€4.80, 25 minutes). The cross-country IR train from Norddeich in Friesland via Cologne, Mainz and Baden-Baden also terminates in Seebrugg.

From Seebrugg, bus No 7319 provides an almost hourly connection to St Blasien (20 minutes). Bus No 7343 makes the trip from St Blasien to Bonndorf, the gateway to the Wutachschlucht (Wutach Gorge).

St Blasien is situated on the B500, which crosses the B31 (Freiburg–Donaueschingen) in Titisee.

Getting Around

It's easy to get around town on foot; should you need a taxi, ring ☎ 907 090. Mountain bikes can be hired from **MTB Zentrum Kalle** (☎ 07675-1074; Grosse Bachwiesen 4), located in Menzenschwand.

WUTACHSCHLUCHT

In a country as developed and densely populated as Germany, few natural paradises remain. The Wutachschlucht (Wutach Gorge) near Bonndorf, sometimes billed as the 'Grand Canyon of the Black Forest', is one of them. It's a lovely ravine with craggy rock faces making a near-vertical rise skywards. Below lies a fertile habitat harbouring about 1200 types of wildflowers, including orchids, rare birds like grey egrets, and countless species of butterflies, beetles and lizards.

Lined by ancient trees, the valley follows the flow of the 90km-long Wutach (loosely translated as 'angry river') which originates as the placid Gutach (literally 'good river') on the Feldberg at 1450m before flowing into the Rhine near Waldshut.

To appreciate the Wutachschlucht in all its splendour and complexity, take the 13km hike from the Schattenmühle in an easterly direction to the Wutachmühle (or vice versa). This can be accomplished in about 4½ hours. If you have the energy, add the 2.5km-long wildly romantic Lotenbach-Klamm (Lotenbach Glen) to your tour. The Bonndorf **tourist office** (☎ 07703-7607; www.bonndorf.de/touristinfo; Schloss-strasse 1; ✋ 9am-noon & 2-6pm Mon-Fri, 10am-noon Sat May-Oct) has maps and details about hiking in the Wutachschlucht.

To get to either trail head, take bus No 7344 from Bonndorf. The bus also stops in Boll about 4km east of the Schattenmühle and 9km west of the Wutachmühle, which is a good place to end your hike if you don't want to walk the entire distance.

Bonndorf itself is served by buses from all directions. If you're coming from Neustadt, take bus No 7258 (40 minutes). From Donaueschingen, bus No 7260 travels to Bonndorf via the Wutachmühle (20 minutes). From St Blasien and the Schluchsee, bus No 7343 cuts west in about one hour.

If you're driving, take the B31 or B500 to Titisee, then the B315 in the direction of Bonndorf.

LAKE CONSTANCE

Lake Constance (Bodensee) is a perfect cure for travellers stranded in landlocked southern Germany. Often called the 'Swabian Sea', this giant bulge in the sinewy course of the Rhine offers a choice of water sports, relaxation and cultural pursuits. It has a circumference of some 273km, of which the southern 72km belong to Switzerland, the eastern 28km to Austria, and the remaining northern and western 173km to Germany. It measures 14km at its widest point and 250m at its deepest level. The distance from Konstanz at its western end to Bregenz in the east is 46km. The snow-capped Swiss peaks provide a breathtaking backdrop when viewed from the German shore. During stormy weather, Lake Constance can get quite dangerous, with huge waves crashing onto the shores.

The Lake Constance region is popular with tourists, and gets extremely crowded in July and August. It may be hard to find a room for the night, and drivers are bound to get very frustrated by the constantly choked roads. Be sure to call ahead to check on room availability, and be prepared to head into the hinterland to find a place to stay. The public transport system is well coordinated and a good alternative to driving a car.

April and May are among the best times to visit Lake Constance because that's when the fruit trees are flowering. Summers are humid, but at least the lake is warm enough for swimming (around 20° to 23°C). The autumn wine harvest is also a pleasant time to come. Winters are often foggy, or misty at best.

Getting Around

Although most of the towns on Lake Constance have a train station (Meersburg is an exception), buses provide the easiest land connections. By car or motorbike, the B31 hugs the northern shore of Lake Constance, but it can get rather busy. By far the most enjoyable way to get around is on the **ferries** (☎ 07531-281 389) which, from March to early November, call several times a day at all the

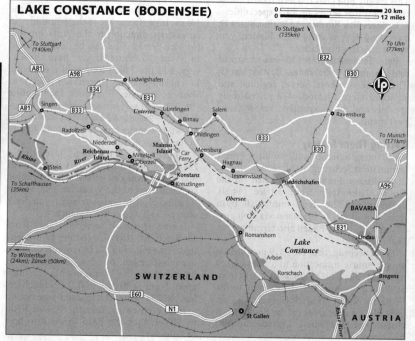

LAKE CONSTANCE (BODENSEE)

To Stuttgart (140km)
To Stuttgart (135km)
To Ulm (77km)

A81
A98
B32
B30
Ludwigshafen
B34
A81
B31
Singen
B33
Überlingen
Salem
Ravensburg
Untersee
Birnau
Radolfzell
Uhldingen
B33
B30
To Munich (171km)
Niederzell
Mainau Island
Meersburg
Reichenau Island
Mittelzell
Car Ferry
Hagnau
A96
Rhine River
Oberzell
Stein
Konstanz
Immenstaad
Friedrichshafen
BAVARIA
To Schaffhausen (35km)
Kreuzlingen
Obersee
B31
Lindau
Car Ferry
Romanshorn
Lake Constance
To Winterthur (24km); Zürich (50km)
Arbon
SWITZERLAND
Rorschach
Bregenz
E60
N1
Rhine River
St Gallen
AUSTRIA

0 — 20 km
0 — 12 miles

BADEN-WÜRTTEMBERG

arger towns on the lake; there is a 50% discount for holders of most rail passes. The three-day BodenseeErlebniskarte (€49/29 adult/concession), is valid from April to October, and allows free travel on all boats and mountain cableways on and around Lake Constance, including its Austrian and Swiss shores, as well as free entry to around 140 tourist attractions and museums. There are also seven-day (€63/95) and 14-day (€89/49) versions.

An international bike track circumnavigates Lake Constance, tracing the shoreline between vineyards and beaches. The route is well signposted but Regio Cart's 1:50,000 *Rund um den Bodensee* cycling/hiking map is useful and available at tourist offices.

KONSTANZ

☎ 07531 / pop 79,000

Konstanz (Constance) is the cultural and economic centre of the Bodensee. Bordering on Switzerland, it has an attractive location on a spit of land separating the Obersee (the main section of lake) from the Untersee. Its picturesque Altstadt never suffered fire or war damage. Konstanz was first settled by the Romans and played a leading role in the Middle Ages when it was the centre of the Duchy of Swabia – whose territory included much of Central Europe – and was also the largest bishopric north of the Alps. The town reached its historical apex when the Council of Constance convened here from 1414 to 1418. The meeting chose a single pope (replacing three others), thereby healing the 'Great Schism' in the Catholic Church. This was the last great moment for the world stage for Konstanz, which then plunged into relative obscurity. The final blow came in 1821 when the bishopric – in existence for 1000 years – was dissolved and moved to Freiburg.

Today, Konstanz is a rather liberal town with little industry. About one in seven inhabitants – affectionately known as *Seehas* (sea hares) – is a student at the local university, which was founded only in 1966. Their presence is felt in a lively pub and restaurant scene, unique in the otherwise rather staid region of Lake Constance.

Orientation & Information

Konstanz is bisected by the Rhine, which flows through a channel linking Obersee and Untersee. On its left (south) bank is the Altstadt, where most sights are located, while the modern quarter is on the right (north) bank. Konstanz has a German and a Swiss train station adjacent to each other on Bahnhofplatz, on the eastern edge of the Altstadt next to the harbour. Most city buses and those bound for destinations in the countryside depart from here also.

Information

If you're staying more than one night, your hotel or pension will give you the *Gästekarte*, which entitles you to unlimited bus rides and various discounts, for instance on the island of Mainau.

The tourist office also sells the three-day BodenseeErlebniskarte. For more details see Getting Around under Lake Constance (p478). The Reisebank is inside the train station. You can also change money at the ticket counter of the Swiss train station.

Ambulance (☎ 192 22, on weekends 07732-100 11)

Clixworx (☎ 991 2111; Bodanstrasse 21) Around the corner from the train station.

English Bookshop (☎ 150 63; Münzgasse 10) Stocks a good selection.

Münz-Waschsalon (☎ 160 27; Hofhalde 3) Offers a good deal on laundry. The owner is extremely chatty, has lots of tips and will even do your wash for you while you go sightseeing.

Tourist office (☎ 133 030; www.konstanz.de/tourismus; Fischmarkt 2; 🕙 9am-7pm Mon-Fri Apr-Oct, 9am-12.30pm & 2-6pm Mon-Fri Nov-Mar) Staff will find accommodation for €2.50. There's also a hotel reservation board and telephone outside the tourist office.

Sights

HARBOUR & WATERFRONT

To reach the harbour, take the passageway beneath the railway tracks just north of the tourist office. The imposing grey stone cube on your left is the **Konzilgebäude** (Council Building). Built in 1388, this was a granary and warehouse before making its mark in history as the place where Pope Martin V was elected. It's a concert hall today.

On a perpetually turning pedestal over the lake, you'll see the newest Konstanz landmark, the **Imperia**, a sculpture of a scantily clad, voluptuous woman. Imperia was allegedly a prostitute who plied her trade in the days of the Council of Constance and was immortalised in a novel by Honoré de Balzac.

A few steps from here is the **Zeppelin Monument**, honouring the airship inventor Count Ferdinand von Zeppelin. He was born in 1838 on the **Insel**, a tiny island a short stroll north through a small park. This handsome structure has housed a swanky hotel since 1875, but began life as a Dominican monastery in 1235. Just past the lobby is the former cloister with 19th-century murals depicting the history of Konstanz.

Practically opposite the Insel is the **Theater**, whose façade sports a comical semi-relief showing the Fool's banishment from the theatre.

The nearby **Rheinbrücke** links the Altstadt and Neustadt. Take a look across at Seestrasse on the opposite shore, with its row of handsome Art Nouveau villas. The one at No 21 houses the city **Casino**.

MÜNSTER

The Council of Constance once held its sessions at the **Münster** (10am-6pm Mon-Sat, 1-6pm Sun), which sits on a slightly raised square marking the highest point in Konstanz's Altstadt. It's a showcase of architectural styles from nine centuries, starting with the original Carolingian church, built in 1000, but collapsed a mere 52 years later. Its reconstruction incorporated the original crypt beneath the choir that's decorated with large gilded copper medallions and – highly unusual for a crypt – bathed in muted daylight streaming in from a little window.

The new church in the Romanesque style still forms the core of today's structure. Between the 12th and 15th centuries, the Gothic vaulted side aisles, with their chains of chapels, were added, as were the masterfully carved oak main portal and choir stalls. The Renaissance brought the organ, which perches on a stone balcony, while the high altar dates from the baroque era. The 19th century gave the church its neo-Gothic spires.

The Münster contains a number of treasures. A highlight is the **Schnegg** (literally 'snail'; 1438) in the northern transept, a vividly decorated spiral staircase. Exit left into the cloister to get to the **Mauritius Rotunda**, with the 13th-century **Heiliges Grab** (Holy Sepulchre), inspired by the one purportedly of Christ in Jerusalem. It's a crown-shaped stone structure festooned with highly emo-

tional and artistic sculptures, including the apostles perched between each of the gables. Time and the elements have taken a toll on the Münster, which has not been without scaffolding since 1961.

NIEDERBURG

Stretching north from the Münster to the Rhine, the Niederburg is the oldest quarter of Konstanz. The site of the original Roman settlement, it was later the quarter of the craftspeople and small merchants. An almost medieval atmosphere still permeates this maze of alleyways lined with centuries-old houses, some of which contain lovely antique shops, snug wine bars or lively restaurants.

At No 15, **Brückengasse Kloster Zoffingen**, founded in 1257 and still in the hands of Dominican nuns, is the only surviving convent in Konstanz. On the Rheinsteig, running parallel with the river, stands the 15th-century **Rheintorturm**, a defensive tower whose upper section is covered by a mantle of wooden planks and topped by a steep tent roof. About 200m further west is the **Pulverturm** (1321), with 2m-thick walls. Nearby in Rheingasse is the **Domprobstei** (1609), a red baroque structure that used to be the residence of the cathedral provosts.

MUSEUMS

The former guildhall of the butchers is now occupied by the newly renovated **Rosgartenmuseum** (900 246; Rosgartenstrasse 5; adult/concession €3/1.50; 10am-6pm Tue-Fri, 10am-5pm Sat & Sun), founded in 1871 and dedicated to regional art and history.

The **Archäologisches Landesmuseum** (Archaeological State Museum; 980 40; Benediktinerplatz 5; adult/concession €3/2; 10am-6pm Tue-Sun), located inside a former monastery, has three floors filled with regional artefacts, models and reconstructions.

Locals are proud of **Sea Life** (128 2727; Hafenstrasse 9; adult/child €10/6.50; 10am-6pm May, Jun & Oct; 10am-5pm Mon-Thu, 10am-6pm Fri & Sat Nov & Apr), a multimedia interpretive centre on the subject of water. Verging on the kitsch, it's redeemed by the fact that it does have educational value and keeps kids occupied with games and treasure hunts. From glaciers to North Sea marine life to the Atlantic Deep Sea tunnel, Sea Life leaves no shell unturned. Greenpeace has a permanent exhibition space, and the centre also houses the Bodensee Natural History Museum.

Sleeping

The tourist office books accommodation for a €2.50 fee (but the electronic booking board with telephone outside the front door is free).

DJH hostel (☎ 322 60; www.jugendherberge-konstanz.de; Zur Allmannshöhe 18; juniors/seniors €19/21.70) Konstanz's hostel has a bland, institutional look. The bonus is that room prices decrease by €3 to €4 after the first night. It's located in a tower in the northern suburb of Allmannsdorf. From the train station, take bus No 4 to Jugendherberge or bus No 1 to Allmannsdorf-Post.

Campingplatz Bodensee (☎ 330 57; service@kanu .de; Fohrenbühlweg 45; tent €4.50-5.75, person €3.50) Built in 1995, this modern camp site is in the northeastern suburb of Staad near the car-ferry port. Perfect for water-sport enthusiasts, it hires out surfboards and canoes.

Campingplatz Klausenhorn (☎ 6372; camping@ ti.konstanz.de; tent €4-10, person €5; ☺ late Mar–Sept) This camp site is on the shore of the Überlinger See in the northern suburb of Dingelsdorf (take bus No 4 to Klausenhorn).

Gästehaus Holzer (☎ 315 46; www.gaestehaus -holzer.de; Fischerstrasse 6; s/d from €40/70; ✕) This little pension has simple but well-outfitted rooms. There are larger and more expensive rooms available.

Sonnenhof (☎ 222 57; www.hotel-sonnenhof-konstanz.de; Otto-Raggenbass-Strasse 3; s/d €41/70) A comfortable guesthouse, Sonnenhof is situated right on the Swiss border. There are singles with shared bathroom for €33.

Hotel Barbarossa (☎ 128 990; www.barbarossa -hotel.com; Obermarkt 8-12; s/d from €38/85; P) Beautifully located on a central square and decorated with panelling and wood floors, the Barbarossa offers comfortable, well-equipped rooms. Larger and more expensive rooms are available, and the car park costs an extra €6 per day.

Steigenberger Inselhotel (☎ 1250; www.konstanz .steigenberger.de Auf der Insel 1; s/d from €131/200; P ✕) This is the town's major blow-out hotel, lodged in a gorgeous 13th-century monastery that happens to be on an island in the middle of Lake Constance. Discreet, classically elegant and equipped with a steam bath and sauna, the hotel is a destination in itself.

Eating

Sedir (☎ 293 52; Hofhalde 11; meals under €6) Sedir is a lively Turkish restaurant serving Turkish pizza, super salads and spiced noodle casseroles. The beams and brick décor add to its relaxed ambience.

Seekuh (☎ 272 32; Konzilstrasse 1; meals around €6) This relaxed student bar with black, white and red décor and a leafy beer garden, serves salads, pasta and pizza. There's occasional live music.

Pan (☎ 254 27; cnr Salmannsweiler & Hohenhausgasse; mains average €8) It looks like a beer hall, but the menu is decidedly Greek and the place is deservedly popular.

Brauhaus Johann Albrecht (☎ 250 45; Konradigasse 2; mains under €10) This is a rambling beer hall with a rustic menu featuring daily specials.

Entertainment

Niederburg-Weinstube (☎ 213 67; Niederburggasse 7) This rustic hole in the wall claims to have 400 regional wines on its menu. The locals start sipping at noon with a Bretzel.

Wessenberg (☎ 919 664; Wessenbergstrasse 41) Wessenberg is a chichi pub continuing to attract an 'in' crowd with its really cool bar and good food.

K9 (☎ 167 13; Pfauengasse 3) This concert venue is perhaps the most happening nightspot in town if you're into grunge and student attractions.

Steg 4 (☎ 174 28; Hafenstrasse 8) Steg 4 is in a revamped warehouse down on the south side of the harbour.

Konstanz Stadttheater (☎ 130050; Konzilstrasse 11) The Stadttheater performs a repertoire of classical and contemporary drama and comedies. About 10% of the local casino's profits are earmarked for the theatre.

Getting There & Away

If you're going to Switzerland, the Thurgauer Tageskarte day pass covers all bus, train and boat travel with links in the triangular zone of Konstanz/St Gallen/ Schaffhausen (€19.60). This pass is available from the tourist office. It includes the ferry from Romanshorn on the Swiss side to Friedrichshafen in Germany.

BOAT

Between March and early November, **Weisse Flotte** (☎ 281 389) offers several departures daily between Konstanz and Bregenz (Austria) at the east end of Lake Constance (€11.40). Boats stop at Meersburg (€3.80, 30 minutes), Friedrichshafen (€7, 1¾ hours), Lindau (€9.80, 3½ hours) and smaller towns in between. A second ferry headed for Überlingen (€7, 1½ hours) also travels via Mainau and Meersburg.

The **Schweizerische Schiffahrtsgesellschaft Untersee und Rhein** (☎ 0041-52-634 0888) provides service to Schaffhausen, Switzerland via Reichenau Island and Stein am Rhein (€19.60 return, three hours), and then a bus to Rhine Falls, Europe's largest waterfalls (CHF 3.50 return, 15 minutes). Boats leave from the harbour.

The frequent car ferry to Meersburg is the best bet to the north shore. Cars cost €4.65 to €9.30, plus €1.70 per person. Bicycles are €0.90 and motorcycles €3.10, including driver. Boats leave from the landing docks in Staad.

BUS
Bus No 7394 provides express service on Monday to Friday to Meersburg (35 minutes) and Friedrichshafen (70 minutes). Bus No 7372 goes to Reichenau Island (20 minutes) from outside the Swiss train station.

CAR & MOTORCYCLE
Konstanz is reached via the B33, which connects with the A81 to/from Stuttgart in Singen. For information on the car ferry to Meersburg, see the Boat section (p481).

TRAIN
Konstanz is connected to Frankfurt-am-Main (€56.80, 4½ hours) by IR and ICE trains every two hours. It is also the southern terminus of the scenic *Schwarzwaldbahn*, which travels hourly through the Black Forest to Offenburg.

To get to towns on the northern shore of Lake Constance – Salem, Friedrichshafen, Lindau – you must change in Singen, which is also where you catch the hourly *Gäubahn* to Stuttgart (€28.40, 2½ hours).

Getting Around
Single tickets on SBG buses around town cost €1.70. Day passes are €2.80, family passes are €4.40 and are valid from 9am Monday to Friday and all day on Saturday and Sunday.

For a taxi, ring ☎ 222 22. Touring and trekking bicycles may be hired from **Kultur-Rädle** (☎ 273 10; Bahnhofplatz 29).

AROUND KONSTANZ
Mainau Island
One of the finest attractions in the Lake Constance region, **Mainau** (☎ 07531-3030; adult/concession €10.50/5; ⊙ 7am-8pm mid-Mar–early-Nov; adult/concession €5.10/3.60; ⊙ 9am-6pm mid-Nov–mid-Mar) is something of a surprise. What was initially the island compound for the large Schloss of the Knights of the Teutonic Order has been transformed into a vast Mediterranean garden complex by the Bernadotte family, who are related to the royal house of Sweden. The current owner, Count Lennart Bernadotte, has worked for more than 50 years to refurbish the island, which takes its name from the German Maienaue (May Meadow).

More than two million visitors a year make their way over a narrow causeway to stroll around 45 hectares of splendid gardens and arboretums, visit the baroque church, or attend special events and concerts. To avoid the crush, it's a good idea to arrive early or late in the day. You can stay later than the official closing time if you want.

The **Tropical Garden** is a lush hothouse brimming with banana trees, bamboo, orchids and other exotic flowers. The **Italian Cascade** integrates bursting patterns of flowers with waterfalls and makes for lovely photographs.

The novel **Butterfly House** is another highlight: you walk through a network of bridges and small canals while butterflies of the world flit and dart obliviously around your head. Also check the new state-of-the-art **Palm House**, erected in late 1999, which is dismantled each winter.

Reichenau Island
☎ 07534 / pop 3500
In 724 AD, a hard-working missionary named Pirmin founded a Benedictine monastery on Reichenau, the largest island at 4.5km by 1.5km in Lake Constance, located in the Untersee section about 12km west of Konstanz. Pirmin soon moved on to found other monasteries in the Upper Rhine area, but the abbots and monks he left behind ensured that, by the end of the 8th century, Reichenau had become

a prominent cultural and artistic centre in southwest Germany. During its heyday from around 820 to 1050, it had more than 100 monks and one of the largest libraries anywhere. The so-called Reichenauer School of Painting produced stunning illuminated manuscripts and vivid frescoes.

Decline set in along with church reforms in the high Middle Ages, and the monastery essentially passed its prime by 1200, though it wasn't dissolved until 1757. Of its many buildings scattered across the island, three surviving churches provide silent testimony to the Golden Age of Reichenau. These three churches were the reason Reichenau was made a Unesco World Heritage Site in December 2000. About two-thirds of the island is taken up by vegetable cultivation, the prime source of income for the islanders. A 2km-long tree-lined causeway connects the island with the mainland, marking the end of the German Avenue road (Deutsche Alleenstrasse).

GETTING THERE & AWAY
The best way to get to and around Reichenau from Konstanz is by taking bus No 7372. Buses leave from the Swiss train station. Reichenau is a stop on the *Schwarzwaldbahn* train, but the station is just off the island.

The ferries from Konstanz to Schaffhausen and from Konstanz to Radolfzell also travel via Reichenau.

MEERSBURG
☎ 07532 / pop 5500
Meersburg is a picture-book romantic village, scenically perched on a rocky plateau overlooking Lake Constance and surrounded by vineyards and orchards. Its historic Oberstadt (Upper Town) has a labyrinth of narrow, car-free lanes that are lined by gorgeous red-tiled, half-timbered houses and stately baroque buildings. There are two castles, the Altes and the Neues Schloss (Old and New Palace), which lord over the bustling Unterstadt (Lower Town), the much more touristy section with a pretty promenade and plane trees.

Located 17km west of Friedrichshafen and reached by ferry from Konstanz, Meersburg makes for an extremely popular day excursion, and in July and August its tiny alleys are choked with visitors. If you're travelling in those months, try to show up early or late in the day to catch some of Meersburg's magic.

Orientation
A steep vineyard separates the Oberstadt from the Unterstadt, and there's a scenic set of steps connecting the two (enter between the Altes and Neues Schloss). The northern boundary of the old part of the Oberstadt is the B33, here called Stettener Strasse.

Information
Cafe Schickeria (☎ 6887; Stettener Strasse, 🕑 12pm-12am) Internet access.
Library (Kirchstrasse 4; 🕑 10am-6pm Tue & Fri, 3-7pm Thu) Internet access.
Main post office (Am Bleicheplatz) Just north of Stettener Strasse.
Tourist office (☎ 431 110; Kirchstrasse 4; www .meersburg.de; 🕑 9am-6.30pm Mon-Fri, 10am-2pm Sat May-Sep, 9am-noon & 2-4.30pm Mon-Fri Oct-Apr) You can pick up the useful *Radtourlaub* bike tour map (€1.25) here.
Volksbank (Marktplatz) Exchanges money and has an ATM.

Sights
ALTES SCHLOSS
Meersburg's landmark is the **Altes Schloss** (☎ 800 00; adult/concession €5.50/3; 🕑 9am-6pm Mar-Oct, 10am-6pm Nov-Feb), overlooking Lake Constance from its lofty Oberstadt perch. Its origin supposedly goes back to the 7th-century Merovingian king Dagobert I, after whom the massive central keep is named. Between 1268 and 1803, the bishops of Konstanz used the castle as a summer residence (they moved in permanently in 1526, after the Reformation).

The place was purchased in 1838 by Baron Joseph von Lassberg, who turned the castle into something of an artists' colony. His sister-in-law, the celebrated German poet Annette von Droste-Hülshoff (1797–1848), resided here for many years, and the Brothers Grimm and Ludwig Uhland were among those who also flocked to Meersburg. It remains a private residence today.

The Altes Schloss is your quintessential medieval castle, complete with defensive walkways, knights' hall, moats, dungeons and subterranean tunnels.

On a self-guided tour (English pamphlet available) you'll see the usual collection of furniture, arms and armoury, but also a frightful 9m-deep prison hole for which the condemned only got a one-way ticket.

BADEN-WÜRTTEMBERG

You'll also pass through Droste-Hülshoff's living quarters, primly furnished in Biedermeier style.

NEUES SCHLOSS

In 1710 Prince-Bishop Johann Franz Schenk von Stauffenberg determined that the Altes Schloss was no longer suitable to represent his exalted office and began building the **Neues Schloss** (☎ 414 071; adult/concession €4/3; ☯ 10am-1pm & 2-6pm Apr-Oct) on the terrace east of the old castle.

Construction continued under his successor, Damian Hugo von Schönborn, who added the impressive staircase designed by Balthasar Neumann (1741), the chapel with stucco by Joseph Anton Feuchtmayer and frescoes by Gottfried Bernhard Göz (1743). The pink baroque palace was finally completed in the late 18th century, only a few years before the Grand Duchy of Baden took possession through secularisation.

Now state-owned, the palace houses the **Municipal Gallery**, with changing exhibits. On the 1st floor is the interesting **Dornier Museum** dedicated to Claude Dornier, the inventor of the seaplane.

OTHER MUSEUMS

Tiny Meersburg has a surprising array of museums outside the two castles. Unless noted otherwise, the museums in Meersburg are closed between November and March.

To learn more about Annette von Droste-Hülshoff, you should visit the exhibit in the **Fürstenhäusle** (☎ 6088; Stettener Strasse 9; adult/concession €3/2; ☯ 10am-12.30pm & 2-5pm Mon-Sat, 2-5pm Sun Apr-Oct). The poet bought this little garden house with the income from her first collection of poems. Though she never actually lived here, she frequently visited it for inspiration. Droste-Hülshoff's portrait, along with several Meersburg landmarks, once graced the DM20 note.

The diminutive but interesting **Weinbaumuseum** (☎ 431 110; Vorburgstrasse 11; admission €2; ☯ 2-5pm Tue, Fri & Sun Apr-Oct) displays historical wine casks, including a giant one that holds more than 50,000l. There's also a wine press from 1607 that remained functional until the 1930s, plus lots of wine-making tools.

Tastings take place here on Wednesday at 6pm and on Friday at 7pm (€7.50/6.50 adult/concession).

Sleeping

The tourist office can book **private rooms** (from €20 per person), free of charge, but the cheapest rooms are outside the Altstadt.

Haus Säntisblick (☎ 9277; tauchschule.mmersburg@t-online.de; Von-Lassberg-Strasse 1; s/d from €30/48; P ⚓) Dive into the Haus Säntisblick, which also houses the Bodensee Scuba School. Inside the canary-yellow building you'll find comfortable rooms.

Camping Seeblick (☎ 07532-5620; www.camping-seeblick.de; Strandbadstrasse 11, Hagnau; tent/person €4.60/3.10) The nearest camp site is in Hagnau, 4km east of Meersburg.

Camping Schloss Kirchberg (☎ 07545-6413; www.camping-kirchberg.de; tent/person €6.50/4) This camp site is in Immenstaad, east of Meersburg.

Gasthaus zum Letzten Heller (☎ 6149; fax 489 65; Daisendorfer Strasse 41; s/d from €31/50; P) This friendly place also has a popular restaurant.

Ferienhof Mohr (☎ 6572; fax 414 205; Stettener Strasse 57; s/d €35/55; P) Simple and bright, its rooms are well maintained. Try tasting the owner's home-made schnapps to put you to sleep.

Gasthof zum Bären (☎ 432 20; www.meersburg.de/baeren; Marktplatz 11; s/d from €46/76; P) If you want to stay in classic surrounds, try this three-star historical hotel in the Oberstadt, with traditionally furnished, comfortable rooms.

Eating

Almost all restaurants and cafés have a daily special priced under €10, often including locally caught *Felchen* (salmon trout).

Burgcafé (☎ 800 00; Altes Schloss; snacks around €6; ☯ 10am-6.30pm, closed Mon) Savour your coffee, cake or ice cream on the terrace of this stately establishment and enjoy the fabulous view.

Bistro 3 Stuben (☎ 800 20; Kirchstrasse 7; mains around €8; ☯ closed Mon) Opposite the tourist office, this bistro serves light bistro fare in a yuppie-inspired contemporary décor. In the same building, a restaurant of the same name (enter on Winzergasse) presents stunning world cuisine at equally stunning prices.

Alemannen-Torkel (☎ 1067; Steigstrasse 16-18; meals around €10) This 300-year-old wine cellar has a plethora of local vintages on offer, and you'll feast like Prince von Stauffenberg in the restaurant upstairs.

Winzerstube zum Becher (☎ 9009; Höllgasse 4; mains from €12; ⊗ closed Mon) In the Oberstadt, this restaurant has a classy chef who infuses traditional Baden dishes with an international flavour. You'll also enjoy the rustic setting.

Getting There & Away

BOAT

From March to November, Meersburg is a stop on the **Weisse Flotte** (☎ 07531-281 389) boat service between Konstanz and Bregenz and Konstanz and Überlingen. Some boats travel via the island of Mainau. The car ferry to Konstanz operates day and night, and is the fastest way across the lake. All boats leave from the ferry harbour in the Unterstadt. For more details, see Getting There & Away under Konstanz (p481).

BUS

Lacking a train station, Meersburg relies on buses for connections with the outside world. On Monday to Friday, express bus No 7394 makes the trip to Konstanz (45 minutes) and Friedrichshafen (30 minutes). The latter is also served more frequently (and on weekends) by bus No 7395. To get to Salem, take bus No 7397. Bus No 7373 connects Meersburg with Ravensburg and Konstanz four times daily from Monday to Saturday (no service on Sunday).

CAR & MOTORCYCLE

Meersburg lies just south of the B31 and is reached via Daisendorfer Strasse. In the Oberstadt, it merges with the B33, which begins in Meersburg and continues northeastwards to Ravensburg.

Getting Around

The best – actually the only – way to get around Meersburg is on foot. Those with motorised wheels must park in a pay car park, but even these can be full in the high season. For excursions, you can hire bicycles at **Hermann Dreher** (☎ 5176, Stadtgraben 5).

AROUND MEERSBURG
Birnau

The rococo pilgrimage church of Birnau is one of the artistic highlights of the Lake Constance region and is a sight worth braving the hordes for. Sitting majestically on a bluff overlooking the lake and surrounded by lush orchards, it looks more like a palace than a church. It was built by Peter Thumb of Vorarlberg, master architect of the rococo, who also gave the world the abbey in St Peter (see p472) and many other churches in the region. He was joined by two other household names of the period, the stucco master Joseph Anton Feuchtmayer and the fresco painter Gottfried Bernhard Göz.

The entrance to the church is truly awe-inspiring, the décor being so intricate and profuse you don't know where to look first. Your gaze is drawn to the ceiling, where Göz worked his usual magic, and there are whimsical details such as the tiny mirror in the cupola fresco.

Birnau is on the B31 about 10km north of Meersburg between Uhldingen and Überlingen. Bus No 7395 from Friedrichshafen and Meersburg stops right at the church. Entry to the church is free.

Schloss Salem

The 7km-long Prälatenweg (Prelates' Path) connects the church at Birnau with its mother church, the former Cistercian abbey of Salem. Founded in 1137, it was the largest, richest monastery in southern Germany. The huge complex, now named **Schloss Salem** (☎ 07553-814 37; adult/concession €5.50/3, children under 16 free; ⊗ 9.30am-6pm Mon-Sat, 10.30am-6pm Apr-Oct), became the property of the Grand Duchy of Baden after secularisation and is still the main residence of the family's descendants. The west wing is occupied by an elite boarding school that was briefly attended by Prince Philip (Duke of Edinburgh and husband of Queen Elizabeth II).

The focal point is the **Münster 1414**, with a Gothic purity that has been diluted by a high altar and 26 alabaster altars fashioned in an early neoclassical style. Of particular note are the study of Abbot Anselm II, with superb stucco ornamentation, as well as the **Kaisersaal**, which contains a bewilderingly detailed amount of sculpture and stucco.

The complex has been turned into something of a low-key amusement park, integrating museums, artisans' workshops, a golf driving range, gardens and various restaurants. German language tours cost €4/7 for one/1½ hours.

Bus No 7397 travels to Salem from Meersburg via Oberuhldingen. From Friedrichshafen, you can catch bus No 7396 or the

Bodensee-Gürtelbahn train, with departures roughly every 30 minutes.

FRIEDRICHSHAFEN
☎ 07541 / pop 57, 500

Friedrichshafen is surely one of Germany's nicer industrial towns, stretched out for 11km along a placid bay of Lake Constance. Its name will forever be associated with the Zeppelin airships, first built here under the stewardship of Count Ferdinand von Zeppelin at the turn of the 20th century.

It's a relatively young town, formed only in 1811 when King Friedrich of Württemberg merged the former imperial city of Buchhorn with the priory of Hofen. In WWII it was blown to smithereens and therefore has little in the way of historical sights. The extraordinary Zeppelin Museum, however, shouldn't be missed.

Orientation & Information
There are two train stations, the Hauptbahnhof and the better-connected Stadtbahnhof. The bus station is outside the Stadtbahnhof. The lakeside is a few metres south across Friedrichstrasse; its promenade is called Uferstrasse until the Gondelhafen, and then Seestrasse (where it terminates at the Zeppelin Museum).

Situated right outside the Stadtbahnhof, the **tourist office** (☎ 300 10; www.friedrichshafen.de; ☒ 9am-5pm Mon-Fri, 10am-noon Sat May-Sep, 9am-noon & 2-5pm Mon-Thu, 9am-noon Fri Oct-Apr) will find accommodation for €3 and has information about biking around the lake. If it's closed, information may also be gathered at the **Schulmuseum** (☎ 326 22; Friedrichstrasse 14), about a five-minute walk west of the train station.

The **Sparkasse** (Charlottenstrasse 2) exchanges currency and has an ATM. The post office is immediately to the right as you exit the Stadtbahnhof. You can wash your clothes at the **City Wash laundrette** (Schwabstrasse 16), and access the Internet at **Netmeeting** (☎ 374 30; Schanzstrasse 16).

Sights
ZEPPELIN MUSEUM
At the eastern end of Friedrichshafen's pleasant, café-lined promenade you'll find the town's top tourist attraction. Inaugurated in 1996 in the reconstructed Hafenbahnhof, exactly 96 years after the first Zeppelin airship was launched, the **Zeppelin**

Museum (☎ 380 10; Seestrasse 22; adult/concessio. €6.50/3; ☒ 10am-6pm Tue-Sun, 10am-5pm Tue-Su winter) is built around a full-scale (33m long) recreated section of the *Hindenburg* at 245m the largest airship ever made. Walk through its reconstructed passenger rooms and examine the filigree of the aluminium framework.

Exhibits, interactive information terminals (in German and English) and a series of short movies provide technical and historical insights. The top floor contains an eclectic art collection.

SCHLOSSKIRCHE
The western end of the promenade is anchored by the twin onion-domed, baroque **Schlosskirche** (Klosterstrasse; ☒ 9am-6pm mid-Apr–Oct), built between 1695 and 1701 by Christian Thumb. It's the only accessible part of the Schloss, still inhabited by the ducal family of Württemberg. The lavish stucco ceiling was destroyed in WWII but re-created in 1950 by Joseph Schnitzer (Schnitzer, by the way, means 'carver'). Also note the vividly carved choir stalls, whose end pieces represent, clockwise from the front left, Moses, St Benedict, an abbot and King David.

Sleeping & Eating
The tourist office will find **private rooms** (from €22). You can call the **hotel hotline** (☎ 194 12) at any time of day. There's also a free automated booking terminal outside the tourist office.

Numerous cafés, snack bars and restaurants line the Seestrasse promenade.

DJH hostel (☎ 724 04; fax 749 86; Lindauer Strasse 3; juniors/seniors €19/21.70) Immediately opposite Campingplatz Dimmler, this hostel is often full, especially in summer, so be sure to call ahead. To get here, take bus No 7587 from Stadtbahnhof.

Campingplatz Fischbach (☎ 420 59; Meersburger Strasse; tent/person €5/4.50) Operates on a first-come, first-served basis in the suburb of Fischbach.

Campingplatz CAP Rotach (☎ /fax 734 21; www .cap-rotach.de; Lindauer Strasse 20; tent/person €6.50/5) Is east of the town centre.

Gasthof Rebstock (☎ 216 94; www.gasthof-rebstock -fn.de; Werastrasse 35; s/d €48/68; **P**) One of the better deals, you'll find small, tidy rooms with few flourishes.

LEGACY OF THE ZEPPELIN

Like many before him, Count Zeppelin (1838–1917) was obsessed with the idea of flying. With his vision and determination, he contributed significantly to the development of modern aircraft when the first Zeppelin made its inaugural flight over Lake Constance in 1900.

Unlike today's nonrigid airships (such as the Goodyear blimp), Zeppelins had an aluminium framework covered by a cotton-linen fairing. The cigar-shaped behemoths were soon used for passenger flights, outfitted as luxuriously and comfortably as ocean liners. The most famous of them all, the *Graf Zeppelin*, made 590 trips, including 114 across the Atlantic and, in 1929, travelled around the world in only 21 days.

The largest airship ever built was the 245m-long *Hindenburg*, which was destroyed in a terrible accident – or possible act of sabotage – while landing in Lakehurst, New Jersey, in 1937, killing 36 passengers and crew.

Over 65 years later, Zeppelins have been revived as a tourist attraction. From April to October or November a regular Zeppelin service carries passengers across Lake Constance for €335 for the one-hour trip (€370 on weekends). Reservations are made through the tourist office in Friedrichshafen and departure is from the Zeppelingelände, Allmannsweilerstrasse 132, Friedrichshafen.

Ringhotel Buchhorner Hof (☎ 2050; www.buchhorn.de; Friedrichstrasse 33; s/d from €80/100; P) This is one of the top places in the town centre, with cleverly decorated rooms, an onsite fitness centre and an impressive restaurant.

Old City (☎ 705 802; Schanzstrasse 7; mains €8.50-14) For Swabian specialities and fish and meat dishes, you could try Old City, situated on the 1st floor of the Hotel CityKrone.

Hotel Goldenes Rad (☎ 2850; Karlstrasse 43; mains from €11) This restaurant has solid regional fare and a pleasant terrace for dining, with fish dishes, meat and poultry.

Getting There & Away
BOAT
Friedrichshafen is a regular stop on the Konstanz–Bregenz route of the **Weisse Flotte** (☎ 07531-281 389). For more details, see Getting There & Away under Konstanz (p481).

Friedrichshafen is also used as the springboard for the **Bodensee-Schiffsbetriebe car ferry** (☎ 923 8389) to Romanshorn in Switzerland, the fastest way to get across the lake. There are departures about every hour between 5.30am and 9.30pm year-round. The trip takes 45 minutes and costs €5.80/2.90/29 adults/children under 16/car.

BUS
On Monday to Friday, a fast way to get to Konstanz, via Meersburg, is on the express bus No 7394 (70 minutes). For the local service to Meersburg and on to Birnau, take bus No 7395. Bus No 7395 makes the trip to Salem in 45 minutes.

CAR & MOTORCYCLE
Friedrichshafen is on the B31 along the northern lake shore and is the starting point of the B30 to Ravensburg.

TRAIN
Friedrichshafen is a stop on the *Bodensee-Gürtelbahn* between Singen and Lindau, as well as the *Südbahn*, which goes to Ulm (€14.40, one hour 20 minutes), Ravensburg (€3.10, 15 minutes) and Lindau (€4, 20 minutes).

Getting Around
The town is compact and easy to get around on foot. Bikes can be hired from **Zweirad Schmid** (☎ 218 70; Ernst-Lehmannstrasse 12).

RAVENSBURG
☎ 0751 / pop 48,000
Half an hour's drive north of Lake Constance, Ravensburg was a Free Imperial City in medieval times and became exceedingly rich from the linen trade. It was also one of the first German cities to mass-produce paper, an industry that would later spawn the Ravensburg publishing house. Spared in the Thirty Years' War, Ravensburg still bears the hallmarks of past glories, but bills itself nowadays as a regional shopping hub.

BADEN-WÜRTTEMBERG

Orientation & Information

The train station and post office are at the western end of the city, a five-minute walk down Eisenbahnstrasse to Marienplatz, the heart of the Altstadt. The hostel is at the southeastern end of the Altstadt, perched on a hill top near the Mehlsack tower.

The **tourist office** (☎ 823 24; www.ravensburg.de; Kirchstrasse 16; ⏰ 8am-noon Mon, 8am-5.30pm Tue-Fri, 9am-noon Sat), just east of Marienplatz, has a free 90-minute walking tour (in German) at 2pm Wednesday and at 4pm Saturday.

House (☎ 351 384, Seelbruckstrasse 1) is a loud café with one Internet access terminal that charges €3.50 per 30 minutes. Buy English-language books and maps at **Ravensbuch** (☎ 163 88; Marienplatz 34).

Sights & Activities

The central **Marienplatz** is the site of a bustling market on Saturday morning. At the western end of the square stands the **Lederhaus**, a 16th-century domain of tanners and shoemakers that has an outrageous Renaissance façade. The teeny Flattbac River gurgles through a canal on the north side of the square, which is dominated by the stepped gable of the late-Gothic **Gewandhaus** and the impressive **Blaserturm**, part of the original city fortifications. The **Rathaus** doesn't look like much from the front, but the northern side is full of stained glass.

The 51m-high Gothic **Blaserturm** in the town centre vies for attention with the similarly 51m-high **Mehlsack** (Flour Sack), so named for its white, bulky form. Between May and September you can climb both **towers** (adult/child €1/0.50; Blaserturm: ⏰ 2-5pm Mon-Fri, noon-4pm Sat; Mehlsack: ⏰ 10am-1pm Sat, closed Jul).

To the north is the **Grünes Tor** (Green Tower), with its intricate tiled roof, and the weighty late-Gothic **Liebfrauenkirche**. The tower was constructed as a defence against soldiers who invaded from the hill-top **Veitsburg**, the 11th-century castle believed to be the birthplace of Heinrich der Löwe. Nowadays the castle houses the hostel and a chic restaurant.

Sleeping & Eating

DJH hostel (☎ 253 63; info@jugendherberge-ravensburg .de; Veitsburg Castle; juniors/seniors €17.30/20) Check-in at this hostel is from 5pm and curfew is at 10pm.

Hotel Garni Baur (☎ 256 16; fax 132 29; Marienplatz 1; s/d €38/70; 🅿 ✕) This is a central hotel with very reasonable rooms decorated in a modern style.

Hotel Residenz (☎ 369 80; www.residenz-ravensburg .de; Herrenstrasse 16; s/d from €70/90; ✕) Hotel Residenz has fine historic rooms, good service and great prices. In its wine room you can sample Ravensburger tipple; the hotel owner runs the sole wine estate in the area.

Humpisgaststätte (☎ 256 98; Marktstrasse 47; meals under €9) This is an earthy pub-eatery, with organic food, schnitzels and Swabian dishes.

Central (☎ 325 33; Marienplatz 48; meals around €9) This trendy option takes centre stage on Marienplatz. It offers reasonably priced Asian-European fusion dishes in rather chic bistro surrounds.

Getting There & Away

Trains leave hourly for Stuttgart (€25, two hours), via Ulm (€11.70, one hour). From Markdorf, near Meersburg, trains run hourly (€3.90, 40 minutes); from Friedrichshafen the ride takes 15 minutes and costs €3.

LINDAU

☎ 08382 / pop 24,000

Lindau hugs a picturesque little island in the northeastern corner of Lake Constance. It occupies the only snippet of Bavarian coastline on the entire lake, although you're unlikely to see any Lederhosen-clad visitors here. The town enjoyed a heady prosperity in the Middle Ages, thanks primarily to its spot on a major north–south trading route. In the early 13th century it became a free imperial city.

The place exudes old-world wealth and romance, and its superb views across to the Alps are worth a thousand postcards. Since 1951, Nobel Prize winners and their colleagues have met in Lindau to promote scientific ideas, rub elbows and book the region's hotels solid at the end of June.

Orientation

You'll find the Hauptbahnhof and bus station, as well as a large pay car park, on the western side of the island; the harbour and its lovely promenade is to the south, while numerous suburbs line the mainland. The heart of the Altstadt is the east–west pedes-

BADEN-WÜRTTEMBERG

trian **Maximilianstrasse**, lined by statuesque town houses.

Information

B@mboo (☎ 942 767; Zeppelinstrasse 6; ⏲ 7pm-3am Tue-Sun; €4.50 per hr) You can surf the Internet here.

Main post office (cnr Maximilianstrasse & Bahnhofplatz) There is also a Postbank here.

Tourist office (☎ 260 030; www.lindau-tourismus.de; Ludwigstrasse 68; ⏲ 9am-1pm & 2-5pm Mon-Fri Nov-Mar; 9am-1pm & 2-6pm Mon Fri 10am-2pm Sat Apr–mid-June & mid-Sep–Oct; 9am-6pm Mon-Fri 10am-2pm Sat & Sun mid-June–mid-Sep)

Volksbank (cnr Maximilianstrasse & Zeppelinstrasse) This bank has an ATM.

Waschsalon (Holdereggenstrasse 21) You can do your laundry here.

Sights
ALTSTADT

The Markt, in the northeast of the island, is dominated by the **Haus zum Cavazzen**, a beautiful baroque construction with murals that appear three-dimensional. It contains the attractive **Stadtmuseum** (☎ 944 073; adult/ concession €2.50/2) with a fine collection of furniture and mechanical instruments, among other exhibits. Visits are by tour only, which are held from 11am to 5pm Tuesday to Friday and Sunday, and 2pm to 5pm Saturday.

Even more impressive are the frescoes of the Passion of Christ, painted by Hans Holbein the Elder, inside the former **Peterskirche** (St Peter's Church; circa 1000), now a war memorial.

Another visual highlight is the **Altes Rathaus** (1436), which has a stepped gable from the 16th century; the almost gaudy murals, however, were added only in 1975 and are based on 19th-century designs. Alongside stands the **Diebsturm** (Brigand's Tower), a tiny jail once adjoining the town fortifications.

The **promenade** in summer offers an almost Mediterranean scene, with a sky bluer than blue, resort hotels and lots of well-heeled tourists soaking up the sun. Out at the harbour gates you'll spot Lindau's signature **lighthouse**, and on the other side – just in case you forget which state you're in – a pillar bearing the Bavarian lion. The **Mangturm** (admission €1), the former lighthouse at the top of the sheltered port, offers a good view towards the Alps.

Activities

Lindau is a paradise for boating, sailing and windsurfing; the tourist office has a list of sports clubs and shops offering equipment hire and instruction.

There are 1½-hour tours (€4) in English at 10am on Monday from May to August. The tours depart from the tourist office.

Weisse Flotte (☎ 07531-281 389) offers a round-trip tour several times a day from Lindau harbour to Bregenz and the mouth of the Rhine (€6.50, one hour).

Sleeping

All the listed hotels are on the island (rather than the mainland).

DJH hostel (☎ 967 10; www.djh-bayern.de; Herbergsweg 11; bed €20) The 240-bed hostel is in a beautiful hotel-like complex. Take bus No 3 from Anheggerstrasse one stop east; remember to call to reserve first.

Park-Camping Lindau am See (☎ 722 36, www .park-camping.de; Frauenhoferstrasse 20; tent/person €5.50/ 5.50) On the water at the Austrian border, this is a nice camp site with a coin-op laundry, supermarket and restaurant. Take bus No 1 or 2 to Anheggerstrasse, then bus No 3 to Leiblachstrasse.

Gasthof Inselgraben (☎ 5481;www.inselgraben.de; Hintere Metzgerstrasse 4-6; s/d €40/76) This is a reasonable deal, though the neat rooms are unimaginatively furnished.

Gasthof Engel (☎ 5240; fax 5644; Schafgasse 4; s/d €45/€85) This guesthouse offers quaint, well-equipped rooms, and has a decent restaurant specialising in fish dishes.

Hotel Bayerischer Hof (☎ 9150; www.bayerischer hof-lindau.de; s/d from €106/114; P ⏲) This classical white building is the pride of the harbour front and idyllic any time of the year. Soothing saunas, comfort cuisine from a fine kitchen, massages and impeccable rooms conspire to wish you could stay forever.

Eating

Café-Bistro Wintergarten (☎ 946 172; Salzgasse 5; meals from €4.50) In an atrium-like chamber, this café serves salads, pasta, veggie casseroles and more.

Alte Post (☎ 934 60; Fischergasse 3; meals from €7.50) Alte Post is the most atmospheric of local restaurants; every nook and cranny tells a story, and there's a huge regulars' table with the carved names of members. The food's excellent and affordable, too.

BADEN-WÜRTTEMBERG

Gasthaus zum Sünfzen (☎ 5865; Maximilianstrasse 1; meals from €9) This is an island institution, with Swabian-Bavarian fare under coffered ceilings and medieval vaults.

Lindauer Hof (☎ 4064; Seepromenade; meals under €10) At the east end of the harbour, Landauer Hof has a great outside section (despite the canned kitsch music), with reasonably priced fish, steaks, pizza, pasta and ice cream.

Turkiyem (Schafgasse 8; doner kebab from €3) This place serves takeaway meals.

Getting There & Away
BOAT
Weisse Flotte (☎ 07531-281 389) boats stop in Lindau daily between March and November en route from Konstanz to Bregenz. For more details, see Getting There & Away earlier under Konstanz (p481).

CAR & MOTORCYCLE
Lindau is on the B31 and also connected to Munich by the A96. The scenic Deutsche Alpenstrasse (German Alpine road), which winds eastward to Berchtesgaden, begins in Lindau.

TRAIN
Lindau has train connections to/from Friedrichshafen several times each hour (€4, 20 to 30 minutes). It is the eastern terminus of the *Bodensee-Gürtelbahn* railway line to Singen and the southern terminus of the *Südbahn* to Ulm (€17.80, 1¾ hours) via Ravensburg (€6.60, 40 minutes).

Getting Around
The island is tiny and perfect for walking. For buses to/from the mainland, singles cost €1.50, a day pass is €3.50 and a week pass is a great deal at just €9.

There are a few metered car parks on the island, but the best bet is to park on the mainland and catch a bus over.

You can hire bicycles at **Fahrrad Station** (☎ 212 61) in the Hauptbahnhof.

Rhineland-Palatinate

CONTENTS

Rhine-Hesse & Palatinate	**493**
Mainz	493
Worms	497
Speyer	500
German Wine Road	502
Ahr Valley & the Eifel	**504**
Remagen	504
Bad Neuenahr-Ahrweiler	504
Altenahr	506
Nürburgring	506
Kloster Maria Laach	506
The Romantic Rhine	**507**
Koblenz	508
Braubach	511
Boppard	511
St Goar	512
St Goarshausen & Loreley	512
Oberwesel	513
Bacharach	513
Bacharach to Bingen	514
Bingen	514
Rüdesheim	515
Around Rüdesheim	516
The Moselle Valley	**516**
Trier	518
Bernkastel-Kues	522
Traben-Trarbach	523
Cochem	524
Around Cochem	525
Hunsrück Mountains	**525**
Idar-Oberstein	525

When the French patched together the state of Rhineland-Palatinate (Rheinland-Pfalz) after WWII from parts of Bavaria, Hesse and Prussia, they joined together formerly disparate territories with only one thing in common – the Rhine. The river meanders for 1320km from the Swiss Alps to Rotterdam, but nowhere has it shaped the land and its people more than along the 290km stretch traversing the Rhineland-Palatinate.

Some of Europe's largest corporations dominate the Rhine banks south of Mainz, the state capital. But also along here, the Middle Ages have left their legacy in the form of a magnificent trio of Romanesque cathedrals at Mainz, Worms and Speyer. Further north is the most picturesque stretch of river, the Romantic Rhine. Its vine-clad slopes, medieval hilltop castles and snug wine villages have drawn artists and tourists here since the 19th century, and Unesco placed the region on its list of World Heritage Sites in 2002.

As the Rhine River flows through the Rhineland-Palatinate, so do Germany's rivers of wine. About two-thirds of the country's entire yield comes from the state's six growing regions: the Ahr Valley, the Moselle-Saar-Ruwer, the Middle Rhine, the Nahe, the Rheinhessen, and the Rheinpfalz with its German Wine Road. Tasting the wonderful wines in ambience-laden wine taverns is a true delight. Some vintners also organise vineyards tours and wine tastings; check with local tourist offices. The local people's *joie de vivre* finds expression in the many wine festivals run by the towns and villages, mostly from August to October.

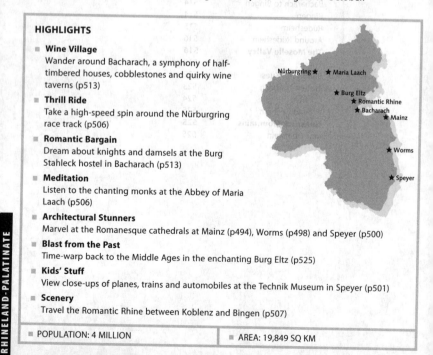

HIGHLIGHTS

- **Wine Village**
  Wander around Bacharach, a symphony of half-timbered houses, cobblestones and quirky wine taverns (p513)

- **Thrill Ride**
  Take a high-speed spin around the Nürburgring race track (p506)

- **Romantic Bargain**
  Dream about knights and damsels at the Burg Stahleck hostel in Bacharach (p513)

- **Meditation**
  Listen to the chanting monks at the Abbey of Maria Laach (p506)

- **Architectural Stunners**
  Marvel at the Romanesque cathedrals at Mainz (p494), Worms (p498) and Speyer (p500)

- **Blast from the Past**
  Time-warp back to the Middle Ages in the enchanting Burg Eltz (p525)

- **Kids' Stuff**
  View close-ups of planes, trains and automobiles at the Technik Museum in Speyer (p501)

- **Scenery**
  Travel the Romantic Rhine between Koblenz and Bingen (p507)

Nürburgring ★   ★ Maria Laach
★ Burg Eltz
★ Romantic Rhine
★ Bacharach
★ Mainz
★ Worms
★ Speyer

| ■ POPULATION: 4 MILLION | ■ AREA: 19,849 SQ KM |

RHINELAND–PALATINATE

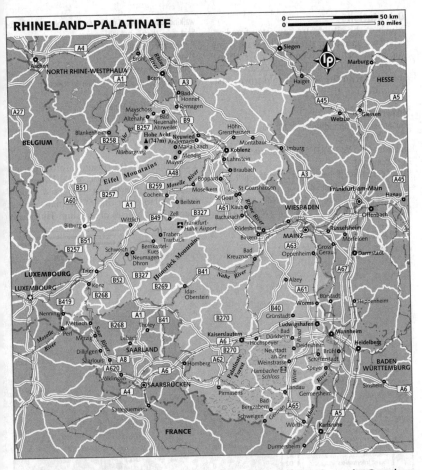

| 0 | | 50 km |
| 0 | | 30 miles |

RHINE-HESSE & PALATINATE

MAINZ

☎ 06131 / pop 184,000

Mainz, the state capital, is a lively city, influenced by French-style *savoir vivre* retained from that country's brief occupation (1798–1814), a large media presence and a sizable university. A stroll along the Rhine and sampling the local wines in the half-timbered taverns of the Altstadt should be as much a part of any Mainz visit as viewing the fabulous cathedral, Chagall's ethereal church windows at St-Stephan-Kirche or

the oldest printed Bibles in the Gutenberg Museum.

The Romans were the first to make use of the strategic location at the confluence of the Main and Rhine Rivers. In 12 BC, under the reign of Emperor Augustus, they founded a military camp called Moguntiacum here as a base for the invasion of Germania. After the Romans, Mainz took a 250-year nap before being awoken by English missionary St Boniface, who established an archbishopric here in AD 746. In the 15th century, native son Johannes Gutenberg ushered in the Information Age by inventing moveable type in Mainz (see the boxed text Johannes Gutenberg on p496).

Orientation

Much of the city centre consists of pedestrianised shopping streets. The walk from the Hauptbahnhof (central train station) to the Dom (cathedral) takes about 20 minutes, with the Altstadt (old town) just beyond.

Information

Gutenberg Buchhandlung (☎ 270 330; Grosse Bleiche 29) Bookshop.

Internet City (☎ 214 882; Christophsstrasse 15; ☼ 10am-8pm)

Main post office (Bahnhofstrasse 2; ☼ 8am-6pm Mon-Fri, 8.30am-12.30pm Sat)

MainzCard (€6/10 individual/family) Entitles bearer to museum admissions (though most are free anyway), a free walking tour, unlimited public transport, plus discounts for boat tours, theatre and other events.

Reisebank (Hauptbahnhof; ☼ 8am-6pm Mon-Fri, 7.30am-noon & 12.30-3pm Sat)

Tourist information (☎ 286 210; www.info-mainz.de; Brückenturm am Rathaus; ☼ 9am-6pm Mon-Fri, 10am-3pm Sat)

Waschcenter (cnr Gärtnergasse & Parcusstrasse; ☼ 6am-11pm Mon-Sat) Laundry.

Sights
DOM

Push through the heavy bronze portals of Mainz' **Dom** (Cathedral; ☎ 223 727; ☼ 9am-6.30pm Mon-Fri, 9am-4pm Sat, 12.45-3pm & 4-6.30pm Sun Apr-Sep) to enter one of Germany's most magnificent houses of worship. This richly

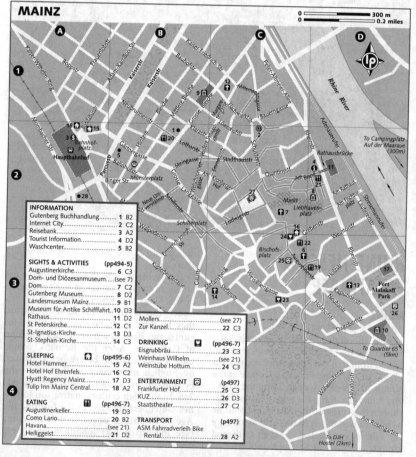

detailed mountain of reddish sandstone, looming above the Markt (market place) and Altstadt, literally experienced a baptism by fire when the original burned down just one day before its consecration in 1066. Most of what you see today is quintessential 12th-century Romanesque. Opening hours are slightly reduced from October to March.

Inside, a solemn ambience pervades the three dimly lit aisles, which culminate in choirs at each end. Of special note are the grandiose memorial tombstones of archbishops and other power mongers from the 13th to 18th centuries. Clinging to the central-nave pillars, they form a veritable portrait gallery. The brightly coloured murals above show scenes from the life of Christ but, despite their medieval appearance, they only date back to the 19th century.

The newly renovated **Dom- und Diözesanmuseum** (☎ 253 344; adult/concession €3/1.50; ◷ 10am-5pm Tue-Sun) shows off the cathedral treasury in the attractive setting of the Gothic cloister. Pride of place goes to a sculpture that formed part of the cathedral's 13th-century rood screen carved by the renowned Master of Naumburg.

OTHER CHURCHES

On a hill, the **St-Stephan-Kirche** (St Stephen's Church; ☎ 231 640; Kleine Weissgasse 12; ◷ 10amnoon & 2-5pm Mon-Sat) would be just another Gothic church were it not for the nine brilliant, stained-glass windows created by the Russian Jewish artist Marc Chagall (1887–1985) in the final years of his life. Bright blue and imbued with a mystical, meditative quality, they serve as a symbol of Jewish-Christian reconciliation.

Mainz also has a trio of stunning baroque churches, which together illustrate the evolution of this architectural style. The classically baroque **Augustinerkirche** (☎ 2660; Augustinerstrasse 34; ◷ 8am-5pm Mon-Fri, 10am-5pm Sat & Sun) dates back to 1768, has never been destroyed and features a delicate ceiling fresco by Johann Baptist Enderle. **St Peterskirche** (☎ 222 035; Peterstrasse 3; ◷ 10am-6pm Mon, Wed & Fri, 8.30am-6.30pm Tue & Thu) shows off the sumptuous glory of the rococo style and is noted for its richly adorned pulpit and altars. **St-Ignatius-Kirche** (☎ 224 264; Kapuzinerstrasse 36; ◷ 8.30am-6pm) marks the transition from rococo to neoclassicism. The sculpture

outside is a copy of the one made by Hans Backoffen (the original is in the Dom- und Diözesanmuseum – see opposite).

GUTENBERG MUSEUM

More than just a tribute to Mainz' most famous son, the **Gutenberg Museum** (☎ 122 640; Liebfrauenplatz 5; adult/concession €3/1.50; ◷ 9am-5pm Tue-Sat, 11am-3pm Sun) chronicles the entire history of printing, also acknowledging the achievements made in Korea, China and Japan long before Gutenberg's invention. Besides historical presses, composing and typesetting machines, you'll encounter a bewildering display of printed books and documents, most notably of course the two copies of the world-famous 42-line Gutenberg Bible kept in a specially designed vault. For a re-creation of Gutenberg's print shop, head to the basement.

LANDESMUSEUM MAINZ

The rich and far-reaching collection of the **Landesmuseum Mainz** (State Museum; ☎ 285 70; Grosse Bleiche 49-51; adult/concession €2.50/1.50; ◷ 10am-8pm Tue, 10am-5pm Wed-Sun), housed in the former prince-elector's stables, traces the region's cultural history from the Stone Age to today. A thorough renovation, underway at the time of writing, should by now be completed. Treasures include the famous **Jupitersäule**, a 1st-century triumphal column from Roman days. The medieval section has the richly festooned façade of a 14th-century trading house, the **Kaufhaus am Brand**. There are also plenty of Dutch and Flemish paintings, precious faïence (porcelain) and Art Nouveau glass. Admission prices rise during special exhibitions.

MUSEUM FÜR ANTIKE SCHIFFFAHRT

Excavations for a hotel in 1981 spectacularly unearthed a rare collection of Roman ships, now housed in the **Museum für Antike Schifffahrt** (Museum of Ancient Navigation; ☎ 286 630; Neutorstrasse 2b; admission free; ◷ 10am-6pm Tue-Sun). On view besides ship models, reliefs and monuments are two full-size replicas along with the remains of five original warships once used to thwart Germanic tribes trying to intrude upon Roman settlements.

Sleeping

The tourist office can make room reservations through its hotline at ☎ 286 2128.

JOHANNES GUTENBERG

Johannes Gutenberg is one of those epochal figures whose contribution to history changed its very course.

The man from Mainz essentially paved the way for the Information Age with his invention of the printing press in the 1430s. To be fair, the Chinese deserve credit for coming up with moveable type long before Gutenberg, but they used it to print on silk not to spread the word, any word. Without Gutenberg, Martin Luther's career as a religious reformer might never have got off the ground and Shakespeare's plays might have been resigned to history's ash heap.

Little is known about the man himself, who was born in Mainz around 1400, trained as a goldsmith and then left for Strasbourg in the late 1420s where he first experimented with print technology. Gutenberg may have sensed that he was onto something big but was too poor to give his visions flight. Back to Mainz he went, in 1448, where he managed to persuade a moneyed entrepreneur, Johann Fust, to lend him 800 gilders to finance his pet project. He soon began cranking out school grammar books and calendars and by 1456 had produced his masterpiece: the world's first printed 42-line Bible (so called because there are 42 lines in each column).

While there's little doubt that Gutenberg made the type for this Bible and built the screw press used in its printing, it's possible that the printing itself was undertaken by Fust and another colleague. Legal records show that Fust sued Gutenberg in 1455 to recover the money he advanced to Gutenberg. But Gutenberg, broke as usual, couldn't repay him in cash, and thus the court ordered that type and press be turned over to Fust. An appointment to the court of the Archbishop of Mainz eventually saved Gutenberg from the poorhouse, though he died nearly penniless in 1468.

Many hotels lower rates on weekends and in summer.

Hotel Hof Ehrenfels (☎ 224 334; fax 237 910; Grebenstrasse 5-7; s/d €55/78; P) The rooms are on the small side and sport décor from around the time of the moon landing, but the location right in the Altstadt, just steps from the Dom and wine taverns, is hard to beat. It has a restaurant downstairs.

Quartier 65 (☎ 277 600; www.quartier65.com; Wormser Strasse 65; s/d €82/98; P X) This sleek, riverside hotel, about 5km south of the town centre, has only six designer rooms, all nonsmoking. Rates include such smile-inducing extras as a glass of sparkling wine at check-in, fluffy bathrobes and slippers, and a gourmet breakfast made from organic local produce.

Hotel Hammer (☎ 965 280; www.hotel-hammer .com; Bahnhofplatz 6; s €71-98, d €86-128; P X X) Newly renovated according to Feng Shui principles, with contemporary furnishings and an upbeat colour scheme, the Hammer is a pleasant place to camp out close to the train station. Standard amenities include a minibar and hair dryers, while the attractively designed sauna is a welcome bonus.

Tulip Inn Mainz Central (☎ 2760; www.goldentulip .com; Bahnhofplatz 8; s €72-108, d €105-149; P X) An air of faded grandeur envelops this hotel,

which in more glamorous times as the Central Hotel Eden hosted stars from film and stage. Rooms have been updated and feature modern amenities, including cable TV and dataports.

Hyatt Regency Mainz (☎ 731 234; www.mainz .regency.hyatt.de; Malakoff-Terrasse 1; s/d from €180; P X X X X) A fine hotel of high international standards, the Hyatt Regency has large, handsomely furnished rooms equipped with all modern communication devices. Its location on the Rhine and the Altstadt periphery is another asset.

Other recommendations:

DJH hostel (☎ 853 32; jh-mainz@djh-info.de; Otto-Brunfels-Schneise 4; d/q €21.90/16.90 per person; P X) Modernised hostel near a city park with two- and four-bed rooms, all with private bathroom. About 3.5km from the Hauptbahnhof. Take bus No 62 or 63.

Campingplatz Auf der Maaraue (☎ 06134-4383; Auf der Maaraue; adult/tent/car €4.20/3.20/2.70) Nicely located at the confluence of the Rhine and Main and close to a public outdoor pool. From the Hauptbahnhof take bus No 6, 54, 55 or 56 to Brückenkopf, then a 10-minute walk.

Eating & Drinking

Weinstube Hottum (☎ 223 370; Grebenstrasse 3; dishes €4-10; ⏱ from 4pm) One of the best of the Altstadt wine taverns, Hottum has cluttered living-room flair, delectable wines and a small menu with typical regional dishes, such as *Pfälzer Pfannkuchen* (pancakes).

Eisgrubbräu (☎ 221 104; Weissliliengasse 1a; mains €4-10) Grab a seat in the warren of vaulted chambers of this local brewery, order a mug of Helles Märzen or Dunkles Pils and settle in for a round of people-watching. The daily all-you-can-eat lunch buffet is good value at €5.10.

Havana (☎ 234 608; Rheinstrasse 49; mains €6-9) Right in the small entertainment zone below the tourist office, Havana seduces with tropical ambience, clever cocktails, and a menu of simple, filling fare infused with Latin flavours. In summer, the action moves outdoors.

Augustinerkeller (☎ 222 662; Augustinerstrasse 26; mains €6-12) This woodsy establishment gets its unique look from walls covered completely in framed historic photographs. The menu is heavy on German staples but also features Alsatian-style *Flammekuche* (a thin layer of pastry topped with cream, onion, bacon and sometimes cheese or mushrooms, and cooked in a wood-fired oven).

Heiliggeist (☎ 232 026; Mailandsgasse 11; mains €6-15, snacks less) If God designed a living room, this may well be what it would look like. Sit beneath the soaring cross-vaulted ceiling of this former chapel and enjoy a drink, snack or full dinner from a menu that travels around the world, from carpaccio and gazpacho to schnitzel.

Mollers (☎ 627 9211; Gutenbergplatz 7; mains €12-28; ☽ closed Wed) In a glass cylinder atop the Staatstheater, Mollers takes 'dining with a view' to new heights. Enjoy bird's-eye views of the Dom and Altstadt enjoying the exquisite seasonal fish, meat and vegetable selections. It's best at night and for Sunday champagne brunch (€20).

Other recommendations are:

Como Lario (☎ 234 028; Neubrunnenstrasse 7; pizza & pasta €6-9, mains €11-19) Mainz' most dependable and popular pizzeria.

Weinhaus Wilhelm (☎ 224 949; Rheinstrasse 51) Wine tavern in one of Mainz' historical buildings.

Zur Kanzel (☎ 237 137; Grebenstrasse 4; mains €11-19; closed Sun) Classy place with nice inner courtyard serving up-market German and international cuisine.

Entertainment

Look in the tourist office, in cafés and in pubs for a copy of the free listings magazines *Fritz* or *Der Mainzer*.

KUZ (☎ 286 860; Dagobertstrasse 20b) Dance parties, live concerts, a summer beer garden with al fresco movie screenings, a world music summer festival, kids' theatre…this happening cultural centre has something for everyone. It's housed in a neat 19th-century red-brick building that began life as a military laundry.

Staatstheater (☎ 285 1222; Gutenbergplatz 7) Mainz' freshly revamped theatre has its own ensemble and stages plays, opera and ballet. Students get a 50% discount.

Frankfurter Hof (☎ 220 438; Augustinerstrasse 55) In the late 1980s, a group of preservation-minded citizens saved this historical building from demolition and turned it into a hugely popular performance venue. Since 1991, it has hosted everyone from up-and-comers to big-name artists like Al Jarreau, Eartha Kitt and Nick Cave.

Getting There & Away

Frankfurt airport is 30km northeast of Mainz and is served by S-Bahn No 8 several times hourly. The airport at Frankfurt-Hahn is 90km west of Mainz and served by shuttle bus from the Hauptbahnhof five times daily (€10, 70 minutes).

Mainz is a major hub for IC trains in all directions. Regional connections include frequent direct trains to Worms (€6.60, 45 minutes), Saarbrücken (€22.60, two hours) and Idar-Oberstein (€9.50, one hour).

Mainz is encircled by a ring road with connections to the A60, A63 and A66.

Getting Around

Mainz operates a joint bus and tram system with Wiesbaden, for which single tickets cost €1.95. Day passes are €4.60 for individuals and €7.70 for groups of up to five. Tickets are available from vending machines and must be stamped before boarding.

ASM Fahrradverleih (☎ 238 620; Binger Strasse 19; day/week €5/20; ☽ 7am-8pm Mon-Fri, 10am-1.30pm Sat) hires out bikes on the ground level of City-Port Parkhaus, near the Hauptbahnhof.

WORMS

☎ 06241 / pop 83,000

Worms (rhymes with 'forms'), one of Germany's oldest cities, has continually played a role in major moments in European history. In AD 413 it became capital of the legendary, if short-lived, Burgundian kingdom whose rise and fall was creatively chronicled in the 12th-century *Nibelungenlied* (see p499), now the subject of an excellent new museum and the annual **Nibelungen-Festspiele** in August.

After the Burgundians, just about every other tribe had a go at ruling Worms, including the Huns, the Alemans and finally the Franks, under whose leader, Charlemagne, the city finally began to flourish. In the Middle Ages, Worms hosted more than 100 sessions of the imperial parliament, called the 'diet', including the one in 1521 at which Luther famously refused to recant his views and was declared an outlaw. A huge memorial now honours the Protestant reformer.

The most poignant reminder of Worms' medieval heyday is its majestic late-Romanesque cathedral. Catholicism dominated, but a Jewish community managed to thrive here from the 11th century to 1933, even earning Worms the moniker 'Little Jerusalem'.

Orientation

Worms' train and bus stations are about 250m northwest of the ring road that encircles the Altstadt. It's about a 10-minute walk from here to the Dom via Wilhelm-Leuschner-Strasse (one of the main shopping streets) and Kämmererstrasse. The tourist office is just east of the Dom.

Information

Internet Café Zwiebel (☎ 411 581; Kämmererstrasse 77; ⊙ 10am-1am Sun-Thu, to 2am Fri-Sat)

Main post office (cnr Ludwigsplatz & Korngasse)

Tourist information (☎ 250 45; www.worms.de; Neumarkt 14; ⊙ 9am-6pm Mon-Fri year round, 9.30am-1.30pm Sat Apr-Oct)

Sights

Ask at the tourist office for a handy free walking tour map.

KAISERDOM

Worms' landmark **Dom St Peter und St Paul** (☎ 6115; ⊙ 9am-6pm Apr-Oct, to 5pm Nov-Mar), with its four towers and two domes, dominates the city skyline. Built in the 11th and 12th centuries in late-Romanesque style, it ranks as one of the greatest accomplishments of medieval architecture.

Inside, the cathedral's lofty dimensions impress as much as the lavish, canopied

high altar (1742) in the east choir designed by the baroque master Balthasar Neumann. A stuffy **crypt** holds the stone sarcophagi of several members of the Salian dynasty of Holy Roman emperors, while the **scale model** in the south transept shows the enormity of the original complex, which until 1689 also encompassed the imperial and bishop's palace north of the Dom.

In the *Nibelungenlied* (see Nibelungen Museum following), the **Kaiserportal** on the north side was the setting of a fierce quarrel between the Burgundian queens Kriemhild and Brunhilde about who had the right to enter the Dom first. Trivial as it may seem, this little interchange ultimately led to their kingdom's downfall. Today, the main entrance is through the Gothic **Südportal** (1300), richly decorated with biblical figures.

JEWISH QUARTER

Few German cities have as many well-preserved Jewish monuments and buildings as Worms. The community was centred in the northeast corner of the Altstadt along Judengasse and its side streets. The Nazis destroyed the original 1034 synagogue, but by 1961 the new **Alte Synagoge** (☎ 853 4707; Synagogenplatz; admission free; ⊙ 10am-12.30pm & 1.30-5pm Apr-Oct, 10am-noon & 2-4pm Nov-Mar), a serene, whitewashed vaulted hall, had risen from its ashes.

Behind the synagogue is the modern **Raschi Haus**, built on the 14th-century foundations of a former dance hall named after Raschi of Troyes, a prominent 11th-century Talmudic scholar. It now holds the **Jüdisches Museum** (☎ 853 4707; Hintere Judengasse 6; adult/concession €1.50/0.75; ⊙ 10am-12.30pm & 1.30-5pm Tue-Sun Apr-Oct, 1.30-4.30pm Nov-Mar), which explains Jewish customs, ceremonies and festivals and also tells the history of the local community. Just east of here is the impressive **Raschitor**, a surviving gate of the town wall that still partially encircles the Altstadt.

Worms' other major Jewish heritage site is the **Heiliger Sand** (⊙ 9am-dusk, to 8pm in summer), Europe's oldest Jewish cemetery. Buried among the 2000 graves is Meir von Rothenburg, one of Germany's leading rabbis. He died in 1293 while a captive of King Rudolf of Habsburg for having attempted to lead a group of would-be emigrants to Palestine. The cemetery is across town on Willy-Brandt-Ring, in the southwest corner of the Altstadt.

NIBELUNGEN MUSEUM

The *Nibelungenlied* is the ultimate tale of love and hate, treasure and treachery, revenge and death with a cast including dwarves, dragons and bloodthirsty *überfraus* (superwomen). Richard Wagner set it to music, Fritz Lang turned it into a masterful silent movie, and the Nazis abused its mythology, seeing in Siegfried the quintessential German hero. The new, state-of-the-art **Nibelungen Museum** (☎ 202 120; Fischerpförtchen 10; adult/child €5.50/3.50; ☯ 10am-5pm Tue-Sun, 9am-10pm Fri) brings the epic to life in a highly entertaining, multimedia exhibit set up in two towers and along the ramparts of the medieval town wall. The best part is in the first tower, where you'll listen to the anonymous poet tell his tale (in flawless English) via a wireless headset, while watching excerpts from Lang's movies. Allow about two hours.

OTHER MUSEUMS

The **Städtisches Museum** (City Museum; ☎ 946 390; Weckerlingplatz 7; adult/student €2/1; ☯ 10am-5pm Tue-Sun), housed in the handsome Andreasstift Kirche, chronicles Worms' turbulent history from prehistoric times onward.

In a pretty park north of the Dom, on the grounds of the former imperial and bishop's palace, is the **Museum Heylshof** (☎ 220 00; Stephansgasse 9; adult/student €2.50/1; ☯ 11am-5pm Tue-Sun May-Sep, 2-5pm Tue-Sat, 11am-5pm Sun Oct-Apr, closed Jan–mid-Feb). Its important private art collection includes Italian, Dutch, French and German paintings from the 15th to the 19th centuries, including works by such heavyweights as Tintoretto, Rubens and Lenbach. The collection of Venetian, Bohemian and German glass is also worth a gander.

Sleeping

The tourist office makes free hotel reservations. When it's closed, an automated system directly outside indicates hotel vacancies and allows unlimited free calls to hotels of interest.

Hotel Kriemhilde (☎ 911 50; www.hotel-kriemhilde.de; Hofgasse 2-4; s/d €46/67; ⓟ) Wake up to the peal of the Dom bells in this friendly, unpretentious inn, a mere stone's throw from the mighty cathedral, which can be seen from the top-floor rooms. Downstairs is a popular restaurant and wine bar (mains €10 to €20).

Hotel Lortze-Eck (☎ 263 49; Schlossergasse 10-14; s/d €46/70; ⓟ) This small, family-run hotel is one of the more stylish choices in Worms. Most rooms are of a decent size and have modern country-style furnishings. Bright colours and tasteful knick-knacks brighten up the public areas. The attached restaurant serves the usual German classics (mains €9 to €14).

Parkhotel Prinz Carl (☎ 3080; www.parkhotel-prinz carl.de; Prinz-Carl-Anlage 10-14; s €68, d €79-98; ⓟ ✗) Housed in a late-19th-century Prussian barracks, Worms' newest hotel has brought a welcome touch of class and international flair to this historic town. Rooms vary in size, but none lack in comfort or style. Facilities include a restaurant and a fitness centre with sauna.

Other recommendations:

DJH hostel (☎ 257 80; jh-worms@djh-info.de; Dechanei-gasse 1; d/q €21.90/16.90 per person; ✗) Unbeatable location right next to the Dom and modernised rooms with private bathroom. Take bus No 1a or 1b from the train station.

Central Hotel (☎ 645 70; www.centralhotel-worms.de; Kämmererstrasse 5; s €50-60, d €80-90; ⓟ ✗) Central and friendly; some rooms are suitable for the wheelchair users.

Eating & Drinking

See Sleeping opposite for additional restaurant recommendations.

Gaststätte zur Schänke (☎ 276 48; Wollstrasse 7-9; mains €4-8) *Flammkuche* the size of wagon wheels are the speciality of this comfortably cluttered wine tavern. The salads, piled high with fresh ingredients, are also a satisfying option.

Hagenbräu (☎ 921 100; Am Rhein 5; mains €5-10) Although this riverside brewery is often crowded with tourists, it's still a solid choice, not in the least for its excellent brew. The menu revolves around a greatest hits of hearty German fare, including sausages, roasted pork loaf and liver dumplings, all made in-house.

Kolb's Biergarten (☎ 234 67; Am Rhein 1; mains €5-10) This cosy tavern a few steps south of Hagenbräu is equally popular, particularly because of its wonderful beer garden.

Rôtisserie Dubs (☎ 06242-2023; Kirchstrasse 6, Rheindürkheim; mains €15-30) The owner-chef here,

Wolfgang Dubs, performs culinary miracles with fresh, seasonal ingredients, complemented by a weighty selection of wines, including his own. It's in Rheindürkheim, a suburb about 10km north of town.

Café Ohne Gleichen (☎ 411 177; Kriemhildenstrasse 11) and **Café TE** (☎ 234 65; Bahnhofstrasse 5) are both happening, student-oriented café-bars near the train station offering cocktails, imaginative décor, and simple, budget-priced meals from morning till midnight. Local bands occasionally pack these places with a variety of sounds.

Getting There & Around
Worms is about 50km south of Mainz and has frequent train connections with Mannheim, a major hub for long-distance trains in all directions. The regional service to Mainz (€6.60, 45 minutes) leaves twice hourly. Going to Speyer requires a change in Ludwigshafen.

All major sights are easily covered on foot, though Worms also has a bus system (single ticket/day pass €1.90/5).

SPEYER
☎ 06232 / pop 50,000
Speyer, about 50km south of Worms, is a dignified town with a compact centre distinguished by a magnificent Romanesque cathedral, a couple of top-rated museums and a well-respected culinary scene. First a Celtic settlement, then a Roman market town, Speyer gained prominence in the Middle Ages under the Salian emperors and hosted 50 sessions of the imperial parliament between 1294 and 1570.

In 1076 the king and later Holy Roman Emperor Heinrich IV – having been excommunicated by Pope Gregory VII – launched his penitence walk to Canossa in Italy from Speyer. He crossed the Alps in the middle of winter, an action that warmed even the heart of the pope, who revoked his excommunication. He lies buried in the Kaiserdom.

Orientation
The Hauptbahnhof is on Bahnhofstrasse, about 1km northwest of the city centre. Most city buses will drop you off at the Altpörtel city gate, from where Speyer's lifeline – the broad, pedestrianised Maximilianstrasse – leads you straight to the Dom in about 10 minutes.

Information
Main post office (Wormer Strasse 4, cnr Grosse Greifenstrasse) Near the Altpörtel.
Tourist information (☎ 142 392; www.speyer.de; Maximilianstrasse 13; ☼ 9am-5pm Mon-Fri year round, 10am-3pm Sat, 10am-2pm Sun Apr-Oct, 10am-noon Sat Nov-Mar)

Sights
KAISERDOM
In 1030 Emperor Konrad II of the Salian dynasty laid the cornerstone of the **Kaiserdom** (☎ 100 9218; ☼ 9am-7pm Mon-Fri, 9am-6pm Sat & Sun Apr-Oct & 9am-5pm Mon-Sat, 1.30-5pm Sun Nov-Mar), whose towers float above Speyer's rooftops like the smokestacks of a giant ocean liner. It's the most majestic of the trio of imperial cathedrals (the other two being in Mainz and Worms) and has been a Unesco World Heritage Site since 1981.

Most startling about the interior are its awesome dimensions (it measures an astonishing 134m in length) and dignified symmetry. The height of the central nave, the clear lines of construction and the unadorned walls all contribute to the solemn atmosphere. Make sure you walk up the staircase to the elevated altar area to get a true sense of its vastness. Another set of steps leads down to the darkly festive **crypt**, whose candy-striped arches recall Moorish architecture. Stuffed into a side room are the austere granite sarcophagi of eight Salian emperors and kings, along with some of their queens. Until 2006 the cathedral will be undergoing a €25 million restoration, but it remains open for visitors.

HISTORISCHES MUSEUM DER PFALZ
Though it may be hard to get excited about regional history museums, the **Historisches Museum der Pfalz** (Historical Museum of the Palatinate; ☎ 620 222; Domplatz; adult/child €7/2.50; ☼ 10am-6pm Tue-Sun) deserves a closer look. Besides hosting world-class special exhibitions, it has a permanent collection that values quality over quantity and presents each artwork in a unique, intimately lit fashion. A combination ticket with Sealife (see p501) is adult/concession €13/6.50.

One of the highlights is the **Goldener Hut von Schifferstadt**, an incredibly ornate, perfectly preserved gilded hat in the shape of a giant thimble that dates back to the Bronze Age. The **Wine Museum** features one of the most unusual exhibits: a bottle containing an unappetizing jellied substance from the 3rd century AD, purported to be the world's oldest wine. Two more floors below is the **cathedral treasury**, where the prized exhibit is Emperor Konrad II's surprisingly simple bronze crown. Note that some exhibits may still be closed for renovations, scheduled for completion in 2004.

TECHNIK MUSEUM

It's easy to spend an entire day wandering among the amazing exhibits of the enormous **Technik Museum** (Technology Museum; ☎ 670 80; Am Technik Museum 1; adult/child €10.50/8.50, IMAX €7.50/5.50, combined ticket €15/10.50; ⏱ 9am-6pm), just a short walk south of the Dom. There are plenty of planes, trains and automobiles to look at, including an original Boeing 747, a U9 submarine and an Antonov-22 transporter, the world's largest prop plane. All can be climbed aboard and explored at leisure. Kids also love the playgrounds, various motion simulators and a 54m slide. Two IMAX theatres form part of the complex as well.

SEALIFE SPEYER

Speyer's newest attraction is an aquarium complex called **Sealife Speyer** (☎ 697 80; Im Hafenbecken 5; adult €10, senior & student €8.50, child 3-14 €7.50; ⏱ 10am-7pm Jul-Sep, 10am-6pm Apr-Jun & Oct, 10am-5pm Nov-Mar), which introduces visitors to the denizens of the Rhine River from its source in the Swiss Alps all the way to the North Sea. Sponsored by a preservation-minded organisation in cooperation with Greenpeace, it's fun but with a serious message about pollution, overfishing and other environmental problems. A combination ticket with the Historisches Museum der Pfalz (see p500) is adult/concession €13/6.50.

MAXIMILIANSTRASSE

Roman troops and medieval emperors once paraded down 'Via Triumphalis' now Speyer's Maximilianstrasse and its main commercial drag. The street is lined with baroque buildings of which the **Rathaus**, with its red façade and lavish rococo interior, and the **Alte Münze** (Old Mint) are worth a look. The road culminates at the **Altpörtel** (adult/concession €1/0.50; ⏱ 10am-noon & 2-4pm Mon-Fri, 10am-5pm Sat & Sun Apr-Oct), the main city gate and only remaining part of the town wall.

You can climb to the viewing gallery and have a quick look at the exhibit of the city's fortifications.

Sleeping

Hotel Zum Augarten (☎ 754 58; www.augarten.de; Rheinhäuser Strasse 52; s €44-50, d €61-70; Ⓟ) A cosy and friendly atmosphere welcomes guests in this small, family-run hotel with charming rooms in contemporary style and pleasing, peach-coloured walls.

Hotel am Technik Museum (☎ 671 00; hotel@technik-museum.de; Am Technik Museum 1; s/d €50/65; Ⓟ ✗) Part of the Technology Museum complex, this place has a central location, adequate comforts and modern rooms to recommend it. Those travelling by campervan can use the **Stellplatz** (campervan park; €18) next door to the hotel.

Hotel Domhof (☎ 132 90; www.domhof.de; Bauhof 3; s €91, d €111-121; Ⓟ ✗) A hotel has stood on these grounds next to the Dom since the Middle Ages, once hosting emperors, kings and councillors. Although completely renovated and brought up to modern standards, an aura of history continues to envelope this deluxe hotel. Its 50 rooms are wrapped around a picturesque, cobbled courtyard.

Other recommendations include:

DJH hostel (☎ 615 97; jh-speyer@djh-info.de; Geibstrasse 5; d/q €21.90/16.90 per person; ✗) Modern hostel with 48 rooms, including 13 doubles, all with private bathroom.

Camping am Bonnetweiher (☎ 422 28; www .wolfshuette.de; Am Rübsamenwühl 31; person €4, tent €3-6) Lakeside camp site about 4km north of the centre.

Hotel Trutzpfaff (☎ 292 529; www.trutzpfaff-hotel .de; Webergasse 5; s/d €49/69) Close to the Dom and with an excellent wine tavern serving Palatine specialities (€5 to €15).

Eating & Drinking

Maximilian (☎ 622 648; Korngasse 15; mains €3-9) Near the Altpörtel, this convivial bistro is a good spot any time of day. Breakfast is served until 2pm, while the menu runs the gamut from soups to Tex-Mex, pasta and salads.

Domhof-Hausbrauerei (☎ 740 55; Grosse Himmelsgasse 6; mains €6-15) Speyer's loveliest beer garden, flooded with red geraniums, is just steps from the Dom and has its own children's playground. The menu features classic German comfort food, some prepared using the home-made brew. In winter, sit inside beneath garlands of hops.

Zum Alten Engel (☎ 709 14; Mühlturmstrasse 7; mains €8-19) This romantic vaulted cellar restaurant pairs a gorgeous setting with refined regional and German cuisine. Enjoy delicious wines along with such dishes as lamb with tarragon sauce or garlic sausages with fried potatoes.

Zweierlei (☎ 611 10; Johannesstrasse 1; mains €9-19; ☙ closed Sun & Mon) This trendy eatery with postmodern décor has an ambitious German nouvelle menu that may include such dishes as dorado fillet with algae and cucumber.

Backmulde (☎ 715 77; Karmeliterstrasse 11-13; mains €15-25; ☙ closed Sun & Mon) Owner-chef Gunter Schmidt has a knack for spinning fresh, local products into gourmet dishes with a Mediterranean flavour and presentation. With an epic wine list, it's considered one of Speyer's finest restaurants. Reservations are advised.

Getting There & Away
Buses depart from the Hauptbahnhof for Ludwigshafen (No 572) and Heidelberg (No 717), but the train is more efficient (even though Speyer is on a minor rail line) and most trips require a change in Ludwigshafen or Schifferstadt. Regional trains to both destinations leave frequently. There is also direct service to Heidelberg via Mannheim, a major hub for ICE and other long-distance trains.

Getting Around
Most sights are within walking distance of each other, but for the foot-weary there's the City-Shuttle minibus (bus No 565), which loops around town at 10-minute intervals from 6am to 8.45pm (day pass €0.50). Bikes are for hire from **Radsport Stiller** (☎ 759 66; Gilgenstrasse 24; €10 per day).

GERMAN WINE ROAD
The German Wine Road (Deutsche Weinstrasse) cuts right through the heart of the Palatinate (Pfalz), a region of gentle forests, ruined castles and Germany's largest contiguous wine-growing area. Starting in Bockenheim, about 15km west of Worms, it winds south 85km to Schweigen on the French border. Blessed with a moderate climate that allows figs, kiwifruit and lemons to thrive, the Weinstrasse is especially pretty during the spring bloom. The **wine festival season** from late summer to autumn

is also a good time to visit. In part because of its proximity to France, the Palatinate is also a renowned culinary destination, with restaurants serving everything from gourmet New German cuisine to traditional regional specialities such as *Saumagen* – a sheep's stomach stuffed with meat, potatoes and spices, boiled, then sliced and briefly fried. Try it – it's not as challenging as it sounds!

Getting There & Away
Neustadt an der Weinstrasse, a central hub from which to start exploring the German Wine Road, has regular train links with Saarbrücken (from €14, 1½ hours) and Karlsruhe (€8.10, one hour). The trip from Speyer requires a change in Schifferstadt. Bad Dürkheim has a direct train link with Ludwigshafen.

Getting Around
The Weinstrasse is best explored under your own steam by car or bicycle (look for the yellow signs sporting a cluster of grapes), although it's possible to cover much of the route by public transport. Local trains connect Neustadt with Deidesheim and Bad Dürkheim to the north every 30 minutes. For towns south of Neustadt, you have to take the bus to Landau and connect to one in the direction of Bad Bergzabern or Schweigen.

Neustadt an der Weinstrasse
☎ 06321 / pop 29,000
Neustadt is mostly a busy, modern town that, to its credit, has preserved a rather charming, largely pedestrianised **Altstadt** teeming with half-timbered houses and anchored by the **Marktplatz**. It's an attractive square flanked by the baroque **Rathaus** and the Gothic **Stiftskirche**, a red-sandstone composition that's been shared by Protestant and Catholic congregations since 1708 (open only during services).

About 4km south of the centre is the **Hambacher Schloss** (Hambacher Castle; ☎ 308 81; admission to grounds free, exhibit adult/student €4.50/1.50; ☙ 10am-6pm Mar-Nov), known as the 'cradle of German Democracy'. It was here that students held massive protests for a free, democratic and united Germany on 27 May 1832, during which the German tricolour flag of black, red and gold was raised for the first time. An exhibition commemorates the event, called the Hambacher Fest. Views over the vineyards and the Rhine plains are best from the tower. Bus No 502 makes the trip here up to 10 times daily.

Neustadt's **tourist office** (☎ 926 892; www.neustadt.pfalz.com; Hetzelplatz 1; 9.30am-6pm Mon-Fri, 10am-noon Sat May-Oct, to 5pm & closed Sat Nov-Apr), right by the Hauptbahnhof, has helpful staff and is stocked with information about the German Wine Road.

SLEEPING & EATING

Neustadt's nicest lodging options are in the Haardt suburb, northwest of the town centre. There are lots of good restaurants here, especially in the Altstadt.

DJH hostel (☎ 2289; jh-neustadt@djh-info.de; Hans-Geiger-Strasse 27; d/q €21.90/16.90 per person;) This is a renovated facility where all rooms have private bathroom.

Mandelhof (☎ 882 20; www.mandelhof.de; Mandelring 11; s €45-55, d €60-80;) Up on a hill overlooking the town, this property has lovely rooms and a gourmet restaurant. A leisurely walk leads to the Wolfsburg ruin.

Hotel Tenner (☎ 9660; www.hotel-tenner.de; Mandelring 216; s €64-87, d €89-98;) Embraced by vineyards, this hotel offers sweeping views of the forest and the Hambacher Schloss. In fine weather, the gourmet breakfast is served on the panoramic terrace.

Novalis Cafe (☎ 2760; Hintergasse 26; mains €3.40-8) Novalis serves snacks and small meals in a setting of eclectic flea-market finds.

Liebstöckel (☎ 313 61; Mittelgasse 22; lunch mains €5.50-7, dinner €7-14) More up-market is Liebstöckel, which has a large beer garden and a meat-heavy menu complemented by a few vegetarian choices.

Deidesheim

☎ 06326 / pop 3650

Diminutive Deidesheim, one of the Weinstrasse's most popular and picturesque villages, centres on the historical Markt with the requisite **Rathaus** and church, in this case the Gothic **Pfarrkirche St Ulrich**. Inside the Rathaus, noted for its neat, canopied open staircase, is a small **Wine Museum** (☎ 981 561; Marktplatz 8; adult/child €2/1; 4-6pm Wed-Sun Mar-Dec).

Deidesheim briefly enjoyed the international limelight when former chancellor Helmut Kohl brought visiting dignitaries

to dine at the **Deidesheimer Hof** (☎ 968 70; Am Marktplatz; fixed price lunch/dinner €18/40), a stuffily stylish hotel-restaurant opposite the Rathaus. A few steps away, the **Deutsches Film- und Fototechnik Museum** (Film & Photography Museum; ☎ 6568; Weinstrasse 33; adult €3, student & senior €2.50; 4-6.30pm Wed-Sun Mar-Dec) travels from wooden boxes to high-tech in its large display of historical cameras and related equipment.

Deidesheim is home to a large number of artists whose studios can be explored along the **Artists' Trail** look for the black 'K' signs. A leaflet available at the tourist office lists details and opening hours.

On Bahnhofstrasse, the whimsical **Geissbockbrunnen** (Goat Fountain) celebrates a quirky local tradition. For centuries, the nearby town of Lambrecht has had to pay an annual tribute of one goat for using pastureland belonging to Deidesheim. The presentation of this goat, and its subsequent auctioning, culminates in the raucous **Goat Festival** held yearly on Pentecost Tuesday.

SLEEPING & EATING

The **tourist office** (☎ 967 70; www.deidesheim.de; Bahnhofstrasse 5; 9am-noon & 2-5pm Mon-Fri year round, 10am-noon Sat Apr-Oct) can help find accommodation.

Gästehaus Ritter von Böhl (☎ 972 201; fax 972 200; Weinstrasse 35; s €43-49, d €66-82;) Integrated within a 15th-century hospital complex, this guesthouse has spacious and modern rooms, all with disabled access.

Turmstübl (☎ 981 081; Turmstrasse 3; mains €5-14) This contemporary, artsy wine-café serves salads and tasty hot dishes.

Gasthaus zur Kanne (☎ 966 00; Weinstrasse 31; mains €10-20) This is one of the best restaurants in town for updated regional cuisine, often creatively infused with French flavours. Sit inside at hand-painted tables or in the leafy inner courtyard.

Bad Dürkheim

☎ 06322 / pop 16,900

Bad Dürkheim is a handsome spa town as famous for its salty thermal springs as it is for the annual **Dürkheimer Wurstmarkt**, the world's largest wine festival, which swamps the little town with visitors on the second and third weekends in September. Most of the action takes place in and around the landmark **Dürkheimer Riesenfass**, a restaurant built in the shape of a giant wine cask for the 1935 fair and hugely popular with tour groups year-round.

South of the cask ensues the **Kurpark**, where most of the town's spa and wellness facilities are located. Choose from an interesting menu of classic and exotic treatments, including full-body massages (€24), an oriental body peeling called Rasul (€16) and milk and oil baths (€21). Or simply unwind in the thermal baths (€7) or the eucalyptus- and lavender-scented air of the Turkish *hammam* (€28). For reservations (required for all but the thermal baths) stop by the **Kurzentrum** (☎ 9640; Kurbrunnenstrasse 14), which shares a building with the **tourist office** (☎ 956 6250; www.bad-duerkheim.de; ⓨ 9am-7pm Mon-Fri, 11am-3pm Sat).

SLEEPING & EATING

Marktschänke (☎ 952 60; www.bd-marktschaenke.de; s €47-62, d €72-77; **P**) Assets include extra-large family rooms, a central location and a restaurant, in summer with a beer garden.

Knaus Camping Park (☎ 613 56; www.knauscamp .de; In den Almen 3; site €6-10, person €5) This camp site is located at the lakeside

Hotel Weingarten (☎ 940 10; www.gerlach-papst .de; Triftweg 11a-13; s €61, d €81-94; **P** **✗**) This is a nice place offering exceptional value for money with lovingly decorated rooms (most with balconies), a large garden and sauna.

Philip's Brasserie (☎ 688 08; Römerplatz 3; mains €13-19) This stylish restaurant has a Mediterranean menu that offers a welcome break from the classic German fare that predominates around town.

AHR VALLEY & THE EIFEL

The Eifel, a rural area of gentle hills, tranquil villages and volcanic lakes, makes for a perfect respite from the mass tourism of the Moselle and Rhine Valleys. Its subtle charms are best sampled during a bike ride or a hike, though it also has a few headline attractions, including a world-class carracing track, a stunning Romanesque abbey and a lovely wine region, the Ahr Valley.

The Ahr River has carved its scenic 90km valley from Blankenheim – in the High Eifel – to the Rhine, which it joins near Remagen. It's one of Germany's few red-wine regions – growing *Spätburgunder* (pinot noir), in particular – with vineyards clinging to steeply terraced slopes along both banks. The quality is high but the yield small, so very few wines ever make it beyond the valley – all the more reason to visit and try them for yourself.

Getting Around

The best way to travel through the Ahr Valley is by the Ahrtalbahn, which serves most villages between Remagen and Altenahr. Trains leave hourly, and the entire distance takes about 35 minutes, costing €4.10. Bus No 841 also travels the route, but it's quite slow. If you're driving, make your way to the B266/B267, which traverses the valley.

Rotweinwanderweg

Hikers will enjoy trekking the scenic **Red Wine Hiking Trail**, which leads right through grape country on its 35km route from Sinzig/Bad Bodendorf to Altenahr. The trail is marked by small signs with grape symbols, and you can walk as far as you like and then return on the Ahrtalbahn. All Ahr Valley tourist offices have a detailed trail description and maps.

REMAGEN

☎ 02642 / pop 14,500

Remagen was founded by the Romans in AD 16 as Rigomagus, but the town would hardly figure in the history books were it not for one fateful day in 1945. As the Allies stampeded across France and Belgium to rid Germany of Nazism, the *Wehrmacht* tried frantically to stave off the attack by destroying all bridges across the Rhine. But the **bridge at Remagen** remained intact long enough for Allied troops to cross the river – and, bye-bye Hitler. The bridge itself is now gone, but one of its surviving towers houses the **Friedensmuseum** (Peace Museum; ☎ 201 46; adult/concession €3.50/1; ⓨ 10am-5pm Mar, Apr & Nov, 10am-6pm May-Oct), with a new expanded and upgraded exhibit about its role in history.

BAD NEUENAHR-AHRWEILER

☎ 02641 / pop 25,000

Bad Neuenahr and Ahrweiler are a bit of an odd couple. The former is an elegant spa town whose healing waters have been sought out by the moneyed and the famous (including Karl Marx and Johannes Brahms) for a century and a half. Ahrweiler, by contrast, is a dreamy medieval village encircled by a town wall and crisscrossed by narrow, pedestrianised lanes lined with half-timbered houses. What the two have in common is wine, which can be enjoyed everywhere at taverns and in estates.

Orientation

Bad Neuenahr is the eastern half of the twin towns. It's a five-minute walk from the train station to the centre via the car-free Poststrasse, the main drag. Ahrweiler is about 3km west. To reach its centre, head west for about 600m from the train station along Wilhelmstrasse and Niederhutstrasse.

Information

Ahrweiler tourist office (☎ 977 350; Markt 21; ☯ 9.30am-5.30pm Mon-Fri, 10am-3pm Sat & Sun Easter-Oct, 9am-5pm Nov-Easter)

Bad Neuenahr tourist office (☎ 977 350; www.bad-neuenahr-ahrweiler.de; Felix-Rütten-Strasse 2; ☯ 9.30am-5.30pm Mon-Fri, 10am-3pm Sat & Sun Easter-Oct, 9am-5pm Nov-Easter)

Kreissparkasse (Markt 5) Bad Neuenahr bank.

Post office (cnr Kölner Strasse & Hauptstrasse) In Bad Neuenahr.

Sights & Activities

BAD NEUENAHR

The focal point of Bad Neuenahr is the stately **Kurhaus**, a *fin de siècle* Art Nouveau confection that contains the **casino** (☎ 757 50; Felix-Rütten-Strasse 1; admission €2.50; ☯ 2pm-2am Sun-Thu, 2pm-3am Fri-Sat), the first to open in post-WWII Germany. Night after night, an elegant crowd (jacket and tie required for men) mingles among the roulette and blackjack tables or tries its luck at the slot machine. Bring your passport.

Neuenahr owes its spa status to its mineral springs, whose soothing qualities are pleasantly experienced in the **Ahr-Therme** (☎ 801 200; Felix-Rütten-Strasse 3; 2 hr €9.70, day pass €13.80; ☯ 9am-11pm). Besides various pools, you'll also get a surge channel, different saunas, massages jets and other pampering tools to enjoy. A sauna is €2 extra, and various discounts are available.

AHRWEILER

Ahrweiler preserves a delightful **old town** full of nicely maintained half-timbered

buildings, with pride of place going to **Haus Wolff** (Niederhutstrasse 146), festooned with a knock-out octagonal oriel. It's almost entirely encircled by the medieval **town wall** with its four surviving gateways. At its heart, on Markt, is the Gothic **Pfarrkirche St Laurentius**, beautifully decorated with floral frescoes from the 14th century and luminous stained-glass windows, some of which show farmers working their vineyards.

Ahrweiler's Roman roots spring to life at the 2nd-century AD **Römische Villa Museum** (Roman Villa Museum; ☎ 5311; Am Silberg 1; adult/concession €3.60/1.80; ☯ 10am-6pm Tue-Fri, 10am-5pm Sat & Sun Apr–mid-Nov) on the northwestern edge of town. Protected by a lofty, light-filled glass and wood structure is a huge complex whose remains reveal the amazing standard of living enjoyed by wealthy Romans. A functional floor heating system and a complete kitchen with stove, oven and smoking pantry are just a couple of the highlights. A detailed English pamphlet is included in the price.

Sleeping & Eating

All places listed here are in Ahrweiler.

DJH hostel (☎ 34924; jh-bad-neuenahr-ahrweiler@djh-info.de; St-Pius-Strasse 7; d/q €21.90/16.90 per person) This snazzy hostel is about halfway between Ahrweiler and Bad Neuenahr and has welcoming rooms with private bathroom.

Hotel Garni Schützenhof (☎ 90283; www.schuetzenhof-ahrweiler.de; Schützenstrasse 1; s/d €50/75; P) Right by the Ahrtor, one of the landmark town gates, this hotel is great for those tired of cramped quarters. Some rooms have balconies, albeit above a noisy street, and the family-friendly downstairs units come with kitchens.

Hotel-Restaurant Hohenzollern (☎ 4268; www.hotelhohenzollern.com; Am Silberg 50; s/d €60/100; P ✗) This casually elegant hillside hotel right on the Rotweinwanderweg, with unbeatable valley views, is the perfect deluxe retreat. Rooms lack no comfort and even fussy diners won't be disappointed by the gourmet restaurant (mains €17 to €30).

Hotel Rodderhof (☎ 3990; www.rodderhof.de; Oberhutstrasse 48; s/d €66/103; P) This is a splendid property sensitively converted from a medieval monastery. Rooms are modern and of a good size and there's also a restaurant and wine tavern with courtyard seating in summer.

Both Bad Neuenahr and Ahrweiler teem with traditional German restaurants and dowdy cafés popular with spa visitors.

Both's (☎ 359 734; Wilhelmstrasse 58-60; light meals under €6) The most happening place in town combines a jazzy bar, beer garden, restaurant and disco with an American-style menu that includes bagels, nachos and salads.

Apbell's (☎ 900 243; Niederhutstrasse 27a; mains €6.50-13) The menu here has something in store for all tastes and wallet sizes. In fine weather, the chestnut-shaded beer garden has the nicest tables.

Eifelstube (☎ 348 50; Ahrhutstrasse 26; mains €9-15, 3-course lunch €20) In the same family since 1905, this is one of Ahrweiler's best restaurants. Sample up-market German and regional specialities while seated in the cosy dining room with exposed-beam ceiling and tiled stove.

ALTENAHR
☎ 02643 / pop 1900
Hemmed in on all sides by craggy peaks giving way to rolling hills and steep vineyards, Altenahr wins top honours as the most romantic location in the Ahr Valley. The landscape is best – and most easily – appreciated by taking a 10-minute uphill walk to **Burg Are** (1100m), whose weather-beaten tower stands guard over the valley. This is also the western terminus of the Rotweinwanderweg. A dozen more trails are accessed either from the village centre or picked up at the top of the **Ditschard**, whose 'peak' at 354m is easily reached by **chair lift** (☎ 8383; up/return €2.50/4; ⏰ from 10am).

Altenahr's **tourist office** (☎ 8448; www.altenahr .de; ⏰ 9am-noon & 2-5pm Mon-Fri, 9am-noon Sat) is inside the Hauptbahnhof.

Sleeping & Eating
DJH hostel (☎ 1880; jh-altenahr@djh-info.de; Langfigtal 8; dm €12.50) Altenahr's hostel is beautifully located in the Langfigtal nature park.

Campingplatz Altenahr (☎ 8503; fax 900 764; Im Pappelauel; tent & car/person €7/4.50; ⏰ Apr-Oct). If you'd like to pitch your tent, head to this camp site.

Hotel-Restaurant Zum Schwarzen Kreuz (☎ 1534; www.zum-schwarzenkreuz.de; s €33-50, d €54-90; ⏸ ✗) In a neat half-timbered building in the heart of town, this place offers original retro flair with flowery wallpaper and shag carpet;

some rooms even have groovy tapestries. The restaurant does regional specialities (mains €9 to €18).

NÜRBURGRING
This historic **Formula 1 race car track** (☎ 02691-302 178; www.nuerburgring.de) has hosted many spectacular races with legendary drivers since its completion in 1927. At 21km its North Loop was not only the longest circuit ever built but also one of the most difficult, earning the respectful moniker 'Green Hell' from racing legend Jackie Stewart. After Niki Lauda's near-fatal crash in 1976, the German Grand Prix moved to the Hockenheimring near Mannheim, but in 1996 Formula 1 returned to the 5km South Loop, built in 1984, with the Grand Prix of Europe.

If you have your own car or motorbike, you can discover your inner Michael (Schumacher, that is) by taking a spin around the North Loop for €14 per round. Those who prefer to let someone else do the driving can take the Ringtaxi for €130 up to three people pile into a 400hp BMW and are 'chauffeured' around the North Loop by a professional driver at speeds of up to 320km/h. It's hugely popular, so make reservations early.

Right by the track is the **Erlebniswelt** (☎ 302 698; adult/child €10/7.50; ⏰ 10am-6pm), an automotive theme park where you'll learn about the history and mythology of the Nürburgring and participate in interactive entertainments and simulators. One hall houses the 1.3km **Kartbahn** (⏰ 11am-9pm), a go-kart track where you get to experience what 60km/h feels like with your tail just 3cm above the asphalt.

The Nürburgring is off the B258, reached via the B257 from Altenahr.

KLOSTER MARIA LAACH
About 25km northwest of Koblenz, the Benedictine **Kloster Maria Laach** (Abbey of Maria Laach; ☎ 02652-590; admission free; ⏰ 5.30am-8pm) is one of the most stunning examples of Romanesque architecture in Germany. Still home to around 60 monks, it enjoys a lovely setting beside a volcanic lake, the Laacher Maar.

The abbey's striking outline is dominated by two central towers – one octagonal, the other square – each of which is flanked by two smaller ones. The interior is surpris-

ngly modest, anchored in the west apse by
the tomb of abbey founder Henry II of Pala-
ine and in the east apse by the high altar.
Above the altar is a wooden canopy, which
n turn is lorded over by an early–20th century, Byzantine-style mosaic of Christ.

Enter via a large portico, an architectural feature not usually found north of the
Alps, and note the quirky carvings on the
capitals. The portico wraps around an inner
courtyard with a Löwenbrunnen (Lion
Fountain), oddly reminiscent of Moorish
architecture.

A free 20-minute film (German only)
takes visitors behind the monastery walls to
reveal that the monks take their motto 'Ora
et Labora' (Pray and Work) very seriously
indeed. Five times each day they take part
in prayer services, which are well worth
attending, if only to listen to the ethereal
chanting.

Maria Laach is accessible by bus No 6031
from Andernach and bus No 6032 from
Niedermendig, the town with the nearest
train station. By car, take the Mendig exit
off the A61 and follow the signs.

THE ROMANTIC RHINE

Between Koblenz and Bingen, the Rhine
carves deeply through the Rhenish slate
mountains, meandering sinuously through
realms of castles and fields of wine in a
deep meditation of wonder and legend.
This is landscape at its most dramatic,
with muscular forested hillsides alternating with craggy cliffs and impossibly steep
terraced vineyards. Idyllic villages appear,
their neat half-timbered houses and proud
church steeples seemingly plucked from the
world of fairy tales.

And above it all lord the famous medieval castles, some ruined, some restored, all
mysterious and vestiges of a time that was
anything but romantic. Most were built by
a mafia of local robber barons – knights,
princes, even bishops – who extorted huge
tolls from merchant ships by blocking their
passage with iron chains. Time and French
troops under Louis XIV laid waste to many
of the castles, but several were restored in
the 19th century when Prussian kings, German poets and British painters discovered
the gorge's timeless beauty. Today, some

have been reincarnated as hotels and, in
the case of Burg Stahleck, as a hostel (see
p513).

In 2002, Unesco awarded World Heritage Site status to these 65km of riverscape,
which is more prosaically known as the
Middle Rhine Valley. As one of Europe's
most popular tourist destinations, it's often
deluged with visitors, especially in summer
and early autumn. The area all but shuts
down in winter.

Hiking & Cycling
The Rhine Valley is great hiking and biking territory, and each tourist office has
specific suggestions and maps for long
and short trips. One hiking option is the

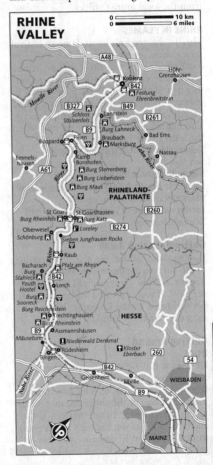

long-distance **Rheinhöhenweg**, which runs parallel to the left river bank between Bonn and Oppenheim, south of Mainz, over a distance of 240km through hills and vineyards. Another path travels along the right bank between the Bonn suburb of Bonn-Beuel and Wiesbaden, for a total of 272km. Trails are marked with an 'R'. Bicycle paths also run parallel to both banks.

Festivals & Events

Every little river village holds at least one wine festival each year, with most of them crammed into August and September, just before harvest time. The brochure *Veranstaltungskalender Rheinland-Pfalz*, with a complete listing of all festivals, is available from the local tourist offices.

RHINE IN FLAMES

This is the region's most famous festival series, held every year in five different locations. Water and fire combine in one spectacular show with castles, boats, monuments and the river banks all swathed in glowing Bengal lights and forming the backdrop to gargantuan firework displays. The following list shows where and when the festivals are held.

Siebengebirge (villages btwn Linz & Bonn) First Saturday in May.
Bingen/Rüdesheim First Saturday in July.
Koblenz to Braubach/Spay Second Saturday in August.
Oberwesel Second Saturday in September.
Loreley rock (St Goar/St Goarshausen; see p512) Third Saturday in September.

Getting There & Away

Koblenz and Mainz are the best starting points for touring the region. For details on how to reach Koblenz, see p511; for Mainz, see p497. If you're pressed for time, you can get a glimpse of the Romantic Rhine on a long day trip from Frankfurt.

Getting Around
BOAT

KD Line (☎ 0261-310 30; www.k-d.com) operates a regular boat service between all Rhine villages on a set timetable. You can travel to the next village or the entire distance. Once you've bought your ticket, you can get on and off as often as you like (eg if you're going from Boppard to Rüdesheim, you can also get off at St Goar, Bacharach and so on).

Many rail passes (such as Eurail) will get you a free ride for normal KD services, but you still need to obtain a ticket. Children up to the age of four travel for free, while those up to age 13 are charged a €3 flat fee. Students get a 50% discount. Travel on your birthday is free. Return tickets usually cost slightly more than one-way tickets.

CAR & MOTORCYCLE

The B9 highway travels along the left bank of the Rhine from Koblenz to Bingen, from where the A60 leads on to Mainz. On the right bank, the B42 hugs the river.

FERRY

Since there are no Rhine bridges between Koblenz and Mainz, the only way to cross the river along this stretch is by ferry. Car ferries operate between Boppard and Filsen/Kamp Bornhofen, St Goar and St Goarshausen, Bacharach and Kaub, Trechtinghausen and Lorch, and Bingen and Rüdesheim. These also carry foot passengers, and additional passenger ferries also make the brief hops. Prices vary slightly but you can figure on around €3 per car, including driver, €1 per additional person and €0.80 per bike.

TRAIN

Train travel is an efficient and convenient way to go village-hopping along the Rhine. Local trains connect all villages along the left river bank between Koblenz and Mainz at least hourly. The entire trip takes 1¾ hours. Some trains stop only at the bigger towns. Koblenz and Mainz are also gateways for trains to Rhine villages on the right bank, though service is less frequent.

KOBLENZ
☎ 0261 / pop 109,000

Koblenz is a modern town with ancient roots going back to the Romans, who founded a military stronghold here around 10 BC. They called it, quite appropriately, Confluentes for its supremely strategic value at the spot where the Moselle merges with the Rhine. Today, Koblenz is the economic centre of the Upper Rhine region and a major tourist hub. The town, itself home to two fabulous castles, is the gateway to the Romantic Rhine and also gives access to the outdoor charms of three low mountain ranges – the Hunsrück, the Eifel and the Westerwald – which converge here as well.

Orientation

Koblenz' core is on the left bank of the Rhine and is bordered by the Moselle to the north. The Altstadt is encircled by the Moselring and the Friedrich-Ebert-Ring roads. The Hauptbahnhof and central bus station are a few hundred metres southwest of this ring on Löhrstrasse. From there, it's about a 10- to 15-minute walk north on Löhrstrasse to the heart of the Altstadt. The landing stages of several boat operators are along the Konrad-Adenauer-Ufer on the Rhine just south of the Deutsches Eck (see p510).

Information

Bouvier Bookshop (☎ 303 370; Löhrstrasse 30)
Main post office (Bahnhofsplatz 16; 7am-7pm Mon-Fri, 7am-2pm Sat)
Main tourist office (☎ 313 04; www.koblenz.de; Bahnhofsplatz 17; 9am-7pm Mon-Fri, from 10am Sat & Sun May-Sep, to 6pm Apr & Oct, to 4pm & closed Sun in winter) Outside the Hauptbahnhof.
Rathaus tourist office (☎ 130 920; Jesuitenplatz) Same opening hours as the main tourist office.
Sparkasse (☎ 3930; Bahnhofstrasse 11) Bank.
Waschcenter (cnr Rizzastrasse & Löhrstrasse; 6am-midnight) Laundry.

Sights

CITY CENTRE WALKING TOUR

Löhrstrasse, which connects the Hauptbahnhof with the Altstadt, is Koblenz' main shopping drag, lined primarily with chain and department stores. Its prettiest spot is the intersection with Altergraben – called **Four Towers** – where each of the 17th-century corner buildings sports a richly detailed façade and an ornately carved and painted oriel.

Turning right on Altergraben takes you to **Am Plan**, a beautiful square that has undergone various incarnations as a butchers' market, a stage for religious plays, a place of execution and an arena for medieval tournaments.

The arched walkway at Am Plan's northeastern end leads to the **Liebfrauenkirche**, built in a harmonious hotchpotch of styles: of Romanesque origin, it has a Gothic choir and baroque onion-domed turrets. Note the painted net vaulting above the central nave. North of here, Florinsmarkt is dominated by the **Florinskirche** and also has the **Mittelrhein-Museum** (☎ 129 2520; Florinsmarkt 15; adult/concession €2.50/1.50; 10.30am-5pm Tue-Sat, 11am-6pm Sun), with eclectic displays reflecting the region's history. The collection of 19th-century landscape paintings of the Romantic Rhine by German and British artists is worth a closer look. For a bit of whimsy, look for the **Augenroller** (eye roller) figure beneath the façade clock, which rolls its eyes and sticks out its tongue on the hour and half-hour. Admission prices rise during special exhibitions.

Stroll a block north to the Moselle, turn right and follow it to the **Deutsches Eck** (see p510). Just south, the **Deutschherrenhaus**, once belonging to the Teutonic Knights, holds the **Ludwig Museum** (☎ 304 040; Danziger Freiheit 1; adult/concession €2.50/1.50; 10.30am-5pm Tue-Sat, 11am-6pm Sun) whose emphasis is on contemporary art, primarily from France. The slender towers of the recently spruced-up **Basilika St Kastor** from the late 12th century come into view just beyond. Conclude your tour with a stroll south along the **Rheinpromenade** to the **Weindorf**, a tourist-oriented but enjoyable cluster of restaurants and wine taverns.

EHRENBREITSTEIN

On the right bank, looming above the confluence of the Rhine and Moselle Rivers, this mighty **fortress** (☎ 974 2450; fortress only adult/concession €1.10/0.50; 10am-5pm) proved indestructible to all but Napoleonic troops, who levelled it in 1801. A few years later, the Prussians took this as a challenge to build one of Europe's strongest fortifications, completed in 1832. Behind the mighty bulwarks is a hostel (see Sleeping, p510), two restaurants and the **Landesmuseum** (☎ 970 31 50; adult/concession €3.10/2, including fortress admission; 9.30am-5pm mid-Mar–mid-Nov), with exhibits about local industries, including tobacco production and wine making. There's also a section about local boy August Horch, the founder of the Audi automotive company.

Ehrenbreitstein is accessible by car, or take bus No 9 or 10 from the Hauptbahnhof to the Obertal bus stop where you can board the chairlift to the castle (adult/concession €3.50/2 one way, €5/3 return). Alternatively, take bus No 9 to the Neudorf/Bergstrasse stop, from where it's a 20-minute walk uphill (follow the signs to the DJH hostel). A Rhine ferry operates daily until around 7pm between Easter and October (adult/child €1/0.50 each way).

DEUTSCHES ECK

The Deutsches Eck is a promontory built on a sandbank right at the rivers' confluence. It derives its name from the Deutscher Ritterorden (Order of Teutonic Knights), which had its headquarters in the 13th-century building now occupied by the Landesmuseum (see earlier). A statue of Kaiser Wilhelm I on horseback, built in the bombastic style of the late 19th century, dominates the spot. After the original was destroyed in WWII, the stone pedestal served as a memorial to German unity until reunification came about in 1990. Since 1993, a replica Kaiser rides high again above this strategic location.

SCHLOSS STOLZENFELS

With its crenellated turrets, ornate gables and fortifications, **Schloss Stolzenfels** (☎ 516 56; adult/concession €2.60/1.30 with guided tour in German; ☺ 9am-6pm Apr-Sep, 9am-5pm Oct-Nov, 9am-4pm Jan-Mar, closed Dec and first work day of week), 5km south of the town centre, exudes the sentimental beauty for which the Romantic Rhine is famed. In 1823, the later Prussian king Friedrich Wilhelm IV fell under its spell and had the castle, which had been ruined by the French, rebuilt as his summer residence. Today, the rooms largely remain as the king left them, with paintings, weapons, armoury and furnishings from the mid-19th century. You'll see all that, along with some fancy murals in the chapel and the Knights' Hall, on the guided tour.

To get there, take bus No 650 from the Hauptbahnhof to the castle parking lot, from where it's a 15-minute walk.

Sleeping

Hotel Hamm (☎ 303 210; www.hotel-hamm.de; St-Josef-Strasse 32-34; s €52-78, d €70-85; P ⊠) Get comfortable in the good-sized rooms, each decorated differently in styles ranging from the traditional to the contemporary. It's in a residential area south of the train station, putting it at a fair distance from the Altstadt.

Contel Koblenz (☎ 406 50; www.contel-koblenz.de; Pastor-Klein-Strasse 19; r €65-90; P ⊠) Children stay free with their parents in this quirky

hotel with its artsy, bright-blue façade. Match your needs to the room or suite, some of which have kitchenettes and waterbeds. It's a block from the Moselle in the Rauental district, west of the Altstadt.

Diehl's Hotel (☎ 970 70; www.diehls-hotel.de; Am Pfaffendorfer Tor 10; s €71-97, d €98-139; P ⊠ 🅿) Watch the sun set over Koblenz from your cosy room at this venerable hotel on the right river bank, below Ehrenbreitstein. Enjoy the same panorama from the indoor pool with adjacent sauna, or the well-respected restaurant with a terrace and excellent breakfast buffet. Take bus No 8, 9 or 10 to Kapuzinerplatz.

Other recommendations are:

DJH hostel (☎ 972 870; jh-koblenz@djh-info.de; 2-/4-bed dm €20.90/15.90 per person; P ⊠) In Ehrenbreitstein, popular with school groups; some rooms have private bathroom.

Campingplatz Rhein-Mosel (☎ 827 19; fax 802 489; Schartwiesenweg 6; person/tent/car €4/2.50/3; ☺ Apr-Oct) On the Moselle opposite the Deutsches Eck and served by ferry.

Eating

Most of Koblenz' restaurants and pubs are in the Altstadt and along the Rhine.

Grand Café (☎ 100 5833; Josef-Görres-Platz; dishes from €4) This popular gathering place, with a cool Art Nouveau glass ceiling, caters for all tastes, moods and budgets all day long. It's busiest at night, when Koblenz' trendy troupes gather for cocktails or even a shuffle on the dance floor. Look for promotions such as after-work happy hours and all-you-can-eat buffets.

Cafe Miljöö (☎ 142 37; Gemüsegasse 12; dishes €4-8) This cosy café is decorated with original art, Hollywood photos and fresh flowers. Breakfast is served until 5pm.

Kaffeewirtschaft (☎ 914 4702; Münzplatz 14; mains €5-11) One of several café-restaurants on hip Münzplatz, Kaffeewirtschaft impresses with its understated designer décor and daily changing specials that make use of whatever is fresh and in season, nonmeat options included.

Weindorf (☎ 316 80; Julius-Wegeler-Strasse 2-4; dishes €5-13) Sure, this little 'wine village' with its cute half-timbered restaurants – rustic to elegant – around a central courtyard often swarms with tourists, but the quality of the food remains high and prices are fair. Only the service needs improving.

Alt Coblenz (☎ 160 656; Am Plan 13; mains €8-8) The most pleasant restaurant on this bustling square, this traditional place has updated its look, menu and attitude and offers an excellent list of regional wines by the glass.

Getting There & Around

Koblenz is served by frequent IC train connections going north to such cities as Bonn and Cologne and south to Mainz, Frankfurt and beyond. Regional trains go to Trier and the Rhine villages. Some of the latter are also served by bus. Bus No 650 goes to Boppard via Schloss Stolzenfels, bus No 6130 to Braubach/Marksburg and bus No 6129 to St Goarshausen/Loreley.

Several highways converge in Koblenz, including the B9 from Cologne/Bonn. The nearest autobahns are the A61 (Koblenz-Nord exit) and the A48/A1 to Trier.

Buses serve all of Koblenz' corners, with most trips within the city costing €1.25. Longer trips (eg to the hostel or Schloss Stolzenfels) cost €1.80, and day passes are €3.70.

BRAUBACH

☎ 02627 / pop 3500

Framed by vineyards and rose gardens, the snug 1300-year-old town of Braubach, about 8km south of Koblenz on the right bank, unfolds against the dramatic backdrop of the **Marksburg** (☎ 206; adult/student/child €4.50/4/3.50; ☼ 10am-5pm Apr-Oct, 11am-4pm Nov-Mar). This hilltop castle's main claim to fame is that it has never been destroyed, thanks to several layers of fortification added by a succession of counts and landgraves. A tour takes in the citadel, the Gothic hall and the large functioning kitchen, plus the grisly torture chamber in the cellar with its hair-raising assortment of pain-inflicting nasties.

Take bus No 6130 from Koblenz' central bus station to Braubach, and then it's a 20-minute walk uphill.

BOPPARD

☎ 06742 / pop 17,000

Boppard, about 20km south of Koblenz, offers many cultural, historical and natural delights and is a worthwhile stop, not least for its scenic location on a sharp horseshoe-shaped bend in the river. Be sure to sample the excellent riesling grown on some of the Rhine's steepest vineyards here. Boppard is also a gateway to fun hikes in the Hunsrück, the forest region linking the Rhine and the Moselle.

Information

Post office (Heerstrasse 177)

Tourist information (☎ 3888; www.boppard.de; Altes Rathaus, Marktplatz; ☼ 8am-5.30pm Mon-Fri, 9am-noon Sat May-Sep, 8am-4pm Mon-Fri Oct-Apr)

Volksbank (Marktplatz 9)

Sights

The central Marktplatz is a good place to start an exploration of Boppard. It's dominated by the twin towers of the **Severuskirche**, an elegant 13th-century church built on the site of Roman military baths. Its delicate wall paintings, a triumphal cross from 1225 and the spiderweb-like vaulted ceilings are all features recommending a visit.

A couple of blocks east, in a 14th-century palace, the **Museum der Stadt Boppard** (☎ 103 69; Burgstrasse; admission free; ☼ 10am-noon & 2-5pm Tue-Sun Apr-Oct) has displays about the town's history and an entire floor dedicated to the bentwood furniture first invented by Michael Thonet (1796–1871), who was born here.

Walk two blocks inland, crossing Oberstrasse, Boppard's main drag, to the **Archaeological Park** (Angertstrasse; admission free), which incorporates 55m of the original Roman camp wall and also contains graves from the Frankish era (7th century) and a section of a medieval store/dance hall.

Activities

For a spectacular view that gives you the illusion of looking at four lakes instead of a single river, take the 20-minute **chairlift ride** (☎ 932 050; up/return €4.20/6.20; ☼ 9.30am-6.30pm Apr-Oct) to the **Vierseenblick** viewpoint.

Even more memorable is the dramatically steep ride on the **Hunsrückbahn** train that travels through five tunnels and across two viaducts on its 8km journey from Boppard to Buchholz (€1.75, 15 minutes). Many people hike back to Boppard from here, but Buchholz is also the starting point of the excellent 17km hike to Brodenbach via the romantic **Ehrbachtal**. In season, a shuttle bus takes you back to town, or else catch a bus to Koblenz Hauptbahnhof and then change to bus No 650 to Boppard.

From April to October the tourist office organises wine tastings with different vintners at 8pm Thursday (€5 for five wines).

Bikes may be hired from **Fahrrad Lüdicke** (☎ 4736; Oberstrasse 105; €6.50/day; 🕙 9am-6pm Mon-Fri, 9am-1pm Sat).

Sleeping & Eating

Hotel Rebstock (☎ 4876; fax 4877; Rheinallee 31; s €31-46, d €46-77) This classic Rhine hotel, next to the museum and across from the car-ferry landing, has comfortable rooms with a good range of modern amenities; many also have river views. The restaurant with covered terrace is top-notch.

Günther Garni (☎ 890 90; www.hotelguenther.de; Rheinallee 40; s €50-82, d €62-88) Watch the boats and barges glide along the mighty Rhine right from your balconied room at this charming waterfront hotel. It's partly owned by an American, making communication a bit easier. The décor is bright and modern. Discounts are offered from November to April.

Campingpark Sonneneck (☎ 2121; www.camping park-sonneneck.de; An der B9; person/tent/car €5.70/3.20/3.20; 🕙 Easter–mid-Oct) Stretching for 2km along the river, about 5km north of Boppard, this camp site has modern facilities and a large pool. Take bus No 650 and ask the driver to drop you off.

Weingut Felsenkeller (☎ 2154; Mühltal 21; snacks €4-7) Right by the chairlift station, this wine tavern sits next to a little stream and has the feel of a private living room.

Weinhaus Heilig Grab (☎ 2371; Zelkesgasse 12; snacks €4-7; 🕙 from 3pm, closed Tue) By the train station, Boppard's oldest wine tavern offers a cosy setting for sipping the local product. In summer, sit outside under a leafy chestnut canopy.

ST GOAR

☎ 06741 / pop 3250

The busy riverside promenade of St Goar, 10km upriver of Boppard, is lorded over by the sprawling ruins of **Burg Rheinfels** (☎ 383; adult/concession €4/2; 🕙 9am-6pm Apr-Oct, 10am-5pm Sat & Sun in good weather Nov-Mar), once the mightiest fortress on the Rhine and a must-see. Built in 1245 by Count Dieter V of Katzenelnbogen as a base for his toll-collecting operation, its size and labyrinthine layout is truly astonishing. Not just children love exploring the subterranean tunnels and mine galleries.

The castle museum provides background information and neat models showing th enormity of the original complex.

Another kid-pleasing stop is the **German Doll & Bear Museum** (☎ 7270; Sonnengasse 8; adult concession/child €3.50/2.50/1.50; 🕙 10am-5pm mid-Mar mid-Jan, 2-5pm Sat & Sun otherwise).

For more information, stop by the **touris office** (☎ 383; www.st-goar.de; Heerstrasse 86; 🕙 8am 12.30pm & 2-5pm Mon-Fri, 10am-noon Sat May-Oct, to 4pr & closed Sat Nov-Apr) right on the pedestrianised main street. Check your email at **Hotel Mon tag** (Heerstrasse 128) and buy your stamps an train tickets at the **TotoLottoTabak Shop** (☎ 93 03; Heerstrasse 93).

Sleeping & Eating

The tourist office can assist with finding accommodation.

DJH hostel (☎ 388; jh-st-goar@djh-info.de; Bismarck weg 17; dm €12.70) This old-fashioned hostel i right below Burg Rheinfels.

Hotel Zur Loreley (☎ 1614; www.hotel-zur-lorele .de; Heerstrasse 87; s/d €44/64, 2-room ste €72; P) A good place to hang your hat, this hotel ha tasteful, modern décor in natural colour and a variety of lodging options to su various space needs.

Traditional eateries in town include **Zu Krone** (☎ 1515; Oberstrasse 38; mains €9-13) in snug half-timbered building, whose ment includes options for kids and vegetarians. A quick drive or 20-minute walk away is the idyllic **Winzerschenke Philipps** (☎ 1606; Gründel bach 49; snacks €4-10; 🕙 from 3pm May-Oct), a wine tavern in a working historic mill with a side business selling organic products.

ST GOARSHAUSEN & LORELEY

☎ 06771 / pop 1150

St Goar's twin town on the right bank o the Rhine – and connected to it by ferry – St Goarshausen is the gateway to the mos anticipated spot along the Romantic Rhine the **Loreley**. Though nothing but a giant slab of slate, this rock owes its fame to a myth ical maiden whose siren songs once lured sailors to their death in the treacherous currents, as poetically captured by Heinrich Heine. A sculpture of the buxom beauty perches lasciviously at the tip of a strip o land jutting into the Rhine.

Views from the top, reached by shuttle bus (€1.25, return €2.50) or via a long stair way, are predictably stunning. The plateau is now part of a landscape park, an EXPO 2000 project, and anchored by a new multimedia **Visitor Centre** (☎ 599 093; ⏰ 10am-6pm Apr-Oct). Exhibits here examine the Loreley myth, the beginnings of Rhine tourism, wine making, shipping and the region's geology, flora and fauna in an engaging, interactive fashion. The adjacent outdoor amphitheatre is a great setting for rock and other concerts.

St Goarshausen is also home to two castles. **Burg Maus** (Mouse Castle) was originally called Peterseck and was built by the archbishop of Trier in an effort to counter Count Dieter's toll practices. In a show of medieval muscle-flexing, the latter responded by building yet another, and much bigger, castle and called it **Burg Katz** (Cat Castle). And so, to highlight the obvious imbalance of power between count and archbishop, Peterseck soon came to be known as Burg Maus. These days, Burg Maus houses an **eagle and falcon station** (☎ 7669; adult/child €6.50/5.50; ⏰ 10am-5pm mid-Mar–Sep), reached by a 20-minute walk from St Goarshausen-Wellmich. Burg Katz is not open to the public.

St Goarshausen has its own **tourist office** (☎ 9100; www.loreley-touristik.de; Bahnhofstrasse 8), which can help with lodging and general information.

OBERWESEL

☎ 06744 / pop 3500

Oberwesel has lost some of its 'romantic' aspects to modern construction and the railway that runs parallel to the river and a section of the otherwise impressive 3km-long medieval **town wall**. The latter wraps around much of the Altstadt and still sports 16 guard towers. Easily spotted on a hillside on the northern end of town is the 14th-century church of **St Martin** (aka the 'white church'), with painted ceilings, a richly sculpted main altar and a tower that once formed part of the fortifications. St Martin is juxtaposed by the **Liebfrauenkirche** in the southern Altstadt, older by about 100 years and known as the 'red church' for the colour of its façade. It boasts an impressive carved gold altar.

Lording above the town is the **Schönburg**, still majestic despite having been ruined. Legend has it that this was once the home of seven beautiful but haughty sisters who

ridiculed and rejected any potential suitors until they were turned into stone and submerged in the Rhine. If you look closely, you can spot the **Sieben Jungfrauen rocks** from the Seven Virgins viewpoint reached via a lovely vineyard trail.

For details, stop by the **tourist office** (☎ 710 624; www.oberwesel.de; Rathausstrasse 3; ⏰ 9am-1pm & 2-6pm Mon-Fri Apr-Oct, 10am-2pm Jul-Aug; reduced hours Nov-Mar).

BACHARACH

☎ 06743 / pop 2400

One of the prettiest of the Rhine villages, tiny Bacharach conceals its considerable charms behind a time-worn town wall. Enter through one of the thick arched gateways to find yourself in a gorgeous medieval village with exquisite **half-timbered mansions** such as the Altes Haus, the Posthof and the Alte Münze, all along Oberstrasse, the main street. Also here is the late Romanesque **Peterskirche**, with some particularly suggestive capstones. Look for the naked woman with snakes sucking her breasts (a warning about the consequences of adultery) at the end of the left aisle. Heading uphill for about 15 minutes takes you to the 12th-century **Burg Stahleck**, now a hostel (see below), and past the filigree ruins of the Gothic **Wernerkapelle**.

Bacharach's **tourist office** (☎ 919 303; www.bacharach.de; Oberstrasse 45; ⏰ 9am-5pm Mon-Fri, 10am-4pm Sat Apr-Oct, 9am-noon Fri Nov-Mar) has handy information about the entire area. The same building, the historical Posthof, also houses the Middle Rhine Visitors Centre and an excellent restaurant.

Sleeping & Eating

Burg Stahleck (☎ 1266; jh-bacharach@djh-info.de; Burg Stahleck; d/q €20.90/15.90 per person; ✕) Bacharach's DJH hostel has a dream setting inside the medieval Burg Stahleck. After a thorough renovation, most rooms now have private bathrooms.

Campingplatz Sonnenstrand (☎ 1752; www.camping-sonnenstrand.de; Strandbadweg 9; person/tent/car €4.20/3/3; ⏰ Apr–mid-Oct) This camp site on the Rhine is about 500m south of town.

Rheinhotel (☎ 1243; www.rhein-hotel-bacharach.de; An der Stadtmauer; s €47-52, d €37-42; 🅿) The modern rooms here are each named after the vineyard they look out upon and are decorated with original artwork by local artists. Some have balconies. The in-house restaurant serves regional dishes (mains €7 to €15).

Zum Grünen Baum (☎ 1208; Oberstrasse 63; snacks €3-6) This unpretentious wine tavern, run by the congenial Bastian family, has some of the best wine in town. You can order the 'wine carousel' 15-wine sampler (€13.50).

Posthof (☎ 599 663; mains €6-15) In the same building as the tourist office, this restaurant serves everything from pork roast to tofu terrine, all made with fresh, local products. On balmy summer nights, the most coveted tables are in the ancient courtyard.

BACHARACH TO BINGEN

Three more castles grace the craggy slopes along the southernmost stretch of the Middle Rhine. First up is **Burg Sooneck** (☎ 06743-6064; adult/concession €2.60/1.30; ☺ 10am-6pm Tue-Sun Easter-Sep, otherwise 10am-5pm, closed Dec), carefully restored in the 19th century and filled with furniture and paintings that once belonged to the Prussian royal family.

Looming above the village of Trechtinghausen, the mighty **Burg Reichenstein** (☎ 06721-6117; adult/child €3.40/2.30; ☺ 9am-6pm Mar-Nov) now harbours a hotel, restaurant and museum with a prized collection of cast-iron oven slabs, hunting trophies, armoury and furnishings.

The last in the trio, and the most picturesque, is the privately owned **Burg Rheinstein** (☎ 06721-6348; adult/child €3.50/2.50; ☺ 9.30am-5.30pm mid-Mar–mid-Nov) with origins in the 9th century, making it one of the oldest Rhine castles. In 1825 it became the first to be converted into a romantic summer residence by Prussian royalty. The still functional drawbridge and a portcullis evoke medieval times, but the interior is mostly in neo-Gothic style. The castle has reduced opening hours from mid-November to mid-March.

BINGEN

☎ 06721 / pop 25,000

Bingen marks the southern terminus of the Middle Rhine region. Thanks to its strategic location at the confluence of the Nahe and Rhine Rivers, the town has been coveted by warriors and merchants since being founded by the Romans in 11 BC. Scarred by war and destruction multiple times, it still remains an attractive place and is considerably less touristy and commercial than some of its neighbours.

Bingen was the birthplace of the writer Stefan George (1868–1933) and, more notably, of Hildegard von Bingen, one of the few seminal female figures in medieval history (see the boxed text on p515).

The town centre spreads out east of the Nahe, with the Hauptbahnhof just off the western bank. The smaller Bahnhof Bingen, near the town centre, only has local trains. City-Linie minibuses shuttle between all major points of interest every 30 minutes (€0.50).

Information

Main post office (Am Fruchtmarkt)
Sparkasse (Mainzer Strasse 26) Bank.
Tourist information (☎ 184 205; www.bingen.de; Rheinkai 21; ☺ 9am-6pm Mon-Fri, 9am-12.30pm Sat Apr-Oct; reduced hours Nov-Mar)

Sights

Bingen's most visible landmark is the medieval **Burg Klopp**, resting on a hilltop above the town centre with good views and the moderately interesting **Heimatmuseum** (☎ 184 110; adult/concession €0.50/0.25; ☺ 11am-5pm Tue-Sun Apr-Oct). If you're pressed for time, it's better spent at the modern **Historisches Museum am Strom** (☎ 991 531; Museumsstrasse 3; adult/concession €3/2; ☺ 10am-5pm Tue-Sun) in a former power station right on the Rhine. Its core exhibit traces the life and achievements of Hildegard von Bingen, with few actual objects but informative panelling in German and English. Another highlight is a set of surgical instruments – from scalpels and cupping glasses to saws – left behind by a Roman doctor in the 2nd century AD. Idealised visions in ink and paint of the Rhine area are the focus of several rooms dedicated to Rhine Romanticism.

Up on Rochus Hill is the neo-Gothic **Rochuskapelle**, a pilgrimage church with a splendid canopied altar showing scenes from the life of Hildegard von Bingen. Run by nuns, the adjacent **Hildegard Forum** (☎ 181 000; Rochusberg 1; admission free; ☺ 2-6pm Tue-Thu, 2-8pm Fri, 11am-6pm Sat & Sun) houses Hildegard exhibits, a restaurant serving wholesome foods made with spelt, Hildegard's favourite grain, and a medieval herb garden.

On an island in the Rhine is the **Mäuseturm** (Mouse Tower), where, according to legend, Bishop Hatto was devoured alive by mice in retaliation for having burned starving peasants begging for grain after a bad harvest. In reality, though, the name is a mutation of *Mautturm*, or toll tower, which was the building's medieval function.

Sleeping & Eating

Hotel-Café Köppel (☎ 147 70; fax 127 51; Kapuzinerstrasse 12; s/d €55/75; P) In the heart of town, this place is buttressed by a café serving home-made cakes and offers comfortable if modest rooms. The few that still have shared bathroom cost €20 less.

Hotel Martinskeller (☎ 134 75; www.hotel-bingen-rhein.com; Martinsstrasse 1-3; s €64-68, d €82-103; P ⊠) This building has gone through stints as a wine store and even a synagogue before becoming, in 1984, a comfortable hotel with a well-respected restaurant. It's done up in country-style with exposed-beam ceilings, heavy furniture and frilly decorations.

Life & Art House (☎ 126 95; Speisemarkt 3; mains €5-10) This is a youthful bistro-cum-gallery in the heart of the pedestrianised zone.

Burg Klopp Restaurant (☎ 156 44; mains €12.50-18) One of Bingen's finest restaurants is right in the castle and serves inspired Mediterranean cuisine, including fish and vegetarian options, in a stylish ambience with lovely city and Rhine views.

RÜDESHEIM

☎ 06722 / pop 10,360

Rüdesheim is the capital of the Rheingau, famous for its superior riesling. It is on the Rhine's right bank, about 25km west of Wiesbaden (which administratively makes it part of Hesse) and connected to Bingen by ferry. Rüdesheim is a quintessential wine town and deluged by day-tripping coach tourists to the tune of three million a year. Their 'shrines' are the wine bars and restaurants along the tunnel-like Drosselgasse, whose half-timbered houses reverberate with music and the laughter of a rollicking crowd. If this is not your scene, you can simply wander beyond these 100m of drunken madness to discover that Rüdesheim is quite a classy place. In December, the town hosts a popular and scenic Christmas market.

For visitor information, go to the **tourist information** (☎ 2962, 194 33; www.ruedesheim.de; Geisenheimer Strasse 22; ⊙ 8.30am-6.30pm Mon-Fri, 11am-5pm Sat May-Oct; reduced hours Nov-Apr).

Sights & Activities

Rüdesheim is too small to avoid the Drosselgasse razzmatazz completely, but one island of calm is **Siegfrieds Mechanisches Musikkabinett** (☎ 492 17; Oberstrasse 29; adult/child €5/2.70; ⊙ 10am-10pm Mar-Dec), a fun collection of

---

HILDEGARD VON BINGEN

She's hip and holistic, a composer, dramatist and a courageous campaigner for the rights of women. She heals with crystals and herbs, her music frequently hits the New Age charts…and she's been dead for more than 800 years.

Hildegard von Bingen was born in 1098 at Bermersheim (near Alzey), the 10th child of a well-off and influential family. At the age of three she experienced the first of the visions that would occur over the course of her extraordinarily long life. As a young girl she entered the convent at Disibodenberg on the Nahe River and eventually became an abbess who founded two abbeys of her own: Rupertsberg, above Bingen, in 1150; and Eibingen, across the Rhine near Rüdesheim, in 1165 (see p516). During her preaching tours – an unprecedented activity for women in medieval times – she lectured both to the clergy and the common people, attacking social injustice and ungodliness.

Pope Eugen III publicly endorsed Hildegard, urging her to write down both her theology and visionary experiences. This she did in a remarkable series of books that encompass ideas as diverse as cosmology, natural history and female orgasm. Her overarching philosophy was that humankind is a distillation of divinity and should comport itself accordingly. Her accomplishments are even more remarkable considering her life-long struggle against feelings of worthlessness and the physical effects of her mysterious visions, which often left her near death.

Hildegard von Bingen was a force of nature who remains as much a cult figure today as she was during her life. She died in 1179.

mechanical musical instruments, such as pianolas, from the 18th and 19th centuries. Many are demonstrated during the guided tour. Just east of here, a steep staircase descends into the **Medieval Torture Museum** (☎ 475 10; Oberstrasse 49; adult/student €5/3.50; ☉ 10am-6pm Apr-Nov) with predictably ghoulish displays.

More welcoming is the **Weinmuseum** (Wine Museum; ☎ 2348; Rheinstrasse 2; adult/concession €3/2; ☉ 9am-6pm mid-Mar–Oct) in the 1000-year-old Brömserburg castle. It has lots of drinking vessels from Roman times onwards, but you'll probably have more fun climbing the tower for great town and river views.

For an even better panorama, head up to the **Niederwald Denkmal** (1883), a bombastic monument starring Germania that celebrates the creation of the German Reich in 1871. You can walk up, but it's faster to glide above the vineyards aboard the **cable car** (☎ 2402; Oberstrasse; adult/child €4/2, return €6/3; ☉ 9.30am-7pm Jun-Sep, reduced hours Oct-May). From the monument, gentle trails lead to the romantic ruin of **Burg Ehrenfels** or to a hunting lodge above the neighbouring village of Assmannshausen, which specialises in red wine. From here you could catch the chairlift down into town, then head back to Rüdesheim by boat.

Sleeping & Eating

DJH hostel (☎ 2711; ruedesheim@djh-hessen.de; Am Kreuzberg; dm junior/senior €15/17.70; P ✗) Rüdesheim's hostel is about a 30-minute walk from the train station (there's no bus) and overlooks the vineyards.

Hotel Germania (☎ 2584; www.hajos.de; Rheinstrasse 10; s €55-95, d €70-118; P) From the outside it looks just like any other traditional Rhine hotel, but inside blows a fresh, youthful breeze. Rooms sport bold colours and creative décor; some have balconies and/or river views. Locals and tourists mix it up in the lively pub, which has a broad selection of beer.

Breuer's Rüdesheimer Schloss (☎ 905 00; www.ruedesheimer-schloss.com; Steingasse 10; s €95-115, d €115-145; P ✗ 🖴) You'd never expect to find a modern, stylish and artsy hotel off the Drosselgasse, but that's just what this place, owned by the Breuer family of quality wine makers, is. Spacious rooms have one-of-a-kind designer furniture, and the roast duck at the downstairs restaurant is excellent.

AROUND RÜDESHEIM
Kloster Eberbach

If you saw the 1986 film *The Name of the Rose*, starring Sean Connery, you've already seen much of this one-time Cistercian **monastery** (☎ 06723-917 80; adult/concession €3.50/1.50; ☉ 10am-6pm Apr-Oct, 11am-5pm Nov-Mar), where a number of scenes were shot. Dating back to the 12th century, the graceful complex went through periods as a lunatic asylum, jail and sheep pen after secularisation in the 19th century. In 1918, it was turned into a state-owned wine estate. Explore the monks' refectory and dormitory, as well as the austere Romanesque basilica, then taste and buy the local wines in the Vinothek.

Eberbach is about 20km from Rüdesheim, but if you're not driving the only way to get here is by taking the train or bus to Eltville, followed by a one-hour signposted walk.

Eibingen

About 2km north of Rüdesheim, Eibingen is the burial place of medieval power-woman, **Hildegard von Bingen** (see the boxed text p515). Her elaborate reliquary shrine, which contains her heart, hair, tongue and skull, is prominently displayed inside the **Parish Church** (☎ 06722-4520; Marienthaler Strasse 3). It attracts pilgrims from around the world, especially on 17 September, the day of her death, when a procession makes its way here from Rüdesheim. The church stands on the site formerly occupied by the second abbey founded by Hildegard in 1165. The nearby new St Hildegard Convent, with around 60 nuns, dates back to 1904.

THE MOSELLE VALLEY

Where other places in Germany demand that you hustle, the Moselle suggests that you just, well…mosey. The German section of the river, which originates in France and traverses Luxembourg, runs 195km northeast from Trier to Koblenz on a slow, winding course, revealing new scenery at every bend.

Exploring the vineyards and wineries of the Moselle Valley is an ideal way to get a taste for German culture, people and – of course – some wonderful wines. Slow down and do some sipping. Europe's steepest vineyards (the Bremmer Valmont) with a 72% grade and Germany's most expensive vineyards (the Bernkasteler Doctor in Bernkastel-Kues) are both on the Moselle.

Cycling

With its gentle curves, the Moselle is great for exploring by bicycle, especially because you can ride on a separate bike path for much of way. The *Moselland-Radwanderführer* (€7.60) has detailed maps and information on bike hire and repair shops, sights, accommodation and other useful hints and tips. It's available at local tourist offices and in bookshops.

An alternative is the ADFC map *Radtourenkarte Mosel-Saarland* (€7.50), which is also useful for hiking.

Between May and October you can take your bike on some of the Moselbahn buses travelling between Trier and Bullay.

Hiking

The Moselle Valley is especially scenic walking country. Expect some steep climbs if you venture away from the river, but the views are worth all the sore muscles. Good hiking maps are available at most good bookshops and tourist offices. The *Moselland-Wanderführer* (€6.60) is a comprehensive guide. A popular long-distance hike is the **Moselhöhenweg**, running on both sides of the Moselle for a total of 390km.

Getting There & Away

The closest airport is Frankfurt-Hahn, which is only 20km from Traben-Trarbach, 30km from Bernkastel-Kues and 50km from Cochem.

Most people start their Moselle exploration either in Trier or in Koblenz. If you have private transport and are coming from the north, however, you might head up the Ahr Valley and cut through the Eifel Mountains. If you're coming from the Saarland, your route will lead you through the Hunsrück Mountains.

Getting Around
BOAT

The river's winding course and a fair number of locks make water travel rather slow. From late April to mid-October, the **KD Line** (☎ 0221-208 8318; www.k-d.com) sails daily between Koblenz and Cochem (€20.40/23.60 one way/return, 5¼ hours), stopping at

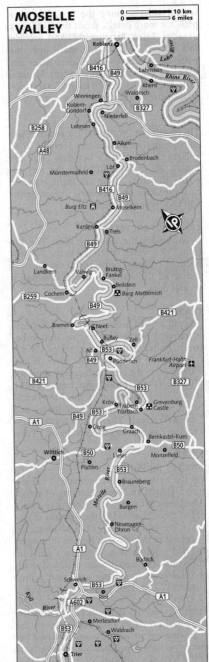

MOSELLE VALLEY

several villages along the way. (See Boat p508 for more details about the KD Line.)

From Trier, **Personenschifffahrt Gebrüder Kolb** (☎ 0651-266 66) is the main operator, with day tours to Bernkastel-Kues and back (€25, all day) daily except Monday from May to October. In most villages, local boat operators offer additional options.

BUS
The **Moselbahn** (☎ 0651-147 750; www.moselbahn .de) operates scheduled bus services to all villages on the Moselle between Trier and Bullay, about three-fifths of the way towards Koblenz. There are eight buses in each direction on weekdays, five on Saturday and three on Sunday.

CAR & MOTORCYCLE
Driving along the Moselle is ideal. The B53 from Trier, which continues as the B49 just north of Traben-Trarbach, follows the river course all the way to Koblenz, crossing it several times.

TRAIN
The rail service between Trier and Koblenz is frequent but, except for the section between Bullay and Koblenz, trains do not travel to the villages on the river. If you want to enjoy the beautiful scenery along the Moselle, take a Moselbahn bus (see Bus, above). One exception is the Moselweinbahn, which shuttles between Bullay and Traben-Trarbach. There's also regular service from Saarbrücken to Koblenz and Trier.

TRIER
☎ 0651 / pop 99,700
On the western edge of Germany, Trier is a true highlight and well deserving of a visit. Along with Worms, it is one of the country's oldest cities, founded by the Romans as Augusta Treverorum in 15 BC and advancing to capital of the Western Roman Empire by the 3rd century. It is home to a fantastic collection of Roman monuments, and architectural gems from later ages, and gained Unesco World Heritage Site status in 1986.

Trier's second heyday came in the 13th century, when its archbishops acquired the rank and power of prince-electors. In the following centuries, the town seesawed between periods of prosperity and poverty. It is the birthplace of Karl Marx (1818–83).

The town is beautifully located on the Moselle and hemmed in by the Eifel and Hunsrück Mountains. Its proximity to Luxembourg and France can be tasted in the local cuisine, and about 18,000 students do their part to infuse a lively spirit.

Trier is an inspiring place that deserves at least a couple of days of exploration. It also makes an excellent base for trips on the Moselle River, to Luxembourg or into the nearby hills. From 24 April to 24 October 2004, Trier hosts the *Landesgartenschau,* a state-sponsored garden show.

Orientation
Trier's major sights cluster in or near the largely pedestrianised city centre, bounded by a ring road on three sides and by the Moselle to the west. The Hauptbahnhof is about 500m southeast of the landmark Porta Nigra and the adjacent tourist office. The Olewig Wine District is about 2km southeast from the centre and served by bus Nos 6, 16 and 26.

Information
BOOKSHOPS
Akademische Buchhandlung Interbook (☎ 979 90; Fleischstrasse 62)

DISCOUNT CARDS
Roman Combination Ticket (adult €6.20, senior & student €3.10, child €2.50) One ticket to the Porta Nigra, Kaiserthermen, Amphitheater and Barbarathermen.
TrierCard (€9/15 individual/family) Entitles bearer to discounted admissions, tours and free public transport for three consecutive days.

INTERNET ACCESS
Cyber-Café (☎ 194 44; Karl-Marx-Strasse 32; ☺ 10am-11pm) The venue doubles as a *Mitfahrzentrale* (ride-sharing agency).

LAUNDRY
Waschcenter (Brückenstrasse 19-21; ☺ 8am-10pm Mon-Sat)

MEDICAL SERVICES
Elisabeth-Hospital (☎ 209 20; Theobaldstrasse 12)
Emergency medical referral service (☎ 455 55)

POST
Branch office (Am Kornmarkt)
Main post office (Hauptbahnhof; ☺ 8am-7pm Mon-Fri, 8am-1pm Sat)

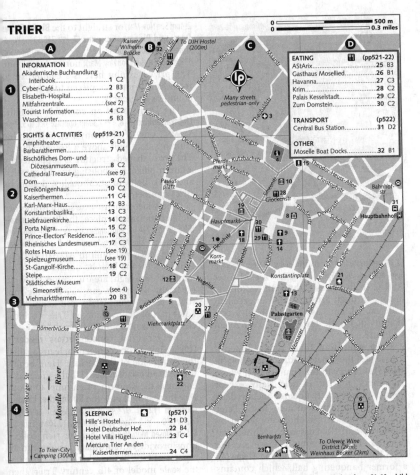

TRIER

INFORMATION
Akademische Buchhandlung
  Interbook....................................1 C2
Cyber-Café....................................2 B3
Elisabeth-Hospital.........................3 C1
Mitfahrzentrale........................(see 2)
Tourist Information.......................4 C2
Waschcenter.................................5 B3

SIGHTS & ACTIVITIES (pp519-21)
Amphitheater................................6 D4
Barbarathermen............................7 A4
Bischöfliches Dom- und
  Diözesanmuseum.......................8 C2
Cathedral Treasury...................(see 9)
Dom...9 C2
Dreikönigenhaus.........................10 C2
Kaiserthermen.............................11 C4
Karl-Marx-Haus...........................12 B3
Konstantinbasilika.......................13 C3
Liebfrauenkirche..........................14 C2
Porta Nigra.................................15 C2
Prince-Electors' Residence...........16 C3
Rheinisches Landesmuseum.........17 C3
Rotes Haus...............................(see 19)
Spielzeugmuseum.....................(see 19)
St-Gangolf-Kirche.......................18 C2
Steipe...19 C2
Städtisches Museum
  Simeonstift..........................(see 4)
Viehmarktthermen......................20 B3

EATING (pp521-22)
AStArix......................................25 B3
Gasthaus Mosellied....................26 B1
Havanna....................................27 C3
Krim..28 C2
Palais Kesselstadt.......................29 C2
Zum Domstein...........................30 C2

TRANSPORT (p522)
Central Bus Station......................31 D2

OTHER
Moselle Boat Docks.....................32 B1

SLEEPING (p521)
Hille's Hostel..............................21 D3
Hotel Deutscher Hof...................22 B4
Hotel Villa Hügel........................23 C4
Mercure Trier An den
  Kaiserthermen.........................24 C4

TOURIST INFORMATION

Tourist office (☎ 978 080; www.trier.de/tourismus;
An der Porta Nigra; ☻ 9am-6pm Mon-Sat, 10am-3pm
Sun Apr-Oct, reduced hours Nov-Mar) Hires out English-
language audiotapes for self-guided city tours (€6).

Sights & Activities
WALKING TOUR

Walk in the footsteps of gladiators, bishops
and artisans on this tour that takes you
through 2000 years of history in about two
hours. Plan extra time for close-up inspec-
tions of the sights that most intrigue you.
The following sights all appear on the walking tour map (Map p520).

Top billing among Trier's Roman monuments belongs to the **Porta Nigra** (1; ☎ 754 24;

Porta-Nigra-Platz; adult €2.10, senior/student €1.60, child
€1; ☻ 9am-6pm Apr-Sep, 9am-5pm Oct-Mar). Blackened by time (hence the name, Latin for
'black gate'), this brooding 2nd-century
city gate is a marvel of engineering and ingenuity. Held together by nothing but iron
rods, its design allowed the Romans to trap
would-be attackers in the central courtyard,
cleverly concealed by innocuous arched
gateways. In the 11th century, Archbishop
Poppo converted the secular structure into
the St Simeonkirche in honour of a Greek
hermit who spent a stint holed up in its
east tower.

St Simeon church spawned a monastery,
which now houses the **Städtisches Museum
Simeonstift** (2; ☎ 718 1459; An der Porta Nigra; adult

RHINELAND-PALATINATE

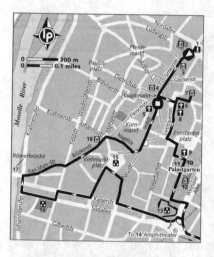

€2.10, senior/student €1.60, child under 10 free; 9am-5pm Apr-Sep, 9am-5pm Tue-Fri, 9am-3pm Sat & Sun Oct-Mar). It illustrates eight centuries of city history through artworks and an excellent scale model, and also has impressive collections of Coptic textiles and East Asian sculpture.

Make your way south along Simeonstrasse past the ornate medieval **Dreikönigenhaus (3)** at No 19 to the Hauptmarkt, where a farmers' market is held daily except Sunday. It's a pretty square, anchored by a festive fountain dedicated to St Peter and the Four Virtues and hemmed in by medieval and Renaissance architectural beauties. Foremost among these are the **Rotes Haus** (Red House); and the **Steipe (4)**, a former banqueting hall, which contains a restaurant and is also the new home of the **Spielzeugmuseum** (Toy Museum; ☎ 758 50; adult/youth/child under 11 €4/2/1.50; 11am-5pm), a major draw for fans of miniature trains, mechanical toys, dolls and other youthful delights. The Gothic **St-Gangolf-Kirche (5)** is reached via a flowery portal.

East of Hauptmarkt looms the fortress-like **Dom (6**; ☎ 979 0790; 6.30am-6pm Apr-Oct, 6.30am-5.30pm Nov-Mar), built above the palace of Helena, the mother of Roman emperor Constantine. The present structure is mostly Romanesque with some Gothic and baroque embellishments. To marvel at the church's incredible wealth, head upstairs to the **cathedral treasury** (adult/child €1.50/0.50; 10am-5pm Mon-Sat, 2-5pm Sun Apr-Oct, 11am-4pm Mon-Sat,

2-4pm Sun Nov-Mar) or straight to the **Bischöfliches Dom- und Diözesanmuseum (7**; ☎ 710 5255; Windstrasse 6-8; adult/student €2/1; 9am-5pm Mon-Sat, 1-5pm Sun, closed Mon Nov-Mar), north of the Dom. The prized exhibit here is a ceiling fresco from Helena's palace pieced together from countless fragments.

The Dom forms an ensemble with the **Liebfrauenkirche (8**; 7.30am-6pm Apr-Oct, to 5.30pm Nov-Mar), one of Germany's earliest Gothic churches and built above a Roman church. The cross-shaped structure is supported by a dozen pillars symbolising the 12 apostles, and has a light, mystical quality, despite its strict symmetry.

Follow Liebfrauenstrasse south to another architectural masterpiece, the **Konstantinbasilika (9**; ☎ 724 68; Konstantinplatz; 10am-6pm Mon-Sat, noon-6pm Sun Apr-Oct; 11am-noon & 3-4pm Tue-Sat, noon-1pm Sun Nov-Mar), built in AD 310 as Constantine's throne hall. Its dimensions (67m long and 36m high) are truly mind-blowing, especially when you consider that the roof structure is completely self-supporting. Later part of the residence of Trier's prince-electors, it is now a Protestant church.

The remaining **prince-electors' residence (10)**, a pink rococo confection, leans against the south side of the basilica. Here begins the stylised **palace garden (11)**, the green axis ending at the Kaiserthermen ruins. On your way there, you'll pass the **Rheinisches Landesmuseum (12**; ☎ 977 40; Weimarer Allee 1; adult/child €5.50/1.50; 9.30am-5pm Mon-Fri, 10.30am-5pm Sat & Sun, closed Mon Nov-Apr), whose rich collections provide extraordinary insight into all aspects of local Roman life. Have a look at the scale model of 4th-century Trier, then delve into rooms filled with tombstones, floor mosaics, coloured glass, rare gold coins and other fine exhibits.

From the museum, it's just a coin toss south to the **Kaiserthermen (13**; ☎ 442 62; Im Palastgarten; adult €2.10, senior/student €1.60, child €1; 9am-6pm Apr-Sep, 9am-5pm Oct-Mar), once a vast thermal bathing complex and yet another Constantine creation. Only the underground heating ducts and sections of the hot pool area survive, but it's still fun to wander among the ruins.

A short walk east is the **Amphitheater (14**; ☎ 730 10; Olewiger Strasse; adult €2.10, senior/student €2.10/1.60, child €1; 9am-6pm Apr-Sep, 9am-5pm Oct-Mar), once capable of holding 20,000 spectators during gladiator tournaments and

DAVID PEEVERS

Burg Eltz (p525), Moselle Valley

IONAS KALTENBACH

Bottles of riesling, Moselle Valley (p516)

Moselle River, Moselle Valley (p516)

DAVID PEEVERS

City skyline, Frankfurt-am-Main (p538)

Römerberg (p541), Frankfurt-am-Main

Street art on Domplatz near Kölner Dom (p578), Cologne

Museum für Sepulkralkultur (Museum of Sepulchral; p563), Kassel

animal fights. A visit includes the dank cellars once used to keep prisoners, caged animals and corpses. Both Kaiserthermen and the Amphitheater serve as staging sites for the **Antikenfestspiele**, an annual open-air festival of tragedy, comedy and opera based on works by ancient Greek and Roman writers. It runs roughly from late June to mid-July.

For more Roman ruins, head west on Kaiserstrasse, right onto Neustrasse and left onto Viehmarktplatz to the **Viehmarktthermen** (**15**; ☎ 9941 1057; adult/senior/student €2.10/1.60/1; 🕑 9am-5pm). Found by accident in the 1980s during construction of a parking garage, the ruins of these Roman baths are sheltered by a dramatic glass cube designed by Cologne architect OM Ungers. True thermal bath devotees still have the **Barbarathermen** (**16**; cnr Südallee & Friedrich-Wilhelm-Strasse; adult €2.10, senior/student €1.60, child €1; 🕑 9am-6pm Apr-Sep, 9am-5pm Oct-Mar), about five minutes southwest of here, to explore. Unfortunately, only bits of the foundation, cellars and floor-heating system survived a 17th-century raid for stones to build a school. Alternatively, head west to the Moselle and the **Römerbrücke (17)**, successor to a 2nd-century bridge of which five of the original seven pylons are still extant.

Wrap up the tour by dropping in at **Karl-Marx-Haus** (**18**; ☎ 970 680; Brückenstrasse 10; adult/concession €2/1; 🕑 1-6pm Mon, 10am-6pm Tue-Sun, reduced hours Nov-Mar) a respectable baroque town house where the author of *Das Kapital* was born in 1818. Marx left town at age 17 to attend universities in Bonn, Berlin and Jena. The permanent exhibition focuses not only on his life and ideas, but also on his associate Friedrich Engels.

Tours

City Walking Tour (adult/child €6/3; 🕑 1.30pm Sat May-Oct) Two-hour tour in English.
Mosel Boat Tours (☎ 266 66; prices €7-25) One-hour to all-day tours, daily from May to October. Departures from the boat docks at Zurlaubener Ufer.
Römer-Express (☎ 9935 9525; adult/child €6/3; 🕑 10am-6pm Apr-Oct, reduced operation Nov-Mar) Thirty-minute trolley-bus tour in three languages.
Wine Tastings (€4.50-8.50; 🕑 10am-6pm) Five local vintners take turns hosting this; ask at the tourist office for a schedule.

Sleeping

Hille's Hostel (☎ 710 2785; www.hilles-hostel-trier.de; Gartenfeldstrasse 7; dm €14, s/d €27/32; 🗷) Original

artwork, a piano lounge and a full kitchen make this independent hostel a great place to stay. The spacious, brightly decorated rooms have private bathrooms. Walk to trains, sights and nightlife.

Weinhaus Becker (☎ 938 080; www.weinhaus-becker.de; Olewiger Strasse 206; s/d €45/80; 🅿) About 2km east of the centre, in the wine district of Olewig, this small hotel pairs down-to-earth accommodation with a Michelin-starred restaurant (four-course meals from €60). Rooms in the back are quieter and bigger, while some street-facing ones have balconies.

Hotel Deutscher Hof (☎ 977 80; www.hotel-deutscher-hof.de; Südallee 25; s €60-85, d €90-110; 🅿 🗷) This centrally located hotel offers a pleasant combination of business and personal flair. The fairly generic rooms feature all modern amenities, and the sauna environment with rooftop terrace is a welcome bonus.

Hotel Villa Hügel (☎ 33066; www.hotel-villa-huegel.de; Bernhardstrasse 14; s €69-82, d €97-133; 🅿 🗷 🖳) Days at this stylish hilltop Art Nouveau villa begin with a lavish champagne breakfast buffet and might end luxuriating in the indoor pool with sauna. Views are great from the terrace and from many of the rooms.

Other recommendations are:
DJH hostel (☎ 146 620; www.djh-info.de; An der Jugendherberge 4; d/q €21.90/16.90 per person; 🅿 🗷) Spick-and-span hostel right on the Moselle; take bus No 12 from the Hauptbahnhof.
Mercure Trier An den Kaiserthermen (☎ 937 70; www.mercure.de; Metzer Allee 6; s €80-90, d €100-126; 🅿 🗷 🖳) Modern, well-run business hotel with weekend and seasonal specials.
Trier-City Camping (☎ 869 21; fax 830 79; Luxemburger Strasse 81) Year-round riverside camp site.

Eating

Palais Kesselstadt (☎ 402 04; Liebfrauenstrasse 10; restaurant mains €18-22, Weinstube daily €3-9; 🕑 closed Sun & Mon) Bring your best table manners when dining on innovative seasonal fare at this sumptuous gourmet restaurant draped in peach and pea colours. Alternatively, just order a snack from the attached self-service wine bar and hunker down beneath the chestnuts with views of the Dom.

Gasthaus Mosellied (☎ 265 88; Zurlaubener Ufer 86; mains €6-15) This is just one of several ambience-laden pubs along Zalaawen, as the locals call this idyllic quarter hugging

RHINELAND-PALATINATE

the Moselle. Balmy summer nights on the terrace are ideal for enjoying hearty meals, best washed down with a cold glass of potent cider known as *Viez*.

Krim (☎ 739 43; Glockenstrasse 7; mains €7-14) This bustling bistro with a beautiful interior wouldn't be out of place in Provence, but here it is in ancient Trier. The chef gets creative from morning till midnight with Mediterranean cuisine, offering snacks to three-course meals.

Zum Domstein (☎ 744 90; Am Hauptmarkt 5; mains €6-17, 5-course Roman dinners €23-32) Feast like the ancient Romans on dishes inspired by a 2000-year-old cookbook discovered during excavations beneath this very restaurant. German fare is also served.

Other recommendations include:

Havanna (☎ 994 2093; Viehmarktplatz 8; mains €7-12) Pizza to schnitzel as Che and Fidel look on. Trendy.

AStArix (☎ 722 39; Karl-Marx-Strasse 11; meals around €5) Popular student hang-out with good pizza and casseroles (enter through the arcade).

Getting There & Away

Trier is about a 60km or 1¼-hour bus ride from Frankfurt-Hahn airport. **Jozi-Reisen** (☎ 06502-5090; adult €12, child to 12 €8) operates shuttle buses to/from the Hauptbahnhof throughout the day. The airport in Luxembourg, about a 30-minute drive away, is served by the **Airport-Liner** (☎ 942 75), a shuttle that must be ordered 48 hours in advance (€12).

Trier has several hourly train connections to Saarbrücken (€12.40, one to 1½ hours) and Koblenz (€15.60, 1½ to two hours). There are also frequent trains to Luxembourg with onward connections to Paris. Regional buses to the Eifel or Hunsrück Mountains leave from outside the Hauptbahnhof.

The city is connected to the A1 and A48 via the short A602 and is also crisscrossed by several Bundesstrassen from all directions.

Getting Around

Trier has a comprehensive public bus system, though the city centre is best explored on foot. Single tickets cost €1.40, day passes are €4. All are sold by bus drivers.

Rental bikes are available from the **Radstation Bahnhof** (☎ 148 856) in the Hauptbahnhof, at the DJH hostel and at Trier-City Camping (see Sleeping, p521). They cost between €6 and €10 per day.

BERNKASTEL-KUES

☎ 06531 / pop 7500

This charming twin town, some 50km downriver from Trier, is the hub of the middle Moselle region and swarms with visitors all summer long. Bernkastel, on the right bank, is a symphony in half-timber and teems with wine taverns. Kues, the birthplace of theologian Nicolas Cusanus (1401–64), has less of a fairy-tale flair but contains the town's most important sights.

The bus station is next to the boat docks in Bernkastel.

Information

Post office (☎ 960 413; Im Viertheil 25)

Sparkasse (☎ 950 480; Am Gestade 3b) Bank.

Tourist information (☎ 4023/24; www.bernkastel.de; Am Gestade 6, Bernkastel; ☻ 8.30am-12.30pm & 1-5pm Mon-Fri, 10am-5pm Sat, 10am-1pm Sun Easter-Oct, to 3.30pm Fri & closed weekends Nov-Easter) Offers Internet access to visitors.

Sights & Activities

Bernkastel's **Markt**, one of the prettiest squares along the Moselle, is a romantic ensemble of half-timbered houses with beautifully decorated gables. Note the **medieval pillory** to the left of the Rathaus. On Karlsstrasse, southwest of the Markt, the tiny **Spitzhäuschen** resembles a giant bird's house with its narrow base topped by a much larger, precariously leaning, upper floor. More such crooked gems line Römerstrasse and its side streets. Also take a look inside the 14th-century **Pfarrkirche St Michael**, whose tower – ringed by a crown of turrets – was originally part of the fortification wall.

A pleasant way to get your heart pumping is by hoofing it up to the **Burgruine Landshut**, a ruined 13th-century castle framed by vineyards, which should take 30 to 60 minutes. You'll be rewarded with glorious river valley views and a cold drink at the café-beer garden. The less robust can catch a ride on the **Burg Landshut-Express** (up/down/return €3.50/2.50/5; ☻ hourly 10am-6pm Easter-Oct).

In Kues, most sights are conveniently grouped in the **St-Nikolaus-Hospital** (☎ 2260; Cusanusstrasse 2; admission free; ☻ 9am-6pm Mon-Fri, 9am-3.30pm Sat), a hospice founded by Cusanus for 33 men (one for every year of Christ's life) over the age of 50. You're free to explore the inner courtyard, Gothic chapel and cloister at leisure, but the treasure-filled library can only be seen on a guided **tour** (€4; ☉ 10.30am Tue & 3pm Fri Apr-Oct).

After you've drunk in all this cultural splendour, it's time to follow up with a visit to the **Mosel-Weinmuseum** (☎ 4141; adult/child €2/1; ☉ 10am-5pm mid-Apr-Oct, 2-5pm Nov-mid-Apr) and, most important to many, a stop at the adjacent **Vinothek** (☉ 10am-5pm mid-Apr-Oct, 2-5pm Nov-mid-Apr). Here, in the hospice's historical cellars, you can get thoroughly acquainted with Moselle wines during an 'all-you-can-drink' wine tasting for €9. Bottles are available for purchase from €5.

Sleeping & Eating
DJH hostel (☎ 2395; jh-bernkastel-kues@djh-info.de; Jugendherbergsstrasse 1; dm €12.30) The local hostel is fairly basic by today's standards and scenically but inconveniently located above town next to Burgruine Landshut.

Campingplatz Kueser Werth (☎ 8200; fax 8282; Am Hafen 2; site/person/car €3.50/4.50/1.50; ☉ Apr-Oct) About 1km upriver on the Kues side.

Camping Schenk (☎ 8176; fax 7681; Hauptstrasse 165; tent & car €4.60, person €4.35; ☉ Easter-Oct) A second camping option, in the district of Wehlen.

Hotel-Restaurant Weinhaus St Maximilian (☎ 965 00; www.hotel-sankt-maximilian.de; Saarallee 12; s €31-44, d €57-52; **P**) Run by a family of wine makers, this place uses Persian carpets, window drapes and crisp tablecloths to build an appealingly old-fashioned ambience.

Hotel Bären (☎ 950 440; www.hotel-baeren.de; Schanzstrasse 9; s €39-86, d €67-98; **P** ✗ 🖵) A new-generation Moselle hotel, the Bären pairs youthful flair with old-fashioned service. The sun-flooded bistro serves light dishes (€4 to €14) and drinks.

Altes Brauhaus (☎ 2552; Gestade 4; mains €7-17) Lunch on the riverside terrace of this tradition-rich restaurant is a treat. The kitchen produces the usual meaty German classics but also does interesting things with shrimp, fish and vegetables.

Getting Around
Hire bikes at **Fun Bike Team** (☎ 940 24; Schanzstrasse 22).

TRABEN-TRARBACH
☎ 06541 / pop 6200
It's hard to imagine today that this peaceful twin town, 24km from Bernkastel-Kues,

was once in the cross hairs of warring factions during the War of the Palatine Succession in the late 17th century. Two ruined fortresses are all that survive from those tumultuous times, which were followed by a long period of prosperity as the town became a centre of wine making and trading. Traben lost its medieval look to three major fires but was well compensated with beautiful Art Nouveau villas, a feature unique to the Moselle. It joined with Trarbach across the river in 1904.

Orientation
Traben, on the left bank, is the commercial centre and home to the tourist office and the train station. It's a five-minute walk south on Bahnstrasse to the town centre.

Information
Kreissparkasse (Bahnstrasse 41, Traben) Bank.
Post office (☎ 7040; Poststrasse, Traben)
Tourist information (☎ 839 80; www.traben-trarbach .de; Bahnstrasse 22; ☉ 9am-6pm Mon-Fri, 11am-5pm Sat Easter-Oct, to 4pm & closed Sat Nov-Easter)

Sights & Activities
The ruined medieval **Grevenburg** sits high in the craggy hills above Trarbach and is reached from Markt via a steep footpath. Because of its strategic importance, the castle changed owners 13 times, found itself under siege six times and was destroyed seven times. No wonder two walls are all that are left of it. Across the river, the giant **Mont Royal** fortress, built by French king Louis XIV as a base from which to expand his hold over the Rhineland, suffered pretty much the same fate.

Learn more about these castles and their roles in history at the **Mittelmosel-Museum** (☎ 9480; Casinostrasse 2; adult/concession €4/2; ☉ closed Mon), housed in a baroque villa famous for once hosting Johann Wolfgang von Goethe.

Of the town's fanciful **Art Nouveau villas**, the most sparkly – and indeed the only one open to the public – is the **Hotel Bellevue** (see p524), easily recognised by its champagne bottle–shaped slate turret. The oak-panelled lobby and especially the coloured windows in the restaurant are prime features of the style brought to town by Berlin architect Bruno Möhring. He also designed the **Brückentor**, on the Trarbach side, the town landmark which houses a wine tavern and gallery.

Traben-Trarbach is also a spa town with hot mineral springs in its district of Bad Wildstein. Experience these healing waters at the **Moseltherme** (☎ 830 30; Wildsteiner Weg; ✆ pool 9am-9pm Mon-Thu, 9am-6pm Sat & Sun, sauna 3-9pm Mon, 3-10pm Tue, 3pm-midnight Wed-Fri, 10am-6pm Sat & Sun), which also offers a menu of massages, aromatherapy and beauty treatments. Day passes to the pool and sauna are €11, while two hours in the pool only are €5.

The tourist office organises daily wine tastings and cellar tours (€6) with different vintners.

Sleeping

Altstadt Café (☎ 810 625; fax 4605; Mittelstrasse 12, Trarbach; s/d/tr €25/48/72) Rooms are plain and simple but of a decent size and clean. The café is in a quiet side street, but there's a bar and beer garden attached.

Hotel Bellevue (☎ 7030; www.bellevue-hotel.de; Am Moselufer; s €71-89, d €120-200; ℗ ☒ ☒) Classy, romantic and historic, this exquisite Art Nouveau hotel is the choicest place to stay in Traben. Perks include bike and canoe hire, pool, sauna and beauty farm and a gourmet restaurant (mains €10 to €18).

Other recommendations are:

DJH hostel (☎ 9278; jh-traben-trarbach@djh-info.de; Hirtenpfad 6; d/q €20.90/15.90 per person) All rooms at this modern hostel have private bathrooms. It's a 15-minute walk from the train station.

Campingplatz Wolf (☎ 9174; Wedenhofstrasse 25; tent/person €5.50/3.80; ✆ mid-Apr–Oct) About 3km south of town.

Campingplatz Rissbach (☎ 3111; Rissbacher Strasse 155; tent/person €6.50/4.80; ✆ mid-Apr–mid-Oct)

Eating

Zum Graifen (☎ 811075; Wolfer Weg 11; light meals under €8) This lovely wine restaurant offers a modern take on Moselle romanticism and serves delicious, freshly prepared light meals. Cap a day of sightseeing off in the sculpture-studded garden overlooking the river or in the candle-lit winter garden amid an eclectic assortment of antiques and bric-a-brac.

Alte Zunftscheune (☎ 9737; Neue Rathausstrasse 13; mains €8-15; ✆ from 5pm, closed Mon) This rustic eatery stuffed with whimsical knick-knacks is a nice place for good wine and grilled meats while seated in the vaulted cellar, small garden or squeezed onto ancient church pews.

Alte Ratschenke (☎ 9357; Kirchstrasse 19; mains €9-16; closed Wed) Dine on classic German cuisine at this friendly restaurant in the only surviving half-timbered house that survived the big fires.

Getting Around

Rent bikes at **Zweirad Wagner** (☎ 1649; Brückenstrasse 42, Trarbach; €7/40 day/week), where staff can also help with repairs.

COCHEM

☎ 02671 / pop 5300

Cochem, another 40km downriver, has all the trappings of a picture-postcard river village, complete with castle, narrow alleyways, half-timbered houses and town gates. But it's almost too cute for comfort and often drowns in day-trippers coming from Koblenz, some 60km away. Cochem's train station is at the northern end of town, from where it's only a short walk down Ravenéstrasse or Moselstrasse to the centre.

Information

Murphy's (☎ 980 107; Endertstrasse 11) Internet access.

Post office (Ravenéstrasse)

Sparkasse (☎ 6010; Brückenstrasse 2) Bank.

Tourist information (☎ 600 40; www.cochem.de; Endertplatz 1; ✆ 9am-5pm Mon-Thu, 9am-6pm Fri Apr-Oct, plus 9am-5pm Sat May-Oct & 10am-noon Sun Jul-Oct, closed weekends & lunch Nov-Mar)

Volksbank (Markt)

Sights & Activities

Cochem's *pièce de résistance* is the **Reichsburg** (☎ 255; adult/child €4/2; ✆ 9am-5pm mid-Mar–Nov), which must be seen on a 40-minute guided tour in German (ask for a free translation sheet). Although it matches everyone's imagined version of a medieval castle, it only dates from the 19th century, the 11th-century original having fallen victim to frenzied Frenchmen in 1689. The walk up to the castle takes about 15 minutes.

For great views of the town and river, catch the chairlift to the **Pinnerkreuz** (☎ 989 063; one way/return €4/5.50; ✆ 9.30am-6.30pm Easter–mid-Nov) leaving from Endertstrasse. It's a pleasant walk back down through the vineyards.

Sleeping & Eating

DJH hostel (☎ 8633; jh-cochem@djh-info.de; Klottener Strasse 9; d/q per person €21.90/15.90) Freshly renovated, this hostel is as good as they get. Rooms are generously sized, well lit and nicely furnished; all have en suite facilities.

Hotel-Pension Garni Villa Tummelchen (☎ 910 520; www.villa-tummelchen.com; Schlossstrasse 22; s €40-55, d €64-84; **P** ⊠) Enjoy the splendid views from the terrace or balconied rooms, nicely decorated in a romantic style. For that complete princess feel, opt for a room with a four-poster bed.

Moselromantikhotel Thul (☎ 914 150; www .hotel-thul.de; s €47-66, d €74-124; **P**) In an idyllic location, close to forest and vineyards, this hotel is a great retreat from Cochem's tourist bustle. Rooms are comfortable but surprisingly uninspired décor, making the café-restaurant, terrace, lounge with fireplace and fitness room with sauna better places to hang out.

Zom Stüffje (☎ 7260; Oberbachstrasse 14; mains €7-18) Tucked away off the main drag uphill from Markt, this cosy eatery is richly decorated in dark timber and murals and serves classic German fare with only a few meat-free selections.

Getting There & Away
Trains to Cochem leave Koblenz several times per hour (€6.80, 30 to 45 minutes). Boats to Beilstein and beyond also leave regularly.

AROUND COCHEM
Beilstein
On the right bank of the Moselle, about 12km upriver from Cochem, Beilstein (population 160) is a pint-size village right out of the world of fairy tales. It's little more than a cluster of houses squeezed into whatever space has not been taken up by steep vineyards.

Beilstein's romantic townscape is further enhanced by the ruined **Burg Metternich**, a hilltop castle reached via a set of steps. There's little to do here but soak up the atmosphere during a stroll through the tiny lanes, taste some wine in one of the many cellars or walk up to the castle.

One of the finest buildings is the **Zehnthauskeller** where, in the Middle Ages, wine delivered as a tithing was stored. It now houses a romantically dark, vaulted wine tavern.

From Cochem, catch bus No 8060 or take the boat.

Burg Eltz
Victor Hugo thought this castle was 'tall, terrific, strange and dark', adding that he'd never seen anything like it. Indeed, **Burg Eltz** (☎ 02672-950 500; adult/concession €6/4.50, entry to treasury adult/child €2.50/1.50; ⊙ 9.30am-5.30pm Apr-Oct), hidden away in the forest above the left bank of the Moselle, epitomizes to many what medieval castles should look like.

The compact and impenetrable exterior is softened by scores of turrets crowning it like candles on a birthday cake. Eight residential towers stand gathered around an oval courtyard.

Burg Eltz has been owned by the same family for almost 1000 years and has never been destroyed. Highlights of the often-crowded guided tour include the **Flag Room**, with its fan vaulted ceiling, and the festive **Knights' Hall**. The **treasury**, which extends four floors beneath the rock, features a rich collection of jewellery, porcelain and priceless weapons.

The only direct access to Eltz, about 30km from either Koblenz or Cochem, is by private vehicle via the village of Münstermaifeld. The castle is about 800m from the car park and is also served by shuttle (€1.50). Alternatively, take a train to the village of Moselkern (from Koblenz €5.10, 30 minutes; from Cochem €3.05, 20 minutes) and follow the trail from the Ringelsteiner Mühle car park for about 40 minutes.

HUNSRÜCK MOUNTAINS

IDAR-OBERSTEIN
☎ 06781 / pop 34,300

Since the Middle Ages, Idar-Oberstein's history has been inextricably linked to gemstone production and trade. Records of agate mining go back to 1454, but the industry really took off in the early 19th century after local adventurers left for South America (especially Brazil), where they harvested raw stones as if they were potatoes, then sent them back home to be processed. The local mines have long since been exhausted, but Idar-Oberstein has remained a major gem-cutting and jewellery-manufacturing centre and is also home to Europe's only combined diamond and gemstone exchange. City streets are lined with shops selling local products as well as minerals of all types.

Orientation

Idar-Oberstein is an unwieldy town. It stretches for about 20km along the steeply forested and narrow valley carved by the Nahe River which, alas, here is almost completely buried beneath the modern town. The train station is in Oberstein and a short walk from the Hauptstrasse, the partly pedestrianised main commercial drag, which leads to Markt, the main square. Most of the major sights are in Idar and the outlying suburbs and are best reached by car, although they're also served by public bus from the Hauptbahnhof.

Information

For visitor information go to the main **tourist information** (☎ 644 21; www.idar-oberstein.de; Georg-Maus-Strasse 2; ☺ 9am-5pm Mon-Thu, 9am-1pm Fri) which also has a **branch office** (Hauptstrasse 436, at Museum Idar-Oberstein; ☺ 9am-5.30pm Apr-Oct, 10am-5.30pm Nov-Mar).

Sights & Activities

Not surprisingly, most of Idar-Oberstein's attractions involve gemstones, and you can learn about every stage of production from raw stone to brilliant bauble.

A major draw in Oberstein is the **Museum Idar-Oberstein** (☎ 246 19; Hauptstrasse 436; adult/child €3.60/2.10; ☺ 9am-5.30pm), near Markt, where visitors in the know make a beeline for the fluorescent room where special lamps produce interesting light effects. Also of note is the collection of crystals and quartz.

Hugging a niche in the rock face above Markt, and reached via 230 steps, is the landmark 15th-century **Felsenkirche** (Chapel in the Rocks; ☎ 228 40; adult/child €2/0.50; ☺ 10am-6pm Apr-Oct), said to be built by a local knight in atonement for the murder of his brother. A steadily trickling well and precious altar are among the most appealing features here.

From the church it's a 20-minute uphill hike through a beech forest to the twin castles of **Burg Bosselstein**, a ruin dating from 1196, and **Schloss Oberstein** (☎ 1320; admission free; ☺ year round). At the top, you'll be rewarded with great views over the town, the Hunsrück Mountains and the Nahe Valley.

In a nature park west of Idar is the **Edelsteinminen Steinkaulenberg** (☎ 474 00; tours adult/child €4/2.50; ☺ 9am-5pm mid-Mar–mid-Nov), the only gemstone mine in Europe open to visitors. Agates were still mined in this glit-

tering underground world until 1870, but nowadays only hobby prospectors dig for treasure in a designated 'miner's tunnel'. For adult/concession €13/5, you can keep whatever agates, amethysts, jasper, crystals or other gemstones you unearth during three hours of digging. Finds are guaranteed, but reservations are required. Nondiggers may visit the mines on a 30-minute guided tour. To get there, take bus No 3 to Strassburgkaserne.

To learn how gemstones were traditionally processed, visit the 17th-century **Historische Weiherschleife** (Historical Pond Mill; ☎ 315 13; Tiefensteiner Strasse 87; adult/child €3/2; ☺ 10am-6pm mid-Mar–mid-Nov, 10am-4pm Mon-Fri mid-Nov–mid-Dec & mid-Feb–mid-Mar), the last of nearly 200 such water-powered cutting mills that once stood along the Idarbach creek. Cutters lying belly-down atop tilting benches demonstrate the sawing, grinding, sanding and polishing procedures – a rather backbreaking way to earn a living. Take bus No 1 to the Weiherschleife stop.

The 9000 exhibits at the **Deutsches Edelsteinmuseum** (☎ 900 980; Hauptstrasse 118, Idar; adult/child €4.20/3.20; ☺ 9am-6pm May-Oct, 10am-5.30pm Nov-Apr, closed Mon in Nov, Jan & Feb) should dazzle even the most, well, jaded of visitors. Highlights include a 12.555 carat topaz from Brazil and copies of the famous Hope and Koh-i-Nor diamonds. Take bus No 1, 2 or 3 to Börse.

Sleeping & Eating

DJH hostel (☎ 243 66; jh-idar-oberstein@djh-info.de; Alte Treibe 23; d/q €20.90/15.90 per person; P ✗) Those travelling on a tight budget might wish to opt for the well-modernised hostel, where each room has a private bathroom.

Naturfreundehaus (☎ 224 50; www.naturfreundehaus-alte-treibe.de; Alte Treibe 25; beds from €10.50; P ✗) Adjacent to the hostel, this is another good budget option.

Edelstein-Hotel (☎ 502 50; www.edelstein-hotel.de; Hauptstrasse 302, Oberstein; s/d €52/75; P ⌨) It's not terribly stylish, but the owners are enthusiastic and helpful, and the handsome pool and sauna area offer a perfect retreat on a rainy day. Some rooms sleep up to four, making this a good choice for families.

Gästehaus Amethyst (☎ 700 01; www.gaestehaus-amethyst.de; Hauptstrasse 324, Oberstein; d €66; P) This pocket-size pension offers much more than meets the eye, such as a spanking-clean sauna, a fitness room and a wine tavern. It's central, the rooms are nicely furnished and filled with amenities, and the owners delightful.

Park Hotel (☎ 509 00; www.parkhotel-idaroberstein .de; Hauptstrasse 185; s €67-125, d €92-180; P ⊠ ⊠) There's a new kid in town and it's as polished as a freshly cut diamond. Classically furnished rooms and suites complement the equally posh public spaces, including two restaurants, a clubby cigar lounge and elegant bar. Choose from three room types. It's halfway between Idar and Oberstein.

Unless you're a vegetarian, you shouldn't leave Idar-Oberstein without trying the local speciality, *Spiessbraten*. This is a large hunk of beef or pork, marinated in raw onion, salt and pepper, then grilled over a beechwood fire, which gives it its characteristic spicy and smoky taste. Almost all local restaurants serve this dish, but the **Badischer Hof** (☎ 240 71; Hauptstrasse 377; mains €9-18) scores high in the popularity department.

Getting There & Around

Idar-Oberstein is about 80km east of Trier and about 90km northeast of Saarbrücken. The airport at Frankfurt-Hahn is about 30km away and served by shuttle bus five times daily (€5.30, one hour). There are direct train connections with Saarbrücken (€10.70, one hour), Mainz (€9.50, one hour) and Frankfurt (€18.40, 1¾ hours). Travel to Trier requires a change in Saarbrücken (€22, two hours). The B41 and the B422 cross in Idar-Oberstein.

Local bus Nos 1, 2, 3 and 4 regularly shuttle between Oberstein and Idar.

SAARLAND

Saarland

CONTENTS

History 530
Saarbrücken 530
Around the Saarland 534

The Saarland is one of the most surprising and overlooked of the German states. Traditionally a land of coal mining and heavy industry, it has undergone thorough economic restructuring, cleaned up its air and streams, and developed a thriving tourism and leisure infrastructure. Its capital, Saarbrücken, is a vibrant city with good museums and a high-quality culinary scene. Rolling hills and forest cover much of the countryside, which can be explored not only by car but also on foot or bicycle along sign-posted long-distance routes. Trails include those following the gentle valley of the Saar River or the challenging grades around St Wendel, a mountain-biker mecca and world cup championship site for that sport.

Archaeology fans can meander in the footsteps of the Romans and Celts who've left their traces all over the state. Even the Saarland's industrial heritage is celebrated rather than ignored in such places as the Völklinger Hütte ironworks. This perfectly preserved monument to the Industrial Age has even garnered protection as a Unesco World Heritage Site.

France and Germany have played ping pong with the Saarland many times, coveting it for its rich supply of coal and other natural resources. In the 20th century alone, the region was under French control twice – after both world wars – until its people eventually voted in favour of returning to Germany.

Although now solidly within German boundaries, the influence of the land of baguette and Piaf is still felt in many ways. Most locals are bilingual and signs in the border towns often sport both languages. The standard greeting is not 'Hallo' but 'Salü', a variation of the French 'Salut'. Their French heritage has softened the Saarlanders who tend to be a rather relaxed sort of folk with an appreciation of good food, wine and company.

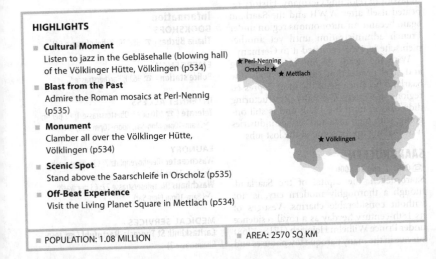

HIGHLIGHTS

- **Cultural Moment**
  Listen to jazz in the Gebläsehalle (blowing hall) of the Völklinger Hütte, Völklingen (p534)

- **Blast from the Past**
  Admire the Roman mosaics at Perl-Nennig (p535)

- **Monument**
  Clamber all over the Völklinger Hütte, Völklingen (p534)

- **Scenic Spot**
  Stand above the Saarschleife in Orscholz (p535)

- **Off-Beat Experience**
  Visit the Living Planet Square in Mettlach (p534)

★ Perl-Nennig
Orscholz ★ ★ Mettlach

★ Völklingen

- POPULATION: 1.08 MILLION
- AREA: 2570 SQ KM

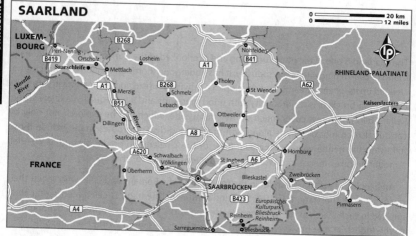

HISTORY

Already settled in Celtic and Roman times, the Saarland was periodically governed by France throughout the Middle Ages. After Napoleon's defeat at Waterloo in 1815, it was divided by Prussia and Bavaria, both of whom wanted the area for its rich pockets of coal to fuel the burgeoning German economy. Under the Treaty of Versailles following WWI Germany lost the Saarland, and it became an independent territory administered by the League of Nations under French guidance. In a referendum held in 1935, however, some 90% of voters decided in favour of rejoining Germany. History repeated itself after WWII and the Saarland again became an autonomous region under French administration until yet another plebiscite in 1955 returned it to Germany.

With the steady decline of coal mining and steel production since the 1960s, the Saarland became one of the most depressed regions in western Germany. Restructuring didn't begin until the 1980s and is still ongoing, with high-tech and service industries now making up for some of the lost jobs.

SAARBRÜCKEN

☎ 0681 / pop 200,000

Saarbrücken, the capital of the Saarland, though a thoroughly modern city, is not without considerable charms. Vestiges of its 18th-century heyday as a royal residence under Prince Wilhelm Heinrich (1718–1768) survive in the many baroque townhouses and churches designed by his prolific and skilled court architect, Friedrich Joachim Stengel. The historic centre around St Johanner Markt (square) brims with excellent restaurants and cafés, and there's a pleasant promenade for strolls along the Saar River.

Orientation

Saarbrücken's centre is fairly compact. It's bisected by the Saar River, which runs southeast to northwest, parallel to the A620. The Hauptbahnhof is at the northwestern end of the centre, with St Johanner Markt about a 15-minute walk away.

Information

BOOKSHOPS

Thalia Bücher (☎ 388 30; Bahnhofstrasse 54)

EMERGENCY

Police station (☎ 9620; Karcherstrasse 5)

INTERNET ACCESS

Telecafé (☎ 910 0677; Obertorstrasse 1; €2 per hr; ☺ 9am-10pm Mon-Sat, noon-10pm Sun)

LAUNDRY

Waschcenter (Beethovenplatz 7; €3.50 per wash; ☺ 7am-11pm Mon-Sat)
Waschhaus (Nauwieserstrasse 22; €3 per wash; ☺ 8am-10pm Mon-Sat)

MEDICAL SERVICES

Caritasklinik St Theresia-Rastpfuhl (☎ 4060; Rheinstrasse 2)

MONEY
Reisebank (Hauptbahnhof; ☾ 7am-7.45pm Mon-Fri, 8.30am-4pm Sat) Also has an ATM.

POST
Main post office (Hauptbahnhof; ☾ 8am-6.30pm Mon-Fri, 9am-1pm Sat)
Branch office (cnr Dudweilerstrasse & Kaiserstrasse)

TOURIST INFORMATION
Tourist Information (☎ 938 090; www.die-region-saarbruecken.de; Saar-Galerie, Reichsstrasse 1; ☾ 9am-6pm Mon-Fri, 10am-4pm Sat)

Sights
NORTHERN SAAR BANK
The heart of Saarbrücken, and its nightlife hub, is the historic **St Johanner Markt**, a stretched-out square anchored by an ornate fountain designed by Stengel and flanked by some of the town's oldest buildings. It's easily reached from the Hauptbahnhof by following first Reichsstrasse, then Bahnhofstrasse south for about 800m. As you cross Betzenstrasse, look left and you'll spot the cathedral-like **Rathaus** (town hall), a neo-Gothic red-brick structure that's a fine example of turn-of-the-20th-century historicist architecture.

Also on St Johanner Markt is the **Stadtgalerie** (☎ 936 830; St Johanner Markt 24; admission free; ☾ 11am-7pm Tue & Thu-Sun, noon-8pm Wed), which presents the latest in contemporary art, including video and performance art. More Stengel awaits a block east and north on Türkenstrasse, this time in the form of the Catholic **Basilika St Johann**.

Heading south on Türkenstrasse, you'll find the massive yellow **Staatstheater** (☎ 322 04; Schillerplatz/Tbilisser Platz 1), a grandiose Nazi-era structure with neoclassical touches. It opened in 1938 with Richard Wagner's *The Flying Dutchman* and today presents opera, ballet, musicals and drama.

A short walk east is one of Saarbrücken's cultural highlights, the **Saarland Museum** (☎ 996 4220; Bismarckstrasse 11-19; adult/senior/student €6/4/2; ☾ 10am-6pm Tue & Thu-Sun, 10am-10pm Wed). It encompasses several collections, including the **Modern Galerie** which tracks the development of European art throughout the 20th-century. It's especially noteworthy for its German Impressionists – such as Slevogt, Corinth and Liebermann – and there are also fine examples by Expression-

ists like Kirchner, Marc and Jawlensky. As the name suggests, the **Alte Sammlung** (Old Collection) across the street goes back further in history with a millennium's worth of paintings, porcelain, tapestries and sculptures from both southwest Germany and the Alsace-Lorraine region of France.

SOUTHERN SAAR BANK
Crossing the Saar River via the Alte Brücke takes you straight to the Stengel-designed baroque **Schlossplatz**, which is orbited by three museums. The dominant building here is the **Saarbrücker Schloss**, which has risen from the ashes more times than an entire flock of phoenixes. It sports elements of several architectural styles, from Renaissance to baroque to neoclassical to a modern glass tower added in the 1980s.

Its basement and a modern adjacent annex houses the **Historisches Museum Saar** (☎ 506 4501; Am Schlossplatz 15; adult/concession €2.50/1.50; ☾ 10am-6pm Tue-Sun, 10am-8pm Thu, noon-6pm Sat), which has interesting exhibits about the region in the 20th century, with a focus on WWI, the Third Reich and the post-WWII years. There's an additional charge for special exhibits. Fans of archaeology will surely be entertained by the exhibits at the **Museum für Vor- und Frühgeschichte** (Museum of Early History & Prehistory; ☎ 954 0515; Am Schlossplatz 16; admission free; ☾ 9am-5pm Tue-Sat, 10am-6pm Sun).

A more curious display awaits at the **Abenteuer Museum** (☎ 517 47; Am Schlossplatz; adult/concession €2/1.50; ☾ 9am-1pm Tue & Wed, 3-7pm Thu & Fri, 10am-2pm 1st Sat of the month) in the **Altes Rathaus** on the square's north side. It's filled with a peculiar assortment of ethnic masks, sculptures and the like collected by adventurer Heinz Rox on his expeditions to Asia, Africa, South America and New Guinea. There's a panoramic view of the river and town from atop the wall to the east of the Schloss.

From the Schloss, head westward along Schlossstrasse to Eisenbahnstrasse and the handsome Ludwigsplatz, yet another Stengel masterpiece flanked by stately baroque townhouses. At the square's centre looms the 1775 **Ludwigskirche** (☾ 3-5pm Tue, 10am-noon Wed, 4-6pm Sat, 11am-noon Sun), which sports a façade festooned with Biblical figures and a pure, brilliant white interior with stylish stucco decoration. If the church is closed, you can sneak a peek through the windows of the vestibule.

SAARLAND

SAARBRÜCKEN

```
0                    200 m
0                    0.1 miles
```

INFORMATION	
Reisebank	1 C2
Saar-Galerie	(see 4)
Telecafé	2 D4
Thalia Bücher	3 C3
Tourist Information	4 B2
Waschcenter	5 C2
Waschhaus	6 D3

SIGHTS & ACTIVITIES	(p531)
Abenteuer Museum	(see 7)
Altes Rathaus	7 B4
Basilika St Johann	8 D4
Der Fahrradladen	9 D3
Historisches Museum Saar	(see 13)
Ludwigskirche	10 B4
Museum für Vor- und	
Frühgeschichte	11 B4
Rathaus	12 C3
Saarbrücker Schloss	13 C4
Saarland Museum (Alte	
Sammlung)	14 D4
Saarland Museum (Moderne	
Galerie)	15 D4
Staatstheater	16 C4
Stadtgalerie	17 C4

SLEEPING	(pp532-3)
Hotel am Triller	18 B4
Hotel Im Fuchs	19 C4
Hotel Madeleine	20 D3
Mercure Kongress Saarbrücken	21 B2

EATING	(p533)
Gasthaus Zum Stiefel	22 C4
Hauck, Das Weinhaus	23 C4
Kerwan	24 C4
Kulturcafé	(see 17)
Stiefelbräu	25 C4

TRANSPORT	(pp533-4)
Boat Landing	26 C4
Central Bus Station	27 B2

Tours

Saarbrücker Personenschifffahrt (☎ 340 84) runs various boat trips from the landing near the Staatstheater, but don't expect too much in the way of scenery. On most Saturdays from May to September, boats travel across the border to Sarreguemines in France (one way/return €10/14). If possible, try to make the trip on Tuesday (offered from mid-June to late August) to catch the town's excellent farmers market. Make advance bookings.

Sleeping
BUDGET

DJH hostel (☎ 330 40; jh-saarbrücken@djh-info.de; Meerwiesertalweg 31; d/q €21.90/16.90 per person) This hostel is on the Prinzenweiher lake in Saarbrücken's green belt, near the university in the northeast of town. It has a playground and barbecue facilities, and anglers can try their luck in the lake. Take bus No 49 or 69 from the Hauptbahnhof or No 19 from Beethovenplatz near the Rathaus to Prinzenweiher (Monday to Friday only).

Campingplatz Saarbrücken (☎ 517 80; Spicherer Berg; tent/person €6/4; ☼ Apr-Sep) This camp site is near the Deutsch-Französischer Garten south of the city centre. Take the bus No 42 from the Hauptbahnhof to Spicherer Weg. It's a five-minute walk from the bus stop and is situated at the edge of the lush Pfaffenwald woods, which make an ideal shaded getaway on a hot summer's day.

MID-RANGE

Mercure Kongress Saarbrücken (☎ 389 00; Hafenstrasse 8; www.mercure.de; s/d €66/79; P X 🖵) Although it caters primarily for the business crowd, this large hotel is worth a mention for offering lots of modern amenities at a great price, unless there's a major event or convention in town.

Hotel Meran (☎ 653 81; www.hotel-meran.de; Mainzer Strasse 69; s €51-77, d €72-93; 🍴) Despite the forebodingly grey façade, the Meran has some nice touches such as a pool and sauna, and fireplace lounge. Rooms are fairly standard; if you want quiet, opt for one facing the inner courtyard.

Hotel Im Fuchs (☎ 936 550; fax 936 5536; Kappenstrasse 12; s/d €52/71; X) Close to St Johanner Markt, this small and old-fashioned hotel is a great option for those planning on in-depth 'research' of the quarter's bars and restaurant scene.

Hotel Madeleine (☎ 322 28; www.hotel-madeleine.de; Cecilienstrasse 5; s €53-65, d €64-75) This central and friendly family-run hotel has 32 smallish rooms that are clean and comfortable, even if they could use a little help in the décor department.

TOP END

Hotel am Triller (☎ 580 000; Trillerweg 57; www.hotel-am-triller.de; s €99-111, d €136, ste €162-260; P X 🖵 🍴) Saarbrücken's most stylish hotel, on a quiet street uphill from Schlossplatz, has airy and artsy public areas and a Franco-German restaurant. The imaginatively designed themed suites, with names like Seventh Heaven and Four Seasons, relegate regular rooms to a distinctly second choice.

Eating

Saarbrücken has a lively and attractive restaurant and bar scene that centres on St Johanner Markt. Local dishes revolve around the humble potato but are well worth trying, including *Hoorische*, which are tasty potato dumplings sometimes stuffed with ground meats, and *Dibbelabbes*, a potato casserole with dried meat and leeks.

Gasthaus Zum Stiefel (☎ 936 45 16; Am Stiefel 2; mains €8-12) Saarbrücken's oldest restaurant brings in a wonderful range of people from students to theatre-goers to tourists. The menu features classic German and local dishes alongside home-spun creations such as the delicious *Bierhähnchen*

(beer chicken). In summer, try scoring a table in the romantic inner courtyard. The drink of choice is beer made by the local Bruch brewery, also served in the more rustic ambience of the next-door brew-pub, Stiefelbräu.

Hauck, Das Weinhaus (☎ 319 19; St Johanner Markt 7; mains €7-10) Wine fans should make a beeline for this delightful restaurant with its thumb-thick wine list and lots of choices by the glass. Olives, cheese and *Flammekuche* (Alsatian 'pizza' topped with cream and onion) are good accompaniments, but more substantial local and French fare is available too.

Kulturcafé (☎ 379 9200; St Johanner Markt 24; snacks €2-8) A café by day, this place attracts a youngish crowd after dark with its world music and stylish ethno-look décor.

Kerwan (☎ 938 57 00; Kappenstrasse 9; mains €4-8) This is the best place in town for Turkish and Lebanese specialities, including a fair number of meatless choices. Take away or eat inside amidst a curious mix of German and oriental décor.

Getting There & Away

AIR

Saarbrücken airport (☎ 06893-832 72) is about 14km east of town and offers mainly holiday charters and short hops within Germany, eg to Berlin-Tempelhof, Hamburg and Leipzig/Halle. Most are operated by locally-based **Cirrus Airlines** (0180-444 4888; www.cirrus-airlines.de), a Lufthansa affiliate.

BUS

The central bus station for local and regional buses is on Bahnhofsplatz outside the Hauptbahnhof. Bus No 40 takes you right to the Völklinger Hütte (see p534).

CAR & MOTORCYCLE

Saarbrücken is bisected by the A620 leading north along the Saar River to Merzig. It's also served by the A6 from Kaiserslautern and the A1 from the Moselle Valley. The B40 and B51 also cross the city.

TRAIN

Saarbrücken has at least hourly connections with Trier (€12.40, one hour), Idar-Oberstein (€10.70, 50 minutes) and Mainz (€22.60, 1¾ hours). Regional services to Völklingen (€2.50, 9 minutes) and Homburg

(€5.20, 30 minutes) leave about every half-hour. RE trains run directly to Frankfurt (€28, 2¼ hours).

Getting Around

Bus R10 makes the trip out to the airport throughout the day (€2.60).

For information on public transport in Saarbrücken, call ☎ 500 3377. Bus and tram tickets within the city cost €1.70 or €6.10 in packs of four. Individual day passes are €3.50, three-/five-person groups pay €4.80/6.60.

You can book a taxi on ☎ 330 33.

Bicycles may be hired from **Der Fahrradladen** (☎ 370 98; Nauwieserstrasse 19). Rates are €12.50 a day, plus €10 for each additional day; weekend rates (Friday to Monday) start at €25. There's a €25 deposit.

AROUND THE SAARLAND
Völklinger Hütte

About 10km northwest of Saarbrücken and on the banks of the Saar, is the former ironworks **Völklingen Hütte** (☎ 06898-910 0100; adult/concession €7.50/6; ☼ 10am-7pm Apr-Oct, 10am-6pm Nov-Mar Gebläsehalle only), one of Europe's great industrial monuments and a highlight of any visit to the Saarland. This giant foundry was in operation from 1872 to 1986 when it was left to succumb to rust and corrosion – like an abandoned set from a version of *Metropolis* that was never filmed. It took only a few years before its historical significance was recognised by none other than Unesco which placed it on its list of World Heritage Sites in 1994.

Today its vast blast furnaces and smelting houses exist not only as a testament to the Machine Age, but the site has also taken on new life as a cultural venue. Its halls regularly host intriguing art and photography exhibitions, including a permanent one in the blast furnace itself with images depicting the harsh life of the local foundrymen. In summer, the sweet sounds of jazz and world-music ring out every Friday night in the Gebläsehalle (blowing hall) with its original red and white tiled floor. Two viewing platforms offer unusual perspectives on this industrial 'cathedral', especially its impressive blast furnace group. Nights are a great time to visit when the entire compound is lit up like a vast science fiction set. Call and ask about times.

Guided tours in German take place at 11am and 3pm daily, or you can hire audioguides with English commentary for €5 and take your own 40-minute tour.

Völklingen is reached at least every 30 minutes by train from Saarbrücken; the ironworks is only a three-minute walk from the train station. Alternatively, take bus No 40 from the Hauptbahnhof. A bistro and beer garden are on the premises (April to November only).

Mettlach
☎ 06864 / pop 11,500

Mettlach, on the Saar River about 50km northwest of Saarbrücken, is at the heart of the prettiest section of the Saarland. For the last 200 years its history has been tied to the ceramics firm of Villeroy & Boch, which moved its factory and administrative headquarters into a former Benedictine Abbey in 1809.

Today it houses a predictably commercial, though not uninteresting, multimedia exhibit called **Keravision** (admission €2.50; ☼ 9am-6pm Mon-Fri, 9.30am-4pm Sat & Sun), which introduces the company's history and products. Tickets also give admission to the Keramikmuseum, under the same roof, with its collection of historical porcelain; it's open the same hours.

Those feeling so inclined can then stock up on discounted ceramics at several factory outlets in town. But before you do so be sure to take a stroll through the abbey park, home of the octagonal 990 **Alter Turm** (Old Tower), the burial place of the town's founder, Merovingian Duke Luitwin. Beside it is a refreshingly quirky walk-in piece of public art called **Living Planet Square**. It consists of a giant bird topiary (the 'Earth Spirit') overlooking six giant tile walls representing the continents, sometimes in a rather, shall we say, 'explicit' fashion. Called the 'World Map of Life', it's purportedly the world's largest ceramic puzzle. As you walk through the installation, your movement activates jungle noises. The work combines the slightly warped visions of multimedia artist André Heller and Stefan Szczesny and was originally shown at the Expo 2000 in Hanover.

Saarschleife Touristik (☎ 06864-8334; www.tourist-info.mettlach.de; Freiherr-vom-Stein-Strasse 64; ☼ 8.30am-4.30pm Mon-Fri) has information about the town and region.

Regional trains head out to Mettlach at least hourly from Saarbrücken (€6.60, 35 minutes). By road, take the Merzig-Schwemlingen exit off the A8 (Saarbrücken-Luxembourg) and then follow the B51 north.

Around Mettlach

The most scenic spot along the Saar River is the **Saarschleife**, where the river makes a spectacular hairpin loop. It's in the community of **Orscholz**, in a large nature park about 5km west of Mettlach (bus No 6300). The best viewing point is in Cloef, just a short walk through the forest from the village. Just look for signs saying Cloef or ask for directions.

If you want to experience the loop from a boat, you can take a 1½-hour cruise offered by **Mettlacher-Personenschifffahrt** (☎ 06864-802 20; adult/concession €7/3.50) with several departures daily from March to December. Boats leave from the docks in Mettlach.

Perl-Nennig

☎ 06866 / pop 6350

Perl-Nennig is right on the border with Luxembourg, about 20km west of Mettlach and 40km south of Trier. It is the Saarland's only wine-growing community and specialises in burgundies. On weekends between April and October, the wine growers open up their cellars for tastings on a rotating basis.

The main historical sight located here is the stunning 160-sq-metre floor **mosaic** in a 3rd-century reconstructed **Roman villa** (☎ 1329; Römerstrasse 11; adult/concession €1.50/0.75; ⏲ 8.30am-noon & 1-6pm Tue-Sun Apr-Sep, 9-11.30am & 1-4pm Tue-Sun Oct-Mar, closed Dec). Composed of three million tiny chips of coloured stone, it's the largest and best preserved such mosaic north of the Alps. It shows scenes from a performance at an amphitheatre. A farmer discovered it by accident while digging in his field in 1852.

The **tourist office** (☎ 1439; fax 1728; Bübinger Strasse 1a; ⏲ 9.30am-12.30pm & 2-5pm Mon-Fri), right by the train station in Nennig, can provide information on the villa, wine tastings and accommodation. It also hires out bicycles.

Perl-Nennig can be reached from Mettlach by bus No 6300. It also makes for an easy excursion from Trier, from where it is served by train at least every two hours (get off at Nennig; €5.50, 40 minutes). If you're travelling in from Saarbrücken, take the train to Merzig, then change to bus No 6300. Drivers can take the A8 from Saarbrücken or the B419 from Trier.

Europäischer Kulturpark Bliesbruck-Reinheim

About 25km southeast of Saarbrücken, in the charming Blies Valley, the **Europäischer Kulturpark Bliesbruck-Reinheim** (European Archaeological Park; ☎ 06843-900 225; Robert-Schuman-Strasse 2; adult/concession €4.60/3.10; ⏲ 10am-6pm Tue-Sun mid-Mar–Oct) stretches across the French-German border over what was a large Gallo-Roman crafts town between the 1st and 4th centuries. Most of the foundations of the artisans' houses, with their ovens, cellars and heating systems, as well as the settlement's thermal baths, are on the French side. The area's most spectacular discovery, the **tomb of a Celtic princess** from 400 AD, was found in 1954 in Reinheim, on the German side of the border. There's a walk-in reconstruction of the necropolis, along with replicas of the jewellery, drinking vessels and other objects found entombed with her body.

Getting to the park from Saarbrücken by public transport is a one-hour journey that requires taking a train to Blieskastel and changing to bus K501. By car, it's country road most of the way.

Hesse

CONTENTS

Frankfurt-am-Main	538
Darmstadt	554
Around Darmstadt	555
Wiesbaden	555
Lahn Valley	558
Marburg	558
Fulda	560
Kassel	561

The Hessians, a Frankish tribe, were among the first people to convert to Lutheranism in the early 16th century. Apart from a brief period of unity under the aegis of Philip the Magnanimous, Hesse (Hessen) remained a motley collection of squabbling principalities and, later, of Prussian administrative districts until it was made a state in 1945. Today it's the fifth most populous of the Bundesländer; the main cities are the economic heavyweight (and nightlife mecca) Frankfurt-am-Main, the charming, deceptively small state capital Wiesbaden, and the park-tastic tourist favourite Kassel.

In general Hesse prides itself on being a forward-looking state, giving equal weight to progress and tradition with generous funding for both arts and sciences and a no-nonsense approach to architecture and conservation. Don't mention the infamous German spelling reform though – like many of its more conservative counterparts, Hesse was pretty strident in resisting the linguistic clean-up in 1997, and the eventual overruling of the local courts still rankles in certain quarters.

Its central position and unrivalled transport connections in Frankfurt bring vast numbers of people through Hesse, and you'll find a highly efficient network of tourist offices and agencies to help you pick the best of the many museums and make the most of the less obvious attractions around the state. The cities may be what draws the crowds, but in areas like the Lahn and Fulda Valleys Hesse boasts enough picturesque towns and landscapes to satisfy countryside cravings, with modern amenities never too far away. Hesse was also the native stomping ground of macabre connoisseurs the Grimm Brothers, and you can follow the Fairy-Tale Road through many of the towns that inspired their best-loved stories.

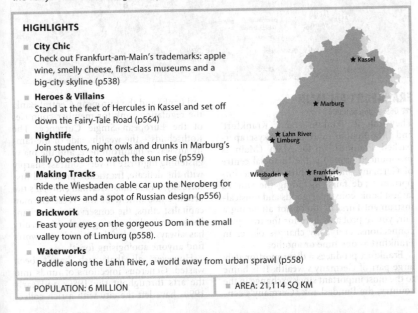

HIGHLIGHTS

- **City Chic**
  Check out Frankfurt-am-Main's trademarks: apple wine, smelly cheese, first-class museums and a big-city skyline (p538)

- **Heroes & Villains**
  Stand at the feet of Hercules in Kassel and set off down the Fairy-Tale Road (p564)

- **Nightlife**
  Join students, night owls and drunks in Marburg's hilly Oberstadt to watch the sun rise (p559)

- **Making Tracks**
  Ride the Wiesbaden cable car up the Neroberg for great views and a spot of Russian design (p556)

- **Brickwork**
  Feast your eyes on the gorgeous Dom in the small valley town of Limburg (p558).

- **Waterworks**
  Paddle along the Lahn River, a world away from urban sprawl (p558)

- POPULATION: 6 MILLION
- AREA: 21,114 SQ KM

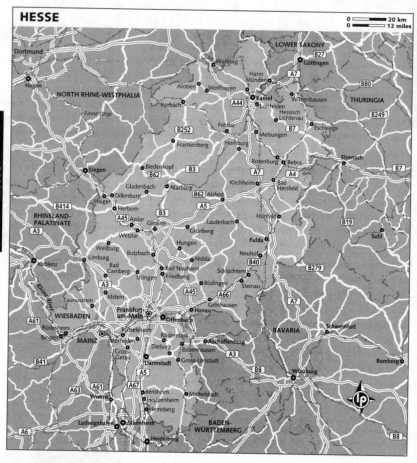

HESSE

FRANKFURT-AM-MAIN

☎ 069 / pop 650,000

They call it 'Bankfurt' and 'Krankfurt' and 'Mainhattan' and more. Skyscraper-packed Frankfurt-on-the-Main (Main is pronounced 'mine') is the financial centre of Germany and plays host to some important trade fairs, including the world's largest book, consumer-goods and musical-instrument fairs. If you're not attending a fair, you're probably here for the transport connections: *everybody* changes planes in Frankfurt at one time or another.

Frankfurt produces a disproportionately large part of Germany's wealth. It is home to the most important stock exchange in the country, the Bundesbank (Germany's cen-

tral bank) and the European Central Bank, the regulating bank for member countries of the European Single Currency. The Rothschilds – the wealthy side of the family anyway – hail from here, and the many glistening high-rise towers contrast sharply with the delicate, frantically preserved historic skylines of most German cities; it's the urban embodiment of the West German capitalist ethos, the conservative merchant banker to Berlin's ageing punk. Modernity has always been 'in' here, and you won't find anyone apologising for it!

However, all that cash hasn't been wasted. Generous injections of funds into the arts throughout the 1980s and early 1990s have left the city with a rich collection of museums second only to Berlin's; in nightlife, too, Frankfurt is the capital's only serious rival, with a thriving dance-music scene centred on the ever-popular techno beat.

Frankfurt's centre is surprisingly compact, and you can pack a lot in to a few days here. Avoid the trade fairs and the transport masses and join the increasing number of travellers visiting the city for its own sake – it may not look as good on the postcards, but this earnest cosmopolitan metropolis could yet become Germany's best city-break destination.

History

The first official mention of Frankfurt was in a document signed by Charlemagne in 794, which granted the town to the convent at St Emmeram – though by then it had been long established as a trading centre. Later, Frankfurt held a place of power in the Holy Roman Empire.

As its market flourished, so did its importance as a trade city; by the 12th century the 'Frankfurt Fair' attracted business from the Mediterranean to the Baltic. Throughout the history of the city and its market, Jews were alternately invited to participate and then killed or driven out in pogroms. Frankfurt was among the first cities to convert to Protestantism.

With the election of Frederick I (Barbarossa) in 1152, Frankfurt became the site of the election and coronation of all German kings. The last German emperor was elected in 1792, and by the time the Holy Roman Empire collapsed in 1806 the region was under French control.

It was in Frankfurt in 1848 that Germany's first-ever parliamentary delegation met at the Paulskirche. Though that parliament was disbanded by the Prussians, Frankfurt was hailed, much later, by US President John F Kennedy as the 'cradle of democracy in Germany'.

By the early 20th century the walled city of Frankfurt had expanded to include a large Jewish quarter at its northeastern end. The ghetto was abysmal, with poor sewerage and filthy conditions, but the city was again tolerant of Jews – until the rise of Nazism.

About 80% of the centre was destroyed by Allied bombing raids in March 1944.

Plans to raze the remains of the Alte Oper (old opera) were vigorously opposed by residents and a reconstruction of it, along with much of the historic city centre, was undertaken. The Römerberg was completed in 1983.

The banking district is a shimmering symbol of Germany's post-war economic redevelopment, when high-rise after high-rise was erected.

Orientation

The Main River flows from east to west, dividing the northern section of the city, its traditional centre, from the southern section, whose focus is the lovely Sachsenhausen district.

Tour boats leave from the north bank of the Main River, the Mainkai, between Alte Brücke and the pedestrian-only Eiserner Steg. The south bank of the Main River is Schaumainkai, called Museumsufer, or the Museum Embankment, for the high concentration of museums there.

The Hauptbahnhof is on the western side of the city, about a 800m from the old city centre. East along Kaiserstrasse is a large square called An der Hauptwache, northeast along Kaiserstrasse. The Hauptwache itself is a lovely baroque building that was once the local police station; now it's a restaurant and café. The area between An der Hauptwache and the Römerberg, the tiny vestige of Frankfurt's original old town, is the city centre.

The pedestrianised Zeil, Frankfurt's main shopping street, runs west to east between the Hauptwache U/S-Bahn station and the Konstablerwache U/S-Bahn station at Kurt-Schumacher-Strasse. East of there, Zeil is open to traffic and leads to the zoo.

Bockenheim, a student area northwest of the centre and due north of the Hauptbahnhof, and Bornheim, a café-laden, cosmopolitan district northeast of the zoo, are some of the neighbourhoods you'll see referred to in listings magazines and tourist brochures. Nordend is traditionally Frankfurt's most liberal district, and contains some of its finest architecture. It lies between populous Bornheim and well-heeled Westend.

The airport is about 15 minutes by train southwest of the city centre.

Information

BOOKSHOPS
British Bookshop (☎ 280 492; Börsenstrasse 17) Largest selection of English-language books in town.
Hugendubel (☎ 289 820; Steinweg 12) Multi-level chain store.
Oscar Wilde Bookshop (☎ 281 260; www.oscar-wilde .de; Alte Gasse 51) Gay and lesbian books and tapes, plus local information.
Schmitt & Hahn Internationale Presse (☎ 319 109; Hauptbahnhof)
Süssmann's Presse & Buch (☎ 131 0751; Zeil 127) Good range of English-language magazines.

CULTURAL CENTRES
Amerika Haus (☎ 971 4480; Staufenstrasse 1) Hugely popular with Germans.
Goethe Institut (☎ 961 2270; Diesterwegplatz 72) The German cultural organisation.

DISCOUNT CARDS
FrankfurtCard (24/48 hours €7.50/9.70) Free public transport, up to 50% reduction at museums, galleries, zoo and airport visitor terraces.

EMERGENCY
Emergency clinic (☎ 4750; Friedberger Landstrasse 430)
English hotline (☎ 192 92) Advice, assistance and information for English speakers.
Fire/ambulance (☎ 112)
Police (☎ 110)
Women's hotline (☎ 709 494; www.frauennotrufe -hessen.de)

INTERNET ACCESS
Unwieldy but free AOL Internet booths can be found in cafés and bars around town:
CyberRyder (☎ 9139 6754; Töngesgasse 31; €1.30 per 15 min; ⏱ 9-1am Mon-Sat, 11am-11pm Sun)
Dolly Busters (Kaiserstrasse 54; €6 per day) Sex shop (!) with late-opening Internet café.
Habib Internet (Kaiserstrasse 70; €3 per hr) One of several Internet/phone places near the Hauptbahnhof.
Telecafe Internet (Grosse Friedberger Strasse 34; €1 per 20 min)

INTERNET RESOURCES
www.frankfurt.de Official Frankfurt website
www.frankfurt-handicap.de Excellent city guide giving detailed information on disabled access to many of Frankfurt's attractions and venues.

LAUNDRY
SB Waschsalon (Wallstrasse; wash €3-4, dry €0.50; ⏱ 6am-11pm) Bockenheim (Grosse Seestrasse 46)

Wasch-Center (Sandweg 41; wash/dry €3/0.50; ⏱ 6am-11pm)

LIBRARIES
Amerika Haus (☎ 971 4480) Excellent reference source on economic and business matters.
Central library (☎ 2123 8080; Zeil 17)
Stadt- und Universitätsbibliothek (☎ 2123 9205; Bockenheimer Warte U-Bahn)

MEDICAL SERVICES
Pharmacies take turns staying open round the clock – check the list in all pharmacy windows or in the *Frankfurter Rundschau* newspaper.
24-hour doctor service (☎ 192 92)
Krankenhaus Sachsenhausen (☎ 660 50; Schulstrasse 31)
Uni-Klinik (☎ 630 11; Theodor-Stern-Kai 7, Sachsenhausen; ⏱ 24hr)

MONEY
Exchange machine (Platform 15, Hauptbahnhof) Foreign currency notes only.
Reisebank (☎ 2427 8591; South exit, Hauptbahnhof; ⏱ 6.30am-10pm)

POST
Deutsche Post Karstadt (Zeil 90) Hauptbahnhof (1st floor, Hauptbahnhof; ⏱ 7am-7.30pm Mon-Fri, 8am-4pm Sat) Airport (Departure hall B; ⏱ 7am-9pm)
DHL (☎ 0800 225 5345; Grüneburgweg 6, Westend; ⏱ 9am-7pm Mon-Fri)

TOURIST INFORMATION
German National Tourist Office (☎ 974 640; www.germany-tourism.de; Beethovenstrasse 69)
Infoline (☎ 2123 8800) Event information in English.
Tourismus + Congress (☎ 2123 0776, room reservations ☎ 2123 0808; www.tcf.frankfurt.de; Kaiserstrasse 56; ⏱ 8am-9pm Mon-Fri, 9am-6pm Sat & Sun) Services for tourists with particular needs and long-stay visitors.
Tourist office Hauptbahnhof (☎ 2123 8849; www .frankfurt.de; ⏱ 8am-9pm Mon-Fri, 9am-6pm Sat & Sun) Römer (☎ 2123 8708; Römerberg 27; ⏱ 9.30am-5.30pm Mon-Fri, 9.30am-4pm Sat & Sun)
Verkehrsinsel (Zeil; ⏱ 9am-8pm Mon-Fri, 9am-4pm Sat) Public transport and general information, plus transport tickets.

TRAVEL AGENCIES
American Express (☎ 210 50; Hauptbahnhof)
Lufthansa (☎ 2828 9596; Level B, Hauptwache U-Bahn)

A Travel (☎ 703 035; Bockenheimer Landstrasse 3) Bornheim (☎ 430 191; Berger Strasse 118) Bornheim ☎ 443 027; Berger Strasse 109).
homas Cook (☎ 9139 7603; frankfurt4@thomascook e; Rossmarkt)

NIVERSITIES
ohann Wolfgang von Goethe Universität
☎ 7981; Bockenheimer Warte)

angers & Annoyances
he area around the Hauptbahnhof is a ase for Frankfurt's trade in sex and illegal rugs. To contain the problem of junkies ublicly shooting up, *Druckräume* ('shootng galleries') have been established in vhich drugs can be taken but not sold and vhere clean needles are distributed (there's ne on Niddastrasse).

However, chances are you *will* see junkes self-medicating (and defecating between arked cars) during your visit. Frequent poice and private security patrols of the staion and the surrounding Bahnhofsviertel keep things under control, but it's always dvisable to use big-city common sense.

The main sex drags here are Elbestrasse and Taunusstrasse, which hold most of the ity's licensed Eros Centres (brothels to is laypeople). On the whole they're more eedy than dangerous, but if these areas will nake you uncomfortable, steer clear. Men should expect at least a few shouts from the street prostitutes.

Sights

MAIN TOWER
A good place to start seeing the sights of Frankfurt is from the **Main Tower** (☎ 3650 4740; www.maintower.helaba.de; Neue Mainzer Strasse 52-58; adult/concession €4.50/3; ☺ 10am-9pm Sun-Thu, 10am-11pm Fri & Sat, weather permitting), a relatively new addition to Frankfurt's skyline and the only high-rise in town with a public viewing platform. At 200m tall, the gallery offers spectacular views of the city. To the southeast you can see the Römerberg, a remake of the original city centre; beyond it, across the river, is Sachsenhausen, an entertainment area with lots of pubs, bars and restaurants. To the north and northwest is the banking district with its ever-changing vista of towers, including the 256m-high peak of the elegant **Messeturm**, which locals call the *Bleistift* (pencil). Its grace comes at the

expense of space – the service shaft takes up half of this slender building's interior. Europe's tallest office block, the 258m-high (298m including the antenna) **Commerzbank Tower**, stands aloof at Kaiserplatz, a stone's throw from the Main Tower.

RÖMERBERG
The Römerberg, west of the Dom, is Frankfurt's old central square, where restored 14th- and 15th-century buildings, including the **Paulskirche** (☎ 281 098; ☺ 10am-5pm Mon-Fri), provide a glimpse of how beautiful the city once was. It's especially lovely during December's Weihnachtsmarkt.

The old town hall, or **Römer**, in the northwestern corner of Römerberg, consists of three recreated step-gabled 15th-century houses. The Römer was the site of celebrations of the election and coronation of emperors during the Holy Roman Empire; today it's the registry office and the office of Frankfurt's mayor. Inside, there are portraits of 52 rulers in the **Kaisersaal** (Imperial Hall; ☎ 2123 4919; adult/concession €2/1; ☺ 10am-noon & 1.30-5pm). Flags flying outside the building indicate the Kaisersaal is being used for official functions, in which case you won't be able to get inside.

Right in the centre of Römerberg is the **Gerechtigkeitsbrunnen**, the 'Font of Justice'. In 1612, at the coronation of Matthias, the fountain ran with wine!

FRANKFURTER DOM
East of Römerberg, the **Frankfurter Dom** (tour adult/concession €3/2; ☺ 9am-noon Mon-Thu, Sat & Sun, 2.30-6pm daily) is behind the **Historischer Garten** (Historical Garden), where you can wander through excavated Roman and Carolingian foundations. Dominated by the elegant 15th-century Gothic-style **tower** (95m; completed in the 1860s), the Dom was one of the few structures left standing after the 1944 raids. Trivia fans and pedants may like to know that it has in fact never been a real cathedral, as there's never been an archbishop here.

At time of writing the tower was still undergoing renovation, with the expected reopening in 2002 long overdue. When work is finally completed, visitors should once again be able to climb to the two viewing platforms at 40m and 75m.

The small **Wahlkapelle** (Voting Chapel) on the cathedral's southern side is where seven electors of the Holy Roman Empire chose the emperor from 1356 onwards. The adjoining **choir** has beautiful wooden stalls.

GOETHE HAUS
Anyone with an interest in German literature should visit the **Goethe Haus** (☎ 138 800; www.goethehaus-frankfurt.de; Grosser Hirschgraben 23-25;

adult/concession €3.50/2.50; ☼ 9am-6pm Mon-Fri, 10am-4pm Sat & Sun), where the great Johann Wolfgang von Goethe was born in 1749. Much of the furniture is reproduction, but some originals remain. There are guided tours in German at 10.30am and 2pm; English tours can be held by arrangement. At other times staff might point out the highlights. Don't

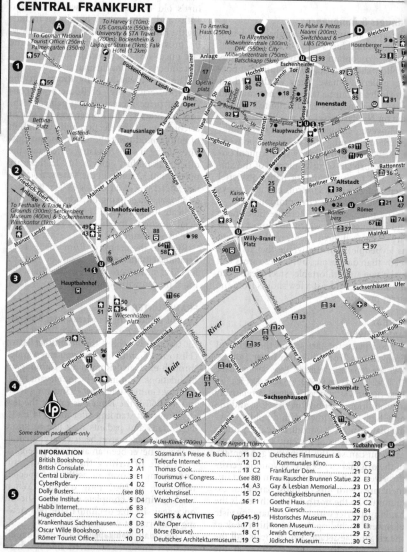

CENTRAL FRANKFURT

INFORMATION
British Bookshop.....................1 C1
British Consulate.....................2 A1
Central Library........................3 E1
CyberRyder............................4 D2
Dolly Busters......................(see 88)
Goethe Institut.......................5 D4
Habib Internet........................6 B3
Hugendubel............................7 C2
Krankenhaus Sachsenhaus..8 D3
Oscar Wilde Bookshop...........9 D1
Römer Tourist Office.............10 D2

Süssmann's Presse & Buch....11 D2
Telecafe Internet....................12 D1
Thomas Cook.........................13 C2
Tourismus + Congress.......(see 88)
Tourist Office.........................14 A3
Verkehrsinsel.........................15 D2
Wasch-Center........................16 F1

SIGHTS & ACTIVITIES   (pp541-5)
Alte Oper..............................17 B1
Börse (Bourse)......................18 C1
Deutsches Architekturmuseum...19 C3

Deutsches Filmmuseum &
  Kommunales Kino...............20 C3
Frankfurter Dom.....................21 D2
Frau Rauscher Brunnen Statue..22 E3
Gay & Lesbian Memorial........23 D1
Gerechtigkeitsbrunnen...........24 D2
Goethe Haus.........................25 C2
Haus Giersch.........................26 B4
Historisches Museum..............27 D3
Ikonen Museum.....................28 E3
Jewish Cemetery...................29 E2
Jüdisches Museum.................30 C3

Some streets pedestrian-only

niss Goethe's original writing desk and the library on the top floor.

ALTE OPER & BÖRSE

Inaugurated in 1880, Frankfurt's lovely Renaissance-style **Alte Oper** (Old Opera House; ☎ 134 0400; Opernplatz 8) was designed by Berlin architect Richard Lucae and stylistically influenced by Gottfried Semper, creator of the famous Semperoper in Dresden.

Destroyed in WWII, the Alte Oper – after a vote saved it from being razed and replaced with 1960s-style cubes – underwent a €110 million renovation. The outside is as original as is possible but the inside is modern. Statues of Goethe and Mozart grace the façade.

Hotel Continental	50 B3
Hotel Excelsior	51 A3
Hotel Ibis Friedensbrücke	52 A4
Hotel Minerva	53 A4
Hotel National	54 A3
Hotel Pension Backer	55 A1
Hotel Zeil	56 E1
Hotel-Pension Gölz	57 A1
Ramada Hotel & Indian House Curry	58 B3
Zur Traube	59 D1

EATING 🍴	(pp548-50)
Affentor Brasserie	60 E3
African Queen	61 A4
Avocado	62 C1
Café Mozart	63 D2
Coconut Groove	64 B3
Di Vino	65 B2
Ginger Brasserie	66 B3
Historisches Restaurant zum Storch	67 D2
HL Markt	68 E3
Iwase	69 D1
Kleinmarkthalle	70 D2
Lagerhaus	71 E4
Lobster	72 E3
Manitou	73 E3
Metropol	74 D2
Plöger	75 C1
Vinum	76 C1
Zu den Zwölf Aposteln	77 D1
Zum Gemalten Haus & Adolf Wagner	78 D4

DRINKING 🍷	(pp550-1)
Affentor Schänke	79 E4
Blaubart Gewölbekeller	80 C1
Café Royal	81 D1
Jazzkeller	82 C1
Living XXL	83 C2
O'Dwyers Pub	84 E3
Sinkkasten	85 D1
Studio Bar	86 D2

ENTERTAINMENT 🎭	(pp551-2)
Blue Angel	87 D1
English Theatre	88 B3
La Gata	89 E3
Oper	90 C3
Stereo Bar	91 E4
Tiger Palast	92 E1
Turm-Palast	93 D1
U 60311	94 C2

TRANSPORT	(pp552-3)
ADAC	95 C1
Mitfahrzentrale	96 A4
Primus-Linie Quay	97 D3

OTHER	
Inlingua	98 B3
Language Alliance	(see 6)

Liebieghaus Museum Alter Plastik	31 C4
Main Tower	32 B2
Museum der Weltkulturen	33 C3
Museum für Angewandte Kunst and Museum für Kunsthandwerk	34 C3
Museum für Kommunikation	35 C4
Museum für Moderne Kunst	36 D2
Museum Judengasse	37 E2
Museum Regionaler Kunst	(see 26)
Paulskirche	38 D2
SB Waschsalon	39 E3
Städel Art Institute	40 C4
Zoo	41 F1

SLEEPING 🛏	(pp546-8)
Arabella Sheraton Grand Hotel	42 E1
Concorde Hotel	43 A3
DJH Hostel	44 E3
Frankfurter Hof	45 C2
Glockshuber	46 A3
Hotel am Dom	47 D2
Hotel am Zoo	48 F1
Hotel Carlton	49 A3

Between Opernplatz and Börsenstrasse is the section of street known as **Fressgasse** (Munch Alley), a somewhat overrated dining area lined with snack bars and restaurants. If you're visiting in September, try to catch the very nice Rheingau wine festival held here.

The old city **Börse** (Stock Exchange; ☎ 210 10; visitors-centre@deutsche-boerse.com; Börsenplatz; ☯ 10.30am-1.30pm Mon-Fri) is open to visitors, who can view a semiactive trading floor from an observation section. Book at least an hour in advance, and bring ID with you. Most of the Bourse's functions and electronic trading systems have moved to new headquarters in the northwestern suburb of Frankfurt-Hausen.

MUSEUMS

Most museums open from 10am to 5pm Tuesday to Sunday and 10am to 8pm Wednesday, and close on Monday. Entry is free on Wednesday in many places – arrive early to beat the school groups in summer.

Museumsufer

A string of museums lines the southern bank of the Main River, also known as Museum Embankment. The pick of the crop is the **Städelsches Kunstinstitut** (Städel Art Institute; ☎ 605 0980; www.staedelmuseum.de; Schaumainkai 63; adult/concession €6/5, free Tue; ☯ 10am-5pm Tue & Fri-Sun, 10am-8pm Wed & Thu). It harbours a world-class collection of works by various artists including Botticelli, Dürer, Van Eyck, Rembrandt, Renoir, Rubens, Vermeer and Cézanne, plus Frankfurt natives such as Hans Holbein.

The **Museum für Kommunikation** (☎ 606 00; Schaumainkai 53; ☯ 9am-5pm Tue-Fri, 11am-6.30pm Sat & Sun) is a touchy-feely museum displaying the history of communication, including tips on how to make invisible ink and decipher codes. It's a winner with kids, and it won't cost you a penny unless you visit the excellent café – on Wednesday and Sunday even the tours are free.

The **Deutsches Architekturmuseum** (☎ 2123 8844; www.dam-online.de; Schaumainkai 43; adult/concession €5/2.50, Wed €2.50/1.25) is something of a disappointment: the permanent collection is just a series of models showing settlements from the Stone Age to the present day, and the rotating exhibits tend to fail on their English translations. Without a single display on the

architecture of Frankfurt itself, this is really a missed opportunity.

By contrast, you'll find the **Deutsches Filmmuseum** (☎ 2123 8830; www.deutsches-filmmuseum.d Schaumainkai 41; adult/concession €2.50/1.30, free We next door a fascinating place. It has a library and film history exhibit, constantly changing exhibitions and extensive archives, plus premieres and special film events (all in their original languages) in the Kommunale Kino; check the programme in any listing magazine (see Entertainment p551).

The **Ikonen-Museum** (Icon Museum; ☎ 2123 626 www.ikonenmuseumfrankfurt.de; Brückenstrasse 3-7; adult concession €2.50/1.25, free Wed) houses a collectio of Russian religious paintings. Admissio includes entry to the neighbouring Russian church.

The **Museum für Angewandte Kunst** and **Museum für Kunsthandwerk** (Museum of Applied Arts Craft Museum; ☎ 2124 4539; Schaumainkai 15-17; adult concession €5/2.50, free Wed; ☯ 10am-8pm Tue-Sun) ar set in lovely gardens with a smart café.

A favourite with school parties, thanks to its Native American displays, the **Museum der Weltkulturen** (Museum of World Cultures; ☎ 212 5913; www.mdw.frankfurt.de; Schaumainkai 29-37; adult concession €3/1.50, free Wed; ☯ 10am-5pm Tue-Fri Sun, 10am-8pm Wed, 2-8pm Sat) also overlooks th river along the Museum Embankment.

The **Liebieghaus Museum Alter Plastik** (Museur of Ancient Sculpture; ☎ 2123 8617; Schaumainkai 71; adult concession €3/2, free Wed) has classical, medieval baroque and Renaissance sculptures and ai exhibition of Egyptian art. Close by is th **Haus Giersch Museum Regionaler Kunst** (Regional Ar Museum; ☎ 6330 4128; www.haus-giersch.de; Schaumain kai 83; adult/concession €4/2; ☯ noon-7pm Tue-Fri, 11am 5pm Sat & Sun), which has regular exhibitions o works by lesser-known Hesse artists.

Other Museums

The triangular **Museum für Moderne Kunst** (Museum of Modern Art; ☎ 2123 0447; www.mmk-frankfur .de; Domstrasse 10; adult/concession €5/2.50, free Wed) dubbed the 'slice of cake' by locals, is ar excellent and imaginatively run exhibition space with a permanent collection containing works by Roy Lichtenstein, Claes Oldenburg and Joseph Beuys. Temporary exhibits showcase local, national and international artists; a 2003 highlight was the first opening of some of Andy Warhol's personal 'time capsules'.

The **Historisches Museum** (☎ 2123 5599; Saalgasse 19; adult/concession €4.20/2.10, free Wed; ☯ 10am-

5pm Tue, Thu & Sun, 4-8pm Wed, 10am-2pm Fri, 1-5pm Sat), just south of Römerberg, is worth visiting, even if you skip the uninspiring permanent exhibition on the Middle Ages in favour of the spectacular model (€0.50) of the city from the 1930s in the foyer. The city centre detail is wonderful; it's especially nice to go on Wednesday when local pensioners, taking advantage of the free admission, stand around and point out places remembered from their youth. In the same foyer is a model of the ruins of the city after the war.

The city has two notable museums on Jewish life in Frankfurt, reminding visitors that the Jewish community here, with 35,000 people, was once one of the largest in Europe. The main **Jüdisches Museum** (☎ 212 3880; www.juedischesmuseum.de; Untermainkai 14-15; adult/concession €2.60/1.30), in the former Rothschildpalais, is a huge place with an exhibit of Jewish life in the city from the Middle Ages to present day, with good detail on well-known Frankfurt Jews persecuted, murdered or exiled by the Nazis. Religious items are also displayed.

The **Museum Judengasse** (☎ 297 7419; Kurt-Schumacher-Strasse 10; adult/concession €1.50/0.70, with Jüdisches Museum €3/1.50, free Sat), along the northeastern boundaries of the old city fortifications, is the annexe to the Jüdisches Museum. On display here are remains of ritual baths and houses from the Jewish ghetto, which was destroyed by the Nazis.

Behind the Museum Judengasse, the western wall of the **Jewish Cemetery** is a remarkable **memorial** studded with metal cubes bearing the names of all the Frankfurt-born Jews murdered during the Holocaust. The cubes allow visitors to place stones or pebbles, a Jewish tradition that shows that a grave is tended and the person not forgotten.

North of here is the highly interactive **Explora** (☎ 788 888; www.exploramuseum.de; Glauburg Platz 1, Nordend; adult/concession €7/5; ☷ 11am-6pm Tue-Sun), a family-oriented science and technology museum with a heavy visual emphasis. The 3D photos of turn-of-the-century Frankfurt are a definite highlight. To get there, get off at Glauburgstrasse U-Bahn.

PALMENGARTEN

A nice place to relax is the botanical **Palmengarten** (Palm Garden; ☎ 2123 3933; Siesmayerstrasse 61; adult/child €4/2). It has rose and for-

mal gardens, a playground for kids, a little pond with rowing boats and a mini-gauge train that puffs round the park (€1/0.50). It's near the German National Tourist Board and the university, one block from Bockenheimer Warte, and Westend is the U-Bahn station.

MONUMENTS

On the corner of Alte Gasse and Schäfergasse, at the heart of the city's main gay and lesbian area, is a **gay and lesbian memorial** (one of only three in Europe) to the many homosexuals persecuted and killed by the Nazis during WWII. It is deliberate that the statue's head is nearly severed from the body.

South of the river, **Frau Rauscher Brunnen** on Klappergasse in Sachsenhausen is a rather less poignant figure: a bulky, bitchy-looking Hausfrau who periodically spews a stream of water about 10m onto the footpath. When the street's busy you'll undoubtedly see pedestrians get drenched. The idea is based on a popular Frankfurt song about apple wine.

FRANKFURT ZOO & AIRPORT

The **zoo** (☎ 2123 3731; Alfred-Brehm-Platz 16; adult/concession €7/3; ☷ 9am-7pm Apr-Oct, 9am-5pm Nov-Mar), with its creative displays, signs and exhibits, is a relief from the cosmopolitan chaos, and even has scheduled tropical storms (11.30am and 3.30pm). Take the U6 to Zoo station.

Just as creative, and beloved by children, are the two visitor terraces at **Frankfurt airport** (Level 3, Terminal 1 & Level 4, Terminal 2; €3/2; ☷ 8am-8.30pm). It's only 11 minutes away from the Hauptbahnhof by S-Bahn (see Getting Around, p553).

Language Courses

Due to the high percentage of foreign residents in Frankfurt-am-Main, there are a number of language schools in the city. The most respected, and expensive, option is the **Goethe Institut** (☎ 961 2270; frankfurt@goethe.de; Diesterwegplatz 72); call for accommodation options.

Inlingua (☎ 242 900; www.inlingua-frankfurt.de; Kaiserstrasse 37) and **Language Alliance** (☎ 253 952; www.languagealliance.de; Kaiserstrasse 74) offer a wide range of intensive afternoon and evening courses, starting from around €140 a month. Accommodation is offered at Stay & Learn (see Sleeping opposite).

Tours

During weekends and holidays the city's **Ebbelwei-Express** (☎ 2132 2425; www.vgf-ffm.de; adult/concession €5/2.50) tram circles Frankfurt, stops at the zoo, Hauptbahnhof, Südbahnhof, Frankensteiner Platz (near the Haus der Jugend) and circles back many times daily.

Kulturothek Frankfurt (☎ 281 010; www.kulturothek.de; adult/concession €7.50/5) runs 2½-hour German-language walking tours on a variety of subjects every Sunday. Show up at 2pm at the agreed meeting point. The price is €90 to €120 for groups of up to 25 people.

The **tourist offices** offer excellent 2½-hour city tours, which include visits to the Historisches Museum and Goethe Haus and a ride up to the Main Tower gallery, leaving at 2pm daily (also 10am April to October) from the Römer and Hauptbahnhof offices. The cost is €25/20/10 per adult/concession/child. There are also themed excursions, like Jewish Frankfurt, Frankfurt architecture and Goethe tours.

Elisabeth Lücke (☎ 06196-457 87; www.elisabeth-luecke.de; €50 per hr) is a private guide who runs tours for individuals or groups in English, German and Spanish on the themes of architecture, the finance world and Jewish life in Frankfurt.

Primus Linie (☎ 133 8370; www.primus-linie.de; ☼ May-Oct) operates short cruises along the Main River (€5.50 to €7.50) and longer Rhine trips to Rüdesheim, Loreley, Seligenstadt and Aschaffenburg, leaving from the docks on the northern embankment near the Eiser Steg bridge.

Festivals & Events

Frankfurt festivals include: **Dippemess**, in March and September, a fun fair with apple wine and food; **Kunsthandwerk Heute** in late May/early June, an arts and handicrafts festival held on Paulsplatz; and the **Sound of Frankfurt** in July, which takes place along the Zeil, with local and visiting groups playing everything from techno to soul, blues and rock. There's also the world-famous **Frankfurt Book Fair** (see the boxed text, following) in the autumn and the **Weihnachtsmarkt** in December, a Christmas fair on Römerberg with mulled wine, choirs and traditional foods.

THE FRANKFURT BOOK FAIR

If you're in publishing, there's no avoiding the world's largest book fair, held in Frankfurt in late September/early October. Over 250,000 publishers, agents, authors, wannabes, drunks, Lonely Planet staffers and other nefarious characters descend on Mainhattan with a vengeance.

It's a scene and a half, and hotels are booked out years in advance, with prices going through the roof. Plan well ahead if you're anywhere near the city round this time.

The fair is only open to the public at the weekend. To get to the Frankfurter Messe, take tram Nos 16 and 19, or S-Bahn No 3, 4 or 5 from the Hauptbahnhof. Day admission is €9; check www.buchmesse.de for more information.

Sleeping
BUDGET

In Frankfurt, 'cheap' can mean paying over €50 for a spartan double room. Weekend rates are the cheapest; during the many busy trade fairs even €60 may turn out to be unrealistic, since most hotels and pensions jack up their rates – in many cases close to double the standard price. But don't give up hope: the tourist office has been known to perform miracles.

The tourist offices can book singles from about €20 to €50. They only book **private rooms** (from €40 per person) during trade fairs. At other times you can contact one of the Mitwohnzentrale offices: **City** (☎ 299 050; www.city-mitwohnzentrale.de; Hanseallee 2), which also has its own apartments; **Mainhattan** (☎ 597 5561; www.mitwohnzentrale-mainhattan.de; Falkensteiner Strasse 68); or the **Allgemeine Mitwohnzentrale** (☎ 9552 0892; allgemmitwohn@t-online.de; Oeder Weg 7).

Most of Frankfurt's low-end accommodation is in the Bahnhofsviertel, the rather sleazy area surrounding the Hauptbahnhof.

DJH hostel (☎ 610 0150; www.jugendherberge-frankfurt.de; Deutschherrnufer 12; dm junior/senior €15/20; ☼ 6-2am; P) The big, bustling DJH Haus der Jugend on the south side of the Main River is within walking distance of the city centre and Sachsenhausen's nightspots, and is wheelchair-accessible throughout. Book

n advance for any visit. From the Haupt-
bahnhof, take bus No 46 to Frankensteiner
Platz or S-Bahn lines No 2, 3, 4, 5, or 6 to
Lokalbahnhof.

Stay & Learn Residence (☎ 253 952; www.room
-frankfurt.de; Kaiserstrasse 74; r €35-45; 🗙 🖳) The
rooms at the busy Language Alliance language school opposite the Hauptbahnhof
are mainly used to house people taking
courses, but are also available for travellers, and are actually a great deal, with a
choice of private and shared bathrooms,
fridges, huge TVs and small shared kitchens
(there's no on-site catering).

Hotel Carlton (☎ 241 8280; www.carlton-hotel.de;
Karlstrasse 11; s/d €55/65) A smart little townhouse, the Carlton is one of the best options
in this area, with cheaper summer rates,
TV, phone, nice linen and even minibars
in the rooms.

Ibis Friedensbrücke (☎ 273 030; Speicherstrasse
3-5; r €69; 🅿 🗙 🖳) This standard business
chain provides the usual accommodation
for the usual clientele, with a few extra leisure facilities and a great riverside location.
Breakfast is €9.

Hotel Am Berg (☎ 612 021; www.hoel-am-berg
-ffm.de; Grethenweg 23; s/d €48/58; 🗙) In Sachsenhausen, this hotel occupies a lovely
sandstone building in the quiet backstreets
a few minutes' walk from the Südbahnhof. The simple rooms come without
breakfast.

Hotel Zeil (☎ 209 7770; www.hotel-zeil.de; Zeil
12; s/d €55/70; 🅿 🗙 🗙) You'll have trouble
beating this price for this location, right on
Frankfurt's main shopping street. Rooms
are unfancy but comfortable, and you
generally feel like you're getting what you
pay for.

Glockshuber (☎ 742 628; Mainzer Landstrasse 120;
s/d €39/60; 🅿 🗙) Glockshuber offers pleasant, clean and bright rooms with shared
bathroom, on a busy road northeast of the
Hauptbahnhof.

Hotel Pension Backer (☎ 747 992; Mendelssohn-
strasse 92; r €25-50; 🅿) A good contender for
cheapest hotel in town, this pension has
spartan but clean rooms with shared bathrooms on each floor.

MID-RANGE
Zur Traube (☎ 280 388; www.art-hotel-zur-traube.de;
Rosenberger Strasse 4; s/d €50/80) It may look like
a rustic guesthouse from the outside, but

inside the effect is pure Turkish brothel:
rooms are done out in shades of purple
with lacy nets over the beds (No 6 is our
favourite), while the bar is a sultry pink
with satin drapes and erotic paintings on
the walls. It's certainly a unique place!

Ramada City Center (☎ 310 810; ramada-frank
furt@t-online.de; Weserstrasse 17; s/d €92/107; 🅿 🗙
🗙) Opposite a Church of Scientology, the
Ramada has far more character than you'd
expect from a chain hotel, with good standard rooms, luxurious superior doubles and
a classy Lebanese restaurant. Prices drop
considerably in summer and at weekends.

Concorde Hotel (☎ 242 4220; www.hotelconcorde
.de; Karlstrasse 9; s/d €80/105; 🗙 🖳) A restored
Art Deco boutique houses this excellent,
understated establishment near the Hauptbahnhof. Weekend rates are a particularly
great deal.

Hotel am Dom (☎ 138 1030; Kannengiessergasse 3;
s €85-90, d €95-110) You can take your pick of
the various immaculate rooms, suites and
apartments here, just a few paces from the
mighty Frankfurter Dom. Unsurprisingly,
it's very popular – book well in advance.

Hotel Continental (☎ 230 341; www.hotelconti
frankfurt.de; Baseler Strasse 56; s €50-85, d €70-120; 🗙)
Deceptively grand-looking thanks to its
top-end neighbours, the 'Conti' is actually an unpretentious mid-range stalwart,
though it more than holds its own as far as
service is concerned.

Falk Hotel (☎ 7191 8870; www.hotel-falk.de; Falk-
strasse 38, Bockenheim; s/d €65/85; 🗙) Surrounded
by bars, cafés and shops, this small hotel
has quiet and pleasant rooms, but prices
double during trade fairs. Take the U-Bahn
to Leipziger Strasse.

Hotel am Zoo (☎ 949 930; www.hotel-am-zoo.com;
Alfred-Brehm-Platz 6; s/d €72/106; 🅿) This is a de-
cent modern pension-style option near the
Zeil and (obviously) the zoo.

Hotel Excelsior (☎ 256 080; www.hotelexcelsior
-frankfurt.de; Mannheimer Strasse 7-9; s €89-110, d €125-
150; 🅿 🗙 🖳) Opposite the Hauptbahnhof,
the Excelsior is a pretty typical high-end
modern business hotel, but with the added
plus of free minibar and Internet access. It's
also a good place to catch a taxi.

Hotel Minerva (☎ 25617600; www.hotelminerva.de;
Stuttgarter Strasse 31; s/d €90/120; 🖳) One of several reasonable hotels nearby, the Minerva
has small but well-equipped, good-looking
rooms, with walk-in deals starting at €60.

TOP END

If you're in Frankfurt on expenses or just feel like splashing out, there are plenty of top-flight options around the city. Even these prices usually double during important fairs – take note if you don't want your receipts sent directly to the Raised Eyebrow Department.

Frankfurter Hof (☎ 215 02; www.frankfurter-hof .steigenberger.de; Kaiserplatz; s €129-405, d €149-455; P ✕ ✕ ➲) One of Frankfurt's two great heavyweights, this hotel has grandiose rooms and great service, plus a lovely courtyard restaurant out the front. Rooms usually come without breakfast, but inclusive weekend deals start at almost half-price, and there are web-only special offers worth checking.

Villa Orange (☎ 405 840; www.villa-orange.de; Hebelstrasse 1, Nordend; s €120-190, d €130-270; P ✕) For a much lighter touch, try this Italian-flavoured 'country' villa, which sports a library, patio and four-poster beds in the spacious rooms. The bar is open 24 hours. It's about 400m north of the centre in the fashionable Nordend district.

Hotel National (☎ 242 6480; www.hotelnational.de; Baseler Strasse 50; s €99-180, d €149-255; P ✕) A good old-fashioned four-star establishment, complete with piano bar, the real selling point here is the unique mix of modern and antique furniture in all areas of the hotel.

Arabella Sheraton Grand Hotel (☎ 298 10; grand hotel.frankfurt@arabellasheraton.com; Konrad-Adenauer-Strasse 7; s/d €325/345; P ✕ ✕ ➲ ➲) The Frankfurter Hof's main rival offers friendly service, extravagant décor and excellent facilities, but relatively boxy rooms. Check for weekend deals.

Eating
BAHNHOFSVIERTEL

The area around the Hauptbahnhof is dominated by southern European, Middle Eastern and Asian eateries. The station itself has plenty of snack and fast-food options.

Coconut Groove (☎ 2710 7999; Kaiserstrasse 53; mains €4.50-24) This funky place is as much cocktail bar as restaurant, with DJs at weekends, but the inventive new-world menu is well worth investigating, making good use of unusual elements like okra and guava-coconut sauce.

Di Vino (☎ 721 308; Zimmerweg 5/8; food from €5) For real Italian character, this is the only

place you need to know. The *paninotec* on one side of the road sells snacks and wine, while the excellent restaurant opposite serves up stylish classics and some of the best tiramisu in town. Reservations are mandatory.

Indian Curry House (☎ 230 690; Weserstrasse 17; dishes €3-7) Popular with insiders, this unassuming spicehouse is full of character and stands out from the shabby Imbisse around it for all the right reasons.

African Queen (Stuttgarter Strasse 23; mains €6-8.50) It's not every day you come across an Eritrean restaurant in Germany. Sophisticated cuisine it ain't, but you will find good filling meals based around traditional *injera* bread, and a lively clientele from both continents.

Ginger Brasserie (☎ 231 771; Windmühlstrasse 14; mains €10-15) A broad spectrum of Asian cooking is on offer here, with changing monthly menus; some experiments are more successful than others (we'll take the Szechuan over the sushi any day).

FRESSGASSE & NORTHERN CENTRE

Known to locals as Fressgasse (Munch Alley), the stretch of Kalbächer Gasse and Grosse Bockenheimer Strasse between Rathenauplatz and Opernplatz has lots of mid-priced restaurants and fast-food places with outdoor tables. The streets northeast of here are also strewn with (generally more interesting) options.

Plöger (☎ 138 7110; Grosse Bockenheimer Strasse 30) Even self-caterers deserve a treat – this fantastic-looking deli, founded in 1935, has some of the finest tinned, smoked and bottled goodies money can buy. Flavoured olive oil, Russian caviar, 1958 cognac, 1943 champagne...try not to drool while browsing.

Vinum (☎ 293 037; Kleine Hochstrasse; mains €6.50-14) Chilli, Wurst and steak are among the hefty dishes on offer here, but it's the vast wine selection that gives this atmospheric cellar its real *raison d'être*. The reds in particular will tackle your tastebuds head-on.

Iwase (☎ 283 992; Vilbeler Strasse 31; mains around €11) An excellent but tiny Japanese restaurant, popular with business types for its generous portions of sushi and miso soup and its €35 set menus.

Zu den Zwölf Aposteln (☎ 288 668; www.12apostel .net; Rosenbergerstrasse 1; mains €9-18) Situated on the corner of Elefantengasse, this is a traditional microbrewery restaurant serving up meat-heavy German and Eastern European meals. Downstairs is an interesting beer cellar, open in the evening.

Avocado (☎ 294 642; resto-avocado@t-online.de; Hochstrasse 27; mains €24.50-27; ✌ noon-2.30pm Mon-Sat, 6-10.30pm Tue-Sat) Treat yourself in style at what must be the best French bistro in town. The menu's a nightmare for the indecisive (try the €57 five-course surprise dinner), the champagne list sparkles with class, and the little outside garden area, completely enshrouded in vines, is as romantic as anything on a summer's night.

ZEIL & RÖMERBERG

Café Mozart (☎ 291 954; Töngesgasse 23; cake from €1) The nearby café is popular with tourists and local old ladies for its cakes and coffee.

Kleinmarkthalle (Off Hasengasse; ✌ 7.30am-6pm Mon-Fri, 7am-3pm Sat) Just south of Zeil, this huge covered hall was the first food market in post-war Frankfurt selling fruit, vegetables, meats, fish and hot food. Stalls have Italian, Turkish, Chinese and German food, and you can get salads and fresh fruit juices as well as wine and beer. The *Gref Völsings Rindswurst* (beef sausage) stand is an institution. At the western end of the hall is a large mural depicting impressions of Frankfurt.

Historisches Restaurant zum Storch (☎ 284 988; cnr Saalgasse & Höllgasse; mains €13-22.50) OK, so

the 'historic' is tacked on to get the tourists in, but this really is a pretty venerable old place, and the regional specialities are top-notch. The terrace has great views of the Dom.

Metropol (☎ 288 287; Weckmarkt 13-15; mains €11-13) Directly outside the Dom (it even caters wedding breakfasts for couples marrying inside), Metropol offers varied and inventive dishes from a changing menu, with some organic produce and special dishes in aid of good causes such as street kids in Cameroon. It's also a great place for coffee or a drink, and stays open late.

SACHSENHAUSEN

Sachsenhausen is everyone-friendly (gays, lesbians, heteros, students, naked men with Walkmans). Virtually every building in the pedestrian area between Grosse Rittergasse and Darmstädter Landstrasse is a bar, restaurant or takeaway; Schweizer Strasse is also full of taverns and eating places.

Lagerhaus (☎ 628 552; Dreieichstrasse 45; mains €6-13) This colourful restaurant/bar is a pillar of the gay scene, and its reasonably priced eclectic menu continues to draw in the crowds; weekend brunches are practically a social event.

Affentor Brasserie (☎ 6616 1473; Paradiesgasse 67; mains €8-15) In a corner dominated by German traditions, this modern brasserie is a bit of a renegade, aiming at French

---

EBBELWOI & HANDKÄSE MIT MUSIK

Frankfurt delicacies are best experienced in the city's traditional taverns, which serve *Ebbelwoi* (Frankfurt dialect for Apfelwein), an alcoholic apple cider, along with local specialities like *Handkäse mit Musik* (hand-cheese with music) and *Frankfurter Grüne Sosse* (Frankfurt green sauce).

The majority of Ebbelwoi taverns are in Alt Sachsenhausen, the area directly behind the youth hostel. In most you'll be served the stuff in *Bembel* jugs; it's something of a tradition to scrunch closer to your neighbours and try to grab some from their pitcher too.

Definitive Ebbelwoi joints include **Solzer** (Berger Strasse 237); the tucked-away **Adolf Wagner** (Schweizer Strasse 69); and the **Affentor Schänke** (Neuer Wall 9), with its tree-shaded terrace. **Im Blauen Bock** (Saalburgstrasse 36, Bornheim) has a firebrand proprietress and all the ingredients of a real classic, though **Zur Sonne** (Berger Strasse 312) is widely considered the best in town.

Handkäse mit Musik is a name you could only hear in Germany. It describes a round cheese marinated in oil and vinegar with onions, served with bread and butter and no fork. As you might imagine, this potent mixture tends to give one a healthy dose of wind – the release of which, ladies and gentlemen, is the 'music' part.

Frankfurter Grüne Sosse is made from parsley, sorrel, dill, burnet, borage, chervil and chives mixed with yoghurt, mayonnaise or sour cream; it's served with potatoes and ox meat or eggs – Goethe's favourite food.

HESSE

sophistication rather than local colour. A well-stocked bar means it can hold its own with the night crowd as well.

Manitou (☎ 6612 7738; Seehofstrasse 6; mains €7-21) For something really different, don your feathered headgear and track down this amazing Native American restaurant, where you can try Apache-style crocodile or bison goulash in surrounds you just have to see for yourself.

Zum Gemalten Haus (☎ 614 559; Schweizer Strasse 67; mains €10-20) This is one of the best places in town to try local specialities like *Handkäse mit Musik* (see boxed text p549), the smelly cheese that keeps on reminding you, and everyone around you, just how charming Frankfurt can be. The colourful façade and the paintings inside elevate it above most of the nearby taverns.

Lobster (☎ 612 920; Wallstrasse 21; mains €15-25) The crustacean moniker is right on the money: this is a seafood specialist in the heart of pork country, with distinct French character coming out in the daily menus and uncomplicated, cosy surrounds.

NORDEND & BORNHEIM

Berger Strasse is the main drag here, boasting a wealth of cafés and bars.

Manolya (☎ 494 0162; Habsburger Allee 6; mains from €5) Sick of döners? Try some of Frankfurt's best-rated Turkish food in this appealing restaurant, with friendly service and super starters.

Eckhaus (☎ 491 197; Bornheimer Landstrasse 45; mains €7.50-11.50) The first pub-restaurant to open in Nordend, Eckhaus has been dishing up large servings of tasty salads and good main courses for over 100 years. Its hallmark is the *Rösti* (shredded potato pancake).

Grössenwahn (☎ 599 356; www.cafe-groessenwahn .de; Lenaustrasse 97; mains €6-14) This is a lively pub-restaurant that serves stylish modern German cuisine with plenty of international extras and a selective wine list. Take the U-Bahn to Glauburgstrasse.

Weisse Lilie (☎ 453 860; Berger Strasse 275; mains €8-15) One of Frankfurt's worst-kept secrets, this tiny Spanish bodega is always crammed full of Rioja buffs and paella aficionados; if you can squeeze in you'll see why.

BOCKENHEIM

Over to the west in bohemian Bockenheim, past the university, Leipziger Strasse branches off from Bockenheimer Landstrasse and becomes a very pleasant shopping and cheap eating area. Take the U6 or U7 to Bockenheimer Warte, Leipziger Strasse or Kirchplatz.

Stattcafé (☎ 708 907; www.stattcafe.de; Grempstrasse 21; meals €2.40-18.20) Near the Kirchplatz U-Bahn station, this café offers vegetarian and meat dishes, good coffee and cakes and a comprehensive range of breakfasts. This is where students pass the time between (or during) lectures.

Prielok (☎ 776 468; Jordanstrasse 3; mains €8-11) Near the university, this is a student favourite thanks to its hearty servings of fairly traditional main dishes.

Joe Penas (☎ 707 5156; www.joepenas.de; Robert-Mayer-Strasse 18; mains €8-16) More Latin vibes, this time Mexican, although the tasty flavoured tequila and margaritas threaten to overshadow the good but unspectacular food.

Andalucia (☎ 773 730; www.restaurante-andalucia .de; Konrad-Brosswitz-Strasse 41; mains €11.50-16.50) This is a quality Spanish restaurant with a menu strong on red meat and seafood dishes, though you can easily make a meal out of the excellent tapas. It's worth booking in advance.

SELF-CATERING

Fresh produce markets are held from 8am to 6pm on Thursday and Friday at Bockenheimer Warte and Südbahnhof respectively. There are supermarkets in the basements of Galeria Kaufhof and Hertie on Zeil, and an **HL Markt** (Elisabethenstrasse 10-12) near the hostel in Sachsenhausen.

Drinking

Studio Bar (☎ 1337 9225; Katharinenpforte 6) A hot favourite in the centre of town, with a café downstairs and shiny futuristic bar upstairs; the roof terrace is *the* place to be in summer. The door policy can be pretty selective at weekends.

Blaubart Gewölbekeller (☎ 282 229; Kaiserhofstrasse 18-20) This bar has a vaulted beer cellar with long tables, bright faces and a hearty atmosphere. It also has a self-service cafeteria section offering a few standard dishes.

Café Royal (www.royal-frankfurt.de; Schäfergasse 10; ⊙ from 7pm Wed-Sun) In the spacious old MGM cinema complex just off Zeil, this is a cool art café and DJ lounge. The attached Royal Kino club has bigger nights at weekends.

Bockenheimer Weinkontor (☎ 702 031; Schlossstrasse 92) A mixed crowd of the young, middle-aged and business-suited all come here to sample various European wines. The building, a 19th-century workshop, has a lovely summer courtyard.

O'Dwyers Pub (☎ 9620 1413; Klappergasse 19) Irish pubs are a mainstay of the drinking landscape in Frankfurt, and this Sachsenhausen joint is a good specimen. On Tuesdays the bar is a U2-free zone!

Entertainment

Frankfurt has an exhaustive choice of evening entertainment options and one of the liveliest club scenes outside Berlin.

The best source of information is the German-language *Journal Frankfurt* (€1.65), available at newsstands and kiosks, with comprehensive monthly listings in German. It also has a section for lesbians and gays.

Fritz, Prinz and *Strandgut* are free listings magazines, available throughout the city. *Partysan* concentrates on club events in the Rhein-Main-Saar area. They are also in German, but use enough English to make them understandable to English-speakers.

CABARET

Tigerpalast (☎ 920 0220; www.tigerpalast.com; Heiligkreuzgasse 16-20) The Tiger Palace has popular cabaret and variety acts, and can be an expensive night out once you've paid for food. Book in advance.

Mousonturm (☎ 4058 9520; www.mousonturm.de; Waldschmidtstrasse 4) In a converted soap factory, the Mousonturm offers dance performances and politically oriented cabaret.

CINEMAS

Films screened in the original language are denoted by 'OF' or 'OmU'. Look for posters in U-Bahn stations; if the description is in English, so is the movie. Listings can also be found at www.kinoservice.de.

Turm-Palast (☎ 281 787; Grosse Eschenheimer Strasse 20) This is a multiscreen cinema that shows new films in their original languages, mostly English. On Sunday nights it gets jam-packed.

Berger Kinos (☎ 945 0330; Berger Strasse 177) A good arthouse venue in Bornheim, with regular festivals and special screenings.

Kino Mal Seh'n (☎ 597 0845; www.malsehnkino.de; Adlerflychtstrasse 6) This tiny repertory cinema

shows all kinds of offbeat movies; its wine bar and living room are equally engaging.

CLUBS & DISCOS

King Kamehameha (☎ 480 0370; www.king-kamehameha.de; Hanauer Landstrasse 192) Frankfurt's number one nightclub has its own '80s house band; prices are high and queues are inevitable. Live concerts Thursdays, dance music at weekends, and the pickiest doormen in town.

U 60311 (☎ 2970 60311; www.u60311.net; Rossmarkt) Techno is the staple diet at this full-on subterranean den. Local institution and Ibiza export the Cocoon Club has its home residency here.

Stereo Bar (☎ 617 116; Abtsgässchen 7) A quirky bar-club with a young following, '70s décor, eclectic music and an aquarium to gaze at.

190 East (☎ 5060 17180; www.190east.de; Hanauer Landstrasse 190) Budding DJs can sniff or swoon at the quality house music here, and nip into the attached record shop to buy their own.

Living XXL (☎ 242 9370; Kaiserstrasse 29) At the base of the European Central Bank tower, Frankfurt's largest club has three bars and a gallery dining room.

Robert Johnson (☎ 821 123; www.robert-johnson.de; Nording 131) Out in the suburb town of Offenbach, this big club attracts some of the best names in German electronic music, including regular nights from the thriving Frankfurt-based Playhouse label.

GAY & LESBIAN VENUES

Fritz, published monthly, has gay listings in every issue. The **Lesben Informations- und Beratungsstelle** (LIBS; ☎ 282 883; www.libs.w4w.net; Alte Gasse 38) provides information and assistance to lesbians; **Rosa Hilfe Ffm** (☎ 194 46) does the same for gay men. **Switchboard** (☎ 283 535; Alte Gasse 36) is an info-café and Aids advice centre. Pick up *Frankfurt von Hinten* (Frankfurt from Behind), a good gay guide, and check out www.frankfurt.gay-web.de. The website uses some English in its city guide.

The gay scene is concentrated around Alte Gasse and Schäfergasse, with plenty of clubs, cafés and bathhouses.

Harvey's (☎ 497 303; www.harveys-frankfurt.de; Bornheimer Landstrasse 64) This restaurant/bar's baroque décor and huge terrace make it a favoured meeting place for a mixed crowd.

HESSE

L.O.F.T.-House (☎ 9434 4841; www.lofthouse.de; Hanauer Landstrasse 181-185) One of Frankfurt's most established gay discos, with live dance groups and ever-changing décor.

Blue Angel (☎ 282 772; www.blueangel-online.de; Brönnerstrasse 17) This is a popular, strictly gay club (men only) with countless events for the party-minded.

Pulse (☎ 1388 6802; www.pulse-frankfurt.de; Bleichstrasse 38a) This is a mixed restaurant, bar and nightclub all rolled into one. Check out the wonderful conservatory/patio out the back.

Lesbian hangouts include **La Gata** (☎ 614 581; Seehofstrasse 3), Frankfurt's only women-only bar, and **Petra's Naomi** (☎ 498 0016; www .petras-naomi.de; Bleichstrasse 38).

ROCK & JAZZ

Batschkapp (☎ 9521 8410; www.batschkapp.de; Maybachstrasse 24) Hosts larger live events and some club nights.

Festhalle (☎ 757 50; Ludwig-Erhard-Anlage 1) Major international acts usually play here.

Sinkkasten (☎ 280 385; Brönnerstrasse 5) Live music with an alternative bent, from '80s covers to soul and roots.

Jazzkeller (☎ 288 537; www.jazzkeller.com; Kleine Bockenheimer Strasse 18a) This cellar jazz venue is hidden in an alley parallel to Goethestrasse, and has a great atmosphere.

Mampf (☎ 448 674; Sandweg 64) This tiny club/pub in Bornheim has some crazy jazz sessions.

THEATRE & CLASSICAL

Theatre, ballet and opera are very strong in Frankfurt; there are more than 30 different venues around town. **Frankfurt Ticket** (☎ 134 0400) takes bookings for the theatres **Kammerspiel** and **Schauspielhaus** (☎ 2123 7101; www.schauspielfrankfurt.de; Neuer Mainzer Strasse 17), as well as the **Oper complex** (Willy-Brandt-Platz) and the three stages at the **Alte Oper** (Opernplatz 8).

English Theatre (☎ 2423 1620; www.english-theatre .org; Kaiserstrasse 52) As the name suggests, you can see English-language plays and musicals here.

Freies Schauspiel Ensemble Philanthropin (☎ 596 9490; Hebelstrasse 15-19, Nordend) This is a slightly offbeat venue with alternative theatre.

TAT (☎ 2123 7555; Bockenheimer Warte) This avant-garde theatre stages highbrow performance art and special events.

Shopping

The shopping in Frankfurt is excellent. It's an ideal place to satisfy any souvenir or last-minute requirements before boarding the plane or train home.

Zeil reputedly attracts more business than any other shopping district in Europe, particularly between the Hauptwache and the Konstablerwache. Serious splurging, however, takes place on the streets immediately south of Fressgasse, where you can browse upmarket fashion boutiques and jewellery stores. Schweizer Strasse in Sachsenhausen and Berger Strasse in Bornheim are other streets with fairly good shopping.

There's a great **flea market** along Museumsufer between 8am and 2pm every Saturday. You'll also find plenty of private art galleries south of the museums, selling work by local and international artists.

Getting There & Away

AIR

Flughafen Frankfurt-am-Main (☎ 01805-372 4636; www.frankfurt-airport.de) is Germany's largest airport, with the highest freight and passenger turnover in continental Europe (London's Heathrow just beats it on passenger numbers).

This high-tech sprawl has two terminals, linked by an elevated railway called the Sky Line. Departure and arrival halls A, B and C are in the old Terminal 1, which handles Lufthansa and Star Alliance flights. Halls D and E are in the new Terminal 2.

Regional train and S-Bahn connections are deep below Terminal 1 in Hall B. IC/EC and ICE trains depart from the new Fernbahnhof, connected to the main terminal building by a walkway. ICE trains run between Hamburg and Stuttgart via Hanover and the airport every two hours, to Berlin via Cologne and Dortmund, and south to Basel. Platforms 1 to 3 are in the regional station and platforms 4 to 7 are in the long-distance train station, where there's also a DB ticket office and service point. All trains leave from the regional station between 5am and 12.30am.

The terminals have a wide range of (horribly expensive) cafés and bars, as well as Dr Müller's – Germany's only airport sex shop/adult movie theatre.

If you're in transit, you can enjoy a hot shower for €4.09 in Hall B; ask at the information counter.

Tree-lined boulevard, Hanover (p633)

DAVID PEEVERS

DAVID PEEVERS

Bremerhaven port (p630), Bremerhaven

Neues Rathaus (p635), Hanover

DAVID PEEVERS

Hamburger Kunsthalle (p693),
Hamburg

Rock concert, Fischmarkt (p691), Hamburg

Speicherstadt (p691), Hamburg

From the UK, Ryanair offers amazingly cheap flights to Frankfurt-Hahn airport – despite the name, this is not even in Hesse, and is actually nearer Koblenz! It's a 110km, 1¾-hour bus journey to Frankfurt city from the terminal (€12).

BUS
Long-distance buses leave from the south side of the Hauptbahnhof, where there's a **Eurolines office** (☎ 230 331) catering for most European destinations; an interesting domestic option is the Romantic Road bus (see Bus p359). German Eurolines services are operated by **Deutsche Touring** (☎ 790 350; Am Römerhof 17).

CAR & MOTORCYCLE
Frankfurt features the Frankfurter Kreuz, Germany's biggest autobahn intersection – modelled, it would seem, after the kind you might find in Los Angeles. All major (and some minor) car-rental companies have offices in the Hauptbahnhof and at the airport.

Känguruh (☎ 596 2035; Eckenheimer Landstrasse 99, Nordend) rents out older-model cars from around €30 per day, including insurance and a generous kilometre allowance. **ADAC** (☎ 01805-101 112; Schillerstrasse 12) has useful information for drivers.

The **Mitfahrzentrale** (☎ 194 40; Baselerplatz; ⏲ 8am-6.30pm Mon-Fri, 8am-4pm Sat, 10am-4pm Sun) arranges lifts; typical fares are Berlin €19, Munich €13 and Kassel €7, plus fees (€2 to €12).

TRAIN
The Hauptbahnhof west of the centre handles more departures and arrivals than any other station in Germany. The information office for connections and tickets is at the head of platform 9; for train information call ☎ 01805-996 633.

Deutsche Bahn's regional saver comes in the form of the hessenticket (€25), which gives the usual full day of regional train travel for up to five people.

Getting Around
TO/FROM THE AIRPORT
S-Bahn line No 8 shuttles between the airport and the Hauptbahnhof (€3.20, 15 minutes), usually continuing to Offenbach via Hauptwache and Konstablerwache.

Bus No 61 runs to the Südbahnhof in Sachsenhausen from Terminal 1, level 1.

Taxis charge about €25 for the trip into town.

BICYCLE
The city is good for cyclists, with designated bike lanes on most streets. Bikes are treated by the law as cars, so watch out for red lights. You can rent bikes from the **Hauptbahnhof** (☎ 2653 4834) or **Radschlag** (☎ 452 064; Hallgartenstrasse 56, Bornheim); Deutsche Bahn's remote-operated **Call-a-Bike** scheme (☎ 07000-522 5522; www.callabike.de) costs €0.06 a minute. See p763 for details of this scheme.

CAR & MOTORCYCLE
Traffic flows smoothly in central Frankfurt, but the one-way system makes it extremely frustrating to get to where you want to go. You're better off parking your vehicle in one of the many car parks (€2 per hour, €2.50 overnight) and proceeding on foot. Throughout the centre you'll see signs giving directions and the number of places left in nearby car parks.

PUBLIC TRANSPORT
Frankfurt's excellent – if expensive – transport network (RMV) integrates all bus, tram, S-Bahn and U-Bahn lines. Single or day tickets can be purchased from the machines at almost any stop. Press *Einzelfahrt Frankfurt* for destinations in zone 50, which takes in most of Frankfurt, excluding the airport. *Kurzstrecken* (short-trip tickets; consult the list on machines) cost €1.55, single tickets €1.95 and a *Tageskarte* (24-hour ticket) €4.60. Weekly passes cost €17.50.

SKATING
It's not usually the best way to get around, but every Tuesday from April to October thousands of inline skaters hit the streets for a sociable 33km to 42km road circuit with police escort. For details click onto www.tns-frankfurt.de.

TAXI
Taxis are quite expensive at €1.90 hire charge plus a minimum of €1 per kilometre. There are taxi ranks throughout the city, or you can call ☎ 792 020, ☎ 634 800 or ☎ 230 01.

DARMSTADT

☎ 06151 / pop 139,000

About 35km south of Frankfurt, Darmstadt is a modest town with a long history of scientific and artistic accomplishments; the Mathildenhöhe, the artists' colony that truly brought the *Jugendstil* (Art Nouveau) into vogue, was founded here. It's an easy side trip from Frankfurt, and if you decide to stay, there are some great nightspots catering for the lively student population.

Orientation

The Hauptbahnhof and Europaplatz complex is at the western end of the city, connected to the Altstadt (Old Town) by a long walk (or quick bus ride on bus No 6, 7, 8, 9 or 10) down Rheinstrasse, which runs directly into Luisenplatz, the expansive French-style square at the pedestrianised heart of the city. The Hessisches Landesmuseum and Schloss museum are right in the centre. The Mathildenhöhe is about 1km east of the centre.

Information

Commerzbank (Rheinstrasse 34)

Gutenberg Buchhandlung (Am Luisenplatz 4) Bookshop.

On-Game (☎ 870 0651; www.multimedia-bistro.de; Europaplatz 1; €3.50-4.50 per hr) Internet access.

Post office (Luisenplatz)

ProRegio (☎ 132 782; www.darmstadt.de; Im Carree 4a; 🕓 9.30am-7pm Mon-Fri, 9.30am-6pm Sat) Tourist information.

Sights

Established in 1899 at the behest of Grand Duke Ernst-Ludwig, the artists' colony at **Mathildenhöhe** churned out some impressive works of Art Nouveau between 1901 and 1914. The **Museum Künstlerkolonie** (Artists' Colony Museum; ☎ 133 385; Olbrichweg/Bauhausweg; adult/concession €3/2; 🕓 10am-5pm Tue-Sun) displays some of these works in its beautiful grounds. Take bus F from the Hauptbahnhof. Also in the grounds is the **Ausstellungsgebäude Mathildenhöhe**, an art gallery with changing exhibitions (€5/3), and a stunning Russian Orthodox **chapel** (1897-99; donation €0.75; 🕓 9am-6pm Apr-Sep, 9am-5pm Oct-Mar), built and designed by Louis Benois for the Russian Tsar Nicholas II after he married Princess Alexandra of Hesse in 1894.

Back in the centre, the **Hessisches Landesmuseum** (Hesse State Museum; ☎ 165 703; Friedensplatz 1; adult/concession/child €2.50/1.20/0.50, free after 4pm; 🕓 10am-5pm Tue, Wed & Thu-Sat, 10am-8pm Wed, 11am-5pm Sun) is one of the oldest art museums in Germany, housing Hessian artworks from 1550 to 1880 and exhibitions on the natural sciences and geology.

The **Schlossmuseum** (☎ 240 35; Marktplatz; adult/concession €2.50/1.50; 🕓 10am-1pm & 2-5pm Mon-Thu, 10am-1pm Sat & Sun) is in a former margrave's residence with an 18th-century castle, and is packed with ornate furnishings, carriages and paintings, including *The Madonna of Jakob Meyer, Mayor of Basle* by Hans Holbein the Younger. The building is now part of the Technische Universität.

Tours

ProRegio organises thematic city tours in German (one/two hours €4.50/6.50); the timetable varies so it's best to check ahead.

Sleeping & Eating

DJH hostel (☎ 452 93; darmstadt@djh-hessen.de; Landgraf-Georg-Strasse 119; junior/senior €17/19.70) In the heart of Darmstadt's nightlife district, DJH Jugendherberge is a stone's throw from the shores of the Woog lake (take bus D from anywhere in the centre of town). There's an outdoor swimming pool next door.

Hotel Ernst-Ludwig (☎ 271 90; Ernst-Ludwig-Strasse 14; s €42-55, d €68-77) More central and more modern, this is an immaculate pension just off Luisenplatz; the huge TVs easily drown out any daytime street noise from the many shoppers outside.

Hotel Prinz Heinrich (☎ 813 70; www.hotel-prinz-heinrich.de; Bleichstrasse 48; s €56.50-75, d €92-107; ⊠) Very traditional and very comfortable, the old-fashioned furniture and atmospheric *Weinstube* (wine room) make this vine-covered establishment near the centre a classic.

City Braustübl (☎ 255 11; Wilhelminerstrasse 31; mains €6-14) A good brewery outlet restaurant offering a range of regional and national dishes to complement the many kinds of local beer. The Darmstädter Brauerei itself is opposite the station, and can be visited.

Drinking & Entertainment

Centralstation (☎ 366 8899; www.centralstation-darmstadt.de; Im Carree) This three-level party paradise not only has a great cocktail bar and restaurant, it's also one of the best live music and cultural centres in the Rhine-Main region.

An Sibin (☎ 204 52; www.ansibin.com; Landgraf-Georg-Strasse 125) This is a great Irish pub and live concert venue with good beer.

Goldene Krone (☎ 213 52; www.goldene-krone.de; Schustergasse 18) This is a Darmstadt institution, drawing a grungy student crowd. It has a cinema, piano room, pool table, club nights, live music and shocking toilets.

Getting There & Away

Frequent S-Bahn trains serve Frankfurt's Hauptbahnhof (€5.90, 20 minutes). The A5 connects Frankfurt and Darmstadt.

AROUND DARMSTADT
Kloster Lorsch

Founded in the 8th century and Unesco-listed in 1991, **Kloster Lorsch** (Lorsch Abbey; ☎ 06251-103 820; www.kloster-lorsch.de; Nibelungenstrasse 35, Lorsch; adult/concession €3/2; ✆ 10am-5pm Tue-Sun) was once one of the most significant religious complexes in Germany and a site of great importance to the Carolingian dynasty. Today it's primarily interesting from an archaeological point of view, as possibly the only monastery site in Europe where the medieval grounds remain undisturbed by modern activity; sadly few of the original buildings have been preserved (the King's Hall and Altenmünster are the most accessible). However, various projects are in progress and the museum centre gives visitors a thorough picture of the abbey's history, as well as displaying fascinating manuscripts like the *Lorsch Pharmacopia*.

Lorsch is easily reached from Darmstadt by train via Bensheim (€7.60, 25 minutes) and by road with the A9 or A30 south. The abbey is a 10-minute walk from the station.

Messel

Another Unesco monument, the Grube Messel (Messel Pit) fossil site contains a wealth of well-preserved animal and plant remains from the Eocene era, around 49 million years ago. It's best known for the specimens of early horses found here, which clearly illustrate the evolution towards the modern beast.

Full excavation began in 1975 and most of the interesting fossils are now held in the Hessisches Landesmuseum in Darmstadt (see p554), the **Senckenberg Museum** (☎ 069-754 20; www.senckenberg.uni-frankfurt.de; Senckenberganlage 25; ✆ 9am-5pm Mon, Tue, Thu & Fri,

9am-8pm Wed, 9am-6pm Sat & Sun) in Frankfurt and Messel's own **museum** (☎ 06159-5119; Langgasse 2; ✆ 2-5pm Tue-Sun May-Oct, 2-4pm Sat & Sun Nov-Apr, 10am-noon Sun year-round). For tours of the site itself, call 06159-71570 or contact the Messel museum.

Messel is about 10km northeast of Darmstadt and is served by regional trains and buses.

WIESBADEN
☎ 0611 / pop 266,000

Once favoured by ailing gentry, Hesse's capital is a historic and attractive spa centre west of Frankfurt and just across the Rhein from Mainz. Goethe spent time here in 1814, and more Russian writers than you can poke a potato at have swanned in over the centuries to partake of the cure. Dostoevsky made a mess of his nerves here during the 1860s, when he amassed huge losses at the city's gambling tables; in 1991 the Russian government reportedly offered to settle his debts, but Wiesbaden graciously wrote them off as a gesture of goodwill.

Wiesbaden still attracts the rich, the famous and the ailing (and the Russians) – it's an appealing spot for travellers, too, and well worth a visit for its charming atmosphere and fine parks. It's quite possible to wander around the compact Altstadt and never realise just how big the modern city actually is!

Orientation

The city centre is a 15-minute walk north from the Hauptbahnhof along Bahnhofstrasse, or you can take bus No 1 or 8.

The cable car up the Neroberg is on the northern edge of the city; the Kurhaus is northeast of the centre. Bus No 1 goes to both.

Information

Channel 13 (☎ 341 9954; www.channel-thirteen.com; Rheinstrasse 123; €2.25 per hr; ✆ 24 hrs) Internet access. Free to US citizens.
Doctor (☎ 461 010, 670 60)
Nemesis (☎ 308 8850; Luisenstrasse 17; €2-2.50 per hr) Internet access.
Reisebank (Hauptbahnhof)
Post office (Kaiser-Friedrich-Ring 81)
Tourist office (☎ 172 9780; www.wiesbaden.de; Marktstrasse 6; ✆ 9am-6pm Mon-Fri, 9am-3pm Sun) Very helpful office with plenty of English material.

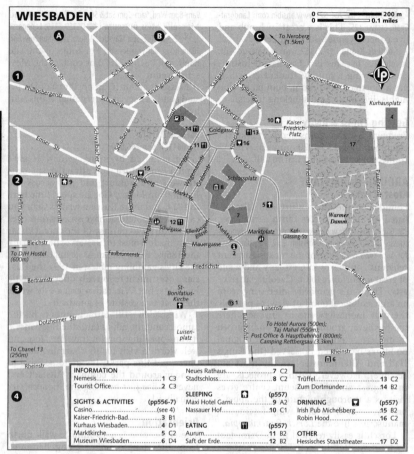

WIESBADEN

INFORMATION		Neues Rathaus................................7 C2		
Nemesis.................................1 C3		Stadtschloss.................................8 C2		Trüffel...................................13 C2
Tourist Office..........................2 C3				Zum Dortmunder....................14 B2
		SLEEPING (p557)		
SIGHTS & ACTIVITIES (pp556-7)		Maxi Hotel Garni.......................9 A2		DRINKING (p557)
Casino..................................(see 4)		Nassauer Hof...........................10 C1		Irish Pub Michelsberg...........15 B2
Kaiser-Friedrich-Bad...............3 B1				Robin Hood............................16 C2
Kurhaus Wiesbaden................4 D1		EATING (p557)		
Marktkirche...........................5 C2		Aurum....................................11 B2		OTHER
Museum Wiesbaden................6 D4		Saft der Erde...........................12 B2		Hessisches Staatstheater.......17 D2

Sights & Activities

The **Schlossplatz** is in the centre of the city and contains the stunning Gothic **Marktkirche** (1852–62) and the **Neues Rathaus** (New Town Hall; 1884–87) surrounding the **Marktbrunnen** (market fountain) originally built in 1537. On the northern side is the neoclassical **Stadtschloss** (1840), built for Duke Wilhelm von Nassau and now the Hessian parliament.

A restored 1888 **cable car** (€1.30) makes the trip up the Neroberg for the **Russian Orthodox Church** (adult/child €0.60/0.30; ☺ 10am-5pm), often mistakenly called the 'Greek Chapel'. It was built between 1847 and 1855 as the burial place of Elizabeth Mikhailovna, wife of Duke Adolf of Nassau; Elizabeth died

here during childbirth in 1845 and Adolf built this five-domed church in her honour, modelled on the Church of the Ascension in Moscow. An impressively bearded custodian turns on atmospheric music when you enter.

Also on the hill are a war memorial, a large swimming pool complex, a café and one of the oldest vineyards in the area (open to visitors). The grassy expanse overlooking the pool and the town is a popular sunbathing spot.

Back in town, **Museum Wiesbaden** (☎ 335 2170; www.museum-wiesbaden.de; Friedrich-Ebert-Allee 2; adult/concession/child €2.50/1.25/0.50, free from 4pm Tue; ☺ 10am-8pm Tue, 10am-5pm Wed-Sun) houses many paintings by Russian expressionist

Alexei Jawlensky, who lived in Wiesbaden from 1921 until his death in 1941.

The **Kurhaus Wiesbaden** (☎ 172 90; Kurhausplatz 1) is a restored classical building (1907) that's been converted into the city's main theatre, convention centre and casino. Men wanting to do a Dostoevsky should pack a jacket and tie. You can view the obscenely lavish rooms with a guide (see Tours below) or just walk up to the desk staff and ask them to let you snoop around.

For the full spa experience, try historic **Kaiser-Friedrich-Bad** (☎ 172 9660; kft@wiesbaden .de; Langgasse 38-40; four hours €17.50; 🕙 10am-10pm Sat-Thu, 10am-midnight Fri). Tuesday is for women only; nudity is compulsory all week.

Tours
The tourist office runs bus and walking tours on Saturdays, leaving from the Theatre Colonnade in front of the Hessisches Staatstheater. Most take in the Kurhaus, Neroberg and the castle at Biebrich, and sometimes include a glass of wine. Bus tours cost €10/5 per adult/child; walks are €6/3. Tours in English are available, and can also be arranged for groups at €62 for up to 30 people.

Sleeping
The thermal waters might heal the body, but Wiesbaden's hotel prices won't help anyone on a budget. To add insult to injury, rates rise around Frankfurt trade fairs as well. Weekends are the cheapest times.

DJH hostel (☎ 486 57; Blücherstrasse 66; junior/senior €19/21.70) Back down to earth, the DJH Jugendherberge is 10 minutes from the city centre; take bus No 14 to Gneisenaustrasse. Despite the unattractive building, it's clean, the staff are helpful, and the cafeteria downstairs serves beer and apple wine.

Camping Rettbergsau (☎ 215 51; www.rettbergsau .de; Shierstein; camp sites €4.50; 🕙 Apr-Sep) This camp site is on the island in the middle of the Rhine. The island is off-limits to cars; take bus No 3, 4 or 38 from anywhere in the centre to Rheinufer Biebrich, then catch the ferry (€2).

Hotel Aurora (☎ 373 728; Untere Albrechtsstrasse 9; s/d €55/80; ✖) A rare bargain, situated on a quiet side street near the Hauptbahnhof. Some small apartments are also available alongside the comfortable standard rooms.

Maxi Hotel Garni (☎ 945 20; www.hotel-max.de; Wellritzstrasse 6; s/d €70/95; Ⓟ) Recently renovated, these are simple but very tasteful rooms in a convenient, if unexciting, location just outside the Altstadt.

Nassauer Hof (☎ 1330; www.nassauer-hof.de; Kaiser-Friedrich-Platz 3-4; s €195-225, d €260-305, ste €370-1100; Ⓟ ✖ 🐾 🌊) Set foot inside the door here and you'll understand why people shell out for rooms here – it's one of Europe's few remaining full-service grand hotels, with a prestigious position and total luxury throughout.

Eating & Drinking
Saft der Erde (☎ 308 2101; Kleine Kirchgasse; drinks from €3) Superb juice bar peddling fantastically named fruit concoctions, soya shakes and the like.

Aurum (☎ 302 880; Goldgasse 16; mains €4-10) One of the many eateries sardined along Goldgasse, this café-bar offers light meals like baked potatoes and apple strudel (€4). You can also drink here till late.

Zum Dortmunder (☎ 302 096; Langgasse 34; mains €8-18) In the centre, this restaurant offers traditional cuisine in a pub atmosphere. The streetside tables, free-flowing beer and convivial ambience make it a local favourite in summer.

Taj Mahal (☎ 373 389; Bahnhofstrasse 52; curries from €13; 🕙) You get all the classics at this upmarket Indian, with a nice terrace and good cheap lunch deals.

Trüffel (☎ 990 550; www.trueffel.net; Webergasse 6-8; mains €10-24) Talk about versatile: this classy but friendly establishment is a deli, bistro, restaurant and hotel all in one place. The upstairs restaurant, with its lovely terrace overlooking the street, is an absolute must.

Irish Pub Michelsberg (☎ 300 849; Michelsberg 15; 🖥) A typical Irish pub, with an appreciative expat/student crowd coming for the live music.

Robin Hood (☎ 301 349; www.robin-wi.de; Häfnergasse 3) They may not be stealing from the rich, but you'll certainly find a bunch of merry men in this well-frequented gay bar-bistro.

Getting There & Around
S-Bahn trains leave every 20 minutes from Frankfurt's Hauptbahnhof (€5.90, 45 minutes). The S8 runs via Frankfurt airport.

HESSE

Passenger boats on Cologne–Mainz routes stop at Wiesbaden, as do cruises to/from Frankfurt and other local destinations.

Wiesbaden is connected to Frankfurt by the A66 Autobahn and is just off the A3, which leads to the Ruhr region.

City buses cost €1.95 for a single ticket or €4.50 for a day pass. The train station is a major hub for buses and you can buy tickets from the machines.

LAHN VALLEY

The majestic valley carved by the Lahn River acts as a natural border between both the Taunus and Westerwald hills, due north of Wiesbaden. It links such eye-catching places as the peninsula town of Weilburg and the historic town of Limburg, before spilling into the Rhine at Lahntal, south of Koblenz. The 44km stretch between Weilburg and Limburg is a particular attraction, both for its cultural and sporting offerings.

Weilburg, almost entwined by the river, is dominated by the 16th-century **Schloss** (☎ 06471-2236; adult/concession €3.50/2.50; ☯ 10am-5pm Tue-Sun), a sprawling rococo complex whose splendid gardens stretch 400m from the craggy hilltop right down to the Lahn River bank. Weilburg is also home to Germany's only **ship tunnel**, a 195m-long structure built in 1847 to save river traffic having to sail around the peninsula. It's a perfect point to embark on a paddle downstream.

Limburg has a timber-framed core that is preserved as a historic monument. Its striking orange-and-white **Dom** (☎ 06431-295 332; tours 11am & 3pm Mon-Fri, 11am Sat, 11.45am Sun) is unlike anything else you'll see in this area, standing on a rocky precipice overlooking the Lahn to the north and the beautiful Altstadt to the south. The **Rathaus** is a well-preserved 14th-century masterpiece and the **Lahnbrücke**, a former toll bridge, is testament to the days when Limburg was a rich merchant town.

A wonderful way to soak up the beauty of these two towns and the surrounding countryside is to hike, bike or boat through the river valley from one to the other. **Velociped** (☎ 06421-245 11; www.velociped.de) organises one- to 11-day 'TriathLahn' tours (€45 to €799), which include maps, hiking routes, lodging, food, kayaks and bicycles. **Lahntours** (☎ 06426-928 00; www.lahntours.de) offers weekend kayaking tours for €135, with

camping in an Indian tepee village with an evening barbecue.

MARBURG

☎ 06421 / pop 77,600

Some 90km north of Frankfurt, Marburg is a university city with a charming Altstadt and the splendid Elisabethkirche, Germany's oldest pure Gothic cathedral. Established in 1527, the Philipps-Universität was Europe's first Protestant university; the Brothers Grimm studied here for a short time, and while their successors may not yet be as illustrious, the student crowds give the town a very friendly buzz at night.

It's also a great place to get fit; much of it is built on a hillside, and staircases and ramps abound. When the toil of the cobblestoned Altstadt becomes too much, you'll find plenty of bars and cafés to relax in.

Orientation

The Lahn River flows south between the Altstadt and the Hauptbahnhof area. The Altstadt rises up the hill on the west bank of the river, divided into a fairly bland Unterstadt at the bottom and the charming old-fashioned Oberstadt on the hillside.

Bahnhofstrasse leads from the Hauptbahnhof to Elisabethstrasse, which takes you south past the Elisabethkirche to a fork in the road; bear right for the Oberstadt and left for the Unterstadt. See the Altstadt Walking Tour later in this section for information about the lifts and a delightful staircase that runs between the two.

The university campus is spread throughout the city, but the Old University building is in the centre of the Altstadt.

Information

Internet TREFF (☎ 924 705; Pilgrimstein; €2 per 30 min; ☯ 11-1am Mon-Sat, 3pm-1am Sun)

Internet World (☎ 690 645; www.internetworld -marburg.de; Bahnhofstrasse 23; €3 per hr; ☯ 10am-9.30pm Mon-Sat, 1-10pm Sun)

Marburg Information (☎ 991 20; www.marburg.de; Pilgrimstein 26; ☯ 9am-6pm Mon-Fri, 10am-2pm Sat)

Post office (Bahnhofstrasse 6)

Sparkasse (Mauerstrasse) Bank.

Uni-Klinikum (☎ 283 697; Baldingerstrasse) Medical services.

Universitätsbuchhandlung (☎ 170 90; Reitgasse 7-9) Bookshop.

Wohlfeile Bücher (☎ 669 19; Neustadt 9) Bookshop.

Sights
ELISABETHKIRCHE

Germany's oldest pure Gothic cathedral was built between 1235 and 1283, though the twin spires weren't finished for another three decades. It's worthwhile going behind the screen to view the **Hohe Chor** (High Choir), the elegant **Elisabethschrein** (Elisabeth Shrine) and **gravestones** (adult/concession €2/1.50; 9am-6pm). You can also join a German-language **tour** (adult/concession €2.50/1.50), or an attendant might take you around for the same fee.

OTHER ATTRACTIONS

The **Universitätsmuseum für Bildende Kunst** (University Fine Arts Museum; ☎ 282 2355; Biegenstrasse 11; 11am-1pm & 2-5pm Tue-Sun), on the east bank of the river, has artworks from the 19th and 20th centuries. The **Marburger Kunstverein Ausstellungshaus und Artothek** (☎ 258 82; Biegenstrasse 1) is the latest addition to Marburg's cultural scene, exhibiting works by contemporary German artists; it also contains a cinema complex.

The former city **botanical gardens**, just to the northwest of the museum, are now open as a public park.

Altstadt Walking Tour

From Elisabethkirche, walk south, take the left jig to Steinweg, which leads up the hill. Steinweg becomes Neustadt and Wettergasse. Turn right when Wettergasse becomes Reitgasse and you'll reach the **Markt**.

In the centre of the Markt is the **Rathaus** (1512). Its beautiful clock strikes hourly with lots of pomp, and there's an odd half-gable on the west side. A market is held here every Saturday morning.

From here, go up the narrow Nikolaistrasse to the **St-Marien-Kirche**, an imposing red-brick church on a terrace with great views over the lower town – this is the place to come for sunrise, particularly at weekends, when you'll often be joined by a motley crowd of students, late-night drinkers, early morning dog walkers, rough sleepers and anyone else who wanders past. You may notice that the church tower is at a slight angle; university legend has it that this will straighten out if a medical student graduates while still a virgin!

Follow the steps up to Landgraf-Philipp-Strasse and the **Landgrafenschloss** (Landgraves'

Castle; ☎ 282 2355; Schloss 1; adult/concession €2.60/1; 10am-6pm Tue-Sun Apr-Oct, 11am-5pm Nov-Mar), a massive stone structure built between 1248 and 1300 that used to be the administrative seat of Hesse. There the **Kulturhistorisches Museum** (Cultural History Museum) and some great views here; concerts are held in the adjacent **Schlosspark** throughout the year.

On the way down, turn left on Ritterstrasse and head to Schlosssteig, where you can see the excavated remains of a medieval **synagogue** under glass. From here, go along Wettergasse and Reitgasse and you'll reach the **Universitätskirche** (1300), a former Dominican monastery, and the **Alte Universität** (1891), still part of the campus and still bustling.

Finally, walk round the church and across the Weidenhäuser Brücke; on the south side of the bridge and the east side of the Lahn is a stand with **rowing boats** (€5 per hour).

To get to the Markt without climbing Steinweg, walk south from Elisabethkirche, bear left at the fork and go along Pilgrimstein. Past the tourist office, free lifts carry you up to Reitgasse from 7am to 1.30am. There's also a monstrously steep stone staircase at Enge Gasse, just north of the tourist office, which was once a sewage sluice.

Tours

The tourist office runs two-hour walking tours round the Elisabethkirche and Landgrafenschloss, leaving from the church at 3pm Saturday (adult/concession €3/2). One-hour tours of the Markt and Altstadt leave from the Rathaus at 3pm Wednesday (adult/concession €3/2; April to October).

Sleeping

Hotels in town are generally expensive. The tourist information office books **private rooms** (from around €20) at no charge.

DJH hostel (☎ 234 61; marburg@djh-hessen.de; Jahnstrasse 1; junior/senior €18/20.70) Downstream from Rudolphsplatz, this is a clean and well-run establishment; staff can help plan outings, rent out canoes and arrange bike hire. From the Auf der Weide bus stop, follow the street left and cross the small bridge; the hostel is straight ahead on the left. Take Bus C.

Campingplatz Lahnaue (☎ 213 31; Trojedamm 47; adult/child €4/2, car/tent €2/3) South of the hostel, this is a fine site right on the river, with plenty of sports facilities in the immediate vicinity.

Gästehaus Einsle (☎ 234 10; Frankfurter Strasse 2a; d €65) On the west side of the Lahn near the hostel, this is about the best value you'll get here. The three apartment-style doubles are a touch twee (think doilies), but they're clean and nicely fitted-out.

Hotel Waldecker Hof (☎ 600 90; waldecker-hof@ t-online.de; Bahnhofstrasse 23; s €68-91, d €85-112; Ⓟ ⊠ ☒) This big hotel near the station has all the character of a traditional pension, complete with random décor such as large wooden dogs at reception. The rooms are variable but you can't argue with the amenities.

Hotel Sorat (☎ 9180; marburg@sorat-hotels.com; Pilgrimstein 29; s €97-137, d €117-157; ⊠ ☒) Typically swish ultra-modern Sorat branch near the tourist office and the Lahn-Center mall, with plenty of away-from-home comforts and champagne breakfast.

Eating

Café Vetter (☎ 258 88; Reitgasse 4; cakes from €1) Still going strong after 90 years, Vetter accompanies its delectable range of cakes and food with a mixed bag of music, stand-up, one-person shows and a regular flea market. The treat of choice for local students.

Café Barfuss (☎ 253 49; Barfüsserstrasse 33; food €3-7) One of our favourite options on busy Barfüsserstrasse, this offbeat place attracts a sociable student crowd and serves up good light and vegetarian dishes until late.

Brasserie (☎ 219 92; Reitgasse 8; mains from €7.50) The best feature of this traditional bistro-café is the summer beer garden, occupying a miniature terrace in front of the St Kilian chapel in the Oberstadt.

Altes Brauhaus (☎ 221 80; Pilgrimstein 34; mains €8.50-11) A fine traditional brewery restaurant serving beer in litres and hearty meals in spades. Options for vegetarians are pointedly minimal.

Atelier (☎ 6960; Elisabethstrasse 12; mains €12.50-18.50) The award-winning house restaurant at the Europäischer Hof hotel is well worth the time and money involved for fans of sophisticated Italian and international cuisine.

Alter Ritter (☎ 628 38; Steinweg 44; mains €13-19) This is a traditional gourmet restaurant with four- and five-course set menus from €30, plus cheaper lunch specials.

Drinking & Entertainment

Pick up the free *Marburger Magazin Express* for listings. The *Kino-Programm* leaflet has film schedules. Both are in German, but are pretty easy for English speakers to decipher.

Filmkunst am Steinweg (☎ 672 69; www.marbur ger-filmkunst.de; Steinweg 4) Every student town needs a good arthouse cinema, and Marburg is no exception – the Kammer, Palette and Atelier screens show blockbusters, classics and offbeat treats for the pickiest of audiences.

Sumo (☎ 941 83; www.sumoclub.de; Temmlerstrasse 7) It's quite a way from the centre, but this is the place to go for serious club nights. Head for Marburg-Süd station.

In the Altstadt, **Delirium** (Steinweg 3) stays open longer than anywhere else and is usually packed. You could also try **Jazz Kneipe Cavete** (☎ 661 57; Steinweg 12), **Mox** (☎ 690 0161; www.moxclub.de; cnr Keizerbach & Pilgrimstein) or salsa nights at **Club Lounge** in the Hotel Sorat.

Getting There & Around

Trains to Marburg run hourly from Frankfurt (€11.30, one hour) and twice an hour from Kassel (€14, 1¼ hours). By car, the quickest way to reach Marburg from Frankfurt is via the A5 heading north towards Giessen. Marburg lies on the B3.

Velociped (☎ 245 11; www.velociped.de; Alte Kasseler Strasse 43) hires out bicycles from €10 per day and can help organise trips to nearby towns, including accommodation.

Bus Nos A1 and 7 operate from the Hauptbahnhof to Rudolphsplatz; tickets cost €1.30.

FULDA

☎ 0661 / pop 64,000

With a large baroque district and many fine and interesting churches, Fulda, an old monastery town one hour from Frankfurt, is definitely worth a visit. It's also a good base for trips into the outlying region, which includes the beautiful Rhön nature park and its highest mountain, the Wasserkuppe, a magnet for hang-gliders, rock-climbers and skiers.

The Hauptbahnhof is at the northeastern end of Bahnhofstrasse, five minutes from the baroque Altstadt, which begins just west of Universitätsplatz. Turn right at Universitätsplatz to get to the Stadtschloss, at the northern end of the Altstadt. The Dom and St-Michaels-Kirche are just west of the Stadtschloss. The bus station is at the southern end of the Hauptbahnhof.

Information

Ärztlicher Notdienst (☎ 192 92; Würtstrasse 1) Emergency doctors.

Café Online (☎ 901 2460; Königstrasse 80-82; €2 per 30min) Internet access.

Commerzbank (Universitätsplatz)

Post office (Heinrich-von-Bibra-Platz)

Tourist Information (☎ 102 1813; www.fulda.de; Bonifatiusplatz 1; ☽ 8.30am-6pm Mon-Fri, 9.30am-4pm Sat, 10am-2pm Sun)

Sights

The **Stadtschloss** (Town castle; ☎ 102 1814; adult/concession €2/1.50; ☽ 10am-6pm Sat-Thu, 2-6pm Fri), built in 1707, was the former residence of the prince abbots and now houses the city administration and a museum. The historic rooms include the Fürstensaal, a grandiose banquet hall, the Spiegelkabinett (Chamber of Mirrors) and a good collection of 18th-century porcelain. From the Green Room there are views over the palace gardens to the **Orangerie**, now part of the Maritim Hotel. On the hill is the baroque Frauen-berg Franciscan Friary; the **church** (☽ 10am-5pm) of this functioning convent is open to the public.

West of the gardens is the remarkable **Michaelskirche** (☎ 820-22; ☽ 10am-6pm Apr-Oct, 2-4pm Nov-Mar), the burial chapel of the Ben-edictine monastic cemetery, with its classic witch's-hat towers. The rotunda dates from the original construction and the pillars in the crypt are from the Carolingian era.

The reconstructed **Dom** (built 1704-12) is across the street on the grounds of the Ratgar Basilica, which stood here from 819 to 1700. Inside is the tomb of St Boniface – the English missionary who died a martyr in 754 – plus amazing paintings of the As-sumption of Mary and the Holy Trinity, and a Gothic relief of Charlemagne (15th cen-tury). There are **organ recitals** (adult/concession €10/7.50) here every Saturday at noon during May, June, September and October.

The **Cathedral Museum** (☎ 872 07; adult/concession €2.10/1.30; ☽ 10am-5.30pm Tue-Sat, 12.30-5.30pm Sun), in the former Stiftskirche, is the highlight of a visit to Fulda. The museum's treasures include Jewish gravestones (in

the artefact-packed front yard), the paint-ing *Christus und die Ehebrecherin* by Lucas Cranach the Elder (1512), the spectacular Silver Altar and a spooky thing reported to be the skull of St Boniface. In the cloak-room, look through the glass floor to the foundations of the original basilica.

Sleeping & Eating

DJH hostel (☎ 733 89; Schirrmannstrasse 31; junior/senior €16/18.70) Clean and friendly, the hostel is southwest of the centre – take bus Nos 50, 52 or 1B to Am Stadion.

Hotel Lenz (☎ 620 40; www.hotel-lenz.de; Leipziger Strasse 122-124; s €53-81, d €79-112; ☒ ☒ ☒) This is named not after the tragic playwright but after the proprietor, who takes per-sonal charge of the excellent restaurant. This engaging place comes into its own at night, when the half-timbered arch façade is stunningly lit from inside.

Hotel Goldener Karpfen (☎ 868 00; www.hotel-goldener-karpfen.de; Simpliziusbrunnen 1-15; s €95-155, d €145-230; ☒ ☒ ☒) This fantastic Romantic hotel offers a playful mix of ancient and modern, with antiques and contemporary furniture throughout. The highly rated restaurant serves up superb regional dishes and two- to five-course 'light' lunches (€16 to €40).

Restaurant Cafe Hauptwache Da Mario (☎ 227 11; Bonifatiusplatz 2; mains €6-15) Sit on the terrace and gaze up at the Dom from this recom-mended Italian restaurant in the baroque former watch house.

Aubergine (☎ 292 6868; Haimbacher Strasse 51; mains from €5; ☒) Watch out for flying pigs – this is that rare creature, a German vegeta-rian restaurant, and a good one at that.

Getting There & Away

There's a regular train service to Fulda from Frankfurt (€11.30, 80 minutes), but the fast-est method is by IC (€19.60, one hour) or ICE train (€25.20, 50 minutes). Fulda can be reached by the A7, which runs north towards Kassel and south to Würzburg.

KASSEL

☎ 0561 / pop 194,000

The term 'architectural crimes' could well have been coined to describe the reconstruc-tion of Kassel, a once lovely city on the Fulda River, 1½ hours north of Frankfurt. The label still fits, but the sprawling town is doing its best to regain some of its former appeal.

Must-sees here include the city's unusual Museum of Death and Wilhelmshöhe, a glorious nature park with waterfalls, a Roman aqueduct, two castles and the massive Herkules monument. There's also a museum dedicated to Wilhelm and Jakob Grimm, who were born in Hesse and began compiling folk stories while living in Kassel.

Every five years Kassel is host to one of Western Europe's most important contemporary art shows, the **Documenta**, founded by art professor Arnold Bode in 1955; lasting 100 days, it attracts up to 700,000 visitors. As if this wasn't enough, the city is bidding against stiff competition for European Capital of Culture 2010.

Orientation

There are two main train stations. ICE, IC and IR trains pull into the new Bahnhof Wilhelmshöhe (known as the ICE-Bahnhof), 3km west of the city centre. The Hauptbahnhof (in name only) is at the western end of the centre at Bahnhofsplatz, and is being developed as a cultural centre.

The mostly pedestrianised centre of the city focuses on Königsplatz and Friedrichsplatz, which are frequently crammed with shoppers, tourists and stalls on special occasions. Wilhelmshöhe and its attractions are all at the western end of Wilhelmshöher Allee, which runs straight as an arrow from the centre to the castle.

Information

Deutsche Bank (Königsplatz)
Doom's World (☎ 400 1031; cnr Königstrasse & Wilhelmshöher Allee; €2 per hr) Internet access.
Freyschmidts Buchhandlung (☎ 729 0210; Königstrasse 23) Bookshop.
Kassel Card (1/3 days €7/10) Free public transport, tours and admission/discounts for attractions.
Kassel Tourist Station (☎ 340 54; www.kassel.de; ICE-Bahnhof; ☺ 9am-6pm Mon-Fri, 9am-1pm Sat) Rathaus (☎ 707 707; kgs@kassel.de; Obere Königstrasse 8) Tourist information.
Post office Centre (Untere Königstrasse 95) Station (ICE-Bahnhof)
Schlosspark Ticket (€10) All Wilhelmshöhe attractions and return journey.
Sparkasse (ICE-Bahnhof) Bank.
Wasch-Treff (Friedrich-Ebert-Strasse 81; ☺ 5am-midnight) Laundry.

Sights
WILHELMSHÖHE

Seven kilometres west of the centre, within the enchanting **Habichtswald** (Hawk Forest) nature park, stands the city's symbol: a massive statue, the Herkules, atop a huge stone pyramid atop an octagonal amphitheatre atop an impressive hill. It should be your first stop.

You can spend an entire day here walking through the forest, down the hiking paths (all levels of difficulty) and, if you avoid the tour buses, it can be a very romantic spot to have a picnic.

Entry to each attraction is charged separately, although various combination tickets are also available.

Wilhelmshöhe is currently applying for Unesco World Heritage status, along with the neighbouring Karlsaue and Wilhelmstal royal gardens.

Herkules

This **statue** (adult/concession €1.80/1.30; ☺ 10am-5pm Mar-Nov), 600m above sea level, was built between 1707 and 1717 as a symbol of the area's power. The scantily clad mythical hero leans nonchalantly on his big club and looks down at the defeated Encelados, but the main attraction here (after 449 steps to the top) is an unbelievable view in all directions.

Facing the town, you'll see Wilhelmshöhe Allee running due west towards the town; until reunification, the hills here formed the border with the GDR. To the south and northwest is the Habichtswald, with over 300km of hiking trails. At the bottom of the hill you'll see Schloss Wilhelmshöhe and, to its south, Löwenburg.

To get here take tram No 3 from the ICE-Bahnhof or town to the terminus and change for bus No 43, which goes right up to the top once or twice an hour from 8am to 8pm.

Schloss Wilhelmshöhe

Home to Elector Wilhelm and later Kaiser Wilhelm II, this palace (1786–98) houses the **Galerie Alter Meister** (Old Masters Gallery; ☎ 937 77; adult/concession €3.50/2.50, free Fri; ☺ 10am-5pm Tue-Sun). It features works by Rembrandt, Rubens, Jordaens, Lucas Cranach the Elder, Dürer and many others.

To reach Schloss Wilhelmshöhe from the ICE-Bahnhof, take tram No 1 to the last stop. From there you can take bus No 23, which makes a loop around the lower regions of the park, or walk to the top, following the well-marked hiking trails.

Schloss Löwenburg
Modelled on a medieval Scottish castle, the **Schloss Löwenburg** (☎ 935 7200; tours adult/concession €3.50/2.50; ☑ 10am-5pm Tue-Sun) is only open to visitors on guided tours, which take in the castle's Rüstkammer (Museum of Armaments) and Ritterzeitsmuseum (Museum of Chivalry).

Fountains
Every Wednesday, Sunday and public holiday from April to October, the **Wasserspiel** takes place along the hillside. Water cascades from Herkules down to about the halfway point, then follows underground passages until it emerges at the **Grosse Fontäne** in a 52m-high jet. The waterworks run from 2.30pm to 3.45pm – follow the crowds. On the first Saturday of the month from June to September, the cascades are illuminated at dusk.

MUSEUMS & GALLERIES
Billed as 'a meditative space for funerary art', Kassel's excellent **Museum für Sepulkralkultur** (Museum of Sepulchral; ☎ 918 930; www.sepulkral museum.de; Weinbergstrasse 25-27; adult/concession €3.50/2.50; ☑ 10am-5pm Tue-Sun, 10am-8pm Wed) is certainly an interesting way to become familiar with German death rituals. Designed to end the taboo of discussing death, the museum's permanent collection consists of headstones, hearses, dancing skeleton bookends and sculptures depicting death.

The **Brüder-Grimm-Museum** (Brothers Grimm Museum; ☎ 103 235; grimm-museum@t-online.de; Brüder-Grimm-Platz 4a; adult/concession €2/1.50; ☑ 10am-5pm Tue-Sun), in the Palais Bellevue, has displays on the brothers' lives, their work (they were well-respected grammarians before turning to fairy stories) and the famous tales themselves, with original manuscripts, portraits and sculptures. *Grimm's Fairy Tales* is now available in almost 200 languages and is read to children all over the world.

Across the street is the **Neue Galerie** (New Gallery; ☎ 709 630; Schöne Aussicht 1; adult/concession €3.50/2.50, free Friday; ☑ 10am-5pm Tue-Sun), housing paintings and sculptures by German artists from 1750 to the present day. Particular attractions include the major Documenta exhibits from 1960 on.

The sharply contoured **Documenta Halle** (☎ 107 521; Du-Ry-Strasse 1) was an architectural contribution designed to mark the ninth Documenta in 1992, and houses changing modern art exhibitions.

Tours
From May to late October, there are two-hour city bus tours – which include Wilhelmshöhe – at 2pm on Saturday (adult/concession €13/9.50), leaving from the Staatstheater bus park. The tourist office also organises a wide range of thematic **walking tours** (adult/concession €6.50/4.50).

Rehbein-Linie (☎ 185 05; www.fahrgastschiffahrt .com) and **Söllner** (☎ 774 670; www.personenschiffahrt .com) run cruises to destinations along the Fulda River from the docks east of town. Prices start at €5.50/3.50 one way.

Sleeping
The tourist office books **private rooms** (from around €20).

DJH hostel (☎ 776 455; kassel@djh-hessen.de; Schenkendorfstrasse 18; junior/senior €18/20.70). Kassel's hostel is one of the best in the country: huge and airy, with good food and activities and friendly, helpful staff. It's 10 minutes' walk from the Hauptbahnhof, or take tram No 4 or 8 to Annastrasse.

Fulda-Camp (☎ 224 33; www.fulda-camp.de; Giessenallee 7; adult/child €4/2, car €3, camp site, €6-11.50). Between Auestadion and the Messehallen on the Fulda River, this is a very peaceful spot. Bus No 25 stops right outside.

Hotel Garni Kö 78 (☎ 716 14; www.koe78.de; Kölnische Strasse 78; s €32-51, d €51-74.50; **P**)) An excellent family-run guesthouse west of the Hauptbahnhof, with cosy rooms, a choice of shared and private bathrooms and a lovely peaceful back garden. Front-facing rooms have balconies.

Hotel Domus (☎ 703 330; www.hotel-domus-kassel .de; Erzbergerstrasse 1-5; s €66-86, d €86-106; **P**)) The emphasis is on service at this traditional-minded place, with different décor and character on each of the three floors; the atrium fountains are a nice touch. Prices include half board and various other extras.

Schlosshotel Wilhelmshöhe (☎ 308 80; schloss hotel@privathotel.net; Schlosspark; s/d €78/106; **P**)) The building lacks the charm of its surroundings, but money can't buy you a better location,

FAIRY-TALE ROAD

The 600km *Märchenstrasse* (Fairy-Tale Road) is one of Germany's most popular tourist routes. It's made up of cities, towns and hamlets in four states (Hesse, Lower Saxony, North Rhine-Westphalia and Bremen), many of them associated with the works of Wilhelm and Jakob Grimm.

The brothers travelled extensively through central Germany in the early 19th century documenting folklore. Their collection of tales – *Kinder- und Hausmärchen* – was first published in 1812 and quickly gained international recognition. It includes such famous tales as *Hansel & Gretel, Cinderella, The Pied Piper, Rapunzel* and scores of others.

Every town, village and hamlet along the Fairy-Tale Road has an information office of sorts. For advance information, contact the **central information office** (☎ 0561-707 707; www.german-fairytale-route.com; Königsplatz 53, Kassel); also helpful is the tourist office in Hamelin.

For an organised tourist route, Fairy-Tale Road transport isn't very well organised. There's no equivalent of the Romantic Road bus and, because the route covers several states, local bus and train services outside the major cities aren't coordinated. The easiest way to travel is by car; the ADAC Weserbergland map covers the area in detail.

There are over 60 stops on the Fairy-Tale Road. Kassel aside, major ones include:

Hanau
The route kicks off east of Frankfurt in the birthplace of Jakob (1785–1863) and Wilhelm (1786–1859) Grimm. A statue honours the town's most famous sons, and there's also a puppet museum featuring some recognisable characters.

Steinau
The Grimm brothers spent their youth here, and the Renaissance Schloss contains exhibits on their work. The Amtshaus, Renaissance palace of the counts of Hanau, was their grand home, and the puppet theatre stages some of their best-known tales.

Marburg
This university town on the Lahn River (see p558) was where the Grimms were educated and began their research into folk tales and stories.

Göttingen
The brothers were professors at the university here (see p666) before being expelled in 1837 for their liberal views. In the summer months, versions of the tales are performed at the woodland stage in Bremke, southeast of Göttingen.

Bad Karlshafen
This meticulously planned white baroque village is a major highlight of the Fairy-Tale Road (see p645).

Bodenwerder
The Rathaus contains an exhibit on the legendary Baron von Münchhausen, said to have been born in the building and (in)famous for telling outrageous tales (see p645).

Hamelin
The biggest stop on the Fairy-Tale Road is the quaint city of Hamelin (Hameln), forever associated with the legend of the Pied Piper (see p644).

Bremen
The route ends in this old Hanseatic city, at the statue of the famous Musicians of Bremen (see p622).

halfway up the Wilhelmshöhe hill and right opposite the Schloss itself.

Hotel Schweizer Hof (☎ 936 90; www.schweizer -hof-kassel.de; Wilhelmshöher Allee 288; s €53-61, d €61-82; **P** **X**) Between Wilhelmshöhe and the ICE-Bahnhof, this is a nice, smart, private place with friendly service and a Chinese restaurant downstairs.

Eating

Mr Jones (☎ 710 818; Goethestrasse 31; mains €2.50-8) A favourite on the local scene, this colourful café-bar does all kinds of light meals, buffet breakfasts and a selection of cheap Indian dishes. DJs spin house tunes at night.

Duck Dich (☎ 312 881; Wilhelmshöher Allee 288a; mains from €5.50) This half-timbered house is home to the cosiest restaurant in Kassel, serving wholesome food and good beer; mind your head on the beams!

Podium (☎ 104 963; Kölnische Strasse 48; mains €8-10) This is a friendly local place near the Hauptbahnhof, with a nice raised terrace area for summer dining. The food is mostly German standards and bistro classics.

Wok (☎ 739 8889; Kölnische Strasse 124; mains €8-10) Wok is a good spot for Thai food, with an extensive menu catering to herbivores as well as carnivores. There's a beer garden out the back.

Zum Ägypter (☎ 180 50; Am Friedrichsplatz 18; mains €9-16) Much like the Pyramids, all the action takes place underground in this Egyptian cellar restaurant, which hosts traditional dancers (of the belly variety) once a month. You can also take Arabic lessons here.

El Erni (☎ 710 018; Parkstrasse 42; mains €12-18) Kassel's finest Spanish restaurant is particularly strong on fish and atmosphere, with chandeliers providing effective mood lighting and a wonderful shrub-shrouded front garden area with real flaming torches to eat by. Just say 'Si'.

Drinking & Entertainment

The Hauptbahnhof, now called the Kultur Bahnhof (or KüBa), is full of cafés and bars, with art openings and sometimes original-language movies. Stop in or check out *KüBa* magazine, available in the city at bars and pubs.

Gleis 1 (☎ 780 160; www.gleis1.de; Hauptbahnhof) Looking more like New York than Hesse, this very cool place is an American-style diner and bar, with club nights and, on some nights, live music.

Hotel Reiss (☎ 788 30; www.hotel-reiss.de; Werner-Hilpert-Strasse 24) Just opposite the Hauptbahnhof, this unassuming hotel is actually Kassel's premier party venue, also incorporating the Arm basement club and Lolita bar. The Bed & Party weekend specials take all the hassle out of getting home afterwards, with an extra-late Sunday check-out.

Cafe-Bar Suspekt (☎ 104 522; Fünffensterstrasse 14) Dim but friendly gay bar; a good place to start exploring the Kassel scene.

Getting There & Away

ICE trains to/from Frankfurt-am-Main stop at the ICE-Bahnhof two to three times an hour (€41.60, 1½ hours); regional trains are less frequent but much cheaper. To Fulda, trains leave twice hourly from the ICE-Bahnhof (€25.20, 30 minutes) or hourly from the Hauptbahnhof (€15.60, 1¼ hours). Marburg trains leave from both ICE-Bahnhof and the Hauptbahnhof (€14, 1¼ hours).

Travellers heading to Paderborn airport can now check in at Kassel Hauptbahnhof.

Getting Around

The local transport authority NVV operates a transport network connecting the entire north Hesse region, with Kassel at its centre. Tickets are available from bus and tram drivers as well as at machines and kiosks (single €2.10, MultiTicket day pass €5). Tram No 1 runs from the ICE-Bahnhof to the centre.

You can rent bicycles from **Fahrradhof** (☎ 313 083; Wilhelmshöher Allee 253); for mountain bikes, head to **Edelmann** (☎ 117 69; Goethestrasse 37-39).

North Rhine-Westphalia

CONTENTS

The Rhineland	**568**
Düsseldorf	568
Xanten	575
Around Xanten	577
Cologne	577
Around Cologne	588
Bonn	588
Around Bonn	594
Aachen	594
Around Aachen	598
The Ruhrgebiet	**598**
Essen	598
Bochum	602
Dortmund	603
Other Ruhrgebiet Attractions	605
Westphalia	**607**
Münster	607
Around Münster	610
Soest	611
Paderborn	613
Sauerland	**615**
Attendorn	616
Altena	616
Winterberg	616
Siegerland	**617**
Siegen	617
Around Siegen	618

Few German states have to contend with as many negative perceptions as North Rhine-Westphalia (Nordrhein-Westfalen). Billowing chimneys and heavy industry, crowded cities, a barren landscape devoid of greenery – these are all stereotypes and outdated images. Not many people realise that forests, fields and lakes cover about 75% of the state; that the cities are pulsating cultural centres; and that high-tech and speciality industries – not coal and steel – form the backbone of North Rhine-Westphalia's economy today. There's a greater density of theatres, orchestras and museums here – many of international stature – than anywhere else in Germany. There are also churches, palaces and castles that bulge with art treasures.

Must-sees include Aachen (Charlemagne's imperial capital) and Cologne with its awe-inspiring Gothic Dom (cathedral) and first-rate art museums. Bonn's museum mile is also worth seeking out, as is the nearby baroque palace of Brühl. Düsseldorf, the state capital, pairs elegance with earthiness that's best experienced on an Altstadt (old town) pub crawl. Meanwhile, Dortmund, Essen and other Ruhrgebiet (Ruhr District) cities have found unique ways to capitalise on their industrial heritage with top-notch venues in unusual settings.

Also off the beaten track are the nature parks of the Sauerland and Siegerland, both popular getaways that Germans have kept largely to themselves. The skylines of the Westphalian towns Soest and Paderborn are studded with the spires of medieval churches packed with priceless art. And were there still an independent Westphalia, Münster, with its great Dom, university and historic centre, would surely be its capital.

NORTH RHINE-WESTPHALIA

HIGHLIGHTS

- **Spiritual Splendour**
  Admire the awe-inspiring Dom (cathedral) of Cologne (p578) and that of Aachen (p595)

- **Party Town**
  Toast your health in Düsseldorf's Altstadt, the 'world's longest bar' (p574)

- **Kids' Stuff**
  Recapture your youth at the theme parks of Phantasialand in Brühl (p588) and Warner Bros Movie World in Bottrop (p606)

- **Off-Beat Adventure**
  Free-climb and dive in a former steel mill in Duisburg, now the Landschaftspark Duisburg-Nord (p606)

- **Quirky Perspective**
  Climb the Tetrahedron in Bottrop for panoramic Ruhrgebiet views (p606)

- **Fitness Fix**
  Cycle from castle to palace to castle in the Münsterland (p610)

★ Münsterland
★ Bottrop
★ Duisburg
★ Düsseldorf
★ Cologne
★ Aachen ★ Brühl

- POPULATION: 17.95 MILLION
- AREA: 34,080 SQ KM

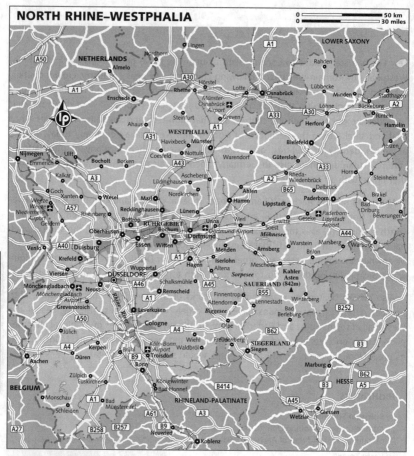

NORTH RHINE–WESTPHALIA

THE RHINELAND

DÜSSELDORF

☎ 0211 / pop 567,000

Düsseldorf, the state capital, is a posh, modern city that retains a charming earthiness and Rhenish *joie de vivre* behind its businesslike façade. This is perfectly reflected in its lively cultural and culinary offerings, and a rollicking bar and nightlife scene. Nowhere is this more true than in and around the Altstadt, the historical quarter hugging the Rhine River, which has been nicknamed 'the longest bar in the world'.

Fans of modern and contemporary art have plenty to look forward to in Düssel-

dorf, which has been an artistic mecca since the reign of Elector Johann Wilhelm II (1679–1716), popularly known as Jan Wellem. His prestigious collection formed the basis of Munich's Alte Pinakothek museum. In 1773 Elector Carl Theodor built upon the tradition with the founding of the *Düsseldorfer Kunstakademie* (Art Academy). Over the years, such major artists as Peter Cornelius, William Schadow, Paul Klee and Joseph Beuys have been at its helm, and it continues to make waves in the art world under its current director Markus Lüpertz. For international avant-garde architecture look no further than the brand-new Medienhafen, a bold adaptation of an old Rhine harbour into a postmodern media centre.

Orientation

The airport is about 6km north of the Altstadt, see p575 for details about getting into town. The Hauptbahnhof (main train station) is on the southeastern edge of the city centre. From here it's about a 20-minute walk along Bismarckstrasse and Blumenstrasse to the Königsallee, with the Altstadt just beyond. Alternatively, take any U-Bahn (underground train) from the Hauptbahnhof to Heinrich-Heine-Allee stop to be right in the heart of things.

Information

DISCOUNT CARDS

Düsseldorf Welcome Card (€9/14/19 per 24/48/72 hr) Buys unlimited public transportation and discounts for museums, tours and cultural venues. The group version, good for three adults or two adults and two kids, costs €18/28/38 per 24/48/72 hours. Get it at hotels or the tourist office.

EMERGENCY

After-hour medical emergencies (☎ 192 92)
Dental emergencies (☎ 666 291)
Municipal Lost & Found (☎ 899 3285)

INTERNET ACCESS

G@rden (☎ 866 160; Rathausufer 8; €1.80 per 30 min; ☽ 11am-1am)
Surf Inn (☎ 139 1213; 3rd fl, Galeria Kaufhof; Königsallee 1-9; €1.50 per 30 min; ☽ 9.30am-8pm Mon-Sat)

MONEY

American Express (☎ 385 00 69; Königsallee 98a)
Reisebank (☎ 364 878; Hauptbahnhof; ☽ 7am-10pm Mon-Sat, 8am-9pm Sun)

POST

Main post office (Konrad-Adenauer-Platz 1; ☽ 8am-8pm Mon-Fri, 9am-2pm Sat)

TOURIST INFORMATION

When major trade shows are in town, the tourist offices usually keep longer hours.
Tourist Office Altstadt (☎ 602 5753; Burgplatz; ☽ noon-6pm)
Tourist Office Finanzkaufhaus (☎ 300 4897; Berliner Allee 33; ☽ 10am-6pm Mon-Sat)
Tourist Office Hauptbahnhof (☎ 172 0222; Immermannstrasse 65b; ☽ 10am-6pm Mon-Sat)

Dangers & Annoyances

The area near the Hauptbahnhof – and especially around Worringer Platz just north of here – attracts a murky element and should be avoided after dark. The same is true of the city parks.

Sights

ALTSTADT

Düsseldorf's old quarter, a largely car-free warren of narrow lanes hugging the Rhine, encapsulates the city's heart and soul. Famous for its raucous nightlife, it's also crammed with boutiques, charming and quiet corners and a smattering of museums and historical sites.

The Altstadt's historic core is on the Marktplatz, framed by the Renaissance **Rathaus** (town hall; 1573) and anchored by a striking **statue of Jan Wellem** on horseback. The artsy elector lies buried a short walk north of here in the mostly baroque (1629) church **Andreaskirche** (Grabbeplatz), decked out in uplifting white and gold with fanciful stucco and 22 life-size sculptures of the apostles and other biblical figures. It's hugely popular for its daily noontime sermons and organ concerts.

A few steps west is the memorial **Mahn- und Gedenkstätte für die Opfer des Nationalsozialismus** (Memorial for the Victims of the Nazi Regime; ☎ 899 6205; Mühlenstrasse 29; admission free; ☽ 11am-5pm Tue-Fri & Sun, 1-5pm Sat), with an interesting exhibit on local persecution and resistance during the Third Reich. Leaflets and audiotapes in English may be borrowed at no charge.

Nearby is the 14th-century **St Lambertus Kirche** (Stiftsplatz), with its peculiar twisted tower and rich interior from a variety of periods. Note the Gothic tabernacle, Renaissance marble tombstones, baroque altars and modern windows.

Just beyond, on Burgplatz, the **Schlossturm** is all that's left of the electors' palace. It now houses the recently updated **Schifffahrt Museum** (Navigation Museum; ☎ 899 4195; adult/concession €2.50/1.50; ☽ 11am-6pm Tue-Sun) with multimedia exhibits chronicling 2000 years of Rhine shipping.

Burgplatz marks the beginning of the broad **Rheinuferpromenade**, whose cafés and benches fill with people in fine weather, giving it an almost Mediterranean flair. It follows the Rhine all the way to the Rheinpark and the 234m **Rheinturm**, with a viewing platform and restaurant at 180m (lift €4). Just beyond is Düsseldorf's new architectural showcase, the Medienhafen (see p571).

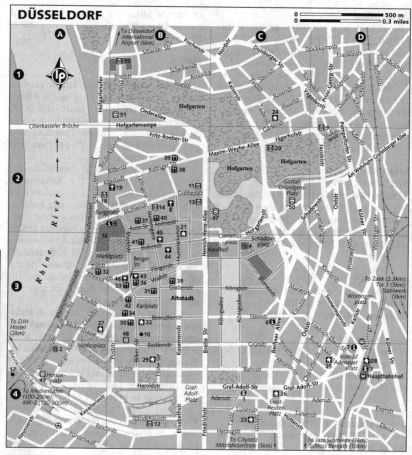

DÜSSELDORF

En route you'll pass by the ornate Palais Nesselrode, which houses two worthwhile museums (one ticket buys admission to both). The **Hetjens Museum** (☎ 899 4210; Schulstrasse 4; adult/concession €3/1.50; 🕑 11am-5pm Tue & Thu-Sun, 11am-9pm Wed) is Germany's only museum dedicated to ceramics. Its displays, spanning 8000 years, provide a surprisingly entertaining survey of this ancient art. Also here is the **Film Museum** (☎ 899 2232), which has the same hours as the Hetjens Museum, and focuses on the evolution of cinema in Germany, one of the industry's birthplaces. Its Black Box cinema presents nonmainstream movies, many in the original with subtitles.

Heinrich Heine fans can get their literary kicks at the **Heinrich Heine Institut** (☎ 899 5571;

Bilker Strasse 12-14; adult/concession €2/1; 🕑 11am-5pm Tue-Fri & Sun, 1-5pm Sat), where letters, portraits, first editions and manuscripts document this famed Düsseldorfer's career. His house at Bolkerstrasse 53 now contains a literary pub called Schnabelewopski (see Drinking p574).

ART MUSEUMS

Düsseldorf's long and fruitful love affair with art finds expression in several high-calibre museums clustered in the northern Altstadt. The **museum kunst palast** (☎ 899 2460; Ehrenhof 5; adult/concession €7/4; 🕑 11am-6pm Tue-Sun) presents European art from the Middle Ages to today, including such delicacies as Rubens' sensual *Venus and Adonis*.

INFORMATION		
American Express	1	C4
G@rden	2	A4
Reisebank	3	D4
Surf Inn	4	C3
Tourist Office Altstadt	5	B2
Tourist Office Finanzkaufhaus	6	C3
Tourist Office Hauptbahnhof	7	D4

SIGHTS & ACTIVITIES	(pp569-72)	
Andreaskirche	8	B2
Goethe Museum	9	D2
Heinrich Heine Institut	10	D3
K20 Kunstsammlung am Grabbeplatz	11	B2
K21 Kunstsammlung im Ständehaus	12	B4
Kunsthalle	13	B2
Mahn- und Gedenkstätte für die Opfer des Nationalsozialismus	14	B2
museum kunst palast	15	B1
Rathaus	16	A3
Rheinturm	17	A4

Schifffahrt Museum	18	A2
Schloss Jägerhof	(see 9)	
Schlossturm	(see 18)	
St Lambertus Church	19	B2
Theatermuseum	20	C2

SLEEPING	(pp572-3)	
Altstadthotel St Georg	21	B3
Carathotel	22	B3
Haus Hillesheim	23	C4
Hotel Berial	24	C1
Hotel Komet	25	D4
Hotel Manhattan	26	C4
Hotel Orangerie	27	A3
Ibis Hotel	28	D4
Schaper Apartment	29	B4

EATING	(pp573-4)	
Bim's Marktwirtschaft	30	B3
Bäckerei Hinkel	31	B3
En de Canon	32	A3
Fischhaus	33	B3

Herr Spoerl Deli	34	B3
Im Füchschen	35	B2
Libanon Express	36	B3
Master Grill	37	B2
Ohme Jupp	38	B2
Pia Eis	39	B3
Tante Anna	40	B2
Waffelladen	41	B3
Zum Schiffchen	42	B3

DRINKING	(p574)	
Et Kabüffke	43	B3
Schnabelewopski	44	B3
Unique-Club	45	B3
Zum Uerige	46	B3

ENTERTAINMENT	(p574)	
Deutsche Oper am Rhein	47	C2
Marionetten-Theater	48	B3
Roncalli's Apollo Varieté	49	A4
Schauspielhaus	50	C2
Tonhalle	51	B1

NORTH RHINE-WESTPHALIA

The dazzling glass collection rivals that of London's Victoria & Albert Museum, with an exceptional range of Art Nouveau items and glass from China, Persia and India.

Top billing goes to the, **K20 Kunstsammlung am Grabbeplatz** (K20 Art Collection on Grabbeplatz; ☎ 838 10; Grabbeplatz 5; adult/concession €6.50/4.50; ☼ 10am-6pm Tue-Fri, 11am-6pm Sat & Sun), housed behind an undulating shiny black façade. Its permanent collection includes paintings and sculpture by every leading light of the 20th century: Picasso, Braque, Chagall and Modigliani among them, along with German Expressionists like Kirchner, Beckmann and Grosz, and a prestigious Paul Klee collection. Admirers of contemporary American artists, such as Rauschenberg and Jasper Johns, as well as Düsseldorf's own Joseph Beuys, will also get their fill. All this is supplemented with special exhibitions of international repute. A combination ticket with K21 (see below) costs €10/8 including audioguide.

Immediately south, the **Kunsthalle** (Art Hall; ☎ 899 6240; Grabbeplatz 4; admission prices vary; ☼ noon-7pm Tue-Sat, 11am-6pm Sun) is an exhibition hall renowned for its outstanding temporary art and photography shows.

For the city's newest art museum, you have to travel to a little park some 1.3km south, where a 19th-century mansion has been reborn as the ultra-contemporary **K21 Kunstsammlung im Ständehaus** (K21 Art Collection in the Ständehaus; ☎ 838 1630; Ständehausstrasse 1; adult/concession €6.50/4.50; ☼ 10am-6pm Tue-Fri, 11am-6pm Sat & Sun). Some of the art here is so new the paint has barely dried. You'll often see mind-bending canvases, photographs, installations and videos by an international

cast of artists including Sigmar Polke, local boy Thomas Schütte, Korean-American Nam June Paik, the sculptor Robert Gober and Bill Viola. Expect to be shocked, entertained and provoked. To understand it all better, invest €1 in an audioguide.

MEDIENHAFEN

South of the Rheinturm (see Altstadt p569), the **Medienhafen** (Media Harbour) is a spectacular showcase of international architecture and a successful example of urban renewal. Once-crumbling warehouses have been restored into state-of-the-art office buildings and cleverly juxtaposed with often dramatic new structures. The most eye-catching is Frank Gehry's **Neuer Zollhof**, an ensemble of three warped and dynamically curving buildings typical of the American's sculptural approach to architecture. Nearby, keep an eye out for Claude Vasconi's **Grand Bateau**, built to resemble an ocean liner. On the other harbour bank, the **Colorium** by London-based William Alsop, with its Mondrian-inspired façade and springboardlike red roof, is another standout, especially at night when it's lit from within. You'll find more whimsy a few doors down where a plain structure is enlivened by an 'invasion' of **Flossies** – giant candy-coloured stick figures clambering all over its façade. Ask about an information booklet (€5) or guided tours at the tourist offices.

KÖNIGSALLEE & HOFGARTEN

Düsseldorf's version of Rodeo Drive or the Ginza strip, the Königsallee (Kö for short) is supposed to epitomise the city's sophistication, lined as it is by expensive designer boutiques on one side and banks and offices on the other. In reality, though, there's little of actual merit – architectural, cultural or otherwise – and it really only exists to help you part with your hard-earned cash.

By all means, though, take a stroll and have a look, but then head on over to the pleasant **Hofgarten** (palace garden) where you can wander among statues of Heinrich Heine, Robert Schumann and other German greats. Thespians will get a kick out of the **Theatermuseum** (☎ 899 6130; Jägerhofstrasse 1; adult/concession €2/1; ۞ 11am-5pm Tue-Sun), which looks back on Düsseldorf's centuries-old theatre tradition and even has a cool collection of marionettes and paper toy theatres. Enter from the park side.

Painted piglet-pink, but otherwise *très* dignified, the nearby **Schloss Jägerhof** (Jägerhof Palace) is a rococo confection dreamed up by leading 18th-century architect Johann Joseph Couven. Inside is the eclectic **Goethe Museum** (☎ 899 6262; Jacobistrasse 2; adult/concession €2/1; ۞ 11am-5pm Tue-Fri & Sun, 1-5pm Sat), whose exhibits capture the spirit of this complex genius as well as of his time. Putting the 'trip' in triptych is an epic oil painting of the classical Walpurgisnacht scene from Faust II by Paul Struck (1974).

SCHLOSS BENRATH
Elector Karl Theodor was a man of deep pockets and good taste, as reflected in his extravagant **pleasure palace and park** (☎ 899 3832; Benrather Schlossallee 104; adult/concession per museum €4/2, for all three €6.50/3.75; ۞ 10am-6pm Tue-Sun mid-Mar–Oct, 11am-5pm Nov–mid-Mar), some 10km south of the city centre. He drew upon the talents of Frenchman Nicolas de Pigage who created this harmonious ensemble of rococo architecture, landscaping and interior decorations. Catch a glimpse of the period's lifestyle on a tour (in German) of the **Museum Corps de Logis**, a highfalutin name for the former residential tract. In 2002 the **Naturkundemuseum** (Museum of Natural History) in the west wing was joined by the **Museum für Europäische Gartenkunst** (Museum of European Garden Art) in the east wing.

Take tram No 701 from Jan-Wellem-Platz or S6 from Hauptbahnhof.

Sleeping
Düsseldorf hotels cater primarily to business travellers, which explains the relative dearth of places that won't cost an arm and a leg and yet offer a decent level of comfort. Prices spike during big trade shows held not only in Düsseldorf but as far away as Cologne and Essen. On the bright side, there are plenty of bargains out there on weekends and in summer. Prices quoted below are applicable outside trade-show times. The tourist office operates a **room reservation hotline** (☎ 01805-172 020; €0.12 per min); although bookings are limited to partner hotels.

BUDGET
Haus Hillesheim (☎ 386 860; www.hotel-hillesheim.de; Jahnstrasse 19; s/d with shared bathroom €25/45, with private bathroom €45/65; P 🖳) This old-timey hotel has been in the same family since 1894 and is now run by a congenial motorcycle aficionado. Room types vary but all are comfortable, have excellent mattresses and such women-friendly amenities as lit make-up mirrors. Rooms facing the garden are quieter.

DJH hostel (☎ 557 310; jh-duesseldorf@djh-rheinland .de; Düsseldorfer Strasse 1; dm/s/d €20.70/25.30/46.60; P 🖂 🖳) This 272-bed hostel is across the Rhine from the Altstadt and has mostly four-bed dorms, about a third with in-room sink. Take U-Bahn No 74, 75, 76 or 77 from the Hauptbahnhof to Luegplatz, from where it's a 10-minute walk south via Kaiser-Wilhelm-Ring.

Hotel Komet (☎ 178 790; www.hotelcomet.de; Bismarckstrasse 93; s/d from €38/50) Occupying two floors of an Art Nouveau building near the Hauptbahnhof, this place may be frill-free but it'll do at a pinch, especially if you're here for a night on the town. Optional breakfast is €6.50 per person.

MID-RANGE
Altstadthotel St Georg (☎ 602 230; Hunsrückenstrasse 22; s/d €65/110; 🖂) Right in the thick of the Altstadt action (there's a cocktail bar on the ground floor), this place wasn't made for light sleepers but has good old-fashioned ambience galore.

Schaper Apartment (☎ 8622 1100; www.schaper -apartment.com; Hohe Strasse 37-41; s €90-135, d €140) If you're in town for three or more nights, you might opt for one of these bright, furnished apartments with pantry kitchens in surroundings of galleries and antique stores. The rooftop garden suite (€235) is the ultimate retreat.

Hotel Berial (☎ 490 0490; www.hotel-berial.de; Gartenstrasse 30; s/d €60/80) A youthful ambience reigns in this hotel right by the Hofgarten, thanks to contemporary furnishings, walls spruced-up with colourful prints and laminate flooring in some of the rooms. Ask about specials.

Ibis Hotel (☎ 167 20; www.ibishotel.com; Konrad-Adenauer-Platz 14; s/d from €68/87; P X) Predictable but not a bad choice in this pricey city, the Ibis is perfectly located for catching an early train.

Hotel Manhattan (☎ 602 225 110; hotel-manhattan@freenet.de; Graf-Adolf-Strasse 39; s €34-89, d €46-131; P 🖳) The grey façade may not be terribly inviting, but inside awaits a modern hotel with cheerful decorations and such extras as a lift and an Internet terminal for guests.

TOP END
Hotel Orangerie (☎ 866 800; www.hotel-orangerie-mcs.de; Bäckergasse 1; s €100-150, d €126-180; X) If you're in town to sample the Altstadt *Gemütlichkeit* (cosy ambience) but like to retire to stylish and modern digs, this hotel might fit the bill. It's in a particularly quiet and picturesque section of the historic quarter.

Carathotel (☎ 130 50; www.carat-hotel.de; Benrather Strasse 7a; s/d from €125/150; X X) This place is packed with suits during the week, but on weekends it's not a bad choice for the leisure crowd. Expect efficiency, amenities and comfort but little character, neither in the rooms (decked out in bland beige) nor from the staff.

Eating
Im Füchschen (☎ 137 470; Ratinger Strasse 28; mains €5-11) Noisy, cavernous, packed – the Füchschen (which translates as 'Little Fox') is all you expect a Rhenish beer hall to be. They make a mean Schweinshaxe (roast pork leg) but there's plenty of less challenging fare on the menu as well.

Tante Anna (☎ 131 163; Andreasstrasse 2; mains €17.50-25, six-course dinners €33-52; 🕑 dinner only, closed Sun) Meals in this history-drenched gourmet restaurant, ensconced in a 16th-century chapel, are truly a special treat. Eat à la carte or choose the set menu, also available for vegetarians.

Herr Spoerl Deli (☎ 323 8211; Benrather Strasse 6a; dishes €3.50-7; 🕑 closed Sun) This young-and-hip deli is famous for its generously sized and freshly made sandwiches, best enjoyed in the quiet courtyard. Soups, quiches and daily blackboard specials are other tempting options.

En de Canon (☎ 329 798; Zollstrasse 7; mains €10-18) Housed in the city's first post station, this is the kind of place where Elector Jan Wellem got drunk with his artist buddies three centuries ago. These days, it's still a classic for local specialities, preferable in summer when the action moves to the jovial beer garden.

Zum Schiffchen (☎ 132 421; Hafenstrasse 5; mains €10-18; 🕑 closed Sun) This is similar to En de Canon but has the distinction of being Düsseldorf's oldest restaurant ('since 1628'). One wonders if the portions were as huge when Napoleon or Heinrich Heine dropped by a few centuries back.

Bim's Marktwirtschaft (☎ 327 185; Benrather Strasse 7; mains €7-14) With its horseshoe-shaped bar and red leather banquettes, Bim's has a vaguely retro look and is great for breakfast, a snack or drinks at night.

THE AUTHOR'S CHOICE

The Altstadt is chock-full of *Imbisse* (snack bars), mostly of the pizza-by-the-slice and doner-kebab variety, which are fine but nothing to write home about. We've ferreted out a few of the places where in-the-know locals feed their cravings. Those with a sweet tooth, for instance, can't escape the magnetism of **Pia Eis** (Kasernenstrasse 1), the best ice-cream parlour around, bar none, with an incredible selection, quick service and modest prices. Another great sugar fix is the **Waffelladen** (Bolkerstrasse 8), an unimaginably tiny waffle kitchen in business for over 40 years. Try one with a little powered sugar or drenched in cherries or other toppings.

Bäckerei Hinkel (several branches, including Hohe Strasse 31) is another institution that has people queuing patiently for their excellent breads and cakes. For more sustenance, try **Master Grill** (Kurze Strasse 4), which does its name justice and is especially famous for its *Schaschlik* (meat and vegetable kebab) – an excellent way to prepare the stomach for an extended pub crawl. For filling up on superb felafel sandwiches, stop by **Libanon Express** (Berger Strasse 21).

Other recommendations:
Ohme Jupp (☎ 326 406; Ratinger Strasse 19; dishes €4-8) Casual, slightly artsy café serving breakfast and blackboard specials.

Fischhaus (☎ 854 9864; Berger Strasse 3-7; mains €9-18)

For tapas, paella and other Iberian fare, head to Schneider-Wibbel-Gasse, just off Bolkerstrasse, which is almost completely given over to Spanish restaurants, from cheap to frivolously pricey.

Drinking

After dark, especially in good weather, the atmosphere in the pedestrianised Altstadt is electric and, occasionally, a bit rowdy. The beverage of choice is Alt, a dark and semisweet beer typical of Düsseldorf.

Zum Uerige (☎ 866 990; Berger Strasse 1) This cavernous warren is the best place to soak it all up. Here the beer flows so quickly from giant copper vats that the waiters – called 'Köbes' – just carry huge trays of brew and plonk down a glass whenever they spy an empty.

Et Kabüffke (☎ 133 269; Flingerstrasse 1) At this tiny, olde-worlde pub, with its cool S-shaped bar built from bottles, you can try *Killepitsch*, a Düsseldorf-made sweet herb schnapps also sold in the shop next door.

Schnabelewopski (☎ 133 200; Bolkerstrasse 53) The former home of Heinrich Heine is now occupied by a charming literary pub, named after a Heine character.

Im Füchschen This is another ambiance-drenched brew-pub with plenty of local colour (see Eating p573).

Entertainment

Check the listings magazines *Prinz* and *Überblick* or the free *Coolibri* for current goings-on in 'D-Town'.

CLUBS & LIVE MUSIC

MK-2 (☎ 601 2847; Kaistrasse 4; ⏰ Tue & Sat) Right in the Medienhafen, MK-2 is best known for its happening Tuesday after-work parties. On weekends, resident and guest DJs play mostly house to get the chic crowd onto the dance floor.

Unique-Club (☎ 323 0990; Bolker Strasse 30; ⏰ closed Mon) Red lights and white leather booths separated by curtains hark back to the days when this Altstadt club was a bordello. Now it's one of the most laid-back

places to get a groove on to funk, nubeats, '60s sounds and soul jazz.

Zakk (☎ 973 0010; Fichtenstrasse 40) Parties, concerts, readings, theatre, discussions – there's always something at this well-established cultural centre in a former factory. A couple of kilometres east of the Hauptbahnhof, the beer garden is a convivial place to spend a balmy summer night.

Tor 3 (☎ 733 6497; Ronsdorfer Strasse 143) Radiohead has played here, as has Paul Weller and even Robbie Williams, but now this mega-sized old factory venue does mostly elaborate theme parties from Milky Nights (R&B and soul) to Italian Nights (Italo pop, soul and dance). It's in the suburb of Flingern, just east of the Hauptbahnhof (take the U75).

Other recommendations:
Stahlwerk (☎ 730 8681; Ronsdorfer Strasse 134; ⏰ Fri & Sat) Huge dance hall with industrial flair, different sounds and theme parties, near Tor 3.

Jazz-Schmiede (☎ 311 0564; Himmelgeisterstrasse 107g; ⏰ closed summer) Beautiful concert hall, even better jazz with national and international talent, 3km south of the Hauptbahnhof. Free Tuesday jam sessions. Enter from Uhlenbergstrasse.

THEATRE & CLASSICAL MUSIC

Düsseldorf has plenty to offer to fans of high-brow pursuits. The main venue for drama and comedies is the **Schauspielhaus** (☎ 369 911; Gustaf-Gründgens-Platz 1), which enjoys a solid reputation nationwide. Opera and musicals make it to the stage at the **Deutsche Oper am Rhein** (☎ 890 80; Heinrich-Heine-Allee 16a), while the imposing domed **Tonhalle** (☎ 899 6123; Ehrenhof 2) is the home base of the Düsseldorfer Symphoniker.

For something entirely different, catch a show at the **Marionetten-Theater** (☎ 328 432; Bilker Strasse 7), which presents charming and beautifully orchestrated operas and fairy tales, many geared to an adult audience. Another popular diversion is **Roncalli's Apollo Varieté** (☎ 828 9090; Haroldstrasse 1), where you'll be entertained by acrobats, jugglers, comedians and other variety acts.

Getting There & Away

AIR

With reconstruction and expansion finally completed in the summer of 2003, Düsseldorf now has an airport to make the city proud. **Düsseldorf International** (☎ 4210; www

.duesseldorf-international.de) is sparkling, state-of-the-art, well-designed and easy to navigate. It has a 24-hour left-luggage office, a Reisebank and car-rental desks. Some airlines that serve the area:

Air Berlin (☎ 01801-737 800)
British Airways (☎ 01805-266 522)
Lufthansa (☎ 01803-803 803)
United Airlines (☎ 069-5007 0387)

BUS

Eurolines (www.eurolines.com) buses provide daily trips to Paris (one way/return €35/62, nine hours) and Warsaw (€56/98, 20 hours), to London twice weekly (€63/102, nine hours) and to Prague three times weekly (€45/77, 13 hours).

CAR & MOTORCYCLE

Autobahns from all directions lead to Düsseldorf city centre; just follow the signs. Parking in the centre is pretty much limited to parking garages, which command €1 to €1.50 an hour. For ride-share opportunities contact **Citynetz Mitfahrzentrale** (☎ 194 44; Kruppstrasse 102).

TRAIN

Düsseldorf is part of a dense S-Bahn network in the Rhine-Ruhr region (the VRR; see Getting Around p598) and regular services run to Cologne and Aachen as well. There are frequent ICE trains to Frankfurt (€58.80, 1¾ hours), Berlin-Zoo (€77.20, four hours) and Munich (€102.40, five hours).

Getting Around
TO/FROM THE AIRPORT

S-Bahn Nos 1 and 7 shuttle between the airport and the Hauptbahnhof every few minutes. A new airport train station has direct ICE, IC and InterRegio service, which significantly cuts travel time to destinations in the Rhine-Ruhr region and beyond. Lufthansa and several other companies allow check-in at the train station. A taxi into town costs about €15.

PUBLIC TRANSPORT

Düsseldorf's network of U-Bahn trains, trams and buses is divided into zones. Prices vary according to how many zones you travel through. Single tickets are €1.80/ 3.40/7.30 for one/two/three zones. Better

value are the four-trip tickets selling for €5.85/11/23.65; day passes (valid for up to five people) cost €6.55/9.55/18. Tickets are available from bus drivers and orange vending machines at stops, and must be validated when boarding.

TAXI
For a taxi, call ☎ 333 33 or ☎ 212 121.

XANTEN
☎ 02801 / pop 24,500

One of Germany's oldest cities, Xanten was founded as a residential settlement by Roman Emperor Trajan around AD 100. Colonia Ulpia Traiana enjoyed a high standard of civilisation and infrastructure and had as many as 15,000 inhabitants, second only to Cologne. Visit the Archaeological Park for a glimpse at life in those days. Xanten's medieval heyday is best symbolised by the majestic Dom and nicely restored centre. The town is also the mythological birthplace of Nibelungen hero Siegfried.

Orientation
The Dom and city centre are about a 10-minute walk northeast of the Hauptbahnhof via Hagenbuschstrasse or Bahnhofstrasse. The Archaeological Park is a further 15 minutes north of here.

Information
For local information, go the **tourist office** (☎ 983 00; www.xanten.de; Kurfürstenstrasse 9; ☽ 9am-6pm Mon-Fri, 10am-4pm Sat & Sun Apr-Oct; 10am-5pm Mon-Fri, 10am-noon Sat & Sun Nov-Mar). It's right in the town centre, close to the Markt (market square) and Dom.

Sights
ALTSTADT

The crown jewel of Xanten's Altstadt is **Dom St Viktor** (Propstei-Kapitel 8), even if its sturdy twin towers are all that remains of the late-Romanesque original. In the 13th century, it was replaced by a flamboyant Gothic structure, complete with flying buttresses. A walled close, called an 'Immunity', frames the large complex, which must be entered through the gate from the Markt .

The vast five-nave interior is filled with art treasures, reflecting the wealth Xanten enjoyed in the Middle Ages. Look for precious carvings, the shrine of St Victor, the city's parton saint, and no fewer than 15 altars. Foremost among them is the **Marienaltar**, halfway down the right aisle, whose base (or predella) features an intricately carved version of the *Tree of Jesse* by Heinrich Douvermann (1535). Other masterpieces include the candelabrum in the central nave, with its **Doppelmadonna** (1500), and the many stone sculptures of the apostles and other saints affixed to the pillars.

Just outside the Dom is the **Regional Museum** (☎ 719 415; Kurfürstenstrasse 7-9; adult/student/child €3/2.50/1.50; ☽ 9am-5pm Tue-Fri, 11am-6pm Sat & Sun May-Sep; slightly reduced hours Oct-Apr). It displays Roman objects gleaned from the nearby excavation site, along with other exhibits chronicling Xanten's history from the Ice Age to today. A combination ticket including the Regional Museum, the Archäologischer Park and the Grosse Thermen (thermal baths) is €7/4.50/3.

ARCHÄOLOGISCHER PARK & GROSSE THERMEN

Colonia Ulpia Traiana was the only Roman settlement north of the Alps that was never built upon. What's left of it can now be seen at the **Archäologischer Park** (Archeological Park; ☎ 2999; Wardter Strasse 2; adult/student/child €5.50/3.50/2 Mar-Nov; €4.50/3/1.50 Dec-Feb; ☽ 9am-6pm Mar-Nov, 10am-4pm Dec-Feb). To help amateurs visualise what a Roman town looked like, it doesn't merely preserve the ancient foundations and ruins but features faithfully reconstructed buildings and roads. Critics have ridiculed the results, and the place does indeed feel like a bit like a Roman theme park – especially in the restaurant, where toga-clad personnel serve 'Roman' fare. But overall, it's been nicely done and is well worth a visit.

A self-guided tour begins at the **Herberge**, an inn that, along with the restaurant, snack bar and furnished rooms, also contains an Info-Center with models and explanatory panels. Next door, the **Badehaus** (bath house) points to the fairly high standard of hygiene enjoyed 2000 years ago. Other highlights include the **Amphitheatre**, which seats about 12,000 people during Xanten's summer festival, and the partly rebuilt **Hafentempel**. Be sure to walk around the back for

a glimpse of the original foundation. At the **Spielehaus** you can play a round of authentic antique board games.

Just west of the park, and included in the admission, are the **Grosse Thermen**, large-scale Roman thermal baths built during the reign of Emperor Hadrian around AD 125. Since 1999 these have been sheltered by an extravagant glass and steel construction.

Sleeping & Eating

By the time you reading this, Xanten's brand-new DJH hostel should have opened at Bankscher Weg next to a large lake and recreational area. For information, call ☎ 0212-591 198.

Hotel-Galerie an de Marspoort (☎ 1057; www .hotel-an-de-marspoort.de; Marsstrasse 78; s €34-40, d €51-63) This artsy Altstadt abode offers good value for money. Expect snug but pleasantly furnished rooms, an abundant breakfast and original art throughout. Some of the cheaper rooms have a shower but no private toilet.

Hotel Neumaier (☎ 715 70; www.minexa.de; Orkstrasse 19-21; s/d €50/75; P) Another central choice, rooms here are decked out in bright colours and feature tiled floors and live plants. The beer garden is great for luxuriating on a summer day, while the restaurant kitchen serves up German fare with the occasional Mediterranean touch (mains €11 to €18).

Café de Fries (☎ 2068; Kurfürstenstrasse 8; dishes €2.50-12; ☽ closed Mon) A Xanten institution for 177 years, this central café presents changing art exhibits and has its own small chocolate museum with historic equipment. It's especially popular for breakfast and is famous for its pancakes.

Getting There & Away

Xanten is 30km from the tiny **Niederrhein airport** (☎ 02837-666 000) in Weeze, served by RyanAir from London/Stansted. Travel into town involves taking the airport shuttle to the train station in Weeze, catching a train to Kleve, then bus No 44 to Xanten.

A branch train line from Duisburg makes the trip out to Xanten hourly (€6.60, 45 minutes). Xanten is on route B57 (Kleve–Dinslaken). If travelling on the A57, take the Alpen exit, then route B58 east to B57 north.

AROUND XANTEN
Kalkar
☎ 02824 / pop 11,500
About 15km north of Xanten, Kalkar boasts a beautiful medieval core anchored by **St Nikolaikirche** (☎ 2380; Jan-Joest-Strasse 6; ☯ 10am-noon & 2-6pm Mon-Fri, 10am-noon & 2-4.15pm Sat, 2-5pm Sun) and its astonishing carved altars. Many were created by artists from the Kalkar School of Woodcarving, founded in the late Middle Ages by wealthy town burghers. Some were sold off in the early 19th century to pay for the church's restoration, leaving nine to be admired.

Top billing goes to the **High Altar**, which depicts the Passion of Christ in dizzying detail. The work was begun in 1490 by Master Arnt of Zwolle, who died before finishing it, a task then undertaken by Jan Halderen and Ludwig Jupan. For a little comic relief, turn around and lift the first seat of the upper choir chair on the right to reveal the relief of a **monkey on a chamberpot**. Another eye-catcher is the **Altar of the Seven Sorrows** by Heinrich Douvermann at the end of the right aisle. Note the oak-carved *Tree of Jesse*, which wraps around the entire altar starting at its base.

Bus No 44 makes the trip from Xanten's train station to Kalkar hourly (Monday to Saturday only).

COLOGNE
☎ 0221 / pop 1,020,000
Cologne (Köln) is not only the largest city in North Rhine-Westphalia (and fourth largest in the country), but it is also one of its most attractive and should be on everyone's must-see list. It spoils visitors with a cornucopia of sightseeing choices and activities: great architecture in its magnificent cathedrals, churches and public buildings; internationally renowned museums with world-class collections; funky boutiques and giant department stores; unique local cuisine and beer; cutting-edge dance clubs; and first-rate theatre and concerts.

Orientation
Köln-Bonn airport is southeast of the city; see Getting Around p587 for details on transport to/from the airport. Cologne's Hauptbahnhof is practically on the Rhine River's western bank, right next to the landmark Dom. The pedestrianised Hohe Strasse –

the main shopping street – runs south of the Dom, as does the Altstadt, which hugs the river bank between the two bridges, Hohenzollernbrücke and Deutzer Brücke. There are also lively bar and restaurants scenes in the student-flavoured Zülpicher Viertel and the more grown-up Belgisches Viertel about 1.5km west of here.

Information
BOOKSHOPS
Gonski (Map pp578-9; ☎ 209 00; Neumarkt 18a)
Mayersche Buchhandlung (Map pp578-9; ☎ 920 1090; Hohe Strasse 68-82 & Neumarkt 2)

DISCOUNT CARDS
Köln Welcome Card (€9/14/19 per 24/48/72 hr) Offers the usual free public transportation and admission discounts; also available for groups of three adults or families (€18/28/39).

EMERGENCY
Dental emergencies (☎ 011 500)
Gay Attack Hotline (☎ 192 28)
Medical emergencies (☎ 192 92)

INTERNET ACCESS
Future Point (Map pp578-9; ☎ 206 7251; Richmodstrasse 13; €1 per 10 min; ☯ 10.30am-9pm Mon-Fri, 11.30am-8pm Sat & Sun) Inside the trendy Café Lichtenberg with coffee, cakes and snacks served beneath cool chandeliers made from shards or kitchen objects.
Surf Inn (Map pp578-9; ☎ 925 3301; 3rd fl, Galeria Kaufhof, Hohe Strasse 41-53; €1 per 15 min; ☯ 9.30am-8pm Mon-Sat)

LAUNDRY
Eco-Express Waschsalon (per load from €2.30, per 10 min of dryer time €0.50; ☯ 6am-11pm Mon-Sat) has branches at Friedrichstrasse 12 (Map p583), Richard-Wagner-Strasse 2 (Map p583), Brüsseler Strasse 62 (Map p583) and Hansaring 68 (Map pp578-9).

MEDICAL SERVICES
Universitätskliniken (☎ 4780; Josef-Stelzmann-Strasse 9) Located 1.6km southeast of Zülpicher Viertel.

MONEY
American Express (Map pp578-9; ☎ 925 9010; Burgmauer 14 ; ☯ 9am-6pm Mon-Fri, 10am-1pm Sat) Also a travel agency.
Reisebank (Map pp578-9; ☎ 134 403; Hauptbahnhof; ☯ 7am-10pm)
Travelex (Map pp578-9; ☎ 202 0817; Burgmauer 4; ☯ 9am-7pm Mon-Fri, 9am-2pm Sat Apr-Oct; 10am-1pm Sat Nov-Mar)

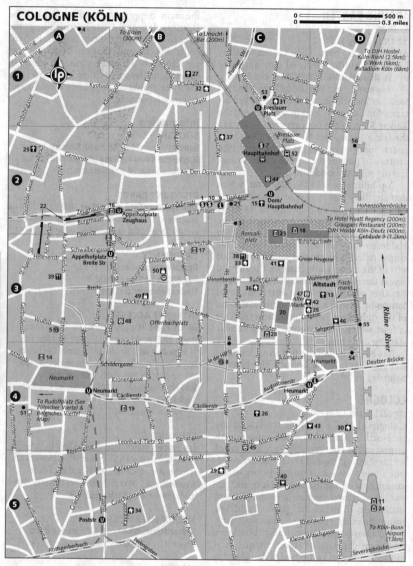

COLOGNE (KÖLN)

0 — 500 m
0 — 0.3 miles

To Bizim (300m)

To Unsicht-Bar (200m)

To DJH Hostel Köln-Riehl (2.5km); E-Werk (6km); Palladium Köln (6km)

Breslauer Platz

Breslauer Platz

Hauptbahnhof

Dom/Hauptbahnhof

Hohenzollernbrücke

To Hotel Hyatt Regency (200m); Graugans Restaurant (200m); DJH Hostel Köln-Deutz (400m); Gebäude 9 (1.2km)

Appelhofplatz Zeughaus

Appelhofplatz Breite Str

Roncalliplatz

Altstadt

Fischmarkt

Alter Markt

Rhine River

Neumarkt

To Rudolfplatz (See Zülpicher Viertel & Belgisches Viertel Map)

Neumarkt

Heumarkt

Heumarkt

Deutzer Brücke

To Köln-Bonn Airport (13km)

NORTH RHINE-WESTPHALIA

POST

Main post office (Map pp578-9; ☎ 925 9290; WDR Arkaden shopping mall, Breite Strasse 6-26; ⏲ 9am-7pm Mon-Fri, 9am-2pm Sat)

TOURIST INFORMATION

Tourist office (Map pp578-9; ☎ 2213 0400; www .koelntourismus.de; Unter Fettenhennen 19; ⏲ 9am-

10pm Mon-Sat, 10am-6pm Sun Jul-Sep, 9am-9pm Mon-Sat, 10am-6pm Sun Oct-Jun)

Sights
KÖLNER DOM

Cologne's geographical and spiritual heart and its main tourist drawcard is the magnificent **Kölner Dom** (Map pp578-9; ⏲ 6am-7.30pm;

INFORMATION
American Express..1 B2
Checkpoint...2 D4
Domforum...3 C2
Eco-Express Waschsalon............................4 A1
Future Point...5 A3
Gonski...(see 14)
Mayersche Buchhandlung..........................6 C3
Reisebank...7 C2
Surf Inn...8 C4
Tourist Office...9 C2
Travelex...10 C2

SIGHTS & ACTIVITIES   (pp578–82)
Deutsches Sport- und
   Olympiamuseum...................................11 D5
Diözesan Museum.................................(see 23)
Domschatzkammer...............................(see 15)
EL-DE Haus...12 B3
Gross St Martin.......................................13 D3
Käthe Kollwitz Museum..........................14 A4
Kölner Dom..15 C2
Kölnisches Stadtmuseum.........................16 B2
Mikwe...(see 20)
Museum für Angewandte Kunst...............17 B3
Museum Ludwig.....................................18 C2
Museum Schnütgen.................................19 B4
Praetorian Palace..................................(see 20)
Rathaus...20 C3

Roman Arch...21 C2
Roman Wall...22 A2
Römerturm...(see 22)
Römisch-Germanisches Museum..............23 C2
Schokoladenmuseum...............................24 D5
St Gereon..25 A2
St Maria im Kapitol.................................26 C4
St Ursula...27 B1
Wallraf-Richartz-Museum – Fondation
   Corboud...28 C3
Zeughaus...(see 16)

SLEEPING   [icon]   (pp582–4)
Heinzelmännchen Hotel............................29 C5
Hotel Allegro...30 D4
Hotel Brandenburger Hof..........................31 C1
Hotel Cristall..32 B1
Hotel Eden am Dom.................................33 C3
Hotel im Wasserturm................................34 B5
Lint Hotel...35 D3
Senats-Hotel...36 C3
Station – Hostel for Backpackers...............37 C2

EATING   [icon]   (pp584–5)
Früh am Dom...38 C3
Moderne Zeiten.......................................39 A3

DRINKING   [icon]   (p585)
Biermuseum...(see 46)

Blue Lounge..40 C5
Brauhaus Sion...41 C3
Flanagan's...42 D3
Malzmühle..43 D4

ENTERTAINMENT   [icons]   (pp586–7)
Alter Wartesaal..44 C2
Chains..45 C4
Kölner Philharmonie.............................(see 18)
Kölnticket..(see 18)
Opernhaus...(see 48)
Papa Joe's Em Streckstump.......................46 D3
Papa Joe's Klimperkasten..........................47 C3
Schauspielhaus..48 B3

SHOPPING   [icon]   (p587)
4711 Perfumery & Gift Shop.....................49 B3
WDR Arkaden..50 B3

TRANSPORT   (pp587–8)
Avis..51 A4
Central Bus Station...................................52 C2
Mitfahr2000..53 C1
Rent-A-Bike..54 D4

OTHER
KD Köln-Düsseldorfer Rheinschifffahrt....55 D3
Köln-Tourist Personenschifffahrt &
   Dampfschifffahrt Colonia......................56 D2

With its soaring twin spires, this is the Mt Everest of cathedrals. It's packed with an amazing array of art treasures and its elegant proportions and dignified ambience leave only the most jaded of visitors untouched.

Building began in 1248 in the French Gothic style but was suspended in 1560 for lack of money. For approximately 300 years, the structure lay half-finished and was even demoted to a horse stable and prison by Napoleon's troops until a generous cash infusion from Prussian King Friedrich Wilhelm IV finally led to its completion in 1880. Luckily, it escaped WWII bombing raids with nary a shrapnel wound and has been a Unesco World Heritage Site since 1996.

This is Germany's largest cathedral. Circle it before heading inside to truly appreciate its dimensions. Note how its lacy spires and flying buttresses create a sensation of lightness and fragility despite its impressive mass and height.

This sensation continues inside where a phalanx of pillars and arches supports the lofty central nave. Soft light filters through the radiant **stained-glass windows**, whose dazzling richness deserves closer inspection. Other highlights include the **Gero Crucifix** (970), notable for its monumental size and an emotional intensity rarely achieved in those early medieval days; the **choir stalls** from 1310, richly carved from oak; and the **altar painting** by local artist Stephan Lochner from around 1450.

The *pièce de résistance*, though, is the **Shrine of the Three Magi** behind the main altar, a richly bejewelled and gilded sarcophagus said to hold the remains of the kings who followed the star to the stable in Bethlehem where Jesus was born. It was spirited out of Milan in 1164 as spoils of war by Emperor Barbarossa's chancellor and instantly turned Cologne into a major pilgrimage site.

To get more out of your visit, invest a mere €0.50 in a pamphlet with basic information or join a guided tour. These are offered in English (adult/concession €4/2) at 10.30am and 2.30pm (2.30pm only on Sunday) and more frequently in German (€3/2). The Domforum information office opposite the main portal has more information.

For an exercise fix, climb the 509 steps up the Dom's **south tower** (adult/concession €2/1, combination ticket with treasury €5/2.50; [clock icon] 9am-6pm May-Sep; 9am-5pm Mar-Apr & Oct; 9am-4pm Nov-Feb) to the base of the stupendous steeple, which dwarfed all buildings in Europe until Gustave Eiffel built a certain tower in Paris. A good excuse to take a breather on your way up is the 24-tonne **Peter Bell** (1923), the largest working bell in the world. As you might imagine, views from the 95m platform are pretty good…

Cologne is proud of its **Domschatzkammer** (Cathedral Treasury; [phone icon] 272 8010; adult/concession €4/2; [clock icon] 10am-6pm), whose many reliquaries, robes, sculptures and liturgical objects are handsomely presented in 13th-century vaulted

NORTH RHINE-WESTPHALIA

rooms on the north side of the Dom. Items to keep an eye out for include a Gothic bishop's staff from 1322.

ROMANESQUE CHURCHES

Cologne's medieval wealth is reflected in its many Romanesque churches, built between 1150 and 1250, many of which survived intact until WWII. About a dozen of those that didn't have since been rebuilt and offer unique architectural and artistic features. If you're pushed for time, try seeing at least a couple of the ones mentioned here.

Winning top honours for most handsome exterior is **Gross St Martin** (Map pp578-9; ☎ 1642 5650; Martinspförtchen; ⏰ 10am-6pm Mon-Sat, 2-4pm Sun), whose ensemble of four slender turrets, grouped around a central spire, towers above Fischmarkt in the Altstadt. Inside, it has a striking clover-leaf choir, similar to the one in **St Maria im Kapitol** (Map pp578-9; ☎ 214 615; Kasinostrasse 6; ⏰ 10am-6pm), whose stand-out treasures include a carved door from around 1050.

The church with the most spectacular interior, though, has to be **St Gereon** (Map pp578-9; ☎ 134 922; Gereonsdriesch 2-4; ⏰ 9am-noon Mon-Sat & 1-6pm daily) with amazing wall frescoes in the choir and baptismal chapel and an impressive four-storey decagonal dome.

If you look at Cologne's coat of arms, you'll see what looks like 11 apostrophes but in fact represents the Christian martyrs St Ursula and 10 virgins. The church of **St Ursula** (Map pp578-9; ☎ 133 400; Ursulaplatz) was built atop the Roman cemetery where the virgins' remains were allegedly found. In the 17th century, the amazing baroque **Goldene Kammer** (Golden Chamber) was built to house their relics. A renovation was supposed to be over with by 2004, but it's best to call ahead.

RÖMISCH-GERMANISCHES MUSEUM

Anyone even remotely interested in Roman history should not skip the extraordinary **Römisch-Germanisches Museum** (Roman Germanic Museum; Map pp578-9; ☎ 2212 4438; Roncalliplatz 4; adult/concession €4.30/2.70; ⏰ 10am-5pm Tue-Sun), right next to the Dom. Sculptures and parts from ruined buildings displayed outside and in the lobby give you a (free) taste of what is the most thorough collection of Roman artefacts found along the Rhine. Inside it's all presented in an appealing fashion that's easily assimilated. Highlights include the giant **Poblicius grave monument** (AD 30–40), the magnificent 3rd-century **Dionysus mosaic** around which the museum was built, and astonishingly well-preserved glass items. Insight into daily Roman life is gained from such items as toys, tweezers, lamps and jewellery, the designs of which have changed surprisingly little since.

MUSEUM LUDWIG

The distinctive building façade and unorthodox roofline signal that the **Museum Ludwig** (Map pp578-9; ☎ 2212 6165; Bischofsgartenstrasse 1; adult/concession €5.80/3.30; ⏰ 10am-6pm Tue-Sun) is no ordinary museum. Considered a European mecca of postmodern art, it offers a thorough overview of all genres – traditional to warped – generated in the 20th century. American pop artists Andy Warhol, Robert Rauschenberg and Jasper Johns are especially well represented, as are German painters Georg Baselitz and AR Penck. But you'll also find plenty of works by those who inspired them: Paul Klee to Marc Chagall, Max Beckmann to Magritte and Dalí, to drop just a few names. It's all rounded off with a unique photography collection from the former Agfa Museum in Leverkusen.

SCHOKOLADEN MUSEUM

Anyone with a sweet tooth will have a fun time at the fabulous **Schokoladen Museum** (Chocolate Museum; ☎ 931 8880; Rheinauhafen 1a; adult/concession €5.50/3; ⏰ 10am-6pm Tue-Fri, 11am-7pm Sat & Sun), a state-of-the-art temple to the art of chocolate-making. A thorough section on the origin and cocoa-growing process (with written explanations in German and English) is followed by a live-production factory tour and an opportunity to sample the final product from a flowing chocolate fountain. Upstairs are departments on the cultural history of chocolate, advertising, and porcelain and other accessories. Stock up on your favourite flavours at the large shop downstairs.

WALLRAF-RICHARTZ-MUSEUM – FONDATION CORBOUD

Ranking as one of the world's finest collections of art from the 13th to the 19th century the **Wallraf-Richartz-Museum** (Map pp578-9; ☎ 2212 1119; Martinstrasse 39; adult/concession €5.80/3.30; ⏰ 10am-8pm Tue, 10am-6pm Wed-Fri, 11am-6pm

Sat & Sun), which previously shared space with the Museum Ludwig, is now housed in a postmodern cube designed by Cologne's own OM Ungers.

Come here to admire medieval works by the Cologne Masters, known for their distinctive use of colour. Dutch and Flemish artists like Rembrandt and Rubens are part of the collection, as are Italians such as Canaletto and Spaniards Murillo and Ribera. The exhibit continues with 19th-century romanticists such as Caspar David Friedrich and Lovis Corinth, and impressionists including Monet, Van Gogh and Renoir. A donation by Swiss collector Gèrard Corboud in 2001 greatly expanded the museum's stock of Impressionist and Post-Impressionist works.

MUSEUM SCHNÜTGEN
Located in the former Church of St Cecilia, the recently renovated and expanded **Museum Schnütgen** (Map pp578-9; ☎ 2212 2310; Cäcilienstrasse 29; adult/concession €3.20/1.90; ☒ 10am-5pm Tue-Fri, 11am-5pm Sat & Sun) houses an overwhelming display of medieval ecclesiastical treasures, including wooden sculptures, manuscripts, textiles and ivory carvings. For even more Christian art, visit the **Diözesan Museum** (Map pp578-9; ☎ 257 7672; Roncalliplatz 2; admission free; ☒ 11am-6pm Fri-Wed), packed with 2000 years' worth of treasures.

DEUTSCHES SPORT- & OLYMPIA MUSEUM
Located in a former warehouse adjacent to the Schokoladen Museum, the **Deutsches Sport- & Olympia Museum** (German Sport & Olympic Games Museum; Map pp578-9; ☎ 336 090; Rheinauhafen 1; adult/concession €4/2; ☒ 10am-6pm Tue-Fri, 11am-7pm Sat & Sun) is an imaginative tribute to the sporting life. It presents exhibits on the subject of sport in all its infinite variety. Permanent departments focus on the evolution of the Olympic Games, exercising in ancient Greece and Rome, and sport as a universal pastime. Interactive displays allowing you to experience a bobsled run or a bike race are especially entertaining.

EL-DE HAUS
Cologne's history during the Nazi era is poignantly documented in the **EL-DE Haus** (Map pp578-9; ☎ 2212 6331; Appellhofplatz 23-25; adult/concession €2.50/1; ☒ 10am-4pm Tue-Fri, 11am-4pm Sat & Sun), which takes its curious name from its builder Leopold Dahmen. In 1935, the Gestapo appropriated the house and moved its local headquarters here, torturing and killing scores of regime opponents and Jews in the basement prison cells. Inscriptions on the cell walls offer a gut-wrenching record of the unspeakable emotional and physical pain endured by inmates.

OTHER MUSEUMS
In a bank branch is the **Käthe Kollwitz Museum** (Map pp578-9; ☎ 227 2363; Neumarkt 18-24; adult/concession €3/1.50; ☒ 10am-6pm Tue-Fri, 11am-6pm Sat & Sun), with its sculptures and stunning black-and-white graphics of the acclaimed socialist artist. Enter through the arcade, then take the glass-bubble lift to the 4th floor.

NORTH RHINE-WESTPHALIA

FOOLS, FLOATS & REVELRY
Carnival in Cologne is one of the best parties in Europe and a thumb in the eye of the German work ethic. Every year at the onset of Lent (late February/early March), a year of painstaking preparation culminates in the 'three crazy days' – actually more like six.

It all starts with *Weiberfastnacht*, the Thursday before Ash Wednesday, when women rule the day (and do things like chop off the ties of their male colleagues/bosses). The party continues through the weekend, with more than 50 parades of ingenious floats and wildly dressed lunatics dancing in the streets. By the time it all comes to a head with the big parade on *Rosenmontag* (Rose Monday), the entire city has come unglued. Those still capable of swaying and singing will live it up one last time on Shrove Tuesday before the curtain comes down on Ash Wednesday.

'If you were at the parade and saw the parade, you weren't at the parade', say the people of Cologne in their inimitable way. Translated, this means that you should be far too busy singing, drinking, roaring the Carnival greeting *'Alaaf!'* and planting a quick *Bützchen* (kiss) on the cheek of whoever strikes your fancy, to notice anything happening around you. Swaying and drinking while sardined in a pub, or following other costumed fools behind a huge bass drum leading to God-only-knows-where, you'll be swept up in one of the greatest parties the world knows.

The **Kölnisches Stadtmuseum** (Cologne City Museum; Map pp578-9; ☎ 2212 5789; Zeughausstrasse 1-3; adult/concession €4.20/2.60; ☼ 10am-8pm Tue, 10am-5pm Wed-Sun), in the medieval former armoury, allows a journey into the history of Cologne. Besides an interesting scale model of the old city, it also has a fine weapons collection and exhibits on carnival traditions.

The **Museum für Angewandte Kunst** (Museum of Applied Arts; Map pp578-9; ☎ 2212 6714; An der Rechtschule; adult/concession €4.20/2.60; ☼ 11am-5pm Tue-Sun, 11am-8pm Wed) traces the development of industrial design from the Middle Ages to today. Furniture, TV screens, tableware and bathroom fixtures are among the objects featured, including some by big-name designers like Mies van der Rohe and Charles Eames.

ROMAN COLOGNE

Remnants from the former Roman settlement lie scattered around town. In front of the Dom is a **Roman arch** (Map pp578-9) from the former town wall. Walk west along Komödienstrasse over Tunisstrasse to reach the **Zeughaus** (Map pp578-9; containing the Kölnisches Stadtmuseum), the Burgmauer side of which was built along the line of the **Roman wall** (Map pp578-9). On the pavement at the west end is a plaque tracing the wall's outline on a modern street plan (other plaques appear around the city near Roman sites). West of here is a complete section of the north wall, which leads to the **Römerturm** (Map pp578-9), a corner tower standing among buildings on the street corner at St-Apern-Strasse. Walk south one block to get to another tower ruin near Helenenstrasse.

On the southern wall of the Römisch-Germanisches Museum are remains of the **Roman harbour street** and two **Roman wells**. The foundations of the **Praetorian** (Map pp578-9; ☎ 2212 2394; adult/concession €1.50/0.75; ☼ 10am-4pm Tue-Fri, 11am-4pm Sat & Sun), beneath Cologne's medieval town hall, are a highlight (enter from Kleine Budengasse). The **Rathaus** (Map pp578-9; ☎ 221 2192; Untere Goldschmied; admission free; ☼ 7.30am-4.45pm Mon-Thu, 7.30am-2pm Fri) itself has a Gothic tower and Renaissance loggia. Below the adjacent square is a medieval **Mikwe** (Map pp578-9; ☼ 8am-4pm Mon-Thu, 8am-noon Fri, 11am-3pm Sat & Sun), a Jewish ritual bath, which can be visited. On weekdays, you can pick up the key inside the Rathaus; on weekends from the ticket office of the Praetorian.

Tours

Guided two-hour city **bus tours** (☎ 979 2570; adult/child aged 6-12 €14/4) in German and English depart from the tourist office up to three times daily.

Rent-A-Bike (Map pp578-9; ☎ 0171-629 8796; Marksmanngasse; tour €15) runs German/English three-hour bicycle tours daily at 1.30pm from April to October. Tours start in the Altstadt right below the Deutzer Brücke.

In the warmer months, several operators offer a variety of boat tours leaving from landing docks below the Konrad-Adenauer-Ufer north of the Hohenzollernbrücke and from the Frankenwerft north of the Deutzer Brücke. The standard one-hour tours cost around €5/2.50 adult/child. Companies offering boat tours include:

Dampfschifffahrt Colonia (Map pp578-9; ☎ 257 4225; Lintgasse 18)

KD Köln (Map pp578-9; ☎ 208 8318; Frankenwerft 35) Boats leave from Konrad-Adenauer-Ufer.

Köln-Tourist Personenschifffahrt (Map pp578-9; ☎ 121 600; Konrad-Adenauer-Ufer)

Sleeping

The tourist office runs a room-finding service for €2.50 per person, but cheap accommodation in Cologne is rare. Prices soar as high as triple the standard rate during major trade shows, held mostly in spring and autumn. Ask about specials on weekends and other times.

BUDGET

Station – Hostel for Backpackers (Map pp578-9; ☎ 912 5301; www.hostel-cologne.de; Marzellenstrasse 44-56; dm €15-16, s/d/tr/q €27/20/18/16.50, d/q with bathroom €25/18.50, all rates per person; ☒ ☐) This recently expanded and upgraded hostel is a great budget base that's a mere hop, skip and a jump from the Hauptbahnhof. A large, welcoming lounge gives way to clean, colourful rooms, some with private bathrooms, sleeping one to six people. The owner and his team are fluent in English and very helpful. There's lots of free stuff, including linen, Internet access, lockers, city maps and guest kitchen. The breakfast buffet is €5.

Hotel Allegro (Map pp578-9; ☎ 240 8260; www .hotel-allegro.com; Thurnmarkt 1-7; s €59-119, d €79-159; ☐ ☒) This is a pleasant option just south of the Altstadt with rooms that sport either a rustic Bavarian, modern or colourful

Mediterranean look. Some have river views, although those at the back are quieter.

Pension Jansen (Map p583; ☎/fax 251 875; Richard-Wagner-Strasse 18; s €31-47, d €57-77) In the Zülpicher Viertel, this hotel is small but cheap and not far from restaurants and nightlife. It's hugely popular and often fully booked, so reserve early.

DJH hostel Köln-Deutz (☎ 814711; jh-koeln-deutz@ djh-rheinland.de; Siegesstrasse 5a; dm €21, s/d €36/56; P ☒ ☐) The big, 506-bed DJH hostel is in Deutz, a 10-minute walk east from the Hauptbahnhof over the Hohenzollern-brücke, or three minutes from Bahnhof Köln-Deutz. All rooms have their own bathroom. Discounts are available in November, January and February.

Other recommendations:

DJH hostel Köln-Riehl (☎ 767 081; jh-koeln-riehl@ djh-rheinland.de; An der Schanz 14; dm €22, s/d €34/54) This hostel is near the Rhine but about 3km north of the city centre in the suburb of Riehl; take the U16 to Boltensternstrasse.

Hotel Brandenburger Hof (Map pp578-9; ☎ 122 889; www.brandenburgerhof.de; Brandenburger Strasse 2; s/d with shared bathroom from €29/46, with private bathroom from €44/68) Nice, cheerful rooms with TV but no telephone.

MID-RANGE

Chelsea Hotel (Map p583; ☎ 207 150; www.hotel -chelsea.de; Jülicher Strasse 1; s €69-100, d €79-110; P ☒ ☐) Those fancying an artsy vibe will be well sheltered in this Belgian Quarter hotel. It has an eye-catching rooftop extension where rooms have a private terrace and stunning views. There's fine modern art throughout, including the gallery and café. Breakfast is €9 per person.

Hotel Cristall (Map pp578-9; ☎ 163 00; www.hotel cristall.de; Ursulaplatz 9-11; s/d from €69/89; P ☒ ☒) This laid-back, yet stylish, hotel gets its character from custom-made furniture and nice design touches throughout. It's close to major sights and popular with creative types. Includes a cocktail bar.

Hopper Hotel Et Cetera (Map p583; ☎ 924 400; www.hopper.de; Brüsseler Strasse 26; s/d from €70/100; P ☒ ☐) Rooms in this former monastery pay homage to monastic simplicity in their clean, uncluttered design but also come with lots of little pampering touches. The sauna and bar, both in the vaulted cellars, are great places for reliving the day's exploits.

Hotel Leonet (Map p583; ☎ 272 300; www.leonet -koeln.de; Rubensstrasse 33; s/d from €90/115; P ☒ ☐)

ZÜLPICHER VIERTEL & BELGISCHES VIERTEL

NORTH RHINE-WESTPHALIA

INFORMATION		
Eco-Express Waschsalon	1	B3
Eco-Express Waschsalon	2	A2
Eco-Express Waschsalon	3	A2

SLEEPING	⌂	(pp582-4)
Chelsea Hotel	4	A2
Hopper Hotel Et Cetera	5	A2
Hotel Leonet	6	B2
Pension Jansen	7	A2

EATING	⑪	(pp584-5)
Alcazar	8	A1
Bagutta	9	B3
Café Feynsinn	10	A3
Café Fleur	11	B2
Engelbät	12	B3
Filmdose	13	B3
Fischermann's	14	A3
Magnus	15	A3
Sprössling	16	B3
Thali	17	B3

DRINKING	☐	(p585)
Café Huber	18	B2
Hallmackenreuther	19	A2
Päffgen	20	B1
Rosebud	21	B3
Spirits	22	B2

ENTERTAINMENT	☐	(pp586-7)
Das Ding	23	B3
Downtown Club	24	A2
Metronom	25	B3
Stadtgarten	26	A1
Vampire	27	B3

TRANSPORT		(pp587-8)
Hertz	28	A1

This solid mid-range option close to the Zülpicher Viertel has a rather extensive wellness area with several saunas, Jacuzzi and a nifty shiatsu massage chair. Rooms are good-sized, decorated in blue hues and have all major modern amenities.

Lint Hotel (Map pp578-9; ☎ 920 550; www.lint -hotel.de; Lintgasse 7; s/d from €80/112) In a quiet, pretty alley in the heart of the Altstadt, this contemporary and innovative hotel has undergone an ecologically sensitive renovation and is completely nonsmoking. A small bistro serves light meals nightly.

Hotel Eden am Dom (Map pp578-9; ☎ 272 920; www.hotel-eden.de; Am Hof 18; s/d €101/130; P X) Largish rooms warmly furnished in reds and yellows make the Eden an attractive and central Altstadt choice. There's a decent Italian restaurant to boot.

Other recommendations:

Heinzelmännchen Hotel (☎ 211 217; fax 215 712; Hohe Pforte 5-7; s € 36-50, d €61-100) Cute place close to a major shopping zone.

Senats-Hotel (Map pp578-9; ☎ 206 20; www.senats -hotel.de; Untere Goldschmied 9-17; s/d from €79/115; P X) Businesslike yet pleasant with good-sized rooms.

TOP END

Hotel Hyatt Regency (☎ 828 1234; www.cologne.hyatt .com; Kennedy-Ufer 2a; s/d from €175/200; P X 🔲 ▣ 🔳) This ultra-posh abode is a favourite with celebrities, politicians and those needing the ultimate in comfort across the river from the Altstadt. If you go for it, get a room facing the river and the awesome Altstadt skyline.

Hotel Im Wasserturm (☎ 200 80; www.hotel-im -wasserturm.de; Kaygasse 2; s/d from €160/195) This is an extremely classy designer hotel cleverly converted from an old water tower, south of Neumarkt. Take the U12, U16 or U18 to Poststrasse.

Eating

RESTAURANTS

Cologne's multiculturalism makes it possible to take a culinary journey around the world. Rhenish specialities and typical German food are best sampled in the beer halls (see Drinking p585).

Graugans (☎ 8281 1771; Kennedy-Ufer 2a; mains €20-30; closed Sun) Dinner here is going to make a serious dent in your wallet, but fans of 'wok-meets-Western' cuisine will probably like what's on the plates at this elegant restaurant inside the Hyatt Regency Hotel. Romantic views of the Dom and the Altstadt skyline and superb wine list.

Alcazar (Map p583; ☎ 515 733; Bismarckstrasse 39; snacks €4-9, mains €9-15) There's no fixed menu at this lively and unpretentious restaurant-pub in the Belgian Quarter, but the eclectic offerings always include soups, salads, vegetarian and meat-based dishes made from seasonal ingredients.

Bizim (☎ 131 581; Weidengasse 47; mains €20-25; closed Sun & Mon) For sophisticated Euro-Turkish food, there's no place like Bizim, north of the Hauptbahnhof, which offers professional preparation and service. It also has excellent Turkish wines from the Bosporus, including a big red called Yakut.

Fischermann's (Map p583; ☎ 801 7790; Rathenau-platz 21; mains €9-16, three-course dinner €22; dinner only) This gorgeous yet unpretentious restaurant wows patrons with competent crossover cuisine that offers nouveau German, Mediterranean and Asian flavour pairings. Perfect for al fresco dining on the spacious outdoor terrace. Popular with gay men and women.

Unsicht-Bar (☎ 200 5010; Im Stavenhof 5-7; three-course dinner €29-41; dinner only, closed Mon) This restaurant, north of the Hauptbahnhof, leaves you completely in the dark – literally so. The complete absence of light is supposed to sharpen your other senses as you indulge in multi-course dinners served by visually-impaired servers. Also in Berlin (p125).

Thali (Map p583; ☎ 239 169; Engelbertstrasse 9; mains €8-13; closed Mon lunch) This unassuming little Zülpicher Viertel restaurant serves some of the best curries and tandoori dishes in town with plenty of choices for vegetarians to feast on. Lunch specials are €5 to €8.

Sprössling (Map p583; ☎ 232 124; Mozartstrasse 9; mains €5-11; closed Tue; X) One of Cologne's few truly vegetarian restaurants, this one has a daily changing menu with Oriental and Italian inflections. A special touch is the flower-festooned courtyard. The Sunday brunch buffet is €11.

Other recommendations:

Engelbät (Map p583; ☎ 246 914; Engelbertstrasse 7; dishes €2-6) Friendly restaurant-pub known for its habit-forming crepes – sweet, meat or vegetarian.

Bagutta (Map p583; ☎ 212 694; Heinsbergstrasse 20a; mains €12-20) Romantic, modern restaurant with outdoor terrace serving mostly Mediterranean cuisine.

CAFÉS

Café Feynsinn (Map p583; ☎ 240 9209; Rathenauplatz 7; mains €8-14) This relaxed neighbourhood favourite sits next to a large park with two playgrounds and serves excellent breakfasts and a surprisingly accomplished menu inspired by Mediterranean and sometimes even Asian cuisine.

Magnus (Map p583; ☎ 241 469; Zülpicher Strasse 48; dishes €3-8) A chatty, student-age crowd fills tables here from breakfast to the wee hours. Pizza, pasta, salads and pancakes provide sustenance. Cocktails are just €4 from 10pm to 1am.

Filmdose (Map p583; ☎ 239 643; Zülpicher Strasse 39; dishes €5-7) Across the street from Magnus, the speciality here is Kölsche Pizza, where the dough is made of potato pancakes. The restaurant is cheerful and cinematic with a long bar and red velvet curtains. Breakfast is served until 6pm.

Moderne Zeiten (Map pp578-9; ☎ 257 5171; Breite Strasse 100; meals €7-10) This long-standing café, across from the WDR radio and TV studios, has good views of the street action and dependable, creative cuisine.

Café Fleur (Map pp578-9; ☎ 244 897; Lindenstrasse 10; dishes €4-10) This is a classic Viennese-style coffeehouse where you can lounge over breakfast, brunch and cakes or simply while away the time pouring over the free periodicals.

Drinking

Cologne is a happening place when it comes to bars, pubs and clubs, with a scene that ranges from grungy and relaxed to upmarket chic. Centres of action include the Altstadt, with its rollicking pubs and beer halls; the Friesenviertel, with the greatest density of places along Friesenwall and Friesenstrasse which feels like a miniature carnival on weekends; the 'Kwartier Lateng' (Cologne dialect for *Quartier Latin*, or student quarter), also known as Zülpicher Viertel, along Zülpicher-, Roon- and Kyffhäuser Strasse; and the Belgisches Viertel (Belgian Quarter); and which has a more grown-up yet still somewhat alternative feel, along Bismarck-, Flandrische- and Maastrichtstrasse.

BEER HALLS

Beer reigns supreme in Cologne with over 20 breweries producing a variety called *Kölsch*, which is relatively light and slightly bitter. Many run their own beer halls where the brew comes in skinny glasses called *Stangen* that hold a mere 200ml. They also serve a selection of stout Rhenish dishes to keep you grounded.

Früh am Dom (Map pp578-9; ☎ 261 30; Am Hof 12-14; breakfast €4-10, mains €5-14) This beer hall–cum-restaurant is in the shadow of the Dom. It serves filling breakfasts and a good range of hearty fare in its warren of rooms or, in summer, outside on a pretty square featuring by a whimsical fountain.

Other choices:

Brauhaus Sion (Map pp578-9; ☎ 257 8540; Unter Taschenmacher 9; mains €8-13) This Altstadt tourist favourite, often jam-packed, serves sausages by the metre.

Malzmühle (Map pp578-9; ☎ 210 117; Heumarkt 6; mains €8-15) Plenty of local colour; customers enjoy beer brewed with organic ingredients.

Päffgen (Map p583; ☎ 135 461; Friesenstrasse 64-66; mains €8.50-14) Considered one of the most original beer halls.

PUBS & BARS

Spirits (Map p583; ☎ 473 3625; Engelbertstrasse 63) Staff at this small, elegant and dimly lit cocktail bar keep their attitude in check and have a generous elbow when pouring drinks.

Rosebud (Map p583; ☎ 240 1455; Heinsbergstrasse 20) This is a popular American-style cocktail bar for the see-and-be-seen scensters with fancy drinks, a mirror-backed bar, complexion-friendly lighting and smooth jazz. Happy hour is 8.30pm until 10pm Monday to Thursday and 10pm until midnight on Sundays.

Hallmackenreuther (Map p583; ☎ 517 970; Brüsseler Platz 9) Named after a character created by German satirist Loriot, this bustling Belgian Quarter bar-restaurant went 1960s retro-style long before the look became all the rage. Most of the clientele, though, weren't born until after that particular decade.

Flanagan's (Map pp578-9; ☎ 257 0674; Alter Markt 36) If you're feeling homesick, you're bound to find some company at this happening Irish pub with live bands, nightly parties and English as the reigning language.

Biermuseum (Map pp578-9; ☎ 257 7802; Buttermarkt 39) You won't find many locals at this place either, but who cares when you've got more than three dozen beer varieties from around the world to keep you in suds.

Entertainment

For an overview of Cologne's main nightlife quarters, see the introduction to Drinking (p585). To find out what's on consult the city's listings magazines *Monatsvorschau* (bilingual, mainstream), *Kölner Illustrierte* (mainstream), *Prinz* (trendy) or *StadtRevue* (alternative), available at newsagents and bookshops.

CLUBS & LIVE MUSIC

Gebäude 9 (☎ 814637; Deutz-Mülheimer Strasse 127) In 1996, this ex factory got a new lease on life as an off-beat cultural venue with an eclectic programme of live concerts, theatre and parties, sometimes all three in one night. Take tram No 3 or 4 to KölnMesse/Osthallen.

Stadtgarten (Map p583; ☎ 9529 9433; Venloer Strasse 40) This is one of the most happening spots in the Belgian Quarter. Right in the middle of a small park, it combines a beer garden, a sleek restaurant serving Mediterranean creations and a downstairs hall for live concerts, dance parties and other events.

Underground (☎ 544 376; Vogelsanger Strasse 200; ✦ closed Mon) This big complex combines a pub and two concert rooms where indie and alternative rock bands hold forth several times a week. Otherwise it's party time with different music nightly (no cover). There's a beer garden in summer. To get here take U3 or U4 to Venloer Strasse/Gürtel.

Metronom (Map p583; ☎ 213 465; Weyerstrasse 59) The intimate setting is ideal for listening to some quality jazz drawn from the American owner's awesome vinyl collection behind the bar. Live music on Tuesday.

Alter Wartesaal (Map pp578-9; ☎ 912 8850; Johannisstrasse 11) Right by the Hauptbahnhof in a former station waiting hall, this is a stylish bar-disco-restaurant combo decked out in noble woods, stucco and marble. The Blue Monday parties, with go-go dancers, are legendary.

Downtown Club (Map p583; ☎ 510 4783; Brabanter Strasse 15; ✦ Thu-Sat) People with day jobs appreciate the Thursday after-work parties from 5pm, while those on a budget are drawn by the modest drink prices, especially during happy hour, and free snacks. Weekends attract the over-25 set for '80s sounds and world music.

Papa Joe's Em Streckstrump (Map pp578-9; ☎ 257 7931; Buttermarkt 37) This Altstadt institution claims to be Germany's oldest jazz pub. Free live concerts and a wicked herb liquor available only here keep the spirits high nightly.

Other recommendations:

Prime Club (☎ 924 460; www.primeclub.de; Luxemburger Strasse 40; ✦ Wed, Fri, Sat) Concerts and parties held south of Zülpicher Platz.

Das Ding (Map p583; ☎ 246 348; Hohenstaufenring 30-32) Student-only dance club (student ID required) with low-key ambience.

Papa Joe's Klimperkasten (Map pp578-9; ☎ 258 2132; Alter Markt 50) A piano player tickles the ivories nightly in this museumlike place with 1920s-style décor.

GAY & LESBIAN COLOGNE

Cologne is one of Germany's gayest cities with two main districts: the so-called 'Bermuda Triangle' around Rudolfplatz, which draws a youngish crowd and turns into nonstop party central on weekends; and the area around Marienplatz, where venues generally attract an older crowd as well as the leather and fetish scenes. The Christopher Street Day celebration regularly brings over a million people to Cologne (dates vary but it's usually in early July), and the Gay & Lesbian Street Festival in June also gets a good turnout.

Schulz, the city's main gay culture and communication centre, is perfect for plugging into the current scene, but unfortunately it was moving to a new location at the time of writing. Check www.schulz-cologne.de for updates. Meanwhile, pick up a copy of the free bilingual gay mag *RIK* for the latest scoops or drop by the information centre **Checkpoint** (Map pp578-9; ☎ 9257 6868; www.checkpoint-cologne.de; Pipinstrasse 7; ✦ 5-9pm Mon-Fri, 1-9pm Sat).

Bars worth checking out include: **Blue Lounge** (☎ 271 7117; Mathiasstrasse 4-6; ✦ Wed-Sun), a smooth dance and cocktail bar for a mixed crowd; **Café Huber** (Map p583; ☎ 245 6030; Schaafenstrasse 51), which organises theme parties for its predominantly young and flamboyant clientele; **Vampire** (Map p583; ☎ 241 1211; Rathenauplatz 5), cleverly covered in hues of red and favoured by lesbians; and the men-only **Chains** (Map pp578-9; ☎ 238 730; Stephanstrasse 4), the city's largest leather-and-fetish bar with house and techno on the turntable and an active darkroom.

To enjoy some of Cologne's biggest and boldest dance parties and live concerts you need to travel out to the suburb of Mülheim north of the city centre, where **E-Werk** (☎ 962 790; Schanzenstrasse 37) and **Palladium Köln** (☎ 967 90; Schanzenstrasse 40) compete for party animals in an industrial section of town.

THEATRE & CLASSICAL MUSIC

Kölner Philharmonie (Map pp578-9; www.koelner-philharmonie.de; Bischofsgartenstrasse 1) Lovers of classical music should not miss a concert here, below the Museum Ludwig. The box office is at **KölnTicket** (☎ 280 280; Roncalliplatz).

Repertory theatre is based at the **Schauspielhaus** (Offenbachplatz). The **Opernhaus** (box office ☎ 2212 8400; Offenbachplatz; www.buehnenkoeln.de) is also here. The box office for both is in the Opernhaus foyer.

Shopping

Cologne is a fantastic place to shop, with lots of eccentric boutiques, designer stores and trendy second-hand shops, plus the usual selection of chain and department stores. Hohe Strasse – which meanders south from the Dom, and then forks off into In der Höhle and Schildergasse, culminating in Neumarkt – is best for mainstream shopping, while Breite Strasse and side streets like Apostelnstrasse have a more eclectic mix of stores from funky to elegant.

If you want to bring something home to mother, consider a bottle of eau de Cologne, the not terribly sophisticated but refreshing perfume created – and still being produced – in its namesake city. The most famous brand is called 4711, after the number of the house where it was invented. The **4711 perfumery & gift shop** (Map 195; cnr Glockengasse & Schwertnergasse) also has a carillon with characters from Prussian lore parading hourly from 9am to 9pm.

Getting There & Away

AIR

Köln-Bonn Airport (☎ 02203-404 001; www.airport-cgn.de) offers connections to around 30 European cities. Airlines include German Wings (to/from London-Stansted), Air Berlin, British Airways, Deutsche BA and Eurowings. See the transport chapter p755 for airline details.

BUS

The bus station (Busbahnhof) is just behind the Hauptbahnhof, on Breslauer Platz. **Eurolines** (www.eurolines.com) buses go to Paris (one way/return €35/62, eight hours) and back daily (some trips overnight) and to Warsaw daily (€55/96, 21 hours). Trips to Prague (€45/77, 12 hours) are scheduled three times a week.

CAR & MOTORCYCLE

Cologne is also a major autobahn hub and is encircled by the immense Kölner Ring, with exits to the A1, A3, A4, A57, A555 and A559 leading in all directions. Note that this ring road is often jammed with traffic.

If you'd like to hitch a ride through a Mitfahrzentrale, try:

Citynetz Mitfahr-Service (☎ 194 44; www.citynetz-mitfahrzentrale.de; Saarstrasse 22) South of Zülpicher Viertel near Barbarossaplatz.

Mitfahr2000 (Map pp578-9; ☎ 194 40; www.mitfahr 2000.de; Maximinenstrasse 2; 🕑 9am-7pm) Near the Hauptbahnhof.

TRAIN

Cologne is a major train hub with regional and main-line train services to Bonn (€5.20, 40 minutes), Düsseldorf (€6.60, 30 minutes) and Aachen (€10.70, one hour) several times an hour. Superfast ICE trains make hourly trips to Frankfurt (€51, 1¼ hours) and Berlin (€80, 4¼ hours), and every two hours to Munich (€99, 4½ hours). Hamburg is served by IC trains (€56, four hours).

Getting Around

TO/FROM THE AIRPORT

Bus No 170 shuttles between Cologne/Bonn airport and the main bus station every 15 minutes from 6am to 11.30pm (€4.65, 20 minutes). Taxis charge about €25.

BICYCLE

Rent-A-Bike (Map pp578-9; ☎ 723 627 or 0171-629 8796; Marksmanngasse) hires out bikes for €2/10 per hour/day or €5 for three hours and also does tours (see Tours p582).

CAR & MOTORCYCLE

Driving in Cologne can be an absolute nightmare. Unless you're careful, you could easily end up in a tunnel or on a bridge

NORTH RHINE-WESTPHALIA

going across the Rhine. Most streets in the centre have residential parking only, so your only option is usually to find an expensive parking garage (from €1.25 an hour). Note that some close at night and charge an overnight fee.

Avis (Map pp578-9; ☎ 234 333; Clemensstrasse 29-31) and **Hertz** (Map p583; ☎ 515 084; Bismarckstrasse 19-21) are among international car-hire agencies with branches in town.

PUBLIC TRANSPORT

Cologne's mix of buses, trams, and U-Bahn and S-Bahn trains is operated by the **Verkehrsverbund Rhein-Sieg** (VRS; ☎ 01803-504 030) in cooperation with Bonn's system.

Short trips within the city cost €1.25, though most require the €2 ticket; 24-hour passes are €5.30. Groups of up to five people can travel with the *Minigruppenkarte* for €7.50. Buy your tickets from the orange ticket machines at stations and aboard trams; be sure to stamp them.

TAXI

Taxis cost €1.55 at flag fall, plus €1.15 per kilometre (€0.10 more at night); add another €0.50 if you order by phone (☎ 28 82 or ☎ 194 10).

AROUND COLOGNE
Brühl
☎ 02232 / pop 40,000

About 15km south of Cologne, Brühl is home to **Schloss Augustusburg** (☎ 440 00; tours adult/student €4/3; 🕐 9am-12.30pm & 1.30-5pm Tue-Fri, 10am-6pm Sat & Sun; closed Mon & Dec-Jan), a major treat for fans of baroque palaces and a Unesco World Heritage Site. It was commissioned by Clemens August (1723–61), the flamboyant archbishop-elector of Cologne, friend of Casanova and himself a lover of women, parties and palaces.

Three of the period's best architects – Johann Conrad Schlaun, François Cuvilliés and Balthasar Neumann – collaborated on this elegant edifice, which is surrounded by a formal French garden. The palace interior, which must be seen on a guided tour, is a dizzying extravaganza incorporating every architectural and decorative element the baroque era had to offer. The most impressive feature is the ceremonial staircase by Neumann. A symphony in stucco, sculpture and faux marble, it is

bathed in muted light and crowned by a multicoloured ceiling fresco by Carlo Carlone.

A short stroll away is the much smaller **Schloss Falkenlust** (adult/concession €3/2; 🕐 see Schloss Augustusburg opposite), used as a private retreat by Clemens August.

Brühl's other big drawcard is **Phantasialand** (☎ 362 00; Berggeiststrasse 31-41; adult/child €24.50/€19.50; 🕐 9am-6pm Apr-Oct, extended summer hours possible), one of Europe's earliest Disneyland-style amusement parks (it turned 35 in 2002) and naturally a winner with children. The park has six themed areas – Chinatown, Old Berlin, Wild West, Mexico, Fantasy and Mystery – each with its own set of rides from roller coasters to gondolas to flight simulators, plus several song and dance shows. To be admitted as a child you have to be shorter than 145cm; any child shorter than 1m is free and if it's your birthday it's free also.

Brühl is regularly served by regional trains from Cologne and Bonn. If you're driving, exit Brühl-Süd from the A553.

BONN
☎ 0228 / pop 311,000

When this friendly, relaxed city on the Rhine became West Germany's 'temporary' capital in 1949 it surprised almost everyone, including its own residents. Soon it was nicknamed 'Federal Village' for its supposed provincialism and lack of sophistication. While Bonn was no world-class capital, these slights were not entirely deserved. Besides large international and student populations, it was – and still is – endowed with several first-rate museums, some packed with the biggest and brightest names in art. Artists, in fact, have played a large role in the city's history. Bonn was the birthplace of Ludwig van Beethoven, the painter August Macke had his studio in town, and composer Robert Schumann lived and was buried here.

Over the last decade, the city has been busy reinventing itself, attracting international organisations and retaining the status of *Bundesstadt* (Federal City), a secondary governmental seat (see the boxed text p591).

Bonn is an easy day trip from Cologne and a good base for exploring some of the sights along this section of the Rhine.

Orientation

Bonn is about 30km south of Cologne and just north of the Siebengebirge nature reserve. The Köln-Bonn airport is about 15km north (see p593 for information on getting to/from the airport). The B9 from Cologne changes names several times within Bonn; it connects the Altstadt with the Bundesviertel

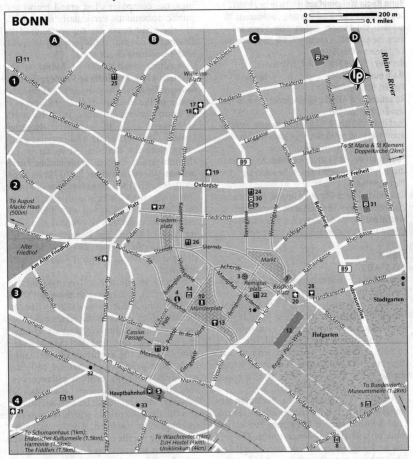

INFORMATION

Bouvier	1 C3
Post Office	(see 14)
Reisebank	2 B4
Surf Inn Internet Café	3 C3
Tourist Office	4 B3
University	(see 12)

SIGHTS & ACTIVITIES (pp590-2)

Akademisches Kunstmuseum	5 D4
Alter Zoll	6 D3
Altes Rathaus	7 C3
Arithmeum	8 D4
Beethoven Haus	9 C2
Beethoven Memorial	10 B3
Frauen Museum	11 A1
Kurfürstliche Residenz	12 C3

Münster Basilika	13 C3
Palais Fürstenberg	14 B3
Rheinisches Landesmuseum	15 A4
Rhine Cruises	(see 6)

SLEEPING (pp592-3)

Best Western Domicil	16 A3
Deutsches Haus	17 B1
Hotel Bergmann	18 B1
Hotel Consul	19 C2
Hotel Löhndorf	20 C3
Hotel Mozart	21 A4

EATING (p593)

Bonner Brasserie	22 C3
Cassius Garten	23 B4
Im Stiefel	24 C2

Klein Bonnum	25 B1
Zum Gequetschten	26 B3

DRINKING (p593)

Brauhaus Bönnsch	27 B2
Zebulon	28 D3

ENTERTAINMENT (p593)

Beethovenhalle	29 D1
Kammermusiksaal	30 C2
Oper Bonn	31 D2

TRANSPORT (pp593-4)

Citynetz Mitfahrzentrale	32 A4
Radstation Bike Rentals	33 B4

NORTH RHINE-WESTPHALIA

(former government district), and continues south to Bad Godesberg and Koblenz.

Information

Bonn Regio WelcomeCard (€9/14/19 for 24/48/72 hours) Unlimited public transportation, admission to 20 museums, plus discounts on tours, thermal baths and more. The group (three adults) or family (two adults, two kids) version is €18/28/38.

Bouvier (☎ 729 010; Am Hof 28) Bookshop.

Main post office (Münsterplatz 17; ⊗ 9am-8pm Mon-Fri, 9am-4pm Sat)

Reisebank (☎ 632 958; Hauptbahnhof; ⊗ 9am-7pm Mon-Fri, 9am-3pm Sat)

Surf Inn (☎ 516 513; 1st fl Sportarena store, Remigius-strasse 6-8; €1.50 per 30 min; ⊗ 9.30am-8pm Mon-Fri, 9.30am-6pm Sat) Internet access.

Tourist office (☎ 77 50 00; www.bonn.de; Windeck-strasse 1; ⊗ 9am-6.30pm Mon-Fri, 9am-4pm Sat, 10am-2pm Sun)

Uniklinikum Bonn (☎ 2870; Sigmund-Freud-Strasse 25) Medical services, 4km south of the Hauptbahnhof.

Waschcenter (cnr Reuterstrasse & Argelanderstrasse) About a 15-minute walk south of the Hauptbahnhof.

Sights

ALTSTADT

A good place to start exploring Bonn's historic centre is on Münsterplatz, dominated by the five soaring spires of the Münster Basilika, whose architecture blends Romanesque and Gothic style elements. It's built on top of the graves of the city's patron saints, two martyred Roman soldiers named Cassius and Florentius, whose shrine is in the crypt. The Romanesque cloister is worth a spin as well.

Also on the square is the **Beethoven Memorial** (1845), largely financed by Franz Liszt who donated a large sum and raised more on a worldwide concert tour. The yellow building behind the statue is the Palais Fürstenberg, now the main post office.

Northeast of here is the Altstadt's other main square, the triangular Markt, easily reached via Remigiusstrasse. It is dominated by the baroque **Altes Rathaus**, standing pretty in pink with silver and gold trim. Politicians from Charles de Gaulle to John F Kennedy have waved to the crowds from its double-sided staircase.

North of the Markt is Bonn's most famous building, the **Beethoven Haus** (☎ 981 7525; Bonngasse 20; adult/concession €4/3; ⊗ 10am-6pm Mon-Sat Apr-Oct, 10am-5pm Nov-Mar; 11am-5pm

Sun year-round) whose modest exterior belies its historic importance as the birthplace of Ludwig van Beethoven (1770–1827). Inside are letters, musical scores, paintings, the composer's last grand piano and public documents. Particularly memorable are the giant brass ear trumpets, used by Beethoven to combat his growing deafness, and a haunting death mask.

A short stroll south of Markt is the palatial 1705 **Kurfürstliche Residenz** (Electoral Residence; Regina-Pacis-Weg), once the immodest home of the electors of Cologne and part of Bonn's university since 1818. Its south side opens up to the expansive **Hofgarten** (Palace Garden), a park and popular gathering place for students. At its far end is the university-owned **Akademisches Kunst-museum** (Academic Art Museum; ☎ 737 738; Am Hofgarten 21; admission €1.50, students free; ⊗ to view copies: 10am-1pm Sun-Fri & 4-6pm Thu; to view originals: 10am-1pm Sun & Tue, 4-6pm Thu; closed Aug) with a large and prestigious collection of original and plaster casts of Greek and Roman statues. It's housed in the former anatomy institute designed by Berlin architect Karl Friedrich Schinkel.

Nearby is another university-affiliated museum, the intriguing **Arithmeum** (☎ 738 771; Lennéstrasse 2; adult/concession €3/2; ⊗ 11am-6pm Tue-Sun), which explores the relationship between science, technology and art. Housed in a minimalist glass and steel cube, the core exhibit traces the evolution of calculating tools from primitive mechanical counting machines to highly evolved microprocessors. It's amazing to see the similarities between ancient calculation techniques and the digital world in which we now live so eloquently displayed. Another floor examines the parallels between the aesthetics of modern art and chip design. Work your way down from the top floor.

North of the Hofgarten across Adenauer-allee, at the **Alter Zoll**, is a small section of the stone ramparts that once encircled Bonn, with great views of the river and the hilly surrounds. The embarkation point for river cruises is here as well.

BUNDESVIERTEL & MUSEUMSMEILE

About 1.5km south of the Altstadt along the B9, Bonn's former government quarter was, from 1949 to 1999, the nerve centre of German political power. These days the Bundesviertel has reinvented itself as the home of UN and other international and federal institutions (see the boxed text below). The airy and modern **Plenary Hall**, for instance, where the *Bundestag* (German parliament) used to convene, now hosts international conferences, while the former **Chancellery** is being renovated as the future home of the Federal Ministry for Economic Cooperation and Development. At least partly retaining their original purposes are the stately **Villa Hammerschmidt**, still a secondary official residence of the federal president, and the neoclassical **Palais Schaumburg**, now serving as the chancellor's Bonn office. Also of note is the **Adenauer Memorial**, a gigantic bronze head with important events in the life of Germany's first post war chancellor engraved on the back.

While a stroll through the old government district is worthwhile, most people come here because of the world-class museums of Bonn's **Museumsmeile** (Museum Mile). One of the most interesting is the **Haus der Geschichte der Bundesrepublik Deutschland** (Forum of Contemporary German History; ☎ 916 50; Willy-Brandt-Allee 14; admission free; ☀ 9am-7pm Tue-Sun). Five levels of rampways present an entertaining multimedia chronology of the entire post-WWII history of Germany – from bombed-out obliteration to the industrialised and unified powerhouse of today.

It's a must for anyone interested in recent German history.

The **Kunstmuseum Bonn** (Bonn Art Museum; ☎ 776 260; Friedrich-Ebert-Allee 2; adult/concession €5/2.50; ☀ 10am-6pm Tue-Sun, 10am-9pm Wed) is known for its 20th-century collection, especially for its armloads of works by August Macke and other Rhenish expressionists, as well as for German art after 1945 (including Beuys, Baselitz and Kiefer). It's all housed in a postmodern building with a generous and light-flooded interior.

Next door, the art exhibition centre **Kunst- und Ausstellungshalle der Bundesrepublik Deutschland** (☎ 917 1200; Friedrich-Ebert-Allee 4; adult/concession €6.50/3.50; ☀ 10am-9pm Tue & Wed, 10am-7pm Thu-Sun) supplements its changing exhibits – many on loan from the world's leading museums – with concerts, film screenings and theatre productions. The building, by Viennese architect Gustav Peichl, is easily recognised by the sky-blue cones jutting from its rooftop garden and a line of 16 columns representing the states of Germany.

The newest museum along here is the **Deutsches Museum Bonn** (☎ 302 255; Ahrstrasse 45; adult/concession €4/2.50; ☀ 10am-6pm Tue-Sun), a small subsidiary of the famous one in Munich. It highlights the accomplishments of German technology since WWII, including inventions such as the airbag, the Trans-Rapid train and the computer tomograph.

NORTH RHINE-WESTPHALIA

BONN IS BACK

Boomtown Bonn? Who would have thought so in 1991 when the federal government decided to move the capital of Germany back to Berlin? Pundits created visions of a veritable ghost town, predicting a return to provincial backwater for the Rhenish city that beat Frankfurt by a hair to become Germany's 'temporary capital' on 10 May 1949. The federal government responded to this potentially destructive scenario with a mega-cash infusion of €1.7 billion to help Bonn forge a new identity. There's plenty of proof that the investment has paid off.

In just over a decade, the city has attracted scores of international organisations and companies, among the most prestigious a dozen UN offices, making it the only UN base in Germany. These offices range from the endearingly named Eurobats, which busies itself protecting bats in Europe, to major players such as the head office of the UN Framework Convention on Climate Change (UNFCCC). A UN campus is being created in the 'Langer Eugen', the office tower that once served members of parliament. The former Plenary Hall nearby has taken on a new role as an international conference centre.

Other facilities in the Bundesviertel (the former government district) have attracted new tenants, including many of the two dozen federal institutions that have moved to Bonn in recent years. And there's even new construction, most notably with the headquarters of the Deutsche Post, a head-turning high-rise designed by Helmut Jahn, as well as new digs for Deutsche Welle and the Center of Advanced European Studies and Research (Caesar). It seems the people of Bonn, ever resilient and savvy, have proved the naysayers wrong.

The fifth museum, the **Museum Koenig** (☎ 912 20; Adenauerallee 160), one of Germany's most well-respected natural history museums, was scheduled for reopening in late 2003. A new permanent exhibit entitled 'Our Blue Planet – Living in Networks' will show how ecological processes differ in various habitats, such as in deserts or rain forests. Call or check with the tourist office for specifics.

OTHER MUSEUMS

In the western Altstadt, the **Rheinisches Landesmuseum** (Rhineland Regional Museum; ☎ 988 10; Colmantstrasse 14-16; adult/child €6.50/3; ☼ 10am-6pm Tues-Sat, to 9pm Wed & Fri, closed Sun) Themed exhibits put the spotlight on various aspects of regional history, culture and art from the Stone Age to the present at this recently renovated museum.

In 1911, the painter August Macke (1887–1914) and his family moved to the top floor of a neoclassical house, northwest of the Hauptbahnhof, now known as the **August-Macke-Haus** (☎ 655 531; Bornheimer Strasse 96; adult/concession €3.50/2.50; ☼ 2.30-6pm Tue-Fri, 11am-5pm Sat & Sun). Macke spent his most productive years in the attic studio, creating well over 400 works, before his early death on the battlefields of WWI. To see his art, visit the Kunstmuseum Bonn.

Fans of Robert Schumann (1810–56) can study pictures, letters and documents in the two memorial rooms devoted to the composer in a former sanatorium that is now the **Schumannhaus** (☎ 773 656; Sebastianstrasse 182; admission free; ☼ 11am-1.30pm & 3-6pm Mon & Wed-Fri) in the suburb of Endenich. Schumann suffered severe depression and checked himself into the asylum in 1854 after a suicide attempt. Take bus No 622, 623, 632 or 635 to Alfred-Bucherer-Strasse. He and his wife Clara are buried in **Alter Friedhof** (Old Cemetery) on Bornheimer Strasse.

The **Frauenmuseum** (Women's Museum; ☎ 691 344; Im Krausfeld 10; adult/concession €4.50/3; ☼ 2-6pm Tue-Sat, 11am-6pm Sun) is one of the world's few museums entirely dedicated to promoting and showcasing the art of women and offers a lively schedule of exhibitions, lectures, readings and performances.

ST MARIA & ST KLEMENS DOPPELKIRCHE

Located on the right bank of the Rhine, in the suburb of Schwarzrheindorf, is this magnificent 'double church'. Originally the family chapel of a local count, **St Maria & St Klemens Doppelkirche** (☎ 461 609; Dixstrasse 41; ☼ 9am-6.30pm Tue-Sat, noon-6.30pm Sun, to 5pm in winter; upper church Sat & Sun only) was later part of a Benedictine monastery (1172–1806). It's a 'double church' because it has two levels: the upper for the nobility, and the lower for the commoners. The beautiful Romanesque architecture is impressive, but the church is especially famous for its extremely well-preserved 12th-century fresco cycles in the lower church. Bus No 550 and 640 both make the trip out here from the Hauptbahnhof (€2, 17 minutes).

Sleeping

The tourist office operates an in-person room-finding service (€2.50 fee). Many properties offer discounts in summer and at weekends, but hike prices during major international conferences and heavy tradeshow activity in nearby Cologne.

DJH hostel (☎ 289 970; jh-bonn@djh-rheinland.de; Haager Weg 42; s/d/q per person €35.30/25.30/21.30; P ✗) A finance-friendly option with nice, functional rooms, a bistro and a garden terrace. Unfortunately, it's inconveniently located on a hillside some 4km south of the Hauptbahnhof (bus No 621).

Hotel Löhndorf (☎ 655 439; www.hotel-loehndorf-bonn.de; Stockenstrasse 6; s/d €69/85) This is a small but comfortable property close to the Hofgarten and the Rhine. Lacy curtains, beds with crisp white linen and dark furniture create good old-fashioned ambience. The cheaper singles must share facilities (€43).

Hotel Mozart (☎ 659 071; fax 659 075; Mozartstrasse 1; s €41-80, d €60-100; P ✗) Housed in an elegant corner building, the Mozart could use a bit more style and creativity within, but at these prices it's still a good choice. It's in a residential quarter, about a five-minute walk south of the Hauptbahnhof.

Hotel Consul (☎ 729 20; www.consul-bonn.de; Oxfordstrasse 12-16; s €99-110, d €135-148; P ✗ ⚄) Though primarily catering for business travellers, this friendly hotel is also a good choice for sightseers, thanks to its quiet yet central location, comfortable rooms and such extras as bike-hire for guests.

Best Western Domicil (☎ 729090; www.domicil-bonn.bestwestern.de; Thomas-Mann-Strasse 24/26; s €132-195, d €160-222; P ✗) Right in the heart of town, this classy hotel sprawls over several buildings grouped around a central courtyard. Choose from the functional-yet-elegant Business Rooms, or the Salon Rooms in softer colours and with ornate ceilings (some with courtyard-facing terraces). A Jacuzzi, sauna, 24-hour reception and lobby bar, and an Italian restaurant are on the premises.

True budget hotels are rare in Bonn. Two basic and clean options:

Hotel Bergmann (☎ 633 891; fax 635 057; Kasernenstrasse 13; s/d with shared bathroom €35/50)

Deutsches Haus (☎ 633 777, 659 055; Kasernenstrasse 19-21; s/d with private bathroom €56/77, with shared bathroom €39/63) Slightly larger and more comfortable than Hotel Bergman.

Eating & Drinking

You'll find a few good, traditional Rhenish restaurants around Markt and more casual student pubs in the northern Altstadt along Breite Strasse, Heerstrasse and Maxstrasse. Another good place to party is on Frongasse, the so-called *Endenicher Kulturmeile* (literally 'Endenich Cultural Mile') in the suburb of Endenich, about 1.5km west of the Altstadt (bus No 634 from Hauptbahnhof to Frongasse).

Harmonie (☎ 614 042; Frongasse 28-30; mains €4-10; ☼ dinner only Mon-Sat, from 10am Sun) This 100-year-old former dance hall has evolved into one of the most beloved spots on the Endenicher Kulturmeile. A low-key, all-age crowd feasts on delicious German and Mediterranean dishes, moving from the cosy pub to the idyllic beer garden in summer. A separate hall has a lively schedule of jazz, blues and rock concerts.

The Fiddlers (☎ 614 161; Frongasse 9; dishes €4-16) Near Harmonie, Bonn's best Irish pub does a lot more than serve foamy Guinness. Tasty fish and chips, made with fresh cod fillet, are the standard bearers of the expansive menu. For the penny-wise, there are nightly drink and food specials.

Brauhaus Bönnsch (☎ 650 610; Sterntorbrücke 4; mains €4-12) This vibrant brew-pub features a gallery of framed historical photographs, including one of Arnold Schwarzenegger as Mr Universe and others featuring famous former Bonn politicians like Willy Brandt. Foodwise, you'll be filling up on sausages, spare ribs, Rhenish-style snacks and other hearty fare.

Im Stiefel (☎ 630 805; Bonngasse 30; mains €7-14) This rustic Rhenish inn makes dependable home-style German cooking. It hosts a sedate crowd that includes its share of tourists, thanks to its location – within earshot of the Beethoven Haus. On Wednesdays, regulars come for the freshly made potato pancakes.

Bonner Brasserie (☎ 655 559; Remigiusplatz 5; mains €5-12) This is the kind of bustling place that manages to be all things to all people, from the breakfast crowd to business lunchers, from shoppers refuelling on coffee and cake to the cool cocktail crowd after dark. Pizza, salads, burgers, steaks and other treats are on the menu.

Zum Gequetschten (☎ 638 104; Sternstrasse 78; mains €8-18) This traditional restaurant-pub is festooned with eye-catching blue tiles and is one of the oldest inns in town. The menu is back-to-basics German, but it's all delicious and portions are huge.

Other recommendations:

Cassius Garten (☎ 652 429; Maximilianstrasse 28, Cassius Arcade; dishes €1.50 per 100g; ☼ closed Sun) Self-service vegetarian buffet.

Klein Bonnum (☎ 638 104; Paulstrasse 5; mains €8-14; ☼ dinner only) Always busy with an intimate courtyard and a creative menu, including lots of freshly made salads.

Zebulon (☎ 657 690; Stockenstrasse 19; dishes €3-8) Popular student pub.

Entertainment

To find out what's on in Bonn, pick up the monthly listings magazines *De Schnüss* or *Bonner Illustrierte* at any newsagent. The central ticket hotline is ☎ 910 4161.

Bonn's entertainment scene is especially strong in the field of classical music. In late September, the city hosts the International Beethoven Festival, with hundreds of concerts held in venues around town. These include the **Kammermusiksaal** (☎ 981 7515; Bonngasse 24-26), an intimate and exquisite hall adjacent to the Beethoven Haus that presents chamber music and soloist recitals; the **Beethovenhalle** (☎ 778 008; Wachsbleiche 17), Bonn's premier concert hall and home of the Orchester der Beethovenhalle; and the **Oper Bonn** (Bonn Opera; ☎ 773 668; Am Boeslagerhof 1). All venues host many other concerts throughout the year.

Getting There & Away

Bonn shares its **Köln-Bonn Airport** (☎ 02203-404 001; www.airport-cgn.de) with Cologne and offers connections within Germany, Europe and beyond. Express bus No 670 makes the trip into town every 30 minutes (€5.20). A taxi to the airport from Bonn costs about €30.

Trains to Cologne (€5.20, 40 minutes) leave several times hourly, and there are also frequent trains to the Ruhrgebiet cities and Koblenz (€7.70, 30 minutes).

Bonn is at the crossroads of several autobahns, including the A565, A555 and A59. The B9 highway cuts north–south through the city. For ride services, you'll find a **Citynetz Mitfahrzentrale** (☎ 693 030; Herwarthstrasse 11) west of the Hauptbahnhof.

Getting Around

Buses, trams and the U-Bahn make up the public transportation system operated by the **VRS** (☎ 01803-504 030), which extends as far as Cologne and is divided into zones. All you need within Bonn is an A-zone ticket, which costs €2 each trip or €5.30 for the 24-hour pass. Tickets must be validated when boarding.

For a taxi, ring ☎ 55 55 55. Bikes may be hired at **Radstation** (☎ 981 4636; Quantiusstrasse 26; €6.50 per day; 🕙 6am-10.30pm Mon-Fri, 7am-10.30pm Sat, 8am-10.30pm Sun), right at the Hauptbahnhof.

AROUND BONN
Siebengebirge

Just south of Bonn, on the right bank of the Rhine, begins the Siebengebirge (Seven Mountains), a low mountain chain that is Germany's oldest nature reserve (1923). More than 200km of hiking trails lead through mostly deciduous forests, often allowing tremendous views of the Rhine, the Eifel and the Westerwald.

The Ölberg (461m) may be the highest of the seven mountains, but the **Drachenfels** (321m) is the most heavily visited. You can reach the summit on foot, by horse carriage, on the back of a mule or by riding the historic cogwheel train that has made the 1.4km climb since 1883 (the station is in Königswinter on Drachenfelsstrasse, just east of the B42). About halfway up the steep slopes, you will pass the neo-Gothic **Drachenburg** and, further uphill, the ruined **Schloss Drachenfels** (1147).

The base for explorations of the **Siebengebirge is Königswinter**, reached from Bonn Hauptbahnhof via the U66 (€2.75). The U-Bahn continues to **Bad Honnef**, the long-time home of the first West German chancellor, Konrad Adenauer. His house in the street named after him has been turned into a **Gedenkstätte Stiftung Bundeskanzler-Adenauer-Haus** (Memorial Site Foundation Chancellor Adenauer House; ☎ 02224-921 234; Konrad-Adenauer-Strasse 8c; admission free; 🕙 10am-4.30pm Tue-Sun).

AACHEN

☎ 0241 / pop 251,000

Hugging the Belgian and Dutch borders, Aachen may be on the 'edge' of Germany, but for many centuries it occupied a central position in the country's history. It owes this distinction to none other than Charlemagne, who chose to establish the capital of his vast Frankish empire here in 794, enticed not only by its strategic location but also by its sulfurous hot springs. These had already inspired the Romans to set up a military camp here some 800 years earlier.

The thermal waters remain one of Aachen's attractions to this day, but even more people flock here to visit the stunning cathedral, which incorporates Charlemagne's original palace chapel. In 1978, it became Germany's first monument to be included on Unesco's list of World Heritage Sites.

Aachen shares borders with the Netherlands and Belgium, giving it a distinctly international and lively vibe that's further enhanced by a large student population.

Orientation

Aachen's compact city centre is contained within two ring roads and is best explored on foot. The inner ring road encloses the Altstadt proper and is called Grabenring because it's composed of segments all ending in 'graben' (meaning 'moat'). The Hauptbahnhof is southeast of the town centre just beyond Alleenring, the outer ring road. To get to the Dom and the Altstadt, head north from the Hauptbahnhof for about 10 to 15 minutes. The bus station is at the northeastern edge of the Grabenring.

Information

Main post office (☎ 4120; Kapuzinerkarree; 🕙 9am-6pm Mon-Fri, 9am-2pm Sat) Inside a shopping mall.

Mayersche Buchhandlung (☎ 474 940; Pontstrasse 131) Bookshop.

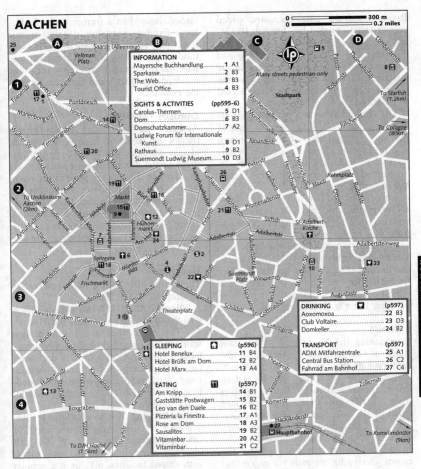

AACHEN

0	300 m
0	0.2 miles

INFORMATION
Mayersche Buchhandlung........1 A1
Sparkasse..................................2 B3
The Web..................................3 B3
Tourist Office..........................4 B3

SIGHTS & ACTIVITIES   (pp595-6)
Carolus-Thermen......................5 D1
Dom...6 B3
Domschatzkammer....................7 A2
Ludwig Forum für Internationale
  Kunst...................................8 D1
Rathaus....................................9 B2
Suermondt Ludwig Museum....10 D3

Many streets pedestrian-only

DRINKING   (p597)
Aoxomoxoa............................22 B3
Club Voltaire..........................23 D3
Domkeller...............................24 B2

TRANSPORT   (p597)
ADM Mitfahrzentrale..............25 A1
Central Bus Station................26 C2
Fahrrad am Bahnhof...............27 C4

SLEEPING   (p596)
Hotel Benelux........................11 B4
Hotel Brülls am Dom..............12 B2
Hotel Marx............................13 A4

EATING   (p597)
Am Knipp...............................14 B1
Gaststätte Postwagen.............15 B2
Leo van den Daele..................16 B2
Pizzeria la Finestra.................17 A1
Rose am Dom.........................18 A3
Sausalitos..............................19 B2
Vitaminbar.............................20 A2
Vitaminbar.............................21 C2

NORTH RHINE-WESTPHALIA

Sparkasse (☎ 4440; Friedrich-Wilhelm-Platz 1-4;
⏰ 8.30am-6pm Mon-Fri, 9am-1pm Sat) Bank.

Tourist office (☎ 180 29 60/61 or 194 33; www
.aachen.de; Elisenbrunnen, Friedrich-Wilhelm-Platz;
⏰ 9am-6pm Mon-Fri, 9am-2pm Sat year-round;
10am-2pm Sun Jul-Sep)

Universitätsklinikum Aachen (☎ 800;
Pauwelsstrasse) Medical services, 2km northwest of
the city centre.

Web (Kleinmarschierstrasse 74-76; €4 per hr; ⏰ 11am-
11pm Sun-Thu, 11am-3am Fri-Sat) Internet access.

Sights
DOM

Aachen's main draw is its **Dom** (☎ 477 090;
Münsterplatz; ⏰ 7am-7pm), with Charlemagne's
exquisite **Pfalzkapelle** (palace chapel) at its

core. One of the best-preserved examples of
Carolingian architecture, the chapel served,
over the course of nearly 600 years, as the
coronation church of some 30 Holy Roman
emperors, starting with Otto I in 936.

Inspired by Byzantine architecture, the
harmoniously proportioned structure consists of an octagonal dome supported by a
16-sided, two-storey ambulatory featuring
antique pillars imported from Italy. A co-
lossal brass **chandelier**, donated by Friedrich
Barbarossa in 1165, swings down from the
dome, which rises to a lofty 31m. For about
four centuries, this was the largest vaulted
structure north of the Alps. Also of note
are the **main altar**, with its 11th-century
gold-plated front depicting scenes of the

Passion; and the jewel-encrusted gilded copper **pulpit** donated by Heinrich II. Unless you join a German-language tour (€2, 45 minutes), you'll only catch a glimpse of Charlemagne's white marble **throne** in the upstairs gallery. Six steps lead up to it – the same number, supposedly, as those that led to the throne of King Solomon.

The chapel has been a popular pilgrimage site since the Middle Ages, because of the cult surrounding Charlemagne and also because of a prized collection of relics said to include Christ's loincloth. To accommodate the flood of pilgrims, a **choir hall** in Gothic style was added in the 14th century. Displayed here is the gilded **shrine of Charlemagne**, which has held the emperor's remains since 1215 following his canonisation. His more modest original Roman sarcophagus is on view in the **Domschatz-kammer** (Cathedral Treasury; ☎ 4770 9127; Klostergasse; adult/concession €2.50/2; ⊙ 10am-1pm Mon, 10am-6pm Tue, Wed & Fri-Sun, 10am-9pm Thu), with one of the richest collections of religious art north of the Alps. Enter from Klostergasse.

RATHAUS

Overlooking the Markt and its fountain statue of Charlemagne is Aachen's 14th-century **Rathaus** (Town hall; ☎ 432 7310; adult/concession €2/1; ⊙ 10am-1pm & 2-5pm). Its eastern tower, the **Granusturm**, is all that survives from Charlemagne's palace, which once stood on this site. Some 50 statues of German rulers, including 31 emperors crowned in Aachen, adorn the building's façade. Inside, an exhibit displays copies of the crown jewels (the originals are in Vienna) as well as the imperial crown and orb and Charlemagne's sword. The **Kaisersaal** (imperial hall) is adorned with massive murals depicting the emperor's life.

MUSEUMS

Aachen has two art museums. The **Suermondt Ludwig Museum** (☎ 479 800; Wilhelmstrasse 18; adult/concession €3/1.50; ⊙ noon-6pm Tue & Thu-Sun, noon-9pm Wed) surveys art from the Middle Ages to modern times. Highlights include portraits by Lucas Cranach and Rubens, and sculptures from the late Middle Ages. Picking up where the Suermondt leaves off is the **Ludwig Forum für Internationales Kunst** (Ludwig Forum for International Art; ☎ 180 70; Jülicherstrasse 97-109; adult/concession €3/1.50; ⊙ noon-6pm Tue-Sun), housed in a former umbrella factory. Exhibits vary but usually include selections of works by such major postmodernists as Warhol, Lichtenstein and Baselitz. Performance art events, including music, dance, poetry and film, complement the exhibits.

CAROLUS-THERMEN

Aachen's state-of-the-art **Carolus-Thermen** (Thermal Baths; ☎ 182 740; Passstrasse 79, Stadtgarten; admission with/without sauna from €9/17; ⊙ 9am-11pm) make a great destination on a rainy day. Or any day, for that matter. Soak in the warm waters, relax to soothing sounds in the warm sands of the exotic 'Karawanserei', or bare all and sweat it out in the sauna. There's even a women-only sauna. A spa, bar and Mediterranean restaurant are also part of the complex.

Sleeping

The tourist office has a room reservation service; call ☎ 180 2950.

DJH hostel (☎ 711 010; jh-aachen@djh-rheinland.de; Maria-Theresia-Allee 260; dm/s/d €20.90/34.20/51.80; ☒) This modernised hostel is about 4km south of the Hauptbahnhof on a hill overlooking the city. Only a third of the rooms have private facilities, but there are special rooms for families and people with disabilities. Take bus No 2 (direction: Preuswald) to the Ronheide stop.

Hotel Marx (☎ 375 41; www.hotel-marx.de; Hubertusstrasse 33-35; s/d with shared bathroom from €35/60, with private bathroom from €50/75; ☒) This old-timey family hotel still has some rooms with shared facilities, making it a popular budget choice. For extra quiet, pick one facing the beautiful garden whose pond even attracts the occasional wild duck family.

Hotel Benelux (☎ 223 43; fax 223 45; Franzstrasse 21-23; s €82-97, d €97-133; ☒) Though on a busy street, this well-run place has quiet, uncluttered rooms and classy, art-filled floors. The rooftop garden with enclosed gazebo is a bonus. Days start with a generous breakfast served tableside.

Hotel Brülls am Dom (☎ 317 04; fax 404 326; Hühnermarkt; s/d €83/102) Within steps of the Dom, this place packs as much comfort into its small and old-fashioned rooms as possible. The doll and knickknack collection cluttering up the downstairs restaurant does not extend to the upper floors.

Eating

Leo van den Daele (☎ 357 24; Büchel 18; dishes €5-8) Of all Aachen's historic coffee houses, this nook-and-cranny café is the one not to be missed. Leather-covered walls, tiled stoves and antique furniture create a quintessential old-world atmosphere.

Sausalitos (☎ 401 9437; Markt 45; mains €5-15) The quasi-Mexican food – nachos, burritos, enchiladas etc – may lack authenticity but the lively cantina setting makes up for such shortcomings. Young crowd, serious cocktails and a good place to get social.

Am Knipp (☎ 333 68; Bergdriesch 3; mains €6-15; ⓨ dinner only, closed Tue) One of Aachen's oldest restaurants (1698), Am Knipp is a showcase of painted tile walls, pewter mugs and copper pots. The menu, though largely German, also makes excursions to Italy and France. In summer, the beer garden is the place to be.

Rose am Dom (☎ 287 82; Fischmarkt 1; mains €12-18) In the former cathedral kitchen, this place combines medieval ambience with modern international cuisine that makes good use of quality seasonal ingredients like trout and chanterelle mushrooms. Outdoor seating in fine weather.

Gaststätte Postwagen (☎ 350 01; Krämerstrasse 2; mains €12-22) You can enjoy the same German dishes – schnitzel, sausages, veal etc – in plenty of other restaurants, but rarely will you find one as snug and convivial as this historic double-decker right next to the Rathaus.

Other recommendations:

Pizzeria la Finestra (☎ 258 45; Pontstrasse 123; pizzas €4.50-9) One of several pizzerias on Pontstrasse.

Vitaminbar (☎ 409 3912; Blondelstrasse 24; dishes €1.50-7) Delicious sandwiches, salads and freshly pressed fruit and vegetable juices. Self-service. There's another branch at Pontstrasse 46.

Drinking

Aachen brims with cafés and pubs catering for a student clientele, many of which are concentrated along Pontstrasse. Other entertainment options include:

Aoxomoxoa (☎ 226 22; Reihstrasse 15; ⓨ from 10pm, closed Sun) This laid-back dance club hums with different music nightly (from rock to house and jazz), charges no cover, and numbers cheap drinks and a friendly, mixed clientele among its assets.

Starfish (☎ 938 900; Liebigstrasse 17; admission €5; ⓨ Fri & Sat) Theme parties à la 'Beach Party'

and 'Men's Strip' keep this place, northeast of the city centre, buzzing on weekend nights. It's huge, with different sounds filling different rooms to suit people of all ages. The admission price includes one drink.

Club Voltaire (☎ 543 427; Friedrichstrasse 9) Voltaire doesn't really wake up until other places go to sleep. A great place to chill in the early morning hours.

Domkeller (☎ 342 65; Am Hof 1) Near the cathedral, this casual pub has drawn students since the 1950s with its woodsy ambience and fair beer prices. In summer, the action spills out onto the picturesque square.

Shopping

Aachen is known for its *Printen*, a crunchy spiced cookie similar to gingerbread. Traditionally log-shaped, Aachen bakeries now churn it out in various shapes, from the Easter Bunny to Santa Claus. One of the best places to buy them is Leo van den Daele (see Eating opposite). The street to go for mainstream shopping is Adalbertstrasse.

Getting There & Away

Aachen is about 90km from the airports at Düsseldorf and Cologne/Bonn. The **Airport Aixpress** (☎ 182 000) shuttles from the bus station to Düsseldorf 12 times daily, and to Cologne/Bonn four times.

Trains to Cologne (€10.70, one hour) run several times hourly, with some proceeding to Dortmund and other Ruhrgebiet cities. Trips to most cities south of Aachen require a change in Cologne.

For drivers, Aachen is easily reached via the A4 (east–west) from Cologne and the A44 (north–south) from Düsseldorf. The B57, B258 and B264 also meet here. For rideshares, contact **ADM Mitfahrzentrale** (☎ 194 40; Roermonder Strasse 4, cnr Ludwigsallee).

Getting Around

Bus Nos 1, 11 and 21 run between the Hauptbahnhof and the town centre. Bus tickets for travel within the area encircled by Alleenring cost a flat €1.40. All of Aachen and the adjoining Dutch communities of Vaals and Kelmis can be covered with a Zone 1 ticket for €1.80. Day passes are €5. Buy tickets from the drivers.

Bicycles can be hired from **Fahrrad am Bahnhof** (☎ 433 2366; Bahnhofsplatz). For a taxi, call ☎ 344 41.

AROUND AACHEN
Kornelimünster

The romantic suburb of Kornelimünster is worth a short excursion. The main attraction here is the **Pfarrkirche St Kornelius** (☎ 02408-6492; Abteigarten 6; ⏰ 10am-1pm & 3-5pm Tue & Wed, 3-6pm Sat & Sun), once part of a Benedictine abbey. Upon its consecration in 817, Charlemagne's son, Ludwig the Pious, bestowed several important relics on the monastery. These are said to include Jesus' shroud, which is among items exhibited to the faithful every seven years. The abbey now functions as a gallery of contemporary art. To get here take the bus No 68 or 166 from the Hauptbahnhof.

THE RUHRGEBIET

Densely populated and with a legacy as Europe's largest industrial and mining region, the Ruhrgebiet doesn't show up in glossy brochures promoting German *Gemütlichkeit*. But to travellers with an open mind, a sense of adventure and a desire to get off the beaten track, it offers a treasure trove of surprises and unique experiences: a former gas tank converted into cutting-edge exhibit space; free-climbing around a blast furnace; a turbine house turned trendy restaurant; dancing in a pit's boiler room; and coal mines designed by Art Nouveau and Bauhaus architects are just a few of the quirky places that give the Ruhrgebiet its edge.

Discount Cards

The **Ruhrpott Card** (adult/child €33/21) gives free public transportation and admission to theme parks, museums, tours and other attractions on any three days. It's available from the tourist offices and other outlets. For information call ☎ 01805-181 6180.

Entertainment

For a thorough listing of hot spots and events throughout the Ruhrgebiet, pick up a copy of *Coolibri* (free and available in bars, restaurants and the tourist offices) or the magazine *Prinz*.

Industrial Heritage Trail

With most of the steel mills, factories and collieries are no longer in operation, the Ruhrgebiet has embraced its heritage by cleverly converting many of its 'cathedrals of industry' into appealing multi-use spaces. About 30 of these venues, museums and lookouts are now linked along a 400km Industrial Heritage Trail that loops around much of the region. The route takes in attractions in major cities including Dortmund, Essen, Duisburg and Bochum, and smaller ones such as Bottrop, Oberhausen and Hagen. If you're motorised or on a bicycle, you can follow the route signs from one site to the next, but most can also be reached by public transport.

For more information, check into www.route-industriekultur.de (in German and English) or stop by the route's **central information office** (☎ 0180-400 0086; ⏰ 10am-7pm Apr-Oct, 10am-5pm Nov-Mar) at the Zeche Zollverein XII (see p599). If you want a detailed Ruhrgebiet guide, pick up excellent *Tour The Ruhr* (€11.50) by British writer Roy Kift and sold at major bookshops and many tourist offices.

Getting Around

Each Ruhrgebiet city has an efficient and comprehensive public transportation system, usually composed of U-Bahns, buses and trams. Cities are also connected to each other by a network of S-Bahn and regional trains, managed by the **Verkehrsverbund Rhein-Ruhr** (VRR; ☎ 0209-194 49). The same tariffs apply within the entire region, which is divided into three zones. Look at the displays on orange ticket vending machines to see which price applies in your case. Single tickets are €1.80/3.40/7.30 for one/two/three zones. Day passes are €6.55/9.55/18 and valid for up to five people travelling together.

ESSEN

☎ 0201 / pop 585,000

Along with Dortmund, Essen is the one of the largest cities in the Ruhrgebiet and the seventh largest in Germany. A settlement developed here around a monastery founded in 852, and it obtained town rights in 1244. In the early 19th century, Essen plunged headlong into the Industrial Age, with the next 150 years dominated by steel and coal production. Essen is the ancestral home of the Krupp family of industrialists (see The Krupp Dynasty p600). All of

Essen's mines and steelworks have closed now, but several energy corporations still maintain their headquarters here. For visitors, Essen has a surprising menu of attractions that includes some fine museums, generous green areas and a lively cultural scene.

Orientation

Essen's sights are rather spread out, but all are accessible by public transport. The Hauptbahnhof Nord (North) exit drops you right onto the centre's main artery, the pedestrianised Kettwiger Strasse. The museum complex and the recreational areas are both south of the station, while the Zeche Zollverein is to the north.

Information

Main post office (Willy-Brandt-Platz 1; 8am-7pm Mon-Fri, 8.30am-3.30pm Sat) Outside the Hauptbahnhof.
Mayersche Buchhandlung (365 670; Am Markt 5-6) Bookshop.
Medical emergencies (192 92)
Police headquarters (8290; Büscherstrasse 2)
Reisebank (202 671; Hauptbahnhof; 7.15am-7.45pm Mon-Fri, 8.15am-4pm Sat, 9.45am-1.15pm Sun)
Surf Inn (812 1449; basement, Galeria Kaufhof, Kettwiger Strasse 1a; €1 per 15 min; 9.30am-8pm Mon-Fri, 9.30am-6pm Sat) Internet access.
Tourist office (194 33 or 887 20 48; www.essen.de; Am Hauptbahnhof 2; 9am-5.30pm Mon-Fri, 10am-1pm Sat)

Sights

CITY CENTRE

Essen's medieval **Münster** (Minster; 220 4206; Burgplatz 2) is an island of quiet engulfed by the commercialism of the Kettwiger Strasse, the pedestrianised main artery of Essen's popular shopping district. Of average architectural appeal, it has one of the world's richest collections of Ottonian works of art from around AD 1000. Inside the church itself is a **seven-armed candelabrum** that stands taller than Michael Jordan and the much venerated **Golden Madonna** with a haunting pair of blue eyes. An admission ticket to the freshly renovated **cathedral treasury** (adult/concession €3/1.50; 10am-5pm Tue-Sat, 11.30am-5pm Sun) separates you from the other prized exhibits, but it's well worth the cash to see such priceless objects as gemstone-encrusted processional crosses and the crown of Otto III.

East of the cathedral, the monumental **Alte Synagoge** (884 5218; Steeler Strasse 29; admission free; 10am-6pm Tue-Sun) is the largest synagogue north of the Alps. Completed in 1913, it survived WWII and now contains an exhibit on life in Essen during the Third Reich.

MUSEUM COMPLEX

Art fans should hop on the U-Bahn No 11, alight at Rüttenscheider Stern and make their way to the amazing **Museum Folkwang** (884 5314; Goethestrasse 41; adult/concession €5/3.50, under 14s free; 10am-6pm Tue-Sun, 10am-midnight Fri). It offers a comprehensive survey of art from the 19th and 20th centuries. From brooding landscapes by Caspar David Friedrich to light-hearted Impressionst works by Monet and Renoir and abstract classics by Mark Rothko and Jackson Pollock, you'll find hardly a big name missing. There's €8 ticket available which also allows admission to the Ruhrlandmuseum.

The focal point of the **Ruhrlandmuseum** (Ruhr Regional Museum; 884 5200; Goethestrasse 41; adult/concession €5/3.50, under 14s free; 10am-6pm Tue-Sun, 10am-midnight Fri) next door is a moderately interesting permanent exhibit on the work and daily life in the Ruhrgebiet during the boom years of the late-19th century.

ZECHE ZOLLVEREIN XII

A key site along the Industrial Heritage Trail is the **Zeche Zollverein XII** (302 0133; www.zollverein.de; Gelsenkirchener Strasse 181), a marvel of efficiency when it opened in 1932 and still a top producer of coal in Europe at its closing in 1986. In 2001 Unesco honoured the Bauhaus-style complex by making it a World Heritage Site. Now a lively creative centre with artist studios, offices, exhibition space, a restaurant and performance venues, Zollverein is a shining example of how to recycle an old industrial site. To get here take tram No 107 from the Hauptbahnhof.

A highlight here is the **Red Dot Design Museum** (301 040; adult €5-6, concession €3, under 12s free; 11am-6pm Tue-Thu, 11am-8pm Sat & Sun) in the former boilerhouse, masterfully adapted by Sir Norman Foster (who also designed the Reichstag cupola in Berlin). In a perfect marriage of space and function, this four-storey maze showcases the best in contemporary design right amid the original fixtures: bathtubs or bike helmets balance on grated walkways, taps dangle from snakelike heating ducts, and an entire bedroom perches atop a large oven. It's wonderfully bizarre, surprising and fascinating.

To learn more about the inner workings of the former mine, join a **guided tour** (adult/concession €5/2.50) in German, led by ex miners who sprinkle their narrative with the odd anecdote from the old days. Tours leave daily from the **visitors centre** (☎ 0180-400 0086; ⏱ 10am-7pm Apr-Oct, 10am-5pm Nov-Mar) in Hall 2. Call for hours and reservations.

VILLA HÜGEL

South of the city centre is Essen's sprawling green belt, which follows the flow of the Ruhr River to the **Baldeney See**, a reservoir popular for windsurfing, sailing and rowing. On its north shore is the **Villa Hügel** (☎ 188 4823; Hügel 1; adult/concession €1/free; ⏱ 10am-6pm Tue-Sun), the estate of the Krupp family from 1873 to 1945. Their former private residence, the Grosses Haus (Large House), now hosts the occasional concert as well as internationally acclaimed art shows (call for hours and admission). On the ground floor of the adjacent Kleines Haus (Small House), a glossy exhibit showcases the achievements of the Krupp corporation and can easily be skipped. Upstairs is a more intriguing chronicle of the family's rise to Germany's most powerful industrial

---

THE KRUPP DYNASTY – MEN OF STEEL

Steel and Krupp are virtual synonyms. So are Krupp and Essen. For it's this bustling Ruhrgebiet city that is the ancestral seat of the Krupp family and the headquarters of one of the most powerful corporations in Europe. (To avoid confusion, Krupp has nothing to do with the company that produces coffee makers and other appliances – that's Krups.)

Through successive driven and obsessive generations, the Krupps amassed a huge private fortune, provided the German weaponry for four major wars and manipulated world economics and politics for their own gain. At the same time, however, they established a relationship between workers and management that's still the basis for today's social contract in industrialised Germany.

It all began rather modestly in 1811 when Friedrich Krupp and two partners founded a company to process 'English cast steel' but, despite minor successes, he left a company mired in debt upon his death in 1826. Enter his son Alfred, then a tender 14, who would go on to become one of the seminal figures of the Industrial Age.

It was through the production of the world's finest steel that the 'Cannon King' galvanised a company that – by 1887 – employed more than 20,000 workers. In an unbroken pattern of dazzling innovation, coupled with ruthless business practices, Krupp produced the wheels and rails for America's railroads and the stainless steel plating on New York's Chrysler building. It gave the world the first diesel engine and the first steam turbine locomotive. And – ultimately – it produced the fearsome weapons that allowed the Wehrmacht to launch the horror of the Blitzkrieg in WWII.

But in another pioneering move, Krupp also provided womb-to-tomb benefits to its workers at a time when the term 'social welfare' had not yet entered the world's vocabulary. Alfred realised that his company's progress and profit came at a price largely borne on the backs of his workers. He created a variety of measures, including company health insurance, a pension scheme, subsidised housing estates and company-owned retail stores.

Krupp will forever be associated, however, with the disastrous period in German history when a maniac from Austria nearly brought the world to its knees. Not only did the corporation supply the hardware for the German war machine, but it also provided much of the financial backing that Hitler needed to build up his political power base. Krupp plants were prime targets for Allied bombers. When the dust had settled, about two thirds of its factories had either been destroyed or damaged. An American military court sentenced Alfred Krupp von Bohlen und Halbach to prison, releasing him in 1951. He resumed the management of the firm in 1953.

An excellent source for an understanding of what the Krupp family has meant to Germany is William Manchester's brilliant chronicle *The Arms of Krupp* (1964).

giants. Its leading role in the manufacturing of guns, cannons and other military equipment, while not emphasised, is included as well. Written explanations are in German only, but free English-language brochures should be available. To get here take the S6 to Essen-Hügel.

Nearby, you can stroll through the same generous salons, halls and galleries where the Krupps once received royalty and Nazi party elite. Note the carved wooden ceilings and grand staircase that leads to a ballroom beneath a dramatic glass vault.

The lavish **park** (8am-8pm) is a pleasant place for a picnic or relaxing.

WERDEN

On the southern Ruhr bank, not far from Villa Hügel, the 1200-year-old suburb of Werden, with its half-timbered houses and cobbled lanes, feels like an anachronism in the Ruhrgebiet. Students of the prestigious Folkwang School for Music, Dance and Drama fill the many pubs, cafés and restaurants, and the DJH hostel is here as well.

Werden's main sight is the 1175 **Abbey of St Liudger** (491 801; Brückstrasse 54; 10am-noon & 3-5pm Tue-Sun), a beautiful late-Romanesque church named for the Frisian missionary buried here. Its interior is now largely baroque. The treasury (€1) contains a hauntingly beautiful bronze crucifix from 1060.

S-Bahn No 6 goes straight to Werden from the Hauptbahnhof.

Sleeping

DJH hostel (491 163; jh-essen@djh-rheinland.de; Pastoratsberg 2; s/d/q per person €28.20/23.10/18;) Essen's expanded and updated hostel is nicely located in Werden. Many rooms have private bathrooms. From Werden's S-Bahn station, take bus No 190, or cross the Ruhr and walk uphill for 10 minutes.

Stadtcamping Essen-Werden (492 978; www.stadtcamping-essen.de; Im Löwental 67; person/tent €4/8) This camp site is riverside, near the Essen-Werden train station served by the S6.

Hotel Zum Deutschen Haus (232 989; deutscheshaus.essen@gmx.de; Kastanienallee 16; s €41-46, d €46-77) This family-operated hotel in the city centre offers pleasant if plain rooms and a *gutbürgerlich* (simple) restaurant downstairs (mains €6 to €12).

Hotel an der Gruga (841 180; www.grugahotel.de; Eduard-Lucas-Strasse 17; s/d €95/116, Sat & Sun

€67/86;) Rooms wrap around a courtyard at this stylish business hotel, which offers exceptional value on weekends. It's south of the centre, within walking distance of nice restaurants. Take U11 to Messe Ost/Gruga.

Hotel Margarethenhöhe (438 60; www.margarethenhoehe.com; Steile Strasse 46; s €118-128, d €148-158;) Essen's nicest hotel is swathed in bold colours, filled with art and intriguing designer touches and comes with a matching restaurant (mains €8 to €20). It's right in the heart of the Margarethenhöhe, a gardenlike workers' colony of small and trim houses built by the Krupp family between 1910 and 1931. Take the U17 to Laubenweg.

Eating

Skip Essen's city centre and head straight to the Rüttenscheid district ('Rü' for short; take the U11 to Martinstrasse). Here pubs and bars rub shoulders with restaurants of all kinds.

Zodiac (771 212; Witteringstrasse 41; mains €8-13; dinner only, closed Thu) Leafy plants and knickknacks from around the world form the setting of this vegetarian restaurant, whose chefs make clever use of seasonal ingredients and exotic spices. Some dishes are suitable for vegans.

raum.eins (455 3747; Rüttenscheider Strasse 154; lunch €4-10, dinner €9-21) A variety of woods and intimate lighting give this restaurant a classy touch that goes well with the new, light and seasonal cuisine. Nice beer garden.

Casino Zollverein (830 240; Gelsenkirchener Strasse 181; mains €12-20; closed Mon) The industrial chic of the colliery's former turbine house creates a suitably eccentric backdrop for this restaurant's bold new world cuisine. Reservations are recommended.

Schote (780 107; Emmastrasse 25; mains €12-25; dinner only, closed Mon) It may look like a little neighbourhood restaurant, but the kitchen's creations – mixing regional and international flavours – draw loyal fans from all over the Ruhrgebiet. There's attentive service, too.

Entertainment

Zeche Carl (834 4410; Wilhelm-Nieswandt-Allee 100; nightly) In the northern suburb of Altenessen, this is an old mine reborn as a trendy cultural centre with live concerts, discos, cabaret, theatre and art exhibits. Tram No 101 or 106 to Karlsplatz.

Mudia Art (☎ 269 8306; Frohnhauser Strasse 75; ⏱ Sat) Essen's premier dance temple is the labyrinthine Mudia Art, located in an old factory. It's high-style, high-energy and high-attitude.

GOP Varieté (☎ 247 9393; Rottstrasse 30; tickets €17-29) At this crowd-pleaser, jugglers, acrobats, ventriloquists and other artistes seize the stage in programmes which change every other month.

Colosseum (☎ 887 2333; Altendofer Strasse 1) Musical theatre is presented at this handsomely converted late-19th-century factory.

Saalbau (☎ 812 2810; Huyssenallee 53) Starting in June 2004, the well-respected Essen Philharmonic Orchestra will move into the newly renovated historical Saalbau.

Of Essen's several high-brow cultural venues, the **Grillo-Theater** (☎ 812 2200; Theaterplatz) presents classic and contemporary drama and comedies, while the **Aalto Musiktheater** (☎ 812 2200; Operplatz 10) is the main venue for opera and ballet. Fans of modern architecture will appreciate the chance to see one of the few buildings outside of Finland designed by Alvar Aalto, who ranks among the 20th century's top architects. It was completed after his death by his widow.

Getting There & Away

ICE trains leave in all directions hourly for such cities as Frankfurt (€63.60, 2¼ hours) and Berlin (€72.60, 3¼ hours). Essen is also efficiently linked to other Ruhrgebiet cities, as well as to Düsseldorf and Cologne, via the VRR network.

The autobahns A40 and A52, which serve Essen, are often clogged because of heavy commuter traffic. For ride-shares contact the **Mitfahrzentrale** (☎ 194 22; Freiheit 5) outside the Hauptbahnhof's south exit.

BOCHUM

☎ 0234 / pop 396,000

Industrial cities are not exactly the stuff of heartfelt anthems, but that didn't stop singer-songwriter Herbert Grönemeyer from rhapsodising about his home town in the 1984 song 'Bochum'. The homage not only boosted Grönemeyer's career but also the image of this classic Ruhrgebiet city, halfway between Essen and Dortmund.

Though indeed no beauty, as one of the lyrics says, Bochum still makes for a worthwhile stop thanks to its two excellent technical museums, the renowned **Zeiss Planetarium Bochum** (☎ 516 060; Castroper Strasse 67; adult/concession €5/2.50; ⏱ showtimes usually 2pm Tue & Thu, 7.30pm Wed & Fri, 3.30pm & 5pm Sat & Sun) and a popular green belt along the Ruhr and the Kemnader Stausee reservoir on the southern edge of town. Also here are two medieval castles, **Burg Blankenstein** (☎ 02324-332 31; admission free) and the **Wasserschloss Kemnade** (☎ 02324-302 68; An der Kemnade 10; admission free; ⏱ 9am-3pm Tue, 1-7pm Wed-Fri, 11am-6pm Sat & Sun). Both castles are frequently served by bus No C31 from the Hauptbahnhof.

For accommodation and eating options drop by the **tourist office** (☎ 963 020; Huestrasse 9; ⏱ 10am-7pm Mon-Fri, 10am-6pm Sat), a short walk north of the Hauptbahnhof main exit.

Sights

DEUTSCHES BERGBAUMUSEUM

Part of the Industrial Heritage Trail, this museum has a turquoise winding tower that soars 68m high, and is dedicated to documenting life *unter Tage* (below ground). The **Deutsches Bergbaumuseum** (German Mining Museum; ☎ 587 70; Am Bergbaumuseum 28; adult/concession €6/3; ⏱ 8.30am-5pm Tue-Fri, 10am-5pm Sat & Sun) is huge and imaginative and touches on every aspect of the industry, including the role of women in mining. Admission includes a trip beneath the earth's surface for a guided tour of a demonstration pit, which shows the tough working conditions miners had to endure. You'll also get to ride up the tower for bird's-eye views of the city and surrounds. To get here, take the U35 from the Hauptbahnhof.

EISENBAHNMUSEUM

A place of pilgrimage for fans of historic 'iron horses', and also part of the Industrial Heritage Trail, is the wonderfully nostalgic **Eisenbahnmuseum** (Train Museum; ☎ 492 516; Dr-C-Otto-Strasse 191; adult/child €5/2.50; ⏱ 10am-5pm Wed & Fri, 10am-1pm Sun Nov-Mar, to 3pm Sun Apr-Oct; closed mid-Dec–mid-Jan). It displays around 180 steam and electric locomotives, coaches and wagons, some dating from as early as 1853. Between April and October, it organises **steam train rides** (one-way/return €7/10) through the Ruhr Valley on the first Sunday of the month.

From the Bochum Hauptbahnhof take tram No 318 to Bochum-Dahlhausen, then walk for 1300m or take the historic shuttle (Sundays only).

Entertainment

Bochum is really best known for its entertainment and raucous nightlife scene that brings in people from as far as Cologne and the Sauerland. More than nine million tickets to the musical *Starlight Express* have been sold since its opening in 1988 and the Schauspielhaus (theatre) has a fine reputation as well. But even more people come to get lost in the city's infamous Bermuda Triangle of bars, clubs and restaurants. The three streets in question are the Kortumstrasse, Viktoriastrasse and Brüderstrasse, all within a five-minute walk of the Hauptbahnhof. New places open up all the time, but Mandragora with its huge beer garden and trendy Sachs have both been around for decades.

DORTMUND

☎ 0231 / pop 587,000

Dortmund, the largest city in the Ruhrgebiet, has two major passions: football (soccer) and beer. Its Bundesliga team, Borussia Dortmund, has been national champion five times – most recently in 1995 and 1996 – and won the coveted Uefa Champions League trophy in 1997. Home games are played in the 69,000-seat Westfalenstadion, Germany's third-largest football stadium, which will also be one of venues of the 2006 World Cup.

If sports don't do it for you, maybe Dortmund's fine brews will. Although only two of the original six major breweries still exist, the city is still Germany's second-largest beer producer (after the Warsteiner brewery in the nearby Sauerland).

Though physically scarred by war, Dortmund is an enjoyable down-to-earth city with a lively cultural and pub scene and interesting sights and museums, as well as a university with 20,000 students.

Orientation

The airport is east of the city (see Getting Around p605 for taxi details). Most attractions are located in the city centre, an area bounded by a ring road made up of segments ending in 'wall'. The Hauptbahnhof and the bus station are on Königswall on the north side of the ring. Cross Königswall from the southern exit of the Hauptbahnhof, then take any road to the pedestrianised Westenhellweg (which turns into Ostenhellweg), the main artery that bisects Dortmund's circular centre.

Information

Dortmund Tourist-Card (€8.90) For overnight guests only, this is good for unlimited public transport, free or reduced museum admission and other discounts on two consecutive days.

Main post office (☎ 01802-3333; Kurfürstenstrasse 2; ⊙ 7.30am-8pm Mon-Fri, 8am-3.30pm Sat) About 75m to the left of the Hauptbahnhof north exit.

Mayersche Buchhandlung(☎ 809 050; Westenhellweg 41) Bookshop.

Sparkasse (☎ 1830; Freistuhl 2) Just south of the Hauptbahnhof.

Städtische Kliniken Mitte (☎ 500; Beurhausstrasse 40) Centrally located hospital.

Tourist office (☎ 502 2174; www.dortmund-tourismus .de; Königswall 18a; ⊙ 9am-6pm Mon-Fri, 9am-1pm Sat) Opposite the Hauptbahnhof south exit.

Web M@nia Café (☎ 189 1848; Kampstrasse 88; €4 per hr; ⊙ 10am-1am Mon-Sat, noon-1am Sun)

Walking Tour

Several of Dortmund's main attractions are conveniently grouped within walking distance of the Hauptbahnhof. Cross Königswall as you leave the train station through the south exit, then head up the sweeping staircase to the Gothic **Petrikirche** (1353) on the pedestrianised shopping artery Westenhellweg. The show-stopper here is the massive Antwerp **altar**, which dates from around 1520 and features 633 individually carved and gilded figurines in scenes depicting the Passion and the Legend of the Cross.

Stroll east on Westenhellweg past the elegant **Krügerpassage**, a shopping arcade built in 1912 in neo-Renaissance style, to the **Reinoldikirche** (1280), named after the city's patron saint who was martyred in Cologne. According to legend, the carriage containing his coffin rolled all the way to Dortmund, stopping in the spot now occupied by the church. Inside is a life-sized statue of the saint opposite another one of Charlemagne. Of outstanding artistic merit is the late Gothic **high altar** (ask nicely in the sacristy for a close-up look).

NORTH RHINE-WESTPHALIA

Across the street, **Marienkirche** is the oldest of Dortmund's Gothic churches. The star exhibit here is the **Marienaltar**, with a delicate triptych (1420) by Conrad von Soest who, despite his name, was actually born in Dortmund. In the northern nave is the equally impressive **Berswordt Altar** (1385). Also note the rather frivolous wood reliefs on the choir stalls and the ethereal St Mary statue (1230).

From here, head south along Kleppingstrasse, then east on Viktoriastrasse to Ostwall, where the **Museum am Ostwall** (☎ 502 3247; Ostwall 7; adult/concession €3/0.75, Sat free; ☷ 10am-5pm Sun & Tue-Fri, 10am-8pm Thu, noon-5pm Sat) specialises in 20th-century art with particular emphasis on Expressionist and avant-garde works created between 1950 and 1970. Admission is more expensive for special exhibits.

Follow Ostwall, which turns into Schwanenwall, north back towards the Hauptbahnhof. Where it meets Hansastrasse is the **Museum für Kunst & Kulturgeschichte** (Museum of Art & Cultural History; ☎ 502 5522; Hansastrasse 3; adult/concession €3/0.75, free Sat; ☷ 10am-5pm Sun & Tue-Fri, 10am-8pm Thu, noon-6pm Sat) in a handsomely renovated former bank building in Art Deco style. Exhibits take visitors from the Stone Age to the present. Highlights include re-created period rooms, a Roman gold treasure and a Romanesque triumphal cross, as well as paintings by stellar artists such as Caspar David Friedrich and Lovis Corinth.

Go through the station to the north exit where, just beyond the cinema complex, is the **Mahn- und Gedenkstätte Steinwache** (☎ 502 5002; Steinstrasse 50; admission free; ☷ 10am-5pm Tue-Sun), a memorial exhibit about Dortmund during the Third Reich. It's housed in a former Gestapo prison that held as many as 65,000 people between 1933 and 1945. A free English-language pamphlet is available.

Industrial Museums

Outside of the city centre are these two excellent Industrial Heritage Trail sites.

The **Zollern II/IV Colliery** (☎ 696 1111; Grubenweg 5; adult/concession €2.60/1.10; ☷ 10am-6pm Tue-Sun) is one of eight former industrial sites that now form the Westphalian Industrial Museum. Considered a 'model mine' when operation began in 1902, it boasted state-of-the-art technology and amazing architectural detail, including a castlelike administra-

tive complex and a machine hall with Art Nouveau features. An innovative exhibit documents the daily lives of the miners and their families, with plenty of interactive and children-oriented programmes. To get here, take the U-Bahn No 47 to Huckarde Bushof, then bus No 462 toward Dortmund-Marten to Industriemuseum Zollern.

The **Deutsche Arbeitsschutzausstellung** (German Occupational Safety and Health Exhibition; ☎ 907 1479; Friedrich-Henkel-Weg 1-25; admission free; ☷ 9am-5pm Tue-Sat, 10am-5pm Sun) may have an unwieldy name but is in fact an intriguing and very hands-on museum that examines how workplace conditions affect our wellbeing. Walk through the 'noise tunnel', experience the vibrations sitting in a fork lift, imagine the stress level of an air traffic controller, and then learn what can be done to prevent damage. To get here take the S-Bahn No 1 to Dortmund-Dorstfeld-Süd.

Sleeping

The tourist office makes free room reservations. Expect rate hikes during major trade shows and discounts on weekends.

DJH hostel (☎ 1400; jhg-dortmund@djh-wl.de; Silberstrasse 24-26; per person shared/private bathroom €21.20/26.80, s €26.20/31.90; P ✗ ▣) This large, central and completely modernised hostel has a variety of basic rooms. Those with private bathroom tend to be bigger and some even have sitting areas.

Akzent-Hotel Esplanade (☎ 585 30; www.akzent .de/Dortmund; Bornstrasse 4, cnr Burgwall; s €59-79, d €59-99; P ✗) Avoid the as-yet-unrenovated, dowdy 'standard' rooms and request a 'comfort' room for more amenities and upbeat flair. All come with such business-traveller essentials as large desks, minibar and telephones with dataports.

Cityhotel Dortmund (☎ 477 9660; www.cityhotel dortmund.de; Silberstrasse 37-43; s/d €79/97; P ▣) This jewel of a hotel hides behind a mousy grey façade on a nondescript street in the city centre. Sprightly Mediterranean colours and a contemporary look extend from the public areas into the fully equipped rooms featuring such extras as water heaters, free bottled water and large TVs. Breakfast is served anytime.

Eating & Drinking

Dortmund's centre brims with pubs and restaurants, making it ideal for sampling the local brews and cuisine. Centres of action include Kleppingstrasse and Alter Markt. Southeast of here is the student-flavoured Kreuzviertel, with Arneckestrasse being one of the main drags (take the U42 to Möllernbrücke).

Hövel's Hausbrauerei (☎ 914 5470; Hoher Wall 5; mains €7-14) Dried hops, shiny copper dishes and blue tiles make for a wonderfully rustic backdrop for trying Bitterbier, the speciality of this historic microbrewery. The menu is custom-made for meat lovers, who will delight in sausages, roast lamb, potato soup and other stick-to-the-ribs fare.

Rigoletto (☎ 150 4431; Kleppingstrasse 9-11; mains €7-15) The panoramic windows attracts the see-and-be-seen crowd but this high-energy place also delivers substance with beautiful décor and a dependable Italian menu. It's easy to fill up on the appetisers and pasta, although the *secondi* (meats and fish) are good also.

Am Alten Markt (☎ 572 217; Markt 3; mains €8-19) One of several restaurants on this large square with outdoor seating in fine weather, the Alter Markt is the place to sample traditional local dishes such as *Pfefferposthast* (beef and onion stew) or *Wirsingroulade* (meat-stuffed cabbage rolls).

Pfefferkorn (☎ 143 644; Hoher Wall 38; mains €9-19) For fun ambience in a classy, nostalgic interior filled with antiques and paintings, head to Pfefferkorn. The kitchen staff whips up everything from crunchy salads to sautéed tiger shrimp and juicy steaks, including many nonmeat options. Also look for special promotions.

Other recommendations:

La Salinas (☎ 586 3637; Kleppingstrasse 9-11; breakfast & snacks €5, tapas €2-10) Next to Rigoletto, same owner, similar concept, only the food is Spanish.

Swabedoo (☎ 141 300; Kleine Beurhausstrasse 26; mains €5-16) Upmarket, colourful Mediterranean-style restaurant near the Kreuzviertel.

Entertainment

Stadtpalais (☎ 165 5430; Hansastrasse 5-7; ☼ Fri & Sat) Dress nicely to get into this trendy dance temple with refined ambience and a high flirt factor. It's a big space with three dance floors, two cocktail bars and a terrace.

Live Station (☎ 914 3625; Königswall 15, Hauptbahnhof; ☼ Fri & Sat) This scene dinosaur still packs them in with a variety of dance parties that often keep going into the wee hours, plus regular live gigs.

Domicil (☎ 523 806; Leopoldstrasse 60) Jazz, world and avant-garde music are the focus of this highly regarded club that's been booking newcomers and established names for a quarter century. A location change was under consideration at the time of writing.

Theater Dortmund (☎ 502 7222; Hiltropwall 15) High-brow drama, opera and musicals are staged at this theatre.

Konzerthaus (☎ 01805-448 044; Brückstrasse 21) Since September 2002, this brand-new concert house has been the home of the city's Philharmonic Orchestra. The architecturally stunning hall with superb acoustics also hosts top-flight guest performers, including Alfred Brendel and The Harlem Gospel Singer.

Luna Varieté & Theater (☎ 01805-976 760; Harkortstrasse 57a) For light-hearted cabaret, magic and comedy shows, visit this theatre, in the Hombruch suburb (take the U42 to Harkortstrasse).

Getting There & Away

Air Berlin has direct flights to **Dortmund airport** (☎ 921 30) from London/Stansted and Berlin/Tegel (see p755 for airline details). Free buses shuttle between the airport and the Holzwickede train station, with regular connections to Dortmund Hauptbahnhof, a major hub with frequent ICE and IC trains in all directions and regional and local trains every few minutes.

Dortmund is on the A1, A2 and A45. The B1 runs right through the city and is the link between the A40 to Essen and the A44 to Kassel. It's very busy and often clogged. For ride-sharing, contact **Mitfahrzentrale** (☎ 194 44; Grüne Strasse 3).

Getting Around

For public transport, see Getting Around p598. For a taxi call ☎ 144 444 or ☎ 194 10. **ADFC** (☎ 136 685; Hausmannstrasse 22, cnr Saarlandstrasse; €8 per 24hr) hires out bikes.

OTHER RUHRGEBIET ATTRACTIONS

The Ruhrgebiet has various places of interest that are part of the Industrial Heritage Trail (see p598), including Gasometer exhibition space in Oberhausen, Landschaftspark Duisburg-Nord in Duisburg and the Tetraeder in Bottrop.

NORTH RHINE-WESTPHALIA

Oberhausen

The city of Oberhausen has one of Germany's most unusual exhibit spaces, the **Gasometer** (☎ 0208-850 3733; www.gasometer.de; Am Grafenbusch 90; adult/concession tower only Tue-Fri €2/1; interior & tower Sat & Sun €3/2; ☼ 10am-5pm Tue & Thu-Sun, 10am-3pm Wed). The same giant barrel-shaped structure that once stored gas to power blast furnaces now hosts high-profile shows featuring international artists such as Christo and Bill Viola. Most run from May to October, but all year long you can ride the glass elevator to a 117m platform with views over the entire western Ruhrgebiet. On weekends, you can also explore the interior with the help of an audioguide (included in the admission price). Prices and hours vary with different exhibits.

Next door is the **Centro**, one of Europe's largest shopping malls with over 200 shops, some 20 restaurants and entertainment, including a multiplex cinema. For kids there's the **Centro Adventure Park** (☎ 0208-456 780; unlimited rides adult/concession €8/11; ☼ 10am-7pm daily mid-Apr–Sep; 10am-7pm Sat, Sun & school holidays Oct–mid-Apr), a small theme park with a pirate ship, a water playground, an English maze and other diversions.

To get here, take any bus or tram going toward Neue Mitte Oberhausen from terminal 1 of the Oberhausen Hauptbahnhof. By car, take the Neue Mitte exit off the A42.

Duisburg

Molten iron used to flow 24/7 from the fiery furnaces of a steel mill in the city of Duisburg. Since the last shift ended in 1985, the vast complex has been recycled as a one-of-a-kind adventure playground, the **Landschaftspark Duisburg-Nord** (Emscherstrasse 71; admission free; ☼ 24hr). You can free-climb its walls, take a diving course in the former gasometer and climb to the top of the blast furnace. There's plenty of green space for strolls, picnics or play, along with flower gardens and even a small farm with a petting zoo. At dusk from Friday to Sunday, a spectacular light show designed by British artist Jonathan Park envelops the blast furnaces, making them look like giant alien spacecraft. To get to the park take tram No 903 toward Hamborn/Meiderich from Duisburg Hauptbahnhof.

The park is home to a **visitors centre** (☎ 0203-429 1942; ☼ 10am-5pm Mon-Thu, 10am-9pm Fri-Sun Apr-Oct, reduced hours in winter) where you can pick up information about the entire heritage trail and find out about guided tours, concerts and other events at the park. Next door, a neat restaurant-bar serves drinks, snacks and full meals.

Just outside the complex is a brand-new **DJH hostel** (☎ 0203-417 900; jh-duisburg-nord@djh -rheinland.de; Lösorter Strasse 133; junior/senior dm €21.10/ 23.80, d €24.20/26.90; Ⓟ 🚫).

Bottrop

TETRAEDER

Egypt has them, so does Mexico and now there's also one in the Ruhrgebiet: a pyramid, right here in the town of Bottrop. The **Tetraeder** (Tetrahedron; admission free; ☼ 24hr) is a 50m-high skeletal construct made from steel pipes and open space. It graces the top of a former slag heap turned attractive landscape park, complete with trees, trails and benches for resting. You can climb the Tetraeder via staircases suspended from steel cables (yes, they swing when the wind's up) and leading to three viewing platforms, an experience not recommended for vertigo sufferers. Views of the surprisingly green yet undeniably industrial landscape are more impressive than conventionally beautiful. At night, the Tetraeder becomes a light installation that can be seen from afar.

Bus No 262 makes the trip out here from Bottrop Hauptbahnhof (get off at Brakerstrasse).

JOSEF ALBERS MUSEUM

An excellent collection of works by this Bottrop-born and Bauhaus-influenced artist is housed at the **Josef Albers Museum** (☎ 297 16; Im Stadtgarten 20; admission free; ☼ 10am-6pm Tue-Sun). Albers spent much of his life in the US and is especially famous for his explorations of colour and spacial relationships, especially of squares.

WARNER BROS MOVIE WORLD

This is Ruhrgebiet's answer to EuroDisney – 'Hollywood in Germany', as the brochures call it – the sprawling **Warner Bros Movie World** (☎ 02045-899 899; www.movieworld.de; Warner Allee 1; adult/senior/child 3-11 €23/20/18.25; ☼ 10am-6pm Mon-Fri, 10am-7pm Sat & Sun Apr-Oct; closed Nov-Mar). Opened by the movie giant Warner Brothers in 1996, it's a collection of thrill rides, restaurants, shops and shows providing 'nonstop entertainment'. Attractions include the Lethal Weapon and Riddlers Revenge rollercoasters, the Bermuda Triangle water ride, Hollywood Boulevard movie magic and a changing roster of live shows. Hours vary; those shown here are the minimum.

The park is in Bottrop-Kirchhellen, about 15km north of Essen. If you arrive by train, you must get off at the Feldhausen stop. There are direct RE connections hourly from Essen (€3.40, 25 minutes). If you're driving, take the Kirchhellen exit off the A31.

WESTPHALIA

MÜNSTER

☎ 0251 / pop 280,000

Münster is an attractive university town and administrative centre in the flatlands of northern Westphalia, an hour's drive north of the Ruhrgebiet cities. Patrician townhouses and baroque city palaces characterise the Altstadt, but perhaps more than anything it's the bicycles – called *Leeze* in local dialect – that give the city its flair. On any given day, some 100,000 of them wheel through Münster's streets, making liberal use of special driving regulations and numerous designated bike paths and parking lots. Germany's fourth-largest university – and its 54,000 students – keep the cobwebs out of this otherwise conservative and Catholic town.

Orientation

Many of Münster's main sights are within the confines of the easy-to-walk Altstadt, a short walk northwest of the Hauptbahnhof via Windhorststrasse. The bus station is right outside the station's west exit. The Altstadt is encircled by the 4.8km *Promenade*, a car-free ring trail built on top of the city's old fortifications; it's hugely popular with bicyclists.

Information

Main post office (☎ 01802-3333; Domplatz; ⏱ 8am-7pm Mon-Fri, 8am-1pm Sat) There is another branch at the Hauptbahnhof.

Main tourist office (☎ 492 2710; www.muenster.de /stadt/tourismus; Klemensstrasse 10; ⏱ 9am-6pm Mon-Fri, 9am-1pm Sat)

Poertgen Herder (☎ 490 140; Salzstrasse 56) Good selection of English books.

Rafaelsklinik (☎ 500 70; Klosterstrasse 72) Medical sevices.

Sparkasse (☎ 5980; Ludgeristrasse; ⏱ 9am-6pm Mon-Fri) Bank.

Surf Inn (☎ 500 2184; 3rd fl, Kaufhof department store, Ludgeristrasse 1; €1 per 15 min; ⏱ 9.30am-8pm Mon-Fri, 9.30am-6pm Sat)

Tourist Office Altes Rathaus (⏱ 10am-5pm Tue-Sat, 10am-4pm Sun)

Sights

DOM ST PAUL

The two massive towers of Münster's cathedral, **Dom St Paul** (Domplatz; ⏱ 10am-6pm) match the proportions of this 110m-long structure and the enormous square it overlooks. The three-nave construction was built in the 13th century on the cusp of the transition from Romanesque to Gothic. Enter from Domplatz through a porch (called the 'Paradise'), richly festooned with apostle sculptures. Inside, a 5m **statue of St Christopher**, the patron saint of travellers, greets visitors (yes, that's a real tree branch in his left hand).

The main attraction inside, though, is the **astronomical clock** (1542) on the right side of the ambulatory. It's a marvel of medieval ingenuity and indicates the time, the position of the sun, the movement of the planets, and the calendar. Crowds gather daily at noon (12.30pm Sunday) when the carillon starts up. Just beyond, a chapel contains the tomb of Clemens August Cardinal von Galen, one of the most outspoken opponents of the Nazi regime.

The **Domkammer** (Treasury; ☎ 424 71; admission €1; ⏱ 11am-4pm Tue-Sun), reached via the cloister, counts an 11th-century gem-studded golden head reliquary of St Paul among its finest pieces.

AROUND DOMPLATZ

A few steps northwest of the Dom, the **Überwasserkirche** (also known as Liebfrauenkirche) is a 14th-century Gothic hall church with handsome stained-glass windows. Its name, which means 'above the water', was inspired by its location adjacent to Münster's tiny stream, the Aa, whose tree-lined promenade invites a stroll.

In the 16th century, the iconoclastic Anabaptists 'cleansed' this church of all sculptures, but fortunately many were saved

NORTH RHINE-WESTPHALIA

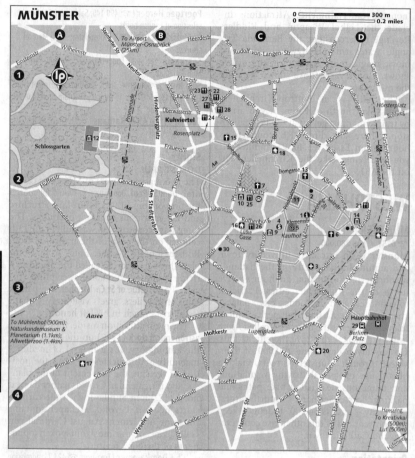

MÜNSTER

INFORMATION		
Main Tourist Office	**1**	C2
Poertgen Herder Bookstore	**2**	D2
Rafaelsklinik	**3**	D3
Sparkasse	**4**	C2
Surf Inn	**5**	C2
Tourist Office Altes Rathaus	(see 11)	

SIGHTS & ACTIVITIES	(pp607-9)	
Clemenskirche	**6**	D2
Dom St Paul	**7**	C2
Domkammer	(see 7)	
Erbdrostenhof	**8**	D2
Friedenssaal	(see 11)	
Graphikmuseum Pablo Picasso	**9**	C2

Landesmuseum	**10**	C2
Rathaus	**11**	C2
Schloss	**12**	A2
St Lamberti Church	**13**	C2
Stadtmuseum	**14**	D2
Stadtweinhaus	(see 11)	
Überwasserkirche	**15**	C2

SLEEPING	(pp609-10)	
Central-Hotel	**16**	C2
DJH Hostel	**17**	A4
Hotel Busche am Dom	**18**	C2
Hotel Mauritzhof	**19**	D2
Ibis Hotel	**20**	D4

EATING		(p610)
Altes Gasthaus Leve	**21**	D2
Cavete	**22**	C1
Das Blaue Haus	**23**	B1
La Torre	**24**	B1
Marktcafé	**25**	C2
Mokka D'Or	**26**	C2
Pinkus Müller	**27**	B1
Rico	**28**	C1

TRANSPORT		(p610)
Central Bus Station	**29**	D3
Citynetz Mitfahrzentrale	**30**	C3
Radstation	(see 29)	

and are now on display in the **Landesmuseum** (Regional Museum; ☎ 590 701; Domplatz 10; adult/concession €2.60/1.10; ⏰ 10am-6pm Tue-Sun). The museum's well-respected art collection includes works by accomplished Westphalian painters, including Conrad von Soest and

Hermann and Ludger tom Ring. Two rooms are dedicated to August Macke, one of the leading German Expressionists.

For an in-depth study of the lithographic work of another 20th-century master, head a short walk south of Domplatz to the **Graphik-**

museum Pablo Picasso (☎ 414 470; Königsstrasse 5; adult/concession €5/4; ⏰ 11am-6pm Tue-Fri, 10am-6pm Sat & Sun), the first German museum dedicated to the Spanish artist. Selections from the collection's nearly 800 graphics, including still lifes and bull-fighting scenes, are shown on a rotating basis.

PRINZIPALMARKT
Münster's main artery is the Prinzipalmarkt, lined by gabled Patrician townhouses with arcades sheltering elegant boutiques and cafés. The most majestic façade along here belongs to the Gothic **Rathaus**, site of the signing of the Peace of Westphalia in 1648, which marked the first step in ending the calamitous Thirty Years' War. The event took place in the freshly restored **Friedenssaal** (Hall of Peace; ☎ 492 2724; admission €1.50; ⏰ 9am-5pm Mon-Fri, 9am-4pm Sat, 10am-1pm Sun), a spectacular hall with intricately carved wood panelling. There's also an odd display of a golden drinking vessel in the shape of a rooster, a mummified hand and a slipper. As you exit, note the adjacent **Stadtweinhaus** (City Wine House), built in 1615, once used for wine storage and now containing a restaurant.

Look north for a fine view of the late-Gothic **St Lamberti Church** (1450). The three iron cages dangling from its slender openwork spire once held the corpses of the Anabaptist leaders Jan van Leyden and his deputies. This Protestant sect, which sought to institute adult baptism and polygamy and to abolish money, was routed in 1535 by troops of the prince-bishop after van Leyden proclaimed Münster the capital of the utopian 'New Jerusalem' with himself as king. He and his cohorts were publicly tortured with red-hot tongs – now on view at the **Stadtmuseum** (Salzstrasse 28) – then stuck in the cages as a warning to all wannabe protestants.

BAROQUE BUILDINGS
The architect that left its mark on Münster more than any other was Johann Conrad Schlaun (1695–1773), a master of the Westphalian baroque, a more subdued, less exuberant style than in vogue in southern Germany. His vision survives in several buildings, mostly notably the exquisite 1757 **Erbdrostenhof** (Salzstrasse 38), built as a residence for a high-powered aristocrat. Nearby the

equally stunning 1753 **Clemenskirche** (Klemensstrasse) boasts a domed, frescoed ceiling supported by turquoise faux-marble pillars. Less pristinely preserved is the 1773 **Schloss** (Schlossplatz), the former residence of the prince-bishops and now the main university building.

OUTSIDE THE ALTSTADT
A 10-minute walk southeast of the Hauptbahnhof takes you to the **Kreativkai**, Münster's redeveloped old harbour. Its handsome brick warehouses now house a theatre, artists studios, a children's book publisher and other offices alongside a fun mix of restaurants, bars and dance clubs (see Eating & Drinking p610). Its edgy charms are best sampled sitting outdoors and watching cargo barges cutting through the Dortmund-Ems canal. Exit the Hauptbahnhof to the east, then follow Bremer Strasse south, cross Hansaring and the area will be on your left.

The Aasee lake, southwest of the Altstadt, is popular for picnics and activities like sailing and windsurfing. Halfway down the lake's western shore is the **Mühlenhof** (☎ 981 200; Theo-Breider-Weg 1; adult/student/child €3/2/1.50; ⏰ 10am-6pm mid-Mar–Oct, reduced hours Nov-Apr), an open-air museum of typical Westphalian buildings, including a mill and bakery. Other lakeside attractions are the **Naturkundemuseum & Planetarium** (Natural History Museum; ☎ 591 05; Sentruper Strasse 285; adult/concession €5.50/3), which has several shows daily, except Monday; and the **Allwetterzoo** (☎ 890 40; Sentruper Strasse 315; adult/concession €11.50/5.75; ⏰ 9am-6pm Apr-Sep, 9am-4pm or 5pm Oct-Mar), where admission includes a new equestrian museum and the dolphin show.

Sleeping
The tourist office operates a **reservation hotline** (☎ 492 2726; ⏰ 8am-10pm).

DJH hostel (☎ 530 280; jhg-muenster@djh-wl.de; Bismarckallee 31; dm/d €21/56; 🅿 🖳) This modernised lakeside hostel has two- and four-bed rooms, including six for people with disabilities. Take bus No 10 or 34 to Hoppendamm, from where it's a 500m walk.

Ibis (☎ 481 30; Engelstrasse 53; s/d €65/74; 🅿 ❌ 🐾) This chain hotel near the train station offers the standard small rooms but, given the good range of amenities, it represents great value for money in central Münster.

Hotel Busche am Dom (☎ 464 44; hotel-busche@t-online.de; Bogenstrasse 10; s €49, d €79-99; [P] [X]) Not much imagination may have gone into the décor at this traditional hotel, but the rooms are clean, the location central and the proprietors friendly.

Central-Hotel (☎ 510 150; www.central-hotel.de; Aegidiistrasse 1; s €85-95, d €100-130; [P] [X]) This small and excellent hotel has so many fans that it's often fully booked. The couple that runs the show know a thing a two about art, as is reflected in the choice of furnishings, décor and general flair.

Mauritzhof (☎ 417 20; www.mauritzhof.de; Eisenbahnstrasse 15-17; s & d €98-121; [P] [X] [X]) Bold colours, clear lines and extravagant designer furniture give this place upmarket ambience. Extras to enjoy include climate-controlled rooms, 24-hour room service and a central location. Breakfast costs €13.

Eating & Drinking

Marktcafé (☎ 575 85; Domplatz 7; mains €5-11) Views of the Dom are gratis at this contemporary café where empty chairs are rare, especially on market days (Wednesday and Saturday). The food is fresh and tasty, and Sunday's brunch buffet (€9.50) is great value.

Mokka D'Or (☎ 482 8591; Rothenburg 14-16; mains €5-15) This trendy bar, restaurant and beer garden, accessed through a little alleyway, is one of Münster's new favourite restaurants. *Panini*, *tramezzini* and other sandwiches for breakfast, satisfying salads for lunch, wood-fired pizza at night – that's *dolce vita* Westphalian style.

Altes Gasthaus Leve (☎ 455 95; Alter Steinweg 37; mains €6-16) Guests have patronised this inn since 1607, making it Münster's oldest. Decorated with painted tiles, oil paintings, copper etchings and other traditional art, it is one of the most ambience-laden places to try typical Westphalian fare like lima-bean stew, fried liverwurst, or sweet and sour beef with onions.

Luf (☎ 674 3444; Hafenweg 46-48; lunch €5-7, dinner €7-14) This party place on the Kreativkai has inexpensive lunch specials, a popular Sunday brunch (€12.50) with childcare, after-work lounges, dinner on the harbour-facing terrace and lots of other activities.

Other recommendations:

Rico (☎ 459 79; Rosenplatz 7; dishes €4-6; ⏱ 11.30am-3.30pm Mon-Sat) Clean and friendly vegetarian, self-service restaurant.

La Torre (☎ 583 95; Rosenplatz 15-17; pizzas €8-11) Tasty pizza with classic to adventurous flavour combos.

The Kuhviertel, north of the Dom, is the traditional student quarter. Kreuzstrasse, especially, is lined with casual pubs conducive to making new friends over inexpensive drinks and small meals. **Cavete** (☎ 457 00; Kreuzstrasse 38; meals €3-8) and **Das Blaue Haus** (☎ 421 51; Kreuzstrasse 16; meals €3-8) are classics. Also here is **Pinkus Müller** (☎ 451 51; Kreuzstrasse 4; mains €10-20; ⏱ closed Sun), a typical Westphalian restaurant that makes its own beer.

Getting There & Away

The **Münster-Osnabrück airport** (☎ 02571-940; www.fmo.de) has direct connections to London and Rome on Air Berlin (see p755 for airline details) and is easily reached by bus with half-hourly departures throughout the day (€4.60, 40 minutes).

Münster is on an IC line with regular fast links to points north and south. Regional trains to the Ruhrgebiet cities also leave frequently. The city is on the A1 from Bremen to Cologne and is the starting point of the A43 direction Wuppertal. It is also at the crossroads of the B51, B54 and B219. Parking in the centre is largely confined to parking garages (from €1 per hour).

For ride-sharing, check the board in the university or call **Citynetz** (☎ 194 44; Aegidiistrasse 20a).

Getting Around

Bus drivers sell single tickets for €1.20 or €1.75, depending on the distance. Day passes are €4.10. For information, call ☎ 01803-504 030.

Better yet, do as the locals do and ride a bike, available for hire at **Radstation** (☎ 484 0170; day/week €6/25; ⏱ 5.30am-11pm Mon-Fri, 7am-11pm Sat & Sun) outside the Hauptbahnhof. The tourist office stocks a palette of biking maps.

AROUND MÜNSTER
Münsterland Castles

Münster is surrounded by the Münsterland, home to about 100 well-preserved Schlöss (castles and palaces), many of them protected by moats. In these rural flatlands, water was often the only way for local rulers to keep out the 'rabble' and rebels.

The region is a dream for cyclists, with over 4000km of well signposted trails (called *Pättkes* in local dialect), including the 100 Schlösser Route (Route of 100 Palaces) which allows you to hop from one castle to the next. Bicycles may be hired in Münster (p610) and at nearly all local train stations.

For route planning, lodging and general information, call the tollfree **Radler Hotline** (☎ 0800-939 2910) or stop by the Münster Tourist Office (see Information p607). German readers will also find useful information on the website of the regional tourist office (www.muensterland-tourismus.de).

The following are snapshots of a quartet of castles that offer the greatest tourist appeal and are relatively accessible from Münster.

BURG HÜLSHOFF

About 10km west of Münster, in Havixbeck, **Burg Hülshoff** (☎ 02534-1052; Schonebeck 6; museum €3; ☯ 9.30am-6pm Feb–mid-Dec) is the birthplace of one of Germany's pre-eminent women of letters, Annette von Droste-Hülshoff (1797–1848). The large red-brick Renaissance chateau is embedded in a lovely – partly groomed, partly romantic – park (admission free), which is especially pleasant in spring. Inside is an unexciting restaurant and a small museum, which is basically a series of rooms furnished as they would have been in the poet's day. Bus Nos 563 and 564 make the trip out here from Münster's city centre, though service is sketchy on weekends.

HAUS RÜSCHHAUS

In 1826 Annette von Droste-Hülshoff moved to the smaller **Haus Rüschhaus** (☎ 02533-1317; adult/concession €3/2; ☯ tours hourly 10am-noon & 2-5pm Tue-Sun May-Oct; fewer tours Nov-Apr) in the Münster suburb of Nienberge, just 3km north of Burg Hülshoff. This was the one-time private home of master architect JC Schlaun (1749), who infused baroque touches into what had been a Westphalian farmhouse. The strictly symmetrical garden makes for a lovely stroll. Take bus No 5 direction Nienberge from Münster's Hauptbahnhof.

BURG VISCHERING

The quintessential medieval moated castle, **Burg Vischering** (☎ 02591-799 00; Berenbrok 1) is

Westphalia's oldest (1271), and the kind that conjures romantic images of knights and damsels. Surrounded by a system of ramparts and ditches, the complex consists of an outer castle and the main castle, connected by a bridge. Inside the main castle is the **Münsterland Museum** (adult/concession €2.50/2; ☯ 10am-12.30pm & 1.30-5.30pm Tue-Sun Apr-Oct; until 4.30pm Nov-Mar).

Burg Vischering is in Lüdinghausen, about 30km south of Münster. Bus Nos S90 and S92 make the trip from Münster's central bus station to Lüdinghausen, but getting to the castle itself can be complicated. Call ☎ 01803-504 030 for route details.

SCHLOSS NORDKIRCHEN

A grandiose baroque red-brick structure sitting on an island and surrounded by a lavish, manicured park, **Schloss Nordkirchen** (☎ 02596-933 402; tours €2; ☯ 11am-6pm Sun May-Sep, 2-4pm Sun Oct-Apr) is accessible via three bridges. This symmetrical palace, nicknamed the 'Westphalian Versailles', was commissioned at the beginning of the 18th century by the prince-bishop of Münster, Christian Friedrich von Plettenberg. Gottfried Laurenz Pictorius began building it in 1703 and Schlaun completed it in 1734. It now houses the state college for financial studies.

On a nice day, the palace is well worth visiting for the gardens and the exterior alone; the interior – with its stuccoed ceilings, the festival hall, the dining room and the other chambers – may only be viewed during guided tours. Admission is possible outside of opening hours by appointment.

Schloss Nordkirchen is 8km southeast of Lüdinghausen in the hamlet of Nordkirchen, which does not have a train station. Consult your bike map to find the route between the two castles.

SOEST

☎ 02921 / pop 48,500

Soest, a placid town of neat, half-timbered houses and a web of idyllic lanes, has largely preserved its medieval appearance. It lies about 45km east of Dortmund and is the northern gateway to the Sauerland (p615). Soest is a 'green' town, not only because of its parks and gardens but also for the unusual green sandstone used in building its churches and other structures. Brimming with works of art, these churches reflect the wealth Soest enjoyed in the Middle Ages as a member of the Hanseatic League, when its products – mostly textiles, salt and corn – were in great demand throughout Europe. They are also what makes Soest a popular destination for day-trippers from the nearby Ruhrgebiet cities and the Sauerland.

Information

Deutsche Bank (Markt 14)

Post office (Hospitalsgasse 3)

Tourist office (☎ 103 1414; www.soest.de; Am Seel 5; ⏰ 9.30am-12.30pm & 2-4.30pm Mon-Fri, 10am-1pm Sat year-round; 11am-1pm Sun Apr-Oct)

Sights

Much of Soest's historic centre is still encircled by the town fortifications from 1180, which today have a parklike appearance and are great for strolling and picnicking. Fans of medieval churches have plenty to keep them busy in Soest. Closest to the Hauptbahnhof is the exquisite late-Gothic (1313) hall church, **St Maria zur Wiese** (Wiesenstrasse; ⏰ 11am-4pm Mon-Sat, noon-4pm Sun), also known as Wiesenkirche and easily recognised by its filigreed neo-Gothic twin spires. Inside it's the beautifully balanced proportions and vibrant stained-glass windows that create a special atmosphere. The most charming window is the **Westphalian Last Supper** over the north portal, which shows Jesus and his followers enjoying Westphalian ham, rye bread and beer.

Just west of here is the smaller **St Maria zur Höhe** (⏰ 10am-5.30pm Mon-Fri, 10am-5pm Sat, noon-5pm Sun Apr-Sep; closes 4pm Oct-Mar), better known as Hohnekirche, a squat, older (1200) and architecturally less accomplished hall church. Its sombreness is brightened by beautiful ceiling frescoes, an altar ascribed to the Westphalian painter known as the Master of Liesborn, and the *Scheibenkreuz*, a huge wooden cross on a circular board more typically found in Scandinavian churches; in fact, it's the only such cross in Germany. Look for the light switch on your left as you enter to shed a little light on the matter.

Three more churches are near Markt. **St Patrokli** (Propst-Nübel-Strasse 2; ⏰ 10am-6pm), a three-nave Romanesque structure (965), is famous for its stout square tower known as the 'Tower of Westphalia'. Note the deli-

cate frescoes (1200) in the apse. Of almost mystical simplicity is the tiny **Nikolaikapelle** (Thomästrasse; ⏰ 11am-noon Wed & Sun) a few steps southeast, where a masterful altar painting by the 15th-century artist Conrad von Soest (born in Dortmund) delights art connoisseurs. Last but not least, there is **St Petri** (Petrikirchhof 10; ⏰ 9.30am-noon & 2-5.30pm Tue-Fri, until 4.30pm Sat, 2-5.30pm Sun), Westphalia's oldest church with origins in the 8th century. It's adorned with wall murals and features an unusual modern altar made from the local green sandstone, glass and brushed stainless steel.

Sleeping

DJH hostel (☎ 162 83; jh-soest@djh-wl.de; Kaiser-Friedrich-Platz 2; junior/senior €13/15.40; Ⓟ ✗) Fully renovated and expanded after 1999 fire, this hostel has some doubles with private bathroom.

Other good choices for spending the night:

Hotel Stadt Soest (☎ 362 20; www.hotel-stadt -soest.de; Brüderstrasse 50; s/d €45/85; Ⓟ) Traditionally furnished but modernised, in the pedestrian zone near the Hauptbahnhof.

Hotel Im Wilden Mann (☎ 150 71; www.im-wilden -mann.de; Markt 11; s/d €54/91; Ⓟ) A landmark hotel with a fine restaurant.

Eating

Bon Tempi (☎ 166 31; Im Theodor-Heuss-Park; mains €10-15) In fine weather, the idyllic park setting next to a duck pond is the biggest selling point of this popular bistro, but the menu convinces too. Come for breakfast, snacks, ice cream, coffee or a full meal.

Brauerei Christ (☎ 155 15; Walburger Strasse 36; mains €8.50-15) A dependable favourite, the Christ has a gorgeous beer garden and a menu that features about 20 schnitzel variations, Westphalian specialties and a few nonmeat choices. Regulars give a big thumbs up to the succulent spare ribs.

Pilgrim Haus (☎ 1828; Jakobistrasse 75; snacks €6-10, mains €14-20; ⏰ dinner only Mon & Wed-Fri) Westphalia's oldest inn has welcomed visitors since 1304. Enjoy upmarket regional cuisine in a museumlike setting filled with gewgaws and anchored by a shiny tiled stove.

Getting There & Away

Soest is easily reached by train from Dortmund (€8.40, 40 minutes) and is also regularly connected to Paderborn (€8.40, 40 minutes) and Münster (€11.20, one hour). There's a regular bus service to the northern Sauerland, including lines to Möhnesee lake (bus No 549, €3.50, 20 minutes), Warstein (bus No 551, €6.50, 1½hours) and Arnsberg (bus No 550, €11.20, one hour). If you're driving, take the Soest exit from the A44. Soest is also at the crossroads of the B1, B229 and B475.

PADERBORN

☎ 05251 / pop 138,500

Paderborn offers an intriguing blend of medieval marvels and high tech, and derives its name from the Pader, Germany's shortest river. It's fed by about 200 springs that surface in the Paderquellgebiet, a little park in the city centre, and merges with the Lippe River after only 4km.

Charlemagne used the royal seat and bishopric he had established here to control the Christianisation of the Saxon tribes. In 799 he received a momentous visit from Pope Leo III, which led to the foundation of the Holy Roman Empire and Charlemagne's coronation as its emperor in Rome. Catholicism characterises Paderborn to this day – churches abound, and religious sculpture and motifs adorn public façades, fountains and parks. Many of the city's 15,000 students are involved in theological studies (economics and technology are other major fields).

Orientation

Paderborn-Lippstadt airport is 20km southwest of the city. For details about getting into town, see Getting There & Away (p615). Paderborn's centre is small enough to explore on foot. The Hauptbahnhof is situated about 1km west of the largely pedestrianised Altstadt. Exit right onto Bahnhofstrasse, then continue straight to Westernstrasse, which leads to Marienplatz (with the tourist office), the Dom and other sights. The Hafenviertel pub quarter is north of here.

Information

Commerzbank (☎ 290 760; Rathausplatz 14)
Main post office (Liliengasse 2; 🕑 9am-6pm Mon-Fri, 9am-1pm Sat) Off Westernstrasse.
St-Vincenz Hospital (☎ 860; Am Bushof 2)
Thalia Bücher (☎ 272 64; Rathausplatz 19) Bookshop.
Tourist office (☎ 882 980; www.paderborn.de; Marienplatz 2a; 🕑 9.30am-6pm Mon-Fri, 9.30am-2pm Sat)

Sights

CITY CENTRE

Paderborn's landmark 1270 Gothic **Dom** (Markt 17), a three-nave hall church, is a good place to start your exploration of the city. As you enter through the southern portal (called 'Paradies'), note the delicate carved sculptures. Inside, main features include the late-Gothic **high altar** and a grand **monument to Bishop Dietrich von Fürstenberg** (d. 1681). The unusual stained-glass windows have an uncanny resemblance to a computer motherboard, a bizarre coincidence considering Paderborn's close ties to the computer industry. The most famous feature is the so-called **Hasenfenster**. Its tracery depicts three rabbits, arranged in such a way that each has two ears, even though there are only three ears in all. This clever illusion gave rise to the following nursery rhyme: 'Count the ears. There are but three. But still each hare has two, you see?' The window is supposed to represent the Holy Trinity and has become the city's symbol. It's in the cloister; look for the signs.

The hall-like **crypt**, one of the largest in Germany, contains the grave and relics of St Liborius, the city's patron saint. To see the famous Liborius shrine, though, head to the **Diözesanmuseum** (☎ 125 216; Markt 17; adult/concession €2.50/1.50; 🕑 10am-6pm Tue-Sun), housed in the incongruously modern structure just outside the Dom. Its surprisingly attractive interior houses an impressive collection of ecclesiastical sculpture and paintings. The Libori shrine is in the basement, near a room filled with prized portable altars. Not to be missed upstairs is the Imad Madonna, an 11th-century lindenwood sculpture.

Exiting the museum, you'll find yourself on Markt. Turn right onto the pedestrian street called Schildern to get to the proud **Rathaus** (1616) with ornate gables, oriels and other decorative touches typical of the Weser Renaissance architectural style. Just south of here is the **Jesuitenkirche** (Rathausplatz), whose curvilinear baroque exterior contrasts with the more subdued Gothic vaulted ceiling and Romanesque arches inside. This mix of styles, however, is typical of Jesuit churches from the late-17th century.

Rathausplatz transitions into Marienplatz, where the attractive **Heisingsche Haus** (Marienplatz), a 17th-century patrician mansion with an elaborate façade, stands adjacent to the tourist office. A short walk north via Am Abdinghof, the 1015 **Abdinghofkirche** (Am Abdinghof) is easily recognised by its twin Romanesque towers. Originally a Benedictine monastery, it's been a Protestant church since 1867. Its whitewashed walls, flat wooden ceiling and completely unadorned interior make it a rather austere place.

At the foot of the Abdinghofkirche lies the **Paderquellgebiet**, a small park perfect for relaxing by the gurgling springs of the Pader source and with nice views of the Dom. This is also the starting point of a lovely walk along the little river to **Schloss Neuhaus**, a moated water palace about 5km northwest.

Following Am Abdinghof east gets you to the north side of the Dom where excavations have unearthed the foundations of the **Carolingian Kaiserpfalz**, Charlemagne's palace where the fateful meeting with Pope Leo took place.

Right behind looms the reconstructed **Ottonian Kaiserpfalz**, a dignified 11th-century palace that now contains a **museum** (☎ 105 10; Am Ikenberg 2; adult/concession €2.50/1.50; ☽ 10am-6pm Tue-Sun) with unearthed items on display. Immediately adjacent is the tiny and beautiful **Bartholomäuskapelle** (☽ 10am-6pm), built in 1017 and the oldest hall church north of the Alps, with otherworldly acoustics.

HEINZ NIXDORF MUSEUMSFORUM (HNF)

Not only techies will enjoy the innovative computer museum **Heinz Nixdorf Museums-Forum** (☎ 306 600; Fürstenallee 7; adult/concession €3/1.50; ☽ 9am-6pm Tue-Fri, 10am-6pm Sat & Sun), one of the world's largest. Established by the founder of Nixdorf Computers, a large German computer company (now merged with Siemens), it presents a fascinating journey through 5000 years of communication and information technology – from cuneiform to cyberspace.

On display are calculating machines, typewriters, cash registers, punch-card systems, manual telephone exchanges, accounting machines and other innovations in the fields of writing, telecommunication and data processing. Many of these are presented in recreated office environments from different ages and countries. The Hall of Fame introduces pioneers like Gottfried Wilhelm Leibniz who, as early as 1672, invented a calculating machine based on the binary system, and Herman Hollerith, the creator of the punch-card system in 1889.

The core of the exhibit focuses on the evolution of computers. A room-sized installation shows the original size of **ENIAC**, a vacuum-tube computer developed for the US Army in the 1940s that became the forerunner of the modern computer. Today, a 6mm x 6mm chip holds the same data.

All exhibits are presented in a fashion that is not intimidating to lay people, with plenty of machines to touch, push and prod. You can also play computer games or experience virtual reality in the Software Theatre.

There's limited English-language panelling and a comprehensive museum guide in English (€5). Lectures, events and symposia supplement the exhibits, though these are usually in German. To get here, take bus 11 to Museumsforum.

Sleeping

DJH hostel (☎ 220 55; Meinwerkstrasse 16; junior/senior Mar-Oct €15/17.70, Nov-Feb €13.30/16; (P) ✗) Right in the Hafenviertel pub quarter, this hostel has no curfew and rooms sleeping four to eight, many with private bathroom. If they're not full, singles and doubles are available for a €2.50 surcharge per person. Take bus No 2 to Detmolder Tor.

Campingplatz Stauterrassen (☎ 05254-4504; www.stauterrassen.de; Auf der Thune 14; tent/person/car €2.50/2/1.50) This is a nicely located camp site about 7km north of central Paderborn. Take bus No 1, 8 or 11 to Schloss Neuhaus, then No 58 to Am Thunhof.

Haus Irma (☎ 233 42; Bachstrasse 9; s/d €37/53; (P)) This snug and central guesthouse near the Paderquellgebiet is a good deal for those needing minimal amenities.

Galerie-Hotel Abdinghof (☎ 122 40; reception@galerie-hotel.de; Bachstrasse 1; s/d €70/87; (P)) In a 1563 stone building overlooking the Paderquellgebiet, this is Paderborn's most original hotel. Rooms are named after famous artists and decorated in styles ranging from country-rustic to elegant-feminine. Original art graces the downstairs café-restaurant.

Hotel StadtHaus (☎ 188 9910; info@hotel-stadthaus.de; Hathumarstrasse 22; s/d €84/102; (P)) Behind a stately, white façade awaits a classy hotel furnished in early–20th century style but equipped with all major amenities. Bold greens and yellows give a contemporary feel to the downstairs restaurant, which serves light, seasonal dishes. There's also a sauna for relaxing.

Eating

The highest concentration of restaurants, student pubs and bars is located in the Hafenviertel quarter in the northern Altstadt along Kisau, Mühlenstrasse, Hathumarstrasse and Ükern.

Café Central (☎ 296 888; Rosenstrasse 13-15; mains €4-9) Burgundy walls, velvet drapes and chandeliers create a fun theatrical atmosphere at this trendy eatery near the tourist office. Come for breakfast, simple café fare or a drink. It's in a passageway off Rosenstrasse in the pedestrian zone.

Café Klatsch (☎ 281 221; Kisau 11; mains €5-11; ☼ from 6pm) Candle-lit and casual, this café has a menu of simple but inspired fare for slim wallets. Options include such filling Mediterranean-style snacks as Spanish potatoes, Greek sandwiches and noodle casseroles.

Deutsches Haus (☎ 221 36; Kisau 9; mains €9-18) Rustic beams and woodsy booths combine with colourful Art Deco lamps at this popular German restaurant. Note the mosaic mural of Gustav Klimt's *The Kiss* next to the flat-screen TV in the bar.

Vertiko (☎ 258 51; Hathumarstrasse 1; mains €12-18) This cute half-timbered house from 1728 is the place to go for modern takes on classic Westphalian dishes. Sit inside beneath beamed ceilings or in the courtyard with view of the Paderquellgebiet.

Getting There & Away

AirBerlin offers direct flights to London-Stansted from the **Paderborn-Lippstadt airport** (☎ 02955-770). Bus Nos 400 and 460 make the trip out from the Hauptbahnhof.

Paderborn has direct IC trains every two hours to Kassel-Wilhelmshöhe (€20, 1¼ hours) and regional connections to Dortmund (€15.40, 1¼ hours) and other Ruhrgebiet cities. Trains to Soest (€7.80, 35 minutes) leave several times hourly.

Paderborn is on the A33, which connects with the A2 in the north and the A44 in the south. The B1, B64, B68 and B480 also go through Paderborn. Those interested in ride-shares should contact the **Mitfahrzentrale** (☎ 194 40; Bahnhofstrasse 10).

SAUERLAND

This gentle mountain range in the southeast of North Rhine-Westphalia is a fine destination for a brief respite and almost completely ignored by international travellers, Dutch visitors notwithstanding. Outdoor enthusiasts will find a good network of hiking and biking trails, lakes for water sports and rivers for fishing. For culture buffs there are museums, tidy half-timbered towns and hilltop castles.

The Sauerland's many lakes and reservoirs are tailor-made for camping and there are literally dozens of sites to choose from. You'll also find all other types of lodging, from hostels to castle hotels. The regional tourist offices listed under Information maintain a room reservation service by phone and online.

Information

Besides these two regional offices (www.sauerland-touristik.de), most towns also have their own local branches.

Hochsauerland Touristik (☎ 02961-943 227; Heinrich-Jansen-Weg 14, 59929 Brilon; ☼ 9am-6pm Mon-Fri, 10am-1pm Sat)

Südsauerland Touristik (☎ 02761-94570; Seminarstrasse 22, 57462 Olpe; ☼ 9am-6pm Mon-Fri, 10am-1pm Sat)

Hiking

More than 12,000km of hiking trails, mostly through dense beech and fir forests, traverse the Sauerland. Maps and trail descriptions are available from the local tourist offices or in bookshops. The newest long-distance trail is the 154km **Rothaarsteig** (www.rothaarsteig.de), which runs from Brilon on the Sauerland's northern edge all the way to the Siegerland. A popular medium-level hike of 5km leads from Winterberg to the peak of the Kahler Asten; views from the tower here (€1) are great.

Getting There & Away

Regular train services – even to the smallest towns – exist, though you may have to make a number of changes to get here. Travelling from the north, you'll most likely have to change in Hagen. Coming from points south usually requires a change in Siegen.

For regional buses into the northern Sauerland, see Getting There & Away (p612).

The A45 cuts through the Sauerland, connecting the Ruhrgebiet with Frankfurt. The area is also easily reached via the A4 from Cologne.

Getting Around

The Sauerland is best explored under your own steam, although, with some planning, it can also be done with public transportation. Once you are based in a town, special buses head for the hiking areas and the surrounding towns. Tickets, route maps and timetables are available from bus drivers and the tourist offices. For extended stays, the Sauerland *Urlauberkarte* (€10) buys unlimited public transportation for three days for two adults and three children.

ATTENDORN
☎ 02722 / pop 24,500

The main attraction of this typical Sauerland town on the northern shore of the Biggesee lake is the **Atta-Höhle** (☎ 937 50; tours adult/child €5.50/4; 9.30am-4.30pm May-Sep; reduced hours Oct-Apr), one of Germany's largest and most impressive stalactite caves. Highlights of the 40-minute tour through this bizarre underground world include a 5m-tall column and an underground lake.

In town, there's the **Church of St John the Baptist**, known locally as 'Sauerland Cathedral', whose main attraction is the 14th-century Pietà. The lower section of the square tower reveals the Romanesque origins of this church, which is otherwise Gothic.

The Biggesee offers lots of opportunities for water sports and also has lake cruises through **Personenschifffahrt Biggesee** (☎ 02761-965 90; Am Hafen 1, Olpe-Sondern; €8/4.50; Apr-Oct).

Attendorn's **tourist office** (☎ 4897; www.atten dorn.net; Rathauspassage; 9am-5.30pm Mon-Fri year-round; 10am-1pm Sat Jun-Sep) can help out with accommodation.

The most memorable place in town to spend the night is the imposing **Burg Schnellenberg** (☎ 6940; www.burg-schnellenberg.de; s/d from €85/120; P X), which offers modern luxuries in amazing medieval ambience. It's worth a visit even without staying.

Those with their own tent will find a scenic spot at **Camping Waldenburger Bucht** (☎ 955 00; www.camping-biggesee.de; Waldenburger

Bucht 11; tent €6.80-10, adult €3.10-3.90; year-round) right on the Biggesee.

ALTENA
☎ 02352 / pop 22,200

Embraced by thick forest and romantically lorded over by a 12th-century castle, Altena is one of the most picturesque Sauerland towns and the birthplace of the youth hostel movement in 1912. The original spartan furnishings have been preserved as a museum on **Burg Altena** (☎ 966 7033; Fritz-Thomee-Strasse 80; adult/concession €5/2.50; 9.30am-5pm Tue-Fri, 11am-6pm Sat & Sun). You can see the dormitory with its wooden triple bunks and straw mattresses and the dank day rooms with a small open kitchen and polished communal tables.

The thick castle walls also harbour the **Museum der Grafschaft Mark**, with a splendid assortment of weapons and armour, furniture, ceramics and glassware. There are interactive exhibits castle life in the Middle Ages. About 300m downhill is the **Deutsches Drahtmuseum** (☎ 927 5910; Fritz-Thomee-Strasse 12), which has hands-on displays on the many facets of wire from its manufacture to its use in industry, communications and art. Both museums are included in the same admission, and keep the same hours, as Burg Altena.

Altena's **tourist office** (☎ 209 295; www.altena -tourismus.de; Lüdenscheider Strasse 22) keeps erratic hours, so call ahead if possible.

You won't have to sleep on straw mattresses but staying at Altena's **DJH hostel** (☎ 235 22; jh-burg.altena@djh-wl.de; Fritz-Thomee Strasse 80; junior/senior €14.70/17.40; X), still inside the old castle, is a nostalgic treat.

WINTERBERG

At 842m, Winterberg, at the foot of the Kahler Asten, is the Sauerland's highest mountain and the region's wintersports centre. In good winters, the season runs from December to March, but for up-to-date snow levels, call the **Snowphone** (☎ 0291-115 30). Expect big crowds after major snow falls, especially on weekends. Equipment-rental shops abound; look for the sign saying 'Skiverleih'.

The **tourist office** (☎ 02981-925 00; www.winter berg.de; Am Kurpark 6) has lots of information, including the handy skiing guide *Loipen und Pisten* (Cross-Country Trails & Downhill Runs).

Besides skiing, a major local attraction is the 1600m-long bobsled run, occasionally the site of German and European championships. Hair-raising trips down the ice canal with an experienced driver cost €75 per person (November to February). Contact **Bobbahn** (☎ 0180-500 7263).

SIEGERLAND

The hills and mountains of the Sauerland continue southward into the Siegerland region, with the city of Siegen as its focal point. Frankfurt, the Ruhrgebiet and Cologne are all about 100km away.

SIEGEN
☎ 0271 / pop 106,000
Historically, Siegen has had strong connections with the House of Nassau-Oranien (Nassau-Orange), which has held the Dutch throne since 1813. Around 1403 the counts of Nassau who ruled the area obtained large territories in the Netherlands; in 1530 they added the principality of Orange in France. The Netherlands became a hereditary monarchy in 1813, and the crown went to Wilhelm Friedrich of the House of Nassau-Oranien. Two palaces and other buildings survive from those glory days in this otherwise modern city that's a major regional commercial hub. Siegen was also the birthplace of Peter Paul Rubens (1577–1640).

Orientation
Siegen's centre slopes up from the Hauptbahnhof in the northwest to the Oberes Schloss in the east, where the Altstadt is at its most scenic.

Information
Commerzbank (☎ 598 20; Bahnhofstrasse 2)
Dresdner Bank (☎ 5831; Bahnhofstrasse 4)
Main post office (Hindenburgstrasse 9)
Siegen tourist office (☎ 404 1316; www.siegen.de; Rathaus, Markt 2; ☼ 8.30am-noon Mon-Fri, 2-4pm Tue, 2-6pm Thu)
Siegerland tourist office (☎ 333 1020; Koblenzer Strasse 73; www.siegerland-wittgenstein-tourismus.de; ☼ 10am-5pm Mon-Fri)

Sights
In 1623 the ruling family of Nassau-Oranien was split into two branches feuding over the

Reformation. This required the construction of a second palace, the baroque **Unteres Schloss**, by the Protestant side, while the Catholic counts continued to live in the 13th-century Oberes Schloss. The Unteres Schloss is a short walk southeast from the Hauptbahnhof. Today, it's primarily used as office space and only the family crypt has survived.

Nearby, a former 19th-century telegraph office is now a showcase of 20th-century art at the new **Museum für Gegenwartskunst** (Museum of Contemporary Art; ☎ 405 7710; Unteres Schloss 1; adult/concession €3.90/2.60; ☼ 11am-6pm Tue-Sun, 11am-8pm Thu). Works in all modern media, from photography to video, film and installations are shown in changing exhibits.

Turning left on Löhrstrasse gets you to the Markt, the heart of the Altstadt and dominated by the late Romanesque **Nikolaikirche**, whose galleried, hexagonal main room is unique in Germany. Also note the baptismal plate, made by Peruvian silversmiths in the 16th century and brought back by the counts of Nassau, who were involved in the colonisation of South America.

From here head up on Burgstrasse to the Oberes Schloss, the one-time home of the Catholic princes. It now houses the **Siegerlandmuseum** (☎ 230 410; Burgstrasse; adult/concession €3/2; ☼ 10am-5pm Tue-Sun) where eight original paintings by Peter Paul Rubens are the highlights.

Sleeping & Eating
Both the local and the regional tourist offices can help with room reservations.
Berghotel Johanneshöhe (☎ 310 008; www.johanneshoehe.de; Wallhausenstrasse 1; s €48-66, d €71-89; **P**) As the name suggests, this upmarket hotel has a hilltop location with nice views of town. The restaurant with old-timey flair specialises in northern French dishes, especially lamb and fish (mains €10 to €20). The hotel is about 1.6km from the train station.
Hotel Bürger (☎ 625 51; www.hotel-buerger.de; Marienborner Strasse 134-136; s/d €57/75; **P**) Behind the inconspicuous façade awaits a comfortable hotel with spacious, bright and nicely furnished rooms, all with private updated bathrooms. Extras include cable TV and minibar.
Piazza (☎ 303 0856; Unteres Schloss 1; lunch €6-11, dinner €15-24) Right inside the Museum of Contemporary Art, this is a cool Bauhaus-style

NORTH RHINE-WESTPHALIA

bistro with modern and light cuisine that mixes German and Mediterranean flavours and techniques.

Schwarzbrenner (☎ 512 21; Untere Metzgerstrasse 29; mains €16-23; ☺ dinner only, closed Mon) One of Siegen's best restaurants transports diners to Spain and Italy with inventive platters featuring fresh, seasonal ingredients. Nice terrace, too.

Getting There & Away

Direct trains depart for Cologne hourly (€14, 1½ hours) and to Frankfurt (€19.40, 1¾ hours) every two hours. Change in Hagen for Dortmund (€19.40, two hours). Siegen is off the A45 connecting the Ruhrgebiet with Frankfurt and is also easily reached from Cologne via the A4.

AROUND SIEGEN
Freudenberg

☎ 02734 / pop 21,700

About 12km north of Siegen, the little town of Freudenberg would be unremarkable were it not for its stunning **Altstadt**, which boasts immaculate half-timbered houses set up in the 17th-century equivalent of a planned community. Built in rows, these houses all point in the same direction, are approximately the same height and sport the same white façades, the same pattern of wooden beams and the same black-slate roofs. Conceptualised by Duke Johann Moritz of Nassau-Oranien, the area is called *Alter Flecken* (literally 'old borough') and was accorded preservation status in 1966.

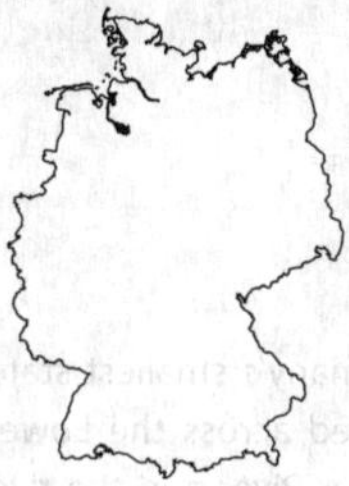

Bremen

CONTENTS

City of Bremen 621
Around Bremen 629

Bremen

Germany's smallest state, Bremen is easy to overlook. It's just two separate flecks of land dotted across the Lower Saxony landscape: industrial Bremerhaven at the mouth of the Weser River and the riverside capital city Bremen, 65km south. The two have been linked politically since 1827, when the mayor of the Hanseatic City of Bremen cleverly snapped up the river delta from Hanover and turned it into a satellite harbour. The port and terminals at Bremerhaven now rank among the country's most important economically, but as a waterside leisure experience, the 404-sq-km 'two-city-state' is often dismissed as Hamburg-lite.

Not true! More compact and easier to get a grip on than its northerly big sister, Bremen is a perfect example of what's called *schön klein* – the German equivalent of 'good things coming in small packages'. The picturesque red-brick city will take you from an Art Nouveau street to a district of winding medieval lanes and an alternative, cool but friendly student quarter, all within minutes. Locals like to boast that Bremen's several science centres, impressive rhododendron park and unusual one-bedroom hotel are all features that Hamburg lacks, while a tight cluster of art galleries near the centre reinforces the small-is-beautiful theme.

Even in the harbour of Bremerhaven, where the ships and port terminal are undeniably on a grand scale, visitors find they can pack a manageable number of sightseeing attractions – including the fabulous German Maritime Museum and the container terminal's viewing platform – into a quick trip.

And when it comes unique brand images, Bremen certainly owes a huge debt to fairy-tale writers the Brothers Grimm. Everywhere you move, the picture of four animals riding piggyback – *The Town Musicians of Bremen* – greets you, staring out from statues, souvenirs and nearly every shop window.

BREMEN

HIGHLIGHTS

★ German Maritime Museum

- **Historic Quarter**
  Explore the medieval Schnoor district (p623)

- **Grand Designs**
  Appreciate the marvellous architecture along Art Nouveau Böttcherstrasse (p622)

- **Wining**
  Down a Beck's beer on the Schlachte promenade (p627)

- **Off-beat Experience**
  Peek in at the blackened mummies in the Dom St Petri's lead cellar (p622)

- **Boat-spotting**
  Admire the ship shapes at the Deutsches Schifffahrtsmuseum (German Maritime Museum; p630)

Schlachte ★ ★ Dom St Petri
Böttcherstrasse ★
★ Schnoor

- POPULATION: 668,000
- AREA: 404 SQ KM

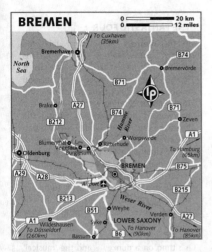

BREMEN
0 ————— 20 km
0 ————— 12 miles

North Sea

To Cuxhaven (35km)
Bremerhaven
B74
Bremervörde
B71
Brake
A27
B74
B71
B212
Hamme River
Zeven
A1
Worpswede
Blumenthal
Vegesack
Burglesum
Ritterhude
To Hamburg (65km)
Oldenburg
BREMEN
B75
A29
A28
Airport
B215
B213
Weser River
B51
Weyhe
Verden
A27
A1
Wildeshausen
Syke
LOWER SAXONY
To Düsseldorf (260km)
Bassum
B6
To Hanover (90km)
To Hanover (85km)

CITY OF BREMEN

☎ 0421 / pop 550,000

The donkey, the dog, the cat and the rooster – if your sole reference point for this metropolis on the Weser River is the fairy tale of four animals on their way here to make their fortune as musicians, then seeing it up close will simply reinforce that truth is more spectacular than fiction. This energetic Hanseatic city has an unexpectedly impressive old town centre, a lovely maritime quarter of snug, winding streets and a once-in-a-lifetime Art Nouveau laneway running from the market to the sea. Bremen citizens, young and old, mingle happily in the restaurants and bars along the waterfront Schlachte promenade and in the more alternative Viertel (district).

And when the wind blows from the southwest you can sniff the town's most famous export, as the hops from the Beck's brewery waft over town.

History

Bremen was known as the 'Rome of the North' during its early history, because after its establishment by Charlemagne in 787, it was used as the main base for Christianising Scandinavia. The city grew by leaps and bounds in the following centuries and by 1358 was ready to join the Hanseatic League. In 1646 it became a free imperial city, a status it still enjoys today as a 'Free Hanseatic City'.

Orientation

Bremen's compact centre is easy to get around on foot. The Altstadt sits just north of the Weser River, south of Wallanlagen park, which in turn is south of the Hauptbahnhof (central train station), and the central bus and tram stations.

To reach the Markt (square) from the stations, bear south (roughly straight ahead as you come out of the train station). Take Bahnhofstrasse to Herdentorsteinweg, continue along the pedestrianised Sögestrasse for another few minutes to Obernstrasse, before turning left (east) into the Markt. The Schlachte promenade lies southwest of the Markt, the Art Nouveau Böttcherstrasse directly south, the Schnoor maritime quarter to the southeast and the art galleries and Ostertorviertel to the east along Ostertorsteinweg.

Information

Branch post office (Bahnhofplatz 21; ☻ 9am-8pm Mon-Fri, 9am-1pm Sat)
Internet Center Bremen (☎ 277 6600; Bahnhofplatz 22-28; €5 per hr)
Main post office (Domsheide 15; ☻ 7am-7pm Mon-Fri, 9am-1pm Sat)
North–West Entdecker Card (€39 for three days)
All tourist offices sell this card, good for unlimited public transport and museum entry.
Police (☎ 3621; Am Wall 201)
Reisebank (Hauptbahnhof)
Schnell und Sauber (Am Dobben 134; €3.50 per wash; ☻ 7am-10pm) Laundry. There's another branch at Vor dem Steintor 105.
Tourist Info Bremen (☎ 01805-101 030, charged at €0.12 per minute; www.bremen-tourism.de; Hauptbahnhof; ☻ 9.30am-6pm Mon-Wed, 9.30am-8pm Thu & Fri, 9.30am-4pm Sat & Sun)
Tourist Info Stands Liebfrauenkirchhof (near the Rathaus; ☻ year-round); Schlachte promenade (☻ Apr-Oct only)

Sights & Activities

MARKT

With tall, old buildings looming over a relatively small space, Bremen's Markt is one of the most striking in northern Germany. The twin towers of the 1200-year-old **Dom St Petri** (St Petri cathedral; see also p622) dominate the northeastern edge, beside the ornate, imposing **Rathaus** (town hall). Although the Rathaus was first erected in 1410, the Weser Renaissance balcony in the middle – crowned by three gables – was added between 1595 and 1618. There are **tours** (in German) of the impressive interior (see Tours p623).

To the northwest of the Markt are the church spires of the **Kirche Unser Lieben Frauen**. Its crypt features some interesting 14th-century murals. Down the western side of the Markt is a row of stately town houses containing bars and restaurants, where you can peer over your coffee at the modern **Haus der Bürgerschaft** (State Assembly; 1966) opposite. The geometrical steel-and-concrete structure has artfully moulded pieces of metal attached to its façade, helping it to blend in with the square's historic feel.

Bremen boasts that the 13m-high **statue of Knight Roland** (1404) before the Rathaus is Germany's tallest representation of this just, freedom-loving knight. However, it's the statue tucked away on the Rathaus' western side, towards the tourist pavilion, that people more readily identify with this city. Sculptor Gerhard Marcks has cast the **Town Musicians of Bremen** (1951) in their famous pose – one on top of the other, on the shoulders of the donkey (see also the boxed text, opposite).

BÖTTCHERSTRASSE

If Bremen's Markt is remarkable, nearby Böttcherstrasse (1931 onwards) is a one-off. An Art Nouveau/Art Deco laneway with a golden entrance, staggered red-brick walls and a wondrously glass-decorated spiral staircase, it's almost comparable with New York's Chrysler Building or London's Eltham Palace as a memorable example of those architectural styles.

This 110m-long street was commissioned by Ludwig Roselius, a merchant who made his fortune by inventing decaffeinated coffee, founding the company Hag in the first half of the 20th century. Most of the design was by Bernhard Hoetger (1874–1959), including the **Lichtbringer** (Bringer of Light; 1936), the golden relief at the northern entrance, showing a scene from the Apocalypse with the Archangel Michael fighting a dragon.

Hoetger was also responsible for the **Haus Atlantis** (now the Bremen Hilton, see p626), with its show-stopping, multicoloured, glass-walled spiral staircase, as well as the **Paula Becker-Modersohn Haus**, with its rounded edges and wall reliefs. Inside the latter is a **museum** (☎ 336 5077; adult/concession €4/2, including admission to the Roselius Haus; ☼ 11am-6pm Tue-Sun) showcasing the art of the early

---

THE FANTASTIC FOUR

In the Brothers Grimm fairy tale, the *Bremer Stadtmusikanten* (Town Musicians of Bremen) never actually make to it Bremen, but having arrived in the city, you might enjoy a quick reminder of what the fuss is about. Starting with a donkey, four overworked, ageing animals fearing the knacker's yard or the Sunday roasting pan run away from their owners. They head for Bremen intending, like many young dreamers, to make their fortune as musicians.

On their first night on the road, they decide to shelter in a house. It turns out to be occupied by robbers, as our heroes discover when they climb on the donkey to peer through the window. The sight of a rooster atop a cat, perched on a dog, which is sitting on a donkey – and the 'musical' accompaniment of braying, barking, meowing and crowing – startles the robbers so much, they flee. The animals remain and make their home 'where you'll probably still find them today'.

From May to early October, this story is charmingly re-enacted in Bremen's **Markt** (☼ noon & 1.30pm Sun). Viewing is free.

---

expressionist painter also known as Paula Modersohn-Becker (1876–1907), a member of the Worpswede artists colony (for details, see p629). Sculptures by Hoetger can also be found upstairs in the museum.

The Paula Becker-Modersohn Haus is connected via a walkway to the **Roselius Haus** (1588), which Hoetger worked around. Inside is Roselius' private collection of medieval art, including paintings by Lucas Cranach the Elder.

Outside, the **Glockenspiel** (Carillon; ☼ hourly noon-6pm May-Dec; noon, 3pm & 6pm Jan-Apr) chimes while a panel honouring great sea explorers, such as Leif Eriksson and Christopher Columbus, rotates.

Böttcherstrasse is all the more enjoyable because it survived a Nazi destruction order. Roselius convinced the authorities to save the 'degenerate' street as a future warning of the depravity of 'cultural Bolshevism'.

DOM ST PETRI

As with Kirche Unser Lieben Frauen, what's most interesting inside this cathedral is underground. Its **Bleikeller** (Lead Cellar; ☎ 365 0441; adult/concession €1.40/1; ⏱ 10am-5pm Mon-Fri, 10am-2pm Sat, noon-5pm Sun Easter-Oct) is certainly unusual and rather macabre, for here you can spy eight mummified corpses in open coffins. The figures include a Swedish countess, a soldier with his mouth opened in a silent scream, and a student who died in a duel in 1705. Nearer the door are a chimpanzee and a cat, whose corpses were put in the cellar to study why corpses do not decompose here. It's uncomfortable viewing, though, and not for the squeamish.

The Bleikeller has its own entrance, to the south of the main door. The 265 steps to the top of the cathedral's **tower** (adult/child €1/0.50; ⏱ Easter-Oct) can also be climbed.

DER SCHNOOR

This is the sort of waterfront cluster of winding cobbled streets found in many a port. The difference is that in Bremen it's not a red-light district (well, not any more) but rather a quaint maze of restaurants, cafés and boutique shops that run the gamut from the interesting to the twee.

The name Schnoor is north German for 'string', and refers to the way the 15th- and 16th-century cottages – once inhabited by fisherfolk, traders and craftspeople – are 'strung' along the alleyways. Even during the day, when overrun with tour groups, this is a fascinating place to explore. At night the crowds thin out, despite the excellent restaurants.

BECK'S BREWERY

You have to feel a little sorry for Beck's. Bottled lagers aren't as fashionable as in the 1990s, and its once distinctive brand name is now more readily associated with a certain footballer playing for Real Madrid. Still, the company is far from crying into its – light, refreshing – beer (also available on tap), and is happy to show you what's pumping out that smell of hops over Bremen during a two-hour tour of the **Beck's Brewery** (☎ 5094 5555; Am Deich; tours €3; ⏱ hourly 10am-5pm Tue-Sat, 10am-3pm Sun). A tour in English leaves at 1.30pm daily. Take tram No 1 or 8 to Am Brill. *Prost!*

MUSEUMS

The **Übersee Museum** (Overseas Museum; ☎ 3619176; Bahnhofplatz 13; adult/concession €5/2.50; ⏱ 10am-6pm Tue-Sun) has long been renowned for its dazzling collection of exotic artefacts brought back from abroad, but it's having a bit of a makeover. A new permanent exhibition will look at the life of oceans, taking its place besides displays ranging from Inuit life to outer space, via a 19th-century Bremen shop. (The restaurant here is also good.)

If you're an art-lover, consider a visit to Bremen's rather short Kulturmeile (Cultural Mile). There's an excellent modern art museum or **Kunsthalle** (☎ 329 080; www.kunsthalle-bremen.de; Am Wall 207; adult/concession €5/2.50, during special exhibitions €8/6; ⏱ 10am-10pm Tue, 10am-6pm Wed-Sun) and two other galleries devoted to Bremen-born lads. The **Gerhard Marcks Haus** (☎ 327 200; Am Wall 208; adult/concession €3/2; ⏱ 10am-6pm Tue-Sun) showcases sculpture, while the **Wilhelm Wagenfeld Haus** (☎ 338 8116; Am Wall 209; adult/concession €5/3; ⏱ 3-9pm Tue, 10am-6pm Wed-Sun) features household objects from this Bauhaus luminary.

OTHER ATTRACTIONS

Bremen has a strong aerospace industry, and space buffs can explore a life-size International Space Station module on a tourist office tour of the **Centre of Aerospace Technology** (adult/concession €16.50/13.50; ⏱ 5pm Fri, 11am, 1pm & 3pm Sat, 11.30am Sun Mar-Dec, 11am & 3pm Sat Jan & Feb), south of the centre. Alternatively, there's the huge new **Space Park Bremen** (☎ 840 000; www.space-park-bremen.de; adult/concession €22/18; ⏱ 10am-6pm Tue-Sun), with simulated space flights and the like. Space is also on the agenda at the eye-catching, oyster-shaped **Universum Science Center** (⏱ 334 60; www.usc-bremen.de; Wiener Strasse 2; adult/child €10/6; 9am-4.30pm Mon-Fri, 9am-7.30pm Wed, 9am-5.30pm Sat & Sun), where you can make virtual trips to the stars, as well as to the ocean floor or the centre of the earth.

Those looking for more rustic appeal could head to the city's typical Dutch **windmill** (Am Wall; admission free; 9.30am-midnight May-Sept, 10am-11pm Oct-Apr) and its restaurant. Plant-lovers shouldn't miss a trip to **botanika** (Rhododendronpark; adult/child €9/6; ⏱ 9am-6pm) and its replicated landscapes from Borneo, the Himalayas and Japan.

Tours

The tourist office organises a plethora of tours, including: city **walking tours** (adult/child under 14 €6.50/free; ⏱ 2pm daily & 11am Sat May-Sep)

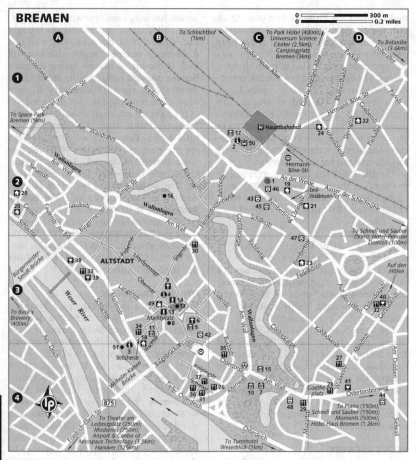

BREMEN

and tours inside the **Rathaus** (adult/child under 14 €4/2; 11am, noon, 3pm & 4pm Mon-Sat, 11am & noon Sun). Contact the Tourist Info Bremen at the Hauptbahnhof for walking tours and the stand on Liebfrauenkirchhof for Rathaus tours. Tours are in German, but English-language guides are available on request for groups on the walking tours.

Hal Över Schreiber Reederei (321 229; www .hal-oever.de) operates a 75-minute **Weser and harbour tour** (adult/child €8/6) up to five times daily between April and October. The meeting point is the Martinianleger (Martini landing) near the south end of Böttcherstrasse. The tourist office has a full schedule of cruises from candlelight cruises, weekend party cruises and cruises to the islands of Helgo-

land and Sylt. Scheduled services also ply the river (see Getting There & Away p628).

Sleeping
BUDGET
The tourist office runs a free same-day hotel room reservation service or you can book a selection of hotels using its website. For private rooms, contact **Bed & Breakfast Bremen** (536 0771).

Bremer Backpacker Hostel (223 8057; www .bremer-backpacker-hostel.de; Emil Waldmann Strasse 5-6; dm €19-23, s/d €30/50) This spotless modern hostel has minimalist bedrooms but plush shared amenities, including a kitchen, laundry, lounge and dining room. Best of all are the extra 'comfort' bathrooms, where you

INFORMATION		
Internet Center Bremen	1	C2
Tourist Info Bremen	2	C2
Tourist Info Stand	3	B4
Tourist Info Stand	4	B3
SIGHTS & ACTIVITIES	**(pp621-3)**	
Bleikeller	5	B3
Dom St Petri	6	B3
Dommuseum	(see 6)	
Gerhard Marcks Haus	7	C4
Glockenspiel	(see 11)	
Haus Atlantis	(see 18)	
Haus der Bürgerschaft	8	B3
Kirche Unser Lieben Frauen	9	B3
Kunsthalle	10	C4
Paula Becker-Modersohn Haus	11	B3
Rathaus	12	B3
Roselius Haus	(see 11)	
Statue of Knight Roland	13	B3
Town Musicians of Bremen Statue	14	B3
Wilhelm Wagenfeld-Haus	15	C4
Windmill	16	B2
Übersee Museum	17	C2

SLEEPING	(pp624-6)	
Bremen Hilton	18	B3
Bremer Backpacker Hostel	19	C2
DJH Hostel	20	A2
Hochzeitshaus	(see 36)	
Hotel Bremer Haus	21	C2
Hotel Bölts am Park	22	D1
Hotel Lichtsinn	23	C3
Hotel Residence	24	D1
Hotel Stadt Bremen	25	A2

EATING	(pp626-7)	
Aioli	26	C4
Bio Biss	27	D4
Café Engel	28	D4
Casablanca	29	C4
Energie Café	30	B3
Katzen Café	31	B4
Malaysia	32	D3
Moto	33	A3
Ratskeller	(see 12)	
Restaurant Flett	34	B3
Salomon's	35	C4
Schnoor Teestübchen	36	B4
Schröter's	37	B4

DRINKING	(p627)	
2raumlounge	(see 40)	
Camarillo	38	A3
Cargo	39	A3
Carnaval	40	D3
Hofmeister	(see 40)	
Litfass	41	D4
Paulaner	(see 38)	

ENTERTAINMENT	(pp627-8)	
Die Glocke	42	B3
La Viva	43	C2
Lagerhaus	44	D4
Neue Welt	45	C2
Rosigen Zeiten	(see 43)	
Schauspielhaus	(see 48)	
Shagall	46	C2
Stubu	47	C3
Theater am Goetheplatz	48	C4

SHOPPING	(p628)	
Hachez	49	B3

TRANSPORT	(pp628-9)	
Central Bus Station	50	C2

OTHER		
Martinianleger	51	B4

can hire a towel and soap and lock yourself in the tub – the backpackers' equivalent of a hotel spa.

Hotel Bölts am Park (☎ 346 110; fax 341 227; Slevogtstrasse 23; s €35-55, d €75-85) This family-run hotel has oodles of character, from the wonderfully old-fashioned breakfast hall to its cosy rooms (some with hall showers and toilets). It's in a leafy residential neighbourhood behind the Hauptbahnhof and is popular, so book ahead.

Hotel-Pension Domizil (☎ 347 8147; fax 342 376; Graf-Moltke-Strasse 42; s €40-50, d €60-75; P) The breakfast room is rustic and sweet, but the bedrooms not so outstanding. However, it does provide decent comfort for the price.

Campingplatz Bremen (☎ 212 002; fax 219 857; Am Stadtwaldsee 1; adult/site/car €4.50/5/2) This camp site is north of the centre, fairly close to the university. Take tram No 5 or 8 to Kulenkampffallee, then bus No 28 to Campingplatz.

Another recommendation:

DJH hostel (☎ 171 369; fax 171 102; Kalkstrasse 6;) The Jugendgästehaus Bremen is due to reopen in the second half of 2004 after major renovations. Ring for prices.

MID-RANGE
Hotel Residence (☎ 348 710; www.hotelresidence.de; Hohlenstrasse 42; s €65-85, d €90-110; P) This century-old terrace has been converted to a charming hotel. The cheaper rooms are a bit snug, but the best doubles – Nos 12 and 22 – have balconies overlooking a quiet street. A sauna, solarium, bar, dining room and London black cab complete the package.

Hotel Lichtsinn (☎ 368 070; www.hotel-lichtsinn .com; Rembertistrasse 11; s/d €80/105; P) Having hosted NASA astronauts and remaining a favourite with thespians, the Lichtsinn is remarkably posh for a three-star hotel. Most rooms have vaguely Regency-style furniture, many with wooden floorboards and Persian carpets. One even features an old German-style four-poster bed.

Hotel Bremer Haus (☎ 329 40; bremerhaus@ online.de; Löningstrasse 16-20; s €75-85, d €90-110; P) Maybe the sticker on the door stating this is one of Germany's 400 best hotels is overdoing it a little, for the rooms are comfortable but boring. You couldn't quibble with the location, though – quiet, yet minutes from the train station.

Turmhotel Weserblick (☎ 949 410; fax 949 4110; Osterdeich 53; s €70-80, d €85-100; P) It looks like an atmospheric old pile from the exterior, but inside the hotel has renovated and extremely spacious rooms, with bare floorboards and Persian carpets. The tower rooms overlooking the river have a kitchen and are more expensive. Take the tram to Sielwall.

The owners of the Weserblick have two others in the same mould (bookable through the same number). There's the central, more upmarket **Hotel Stadt Bremen** (Heinkenstrasse 3-5; s €80-85, d €95-105; P), where some rooms come with a TV in the bathroom for busy execs and the like, or the cheaper **Hotel Haus Bremen** (Verdener Strasse 47; s €50-60, d €70-80) slightly further out (and east of the centre); take tram No 3 to Verdener Strasse.

THE SMALLEST HOTEL IN THE WORLD...PROBABLY

If you've ever struggled to open a suitcase in a hotel room where you can touch all four walls from your bed, Bremen's claim to having possibly the world's tiniest hotel won't immediately impress you. Small isn't usually beautiful in the world of tourist accommodation; however, hang about, because in the Schnoor quarter's **Hochzeitshaus** (Wedding House; ☎ 0170-461 8333; info@hochzeitshaus-bremen.de; Wüste Stätte 5; 1/2 nights €320/520) it is. Aimed at loved-up couples willing to pay to have an entire hotel to themselves, this renovated medieval house has just one bedroom, occupying the entire upper floor, with a bathroom and whirlpool tub on the level below, and a kitchen beneath (should you really want to come back to earth during your romantic sojourn).

According to the owners, wedding houses were common in medieval cities, because couples coming from the country to get married in the cathedral needed somewhere to stay – and consummate the marriage – before returning home. So as they hang out the 'Do not disturb' sign on their narrow three-storey abode, guests can take extra pleasure in the knowledge that they're carrying on a long tradition.

TOP END

Bremen Hilton (☎ 336 960; info_bremen@hilton.com; Böttcherstrasse 2; s €135-195, d €160-220; P X) Occupying the Atlantis House in the Art Nouveau Böttcherstrasse and therefore having a phantasmagorical spiral staircase out back means this is unlike any other in the ubiquitous chain. It's even trying to break out of the identikit mould with newly renovated, light-coloured and stylish rooms.

Park Hotel (☎ 34080; www.park-hotel-bremen.de; Im Bürgerpark; s €155-220, d €205-275; P X) This domed mansion surrounded by parkland and overlooking a lake is extravagance itself. There are excellent spa and beauty facilities, and as in the famous Ritz-Carlton in Singapore, there's a bathroom where you can watch the world below through the window beside the tub.

Eating
TOWN CENTRE

Energie Café (☎ 277 2510; cnr Sögestrasse & Am Wall; mains €5.50-12; 9am-9pm or later, Mon-Sat) The food's good, including cut-price lunches, but it's the little touches that make this half retro, half futuristic café run by utility company SWB Enordia so enjoyable. A classic movie plays in a corner, and you receive a witty brochure reminiscent of the classic 'Point it' picture phrasebook on paying.

Restaurant Flett (☎ 320 995; Böttcherstrasse 3-5; mains €6.50-10.50) If you don't like crowds, it's best to test this restaurant during a late lunch. Its light touch means a gentle introduction to local specialities, like *Labskaus* (a hash of beef or pork with potatoes,

onion and herring) or *Knipp* (fried hash and oats). Plus the photo-bedecked room itself is great.

Ratskeller (☎ 321 676; Marktplatz; mains €11-17) Normally you choose wine to match your food. Here, in this atmospheric cellar restaurant, that's reversed. Regional and international cuisine accompanies your pick of an award-winning selection of more than 650 different wines. The high-ceiling room itself has inspired a poem by Heinrich Heine, and even a book.

Salomon's (☎ 244 1771; Ostertorstrasse 11-13; mains €12-19) The modern designer restaurant in this eatery/bar/club complex in a former law courts building is posh enough to impress a business partner or date. Alternatively, there are a few bench seats where you won't feel uncomfortable treating just yourself. Food ranges from Italian to Japanese (see also Drinking p627).

SCHLACHTE

Moto (☎ 302 113; Schlachte 22; mains €4.50-11) A minimalist Japanese interior marks out this restaurant from some of the more carnival, neon-lit places along this strip. The cuisine is broadly Asian, with sushi sets and tofu joined by dim sum and Malaysian noodles.

SCHNOOR

Aioli (☎ 323 839; Schnoor 3-4; mains €7.50-14, tapas €3.50-8.50) This buzzy Spanish restaurant and tapas bar serves truly delicious food. Eat upstairs if you prefer to take in the atmosphere of this medieval fisherman's house in a less hectic environment.

Katzen Café (☎ 326 621; Schnoor 38; mains €6.50-15) Festooned with large pots of white flowers and red tablecloths, there's a kind of French, Moulin Rouge tone to this basement restaurant and its sunken, open-air terrace. Oysters, bouillabaisse, Norwegian wild salmon and other fish are all available, or plump for the €25 set menu.

Schröter's (☎ 326 677; Schnoor 13; mains €11-17) A modern bistro, with artful decoration, Schröter's is known for its antipasti and has plenty of Mediterranean mains, from risotto to fish. The Toulouse-Lautrec upstairs, decorated with plenty of copies of the painter's pictures, is more formal.

DAS VIERTEL

This arty, student neighbourhood is where to head for cheap eats.

Piano (☎ 785 46; Fehrfeld 64; meals €5.50-11) A popular meeting place where students mooch over coffee and free newspapers, Piano serves a range of down-to-earth fare from pizzas to the occasional apricot curry. The eclectic room combines Italian garden-style statues with a lovely Art Deco bar.

Café Engel (☎ 766 15; Ostertorsteinweg 31; meals €5.50-10) Housed in a former pharmacy, this is a popular hang-out that matches black-and-white tiled floors with dark wood furniture and offers two-course daily specials.

The narrow courtyard off Auf den Höfen in das Viertel has several restaurants, including **Malaysia** (☎ 769 77; Auf den Höfen; mains €9-18). A few years ago, the *Feinschmecker* gastronomic magazine named this the best Asian restaurant in Germany, but when we visited it was all but deserted. Our verdict? Delicious, but possibly too spicy for German tastes. Still, when the restaurant is empty, the service is attentive.

Also recommended:

Casablanca (☎ 326 429; Ostertorsteinweg 59; mains €6.50-9.50) Famed for its Sunday brunch.

Bio Biss (☎ 703 044; Wulwesstrasse 18; meals €5.50-7.50) Organic vegetarian and meat dishes.

CAFÉS

Schnoor Teestübchen (☎ 326 091; Wüste Stätte 1) If you can ignore the hint of twee tourist shop about it, here's a great place to indulge in Frisian tea-drinking rituals – putting huge crystals of sugar into your cup with tongs or twirling honey into your char. Some local blends are wonderfully smooth, too.

Drinking

Bremen has scores more bars and clubs than we'd ever have space for, so check listings mags *Bremer* (€2.30), *Prinz* (€1), *Bremen 4U* (free) or *Big* (free). For drinking, however, the choice is basically threefold: the newer and mainstream Schlachte promenade; the convivial, slightly more alternative Auf den Höfen; or the studenty, quite grungy Ostertorsteinweg.

Cargo (☎ 169 5599; Schlachte 15-18) This enormous, modern bistro is mega-popular, but you're best sticking to beer, cocktails or some rather fine wine, as even on the kindest interpretation the food is overpriced.

Camarillo (☎ 169 5454; Schlachte 30) One of the less lairy bars on Schlachte, this is an elegant venue with a cool-looking but relaxed crowd with a chilled urban vibe.

Paulaner (☎ 169 0694; Schlachte 30) The trad German option along the promenade, with lots of local beer from which to choose. Service can be slow, however.

Hofmeister (☎ 703 692; Auf den Höfen) Grab yourself a perch in this cocktail bar and restaurant's 1st-floor Wintergarten and watch the world go by below. There are DJs on Friday and Saturday nights.

2raumlounge (☎ 745 77; Auf den Höfen) Despite its trendy 1970s retro-décor, 2raumlounge isn't as intimidatingly hip as it looks. The eclectic mix of beautiful people, uni students and even the occasional suit gives it a relaxed air.

Carnaval (☎ 704 539; Auf den Höfen) A large (not quite as large as Rio's) figure of Christ with arms extended watches over the caipirinha drinkers in this colourful Brazilian bar.

Litfass (☎ 703 292; Ostertorsteinweg 22) Like a little drinking capsule, this dimly lit, long, thin bar is crammed and popular. In summer, there's also the added attraction of a leafy spot on the pavement.

Salomon's (☎ 244 1771; Ostertorstrasse 11-13) There's a pale orange glow over the leather lounge chairs and stools for a mixed crowd of older after-workers and young hip things (see also Eating p626).

Entertainment
DISCOS & CLUBS

Two of Bremen's top clubs are former cinemas. Also look out for special summer club nights atop the city's parking garages – the latest thing.

BREMEN

Modernes (☎ 505 553; Neustadtwall 28) South of the river in Neustadt, this converted older movie theatre also hosts live music. The centrepiece is the domed roof that can be opened to let in some much-needed air towards the end of the evening – a highlight for the attractive crowd.

Moments (☎ 780 07; Vor dem Steintor 65) Way out east on Ostertorsteinweg, this is little more than a long bar with a small dance floor attached. And yet it has some interesting offerings, including Turkish pop.

La Viva (cnr Rembertiring & Auf der Brake) A recently transformed multiplex, this massive 1400-sq-m underground space is has one main dance floor and two smaller rooms. People will queue patiently in the rain to get into one of its dance-chart party evenings.

La Viva is on a street of wall-to-wall clubs, including the packed **Stubu** (☎ 326 398; Rembertiring 21), a small, low-ceilinged, red-tiled basement club that is open every night; **Rosigen Zeiten** (☎ 327 787; Rembertiring 1); and the popular, but very young **Neue Welt** (☎ 277 1340; Rembertiring 7/9). These all have varied programmes ranging from indie pop to house, so check weekly listings.

CULTURAL CENTRES

Schlachthof (☎ 377 750; Findorffstrasse 51) In a 19th-century slaughterhouse northwest of the Hauptbahnhof, this place has ethnic and world-music concerts and also theatre, cabaret and variety, complemented by exhibits and a café.

Lagerhaus (☎ 702 168; Schildstrasse 12-19) As in many cultural centres in Germany, despite the enviable schedule of theatre, dance parties, movies, live concerts and more, this mainly functions as a great place for a drink.

THEATRE & CLASSICAL MUSIC

The *Frankfurter Allgemeine Zeitung* rates Bremen's theatre scene as one of Germany's liveliest. The tourist office has further listings and sells tickets.

Die Glocke (☎ 336 699; Domsheide) Bremen's new concert hall is home to its own two orchestras as well as a changing array of visiting orchestras. The acoustics are excellent.

Theater am Leibnizplatz (☎ 500 333; Am Leibnizplatz) The resident, and highly acclaimed, Bremer Shakespeare Company mixes the Bard (in German) with fairy tales and

works by contemporary playwrights like Conor McPherson *(The Weir)*. Take tram No 4, 5 or 6.

Theater am Goetheplatz (☎ 365 30; Goetheplatz) One of the country's most famous film directors, Rainer Werner Fassbinder, spent time honing his craft with this company. The main theatre stages opera, operettas and musicals. In the attached **Schauspielhaus** (☎ 365 3333; Ostertorsteinweg 57a) you'll find updated classics and avant-garde drama. Take tram No 2 or 3 for both venues.

Shopping

It's fun to reacquaint yourself with the fairy tale of *The Town Musicians of Bremen* (see the boxed text on p622) by one of the many English-language editions. Apart from that, the most obvious buy in Bremen is sweets. **Hachez** (☎ 339 8898; Am Markt 1) is a good port of call, as the local purveyor of chocolate and specialities like *Kluten* (peppermint sticks covered in dark chocolate).

Both Böttcherstrasse and the Schnoor Viertel are chock-full of interesting jewellery, from antique silver and oodles of amber to modern designer pieces. Ostertorsteinweg, in Das Viertel, is the place to look for funky streetwear.

There are also two flea markets: one along the north bank of the Weser, roughly between Bürgermeister-Smidt-Brücke and the bridge at Balgebrückstrasse (open 8am to 4pm Saturday year-round), and the other on the Bürgerweide, north of the Hauptbahnhof (open 7am to 2pm most Sundays; check exact dates at the tourist office).

Getting There & Away

AIR

Bremen's small international **airport** (☎ 559 50) is about 3.5km south of the centre and has flights to destinations in Germany and Europe. The airline offices here include low-cost carrier **Air Berlin** (☎ 0421-552 035), **British Airways** (☎ 01805-266 522) and **Lufthansa Airlines** (☎ 01803-803 803).

BOAT

Hal Över Schreiber Reederei (☎ 321 229; www.hal-oever.de) operates scheduled services along the Weser between April and September. Boats from Bremen to Bremerhaven (one way/return €13/21, 3½ hours), with numerous stops en route, depart at 8.30am every

Wednesday, Thursday and Saturday, and 9.30am on Sunday. Shorter trips ending at Brake (€8.50/14, 2½ hours) depart on Tuesday at 12.30pm. Students and children pay half-price.

BUS
Eurolines (☎ 040 247 160) runs from Bremen to Amsterdam (one way/return €37.50/57.50, five hours) and onwards to London (€68/110, 18 hours, including transfers).

CAR & MOTORCYCLE
The A1 (from Hamburg to Osnabrück) and the A27/A7 (Bremerhaven to Hanover) intersect in Bremen. The city is also on the B6 and B75. All major car-rental agencies have branches at the airport, including **Avis** (☎ 558 055), **Hertz** (☎ 555 350) and **Budget** (☎ 597 0018).

TRAIN
Bremen has hourly IC train connections to Dortmund (€34.50, 1¾ hours) and Frankfurt (€86, 3¾ hours). Trains to Hamburg (€16.50, 1½ hours) leave several times hourly. For Berlin (€69.50, 3½ hours), change in Hanover.

Getting Around
Tram No 6 travels between the Hauptbahnhof and the airport (€1.90, 20 minutes). A **taxi** (☎ 140 14, 144 33) costs about €12.

Verkehrsverbund Bremen/Niedersachsen (☎ 01 805-826 826) operates buses and trams. Main hubs are in front of the Hauptbahnhof and at Domsheide near the Rathaus. Short trips cost €0.80, while a €1.90 ticket covers most of the Bremen city area. Four-trip tickets are €5.80 and the Tageskarte (Day Pass) €4.60.

Bremen is a bicycle-friendly town, with lots of specially designated bike paths. The **Fahrradstation** (☎ 302 114) just outside the Hauptbahnhof has bikes for €7.50 for 24 hours and €17.50 for three days, plus a €25 deposit (bring your passport).

AROUND BREMEN
Bremen-Nord
The communities comprising Bremen-Nord – Burglesum, Vegesack and Blumenthal – have retained more of their working maritime identity than Bremen proper. Old traditions are still alive in these villages on the Weser River, where merchant ships were built and hardy whalers set out for the Arctic.

Sightseeing attractions include the **Tall Ship 'Deutschland'** (☎ 658 7373; Friedrich-Klippert-Strasse 1, Vegesack; adult/child €1.50/1.10; ⏱ 11.30am-5.30pm Tue-Fri, 10am-6pm Sat & Sun May-Sep, 10am-5pm Sat & Sun Oct-Apr), a restored, fully rigged windjammer still used as a training ship for sailors and as a museum. It lies at anchor in the mouth of the Lesum River in Vegesack.

To get to Bremen-Nord, take the Stadt-Express train from Bremen's Hauptbahnhof to Bahnhof Vegesack.

Worpswede
☎ 04792 / pop 9000
Readers of 1903 monograph *Worpswede* by leading German writer and poet Rainer Maria Rilke might be a little surprised to learn that the artistic colony profiled therein has had such a long-lasting legacy. However, as the continued density of studios and galleries in Worpswede shows, this pretty Niedersachsen village near Bremen continues to cast its spell on artists from all fields.

To be more accurate, it's the barren, melancholic landscape around Worpswede that has attracted writers and artists down the years. Dramatic clouds and moody light over the **Teufelsmoor** (Devil's Moor) peat bog and the 55m-tall **Weyerberg sand dune** at its heart provided the inspiration for Fritz Mackensen, Otto Modersohn, Fritz Overbeck, Heinrich Vogeler and Hans am Ende, the members of the original 1889 colony.

Gaining fame through their exhibition at the Glaspalast in Munich in 1895, these five soon found themselves joined by others, including the future co-creator of Bremen's Böttcherstrasse, Bernhard Hoetger, Rilke himself and Paula Modersohn-Becker, who is now buried in the village cemetery. (For more on Hoetger and Modersohn-Becker see p622.)

The creative heart of the colony was the **Barkenhof** (Ostendorfer Strasse 10), a half-timbered structure remodelled in Art Nouveau style by its owner Heinrich Vogeler. Vogeler's Art Nouveau **train station** is also worth viewing. The rail line closed in 1978, and the structure is now a restaurant. The **Grosse Kunstschau** (☎ 1302; Lindenallee 3; adult/concession €2.50/1.50; ⏱ 10am-6pm) shows works by original colony members.

The **Worpswede tourist office** (☎ 950 121; info@ worpswede.de; Bergstrasse 13; ☺ 9am-1pm & 2-5pm Mon-Fri, 10am-3pm Sat & Sun, restricted hours in winter) can suggest walks and cycling routes, including the 20km signposted Teufelsmoor–Rundweg bike route. The moors surrounding Worpswede are an important wetland for wild geese, ducks, cranes and other birds.

GETTING THERE & AROUND
To travel the 30km to Worpswede from Bremen, take bus No 670 from the central bus station, which makes the 50-minute trip about every 1½ hours. **Personenschiffahrt Ruth Haferkamp** (☎ 04404-3514) offers boat trips from Bremen-Vegesack (one way/return €10.25/14, 2½ hours) via the Lesum and Hamme Rivers at 9.15am every Wednesday and Sunday from May to September. From late June to early August, there's an additional boat on Thursday. You can always take the bus back to Bremen.

Fahrradladen Eckhard Eyl (☎ 4301; Finddorfstrasse 28) hires out bikes.

BREMERHAVEN
☎ 0471 / pop 130,000
Bremerhaven is a boy's-own adventure for anyone who likes industrial machinery and has dreamt of running away to sea. The city *is* its port, where one of the world's largest and most modern container terminals handles nearly 1.3 million crates annually. Year-round, you can climb the viewing platform near the terminal in the North Harbour to watch ships berth and the accompanying giant hive of activity.

Alternatively, soak up the atmosphere as international crews swarm all over town. More than six million emigrants passed this way in the 19th and 20th centuries on their way to new homes in the USA and other countries.

ORIENTATION
To reach the centre, turn right out of the train station, then left almost immediately into Bismarckstrasse. Continue until Elbinger Platz, where you need to head diagonally right (northwest) into Columbusstrasse. The tourist office is in the radar tower you see to your left as you approach the Deutsches Schifffahrtsmuseum. The information pavilion runs parallel to Columbusstrasse, taking a right turn off

the street. Alternatively, take bus No 501, 509 or 511.

INFORMATION
Bremerhaven tourist office (☎ 946 4610; touristik@ bremerhaven.de; Van-Ronzelen-Strasse 2; ☺ 8am-4pm Mon-Fri, 8am-6pm in summer)

Information pavilion (☎ 430 00; Columbus-Center, Obere Bürger 17; ☺ 9.30am-6pm Mon-Wed, 9.30am-8pm Thu & Fri, 9.30am-4pm Sat)

SIGHTS & ACTIVITIES
Bremerhaven's main draw is the magnificent **Deutsches Schifffahrtsmuseum** (German Maritime Museum; ☎ 482 070; Hans-Scharoun-Platz 1; adult/concession €4/2.50; ☺ 10am-6pm daily Apr-Oct, closed Mon Nov-Mar). Documenting the evolution of shipbuilding, its collection of 500 ship models includes whalers, brigantines, three-masters and steamers. Inside, where the museum's floors are made to resemble the decks of a passenger liner, watch out for the reconstruction of the *Bremer Hansekogge*, a merchant boat from 1380, whose hull was partially reassembled over years from pieces rescued from the briny deep. Take bus No 501, 509 or 511.

Another excellent stop is the **Morgenstern Museum** (☎ 201 38; An der Geeste; adult/concession €3.20/2.50; ☺ 10am-6pm Tue-Sun), which brings to life the port's early history with such exhibits as an old harbour pub. It also has a database of emigrants.

Near the tourist office and (climbable) radar tower is an **Auswandereraustelling** (Emigration exhibition; ☎ 308 1608; Deichpromenade; adult/ concession €2.50/1.50; ☺ 10am-6pm Apr-Oct).

Reaching the container terminal's **viewing platform** by public transport is tricky, and it's a long walk. Bus No 512 leaves from Rotersand (bus No 505, 506 or 509 from the train station), but only between 6am and 8am, and 2pm and 3pm. Ask the tourist office about its double-decker Hafenbus (€8), which runs past the viewing platform from April to November.

GETTING THERE & AROUND
Frequent trains from Bremen to Bremerhaven take about one hour (€8.80). By car, Bremerhaven is quickly reached via the A27 from Bremen; get off at the Bremerhaven-Mitte exit. An alternative is a leisurely boat ride from Bremen (see Getting There & Away p628).

Lower Saxony

CONTENTS

Hanover	**633**
History	633
Orientation	634
Information	634
Dangers & Annoyances	635
Sights & Activities	635
Festivals & Events	638
Sleeping	639
Eating	640
Drinking	641
Entertainment	641
Shopping	643
Getting There & Away	643
Getting Around	643
Fairy-Tale Road – South	**643**
Hamelin	644
Bodenwerder	645
Bad Karlshafen	645
Lüneburger Heide	**646**
Celle	646
Bergen-Belsen	650
Lüneburg	651
Around Lüneburg	654
South & East of Hanover	**655**
Hildesheim	655
Braunschweig	657
Wolfenbüttel	662
Wolfsburg	663
Göttingen	666
West of Hanover	**671**
Osnabrück	671
Oldenburg	673
Emden & Around	675
Jever	676
East Frisian Islands	**678**
Wangerooge	679
Spiekeroog	679
Langeoog	679
Baltrum	680
Norderney	680
Juist	681
Borkum	681

From the uplifting grandeur of Hanover's baroque Herrenhäuser Gardens to the sobering fields of Bergen-Belsen, and from the space-age curves of the new Volkswagen cars in Wolfsburg's Autostadt to the fairy-tale medieval curlicues on the houses in Hamelin, Lower Saxony (Niedersachsen), is a veritable potpourri. Tourism authorities like to make much of the many clusters of half-timbered houses you find in the second largest state after Bavaria. It's true that lovers of quaint, historic towns will find themselves in heaven visiting places like Celle, Hildesheim and Wolfenbüttel. However, less publicised treasures, like Daniel Libeskind's archmodern Felix-Nussbaum-Haus in Osnabrück or the world-beating collection of porcelain and knick-knacks at Braunschweig's Herzog Anton Ulrich Museum also have the capacity to move or delight.

As the state capital, Hanover (Hannover) has a no-nonsense reputation as a business-minded host of enormous trade fairs, including Cebit and the Hannover Messe. But even it has an artistic side, with works by French artist and honorary Hanoverian Niki de Saint Phalle dotted across its landscape and museums.

It's not just culture-vultures, however, who will feel happy here. There are plenty of breathtaking destinations for nature lovers and sporty types. You can cycle along the gently rolling banks of the Weser River or journey into the Lüneburg Heath. Further north, there's the chance to canoe along canals or cycle across the flat landscape of Friesland.

HIGHLIGHTS

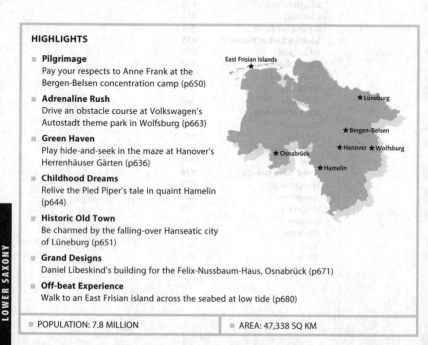

- **Pilgrimage**
  Pay your respects to Anne Frank at the Bergen-Belsen concentration camp (p650)

- **Adrenaline Rush**
  Drive an obstacle course at Volkswagen's Autostadt theme park in Wolfsburg (p663)

- **Green Haven**
  Play hide-and-seek in the maze at Hanover's Herrenhäuser Gärten (p636)

- **Childhood Dreams**
  Relive the Pied Piper's tale in quaint Hamelin (p644)

- **Historic Old Town**
  Be charmed by the falling-over Hanseatic city of Lüneburg (p651)

- **Grand Designs**
  Daniel Libeskind's building for the Felix-Nussbaum-Haus, Osnabrück (p671)

- **Off-beat Experience**
  Walk to an East Frisian island across the seabed at low tide (p680)

East Frisian Islands
★ Lüneburg
★ Bergen-Belsen
★ Osnabrück ★ Hanover ★ Wolfsburg
★ Hamelin

- POPULATION: 7.8 MILLION
- AREA: 47,338 SQ KM

HANOVER

☎ 0511 / pop 520,000

'I feel sorry for him,' was the reaction of Italian prime minister Silvio Berlusconi when he learned in 2003 that, in response to anti-German jokes from himself and another Italian MP, German chancellor Gerhard Schröder had cancelled his holiday on the Adriatic coast and was taking a 'balcony holiday' at home in Hanover instead.

Well, easy on the sympathy, Silvio; it's really not so grim up north. Sure, Hanover's *raison d'être* remains as a host to trade fairs, and wits like TV personality Harald Schmidt (a German David Letterman) will always get laughs dismissing it as 'the Autobahn exit between Göttingen and Walsrode'. However, Lower Saxony's state capital also boasts acres of greenery.

The compact centre, only partially reconstructed in a medieval style after WWII bombing, is adjoined to the east by the Eilenreide forest. The baroque Herrenhäuser Gärten (gardens) and their sparkly new Niki de Saint Phalle Grotto lie to the northwest, while you can enjoy a few museums en route to the southern Maschsee lake.

(All this said, we still bet Herr Schröder was relieved when things were patched up pronto with his beloved Italy.)

HISTORY

Hanover was established around 1100 and became the residence of Heinrich der Löwe later that century. An early Hanseatic city, it developed into a prosperous seat of royalty and a major power by the Reformation.

It has links with Britain through a series of marriages. In 1714 the eldest son of Electress Sophie of Hanover – a granddaughter of James I of England (James VI of Scotland) – ascended the British throne as George I while simultaneously ruling Hanover. This British–German union lasted until 1837.

In 1943, up to 80% of the centre and 50% of the entire city was destroyed by Allied bombing. The rebuilding plan included creating sections of reconstructed half-timbered houses and painstakingly rebuilding the city's prewar gems, such as the Opernhaus (Opera House), the Marktkirche and the Neues Rathaus (New Town Hall).

A few years ago, Hanover was hoping to be at the centre of world attention as the host of Expo 2000. However, only 18 million visitors turned up – less than half the number expected. Despite this, announcements at the Hauptbahnhof continued to welcome visitors to 'Hanover, the Expo City' for several years after the event. Being one of the 12 German host cities for the FIFA football World Cup in 2006 will at least give the city something new to boast about.

ALL THE FUN OF THE TRADE FAIR

Coming to Hanover for a trade fair or *Messe*? You're part of a time-honoured tradition. The first export fair was held in August 1947 in the midst of all the rubble from WWII. As most hotels had been destroyed, the mayor made an appeal to citizens to provide beds for foreign guests. The people did, the money came and it's become a tradition; about a third more beds are available in private flats at fair-time (the only time they're offered) than in hotels.

The pre-eminent fair today is CeBit, a telecommunications and office information gathering that organisers claim is 'the largest trade show of any kind, anywhere in the world'. It's held every March and during the dotcom boom of the late 1990s had as many as 800,000 attendees. (More recent shows have attracted smaller crowds of around half a million visitors.) Another biggie is Hannover Messe, an industrial show in late April.

The Messegelände, the main trade fairgrounds, are in the city's southwest, served by tram/U-Bahn No 8 (and during fair times No 18) as well as IC and ICE trains. Tram/U-Bahn No 6 serves the eastern part of the fairgrounds near the former Expo site.

During major fairs there's a full-service tourist office at the airport and an information pavilion at the fairgrounds, in addition to the main tourist office (see Information, p635).

Pressure on accommodation means you really need to book ahead – and be prepared for phenomenal price hikes too. Indeed some visitors choose to stay instead in Hildesheim, Celle (both of which up their own prices during these times) or even in Hamburg, and commute.

To organise a private room or hotel in Hanover, call ☎ 1234 5555.

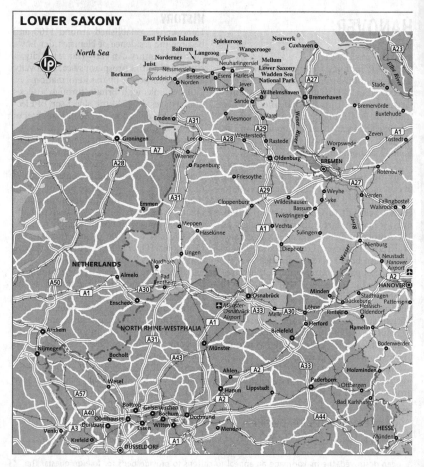

LOWER SAXONY

ORIENTATION

The Hauptbahnhof (central train station) is on the northeastern edge of the city centre. The centre contains one of the largest pedestrianised areas in Germany, focusing on Georgstrasse and Bahnhofstrasse. Bahnhofstrasse heads southwest from the Hauptbahnhof, and Georgstrasse runs west–east from Steintor via the Kröpcke square to Georgsplatz. There's a recently renovated subterranean shopping strip running below Bahnhofstrasse from the Hauptbahnhof to just south of Kröpcke, called the Niki de Saint Phalle Promenade (formerly the rundown Passerelle).

The Herrenhäuser Gärten are about 4km northwest of the city centre. The Messege-

lände, the main trade fairgrounds, are in the city's southwest (see the boxed text All the Fun of the Trade Fair, p633).

INFORMATION
Bookshops
Decius Buchhandlung (☎ 364 7610; Marktstrasse 52)
Schmorl uv Seefeld (☎ 367 50; Bahnhofstrasse 14)

Discount Cards
HannoverCard (€8/12 for 1/3 days) Offers unlimited public transport and discounted or free admission to museums etc.

Emergency
Medical emergency service (☎ 314 044)
Police (Raschplatz) Beneath the overpass on the north side of the Hauptbahnhof.

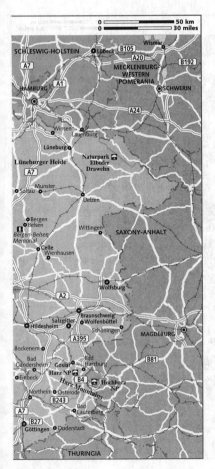

Internet Access
Internet Café Linuxs (☎ 353 0140; Lange Laube 27)

Laundry
Schnell & Sauber (cnr Friesenstrasse & Eichstrasse; ☺ 7am-10pm)

Libraries
Stadtbibliothek (City library; ☎ 1684 2169; Hildesheimer Strasse 29)

Medical Services
Hospital (☎ 304 31; Marienstrasse 37)

Money
There are several ATMs and a late-opening Reisebank in the Hauptbahnhof.

American Express (☎ 363 428; Georgstrasse 54)
Commerzbank (☎ 386 920; Rathenausstrasse 16a)
Hypovereinsbank (☎ 366 40; Rathenausstrasse 5-6)

Post
Main post office (Kurt Schumacher Strasse 4; ☺ 9am-8pm Mon-Fri, 9am-4pm Sat)

Tourist Information
Tourist brochures are also available from the Neues Rathaus (see Sights & Activities below).
Hannover Tourismus Service (☎ 1684 9700 information, 1234 555 room reservations; www.hannover.de; Ernst-August-Platz 2; ☺ 9am-6pm Mon-Fri, 9.30am-3pm Sat)

Travel Agencies
American Express (☎ 363 428; Georgstrasse 54)
Explorer (☎ 307 7200; Röselerstrasse 1) Discount agency.

DANGERS & ANNOYANCES
The area around the Hauptbahnhof feels a bit dodgy after dark; there's a huge police presence, but you should still use common sense. The red-light districts around Steintor, to the southwest of the station and Ludwigstrasse to its north, have been partly reclaimed by clubs and hotels, but it's still a good idea to stay reasonably vigilant in these areas at night.

SIGHTS & ACTIVITIES
Roter Faden
The city has painted a *Roter Faden* (red line) on pavements around the centre. Follow it with the help of the multilingual *Red Thread Guide* (€2), available from the tourist office, for a quick 4.2km, do-it-yourself tour of the city's main highlights.

Neues Rathaus
An excellent way to get your bearings in Hanover is to visit the Neues Rathaus (built in 1901–13) and travel 98m to the top in the **curved lift** (elevator; adult/concession €2/1.50; ☺ 10am-6pm Apr-Nov) inside its green dome. There are several viewing platforms here, and while it's a novelty taking a lift that slants to stay within the dome, it's only on descent that you feel any gravitational swing. The cabin can take only five people at a time, however, so queues are inevitable.

In the downstairs lobby are four city models showing Hanover from the Middle

LOWER SAXONY

HANOVER

0   300 m
0   0.2 miles

To Schwule
Sau (1km);
Christuskirche
Engel-
bosteler
Damm

To Basil (1.6km);
Airport (10.5km)   Friedastr

To Gästeresidenz
Pelikanviertel &
Arabella Sheraton
Pelikan (3km)

Postkamp

Hauptbahnhof

Raschplatz-hochstr

Hauptbahnhof

Rasch-
platz

Ernst-
August-
platz

Steintor

Kröpcke

Niki de Sainte
Phalle Promenade

Galerie
Luise

To Herrenhäuser
Gärten (4km);
Stern's Restaurant
im Georgenhof (3.5km);
Musiktheater Bad

Heiligerstr

Georgstr

To Hotel
Leisewitz (400m);
Hotel Elisabetha
(600m); Congress
Hotel am
Stadtpark (1.3km)

Marthenia-Theaterstr

To Backpacker
Gästehaus (200m);
TaK (800m);
Faust (1.2km)

Kramerstr

Blumenstr

Sophienstr

Hedwigstr

Markthalle

Windmühlenstr

Georgs-
platz

Warmbüchen-
kamp

Arnswaldtstr

Marienstrasse

To Café Glocksee (200m);
Capitol (400m); Gig
Neue Welt (800m); Jazz
Club Hannover (1.5km)

Friedrichswall

Breite Str

Aegidientorplatz

Marienstr

Waterloo

Waterloo-
platz

Hardenbergstr

Tramm-
platz

Bleichenstr

Gustav-Bratke-
Allee

To Campingplatz
Arnumer See

Am Schützenplatz

To Niedersachsenstadion
Football Arena (300m);
DJH Hostel (1.2km)

Masch Pond

To Sprengel
Museum (100m);
Maschsee (150m);
Pier 51 (800m)

To Hotel Wiehberg (4.5km);
Expo Grounds & Preussag Arena
(7.5km); Trade Fair Grounds (9.5km)

Schlägerstrasse

Ages to today. Comparing the models from 1939 and 1945 drives home the dramatic extent of WWII devastation.

To get there, take tram/U-Bahn No 10 to Aegidientorplatz.

Herrenhäuser Gärten

Largely modelled on the gardens at Versailles, the **Herrenhäuser Gärten** (☎ 1684 7576; www.he rrenhaeuser-gaerten.de; ☼ 9am-sunset) truly rank among Hanover's most memorable attractions. You need a couple of hours to do them justice, but they combine several treats.

Firstly, the Grosser Garten (Large Garden), Berggarten (Mountain Garden) and Georgengarten (Georgian garden), are prime examples of why Hanover calls itself a city 'in green'. Then, the statues, fountains and coloured tile walls of the **Niki de Saint Phalle Grotto** (opened after her death in 2002) provide a magical showcase of the artist's work that could one day outshine Die Nanas (see p637).

Finally, those interested in the English monarchy can ponder the links with local royals during a visit to the on-site **Fürstenhaus Herrenhausen-Museum** (☎ 750 947; Alte Herrenhäuser Strasse 14; adult/concession €3/1.75; ☼ 10am-6pm Apr-Sep & 10am-5pm Oct-Mar, closed Mon). Admission costs more during special exhibitions.

With its fountains, neat flowerbeds, trimmed hedges and shaped lawns, the 300-year-old **Grosser Garten** (combined admission with Berggarten adult/child €4/free Apr-early Oct, free mid-

INFORMATION			
American Express	**1** C3	Waterloo Memorial	**23** A4
Commerzbank	**2** B2	**SLEEPING** 🏠 (pp639–40)	
Decius Buchhandlung	**3** B3	City Hotel Flamme	**24** C1
Explorer	**4** B3	City Hotel	**25** B3
Hannover Tourismus Service (HTS)	**5** B2	Concorde Hotel Berlin	**26** D2
Hospital	**6** D3	Hotel Alpha	**27** C1
Hypovereinsbank	(see 2)	Hotel Flora-Garni	**28** D1
Internet Café Linuxs	**7** A2	Hotel Königshof am Funkturm	**29** C1
Reisebank	**8** C2	Hotel Rex	**30** A2
Schmorl uv Seefeldís	**9** B2	Luisenhof	**31** C2
Schnell & Sauber	**10** D1	Lühmanns Hotel am Rathaus	**32** C4
Stadtbibliothek	**11** C4		
		EATING 🍴 (pp640–1)	
SIGHTS & ACTIVITIES (pp635–8)		Biesler	**33** C3
Aegidienkirche Memorial	**12** B3	Der Gartensaal	**34** B4
Altes Rathaus	**13** B3	Georxx	**35** C3
Ballhof	**14** B3	Hiller	**36** D3
Die Nanas	**15** A3	Holländische Kakaostube	**37** B3
Historisches Museum	**16** A3	Maestro	**38** C3
Kestner Gesellschaft	**17** A2	Markthalle	**39** B3
Kestner Museum	**18** B4		
Marktkirche	**19** B3	**DRINKING** 🍷 (p641)	
Neues Rathaus	**20** B4	Brauhaus Ernst August	**40** B3
Niedersächsisches Landesmuseum	**21** C4	Cuabar	**41** C2
Oskar-Winter-Brunnen	**22** A3	Discothek Vulcano	**42** A2
Peace Bell	(see 12)	Market Bar & Kitchen	**43** B2

Marlene Bar & Bühne	**44** C3		
ENTERTAINMENT 🎭 (pp641–3)			
Anzeiger Hochhaus	**45** A2		
Café Konrad	**46** B3		
Diablo Latino	**47** C2		
Eve Club	(see 49)		
GOP Varieté	**48** B3		
Heartbreak Hotel	**49** A2		
Kiez Club	**50** A2		
Kino im Künstlerhaus	**51** C3		
Kulturzentrum Pavilion	**52** C1		
Neues Theater	**53** C3		
Opernhaus	**54** C3		
Osho Diskothek	**55** C1		
Palo Palo	**56** C1		
Sansibar	(see 50)		
Schauspielhaus	**57** C3		
Shark Club	(see 49)		
Theater am Aegi	**58** C4		
SHOPPING 🛍 (p643)			
Flea Market	**59** A3		
TRANSPORT (p643)			
ADAC	**60** B2		
Central Bus Station	**61** C1		

Oct–Mar) is reminiscent of Versailles. There's a maze near the northern entrance, while the **Grosse Fontäne** (Big Fountain) at the southern end jets water up to 80m high. In summer, there are **Wasserspiele** (Water games; 🕙 11am-noon & 3-5pm Mon-Fri, 11am-noon & 2-5pm Sat & Sun Apr-early Oct) when all fountains are synchronised. During the **Illuminations** (🕙 9pm Fri-Sun, Jun-Aug) the gardens and fountains are atmospherically lit at night. Meanwhile there are summer concerts, dramas and more. Call or check the Herrenhäuser website for details.

North of the Grosser Garten lies the **Berggarten** (admission €2 year round, combined admission with Grosser Garten adult/child €4/free Apr-early Oct), with its great assortment of flora from around the world. Also here is the **Regenwaldhaus** (Tropical Rainforest House; ☎ 1260 420; Herrenhäuser Strasse 4a; adult/concession €8.50/5.50; 🕙 9am-8pm Sun-Thu, 9am-11pm Fri & Sat). Inside there's a fairly gimmicky and contrived virtual 'journey' to the Amazon. Things are much more pleasant in the attached tropical greenhouse.

Amid the lake-dotted **Georgengarten** (admission free), you'll find the **Wilhelm-Busch-Museum** (☎ 1699 9916; adult/concession €4/2; 🕙 10am-5pm Tue-Fri, 10am-6pm Sat & Sun) containing a wealth of caricature, including works by Busch, Honoré Daumier and William Hogarth.

To get to the gardens, take tram/U-Bahn Nos 4 and 5 from the Hauptbahnhof.

Die Nanas

Highly controversial when installed beside the River Leine in 1974, these three volup-

tuous, fluorescent-coloured, earth-mama **sculptures** by French artist Niki de Saint Phalle have since won a place in Hanover's heart. Indeed, the Nanas 'Sophie', 'Charlotte', and 'Caroline' have become the city's most recognisable landmarks, and they made De Saint Phalle famous. Devout fans of her work will find a direct trip to Leibnizufer (U-Bahn: Markthalle Landtag) rewarding. Others could be left thinking 'Is that it?' – especially as one sculpture might still be away for repairs. In that case, wait until Saturday, when the extra attraction of a flea market takes place at the Nanas' feet.

Sprengel Museum

It's the building as much as the curatorial policy that puts the **Sprengel Museum** (☎ 1684 3875; www.sprengel-museum.de; Kurt Schwitters Platz; adult/concession/under 12 €6/3.50/free; 🕙 10am-6pm Tue-Sun, 10am-8pm Tue) in such high esteem. Its huge interior spaces are brilliant for displaying its modern figurative, abstract and conceptual art, including a few works by Nolde, Chagall and Picasso. At the core of the collection are 300 works by Niki de Saint Phalle, a selection of which is usually on show. Take bus No 131 from in front of the Hauptbahnhof to the Sprengelmuseum/ Machsee stop.

Maschsee

This artificial lake, built by the unemployed in one of the earliest Nazi-led public works projects, is today one of the city's favourite spots for boating and swimming. It's certainly the most central at just half an hour's walk away; otherwise take bus No 131 to Sprengelmuseum/Machsee.

A **ferry** (☎ 0172-541 5525; crossing €3/1.50, tour €6/3) plies the lake from Easter to October in good weather, and there are sailing, pedal and rowing boats for hire. On the southeast bank, there's a free swimming beach, or **Strandbad** (☉ May-Aug), while in-line skaters glide by under the neighbouring trees.

Altstadt

Some of it is a postwar fake, but parts of Hanover's Altstadt (old town) still look appealingly quaint. The red-brick, Gothic **Marktkirche** (1349–59) in the market square has original elements, as do both the **Altes Rathaus** (begun 1455) across the market, and the nearby **Ballhof** (1649–64), a hall originally built for 17th-century badminton-type games.

However, the city re-created an entire row of **half-timbered houses** lining Kramer-strasse and Burgstrasse between the Marktkirche and the Historisches Museum (see Other Museums following). The Renaissance façade of the Leibnizhaus next to the museum is also a reconstruction; the house was once the home of mathematician and philosopher Gottfried Wilhelm Leibniz (1646–1716).

In front of the Leibnizhaus is the **Oskar-Winter-Brunnen** (Oskar Winter Fountain). If you make a wish and turn the small brass ring embedded in the ironwork three times, local lore has it that the wish will come true.

Other Museums

It's always worth checking listings for the **Kestner Gesellschaft** (Kestner Society; ☎ 701 200; Goseriede 11; adult/concession €5/2.50; ☉ 10am-7pm Tue-Sun, 10am-9pm Thu). Having exhibited works by Otto Dix, Georg Grosz, Wassily Kandinsky and Paul Klee before they became famous, the society is still originating shows that later tour Europe. Its wonderfully light, high-ceilinged premises were once a bathhouse.

Despite other interesting bits and pieces, for many overseas visitors the highlight of Hanover's **Historisches Museum** (Historical Museum; ☎ 1684 3052; Pferdestrasse 6; adult/concession €3/2; ☉ 10am-8pm Tue, 10am-4pm Wed-Fri, 10am-6pm Sat & Sun) will be the royal family's original

gilded stagecoaches, plus details of links to other European royalty.

Likewise, it's the upstairs exhibition of 12th- to 20th-century European painting, including works by Lucas Cranach the Elder and from Rembrandt's atelier, that has the widest appeal at the **Niedersächsisches Landesmuseum** (State Museum; ☎ 980 75; Willy-Brandt-Allee 5; adult/concession/child €5/3.50/1.50; ☉ 10am-5pm Tue-Sun, 10am-7pm Thu). The ethnological artefacts from tribal societies, the early history of the Hanover area and 'Vivarium' of live fish are more geared towards locals. Take bus No 131 from the Hauptbahnhof to Bleichenstrasse.

Finally, since its outstanding Egyptian collection suffered water damage and was removed from display, the **Kestner Museum** (☎ 1684 2120; Trammplatz 3; adult/concession €2.50/1.50, free on Fri or if under 12; ☉ 11am-6pm, 11am-8pm Wed, closed Mon) has had to rely mainly on rotating exhibitions. It's not known when the Egyptian artefacts will return, but **decorative art** from the Middle Ages, plus coins and medals from down the ages remain on view.

War Memorials

In a city so devastated by war, it's not surprising to find a **peace bell**. Donated by sister city Hiroshima, it lies inside a steel-cross **Memorial to Our Dead** on Breite Strasse near the corner of Osterstrasse. Every 6 August at 8.15am, the date and time of the atomic detonation at Hiroshima, a delegation from both cities meets here to ring the bell. The neighbouring **Aegidienkirche Memorial** (1350), bashed by artillery in 1943, was being renovated at the time of writing.

The winged angel **Waterloo Memorial** you see south of the Altstadt and west of the Neues Rathaus commemorates the German forces who fought at Waterloo.

FESTIVALS & EVENTS

The annual **Maschsee festival**, with drinking, performances and an enormous fireworks display, runs annually in early August. The international **fireworks festival** and competition at Herrenhäuser Gärten is another big summer event, as is the **Riflemen's Festival** – Germany's largest – in early July. People also come from afar for the **International Jazz Festival**, held around Ascension Day in May/June.

SLEEPING

The tourist office books rooms for a €6.50 fee. The prices given here are those outside trade-show periods. During shows, they at least double or, for major fairs, sometimes triple and quadruple. Given that it's also difficult to get a room at these times, it's imperative to know whether you're arriving during a major fair. Check on the city website (www.hannover.de), under Tourist Information, Event Preview, Fairs and Conferences. Private rooms are only available during trade shows (see the boxed text All the Fun of the Fair, p633).

Budget

DJH hostel (☎ 131 7674; jh-hannover@djh-hannover.de, Ferdinand-Wilhelm-Fricke-Weg 1; junior/senior €16.60/ 19.30; ℗ 🖳) This huge, very modern Jugendherberge overlooks a scenic stretch of river, and on the whole the facilities are very good, despite minor irritations like overflowing showers. From the U-Bahn stop (U-Bahn No 3 or 7, Fischerhof stop), cross the road (away from the road bridge) and follow the DJH signs to the river over the red suspension Lodemannbrücke bridge and turn right.

Backpacker Gästehaus (☎ 131 9919; www.back packerhannover.de; Lenausstrasse 12a; dm €18; ℗ 🖳) This friendly private hostel is more conveniently located than the DJH hostel and reasonably comfortable too. Take U-Bahn No 10 to Goetheplatz, and once on Lenausstrasse (across Goetheplatz), ring the doorbell at No 12 and wait; the hostel itself is located through the courtyard.

Campingplatz Arnumer See (☎ 05101-3534; fax 05136-815 88; Osterbruchweg 3, Arnum-Hemmingen; tent/person/car €3.60/5/1.80) Pleasantly located on leafy lakeside grounds south of the city, this site has modern facilities. Take bus No 364 or 384 from the bus station to Arnum Mitte, and then it's a five-minute walk. By car or motorcycle take A7 south to Laatzen, or B3 from Arnum and follow the signs.

Hotel Leisewitz (☎ 288 7940; webmaster@hotel -leisewitz.de; Leisewitzerstrasse 11; s €45-60, d €65-75; ℗) Though not one for Nordic minimalists perhaps, as the mish-mash of décor is busier than a *Big Brother* voting line on final eviction night, most people will be won over by this small hotel's individuality. In this leafy street, you're a near neighbour to Gerhard Schröder, too. To get there take

bus No 128 from the Hauptbahnhof to Plathnerstrasse.

Gästeresidenz PelikanViertel (☎ 399 90; fax 399 9444; Pelikanstrasse 11; s/d €45/65; ℗) Clean, simple but stylish, this modern 200-bed facility offers superb value. All rooms have private bathroom, desk, phone, TV and kitchenette. It's not particularly central but is near the Eilenreide forest - take U-Bahn No 9 to Pelikanstrasse.

Other recommendations include:

Hotel Elisabetha (☎ 856 930; fax 856 9385; Hindenburgerstrasse 16; s €40-50, d €55-80) Friendly owners and adequate rooms, most with shared bathroom. Bus No 128 to Friedenstrasse.

Hotel Flora-Garni (☎ 383 910; fax 383 9191; Heinrichstrasse 36; singles €35-45, d €50-75) Conveniently located. Some rooms without private bathroom.

Mid-Range

Lühmanns Hotel am Rathaus (☎ 326 268; fax 3262 6968; Friedrichswall 21; s €60-85, d €80-120; ✗) Despite its frontage on a main road, this is one of the best mid-range options in town – central, with friendly owners and well-decorated rooms, each slightly different. If noise, even through double-glazing, bugs you, take a room at the back.

Hotel Wiehberg (☎ 879 990; info@hotel-wiehberg .de; Wiehbergstrasse 55a; s/d €70/90; ℗ ✗) The interior of this historic villa, out in a leafy residential neighbourhood, was remodelled in 1993, and the result is individual and unusual. Guests can rearrange the low, Japanese-style white beds around the room as they please, while bathrooms were designed by Porsche. Take S-Bahn No 1 or 2 to Dorfstrasse.

City Hotel (☎ 360 70; cityhotelh@aol.com; Limburgstrasse 3; s €50-70, d €60-100; ✗) The single rooms, with their striped curtains and bed bases, trade elegance and chic for space: they really are quite compact. Fortunately, the doubles are slightly better proportioned. In the pedestrianised zone, this efficient, modern hotel is central but quiet.

As a warning, quite a few of Hanover's good mid-range options are in slightly seedy areas. However, although you'll see one or two sex shops, even as a lone woman, you're unlikely to get hassled.

Hotel Rex (☎ 123 5870; info@hotelrex.hannover.de; Goethestrasse 2; s/d €60/85; ✗) Most guests are business travellers, apparently, but this hotel is also perfect for groovers who appreciate comfort as well as a bit of edge. The modern rooms are spacious and spotless, while the hotel lies across the road from the city's hippest clubs, in an area that's still partly a red-light district.

City Hotel Flamme (☎ 388 8004; info@cityhotel flamme.de; Lammstrasse 3; s €55-65, d €70-85; P ✗) The rooms of this relaxed hotel-pension open onto balconies facing a large, high-ceilinged internal courtyard – which has an eating area and glassed-in front wall. If you don't like the area around the train station, they will pick you up from there for free; and you can forgo breakfast if you wish to pay slightly less. Parking is €6.

Hotel Königshof am Funkturm (☎ 339 80; info@ koenigshof-hannover.de; Friesenstrasse 65; s €60-110, d €70-125; P ✗) An eclectic mix of religious statues and ethnic sculptures (plus a Rolls Royce) greet you as you walk past the lone sex shop next door onto the Persian carpets here. This rambling abode has an older, cheaper wing out the back – where the bathrooms are huge – and a modern wing with 'comfort', 'business' and 'deluxe' rooms. Parking is €5.50.

Hotel Alpha (☎ 341 535; www.hotelalpha.de; Friesenstrasse 19; s/d €90/120; ✗) Although it's in a more salubrious section of the same street, the Alpha is like Hotel Königshof in having quirky decorations. This time, however, the statues and marionettes are sweeter and more bucolic. There's a trompe l'oeil of an Italian piazza in the breakfast room and the rooms are lovely and homey.

Concorde Hotel Berlin (☎ 410 2800; berlin@con corde-hotel.de; Königstrasse 12; s/d €100/120; P ✗) Being located on top of offices cuts down noise from the fairly central street, and the rooms at the top of this business-oriented hotel offer great views. Weekend rates start at €85/100 for singles/doubles.

Top End

Congress Hotel am Stadtpark (☎ 280 50; info@ congress-hotel-hannover.de; Clausewitzstrasse 6; s €100-140, d €100-170; P ✗ ⚑) On the edge of the city park, this hotel is next to the Congress Centrum. Its unique selling point is on the 17th floor: Hanover's highest swimming pool (with sauna and solarium).

Luisenhof (☎ 304 40; info@kastens-luisenhof.de; Luisenstrasse 1-3; s €115-165, d €140-220; P ✗ ⚑) It's reputed that Peter Ustinov insists on staying here in Hanover, or he refuses to come at all. True or not, the rumour's easy to believe: this opulent *grande dame* of luxury hotels could easily provide the backdrop to one of the Agatha Christie-type period pieces in which the actor has regularly appeared.

Arabella Sheraton Pelikan (☎ 909 30; pelikan hotel@arabellasheraton.com; Podbielskitrasse 145; s €100-125, d €130-155; P ✗) With tall windows and minimalist furniture, the light-filled rooms in this design hotel aim for a loft ambience. A favourite with the stars, the Arabella Sheraton is set in leafy suburbs on a former factory site that's been redeveloped with shops and bars. The hotel also owns the renowned restaurant 5th Avenue plus Harry's New York bar. Weekend rates start at €90 for singles/doubles.

EATING

Cafés

Holländische Kakaostube (☎ 304 100; Ständehaus strasse 2-3; breakfast €3-8, hot drinks €1.80-4.50; ✇ closed from 6pm & Sun) With the blue-and-white square-patterned floor matching the Delft pottery, and a curved ship's staircase and maritime paintings creating a subtly nautical feel, this historic Dutch coffee house has many fans, young and old. Stained glass, windmill figures, daintily swirled cakes and great hot chocolate all contribute to the theme.

Der Gartensaal (☎ 1684 8888; Neues Rathaus, Trammplatz 2; ✇ closed from 6pm) This is simply a great place to sit and have a summer afternoon coffee and cake overlooking the central Stadtpark. (The meals ain't so great.)

Quick Eats

Markthalle (cnr Karmarschstrasse & Leinstrasse; ✇ 7am-8pm Mon-Wed, 7am-10pm Thu & Fri, 7am-4pm Sat) South of the Marktkirche, this is a bargain paradise for hungry gourmets, including vegetarians. It has dozens of stalls selling a huge array of food, and on weekdays it's a major networking spot for local yuppies. There are places here selling sausage and meats, doner kebab, pizza, spices, teas, cakes, bread…it's wonderful. Stock up on hams, meats, cheeses and bottles of Italian wine.

Restaurants

Maestro (☎ 300 8575; Sophienstrasse 2; mains €4.50-8) It's surprising that this cafe in the Künstlerhaus basement isn't more popular. True, the evening menu of pasta, salads and steaks isn't terribly innovative, but the daily, all-you-can-eat vegetarian buffet (€7.50) is great value, and the part Art Deco, part religious cloister decoration is wonderfully atmospheric.

Georxx (☎ 306 147; Georgsplatz 3; mains €7.50-12) Local hipsters visit this Mediterranean-style bistro solely for coffee or champagne, but Georxx also attracts a wide range of customers with its unexpectedly tasty meals. The fresh, herby pizzas are a lip-smacking case in point. In fact, it's hard to go wrong here. Breakfast is served until 5pm.

Pier 51 (☎ 807 1800; Rudolf von Bennigsen Ufer 51; mains €6-18) Walled with glass and jutting out over the Maschsee, Pier 51 enjoys the best outlook of any Hanoverian restaurant. Fittingly, the menu is strong on fish, although you can also choose pasta or meat. In summer, there's an outside 'Piergarten', decked out with the old-fashioned *Strandkörbe* (straw basket seats) that you see on German beaches.

Hiller (☎ 321 288; Blumenstrasse 3; mains €6-12, set menus €7.50-21; ☺ closed Sun) If it ain't broke, don't fix it: Germany's oldest vegetarian restaurant – or so the proprietors claim – is still going strong with its traditional veggie food and no-smoking policy.

Basil (☎ 622 636; Dragonerstrasse 30; mains €12-20; ☺ dinner only, closed Sun & Mon) This former stables to the north of town now houses a fabulous chi-chi restaurant, with a high ceiling and pressed tablecloths. It's formal enough that you don't want to turn up in jeans and a T-shirt. Take tram No 1, 2 or 8 from the Hauptbahnhof to Dragonerstrasse.

Biesler (☎ 321 033; Sophienstrasse 6; Königstrasse 7; mains €15-19; ☺ closed Sun & Mon) One of the oldest eateries in the city likes to mix the ancient and the modern on its menu. So, alongside international fare such as king prawn curry, each day it serves a different traditional German dish, such as roast calves' liver with apple and onion.

Stern's Restaurant im Georgenhof (☎ 702 244; Herrenhäuser Kirchweg 20; mains €20-30) When things are cooking here, they're really cooking, with wonderful *haute cuisine* that might include wild salmon medallions in orange sauce or veal kidneys in a tarragon-mustard sauce. There's a garden terrace attached to the charmingly old-fashioned

dining room. Take tram No 4 or 5 from the Hauptbahnhof to Parkhaus, then turn right (east) along Herrenhäuser Kirchweg.

DRINKING

Many of the cultural centres and rock and jazz venues listed under Entertainment (see following) are also good places to go for just a drink.

Brauhaus Ernst August (☎ 365 950; Schmiedestrasse 13) A Hanover institution, this sprawling brew-pub makes a refreshing unfiltered Pilsner called Hannöversch. A party atmosphere reigns nightly, helped along by a varied roster of live bands.

Market Bar & Kitchen (☎ 169 4910; Goseriede 4) As a restaurant it's somewhat overpriced, but the high ceiling and huge hall of this modern bistro (originally conceived in Hamburg) makes a great place for a drink.

Cuabar (☎ 3539 8730; Ernst-August-Platz 1) In most other cities, a chic and trendy cocktail bar in the train station would be an oxymoron, but all the clubs at the back of Hanover's Hauptbahnhof have set a precedent and Cuabar reels in the punters.

ENTERTAINMENT

For listings, check out *Prinz* (€1) or the free *MagaScene* (both in German).

Cinemas

Anzeiger Hochhaus (☎ 144 54; Goseriede 9) This spacious, arthouse cinema is on the top floor of a magnificent Art Deco building and the views of the city are sometimes just as compelling as the film. Check listing times, as the box office only opens just before screenings.

Kino im Künstlerhaus (☎ 168 4732; Sophienstrasse 2) There's also a good range of foreign films with German subtitles in this down-to-earth studenty place.

Cultural Centres

Faust (☎ 455 001; Zur Bettfedernfabrik 1-3, Linden) In the buildings and grounds of a former factory, this venue has become a pivotal part of the Hanover scene. There's a pub/bar, Mephisto, and a beer garden. However, it's most renowned for its 1960s concert hall. To get there, take U-Bahn No 10 to Leinaustrasse.

Musiktheater Bad (☎ 169 4138; Am Grossen Garten 60) In this large old yellow building and its surrounding grounds, you'll find a mixed bag of live music and dance offerings. It's great in summer when there's an outdoor stage.

Kulturzentrum Pavilion (☎ 344 558; Lister Meile 4) More a countercultural centre than a cultural centre, this industrial-looking place has jazz, off-beat rock, world music and even theatre.

Discos & Clubs

Café Glocksee (☎ 161 4712; Glockseestrasse 35) Part club, part live-music venue, the Glocksee has everything from techno and trance DJs to gigs by the Frank Popp Ensemble or Argentinian punk rockers. Its courtyard out the back makes it hugely popular in summer.

One of Hanover's hottest scenes is around the former red-light district of Steintor (cheekily nicknamed Stöhntor in German, meaning 'Moaning Gate'). Here you'll find the stylish **Kiez Club** (☎ 353 5699; Scholvinstrasse 4), **Sansibar** (☎ 0177-500 6006; Scholvinstrasse 7) and **Shark Club** (Reuterstrasse 5). Be a little careful about the **Eve Club** (Reuterstrasse 3-4); from Thursday to Sunday a cool crowd comes for funk, jazz and so on, but we can't vouch for it on other nights.

If you're not having any of this 'the red-light district is trendy' lark, try the older, concrete environs of Raschplatz behind the train station. **Diablo Latino** (☎ 341 025; Raschplatz 1h) is the city's most famous Latin club. See-and-be-seen **Palo Palo** (☎ 331 073; Raschplatz 8a) and **Osho Diskothek** (☎ 342 217; Raschplatz 7l) play a mix of classic disco hits for the over-25s.

Gay & Lesbian Venues

More information can be found at hann over.gay-web.de.

Schwule Sau (☎ 700 0525; Schaufelder Strasse 30a) This alternative gay and lesbian centre regularly hosts concerts, theatres and club nights. Take tram/U-Bahn No 11 or 6 to Kopernikusstrasse.

Discothek Vulcano (Lange Laube 24) Even in the main room, there's quite a masculine slant, with occasional underwear parties and men-only evenings. The cruisy jeans and leather 'Backstairs' bar is strictly for men.

Other venues and events to look out for include the lesbian and gay hang-out **Café Konrad** (☎ 323 666; Knochenhauerstrasse 34) or the twice-monthly **Blaue Engel parties** (☎ 321 879; www.thenextgeneration.net in German), an excellent

'Queerbeat' night for gays, lesbians and friends, with everything from pop to house on rotation.

Rock & Jazz

Capitol (☎ 444 066; Schwarzer Bär 2) This former movie theatre has rock, pop, house, soul and more on weekends and frequently during the week. Take tram/U-Bahn No 3, 7 or 9 to Schwarzer Bär.

Heartbreak Hotel (☎ 328 061; Reuterstrasse 5) You have to smile at a place that reserves a parking space for Elvis outside, which is just one reason why this scurrilous little live-music venue and not-just-for-old-rockers club managed to become so cool.

Gig Neue Welt (☎ 453 486; Lindener Markt 1) This chi-chi venue in a historic house is divided into three spaces: the Jazz-Café, as well as serving food, has black music, funk and jazz evenings; the Gig-Lounge specialises in soul; and the main room downstairs is for major events. Take U-Bahn No 9 to Lindener Marktplatz.

Jazz Club Hannover (☎ 454 455; Am Lindener Berge 38) This club is unadorned, but takes its music very, very seriously.

Preussag Arena (☎ 954 370; Expo Plaza 7) Nowadays, when old-established megastars like David Bowie blow into town, they're usually found performing here. Take U-Bahn No 6 to Messe Ost.

Sport

Football has always been a leading spectator sport in Hanover and the city's 60,000-capacity stadium, the Niedersachsenstadion (also known as the AWB Arena), has been given a €64 million makeover for the 2006 Fifa World Cup.

It's just west of the Machsee. Take bus No 131 to the stop Niedersachsenstadion.

Theatre & Classical Music

Opernhaus (☎ 268 6240; Opernplatz 1) The star in Hanover's cultural firmament, the 19th-century Opera House was lovingly restored after suffering WWII damage and now hosts classical music performances as well as opera.

GOP Varieté (☎ 301 8760; Georgstrasse 36) This is an old-school type of variety theatre with dancing, acrobatics, circus-style acts, magic, music and more, housed in the Georgspalast.

Those interested in seeing some cabaret should make tracks for **TaK** (☎ 445 562; Stephanusstrasse 29) or **Marlene Bar & Bühne** (☎ 368 1687; cnr Alexanderstrasse & Prinzenstrasse), while German speakers into more serious drama should check out what's on at **Schauspielhaus** (☎ 168 6710; Prinzenstrasse 9) or the **Neues Theater** (☎ 363 001; Georgstrasse 54). Comedies and musical theatre are performed at **Theater am Aegi** (☎ 989 3333; Aegidientorplatz).

SHOPPING

Hanover's compact city centre makes it ideal for shopping, although most of what you will find is modern, international fashion. A pedestrianised zone full of shops extends south from the Hauptbahnhof, along Bahnhofstrasse, Georgstrasse and Karmarschstrasse. The formerly dingy Passerelle has been given a thorough clean-up. Renamed the **Niki de Sainte Phalle Promenade**, it's now a good place to browse.

There's a regular **flea market** (Hohen Ufer; ☼ 7am-1pm Sat) behind the Historisches Museum, along the Leine River Canal near Die Nanas.

GETTING THERE & AWAY
Air
Hanover airport (☎ 977 1223) has efficient transport to the city and the fairgrounds. Airlines servicing the area include:
Air Berlin (☎ 01805-737 800)
British Airways (☎ 721 076)
Lufthansa Airlines (☎ 0180-380 3803)
Scandinavian Airlines (SAS; ☎ 0180-323 4023)

Car
Nearby autobahns run to Hamburg, Munich, Frankfurt and Berlin, with good connections to Bremen, Cologne, Amsterdam and Brussels. Major car-rental firms are in the Hauptbahnhof, including **Sixt** (general reservation ☎ 01805-252 525, local 363 830) and **Avis** (general reservation ☎ 0180-555 77, local 322 610).

ADAC (☎ 124 560; Nordmannpassage 4) provides motoring information.

Train
Hanover is also a major rail hub. ICE trains to/from Hamburg (€29.20, 1½ hours), Munich (€89.20, 4½ hours), Frankfurt (€62.20, 2½ hours) and Berlin (€48.20, 1½ hours) leave virtually every one or two hours from 5am or 6am.

GETTING AROUND
Hanover is eminently walkable: it's only a 20-minute stroll from the Hauptbahnhof to the Sprengel Museum and the northern end of the Maschsee. The S-Bahn No 5 makes the trip from the airport to the Hauptbahnhof in 16 minutes (€2.90). To get to the fairgrounds, switch to the U-Bahn No 8 (17 minutes).

The Hanover transit system of buses and combination tram/U-Bahn line (the trams go underground in the city centre and pop up later) is run by **Üstra** (☎ 01803-194 49). There are three zones: Hannover, Umland and Region. Single tickets are Hannover/ Umland/Region €1.80/2.30/2.90, while day passes cost €3.20/4.20/5.20.

A taxi from the centre to the fairgrounds costs about €17.50; from the airport it's about €35. For a taxi call ☎ 8484.

FAIRY-TALE ROAD – SOUTH

This stretch of the Fairy-Tale Road, or *Märchenstrasse* (see the boxed text Fairy-Tale Road, p564) is one of the prettiest. Connecting Hamelin, Boderwerder and Bad Karlshafen, it hugs the Weser River for much of the way. South of Bodenwerder, the river is flanked to the east by the Solling-Vogler Naturpark, which is a great spot for hikers and cyclists. Hamelin is charming, if touristy, Bodenwerder worth a quick stopover and beautiful Bad Karlshafen a place where you can imagine people arrive and never leave.

Getting There & Away
What is a simple journey by car – take the B83 to/from Hamelin or Bad Karlshafen – requires a little planning with public transport. From Hamelin's Hauptbahnhof, bus No 520 follows the Weser to/from Holzminden via Bodenwerder several times daily (€9.20). From Holzminden trains leave hourly to Bad Karlshafen (€5.75), via Ottbergen. Direct trains run every two hours from Bad Karlshafen to Göttingen (€6.95, one hour).

Plans to reschedule summer boat services will make it possible to travel from Hamelin to Bad Karlshafen, via Bodenwerder, along

LOWER SAXONY

the Weser all in the same day. Ring **Oberweser Dampfschiffahrt** (☎ 05151-939 999) or ask at the Hamelin tourist office for details.

See Getting There & Around p645, for details on bike hire.

HAMELIN
☎ 05151 / pop 59,000

Although it supposedly got rid of all its rats when the Pied Piper *(Der Rattenfänger)* lured them into the Weser River in the 13th century – and then lost all its children when it refused to pay the piper – Hamelin (Hameln) still seems to be enjoying a rodent plague. Enjoying is the right word: this quaint, ornate town revels in *The Pied Piper of Hamelin* fairy tale with rat-shaped bread, fluffy rat toys…rat everything really. And the Pied Piper himself can be seen in various tourist guide guises, mesmerising onlookers with haunting tunes.

Orientation

On the eastern bank of the Weser River lies Hamelin's circular Altstadt. The main streets are Osterstrasse, which runs east–west, and Bäckerstrasse, the north–south axis.

The Hauptbahnhof is about 800m east of the centre. Turn right out of the station square, follow Bahnhofstrasse to Diesterstrasse and turn left. Diesterstrasse becomes Diesterallee and then Osterstrasse. Alternatively, bus Nos 2, 3, 4, 12, 21, 33 and 34 will drop you opposite the tourist office.

Counters at the Hauptbahnhof stock a monthly events booklet, which has a good town map.

Information

Hameln Tourist Information (☎ 957 823; www .hameln.de/touristinfo; Diesterallee 1; 🕑 9am-6pm Mon-Fri year-round; 9.30am-4pm Sat, 9.30am-1pm Sun May-Sep, 9.30am-1pm Sat Oct-Apr) On the eastern edge of the Altstadt.
Main post office (Stubenstrasse 1A) Near the river.

Sights

The best way to explore is to follow the **Pied Piper trail** – the line of white rats drawn on the pavements. There are information posts at various points. They're in German, but at least you know when to stop to admire the various restored 16th- to 18th-century half-timbered houses.

The ornamental Weser Renaissance style prevalent throughout Hamelin's Altstadt has a strong Italian influence. The **Rattenfängerhaus** (Rat Catcher's House; Osterstrasse 28), from 1602, is the finest example, with its typically steep and richly decorated gable. The **Leistehaus** (1585–89) now houses a **museum** (☎ 202 215; Osterstrasse 8-9; admission €2; 🕑 10am-4.30pm Tue-Sun), with exhibits ranging from the town's history through to ceramics, children's toys and, of course, the Pied Piper. Also not to be missed is the **Hochzeitshaus** (1610–17) at the Markt (square) end of Osterstrasse. The **Rattenfänger Glockenspiel** at the far end chimes daily at 9.35am and 11.35am, while a **carousel of Pied Piper figures** twirls at 1.05pm, 3.35pm and 5.35pm.

During summer, ask the tourist office about the **open-air light displays** on Sunday evening and the comic musical *Rats* on Wednesday afternoon.

From late April to early October, there are **one-hour cruises** (adult/child €6/3) on the Weser River. They run six times daily between 10am and 4.15pm. Contact **Oberweser Dampfschiffahrt** (☎ 939 999), upstairs from the tourist office.

Sleeping & Eating

DJH hostel (☎ 3425; jh-hameln@djh-hannover.de; Fischbeckerstrasse 33; junior/senior €14/16.70) This clean and relatively modern Jugendherberge enjoys river views out the back. At night light from the halls pours into some rooms rather disturbingly, though. Take bus No 2 from the Hauptbahnhof to Wehler Weg.

Fährhaus an der Weser (☎ 611 67; www.camp ingplatz-faehrhaus-hameln.de in German; Uferstrasse 80; adult/tent/car €4.50/3/1) This year-round camp site is across the river from the Altstadt and 10 minutes' walk north. There's a beer garden and Greek restaurant.

Hotel Garni Altstadtwiege (☎ 278 54; fax 272 15; Neue Marktstrasse 10; s €40-45; d €65-90; **P**) This red-brick building doesn't look much from outside, but the cute, individually decorated rooms have stained-glass windows or country-cottage effects. No 14 has a four-poster bed and No 12 a raised single bed where you climb steps to retire for the night.

Hotel zur Krone (☎ 9070; www.hotelzurkrone.de in German; Osterstrasse 30; s €65-80, d €90-95; **P** 🗙) Rooms are modern in this central hotel, but if you drive up to the uninspiring rear

Kopmanshof entry to get to the basement garage, don't forget to look at the quaint half-timbered façade on Osterstrasse.

Hotel-Garni Christinenhof (☎ 950 80; www.christ inenhof-hameln.de; Alte Marktstrasse 18; s/d €80/100; Ⓟ 🏊) Discreet and elegant, the Christinenhof's real hit is its small swimming pool in a vaulted cellar.

Rattenfängerhaus (☎ 3888; Osterstrasse 28; mains €6.50-15) Behind the ornate façade is a warm, cosy restaurant serving traditional German fare dressed up with lots of rat-related names. There's also a humorously named 'Girly Teller' (girly dish) of fish and chips for kids.

Ambrosia (☎ 253 93; Neu Marktstrasse 18; mains €5-20) The aromas of this restaurant's Italian and Greek food waft down the street, mesmerising diners just as the Pied Piper's tunes do.

Museumscafé im Stiftsherrenhaus (☎ 215 53; Osterstrasse 8; €7-13) There are light seasonal meals here, or stop by for some marzipan-filled *Rattenfängertorte* (rat-catcher, or Pied Piper, cake).

Getting There & Around

Frequent S-Bahn trains head to Hamelin from Hanover (€8.10, 45 minutes). By car, take the B217 to/from Hanover. See Getting There & Away p643 earlier in this section for bus and boat links.

Bikes can be hired from the **Troches Fahrrad Shop** (☎ 136 70; Kreuzstrasse 7; per day/weekend €8/14).

BODENWERDER
☎ 05533 / pop 6800

One of history's most shameless tellers of tall tales, Bodenwerder's favourite son gave his name to a psychological condition – Münchhausen's syndrome, or compulsive exaggeration of physical illness – and inspired Terry Gilliam's cult movie *The Adventures of Baron Munchhausen*. The 'liar baron' (1720–1797) would regale dinner guests with his Crimean adventures, claiming he had, for example, tied his horse to a church steeple during a snow drift, ridden around a dining table without breaking one teacup and once attempted to spy on a battlefield enemy by hitching a lift on a cannonball.

Honestly though, you'd learn more from a book about this wonderful character, and Bodenwerder merits only a very brief

stopover. There are no trains to Bodenwerder; see Getting There & Away p643 for transport information. The village is small and walkable.

Information

For local information go to **Tourist Information Bodenwerder** (☎ 405 41; touristinformation@ bodenwerder.de; Weserstrasse 3; ☼ 9am-12.30pm & 2.30-6pm Mon-Fri year round, 9am-1pm Sat Apr-Oct)

Sights

The relatively new **Münchhausen Museum** (☎ 409 147; Münchhausenplatz 1; adult/child €2/1.50; ☼ 10am-noon & 2-5pm Apr-Oct) is a bit static for such a lively subject. There's a cannonball to illustrate the baron's most famous tale, and paintings and displays of Münchhausen books in umpteen languages. At present, the best you can do is buy the English-language *Tall Tales of Baron Münchhausen* (€2.30) from the museum or tourist office. From April to October, German storytellers relate Münchhausen tales for €1 (10am-noon and 2-4pm daily), but English stories can only be arranged for groups – call the tourist office.

In the garden nearby, the **statue** of the baron riding half a horse relates to an episode where the baron noticed his horse seemed a bit thirsty, and then realised the animal had been cut in two by a descending town gate, so the water was pouring right through. (In the story the horse is sewn back together and lives happily ever after.)

Across the road, the **ship's engine**, which you throw into motion by putting money in the slot, also belongs to the wacky world one associates with the baron.

BAD KARLSHAFEN
☎ 05672 / pop 4700

With its orderly streets of whitewashed baroque buildings, the beautiful spa town of Bad Karlshafen looks more French than German. That's not surprising, given that Huguenot refugees helped the local earl Karl build the town in the late 18th century. It was planned with an impressive harbour and a canal connecting the Weser with the Rhine to attract trade. But the earl died before his designs were completed and all that exists today is a tiny Hafenbecken (harbour basin) trafficked only by white swans.

LOWER SAXONY

Bad Karlshafen is strictly in Hesse, but it's at the end of the Fairy-Tale Road, just across the Lower Saxony border.

Orientation & Information

Most of the town lies on the south bank of the Weser River, with the Hafenbecken and surrounding square, Hafenplatz, at its western end. Bad Karlshafen is small and walkable. To reach the **tourist office** (☎ 999 924; fax 999 925; Hafenplatz 8; ☺ 9am-noon & 2-5.30pm Mon-Fri, 9.30am-noon Sat, 2.30-5pm Sun May-Oct, 9am-noon & 2-4pm Mon-Fri Nov-Apr) from the Hauptbahnhof follow the only road exiting the station for a few minutes and cross the bridge, right, over the river. Turn right again on the other side and continue straight ahead to Hafenplatz.

For information on transport here see Getting There & Away, p643.

Sights

Take a stroll around the **Hafenbecken**. On the northeast side is the **Deutsches Huguenotten Museum** (German Huguenot Museum; ☎ 1410; Hafenplatz 9a; adult/concession €2/1; ☺ 9am-1pm & 2-6pm Tue-Sat, 11am-6pm Sun, mid-Feb–Dec) containing maps, copperplate etchings and other exhibits explaining the history of the Huguenots in Germany.

Sleeping

DJH hostel (☎ 338; fax 8361; Winnefelder Strasse 7; junior/senior €15.50/18.20; ℗) It's worth the short, uphill walk from the train station (both the first and second left turns out of the train station will get you there), for the Hermann-Wenning-Jugendherberge, as it's clean, modern and does great breakfasts. Some rooms enjoy dreamy views over Bad Karlshafen's rooftops and surrounding hills.

Am Rechten Weserufer (☎ 710; fax 1350; adult/tent/car €3.50/2/1) This camp site enjoys a prime position on the northern riverbank, just south of the train station. It overlooks the town centre.

Hotel-Pension Haus Fuhrhop (☎ 404; fax 314; Friedrichstrasse 15; s/d €35/65). The rooms have a lot of character in this charming pension. The street is the first left after you've crossed the bridge.

Hotel zum Schwan (☎ 104 445; fax 1046; Conradistrasse 3-4; s/d €40/80; ℗) Although Earl Karl's former hunting lodge is now a bit creaky,

this atmospheric hotel inside is still one of the town's best. It overlooks the Hafenbecken (and honking swans), and its rococo dining room is a perfect museum piece. Parking is €5.

LÜNEBURGER HEIDE

North of Hanover along the sprawling Lüneburger Heide lies a land of beautiful villages and natural allure. The region is packed with history. Lower Saxony was ruled from here before the court moved to Hamburg, and royal treasures and sagas, along with exquisitely preserved buildings, await you in Celle. In Lüneburg, whose riches came from the salt trade in the Middle Ages, you can see fascinating museums, and the largest Rathaus in Germany to have survived from the Middle Ages.

The area in between, along the Lüneburger Heide, can be covered on foot, by bike or in a boat, and there are plenty of hay hotels (see the boxed text A Roll in the Hay, p654) and camp sites along the way. This is one of northern Germany's most rewarding areas; at the very least you should try to visit the two main cities, Celle and Lüneburg.

CELLE

☎ 05141 / pop 72,000

Celle's not shy about its looks, claiming to be Germany's most beautiful town. Some visitors might even agree. Its white-and-pink wedding-cake palace is small but perfectly formed, while the façades of many of its 16th-century half-timbered buildings are inscribed with mottos that show they're than just a pretty face. 'With Gentle Hand, God Giveth and God Taketh Away' and 'Work Harder' are two of the thoughts passed on to posterity by the pious, hard-working folk who built these homes.

Orientation

The mainly pedestrianised Altstadt is about a 15-minute walk east of the Hauptbahnhof, reached by the rather unattractive Bahnhofstrasse. Turning left at its end will take you to the palace after 100m. From here, Stechbahn leads east to the tourist office within another 100m. The Aller River flows around the northern section of the Altstadt, with a tributary encircling it to the south. Just south of the Altstadt is the Französischer Garten (French Garden).

Information

Main post office (Rundstrasse 7) Diagonally opposite the Schloss.

Sparkasse (☎ 9130; Schlossplatz 10) Bank.

Tourismus Region Celle (☎ 1212; info@tourismus -region-celle.de; Markt 14; ☜ 9am-7pm Mon-Fri, 9am-4pm Sat, 11am-2pm Sun May-Oct, 9am-5pm Mon-Fri, 10am-1pm Sat Nov-Apr) Runs **guided tours** in German (€3.50; ☜ 2.30pm Mon-Sat, 11am Sun May-Oct, 2pm Sat, 11am Sun Nov-Apr) and organises horse-drawn carriage rides (from €5 per person).

Sights

SCHLOSS

Beautifully proportioned and magnificently restored is Celle's **Schloss** (Ducal Palace; ☎ 123 73; Schlossplatz; tours adult/concession €3/2; ☜ tours hourly 11am-4pm Tue-Sun Apr-Oct, 11am & 3pm Tue-Sun Nov-Mar). It can only be visited on guided tours (in German), but there are explanatory brochures in English you can buy for €2 to €3. There are frequent supplementary tours to meet demand, including on weekends.

Built in 1292 by Otto Der Strenge (Otto the Strict) as a town fortification, the building was expanded and turned into a residence in 1378. The last duke to live here was Georg Wilhelm (1624–1705), and the last royal was the exiled Queen Caroline-Mathilde of Denmark, who died here in 1775 (see the boxed text The Sad Tale of Queen Caroline, below).

Schloss highlights include the magnificent baroque theatre, the private apartment of Caroline Mathilde and, above all, the chapel. Its original Gothic form is evident in the high windows and vaulted ceiling, but the rest of the intricate interior is pure Renaissance. The duke's pew was above; the shutters were added later so his highness could snooze during the three-hour services.

In the left-hand corner closest to the glass is the chapel's prize – *Temptation*, showing a woman (the New Church), surrounded by devils in various forms trying to lead her astray. However, she is saved by an angel descending from heaven.

BOMANN MUSEUM

Across from the palace, you'll find the regional history and modern art **Bomann Museum** (☎ 123 72; Schlossplatz 7; adult/concession €3/2, including entry to the palace's east wing; ☜ 10am-5pm Tue-Sun). It's housed in an enchanting series of buildings spanning most of Celle's architectural periods, from Gothic half-timbered to Renaissance, baroque and modern 20th century. The historic museum is in the older building; the modern art collection and rotating exhibitions are in the new wing. An affiliated exhibition in the east wing of the Schloss shows the history of the Kingdom of Hanover.

ALTSTADT

The heart of the Altstadt is the Renaissance **Altes Rathaus** (1561–79) in the Markt,

---

THE SAD TALE OF QUEEN CAROLINE

Queen Caroline-Mathilde of Denmark was the last royal to live in Celle Schloss (palace), after being exiled there by her brother, England's George III. How an English-born queen of Denmark came to live in a German castle by order of an English king is a convoluted story, but a good and gory one nevertheless.

Caroline's husband, King Christian VII of Denmark (1749–1808), was schizophrenic and placed under the care of expatriate German physician Dr Struensee (1737–72). Struensee did his job so well that, Rasputin-like, he managed to take over the country's day-to-day running. His actions to liberate serfs and create freedom of the press raised eyebrows, but the doctor really overstepped the mark by sleeping with the king's wife.

When Caroline gave birth to a daughter by Struensee, he was arrested. First they cut off his right hand, then they beheaded him and then quartered him, cutting his torso into four parts. These and his head were placed on stakes as a public warning.

Caroline was placed under house arrest at Kronborg, near Copenhagen and only released after appeals from George III, who then put her out of harm's reach in the disused Celle castle.

For the next three years she wrote to her brother repeatedly, begging to return to England. But she died of a fever in Celle in 1775, a few weeks before turning 24.

with one of those trompe l'oeil façades that makes flat bricks look raised. At the northern end there's a wonderful Weser Renaissance stepped gable, topped with a golden weather vane above the ducal coat of arms. On the south side, at the door to the tourist office, are two whipping posts with shackles, used from 1786 to 1850. Prisoners guilty of minor offences were shackled by the neck to the posts for up to 12 hours; although prisoners weren't whipped, this was long enough to allow their neighbours to insult them, throw eggs and apples, and spit at them.

Just west of the Rathaus is the 13th-century Gothic **Stadtkirche** (☎ 7735, 550 345; tower admission adult/concession €1/0.50; 🕑 10am-6pm Tue-Sat, tower 10am-11.45am, 12.45-4.45pm Tue-Sat Apr-Oct). You can climb up the 235 steps to the top of the church steeple (which dates from 1913) for a view of the city, or just watch as the city trumpeter climbs the 220 steps to the white tower below the steeple for a trumpet fanfare in all four directions. The ascent takes place at 8.15am and 5.05pm Monday to Saturday (9am and 7.15pm on Sunday).

Inside the church is a magnificent organ once played by Johann Sebastian Bach. It is smothered in gold leaf and other decoration and has carved faces on the pipes. Services are held year round on Sunday at 10am.

Jousting tournaments were held in front of the church on the **Stechbahn**. The little horseshoe on the corner on the north side of the street marks the spot where a duke was slain during a tournament; step on it and make a wish, and local lore holds that it will come true.

SYNAGOGUE

Dating back to 1740, Celle's **synagogue** (☎ 550 714; Im Kreise 24; admission free; 🕑 3-5pm Tue-Thu, 9-11am Fri, 11am-1pm Sun) is the oldest in northern Germany. Partially destroyed during Kristallnacht (see the boxed text The Night of Broken Glass, p34), it looks just like any other half-timbered house from the outside, but a new Jewish congregation formed in 1997 and services are held regularly. Changing exhibitions on Jewish history take place next door.

Guided tours for groups can be organised. The exact price depends on the size of the group, but bank on around €45. The synagogue is at the southeastern end of the Altstadt, just off Wehlstrasse.

OTHER ATTRACTIONS

If you stand at the tourist office door and walk straight down Poststrasse (past the statue of a man in shackles), one block on, you'll find one of Celle's most magnificent buildings, the ornate **Hoppener Haus** (1532), on the corner of Runde Strasse.

Another block in the same direction (south), there's a small dark-blue **Trinkwasser** (drinking tap) behind the fountain on Bergstrasse. Stand before the tap, look up at the tiny alley between the two buildings there and you'll see a little box with a window. This was a **baroque toilet**. It's less glamorous than the name implies; waste would flush directly down into the alley.

Retrace your steps to the corner of Poststrasse and Zöllnerstrasse, and turn right into Zöllnerstrasse. This way, you'll pass **No 37** (built in 1570, now the shop Reformhaus), with its heart-warming inscription on the upper gable, 'Work! No chatting, talking or gossiping!'. Turn left into Rabengasse, and you'll come to Neue Strasse. Highlights here include the **Green House** (1478) with the crooked beam at No 32 and the **Fairy-Tale House** at No 11. The façade of the latter is decorated with characters such as a jackass crapping gold pieces.

If you'd like to continue walking, Celle also has a lovely **French Garden** at the southern end of the Altstadt.

Sleeping

The tourist office books private rooms free of charge.

DJH hostel (☎ 532 08; jh-celle@djh-hannover.de; Weghausstrasse 2; junior/senior €15/17; Ⓟ) This Jugendherberge has very gloomy lighting in its hallways, although the rooms are clean and comfortable. It's in a fairly rustic part of town; follow the signposts from the Hauptbahnhof (when you cross the railway line into Bremer Weg, continue straight ahead until you come to the next, distant sign) or take bus No 3 to the Boye stop.

Camping Silbersee (☎ 312 23; silbersee@celler-land.de, Zum Silbersee 19; adult/car & tent €2.90/5.10) This is the nicest and closest camp site, about 4km from the centre. Take bus No 6 from Schlossplatz to the terminus.

Hotel Zur Herberge (☎ 208 141; www.nacelle.de; Hohe Wende 14; s/d €35/60; P) Seemingly straight from the Ikea showroom, this charming hotel offers excellent value for money. There are nine rooms with TV, phone and bathroom, and a communal self-service kitchen corner for coffee and beer. It's a little out of the way, but bus no 12 from the Hauptbahnhof will get you there (stop: Harburger Herrstrasse).

Hotel am Hehlentor (☎ 885 6900; www.hotel-am -hehlentor.de; Nordwall 62-63; s €45-55, d €65-80; P) The mix of white, grey and green gives the rooms a slightly murky underwater feeling, but they are clean and comfortable. Although this 18th-century building wraps around an inner courtyard and accommodation at the back is quiet, be warned that the front rooms face a main street.

Hotel Utspann (☎ 927 20; www.utspann.de; Im Kreise 13; s €70, d €85-95; P) In a class of its own, as the 'thanks' from German luminaries and others attest, this hotel is spread across three half-timbered houses, which the owners have fitted out with quirky individual rooms. Surrounded by filled bookcases, copper kettles full of dried flowers, macramé wall hangings, bed canopies and other truly homey touches, you'll feel like you're staying as a friend of the family.

Celler Hof (☎ 911 960; www.cellerhof.bestwestern .de; Stechbahn 11; s €65, d €90-100; P ✗) The rooms are a lot smaller and less interesting than in some other Best Western hotels, but you're paying for the super-central location here – opposite the Stadtkirche and minutes from the Schloss. A fitness room and sauna are also on site. Parking is €10.

Hotel Furstenhof (☎ 201 140; www.fuerstenhof.de; Hannoversche Strasse 55/56; s €110-160, d €180-240; P) On the one hand, the rooms of this former baroque palace still echo its noble history. On the other, all mod cons are provided, from TV, phone, modem plugs and minibar to hairdryers, sauna and solarium.

Eating

Pasta (☎ 483 460; Neue Strasse 37; mains €4.50-8; ⊙ closed Sun) Behind this tiny deli restaurant lies a simple, but ingenious, idea. You combine your favourite fresh pasta (fettuccine, ravioli etc) with your choice from a long list of home-made sauces. Lunch-time suits and leisurely diners happily perch on high stools around the open kitchen to partake,

then slap down generous tips alongside a vow to return.

Zum Ältesten Haus (☎ 246 01; Neue Strasse 27; mains €5-18) German to the neat fringes of its pink tablecloths, this is the best place in town to try local specialities such as *Celler Rohe Roulade*, rolled, thinly sliced raw beef in a mustard marinade or *Herzogen Pfanne*, Heide-style roast lamb with cranberries, stuffed pears, green beans and fried potatoes.

India Haus (☎ 485 152; Neue Strasse 34; mains €7-12) Not the best Indian ever tasted, but pretty darn good for Germany. Besides, the combination of sub-continental interior décor and traditional, exposed medieval beams presents a surprisingly harmonious mix.

For quick meals, try **Schlosscafé Vis à Vis** (☎ 925 790; Schlossplatz; breakfast €3.50-12, mains €4.50-8; ⊙ closed from 6.30pm), which has pasta, salads, jacket potatoes and the like, or **H Kielhorn** (☎ 228 15; Brandplatz 2; meals €2.50-5; ⊙ Mon-Fri 8.30am-6pm, from 7am Wed, 7am-1pm Sat) a butcher's shop-cum-*Imbiss* (stand-up food stall) with hearty soups, sausages and potatoes.

Entertainment

If you're staying longer than most, check out the bar information in the German-language monthly *Celle Szene*.

Schlosstheater (Schlossplatz; tickets ☎ 127 14) This theatre gets a lot of attention because its theatre is in the picture-book pretty palace. However, programme times for plays and concerts are erratic, as are ticket prices, so check with the tourist office.

Shopping

Weinhandlung Bornhöft (☎ 6800; Zöllnerstrasse 29) You can buy souvenirs of the local hooch, the 58% alcohol Ratzeputz here. The liquor is brewed from ginger.

Getting There & Away

Celle is within easy reach of Hanover, with three trains an hour making the trip (from €6.90) in anything from 19 minutes (ICE) to 45 minutes (S-Bahn). There's also a frequent direct service to/from Lüneburg (€12.40, 45 minutes).

If you're driving, take the B3 straight into the centre.

Getting Around

City bus Nos 2, 3 and 4 run between the Hauptbahnhof and Schlossplatz, the two main stations. Single tickets are €1.20, while six-ticket strips are €5.90.

For a taxi call ☎ 444 44 or ☎ 280 01. Hire bikes from **Johcoby** (☎ 254 89; Bahnhofstrasse 27).

BERGEN-BELSEN

Whether you leave in tears or stricken by the inhumanity of humans – or both – it's difficult to remain unmoved by a visit to **Bergen-Belsen** (☎ 05051-6011; www.bergenbelsen.de; Lohheide; admission free; ☯ 9am-6pm). The most infamous Nazi concentration camp on German soil (the largest was at Auschwitz-Birkenau, near Kraków in Poland), it's the cemetery of more than 70,000 Jews, Soviet soldiers, political hostages and other prisoners. Among them lies Anne Frank, whose posthumously published diary, *The Diary of Anne Frank* (1947), recounting two years of hiding in an Amsterdam attic with her German Jewish family, became a modern classic.

Unlike at Auschwitz, absolutely none of the camp remains and you largely see a meadow, which in summer is covered in purple heather. Yet what could in other circumstances be a peaceful spot is palpably poisoned by the torture and killing that occurred on this soil. (The sounds of military aircraft and small-arms fire from the NATO base next door only add to the gloom.)

Inside the **Documentation Centre** just outside the cemetery gates, there's a small exhibition outlining the history of the concentration camps in general and of Bergen-Belsen in particular, plus a theatre showing a 25-minute documentary. Both include awful scenes of the several thousand unburied bodies and emaciated survivors that greeted the British forces who liberated the camp in April 1945. The film includes moving testimony from one of the cameramen. Screenings are hourly from 10am to 5pm daily, but rotate between different languages.

Inside the centre, there's also a book of names of those who were interned here, as well as a shelf of guides, books for sale about Bergen-Belsen and *The Diary of Anne Frank*. There's a free *Guide for Visitors to the Belsen Memorial*, or you can buy a fully illustrated guide (€2.50) in several languages.

Bergen-Belsen began its existence in 1940 as a POW camp, but was partly taken over by the SS from April 1943, to hold Jews hostage in exchange for German POWs held abroad. Many Russian and Allied soldiers, then later Jews, Poles, homosexuals and Romanian Gypsies all suffered here – beaten, tortured, gassed, starved or worked to death, and used as medical guinea pigs. Too many remain here, under large lumps of grass-covered earth that reveal their true identity as mass graves by signs indicating approximately how many people lie in each – 1000, 2000, 5000, an unknown number…

Tens of thousands of prisoners from other camps near the front line were brought to Belsen in the last months of WWII, causing overcrowding, an outbreak of disease and even more deaths. Despite the SS' best attempts to hide the evidence of their inhumane practices, forcing prisoners to bury or incinerate their deceased colleagues, thousands of corpses still littered the compound on 15 April 1945 when British troops entered the camp. Today's graves were initially identified or dug at that time.

Also here in the several hectares of cemetery is a large stone **obelisk and memorial**, with inscriptions to all victims, a **cross** on the spot of a memorial initially raised by Polish prisoners and the **Haus der Stille**, where you can retreat for quiet contemplation. A **gravestone for Anne Frank** and her sister, Margot, has also been erected (not too far from the cemetery gates, on the way to the obelisk). The entire family was initially sent to Auschwitz when their hiding place in Amsterdam was betrayed to police, but the sisters were later transferred to Belsen. Although no-one knows where Anne lies exactly, many pay tribute to their 15-year-old heroine at this gravestone. Other monuments to various victim groups, including a **Soviet memorial**, are dotted across the complex.

After WWII, Allied forces used the troop barracks here as a displaced persons' (DP) camp, for those waiting to emigrate to a third country (including many Jews who went to Israel after its establishment in 1948). The DP camp was closed in September 1950.

Getting There & Away

It's easy to reach Bergen-Belsen by car but tricky by public transport.

If you're driving from Celle, take Hehlentorstrasse north over the Aller River and follow Harburger Strasse north out of the city. This is the B3; continue northwest to the town of Bergen and follow the signs to Belsen.

By public transport, there are only three direct buses daily, Monday to Friday, and none on weekends. You need to catch bus No 11 (€4.80 each way, one hour) from the ZOB, which is under the huge car park opposite the Celle Hauptbahnhof. Buses leave here at 12.05pm, 1.40pm and 3.45pm. However, the 1.40pm bus is scheduled for school days and won't turn up during holidays. The only direct bus back leaves the camp at 4.54pm. For further details, call **CeBus** (☎ 05141-487 080) or ask at the Celle tourist office.

One alternative is to take the frequent bus No 12 to the village of Bergen. From there, a **taxi** (☎ 05051-5555) to the camp will cost about €12. There's a phone at the camp if you need to call a taxi when leaving.

LÜNEBURG

☎ 04131 / pop 66,000

An off-kilter church steeple, buildings leaning on each other and houses with swollen 'beer-belly' façades: it's as if the charming town of Lüneburg has drunk too much of the Pilsener lager it used to brew.

Of course, the city's wobbly angles and uneven pavements have a more prosaic cause. For centuries until 1980, Lüneburg was a salt-mining town, and as this 'white gold' was extracted from the earth, shifting ground and subsidence caused many buildings to tilt sideways. Inadequate drying of the plaster used in the now-swollen façades merely added to this asymmetry.

Still, the lopsidedness of its pretty stepped gables and Hanseatic architecture means Lüneburg has both looks and character. It's a memorable gateway to the surrounding heath.

Orientation

The Hauptbahnhof is to the east, while the city centre is to the west, of the Ilmenau River. To reach the Markt by foot, turn left when leaving the station, go through the bus station and down the steps to your right, before heading right towards the wobbly steeple of the St Johanniskirche into Altenbrückertorstrasse. This street leads across

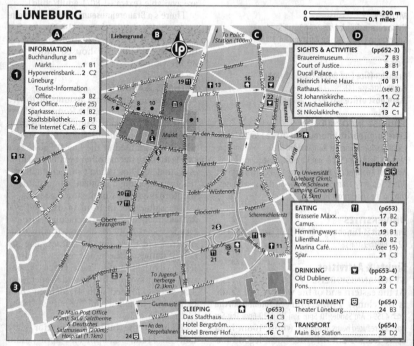

LÜNEBURG

INFORMATION	
Buchhandlung am Markt	1 B1
Hypovereinsbank	2 C2
Lüneburg Tourist-Information Office	3 B2
Post Office	(see 25)
Sparkasse	4 B2
Stadtsbibliothek	5 B1
The Internet Café	6 C3

SIGHTS & ACTIVITIES	(pp652-3)
Brauereimuseum	7 B3
Court of Justice	8 B1
Ducal Palace	9 B1
Heinrich Heine Haus	10 B1
Rathaus	(see 3)
St Johanniskirche	11 C2
St Michaelikirche	12 A2
St Nikolaikirche	13 C1

EATING	🍴	(p653)
Brasserie Mäxx		17 B2
Camus		18 C3
Hemmingways		19 B1
Lilienthal		20 B2
Marina Café		(see 15)
Spar		21 C3

DRINKING	🍺	(pp653-4)
Old Dubliner		22 C1
Pons		23 C1

ENTERTAINMENT	🎭	(p654)
Theater Lüneburg		24 B3

TRANSPORT		(p654)
Main Bus Station		25 D2

SLEEPING	🛏	(p653)
Das Stadthaus		14 C3
Hotel Bergström		15 C2
Hotel Bremer Hof		16 C1

LOWER SAXONY

the river to Am Sande. Turn right at Kleine Bäckerstrasse, and the Markt is the third on your left.

The Deutsches Salzmuseum (German Salt Museum) is in the southwest corner of the pedestrianised Altstadt, south of Lamberti Platz. Universität Lüneburg is 3km south of the centre.

Information

BOOKSHOPS
Buchhandlung am Markt (☎ 450 08; Bardowicker Strasse 1) Has a good travel section.

EMERGENCY
Police (☎ 110; Auf der Hude 1)

INTERNET ACCESS
The Internet Café (☎ 221 326; Am Sande 10)

LIBRARIES
Stadtbibliothek (City Library; Am Marienplatz; ☎ 309 619) Has some English literature.

MEDICAL SERVICES
Stadt Krankenhaus (Hospital; ☎ 770; Bögelstrasse 1)

MONEY
Hypovereinsbank (☎ 748 50; Am Sande 48)
Sparkasse (☎ 2880; An der Münze 4, Markt)

POST
Branch office (☎ 840 927; Hauptbahnhof, Bahnhofstrasse 14)
Main post office (☎ 7270; Sülztor 21)

TOURIST INFORMATION
Lüneburg Tourist-Information Office (☎ 207 6620; touristik@lueneburg.de; Rathaus, Am Markt; ☏ 9am-5pm Mon-Fri, 9am-4pm Sat & Sun May-Oct, closed Sun Nov-Apr) Arranges city **tours** (11am Apr-Oct, plus 2pm Sat Aug & Sep, only 11am Sat & Sun Nov-Mar). Also organises trips to the Lüneburger Heide.

UNIVERSITIES
Universität Lüneburg (☎ 781 260) Take bus No 11 or 12 to Blücherstrasse.

Sights & Activities
ST JOHANNISKIRCHE
At the eastern end of the wobbly Am Sande is the clunky 14th-century **St Johanniskirche** (☎ 43594; Am Sande; 10-5pm Sun-Wed, 10-6pm Thu-Sat Apr-Oct, reduced hours in winter), whose 106m-high spire leans 2.2m off true. Local legend has

it that the architect was so upset by this leaning steeple that he tried to do himself in by jumping off it. However, he merely bounced down the steeple, its angle slowing his descent, and landed safely in a full hay cart. To celebrate what seemed to be divine intervention, the architect made his way to the pub. He told the story over and over again, drinking until he fell and hit his head on the corner of a table, killing himself instantly.

The inside of the church is almost as good as the legend; there's an impressive organ and stained-glass windows, both ancient and modern.

MUSEUMS
At the **Deutsches Salzmuseum** (☎ 450 69; Sülfmeisterstrasse 1; adult/child/student €4/2.50/2.70; ☏ 9am-5pm Mon-Fri, 10am-5pm Sat & Sun May-Sep, 10am-5pm Oct-Apr) you get to descend into the salt cellars, emerge into a salt-panning room and generally, if you speak German, learn about how Lüneberg's precious food preservative made it an important player in the Hanseatic League. One-hour German-language tours are available (extra €1.80/1 adult/child).

There's a **Brauereimuseum** (☎ 448 04; Heiligengeiststrasse 39; admission free; ☏ 1-4.30pm Tue-Sun) looking at the history of beer-making in this city, which once housed more than 80 breweries.

RATHAUS & MARKT
Many sources mistakenly assume the town's name came from Luna, the Roman goddess of the moon. In reality, Lüneburg hails from the Saxon word *hliuni* (meaning refuge), which was granted at the Ducal Palace (see p653) to those fleeing other territories. However, that small fact didn't stop city authorities from erecting a **fountain** with a statue of the Roman goddess in the town's Markt.

The statue sits in front of the medieval **Rathaus**, which has a spectacular baroque façade added in 1720, decorated with coats of arms and three tiers of statues. The top row of statues on the façade represents (from left to right): Strength, Trade, Peace (the one with the big sword), Justice and Moderation. The steeple, topped with 41 Meissen china bells, was installed on the city's 1000th birthday in 1956.

Tours of the building's interior leave daily at 11am, 12.30pm and 3pm (adult/

concession €3/2) from the entrance on Am Ochsenmarkt.

Other buildings around the Markt include the **Court of Justice**, the little gated-in, grotto-like area with paintings depicting scenes of justice being carried out throughout the centuries; and the former **Ducal Palace**, now a courthouse. West of that, on the corner of Burmeisterstrasse and Am Ochsenmarkt, is the home of the parents of poet Heinrich Heine. Heine, who hated Lüneburg, wrote the *Loreley* here (for more on the Loreley rock, see p512).

CARRIAGE RIDES & CYCLING

The Markt is the departure point for regular **horse-drawn carriage rides** (☎ 04178-8542; €9; ⏰ 11.30am, 1pm & 2.30pm Tue, Thu & Fri). Call ahead or simply turn up.

Many tourists come to the Lüneburger Heide to go cycling, and the tourist office has dozens of different pamphlets outlining routes. One to ask about in particular is the **Elbetour Cycling Trail** between the Rathaus in Lüneburg and Neetze, passing the Naturpark Elbufer-Drawehn (see p654).

SPA BATHS

Another pleasant way to while away time is to luxuriate in Lüneburg's **SaLü Salztherme** (Spa baths; ☎ 723 110; Uelzener Strasse 1-5; ⏰ 10am-11pm Mon-Sat, 8am-9pm Sun). Prices start at €7.50 for two hours.

Sleeping

The tourist office can book private rooms, but ask individual hotels about special deals during low seasons.

DJH hostel (☎ 418 64; Soltauer Strasse 133) Lüneburg's Jugendherberge was due to reopen in October 2004 after major renovations, but do ring to check that's happened if you're arriving around this time. Take bus No 11 or 12 from the bus station to Scharnhorststrasse.

Rote Schleuse Lüneburg (☎ 791 500; adult/car & tent €4/5.20) This camp site is about 3.5km south of the centre and offers a woodsy terrain scattered with fruit trees. Take bus No 605 or 1977 from Am Sande (direction: Deutschebern/Uelzen).

Das Stadthaus (☎ 444 38; fax 404 198; Am Sande 25; s €50-70, d €80-95) This hotel near St Johanniskirche is another good option. Its rooms are unfussy and very pleasant, if not exactly huge.

Hotel Bremer Hof (☎ 2240; info@bremer-hof.de; Lüner Strasse 12-13; s €50-100, d €80-125; **P**) This excellent family-run hotel near the Nikolaikirche caters to a wide range of budgets, with older accommodation in the concrete block at the back of the courtyard and more comfortable rooms in the historic main house. Room 76, with its huge exposed ceiling beams, is probably the most stunning. Parking is €5.

Hotel Bergström (☎ 3080; info@bergstroem.de; Bei der Lüner Mühle; s €125-145, d €145-165; **P** ✗) Set in half a dozen warehouse buildings and an old mill around a weir in the Ilmenau River, this wonderful luxury hotel feels like its own dockside village. The rooms in the 'Lüner Mühle' are the newest and flashiest, but the water tower over the bridge has a 'fairy-tale' suite. Parking is €8.50.

Eating

Camus (☎ 428 20; Am Sande 30; mains €6.50-10) This is a clean and crisp brasserie-type establishment, with lots of well-priced modern international fare with an Italian angle, and quite a few veggie dishes.

Hotel Bremer Hof (☎ 2240; Lüner Strasse 12-13; mains €6-17) Light and airy, with a lot of blue, the atmospheric restaurant here is strong on local specialities, including lamb from the heath, or *Heidschnucke*. Among other dishes, there are lamb steaks (€20), lamb's liver (€11) and rack of lamb (€52 for two).

Marina Café (☎ 3080; Bei der Lüner Mühle; mains €25-35) The view over the Ilmenau would be reason enough for coming to the upmarket restaurant of the Hotel Bergström, but the daily changing menu of international cuisine is also pretty good. For those who want to spend a little less but enjoy the views, there's also a pleasant warehouse coffee shop attached to the hotel.

Spar (Am Sande 8) For self-catering, try this convenient supermarket.

Schröderstrasse, south of the Rathaus, has wall-to-wall cafés and is a good place to grab a quick bite to eat. Try **Lilienthal** (☎ 401 144; Schröderstrasse 5a; mains €4.50-10), which serves pizzas, wraps, snacks and grills, or **Brasserie Mäxx** (☎ 732 505; Schröderstrasse 6; mains €5-10) which has a pretty similar menu.

Drinking

Lüneburg is a vibrant university town, and the best place to head for a drink is the riverside lane Am Stintmarkt, nicknamed the 'Stint' by students.

Hemmingways (☎ 232 255; Bardowicker Strasse 27-28) A good option for a drink, with cocktail nights, ladies' nights, men's nights and a general feeling of bonhomie. There's also a limited menu of American and Mexican food and a good Sunday brunch buffet.

Good venues on Am Stintmarkt include **Old Dubliner** (☎ 381 86; Am Stintmarkt 2) and **Pons** (☎ 224 935; Salzstrasse am Wasser 1), which is at the far end of Am Stintmarkt.

Entertainment

Regular classical concerts and recitals are held in **St Johanniskirche** (see p652), **St Nikolaikirche** (cnr Lüner Strasse & Koffmanstrasse) and **St Michaeliskirche** (cnr Johann-Sebastian-Bach-Platz), but Lüneburg also has a healthy theatre scene. Try **Theater Lüneburg** (☎ 421 00; An den Reeperbahnen 3) for German-language drama, as well as musicals, opera and classical music concerts.

Getting There & Away

There are frequent train services to Hanover (€18.40, one hour), Celle (€12.40, 45 minutes), Schwerin (€14.80, 1½ hours) and Hamburg (€6.60, 30 minutes).

If you're driving from Hamburg, take the A7 south to the B250. From Schwerin take the B6 south to the A24 west and then exit No 7 (Talkau). From there, turn south on the B209, and you'll eventually get to town. From Hanover, take the A7 north to the B209.

Getting Around

Buses leave from the ZOB central bus station at the Hauptbahnhof and from the bus centre on Am Sande. Most services stop running at around 7pm. Single tickets are €1.60; day tickets cost €3.20.

For a taxi, call ☎ 194 10.

You can hire bicycles at the **Hauptbahnhof** (☎ 557 77; €7.50/15 per day/weekend).

AROUND LÜNEBURG
Naturpark Elbufer-Drawehn

Some 20km east of Lüneburg, in a wetland area of the Lüneburger Heide, are Bleckede and the Naturpark Elbufer-Drawehn. The nature reserve is a haven for birdlife such as white storks, wild geese and cranes, running for 85km along the Elbe River.

Cyclists and hikers will be well rewarded by this picturesque and interesting wetland, and if you don't have your own bike, you can hire one in Lüneburg or Bleckede. If you intend to come out here, drop by the tourist office in Lüneburg first, which is well stocked with brochures on accommodation and activities.

With its half-timbered houses, pretty **Bleckede** is a good starting point for trips in the Naturpark. The **tourist office** (☎ 05852-390 788; fax 05852-33 03; Elbtal-Haus, Laünburger Strasse 15; ☻ noon-4pm Wed-Fri, noon-6pm Sat & Sun Apr-Oct, noon-5pm Fri-Sun Nov-Mar) has information on walks, boat trips and other activities, plus it can help with accommodation.

GETTING THERE & AROUND

No trains run to Bleckede, but buses leave at least hourly from Lüneburg at Am Sande or the Hauptbahnhof (€4.80, 45 minutes; no bikes permitted).

If you're going by car, the B216 leads to the turn-off to Bleckede. A car ferry crosses the river here and in Neu Darchau to the south.

See Getting Around opposite, for bike hire from Lüneburg. Bikes can be hired in Bleckede at **Fahrradverleih Weber** (☎ 05852-12 72; Breite Strasse 6).

A ROLL IN THE HAY

Lower Saxony has an excellent network of farm accommodation and several **Heu Hotels** (literally 'hay hotels'), where farmers have set up straw bunks in their barns and rent them out for a small fee. They're an interesting way to spend time in the countryside, and are usually much more comfortable (if odorous) than they sound. Some have horse riding, swimming lakes, sledding in winter and other activities. While some are bare-bones, all are heated in winter and many get downright luxurious. Check with tourist offices in the region for listings. The two best centres for finding country accommodation in the Lüneburger Heide are Celle and Lüneburg itself.

Urlaub und Freizeit auf dem Lande (Holidays & Leisure in the Country; ☎ 04231-966 50; info@bauernhofferien.de) is also a useful source of information, though it doesn't handle bookings.

SOUTH & EAST OF HANOVER

HILDESHEIM

☎ 05121 / pop 106,000

Two things in particular have day-trippers flocking to this former bishopric and market city: a picture-book 'medieval' town centre that's a glorious fake and the genuinely ancient cathedral door bas-reliefs, which were cleverly saved from the WWII firebombing that razed Hildesheim to the ground on 22 March 1945. A legendary '1000-year-old' rosebush that re-emerged from the ashes of this attack also attracts pilgrims.

Orientation

The central Markt is 750m south of the Hauptbahnhof. To walk there from the station, take the pedestrianised Bernwardstrasse, which becomes Almsstrasse and Hoher Weg. Turning left, or east, from Hoher Weg into either Markstrasse or Rathaustrasse will lead you to Hildesheim's stunning centre, and the tourist office.

Continuing along Hoher Weg, instead of turning left for the tourist office, you hit Schuhstrasse, a central bus stop. To the right (west), the road heads to the cathedral and the Roemer- und Pelizaeus-Museum. Straight ahead across Schuhstrasse you'll find the drinking strip of Friesenstrasse and, 10 minutes further south, the old Jewish quarter.

Information

Commerzbank (☎ 169 10; Almssstrasse 29-30)
Main post office (Bahnhofsplatz 3-4)
Tourist Office Hildesheim (☎ 179 80; www.hilde sheim.com; Rathausstrasse 20; ☿ 9.30am-5pm Mon-Fri, 9.30am-4pm Sat) Organises **tours** (€3.50; ☿ 2pm daily, plus 9.30am Sat Apr-Oct) in German, and sells the *Hildesheimer Rosenroute* (€1), a guide to the city's buildings and their history.

Sights & Activities

MARKT

The town's central market place was reconstructed in traditional style during the 1980s, after locals decided they could no longer stand the typical 'German postwar hideous' style in which the town was originally repaired. However, knowing that the **Markt** is about as old as *The Simpsons* barely tempers its appeal. People still 'ooh' and 'aah', as they gaze around, particularly at the (clockwise from north) **Rokokohaus**, **Wollenweberhaus**, **Wedekindhaus**, **Knochenhauerhaus** (Butchers' Guild Hall), and **Bäckeramtshaus** (Bakers' Guild Hall). In many cases, you can see behind the façade, too: the Rokokohaus is now home to the Meridien hotel, the Knochenhauerhaus houses a restaurant and there's also a local history **museum** (☎ 301 163; Markt 7-8; adult/concession €2/1; ☿ 10am-6pm Tue-Sun).

The only original feature is the **Marktbrunnen**, the fountain in front of the **Rathaus** on the east side of the square (bells play folk songs at noon, 1pm and 5pm daily).

DOM

There's a tiny entrance fee to see the **Tausendjähriger Rosenstock** (1000-year-old rosebush; adult/concession €0.50/0.30) in the cloister of the **Hildesheim Dom** (Hildesheim Cathedral; ☎ 179 1760; Domhof; ☿ 9.30am-5pm Mon-Sat, noon-5pm Sun May-Oct, 10am-4pm Mon-Fri, 9.30am-3pm Sat, noon-5pm Sun Nov-Apr). However the bas-reliefs on the cathedral's almost 5m-high **Bernwardstüren** (Bernward bronze doors) have much greater visual impact, and they aren't pay-per-view.

The allure of the rosebush lies in its supposed history as the very one on which Emperor Ludwig the Pious left his cloak and other effects in AD 815, where they miraculously stayed safe from theft. And its phoenix-like rise from the burnt-out cathedral remains after 1945 has only added to the bush's mystique.

Ultimately, though, it looks much like any other rose: something you couldn't say about the remarkable cathedral doors. Saved only because a concerned wartime prelate insisted they be stashed in a basement for safe-keeping, their exquisitely executed, three-dimensional reliefs of various historical and biblical tales are now under Unesco protection.

The church's **wheel-shaped chandelier** and the **Christussäule** (Column of Christ) are also original, and if you're really keen, there's an attached **Dom-Museum** (☎ 179 163; Domhof; adult/concession €3/2; ☿ 10am-5pm Tue-Sat, noon-5pm Sun), with rotating exhibitions and the cathedral treasury.

LOWER SAXONY

OTHER CHURCHES

Like the cathedral doors, the Romanesque **St Michaeliskirche** (☎ 344 10; Michaelisplatz; admission free; ✆ 8am-6pm Mon-Sat, noon-6pm Sun Apr-Oct, 9am-4pm Mon-Sat, noon-4pm Sun Nov-Mar) is also under Unesco protection. Built in 1022 and reconstructed after extensive war damage, its most stunning features are its striped columns and detailed ceiling mural. The church is north of the Dom.

Off Hoher Weg is **St Andreaskirche** (☎ 364 37; Andreasplatz; adult/concession €1.50/1; tower ✆ 9am-6pm Mon-Fri, 9am-4pm Sat, 11.30am-4pm Sun Apr-Sep) whose lofty spire offers a sweeping view. There are 364 steps to the top.

LAPPENBERG

The former **Jewish Quarter** in and around Lappenberg Square is the oldest section of town. Most of it remains because, while local fire crews let the synagogue burn to the ground on Kristallnacht in November 1938, they rescued other houses around the square. These included the former **Jewish school**, now owned by St Godehard's Church, on the corner. In 1988, on the 50th anniversary, a memorial was installed on the site of the synagogue, following the outline of its foundations and topped by a model of Jerusalem.

While down this way, take time to check out the quaint **Wernesches Haus** on Hinterer Brühl, which is one of the oldest buildings in Hildesheim.

ROEMER- UND PELIZAEUS-MUSEUM

One of Europe's best collections of Egyptian art and artefacts is found in the **Roemer- und Pelizaeus-Museum** (☎ 936 90; www.rpmuseum.de, in German; Am Steine 1-2; adult/concession/child €6/5/3; ✆ 9am-6pm Mon-Fri, 10am-6pm Sat & Sun). There are dozens of mummies, scrolls, statues and wall hangings, but the life-size re-creation of an Egyptian tomb is a particular highlight. Admission costs more during special exhibitions.

Sleeping

Its proximity to Hanover means Hildesheim often takes overspill guests during trade fairs, when accommodation prices rise phenomenally.

DJH hostel (☎ 427 17; jh-hildesheim@djh-hannover .de; Schirrmannweg 4; junior/senior €15/17.70; P ⌨) Modern, comfortable and serving a decent breakfast, this hillside Jugendherberge has wonderful views over town. The downside, for those without a car, is getting there. From the train station you need to catch a bus (No 1 or 2) to Schuhstrasse, changing to a No 4 in the direction of Im Koken-Hof. Even then the Triftstrasse stop is 750m down the hill. The doors close at 10pm.

Gästehaus Klocke (☎ 179 213; www.gaestehaus -klocke.de; Humboldtstrasse 11; s €45-55, d €75-80) This is a quirky gem, which feels a bit like a mini-castle upon entering, as its high-ceilinged stairwell has a landing with a stained-glass window, chess set and chairs. The rooms aren't quite as amazing but have character nevertheless. The hotel is just south over the canal from the Jewish quarter.

Gästehaus-Café Timphus (☎ 346 86; timphus-cond itorei-hotel@t-online.de; Braunschweiger Strasse 90/91; s €50-65, d €75-85) The set-up here feels like being in your own apartment building, as the clean, modern rooms have their own unmarked entrance hall, next door to the patisserie that owns them. You need to arrive before 6pm to collect the key from the patisserie.

Hotel Bürgermeisterkapelle (☎ 140 21; www .hotelbuergermeisterkapelle.de; Rathausstrasse 8; s €55-65, d €85-95; P). The more expensive rooms in this central, historic hotel have been renovated in a modern style. There's also a great dining room upstairs.

The trade fair markets mean there are several top-end hotels in Hildesheim.

Dorint Sülte Hotel (☎ 171 70; info.hajhil@dorint .com; Bahnhofsallee 38; s €120-130, d €140-165; P ✗) has taken its spacious stone cloister building and imbued it with cosy designer chic. In summer prices start at €80.

Meridien Hotel (☎ 300 600; www.lemeridien-hilde sheim.com; Markt 4; s €140-155, d €155-175; ✗) This hotel has an establishment feel appropriate to its Rokokohaus location. Summer prices start at €100.

Ask the tourist office about camping outside town.

Eating

Knochenhauer-Amsthaus (☎ 323 23; Markt 7; mains €5.50-18) Like every restaurant in and around the Markt, this place is a bit touristy. However, it does compensate with an interesting interior, reconstructed in medieval style. The decent German food not only includes schnitzels and steaks, but a variety of roasts, one of which is sautéed in beer.

Noah (☎ 691 530; Hohnsen 28; mains €7.50-18) This airy, glass-walled bistro faces a lake and serves Mediterranean-influenced modern cuisine, including salads, pasta, risotto and, fittingly, fish. Take bus No 2 to Theodor Storm Strasse/Ochtersum.

Schlegel (☎ 331 33; Am Steine 4-6; mains €9.50-19; ⓨ dinner, closed Sun) The lopsided walls of this rose-covered, 500-year-old house hunkering beside the Roemer- und Pelizaeus-Museum just add to the sheer magic of the place. Inside, there's a group of historic rooms and, in one corner, one round, glass-topped table fashioned from a well, where you dine overlooking the water far beneath. As the ever-changing international cuisine is also exceptional, it's advisable to book.

Paulaner im Kniep (☎ 360 13; Markstrasse 4; mains €3.50-14) If you're after a faster and more functional feed, head here for Bavarian fare.

Café-Brasserie Hindenburg, Chapeau Claque and Limerick (see Drinking below) also serve reasonably priced food, including veggie options, during the day.

Drinking

There's a popular, if slightly tacky, drinking strip just behind Schuhstrasse, along Friesenstrasse, including **Marmaris** (☎ 133 865; Friesenstrasse 19) and the **Two Pence Pub** (☎ 353 58; Friesenstrasse 6). The **Café-Brasserie Hindenburg** (☎ 399 27; Hindenburgplatz 3) is just round the corner at the eastern end.

For somewhere a little more relaxed, try **Limerick** (☎ 133 876; Kläperhagen 6). Head to **Chapeau Claque** (☎ 133 676; Osterstrasse 58) for a café with good background music, or try **Thav** (☎ 132 829; Güntherstrasse 21), which also has club evenings.

Getting There & Around

Frequent regional train services operate between Hildesheim and Hanover (€5.50, 30 minutes), while ICE trains head to Braunschweig (€12.60, 25 minutes) and Göttingen (€22, 30 minutes).

For those under there own steam, the A7 runs right by town from the city of Hanover.

Most sights in Hildesheim are within walking distance, but buses will take you to outlying restaurants and accommodation, as indicated. Single tickets cost €1.50, or €6.50 for six. The tourist office can help with bike hire.

BRAUNSCHWEIG
☎ 0531 / pop 253,000

Its continued self-description as 'the town of Heinrich der Löwe' – something which was true when the Lion King, Henry, lived here in the 12th century – gives the impression Braunschweig (Brunswick) hasn't really found its niche in the modern world. An amalgam of five separate settlements, it has something of a hotch-potch character, and having spent much of its recent history in the shadow of the former Iron Curtain can't have helped.

Still, Lower Saxony's second-largest city is in possession of one of Germany's most amazing collections of porcelain, painting and other *objets d'art* from more than two millennia. A few medieval buildings survived heavy WWII bombing and there's some nice parkland. Winning its bid to become European City of Culture in 2010 would provide a deserved confidence boost.

Orientation

Once you get to the compact old town centre, you rarely need to leave, as most sights are here. To arrive from the Hauptbahnhof, some 1.5km southeast, walk up Kurt-Schumacher-Strasse until John-F-Kennedy-Platz, right into Auguststrasse and Bohlweg, and then left into Damm. Or, as it's a long walk, take tram No 1 or 2 or bus No 420. The boundaries of the centre form a distorted rectangle, with Lange Strasse to the north, Bohlweg to the east, Konrad-Adenauer-Strasse to the south and Güldenstrasse to the west. A moat surrounds the centre, lending it the compact character of an island. A one-way system on the east side (see Getting Around, p662) may cause problems if you're driving. The heart of the pedestrianised shopping district is Kohlmarkt.

Information

Buchhandlung Karl Pfankuch (☎ 453 03; Burgpassage mall, between Damm and Kleine Burg) Excellent collection of English-language books.
Citibank (☎ 400 007; Steinweg 1)
Commerzbank (☎ 480 950; Bohlweg 33)
Flugbörse (☎ 448 54; Hagenbrücke 15) Travel agency.
Main post office (Berliner Platz 12-16) Near the Hauptbahnhof.
Post (Friedrich-Wilhelm-Strasse 3)
SB Waschsalon (Goslarsche Strasse 22) Laundry, about 2km west of the centre.

Tourist Service Braunschweig (☎ 273 550; www.braunschweig.de; Vor der Burg 1; ⊗ 9.30am-6pm Mon-Fri, 10am-2pm Sat year round, 10am-12.30pm Sun May-Oct) Organises city tours year round at 2pm

Saturday (€5) and 10.30am Sunday May to October, or monthly evening Mumme-Bummel tours (€9), including a shot of the local, nonalcoholic drink Mumme.

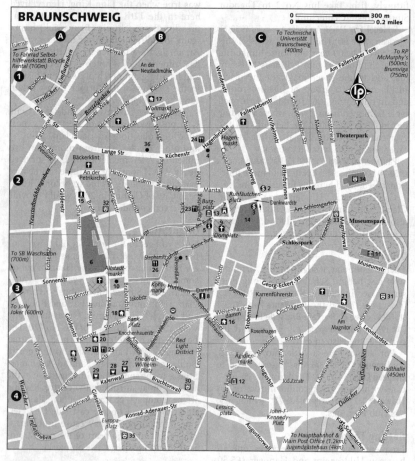

BRAUNSCHWEIG

0 ——— 300 m
0 ——— 0.2 miles

INFORMATION			SLEEPING	⊡	(p660)		Brodocz......................................26	B3
Buchhandlung Karl Pfankuch...............1	B3		Best Western Stadtpalais.................16	C3				
Citibank.......................................2	C2		CVJM Hotel am Wollmarkt...............17	B1		**DRINKING**	⊡	(p661)
Commerzbank................................3	C2		Frühlings Hotel.............................18	B3		Atlantis......................................27	B4
Flugbörse.....................................4	B2		Haus zur Hanse............................19	A4		Liro Dando..................................28	B4
Tourist Service Braunschweig............5	C2		Hotel Ritter St Georg......................20	A3		Merz..29	A4
			Stadthotel Magnitor........................21	D3		Viel Harmonie.........................(see 18)	
SIGHTS & ACTIVITIES		(pp659-60)						
Altstadt Rathaus............................6	A3		**EATING**	⊞	(pp660-1)		**ENTERTAINMENT**	⊡	(p661)
Burg Dankwarderode......................7	C2		Gewandhaus...........................(see 10)				Brain Klub...................................30	B4
Cats Statue..................................8	B3		Hansestube/Boom...................(see 19)				Die Brücke..................................31	D3
Dom...9	C2		Knochenhauer.............................22	A4		LOT-Theater...............................32	A2
Gewandhaus...............................10	B3		Mutter Habenicht.........................23	B2		Staatstheater Kleines Haus.............33	D2
Herzog Anton Ulrich Museum.........11	D3		Penny Markt...............................24	B2		Staatstheater...............................34	D2
Jewish Museum...........................12	C4		Restaurant Ritter St Georg..........(see 20)				VW Halle....................................35	B4
Landesmuseum............................13	B2		Stechinelliis Kartoffel-Keller.........(see 10)				
Neues Rathaus............................14	C2		Tandir..25	A4		**TRANSPORT**		(p662)
Till Eulenspiegel Brunnen...............15	A2		Vegetarisches Vollwert Restaurant				ADAC..36	B2

Dangers & Annoyances

The city's red-light district is in the alley connecting Wallstrasse with the intersection of Leopoldstrasse and Friedrich-Wilhelm-Strasse. Although it's not considered unsafe, women are advised not to go unless they're prepared to be harassed.

Sights & Activities

HERZOG ANTON ULRICH MUSEUM

Like author Bruce Chatwin's compulsive collector *Utz*, Braunschweig's famous duke Anton Ulrich had an eye for miniature porcelain figures – as well for crockery, furniture and all types of painting, from Chinese to European. This makes the **Herzog Anton Ulrich Museum** (☎ 122 50; Museumstrasse 1; combined admission with Burg Dankwarderode adult/concession €2.50/1.30; ☺ 10am-5pm Tue-Sun, 1-8pm Wed) not only the jewel in Braunschweig's crown, but also one of the best regional museums of art in Germany. Artefacts, including an ancient Roman onyx cup that survived some escapades through the years, and the most complete museum collection of Fürstenburg porcelain anywhere, are on one floor. Dutch, French and Italian paintings, with works by artists like Rubens, Rembrandt and Vermeer, are on the floor below.

The only pain is that funding and staffing shortages mean only one floor is open at any given period. So, within the general opening hours, the painting floor will be open for a block of one or two hours, followed by the artefacts floor for the following few hours. Ring ahead, or be prepared to spend some time between floors in the pleasant café.

BURG DANKWARDERODE

Heinrich's former **castle** (☎ 122 50; Burgplatz; adult/concession €2.50/1.30; ☺ 10am-5pm Tue-Sun, 1-8pm Wed) is now the medieval section of the Herzog Anton Ulrich Museum, and the same ticket admits you to both. Here the highlight is the huge, spectacularly adorned **Knights' Hall** on the upper floor, although some of the golden sculptures of arms, medieval capes and the original **lion statue**, copies of which stand all over town, are more impressive than you might expect. Sadly there's the same staggered opening here; while one floor is open, the other is shut. Call ahead for exact times and details.

LANDESMUSEUM

Similar to, but much better than, Hanover's Historisches Museum, the **Landesmuseum** (State Museum; ☎ 121 50; Burgplatz; adult/concession €3/1.50; ☺ 10am-5pm Tue, Wed & Fri-Sun, 10am-8pm Thu) covers German history from a local perspective. Ongoing renovations will mean changes, but the collection will certainly continue to include *zweihundert Milliarden* (200 billion) and *zwanzig Millionen* (20 million) mark notes from the inflationary days of the Weimar Republic, Nazi posters, a Trabant car and so on. Hopefully, the huge statue of Heinrich der Löwe made from nails to commemorate fallen WWI soldiers and the excellent audiovisual show of the battle of Sieverhausen will also remain.

DOM ST BLASII

In the crypt under **Dom St Blasii** (St Blasius Cathedral; ☎ 243 350; Domplatz 5; ☺ 10am-5pm, closed 1-3pm Jan-Easter), the city's Romanesque and Gothic Dom (1173–95), is the tomb of Heinrich der Löwe and Mathilde – an Englishwoman who was, depending on whom you believe, either his wife or (more likely) his consort. Turn right at the bottom of the stairs for the tomb. Admission to the cathedral is free, and €1 to the crypt.

The Dom holds brief services at 5pm weekdays with organ music. There are Protestant services at 10am on Sunday.

JEWISH MUSEUM

In the former monastery of the **Aegidienkirche**, on Mönchstrasse at the southeastern end of the centre, is Braunschweig's small **Jewish Museum** (☎ 1215 2661; Hinter Aegidien; adult/concession €3.50/2; ☺ 10am-5pm Tue, Wed & Fri-Sun, 10am-8pm Thu). The centrepiece is the reconstructed interior of the destroyed synagogue of the village of Hornburg, accompanied by one of its Torah scrolls.

OTHER ATTRACTIONS

Of the several market places in Braunschweig, each representing an original township, the Altstadt Markt is the most appealing, with the step-gabled Renaissance **Gewandhaus** (1303, façade 1590) and the Gothic **Altstadt Rathaus**. Inside the Rathaus is the magnificent Dornse meeting hall. Across town, behind Burg Dankwarderode, the neo-Gothic **Neues Rathaus** (1894–1900) also has a pretty riotous façade.

Kids will like the playful **cats statue** on the corner of Damm and Kattreppeln and the lovely **Till Eulenspiegel Brunnen** at Bäckerklint, with Till sitting above owls and monkeys.

Sleeping

If travelling in summer, contact the tourist office: it has great deals where you might pay €50/80 per single/double for four-star accommodation. Several hotels were closed for renovation or other reasons at the time of writing, so you might want also to ask the tourist office whether the historic Hotel Ritter St Georg, for example, has reopened. Budget travellers might want to try for a **private room** (☎ 695 550; braunschweig@bedandbreakfast.de).

Jugendgästehaus (☎ 264 320; fax 264 3270; Salzdahlumer Strasse 170; dorms €14-17) This non-DJH hostel is a bit out of the way and not the flashiest in the world; however the staff are pleasant and friendly. Take bus No 411, 422, 431 or 439 to Krankenhaus.

Frühlings-Hotel (☎ 243 210; www.fruehlingshotel .de; Bankplatz 7; s €45-110, d €70-145; P) First impressions count, so this central hotel's pleasant modern reception area and dining room is a winner. Upstairs though, there are three categories of room, and the cheapest of these are a little old-fashioned and dark. The nicer accommodation, decorated in a light-coloured Ikea style, starts from €55/85 for a single/double. Parking is €5.

CVJM Hotel am Wollmarkt (☎ 244 400; www .hotelamwollmarkt.de; Wollmarkt 9-12; s €55-60, d €85-90; P) This YMCA-run hotel is just north of the centre and has pretty standard, but clean and comfortable, rooms. The staff are welcoming and there's always the chance to challenge fellow guests to a game of table football in the communal lounge. Weekend rates are a fraction cheaper.

Stadthotel Magnitor (☎ 471 30; www.stadthotel -magni.de in German; Am Magnitor 1; s €75-85, d €105-120) For our money, this 500-year-old black-and-white, half-timbered building in the pedestrianised Magniviertel quarter is the place to stay in Braunschweig. Charming, light-filled rooms successfully merge rustic and the modern (including modem plugs), while staff make you feel like one of the family. If you want a discount – and a good laugh – plump for one of the front rooms, whose very low ceilings date from the Middle Ages. Or come at the weekend, when singles/doubles start from €60/85.

Haus zur Hanse (☎ 243 900; www.haus-zur-hanse .de; Güldenstrasse 7; s/d €80/95) Another historic old house with converted modern rooms, Haus zur Hanse is more masculine and formal than Stadthotel Magnitor. It features a brilliant restaurant (see Hansestube/Boom in the following Eating section), but suffers a little from being on a fairly busy road, so come in winter, when you can keep the windows closed, or ask for a room at the back.

Best Western Stadtpalais (☎ 241 024; www.pal ais-braunschweig.bestwestern.de; Hinter Liebfrauen 1a; s €100-130, d €120-150; P ☒) With plenty of cream-coloured luxury and enough character to keep it from feeling sterile, this former 18th-century palace keeps the fussiest of travellers happy. Okay, those on business might find the desk space a trifle cramped, but the Best Western is in a quieter location than some other chain hotels here. Weekend discounts are available.

Eating

QUICK EATS & SELF-CATERING

Tandir (☎ 165 67; Südstrasse 24) There are lots of Turkish places in the central pedestrianised zones, but Tandir really pulls in the customers with its lavish displays of *pide* (flat bread), salads, fried vegetable dishes and baklava. And there are five kinds of doners.

A **Penny Markt** supermarket is on Hagenbrücke. Fresh produce markets are held on Wednesday and Saturday mornings on the Altstadt Markt.

RESTAURANTS

Mutter Habenicht (☎ 459 56; Papenstieg 3; mains €5.50-15) This 'Mother Hubbard' sure doesn't have a bare cupboard, as she dishes up filling portions of schnitzels and spare ribs. Asian curries and seasonal specialities like *Pfefferlinge* (chanterelle mushrooms) or *Spargel* (white asparagus) are also served in the dimly lit, bric-a-brac-filled front room, or in the small beer garden out the back.

Knochenhauer (☎ 480 3503; Altes Knochenhauerstrasse 11; mains €4-13 ☽ evenings only) The bistro/bar of choice among Braunschweig's hip, casual set, Knochenhauer just buzzes on a summer eve with friends getting together for an international melange of pasta, salads and other dishes. There are also DJs on Friday and Saturday night.

Vegetarisches Vollwert Restaurant Brodocz (☎ 422 36; Stephanstrasse 1; mains €6.50-15; ☽ Mon-Sat)

From the venerable Eastern European tradition comes one of those 'vegetarian' restaurants that also serve meat. Oh well, whatever. In any case, the food – including ratatouille, mushrooms, tofu and beef – is truly delicious, even if the well-intentioned but muddled service leaves something to be desired.

Gewandhaus & Stechinelli's Kartoffel-Keller (☎ 242 777; Altstadtmarkt 1-2; mains €4-21) These adjacent basement restaurants are run jointly and although they look different (Stechnelli's is more casual), they partly share the same menu. In both, you'll get lots of potato dishes; in the Gewandhaus there are more quality meat dishes. Try the potato *Schnapps* with *Gedöns* (small fried potato cakes with apple and berry sauce) as a starter.

Restaurant Ritter St Georg (☎ 618 0100; Altes Knochenhauerstrasse 12; mains €14-19; ❤ Tue-Sat) When lunching or dining in this lovely historic restaurant, it's hard to know what to concentrate on: the rough-hewn walls and faded medieval decoration on the ceiling and beams or the wonderful cuisine, with its Italian, German and Asian influences.

Hansestube/Boom (☎ 243 900; Güldenstrasse 7; mains €8-18) There's a seasonally changing menu at Braunschweig's best restaurant, where the largely Italian menu might include things like home-made squid-ink ravioli filled with salmon, or rack of lamb stuffed with pistachio, mustard and sesame. The room is divided into an elegant dining area with lots of glass and dark wood (Hansestube), beside a more informal bistro (Boom).

Drinking

More listings can be found in *Cocktail*, *Subway*, or *Da Capo*. Also try the tourist office's German-language brochure *Braunschweig Bietet*.

Merz (☎ 181 28; Gieselerstrasse 3) Spacious and relaxed, with table football, an attached weekend club (Schwanensee) playing house and soul classics, and a lovely beer garden, Merz is enduringly popular on the Braunschweig scene. Snacks are also served.

Liro Dando (☎ 157 09; Kalenwall 3) There's a slightly trendier crew here than at Merz, although among all the scruffy chic students you do see the occasional dad.

Viel Harmonie (☎ 416 11; Bankplatz 7) There's not always a harmonious attitude from the

staff here, but the friendly buzz from the punters more than compensates. On summer evenings, tables even spill over to the pavement across the road.

Entertainment
DISCOS & CLUBS

Atlantis (☎ 123 3237; Kalenwall 3) Extremely handy for the stretch of bars along Kalenwall and around, this youngish, up-for-it, good-time club has top chart hits, and classic '70s, '80s and black music nights.

Jolly Joker (☎ 281 4660; Broitzemerstrasse 220) More than 20 years old and still going strong, this mainstream club had a major renovation at the end of 2001, so it's no longer as grimy as it once apparently was. Expect top 100 dance-chart hits. The same complex also houses a cinema.

Brain Klub (☎ 408 62; Bruchtorwall 12) Its bright blue exterior and industrial-looking interior are not the only thing that mark the Brain Klub out. It also has a harder edge than many Braunschweig clubs, playing everything from dance, techno and old school hip hop to nu school drum 'n' bass, with a bit of reggae mixed in.

FOLK & ROCK

There's quite a dreamy side to Braunschweig's live music scene.

Brunsviga (☎ 238 040; Karlstrasse 35) Modern music, jazz, cabaret, classical and folk guitar, and even flamenco (but not rock).

RP McMurphy's (☎ 336 090; Bültenweg 10) Regular live Irish folk music is played here.

When big international rock acts come to town, they're likely to perform at the **VW Halle** (☎ 707 70; Europaplatz 1) on the south side of town or maybe at the **Stadthalle** (see Theatre & Classical Music below).

THEATRE & CLASSICAL MUSIC

Dom (☎ 243 3350; Domplatz 5) Regular choral and organ concerts take place here.

Stadthalle (☎ 707 70; Leonhardplatz) The Philharmonisches Staatsorchestra performs at this city hall.

German-speaking theatre fans should check listings for the **Staatstheater** (☎ 123 40; Am Theater), and its smaller stage **Staatstheater Kleines Haus** (☎ 123 40; Magnitorwall 18). Alternatively, there's the more innovative **LOT-Theater** (☎ 173 03; Kaffeetwete 4a) or the cabaret-style **Die Brücke** (☎ 470 4861; Steintorwall 3).

Getting There & Away

There are regular IC trains to Hanover (€13.20, 35 minutes) and Leipzig (€32, 2½ hours), and ICE trains to Frankfurt (€62.60, 2¾ hours) and Berlin (€41.80, 1½ hours).

The A2 runs east–west between Hanover and Magdeburg across the northern end of the city. This connects with the A39 about 25km east of the city, which heads north to Wolfsburg. The A39 also heads south from the city.

ADAC (☎ 261 530; Lange Strasse 63) provides motoring information.

Getting Around

Braunschweig is the heart of an integrated transport network that extends throughout the region and as far south as the Harz Mountains. Bus and tram ticket prices are determined by time, not distance: 90-minute tickets cost €1.70, and 24-hour tickets cost €4.20.

Roads aren't in pristine condition, and parking enforcement is stringent in the centre. If driving, watch the one-way system that kicks in just north of the corner of Bohlweg and Ritterbrunnen.

A taxi from the Hauptbahnhof to the centre will set you back about €7.

Hire bicycles at **Fahrrad Selbsthilfewerkstatt** (☎ 576 636; Eulenstrasse 5; from €2 per day).

WOLFENBÜTTEL

☎ 05331 / pop 55,500

'Alles mit Bedacht' (take your time) is the motto of this friendly, charming little city, about 10 minutes by train from Braunschweig, but worlds away in attitude. First mentioned in 1118, Wolfenbüttel was virtually untouched by WWII, and it's almost a time capsule of half-timbered houses – there are over 600 of them, nearly all beautifully restored.

Orientation & Information

The Hauptbahnhof is a five-minute walk southwest of Stadtmarkt, the town centre. To get to the **Tourist Information Wölfenbüttel** (☎ 862 80; touristinfo@wolfenbuettel.com; Stadtmarkt 7; ☼ 9am-5pm Mon-Fri) in Stadtmarkt take Bahnhofstrasse north to Kommisstrasse. This joins Kornmarkt, the main bus transfer point. Stadtmarkt is just to the north. The Schloss and Herzog August Bibliothek are west of here.

Sights

The tourist office brochure *A walk through historic Wolfenbüttel* (€1) is an excellent guide. It starts at Wolfenbüttel's pretty **Schloss**, and deservedly so, because the **Schloss Museum** (☎ 924 60; Schlossplatz 13; adult/concession/family €3/2/4, free for children; ☼ 10am-5pm Tue-Sun) is the town's most remarkable attraction. The living quarters of the former residents, the dukes of Braunschweig-Lüneburg, have been preserved in all their glory of intricate inlaid wood, ivory walls, brocade curtains and chairs.

Meanwhile, the **Herzog August Bibliothek** (☎ 808 214; Lessingplatz 1; adult/concession €3/2; ☼ 10am-5pm Tue-Sun) across the square is another must for bibliophiles. Not only is this hushed place one of the world's best reference libraries for 17th-century books (if you're a member that is), its collection of 800,000 volumes also includes what's billed as the 'world's most expensive book' (€17.50 million). This is the *Welfen Evangelial*, a gospel book once owned by Heinrich der Löwe. The original is only on show in September every second year, but a pretty impressive facsimile is permanently displayed in the vault on the first floor. The library's founder, Duke August the Younger, developed an inventive cataloguing system that included, among other things, arranging the books by height. Downstairs there's a huge collection of book illustrations, including works by Chagall, Dali, Braque and Picasso, but only some are on display at any given time. Maps and globes are also found here.

Between the Schloss and the library is **Lessinghaus** (☎ 808 214; Am Schlossplatz; adult/concession €3/2; ☼ 10am-5pm Tue-Sun), a museum dedicated to the writer Gotthold Lessing, who lived and wrote his apocryphal *Nathan der Weise* (Nathan the Wise) here. The gabled pink building across the street was once the **Zeughaus** (armoury), but it is now used to store the library's catalogue.

From Schlossplatz, the walk suggested in the brochure continues east along Löwenstrasse to Krambuden and north up Kleiner Zimmerhof to **Klein Venedig** (Little Venice), one of the few tangible remnants of the extensive canal system built by Dutch workers in Wölfenbüttel in the late 16th century. From there the brochure continues to guide you past historic courtyards, buildings and squares. The entire walk takes around one hour (2km), excluding visits.

Sleeping & Eating

Wölfenbuttel is best visited as day trip from Braunschweig. If you decide to stay it has a Jugendgästehaus and several hotels; no central hotel is particularly outstanding. The tourist office can help with details and bookings.

Try **Historischer Ratskeller** (☎ 984 711; Stadtmarkt 2-4; mains €7.50-18; ⏱ Tue-Sun) for vegetable dishes such as ratatouille alongside traditional German fare, or **Leibnizhaus** (☎ 856 230; Schlossplatz 5/6; mains €6.50-19) for pizza, pasta, antipasti and other Italian fare in a charming courtyard garden. The latter is a little tricky to find, because it's in the northern part of Schlossplatz opposite/behind the pink Zeughaus.

Getting There & Away

Trains connect Wolfenbüttel with Braunschweig's Hauptbahnhof (€2.35, 10 minutes) twice an hour.

WOLFSBURG

☎ 05361 / pop 124,000

There's no doubt in Wolfsburg that Volkswagen is king – from the huge VW emblem adorning the company's global headquarters (and an imposing factory the size of a small country) to the insignia on almost every vehicle. 'Golfsburg', as it's nicknamed after one of the car manufacturer's most successful models, does a nice sideline in modern architecture and has a pretty castle. But here in 'the capital of Volkswagen', a brave-new-world theme park called Autostadt is top of the bill.

Orientation

Wolfsburg's centre is just southeast of the Hauptbahnhof. Head diagonally left out of the train station to the partly pedestrianised main drag, Porschestrasse, and continue south. Autostadt is north across the river from the train station; there's a clearly marked footbridge. The Schloss is five minutes northeast behind Autostadt.

Information

Citibank (☎ 120 35; Porschestrasse 19)
Main post office (Porschestrasse 22-24)
Sparkasse (☎ 174 17; Porchestrasse 70) Bank.

Wolfsburg tourist office (☎ 143 33; infopavilion@ wolfsburg.de; Willy Brandt Platz 5; ⏱ 9am-6pm Mon-Fri, 9am-4pm Sat) Adjacent to the Hauptbahnhof.

Sights & Activities

AUTOSTADT

There's only one fairground ride in this Disneyland of the auto world, and that's into the neighbouring Volkswagen factory, the world's largest car plant. Otherwise, exhibition pavilions account for most of the experience that's **Autostadt** (Car City; ☎ 0800-2886 782 38; www.autostadt.de; Stadtbrücke; adult/concession/ child €14/11/6; ⏱ 9am-8pm Apr-Oct, 9am-6pm Nov-Mar). VW's original plan was for a stylish place for customers to pick up new vehicles, and Autostadt has a centre for that, but across its 25 hectares as many as 12,000 visitors per day also swarm over its models and watch ads for the VW group. Indeed, in pavilions devoted to individual marques, including VW itself, Audi, Bentley, Lamborghini, Seat and Skoda, advertising is mainly what you get. (The Lamborghini and Audi pavilions are possibly the best.)

A broader view of automotive design and engineering is given in the first building you enter, the Konzernforum, while the neighbouring Zeithaus looks back at the history of the Beetle (see the boxed text A Bug's Life, p664) and other VW models. Many exhibits are interactive and most have signage in German and English.

The queues can get quite long for the 45-minute shuttle tours of the Volkswagen factory (included in the admission price), and staff will sometimes ask you to come back at a certain time, after they've cleared the backlog. From Monday to Friday, German-language tours leave at 15-minute intervals except during factory break times, and there's a tour in English at 1.30pm. However, because the factory is larger than Monaco, and because tours rotate through different workshop sections, it's pot luck whether you'll see one of the 3000 cars a day rolling off the assembly line or something less interesting like metal-pressing.

There are exciting obstacle courses and safety training if you have a valid licence and are comfortable with a left-hand drive car. Ring ahead to organise an English-speaking instructor.

The Autostadt counter at the tourist office is there for VW customers picking up cars, rather than for the benefit of visitors – although it will help if you get stuck.

AUTOMUSEUM

After the whizz-bang, showbiz aplomb of Autostadt, its sister **AutoMuseum** (☎ 520 71; Dieselstrasse 35; adult/concession/family €6/3/15; ☯ 10am-5pm, closed 24 Dec-1 Jan) is pretty low-key. Immensely interesting, however, is a line of ads leading to a collection of VW cars. Firstly, the ads (in German) make you realise how central the 'cheeky chappie' persona they cultivated was to the Beetle's success. Then you're confronted by a room full of that personality – from one of the vehicles used in the *Herbie, the Love Bug* movie to a white, see-through, iron-lace Beetle built by Mexican factory workers for the wedding of some colleagues. The original 1938 Cabriolet presented to Adolf Hitler on his 50th birthday is here, as are amphibious Beetles, and a few Passats and Golfs, too. Take bus No 208 from the main bus station at the northern end of Porchestrasse to Automuseum.

SCHLOSS WOLFSBURG

In historic contrast to Autostadt's space-age sheen, Wolfsburg's castle dates from 1600 and today houses the **Stadt Museum** (☎ 828 530; Schlossstrasse 8; adult/concession €1.50/0.50, free admission after 1pm Tue; ☯ 10am-8pm Tue, 10am-5pm Wed-Fri, 1-6pm Sat, 10am-6pm Sun). It has a display of the city's history from 1938 to 1955, a small regional history museum and two **art galleries** that host rotating exhibitions. A courtyard is the site of the **Wolfsburg Summer Festival** in June, and other concerts are held in the grounds during summer.

CITY CENTRE

Next to the train station, Wolfsburg's striking new **Phaeno Science Center** (opening late 2005) has been taking shape since 2003, in accordance with a typically cutting-edge design by renowned British-based architect Zaha Hadid. As you walk down Porschestrasse, you'll come to another great building, the **Kunstmuseum** (Art Museum; ☎ 266 90; Porschestrasse 53; adult/concession €6/3; ☯ 11am-8pm Tue, 11am-6pm Wed-Sun), which is home to temporary exhibitions of modern art. On the hill just southwest of the southern end of Porschestrasse is **Planetarium Wolfsburg** (☎ 219 39; Uhlandweg 2; adult/concession/family €4/2.50/10), built in 1982 after VW bartered Golfs for Zeiss projectors with the GDR.

A BUG'S LIFE

Cast-iron proof that Germans *do* have a sense of humour, the Volkswagen Beetle is truly greater than the sum of its parts. After all, the parts in question initially comprised little more than an air-cooled, 24-horsepower engine (maximum speed: 100km/h) chucked in the back of a comically half-egg-shaped chassis. Yet somehow this rudimentary mechanical assembly added up to a global icon – a symbol of Germany's postwar *Wirtschaftswunder* (economic miracle) that owners the world over fondly thought of as one of the family.

Indeed, it's a testament to the vehicle's ability to run on the smell of an oily rag while rarely breaking down that few would even begrudge its Nazi antecedents. Yes, in 1934 Adolf Hitler asked Ferdinand Porsche to design a 'Volkswagen' (people's car) affordable for every German household and, yes, the *Käfer* (bug) was the result. However, Beetle production only really began in the new Wolfsburg factory under British occupation in 1946.

Did the company realise then what a hit it had on its hands? By the early 1960s, the chugging, spluttering sound of VW engines could be heard across 145 nations.

Urged on by ads to 'Think Small', North Americans were particularly bitten by the bug, and this durable, cut-price vehicle became a permanent fixture on the hippie scene. Later in Europe, the Golf model cars that superseded the Beetle in the 1970s and 1980s would prove a phenomenal success. (While Douglas Coupland talked about *Generation X*, the German equivalent, as identified by best-selling author Florian Illies in 2000, is *Generation Golf*). However the US never warmed to the usurper, pushing VW to introduce a sleek, trendy, state-of-the-art New Beetle in 1998.

Meanwhile, the last bucket-of-bolts old Beetle – essentially the same beast despite improvements – rolled off the assembly line in Mexico on 31 July 2003, the 21,529,464th of its breed. VW hadn't sold the car in Western markets for decades, but tears were shed that night in Germany.

It's got laser and rock shows, star shows and spoken-word performances (like *The Little Prince*) set to the stars. Call ahead, as showtimes vary.

Next to it is the city's historic landmark, the **Esso Station**, built in 1951 and now restored to its original splendour.

FALLERSLEBEN

Keen students of history who speak German might want to visit this part of town with its many 18th-century half-timbered houses and **Fallersleben Schloss**, where the **Hoffmann Museum** (☎ 05362-526 23; adult/concession/family €1.50/0.50/3; 🕙 10am-5pm Tue-Fri, 1-6pm Sat, 10am-6pm Sun) is located. The museum is dedicated to Fallersleben's native son, August Heinrich Hoffman (1798–1874), who in 1841 wrote the lyrics that would become the German national anthem (music courtesy of Joseph Hayden). There's discussion of how the words '*über alles*' (above everything) were simply a call for an end to petty inter-German fiefdoms and how they were expunged after the Third Reich's nationalistic excesses. Take bus No 206 or 214 to Fallersleben from the main bus station at the northern end of Porchestrasse.

Sleeping

Wolfsburg is geared towards business travellers, and while facilities like modem ports are standard, single rooms far outnumber doubles.

DJH hostel (☎ 133 37; fax 166 30; Lessingstrasse 60; junior/senior €15/17.70; **P** 🖳) Everything feels a little cramped in this fairly old, but extremely central, hostel.

Global Inn (☎ 2700; www.globalinn.de; Kleistrasse 46; s €45-65, d €90; **P** 🗙) Its 172 rooms (including apartments for longer stays) are popular with employees of Volkswagen affiliates, so you should book ahead. The central location and value for money make it worth the extra planning; while some cheaper singles are pretty small, they simply can't offer anything less than the corporate standard here. The in-house Italian restaurant is mega-popular, too.

Hotel Goya (☎ 266 00; info@goya-hotel.de; Postrasse 34; s €70-89, d €85-100; **P**) There's a friendly familiar feel at this smaller hotel, which has guests returning regularly. The rooms provide pristine standards rather than character.

Ritz-Carlton (☎ 607 000; www.ritzcarlton.com; Stadtbrücke; rooms from €280; **P** 🗙 🐾) With natural tones of camel, cream and brown plus every luxury, this expansive, semi-colosseum-shaped landmark in the middle of Autostadt is where lucky visitors to Wolfsburg get to stay.

Other recommendations are:

Hotel Jäger (☎ 390 90; www.home.wolfsburg.de /hotel-jaeger in German; Eulenweg 3-5; s/d €60/100; **P**) Charm meets top business facilities. Not exactly central, though.

Penthouse Hotel (☎ 2710; www.penthouse-hotel.de; Schachtweg 22; s €60-65, d €80-95) Apartments with basic kitchens for short or long stays. Rates go down to €35/50 for singles/doubles after a month.

Eating
RESTAURANTS

Atelier Café (☎ 122 19; An der St Annenkirche; mains €3.50-12; 🕙 closed Tue) Summer breakfasts are the best here because you can sit in the lovely courtyard in the historic inner-city district of Hesslingen, five minutes east of Porschestrasse. You can also head inside the half-timbered house, where three meals a day are served in a modern industrial-style bistro of concrete, glass and steel. Tricky to find, the café is best reached by turning right into the alleyway off Hesslinger Strasse just after No 18 and the bus stop. Follow the dirt path round to the left and you should see the sign.

Aalto Bistro (☎ 891 689; Porschestrasse 1; €3.50-8.50) This is only part of the Kulturhaus, designed by star Finnish architect Alvar Aalto, that most visitors will get to see. It serves brilliantly priced pizzas, pasta and seafood in a modern bistro environment.

Walino (☎ 255 99; Kunstmuseum, Porschestrasse 53; €6-16; 🕙 closed Mon) The Kunstmuseum's loft-style restaurant offers a lovely view over the southern end of town. Upmarket international cuisine is served, from chicken breast in coconut sauce to roast lamb on Mediterranean vegetables.

Altes Brauhaus (☎ 053362-31 40; Schlossplatz, Fallersleben; mains €7-14) If you're visiting the Hoffman museum in Fallersleben or simply dying for some genuine German beer-hall atmosphere, come here. There's good house brew (from €3.10) and hearty fare including salads, sausages, potatoes and sauerkraut.

Some **Autostadt restaurants** (☎ 406 100) stay open later than the park itself, so within two hours of the park's closing time, you can buy an *Abendkarte* (evening ticket, €6) and your admission fee is credited towards your restaurant meal. The restaurants are all operated by Mövenpick, but have differences. Fabulous buffets are served in the busy Lagune, but if you wish to go more upmarket try Chardonnay. The casual Tachometer, and more formal Stadtcafé have good views of the park. It's only a shame the diner-style food is so average at Cylinder, because the car-interior décor is so enticing.

SELF-CATERING
Penny Markt (Porschestrasse 74) is a cheap place to shop. A **fresh produce market** (Porschestrasse) does a busy trade on both Wednesday and Saturday mornings.

Drinking & Entertainment
Wolfsburgers do much of their drinking in Kaufhof – not the department store, but a small strip of bars, pubs and a few eateries west of Porschestrasse. Establishments here range from the more traditional **Alt Berlin** (☎ 135 58; Kaufhof 2), which attracts an older crowd, to the trendier **Wunderbar** (☎ 133 47; Kaufhof 21) and **Lupus** (☎ 892 100; Kaufhof 16) at the other end of the strip.

For more German-language entertainment listings, check *Wo und Was*, *Indigo* or even ask for the tourist office's *Jugend in Wolfsburg* brochure.

Getting There & Away
There are frequent ICE train services from Wolfsburg to Braunschweig (€11, 15 minutes), Hanover (€19, 30 minutes) and Berlin (€37.80, one hour). Regional trains, especially to Braunschweig (€3.50, 24 minutes) are cheaper.

From Braunschweig, take the A2 east to the A39 north, which brings you right into town. Alternatively, take the B248 north to the A39.

Getting Around
Single bus tickets, valid for 90 minutes, cost €1.70. Blocks of four are sold for €5.80 and a day pass costs €4. The major bus transfer point (ZOB) is at the northern end of Porschestrasse. Bus Nos 206 and 214 go regularly to Fallersleben from here.

A free shuttle called City Mobil runs from the Hauptbahnhof down Porsches-

trasse with stops at Kaufhof, the Südkopf Center (a shopping centre) and the Kunstmuseum from 8am to 5.30pm Monday to Friday and 10am to 4pm Saturday.

Once you leave the pedestrianised centre, distances become difficult to cover easily by foot. In every sense, Wolfsburg was built for cars. The car park behind the Planetarium is free. Vehicles can be hired from **Europcar** (☎ 815 70; Dieselstrasse 19).

There are taxi ranks at the Hauptbahnhof and at the northern end of Porschestrasse. Alternatively, call **City Taxi** (☎ 230 223).

GÖTTINGEN
☎ 0551 / pop 134,000
It hurts one's brain just to think about Göttingen, a university town that's sent some 40 Nobel Prize winners into the world. The Georg-August Universität has been a pillar of the community since 1734, and as well as all those award-winning doctors and scientists, fairy-tale writers Brothers Grimm (as German language teachers) and Prussian chancellor Otto von Bismarck (as a student) could also be expected at a timeless alumni evening.

Happily, in the flesh Göttingen turns out to be an atmospheric and typical student haunt. Much is made of the iconic statue of Gänseliesel (the little goose girl) being the most kissed in the world, thanks to the custom among graduating doctoral students to peck her on the cheek. For most of the year, however, Gänseliesel remains neglected, while the university's 25,000 students major in having a good time.

Orientation
The circular city centre is surrounded by the ruins of an 18th-century wall and is divided by the Leinekanal (Leine Canal), an arm of the Leine River. The centre has a large pedestrianised mall, the hub of which is the Markt, a 10-minute walk east of the Bahnhof.

Information
Akademische Buchhandlung Calvör (☎ 484 800; Weender Strasse 58) Has English-language books.
Computerwerk (☎ 531 7943; Düstere Strasse 20; €5 per hr, or €2 after 8pm) Internet access.
Deuerlich'sche Buchhandlung (☎ 495 000; Weender Strasse 33) Also carries English-language books.
Main post office (Heinrich von Stephanstrasse 1-5)

GÖTTINGEN

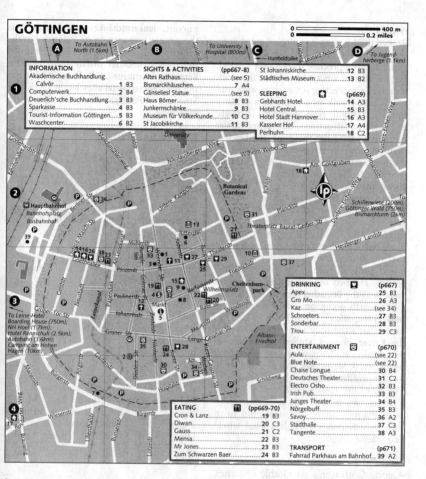

INFORMATION	
Akademische Buchhandlung Calvör	1 B3
Computerwerk	2 B4
Deuerlich'sche Buchhandlung	3 B3
Sparkasse	4 B3
Tourist-Information Göttingen	5 B3
Waschcenter	6 B2

SIGHTS & ACTIVITIES	(pp667-8)
Altes Rathaus	(see 5)
Bismarckhäuschen	7 A4
Gänseliesl Statue	(see 5)
Haus Börner	8 B3
Junkernschänke	9 B3
Museum für Völkerkunde	10 C3
St Jacobikirche	11 B3
St Johanniskirche	12 B3
Städtisches Museum	13 B2

SLEEPING	(p669)
Gebhards Hotel	14 A3
Hotel Central	15 B3
Hotel Stadt Hannover	16 A3
Kasseler Hof	17 A4
Perlhuhn	18 C2

DRINKING	(p667)
Apex	25 B3
Gro Mo	26 A3
Kaz	(see 34)
Schroeters	27 B3
Sonderbar	28 B3
Trou	29 C3

ENTERTAINMENT	(p670)
Aula	(see 22)
Blue Note	(see 22)
Chaise Longue	30 B4
Deutsches Theater	31 C2
Electro Osho	32 B3
Irish Pub	33 B3
Junges Theater	34 B4
Nörgelbuff	35 B3
Savoy	36 A2
Stadthalle	37 B3
Tangente	38 A3

EATING	(pp669-70)
Cron & Lanz	19 B3
Diwan	20 C3
Gauss	21 C2
Mensa	22 B3
Mr Jones	23 B3
Zum Schwarzen Baer	24 B3

TRANSPORT	(p671)
Fahrrad Parkhaus am Bahnhof	39 A2

Post (Groner Strasse 15)

Sparkasse (☎ 4050; Weender Strasse 13) Bank.

Tourist-Information Göttingen (☎ 499 800; www.goettingen.de; Altes Rathaus, Markt 9; ☾ 9.30am-6pm Mon-Fri, 10am-4pm Sat & Sun Apr-Oct, to 1pm Sat, closed Sun Nov-Mar) Sells the Gö-Card (one/three days €5/9), providing free bus travel and reduced admission/tour prices.

Universitätsklinikum (University hospital; ☎ 390; Robert-Koch-Strasse 40) Medical services.

Waschcenter (Ritterplan 4; ☾ 7am-10pm Mon-Fri) Laundry.

Sights & Activities
AROUND THE MARKT

Most people will head to the Markt pretty soon after arrival either to visit the tour-ist office or to see the city's symbol, the **Gänseliesel** statue and fountain. In truth, the demure little goose girl (with geese) is a tad disappointing. After all you hear about her being the 'most kissed girl in the world', the bronze statue doesn't even have par-ticularly shiny cheeks from all that human contact.

Don't despair though, because the inter-ior of the nearby **Altes Rathaus** (☾ 9.30am-6pm Mon-Fri, 10am-4pm Sat & Sun Apr-Oct, to 1pm Sat, closed Sun Nov-Mar), built in 1270, is impressive. It once housed the merchants' guild, and the rich decorations later added to its Great Hall include frescoes of the coats of arms of the Hanseatic cities and local bigwigs, grafted onto historic scenes.

LOWER SAXONY

WALKS

Rather than having any urgent must-sees, Göttingen is a mosaic of attractions that you'll most appreciate by walking around. Having existed since 953 at least, the town long had a protective network of walls and moats, and a walk around the 18th-century ramparts is highly recommended. These are not brick constructions, but rather earthy hummocks left from that time. It takes less than an hour to circumnavigate the city, the best starting point being the entrance near Cheltenham Park. This takes you past **Bismarckhäuschen** (Bismarck's Cottage; ☎ 485 844; im Hainberg; admission free; ☼ 10am-1pm Tue, 3-5pm Thu & Sat), where the town fathers reputedly banished 18-year-old Otto for rowdy behaviour in 1833. This incident is probably apocryphal, but it's a matter of historical record that the future Iron Chancellor was later found guilty of witnessing an illegal duel. Nearby are two old **water mills**. The walk ends near the **Deutsches Theater** (see p670).

It's worth going on a tourist office **city walking tour** (€5; ☼ 11.30pm Fri-Sun Apr-Oct), because that's the only way you get to visit the **Karzer** (former student cells) where, historically, students were sent when they misbehaved. Many used charcoal and chalk to etch profiles that are still well preserved. The brochure *Göttingen Komplett* (€3.50) outlines two other walks to do on your own. Plaques on buildings around town show which famous scholars lived where and when.

CHURCHES

Among Göttingen's six Gothic churches, the most remarkable is the **St Jacobikirche** (1361) on Weender Strasse. It's not just the red, white and grey angular striped columns that catch your attention, but the stained-glass windows. ('What happened? Were they broken in a recent storm?' we asked. 'No,' came the reply. 'It's contemporary art, stupid.' Upon which, we decided that the windows, by Frankfurt artist Johannes Schreiter, were actually rather striking). One of the twin towers of **St Johanniskirche**, behind the Altes Rathaus, can be climbed (admission €1; ☼ 2-4pm Sat).

HALF-TIMBERED HOUSES

Looking at some of Göttingen's half-timbered buildings is another interesting pursuit. **Junkernschänke** (Barfüsserstrasse 5) is the prettiest, thanks to its colourful 16th-century Renaissance façade; and just down the road is another ornate number, **Haus Börner** (Barfüsserstrasse 12). Built in 1536 it has the busy **Börnerviertel** alley behind it. Kurze Strasse and Paulinerstrasse are also worth exploring.

PARKS & GARDENS

In the shadow of the old ramparts, the small **Botanische Gärten** (Botanical Gardens; ☎ 395 753; Untere Karspüle 2; admission free; ☼ 8am-6pm Mon-Fri, 8am-3pm Sat & Sun) were Germany's first, and there's a section devoted to mountain plants – the Andes, the Alps etc. The **tropical greenhouses** (☼ 9am-noon & 1.30-2.45pm) are highly recommended in winter.

A 20-minute walk east of the Markt is the **Schillerwiese**, a large park that backs onto forest and has minigolf. To reach it, follow Herzberger Landstrasse east, then turn right into Merkelstrasse.

To enter **Göttinger Wald** (Göttinger Forest), continue along Herzberger Landstrasse near where it forms a hairpin bend, and turn into Borheckstrasse. From there, a bitumen track open to hikers and cyclists winds towards Hainholzhof-Kehr, a hotel and restaurant another 45 minutes away. Another option is to take bus No 1 to Zietenterrassen from Markt and walk northwest back through the forest into town. From the terminus a path leads to **Bismarckturm** (adult/concession €1/0.25; ☼ 11am-6pm weekends & holidays Apr-Sep). This stone tower has spectacular views over the Leine Valley.

MUSEUMS

If you're in town long enough, you might like to catch up on local history at the **Städtisches Museum** (☎ 400 2843; Ritterplan 7-8; adult/concession €1.50/0.50; ☼ 10am-5pm Tue-Fri, 11am-5pm Sat & Sun).

Alternatively, you can see objects brought back from the Pacific by Captain Cook, and other ethnographic art at the **Museum für Völkerkunde** (Museum of Ethnology; ☎ 397 892; Theaterplatz 15, adult/concession €2.50/1; ☼ 10am-1pm Sun). You can see the museum at other times by prior arrangement.

Festivals & Events

The **Händel Festival**, held over several days in late May and early June, is a must for those keen on music. Inquire about tickets at the tourist office.

Sleeping

DJH hostel (☎ 576 22; jh-goettingen@djh-hannover.de; Habichtsweg 2; junior/senior €15/17.70; P ⌨) This large Jugendherberge is a slightly older model but with lots of facilites, including a laundry, café, games room and grill area. It's in a pleasant spot on the outskirts of town, reached by bus No 9 from the Bahnhof or bus No 6 from downtown.

Camping am Hohen Hagen (☎ 05502-2147; fax 05502-472 39; Hoher-Hagen-Strasse; adult/tent/car €5/1.50/1.50) This year-round camp site is in Dransfeld, about 10km west of town. It sports laundry machines and a small shop. Bus No 120 from the train station will get you there.

Kasseler Hof (☎ 720 812; fax 770 3429; Rosdorfer Weg 26; s €35-55, d €65-85; P ✗) The shared bathrooms here aren't enormously appealing, so it's worth the extra to go for a room with its own facilities. All in all, however, this is a sweet little budget hotel, tucked away in a quiet corner not too far from town. Nice restaurant, too.

Perlhuhn (☎ 551 10; webmaster@perlhuhn.de; Am Goldgraben 22; s/d €55/80) This tiny B&B offers two unforgettable apartments themed from the golden age of travel. One combines an aircraft living room with an Africa bedroom, the other a captain's living room (with a ship's propeller as an elegant table base) and a pirate's bedroom. Am Goldgraben is between the Stadthalle and the Max-Planck-Institute für Geschichte.

Hotel Central (☎ 571 57; info@hotel-central.com; Jüdenstrasse 12; s €50-100, d €80-115; P ✗) The modern design here somehow manages to combine Nordic (clean lines) and Iberian (lots of colour) style, with the odd exposed brick wall, Persian rug and black leather sofa thrown in. The atmosphere is much more straightforward – simply cosy and friendly.

Hotel Stadt Hannover (☎ 547 960; info@hotelstadthannover.de; Goetheallee 21; s €65-85, d €95-115; P ✗) Although the rooms are a lot more modern and generic than the etched glass door and quaint entrance hall might lead you to believe, this is a well-run operation. Smoking rooms are cordoned off from non-smoking rooms by a fire door, some rooms have baths not just showers, and the owners speak excellent English.

Gebhards Hotel (☎ 496 80; gebhards@romantik hotels.com; Goetheallee 22-23; s €90-120; d €130-170; ✗) This hotel is a model of quaint elegance with Art Deco wall panels and lights in some rooms, and one of the city's poshest restaurants.

Business-orientated hotels worth checking out:

Leine-Hotel Boarding House (☎ 505 10; info@leinehotel-goe.de; Groner Landstrasse 55; s €55-70; d €85-110; P ✗)

Hotel Rennschuh (☎ 900 90; hotel@rennschuh.de; Kasseler Landstrasse 93; s €45-50, d €70-75; P ☎)

NH Hotel (☎ 900 50; nhgoettingen@nh-hotel.com; Kasseler Landstrasse 25c; s €65-200, d €85-195; P ✗) Four-star. Sometimes has cheap summer deals.

Eating

Diwan (☎ 560 85; Rote Strasse 11; mains €7-15) When a Turkish restaurant is posher than the norm it usually calls itself Anatolian. And so does Diwan. In a land where common knowledge of Turkish cuisine stops at doner kebabs, it serves a wide range of grills and casseroles (some vegetarian) – in a fairly traditional German setting.

Zum Schwarzen Baer (☎ 573 20; Kurze Strasse 12; mains €9-15; ✹ closed Sun evening & Mon) The snug dining room in this original 500-year-old building has timbered beams and stained glass, and fulfils every dream of dining in Germany. The menu doesn't stray from the theme, with traditional dishes like wild boar in cranberry sauce and *Göttinger Kutscherteller*, an assortment of different cuts of meat with fried potatoes.

Gaudi (☎ 531 3001; Börnerviertel, Barfüsserstrasse 12-13; mains €15-19) The menu has more French, German and Italian influences than the name might hint, but the multicoloured interior design is typically Spanish.

Gauss (☎ 566 16; Oberer Karspüle 22; mains €16-26; ✹ evening only, closed Sun) Although this upmarket cellar restaurant was opened in Göttingen in 1998, it's now getting national attention since the head chef (a woman) began cooking on TV. The menu's a constantly changing one of modern German cuisine. Enter from Theaterstrasse.

Cron & Lanz (☎ 560 22; Weender Strasse 25; coffee/cake from €1.90/2.55) The windows of this ornate Viennese-style café are lined with such artfully arranged cream cakes it's hard to resist. The breakfasts, however, can easily be skipped.

The *Mensas* at Wilhelmplatz and on campus at Platz der Göttinger Sieben offer excellent value for students and their guests.

Drinking

This is an area where Göttingen comes into its own.

Sistaz (☎ 820 7472; Börnerviertel, Barfüsserstrasse 12-13) This funky bar combines '70s retro interior décor with courtyard seating, and attracts a cool, relaxed crowd of varying ages. (The name might imply a lesbian bar, but it's not.) Sadly, the morning after things aren't so hot, when you might find yourself waiting more than half an hour for breakfast.

Schroeters (☎ 556 47; Judenstrasse 29) This hip, studenty place touts itself as a 'bar-café-lounge', and some patrons do seem to treat it as their front room, spending hours drinking and chatting. Football is screened some nights, while DJs spin discs on others.

Sonderbar (☎ 431 43; Kurze Strasse 9) This tiny, striped bar lives up to its name, meaning 'strange'. Punks, drunks, night owls, and even upright citizens all while away the time here before the bar finally shuts at 5am. Every day of the week, that is. If Tom Waits isn't playing in the background, he should be.

Mr Jones (☎ 531 4500; Goetheallee 8) This sunny, slightly American-style bar and restaurant (best to avoid the Indian menu) is usually the most packed along a busy strip.

Gro Mo (☎ 488 9232; Goetheallee 13a) This place is also popular. Besides alcoholic beverages, it does huge bowls of coffee.

Trou (☎ 439 71; Burgstrasse 20) This tucked-away cellar bar is such an institution that patrons sometimes stop and stare at strangers who venture in.

Some longer-standing Göttingen favourites to fall back on include the cultural centres **Apex** (☎ 447 71; Burgstrasse 46) and **Kaz** (☎ 530 62; Hospitalstrasse 6), attached to the Junges Theater.

Entertainment

Göttingen nightlife kicks off late. Live-music venues don't get going until 10pm, clubs until well past midnight. Check German-language *Trends & Fun* or *Scene Inside* for individual gigs and club nights.

DISCOS & CLUBS

Savoy (☎ 531 5353; Berlinerstrasse 5) Definitely the most glam – and popular – Göttingen club, this mainstream/house venue is full of shiny, sleek things mainly in upmarket casual gear like Puma shoes and Stussi (although some women really vamp it up). The main dance floor is in the middle of a decent-sized if not huge room (with go-go podium), plus there's a chilled lounge downstairs.

Chaise Longue (☎ 820 7799; Nikolaistrasse 1b) The three floors of this urban club are full of baggy-trousered young lads and their better-dressed better halves. The DJs spin hip-hop, jungle, R & B, house and similar flavas.

Electro Osho (☎ 517 7976; Weender Strasse 38) This small club, at the end of an arcade next to a mobile-phone shop, used to be part of the oldies Disco chain that has an outlet in Hanover. However, only the name remains. The music policy here now focuses on drum 'n' bass and techno.

Tangente (☎ 463 76; Goetheallee 8a) Tangente is the top disco in town for a slightly older crowd, and famous for its 'Zartbitter' rock parties (from Britpop to Nu-metal) on the first Wednesday of each month.

ROCK & JAZZ

Nörgelbuff (☎ 438 85; Groner Strasse 23) This cosy blues/rock venue is a Göttingen institution, having hosted some stars in its time, and opening on weeknights as well as weekends in recent years.

Blue Note (☎ 469 07; Wilhelmsplatz 3) This is another venue to look out for in listings guides. It's right next to the *Mensa*, and has regular live bands and theme dance nights (eg salsa, tropical).

Irish Pub (☎ 456 64; Mühlenstrasse 4) If you're just in the mood for a cover band, you'll often find them here.

THEATRE & CLASSICAL MUSIC

Deutsches Theater (☎ 496 90; Theaterplatz 11) This is the premier mainstream theatre in the city of Göttingen.

Junges Theater (☎ 495 0150; Hospitalstrasse 6) The Junges Theater is more innovative and draws a young crowd.

Classical-music concerts are held regularly in the **Stadthalle** (☎ 999 580; Albaniplatz) and in the **Aula**, a beautifully appointed hall upstairs on Wilhelmsplatz. At 6pm on Friday nights, you can attend organ recitals at **St Jacobikirche** (admission by donation).

Getting There & Away

BUS
Buses leave from the terminus alongside the station to surrounding towns and to the Harz Mountains, but train services are more convenient.

CAR & MOTORCYCLE
Göttingen is on the A7 running north–south. The closest entrance is 3km southwest along Kasseler Landstrasse, an extension of Groner Landstrasse. The Fairy-Tale Road (B27) runs southwest to the Weser River and northeast to the Harz Mountains.

TRAIN
There are frequent direct ICE services to Kassel (€17.20, 20 minutes), Frankfurt (€47, 1¾ hours), Munich (€76.80, four hours), Hanover (€27.40, 30 minutes), Hamburg (€49.40, two hours) and Berlin (€55.40, 2¾ hours). Indirect regional services run to Weimar via Erfurt (€21.40, 2½ hours). Regional trains leave hourly for Goslar (€12.40, one hour).

Getting Around
Single bus tickets cost €1.60, batches of four tickets go for €4.60 (both valid for 60 minutes), and 24-hour tickets are €3.80.

There are taxi ranks at the Hauptbahnhof and behind the Altes Rathaus. To call one, ring ☎ 340 34.

Bikes can be hired from **Fahrrad Parkhaus am Bahnhof** (☎ 599 94; Am Bahnhof; €7 per day).

WEST OF HANOVER

OSNABRÜCK
☎ 0541 / pop 160,000

'Zum Glück komm' ich aus Osnabrück', locals boast of their good luck to come from this city; and that's something you most understand at night, when the coloured globes – blue, green, purple, yellow and red – of the old town's street lamps cast a low, carnival-like glow over its narrow brick pavements and half-timbered houses.

But this historic heartland is now offset by a contemporary building that has overtaken interest in native son Erich Maria Remarque, author of the WWI classic *All Quiet on the Western Front*, and truly eclipsed Osnabrück's claim to

be where the Thirty Years' War ended in 1648. The construction in question is the Felix-Nussbaum-Haus, by the man whose designs are to be erected on the site of New York's former World Trade Center, Daniel Libeskind.

Orientation
Osnabrück's egg-shaped city centre is divided into the northern Altstadt and the southern Neustadt, with the east–west Neumarkt drawing a line across the middle. The Hauptbahnhof is on the town's eastern edge. To reach the centre from the station takes about 15 minutes, going straight ahead along Möserstrasse, turning left at the Kaufhof building into Wittekindstrasse and then right into Grosser Strasse. When you come to the Domhof, continue left along Krahnstrasse to the tourist office.

The DB Service desk at the station stocks free town maps.

Information
There's an ATM in the Hauptbahnhof.
Main post office (Theodor-Heuss-Platz 6-9)
Marketing & Tourismus Osnabrück (☎ 323 2202, room reservations 951 1195; www.osnabrueck.de in German; Krahnstrasse 58; ◷ 9.30am-6pm Mon-Fri, 10am-4pm Sat)
Sparkasse (☎ 3240; Krahnstrasse 9-10) Bank.

Sights
FELIX-NUSSBAUM-HAUS
Shaped like an interconnected series of concrete shards, with slit windows and sloping floors, the **Felix-Nussbaum-Haus** (☎ 323 2237; Heger-Tor-Wall 28; adult/concession €4/2; ◷ 10am-6pm Tue-Thu, 11am-6pm Fri-Sun) is an older sister to Libeskind's famous building for the Jewish Museum Berlin. The Osnabrück-born Jewish painter Felix Nussbaum (1904–44) wasn't a great original; his work has shades of Van Gogh and Henri Rousseau, but Libeskind's 1988 building lifts it to a great height. According to signs in German and English, Nussbaum fell into despair during wartime exile, and as you view some of his last works before he was sent to Auschwitz, you find yourself heading down the slope of a long, darkening corridor.

We hope the staff's tendency to follow and watch visitors like hawks on the day we were there isn't policy; it can spoil much of the effect. Included in the admission price is entry to the rest of the **Kulturgeschichtliche Museum** (Cultural History Museum; ☎ 323 2237; Heger-Tor-Wall 28; adult/concession €4/2; ☺ 10am-6pm Tue-Thu, 11am-6pm Fri-Sun), which has information on Osnabrück's history and changing temporary exhibitions.

MARKT & AROUND

It was on the **Rathaus** (admission free; ☺ 9am-5pm Mon-Fri, 9am-4pm Sat, 10am-4pm Sun) steps that the Peace of Westphalia was proclaimed on 25 October 1648, ending the Thirty Years' War. The preceding peace negotiations were conducted partly in Münster, about 60km south, and partly in the Rathaus' **Friedenssaal** (peace hall). On the left as you enter the Rathaus are portraits of the negotiators on its walls. Also have a look in the **Schatzkammer** (Treasure Chamber), especially at the 13th-century *Kaiserpokal* (Kaiser goblet).

The four richly ornamented cross gables of the **Marienkirche** loom above the square, painstakingly rebuilt after burning down during WWII. Opposite, the small **Erich Maria Remarque Friedenszentrum** (Erich Maria Remarque Peace Centre; ☎ 323 2109; Markt 6; admission free; ☺ 10am-1pm & 3-5pm Tue-Fri, 10am-1pm Sat, 11am-5pm first Sun of month) uses photos and documents to chronicle the writer's life (1898–1970) and work.

Various **half-timbered houses** survived WWII. At Bierstrasse 24 is the baroque **Walhalla** (see Sleeping, opposite), with a portal flanked by cheeky cherubs. At Krahnstrasse 4 you'll find a beautiful house (1533), with **Café Läer** taking up the ground floor (see Eating, p673). The best of the bunch is the Renaissance **Haus Willmann** (1586), at No 7, with its carved circular motifs and small relief of Adam and Eve.

A short walk north along Natruper-Tor-Wall gets you to the **Bockturm** (adult/concession €2/1; ☺ 11am-5pm Sun), the oldest tower of the former city wall. This contains a hairraising collection of torture implements, dating from Osnabrück's medieval witch trials.

DOM ST PETER

The bulky **cathedral** (☎ 318 481; Domplatz; ☺ 7am-7.30pm) in the eastern Altstadt is distinctive for its two towers: the slender Romanesque tower and the much bigger Gothic one added to house new and bigger church bells. In the chapel on your left as you enter is the 13th-century bronze baptismal font. It's shaped as a bucket perched on feet so that a little fire could be built underneath to heat the water.

Take a look at the wrought-iron gates, with their unusual vanishing point perspective, at the entrance to the square ambulatory. The cathedral boasts the largest cross in Lower Saxony and has more treasures in its **Diözesan Museum**, reached via the cloister.

Sleeping

Intour Hotel (☎ 466 43; fax 434 239; Maschstrasse 10; s €30-50, d €65-85; P) The homey rooms here are light, bright and good value for the price, but the abiding memory you take away is of the owners' very sweet part terrier/part German Shepherd dog.

Dom Hotel (☎ 358 350; www.dom-hotel-osnabrueck .de; Kleine Domsfreiheit 5; s €45-60, d €70-100; P) There are two categories of room in this hotel: new and renovated, but they're both clean and comfortable, if not particularly atmospheric. Parking is €5.

Hotel Walhalla (☎ 349 10; fax 349 1144; Bierstrasse 24; s €80-85, d €100-110; P) Partly housed in a historic half-timbered building, this hotel has older rooms but modern conveniences. It met the approval of the Swedish royal family, has been graced by the Dalai Lama's presence, and other guests repeatedly say on leaving that they've enjoyed their stay. Parking is €10.

Steinberger Hotel Remarque (☎ 609 60; www .osnabrueck.steinberger.de in German; Natruper-Tor-Wall 1; s €105-130, d €120-145; P ✗) Portraits and mementos of Erich Maria Remarque offset the glass lifts and pale Mediterranean colours of this modern four-star hotel. The location, on a small hill just outside the Altstadt ring, combines relative quiet with convenience. Weekend prices start at €85/105 for a single/double; parking is €10.

There are two hostels: the central, friendly **Penthouse Backpackers** (☎ 600 9606; Möserstrasse 19; dorms €14-15), with its rooftop terrace, and the more modern-looking **DJH hostel** (☎ 542 84; jh-osnabrueck@djh-unterweser-ems.de; Iburger Strasse 183a; junior/senior €15.40/18.10), which is more of a schlep to reach. Take bus No 62 or Nos 463 to 468 to Kinderhospital.

Ask the tourist office about camping, about 5km northeast of town.

Eating

Weinkrüger (☎ 233 53; Marienstrasse 18; mains €7-19; ⏰ evening only Mon-Fri, noon-1am Sat & Sun) Behind a lovely ornate façade and hanging sign, you'll find this large, but somehow cosy restaurant/wine bar over a couple of floors, serving German and international cuisine. Sunday brunch is a speciality as is, obviously, wine.

Hausbrauerei Rampendahl (☎ 245 35; Hasestrasse 35; lunch €5.25, mains €8-20) The restaurant here serves one set dish from noon, before breaking out the other traditional German food after 6pm. Special beers are brewed on the premises (including the potent Rampendahl Spezial), as are brandies. Set menus cost €20 to €25.

La Vie (☎ 331 150; Krahnstrasse 35; mains €20-30; ⏰ closed Sun & Mon) The most chi-chi establishment in town has gourmet Mediterranean food and a wine list offering more than 900 choices. The attached bistro is more informal and cheaper (mains €10 to €18).

Arabesque (☎ 260 363; Osterberger Reihe 12; mains €3-7.50) A palace among doner kebab shops, spacious Arabesque has some traditional Arab seating, little tucked-away niches and a desert trompe l'oeil on one wall. *Baba ganoush* (eggplant dip), home-made falafels and other really delicious fare are on the menu; in the evening you can try an apple-flavoured smoke on a hookah pipe.

Café Läer (☎ 222 44; Krahnstrasse 4; snacks €4-4.50) The décor inside this historic building is more bare-stone-walls medieval than plush, opulent *belle époque* café. However, the mezzanine floor is a great place to sit while having coffee and cake.

Osnabrück has a wonderful range of pubs (most open in the evening only) that also serve simple, inexpensive food. These include the traditional food haven of **Grüne Gans** (☎ 239 14; Grosse Gildewart 15; mains €3-8) and **Uni-Keller** (☎ 216 98; Neuer Graben 29; pizzas €3.50-6.50). The latter is a student pub in the west-wing cellars of the Schloss (now part of the university) and has a long list of pizzas, as well as some salads.

Drinking

For pubs that also serve food, see Eating above.

Grüner Jäger (☎ 273 60; An der Katherinenkirche 1) Right near Arabesque (see Eating earlier) is a popular student hang-out, with a covered-

in beer-garden, and an enthusiastically played table-football.

Zwiebel (☎ 236 73; Heger Strasse 34) Through the low-ceiling front room and out the back, 'Onion' does sell onion cake, but it's the quirky decoration in this back room, with a rocking horse, old metal-plate ads for coffee and even a Marx Brothers photo, that makes the place stand out.

Two other decent pubs are **Stiefel** (☎ 226 76; Heger Strasse 4) and **Irish Pub Remise** (☎ 239 22; Rolandsmauer 23).

Entertainment

Lagerhalle (☎ 338 740; Rolandsmauer 26) Although this large alternative cultural centre has a grab-bag of concerts, disco nights, movies, poetry readings and talks, many also come here merely for a drink.

Stadtheater (☎ 323 3314; Domhof 10/11) Osnabrück's theatre offers classical concerts, ballet and drama.

Getting There & Away

The low-cost carrier **Air Berlin** (www.airberlin.com) flies to Münster-Osnabrück airport from countries including England (London Stansted), Greece, Italy, Portugal and Spain. The airport is 30km southwest of the centre.

Hourly IC/EC trains go to Hamburg (€35.60, 1¾ hours), Cologne (€37.15, 2½ hours) and Dortmund (€21.15, 55 minutes). Regional (IR) trains to Hanover (€18.60, 1¾ hours) also leave hourly or half-hourly.

Osnabrück is well connected by road via the A1 (Bremen to Dortmund) and the B51, B65 and B68.

Getting Around

Single tickets cost €1.25, or €3.85 for batches of four tickets. The best deal is the 9-Uhr Tageskarte (one-day ticket) for €2.70.

A taxi can be summoned by calling ☎ 277 81 or ☎ 320 11.

To hire a bicycle, try **Pedals Fahrradstation** (☎ 259 131; Hauptbahnhof; €6 a day).

OLDENBURG

☎ 0441 / pop 154,000

Being shuffled between Danish and German rule has left the relaxed capital of the Weser-Ems region with a somewhat mixed identity. Most of its medieval buildings were destroyed in a huge fire in 1676, while others were later refashioned at various stages according to the prevailing architectural style of the time. Count Peter Friedrich Ludwig began redecorating the town in a neoclassical style in 1785, evidence of which still survives in the Schlosspark, its promenade and other nearby buildings.

Oldenburg is also home to the world's oldest savings bank, the Sparkasse (1786) – which is probably of little consequence to the town's 12,000 students. What little money they possess is more probably spent in the bars on Wallstrasse or around one of Germany's earliest pedestrianised shopping precincts.

Orientation

Oldenburg's pedestrianised core is bounded by Heiligengeistwall to the north, Theaterwall to the west and Schlosswall to the south. Turn right after you exit from the 'Stadtmitte' side of the Hauptbahnhof (Bahnhof Sud), which takes you along Mosiestrasse. Turn left into Osterstrasse, which takes you to Achtenstrasse in the city centre. Make a dog-leg right-left turn to find Wallstrasse and the tourist office.

Information

Landessparkasse der Oldenburg (☎ 925 470; Achternstrasse 11) Bank.

Main post office (Bahnhofsplatz 10)

Oldenburg Tourismus (☎ 361 6130; info@oldenburg.de; Wallstrasse 14; ☯ 10am-6pm Mon-Fri, 10am-1pm Sat)

Sights

SCHLOSSPLATZ

The pale-yellow Renaissance/baroque **Schloss** (1607) at the southern end of the Altstadt shopping district was once home to the counts and dukes of Oldenburg, part of whose family had governed Denmark for a time in the 15th century.

Inside is the **Landesmuseum Oldenburg** (Oldenburg State Museum; ☎ 220 7300; combined admission with Augusteum adult/concession €3/1.50; ☯ 9am-5pm Tue-Fri, 9am-8pm Thu, 10am-5pm Sat & Sun), one of Germany's better regional museums, chronicling the history of the area from the Middle Ages to the 1950s. The collection of paintings, sculpture and everyday items is set against a background of regal rooms, particularly on the first floor. Here you find the remarkable Idyllenzimmer with 44 paintings by court artist Heinrich Wilhelm Tischbein, a friend of Goethe.

Behind the Schloss is the sprawling **English-style Schlosspark**. The neoclassical building you see across the square from the Schloss is **Die Wache** (1839), once a city guardhouse but now part of a bank.

The museum's collection of 20th-century art has been farmed out to the **Augusteum** (☎ 220 7300; Elisabethstrasse 1; combined admission with Landesmuseum Oldenburg adult/concession €3/1.50; ☯ 9am-5pm Tue-Fri, 9am-8pm Thu, 10am-5pm Sat & Sun). Showcased here are works by Erich Heckel, Ernst Ludwig Kirchner, August Macke and others.

AROUND MARKT

When part of the 13th-century Gothic **Lambertikirche** (☎ 174 64; Markt; admission free; ☯ 11am-12.30pm & 2.30-5pm Tue-Fri, 10am-12.30pm Sat) collapsed in 1791, Duke Peter Friedrich Ludwig used the stones to rebuild the church in neoclassical style. Based on the Pantheon in Rome, the interior of this square building features a large galleried rotunda with Ionic columns that support a giant cupola. By the late 19th century, however, the entire edifice had been encased in a neo-Gothic, red-brick shell with its five landmark spires.

Opposite the 19th-century, medieval-style **Altes Rathaus** (☎ 235 2253; Markt; admission free; ☯ 8am-4pm Mon-Thu, 8am-1pm Fri) is the **Haus Degode** (1502), one of the few genuinely medieval buildings to survive the fire of 1676.

Sleeping

The tourist office can help with private rooms or provide information on camping, north of town.

DJH hostel (☎ 871 35; Alexanderstrasse 65; junior/senior €15/17.70; ℗) This hostel makes up for being rather old and very dimly lit by having a few comfy bathrooms with tubs. It's about 20 minutes by foot north of the Hauptbahnhof, or take bus No 302 or 303 to Von-Finckh-Strasse.

Hotel Tafelfreuden (☎ 832 27; www.tafelfreuden-hotel.de; Alexanderstrasse 23; s €60-70, d €85-95; ℗) Really the only interesting hotel in town, this has eight distinctively themed rooms. Some of the singles, such as England and Japan are tiny, if cleverly organised, but larger boudoirs like the 'Orient' and 'Afrika' and 'Unter Wasser' (underwater) are real treasures.

If you get stuck, try:

Hotel Wieting (☎ 924 005; www.hotel-wieting.de in German; Damm 29; s €70-85, d €90-110; P ⊠) Business-orientated without sacrificing personality. Parking costs €3.50.

Trend Hotel (☎ 961 10; www.trendhotel-ol.de in German; Jürnweg 5; s/d €50/75; P) Modern, and offers excellent value for money, but is a bit out of town.

Eating

For drinking and eating options in addition to those listed here, continue past the Baldini Grand Café along the pedestrianised Wallstrasse.

Baldini Grand Café (☎ 925 0605; Wallstrasse 1; meals €5-20) This extravagantly beautiful and spacious Art Deco wonder is as popular for its luxuriant décor as its food. Come in the late afternoon when the sun casts a golden glow on the upper floor.

Chianti Classico (☎ 120 88; Achternstrasse 40; pasta/pizza €5.50-8.50, mains €9.50-18) In a crooked, half-timbered house tucked away in an alley, this restaurant serves good Italian food – pasta, pizzas, *pesce* (fish) – in a wonderfully romantic atmosphere.

Getting There & Away

There are trains at least once an hour to Bremen (€5.80, 30 minutes) and Osnabrück (€15.80, 1¾ hours). From Oldenburg, there are trains north to Emden and beyond.

Oldenburg is at the crossroads of the A29 to/from Wilhelmshaven and the A28 (Bremen-Dutch border).

Getting Around

Single bus tickets (valid for one hour) for the entire city cost €1.60; short trips are only €1.15, and day passes €4.60. Buy your tickets from the driver.

For taxis, call ☎ 225 25.

Bikes can be hired from **Fahrradstation** (☎ 218 8240; Bahnhof-Nord; €7/17 1/3 days).

EMDEN & AROUND

☎ 04921 / pop 50,000

You're almost in Holland here, and it shows – from the flat landscape, dikes and windmills around Emden to the lackadaisical manner in which locals pedal their bikes across canal bridges and past red-brick Lego-like houses into town itself. People greet you with a 'Moin', or 'Moin Moin', and they're generally proud of the local *Plattdütsch* dialect, even if they don't always speak it. It sounds

like a combination of English, German and – guess what? – Dutch.

Orientation

Emden's train and bus stations are about a 10-minute walk west of the city centre. As you exit, take the road heading right, which will lead to Grosse Strasse and the small medieval harbour called Ratsdelft.

Information

Commerzbank (☎ 800 30; Am Delft 24) Most banks here close at lunch time.

Main post office (Bahnhofsplatz 9)

Tourist-Information Emden (☎ 974 00; info@emden-touristik.de; Am Stadtgarten; ☺ 9am-6pm Mon-Fri, 10am-1pm Sat, 11am-1pm Sun May-Sep, 9am-1pm & 3-5.30pm Mon-Fri, 10am-1pm Sat Oct-Apr) Just north of the central Ratsdelft harbour, near the car park and taxi stand.

Sights & Activities

KUNSTHALLE

If you're a culture vulture finding yourself surrounded by nature lovers in Emden, this is your revenge! You'd have to be keen to detour into this fairly far-flung region just for its **Kunsthalle** (☎ 975 050; Hinter dem Rahmen 13; adult/concession €4.50/2.50; ☺ 10am-8pm Tue, 10am-5pm Wed-Fri, 11am-5pm Sat & Sun). However, it does have a fascinating collection of 20th-century art. It comes mostly courtesy of local boy Henri Nannen, founder of the magazine *Stern* (a glossy newsweekly à la *Time* or *Newsweek*), who, upon retirement, made his private collection available to the town.

Inside, its white-and-exposed-timber, light-flooded rooms show off a range of big, bold canvases. There are works by Max Beckmann, Erich Heckel, Alex Jawlensky, Oskar Kokoschka, Franz Marc, Emil Nolde and Max Pechstein although most names will be more familiar to art connoisseurs. Part of the space is used for travelling exhibitions. Three times a year, the museum closes its doors for a week while exhibitions are changed.

Follow the signs from the tourist office.

OTHER ATTRACTIONS

Normally, Emden's **Ostfriesisches Landesmuseum** (Regional History Museum; ☎ 872 057; Rathaus, Neutorstrasse) would rate as an attraction in its own right, but it's closed for refurbishment until late 2005. At the time of writing there was no word on how the gallery of old Dutch masters and other artefacts would now be presented.

Meanwhile, the labyrinth of WWII civilian bunkers at the **Bunkermuseum** (☎ 322 25; Holzsägerstrasse; adult/child €2/1; ☺ 10am-1pm & 3-5pm Mon-Fri year round, 10am-1pm Sat & Sun May-Oct) includes testimony from those who sheltered here, offering a moving insight into part of recent history.

Some 6km north of Emden, along the B70, stands what claims to be the world's most crooked church. That's nothing to do with the administration of the church of **Suurhusen** (1262), but a comment on its tilting tower. Currently leaning 2.43m off true, it allegedly outdoes even the famous tower in Pisa by 4.7cm. The overhang is the result of the decreasing groundwater levels in the peat-rich soil.

CYCLING & BOATING
The flatlands around Emden are perfect for cycling, and the tourist office has plenty of maps. (See Getting There & Around, opposite.)

Another good way to travel is by water. **Kanuverlieh am Wasserturm** (☎ 04921-974 97; Am Wasserturm) has canoes for hire, or ask at the tourist office.

Tours
Harbour cruises run by **EMS** (☎ 890 70; www.ag -ems.de in German) leave several times daily between March and October from the Delfttreppe steps in the harbour (€6.25/3). The company also runs services to the North Frisian Island of Helgoland (see p733).

Meanwhile, canal tours (€4/2) leave from the quay at the Kunsthalle between April and October on weekdays at 11am and 3pm, and on Sunday at noon and 3pm.

Sleeping & Eating
The tourist office will book rooms, including private rooms, for no charge.

DJH hostel (☎ 237 97; fax 321 61; An der Kesselschleuse 5, off Thorner Strasse; junior/senior €15/17.70; ☺ closed Dec & Jan; **P**) Its lovely canal-side location gives this decent hostel a relaxed caravan-park feel. Be warned, however, that it's very popular with school groups. A 15-minute walk east of the centre, it can also be reached on bus No 3003 to Realschule/Am Herrentor from the train station or downtown.

Hotel am Boltentor (☎ 972 70; fax 972 733; Hinter den Rahmen 10; s/d €65/85; **P**) Hidden by trees from the main road nearby and just a minute from the Kunsthalle, this homey hotel has possibly the best location in town, plus comfy and well-equipped rooms.

Heerens Hotel (☎ 237 40; fax 231 58; Friedrich-Ebert-Strasse 67; s €50-80, €90-105; **P**) The generously sized rooms here are slightly older, but the hotel comes highly rated for its service and restaurant.

Goldener Adler (☎ 927 30; Neutorstrasse 5; mains €11-19) This is one of the best places in town to try Frisian cuisine, from Matjes herrings to the *Käpitansfrühstück* (captain's breakfast) of smoked salmon, North Sea shrimp, scrambled eggs and fried potato. This extremely central hotel also has very nice, if sometimes a little noisy, rooms (singles €65-70, doubles €80-85).

Restaurant Café Feuerschiff (☎ 929 200; Ratsdelft; mains €9-16) Aboard the ship moored in the central harbour in front of the Goldener Adler, this restaurant has great views from the deck, and more local specialities than you can shake a fried herring at. Or you can just come for cake and East Frisian tea.

Kunsthalle (☎ 975 050; Hinter dem Rahmen 13) The museum café is just opposite the main building, beside the canal. As well as light snacks and salads (€5 to €10), it also does delicious cakes. It closes at 6pm.

For other eating options try the busy Neuer Markt.

Getting There & Around
Emden is connected by rail to Oldenburg (€12.40, 70 minutes), Bremen (€17.60, 1¾ hours) and Hamburg (€30.40, three hours, change in Bremen). Despite its relative remoteness, Emden is easily and quickly reached via the A31, which connects with the A28 from Oldenburg and Bremen. The B70/B210 runs north from Emden to other towns in Friesland and to the coast.

Emden is small enough to be explored on foot but also has a bus system (€1 per trip). The best transport method is the bicycle; for hirage contact **Oltmanns** (☎ 314 44; Grosse Strasse 53-57; €8 a day).

JEVER
☎ 04461 / pop 13,000
Many will know this town's name from the label of its famous Pilsener beer, but the

capital of Friesland region has a secondary motif. The face of 'Fräulein Maria' peers out from attractions and shop windows alike. She was the last of the so-called *Häuptlinge* (chieftains) to rule the town in the Middle Ages, and although Russia's Catherine the Great got her mitts on Jever for a time in the 18th century, locals always preferred their home-grown queen. Having died unmarried and a virgin, Maria is the German equivalent of England's (in truth more worldly) Elizabeth I.

With its Russian-looking castle, Jever itself is worth a brief visit, perhaps en route to the East Frisian Islands.

Orientation

Most of Jever's attractions are within a few hundred metres of each other in the eastern section of the Altstadt around the Schloss. There are map boards at the small train station. Follow the signs to the centre along Schlossstrasse to the beginning of the pedestrianised streets. Continue along the cobbled streets until you come across yet more signposts.

East, West, Friesland's Best

Like Bavarians, the people in northwest Germany have a reputation for being 'different'. Frieslanders, as they're called, have their own language – *Plattdütsch* – and are rather partial to a cup of tea (reputedly drinking 25% of Germany's tea imports). Although merely a geographical area today, Friesland was once a political entity, a league of seven states stretching from the northern Netherlands to the Danish coast. Roughly speaking, the eastern part of the Netherlands was Westfriesland (Western Frisia), northwest Germany was Ostfriesland (Eastern Frisia) and the area around the Danish border was Nordfriesland (Northern Frisia).

In the 16th century, Jeverland, the region around Jever, seceded from Ostfriesland and remained separate as it fell into the hands of the Dukes of Oldenburg and subsequently Russia. In modern times, however, Jeverland was rechristened Friesland, leading to the odd situation today where Ostfriesland (Eastern Frisia), around Emden, actually lies *west* of Friesland.

Information

Landessparkasse (☎ 9400; Alter Markt 4) Bank.

Tourist Information Jever (☎ 710 10; tourist-info@stadt-jever.de; Alter Markt 18; ⌚ 10am-6pm Mon-Fri, 10am-2pm Sat May-Sep, 9am-5pm Mon-Thu, 9am-1pm Fri Oct-Apr)

Sights & Activities

SCHLOSS

Looking like a prop from the film *Doctor Zhivago*, the Russian onion-shaped spire is the first thing that strikes you about Jever's 14th-century **Schloss** (☎ 2106; adult/concession €3/2; ⌚ 10am-6pm Mar–mid-Jan, closed Mon except in July & Aug). It was added during the Russian reign, to a building built by Fräulein Maria's grandfather, chieftain Edo Wiemken the Elder. Today the palace houses the **Kulturhistorische Museum des Jeverlandes**, a cultural-history museum with objects chronicling the daily life and craft of the Frieslanders, including a vast porcelain collection.

The *pièce de résistance* is the magnificent **audience hall**, with a carved, coffered, oak ceiling of great intricacy. Fräulein Maria retained the Antwerp sculptor Cornelis Floris to create this 80-sq-metre Renaissance masterpiece. Major renovations have been underway, so entrance prices might rise.

FRIESISCHES BRAUHAUS ZU JEVER

A brewery that has been producing dry Pilsener since 1848 is worth a visit, and the **Friesisches Brauhaus** (☎ 137 11; Elisabethufer 18; tours €6.50; ⌚ tours hourly 9.30am-4.30pm Mon-Fri) now allows visitors a peek behind the scenes. Tours travel through the production and bottling facilities, as well as a small museum. Reservations are necessary.

OTHER ATTRACTIONS

Many of Jever's sights are in some way connected to Fräulein Maria. The most spectacular is in the **Stadtkirche** (☎ 933 80; Am Kirchplatz 13; ⌚ 8am-6pm), where you'll find the lavish **memorial tomb** of her father, Edo von Wiemken (1468–1511). The tomb is another opus by Cornelis Floris and miraculously survived eight fires. The church itself succumbed to the flames and was rebuilt in a rather modern way; the main nave is opposite the tomb, which is now behind glass.

Near the tourist office, you'll see a **statue of Fräulein Maria**. Her image also joins that of her father and other historic figures in the town's **Glockenspiel** (☉ 11am, noon, 3pm, 4pm, 5pm & 6pm), opposite the tourist office on the façade of the Hof von Oldenburg.

Alternatively, an interesting Frisian craft is on show at the **Blaudruckerei shop** (☎ 713 88; Kattrepel 3; ☉ 10am-1pm, 2-6pm Mon-Fri, 10am-1pm Sat). This is owned by former teacher Georg Stark, who 20 years ago revived the long-lost art and tradition of Blaudruckerei, a printing and dying process whose results vaguely resemble batik. Using original wooden embossing stamps he finds in old barns, at flea markets, antique shops and secret places, Stark prints everything from tablecloths to jeans in his workshop.

Sleeping

Jever's tourist office can make room reservations at some, but not all, Jever hotels, or book private rooms.

DJH hostel (☎ 3590; Mooshütter Weg 12; junior/senior 12.70/15.40) Jever's recently renovated Jugendherberge is on a leafy residential street, within walking distance of both the centre and train station. Check the map board at the station for directions.

Hotel Pension Stöber (☎ 5580; www.hotel-stoeber .de in German; Hohnholzstrasse 10; s €35-40, d €60-70; P) In a leafy neighbourhood south of the centre, this whitewashed building has rustic rooms that inspire country-manor fantasies.

Am Elisabethufer (☎ 949 640; info@jever-hotel -pension.de; Elisabethufer 9a; s €35-40, d €60-70; P) In a typically Frisian brown-brick building with a steep roof, this hotel-pension has a fairly central location and pleasant rooms.

Im Schützenhof (☎ 9370; www.schuetzenhof-jever .de in German; Schützenhofstrasse 47; s €45-50, d €75-80; P) A more upmarket choice a little south of the centre, this hotel has comfortable modern rooms. It's favoured for local celebrations because of its excellent restaurant, Zitronengras.

Eating & Drinking

Haus der Getreuen (☎ 3010; Schlachtstrasse 1; mains €10-18) One of the nicest eateries in town, with a historic dining room and outside seating, Haus der Getreuen is famous for regional dishes, especially fish.

Balu (☎ 700 709; Kattrepel 1a; mains €9-17) An African restaurant in semirural Germany? What a pleasant surprise. With white walls and tasteful ethnic decoration, Balu mixes dishes like *joliffe* rice, *jambo*, yams and

plantains with more familiar Tex-mex and Italian fare.

Bier Akademie (☎ 5436; Bahnhofstrasse 44) Although it's on the corner of a rather unattractive shopping centre, inside the wood-lined Bier Akademie turns out to be an excellent place to educate yourself in the ways of Jever Pilsener and dozens of other beers.

Getting There & Around

The train trip to Jever from Bremen involves a change in Sande (€14.40, 1½ hours). By road, Jever is take the exit to the B210 from the A29 (direction: Wilhelmshaven).

Jever is small enough to explore on foot, and you can hire bicycles at **Rainer's Zweirad-Shop** (☎ 735 98; Grosse Wasserpfortstrasse 14).

EAST FRISIAN ISLANDS

Trying to remember the sequence of the seven East Frisian Islands, Germans – with a wink of the eye – recite the following mnemonic device: 'Welcher Seemann liegt bei Nanni im Bett?' (which translates rather saucily as 'Which seaman is lying in bed with Nanni?').

Lined up in an archipelago off the coast of Lower Saxony like diamonds in a tiara, the islands are (east to west): Wangerooge, Spiekeroog, Langeoog, Baltrum, Norderney, Juist and Borkum. Their long sandy beaches, open spaces and sea air make them both a nature lovers' paradise and a perfect retreat for those escaping the stresses of the world. Like their North Frisian cousins Sylt, Amrum and Föhr (see p728), the islands are part of the Wadden Sea (Wattenmeer) National Park.

The main season runs from mid-May to September. Beware, however, that the opening hours of tourist offices in nearby coastal towns change frequently and without notice. Call ahead if possible.

Resort Tax

Each of the East Frisian Islands charge a *Kurtaxe* (resort tax), entitling you to entry onto the beach and offering small discounts for museums etc. It's a small amount, typically €3 a day, and if you're staying overnight it's simply added to your hotel bill. Remind your hotel to give you your pass should they forget.

Getting There & Away

Most ferries sail according to tide times, rather than on a regular schedule, so it's best to call the ferry operator or Deutsche Bahn (DB) for information on departure times on a certain day. Tickets are generally offered either as returns for those staying on the island (sometimes valid for up to two months) or usually cheaper same-day returns.

In most cases (apart from Borkum, Norderney and Juist) you will need to change from the train to a bus at some point to reach the harbour from where the ferry leaves. Sometimes those are shuttle buses operated by the ferry company, or scheduled services from **Weser-Ems Bus** (☎ 01805-194 49; www.weser-ems-bus.de in German). For more details, see Getting There & Away under each island.

Getting Around

Only Borkum and Norderney allow cars, so heading elsewhere means you'll need to leave your vehicle in a car park near the ferry pier (about €3 per 12 hours).

WANGEROOGE

Crunching the sand between your toes and watching huge tanker ships lumber in and out of the ports at Bremerhaven, Hamburg and Wilhelmshaven, it's easy to feel like a willing castaway on Wangerooge – despite the many other visitors.

There are two information centres: the **Kurverwaltung** (spa administration; ☎ 04469-990; fax 991 14; Strandpromenade 3; ⏰ 9am-3.30pm Mon-Fri, 9am-noon Sat & Sun Apr-Oct, 9am-noon Mon-Fri Nov-Mar) and the **Verkehrsverein** (☎ 04469-948 811; vvwev@t-online.de; Hauptbahnhof), which handles room reservations as well.

If you're feeling active you can climb the historic **39m-tall lighthouse**, take to the sea-water adventure pool or indulge in a long list of sports activities. For more of a learning experience, head to the bird sanctuaries or the **Wattenmeer Information Centre** (☎ 04469-83 97; admission free; ⏰ 9am-1pm & 2-6pm Mon-Fri, 10am-noon & 3-6pm Sat & Sun) in the Rosenhaus.

Getting There & Away

The ferry to Wangerooge leaves from Harlesiel two to five times daily (1½ hours), depending on the tides. An open return ticket costs €25 (two-month time limit), and a same-day return ticket is €17. This includes the tram shuttle to the village on the island (4km). Large pieces of luggage are an extra €2.50 each, and a bike €10 each way. The ferry is operated by DB (☎ 04464-949 411).

To reach Harlesiel, take bus No 211 from Jever.

SPIEKEROOG

Rolling dunes dominate the landscape of minuscule Spiekeroog; about two-thirds of its 17.4 sq km is taken up by these sandy hills. It's the tranquillity of this rustic island that draws people, although you can distract yourself with the pint-sized **Alte Inselkirche** (☎ 04976-257; ⏰ 4-5pm Mon, 11am-noon Wed, 5-6pm Fri), built in 1696, a church with a surprising interior: a flat, wooden ceiling painted with red stars, and model wooden ships dangling down into the hall. There's also a **Spanish pietà** that washed ashore.

The **tourist office** (☎ 04976-919 3101; www.spiekeroog.de in German; Noorderpad 25; ⏰ 9am-12.30pm & 2-5pm Mon-Fri, 9am-noon Sat Apr-Oct, 9am-12.30pm Mon-Fri Nov-Mar) has a dedicated phone line for room reservations (☎ 04976-919 325).

Spiekeroog is not only car-free but discourages bicycles too.

Getting There & Away

Neuharlingersiel to Spiekeroog takes 40-55 minutes. Ferry departure times depend on the tides, so same-day returns aren't always possible. Prices are €10 each way or €16 for same-day return tickets. Each piece of luggage over the two-bag limit is an extra €2 return. Call ☎ 04974-214 for details and tickets.

To get to the ferry by train, you must change to a bus in Esens or Norden.

LANGEOOG

Floods and pirates make up the story of Langeoog, whose population was reduced to a total of two following a horrendous storm in 1721. But by 1830 it had recovered sufficiently to become a resort town.

The island boasts the highest elevation in East Friesland – the 20m-high **Melkhörndüne** – and the **grave** of Lale Anderson, famous for being the first singer to record the WWII song 'Lili Marleen'. Nautical tradition is showcased in the **Schiffahrtsmuseum** (☎ 04972-693 211; adult/concession €1.50/0.75; ⏰ 10am-noon & 3-5pm Mon-Thu, 10am-noon Fri & Sat), although the original **sea rescue ship** (admission free; ☉ 10am-noon & 3-5pm Mon-Thu, 10am-noon Fri & Sat) also on view is perhaps more interesting. In sunshine, the 14km-long beach is clearly the biggest attraction.

Langeoog's **tourist office** (☎ 04972-6930;standesamt@langeoog.de; Hauptstrasse 28, ☉ 8am-12.30pm & 2-5pm Mon-Thu, 8am-12.30pm Fri, plus 3-5pm Fri & 10am-noon Sat in July & Aug) is in the Rathaus. For room reservations, call ☎ 04972-69 3201 or email zimmernachweis@langeoog.de.

Getting There & Away
The ferry shuttles between Bensersiel and Langeoog up to nine times daily. The trip takes about one hour and costs €19 return, or €17 for a same-day return. Luggage is €2.50 per piece, bikes €15 return. For details, call ☎ 04971-928 90 or email schiffahrt@langeoog.de.

To get to Bensersiel by train, you must change to a shuttle bus in Esens or Norden.

BALTRUM
The smallest inhabited East Frisian Island, Baltrum is just 1km wide and 5km long and peppered with dunes and salty marshland. It's so tiny that villagers don't bother with street names but make do with house numbers instead. Numbers have been allocated on a chronological basis; house Nos 1 to 4 no longer exist so the oldest is now No 5.

There's little to do except go on walks or to the beach, or visit the exhibition on the National Park environment in **house No 177** (☎ 04939-469; admission free; ☉ 9am-noon & 2-7pm Mon-Fri). As the island closest to the mainland, Baltrum is the most popular destination for *Wattwanderungen* guided tours (see the boxed text Walking to the Islands, below).

The **Kurverwaltung** (☎ 04939-800; gemeinde@baltrum.de; House No 130; ☉ 8.30am-noon & 2-4pm Mon-Thu, 8.30am-noon Fri) can provide information. For room reservations, contact ☎ 01805-914 003; zimmernachweis@baltrum.de.

Getting There & Away
Ferries (and *Wattwanderungen*) leave from Nessmersiel. Ferries take 30 minutes. Departures depend on the tides, which means day trips aren't always possible. Single tickets are €10. Bikes are €4 each way and luggage is usually free. More details are available from ☎ 04939-913 00.

To get to Nessmersiel change from the train in Norden to a bus.

NORDERNEY
Norderney is the 'Queen of the East Frisian Islands' and has been wooed by a long line

---

Walking to the Islands

When the tide recedes on Germany's North Sea coast, it exposes the mudflats connecting the mainland to the East Frisian Islands, and that's when hikers and nature lovers make their way barefoot to Baltrum and its sister 'isles'. It's a minimum two-hour journey, wallowing in mud or wading knee-deep in seawater, but it's one of the most popular outdoor activities in this flat, mountainless region.

Wattwandern, as such trekking through the Wadden Sea National Park is called, can be dangerous. You need to know which fordable channels are left by the receding sea, and must be able to cope with the enveloping fog that, even in summer, can blow in within minutes. Therefore, the crossing should only be undertaken with a guide. Once you've safely reached your destination – and can now boast that you've walked to an island – you get to wait for the ferry to take you back while watching the sea rise swiftly over your trail.

As a kind of 'horizontal alpinism', *Wattwandern* (*Wadlopen* in the Netherlands) is far too dirty and strenuous to really be compared to walking on water. But the fresh sea air and the workout you've given your body does make you feel pretty holy.

Tourist offices in Jever and Emden can provide details of state-approved guides, including **Martin Rieken** (☎ 04941-8260; www.wattfuehrer-rieken.de in German), or **Eiltraut and Ulrich Kunth** (☎ 04933-1027; www.wattwanderung-kunth.de in German). English-speaking guides can be contacted at info@wattwandern.de.

Tours cost about €20, including the ferry ride back. Necessary gear includes shorts or short trousers and possibly socks or trainers (although many guides recommend going barefoot). In winter, gumboots are necessary.

of royal suitors, starting with Friedrich Wilhelm II of Prussia in 1797. He gave his blessing to the founding of Germany's first North Sea resort here. Georg V of Hanover liked Norderney so much that he made it his summer residence. Otto von Bismarck came here in 1844.

Norderney's **tourist office** (☎ 04932-918 50; fax 04932-824 94; Bülowallee 5; �ువ 9am-6pm mid-May–Sep, 9am-12.30pm & 2-6pm Mon-Fri, 9am-12.30pm Sat Oct-Apr) also handles room reservations (☎ 01805-667 331).

The island's **lavish gardens**, **parks** and majestic architecture date back to this era of visits by the high and mighty. The red-brick post office and the **Kurhaus** (the town's central building), with its columns and arches, and the many neoclassical homes give Norderney a glamorous flair. One particular attraction is **Die Welle** (☎ 04932-8910; Kurplatz; adult/concession €10/5; �ువ 9am-7pm Mon-Fri, 9am-6pm Sat & Sun), an indoor, ocean-water wave and fun pool. There's also an outdoor pool at Weststrand. The **Nationalpark-Haus** (admission free; �ువ 9am-6pm Tue-Sun) is directly on the harbour.

Getting There & Away

To get to Norderney you have to catch the ferry in Norddeich, which offers roughly hourly departures from 6am-8pm daily (50 minutes). Prices are €13.50 or €14.50 same-day return (including *Kurtaxe*). Bikes are €5. Details are available at ☎ 04931-98 70. There's a train service to Norddeich Mole, the ferry landing stage.

JUIST

Juist, shaped like a snake, is 17km long and only 500m wide. The only ways to travel are by bike, horse-drawn carriage or on your own two feet. What makes Juist special is what is not here: no high-rises, cars or shopping malls. Instead, you're often alone with the screeching seagulls, the wild sea and the howling winds. Forest, brambles and elderberry bushes blanket large sections of the island.

One peculiarity of Juist is the idyllic **Hammersee** – the only freshwater lake on all the islands, and also a bird sanctuary. There's also the **Juister Küstenmuseum** (Coastal Museum; ☎ 04935-1488; adult/concession €2/1.25; �ువ 9am-12.30pm & 2.30-5.30pm Mon-Sat) on Loogster Pad.

Juist's **tourist office** (☎ 04935-8090; www.juist.de in German; Friesenstrasse 18; �ువ 8.30-5pm Mon-Fri, 10am-

noon Sat) has a separate number for room reservations (☎ 04935-809 222).

Getting There & Away

Ferries to Juist depart from Norddeich and take 1½ hours. The cost is €22.50 return (including *Kurtaxe*) or €16.50 for same-day returns. Bikes cost €10. For more detailed information contact ☎ 04931-9870 or any DB office.

Trains from Emden (and beyond) travel straight to the landing dock in Norddeich Mole.

BORKUM

The largest of the East Frisian Islands is also one of the most popular. Until ripped it was apart by a flood in the 12th century, Borkum was even larger than today. For many centuries, the men of Borkum made a living as seafarers and whalers. Reminders of those brutal days are the whalebones that you'll occasionally see, stacked up side by side, as garden fences. It wasn't until 1830 that the locals realised that tourism was a safer way to earn a living.

To learn about the whaling era and other stages in the life of Borkum, visit the **Heimatmuseum** (Local History Museum; ☎ 04922-4860; adult/concession €3/1.50; �ువ 10am-noon & 3-5pm Tue-Sun) at the foot of the old lighthouse. Also of interest is the museum fire ship *Borkumriff*, with its exhibition on the Wadden Sea National Park.

Borkum has a **Kurverwaltung** (☎ 04922-9330; kurverwaltung@borkum.de; Goethestrasse 1). It's open on weekdays, timed to coincide with ferry arrivals/departures. There's a **tourist office** (☎ 04922-933 117; Hauptbahnhof; �ువ 9am-5.30pm Mon-Fri, 10am-noon & 2-4pm Sat & Sun), which also handles room reservations.

Getting There & Away

The embarkation point for ferries to Borkum is Emden. You can either take the car ferry, which takes two hours, or the catamaran, which crosses in an hour. Car-ferry tickets are €26 return, or €14 for a same-day return. Weekend return tickets are €15 (valid from Friday after 3pm to Sunday). Tickets for the catamaran are €41.40 return. Transporting a car costs €100 to €120 return, while a bike costs €10. For information, call ☎ 01805-024 367 or go to www.ag-ems.de (in German).

Hamburg

CONTENTS

History	684
Orientation	684
Information	685
Dangers & Annoyances	685
Sights	688
Activities	695
Tours	695
Festivals & Events	696
Sleeping	696
Eating	700
Drinking	702
Entertainment	703
Shopping	705
Getting There & Away	705
Getting Around	706
Around Hamburg	**707**
Altes Land	707
Stade	707
Buxtehude	708
Hamburg Wadden Sea	
National Park	708

Although it comes second to Berlin in the league of largest German cities, Hamburg is no also-ran. Indeed, had it not been so obsessed with minding its own lucrative business, this thriving 'harbourpolis' and powerful media capital might have been the sort of deputy to rival the boss. Instead, the Hanseatic City of Hamburg has used its ports and long-standing duty-free status to act as a gateway to the outside world – thereby becoming Germany's wealthiest spot and one of the richest in Europe.

The consequences of its enormous international trade permeate the city-state. On the one hand, there's a conservatism among the upper classes, who are focused above all on commercial benefit. On the other, there's a multiculturalism and free-wheeling liberalism on the streets, as foreigners and sailors have docked with this, the mother ship. Shipping, TV and newspaper magnates can be seen driving their Porsches up to lavish mansions in Blankenese, Harvestehude or Winterhude, while immigrant workers mingle with students among the Portuguese, Turkish and Asian eateries of vibrant St Pauli or the Schanzenviertel.

In the commercial hub of the Merchant's District, huge red-brick buildings shaped like ocean liners house some of the city's most venerable companies. Elsewhere, so-called *Ich AGs* ('Me Inc's, or one-person start-ups) – dotcom survivors or the result of recession-related job loss – have colonised former warehouses down at the docks.

Hamburg's location on a series of lakes and waterways makes it a popular tourist destination, as visitors cruise by the neo-Gothic Speicherstadt or haggle at the rowdy fish market, often against a backdrop of mournful foghorns as ships navigate the Elbe in drizzly *Schmuddelwetter* (foul weather). But the city's red-light district remains the best known. 'Which way to the Reeperbahn?' is a question you'll frequently hear.

HIGHLIGHTS

- **Bar-Hopping**
  Down a drink or two along the Reeperbahn and through St Pauli (p702)

- **Shopping**
  Catch the sights, sounds and smells on Sunday morning at the boisterous Fischmarkt in St Pauli (p691)

- **Boating**
  Float through the Speicherstadt canals or on the Alster lakes (p696)

- **Dining**
  Eat in style at Altona or Övelgönne overlooking the Elbe (p701)

- **Museums**
  View pre-eminent arts and crafts at Museum für Kunst und Gewerbe (p693)

- **Off-beat Experience**
  Get a small taste of what it's like to be blind at the pitch-black Dialog im Dunkeln exhibition in Speicherstadt (p691)

Altona ★★ Reeperbahn
Övelgönne ★★ ★★ Alster Lakes
  St Pauli ★★ ★ Museum für Kunst und Gewerbe
  Fischmarkt ★ Speicherstadt

| TELEPHONE CODE: 040 | POPULATION: 1.7 MILLION | AREA: 755 SQ KM |

HAMBURG

HISTORY

Hamburg's commercial character was forged in 1189, when local noble Count Adolf III persuaded Emperor Friedrich I (Barbarossa) to grant the city free trading rights and an exemption from customs duties. This helped transform the former missionary settlement and 9th-century moated fortress of Hammaburg into an important port and member of the Hanseatic League.

In a letter from 1831, treasurer of Glasgow John Strang described Hamburg as the world's 'most mercantile city'. That mercantile city suffered a major setback shortly afterwards in 1842, when the Great Fire destroyed one third of its buildings. However, it managed to recover in time to join the German Reich in 1871. This, however, saw it involved in two World Wars even less kind than the Great Fire. After WWI, most of Hamburg's merchant shipping fleet (almost 1500 ships) was forfeited to the Allies as reparation. During WWII, more than half of Hamburg's housing, 80% of its port and 40% of its industry were left as rubble, and tens of thousands of civilians were killed.

In the postwar years, Hamburg showed its usual resilience to participate in Germany's economic miracle or *Wirtschaftswunder*. Its harbour and media industries are now the backbone of its wealth. More than 6200 companies in the fields of publishing, advertising, film, radio, TV and music are based in the city. The print media are especially prolific: 15 out of 20 of the largest German publications are produced here, including news magazines *Stern* and *Der Spiegel* and the newspaper *Die Zeit*.

About 15% to 20% of the population are immigrants, giving the city an exciting, international flavour.

ORIENTATION

Like Venice and Amsterdam, Hamburg is shaped by water. Three rivers – the Elbe, the Alster and the Bille – traverse it, as does a grid of narrow canals called *Fleete*. The Binnenalster and Aussenalster (Inner and Outer Alster lakes) in the city centre accentuate the maritime feel.

Most major attractions cluster in the half-moon–shaped city centre, which arches north of the Elbe and is bordered by a ring

road following the former fortifications. The area is bisected diagonally by the Alsterfleet, the canal that once separated the now almost seamless Altstadt (old town) and Neustadt (new town).

The Hauptbahnhof (central bus station) is on Glockengiesserwall on the centre's northeastern edge, with the Busbahnhof behind it to the southeast. Three other stations lie west (Altona), south (Harburg) and north (Dammtor) of the centre. The spiky top of the TV Tower and the bronze helmetlike Michaeliskirche spire provide handy visual reference points.

This sprawling city consists of distinct neighbourhoods. East of the Hauptbahnhof is St Georg, a red-light district that's starting to become gentrified. It's also the hub of the city's gay scene. West of the centre lies St Pauli, home to the Reeperbahn, as well as lots of mainstream clubs and bars. Further west St Pauli merges with lively Altona district; to its north you'll find the trendy creative neighbour of the Schanzenviertel.

The city's most select neighbourhoods hug the 160-hectare Aussenalster north of the city centre, with Winterhude and Uhlenhorst on the eastern and Harvestehude and Rotherbaum on the western shores. The Universitätsviertel (University Quarter) takes up the western section of Rotherbaum.

The tourist offices can provide city maps (€0.30).

INFORMATION
Bookshops
Dr Götze Land und Karte (Map pp686-8; ☎ 3574 6310; Alstertor 14-18) For maps.
Heinrich-Heine-Buchhandlung (Map pp686-8; ☎ 441 1330; Grindelallee 26) Good selection of English books.
Thalia Bücher (Map pp686-8; ☎ 3020 7160; Grosse Bleichen 19) Also has English books.

Discount Cards
The tourist office, some hostels and hotels all sell discount cards in Hamburg.
Hamburg Card Offers unlimited public transport and slightly discounted admission to some museums, attractions and tours. The Day Card, valid after 6pm on the day of purchase and the entire next day, costs €7 (valid for one adult and up to three children under 12) or €13 (for groups of up to five people). The Multiple Day Card is valid on the day of purchase and the following two days (€14.50/23).
Power Pass The best deal for those under 30. Costs €6.70 the first day and €3 for each additional day, up to a week. Besides unlimited public transport, it offers great discounts, plus savings coupons good for drinks, movie tickets and nightclubs.

Emergency
Fundbüro (Lost & Found; Map pp686-8; ☎ 428 411 735; Bäckerbreitergang 73; ☒ Mon-Thu, excluding Wed afternoon) Turn up in person – don't ring – about lost wallets and the like.
Police (☎ 110; Hauptbahnhof, Kirchenallee exit, Davidwache at Spielbudenplatz 31) Also at other locations around the city.

Internet Access
Internet Café (☎ 2800 3898; Adenauerallee 10; €2 per hr; ☒ 10am-midnight Mon-Sat, 10am-1pm Sun) Take S/U-Bahn to Hauptbahnhof.
Tele-Time (Map pp686-8; ☎ 4131 4730; Schulterblatt 39; €3 per hr; ☒ 10am-midnight) Take U-Bahn to Feldstrasse or Sternschanze.

Laundry
Some inner-city laundrettes in Hamburg act as unofficial safe havens for homeless people, so turning up too early in the day can be distressing both to them and to you.
Schnell and Sauber (Am Neuer Pferdemarkt 27; ☒ 6am-11pm) Take U-Bahn to Feldstrasse. Also at Nobistor 34 and Grindelallee 138.

Medical Services
Ärtzlicher Notfalldienst Hamburg (☎ 228 022) For 24-hour medical advice.

Internationale Apotheke (Map pp686-8; ☎ 309 6060; Ballindamm 39)
Senator Apotheke (Map p698; ☎ 327 527; Hachmannplatz 14/Hauptbahnhof, Kirchenallee exit) International pharmacy.

Money
All major banks operate exchange counters during normal opening hours (until 4pm Monday to Friday, until 6pm Thursday). Outside the centre, branches may close at lunchtime. There are about half a dozen cash machines at the Hauptbahnhof and several at the airport.
AGW Wechselstube (Map p698; ☎ 280 2331; Steindamm 1; ☒ 8am-8pm Mon-Fri, 9am-4pm Sat) Charges no commission on cash. Also on the Reeperbahn (Map pp686-8; ☎ 314 445; ☒ 4-10pm), next to McDonald's.
American Express (Map pp686-8; ☎ 3039 3811; Rathausmarkt 10; ☒ 9.30am-6pm Mon-Fri, 10am-3pm Sat)

Post
Post office (Map p698; Hauptbahnhof, Kirchenallee exit; ☒ 8.30am-6pm Mon-Fri, 8.30am-noon Sat)
Post office (Map pp686-8; Dammtorstrasse 14; ☒ 8.30am-6pm Mon-Fri, 9am-noon Sat)

Tourist Information
The tourist office organises a multitude of tours, as well as the services below.
Hamburg Hotline (☎ 3005 1300; ☒ 8am-8pm) For room reservations (€4) and tickets, ask for an English-speaking operator.
Hamburg Tourismus Hauptbahnhof (Map p698; ☎ 3005 1200; www.hamburg-tourismus.de; Kirchenallee exit; ☒ 7am-10pm); Landungsbrücken, between piers 4 and 5 (Map pp686-8; ☒ 8am-8pm Apr-Sep, 10am-5.30pm Oct-Mar); airport (☎ 5075 1010; ☒ 6am-11pm).
Information booths Dammtor train station (☒ 8am-8pm Mon-Fri, 10am-5pm Sat); near the Alster ferry departure point (☒ 9am-6.30pm Apr-Oct, 10am-6pm Nov-Mar)

DANGERS & ANNOYANCES
Overall, Hamburg is a safe city with little crime. Junkies and pushers congregate at several places, most notably at the Kirchenallee exit of the Hauptbahnhof, at Hansaplatz in St Georg and in Sternschanzenpark in the Schanzenviertel. Since these areas cannot always be avoided, it pays to be careful around them. Prostitutes work throughout St Pauli and on Steindamm and adjacent streets in St Georg.

HAMBURG

HAMBURG

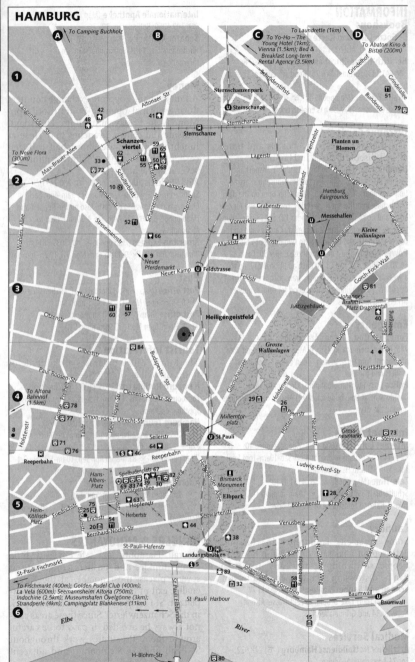

A To Camping Buchholz

B

C To Yo-Ho – The
Young Hotel (1km);
Vienna (1.5km); Bed &
Breakfast Long-term
Rental Agency (3.5km)

To Laundrette (1km)

D To Abaton Kino &
Bistro (200m)

Grindelhof

Grindelallee

51
79
Bundestr

1

Altonaer Str

Sternschanzenpark

U Sternschanze

Sternschanze

Sternschanze

42
48
41

Schanzen-
viertel

Langenfelder Str

Max-Brauer-Allee

To Neue Flora
(300m)

Wohlers Allee

Lagerstr

Planten un
Blomen

St Petersburger Str

Hamburg
Fairgrounds

Karolinenstr

Renzelstr

Schulterblatt

59
65
62
55
50
68
33
72

10

Lippmannstr

Stresemannstr

Kampstr

Grabenstr

Vorwerkstr

Glashüttenstr

U Messehallen

Kleine
Wallanlagen

Holstenplatz

U

U

2

52
66

Clemensstr

9
Neuer
Pferdemarkt

Neuer Kamp

U Feldstrasse

Feldstr

Markstr

87

Gorch-Fock-Wall

81

3

Thadenstr

Otzenstr

60
57

Budapester Str

Heiligengeistfeld

Justizgebäude

Johannes-
Brahms-
Platz

Dragonerstall

40

Gilbertstr

84

21

Grosse
Wallanlagen

Glacischaussee

Pilatuspool

Kaiser-Wilhelm-Str

4

Neustädter Str

Paul-Roosen-Str

To Altona
Bahnhof
(1.5km)

Clemens-Schultz-Str

Simon-von-Utrecht-Str

Hein-Hoyer-Str

Talstr

78
77
71
76

Holstenstr

8

Grosse Freiheit

Millerntor-
platz

29
26

Holstenwall

Hütten

Neanderstr

Wexstr

Grossneumarkt

73
Alter Steinweg

4

Seilerstr

64

U St Pauli

1
46

Reeperbahn

Reeperbahn

Ludwig-Erhard-Str

5

Hein-
Köllisch-
Platz

Hans-
Albers-
Platz

Spielbudenplatz
69
83
74
39
30
82
67

Davidstr

Kastanienallee

75
25
63
20
54

Erichstr

Hopfenstr

Herbertstr

Bernhard-Nocht-Str

Friedrichstr

Balduinstr

Hein-Hoyer-Str

Zirkusweg

Helgoländer Allee

**Bismarck
Monument**

Elbpark

44

38

Seewartenstr

Venusberg

Böhmkenstr

28
27
Krayenkamp

Neuer Pferdemarkt

Neuer Neustädter Weg

Stubbenhuk

Herrengraben

Schaartor

St-Pauli-Hafenstr

Ditmar-Koel-Str

U Landungsbrücken

6

St-Pauli-Fischmarkt

To Fischmarkt (400m); Golden Pudel Club (400m);
La Vela (600m); Seemannsheim Altona (750m);
Indochine (2.5km); Museumshafen Övelgönne (3km);
Strandperle (4km); Campingplatz Blankenese (11km)

Elbe

St Pauli-Elbtunnel

5

89

32

St Pauli Harbour

River

H-Blohm-Str

80

Johannisbollwerk

Vorsetzen

Baumwall

58

15

U Baumwall

Baumwall

Rambachstr

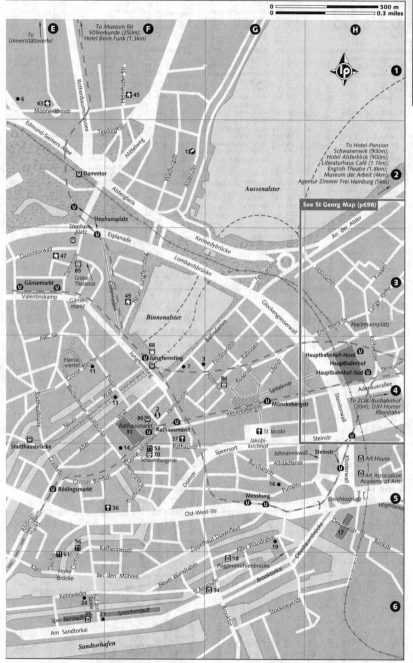

0   500 m
0   0.3 miles

To Museum für
Völkerkunde (250m);
Hotel Beim Funk (1.3km)

To
Universitätsviertel

6   43   Moorweidenstr

Edmund-Siemers-Allee

Tesdorpstr

Rothenbaumchaussee

Heimhuder Str

45

Mittelweg

Warburgstr

Alsterufer

1

Dammtor

Alsterglacis

Aussenalster

To Hotel-Pension
Schwanenwik (900m);
Hotel Alsterblick (900m);
Literaturhaus Café (1.1km);
English Theatre (1.8km);
Museum der Arbeit (4km);
Agentur Zimmer Frei Hamburg (5km)

Stephansplatz

Stephans-
platz   Esplanade   Kennedybrücke

Dammtorwall   47   Lombardsbrücke

85   Grosse
Theaterstr

Gänsemarkt

Valentinskamp

Gänse-
markt

49

Binnenalster

See St Georg Map (p698)

An der Alster

Holzdamm

Koppel

Lange Reihe

Ernst-Merck-Str   Hachmannplatz

Kirchenallee

ABC-Str.

Hanse-
viertel

Büschen

11

Grosse

Neuer

Stadthausbrücke

Poststr

Bleichenbrücke

Adolphsbrücke

Wall

13

Neuer Jungfernstieg

Colonnaden

Jungfernstieg

88   Jungfernstieg

3

7

Ballindamm

Ferdinandstr

Alstertor

Rosenstr

Raboisen

Lilienstr

86

Spitalerstr

Hermannstr

Glockengiesserwall

Hauptbahnhof-Nord

Hauptbahnhof

Hauptbahnhof-Süd

Steindamm

Steintorwall

Adenauerallee

To ZOB/Busbahnhof
(20m); DJH Horner
Rennbahn

2

90

Rathausmarkt

31   Rathausmarkt

14

Alter

Grosse
Burstah

Rödingsmarkt

Stadthausbrücke

Neuer Burstah

Hermannstr

Mönckebergstr   Mönckebergstr

37

Rathausstr

53

70   Schauenburgerstr

Speersort

St Jacobi

Jakobi-
kirchhof

Steinstr

Steinstr

Art House

Art Association
Academy of Arts

36

Tongstrasse

Grosser Burstah

Domstr

Burchardstr

Altstädterstr

Johanniswall

16   Pumpen

Messburg

Ost-West-Str

Deichtorplatz

Högerdamm

Bankstr

Deichtorstr

Klosterwall

56

61

Katherinenstr

Dovenfleet

Zippelhaus

Alter Wandrahm

19

17

Kajen

Cremon

Hohe
Brücke

Bei den Mühren

Neuer Wandrahm

18

Poggenmühlenbrücke

Brooktorkai

Oberbaumbrücke

Deichstr

Rödings-
markt

Kehrwieder

Auf dem
Sande

24

35   23   Speicherstadt

Speicherstadt

Am Sandtorkai

St Annen

34

Brooktor

Stockmeyerstr

Sandtorhafen

E   F   G   H
1
2
3
4
5
6

INFORMATION		
AGW Wechselstube	1	B5
American Express	2	F4
Dr Götze Land und Karte	3	F4
Fundbüro	4	D4
Hamburg Tourismus	5	B6
Heinrich-Heine-Buchhandlung	6	E1
International Pharmacy	7	F4
Schnell and Sauber	8	A4
Schnell and Sauber	9	B3
Tele-Time	10	B2
Thalia Bücher	11	E4
US Consulate	12	F2

SIGHTS & ACTIVITIES	(pp688-95)	
Alsterarkaden	13	E4
Börse	14	F5
Cap San Diego	15	D6
Chile Haus	16	G5
Condomerie	(see 74)	
Deichtorhallen	17	H5
Deutsches Zollmuseum	18	G6
Dialog im Dunkeln	19	G5
Erotic Art Museum	20	A5
Footbal Stadium William-Koch-Stadion	21	B3
Grosse Freiheit 36/Kaiserkeller	22	A4
HafenCity Info Center	23	E6
Hamburg Dungeon	24	E6
Harry's Hamburger Hafenbasar	25	A5
Johannes Brahms Museum	26	C4
Krameramtswohnungen	27	D5
Michaeliskirche	28	D5
Museum für Hamburgische Geschichte	29	C4
Panoptikum	30	B5
Rathaus	31	F4
Rickmer Rickmers	32	C6

Rote Flora	33	A2
Speicherstadtmuseum	34	G6
Spicy's Gewürzmuseum	35	E6
St Nikolai	36	F5
St Petri	37	F4

SLEEPING	⌂ (pp696-700)	
DJH Auf dem Stintfang	38	C5
Florida – The Art Hotel	39	B5
Frauenhotel Hanseatin	40	D3
Fritz Hotel	41	B1
Home Company	42	A1
Hotel Bellmoor	(see 43)	
Hotel Fresena	43	E1
Hotel Hafen	44	B5
Hotel Heimhude	45	F1
Hotel Monopol	46	B5
Hotel SIDE	47	E3
InstantSleep Backpacker Hostel	48	A1
Raffles Hotel Vier Jahreszeiten	49	F3
Schanzenstern	50	B2

EATING	🍴 (pp700-2)	
Balutschi	51	D1
Bok	52	B2
Café Paris	53	F5
Kochsalon	54	B5
Lokma	55	B2
Nido	56	E5
Nil	57	B3
Saliba	58	C6
Shikara	59	B2
Suryel	60	B3
Ti Breizh	61	E6

DRINKING	🍸 (pp702-3)	
Bedford Café	62	B2

Better Days Project	63	B5
Café Keese	64	B4
Dual	65	B2
Mandalay	66	B3
Meanie Bar	67	B5
Nachtasyl	(see 86)	

ENTERTAINMENT	🎭 (pp703-5)	
3001	68	B2
Angie's Nightclub	69	B5
Banque Nationale	70	F5
Betty Ford Klinik	71	A4
Café Unter den Linden	72	A2
Cotton Club	73	D4
Docks	74	B5
EDK	75	A5
Glam	76	A5
Grosse Freiheit 36/Kaiserkeller	77	A4
Grünspan	78	A4
Logo	79	D1
Musikaltheater im Hafen	80	C6
Musikhalle	81	D3
Operettenhaus	82	B5
Schmidt Theater	83	B5
Schmidt's Tivoli	(see 83)	
Spundloch	84	B4
Staatsoper	85	E3
Thalia Theater	86	G4

SHOPPING	🛍 (p705)	
Marktstrasse	87	C3

TRANSPORT		
ATG Alster-Touristik Landing Stage	88	F4
Hadag Landing Stages	89	C6
Rathaus Bus Station	90	F4

SIGHTS

St Pauli Walking Tour

Let's be frank, and start in the district that at least intrigues if not interests most visitors: the sleazy, sexedelic Reeperbahn. It's on such a scale as to be described as the Champ-Élysées of red-light districts, and it's even more of a draw than Amsterdam's equivalent scene. It slowly starts to awaken after about 4pm, and if you alight at the Reeperbahn S-Bahn station several hours later, you'll be sharing the street with thousands of others (see boxed text Sex & the Hanseatic City p689).

Just north of the S-Bahn station is the **Grosse Freiheit** (literally 'Great Freedom') street, with its bright lights, dark doorways and live sex nightclubs. Smarmy doormen try to lure the passing crowd into places like Tabu and Safari. If you're interested, ask about the conditions of entry. Admission tends to be fairly low (around €5), but it's the mandatory drink minimum (usually at least €20) that drives up the cost. Ask at the bar how much drinks cost; there have been reports of people being charged nearly €100 for a couple of watery cocktails.

The Star Club, eternally associated with the Beatles (see the boxed text Beatles in Hamburg – Forever p703), once stood at

Grosse Freiheit 39 but is long gone. The Fab Four also played in the basement **Kaiserkeller** (1; Grosse Freiheit 36), which still exists (see Live Music p704).

Back on the Reeperbahn, head east past sex shops, peep shows and dubious hotels, then cross the street where, on the corner with Davidstrasse, stands the **Davidwache** (2; 1914). This brick building, festooned with ornate ceramic tiles, is the base for 150 police who maintain St Pauli's reputation as the safest area in Hamburg.

Continue south on Davidstrasse where, after 50m, you'll see a metal wall on the right barring views into Herbertstrasse, a block-long bordello that's off-limits to men under 18 and to women of all ages.

Take the next right, Erichstrasse. Continue to the corner with Balduinstrasse,

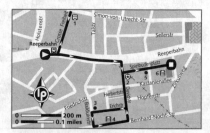

where you'll find **Harry's Hamburger Hafenbasar** (3; ☎ 312 482; www.hafenbasar.de; Balduinstrasse 18; adult/child €2.50/1.50; ☻ noon-6pm Tue-Sun), a treasure trove of African figures, Asian masks and ephemera acquired by now deceased collector Harry Rosenberg. The admission fee is redeemable against purchase of more than €5. The shop also offers good insider tours, in English, of the secrets of the St Pauli district.

Exiting the store head left down Balduinstrasse, turn left into Bernhard-Nocht-Strasse and continue to the **Erotic Art Museum** (4; ☎ 317 4757; www.eroticartmuseum.de; Bernhard-Nocht-Strasse 69; admission €8; ☻ 10am-midnight). It does exactly what it says on the tin: presents erotic art from S&M to (mainly) soft, soft porn.

Turn back left up Davidstrasse and right at the Davidwache into Spielbudenplatz, the site of St Pauli's more 'respectable' bars and clubs. At Spielbudenplatz 18, people gather outside the **Condomerie (5)**, with its extensive collection of prophylactics and sex toys. They're usually gawping at the gargantuan (and nowadays slightly grubby) condom in the window, to which the shop owner has appended an offer of a €100 gift voucher to any gentleman who can properly fit it. They

say the prize has been awarded twice. Ouch. The **Panoptikum** (6; ☎ 310 317; Spielbudenplatz 3; adult/concession €4/2.50; ☻ 11am-9pm Mon-Fri, 11am-midnight Sat, 10am-9pm Sun; closed mid-Jan–early-Feb) of wax figures here is pretty cheesy.

Port of Hamburg   Map pp686–8
South of St Pauli lies one of the largest ports in Europe. Each year about 12,000 ships deliver and take on some 70 million tonnes of goods here. The port sprawls over 75 sq km, accounting for 12% of Hamburg's entire surface area. Harbour cruises (p696) give you a good overview. Climbing the steps above the Landungsbrücken U/S-Bahn stop to the Stintfang stone balcony also offers an interesting snapshot.

At St Pauli's Landungsbrücken, mostly nowadays simply known as Landungsbrücken (landing piers) lies the **Rickmer Rickmers** (☎ 319 5959; adult/child €3/2; ☻ 10am-5.30pm last entry), a three-masted steel windjammer from 1896 that is now a museum ship and restaurant. The 10,000-tonne **Cap San Diego** (☎ 364 209; adult/child €4/2) nearby hosts some interesting temporary exhibitions on immigration and shipping.

Just west of the St Pauli landing piers stands a grey structure topped by a copper

---

SEX AND THE HANSEATIC CITY

The character of Hamburg's St Pauli district and its main artery, the Reeperbahn, is unique. Where else will you find live sex shows and a wax museum filled with stiff Germans – all on the same street?

On a busy night there might be as many as 40,000 people cruising the rip-roaring collection of bars, sex clubs, variety acts, restaurants, pubs and cafés collectively known as the 'Kiez'. The abstemious and celibate St Paul, for whom Hamburg's 'sin centre' is named, wouldn't have taken kindly to such displays, but the sightseers come from all walks of life.

Although it was long established as a party place for incoming sailors, the area's popularity peaked in the liberated 1960s when the Beatles cut their musical teeth at the legendary – now defunct – Star Club. Prostitution boomed along the lurid, spidery streets spilling off the Reeperbahn. But then a wave of hard crime and drugs sent St Pauli on a downward spiral, and rip-offs became commonplace (with cheap wine served from expensive bottles, as just one example). Germany's *Sündenmeile* (Sin Mile) had to reinvent itself to survive – which it did.

The answer, as always in Hamburg, was greater commercialisation, as another layer of attractions was added as the No 1 attraction for tourists. In recent years, musicals like *Cats* and *Mamma Mia* have played to sold-out houses on the eastern edge, and stylish nightclubs, bars and even restaurants keep a hip, moneyed clientele entertained until dawn.

The sex industry is still in full swing as girls line up with almost military precision along some streets. However, some of the rougher edges are gone; for example, pimps no longer loiter and leer. With its flashing neon lights and raucous crowds, the Reeperbahn today seems nothing more than a nightly carnival to some visitors. For others, it's a place to observe the seedy *Taxi Driver* underbelly of the city.

cupola. This is the entrance to the **St Pauli Elbtunnel** (1911), a 426m-long passageway beneath the Elbe River. It is still used, although most cars take the New Elbe Tunnel further west. Cars and pedestrians descend some 20m in a lift, make their way through the tiled tube, then ride back up on the other end.

The view back across the Elbe to the port and the city skyline is interesting (turn left as you exit).

Altstadt Walking Tour

From the Hauptbahnhof, head west down the pedestrianised Spitalerstrasse and past the 12th-century **St Petri** (**1**; ☎ 324 438; Mönckebergstrasse), rebuilt in neo-Gothic style after the Great Fire of 1842. A little further on to your right is the neo-Renaissance **Rathaus** (**2**), where you can make a first stop and take a **guided tour** (☎ 428 312 470; Rathausmarkt; adult/child €1.50/0.50; ❧ hourly 10.15am-3.15pm Mon-Thu, 10.15am-1pm Fri-Sun). The 40-minute journey through the 1897 building only has time for a small percentage of the 647 rooms, but includes the opulent Emperor's Hall

and the Great Hall, with its spectacular coffered ceiling.

To the north of the Rathaus (to your right as you face the building) you'll see the **Alsterarkaden** (**3**), an elegant row of Renaissance-style arcades sheltering shops and cafés. This arcade runs parallel to the Alsterfleet canal, which merges with the Binnenalster, the smaller of the two city lakes and departure point for lake cruises (see Cruises p696).

Take time to do a leisurely lap through the Alsterarkaden, bringing you back to Rathaus. Head across the cobbled square to the Grosse Johannisstrasse and turn right. A few minutes later, at the corner with Börsenbrücke, you'll come across the **Börse** (**4**; ☎ 361 3020; Adolphsplatz; free tours; call for hours), Germany's oldest stock exchange.

Turn left at Börsenbrücke, which takes you to the historic **Trostbrücke**, the oldest bridge linking the Altstadt and Neustadt. It features statues of Ansgar, Hamburg's first archbishop (801–65), and Neustadt founder Count Adolf III. Just beyond is the blackened remains of **St Nikolai** (**5**), now

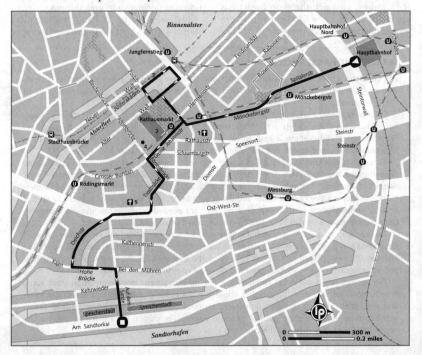

HAMBURG'S UNIQUE FISH MARKET

Every Sunday morning, in the wee hours, an unusual ritual unfolds along the banks of the Elbe, just a few hundred metres south of the Reeperbahn. A fleet of small trucks roars onto the cobbled pavement. Hardy types with hands the size of baseball gloves emerge from the driver's cabins and set out to turn their vehicles into stores on wheels. They artfully arrange their bananas, apples, cauliflower and whatever else the earth has yielded that week. Others pile up slippery eels, smoked fish fillets and fresh shrimp in tasteful displays. In another corner, cacti, flowers and leafy plants begin to wait for customers. It's not yet 5am as the first of them begin to trundle in, their brains boozy, their eyes red, their moods hyper from a night of partying in St Pauli. May the trading begin.

The Fischmarkt in St Pauli has been a Hamburg institution since 1703 and still defines the city's life and spirit. Locals of every age and walk of life join curious tourists as the beer flows and you can buy everything from cheap sweatshirts and tulips to a hearty breakfast or a scorched bratwurst.

The undisputed stars of the event – and great, free entertainment – are the boisterous *Marktschreier* (market criers) who hawk their wares at the top of their lungs. With lascivious winks and leering innuendo, characters like Aal-Dieter or Banana-Harry boast of the quality and size of their product. 'Don't be shy, little girl', they might say to a rotund 60-year-old, waggling a piece of eel in front of her face. But nobody minds the vulgar come-ons. Almost always, the 'girl' blushes before taking a hearty bite as the crowd cheers her on. It's all just part of the show.

More entertainment takes place in the adjoining Fischauktionshalle (Fish Auction Hall), where a live band cranks out cover versions of ancient German pop songs to which everyone seems to know the words. Down in the pit, the beer flows and sausage fumes waft through the air as if it were 8pm and not just past dawn. For those who actually know what time it is, breakfast is served on the gallery, away from the crooners.

Hamburg life thrives here – at the edge of the river – in the good stink of mud and oil and fish. If Bruegel were to paint a picture of Hamburg life, this is where he'd set up his easel.

The Fischmarkt takes place from 5am to 10am on Sunday (from 7am October to March).

an antiwar memorial. What you see today was all that was left by Allied bombers during WWII, and there's an **exhibition** (adult/child €2/1; ⊗ 11am-5pm) under the glass pyramid on-site, with some chilling photos of the bombed-out city.

The Great Fire broke out in **Deichstrasse**, which runs south off Ost-West-Strasse and features a few restored 18th-century homes. Continue south down the street, then turn left (east) and cross the canal at Auf dem Sande for an exploration of the Speicherstadt.

SPEICHERSTADT

The seven-storey, red-brick warehouses lining the Elbe archipelago across from Deichtorhallen are a well-recognised Hamburg symbol, stretching as they do to Baumwall, the world's largest continuous warehouse complex. Their neo-Gothic gables and green copper roofs are reflected in the narrow canals lacing this free-port zone.

Such a separate free port became necessary when Hamburg joined the German Customs Federation on signing up for the German Reich in 1871. An older neighbourhood was demolished – and 24,000 people displaced – to make room for the construction of the Speicherstadt from 1885 to 1927. Today, goods such as coffee, tea, computers and oriental carpets are still hoisted into the storerooms via pulleys and remain there customs-free until the owner decides to sell.

This being the postindustrial age, however, many of the warehouses have been put to a secondary use. There are eight museums down here, including the remarkable **Dialog im Dunkeln** (6; Dialogue in the Darkness; ☎ 0700 4433 200; www.dialog-im-dunkeln.de; Alter Wandrahm; adult/concession €10/7; ⊗ 9am-5pm Tue-Fri, noon-7pm Sat & Sun). This pitch-black journey, with a blind guide, through re-created jungle, country and urban landscapes gives a brief but memorable impression of what it's like not to see. This long-running exhibition might close in late 2005, but you need to ring ahead in any case to book, so check then. Ask for a guide who speaks some English.

The schlock-horror **Hamburg Dungeon** (7; ☎ 3600 5500 for info, 3005 1512 for tickets; Kehrwieder 2; adult/child €13/9.50; ☽ 11am-6pm last entry) is mega-popular, but you might want to head for the **Speicherstadtmuseum** (8; ☎ 321 191; St Annenufer 2; adult/concession €2.50/1.50; ☽ 10am-5pm Tue-Sun), which relates the area's history (in German), or the sweet-smelling **Spicy's Gewürzmuseum** (9; Spice and Herb Museum; ☎ 367 989; Am Sandtorkai 32; adult/concession €3/2; ☽ 10am-5pm Tue-Sun). The most exciting thing about the **Deutsches Zollmuseum** (10; German Customs Museum; ☎ 3397 6386; Alter Wandrahm 15; admission free; ☽ 10am-5pm Tue-Sun) is the chunk of Berlin Wall outside.

The long-abandoned 155 hectares behind the Speicherstadt are finally being redeveloped, in an enormous London Docklands–style inner-city regeneration project called HafenCity (harbour city). Brochures (in German and English), architectural models and installations can be found at the **HafenCity InfoCenter** (11; ☎ 3690 1799; Am Sandtorkai 30; admission free; ☽ 10am-6pm Tue-Sun), where there's also a café.

One of the loveliest views of the Speicherstadt is from the Poggenmühlenbrücke and the area is beautifully lit at night. To leave the Speicherstadt, head north from here, cross Ost-West-Strasse and turn right on Pumpen.

MERCHANT'S DISTRICT

Now you are in the Merchant's District, Hamburg's commercial heartland. It's characterised by mighty red-brick edifices designed to look like ocean liners, including Hamburg's single most famous building, the magnificent **Chile Haus** (12; 1924). Drawn up by architect Fritz Höger for a merchant who derived his wealth from trading with Chile, and located between Burchardstrasse and Messberg, this reddish-brown brick building has staggered balconies to look like ship decks and curved walls meeting in the shape of a ship's bow. To fully appreciate the building's eccentric form, walk to the corner of Burchardstrasse and Johanniswall and look back.

Neustadt Walking Tour

This tour starts at the **Michaeliskirche** (1; ☎ 3767 8100; Krayenkamp; admission free; ☽ 9am-5.30pm Mon-Sat, 11am-5.30pm Sun Apr-Sep, 10am-5pm

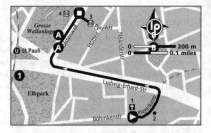

Mon-Sat, 11.30am-5pm Sun Oct-Mar), Hamburg's most prominent landmark. Popularly known as 'Michael', its distinctive tower presides over northern Germany's largest Protestant baroque church. A white-and-gold interior sports a curved upstairs gallery. Organ concerts here often draw capacity crowds of 2500 people. Views from the tower, reached by a **lift** (adult/child €2.50/1.75), help you grasp the city layout. A multivision show on Hamburg's history (in German) or a crypt visit can be skipped.

Below the church, in a tiny alley off Krayenkamp 10, are the **Krameramtswohnungen** (2; ☎ 3750 1988; adult/concession €1/0.50, half-price Fri; ☽ 10am-5pm Tue-Sun), a row of tiny half-timbered houses from the 17th century that, for nearly 200 years, were almshouses for the widows of members of the Guild of Small Shopkeepers. Taken over by the city in 1863, they became seniors' homes until 1969 and are now just a tourist attraction. Only one home is a museum; others are shops or restaurants.

Follow Krayenkamp north to Ludwig-Erhard-Strasse, head west, then north on Holstenwall to get to cobbled **Peterstrasse**, with its restored baroque houses. One harbours the **Johannes Brahms Museum** (3; ☎ 452 158; Peterstrasse 39; admission €2.50; ☽ 10am-1pm Tue & Thu). It's a tribute to the composer, who was born in the city.

On the west side of Holstenwall is the **Museum für Hamburgische Geschichte** (4; Museum of Hamburg History; ☎ 428 412 380; www.hamburgmuseum.de; Holstenwall 24; adult/concession €7.50/4, all €4 on Fri; ☽ 10am-5pm Tue-Sat, 10am-6pm Sun), which kids of all ages will find a treat. It's chock-full of intricate ship models, has a large model-train set (only open at certain times; ring ahead) and even includes the actual bridge of the steamship *Werner*, which you can clamber over. Furthermore, it chronicles the city's evolution, revealing little titbits about its Masonic societies and the fact that the Reeperbahn was once the home of ropemakers ('*Reep*' means rope). Most exhibits have English annotations.

Art Museums

Keep an eye out for special exhibitions in the other smaller museums along Hamburg's **Kunstmeile** (Art Mile), extending from Glockengiesserwall to Deichtorstrasse between the Alster lakes and the Elbe. In particular, the converted market halls of the wonderful **Deichtorhallen** (Map pp686-8; ☎ 321 030; Deichtorstrasse 1-2; ◷ 11am-6pm Tue-Fri, 10am-6pm Sat & Sun) show international touring exhibitions of contemporary art – Warhol, Lichtenstein, Haring etc – as well as photography by Helmut Newton, Annie Leibowitz and other prominent shooters.

HAMBURGER KUNSTHALLE

A solid, well-presented collection has gained **Hamburger Kunsthalle** (Map p698; ☎ 428 542 612; www.hamburger-kunsthalle.de; Glockengiesserwall; adult/concession €7.50/5, higher during special exhibits; ◷ 10am-6pm, 10am-9pm Thu) the reputation as one of the best art museums in Germany. In its main building, you'll find works ranging from medieval portraiture to 20th-century classics, such as Beckmann, Klee, Kokoschka, Munch and Nolde. There's also a memorable set of 19th-century German paintings, including one room of landscapes by Caspar David Friedrich.

Traverse the underground passage from the old building's café and you'll emerge into the stark white **Galerie der Gegenwart** (Map p698). Here works come from German artists like Rebecca Horn, Georg Baselitz and Gerhard Richter, as well as international artists like Nan Goldin, David Hockney, Jeff Koons, Barbara Kruger and Gillian Wearing. But while admiring the art, don't forget to look out the gallery's huge picture windows at the Binnenalster and the city.

There's a free pamphlet laying out the general galleries, or another (€1) with individual highlights, available from the ticket office.

MUSEUM FÜR KUNST UND GEWERBE

Critics are divided over which is Hamburg's pre-eminent art gallery: the Kunsthalle (see above) or the **Museum für Kunst und Gewerbe** (Museum of Arts & Crafts; Map p698; ☎ 428 542 732; www.mkg-hamburg.de; Steintorplatz 1; adult/concession €8.20/4.10, all €4.10 from 5pm Thu; ◷ 10am-6pm Tue, Wed & Fri-Sun, 10am-9pm Thu). Well, this one's more fun, at least. Its vast collection of sculpture, furniture, jewellery, porcelain, musical instruments and household objects runs the gamut from Italian to Islamic, from Japanese to Viennese and from medieval to pop-art eye-candy.

There are period rooms, including an Art Nouveau salon from the 1900 Paris World Fair and a room designed by Belgian architect Henry van der Velde, plus sections on modern poster design, graphic design and Italian design from the 1950s to 1990s (with Bakelite, space-age shaped TVs!). Cabinets of magazine covers not only give you the chance to look back on *Colors* and *Wallpaper**, but also to discover local publications like the much-acclaimed *Brand Eins*.

The museum café, Destille, is integrated into the exhibition space and the shop is brilliant.

Other Museums

MUSEUM FÜR VÖLKERKUNDE

A perfect example of sea-going Hamburg's acute awareness of the outside world, the **Museum für Völkerkunde** (Museum of Ethnology; ☎ 01805-308 888; www.voelkerkundemuseum.com; Rothenbaumchaussee 64; adult/concession €6/3, all €3 Fri; ◷ 10am-6pm Tue, Wed & Fri-Sun, 10am-9pm Thu) is outstanding in two respects. Firstly, the exhibits themselves are stunning, particularly the domed room at the top of the entrance hall's steps, with its carved wooden canoes and giant sculptures from Papua New Guinea. Secondly, the approach is refreshingly open-minded and not at all patronising. Modern artefacts and issues from Africa, Asia and the South Pacific are presented alongside traditional masks, jewellery, costumes and musical instruments. There's also a complete, intricately carved Maori meeting hall open from 1.30pm every day. Take the U1 to Hallerstrasse.

MUSEUM DER ARBEIT

Other good exhibits are found at the **Museum der Arbeit** (Museum of Work; ☎ 428 322 364; Maurienstrasse 19; adult/concession €4/3, half-price Fri; ◷ 1-9pm Mon, 10am-5pm Tue-Sat, 10am-6pm Sun). Chronicling the development of the workplace in the Hamburg area, it has a focus on the changing rights and roles of working men and women. There's also a section on printing, appropriate for this media city. The museum is on the grounds of the former New York-Hamburg Rubber Company. Take the U2/U3/S1 to Barmbek.

Schanzenviertel & Karolinenviertel **Map pp686-8**

North of St Pauli lie the Schanzenviertel and Karolinenviertel. Once home to Hamburg's counter-cultural scene, they have been gentrified in recent years. You'll probably visit this area, bordered by the U-Bahn Feldstrasse, S/U-Bahn Sternschanze and Stresemannstrasse, because you're staying here, shopping here or enjoying one of its restaurants or bars. However, if you just want to explore, you'll find two lively quarters, where creative media types mix with students among a landscape of doner kebab shops, Italian and Portuguese cafés and funky clothing stores.

One of the most outstanding remnants of the area's rougher days is the graffiti-covered building on Schulterblatt that looks one step away from demolition. This is the **Rote Flora**, now an alternative culture centre and drug-dealing hub, but once the famous Flora Theatre. (Sternschanzenpark also remains a stomping ground of drug dealers and junkies and is best avoided.)

Altona & Övelgönne **Map p694**

These western quarters show another side to the Elbe River, and they're united in their reputation as great places to dine (see p701). However, you will also find a few worthwhile museums.

Altona is a fashionable place to live for young professionals. It has a small-town feel quite distinct from the rest of Hamburg, and for good reason. From 1640 to 1867, it was a separate city that belonged to Denmark, then to Prussia and only became part of Hamburg in 1937.

As you exit Altona train station from the east (Ottenser Hauptstrasse exit) and turn and walk south (left), you'll come across the **Platz der Republik**, a rectangular park bordered by the stately **Altona Rathaus** (1898) to the south and Museumstrasse along its western side. Also here is the **Altona Museum/North German State Museum** (☎ 428 111 514; Museumstrasse 23; adult/concession €6/3; 🕑 10am-6pm Tue-Sun) with a focus on art and cultural history. The exhib-

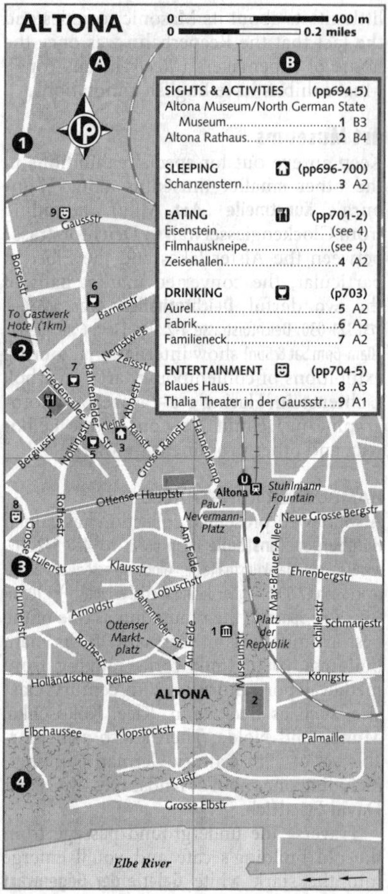

its include model ships, harpoons, scrimshaw and other nautical memorabilia. An entire room is filled with an impressive display of bowsprits. The museum restaurant is inside an authentic 19th-century farmhouse.

Continuing south and turning left (east) behind the Rathaus, you step onto **Palmaille**, a beautiful boulevard lined with linden trees and elegant, neoclassical merchant houses built between 1790 and 1825. The street's name derives from the Italian *palla* for 'ball' and *maglio* for 'bat' as it was originally intended as a playing field. Turning right (west) behind the Rathaus takes you onto the grand thoroughfare of Elbchaussee. Heading straight ahead down Kaistrasse takes you to Övelgönne.

Once home to captains who plied their trade on the Elbe River and North Sea, Övelgönne has a pleasant riverside walkway and several waterfront restaurants. Here, you'll also find the **Museumshafen Övelgönne** (☎ 390 0079; Neumühlen ferry landing; ☽ 24hr), where some 20 working and fishing vessels dating from the 1890s to 1930s bob in the water. All found as wrecks, they've been restored (placards on the pier provide background on each).

You can reach Övelgönne by bus No 112 from Altona train station, which originally leaves from the bus terminal near the Hauptbahnhof.

Blankenese

The people of Hamburg say that the better you're doing in life, the further west in the city you live. If those who reside in Övelgönne (see p694) are making it, those in Blankenese have arrived – this former fishing village and haven for cut-throats now boasts some of the most expensive property in Germany.

This hillside labyrinth of narrow, cobbled streets, lined with fine houses, is for what the area is best known; there's a network of **58 stairways** with 4864 steps. The best views of the Elbe (nearly 3km wide here) and the container ships putting out to sea are enjoyed from the 75m-high **Süllberg** hill (head through the restaurant at the summit).

To get to Blankenese, take the S1. Exiting the station, turn right and continue to the front bus stop, where you'll see a map of the area, and a street sign pointing to the stairs area. It's easiest to catch the tiny bus No 48, which leaves this stop every 10 minutes from 8am to 7pm (then half-hourly to midnight). Getting off at Weseberg – having passed the clutch of beachfront restaurants and cafés and reached the summit of the following hill – you'll see a sign pointing to the nearby Süllberg. Alternatively, you can alight at Krögers Treppe and head up the Bornholldt Treppe and Süllbergsweg – or get off once the road starts winding and just explore.

ACTIVITIES
Boating

Sailing, rowing and pedal boats are for hire along the Alster lakes in summer. Prices start at €18 per hour for two people. Try **Kapitän Prüsse** (☎ 280 3131; An der Alster 47) at the sailing club. See also Cruises p696.

Cycling

The paved path around the Aussenalster is a popular route (also good for walking or inline skating), while another takes you along the Elbe banks from St Pauli to Blankenese and Wedel past gorgeous homes and forests (20km each way).

The excellent *Fahrradtourenkarte für Hamburg*, available at Dr Götze Land und Karte (see Bookshops p685), contains more ideas and itineraries. If you want to hire a bike, try **Fahrradladen St Georg** (Map p698; ☎ 243 908; Schmilinskystrasse 6), which charges €8 a day and requires a €50 deposit.

Spectator Sports

Hamburg opened its new **Stadion Hamburg** (AOL Arena; Sylvesterallee 7, Bahrenfeld) in 2000, in readiness for the FIFA World Cup in 2006. The €97 million, 55,000-seat football stadium is in the city's northwest, just off the E45/7/27 by car. Alternatively, take the S-Bahn (line 3 or 21) to Stellingen.

Favourite local team FC St Pauli plays at home in the **William Koch Stadion** (☎ 3179 6112 for tickets; Heiligengeistfeld). The nearest U-Bahn station is Feldstrasse.

TOURS
Bus Tours

First-time visitors might consider a guided bus tour to gain an overview. Companies listed here are just tasters; for more options, check with the tourist office or read the board where the buses leave at the Hauptbahnhof.

Top-Tour Hamburg (adult/child under 14 €12/6.50; ☽ every 30 minutes 9.30am-4.30pm, 11am-3pm in winter) runs double-decker buses that take you to the leading sights in 1½-hour city sightseeing tours in German and English. Not only can you add a port cruise for an extra €7, but you can also jump on and off the bus at various points, such as the Rathaus and St Michaeliskirche, and catch the next bus for greater flexibility. Tours depart from the Kirchenallee exit of the Hauptbahnhof or from Landungsbrücken.

An unashamedly touristy way to travel is on the 1920s **Hummelbahn Trolley** (☎ 792 8979; adult/teenager/child under 12 €13/11/free). Tours run hourly from 10am to 5pm between April and October, and three times daily throughout the rest of the year. Hummelbahn also operates **double-decker bus tours** (adult/child under 12 €13/free; 9am-4pm daily year-round) leaving on the hour.

Cruises

Taking a cruise on one of Hamburg's lakes or canals is one of the best ways to appreciate the beauty of the city.

LAKES & CANALS

ATG Alster-Touristik (Map pp686-8; ☎ 3574 2419; www.alstertouristik.de) runs tours and ferries from its landing stage at Jungfernstieg. Options include the 50-minute **Alster Tour** (€9; ⏰ every half-hour 10am-6pm Apr-Sep, otherwise 4 times daily), covering both lakes; the two-hour **Canal Tour** (€11; ⏰ 3-6 times daily, depending on season), which floats past stately villas and gardens; and the two-hour **Fleet Tour** (€13; ⏰ 3 times daily Apr-Oct), which heads from the Binnenalster to the Elbe and Speicherstadt. Free English-language pamphlets and taped commentaries are available for the Alster and Fleet Tours. Kids under 16 pay half-price.

Hourly ferries call at nine stops on the Aussenalster and the river itself (€1.10 per stop or €7 for the entire trip). Longer cruises include romantic twilight cruises.

Other sightseeing alternatives include tours on wooden boats, called Barkassen, which are small enough to travel through the canals of the Speicherstadt (about €10). Operators tout for business around the Speicherstadt.

PORT

Various operators on the piers at Landungsbrücken offer port cruises, and sometimes it's best just to wander around and peruse the offers.

A leading operator is **Hadag** (Map pp686-8; ☎ 311 7070), whose boats depart from Landungsbrücken – usually from Brücke (pier) 2 – between April and early October. Its ferry service down the Elbe to Övelgönne takes 10 minutes (€1.45 one way); to Blankenese costs €3 extra, but requires two changes. Hadag also offers a one-hour **steamer tour** (adult/child €8.50/4.50).

For harbour tours with English commentary, call **Abeche** (☎ 3178 2231; adult/child €9/5; ⏰ noon daily Mar-Nov). Tours depart from Brücke 1.

For trips to Helgoland, see Getting There & Away (p705).

FESTIVALS & EVENTS

Among Hamburg's many yearly events is the **Hamburger Dom**, held in late March, late July and late November. Established in 1329, it is one of Europe's largest and oldest fun fairs. It is held on Heiligengeistfeld, a vast field between St Pauli and Schanzenviertel, and attracts millions of visitors. The wild **Hafengeburtstag** (Harbour Birthday) commemorates the day Emperor Barbarossa granted Hamburg customs exemption (see History p684). It runs for five days from 7 May.

SLEEPING

Bargains are rare in Hamburg and decent, central accommodation will usually cost at least €60/100 for singles/doubles. Except where noted, prices listed below include breakfast.

Budget

DJH HOSTELS

Hamburg's two DJH hostels often fill up with school groups. Reservations are especially useful between June and September.

DJH Auf dem Stintfang (Map pp686-8; ☎ 313 488; jh-stintfang@t-online.de; Alfred Wegener Weg 5; juniors €17.50-21.50, seniors €19.70-24.20) Modern, well equipped and clean, this hostel is superbly located above the Landungsbrücken overlooking the Elbe and harbour. On the downside, you'll be treated like one of the many school pupils who regularly stay here in large noisy groups. (This includes being locked out from 10am to 12.30pm while rooms are cleaned.) Coming from Landungsbrücken U-Bahn, you'll have to haul your luggage up 100 stairs, so some prefer the short walk, with its more gradual incline, from St Pauli U-Bahn when they arrive.

DJH Horner Rennbahn (☎ 651 1671; jgh-hamburg@ t-online.de; Rennbahnstrasse 100; juniors €18.50-24.15, seniors €21.20-26.85) This modern 271-bed facility is a lot less central and much more family-oriented, although it also hosts school groups. Take the U3 to Horner Rennbahn, and then walk for 10 minutes north past the racecourse and leisure centre.

INDEPENDENT HOSTELS

Schanzenstern (Map pp686-8; ☎ 439 8441; www .schanzenstern.de; Bartelsstrasse 12; dm/s/d €17/35/50) This former Mont Blanc pen factory has clean if sparse rooms (breakfast €6 extra), but the staff can be a little offhand. If all rooms are booked here, there's an offshoot in **Altona** (☎ 3991 9191; Kleine Rainerstrasse 24-26; s/d/tr €40/60/75; S-Bahn Altona).

InstantSleep Backpacker Hostel (Map pp686-8; ☎ 4318 2310; backpackerhostel@instantsleep.de; Max-Brauer-Allee 277; beds €15-26, plus €2 for sheets; 🖳) Slightly shabbier and more spartan than the DJH hostels, but then also more relaxed, friendlier and cheaper, InstantSleep is just minutes from the bars of the Schanzenviertel. Singles, doubles, triples and smaller dorms have colourful wall decorations, from green stripes to golden Buddhas, and there's one huge 'hall of dreams' dormitory with 25 of the lowest-priced beds.

GUESTHOUSES

Seemannsheim Altona (Seaman's Home Altona; ☎ 306 220; www.seemannsmission.de; Grosse Elbestrasse 132; s/d with shared bathroom €35/60) In this maritime city, why not lodge in the same building as sailors between trips? While the rooms are pretty well of the same standard as the much larger DJH hostels, there are no dorms or strict rules. With a friendly atmosphere – even quite a few women stay – and great harbour views from the front rooms, this is rather a gem. (Don't confuse it with the Seemannsheim near St Michaeliskirche, however, as that's not so nice.) Take the S-Bahn to Königstrasse.

HOTELS & PENSIONS

The are many cheap hotels in St Georg, east of the Hauptbahnhof, but be aware that these include Stundenhotels that rent rooms 'by the hour' to prostitutes and their clients. Places listed below, or in the tourist office hotel brochure, ought to be safe.

Hotel-Pension Schwanenwik (☎ 220 0918; www .hotel-schwanenwik.de; Schwanenwik 29; s/d with shared bathroom €45/65, with private bathroom €75/90; 🅿) Accommodation with private bathrooms spills over into the mid-range category, and that higher standard is evident throughout this private hotel. All rooms have TV, phone and modem plug, while stocks of fluffy towels make the spotless shared bathrooms feel more like spas. The break-fast room overlooks the Aussenalster. Take bus No 6 Mundsburger Brücke. Parking costs €7.

Hotel-Pension Annenhof (Map p698; ☎ 243 426; info@hotelannenhof.de; Lange Reihe 23; s €35-45, d €60-80) Behind the grubby façade lie 13 simple but attractive rooms, with polished wooden floorboards and walls in different, bright colours. Even though a few have shower cabins rather than proper bathrooms, they're still a great deal. Breakfast isn't served, but there are dozens of cafés in this increasingly gentrified part of St Georg.

Florida – The Art Hotel (Map pp686-8; ☎ 314 393; Spielbudenplatz 22; s/d with shared bathroom €40/80) The rooms here would be simple concrete boxes had they not been individually themed. So if you don't mind your cool, kitsch décor with a slight underlying shabbiness, this youthful hotel offers good value. (A new set of themes was being developed at the time of writing, so ring to check what's on offer.) Take S-Bahn to Reeperbahn or U-Bahn to St Pauli.

Eden Hotel (Map p698; ☎ 248 480; fax 241 521; Ellmenreichstrasse 20; s/d with shared bathroom €45/65, with private bathroom from €75/105) It's not bad snagging a cheaper room (phone, washbasin) here. Overall, the hotel caters to the standard of the pricier accommodation, and if you tire of trekking down the hall to wash, you can always upgrade. The location is convenient, if somewhat sleazy. Take S/U-Bahn to Hauptbahnhof.

PRIVATE ROOMS & LONG-TERM RENTALS

Long-term room rentals should cost from €280 to €400 per month. Furnished apartments start at €400, plus about 25% commission and 16% tax.

Agencies worth trying are **Agentur 'Zimmer Frei Hamburg'** (☎ 2787 7777; fax 2787 7779; Steilshooperstrasse 186), **Bed & Breakfast** (☎ 491 5666; fax 491 4212; Müggenkampstrasse 35) and the **HomeCompany** (☎ 194 45; hamburg@homecompany.de; Schulterblatt 112).

CAMPING

Camping Buchholz (☎ 540 4532; Kieler Strasse 374; tent €7.50-10, person €4) In the suburb of Stellingen, this year-round camp site is a 10-minute walk from U-Bahn Hagenbecks Tierpark (U2). You can also take bus No 183 from the Altona train station, which runs down Kieler Strasse. Warm showers are €0.75.

Campingplatz Blankenese (☎ 812 949; Falkensteiner Ufer; tent/person €7/5) Less convenient, but more scenic, this camp site (open March to October) is on the Elbe banks. Take the S1 to Blankenese, then bus No 189 (direction: Wedel) to Tindtsthaler Weg; then it's a 10-minute walk down to the shore.

Mid-Range
ST GEORG   Map p698
These hotels are all within walking distance of the Hauptbahnhof.

Hotel Wedina (☎ 280 8900; info@wedina.de; Gurlittstrasse 23; s €85-120, d €105-180; **P**) It's not often that the person behind the desk is wearing jeans and trainers, but this hotel is youngish and relaxed. Set in four different houses (including the group- and family-friendly red-walled house and the Alpine minimalist green-walled house), it's a favourite of models and media types. A small 'library' of books written (and signed) by past guests includes works by Will Self, Margaret Atwood and Jonathan Safran Foer.

Hotel Village (☎ 480 6490; reserv@hotel-village.de; Steindamm 4; s €65-70, d €90-95) Va-va-voom! This over-the-top former bordello attracts a mix of gay and straight guests, while rock stars like Nena have often borrowed the place for photo-shoots. Each boudoir is unique, with various kitsch mixes of red velvet, gold flock wallpaper, tiger prints, brocade curtains and blue-neon-lit bathrooms. (Beware, though, that Steindamm is full of sex shops.)

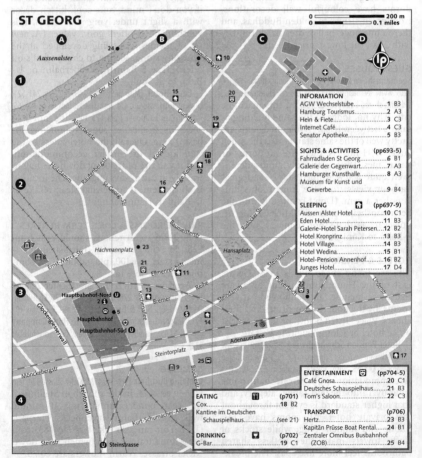

ST GEORG			0 ——————— 200 m
			0 ——— 0.1 miles

INFORMATION	
AGW Wechselstube	1 B3
Hamburg Tourismus	2 A3
Hein & Fiete	3 C3
Internet Café	4 C3
Senator Apotheke	5 B3

SIGHTS & ACTIVITIES	(pp693-5)
Fahrradladen St Georg	6 B1
Galerie der Gegenwart	7 A3
Hamburger Kunsthalle	8 A3
Museum für Kunst und	
Gewerbe	9 B4

SLEEPING	(pp697-9)
Aussen Alster Hotel	10 C1
Eden Hotel	11 B3
Galerie-Hotel Sarah Petersen	12 B2
Hotel Kronprinz	13 B3
Hotel Village	14 B3
Hotel Wedina	15 B1
Hotel-Pension Annenhof	16 B2
Junges Hotel	17 D4

ENTERTAINMENT	(pp704-5)
Café Gnosa	20 C1
Deutsches Schauspielhaus	21 B3
Tom's Saloon	22 C3

EATING	(p701)
Cox	18 B2
Kantine im Deutschen	
Schauspielhaus	(see 21)

DRINKING	(p702)
G-Bar	19 C1

TRANSPORT	(p706)
Hertz	23 B3
Kapitän Prüsse Boat Rental	24 B1
Zentraler Omnibus Busbahnhof	
(ZOB)	25 B4

Galerie-Hotel Sarah Petersen (☎ 249 826, 0174-146 4832; www.galerie-hotel-sarah-petersen.de; Lange Reihe 50; s €70-140, d €85-150; ✗ 🖵) Part private pension, part artists salon, this tiny establishment attracts business travellers and tourists alike. Frau Petersen herself often presides over breakfast (an extra €10), and has decorated each room individually, from 1950s French to classic Biedermeier. You can tour them virtually on the website. One with an external bathroom is much cheaper at €45/60 a single/double. Book ahead.

Junges Hotel (☎ 419 230; www.junges-hotel.de; Kurt-Schumacher-Allee 14; s/d €95/110; Ⓟ) This is particularly fun for young families, where kids under 12 stay free and the extra beds to accommodate them in their parents' room drop down from the wall as in a train sleeper compartment. (This also works for groups of adults, but costs €25 for each extra person in the double room.) Yellow, orange and flesh-pink window panels brighten the day.

Hotel Kronprinz (☎ 271 4070; www.kronprinz-hamburg.de; Kirchenallee 49; s €70-80, d €90-100) Neither hip nor trendy, the friendly Kronprinz is just surprisingly pleasant for a three-star hotel opposite the central train station. Persian rugs and lots of blue manage to camouflage some slightly older touches.

ALSTER LAKES
Hotel Alsterblick (☎ 2294 8989; www.hotel-alsterblick.de; Schwanenwik 30; s €65-125, d €110-145) With parquet floors and blue, red or yellow room furnishings, this boutique hotel manages to feel both warm and uncluttered. The more expensive rooms are larger, but all guests can enjoy the lovely lake view from the breakfast room window.

Aussen Alster Hotel (Map p698; ☎ 241 557; info@aussen-alster.de; Schmilinskystrasse 11; s €90-105, d €130-155) Near (but not on) the waterfront, this uncluttered modern hotel has a personal atmosphere and is decorated in shades of white and pale green. There's a lovely garden, a sauna, and bike and boat hire.

NEUSTADT
Frauenhotel Hanseatin (Map pp686-8; ☎ 341 345; www.hotel-hanseatin.de; Dragonerstall 11; s/d with shared bathroom €50/85, with private bathroom from €65/100) Simple rooms – with wooden floors, cosy bed coverings and small but Japanese 'wet' bathrooms – typify this women-only hotel. Hairdryers and TV can be made available

for no extra cost, and there's a Frauencafé attached.

SCHANZENVIERTEL & ST PAULI
Map pp686-8

Fritz Hotel (☎ 8222 2830; www.fritzhotel.com; Schanzenstrasse 101-103; s/d from €60/90) This conveniently located, friendly and urbane hotel offers excellent value for money with stylish but restrained rooms. Each is furnished in white, cream and grey, with a dash of red. Touches we like: desks on wheels, flowers, Molton Brown toiletries and a bottle of Hamburg's Fritz-Kola humorously placed in the minibar. No breakfast is served, however. Go to S/U-Bahn Sternschanze.

Hotel Monopol (☎ 311770; www.monopol-hamburg.de; Reeperbahn 48; s €60-65, d €75-85; Ⓟ) From musicians to stag parties, many visitors wanting to cling to the Reeperbahn will find this an obvious choice. The rooms are older, but not terrible, and the hotel simply oozes rock 'n' roll attitude, as 'Do not disturb' signs line the halls all day. Past guests range from bands Public Enemy and Him to cyclist Jan Ullrich. Go to S-Bahn Reeperbahn.

Hotel Hafen (☎ 3111 3600; www.hotel-hamburg.de; Seewartenstrasse 9; s & d €100-200; Ⓟ) Modern rooms added to this former seaman's home (and its ornate stair rails) make a nice mix, and the views above the Landungsbrücken are even better than imagined. Unfortunately, although the hotel is enormous, you can't book a room with a view, but only make a request. Still, there's always the 14th-floor Towerbar for gawping (it's open to nonguests, too). Parking is €7. Go to S/U-Bahn to Landungsbrücken.

UNIVERSITÄTSVIERTEL
Yo-Ho – The Young Hotel (☎ 284 1910; www.yoho-hamburg.de; Moorkamp 5; s/d €80/90; Ⓟ) People under 26 get €20 off the regular rates listed, but this stylish hotel appeals to all ages. After a good night's sleep in your elegant, sparse room (slightly Japanese-looking, in shades of camel and white), you can wander down to eat breakfast (€10 extra) on a long table in the impressive Occidental Lounge. There's also a Syrian restaurant, Mazza, open evenings. Go to U-Bahn Schlump/Christuskirche.

Hotel Fresena (Map pp686-8; ☎ 410 4892; www.hotelfresena.de; Moorweidenstrasse 34; s with shared bathroom €60-65, with private bathroom €75-80, d €100;

P ⊠) With 1970s graphic-design posters, bright walls, and simple, vaguely Oriental modern touches added to a lovingly looked-after building, this is one of the best choices in the five-floor, five-pension Dammtorpalais. It has an aura of calm and health – an impression reinforced by the largely nonsmoking policy. Go to S-Bahn Dammtor.

Hotel Bellmoor (Map pp686-8; ☎ 413 3110; hotel bellmoor@t-online.de; Moorweidenstrasse 34; s/d €80/100; P) It's the single rooms that really stand out here, although the doubles are pleasant, too. Numbers 14 and 34 feature Art Nouveau-ish bathrooms with stained-glass windows and tiled tubs. Number 10, the former maid's room, is in the refurbished attic. The breakfast lounge offers a great view over Hamburg's rooftops, and the staff are cheerful and friendly. Go to S-Bahn Dammtor.

Hotel Beim Funk (☎ 450 3000; www.hotel-beim -funk.de; Rothenbaumchaussee 138; s €70-85, d €90-110; P) This hotel has four huge rooms with views over the back garden or a balcony, plus 11 other cosy numbers, with features like chandeliers, gold-tinted wallpaper, patterned bed throws or a cactus mural in the bathroom. It's next door to the NDR TV studios. Go to U-Bahn Klosterstern.

Hotel Heimhude (Map pp686-8; ☎ 413 3300; hotel .heimhude.hamburg@t-online.de; Heimhuder Strasse 16; s €70, d €95-130; P) This quiet, elegant abode is popular with university visitors. Furnishings are traditional and masculine, with leather sofas and striped camel-and-black chairs. One smaller single costs €55. Go to S-Bahn Dammtor.

Top End

Gastwerk Hotel (☎ 890 620; www.gasthof-hotel.de; Beim Alten Gaswerk 3, Daimlerstrasse, Altona; s & d €130-165; P ⊠ ❄ ♨) Hamburg's most famous design hotel is more user-friendly than it sounds. Although it's fashioned from a former gasworks, furnishings in colours such as aubergine and brown offset the exposed steel and concrete to give it a warm feel. Go to U/S-Bahn to Altona, then take bus No 2 to Stresemannstrasse.

Hotel SIDE (Map pp686-8; ☎ 309 990; www.side -hamburg.de; Drehbahn 49; s & d €190-230; P ❄) If style hotels are passé, they don't believe it at SIDE, where interior designer Matteo Thun has created a tasteful millionaire's bach-

elor pad. White walls are decorated with colourful light strips, while 1950s-style, saucers-from-outer-space sofas are strewn across the 8th-floor lounge. The dead-chic reception area and most rooms (excluding the suites) are more sober than this. Go to U-Bahn Stephansplatz/Gänsemarkt.

Raffles Hotel Vier Jahreszeiten (Map pp686-8; ☎ 349 40; www.raffles-hvj.de; Neuer Jungfernstieg 9-14; s €215-290, d €265-340; P ❄) The fame of this palatial hotel stretches well beyond the shores of the Binnenalster that it overlooks. So you probably won't want to just stay in your richly traditional room here, but impress friends or colleagues by inviting them for afternoon tea in the opulent *Wohnhalle*. Breakfast costs an extra €14 to €22, and parking is €17. Go to U-Bahn Jungfernstieg.

EATING

As in any port city, the restaurants are international indeed, and there's a particularly strong vein of Portuguese cuisine. But of course, there are also local specialities: *Aalsuppe* (eel soup) is a sweet and sour soup made with dried fruit, ham, vegetables, lots of herbs and, yes, even some eel, and *Labskaus* consists of boiled marinated beef put through the grinder with mashed potatoes and herring and served with a fried egg, red beets and pickles.

City Centre & Port   Map pp686-8

Nido (☎ 5131 0317; Cremon 35; mains €18-20; ♨ closed lunch Sat & all day Sun) Sushi or Wiener schnitzel? This restaurant has critics drooling with its unusual decision to offer both Japanese and Austrian cuisine. But if the food and square crockery are immensely appealing, so too is the room. Low-ceilinged and vaguely reminiscent of Hamburg's merchant past, it overlooks the Alsterfleet canal.

Sagres (☎ 371 201; Vorsetzen 53; mains €6.50-12) Cheerfully maritime-themed, Sagres is one of the most accessible and better Portuguese restaurants near the waterfront in the touristy Landungsbrücken area. Offerings include tapas, paella, sardines, octopus, meat and many varieties of freshly caught fish.

Ti Breizh (☎ 3751 7815; Deichstrasse 39; mains €6.50-11; ♨ closed Mon) Even if you don't like crepes, this simple Breton restaurant will have you thinking you do. Tuck into a thin, delicious savoury number folded into a perfect square while watching the kids at the next table fight over who gets the bigger Nutella pancake.

Café Paris (☎ 3252 7777; Rathausstrasse 4; mains €6.50-15) Join the chattering crowds ordering French delicacies and looking up at the wonderful high ceilings and tiled murals of this atmospheric café.

St Georg
Map p698

Cox (☎ 249 422; Lange Reihe 68; mains €16-20; ☺ closed lunch Sat & Sun) Indicative of the gentrification of sleazy St Georg, Cox is an upmarket French-style bistro serving modern international cuisine. Fish might come in saffron sauce with pumpkin ravioli, or in lemon caper sauce on parsley risotto.

Kantine im Deutschen Schauspielhaus (Kirchenallee 39; mains €4.50-7; ☺ Mon-Fri) Battered red velour banquettes and leather chairs are patched up with yellow-and-black striped emergency tape in this atmospheric basement caff. At lunch, actors and office workers listen through the hum for the wandering waiter to shout out the name of their order (usually a pasta, salad or cheap grill).

Alster Lakes

Literaturhaus Café (☎ 220 1300; Schwanenwik 38; mains €9-15) Authors do public readings in this building, but otherwise the major draw is the golden baroque café and its huge chandeliers. Bistro fare – antipasti, risotto, tarts, salads and roasts – is served, but it's worth coming for just a coffee (and to gawp) after a walk around the Aussenalster.

Schanzenviertel & St Pauli
Map pp686-8

Nil (☎ 439 7823; Neuer Pferdemarkt 5; mains €12-19; ☺ Wed-Mon evening) The tables on the mezzanine floor overlooking the bar are understandably the most popular in this classy restaurant. The modern international food and excellent service have kept it among the city's best restaurants for many years.

Bok (☎ 4318 3597; Schulterblatt 3; mains €9-15; ☺ closed Sun) We counted four Bok outlets in the same number of streets in Schanzenviertel, but this has the nicest ambience. The burgeoning empire is testament to the minichain's good food: duck makes a frequent appearance on the pan-Asian (Thai, Korean and Japanese) menu.

Suryel (☎ 439 8422; Thadenstrasse 1; mains €6.50-11; ☺ closed Sun) The colourful mosaic tiles draw you in to this veggie restaurant; the food keeps you interested. Pastas and other staples are joined by changing specials, maybe including meat-free versions of local specialities, like sweet-potato *Labskaus* or tofu *Wurst* (sausage). And if you want to go tenpin bowling afterwards, Big-Lebowski-style – as you do – there's an alley in the basement.

Kochsalon (☎ 3179 6070; Bernhard-Nocht-Strasse 95; meals under €10; ☺ closed Sun) For reasonably priced midnight snacks near the Reeperbahn try Kochsalon possibly the only *Imbiss* (stand-up food stall) in town with DJ decks/turntables.

The Schanzenviertel is perfect for foodies on a budget, and **Shikara** (☎ 430 2353; Susannstrasse 20) and **Lokma** (☎ 432 2527; cnr Bartelsstrasse & Susannenstrasse) are just a few of many outlets offering meals under €10.

Universitätsviertel

Vienna (☎ 439 9182; Fettstrasse 2; mains €8.50-19; ☺ Tue-Sat evening) A bit of a secret place where you can't book and where the restaurant itself hides without a sign behind an overgrown garden. The changing menu of modern German/international fare makes it worth it, though. Try to arrive early, around 7.30pm. Go to U-Bahn Christuskirche.

Abaton-Bistro (☎ 457 771; Grindelhof 14a; mains €4.50-8; ☺ from 11am Mon-Fri, from 4pm Sat & Sun) Reinvented as a trendy-looking but low-key Italian trattoria, this attracts office workers as well as the students who happily return, even though the beloved bio-bistro once on this site is gone.

Balutschi (☎ 452 479; Grindelallee 33; meals €7.50-14) Out the back, there's an over-the-top *Arabian Nights* decorated grotto, where you remove your shoes and sit on carpets and low benches. At lunch, however, most customers seem to scarf up the very tasty Pakistani cuisine at tables in the plainer main room. Specials then are as little as €4.50 to €5.50.

Altona & Övelgönne

First it was the restaurants in Altona's Zeisehallen, a converted ship propeller factory, that had Hamburg foodies excited (see following reviews for Eisenstein and Filmhauskneipe), but now the city's 'in' dining stretch has moved to the Altona and Övelgönne riverfronts. If the headline restaurants below don't suit, just wander west along Grosse Elbstrasse.

La Vela (☎ 3869 9393; Grosse Elbstrasse; mains €9.50-19) The crowd is loud, and happy to have a front row seat (one of the best in Hamburg) as cruise ships and tankers head out on the Elbe River. The Italian menu is fairly sparse, with about a dozen choices, but the food is delicious enough to distract you from the view. Go to S-Bahn Königstrasse.

Indochine (☎ 3980 7880; Neuemühlen 11; mains €13-21) While waiting for your table and tasty Vietnamese/Laotian/Southeast Asian meal in this huge riverfront glass cube, join the smartly dressed after-work set for a drink under huge chandeliers that glow purple from the bar's ultra-violet light. Book ahead, or you won't get a table to wait for. Take bus No 112 to Neuemühlen Kirchenweg.

Eisenstein (Map p694; ☎ 390 4606; Friedensallee 9; mains €9-23) This hip Italian restaurant inside Altona's Zeisehallen is a postmodern symphony of stone, steel and wood wrapped around the brick chimney of an old ship propeller factory. It reputedly turns out the best wood-fired pizzas in town. Go to S/U-Bahn Altona.

Filmhauskneipe (Map p694; ☎ 393 467; Friedensallee 9; mains €6.50-14) There's a relaxed vibe and good wholesome Mediterranean food at this caff. It's said to attract film executives, but film fans, families and groovy young things meeting their mums (shhh) are really more the order of the day. Go to S/U-Bahn Altona.

Strandperle (Schulberg 2; ☉ daily spring-autumn) This popular riverbank kiosk is super-cool, but also very funny. What *won't* Hamburg hipsters ignore to have a strip of beach when they've closed their eyes here to glass, dirty sand and a hulking great container port across the river? Still, the people-watching is tops, as patrons linger over the MOPO (*Hamburger Morgenpost* newspaper) with a snack, coffee, beer or local Fritz-Kola. Walk for five minutes straight ahead (west) along the little lane from the Bus No 112 terminus.

DRINKING

For a fuller assessment of the enormous bar scene, check out *Hamburg Pur*, *Prinz*, *Oxmox* or *Szene*.

Nachtasyl (Map pp686-8; ☎ 814 444; Alstertor 1; ☉ from 7pm nightly) 'Just 65 more stairs', 'just 48 more stairs' the signs exhort you as you puff 101 steps to the top. Had you any breath left, it would then be taken by the high-arched ceiling and embossed wallpaper of the Thalia Theater's bar – the most attractive in the city centre and with reasonably priced drinks. Events sometimes mean a cover charge.

G-Bar (Map p698; ☎ 2880 4868; Lange Reihe 81; ☉ from noon) One of the nicest of the trendy bars that has sprung up lately in once-sleazy St Georg, the G-Bar glows with violet and rose light strips on its white walls. Like many establishments here it has a solid gay clientele, but the well-turned-out crowd is definitely mixed.

Bedford Café (Map pp686-8; ☎ 4318 8332; Schulterblatt 72; ☉ from 10am) You won't recognise it by the generic sign but by the swarms of people milling around outside its packed interior, even on a chilly autumn eve. It's the mainstay of the Schanzenviertel scene.

Dual (Map pp686-8; ☎ 4320 8829; Schanzenstrasse 53; ☉ from 11am daily) The orange, 1970s retro lighting that's quite popular in Hamburg gives this a slightly hip feel, but the punters are young, relaxed and down-to-earth. Dual is a cool but unpretentious place.

Mandalay (Map pp686-8; ☎ 4321 4922; Neuer Pferdemarkt 13; from 10pm Wed-Sun) The most chichi bar in the Schanzenviertel, beautiful Mandalay is worth visiting just to look. At one end, sleek patrons come to see and be seen on the wood laminate benches around the glowing bar. The gold wallpaper lines the way to a small dance floor at the other end.

Meanie Bar (Map pp686-8; ☎ 319 6087; Spielbudenplatz 5; ☉ from 9pm nightly) With cheapish 1970s chairs and stools, sticky wooden floors, nightly DJs and a crush of people having an unbelievably good time, the grungy Meanie Bar is loved.

Better Days Project (Map pp686-8; ☎ 3179 2512; Hopfenstrasse 34; ☉ from 10pm Wed-Sat) Behind the narrow, concrete bar infused with a neon glow, the back rooms explode into an appealing potpourri of glitter wallpaper, stark geometrically patterned sofa and customised art. The attached living room (entry door two steps down Hopfenstrasse, away from Davidstrasse) has white sofas and bulbous lights.

Café Keese (Map pp686-8; ☎ 310 805; Reeperbahn 19; ☉ from noon Wed-Mon) Its days of ballroom dancing and table telephones are over, but the famous Keese retains a small disco floor of multicoloured squares at its heart. Low lighting and orangey-red furnishings give it a womblike feel. Drinks are overpriced, but that's par for the course along this strip.

Aurel (Map p694; ☎ 390 2727; Bahrenfelder Strasse 15; ☼ from 11am daily) A long-standing favourite in Altona is this snug bar with an eccentric back room where Stone Age meets baroque. Happy hour runs 5pm to 9pm, when cocktails cost a mere €4.

Blaues Haus (Map p694; ☎ 3990 5842; Grosse Brunnenstrasse 55; ☼ from 9pm nightly in summer, 10pm in winter) Behind the cobalt blue façade lies an interior blending cowhide-covered bar stools with Madonna altars.

Familieneck (Map p694; ☎ 390 7497; Friedensallee 2; ☼ from 6pm nightly) The background music tends towards trance and trip-hop in this mellow Altona bar.

ENTERTAINMENT
Cinemas
Several cinemas screen movies in the original language with subtitles. Look for the acronym 'OmU' (Original mit Untertiteln). Venues include **Abaton Kino** (☎ 4132 0320; cnr Grindelhof & Allende Platz, Universitätsviertel) and **3001** (Map pp686-8; ☎ 437 679; Schanzenstrasse 75, Schanzenviertel). Movies usually cost €5.50 during the week, and €7.50 at weekends.

Discos & Clubs
Angie's Nightclub (Map pp686-8; ☎ 3177 8816; Spielbudenplatz 27; ☼ from 10pm Wed-Sat) When many

---

THE BEATLES IN HAMBURG – FOREVER

'I was born in Liverpool, but I grew up in Hamburg.' – John Lennon

It was the summer of 1960 and a fledgling band from Liverpool had been assured a paying gig in Hamburg, if only they could come up with a drummer in time. After a frantic search, Pete Best joined John, Paul, George and Stuart (Sutcliffe) in August that year.

Within days, the band opened at the Indra Club on the notorious Grosse Freiheit to a seedy crowd of drunks and whores. After being egged on by the club's burly owner to 'Put on a show', John went wild, screaming, leaping and shouting, even performing in his underwear and with a toilet seat around his neck.

After 48 consecutive nights of six-hour sessions, the Beatles' innate musical genius had been honed. The magnetism of the group that would rock the world began drawing huge crowds. When police shut down the Indra they moved a block south to the Kaiserkeller – and the crowds moved with them.

At the Kaiserkeller, the Beatles alternated with a band called Rory Storm and The Hurricanes, whose drummer was one Ringo Starr. But they hardly had time to get to know each other, before an underage George was deported in November, and Paul and Pete were arrested for attempted arson. All three escaped the German authorities and, leaving Stuart behind in Hamburg, returned to England. There, as 'The Beatles: Direct from Hamburg' they had their Merseyside breakthrough.

In 1961 the Beatles returned to Hamburg, this time to the Top Ten Club on the Reeperbahn. During their 92-night stint here, they made their first professional recording as back-up for rocker Tony Sheridan. Around this time, manager extraordinaire Brian Epstein and the recording genius (now Sir) George Martin arrived on the scene. The Beatles' recording contract with German producer Bert Kaempfert was bought out and they began their career with EMI, with one proviso: exit Pete Best, enter Ringo, a more professional drummer. Later that same year, Stuart Sutcliffe quit the band, but sadly not long afterwards died of a brain haemorrhage.

In the spring of 1962 the final constellation of the Beatles was to log 172 hours of performance over 48 nights at Hamburg's Star Club. But with their star in the ascendancy in England, they began to shuttle off more regularly for home and foreign shores. To usher in the New Year of 1963, the Beatles gave their final concert at the Star Club, immortalised in what would become known as the 'Star Club Tapes'.

The Beatles returned occasionally to Hamburg in later years. But it was the combined 800 hours of live performance on grimy German stages in the city's red-light district that burned away the rough edges of four Liverpool boys to reveal their lasting brilliance.

HAMBURG

visitors think of Hamburg nightlife, they immediately think of Angie's. Floy, 'the white queen of soul', plays live as guests sip cocktails. But you never know what might happen: Nick Cave could get up and dance to 'I can't get no satisfaction' or some other famous guest take the microphone.

Golden Pudel Club (☎ 319 5336; Fischmarkt 27; ⏰ from 10pm nightly) A very ramshackle yellow hut, once belonging to a fisherman, houses this seminal bar and club near the waterfront. It attracts a wide mix of locals and tourists, and the music – from punk to disco, via techno, hip hop and house – is just as eclectic. Take bus No 112 to Hafentreppe.

Betty Ford Klinik (Map pp686-8; ☎ 7421 4660; Grosse Freiheit 6; ⏰ from 11pm Thu-Sat) Who can resist the invitation to get sozzled at the Betty Ford Klinik? Certainly not the young crowd who pack out this place for its cocktails and happy, upbeat house. Industrial (lack of) design meets minimal medical theme.

Banque Nationale (Map pp686-8; ☎ 3571 4600; Schauenburgerstrasse 42; ⏰ from 11pm Fri & Sat) You need to look like a million dollars to get into this chic club, which is fitting as it's in a former bank vault. Hamburg's beautiful people move their bodies to house and techno between the metal doors and safes.

Glam (Map pp686-8; Reeperbahn 136; ⏰ from 11pm Fri & Sat) One of the newer clubs in town – recognisable for all the glitzy silver dots over its front portal – sports a larger ballroom and smaller basement club. Friday nights have been given over to Unique Records, playing funk, acid jazz and the like. Saturdays are more disco-oriented.

Grünspan (Map pp686-8; ☎ 313 616; Grosse Freiheit 58; ⏰ from 10pm Fri & Sat) At the other end of the spectrum, Europe's oldest disco has had a recent relaunch, with a revamped main room. But, with what it claims is 'Hamburg's phattest PA', regular live gigs will continue.

Gay & Lesbian Venues

Hamburg has a thriving gay and lesbian scene; find out more at the gay centre **Hein & Fiete** (Map p698; ☎ 240 333; Pulverteich 21; ⏰ 4-9pm Mon-Fri, 4-7pm Sat) in St Georg, or look for free listings magazine *hinnerk* (found in many venues listed in this section).

Café Gnosa (Map p698; ☎ 243 034; Lange Reihe 93) This attractive olde worlde café, with its vaguely erotic, vaguely abstract art, is

hugely popular and a good starting point for gay and lesbian visitors to Hamburg. It stocks *hinnerk*.

Café Unter den Linden (Map pp686-8; ☎ 438 140; Juliusstrasse 16) In the Schanzenviertel, this is another gay hang-out with big bowls of coffee, delectable cakes and bistro fare.

EDK (Map pp686-8; ☎ 312 914; Gerhardstrasse 3) 'Small is beautiful' says the sign outside, and for the gays, lesbians and friends who come to this techno/house club it certainly is.

Tom's Saloon (Map p698; ☎ 280 3056; Pulverteich 17) *The* leather and fetish bar in town, with nightly cruising and a dark room.

Spundloch (Map pp686-8; ☎ 310 798; Paulinenstrasse 19) This is one of Hamburg's oldest discos where the crowd is mixed, gay and straight.

Also look out for popular nights in **Fabrik** (Gay Factory), **Banque Nationale** (Camp 77) – see Live Music below – and the **Kantine im Deutschen Schauspielhaus** (Gaykantine; see Eating p701).

Live Music

Grosse Freiheit 36/Kaiserkeller (Map pp686-8; ☎ 317 7780; Grosse Freiheit 36; ⏰ Grosse Freiheit: from 10pm Fri & Sat, Kaiserkeller: from 10pm nightly) Wedged between live sex theatres and peep shows, this alternative venue hosts an eclectic mix of pop and rock concerts, from the likes of Blur to Ben Harper, The Cramps and Kosheen. The Beatles once played in the basement Kaiserkeller (see the boxed text The Beatles in Hamburg – Forever p703), where there's now range of goth, student and cheap-champagne nights.

Docks (Map pp686-8; ☎ 3178 8311; Spielbudenplatz 19; ⏰ from 10pm Thu-Sun) The acoustics aren't perfect, but that hasn't stopped the likes of Blondie and Wales' Stereophonics playing here. The crowd tends towards the teenage, attracted on Thursdays by cheap drinks.

Logo (☎ 362 622; Grindelallee 5) This black concrete block of a building in the Universitätsviertel is the best place to catch touring American or British alternative/underground bands, or even Australian stars like Powderfinger.

Fabrik (Map p694; ☎ 391 070; Barnerstrasse 36) In Altona, Fabrik is an unusual venue in a former foundry, now painted pink and sporting a crane jutting from its roof. On most nights, the emphasis is on world music, but blues and jazz greats have performed here at the annual jazz festival.

Cotton Club (Map pp686-8; ☎ 343 878; Alter Steinweg 10; ⏰ from 10pm nightly) The best place for jazz is this joint in the city centre.

Musicals

Operettenhaus (Map pp686-8; ☎ 01805-114 113; Spielbudenplatz 1) Big glossy musicals like *Mamma Mia* and *Cats* are staged here. It's a good idea to book ahead.

Neue Flora (☎ 0180-544 44; Stresemannstrasse 159a) One of Europe's largest theatres was built to bring Andrew Lloyd Weber's *Phantom of the Opera* to Hamburg. More recently, it has reverberated to the strains of *Mozart, Titanic* and *Tanz der Vampire*.

Musikaltheater im Hafen (Map pp686-8; ☎ 0180-519 97; Norderelbstrasse 6) The yellow tent resembling a giant bee situated in the free port area hosts *The Lion King*. A shuttle service takes you there from Pier 1 of the Landungsbrücken.

Opera & Classical Music

Staatsoper (Map pp686-8; ☎ 356 868; Grosse Theaterstrasse 34) The citizen-founded Staatsoper is among the most respected opera houses in the world. Performances often sell out, but you can try the **Hamburg Hotline** (☎ 3005 1300) or go to the box office at Grosse Theaterstrasse 35, about 50m from the opera house.

Musikhalle (Map pp686-8; ☎ 346 920; Dammtorwall 46) The premier address for classical concerts is housed in a splendid neo baroque edifice. It's the home of the State Philharmonic Orchestra, the North German Broadcasting Network Symphony Orchestra and the Hamburg Symphonics.

Theatre

Deutsches Schauspielhaus (Map p698; ☎ 248 713; Kirchenallee 39) The video adverts on the TV outside the Schauspielhaus convey the contained chaos and excitement of this, one of Germany's leading stages. The programme demonstrates a huge fondness for Ibsen, alongside Shakespeare and Faulkner, modern works like *Trainspotting* and *The Vagina Monologues*, and experimental productions.

Thalia Theater (Map pp686-8; ☎ 3281 4444; Alstertor 1) Also with a stellar reputation, this is an intimate, galleried venue with a central stage and cutting-edge adaptations of clas-

sics. It has an offshoot in Ottensen, Thalia in der Gauss Strasse, where new works and book readings are performed.

English Theatre (☎ 227 7089; Lerchenfeld 14) A cast of predominantly British actors performs light fare like mysteries and comedies at this venue in Winterhude. Go to U-Bahn Mundsberg.

Schmidt Theater (Map pp686-8; ☎ 3177 8899; Spielbudenplatz 24) This plush former ballroom now stages a cornucopia of very saucy musical reviews, comedies, soap operas and variety shows. Late shows at midnight follow the main performance, and there's a smaller cabaret venue, Schmidt's Tivoli, attached.

SHOPPING

Central Hamburg has two main shopping districts. East of the Hauptbahnhof, along Spitalerstrasse and Mönckebergstrasse (known as the 'Mö'), you'll find the large department stores and mainstream boutiques. However, more elegant shops are located within the triangle created by Jungfernstieg, Fuhlentwiete and Neuer Wall. Most of them are in a network of 11 shopping arcades.

For second-hand shopping, try the Schanzenviertel or Karolinenviertel, particularly **Marktstrasse** (Map pp686-8).

In Altona, along Ottenser Hauptstrasse, hip clothing stores mingle with Turkish vendors.

GETTING THERE & AWAY
Air

Hamburg airport (Map p684; ☎ 50 750; www.ham .airport.de; Fuhlsbüttel) serves cities within Germany and Europe. **Lufthansa** (☎ 01803-803 803; Terminal 4), **British Airways** (☎ 01805-735 522; Terminal 4), **Air France** (☎ 5075 2325; Terminal 4) and low-cost carrier **Air Berlin** (☎ 01801-737 800; Terminal 1) all fly from here.

Low-cost carrier Ryanair flies from Stansted airport in London to Hamburg-Lübeck airport, with coordinated shuttle buses to central Hamburg (€8, 1¼ hours). For details, see Air p720.

Boat

For boats going to Stade, see Getting There & Away p708.

Förde Reederei Seetouristik (☎ 0180-320 2025; www.frs.de) operates services to Helgoland. Between May and October, you can catch the fast 'Halunder Jet' (€64 to €81 return, depending on month) from Landungsbrücken, Pier 4. Every Saturday in July and August, the larger 'Wappen von Hamburg' (€40 return) makes a day trip.

Bus

The **Zentral Omnibus Busbahnhof** (ZOB, central bus station; Map p698; ☎ 247 5765; Adenauer Allee 78; ⏱ 6.30am-9pm) is southeast of the Hauptbahnhof. Travel agencies are in Haus B near the boarding gates. **Autokraft** (☎ 208 8660) travels to Berlin eight or more times daily for €23/30 one way/return. **Eurolines** (☎ 4024 7106) has buses to Amsterdam (€36/56), Copenhagen (€37/67), London (€71/114), Paris (€59/106), Prague (€53/96) and Warsaw (€44/75). Students and those aged under 26 or over 60 get a 10% discount. **Gulliver's** (☎ 253 289 278) is one of several Eastern European specialists you'll find in the building.

Car & Motorcycle

The autobahns of the A1 (Bremen–Lübeck) and A7 (Hanover–Kiel) cross south of the Elbe River. Three concentric ring roads manage traffic flow. For ride-shares, try the **Mitfahrzentrale** (☎ 194 40; Ernst-Merck-Strasse 8).

Train

Hamburg has four train stations: the Hauptbahnhof, Dammtor, Altona and Harburg. Many of the long-distance trains originate in Altona and stop at both Dammtor and the Hauptbahnhof before heading out of the city. Remember this as you read the timetables or you may end up at the wrong station.

There are several trains hourly to Lübeck (€9, 45 minutes), Kiel (€15.20, 1½ hours), Hanover (€29.20, 1½ hours) and Bremen (€16.80, 1½ hours). A direct service to Westerland on Sylt Island leaves every two hours (€27, 2¾ hours).

There are direct IC connections to Berlin-Zoo (€41.40, 2½ hours) and Cologne (€56.20, four hours). Frankfurt is served hourly by the ICE train (€80.80, 3½ hours), as is Munich (€107, six hours). There's a direct service to Copenhagen several times a day, but the only direct train to Paris is the night train (otherwise, change in Cologne). Going to Warsaw requires a change at Berlin-Zoo.

Plenty of lockers are available for €1 to €2 at all stations.

GETTING AROUND
To/From the Airport

Privately run **airport buses** (☎ 227 1060; €4.60; every 15 min 5am-7pm, every 20 min 7-9.20pm) make the 25-minute trip to the airport from the Hauptbahnhof. There's also an airport bus from the Altona station every 30 minutes (€4.95). You can also take the U1 or S1 to Ohlsdorf (1.45), then change to the **HHV Airport Express/bus No 110** (☎ 194 49; €2.40; leaving every 10 min). A taxi from the Hauptbahnhof takes about 20 minutes and costs around €20.

Car & Motorcycle

Driving around Hamburg is easy. Major thoroughfares cutting across town in all directions are well signposted. Parking is expensive, however, especially in the city centre. Expect to pay about €2 an hour at meters or in parking garages.

All major car-hire agencies have branches in Hamburg. **Budget** (☎ 01805-244 388) and **Europcar** (☎ 01805-5000) are both at the train station and airport. The city office of **Hertz** (☎ 01805-333 535; Kirchenallee 34-36) is just opposite the Hauptbahnhof. Local agencies include **Star Car** (☎ 468 8300) or **Profi Rent** (☎ 656 9595), both with cars available from around €25 to €30 per day or €50 per weekend.

Public Transport

The **HVV** (☎ 194 49) operates buses, ferries, U-Bahn and S-Bahn, and has several offices, including at the Hauptbahnhof and at Jungfernstieg station.

The city is divided into zones. The Nahbereich (central area) covers the city centre, roughly between St Pauli and the Hauptbahnhof. The Grossbereich (Greater Hamburg area) covers the city centre plus outlying communities like Blankenese. The Gesamtbereich (Hamburg State) covers the entire Hamburg area.

Tickets for the S/U-Bahn must be purchased from machines at station entrances; bus tickets are available from the driver. Single journeys cost €1.45 for the Nahbereich, €2.30 for the Grossbereich and €6 for the Gesamtbereich. Children's tickets cost €0.85 for the Nahbereich and Grossbereich, and €1.70 for the Gesamtbereich. The express Schnellbus or 1st-class S-Bahn supplement is €1.05 for trips within the Grossbereich; otherwise it's €2.10.

There are several types of day passes (*Tageskarte*), although none of these are available solely for the Nahbereich. Passes for unlimited travel after 9am on weekdays and all day on weekends cost €4.45/11.40 within the Grossbereich/Gesamtbereich. Other all-day passes (allowing you to take three children with you) cost €5.25/13 for the Grossbereich/Gesamtbereich. Passes for groups of up to five people cost €7.40/17.70. A three-day pass (available only for the Grossbereich) is €12.70. Weekly cards (valid from Monday through Sunday) cost from €12.80 to €39.

Bikes may be taken onto S/U-Bahn trains, buses and ferries outside rush hours (6am to 9am and 4pm to 6pm). The fine for riding without a valid ticket is €50 and checks are fairly frequent.

Service is suspended from 1am to 4am when the night bus network takes over, converging on the main city bus station at Rathausmarkt.

Taxi

You can book a taxi through ☎ 441 011 or ☎ 666 666.

AROUND HAMBURG

ALTES LAND

South of the Elbe, roughly bordered by Stade and Buxtehude, is 'Hamburg's fruit basket', the Altes Land. Fruit orchards blanket this fertile area, which was reclaimed from marshy ground by Dutch experts in the Middle Ages. Farms, thatched and panelled houses, windmills and dykes characterise this stretch of land that's best in May when trees are blossoming. Its centre is the little town of **Jork**, which can be reached from Hamburg by taking the S3 to Neugraben and then bus No 257.

In fine weather, cycling is the most pleasant way to explore. The Obstmarschenweg is a particularly scenic bike path, following the Elbe. You can also travel here by boat. **Hadag** (☎ 040-311 7070) cruises to Lühe from Landungsbrücken, Pier 2, several times daily from April to October. The trip takes about 90 minutes and costs €6.10 each way. Between April and November, the **Elbe-City-Jet** (☎ 04142-811 70) to Stadersand also stops at Lühe (€6/12 one way/return, 35 minutes).

STADE

☎ 04141 / pop 45,000

Stade is a little piece of Sweden in Germany. At least 1000 years old, most of its buildings were destroyed in a major fire in 1659 and rebuilt under Swedish occupation after the Thirty Years' War. Picturesque and quaint, it provides a wonderful contrast to Hamburg for a day.

Orientation

Stade's train station is located southwest of the Altstadt, which is encircled by a moat and a ring road. If you cross the moat via Bahnhofstrasse, then continue northeast on the other side via pedestrianised Holzstrasse to Pferdemarkt, you'll reach the tourist office.

Information

For tourist information go to **Stade Tourismus** (☎ 409 170; stade.tourismus-gmbh@stade.de; Zeughaus, Pferdemarkt; ☺ 10am-6pm Mon-Fri, 10am-2pm Sat).

Sights

Stade's oldest church is the **Church of Sts Cosmas and Damiani** on Hökerstrasse. It's easily recognised for its octagonal tower crowned by a baroque helmet. The organ was the first work of local son (and, later, master organ-builder) Arp Schnitger. Hökerstrasse ends at Fischmarkt, which marks one end of the **Alter Hafen**, the canal-like harbour and the prettiest part of the Altstadt.

Beautiful historic houses line the harbour: those on Wasser Ost were once owned by sea captains; the ones on the opposite, western, side were merchants' homes. The **Kunsthaus** (☎ 448 24; Wasser West 7; adult/concession €1/0.50; ☺ 10am-5pm Tue-Fri, 10am-6pm Sat & Sun) contains an exquisite collection of works by painters from the Worpswede artist colony, including Paula Modersohn-Becker, Fritz Mackensen and Fritz Overbeck (see Worpswede p629).

The **Bürgermeister-Hintze-Haus**, a lacy stucco confection with tall gables and a fancy portal, is at No 23. The large building at the harbour's northern end is the **Schwedenspeicher** (☎ 32 22; Wasser West 39; adult/concession €1.50/0.50; ☺ 10am-5pm Tue-Fri, 10am-6pm Sat & Sun), used as a food warehouse by the Swedish garrison during its occupation of Stade. It is now a regional history museum.

Getting There & Away

There's a train service from Hamburg every 30 minutes (€8.10, one hour). If you are coming from Bremen, change at Hamburg-Harburg (€20.40, 1½ hours). If you're driving from Hamburg, take the B73; from Bremen, you can reach Stade via the B74.

From Hamburg, **Elbe-City-Jet** (☎ 04142-811 70) leaves Landungsbrücken, Pier 4, four times daily between April and November heading to Stadersand (one way/return €8/ 15, one hour). From there, bus No 6 takes you to Pferdemarkt in the town centre.

BUXTEHUDE

☎ 04161 / pop 36,000

A picturesque harbour-cum-canal called the Fleth is the centrepiece of this town on the Este River, about 30km to Hamburg's west.

Information

When the **Buxtehude Tourist Office** (☎ 501 297; stadtinformation@buxtehude.de; Am Stavenort 2; 🕑 9.30am-noon & 1-5pm Mon-Fri, to 6pm Wed, 9.30am-noon Sat) is closed, general information and brochures are available from the museum desk in the same building.

Sights

The **Fleth**, a Dutch-style (ie canal-like) harbour in the western Altstadt, is lined with cafés and restaurants, and is a nice place for a stroll. It dates back to the town's founding in 1285 and until 1962 was used by light cargo ships. One of them, the **Ewer Margareta** (1897), is permanently moored here. Also here is the **Flethmühle**, a mill that's now been converted into apartments and shops.

One block east of the Fleth, on the corner of Breite Strasse and the Markt, stands the ivy-clad **Rathaus**, a red-brick edifice with a monumental sandstone portal and copper roof. Built in 1911, it replaced its 15th-century predecessor, which was destroyed by fire. North of here, the spires of **St Petri** come into view. Inside, the star attractions are the sumptuous baroque pulpit supported by a statue of Atlas and the late-Gothic **Halephagen Altar** below the organ, with scenes from the Passion of

Christ. If the church is closed, pick up the key from the **Buxtehude Museum** (☎ 50 1241; Am Stavenort 2; adult/concession €1/0.50; 🕑 1.30-5.30pm Tue-Fri, 10.30am-5.30pm Sat & Sun) about 50m to the east. The museum focuses on regional history and also has special exhibits.

Getting There & Away

Buxtehude is easily reached by the same train connecting Hamburg Hauptbahnhof with Stade and Cuxhaven (€5.50, 45 minutes). Drivers from Hamburg should catch the B73 west to Buxtehude. From Bremen, take the Rade exit off the A1, then travel via the B3 to the B73.

HAMBURG WADDEN SEA NATIONAL PARK

The area at the mouth of the Elbe River forms the smallest of Germany's three mud-flat national parks, and although the nearest jumping point is the Lower Saxony town of Cuxhaven, the park itself belongs to Hamburg. The protected area consists of the seabed around the river delta, as well as three islands: the meadow-covered Neuwerk, the dune-covered Scharhörn and the artificially created Nigehörn.

As in the Schleswig-Holstein Wadden Sea National Park (p728) and the Lower Saxony Wadden Sea National Park (p678), the main activities include climbing dunes, hiking along dykes, seal-spotting and Watt-wandern (p680) at low tide. However, here in the Hamburg Wadden Sea National Park, you can also take a horse-and-carriage ride across the seabed at low tide or hunt for amber.

For further details contact the **Nordseeheilbad Cuxhaven** (☎ 04721-4040 or 01805 601 500; info@ tourismus.cuxhaven.de; Cuxhavener Strasse 92; 🕑 9am-5pm Mon-Fri, 9am-1pm Sat Apr-Oct; 9am-4pm Mon-Fri, 9am-1pm Sat Nov-Mar) or the **Nationalparkverwaltung** (☎ 04721-69271; Nationalpark-Station, Turmwurt, Neuwerk).

About two trains an hour leave Hamburg for Cuxhaven (€16.60, two hours). **Reederei Cassen Eils** (☎ 04721-322 11; info@helgolandreisen.de; Bei der Alten Lieber 12, Cuxhaven) has ferries daily between April and October to the island of Neuwerk (adult one way/return €12/17).

Schleswig-Holstein

CONTENTS

Kiel	711
Around Kiel	714
Lübeck	714
Around Lübeck	721
Schleswig	721
Flensburg	724
Around Flensburg	726
Husum	726
Around Husum	728
North Frisian Islands	**728**
Sylt	728
Amrum	732
Föhr	733
Helgoland	733

SCHLESWIG-HOLSTEIN

Sandwiched between the North and Baltic Seas, Schleswig-Holstein is Germany's answer to the Côte d'Azur. Of course, the northern European weather often makes it a pretty funny sort of answer, as cold winds and dark clouds race in across the wide horizons of this flat peninsula. But that doesn't prevent the local publication of coffee-table books filled with photos of jaunty red-and-white striped lighthouses, sandy beaches at sunset and wildlife from seagulls to seals. Nor does the upside-down weather deter German holidaymakers, who make the most of the summer by sailing to the islands off shore and frolicking in the surrounding waters. Even in October, people are still on the beaches, shivering inside *Strandkörbe* (straw sheltered seats) in a picture of kitschy, warped English-style 'oops, how's-your-Vater' seaside humour.

No, whether on the coast or in the agricultural hinterlands covering 70% of this sparsely populated state, it's been left to artists to embrace – rather than to determinedly try to ignore – the moodier side of Schleswig-Holstein's beauty. Painter Emile Nolde swirled his brushes into stormy oil-paint waves, the aptly named Theodor Storm set his classic novella, *Der Schimmelreiter* (The Rider on the White Horse), along the Husum coast, and contemporary literary giant Günter Grass moved to Lübeck years ago.

Lübeck, one of Germany's best-preserved medieval towns, is reason alone to visit. Elsewhere throughout Schleswig-Holstein you'll find remnants of a Viking past and centuries of Danish rule, (which ended in 1864), but Hanseatic Lübeck overshadows even these.

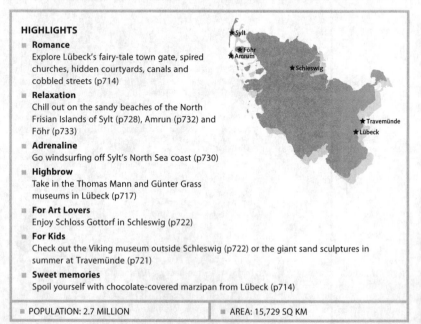

HIGHLIGHTS

- **Romance**
  Explore Lübeck's fairy-tale town gate, spired churches, hidden courtyards, canals and cobbled streets (p714)

- **Relaxation**
  Chill out on the sandy beaches of the North Frisian Islands of Sylt (p728), Amrun (p732) and Föhr (p733)

- **Adrenaline**
  Go windsurfing off Sylt's North Sea coast (p730)

- **Highbrow**
  Take in the Thomas Mann and Günter Grass museums in Lübeck (p717)

- **For Art Lovers**
  Enjoy Schloss Gottorf in Schleswig (p722)

- **For Kids**
  Check out the Viking museum outside Schleswig (p722) or the giant sand sculptures in summer at Travemünde (p721)

- **Sweet memories**
  Spoil yourself with chocolate-covered marzipan from Lübeck (p714)

- POPULATION: 2.7 MILLION
- AREA: 15,729 SQ KM

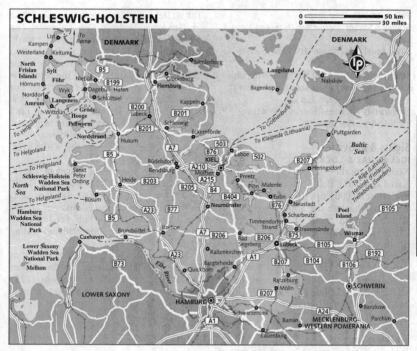

SCHLESWIG-HOLSTEIN

KIEL

☎ 0431 / pop 233,800

You get a real sense of romance watching the huge, overnight ferries from Scandinavia arrive along Kiel's firth of a morning, bringing in 2.5 million passengers a year. However, when you turn your gaze inland, Schleswig-Holstein's capital appears more functional than picturesque; only the tower of the old Rathaus (town hall) stands out among the rows of concrete blocks.

This lack of aesthetics is down to the 18km-long firth itself. It made Kiel one of Germany's most important harbours and a target for Allied bombers during WWII. By war's end, this busy base of U-Boot (submarine) activity was left 80% in ruins and had to be hastily rebuilt.

All of which is why modern-day Kiel keeps its eyes firmly fixed on the water, its most attractive aspect by far. The city's been a long-time host of sailing regattas, including Olympic sailing events in both 1936 and 1972. And the international Kieler Woche sailing spectacle has been taking place for more than 120 years.

Orientation

Kiel's main thoroughfare is the pedestrianised Holstenstrasse, about 100m inland from the firth. It runs between the Sophienhof, a huge indoor shopping mall opposite the Hauptbahnhof (central train station) on Sophienblatt, to Kieler Schloss (castle) about 1.5km north. The central bus station is just to the north of the Hauptbahnhof, through the 'City/Fernbus' exit leading to Auguste-Viktoria-Strasse.

The Deutsche Bahn (DB) service counter inside the Hauptbahnhof has maps of central Kiel.

Information

There's an ATM inside the Hauptbahnhof.

Bordesholmer Sparkasse (☎ 663 080; Sophienblatt 44-46) Bank.

Fabulus (☎ 663 5350; Holstentörn Passage, Sophienhof) Stocks English-language books.

Internet Café Rainforest (☎ 519 2500; Bergstrasse 17; per hr €2)

Kieler Volksbank (☎ 660 10; Raiffeisenstrasse 1)

Main post office (Stresemannplatz 5) Around the corner from the tourist office.

Police (☎ 5981; Gartenstrasse 7)

Schnell & Sauber (Knooper Weg 27; ⏰ 6am-11pm) Laundry.

Silver Angel Café (☎ 888 1919; Schlossstrasse 16; €3-4 per hr) Internet access.

Tourist Information Kiel (☎ 01805-656 700; info@kiel-tourist.de; Neues Rathaus, Andreas-Gayk-Strasse 31; ⏰ 9am-6pm Mon-Fri, 9am-3pm Sat)

Universitäts-Klinikum (University Medical Clinic; ☎ 5970; Brunswiker Strasse 10)

Sights & Activities
KIEL CANAL & LOCKS

Kiel is where the 99km-long Nord-Ostsee-Kanal enters the Baltic Sea from the North Sea. Some 60,000 ships pass through it every year, and through the *Schleusen* (locks) at Holtenau, 6km north of the city centre. There's a **viewing platform** (adult/concession €1.50/1) on the southern side of the canal. Tours of the **locks** (☎ 360 30; adult/concession €2.30/1.50) depart at 9am, 11am, 1pm and 3pm daily from the northern side of the canal. To get to the locks, take bus No 11 to Wik, then head for the small ferry that crosses this section of canal.

Walking Tour

It doesn't take long to see the sights of central Kiel. This walk covers 3.5km and takes between 60 and 90 minutes, excluding museum and other visits. Cross Sophienblatt from the Hauptbahnhof, head into the Sophienhof mall, turn right (north) and then follow this through Karstadt on to Holstenstrasse. Continue straight ahead (north). Left along Fleethörn (the street between Cubus and Commerzbank) is the **Altes Rathaus**, with its 106m tower (ask the tourist office about the €3 guided tours through the building and up the tower).

Further north along Holstenstrasse lies Alter Markt (old square) and the **Nikolaikirche** (Church of St Nicholas), whose huge triumphal cross (1490) deserves a quick look. Outside stands the Ernst Barlach statue **Der Geistkämpfer** (Ghost Fighter), which was removed during the Third Reich as 'degenerate art', but later found buried in the Lüneburg Heath.

Dänische Strasse, at the far left corner of Alter Markt from the church (northwest), is one of the more successfully restored sections of old Kiel. Here you'll find lots of designer boutiques, alongside the **Stadtmuseum**

(☎ 901 3425; Dänische Strasse 19; adult/concession €1/0.50; ⏰ 10am-6pm Tue-Sun Apr-Oct, 10am-5pm Nov-Mar). The **Schloss** (castle) is only a short distance north. The west wing is the only original section still surviving. North of here, across the Schlossgarten park, stands the **Kunsthalle** (☎ 880 5756; www.kunsthalle-kiel.de; Düsternbrooker Weg; adult/concession €5/3; ⏰ 10am-6pm Tue-Sun, 10am-8pm Wed). It has a section dedicated to Emil Nolde, as well as contemporary works by Antony Gormley and Bridget Riley.

Across the road from the Kunsthalle, under the pedestrian bridge, is a sign to the popular waterfront **aquarium** (☎ 600 1637; Düsternbrooker Weg 20; adult/concession €1.60/1; ⏰ 9am-7pm Apr-Oct, 9am-5pm Nov-Mar). The seals in the tank outside (no admission) are the big draw, especially for kids. Feedings take place at 10am and 2.30pm daily, excluding Friday.

Finally, return south along the waterfront to the **Schiffahrtsmuseum** (Maritime Museum; ☎ 901 3428; Am Wall 65; adult/concession €1/0.50; ⏰ 10am-6pm Apr-Oct, 10am-5pm Nov-Mar). Atmospherically located in a former fish market, the maritime museum has its own pier, where three historic ships are moored from April to October.

Tours

One of the best ways to enjoy Kiel is to take a trip through the Nord-Ostsee-Kanal to Rendsburg and back. These cost €22.50/14.50 (adult/child), and are held on Wednesday and Sunday from June to September. On certain days, Sylt's **Adler-Schiffe** (☎ 04651-987 00; www.adler-schiffe.de) also runs trips through the canal on an historic steam ship, *Freya*. Contact the tourist office for bookings.

Festivals & Events

Kiel's most famous event is **Kieler Woche** (Kiel Week; ☎ 679 100) held during the last full week of June. It's a giant festival revolving around a series of yachting regattas, and attended by more than 4000 of the world's sailing elite and half a million spectators. Even if you're not into boats, it's one nonstop party – so you need to book ahead.

Sleeping

The tourist office doesn't charge for booking accommodation. The nearest camp site is 15km away and a fair way from public transport.

A MUSICAL INTERLUDE

The gentle lowing of cattle is the sound one most expects to hear emanating from a barn, but during the statewide **Schleswig-Holstein Music Festival** (www.shmf.de) in late summer you might find yourself down on the farm listening to a chamber orchestra instead. Over seven weeks, leading international musicians and promising young talents perform some 150 concerts in 55 venues throughout Schleswig-Holstein and Hamburg, ranging from the castle in Kiel and music academy in Lübeck to churches, warehouses and animal stalls, and sometimes even ferries to the North Frisian islands.

Each year, the festival takes a different country as a theme (in 2004, for example, the Czech Republic) and, although performances are largely classical, you'll also find pop, rock and jazz on the menu. Tourist offices throughout the state, and in Hamburg, can help with details.

DJH hostel (☎ 731 488; jhkiel@djh-nordmark.de; Johannesstrasse 1; junior/senior €16.20/18.90) On a hill across the firth from the Hauptbahnhof, this 30-year-old red-brick hostel has great night-time views of Kiel. To walk here, cross the pedestrian drawbridge behind the Hauptbahnhof. At the very end of the path veer left, following the road round to the first intersection and turn left again. Some 30m onwards, cross the main road at the cycle sign. Continue to the right as you take the stairs up the hill. Or take Bus No 11 or 12 to Kieler Strasse.

Hotel Nordic (☎ 986 800; www.nordichotel.de; Muhliusstrasse 95; s €55-60, d €80-85; P ⬚) Newly renovated rooms with various Picasso themes, and reasonable minibar and phone prices, make this hotel so popular with budget business travellers that you need to book ahead during the week.

Hotel Berliner Hof (☎ 663 40; www.berlinerhof -kiel.de; Ringstrasse 6; s €60-75, d €90-95; P ✗) Although completely modern, this central hotel has a touch of olde-worlde class. Above the faux marble floor, red leather lounges and Persian rugs in reception, there are two main types of room: a newer, lighter variety, and a cheaper, slightly older type. Accommodation for people with disabilities is available.

For good views of the firth, try the **Hotel Maritim Bellevue** (☎ 389 40; www.maritim.de; Bismarckallee2, Kiel-Düsternbrook; s €95-195, d €135-270; P). The similarly upmarket **Steigenberger Hotel Conti-Hansa** (☎ 511 50; www.kiel.steigenberge r.de; Schlossgarten 7; s €130-180, d €155-205; P ⬚) is more centrally located; parking costs €12.

Eating & Drinking

Frizz (☎ 805 660; Olshausenstrasse 8; mains €7-13) This small bistro near the university serves everything from pizza and pasta to veggie wok dishes and chicken curry.

Schöne Aussichten (☎ 210 8585; Düsternbrooker Weg 16; mains €8.50-17) Overlooking a pleasant stretch of firth, the modern bistro-style restaurant of the Kiel sailing club serves delicious pasta, fish and meat. It's officially open daily, but sometimes shuts without warning in winter.

Ratskeller (☎ 971 0005; Rathaus; mains €9-18) The Ratskeller is great on a cold winter's day. That's when the rustic room is cosiest and the regional specialities so warming that you don't care whether that inch of fat on your *Holsteiner Sauerfleisch* (a local pork speciality) might damage your arteries. Veggie mains include spinach strudel.

Lüneburg-Haus (☎ 982 600; Dänische Strasse 22; mains €10-22; ⏰ closed Mon) Despite the designer touches, there are still historic hints in this lovely century-old restaurant, and the mix of delicious regional cuisine and modern international dishes leaves lasting culinary memories.

Tucholsky/H. Boll (☎ 557 8637; Bergstrasse 17) A very popular haunt, this is an alternative student bar, pool hall and indie club, which also serves cheap food. Apart from the attached Internet café (see Internet Access p711), the entire centre is only open evenings.

O'Dwyer's Irish Pub (☎ 556 227; Bergstrasse 15) Just across the intersection, this pub is a true winner when it comes to conviviality and Guinness.

You'll also pick up reasonably priced meals at many of Kiel's numerous watering holes, such as the traditional brewery **Kieler Brauerei** (☎ 906 290; Alter Markt 9), the legendary student pub **Oblomov** (☎ 801 467; Hansastrasse 82; ⏰ lunch onwards) or **Forstbaumschule** (☎ 333 496; Dvelsbeker Weg 46), which is a huge beer garden in a park about 3.5km north of the city centre.

SCHLESWIG-HOLSTEIN

Getting There & Away

AIR

Air connections run through Hamburg airport, south of Kiel. The 'Kielius' airport bus (€14 one way) heads directly from Kiel's central bus station to Hamburg airport 17 times a day; it's operated by **Autokraft** (☎ 666 2222).

BOAT

See the Transport chapter for details of ferry services from Kiel to Norway (p762) and Sweden (p762).

For daily services to Klaipeda in Lithuania contact **Lisco** (☎ 2097 6420; www.lisco-baltic -service.de).

BUS

Interglobus Reisen (☎ 666 1787; ☺ 2-5pm Mon-Fri), located in the central bus station, has daily buses to Poland. Many other services head from the central bus station to towns in Schleswig-Holstein, although the train is usually more convenient.

CAR & MOTORCYCLE

Kiel is connected with the rest of Germany via the A210 and A215, which merge with the A7 to Hamburg and beyond. The B4, B76, B404, B502 and B503 also converge here.

TRAIN

Numerous trains shuttle between Kiel, Hamburg-Altona and Hamburg Hauptbahnhof (€15.20, 1½ hours). Trains to Lübeck leave hourly (€12.90, 1¼ hours). There are regular local connections to Schleswig, Husum, Schwerin and Flensburg.

Getting Around

Bus trips cost €1.90 one way or €5.30 for a day card. For a taxi, call ☎ 680 101.

A **ferry service** (☎ 594 1263) along Kiel Firth operates daily until around 6pm (to 5pm on weekends) from the Bahnhofbrücke pier behind the Hauptbahnhof. Short journeys cost €2.45, and the trip to Laboe is €3.20.

AROUND KIEL

Laboe

At the mouth of the Kiel Firth, on its eastern bank, lies the village of Laboe. It is home to a **U-Boot** (☎ 04343-427 00; adult/concession €2.10/ 1.50; ☺ 9.30am-6pm Apr-Oct, 9.30am-4pm Nov-Mar)

and associated **Marine Ehrenmal** (adult/concession €2.80/1.80). The sub is the kind featured in Wolfgang Petersen's seminal film *Das Boot* (1981), and actually served during WWII. It's now a museum where you can climb through its claustrophobic interior. Next to the sub is a naval memorial built in the shape of a ship's stern and housing a **navigation museum**. In fine weather, you can see Denmark from atop the 80m tower, but be warned that the exhibition doesn't have quite the same soul-searching attitude that accompanies most German exhibitions on WWI or WWII. From Kiel, take the ferry (see Getting Around p714) or bus No 100 or 101.

Schleswig-Holsteinisches Freilichtmuseum

South of Kiel, in Molfsee, is the **Schleswig-Holsteinisches Freilichtmuseum** (Schleswig-Holstein Open-Air Museum; ☎ 0431-659 660; Alte Hamburger Landstrasse 97; adult/concession €4.50/3.50; ☺ 9am-5pm Apr-Oct, 9am-6pm mid-Jun–Aug, 11am-4pm Sun & holidays Nov-Mar) This open-air museum features some 70 traditional houses typical of the region, relocated from around the state. The houses, some of them furnished, provide a thorough introduction to the northern way of life. Take bus No 500/504 from Kiel's central bus station.

LÜBECK

☎ 0451 / pop 213,000

Oh, how the mighty are fallen! But Lübeck doesn't look like she cares. The centre of the powerful Hanseatic League, or 'Queen of the Hanse' (see the League of Gentleman boxed text p716), is now merely a provincial city, albeit with a picture-book appearance.

Yet what a fairy tale it seems. The two pointed cylindrical towers of the landmark Holstentor (gate) lean together across the stepped gable that joins them, behind which the streets are lined with medieval merchants' homes and spired churches forming Lübeck's so-called 'crown'. It's no surprise to learn that this 12th-century gem, including more than 1000 historical buildings, has been on Unesco's World Heritage List since 1987. It looks so good you could eat it – especially the red-foil-wrapped displays of its famous marzipan, which you actually can.

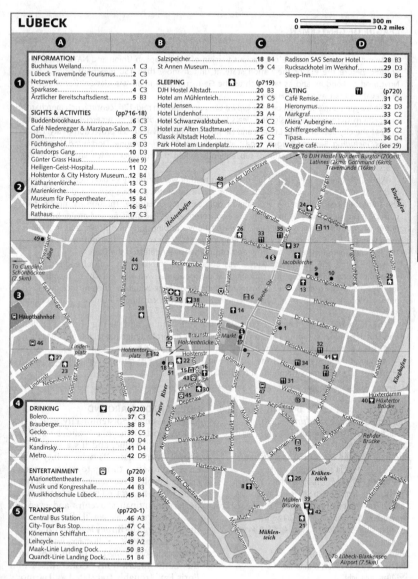

LÜBECK

0 ————————— 300 m
0 ————————— 0.2 miles

INFORMATION
Buchhaus Weiland.............................1 C3
Lübeck Travemünde Tourismus.........2 C3
Netzwerk...3 C4
Sparkasse..4 C3
Ärztlicher Bereitschaftsdienst...........5 B3

SIGHTS & ACTIVITIES   (pp716-18)
Buddenbrookhaus.............................6 C3
Café Niederegger & Marzipan-Salon..7 C3
Dom...8 C5
Füchtingshof......................................9 D3
Glandorps Gang...............................10 D3
Günter Grass Haus.......................(see 9)
Heiligen-Geist-Hospital....................11 D2
Holstentor & City History Museum...12 B4
Katharinenkirche..............................13 C3
Marienkirche....................................14 C3
Museum für Puppentheater..............15 B4
Petrikirche.......................................16 B4
Rathaus..17 C3

Salzspeicher.....................................18 B4
St Annen Museum............................19 C4

SLEEPING   (p719)
DJH Hostel Altstadt..........................20 B3
Hotel am Mühlenteich......................21 C5
Hotel Jensen....................................22 B4
Hotel Lindenhof...............................23 A4
Hotel Schwarzwaldstuben................24 C2
Hotel zur Alten Stadtmauer..............25 C5
Klassik Altstadt Hotel.......................26 C2
Park Hotel am Lindenplatz...............27 A4

Radisson SAS Senator Hotel.............28 B3
Rucksackhotel im Werkhof...............29 D3
Sleep-Inn...30 B4

EATING   (p720)
Café Remise.....................................31 C4
Hieronymus......................................32 D3
Markgraf..33 C2
Miera' Aubergine.............................34 C4
Schiffergesellschaft..........................35 C2
Tipasa..36 D4
Veggie café..................................(see 29)

DRINKING   (p720)
Bolero..37 C3
Brauberger.......................................38 B3
Gecko..39 C5
Hüx...40 D4
Kandinsky...41 D4
Metro...42 D5

ENTERTAINMENT   (p720)
Marionettentheater..........................43 B4
Musik und Kongresshalle..................44 B3
Musikhochschule Lübeck..................45 B4

TRANSPORT   (pp720-1)
Central Bus Station..........................46 A3
City-Tour Bus Stop...........................47 C4
Könemann Schiffahrt.......................48 C2
Leihcycle...49 A2
Maak-Linie Landing Dock.................50 B3
Quandt-Linie Landing Dock.............51 B4

To DJH Hostel Vor dem Burgtor (700m);
Latlines (2km); Gothmund (6km);
Travemünde (16km)

To Camping
Schönböcken
(2.5km)

To DJH Hostel Vor dem Burgtor (700m);

To Lübeck-Blankensee
Airport (7.5km)

Orientation

Lübeck's Altstadt is on an island ringed by the canalised Trave River. The Holstentor forms the western gateway to the Altstadt, with the Hauptbahnhof and central bus station only several hundred metres west of here. There's a map on a billboard just across from the Hauptbahnhof exit, and others dotted around town, making it hard to get lost.

Information

There's an ATM at the Hauptbahnhof and others all over town. Both the tourist office and the Info-booth sell the Lübeck-Travemünde HappyDay Card (€5/10 for

LEAGUE OF GENTLEMEN

As a trading bloc that could raise an army to safeguard its commercial interests, the medieval Hanseatic League was a more pugnacious version of the European Union and NATO combined. Formed before the era of the nation state, it united more than 150 merchant cities – from Novgorod to London, and as far south as the German Alps – in an 'association' (for which the medieval German word was 'Hanse').

The league wasn't so much born as grown organically. In the mid-12th century, rich merchants in Northern Germany began signing deals to safeguard each others' commercial shipping, and in 1241 the city authorities of Lübeck and Hamburg completed a mutual protection treaty. Other towns, including Bergen, Bruges, Riga, Tallinn, Braunschweig, Cologne, Dortmund, Lüneburg, Magdeburg, Rostock and Stralsund, subsequently joined the compact, which lasted some 500 years.

While its initial aim was simply to ensure that neither war nor piracy would interrupt shipping and trade in the North Sea and Baltic regions, by virtue of its collective power and monopolies the Hanseatic League became a dominant political force in Europe. Through its meetings in Lübeck, it dictated policy by fixing the prices of commodities like grain, fur and ore, or by threatening to withhold trading privileges. It wasn't above bribing foreign officials, and in 1368 it even went to war. Challenged by Danish King Valdemar IV for control of the southwestern Baltic, the league's members raised an army and comprehensively defeated the Danes.

All the same, the Hanseatic League was a bastion of stability in a time of endless feudal squabbles and religious ruptures. Commercial prosperity sat well with citizens of member cities. Plus, its far geographical reach fostered political exchange between different societies. Even author Thomas Mann, born in Lübeck, admired its power in creating 'a humane, cosmopolitan society'.

The Hanseatic League began to crumble in the 16th century, with the rise of strong English and Dutch national authorities and an increasing focus on protecting national interests. The ruin and chaos of the Thirty Years' War in the 17th century delivered the final blow.

Although the league met for the last time in 1669, three of its bastions still call themselves Hanseatic cities: Bremen, Hamburg and Lübeck.

one/three days), and a book of tours and tips called *Lübeck rundum* (€2.90).

Ärztlicher Bereitschaftsdienst (☎ 710 81; An der Untertrave 98) Medical services.

Buchhaus Weiland (☎ 160 060; Königstrasse 67a) Stocks a selection of foreign-language books.

Info-booth (☎ 864 675; Hauptbahnhof; ☷ 2-6pm Mon-Fri, 10am-1pm & 2-6pm Sat) Tourist information.

Lübeck Travemünde Tourismus (☎ 01805-882 233; www.luebeck-tourismus.de; Breite Strasse 62; ☷ office 10am-6pm Mon-Fri, 10am-4pm Sat; phone line 8am-10pm)

Main post office (Königstrasse 46)

Netzwerk (☎ 396 8060; Wahmstrasse 58; ☷ 10am-midnight)

Police (☎ 1311; Mengstrasse 20)

Sparkasse (☎ 1470; Breite Strasse 18-28)

Sights & Activities

Lübeck has good English signposting, with information on the sides of landmarks and in museums. Some churches also have multilingual electronic information points.

HOLSTENTOR & AROUND

Lübeck's small Holstentor city gate is one of the most Disneylike realities you'll see this side of Prague, and it's a sight where people sit and stare. Its twin, pointy-roofed circular towers, tilting together across a stepped gable, have made it a true German icon, which has graced postcards, paintings, posters, marzipan souvenirs and even the old DM50 note, as you'll discover inside the engaging **City History Museum** (☎ 122 4129; adult/concession €4/3.50; ☷ 10am-6pm Tue-Sun Apr-Sep, 10am-4pm Tue-Sun Oct-Mar). Built in 1464, with the Latin inscriptions 'Concordia Domi Foris Pax' (roughly translated as 'Harmony within, peace abroad') on one side, and 'SPQL' (Senate and People of Lübeck) on the reverse, the gate began to lean because of swampy soil underneath. In the 19th century, a narrow city council majority elected to restore rather than destroy it, and it required further strengthening in the 20th century.

East of the Holstentor stand six gabled brick buildings. These are the **Salzspeicher**, once used to store salt transported from Lüneburg, which was then bartered for furs from Scandinavia and used to preserve the herrings that formed a substantial chunk of Lübeck's Hanseatic trade. Across the scenic canal and Holstenbrücke (bridge), you can see the tower of the **Petrikirche**. Inside is a **viewing lift** (adult/concession €2/1.50; ⏲ 9am-7pm Mar-Oct, 11am-4pm Nov, closed Jan & Feb), which is well worth the ride.

Nearby is the **Museum für Puppentheater** (☎ 786 26; Kolk 14; adult/concession/child €3/2.50/1.50; ⏲ 10am-6pm), a private collection of some 1200 puppets, props, posters and more, from Europe, Asia and Africa.

MARKT & AROUND

Sometimes described as a 'fairy tale in stone', Lübeck's **Rathaus** (☎ 122 1005) is regarded as one of the most beautiful in Germany. Unfortunately, it's become a little grubby and its impact is somewhat limited by new buildings around the marketplace, which block previously open views. The oldest part of the L-shaped building dates from 1230. The free-standing wall facing the Markt from the northern wing was added in 1435; the cream-coloured arcades and the elaborate staircase on the Breite Strasse side are Renaissance embellishments.

The Rathaus interior can only be seen on a guided tour, which costs €2.60/1.60 (adult/concession), at 11am, noon and 3pm Monday to Friday (call ahead). A highlight is the Audienzsaal (Audience Hall), a light-flooded hall decked out in festive rococo.

North of the Rathaus rise the 125m twin spires of Germany's third-largest church, the **Marienkirche** (⏲ 10am-6pm). Despite floral ceiling ornamentation and a few Gothic frescoes, it's best known for its shattered church bells, which have been left as a peace memorial where they fell during a WWII bombing raid in 1942. Turn left upon entering the church and go to the end of the aisle. Other highlights include the world's largest mechanical organ and an ornate astronomical clock directly opposite the entrance. The church's famous *Totentanz* (macabre dance) frieze was destroyed during the war, but has been given a modern twist in the stained-glass windows near the clock. Back outside, don't miss the cheeky

little devil statue sitting on a stone to the right of the main entrance; his saga is explained there in English.

While around the Markt, stop at **Café Niederegger** (☎ 530 1126; Breite Strasse 89; ⏲ 7am-7pm Mon-Fri, 9am-6pm Sat, 10am-6pm Sun) for some marzipan, the almond sweet from Arabia, which Lübeck confectioners have excelled at making for centuries. Even if you're not buying, the stop is a feast for the eyes. Upstairs is the **Marzipan-Salon** (admission free), with a small museum outlining (in German) the history of what in medieval Europe was considered a medicament, not a sweet.

LITERARY MUSEUMS

There must be something in the water in Lübeck, or maybe it's all that marzipan, for the city has connections to two Nobel Prize–winning authors.

The winner of the 1929 Nobel Prize for Literature, Thomas Mann, was born in Lübeck in 1875 and his family's former home is now the **Buddenbrookhaus** (☎ 122 4190; www.buddenbrookhaus.de; Mengstrasse 4; adult/concession €6/3.60; ⏲ 10am-6pm Apr-Oct, 10am-5pm Nov-Mar). Named after Thomas's novel of a wealthy Lübeck family in decline, *The Buddenbrooks* (1901), this award-winning museum is a monument not only to the author of such classics as *Der Tod in Venedig* (Death in Venice) and *Der Zauberberg* (The Magic Mountain), but also to his brother Heinrich, who wrote the story that became the Marlene Dietrich film *Der Blaue Engel* (The Blue Angel). There's a rundown of the rather tragic family history, too.

While born in Danzig (now Gdansk), Günter Grass had been living just outside Lübeck for 13 years when he collected his Nobel Prize in 1999. But Germany's postwar literary colossus – the author of, among many other works, 1959's searing *The Tin Drum* (Die Blechtrommel) – initially trained as an artist, and has always continued to draw and sculpt. So the **Günter Grass-Haus** (☎ 122 4192; www.guenter-grass-haus.de; Glockengiesserstrasse 21; adult/concession €3.0/2.20; ⏲ 10am-6pm Apr-Oct, 10am-5pm Nov-Mar) is one of the most aesthetically inviting literary museums you'll ever see. The author's *leitmotifs* – flounders, rats, snails and eels – are brought to life in bronze and charcoal, as well as in prose, offering a fascinating insight into his creative genius. Here, you can view a copy of the first typewritten page of *Die Blechtrommel*, while the man himself occasionally appears for readings and other events.

Both museums have extensive English annotations and the Buddenbrookhaus in particular houses a great shop. A combination entry ticket costs €8/5 (adult/concession).

NORTHERN & EASTERN ALTSTADT

In the Middle Ages, this charming section of Lübeck was home to craftspeople and artisans. When demand for housing outgrew the available space, tiny single-storey homes were built in courtyards behind existing rows of houses and made accessible via little walkways from the street. Almost 90 such *Gänge* (walkways) and *Höfe* (courtyards) still exist, among them charitable housing estates built for the poor, the so-called *Stiftsgänge* and *Stiftshöfe*. The most famous of the latter are the beautiful **Füchtingshof** (Glockengiesserstrasse 25; 9am-noon & 3-6pm) and the **Glandorps Gang** (Glockengiesserstrasse 41-51), which you can peer into.

At the corner of Glockengiesserstrasse and Königstrasse is the towerless **Katharinenkirche** (admission €0.50; 10am-1pm & 2-5pm Tue-Sun Apr-Sep). Its main attractions are the sculptures by Ernst Barlach and Gerhard Marcks set in niches in the façade, and *The Resurrection of Lazarus* by Tintoretto inside.

North along Königstrasse you reach the **Heiligen-Geist-Hospital** (admission free; 10am-5pm Tue-Sun, to 4pm in winter) the oldest hospital in Germany (1227) and now the site of Lübeck's popular Christmas market. Four slender octagonal spires alternating with gables dominate its distinctive exterior. Inside you pass through an early-Gothic hall church before entering the hospital hallway, where you'll see the little chambers that were built around 1820 to give the sick and old a certain degree of privacy.

DOM & ST ANNEN MUSEUM

The cathedral's foundation stone was laid in 1173 by Heinrich der Löwe when he took over Lübeck, which means that the **Dom** (10am-6pm Mon-Sat, noon-6pm Sun) is the oldest church in town. However, while its 17m-high **Triumphal Cross**, by Bernt Notke, is undoubtedly impressive, the white walls impart a slightly spartan feel and many

visitors will prefer the Marienkirche. Incidentally, if you approach the Dom from the northeast, you have to go through *Hölle* (hell) and *Fegefeuer* (purgatory) – the actual names of the streets – to see **Paradies**, the lavish vestibule to the Dom.

The approach to the Dom from the south is more scenic if less literary. If you head south along An der Obertrave, you pass the idyllic painters' quarter, where people sit on garden benches among blooming flowers in summer, looking out at the houses and white picket fences across the water. There are plenty of courtyards here, too.

More ecclesiastical art, including Hans Memling's Passion Altar (1491), is found in the **St Annen Museum** (122 4137; St-Annen-Strasse 15; adult/concession €4/3.50; 10am-5pm Tue-Sun Apr-Sep, 10am-4pm Tue-Sun Oct-Mar). The building also houses historical rooms and knick-knacks, as well as contemporary art in its modern Kunsthalle wing. Among the permanent collection is, rather surprisingly, an Andy Warhol print of Lübeck's Holstentor.

GOTHMUND

There's a charming fishers' village on Lübeck's outskirts called Gothmund. Take bus No 12 (leaving three times an hour from Lübeck's central bus station) to the last stop. The fishermen's cottages are at the end (north) of the road. Stroll along Fischerweg, a path running in front of the cottages, or take the same path west, which leads through a nature reserve beside the Trave River.

Tours

A boat tour of the canals encircling the Altstadt really shouldn't be missed; you start off viewing an industrial harbour, but soon move to beautiful leafy surrounds. **Maak-Linie** (706 3859; www.maak-linie.de) runs good one-hour tours, leaving from the north of the Holstentorbrücke. **Quandt-Linie** (777 99; www.quandt-linie.de) leaves from just south of the bridge. Boats are scheduled to leave every half-hour, although many wait until they're half-full. Prices are adult/student/child €7/5.50/3.50.

Guided two-hour city **walking tours** (in German; €5) depart from the tourist office on Breite Strasse. Call ahead for tour times.

City-Tour (adult/concession €4.60/3.10; hourly 10am-4pm mid-Apr–Sep) operates 45-minute tours in open double-decker buses from the corner of Kohlmarkt and Wahmstrasse.

Sleeping

To best experience historic Lübeck, stay in one of the restored *Gänghäuser* (see p718) in the courtyards away from the street. They usually cost €50 to €70 per night for two people, but there's often a three-night minimum. The tourist office can help with booking these and other accommodation, but for the Gänghäuser you really should ring ahead.

BUDGET

DJH Jugendgästehaus Altstadt (☎ 702 0399; jgh luebeck@djh-nordmark.de; Mengstrasse 33; junior/senior €17.40/20.10) Although not as new and spotless as the DJH Vor der Burgtor (see later in this section), this hostel is cosier and more central. Accommodation, in one- to four-bed rooms, is comfortable enough. Rates drop slightly after one night.

Rucksackhotel im Werkhof (☎ 706 892; fax 707 3429; Kanalstrasse 70; dm €13-17, d €34-40; 🖳) Informal and relaxed, this 28-bed private hostel is a favourite with independent-minded backpackers. Dorms have up to eight beds. There are cooking facilities, and guests get breakfast in the adjoining veggie café, which is also open to the public. To get here, take bus No 8 to Falkenstrasse.

Campingplatz Schönböcken (☎ 893 090; fax 892 287; Steinrader Damm 12; tent/person/car €4.50/3.50/1; 🗓 Apr-Oct) This modern camp site has a kiosk, entertainment room and children's playground. It's 15 minutes by bus west of the city centre (take bus No 7).

Hotel zur Alten Stadtmauer (☎ 737 02; www .hotelstadtmauer.de; An der Mauer 57; s/d with shared bathroom from €35/60, with private bathroom from €40/70; 🅿) By keeping it simple, with wooden floorboards and plain furniture, this 25-room hotel offers very reasonable rooms for the price. Good lighting and touches of yellow (or occasionally red) give it a cheerful atmosphere.

Hotel Schwarzwaldstuben (☎ 777 15; fax 705 414; Koberg 2-15; s €50-55, d €75-80; 🅿) This is a bit smoky and old-fashioned downstairs, but has charming Bavarian farmhouse–style rooms.

Also recommended:
Hotel am Mühlenteich (☎ 777 71; www.muelenteich .com; Mühlenbrücke 6; s €50, d €70-75; 🅿) Centrally located, simple but comfortable.

DJH Hostel Vor dem Burgtor (☎ 334 33; jhluebeck@ djh-nordmark.de; Am Gertrudenkirchhof 4; junior/senior €24.40/27.10; 🅿 🖳) Huge and popular with school groups; just outside the Altstadt. Prices drop by €1.30 for three nights or more. To get here, take bus No 1, 3, 11, 12 or 31 to Gustav-Radbruch-Platz.

Sleep-Inn (☎ 719 20; www.cvjm-luebeck.de; Grosse Petersgrube 11; dm €10, d €40; 🗓 mid-Jan–mid-Dec.) Pretty basic, but central and with a nice bar. Breakfast costs an additional €4.

MID-RANGE

Hotel Lindenhof (☎ 872 100; www.lindenhof-luebeck .de;Lindenstrasse 1a; s €65-80, d €85-110; 🅿 ✗) One of those (rare) hotels where everything just feels right, Lindenhof has well-designed, if sometimes small, rooms and offers a healthy breakfast buffet. Little extras, like free biscuits and newspapers, plus a 6am to midnight snack service, add up to premium three-star service. Rooms at the back are quieter.

Hotel Jensen (☎ 702 490; www.hotel-jensen.de; An der Obertrave 4-5; s €65-85, d €85-110) Across the Trave River from the Salzspeicher, this fairly traditionally furnished hotel enjoys good views and a pivotal location. The food in its restaurant, Yachtzimmer, is also superb.

Park Hotel am Lindenplatz (☎ 871 970; www .parkhotel-luebeck.de; Lindenplatz 2; s €60-80, d €80-110; 🅿) Art Deco overtones distinguish the public areas of this small, friendly hotel. With their low lighting, the rooms, like Lübeck itself, are ideal for a romantic interlude. Parking costs an additional €5.

TOP END

Klassik Altstadt Hotel (☎ 702 980; www-klassik-alt stadt-hotel.de; Fischergrube 52; s €70-95, d €75-125; 🅿 ✗) The rooms in this pleasant hotel in the Altstadt have art installations and have been designed according to feng shui principles. They're understandably popular, so you need to book ahead.

Radisson SAS Senator Hotel (☎ 1420; www.sen atorhotel.de, Willy-Brandt-Allee 6; s €140-145, d €180-190; 🅿 ✗ 🐾 🖳 🖳) With three rectangular brick buildings leaning out on stilts into the Trave River, the funky Senator Hotel looks like something from *War of the Worlds*. The front rooms with the best views of the Altstadt tend to be singles, but everyone can enjoy the outlook from the waterside restaurant and bar. Parking costs an additional €10.

Eating

Tipasa (☎ 706 0451; Schluhmacherstrasse 14; mains €4.50-8.50) Faux caveman frescoes of animals and Aboriginal dot paintings greet the young crowds of students who come here for budget-priced meat, fish and vegetarian dishes, particularly the excellent pizza.

Hieronymus (☎ 706 3017; Fleischhauerstrasse 81; mains €5.50-12) Yet another restaurant in a 17th-century building, Hieronymus has offset its chunky wooden beams by planting ivy in the recesses of its yellow Mediterranean walls. The atmosphere's relaxed, and the food cheap and filling. Lunch specials, served until 5pm weekdays, cost up to €6.50.

Café Remise (☎ 777 73; Wahmstrasse 43-45; mains €6.50-12) This trendy café has sparse décor and a bistro menu of salads, pasta, and both German and Italian-influenced main dishes.

Miera' Aubergine (☎ 772 12; Hüxstrasse 57; mains €8-19; ☻ delicatessen/bistro 10am-12am, restaurant Tue-Sat evenings) You can eat antipasti for lunch in the delicatessen/bistro or dine in the restaurant on more formal Italian food, ranging from pumpkin risotto to beef in gorgonzola sauce.

Markgraf (☎ 706 0343; Fischergrube 18; mains €14-21; ☻ dinner Tue-Sun) While Schiffergesell-schaft can be touristy, this similarly historic restaurant is elegance itself. White table-cloths and silverware are laid out under the chandeliers and black ceiling beams of this 14th-century house. The modern German cuisine has Mediterranean and Asian influences.

Schiffergesellschaft (☎ 767 76; Breite Strasse 2; mains €10.50-23) Ships' lanterns, models of 17th-century ships and orange Chinese-style lamps with revolving maritime silhouettes hang from the painted and wooden-beamed ceiling in this low-lit former sailors' guild-hall. As you sit on long benches resembling church pews, staff in long white aprons bring you Frisian specialities.

Drinking

Tradition is the vibe at **Brauberger** (☎ 702 0606; Alfstrasse 36; ☻ closed Sun), where it's been serving its own beer since 1225. For a more modern, trendier environment, head to postindustrial **Gecko** (☎ 714 44; Mühlenbrücke 9), Mexican restaurant-cum-bar **Bolero** (☎ 707 9140; Breite Strasse 1), happening **Kandinsky** (☎ 702 0661; Fleischhauerstrasse 89) or **Metro** (☎ 702 0698; Mühlenbrücke 11), whose chairs, curved ceilings and vintage ads of a French café are meant to invoke the tunnels of the Paris Metro.

Entertainment

Local listings magazines include *Piste* and *Ultimo*. The tourist offices' *Lübeck rundum* (€2.90) is also useful.

CLASSICAL MUSIC

Organ concerts are held, most famously, in the Marienkirche, but also in the Jacobi-kirche on Königstrasse. Ask at the tourist offices or call ☎ 397 700.

Musikhochschule Lübeck (☎ 150 50; Grosse Petersgrube 17-29) This music academy puts on a number of high-calibre concerts throughout the summer and winter semesters, which are mostly free.

Musik und Kongresshalle (☎ 790 40; Willy-Brandt-Allee 10) This new monolith across from the Altstadt is where major international names now play when in town.

ROCK & JAZZ

Werkhof (☎ 757 18; Kanalstrasse 70) This is one of Lübeck's premier concert venues – from rock and blues to flamenco.

Hüx (☎ 766 33; Hüxterdamm 14) Playing funk and soul to pop and house, Hüx is proving to be a nightlife institution after years and years.

Dr Jazz (☎ 705 909; An der Untertrave 1) Under the motto of 'make jazz not war', this venue's schedule of interesting performers makes it the top place in Lübeck for serious jazz lovers.

THEATRE

Marionettentheater (☎ 700 60; Im Kolk 20-22; tickets €5-12; ☻ Tue-Sun) This terrific puppet theatre puts on a children's show at 3pm, and another for adults on some Thursdays and every Saturday at 7.30pm.

Theater Lübeck (☎ 745 52; Beckergrube 10-14) Housed in an Art Nouveau building, this is the place to go for drama, musicals, dance, theatre and more.

Getting There & Away

AIR

Low-cost carrier **Ryanair** (www.ryanair.com) flies from London to Lübeck-Blankensee and calls it Hamburg-Lübeck. That's because synchronised shuttle buses take passengers straight to Hamburg (one way €8, 1¼ hours). Alternatively, scheduled bus No 6 takes passengers into Lübeck's Hauptbahnhof and central bus station.

BOAT

See the Transport chapter for details of ferry services from Travemünde (p721), near Lübeck, to Finland (p762) and Sweden (p762).

Latlines (☎ 709 9697; www.latlines.de; Luisenstrasse 13, Lübeck Siems) sails to Riga. A one-way trip costs €80 per passenger or €100 for a car and five passengers.

BUS

Regional buses stop opposite the local buses on Hansestrasse, around the corner from the Hauptbahnhof. Kraftomnibusse services to/from Wismar terminate here, as do the Autokraft buses to/from Hamburg, Schwerin, Kiel, Rostock and Berlin.

CAR & MOTORCYCLE

Lübeck is reached via the A1 from Hamburg. The town also lies at the crossroads of the B75, the B104 to Schwerin, the B206 to Bad Segeberg and the B207 to Ratzeburg.

TRAIN

Lübeck has connections every hour to Hamburg (€9, 45 minutes), Kiel (€12.90, 1½ hours), and Rostock (€18.80, two hours) via Bad Kleinen.

Getting Around

Lübeck's centre is easily walkable, and since some streets (Königstrasse and east) in the Altstadt are off limits to all but hotel guests' vehicles between 11.30am and 6pm (from 10am on Saturday), many people just park their cars and go on foot.

Alternatively, bus tickets for three stops cost €1.35, single tickets €1.65 and day cards €5.60. The last two are valid for Travemünde and Gothmund.

Leihcycle (☎ 426 60; Schwartauer Allee 39) hires out bikes.

AROUND LÜBECK
Travemünde

Bought by Lübeck in 1329 to secure control over the shipping into Lübeck harbour, Travemünde is now a popular, down-to-

earth coastal playground. With 4.5km of sandy beaches at the point where the Trave River flows into the Baltic Sea, water sports are the main draw. However, there's also an annual **sand sculpture festival** (www.sandworld.de) in July and August.

Lübeck's tourist office (see p715) has an office at Nordermole in the large Aqua Top swimming baths complex at Strandpromenade 1b and can help with accommodation. Camping is particularly fun, with two beachfront camp sites, but there's a hostel, hotels and private rooms, too.

Könemann Schiffahrt (☎ 280 1635; www.koenemannschiffahrt.de; Drehbrücke/Teerhofinsel14a) has ferries from Lübeck (one way/return €7/12) three times daily in season. Otherwise, regular trains connect Lübeck to Travemünde, which has three train stations: Skandinavienkai (for ferries), Hafenbahnhof and Strandbahnhof (for the beach and tourist office). Bus Nos 30 and 31 provide direct services from Lübeck's central bus station. The B75 leads northeast from Lübeck to Travemünde.

SCHLESWIG
☎ 04621 / pop 25,500

Two thousand years old in 2004, Schleswig is a regional pillar, literally and figuratively. Literally, because of the tall cathedral spire that distinguishes this attractive town on the shores of the long, narrow Schlei fjord; and figuratively, because this area was once a Viking centre of power, and later the seat of the Dukes of Gottorf between the 16th and 18th centuries.

The Gottorfs' former castle houses a stunning exhibition that Germans themselves make an effort to see, but the tiny fishing village of Holm and the nearby Viking museum make Schleswig worth a full day's detour.

Orientation

Schleswig's Hauptbahnhof is about 1km south of Schloss Gottorf and 3km from the town. Most buses from the Hauptbahnhof will take you into town, while the long footpath from the train station to the Schloss, and onwards into town, is very clearly marked. In town, the central bus station is on the corner of Königstrasse and Plessenstrasse, with the tourist office, Dom and Altstadt just to the southeast.

Information

Commerzbank (☎ 8560; Postrasse 2) Located just off Stadtweg.

Post office (Poststrasse 1a)

SchleswigCard (adult/family €7.50/17.50) This one-day discount card is available at the tourist office.

Tourist office (☎ 981 616; touristinformation@ schleswig.de; Plessenstrasse 7; ⏰ 9.30am-5.30pm Mon-Fri, 9.30am-12.30pm Sat May-Sep, 10am-4pm Mon-Thu, 10am-1pm Fri Oct-Apr) There's a hotel board and phone outside this office for late arrivals.

Sights & Activities

SCHLOSS GOTTORF

Housed in the Dukes of Gottorf's 12th-century castle since its former home in Kiel was bombed during WWII is the **Schleswig-Holstein Landesmuseum** (☎ 8130; www.schloss-gott orf.de; adult/concession €5/2.50; ⏰ 10am-6pm Apr-Oct, 10.30am-4pm Tue-Sun Nov-Mar) is among the state's biggest drawcards. That's little wonder, since it truly has something for nearly everyone. The Historisches Rundgang (historical tour) to the left of the main entrance takes you through rich treasures, from a roomful of paintings by Lucas Cranach the Elder to a wood-panelled 17th-century wine tavern from Lübeck. In this section also is the rococo **Plöner Saal**, with faïence from the Baltic region, and the stunning **Schlosskapelle** (room 26) – a true highlight. Next door there's also the impressive **Hirsch-saal**, the former banquet hall named for the bas-reliefs of deer on the walls.

On the 1st floor, through a staircase just right of the main entrance, is the ornate **Jugendstil Abteilung** (Art Nouveau department; ⏰ closed 1-2pm), which features chairs by Henry van de Velde and Joseph Hoffman, crockery by Juta Sikka, and objets d'art by Peter Behrens and Wenzel Hablik.

The grounds are dotted with sculptures and several smaller buildings. The best is the **Stiftung Rolf Horn**, with an outstanding collection of 20th-century paintings, sketches, lithographs and woodcuts from various German artists, including Emil Nolde, Ernst Balach, Ludwig Kirchner, Erich Heckel, Christian Rohlfs and Otto Müller.

The **Nydam-Boot**, a reconstructed and preserved 28-oar rowing boat from 350 BC, is housed in another hall.

More museum features are outlined in an English-language guide (€2.50/8 for the abridged/complete edition). There's a café and restaurant on site.

HOLM

This traditional fishing village southeast of the Altstadt looks even cuter than it sounds – a kind of mini-me of medieval towns. It sits on a peninsula that until 1935 was an island, and its centrepiece is an almost **toy-sized chapel** in the middle of a small cemetery, which is in turn ringed by a cobbled road and tiny fisherman's houses. Only residents of Holm may be buried here.

At the end of some streets, you can glimpse the waters of the Schlei Fjord, where several fishermen continue to haul in eel, perch, salmon and herring. The **Johanniskloster** (Convent; ☎ 242 36; Süderholmstrasse) can be seen on a guided tour with the prioress (call ahead) or on an official walking tour of Holm (contact the tourist office).

WIKINGER MUSEUM

Haithabu, south of the Schlei Fjord, was northern Europe's most important economic hub during the 9th century, and the **Wikinger Museum** (Viking Museum; ☎ 813 222; www.schloss-gottorf.de; adult/concession/family €3/2/7; ⏰ 9am-5pm daily Apr-Oct, 10am-4pm Tue-Sun Nov-Mar) does a good job of bringing those times back to life. Not only is there a reconstructed 30m-long Viking longboat inside and permanent exhibits, but at certain times the museum also hosts a Messe (fair), when artisans act as blacksmiths or silversmiths and there are demonstrations of crafts such as baking and pottery. Meanwhile, you can sample wild boar and other traditional dishes in the restaurant.

The museum is about 3km from Schleswig's Hauptbahnhof (bus No 4810) and east of the B76 between Schleswig and Kiel. For ferry service across the Schlei to Haithabu, see Getting Around (p723).

DOM ST PETRI

With its steeple towering above the town, the **Dom St Petri** (☎ 253 67; Süderdomstrasse 2; ⏰ 9am-5pm Mon-Sat, 1.30-5pm Sun May-Sep; 10am-4pm Mon-Sat, 1.30-4pm Sun Oct-Apr) provides an excellent point of orientation. It's also home to the intricate **Bordesholmer Altar** (1521), a carving by Hans Brüggemann. The 12.6m x 7.14m altar, on the wall furthest from the entrance, shows more than 400 figures in

24 scenes relating the story of the Passion of Christ – the result of extraordinary craftsmanship and patience.

English pamphlets (€0.30) describe lesser cathedral features.

Tours

Schleischiffahrt A Bischoff (☎ 233 19) operates a scheduled service along the Schlei from mid-June to early September. Boats depart daily, except Tuesday (one way/return €4/7, approximately 1½ hours), from the Schleihallenbrücke near Schloss Gottorf and travel as far as Ulsnis, about 15km to the northeast, which has a beautiful Romanesque church. Trips from Schleswig all the way to the mouth of the Schlei into the Baltic Sea, just beyond Kappeln, are offered on Tuesday (one way/return €7/11.50, 3½ hours). Children up to age 12 pay half-price. The company also runs three-hour excursions (€7) on the Schlei every Sunday, Wednesday, Thursday and holidays from May to mid-June and most of September.

Sleeping

The tourist office can help you book accommodation, including private rooms.

DJH hostel (☎ 238 93; jhschleswig@djh-nordmark.de; Spielkoppel 1; junior/senior €13.50/16.20) This modern, recently renovated hostel is set well back from the Schlei, but isn't too difficult to reach. Take a bus from the Hauptbahnhof to the Stadttheater stop, then follow the signs.

Campingplatz Haithabu (☎ 324 50; adult/tent/car €3.50/5.50/2; Mar-Oct) This camp site is right on the southern shore of the Schlei in Haddeby, with a great view of the Schleswig skyline. Take bus No 4810 to get here.

Hotel-Restaurant Schleiblick (☎ /fax 234 68; Hafengang 4; s/d €40/65) On a quiet street, but just around the corner from the harbour and from Holm, this cute, grandmotherly hotel is a pretty good budget deal.

Hotel Olschewski's (☎ 255 77; hotelolschewski@foni.net; Hafenstrasse 40; s €55-70, d €80-90) Right on the harbour, housed in pretty white A-line buildings that gleam in the sunshine, this hotel is comfortable, convenient and arguably the best choice in town. There are only eight rooms, however, so book ahead.

Zollhaus (☎ 239 47; www.zollhaus-schleswig-de; Lollfuss 110; s €65-75, d €80-90; P) Although it doesn't enjoy a waterside location, this is definitely one of the nicest hotels in town,

with modern designer touches added to an historic building, and a good restaurant.

Eating

Schleimöve (☎ 243 09; Süderholmstrasse 8; mains €11-18) This maritime restaurant rounds off the perfect Schleswig morning or afternoon. On the edges of the main 'square' in pint-sized Holm, it serves platters combining different types of fresh fish, from salmon and perch to North Sea shrimp and, for more adventurous gourmets, eel.

Senatorkroog (☎ 222 90; Rathausmarkt 9-10; mains €9-15) If Schleimöve is booked out, this also gives you the chance to sample a melange of different local fish. The 1884 building creates an interesting atmosphere.

Café im Speicher (☎ 991 960; Am Hafen 5; mains €8.50-14.50) The immediate surrounds are a little industrial. However, once you get onto the 2nd or 3rd Mediterranean-decorated floor of this converted warehouse, there are great views across the Schlei to accompany your coffee and cake or your fishy meal. Snacks cost around €4.50.

Panorama (☎ 245 80; Plessenstrasse 15; mains €4.50-13.50) The tasty wood-fired pizza provides an antidote for strict vegetarians or those tired of seafood. Lunch specials cost €4.50 to €5.50.

Getting There & Away

Direct trains to Hamburg (€18, 1½ hours) run every two hours, while trains to Flensburg (€5.50, 30 minutes) leave several times hourly. There's also an hourly link to Husum (€5.50, 30 minutes) and Kiel (€8.10, 50 minutes).

There are several daily buses, with restricted service on weekends, to Kiel (No 4810), Flensburg (No 4810) and Husum (No 1046). If you're driving, take the A7 (Hamburg-Flensburg) to the Schuby exit, then continue east on the B201.

Getting Around

Tickets for Schleswig's bus system cost €1.15 per trip. Bike rental outlets include **Splettstösser** (☎ 241 02; Bismarckstrasse 13), with bikes from €4.50 per day. Ferries cross the Schlei channel from the Hafen (just south of the Cathedral) to Haithabu from 11.30pm to 5.30pm daily between May and September (adult one way/return €1.90/3.30, child €1.40/2.20).

FLENSBURG

☎ 0461 / pop 90,000

To this day, Flensburg is still sometimes called 'Rumstadt', in reference to its prosperous 18th-century trade in liquor with the Caribbean. If that weren't enough, it has something of a skeleton in its closet. This was the last seat of power of the Third Reich, when a cornered Hitler handed power to Admiral Karl Dönitz shortly before VE Day in WWII (see the boxed text below).

In reality, however, this quiet town on the Flensburg Firth is less exotic than its colourful history would suggest. It makes a pleasant staging post on the way to Denmark (it's right near the border) and is a good spot to chill out. The beautiful Waterschloss in Glücksberg (see p726) is also within easy reach.

Orientation

Most attractions are near the pedestrian zone that runs north–south parallel to, but one street back from, the western bank of the firth. From the train station take a bus to the central bus station. You'll find the tourist office on the northwestern corner of the central bus station (straight ahead on the left as you get off the bus), with the firth lying straight ahead along Norder-hofenden (which becomes Schiffsbrücke). The pedestrian zone is just inland; turn left

at the tourist office into Rathausstrasse and right into Grosse Strasse (which becomes Norderstrasse).

To walk from the train station, which takes 10 to 15 minutes, take the exit straight ahead on your left, past the statues carved from tree trunks. Follow Bahnhofstrasse round to the left until you reach the first major crossroad. Veer left (west) across the street towards Rote Strasse. This leads into Südermarkt, which becomes Holm and then Grosse Strasse.

Information

For late arrivals, there's a hotel board and map at the train station.

Flensburg-Info (☎ 909 09 20; www.flensburg.de; Europa-Haus; ☺ 9am-6.30pm Mon-Sat) Located in the central bus station.

Flensburger Sparkasse (☎ 150 000; Holm 22)

Main post office (Bahnhofstrasse 40)

NetFun Center (Hafermarkt 8; per hr €4; ☺ 2-10pm) Offers Internet access. To get here, head south from the central bus station, turn left off Süderhofenden and continue along Angelburger Strasse.

Post office (Schiffsbrückstrasse 2)

Sights

Art lovers should follow Rathausstrasse from the tourist office to the hilltop **Museumsberg Flensburg** (Municipal Museum; ☎ 852 956; Museumsberg 1; adult/concession €3.50/1.50; ☺ 10am-5pm Tue-Sun Apr-Oct, 10am-4pm Tue-Sun Nov-Mar). Here you'll find

---

THE LAST 'FÜHRER'

In 1945, with the Russians advancing from the east and British and American armies closing in from the west, Flensburg became the final seat of government for the disintegrating Nazi regime.

In the final weeks of WWII, Hitler, broken, paranoid and scribbling his final testament in a Berlin bunker, suddenly decided against appointing either of his two henchman, Himmler or Goebbels, to succeed him and opted instead for Admiral Karl Dönitz. Conveniently, the admiral was based in Schleswig-Holstein, one of the few regions of Germany not occupied when Hitler committed suicide on 30 April 1945.

Dönitz had earned a reputation as the ruthless commander of the German naval fleet, having developed the tactic of using submarine 'packs' to attack Allied (and several neutral) merchant ships. But he was an unquestionably patriotic seaman, rather than a Third Reich ideologue and neither wanted nor felt up to the job of Führer. He moved German Naval Command to the Naval Academy at nearby Mürwik and the government to the passenger liner Patria, then moored in Flensburg harbour. But six days after taking charge on 2 May, he declared Germany's surrender.

His brief brush with power was not the end of the matter for Dönitz, who in 1946 was found guilty at Nuremberg of war crimes as a submarine commander. Flensburg, understandably, does not make a big deal of this period of its history.

watercolours, postcards and a few paintings by Emil Nolde that really are worth seeing, especially when complemented by excellent Art Nouveau works by Flensburg-born Hans Christiansen. Keep your ticket, as it's good for all city museums.

Those wanting to investigate the rum trade in Flensburg could start with the **Schiffahrtsmuseum** (Maritime Museum; ☎ 852 970; Schiffbrücke 39; adult/concession €3.50/1.50; ☒ 10am-5pm Tue-Sun Apr-Oct, 10am-4pm Tue-Sun Nov-Mar), where there's a **Rum Museum** in the basement. There are German and Danish descriptions of how ships from then Danish-ruled Flensburg began taking supplies to the Danish West Indies (St Thomas, St Jan and St Croix) in 1755 in exchange for sugar and rum. However, the bottles of differently labelled rums present a colourful tableau, and you can buy a sample upstairs.

At the Schiffahrtsmuseum (or the tourist office) you can also pick up a free *Käpitans Weg* brochure – or buy a more detailed version in German (€1.50). This tour follows a captain's route while preparing for a trip to the Caribbean. It's marked with roadside information boards and visits several of the town's *Kaufmannshöfe* (merchants' courtyards).

These complexes were designed to make it easier to load goods. They typically consisted of a tall warehouse on the harbour side, behind which was a series of low workshops, wrapped around a central courtyard and leading to the merchant's living quarters (and sometimes offices), which faced the main street. Just off Grosse Strasse 24 is a courtyard that houses the attractive **Westindienspeicher** (West Indian warehouse). If you continue south along Grosse Strasse it becomes Holm, where at No 17, you also find the **Borgerforeningen Hof**.

The prettiest courtyards can be found off picturesque **Rote Strasse** (continue south along Holm through Súdermarkt). While here, you have a chance to buy some rum at **Weinhaus Braasch** (☎ 141 600; www.braasch-rum.de; Rote Strasse 26-28).

If you have time during your explorations, pop by the **Nordertor** (1595), one of the few surviving town gates in Schleswig-Holstein. It's at the northern tip of Norderstrasse not far from the Schiffahrtrsmuseum.

The best-looking Flensburg church is the **Marienkirche**, where Grosse Strasse becomes Norderstrasse. It features medieval frescoes, modern stained-glass windows and, most impressively, a sumptuous high altar (1598) by Hans Ringerink. He was also responsible for the Renaissance organ in the **Nikolaikirche** (Südermarkt). The Danish **Heiliggeistkirche** (Grosse Strasse 43) is decorated with late-medieval frescoes and a baroque altar.

Activities
Ask the tourist office about hikes along the popular Gendarmenpfad trail just over the Danish border. Along it lies the Schusterkate, northern Europe's smallest border post and the only bridge connecting Germany and Denmark.

Tours
Nordlische Seetouristik (☎ 617 10; info@nordlicht-reisen.de; adult/child €4/3) operates boat cruises to Glücksburg, departing from Schiffbrücke, up to five times daily from May to September and less frequently in winter. The tourist office can provide information about short trips around the harbour.

Sleeping
The tourist office has a free booking service for accommodation, including private rooms.

DJH hostel (☎ 377 42; jhflensburg@djh-nordmark.de; Fichtestrasse 16; junior/senior €13.50/16.20; Ⓟ) A pretty decent if unremarkable hostel, this is popular with sporting teams. To get to here, take bus No 3, 5 or 7 from the central bus station to the Stadion stop.

Campingplatz Jarplund (☎ 932 34; tent & car/ person €7/3.50; ☒ Apr-Oct) This camp site is on the B76 south of Flensburg.

Etap Hotel (☎ 480 8920; www.etaphotel.com; Süderhofenden 14; s/d €35/40; Ⓟ ☒ ☐) Unusually for Etap, the McDonalds of the hotel world, this is very centrally located (beside the main city bus station), but all the other typical features are in place: slightly garish colours, capsule bathrooms…and a damned good price for clean, modern, comfortable, self-contained rooms. Breakfast costs an extra €5; parking is also €5.

Hotel Flensburger Hof (☎ 141 990; www.flensburger-hof.de; Süderhofenden 38; s €75-80, d €100; Ⓟ ☒) Even without a harbour view, this is definitely one of the best privately owned hotels in town. Traditional-looking furniture combines with comfy beds and mod cons from hairdryers to ISDN modem plugs. Book ahead. Parking costs an additional €5.

Mercure (☎ 841 10; h2825@accor-hotels.com; Norderhofenden 6-9; r €60-120; P ✕) This bland but reliably comfortable hotel is well located at the southern tip of the firth.

Intermar Ostsee Hotel Glücksberg (☎ 04631-495 00; www.intermar.de; Förderstrasse 2-4; s €80-105, d €120-150; P) To really pamper yourself, head north of town, where this concrete hotel reveals a stylish interior, a well-equipped spa and great views of the Flensburg firth. Parking costs an additional €5.

Eating & Drinking

Weinstube (☎ 128 76; Rote Strasse 24; meals €3.50-13; ☺ Mon-Sat evening) This quaint, half-timbered bar is in one of Flensburg's prettiest medieval merchants' courtyards. Cuban black bean soup is a quirky touch on its sparse menu.

Piet Henningsen (☎ 245 76; Schiffbrücke 20; mains €12-25) Not only highly rated for its North Frisian seafood, Piet Henningsen also provides memorable, over-the-top surrounds, with ship models, empty rum bottles and even, er, a stuffed crocodile hanging from the ceiling, while a leopard's skin, African statues and other bric-a-brac adorn the walls.

Hansens Brauerei (☎ 222 10; Schiffbrücke 16; meals €7-12) For hearty fare and beer made on the premises, head here.

The main pedestrianised street is lined with places to eat, including versatile, bistro-style **Cafe Extrablatt** (☎ 182 9874; Grosse Strasse 61; meals €6-12) and **Cafe Central** (☎ 150 9100; Grosse Strasse 83; meals €4.50-10).

Getting There & Around

Flensburg has rail connections with Kiel (€12.90, 1½ hours), Hamburg (€22.50, 1¾ hours) and Schleswig (€5.50, 30 minutes). Trips to Husum (€8.10, 1½ hours) require a change at Jübek.

Autokraft (☎ 903 390) has regular bus services to Schleswig, Kiel and Husum, all leaving from the central bus station.

Flensburg is at the beginning of the A7, which leads south to Hamburg, Hanover and beyond. The town can also be reached via the B76, B199 and B200.

You can easily cover Flensburg on foot.

AROUND FLENSBURG
Glücksburg

This small spa town 10km northeast of Flensburg is known for its horseshoe-shaped Renaissance **Wasserschloss** (Moated Palace; ☎ 2213; adult/concession €4/3; ☺ 10am-5pm daily May-Sep; 10am-4pm Tue-Sun Apr & Oct; 10am-4pm Sat & Sun Nov-Mar; 10am-4pm daily 17-30 Dec), which appears to float in the middle of a large lake.

Highlights include the lavish baroque palace chapel on the ground floor, and the two sweeping staircases that lead to the upper floors and the family's private quarters, with the **Kaiserin Salon** (Empress' Salon) and **Kaiserin Schlafzimmer** (Empress' bedroom). Also look out for the **Gobelin tapestries** (1740) in the Weisser Saal (White Hall).

If it's a nice day, visit the **Rosengarten** (admission €2.50). The more than 400 varieties of roses in this garden mostly bloom around the end of June.

Bus No 21 goes hourly between to Glücksburg (€1.95 each way) from Flensburg's central bus station. For information on boat services to Glücksburg, see Tours p725.

HUSUM
☎ 04841 / pop 21,000

The 19th-century German novelist and poet Theodor Storm (1817–88) called his hometown 'the grey town by the sea'. That's a little harsh, especially in late March and early April when millions of purple crocuses bloom in Husum's Schlosspark. Storm's fans will want to see where some of his books were written, including the seminal North Frisian novella *Der Schimmelreiter* (The Rider on the White Horse). Others will find Husum a convenient – if, OK, not astoundingly beautiful – launching pad for explorations of the islets known as Halligen and other parts of the coast.

Orientation

Husum is compact and extremely well signposted. The Hauptbahnhof lies 700m south of the city centre. Head north along Herzog-Adolf-Strasse (passing the library, the Nordfriesisches Museum and the central bus station) and turn left at Ludwig-Nissen-Strasse, following the sign saying Zentrum, to the *Binnenhafen* (inner harbour); the *Aussenhafen* (outer harbour) is just west of here. Alternatively, continue north along Herzog-Adolf-Strasse and turn left into Nordstrasse for the Markt, Grossstrasse and tourist office.

Information

The tourist office sells the discount card, Museumsverbundkarte (€6), for entry to all museums.

Husum Tourismus (☎ 898 70; tourist@husum.de; Historisches Rathaus, Grossstrasse 27; ◷ 9am-6pm Mon-Fri, 10am-4pm Sat Apr-Oct, 9am-5pm Mon-Fri Nov-Mar)

Post office (Grossstrasse 5)

Sparkasse (☎ 8998 5555; Grosstrasse 7-11)

Zentralbücherei (☎ 891 86; Herzog-Adolf-Strasse 5; ◷ 10am-1.30pm & 2.30-6.30pm Mon, Tue, Thu & Fri, 10am-12.30pm Sat; €2 per hr) Offers Internet access.

Sights

At the tourist office and at most museums, you can pick up a copy of the *Kulturpfad der Stadt Husum* brochure, which provides a handy map and short description of the town's main sights. Many focus on Theodor Storm, right down to the **fountain** in the middle of the Markt, which shows Tine, a young Frisian woman who figures in a Storm novella. Even the **Marienkirche** (1829) featured in a couple of his novellas. The church tower is supposed to symbolise a lighthouse, while inside you'll find fairly plain neoclassical architecture.

In early spring, the **Schlosspark**, with millions of blooming crocuses, is the town's most colourful sight.

For trips to the Halligen, see p728.

MUSEUMS

The tourist office and individual museums offer the *Museen in Husum* brochure and sell the Museumsverbundkarte (€6) for entry to all museums, including: the **Schifffahrtsmuseum Nordfriesland** (Maritime Museum of North Friesland; ☎ 5257; www.schifffahrtsmuseum-nf.de; Am Zingel 15; adult/concession €2.60/1; ◷ 10am-5pm Apr-Oct, 11am-4pm Nov-Mar), with its lovingly preserved 16th-century wooden sailing boat; the historical **Nordfriesisches Museum Ludwig-Nissen-Haus** (☎ 2545; www.nissenhaus.de; Herzog-Adolf-Strasse 25; adult/concession €3/1; ◷ 10am-5pm Apr-Oct, 10am-4pm Tue-Fri & Sun, Nov-Mar); and the 16th-century **Schloss vor Husum** (☎ 897 3130; Schloss Strasse; adult/concession €3/1; ◷ 11am-5pm Tue-Sun Apr-Oct).

However, the **Theodor-Storm-Haus** (☎ 666 270; www.storm-gesellschaft.de; Wasserreihe 31; adult/concession €2/1.50; ◷ 10am-5pm Tue-Fri, 11am-5pm

Sat, 2-5pm Sun & Mon Apr-Oct, 2-5pm Tue, Thu & Sat Nov-Mar) is the exhibition most visitors want to see first. And even if you've never heard of Storm, its well-placed literary snippets and biographical titbits will whet your appetite to learn more about this author, poet and proud Schleswig-Holstein citizen. A pamphlet in English provides a brief commentary.

As an Aladdin's cave of prams, teddy bears, toys, advertising signs, pipes and general smoking paraphernalia, the **Tabak-und Kindermuseum** (Tobacco & Children's Museum; ☎ 612 76; Wasserreihe 52; adult/child €3/1.50; ◷ 3.30-5.30pm) is a long-standing local curiosity. However, eccentric owner Herbert 'Flohi' Schwermer (b. 1918) has reduced opening times because of his age, and it might even be shut during advertised hours.

Sleeping

Holiday apartments, easily booked through the tourist office, are generally cheaper than hotels, though some have minimum three-night stays in the high season (April to October), when prices also rise. Private rooms are available.

DJH hostel (☎ 2714; jhhusum@djh-nordmark.de; Schobüller Strasse 34; junior/senior €14.50/17.20; P) Husum's hostel is set in a typical, and very atmospheric, Frisian building northwest of the city centre; take bus No 1051 from the central bus station to Westerkampweg. It closes during the off season, so ring ahead.

Nordseecamping zum Seehund (☎ 3999; fax 654 89; Lündenbergweg 4; tent & car/person €7/3) The most accessible of three camp sites around Husum is in Simonsberg, about 7km southwest of Husum (take bus No 1073 or 1077).

Hotel Hinrichsen (☎ 890 70; www.hotel-hinrichsen.de; Süderstrasse 35; s €45-50, d €65-75; P) There's a friendly welcome at this privately run hotel, with modern rooms. Even if the bathrooms are largely moulded-plastic constructions, the wonderful breakfasts soon make up for it.

Hotel Altes Gymnasium (☎ 8330; www.altes-gymnasium.de; Süderstrasse 6; s €110-135, d €135-200; P) This five-star hotel is a splendidly atmospheric former high school, with Persian carpets, flagstones, tapestries and chandeliers in the entrance hall, plus spacious luxury rooms. But it's hardly worth it unless you can get accommodation in the older building, rather than the new wing. Good weekend packages are available.

Other good mid-range hotels include:

Hotel am Schlosspark (☎ 202 224; fax 620 62; Hinter der Neustadt 76-86; s/d from €50/70; **P**) Whitewashed, laid out like a sprawling motel, and popular with groups.

Hotel Thomas (☎ 662 00; www.thomas-hotel.de; Zingel 7-9; s €50-95, d €80-110) Some of the modern rooms here have harbour views.

Theodor-Storm-Hotel (☎ 896 60; www.bestwestern.de; Neustadt 60-68; s €70-85, d €80-110; **P**) Upmarket, with its own brewery (open nightly). Parking is an additional €8.

Eating

Restaurantschiff MS Nordertor (☎ 4841; Binnenhafen; mains €6.50-17) Moored in the muddy inner harbour, this restaurant ship has oodles of rustic character. The cuisine is typical for Husum, ranging from salmon, mussel, matjes herring and *Labskaus* (beef or pork with potatoes, onion and herring) to schnitzels and steaks. Coffee and cake are also served.

Friesenkrog (☎ 811 59; Kleikuhle 6; mains €9-16) Friesenkrog is a rustic eatery, this time for landlubbers. Eel makes a few appearances on the fishy menu.

For fast food, grab a fish sandwich from **Ewald's Fischmarkt** (☎ 839 770; Hafenstrasse 1; sandwiches €2-3) or head across the road to **Fischhaus Loof** (☎ 2034; Kleikuhle 7; meals €5-10) for jacket potatoes filled with Husumer Krabben (tiny brown shrimp), among other things.

Getting There & Away

There are direct hourly train connections to Kiel (€12.90, 1½ hours), Hamburg-Altona (€22.50, 2½ hours) and Schleswig (€5.50, 30 minutes), plus several links daily to Westerland on Sylt (€10.70, one hour).

Husum has many bus connections with other towns in North Friesland, but the service is irregular. For detailed information, call ☎ 7870.

Husum is at the crossroads of the B5, the B200 and the B201.

There are high-speed boats from Amrun to Nordstrand (€18.50) and from Sylt to Nordstrand (€24) daily from April to October. They connect with a bus to Husum.

AROUND HUSUM
Halligen

Is it an island? Is it a sandbank? No, it's a *Hallig*, one of about 10 tiny wafer-flat 'islets' scattered across the Schleswig-Holstein Wadden Sea National Park (Nationalpark Schleswig-Holsteinisches Wattenmeer). In the Middle Ages, some 50 Halligen existed, but the sea has swallowed up most. Life here is rough and in constant conflict with the tides. Up to 60 times a year, floods drown the beaches and meadows, leaving the few reed-thatched farms stranded on the artificial knolls, or 'wharves', that they're built on. (An aerial shot of such stranded farms is a favourite postcard image.)

Most people, however, just experience the islets on day excursions. The prettiest destination is **Hallig Hooge**, which once sheltered a Danish king from a storm in the handsome **Königshaus**, with its blue and white tiles and baroque ceiling fresco. Other popular Halligen include Langeness and Gröde.

From Husum, **Wilhelm Schmid GmbH** (☎ 04841-2014 2016) offers boat tours to the Halligen during the high season. The ride can be quite rough on windy days. Boats leave from the Aussenhafen in Husum, and trips cost €8 to €16. Some boats pass sandbanks with seal colonies.

The Husum tourist office has brochures on various other operators, some of whom leave from Schlüttsiel, about 35km north. If you're driving to Schlüttsiel, take the B5; bus No 1041 makes several runs daily from Husum to the landing docks.

Some Halligen can also be reached from the North Frisian Islands (see p730).

NORTH FRISIAN ISLANDS

Nature is the major draw of the North Frisian Islands, which lie west of the German mainland in the North Sea. They are surrounded by Schleswig-Holstein Wadden Sea National Park (*Watt* of 'Wattensee' means 'mud-flats'), founded in 1985, which stretches down the whole west coast of Schleswig-Holstein.

SYLT
☎ 04651 / pop 21,000

The island of Sylt is shaped a bit like an anchor attached to the mainland. On its west coast, the fierce surf of the North Sea gnaws mercilessly at the changing shoreline. The wind can be so strong that the world's best windsurfers meet here each September for the final Surf World Cup of the tour. By contrast, Sylt's eastern Wadden Sea shore is tranquil and serene. The shallow ocean retreats twice daily with the tides, exposing the muddy sea bottom. In Sylt's north, you'll find wide expanses of shifting dunes with candy-striped lighthouses above fields of gleaming yellow rape flower. Everywhere you go there are typical Frisian homes, thatched with reeds and surrounded by heath.

For the past 40 years, Sylt has also been the preferred playground of the German jet set, providing gossip for Germany's tabloid press. These days, the couplings and triplings are more discreet than they once were, but the glut of fancy restaurants, designer boutiques, ritzy homes and luxury cars prove that the moneyed set has not disappeared.

It's easy enough, though, to leave the glamour and crowds behind and get comfortably lost on the beach, in the dunes or on a bike trail.

Orientation

Sylt is 38.5km long and measures only 700m at its narrowest point. The largest town and commercial hub is Westerland in the centre. At the northern end is List, Germany's northernmost town, while Hörnum is at the southern tip. Sylt is connected to the mainland by a train-only causeway, though you can take your car on board. For details, see Getting There & Away (p732). The train station is in Westerland.

Information

All communities on Sylt charge visitors a *Kurtaxe* (resort tax), usually €2.50 to €3.50 (but up to €6 in Kampen). In return you receive a *Kurkarte* (resort card), which you need to get onto the beach but also entitles you to small discounts at museums. If you're staying overnight, your hotel will automatically obtain a pass for you (adding the *Kurtaxe* to the room rate). Day-trippers will need to buy a *Tageskarte* (day pass) from the kiosks at entrances to the beach.

There are various ATMs around town. While local tourist offices are listed under each village in this section, those listed here can provide islandwide information.

Bädergemeinschaft Sylt (☎ 820 20; info@sylt-touris mus.de; Stephanstrasse 6; ☻ 10am-5pm daily Apr-Oct, 10am-5pm Mon-Fri Nov-Mar) Offers tourist information.
Commerzbank (☎ 988 10; Strandstrasse 18, Westerland)
Main post office (Kjeirstrasse 17, Westerland)
Syltfoto (Kirchenweg 3-5, Westerland; €4 per hr) Offers Internet access.
Sylt Tourismus Zentrale (☎ 6026; fax 281 80; Keitumer Landstrasse 10b; ☻ 9am-6pm Mon-Sat) Just outside town in Tinnum. Offers tourist information.
Volksbank (☎ 9310; Friedrichstrasse 18, Westerland)

Sights
WESTERLAND
Westerland, the largest town on the island, is the Miami Beach of Sylt. In the centre, the view of the sea is sadly blocked by chunky high-rises, but there's a nice promenade along the beach. The pedestrianised Friedrichstrasse is the main shopping and eating drag.

Westerland became Sylt's first resort back in the mid-19th century, its people having moved here much earlier from a little village to the east called Eidum. Don't look for it on the map, though; in 1436 it was swallowed up by the sea during a horrendous storm. Miraculously, the wily villagers managed to save their little church's altar, which can today be admired in the **Alte Dorfkirche** on Kirchenweg to the east of the train station.

If the **Tourismus-Service Westerland** (☎ 9980; www.westerland.de; Strandstrasse 35) is shut, you can still check accommodation options on a hotel board just outside the train station.

For tours, check out the **Info-Pavillon** (☎ 846 1029; ☻ 9am-4pm in summer, reduced hours in winter) on the train station forecourt.

KAMPEN
If Westerland is the Miami Beach of Sylt, Kampen is its St Tropez. This quiet little village is the island's ritziest, as you immediately realise by the Hermès, Cartier, Joop! and Louis Vuitton boutiques ensconced in the traditional reed-thatched houses. Kampen attracts aristocrats and celebrities, from megastars like Boris Becker, Claudia Schiffer and Ralf Schumacher to German D-list celebrities. All come to see and be seen in summer along the main promenade of Stroenwai, which is better known as Whiskey Alley.

Kampen is home to the island's oldest **lighthouse** (1855), which rises 60m above sea level. Locals have baptised it 'Christian' in honour of all the Danish kings by that name who ruled the island until 1866. There's also the **Uwe Dune**, at 52.5m Sylt's highest natural elevation. You can climb the wooden steps to the top for a 360° view over Sylt and, on a good day, to the neighbouring islands of Amrum and Föhr.

Look out for the quirky illustrated map of the 'in' restaurants, bars and clubs produced by **Tourismus-Service Kampen** (☎ 469 80; info@kampen.de; Hauptstrasse 12; ☺ 10am-5pm Mon-Fri, 10am-1pm Sat).

KEITUM

Keitum is the island's prettiest village, where you'll find quiet streets flanked by old chestnut trees and lush gardens. Historic reed-thatched houses (some the former homes of retired sea captains) abound.

In the old days, Keitum was Sylt's most important harbour, and there's plenty of nautical history, from the **Sylter Heimatmuseum** (☎ 328 05; Am Kliff 19; admission €2; ☺ 10am-5pm daily Apr-Oct, 1-4pm Thu-Sun Nov-Mar) to the historic **Altfriesisches Haus** (☎ 328 05; Am Kliff 13; admission €1.50; ☺ 10am-5pm Apr-Oct, 1-4pm Thu-Sun Nov-Mar). The late-Romanesque sailors' church of **St Severin** is known for its Gothic altar and pulpit, as well as for its romantic candlelight concerts.

The **Touristbüro Keitum** (☎ 337 33; fax 337 37; Am Tipkenhoog 5; ☺ 8.45am-noon & 1.45-5pm Mon-Fri) can help you with further details.

LIST

According to the tourist brochures everything here is 'Germany's northernmost' – harbour, beach, restaurant etc... It's a windswept, tranquil land's end, but things usually liven up in the harbour when the ferry from Rømø deposits its load of day-tripping Danes in search of cheap drink. Looking towards Denmark, you can also see one of the many wind farms taking advantage of the stiff breezes in this part of the world.

North of List is the privately owned Ellenbogen (literally 'elbow'). Two families own this banana-shaped peninsula, which has 35m-high moving dunes and beaches that are unfortunately off limits for swimming because of dangerous currents. It's

under a nature-preservation order and you must pay a toll at the entrance.

More information is available from the **Kurverwaltung List** (☎ 952 00; www.list.de; Am Brünk 1; ☺ 9am-noon & 2-4.15pm Mon-Fri, 10am-noon Sat Apr-Sep; reduced hours Oct-Mar).

Activities

Windsurfing off Sylt is known as the most radical you'll get on the World Cup tour, with 'gnarly' winds and waves, but it's not so difficult that beginners should be deterred. **Surf Schule Westerland** (☎ 271 72; Brandenburger Strasse 15) can help you take your first steps and also rents out equipment. There are lots of other sporting opportunities on Westerland's beach, including the super-strength **bungee-trampoline** (operating May to October), where you bungee upwards, often in groups.

Towards List is the extremely popular **Wanderdünengebiet**, where people hike between the grass-covered dunes. Also here is List's **beach-side sauna** (☎ 877 174; admission €14; ☺ 11am-5pm Easter-Oct). The idea is to heat up and then run naked into the chilly North Sea! To get to the sauna, take the road to Ellenbogen, which branches off the main island road about 4km southwest of List. You will see a sign for the sauna on the left.

There's a long list of boat trips, including day cruises to nearby Amrun and Föhr, the Halligen islets and sea-lion colonies, as well as on mock pirate ships for the kiddies. Contact **Adler-Schiffe** (☎ 987 00; www.adler-schiffe.de; Boysenstrasse 13, Westerland) for details and prices.

Wattwandern at low tide (see Walking to the Islands p680) is also possible here. The best trek is between the islands of Amrum and Föhr, a full-day excursion (€24) involving several boat and bus trips to get there and back. Contact Adler-Schiffe or the Info-Pavillon (p729) at the Westerland train station.

Alternatively, try horse riding across the Wadden Sea at low tide or along the dykes. **Reitstall Hoffmann** (☎ 315 63; Keitum) has group rides starting at €15 for two hours.

For more passive entertainment, **SVG** (☎ 836 6100) offers several bus tours of the island at 1pm or 2pm daily in December and January, plus 11am daily from April to November. Costs are €9.50 to €11.50 per adult and €7.50 to €8 per child. Ask at the central bus station behind the train station.

Alternatively, visit the indoor water park and health spa **Sylter Welle** (☎ 0180-500 9980; Strandstrasse, Westerland; admission with/without sauna €14/9; ☾ 10am-9pm Mon, 10am-10pm Tue-Sun) for a bit of sybaritic self-indulgence.

Sleeping

If you're planning a stay of three days or longer, renting a holiday flat can cost as little as €30 a day in the low season and €45 in the high season (May to September). Private rooms are another option – contact the tourist office for assistance.

BUDGET

DJH hostel (☎ 870 397; jhlist@djh-nordmark.de; List-Mövenberg; junior/senior €15/17.70; ☾ closed Nov-Dec; P) The very picture of a beach idyll, this hostel is nestled among the dunes about 2km northeast of List and just 800m from the North Sea. Buses run from Westerland to List-Schule, and between April and September there's a shuttle to the hostel itself. Otherwise, it's a 2.5km trek. It's not always open from January to April, so you need to ring ahead.

DJH hostel (☎ 880 294; jhhoernum@djh-nodrmark .de; Friesenplatz 2, Hörnum; junior/senior €15/17.70; P) Not quite as scenically located, but very handy for ferries and day cruises. Take the bus from Westerland to the Hörnum-Nord stop, from where it's about a 1km walk.

Friesenhaus Maybach (☎ /fax 6775; Maybach-strasse 26, Westerland; s €44-55, d €75-85; P) This sweet-looking Frisian-style house has a lovely, relaxing garden, yet is close to the centre of town.

Sylt has half a dozen camp sites. **Camping-platz Kampen** (☎ 420 86; Möwenweg, Kampen; 1 person & tent €7.50, 2 people & tent €11; ☾ Easter–mid-Oct), located among dunes at the southern end of Kampen, is about the nicest, and **Camp-ingplatz Westerland** (☎ 994 499; Rantumer Strasse, Westerland; tent/person/car €8/3.50/2.50; ☾ Apr-Oct) is the largest.

MID-RANGE

Hotel Gutenberg (☎ 988 80; www.hotel-gutenberg.de; Friedrichstrasse 22, Westerland; s €40-70, d €70-135; ✗) Some of the cheaper rooms, which have shared bathroom and toilet, equate in price to the budget places on the island. However, even they are of a three-star standard, with blonde or sea-green stained wood furniture, TV and phone. There's also a great breakfast. And unlike most mid-range hotels on Sylt, the Gutenberg accepts credit cards.

Hotel Wünschmann (☎ 5025; www.hotel-wuen schmann.de; Andreas-Dirks-Strasse, Westerland; s €80-140, d €120-250; P) This hotel's foyer has a modern designer ambience and more traditionally decorated rooms, some with balconies overlooking the sea.

TOP END

Hotel Benen-Diken-Hof (☎ 938 30; www.hotel-benen -diken-hof.de; Süderstrasse 3-5, Keitum; s €125-170, d €155-255) To really pamper yourself head for this reed-thatched hotel and its marvellous spa.

Eating

Kupferkanne (☎ 410 10; Stapelhooger Wai, Kampen; meals €5.50-9) This *Alice in Wonderland*–style café is largely situated outdoors, with wooden tables surrounded by a maze of low hedges, brambles and trees, above which you can still peer down the hill to the Wadden Sea. Meals are in the attached Frisian house, but most people just stop by for the trademark giant cup of coffee and equally huge slice of cake.

Gosch (fish sandwiches €2-3.50, meals €6-10) This fast-fish chain has now colonised places like Hamburg, Berlin and Hanover, but it originated in Sylt and remains here in force.

Toni's Restaurant (☎ 258 10; Norderstrasse 3, Westerland; mains €6-13) Toni's has good, inexpensive fare, from steaks to schnitzels, but there's little for vegetarians.

Sansibar (☎ 964 646; mains €12-18) This place is on the beach north of Hörnum. It looks like a shack, but having a drink or dinner on its terrace at sunset, with a view of the crashing waves, ranks as a Sylt highlight.

Alte Friesenstube (☎ 1228; Gaadt 4, Westerland; mains €14-21; ☾ Tue-Sun) This is one of those rustic restaurants that Germans do so well: the low-ceilinged, 17th-century building is lined with decorative wall tiles. Although the handwritten menu is in *plattdütsch* dialect, the staff can explain most of it in English.

Gogärtchen (☎ 412 42; Stroenwai, Kampen; mains €18-28) *The* place to see and be seen on Sylt, thatch-roofed Gogärtchen is renowned as a favourite of the nation's holidaying glitterati.

But even if your knowledge of German celebrity starts and ends at the Shumachers and Schiffers, the modern German cuisine from award-winning chef Thomas Fischer is a gourmet experience worth coming for in itself.

Vegetarians should try Italian bistro **Diavolo** (☎ 995 508; Friedrichstrasse 22, Westerland; mains €7.50-13) or **Blum's** (☎ 294 20; Neue Strasse 4, Westerland; meals from €5), which despite being a fish outlet, also has a salad buffet at lunch.

Getting There & Away

There are daily flights between Westerland airport and Frankfurt and Munich, and several weekly flights from other German cities.

Sylt is connected to the mainland by the Hindenburgdamm, a narrow causeway exclusively for trains. Between 13 and 18 passenger trains a day make the direct three-hour trek from Hamburg-Altona to Westerland (€32).

If travelling by car, you must load it onto a **car train** (☎ 04651-995 0565; www.syltshuttle.de; one way/return including all passengers €42/78) in the town of Niebüll. There are constant daily crossings (usually at least once an hour) in both directions, and no reservations can be made. Cheaper returns (€65) are available from Tuesday to Thursday.

Another cheap alternative is to drive across the Danish border to Rømø, and put your car on the ferry to List on Sylt's northern tip. The trip takes one hour, and costs from €55.50 return, including all passengers. **RSL** (☎ 0180-310 3030; www.sylt-faehre.de) operates five daily ferries year-round (up to 12 from May to mid-September) in either direction.

Adler-Schiffe (☎ 987 00; www.adler-schiffe.de; Boysenstrasse 13, Westerland; return adult/child €20/10.50) offers day cruises to the neighbouring islands of Amrum and Föhr from the harbour in Hörnum, and has quicker journeys on its *Adler Express* ship.

Getting Around

Sylt is well covered by **buses** (☎ 7027). The main north–south connections run at 20-minute intervals during the day. There are seven price zones, from €1.30 to €5.60. Some buses have bicycle hangers.

Cycling is extremely popular and *Fahrradverleih* (bike-hire) outlets abound. In

Westerland, the most convenient place is **Fahrrad am Bahnhof** (☎ 5803; Platform No 1, Hauptbahnhof); however, **Tieves** (☎ 870 226; Listlandstrasse 15, List), at the north of the island, also offers bike-hire.

AMRUM

☎ 04682 / pop 2100

Amrum is the smallest North Frisian Island – you can walk around it in a day. Yet it is also, arguably, the prettiest, blessed with the glorious Kniepsand – 12km of fine, white sand, sometimes up to 1km wide – that takes up half the island. Its harmonious patchwork of dunes, woods, heath and marsh make it the perfect place for a retreat. Many, however, simply visit on day trips. Besides the central village of Wittdün, there are Nebel, Norddorf, Steenodde and Süddorf.

Wittdün has northern Germany's tallest **lighthouse** (admission €1.50; ☉ 9.30am-12.30pm Mon-Fri Apr-Oct; Wed only Nov-Mar), which, at 63m, affords a spectacular view of the island and across to Sylt and Föhr.

Much of Amrum is under protection, so you must stick to the marked paths. However, there are some fine walks, including the 10km walk from the lighthouse to Norddorf through the pine forest, or the 8km return hike from Norddorf along the beach to the tranquil **Ood Nature Reserve**, an ideal place to observe bird life.

The **tourist office** (☎ 194 33; fax 940 394; ferry landing, Wittdün) can provide information on accommodation on the island, which offers **camping** (☎ 2254; fax 4348; Wittdün), a **hostel** (☎ 2010; fax 1747; Mittelstrasse 1) and several hotels. The tourist office can provide details on joining hikes across the Watt (see p730) to Föhr.

Getting There & Around

To reach Amrum from the mainland, take the ferry operated by **WDR** (☎ 800; www.wdr-wyk.de) from Dagebüll Hafen (see p733). The one-way trip to Wittdün takes 1½ hours and costs €7.90/14.40 one way/return.

For information on getting to Amrum from Sylt, see opposite.

Buses travel at 30-minute intervals (hourly in winter) along the island spine from the ferry terminal in Wittdün to Norddorf. There are bike-rental places in every village.

FÖHR

☎ 04681 / pop 10,000

Föhr is known as the green isle, although there's also a good sandy beach in the south. Its main village Wyk has plenty of windmills. In the north you'll find 16 tiny Frisian hamlets tucked behind dikes that stand up to 7m tall. In the old days, Föhr's men went out to sea to hunt whales, an epoch you can learn more about at the **Friesenmuseum** (☎ 2571; Rebbelstieg 34, Wyk; adult/concession €3.50/2; ☺ 10am-5pm Tue-Sun Mar-Oct, 2-5pm Tue-Sun Nov-Feb).

The church of **St Johannis** in Nieblum dates from the 12th century and is sometimes called the 'Frisian Cathedral' because it seats up to 1000 people (ask about guided tours at the tourist office).

The **Föhr information service** (☎ 3040; fax 3068; Wyk harbour) can help with accommodation. Föhr does not have a camp site.

Getting There & Away

To get to Föhr from the mainland, you catch a ferry operated by **WDR** (☎ 800; www.wdr -wyk.de) from Dagebüll Hafen (reached via Niebüll). Up to 10 boats make the trip daily in the high season. One-way trips to Wyk (45 minutes) cost €5.20; same-day return is €9.70. Bikes are an extra €3.90, while cars (prior reservation necessary) cost €50.

For information on getting to Föhr from Sylt, see Getting There & Away (p732).

Getting Around

There's an hourly bus service to all villages on Föhr (less frequent in winter). There are bike-rental outlets in every village.

HELGOLAND

☎ 04725 / pop 1650

Its former rulers, the British, really got the better part of the deal in 1891 when they swapped Helgoland for then German-ruled Zanzibar, but Germans today are enormously fond of this North Sea outcrop. They laud its fresh air and warm weather, courtesy of the gulf stream, and even cynics have to admit there's something impressive about this lonesome wedge of red rock.

Beyond the 80m 'Lange Anna' (Long Anna) stretch of rock on the island's southwest edge, there are WWII bunkers and tunnels to explore. And as the island is still covered by an agreement made in 1840 and economically isn't part of the EU, most visitors indulge in a little duty-free shopping in the outlets lining the main drag, Lung Wai (literally 'long way'). To swim, they head to neighbouring **Düne**, a blip in the ocean that is popular with nudists. Little boats make regular trips from the landing stage in Helgoland.

The **Kurverwaltung** (☎ 81430; info@helgoland.de, zimmervermittlung@helgoland.de for room reservations; Im Rathaus, Lung Wai 28; ☺ 9am-5pm Mon-Fri, 11.30am-5pm Sat & Sun May-Sep, reduced hours winter) can help find a room.

Accommodation includes a **camp site** (☎ 7695; fax 7251; adult/tent €3.10/5.20), a **DJH hostel** (☎ 341; haus-der-jugend-helgoland@t-online.de; junior/senior €14.30/17; ☺ Apr-Oct) and a bungalow village on Düne Island, but you should always book ahead.

Getting There & Away

WDR (☎ 04681-801 47; www.wdr-wyk.de) has day cruises that leave from Hörnum on Sylt and go to Helgoland twice weekly from June to September (adult €26), and weekly in April and May. Ferries also travel to Helgoland from Dagebüll, Husum, Büsum, Cuxhaven, Bremerhaven, Borkum, Emden, Hamburg and Wilhelmshaven.

Directory

CONTENTS

Accommodation	734
Activities	737
Business Hours	739
Children	739
Climate Charts	740
Courses	741
Customs	742
Dangers & Annoyances	742
Disabled Travellers	743
Discount Cards	743
Embassies & Consulates	744
Festivals & Events	745
Food	746
Gay & Lesbian Travellers	746
Holidays	746
Insurance	747
Internet Access	747
Legal Matters	748
Maps	748
Money	748
Photography	749
Post	750
Solo Travellers	751
Telephone	751
Time	752
Tourist Information	752
Visas	753
Women Travellers	753
Work	754

ACCOMMODATION

Accommodation in Germany is generally comfortable and well organised. If you have no advance booking, head to the local tourist office where staff can help you find lodging, sometimes for a small fee. If the office is closed, vacancies may be posted in the window or a display case. Some branches have electronic reservation boards or touch terminals that connect you directly to local establishments.

When making a room reservation on the telephone, always tell the receptionist what time they can expect you and stick to your plan or ring again. Many well-meaning visitors have lost rooms by showing up late.

In this book, we list a wide range of accommodation options, from budget to mid-range to top-end properties. The budget category comprises camp sites, hostels, and simple pensions and hotels where rooms may not always have private bathrooms. Rates rarely exceed €60 for a double room, although in major cities and expensive tourist resorts, the threshold may go up to €80.

Mid-range properties generally offer the best value for money. Expect to pay between €70 and €130 for a clean, comfortable and decent-sized room with at least a

PRACTICALITIES

- Electrical supply is at 220V AC, 50 Hz.
- Widely read daily newspapers include the Munich-based *Süddeutsche Zeitung*, the *Frankfurter Rundschau* and Berlin's *Der Tagesspiegel* (all quite centrist), as well as the more conservative *Frankfurter Allgemeine Zeitung*. *Die Zeit* is an excellent weekly with in-depth reporting.
- *Der Spiegel* and *Focus* magazines offer investigative journalism, while *Stern* takes a more populist approach.
- Radio stations are regional with most featuring a mixed format of news, talk and music.
- Bills include a service charge, but most people tip from 5% to 10%.
- Germany uses the metric system (see conversion chart on inside front cover).
- The GSM 900/1800 system is used for mobile phones (compatible with Europe and Australia, but not the US or Japan).
- The PAL system (not compatible with NTSC or SECAM) is used for videos.
- For women's clothing sizes, a German size 36 equals size 8 in the US and size 10 in the UK, then increases in increments of two, making size 38 a US 10 and UK 12.

modicum of style, a private bathroom, TV and direct-dial telephone.

Hotels at the top end (over €130) offer an international standard of amenities and perhaps a scenic location, special décor or historical ambience. Some may also have pools, saunas, business centres or other upmarket facilities. Unless you're going to use these, though, it's rarely worth the extra cost over most mid-range hotels. Hotels in this category usually have rooms equipped for travellers who use wheelchairs.

Prices listed in this book are generally the official ones supplied by the properties. They do not – and in fact cannot – take into account special promotional rates that may become available at any given time. Business hotels, for instance, often drop prices at weekends. It may also pay to check hotel websites (listed throughout this book) for discount rates or packages. On the flip side, higher rates may apply in big cities during major trade shows.

Unless noted, rates quoted include breakfast, which is usually a generous all-you-can-eat buffet. Hotels and pensions with attached restaurants may offer half board (breakfast and dinner) or even full board (breakfast, lunch and dinner).

If you're driving, note that most city hotels don't have their own parking facilities. Street parking may be elusive, requiring you to leave your car in an expensive public garage that may or may not be close to the hotel. Top-end hotels usually offer on-site or valet parking for an extra fee.

Kurtaxe

A nightly *Kurtaxe* (resort tax) is charged to overnight guests in most resorts and spas. This may be a nominal €0.25 or a hefty €3 per night and is usually not included in the quoted room rate. Paying the tax is compulsory and usually gets you a *Kurkarte* (resort card), which is good for small discounts to museums or concerts and other events.

Camping

Camping is a viable budget option and sites are ubiquitous and generally well maintained, although they do get jammed in summer. The nicest ones are in such scenic settings as national parks, lake reserves or along riverbanks. Having your own trans-

port is definitely an asset, as many sites are in remote locales that are not, or are only poorly, served by public transport.

The season generally runs from May to September, although some campsites remain open year-round. Popular places are booked up far in advance, but there's always the chance that you might benefit from last-minute cancellations.

Facilities vary widely from simple sites with communal sinks, toilets and cold showers to fully fledged resorts with swimming pools, playgrounds, shops, restaurants and other creature comforts. Some rent out cabins, caravans or rooms.

Nightly costs vary, but €2.50 to €5 is common for tent sites. Many then charge around €3.50 per person and €2 per car. There may be additional fees for hot showers, resort tax, electricity and sewage disposal. Having a Camping Card International (see Discount Cards p743) often shaves a bit off the final tally.

Ecologically responsible camp sites, such as those using alternative energy or water sources, are awarded the Green Leaf symbol by the ADAC motoring association, which also publishes the comprehensive guide, *ADAC Camping & Caravaning Führer*, available in bookshops.

Camping on public land is not permitted. Pitching a tent on private property requires the consent of the landowner.

Farm Holidays

A holiday on a working farm (*Urlaub auf dem Bauernhof*) is an excellent way for city slickers to get close to nature in relative comfort, and is a big hit with families. Kids get to meet their favourite barnyard animals up close and personal and to help out with everyday chores. The grownups can enjoy the jovial hospitality and home-made farm products of their hosts. Accommodation ranges from plain rooms with shared facilities to fully furnished holiday flats. Some farmers may impose a minimum stay, perhaps three days or a week. There are stays on organic, dairy and equestrian farms as well as wine estates throughout the country. The best establishments are quality-controlled by the *Deutsche Landwirtschafts-Gesellschaft* (German Agricultural Association). To learn more, check www.landtourismus.de.

Holiday Flats

Renting a furnished apartment is a popular form of holiday accommodation in Germany, especially with budget-minded self-caterers, families and small groups. Tourist offices have lists of holiday flats (*Ferien-wohnungen* or *Ferien-Appartements*). Some pensions, inns and even farmhouses also rent out apartments. Most owners impose a minimum rental period of three days to a week, although some may be willing to rent for shorter periods at a higher rate.

Hostels

DJH HOSTELS

Here's a piece of trivia that might come in handy at your next cocktail party: the first youth hostel opened in Germany in 1912 on Burg Altena in the Sauerland. Since then the concept has, of course, taken the world by storm, with over 600 Hostelling International–affiliated hostels in Germany alone, where they are run by the *Deutsches Jugendherbergswerk* – denoted as 'DJH' throughout this book.

Once places of 'monastic' charm, most hostels have recently been spruced up and now boast smaller dorms as well as private rooms for couples, families and small groups, often with private bathrooms. Some occupy such unique locations as hulking medieval castles. Amenities vary widely but the better ones offer Internet access, on-site cafés and even indoor pools. Almost all can accommodate mobility-impaired travellers. Curfews and daytime lockouts are becoming less common, especially in urban areas. Hostels are generally open year-round. In May/June and October, they often swarm with hormone-crazed German teens on school outings.

Staying at a DJH hostel requires membership in your home country's HI association. Non-members can still get a bed by buying a Hostelling International Card for €15.50 (valid for one year) or individual 'Welcome Stamps' costing €3.10 per night. Both are available at any DJH hostel.

Overnight rates in dorms range from €12 to €25 and include linen and breakfast; lunch and supper cost around €5 extra each. Some hostels charge more for so-called 'seniors', ie people over 26. Bavarian hostels generally only accept juniors but make exceptions for families and single parents over 26 travelling with at least one underage child.

DJH hostels were planning a price review for 2004, so expect prices to vary slightly from those recorded at the time of writing.

There is no central reservation service, but over 200 German hostels can now be booked online either on the DJH's website (www.djh.de; German only) or on the Hostelling International website (www.iyhf.org; in English). Alternatively, just contact the hostel directly by phone.

INDEPENDENT HOSTELS

Independent hostels are increasingly common in the larger cities, especially in Berlin but also in Munich, Dresden, Cologne, Nuremberg, Hamburg and elsewhere. While DJH hostels tend to draw more of a German crowd, these alternative places are great for meeting travellers from all over the world. Typical facilities include communal kitchens, bars, cafés, TV lounges, lockers, Internet terminals and laundry. Staff tend to be youthful, energetic, eager to help and multilingual. Besides mixed dorms popular with backpackers, many of these hostels now also offer private rooms, sometimes with en suite bathrooms, to accommodate couples, families and small groups. Rates sometimes include bed linen but not usually breakfast. Useful websites include www.hostels.com and www.hostels.net, which also allow you to make bookings.

Hotels

German hotels range from luxurious international chains to comfortable mid-range hotels and small family-run establishments. Those that serve breakfast only are called Hotel Garni. An official classification system exists, based on a scale of one to five stars, but it's voluntary and most hotels choose not to participate. Even so, this being Germany, you can generally expect even the cheapest places to be spotlessly clean, comfortable and well run. Rooms usually have television, often with cable or satellite reception, and direct-dial phones are common in all but budget places. Rooms in newer or recently renovated hotels often feature minibars, hairdryers and alarm clocks. So-called 'wellness' areas with a sauna, spa and fitness equipment are increasingly common, even in mid-range hotels.

In most older, privately run hotels, rooms vary dramatically in terms of size, décor and amenities. In the cheapest ones you must share facilities, while others may come with a shower cubicle installed but no private toilet; only the priciest have en suite bathrooms. If possible, ask to see several rooms before committing.

Long-Term Rentals

If you're going to stay in any particular city for a month or longer, you might consider renting a room or a flat through a *Mitwohnzentrale* (flat-sharing agency). These match up visitors with fully furnished vacant flats, houses or rooms in shared houses. Rates vary by agency, city and type of accommodation but, generally speaking, a room in a flat goes for about €300 to €400 per month and a one-bedroom flat ranges from €400 to €650, excluding commission and VAT (16%). The final tally almost always comes to less than what you'd pay for a similar standard in a hotel. Even if you're not staying for an entire month, it may still work out cheaper to pay the monthly rent and leave early.

Home Company (www.home-company.de) is a nationwide network of agencies; its website has all the details, also in English.

Pensions, Inns & Private Rooms

These types of lodging are considerably smaller, less formal and cheaper than hotels. You can expect clean rooms but only minimal amenities: maybe a radio, sometimes a TV, but almost never a phone. Facilities are often, but not always, shared. What rooms lack in amenities, they sometimes make up for in charm and authenticity, often augmented by friendly and helpful hosts who take a personal interest in ensuring that you enjoy your stay. Rates always include breakfast.

Throughout the country, pensions *(Pensionen)* are common, while inns *(Gasthof, Gaststätte* or *Gasthaus)* are more prevalent in rural areas. The latter two usually operate their own restaurant serving regional and German food to a loyal local clientele.

Private rooms are most prevalent in resort towns, where locals like to pad their income by renting one or two rooms in their homes. You won't have as much privacy as you would in more formal places,

but you will get a glimpse into how local people live.

The tourist offices keep lists of available rooms or you can simply look for signs saying 'Zimmer Frei' (rooms available) in houses or shop windows. Some landlords refuse to rent for a single night or, if they do, may charge a little extra. It's a good idea to say right up front how long you intend to stay.

ACTIVITIES
Cycling

Pedalling around Germany is extremely popular, with over 200 long-distance routes totalling some 40,000km crisscrossing some of the country's most scenic terrain. Routes are signposted and are often a combination of lightly travelled back roads, forestry access roads and dedicated bike lanes. Trails run from easy to strenuous, meandering through river valleys, traversing nature preserves or venturing into challenging mountain terrain.

For inspiration, check out www.germany -tourism.de/biking (in English) or, if you read German, consult the *Radfernwege in Deutschland* guide, published by the national cycling organisation **ADFC** (☎ 0421-346 290; www.adfc.de), available in bookshops and on its website (in German only).

For day tours, staff at the local tourist offices normally serve as founts of information. They also sell route maps and can refer you to local bicycle-hire outfits, many of which are also listed throughout this book.

Here's just a smattering of long-distance routes to whet your appetite:

Boden–Königsweg (399km) Runs along the foot of the Alps from Lindau on Lake Constance to Berchtesgaden by the Austrian border with magnificent views of the mountains.

Elbe Cycle Trail (860km) Follows the Elbe River from Saxon Switzerland to Hamburg through wine country, heath and marshland; the Elbe Riverside Biosphere Reserve; and cities such as Dresden, Dessau and Wittenberg.

Nahe–Hunsrück–Moselle Cycle Route (207km) Runs from Bingen on the Rhine to Trier on the Moselle via the Hunsrück – a sparsely populated, hilly forest region.

Romantic Road (347km) Passes through medieval towns and gorgeous scenery and by romantic castles on its route from Würzburg to Füssen.

Saarland Cycle Route (350km) Loops around this small state close to the French border, along the Saar River and into the hilly countryside.

Hiking & Mountaineering

From the Wattenmeer mudflats to the snowcapped Alpine peaks, there isn't a region in Germany not traversed by hiking and walking trails. The Black Forest, the Harz Mountains, the Bavarian Forest, Saxon Switzerland, the Thuringian Forest and the Sauerland are among the most popular regions to explore on foot. Some of the nicest routes lead through national and nature parks or biosphere reserves.

Trails are usually marked with signs or symbols, which are often painted on tree trunks. To find a route matching your fitness level and time frame, talk to the staff at the local tourist offices, who will also supply you with maps and tips.

The Bavarian Alps, naturally, are the centre of mountaineering in Germany. You can go out on day hikes or plan multiday treks from hut to hut. Always check local weather conditions before setting out and take all precautions concerning clothing and provisions. And without fail, let someone know where you're going. For potential problems and how to deal with hypothermia, see p774.

The **Deutscher Alpenverein** (German Alpine Club; ☎ 089-140 030; www.alpenverein.de; Von-Kahr-Strasse 2-4; 80997 Munich) is a good resource for information on walking and mountaineering, and has over 350 local chapters throughout Germany. It also maintains numerous Alpine mountain huts, many of them open to the public, where you can spend the night and get a meal. Their website is in German only.

The **Deutscher Wanderverband** (German Hiking Federation; ☎ 0561-938 730; www.dt-wanderverband .de; Wilhelmshöher Allee 157-9, 34121 Kassel) is the umbrella organisation of all local and regional hiking clubs. It co-publishes an excellent hiking website filled with routes, tips and maps at www.wanderbares-deutschland.de, but, alas, it's in German only.

Horse Riding

Anyone with a passion for horse riding will have no trouble saddling up in Germany. All over the country, you'll find dozens of riding stables (Reiterhöfe), pony riding stables (Ponyhöfe), stud farms (Gestüte) and farms with horses. Options include riding excursions, jumping and lessons from beginners' to dressage. A good website for planning purposes is www.reiten.de (also in English).

River Cruises

A relaxing way of seeing some of the most scenic spots in Germany is by cruising its great rivers: the Rhine, Moselle, Danube and Elbe. A small fleet of luxurious 'floating hotels' offers all-inclusive trips, with meals and some drinks, English-speaking guides, escorted sightseeing wherever the boat docks, and coach excursions to nearby towns. Trips last from five to 14 days with typical routes being Amsterdam to Basel, Hamburg to Dresden and Nuremberg to Vienna. Prices depend on the season, cabin location and other factors, but you can figure at least €120 to €160 per day aboard. For details check with your travel agent or the following US-based operators:

Amadeus Waterways (☎ 800-380-3865; www.ama deuswaterways.com)
Brendan Tours (☎ 800-421-8446; www.brendan vacations.com)
Globus Tours (☎ 800-942-3301; www.globus-tour.com)
Peter Deilmann Cruises (☎ 800-348-8287; www.deil mann-cruises.com)
Uniworld (☎ 800-360-9660; www.uniworld.com)
Viking River Cruises (☎ 877-227-1234; www.viking rivercruises.com)

Skiing

Modern ski lifts, trails from 'Sesame Street' to 'Death Tunnel', breathtaking scenery, cosy mountain huts, steaming mulled wine, hearty dinners by a crackling fire – all these are the hallmarks of a German skiing vacation. The Bavarian Alps, only an hour's drive south of Munich, offer the country's best slopes and most reliable snow conditions. The Olympic Games town of Garmisch-Partenkirchen (p378) has world-class facilities and is hugely popular with the international set, but nearby Mittenwald (p381) is cheaper and, many say, more charming. Oberstdorf (p382) in the Allgäu Alps is another good base.

There's also plenty of skiing and snowboarding to be done elsewhere in the country, where the mountains may not soar as high but the crowds are smaller, prices lower and the atmosphere more relaxed. Among Germany's low mountain ranges, the Bavarian Forest (p420) has the most reliable snow levels with good downhill action on the Grosser Arber mountain and wonderful Nordic skiing in the Bavarian Forest National Park. In snowy winters, the Sauerland in North Rhine-Westphalia (p615), the Black Forest (p454), the Harz (p262) and the Thuringian Forest (p223) also attract scores of ski hounds.

At higher elevations, the season generally runs from late November/early December to March. All winter resorts have equipment-hire facilities. The lowest daily rate for downhill gear is about €10, with discounts for longer hiring periods. Cross-country equipment costs slightly less. Daily ski-lift passes start at around €17.

For more information, contact the **Deutscher Skiverband** (German Skiing Federation; ☎ 089-8579 0213; www.ski-online.de; Hubertusstrasse 1, 82152 Munich).

Spas & Saunas

Germans love to sweat it out, and most public baths (*Stadtbäder*) have sauna facilities, usually with fixed hours for men and women, although most sessions are mixed. Prices start at about €6 per session. Note that not a stitch of clothing is worn, so leave your modesty in the locker. Bring, or hire, a towel.

Booking a regimen of sauna, bath, massage and exercise in a spa resort (*Kurort*) is also popular. The local spa centres (*Kurzentrum*) or spa administrations (*Kurverwaltung*) have price lists for services. Expect to pay upwards of €20 for a full massage. Sauna/massage combinations are popular, as are a wide range of beauty and health treatments. Most can usually be booked on short notice.

Water Sports

Germany's coasts, lakes, rivers and canals are all popular playgrounds for water-based pursuits. Canoeing and kayaking are popular in such places as the Spreewald (p153) in Brandenburg and the Altmühltal Nature Park (p404) in Bavaria. Boating is excellent in Müritz National Park (p294), Mecklenburg-Western Pomerania, while sailors should head for the North Sea and Baltic Sea or lakes such as the Starnberger (p356) or the Chiemsee (p354) in Bavaria. The nearby Walchensee is a famous windsurfing mecca.

BUSINESS HOURS

Official shop trading hours in Germany have become more relaxed in recent years,

with shops now allowed to keep doors open until 8pm Monday to Saturday. Actual hours, though, vary significantly. In rural areas and city suburbs, shop owners usually lock doors at 6pm or 6.30pm Monday to Friday and at 2pm or 4pm on Saturday. Some establishments also observe a two- or three-hour lunch break. After hours, you can stock up on basics at train station shops and petrol stations, albeit at inflated prices. Many bakeries open for three hours on Sunday morning and for two hours on Sunday afternoon.

Bank hours are from 8.30am to 4pm Monday to Friday, with smaller branches closing for lunch from around 1pm to 2.30pm and most staying open until 5.30pm or 6.30pm on Thursday. There's a similar variation with post offices; the main branches are usually the only ones offering extended weekday and Saturday hours (also see Post p750).

Service-oriented businesses such as travel agencies are usually open from 9am to 6pm Monday to Friday and until 1pm or 2pm on Saturday. Government offices, on the other hand, close for the weekend as early as 1pm on Friday. Many museums are still closed on Monday, although this is fortunately changing, especially in the cities; many stay open late one evening a week.

Restaurant hours vary greatly, but many still close in the afternoon, stop serving food at about 9.30pm and observe a closing day (*Ruhetag*). Again, this rule generally does not apply in big cities where there's no shortage of eateries selling food all day long and until late in the evening.

Bars tend to open around 6pm, although some now lure the after-work crowd with happy hour starting as early as 3pm or 4pm. In cities without closing hours, such as Hamburg and Berlin, bars stay open until the wee hours if business is good; otherwise, 1am or 2am are typical closing times. Clubs don't really get going before 11pm or midnight and often keep buzzing until sunrise.

All shops, banks, government departments and post offices are closed on public holidays.

CHILDREN
Practicalities

Successful travel with young children requires planning and effort. Don't try to overdo things by packing too much into the time available. Involve the kids in the planning, and balance that visit to the art museum with a trip to the zoo or time spent on a playground. Lonely Planet's *Travel with Children* by Cathy Lanigan offers a wealth of tips and tricks to make travelling with tots child's play.

In Germany, children's discounts are widely available for everything from museum admissions to bus fares and hotel accommodation. The definition of 'child' varies, though. Some places consider anyone under 18 eligible for discounts, while others put the cut-off at age six.

Most car-hire firms have children's safety seats for hire from about €5 per day, but it is essential that you book them in advance. Highchairs are standard in most restaurants and cots (cribs) in most hotels, but numbers are limited.

Childcare and babysitters are widely available. Check the Yellow Pages under *Babysittervermittlung* or, better yet, ask your hotel's reception staff for a referral.

The choice of baby food, infant formulas, soy and cow's milk, disposable nappies (diapers) and the like is great in German supermarkets, but keep in mind their restricted opening hours (see Business Hours p739). Run out of nappies on Saturday afternoon and you're facing a very long and messy weekend.

Bringing your kids, even toddlers, along to casual restaurants is perfectly acceptable, though you might raise eyebrows at upmarket ones, especially at dinner time. See Whining & Dining (p83) for more on the subject. Breastfeeding in public is practised, especially in the cities, although most women are discreet about it.

Sights & Activities

It's easy to keep the kids entertained no matter where you travel in Germany. The countryside, of course, beckons with all kinds of outdoor activities – from swimming and hiking to horseback riding and canoeing – that are sure to leave the little ones exhausted and ready for sleep by the day's end. Farm holidays are an excellent way for city kids to get a full nature immersion (see p735). Germany's legend-shrouded castles, including the medieval fortresses along the Romantic Rhine (p507), the Wartburg in Thuringia (p224) or dreamy Neu-

schwanstein in Bavaria (p375), are sure to fuel the imagination of many a Harry Potter–oriented youngster.

Theme parks are also perennially popular playgrounds, including Phantasialand in Brühl (p588), Europa Park Rust in the Black Forest (p472), the Space Park Bremen (p623) and the CentrO Adventure Park in the Ruhrgebiet (p606). Older kids might enjoy a bit of Hollywood magic made in Germany at Bavaria Filmstadt (Bavaria Filmpark) in Munich (p339), Filmpark Babelsberg (UFA film studios) in Potsdam near Berlin (p149) and Warner Brothers Movie World in the Ruhrgebiet (p606).

Even in the cities, possibilities for keeping kids occupied abound. Take them to parks, playgrounds, public pools or to such kid-friendly museums as the Schokoladen Museum (Chocolate Museum) in Cologne (p580), the Spielzeugmuseum (Toy Museum) in Nuremberg (p389) or the technology museums in Munich (Deutsches Museum; p337), Speyer (Technik Museum; p501) and Berlin (Deutsches Technikmuseum; p113). Münster (Allwetterzoo; p609) and Berlin (Berlin Zoo; p114) are among those cities with excellent zoos.

CLIMATE CHARTS

The German weather is highly capricious: on any given day it can be cold or warm, sunny or rainy, windy or calm – or any combination thereof. Meteorologists blame this lack of stability on colliding maritime and continental air masses, but for visitors this simply means packing a wardrobe that's as flexible as possible.

The weather tends to be most stable in summer, which is rarely suffocatingly hot (usually around 25°C), the prolonged heat wave of 2003 notwithstanding. Humidity levels are usually quite high, making afternoon thunderstorms fairly common. Spring is a beautiful season but it can be slow to arrive, even if jackets are sometimes stripped off as early as April. An Indian summer might keep beer gardens open through October. In a harsh winter, temperatures can plunge well below 0°C and remain there for several weeks. Brrr! At the higher elevations, snowfall is possible starting in November.

Germans have a few indigenous expressions for their weather patterns. A brief

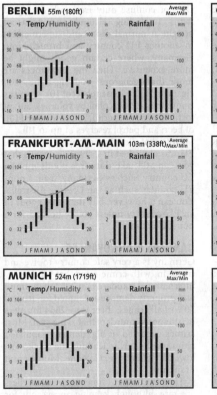

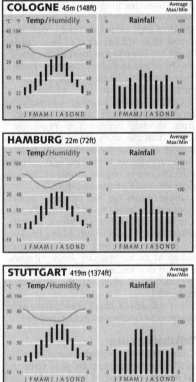

cool period that occurs regularly in May is called *die drei Eisheiligen* (the three ice saints). *Schafskälte* (loosely a 'sheep's cold spell') corresponds with shearing time in June. *Altweibersommer* (old maid's summer) is an Indian summer, while mild weather between Christmas and New Year is called *Weihnachtstauwetter* (Christmas thaw weather).

COURSES

A wide variety of courses is offered in Germany, including hands-on sessions in pottery, sculpture, cooking and skiing that require no special language skills. The best sources of information for these courses are the local or regional tourist offices, particularly in popular resort areas. Local newspapers are another good place to look.

Foreigners who want to study at a German university do not have to pay more than the standard student guild and administration fees paid by Germans. However, you will have to take a language-proficiency test, known as the DSH. The only exemptions are if you can show certain Goethe Institut certificates or have qualified for university entrance at a German school. Information can be obtained from the **Deutscher Akademischer Austauschdienst** (DAAD; ☎ 0228-8820; www.daad.de; Kennedyallee 50) in Bonn.

Universities also offer a wide range of summer courses, a few of which are held in English or are aimed at foreigners wishing to improve their German. Most courses include accommodation in student hostels. The DAAD publishes a multilingual *Sommerkurse in Deutschland* booklet with useful course descriptions, locations and prices.

Goethe Institut

The Goethe Institut is a government-subsidised nonprofit organisation promoting German language and culture abroad.

Aside from teaching German to all those who dare to study it, it also presents thousands of high-calibre cultural events year-round at its 125 branches in 76 countries. There are branches in most of the world's major cities, including London, Dublin, New York, Wellington, Cape Town, Toronto and Melbourne.

Goethe Institut language courses cater for all age groups and stages of proficiency – from absolute beginners to professional levels. You can study for just three hours a week or go for the intensive 25-hour-a-week programme. Some local branches also offer courses in conversational or business German, and German literature.

Programmes for full language immersion, are also available at 16 centres within Germany: Berlin, Bonn, Bremen, Dresden, Düsseldorf, Frankfurt-am-Main, Freiburg im Breisgau, Göttingen, Hamburg, Mannheim, Munich, Murnau, Prien, Rothenburg ob der Tauber, Schwäbisch Hall and Weimar, plus Heidelberg (though in summer only).

For full details, check www.goethe.de or contact the Goethe Institut nearest you.

Volkshochschulen

Courses offered at Volkshochschulen (VHS; adult education centres) are good value and are open to everyone. Most reasonably sized towns have their own VHS, which might offer anything from Japanese origami to language courses. The length of courses varies from several hours to several months. One popular option is to combine au pair work with a German course.

CUSTOMS

Articles that you take to Germany for your personal use may be imported free of duty and tax with some conditions. The following allowances apply to duty-free goods purchased in a non-European Union (EU) country:

Alcohol 1L of strong liquor or 2L of less than 22% alcohol by volume and 2L of wine (if over age 17)

Coffee & Tea 500g of coffee or 200g of coffee extracts and 100g of tea or 40g tea extracts (if over age 15)

Perfume 50g of perfume or scent and 0.25L of eau de toilette

Tobacco 200 cigarettes or 100 cigarillos or 50 cigars or 250g of loose tobacco (if over age 17)

Additional products Up to a value of €175

Do not confuse duty free with duty-paid items (including alcohol and tobacco) bought at normal shops and supermarkets in another EU country and brought into Germany, where certain goods might be more expensive. Then the allowances are more than generous: 800 cigarettes, 200 cigars or 1kg of loose tobacco; 10L of spirits (more than 22% alcohol by volume), 20L of fortified wine or apéritif, 90L of wine or 110L of beer; and petrol reserves of up to 10L.

Note that duty-free shopping within the EU was abolished in 1999. This means that you can still take duty-free goods into an EU country, such as Germany, from a non-EU country such as the USA or Australia. You can't, however, buy duty-free goods in an EU-country unless you're headed for a non-EU country.

DANGERS & ANNOYANCES

Germany is a very safe country to live and travel in, with crime rates that are low by international standards. In 2002 theft, fraud and property damage accounted for around 70% of all crimes; there were 2664 murders or attempted murders that same year. Most crimes occurred in big, densely populated cities, with Berlin leading the pack, followed by Hamburg, Cologne, Munich and Frankfurt.

Theft and other crimes against travellers are rare, although keeping an eye out for pickpockets in crowded places is always wise. Train stations tend to be magnets for the destitute and drug-dependent who might harass you or make you feel otherwise uncomfortable, especially at night. City parks should also be avoided after dark.

Encounters with groups of intoxicated soccer fans, especially those whose team was on the losing side, can lead to unprovoked confrontations. Skinheads, called *Glatzen* (literally 'baldies'), are another potential source of conflict as they too tend to have sudden violent outbursts, especially against people they perceive as 'foreign-looking'. These individuals have also been known to infiltrate otherwise peaceful political demonstrations and to provoke fights simply for their own amusement. Because of their erratic and unpredictable behaviour, keeping your distance from such hooligans is simply a smart move. If you do find yourself in a threatening situation, try not to provoke these people; get away from the scene as fast as possible and notify the police.

DISABLED TRAVELLERS

Overall, Germany caters well for the needs of people with disabilities (*Behinderte*), especially people who use wheelchairs. You'll find access ramps and/or lifts in many public buildings, including train stations, museums, theatres and cinemas. Newer hotels have rooms for mobility-impaired guests with extra-wide doors and spacious bathrooms. However, other disabilities (such as blindness or deafness) are not as well catered for, and German organisations representing people with disabilities continue to lobby for improvements.

The web page of the **German National Tourism Office** (www.germany-tourism.de) has an entire section dedicated to information about vacationing in Germany with a disability (under Travel Tips) with helpful links. Many local and regional tourism offices also have special brochures for people with disabilities.

The Deutsche Bahn operates a **Mobility Service Centre** (☎ 01805-512 512, €0.12 per min; ☉ 8am-8pm Mon-Fri, 8am-2pm Sat) whose operators can answer questions about station and train access, and can help you plan a route requiring minimal train changes. With one day's notice, they can also arrange for someone to meet you at the station and assist you in any way necessary. Generally, all ICE trains and most IC/EC, IR and S-Bahn trains can accommodate people in wheelchairs. Guide dogs are allowed on all trains.

DB's website (www.bahn.de) has extensive information in English (link to International Guests) for travellers with disabilities. Special brochures are also available at train stations.

In cities, U-Bahns and buses are becoming increasingly wheelchair-friendly as well. For details, call the numbers of the local transport organisations listed throughout this book.

Here's a short list of organisations and tour operators that specialise in the needs of disabled travellers:

Access-Able Travel Source (in the US ☎ 303-232 2979; www.access-able.com) Operates an excellent website with many links.

Access Travel (in the UK ☎ 01942-888 844; www .access-travel.co.uk) Tour operator specialising in holidays for travellers with disabilities.

E-Bility (in Australia ☎ 02-9810 2216; www.e-bility .com) Australia-based destination website with disability-related information, services and products.

Mobility International (in the US ☎ 541-343 1284; www.miusa.org; in the UK ☎ 020-7403 5688) Advises travellers on mobility issues and runs an educational exchange programme.

Natko (National Tourism Coordination Agency for All People; ☎ 06131-250 410; home@natko.de; www.natko .de; Kötherhofstrasse 4, Mainz) Central clearing house for inquiries about travelling in Germany as a person with a disability. Has lots of links to local agencies.

Rolling Mobile (in Germany ☎ 07031-750 907; www.rolli-mobil.de) Germany-based company that hires out wheelchair-accessible motorhomes and Paravans (reconfigured Chrysler Voyager minivans) for self-driving or riding.

DISCOUNT CARDS
Camping Card International

These cards are available from your local automobile association or camping federation and can sometimes get you discounted rates at camp sites in Germany. They also incorporate third-party insurance for damage you may cause.

Student & Youth Cards

An International Student Identity Card (ISIC) can pay for itself through discounts on many forms of transportation and admissions to museums, sights and entertainment venues. If you're a full-time teacher, the International Teacher Identity Card (ITIC) offers much the same. Both are plastic ID-style cards with your photograph.

If you're under 26 but not a student, you can apply for an IYTC (International Youth Travel Card) issued by the ISTC (International Student Travel Confederation), or the €26 card, which goes under different names in various countries. Both give much the same discounts and benefits as an ISIC and ITIC.

All these cards are available at student unions, hostelling organisations or youth-oriented travel agencies. They do not automatically entitle you to discounts, and some companies and institutions refuse to recognise them altogether, but you won't find out until you flash the card.

Welcome Cards

Many German cities now offer Welcome Cards, which entitle visitors to discounted admission to museums, sights and tours, plus unlimited trips on the local public transportation network during the period of their validity – usually one, two or three consecutive days. Some cities have cards for individuals, families or groups. They can be good value if you plan on taking advantage of most of the benefits and don't qualify for any of the usual student, senior, child or family discounts.

Other types of visitor-oriented discount cards are also available. You'll find these listed under Information throughout this book.

EMBASSIES & CONSULATES
Your Own Embassy

It's important to realise what your own embassy – the embassy of the country of which you are a citizen – can and can't do to help you if you get into trouble. Generally speaking, it won't be much help in emergencies if the trouble you're in is even remotely your own fault. Remember that you are bound by the laws of the country you are in. Your embassy will not be sympathetic if you end up in jail after committing a crime locally, even if such actions are legal in your own country.

In genuine emergencies you might get some assistance, but only if other channels have been exhausted. For example, if you need to get home urgently, a free ticket home is exceedingly unlikely – the embassy would expect you to have insurance. If you have all your money and documents stolen, it might assist with getting a new passport, but a loan for onward travel is out of the question.

Some embassies used to keep letters for travellers or have a small reading room with home newspapers, but these days the mail-holding service has usually been stopped and even newspapers tend to be out of date.

German Embassies

Germany has diplomatic representation in almost every country in the world. Note that visas and other travel-related services are usually handled by the consular divisions. Contact the embassies listed here to find out the location of the consulate nearest you.

Australia (☎ 02-6270 1911; fax 6270 1951; www.german embassy.org.au; 119 Empire Circuit, Yarralumla, ACT 2600)

Canada (☎ 613-232 1101; fax 594 9330; www.german embassyottawa.org; 1 Waverley St, Ottawa, Ont K2P 0T8)

France (☎ 01 53 83 45 00; fax 01 43 59 74 18; www.amb-allemagne.fr; 13-15 Ave Franklin Roosevelt, 75008 Paris)

Ireland (☎ 01-269 3011; fax 269 3946; www.german embassy.ie; 31 Trimleston Ave, Booterstown, Dublin)

Japan (☎ 03-5791 7700; fax 3473 4243; www .germanembassy-japan.org; 4-5-10 Minato-ku, Tokyo 106-0047)

New Zealand (☎ 04-473 6063; fax 473 6069; www.deutschebotschaftwellington.co.nz; 90-92 Hobson St, Wellington)

Russia (☎ 095-937 9500; fax 938 2354; www.deutsche botschaft-moskau.ru; Ulitsa Mosfilmovskaya 56, 119285 Moscow)

South Africa (☎ 012-427 8900; fax 343 9401; GermanyEmbassyPretoria@gonet.co.za; 180 Blackwood St, Arcadia, Pretoria 0083)

Switzerland (☎ 031-359 4111; fax 359 4444; www .deutsche-botschaft.ch; Willadingweg 83; 3006 Bern)

UK (☎ 020-7824 1300; fax 7824 1435; www.german -embassy.org.uk; 23 Belgrave Square, London SW1X 8PZ)

USA (☎ 202-298 8140; fax 298 4249; www.germany -info.org; 4645 Reservoir Rd NW, Washington, DC 20007-1998)

Embassies & Consulates in Germany

Nearly all countries now have their embassies in Berlin, but many also maintain consulates around the country in such cities as Frankfurt, Hamburg, Düsseldorf and Munich. If you're not in Berlin, call the embassy number listed here to find out which one is closest to your location.

Australia (Map pp98-9; ☎ 030-880 0880; fax 880 088 210; www.australian-embassy.de; Wallstrasse 76-78, Berlin)

Canada (Map pp98-9; ☎ 030-203 120; fax 2031 2590; www.kanada-info.de; Friedrichstrasse 95, Berlin)

Czech Republic (Map pp98-9; ☎ 030-22 63 80; fax 229 4033; www.mzv.cz/berlin; Wilhelmstrasse 44, Berlin)

France (Map pp98-9; ☎ 030-590 039 000; fax 590 039 110; www.botschaft-frankreich.de; Pariser Platz 5, Berlin)

Ireland (Map pp98-9; ☎ 030-220 720; fax 2207 2299; www.botschaft-irland.de; Friedrichstrasse 200, Berlin)

Italy (Map pp98-9; ☎ 030-254 400; fax 254 4100; www.botschaft-italien.de; Hiroshimastrasse 1, Berlin)

Japan (Map pp98-9; ☎ 030-210 940; fax 2109 4222; www.botschaft-japan.de; Hiroshimastrasse 6, Berlin)

Netherlands (Map pp98-9; ☎ 030-209 560; fax 2095 6441; www.dutchembassy.de; Friedrichstrasse 95, Berlin)

New Zealand (Map pp98-9; ☎ 030-206 210; fax 2062 1114; nzemb@t-online.de; Friedrichstrasse 60, Berlin)

Poland (☎ 030-223 130; fax 2231 3155; www .botschaft-polen.de; Lassenstrasse 19-21, Berlin)

Russia (Map pp98-9; ☎ 030-229 1110; fax 229 9397; www.russische-botschaft.de; Unter den Linden 63-65, Berlin)

South Africa (Map pp98-9; ☎ 030-220 730; fax 2207 3190; www.suedafrika.org; Tiergartenstrasse 18, Berlin)

Switzerland (Map pp98-9; ☎ 030-390 4000; fax 391 1030; www.botschaft-schweiz.de; Otto-Von-Bismarck-Allee 4a, Berlin)

UK (Map pp98-9; ☎ 030-204 570; fax 2045 7578; www.britischebotschaft.de; Wilhelmstrasse 70, Berlin)

USA (Map pp98-9; ☎ 030-238 51 74; fax 238 62 90; www.us-botschaft.de; Neustädtische Kirchstrasse 4-5, Berlin); Consulate (☎ 030-832 9233; fax 8305 1215; Clayallee 170, Berlin); Visa Information Service (☎ 0190-8500 5800 automated, ☎ 0190-850 055 live operator, €1.86 per min)

FESTIVALS & EVENTS

Germany has a packed schedule of festivals and special events. Mentioned here are those celebrated either throughout the nation or in specific regions. Festivities taking place in particular towns, such as the Munich Oktoberfest or the Dürkheimer Wurstmarkt, are covered in the destination chapters throughout this book.

JANUARY & FEBRUARY

Karneval/Fasching (Carnival) The season before Lent is celebrated with costumed street partying, parades, satirical shows and general revelry, mostly in cities along the Rhine such as Düsseldorf, Cologne and Mainz, but also in the Black Forest and Munich. See the boxed text on p581.

Valentinstag (Valentine's Day) February 14 as the day of love has a long tradition in the US, UK and France, but the Germans caught the love bug only in the last 20 years or so.

MARCH & APRIL

April Fool's Day 1 April is alive and well in Germany; watch out or you may become the target of an *Aprilscherz* (joke).

Walpurgisnacht Celebrated on April 30 throughout the Harz, this festival of pagan origin has villages roaring to life; young and old dress up as witches and warlocks and parade through the streets singing and dancing. For more, see the boxed text on p281.

MAY

Maifest This festival celebrates the end of winter with villagers chopping down a tree *(Maibaum)*, decorating it with guild signs and ribbons, and staging a merry revelry with traditional costumes, singing and dancing, usually on the eve of May 1 *(Tanz in den Mai)*.

Muttertag (Mother's Day) Mothers are honoured on the second Sunday of May, much to the delight of florists, sweet shops and greeting card companies.

JUNE

Vatertag (Father's Day) Celebrated on Ascension Day since the 1930s, Vatertag has been an excuse for fathers – and those that wanna be – to head out into the countryside or the nearest pub and get seriously liquored up with the blessing of the missus.

Christopher Street Day Major gay celebration with wild street parades and raucous partying, especially in Berlin, Cologne and Hamburg but also in Dresden, Munich, Stuttgart and Frankfurt; dates vary, check www.csd-germany.de.

JULY & AUGUST

Schützenfest (Marksmen's Festivals) Over a million Germans (almost all men, naturally) belong to shooting clubs and show off their skills at these festivals where one of them will be crowned *Schützenkönig* (king of the marksmen); the biggest one takes place in July in Hanover, but Düsseldorf has one of the oldest.

Weinfeste As soon as the grapes have been harvested, the wine festival season starts with wine tastings, folkloric parades, fireworks and the election of local and regional wine queens. The Dürkheimer Wurstmarkt (p503) is one of the biggest and most famous.

SEPTEMBER, OCTOBER & NOVEMBER

Erntedankfest (Harvest Festival) This festival thanking God for the harvest is celebrated in late September/early October with church altars decorated with fruit, vegetables, grain and other products of nature. Some communities stage processions *(Erntedankzug)* featuring wagons piled high with produce and villagers dressed in folkloric garments.

St Martinstag Celebrated on 10–11 November, this festival honours a 4th-century saint known for his humility and generosity with a lantern procession and a re-enactment of the scene where St Martin famously cuts his coat in half to share with a beggar. This is followed by a big feast of stuffed, roasted goose.

DECEMBER

Nikolaustag On the eve of 5 December, German children put their boots outside the door hoping that St Nick will fill them with sweets and small toys overnight. Ill-behaved children, though, may find only a prickly rod left behind by St Nick's helper, Knecht Ruprecht.

Christmas Markets Mulled wine, spicy gingerbread cookies, shimmering ornaments – these and lots more are typical features of German Christmas markets held from late November until December 24. The Christkindlmarkt in Nuremberg is especially famous.

Silvester The German New Year's Eve is called Silvester in honour of the 4th-century pope under whom the Romans adopted Christianity as their official religion; there's partying all night long, and the new year is greeted with fireworks launched by thousands of amateur pyromaniacs.

FOOD

Though traditionally a meat-and-potatoes country, the cuisine available in Germany is becoming lighter, healthier and more international. For the full rundown, see the Food & Drinks chapter (p74).

In this guide we've included eating options to match all tastes and travel budgets. Budget eateries include takeaways, cafés, *Imbisse* (snack bars) and cheap restaurants where you can expect to fill up for under €8. At mid-range establishments, you get tablecloths, full menus, beer and wine lists and a bill that shouldn't exceed €25 per person, including one alcoholic drink. Top-end places are usually full gourmet affairs with fussy service, creative and freshly prepared food, and matching wine lists. Main courses alone can cost €25 or more; the best deals are usually set menus which hover near the €50 mark for three or four courses, excluding wine.

GAY & LESBIAN TRAVELLERS

Germans are fairly tolerant of homosexuality, but gays *(Schwule)* and lesbians *(Lesben)* still don't enjoy quite the same social acceptance as in certain other northern European countries. As elsewhere, cities are more liberal than rural areas, and younger people more tolerant than older generations.

Berlin is by far the gayest city in Germany, if not in all of Europe, but Cologne also has a lively scene and there are smaller but still vibrant ones in Hamburg, Frankfurt and Munich. In those cities gay couples holding hands or kissing in public is becoming more common and raises fewer eyebrows. Discrimination is more likely in eastern Germany and in the conservative south where gays and lesbians tend to keep a low profile.

Germany's gay movement took a huge step forward in 2001 with the passing of the *Life Partnership Act*, sometimes called

the 'gay marriage'. It gives homosexual couples the right to register their partnership at the registry office and to enjoy many of the same rights, duties and protections as married couples.

Local gay and lesbian magazines and centres are listed throughout this book. Online sites about things gay in Germany abound, but most are in German only. Try www.gayscape.com, an online guide and directory with hundreds of links, or go directly to www.eurogay.de, www.justbegay.de and http://stadt.gay-web.de. Sites specifically for women are www.dykeworld.de and www.lesarion.de. A site specialising in gay travel is www.tomontour.de. National publications include *Lespress* (www.lespress.de) and *L.Mag* for lesbians and *Du & Ich* (www.du-und-ich.net) for young gay men.

For details about the Berlin scene, refer to the boxed text on p130.

National help and support organisations include:

Deutsche AIDS-Hilfe (German AIDS Help; ☎ 030-690 0870; Dieffenbachstrasse 33, Berlin) Political interest group fighting for the rights of the HIV-positive.

Lesben- und Schwulenverband Deutschland (German Lesbian & Gay Federation; ☎ 0221-925 9610; www.lsvd.de; Pipinstrasse 7, Cologne) Fights for gay and lesbian rights, and legal and social equality.

HOLIDAYS
Public Holidays

Germany observes nine religious and two secular holidays nationwide. States with predominantly Catholic populations also celebrate Epiphany (6 January), Corpus Christi (10 days after Pentecost), Assumption Day (15 August) and All Saints' Day (1 November). Reformation Day (31 October) is only observed in eastern Germany. Public holidays are:

New Year's Day 1 January
Easter (Good Friday, Easter Sunday and Easter Monday) March/April
Ascension Day 40 days after Easter
Labour Day 1 May
Whit/Pentecost Sunday & Monday May/June
Day of German Unity 3 October
Christmas Day 25 December
Boxing Day 26 December

School Holidays

Since it's up to each state to set school holidays, there's quite a bit of variation in the exact dates and length. In general, though, kids get six weeks off in summer and two weeks each around Christmas and Easter and in October. In some states, schools are also closed for a few days in February and around Whitsun/Pentecost.

Traffic is worst at the beginning of school holidays in population-rich states like North Rhine-Westphalia and can become a nightmare if several states let out their schools at the same time.

Germans are big fans of miniholidays close to public holidays, especially those in spring like Ascension Day, Labour Day, Corpus Christi and Whit/Pentecost. Expect heavy crowds on the roads, in the towns, on boats, in beer gardens and everywhere else.

INSURANCE

Make sure you take out a comprehensive travel insurance policy that covers you for medical expenses and luggage theft or loss, and for cancellations of, or delays in, your travel arrangements. Check your existing insurance policies at home (medical, renters, homeowners etc), since some may already provide worldwide coverage, in which case you only need to protect yourself against other problems. Buy insurance as early as possible, or else you may not be covered for delays to your flight caused by strikes or other industrial action.

Your travel agent should be able to help you wade through the bewildering variety of policies and to explain the finer points. Some, for instance, specifically exclude 'dangerous activities' like scuba diving, motorcycling and even trekking. If these activities are on your agenda, search for policies that include them.

While you may find a policy that pays doctors or hospitals directly, be aware that many healthcare providers still demand payment at the time of service from non-locals. Except in emergencies, it's wise to call around for a doctor willing to accept your insurance. Check your policy for what supporting documentation you need to file a claim and be sure to keep all receipts. Some policies ask you to call back (reverse charges) to a centre in your home country for an immediate assessment of your problem.

Some credit cards offer limited travel accident insurance or other travel benefits if you use them to pay for your airline ticket.

Ask your credit card company what it's prepared to cover.

For additional insurance information, see the Health chapter (p773) and the Transport chapter (p766).

INTERNET ACCESS

Cybercafés are listed under Information in the regional chapters of this guide. Buying online time costs around €2.50 to €5 per hour. Accessing free web-based email accounts such as Yahoo (www.yahoo.com) or Hotmail (www.hotmail.com) is usually no problem, but in order to access a specific account of your own, you'll need to know your incoming (POP or IMAP) mail server name, your account name and your password. Your ISP or network supervisor will be able to give you these. With this information, you should be able to access your Internet mail account from any Net-connected machine in the world, provided it runs some kind of email software (Netscape and Internet Explorer both have mail modules).

A global communication service with an online travel vault where you can securely store all your important documents can be found at www.ekno.lonelyplanet.com.

If you're travelling with a notebook or hand-held computer, make sure that the AC adaptor is compatible with 220 voltage (most are); you may also need a plug adaptor for German electrical outlets. To ensure that your PC-card modem will work in Germany, check that your computer has a reputable 'global' modem installed. If you're spending a long time in Germany, it may be worth buying a local PC-card modem. Before going online, find out whether you're dealing with an analogue or a digital line. Digital lines contain over-currents and are not compatible with analogue modems, but converters exist to remedy this problem.

The most common modem plug used in Germany is the TAE-N. It has larger notches in some places than phone plugs, so it's useful to carry an adapter with three inputs (one for the modem plug) that can be plugged into most telephone sockets. You can buy them anywhere in Germany for a couple of euros. International adapters for German telephone plugs usually accept US RJ-11 plugs, but these are not stocked by all electronics shops, so it's advisable to shop around at home first or seek out a specialist shop in large German cities. Some mid-range and upmarket hotels have telephone sockets that accept RJ-11.

Hardwired telephones (ie wired to the wall) or complex telephone systems requiring you to adjust your modem string will sometimes be a problem.

For more information on travelling with a portable computer, see www.teleadapt.com.

LEGAL MATTERS

German police are well trained, fairly 'enlightened' and usually treat tourists with respect. Most can speak some English, though you may encounter communication problems in rural areas or in eastern Germany. By German law, you must carry some form of picture identification like your passport, national identity card or driving licence.

Reporting theft to the police is usually a simple, if occasionally time-consuming, matter. Remember that the first thing to do is show some form of identification.

If driving in Germany, you should carry your driving licence and obey road rules carefully (see Road Rules p768). Penalties for drinking and driving are stiff. The permissible blood-alcohol limit is 0.05%; drivers caught exceeding this amount are subject to stiff fines, a confiscated licence and even jail time. The legal driving age is 18.

The sensible thing is to avoid illegal drugs entirely, as penalties can be harsh. Travellers coming from the Netherlands should be aware that German authorities are less liberal in this regard than their Dutch cousins. Despite the abolition of border formalities, customs officers and guards still spot-check passengers on trains and also on roads on both sides of the border. Though treated as a minor offence, the possession of even small quantities of cannabis for personal use remains illegal; if you are caught it may involve a court appearance. In practice, though, the courts often waive prosecution if it's a first offence involving only a small amount of cannabis. The definition of 'small', however, is up to the judge, so there are no guarantees. Most other drugs are treated more seriously.

If you are arrested, you have the right to make a phone call and are presumed innocent until proven guilty. For a referral to a lawyer, contact your embassy.

With some restrictions, the age of consent is 14, both for heterosexual and homosexual activity.

MAPS

Maps made in Germany are among the best in the world. Most tourist offices distribute free (but often very basic) city maps, but if you're driving around Germany, you'll need a detailed road map or atlas. The two German auto associations, Allgemeiner Deutscher Automobil Club (ADAC) and Automobilclub von Deutschland (AvD), produce excellent road maps. Also good are those published by Falkplan, with a patented folding system, and the one-sheet maps by Hallwag or RV Verlag. Bookshops and tourist offices usually stock a good assortment of maps and you may find a limited selection at newsagents and petrol stations.

Lonely Planet produces compact, laminated maps of both Berlin and Frankfurt.

MONEY

The euro has been the official currency of Germany and 11 other European nations since 1 January 1999, but coins and notes didn't go into circulation until 1 January 2002. There are seven euro notes (five, 10, 20, 50, 100, 200 and 500 euros) and eight coins (one and two euro coins, and one, two, five, 10, 20 and 50 cent coins).

Thanks to an unstable world economy, wars and other factors, the value of the euro has seen some rather severe fluctuation, especially against the US dollar, since its introduction. The exchange-rate table on the inside front cover can only offer some guidelines. For current rates, check with your bank or online at www.xe.com/ucc or www.oanda.com.

You can exchange money at banks, post offices, foreign-exchange counters at the airport and train stations or at American Express branches. Currency-exchange machines are convenient but usually don't give good rates. Rates are quite good and service swift and unbureaucratic at Reisebank (www.reisebank.de) offices at large train stations; look for branches listed throughout this book.

For an overview of how much things cost in Germany, see Costs (p9).

ATMs

Automatic teller machines, found at most banks, are convenient for obtaining cash from a bank account back home. They're usually accessible 24 hours a day, but occasionally you may have to swipe your card through a magnetic slot to gain entry to a secure area.

Most banks in Germany are affiliated with several international ATM networks, the most common being Cirrus, Plus, Star and Maestro. Check the fees and availability of services with your bank before you leave. Always keep the number handy for reporting lost or stolen cards.

Most ATMs also allow you to withdraw money using a credit card, but this can be quite expensive because, in addition to a withdrawal fee, you'll be charged interest immediately (in other words, there's no grace period as with purchases).

Cash

Cash is still king in Germany, so you can't really avoid having at least some notes and coins, say €100 or so, on you at all times. Plan to pay in cash almost everywhere (see Credit Cards below for likely exceptions). Remember that banks only exchange foreign paper money and not coins.

It's not a bad idea to have a few euros in your wallet when arriving in Germany in case you can't get to an exchange facility or ATM right away. Your bank or local American Express or Thomas Cook branches should be able change your local currency into euros.

Credit Cards

Germany still lags behind other European countries in credit card use, even though major cards (eg MasterCard, Visa and American Express) are gaining in acceptance, especially in cities and at petrol stations, large shops and major hotels. However, it's best not to assume that you can pay with a card – always inquire first. Some shops may require a minimum purchase, while others may refuse to accept a card even if the credit card company's logo is displayed in their window.

Even so, credit cards are vital in emergencies and also useful for hiring a car and booking train and other sorts of tickets over the phone or Internet.

International Transfers

You will need an account at a German bank for bank-to-bank transfers. As an alternative, Western Union and Money-Gram offer fast international cash transfers through agent banks such as Reisebank, American Express and Travelex. Cash sent becomes available as soon as the order has been entered into the computer system (ie instantly). Commissions are paid by the person initiating the transfer; how much varies from country to country but is usually from 10% to 15%.

Travellers Cheques

Travellers cheques, which can be replaced if lost or stolen, are hardly accepted anywhere in Germany, even if denominated in euro. They usually must be cashed at a bank or exchange outlet (bring a passport). The Reisebank charges €3 for amounts up to €50, and 1% or a minimum of €4 for higher transactions. Cheques issued by American Express can be cashed free of charge at their offices. Always keep a record of the cheque numbers separate from the cheques themselves.

PHOTOGRAPHY

Germany is a photographer's dream, with its gorgeous countryside, fabulous architecture, quaint villages, exciting cities, lordly cathedrals, lively cafés and picture-perfect castles, palaces and old towns. A good general reference guide is Lonely Planet's *Travel Photography* by Richard I'Anson.

Film & Equipment

German photographic equipment is among the best in the world, and all makes and types are readily available, as are those manufactured in other countries. Print film is sold at supermarkets and chemists (drugstores), but for black-and-white and slide film you'll have to go to a photographic shop, which can be hard to find outside the cities.

For general-purpose shooting – for either prints or slides – 100 and 200 ASA film are just about the most useful and versatile, as they give you good colour and enough speed to capture most situations on film. If you plan to shoot in dark areas or in brightly lit night scenes without a tripod, switch to 400 ASA.

The best and most widely available films are made by Fuji, Kodak and Agfa. Film of any type is inexpensive in Germany, so there's no need to stock up at home. For a roll of 36-exposure standard print film, expect to pay around €3, while quality slide film should cost from €5 to €7. The cost goes down if you buy in multipacks. Big chain electronics stores like Saturn or MediaMarkt tend to have the best prices for film.

Occasionally, processing is included with the purchase of the film, which is a great deal if you have the time to take it back to the shop where you bought it. With slide film, unless you specify that you want the images framed (gerahmt), you will get them back unframed.

Batteries for your camera are widely available, but it's always best to carry a spare to avoid disappointment in case your camera dies right after you've reached the mountaintop. If you're buying a new camera for your trip, do so several weeks before you leave and practise using it.

Chemists and supermarkets are cheap places to get your film processed, provided you don't need professional-quality developing. Standard developing for print film is about €2, plus €0.20 for each 10cm by 15cm print (allow about four days), and about €0.30 per print for overnight service. Processing slide film costs about €1.75 in these shops; if you want it mounted, your total comes to about €3.50. All prices quoted are for rolls of 36.

Photographing People
Germans tend to be deferential around photographers and will make a point of not walking in front of your camera, even if you want them to. No-one seems to mind being photographed in the context of an overall scene, but if you want a close-up shot, you should ask first.

Technical Tips
When the sun is high in the sky, photographs tend to emphasise shadows and wash out highlights. It's best to take photos during the early morning or the late afternoon when light is softer. This is especially true of landscape photography.

A polarising filter is a very useful piece of gear, as it deepens the blue of the sky and

water, can eliminate many reflections and makes clouds appear quite dramatic. It's best used to photograph scenes in nature, but don't overdo it: using one at high altitudes where the sky is already deep blue can result in pictures with a nearly black and unrealistic sky. The effect of a polariser is strongest when you point your camera 90° away from the sun.

In forests you'll find that light levels are surprisingly low, and fast film or using your camera's fill-flash function may be helpful. A monopod or lightweight tripod is an invaluable piece of gear for 'steadying up' your camera for slow exposure times or when using a telephoto lens.

Film can be damaged by excessive heat. Don't leave your camera and film in the car on a hot day, and avoid placing your camera on the dash while you are driving.

Frame-filling expanses of snow come out a bit grey unless you deliberately overexpose about one to two stops. Extreme cold can play tricks with exposure, so 'bracket' your best pictures with additional shots about one stop under and overexposed.

POST
Main post offices in larger cities are usually open from 8am to 6pm Monday to Friday and till noon or 2pm on Saturday. Occasionally, there will be a late counter offering limited services until 8pm, and until 4pm on Saturday. Branch offices in the suburbs, or those in small towns and villages, close during lunchtime and at 5pm or 5.30pm. You'll often find the main post office at or near the main train station.

Stamps are officially sold at post offices only, though hotel staff and souvenir and postcard shops in tourist resorts may also carry some.

Letters sent within Germany take one to two days for delivery; those addressed to destinations within Europe or to North America take four to six days, and to Australasia five to seven days.

Postal Rates
Within Germany and the EU, standard-sized postcards cost €0.45, a 20g letter is €0.55 and a 50g letter is €1. Postcards to North America and Australasia cost €1, a 20g airmail letter is €1.55 and a 50g airmail letter is €2. A surcharge applies if the post-

card or letter is oversized. German postal workers can be very finicky about this and may measure any letter that looks even remotely nonstandard.

Sending a parcel up to 2kg within Germany costs €4.10. Surface-mail parcels up to 2kg within Europe are €8.20 and to destinations elsewhere €12.30. Airmail parcels up to 1kg are €10.30/21 within Europe/elsewhere; parcels over 1kg cost €14.30/29.70.

Sending & Receiving Mail

Mail can be sent poste restante to any post office (select one, then inquire about the exact address). There is no charge, but German post offices will hold mail for only two weeks, so plan your drops carefully. Ask those sending you mail to clearly mark the letter or package *Postlagernd* and to write your name, followed by the address of the post office. Bring your passport or other photo ID when picking up mail.

You can also have mail sent to American Express offices in large cities, a free service if you have an American Express card or travellers cheques (otherwise it costs €2 per item). Make sure that the words 'Client's Mail' appear somewhere on the envelope. American Express holds mail for 30 days, but won't accept registered mail or parcels.

SOLO TRAVELLERS

Travelling alone is not for everybody, but it does give you the freedom to do anything or go anywhere you want whenever you want. There are many ways to ease the sense of isolation that comes with travelling solo, such as keeping a daily journal, buying cheap phonecards to stay in touch with friends and family back home, and of course meeting locals and other travellers.

Meeting Germans is not always easy because they tend to be a rather reserved bunch and are unlikely to initiate contact with strangers. This shouldn't stop you from striking up a conversation, though, since most will quite happily respond and even be extra-helpful once they find out you're a traveller. Asking for directions or a restaurant recommendation is always an innocuous way to approach someone. Women don't need to be afraid of taking the first step either, even with men. Unless

you're overtly coquettish, it most likely won't be interpreted as a sexual advance.

Germans are cliquish, meaning it's generally easier to make contact with individuals than with people in groups. And don't let your lack of German deter you. Young people especially speak at least some English and many are keen to practise it.

Among the best places for hooking up with other travellers are hostels, especially the independent kind that are more gregarious and international than the DJH hostels. Unless you're a total loner, you'll soon find people with whom to share travel tips or go sightseeing, bar-hopping or out to dinner. Guided English-language walking tours, major tourist attractions, Internet cafés and cultural centres like the British Council are also good places to hook up with other travellers or expat locals.

TELEPHONE

Most public pay phones no longer accept coins but only Deutsche Telecom (DT) phonecards, which are available in denominations of €5, €10 and €20 from post offices, newsagents, some tourist offices and public transport offices.

DT phonecards are OK for local calls, but for calling long-distance within Germany or internationally, you'll usually get better rates with prepaid cards issued by private companies and commonly sold at news kiosks and discount telephone call shops.

With these, calls can be made from any phone, usually including pay phones, by first dialling a toll-free access number, followed by a PIN listed on the card itself followed by the number. Beware of cards with hidden charges such as an 'activation fee' or a per-call connection fee. Reliable ones include those available from Reisebank outlets, which charge €0.06 cents a minute for calls made within Germany or to such countries as the UK, the US, Australia, New Zealand, Ireland, Italy, the Netherlands and a few others. Calls to other countries cost more but rates are still competitive.

Fax

If you're staying at upmarket hotels, fax transmissions are generally not a problem. There's usually no fee for receiving faxes, though sending them can cost you a bundle, so it pays to check in advance.

Faxes can also be sent from copy shops and Internet cafés. If you carry a laptop with a fax modem, you only pay for the cost of the telephone call (keep in mind that hotel phone rates are exorbitant).

Mobile Phone

Germany uses GSM 900/1800, which is compatible with the rest of Europe and Australia, but not with the North American GSM 1900 or the totally different system in Japan (though some North Americans have GSM 1900/900 phones that do work here).

Note that calls made *to* mobile phones cost a lot more than those to a stationary number, though how much more depends on the service used by the mobile-phone provider. Most mobile phone numbers begin with 017 or 016.

If you want the convenience of a mobile in Germany, the simplest solution may be to go to any telecom shop, such as T-Online or Debitel, buy the cheapest mobile phone you can find and load it up with a prepaid chip card for airtime, which can be recharged as needed. There are no contracts or billing hassles.

Airport Communications Service (☎ 069-6959 1163; www.aircom.de) at Frankfurt Airport hires out mobile phones for use in Germany/Europe for €13/15 per day (includes €6.50/8.50 daily call credits), or less for longer periods. The deposit is €500 to €1000. The office is in the shopping arcade of Frankfurt Airport Center 1, Terminal 1. Within Germany, incoming calls are free and outgoing calls cost €0.54 per minute.

Phone Codes

German phone numbers consist of an area code, which always starts with 0 and can be anything from three to six digits long, plus a local number. Numbers within the same city don't require the area code.

To call Germany from abroad, dial your country's international access code, then 49 (Germany's country code), then the area code (dropping the initial 0) followed by the phone number. The international access code from Germany is ☎ 00.

For directory assistance within Germany, dial ☎ 118 33 (☎ 118 37 for information in English), which is charged at a base rate of €0.25 plus €0.99 per minute. For numbers

outside Germany, call ☎ 118 34, which will cost you €0.55 for every 20 seconds.

Numbers starting with 0800 are toll free, 018 05 numbers are charged at €0.12 per minute, 018 03 numbers cost €0.09 cents per minute and 0190 numbers cost €0.62 per minute. Direct-dialled calls made from hotel rooms are also often charged at a premium.

An operator can be reached on ☎ 0180-200 1033. Reverse-charge (collect) calls through this number can only be made to some countries, but it's much cheaper to use the home-direct services. For these dial ☎ 0800 plus: USA 888 0013 (Sprint), 225 5288 (AT&T) or 888 8000 (MCI); Canada 080 1014; UK 0800 044; or Australia 0800 061 (Telstra).

TIME

Throughout Germany, clocks are set to Central European Time (GMT/UTC plus one hour). Daylight-saving time comes into effect at 2am on the last Sunday in March, when clocks are put forward one hour and ends on the last Sunday in October. Without taking daylight-saving times into account, when it's noon in Berlin, it's 11am in London, 6am in New York, 3am in San Francisco, 8pm in Tokyo, 9pm in Sydney and 11pm in Auckland. Official times (eg shop hours, train schedules, film screenings) are usually indicated by the 24-hour clock, eg 6.30pm is 18.30. Refer to the time-zone world map on p775 for additional data.

TOURIST INFORMATION
Local Tourist Offices

Just about every city, town and village in Germany has a tourist office, which may also be called *Verkehrsverein* or *Verkehrsamt, Fremdenverkehrsverein* or *Fremdenverkehrsamt* or, in spa or resort towns, *Kurverwaltung*. Most maintain walk-in offices where you can pick up information, maps and often book a room, sometimes for a small fee. Addresses are listed throughout this book in the Information section of each town.

Tourist offices in big cities and resort areas usually have English-language brochures. With few exceptions, there's at least one staff member more or less fluent in English and willing to make the effort to help you.

The **German National Tourist Office** (GNTO; ☎ 069-974 640; www.germany-tourism.de; headquarters Beethovenstrasse 69, 60325, Frankfurt-am-Main) has representative offices abroad.

Tourist Offices Abroad

If you have questions or would like to receive printed material about Germany before leaving, contact the GNTO branch in or closest to your home country:

Austria (☎ 01-513 27 92; deutschland.reisen@d-z-t.com; Schubertring 12, 1010 Vienna)

Belgium (☎ 02-245 9700; gntobru@d-z-t.com; Gulledelle 92 Val d'Or, 1200 Brussels)

Canada (☎ 416-968 1685; www.cometogermany.com; 480 University Ave, Toronto, Ontario M5G 1V2)

France (☎ 01 40 20 07 46; www.allemagne-tourisme .com; 47 Ave de l'Opéra, 75002 Paris)

Italy (☎ 02-8474 4444; www.vacanzeingermania.com; CP 10009, 20110 Milano Isola)

Japan (☎ 03-3586 0380; www.visit-germany.jp; 7-5-56 Akasaka, Minato-ku, Tokyo 107-0052)

Netherlands (☎ 020-697 8066; www.duitsverkeers bureau.nl; Hoogoorddreef 76, 1101 BG Amsterdam ZO)

Spain (☎ 91-429 3551; www.alemania-turismo.com; San Agustin 2, 1era derecha, Plaza de las Cortes, 28014 Madrid)

Switzerland (☎ 01-213 22 00; gntozrh@d-z-t.com; Talstrasse 62, 8001 Zurich)

UK (☎ 020-7317 0908; gntolon@d-z-t.com; PO Box 2695, London W1A 3TN)

USA (☎ 212-661-7200; www.cometogermany.com; Chanin Bldg, 122 East 42nd St, 52nd Floor, New York, NY 10168-0072)

VISAS

European Union (EU) nationals and those from certain other European countries, including Switzerland and Poland, require only a passport or their national identity card to enter and stay in Germany. Citizens of Australia, Canada, Israel, Japan, New Zealand and the US are among those countries that need only a valid passport (no visa) if entering as tourists for up to three months.

Nationals from most other countries need a so-called Schengen Visa, named after a treaty signed in 1995 in the Luxembourg town by that name by seven European Union countries to end internal border checkpoints and passport controls. Other countries later joined, bringing the total to 15. They are: Austria, Belgium, Denmark, Finland, France, Germany, Iceland, Italy, Greece, Luxembourg, Netherlands, Norway, Portugal, Spain and Sweden. With

a Schengen Visa, you may enter any one of these countries and then travel freely throughout the entire zone. Apply with the embassy or consulate of the country that is your primary destination. A Schengen Visa is valid for stays up to 90 days. For full details, see www.eurovisa.info.

Residency status in any Schengen country makes a visa unnecessary, regardless of your nationality.

Three-month tourist visas are issued by German embassies or consulates. Applications usually take between two and 10 days to process but it's always best to inquire as early as possible. You'll need a valid passport and must demonstrate that you have sufficient funds to finance your stay. Visa fees vary depending on the country. See p755 for more information on passports.

WOMEN TRAVELLERS

Younger German women especially are quite outspoken and emancipated, but self-confidence hasn't yet translated into equality in the workplace where women are often still kept out of middle- and top-level management positions, have a harder time finding a job that matches their qualifications, and receive lower pay than men for equal work. Sexual harassment in the workplace is more commonplace and tolerated here than in countries like the USA and Australia.

Safety Precautions

Germany is generally a safe place for women to travel, even alone and even in the cities. Of course, this doesn't mean you can let your guard down and trust your life to every stranger. Simply use the same common sense that you would at home.

Getting hassled in the streets happens infrequently and is usually limited to wolf-whistles and unwanted stares. In crowded situations, ie on public transport or at events, groping is a rare possibility.

Going alone to cafés and restaurants is perfectly acceptable, even at night. In the cities at least, bars and clubs don't have to be off-limits either. If you don't want company, most men will respect a firm but polite 'no thank you'. If someone continues to harass you, protesting loudly will often make the offender slink away with embarrassment – or will at least draw attention to your predicament.

Physical attack is very unlikely but, of course, it does happen. If you are assaulted, call the police immediately (☎ 110) or, if you're too traumatised to do that, contact a women's crisis centre whose staff will provide all kinds of emotional and practical support. Listed here are the hotlines in the bigger cities. Note that these offices are not usually staffed around the clock, but you're free to call any office from anywhere.

Berlin ☎ 030-251 2828 or 615 4243 or 216 8888
Bremen ☎ 0421-151 81 or 151 00
Cologne ☎ 0221-562 035
Frankfurt-am-Main ☎ 069-709 494
Hamburg ☎ 040-255 566
Hanover ☎ 0511-698 646 or 332 112
Leipzig ☎ 0341-306 5246
Munich ☎ 089-763 737 or 721 1715
Nuremberg ☎ 0911-284 400
Stuttgart ☎ 0711-285 9001 or 296 432

WORK

Non-EU citizens cannot work legally in Germany without a residence permit (*Aufenthaltserlaubnis*) and a work permit (*Arbeitserlaubnis*). EU citizens don't need a work permit but they must have a residence permit, although obtaining one is a mere formality.

Nationals from EU countries, Australia, Canada, New Zealand, USA, Israel and Japan may get a residence permit from the *Ausländerbehörde* (Foreigners' Office) *after* their arrival in Germany. Everyone else must file an application for one with a German embassy or consulate in their home country before coming to Germany. Work permits are issued by the *Arbeitsamt* (National Employment Office) after you get here.

Obtaining these permits is tedious and practically impossible for most people. However, Germany's lack of skilled professionals, most notably in information technology, led to the introduction of a temporary work visa (the so-called Greencard) for IT specialities in 1999. Although this particular scheme will expire by the end of 2004, starting in 2005 new reforms will enable qualified workers in any field (not just IT) to obtain work permits in Germany as long as they can demonstrate that there are no qualified Germans to fill the job. For more details, see www.germany-info.org (in English) or contact the German embassy or consulate in your country.

Finding work in Germany is no easy task, largely because of the country's lingering high unemployment rate. One place to start looking for a job is the **Zentrale Arbeitsvermittlung** (Central Placement Office; ☎ 0228-7130; fax 0228-7130), which maintains job banks that list full-time and part-time positions, as well as internships, at www.arbeitsamt.de (German language only). Information can also be obtained from local Arbeitsamt offices in most towns. Between May and September, they may be contacted for help with finding seasonal job opportunities.

Private placement agencies, temp agencies and the classified sections of major newspapers are also routes to take in finding employment.

Au Pair

Work as an au pair is relatively easy to find and can be done legally even by non-EU citizens. There's no need to speak fluent German, although most families require at least rudimentary language skills. A useful guide is *The Au Pair and Nanny's Guide to Working Abroad* by Susan Griffith & Sharon Legg.

Teaching English

You may be able to find work teaching English at language schools or privately, but you will still need work and residency permits, as well as valid health insurance at all times. Teaching English is certainly no way to get rich, but it might help to keep your head above water or prolong a trip. The hourly rate varies dramatically – from €15 per hour to about €40 for qualified people in large cities. Local papers are the best way to advertise, but notice boards at universities, photocopy shops or even local supermarkets are also good place to start.

Working Holidays

Citizens of Australia, New Zealand and Canada between the ages of 18 and 30 may apply for a Working Holiday Visa, which entitles them to work any job anywhere in Germany for up to 90 days in a 12-month period. There are no educational or language prerequisites, but you must show proof of health insurance valid in Germany and of sufficient funds for the duration of your stay (about €300 a month, although this varies). The German embassies in those countries have full details (see German Embassies p744).

Transport

Getting There & Away	**755**
Entering the Country	755
Air	755
Land	759
Lake	761
Sea	761
Getting Around	**763**
Air	763
Bicycle	763
Boat	764
Bus	764
Car & Motorcycle	765
Hitching	768
Local Transport	769
Train	769

GETTING THERE & AWAY

ENTERING THE COUNTRY

Arriving in Germany is usually a very straightforward procedure. There are no border checkpoints between Germany and other EU countries. If you're arriving from a non-EU country, you'll have to show your passport and visa (if required, see Visas, p753) and clear customs.

Passport

Passports must be valid for at least six months after the end of you trip. Citizens of most Western countries can enter Germany without a visa; other nationals may need a Schengen Visa; see Visas p753 for details.

AIR
Airports

Frankfurt International Airport (FRA; ☎ 01805-372 4636; www.frankfurt-airport.de) is the main gateway for transcontinental flights, although **Düsseldorf** (DUS; ☎ 0211-4210; www.duesseldorf-international.de) and **Munich** (MUC; ☎ 089-975 00; www.munich-airport.de) also receive their share of overseas air traffic. There are also size-

able airports in **Hamburg** (HAM; ☎ 50 750; www.ham.airport.de), **Cologne/Bonn** (CGN; ☎ 02203-404 001; www.airport-cgn.de) and **Stuttgart** (STR; ☎ 94 80; www.flughafen-stuttgart.de), and smaller ones in such cities as Bremen, Dresden, Erfurt, Hanover, Leipzig, Münster-Osnabrück and Nuremberg.

Some of Europe's new budget airlines – Ryan Air in particular – keep their fares low by flying to some pretty odd and remote airports, some of which are little more than recycled military airstrips. The biggest of these is **Frankfurt-Hahn** (HNN; ☎ 06543-509 200; www.hahn-airport.de), which is actually near the Moselle River, about 110km northwest of Frankfurt proper.

For details about individual German airports, including getting to and from information, see the destination chapters.

Airlines
NATIONAL CARRIERS

Most of the world's major airlines serve Frankfurt at the very least. The following list contains telephone numbers in Germany for reservations, changes to flights, and information. For contact information in your home country, see the airline's website. Airlines flying to and from Germany:

Aeroflot (SU; ☎ 0211-320 491; www.aeroflot.com)
Air Canada (AC; ☎ 01805-0247 226; www.aircanada.ca)
Air France (AF; ☎ 01805-830 830; www.airfrance.com)
Air New Zealand (NZ; ☎ 0800-5494 5494; www.airnz.co.nz)
Alitalia (AZ; ☎ 01805-074 747; www.alitalia.com)
American Airlines (AA; ☎ 0180-324-2324; www.aa.com)

THINGS CHANGE...

The information in this chapter is particularly vulnerable to change. Check directly with the airline or a travel agent to make sure you understand how a fare (and ticket you may buy) works and be aware of the security requirements for international travel. Shop carefully. The details given in this chapter should be regarded as pointers and are not a substitute for your own careful, up-to-date research.

British Airways (BA; ☎ 01805-266 522; www
.britishairways.com)
Cathay Pacific Airways (CX; ☎ 069-7100 8800;
www.cathaypacific.com)
Continental Air Lines (CO; ☎ 0180-321 2610; www
.continental.com)
Delta Air Lines (DL; ☎ 0180-333 7880; www.delta.com)
Iberia (IB; ☎ 01803-000 613; www.iberia.com)
KLM (KL; ☎ 01805-254 750; www.klm.com)
LTU (LT; ☎ 0211-941 8888; www.ltu.de)
Lufthansa (LH; ☎ 01803-803 803; www.lufthansa.de)
Malev Hungarian Airlines (MA; ☎ 069-238 5800;
www.malev.hu)
Olympic Airways (OA; ☎ 0211-849 41; www.olympic
-airways.gr)
Qantas Airways (QF; ☎ 01805-250 620;
www.qantas.com.au)
Scandinavian Airlines/SAS (SK; ☎ 01803-234 023;
www.scandinavian.net)
Singapore Airlines (SQ; ☎ 069-719 5200; www
.singaporeair.com)
South African Airways (SA; ☎ 069-2998 0320;
www.flysaa.com)
Swiss (LX; ☎ 01803-000 334; www.swiss.com)
Turkish Airlines (TK; ☎ 0211-373 062; www
.turkishairlines.de)
United Airlines (UA; ☎ 069-5007 0387; www.ual.com)

LOW-COST AIRLINES

Budget airlines have proliferated in Europe, especially in the UK, in recent years. Tickets must usually be booked directly with the airline, which is best done online. Phone reservations usually incur a surcharge of €5 to €10.

Below is an overview of airlines currently offering flights to Germany. Note that some adjust their flight plans seasonally, so not all connections may be available year round. We've listed call centres in Germany and the airline's home country; check the website to see if there's also one in your country:

Air Berlin (AB; ☎ 01805-737 800; www.airberlin.com)
Flies between London-Stansted and Berlin-Tegel, Dortmund, Düsseldorf, Hamburg, Hanover, Mönchengladbach and Paderborn. Also has many flights to/from Barcelona, Madrid, Milan, Rome and other southern European airports.

bmibaby (WW; ☎ 01805-0264 2229 in Germany, 0870-264-2229 in the UK; www.bmibaby.com) Has flights from East Midlands and Cardiff airports to Munich.

Deutsche BA (DI; ☎ 01805-359 3222 in Germany; www.flydba.com) London-Gatwick to Berlin-Tegel, and also from Venice and Nice to Hamburg and Berlin-Tegel.

> **DEPARTURE TAX**
>
> A departure tax of around €4 to €6 per person and airport security fees are included in the price of an airline ticket purchased in Germany. You shouldn't have to pay any more fees at the airport.

---

duo (VB; ☎ 0711-490 813 040 in Germany, 0817-7000 700 in the UK ; www.duo.com) Birmingham to Berlin-Tegel, Cologne and Stuttgart.

easy Jet (U2; ☎ 01803-654 321 in Germany, 0871 7500 100 in the UK; www.easyjet.com) London-Stansted to Munich.

German Wings (4U; ☎ 01805-955 855 in Germany, 0208-321 7255 in the UK; www.germanwings.com) Flights to Cologne/Bonn from London, Edinburgh and Milan. Also has flights to Cologne and Stuttgart from Madrid, Barcelona, Rome, Budapest and Prague.

Germania Express (ST; ☎ 01805-737 100 in Germany, 01292-511 000 in the UK; www.gexx.com) Flies to Berlin-Tegel from such destinations as Glasgow-Prestwick, Moskow-Domodedovo and Lisbon.

Hapag Lloyd Express (HLX; ☎ 0180-509 3509; www.hlx.com) Flies to Hanover, Cologne and Stuttgart mostly from Italian and Spanish cities, including Milan, Naples, Rome and Barcelona.

Ryan Air (FR; ☎ 0190 170 100 in Germany, €0.62/min; 0871-246 016 in the UK; www.ryanair.com) Flies from London-Stansted to Frankfurt-Hahn, Berlin-Schönefeld, Hamburg-Lübeck, Karlsruhe-Baden-Baden, Friedrichhafen and Leipzig-Altenburg. Also has flights from Glasgow-Prestwick, Bournemouth, Shannon, Kerry and major Scandinavian and Italian cities to Frankfurt-Hahn.

Sky Europe (NE; ☎ 069-5098 5222 in Germany, 02-4850 1111 in Slovakia; www.skyeurope.com) Eastern European start-up flies to Stuttgart and Berlin-Tempelhof from Bratislava.

V Bird (☎ 0190-172 500; www.v-bird.com) Based at Niederrhein airport near Xanten in North Rhine-Westphalia, this new airline's destinations include Copenhagen, Helsinki, Vienna, Rome, Nice, Munich and Berlin-Schönefeld.

Volareweb.com (☎ 0800 101 4169 in Germany; 899 700 007 in Italy; www.volareweb.com) Italian airline with service to Frankfurt-Hahn from Venice, and Brindisi, and to Berlin-Schönefeld from Milan, Rome and Brindisi.

Tickets

Since the aeroplane ticket eats the single biggest chunk out of most people's travel budget, it's wise to spend a little time shopping around. Basically, timing is key when it comes to snapping up cheap fares. As a rule of thumb, you can save a bundle by booking as early as possible (at least three weeks, more during the summer) and by travelling midweek (Tuesday to Thursday) and in the off-season (October to March/April in the case of Germany). Departures in the evening may also be less costly than the daytime flights ever popular with the suit brigades. Some airlines offer lower fares if you stay over a Saturday.

Your best friend in ferreting out bargain fares is the Internet. Discount online agencies such as www.travelocity.com and www.expedia.com should be your first stop, but also check the airlines' own websites for promotional fares, which may have to be booked online. This is especially important with most of the low-frills carriers such as Ryan Air and easyJet, which only sell to travellers directly and don't even show up in the computerised systems used by travel agencies.

If you're North America–based and aren't picky about the airline or departure times, you could easily snag a rock-bottom ticket through Priceline (www.priceline.com). You name the fare you're willing to pay and then sit back and see if an airline takes the bite.

Another way to learn about late-breaking bargain fares is by signing on to airlines' free email newsletters, which are usually sent out weekly. Even the old-fashioned newspaper can yield bargains, especially in times of fare wars when airlines plaster the travel sections with giant ads.

Speaking of old-fashioned, if you prefer to make your bookings at a brick-and-mortar agency, STA Travel and Flight Centre, both with worldwide branches, are among the most established companies with extra-special deals for students and anyone under 26. Travel agents are also an invaluable resource in planning a complex travel itinerary.

COURIER FLIGHTS

If you're on a flexible schedule and travelling solo, flying as a courier can be an inexpensive way to go. Couriers accompany freight to its destination in exchange for a discounted ticket. You don't have to handle any shipment personally but simply deliver the freight papers to a representative of the courier company at your destination. Your luggage is limited to what you can carry on

and there may also be other restrictions, such as the length of your stay.

Most courier flights to Europe originate in the US, although some also depart from New Zealand, Australia and Asian cities. Almost all go to London, from where you must organise your own onward trip to Germany.

International Association of Air Travel Couriers (IAATC; ☎ 352-475-1584; www.courier.org) and **Air Courier Association** (ACA; ☎ 800-282-1202; www.aircourier.org) are both US-based organisations that keep track of routes offered by courier companies. For an annual membership fee (US$45 and US$39, respectively) you gain access to their database of upcoming flights.

From Australia

Many airlines compete for business between Australia and Europe, with fares starting at about A$2300/2000 in high/low season. With Europe almost halfway around the globe, a Round-the-World (RTW) ticket may work out to be cheaper than a regular return fare. Some travel agencies, particularly smaller ones, advertise cheap airfares in the travel sections of weekend newspapers, such as the Melbourne *Age* and the *Sydney Morning Herald*.

STA Travel (☎ 1300 733 035; www.statravel.com.au) has branches throughout the country, as does **Flight Centre** (☎ 133 133; www.flightcentre.com.au). For online bookings, try www.travel.com.au.

From Canada

Lufthansa and Air Canada fly to Frankfurt from all major Canadian airports, with prices starting at C$1500/800 in high/low season. **Travel Cuts** (☎ 800-667-2887; www.travelcuts.com) is Canada's national student travel agency. The *Globe & Mail*, the Toronto *Star* and the Vancouver *Sun* carry travel agencies' advertisements and are a good place to look for cheap fares. For online bookings try www.expedia.ca and www.travelocity.ca.

From Continental Europe

Air Berlin, German Wings and Ryan Air are among the budget airlines that connect European cities with German airports. One-way fares to Berlin can be as low as €99 from Madrid or Barcelona, €39 from Milan or €59 from Rome. See Low-Cost Carriers (p756) for a summary of routes.

National carriers such as Air France, Alitalia, Iberia, SAS and, of course, Lufthansa offer numerous flights to all major German airports and may well offer some sort of deal, so shop around.

Recommended travel agencies include **CTS Viaggi** (☎ 06 462 0431; www.cts.it) in Italy, and **Barcelo Viajes** (☎ 902 116 226; www.barceloviajes.com) and **Nouvelles Frontières** (☎ 90 217 09 79; www .nouvelles-frontieres.es) in Spain. In France, try the following:

Anyway (☎ 0892 893 892; www.anyway.fr)
Lastminute (☎ 0892 705 000; www.lastminute.fr)
Nouvelles Frontières (☎ 0825 000 747; www .nouvelles-frontieres.fr)
OTU Voyages (☎ 0820 817 817, €0.12 per min; www.otu.fr) This agency specialises in student and youth travellers.
Voyageurs du Monde (☎ 01 40 15 11 15; www .vdm.com)

From New Zealand
RTW fares usually offer the best value for travel to Germany from New Zealand. Depending on which airline you choose, you may fly across Asia, with possible stopovers in India, Bangkok or Singapore, or across the USA, with possible stopovers in Honolulu, Los Angeles or one of the Pacific Islands. Prices are similar to those from Australia.

The travel section of the *New Zealand Herald* carries adverts from travel agencies. Both **Flight Centre** (☎ 0800 243 544; www .flightcentre.co.nz) and **STA Travel** (☎ 0508 782 872; www.statravel.co.nz) have branches throughout the country. The site www.travel.co.nz is recommended for online bookings.

From the UK & Ireland
Travel to Germany from the UK and Ireland has become very inexpensive thanks to the flood of low-cost carriers that has swept in over the past few years. Rock-bottom fares start as low as £15 one way, including airport taxes, although these tickets are naturally snapped up quickly. For details about which airlines fly where in Germany, see Low-Cost Carriers (p756).

The dominant national carriers are Lufthansa and British Airways with umpteen flights connecting all major airports in all three countries. Standard fares are higher, of course, but this generally buys you greater flexibility, probably more con-

venient departure times, better service, fewer restrictions and shorter commutes to/from airports. Also look for special deals online or in the travel pages of the weekend broadsheet newspapers, in *Time Out*, the *Evening Standard* and the free magazine *TNT*.

Recommended travel agencies include the following:
Bridge the World (☎ 0870 444 7474; www.b-t-w.co.uk)
Flightbookers (☎ 0870 010 7000; www.ebookers.com)
Flight Centre (☎ 0870 890 8099; www.flightcentre.co.uk)
North-South Travel (☎ 01245-608 291; www.north southtravel.co.uk) North-South Travel donates part of its profit to projects in the developing world.
Quest Travel (☎ 0870 442 3542; www.questtravel.com)
STA Travel (☎ 0870 160 0599; www.statravel.co.uk)
Trailfinders (www.trailfinders.co.uk)
Travel Bag (☎ 0870 890 1456; www.travelbag.co.uk)

From the USA
Flights to Germany from major cities in the US abound and bargains are often available. Most flights land in Frankfurt, where you catch a connecting domestic flight.

Lufthansa has flights to Frankfurt from 14 US cities, including Atlanta, Boston, Chicago, Houston, Los Angeles, Miami, New York, San Francisco and Washington DC. Major US carriers serving Frankfurt are Delta, US Airways, American, United, Northwest (with KLM) and Continental.

There are also direct flights to Munich from Atlanta, Chicago, New York, Philadelphia, San Francisco and Washington DC. Düsseldorf is served by LTU from such airports as Miami and Los Angeles (summer only).

Airfares rise and fall in a cyclical pattern. The lowest fares are available from early November to mid-December and then again from mid-January to Easter, gradually rising in the following months. Peak months are July and August, after which prices start dropping again. The cheapest fares are around US$700/400 return in high/low season from New York, US$800/ 450 from Chicago and US$1000/500 from Los Angeles.

If you're flexible with your travel dates, flying stand-by may save you a bundle. Fares offered through **Air Hitch** (☎ 877-247-4482; www.air-hitch.org) can be as low as US$130 one way from east coast cities and US$230 from the west coast. Flights may not get you exactly where you want to go in Germany, but the savings could be so huge that it's worth booking a connecting flight or buying a train ticket.

STA Travel (☎ 800-781-4040; www.statravel.com) and **FlightCentre** (☎ 866-967-5351; www.flightcentre .us) are both reliable budget travel agencies offering online bookings and brick-and-mortar branches throughout the country. To scour the web for cheap fares, you might also try:

www.cheaptickets.com
www.expedia.com
www.lowestfare.com
www.orbitz.com
www.travelocity.com
www.sidestep.com Travel search engine that searches dozens of online agencies simultaneously.

LAND
Bus
BERLIN LINIEN BUS
Berlin-based **Berlin Linien Bus** (www.berlinlinien bus.de) has frequent service between German cities, especially Berlin, and the rest of Europe, including many Eastern European destinations. See also Bus p764.

Following are a few sample single/return fares:

Route	Fare	Duration
Berlin–Amsterdam	€49/89	9 hrs
Berlin–Moscow	€66/113	10½ hrs
Berlin–Prague	€32/50	6½ hrs
Cologne–St Petersburg	€95/148	24 hrs
Dresden–Budapest	€52/93	13½ hrs
Hamburg–Bratislava	€61/104	19 hrs

BUSABOUT
A UK-based company, **Busabout** (☎ 0207-950 1661 in the UK; www.busabout.com) runs coaches along interlocking European circuits. In Germany, buses make stops in Berlin, Dresden, Frankfurt and Munich. There is no upper age limit, but those under 26, students and teachers qualify for lower rates. Two types of passes are available:

Consecutive Pass buys unlimited travel within a specific period of time and costs £359/509 (€599/839) for one/two months at the full fare or £319/459 (€429/759) with the discount.

Flexi Pass allows travel for a set number of days within a certain period, for instance seven days within one month (full-fare/discount £219/199 or €359/329) or 12 days within two months (£349/309 or €579/509).

For other options or to buy a pass, check the website. Passes are also available from such travel agencies as STA Travel and Flight Centre.

In many cities, buses drop off and pick up at centrally located hostels.

EUROLINES
The umbrella organisation of 31 European coach operators, **Eurolines** (www.eurolines.com) serves 500 destinations in 30 countries across Europe, including most major German cities. Its website has links to each national company's site with detailed fare and route information, promotional offers, contact numbers and, in many cases, an online booking system. Children between the ages of four and 12 pay half price and there's a 10% discount for teens, students and seniors.

In Germany, Eurolines is represented by **Deutsche Touring** (☎ 069-790 350; www.deutsche -touring.com) company, which sells tickets only through Deutsche Bahn travel agencies inside the Reisezentrum ticket offices found at major train stations and through DER agencies (look for the Deutsche Bahn logo).

Sample standard one-way/return fares and trip durations are:

Route	Price	Duration
Amsterdam–Berlin	€49/89	10 hrs
Brussels–Frankfurt	€32/54	5¼ hrs
London–Cologne	£50/67	13 hrs
London–Munich	£60/81	19½ hrs
Prague–Freiburg	CZK 1700/3050	13 hrs
Venice–Cologne	€106/180	20 hrs

For frequent travellers, there's the **Eurolines Pass**, which allows for unlimited travel within a 15/30/60-day period between 31 European cities, including Berlin, Cologne, Frankfurt, Hamburg and Munich. From June to mid-September, the cost is €285/ 425/490 (£174/259/299) for full-fare passes and €185/250/310 (£145/209/229) for discounted passes. The rest of the year, full-fare rates drop to €245/345/380 (£135/189/239), while discount passes are €220/310/390 (£113/153/189). Make reservations for onward journeys at least 24 hours in advance, preferably earlier during the busy summer season.

TRANSPORT

GULLIVER'S

Gulliver's (☎ 030-3110 2110 in Berlin, 00800-4855 4837 from outside Germany; www.gullivers.de), another Berlin-based company, covers a good range of international destinations to and from Berlin, Hamburg, Hanover, Nuremberg, Munich and Dresden. Services include Berlin–Amsterdam (€49/89 one way/return, nine hours), Bremen–Krakow (€66/106, 18 hours) and Dresden–Vienna (€38/68, seven hours). Children aged four to 12 pay half price; students and those under 26 or over 60 get about 20% off the standard fare.

Car & Motorcycle

Travelling to Germany with your own car or motorcycle is easy. All you need is a valid driving licence, your car registration certificate and proof of insurance. Foreign cars must display a nationality sticker unless they have official Euro-Plates (number plates that include their country's Euro symbol).

The main gateways to southern Germany are Munich, Freiburg and Passau. Coming from Poland or the Czech Republic may entail delays at the border, although this is likely to change now that those countries have become members of the EU. For information on driving within Germany see p765.

Coming from the UK, high-speed **Eurotunnel** (☎ 08705-35 35 35 in the UK; www.eurotunnel.com) shuttle trains whisk cars, motorbikes, bicycles and coaches in 35 minutes from Folkestone through the Channel Tunnel to Coquelles, 5km southwest of Calais, in soundproofed and air-conditioned comfort. From there, you can be in Germany in about three hours.

Shuttles run 24 hours a day, every day of the year, with up to five departures an hour during peak periods (one an hour from 1am to 5pm). Many different price schemes exist, depending on the day and time of travel, the length of your stay, how early you book and how much flexibility you need. The standard short-stay return fare (stays of between two and five days) is £197 (€288) for cars and £98 (€143) for motorcycles. The rate goes up to €463/230 (£317/158) for stays over five days. For full details, including promotional fares, check the website.

For details about bringing your car across the Channel by ferry, see Sea p762.

Hitching & Ride Services

Lonely Planet does not recommend hitching, but travellers intending to hitch shouldn't have too many problems getting to and from Germany via the main autobahns and highways. See Hitching p768 for a discussion of the potential risks.

Aside from hitching, the cheapest way to get to or away from Germany is as a paying passenger in a private car. In Germany, such rides are arranged by *Mitfahrzentralen* (rideshare agencies) found in all major cities and many smaller ones as well (see listings in the destination chapters throughout this guide). Most belong to umbrella networks like **ADM** (☎ 194 40; www.mitfahrzentralen.de) or **Citynetz** (☎ 01805-194 444; www.citynetz-mitfahrzentrale.de). Women wanting to share a ride with other women only could check www.she-drives.de (German only).

Fares comprise a commission to the agency and a per-kilometre charge to the driver. Expect to pay about €16 (one way) Hamburg–Berlin, €50 Berlin–Paris and €23 Munich–Vienna.

The people answering the phone at Mitfahrzentrale offices usually speak English. If you arrange a ride a few days in advance, it's a good idea to call the driver the night before and again on the departure morning to make sure they're definitely going.

Train

Long-distance trains connecting major German cities with those in other countries are called EuroCity (EC) trains. The most comfortable travel option is to take an overnight train. You can choose between *Schlafwagen* (sleepers), which are comfortable compartments for up to three people, with washbasin; *Liegewagen* (couchettes), which sleep between four and six people; and *Sitzwagen* (seat carriage), which have roomy, reclinable seats. For full details, contact DB's night train specialists (☎ 01805-141 514 in Germany; www.nachtzugreise.de).

On daytime trains, reservations (€2.60) are highly recommended, especially during the peak summer season and around major holidays. They can be made as late as a few minutes before departure.

EURAIL PASS

Eurail Passes (www.eurail.com) are convenient and good value if you're covering lots of territory in a limited time. They're valid for unlimited travel on national railways (and some private lines) in 17 European countries and also cover many ferries, eg from Finland to Germany, as well as KD Line's river cruises on the Rhine and Moselle. Available only to non-residents of Europe, they should be bought before leaving your home country, although a limited number of outlets, listed on the website, also sell them in Europe.

The standard Eurailpass provides unlimited 1st class travel and costs US$588/762 for 15/21 days and US$946/1338/1654 for one/two/three months of travel. If you're under 26, you qualify for the Eurailpass Youth and prices drop to US$414/534/664/938/1160.

A variety of other options, such as group passes and flexi passes are available as well. Children under age four travel free; those between ages four and 11 pay half price.

The Eurail website has full details, including links to agencies all over the world selling these passes.

EUROSTAR

The Channel Tunnel has opened up a land link between Britain and the continent. The **Eurostar** (www.eurostar.com) needs only two hours and 20 minutes to travel from London to Brussels, where you can change to regular or other high-speed trains, such as the French Thalys to or the ICE train, to destinations in Germany.

Eurostar has a complicated and variable price structure, depending on such factors as class, time of day and season. Children, rail-pass holders, and those aged between 12 and 25 and over 60 qualify for discounts. Numerous promotions and special packages become available all the time. You can buy Eurostar tickets from travel agencies, major train stations or on the Eurostar website.

INTERRAIL & EURO DOMINO PASSES

If you've been a permanent resident of a European or North African country for at least six months, you qualify for the InterRail Pass. It divides Europe into eight zones (Germany shares one with Denmark, Austria and Switzerland) and is available for 12 or 22 days of unlimited travel in any one zone, or longer for travel in more zones. Prices for those under/over 25 are

> ### SECURITY
> In recent years, the number of crimes committed on trains – especially at night – has increased. There have been horror stories of passengers getting robbed after being drugged or made unconscious with gas blown in through the ventilation ducts. While this should not stop you from using the train, it pays to be aware and to take a few precautions. Never leave your baggage out of sight, especially the bag holding your personal documents, tickets and money. Lock your suitcases, backpacks or bags; better yet, buy a lock and fasten them to the luggage rack. In general, travel in the daytime is safer, though it's easier to catch some sleep (and save accommodation costs) on night trains. If you travel at night, at least try to lock the compartment, if possible. If you're travelling in a sleeping compartment (as opposed to a couchette), it will be lockable and only the attendant will have a key. Women can request a berth in single-sex compartments.

€182/266 for 11 days and €219/318 for 22 days in one zone.

The EuroDomino Pass is good for three to eight days of travel within one month in 27 European countries. It costs €135/180 for under/over 25 for three days, with each additional day priced at €13/18. Prices vary slightly by country where you buy this pass.

Both passes are sold at major train stations throughout Europe.

LAKE

The Romanshorn–Friedrichshafen car ferry provides the quickest way across Lake Constance between Switzerland and Germany. It's operated year round by **Schweizerische Bodensee-Schiffahrtsgesellschaft** (☎ 071-466 7888 in Switzerland), takes 40 minutes and costs €5.80. Bicycles are €3.80.

SEA

Germany's main ferry ports are Kiel, Lübeck and Travemünde in Schleswig-Holstein, and Rostock and Sassnitz (Rügen Island) in Mecklenburg-Western Pomerania. All have services to Scandinavia. Ferries to the UK leave from Cuxhaven in Schleswig-Holstein. Return tickets are often cheaper than two one-way tickets. Keep in mind that prices fluctuate dramatically according to the season, the day and time of departure and, for overnight ferries, cabin amenities. All prices quoted are for one-way fares. For additional information, see Getting There & Away in the individual port towns.

From Denmark
GEDSER–ROSTOCK
Scandlines (☎ 01805-722 635 4637 in Germany; www.scandlines.de) runs year-round ferries at least eight times daily between Rostock and Gedser, about 100km south of Copenhagen. The trip (two hours) costs €84 from Friday to Sunday, mid-June to August for cars up to 6m in length (€62 at all other times). Walk-on passengers pay €5/8 in low season/high season. The fare for one person with bicycle is €11 year round.

RØDBY–PUTTGARDEN
Scandlines operates a 45-minute service every half-hour for €47 for a regular car and up to nine passengers. Foot passengers pay €6 from mid-June to August and €3 at other times. It's €8 if you bring a bicycle.

RØNNE–SASSNITZ
From March to October, Scandlines operates daily ferries to/from this town on Bornholm Island. The trip takes 3¾ hours and costs €100/150 for midweek/weekend travel from mid-June to August and €65 at other times. Foot passengers pay €12/17; bicycles are €5 extra.

From Finland
HELSINKI–ROSTOCK (VIA TALLIN)
Silja Line (☎ 0451-589 90 in Rostock; www.silja.com) plys this route from June to mid-September. The journey between Helsinki and Rostock takes 24 hours. Prices start at €67 for a chair, rising to €538 for a swish single cabin.

HELSINKI–TRAVEMÜNDE
Finnlines (☎ 0451-150 7443 in Lübeck, 09-251 0200 in Helsinki; www.ferrycenter.fi) goes to Travemünde (near Lübeck) daily year round. Fares start at €190 per berth.

From Norway
OSLO–KIEL
Color Line (☎ 0431-730 0300 in Kiel; www.colorline.de) makes this 20-hour journey almost daily.

The fare, including a berth in the most basic two-bed cabin, is around €150. Students pay half-price in the off season.

From Sweden
GOTHENBURG–KIEL
The daily overnight ferry run by **Stena Line** (☎ 0431-9099 in Kiel; www.stenaline.com) takes 13½ hours and costs €40 to €75 for foot passengers, depending on the season. Single sleeping berths in four-bunk cabins start at €19.

TRELLEBORG–ROSTOCK
This **Scandlines** (☎ 01805-722 635 4637 in Germany; www.scandlines.de) service runs once or twice daily, takes between 5¾ and 6½ hours and costs €115/135 midweek/weekend from mid-June to August and €95/110 day/night trips otherwise. Foot passengers pay €15/20 low/high season, or €16/22 if you bring a bike.

TT-Line (☎ 040-360 1442 in Hamburg; www.ttline.de) makes the same crossing in about 5½ hours. The complicated tariffs vary according to number of people and date of travel; a tourist car with up to five people starts at around €119, while walk-ons pay about €22.

TRELLEBORG–SASSNITZ
Scandlines operates a quick ferry to Sweden, popular with day-trippers. There are five departures daily and the trip takes 3¾ hours. Cars up to 6m cost €90/105 midweek/weekend from mid-June to August and €85 the rest of the year. The fare for passengers only is €10/15 low/high season and €14/20 for those bringing a bicycle.

TRELLEBORG–TRAVEMÜNDE
TT-Line also operates up to five ferries daily on this route, which takes seven hours and costs from €18 for foot passengers. Cars, including all passengers, start at €98. Students, seniors and children pay half-price. Bicycles are €5.

From The UK
HARWICH–CUXHAVEN
The car ferry **DFDS Seaways** (☎ 08705-333 000 in the UK; www.dfdsseaways.com) operates year round at least three times weekly and takes 19½ hours. One-way fares for a passenger in a four-berth inner cabin start from £60 in the low season (around November to April) and rise to £85 in July and August. Friday and Saturday departures pay a £10

supplement. Bicycles are free. Various discounts are available for children, seniors and students.

VIA CALAIS (FRANCE)

Depending on where you're headed in Germany, travelling by ferry via Calais may be the cheapest and most convenient option. **Hoverspeed** (☎ 0870-240 8070; www.hoverspeed.co.uk) operates Seacat catamarans that cross the channel from Dover in about one hour. The fare is a flat £26 for foot passengers and from £133 for cars (including driver and two passengers) or £81 for motorbikes (including two people). Check the website for deals, discounts and bookings.

Calais is about 400km from Cologne and 450km from Trier on the Moselle.

GETTING AROUND

AIR

Most large and many smaller German cities have their own airports (also see Airports p755) and numerous carriers operate domestic flights within Germany. Lufthansa, of course, has the densest route network, especially now that it has teamed up with five smaller airlines – Augsburg Air, Air Dolomiti, Contact Air, Eurowings and Lufthansa City Line – operating as Lufthansa Regional. Other airlines offering domestic flights include Air Berlin, Cirrus Air, Deutsche BA and German Wings.

Unless you're flying from one end of the country to the other, say Berlin–Munich or Hamburg–Munich, planes are only marginally quicker than trains if you factor in the time it takes to get to/from the airports. Fares have become more competitive in recent years but generally prices are still pretty steep and designed with business travellers in mind. With some research, though, you may be able to unearth some good deals, either with the help of a travel agent or on the Internet. For instance, at the time of writing Lufthansa offered €92 tickets on flights anywhere within Germany, while Air Berlin had €69 fares from Nuremberg to Hamburg or Dortmund.

BICYCLE

Bicycle touring (Radwandern) through Germany is fun, popular and eminently feasible, in large part because of a dense network of lightly travelled secondary roads and dedicated bike paths. Even in the cities, you'll often find special bike lanes and pavements separated into sections for pedestrians and cyclists. Bicycles are strictly *verboten* on the autobahns.

Germany has over 200 well-signposted long-distance routes. For details, see Cycling p737.

Hire & Purchase

Practically every town in Germany has a bicycle-hire station (usually at or near the Hauptbahnhof – central train station) or a bike shop that has two-wheelers for hire. Most have a selection of city, cruising and mountain bikes, with prices ranging from €10 to €25 per day and €35 to €85 per week. A minimum deposit of €50 and/or ID is required. Some outfits also offer repair service or bicycle storage facilities.

A **call-a-bike** (www.callabike.de) scheme is currently in place in Berlin, Frankfurt and Munich. Basically, these are bikes with electronic locks parked on racks around town (particularly outside stations); to use one you phone up, give your credit card details, and they give you the code to unlock the bike and start the timer. When you're finished with it you lock it to something (preferably an official city centre rack), phone up again with the receipt number from the timer display and tell them where you parked it. You'll be charged a minimum of €5 for the service.

Hotels, especially in resort areas, sometimes keep a stable of bicycles for their guests, often at no charge.

If you plan to spend several weeks or longer in the saddle, buying a second-hand bike may work out cheaper than renting one or easier than bringing your own. Good reconditioned models start at €100. The hire stations sometimes sell used bicycles or may be able to steer you to a good place locally. You might also give the classified sections of daily newspapers and listings magazines a try, or check the notice boards at universities or hostels.

Transportation

You can take a bicycle with you on most Deutsche Bahn trains, though you'll have to buy a separate ticket (*Fahrradkarte*).

On all long-distance trains, including IC, IR, D and some ICE trains, these cost €8 and advance bookings are necessary. The cost on IRE, RE, RB and S-Bahn is €3 per trip but on certain lines it is free. If bought in combination with one of the saver tickets, such as a Länderticket or the Schönes-Wochenende-Ticket (see Costs p771), the €3 fee is good for multiple trips within one day. For full details, contact the **DB Radfahrer-Hotline** (☎ 01805-151 415; www.bahn.de). DB also publishes the useful free brochure *Bahn & Bike* (in German), which lists the free lines and all stations where you can rent bikes. It's also available for downloading.

With three-day advance notice, you can take bicycles on the Europabus (see Bus opposite). The cost is €6 for journeys up to 12 stops or €12 for longer trips. Many regional companies use buses with special bike racks. Bicycles are also allowed on practically all boat services on lakes and rivers.

BOAT

Travelling by boat is leisurely and relaxing but really more about sightseeing than getting from A to B. From April to October, boat operators in towns and villages on Germany's rivers and lakes run scenic cruises that last from one hour to all day.

For basic transport, boats are primarily used when travelling to or between the East Frisian Islands in Lower Saxony; the North Frisian Islands in Schleswig-Holstein; Helgoland, which also belongs to Schleswig-Holstein; and the islands of Poel, Rügen and Hiddensee in Mecklenburg-Western Pomerania.

KD Line has scheduled boat services on short sections of the Rhine and the Moselle. Ferries connect towns on such major lakes as the Chiemsee and Lake Starnberg in Bavaria and Lake Constance in Baden-Württemberg.

For details, see the individual entries in the destination chapters. See also River Cruises p738.

BUS

Basically, wherever there is a train, take it. Buses are generally much slower and less dependable, less efficient and less comfortable than trains. There are, however, some regions where the terrain makes train travel

more difficult or impossible; the Harz Mountains, sections of the Bavarian Forest and the Alpine foothills are among such areas.

Germany does not have a nationwide bus system, meaning that separate bus companies, each with their own tariffs and schedules, operate in the different regions.

In cities, buses converge at the central bus station (*Busbahnhof* or *Zentraler Omnibus Bahnhof/ZOB*), which is usually close or adjacent to the Hauptbahnhof. Tickets are available directly from the bus companies, which often have offices or kiosks at the bus station, or from the driver on board. Ask about special fare deals, such as day passes, weekly passes or special tourist tickets.

The frequency of service varies dramatically, depending on the destination. It can be as little as three buses daily, and sometimes even fewer at weekends. Routes geared to commuters suspend operation on weekends altogether. If you depend on buses to get around, always keep this in mind or risk finding yourself stuck in a remote place at the weekend.

Berlin Linien Bus

An umbrella for several German bus operators, **Berlin Linien Bus** (www.berlinlinienbus.de) has 30 national bus routes connecting Berlin with all corners of Germany. Destinations include major cities, such as Munich, Düsseldorf and Frankfurt, and holiday regions such as the Harz and the Bavarian Forest. One of the most popular routes is the express bus to Hamburg which makes the journey from Berlin in three hours 10 minutes up to eight times daily (€23/37 one way/return).

Tickets are available online or from travel agencies and should be booked at least three days before the travel date, although short-term bookings are possible as well. Children aged 12 and under travelling with at least one parent or grandparent are free, and discounts are available for young people between 13 and 26, students, seniors over 60 and groups of six or more. Sample full one-way/return fares to/from Berlin are Munich €68/79, Goslar (Harz) €34/37, Düsseldorf €63/71 and Frankfurt €59/76.

Europabus

Deutsche Touring (☎ 069-790 350; www.deutsche-touring.com), a subsidiary of Deutsche Bahn, offers Europabus coach services geared toward travellers on three routes within Germany. By far the most popular one, EB190, goes along the Romantic Road from Frankfurt to Füssen (April to October), while EB189 follows a segment of the Castle Road from Mannheim to Rothenburg via Heidelberg (May to September). EB178 travels through the Black Forest from Reutlingen and ends up in Strasbourg across the French border (year round).

There's one coach in either direction daily. You can break the journey as often as you'd like, but plan your stops carefully as you'll have to wait a full day for the next bus to come around (reserve a seat before disembarking). In Rothenburg, you can connect to buses headed for Munich or to Mannheim.

Tickets are available either for the entire distance or for shorter segments between any of the stops. Eurail and German Rail pass holders get a 60% discount; InterRail card holders, seniors and children aged four to 12 pay half price; and students and those under 26 qualify for 10% off. For prices and other details, see Bus p359.

CAR & MOTORCYCLE

Motoring around Germany is an enjoyable and flexible way to see the country. German roads are generally so excellent that you're less likely to spot a pothole than a UFO. The country's pride and joy are its 11,000km of *Autobahnen* (motorways, freeways), which extend to all nooks and crannies of the land. These are supplemented by an extensive network of *Bundesstrassen* (secondary roads, highways). No tolls are charged on public roads.

Along each autobahn, you'll find elaborate service areas every 40km to 60km with petrol stations, toilet facilities and restaurants; many are open 24 hours. Even more frequent are rest stops (*Rastplatz*), which usually have picnic tables and often facilities as well. If your car breaks down, you can call for help from an emergency call box, which are spaced about 2km apart. Simply lift the metal flap and follow the (pictorial) instructions.

Seat belts are mandatory for all passengers in the front and back seats. If you're caught without it on, you'll be fined €30;

TRANSPORT

Road Distances (km)

	Bamberg	Berlin	Bonn	Bremen	Cologne	Dresden	Erfurt	Essen	Frankfurt-am-Main	Freiburg im Breisgau	Hamburg	Hanover	Koblenz	Leipzig	Mainz	Munich	Nuremberg	Rostock	Saarbrücken	Stuttgart	Würzburg
Bamberg	---																				
Berlin	395	---																			
Bonn	353	596	---																		
Bremen	471	376	335	---																	
Cologne	377	558	28	307	---																
Dresden	275	187	549	460	565	---															
Erfurt	147	277	335	332	351	216	---														
Essen	416	514	105	246	69	547	336	---													
Frankfurt-am-Main	196	507	177	407	347	451	238	396	---												
Freiburg im Breisgau	388	778	393	673	419	662	509	488	269	---											
Hamburg	502	282	476	115	413	453	354	356	482	750	---										
Hanover	354	273	314	115	288	357	213	243	327	593	150	---									
Koblenz	300	564	61	392	88	508	295	153	106	332	492	344	---								
Leipzig	240	160	591	354	472	109	123	438	359	627	354	250	415	---							
Mainz	226	542	142	437	166	487	273	228	39	261	512	357	80	394	---						
Munich	225	576	561	696	569	457	371	646	392	332	777	629	473	422	394	---					
Nuremberg	60	425	412	531	397	304	206	446	216	355	561	417	320	270	246	157	---				
Rostock	580	226	614	290	587	408	430	532	613	882	175	300	641	357	645	762	609	---			
Saarbrücken	359	688	215	552	243	633	419	312	182	267	657	503	165	540	146	423	349	792	---		
Stuttgart	222	613	318	591	345	492	350	410	183	167	650	495	258	457	180	228	182	780	212	---	
Würzburg	82	475	271	463	294	358	208	339	114	305	504	350	217	320	143	257	102	656	276	141	---

if you're in an accident, not wearing a seatbelt may invalidate your insurance. Children need a child seat if under four years old and a seat cushion if under 12; they may not ride in the front until age 13. Motorcyclists must wear a helmet. The use of hand-held mobile phones while driving is very much *verboten*.

Germany's main motoring organisation is the **Allgemeiner Deutscher Automobil Club** (ADAC; ☎ 0180-222 2222 for roadside assistance; www .adac.de) with offices in all major cities and many smaller ones. ADAC's services, including an excellent roadside assistance programme, are also available to members of its affiliates, including American and Australian AAA, Canadian CAA and British AA. Technicians may not speak English, but gestures work very well – impersonate the sound your heap was making before it died, and the mechanic will probably figure it out directly or work it out with the help of a multilingual auto-part dictionary.

Driving Licence

Drivers must have a valid driving licence. You are not required to carry an International Driving Permit (IDP), but having one helps Germans make sense of your unfamiliar local licence (but make sure you take that with you, too) and simplifies the car and motorcycle rental process. IDPs are valid for one year and are issued for a small fee from your local automobile association – bring a passport photo and your regular licence.

Hire

In general, in order to hire a car in Germany you'll need to be at least 21 years old and hold a valid driving licence (an international licence is not necessary) and a major credit card. Amex, Diners Club, Visa and Euro Card/MasterCard are almost always accepted; JCB (Japan Credit Bank) is good only sometimes at airports, and they'll almost never take a Discover Card unless you've prepaid in the USA. There may be a supplement for additional driver(s). Safety seats for children under four are required and cost from €4.50 per day.

The main international companies operating in Germany are:

Avis (☎ 0180-555 7755; www.avis.com)
Budget (www.budget.com)

E-Sixt (☎ 0180-526 0250; www.esixt.de)
Europcar (☎ 0180-580 00; www.europcar.com)
Hertz (☎ 0180-533 3535; www.hertz.com)

Smaller local agencies sometimes offer better prices, so it's worth checking into that as well. Hertz doesn't rent to anyone under 25.

Prebooked and prepaid packages, arranged in your home country, usually work out much cheaper than on-the-spot rentals. The same is true of fly/drive packages. Check the rental and airline companies' websites, ask a travel agent, or scan such travel websites as www.travelocity.com or www.orbitz.com for deals.

Auto Europe (☎ 0800-550 0077; www.autoeurope .com) and **Holiday Autos** (☎ 01805-179 191; www .holidayautos.com) are car-rental brokers that have negotiated often very favourable rates with major international rental agencies.

All phone numbers listed here are in Germany. See the websites for contact numbers in your country.

Insurance

German law requires that all registered automobiles carry third-party liability insurance. You could get seriously screwed by driving uninsured or even underinsured. Germans are very fussy about their cars, and even nudging another vehicle's bumper when trying to get out of a parking space may well result in you having to foot the bill for an entire new one.

When renting a car, liability insurance may be calculated separately from the rental price. Always confirm on rental that you have this insurance.

Collision damage waiver (CDW) is protection for the car if you cause an accident. It reduces or eliminates the amount you'll have to reimburse the rental company. Although expensive, never drive without this either. The cost varies from company to company and their driver-age conditions and cars. Weekend deals sometimes include CDW, making them good value.

Certain credit cards, especially the gold and platinum versions, cover CDW if you use the card to pay for the entire rental and decline the policy offered by the rental company. Always check with your card issuer to see what coverage they offer in Germany.

Personal accident insurance (PAI) covers you and your passenger(s) for medical costs incurred as the result of an accident. If your health insurance from home does this as well, save yourself the €5 to €10 per day.

Purchase

Unless you're staying put in Germany for a while, buying a car here is more hassle than it's worth due to the costs and paperwork.

Non-German citizens must have a legal residency permit *(Aufenthaltsgenehmigung)* in order to register a car. Obtaining one is a mere formality for EU citizens, but very difficult for everyone else (for more on residency permits see Work p754).

If buying a used car from a private owner, the most important thing to consider,

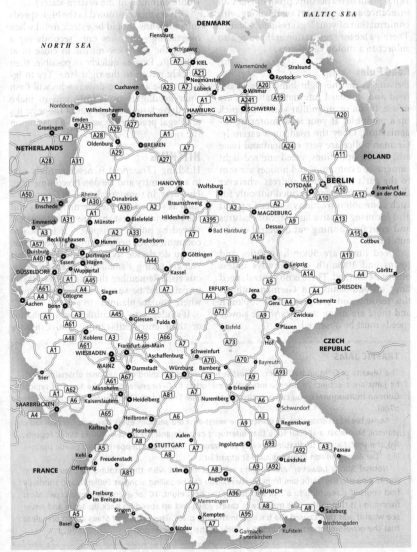

besides age and mileage, is the date of the next safety inspection by the Technical Control Board (TÜV). Cars must be inspected every two years in order to be kept legally on the road. Those bought at a dealership should be TÜV-free for two years and the dealer should register it for you. Everyone else must report immediately to the local motor vehicle office (*KFZ-Zulassungsstelle*). Bring proof of ownership, proof of German insurance and a passport or ID along with confirmation of your legal residency status. There's a fee for registration and you're also subject to a motor vehicle tax.

Road Rules

Driving is on the right-hand side of the road and standard international signs are in use. If you're unfamiliar with these, pick up a pamphlet at your local motoring organisation. Obey the road rules carefully: German police are very efficient and issue stiff on-the-spot fines; speed and red-light cameras are common, and notices are sent to the car's registration address wherever that may be. You can be fined not only for such common infractions as speeding, but also for using abusive language or gestures and even for running out of petrol on the autobahn.

Speed limits are 50km/h in cities and towns and 100km/h on highways unless otherwise marked. There is no general speed limit on autobahns, but German authorities recommend a top speed of 130km/h and there are many stretches where slower speeds must be observed.

The highest permissible blood-alcohol level for drivers is 0.05%, roughly the equivalent of one glass of wine or two small beers.

Pedestrians at crossings have absolute right of way over all motor vehicles. Similarly, you must give right of way to cyclists in bicycle lanes when you're turning. Right turns at a red light are only legal if there's also a green arrow pointing to the right (more common in the eastern states).

Drivers unaccustomed to the high speeds on autobahns should be extra careful when overtaking – it takes only seconds for a car in the rear-view mirror to close in at 200km/h. Pass as quickly as possible, then quickly return to the right lane. Try to ignore those annoying drivers who will flash their headlights or tailgate you to make you drive faster and get out of the way; it's an illegal practice anyway, as is passing on the right.

HITCHING

Hitching *(Trampen)* is never entirely safe in any country and we don't recommend it. However, in some rural areas in Germany – such as sections of the Alpine foothills and the Bavarian Forest that are not adequately served by public transport – it is not uncommon to see people thumbing for a ride. If you do decide to hitch, understand that you are taking a small but potentially serious risk. Remember that it's safer to travel in pairs and be sure to let someone know where you are planning to go.

It's illegal to hitchhike on autobahns or their entry/exit ramps. You can save

---

TRAFFIC JAMS

The severity of German traffic jams *(Staus)* seems to be something of a national obsession. Traffic jams are a subject of intense interest to motorists in Germany and are the focus of typical German thoroughness; you can actually get an annual Traffic Jam Calendar from the ADAC (see p766).

Some breakfast shows on TV present the worst-afflicted sections every day, and German radio stations broadcast a special tone that interrupts cassette and CD players during traffic reports. Ask the rental agent to disable it unless you want all your music peppered with poetic phrases like, *'Die Autobahn von Frankfurt nach Stuttgart ist...'*

Normal Staus, however, are nothing when compared with the astounding *Stau aus dem Nichts* (literally, the traffic jam from nowhere). You can be sailing along at 180km/h and suddenly find yourself screeching to a halt and taking the next eight, 10...or even 30km at a crawl. Most frustrating is that in the vast majority of cases, you'll end up speeding back up again and never see what it was that caused the back-up in the first place. These types of Staus are so prevalent that the government actually funded a study of the phenomenon!

yourself a lot of trouble by arranging a lift through a *Mitfahrzentrale* (see Hitching & Ride Services p760).

LOCAL TRANSPORT

Most German cities have efficient, frequent and punctual public transportation systems. In the bigger cities, they may integrate buses, trams, and U-Bahn (underground) and S-Bahn (suburban) trains. Tickets are available from vending machines at train stations and tram or bus stops. Fares may be determined by zones or time travelled, or sometimes both. Multiticket strips or day passes generally offer better value than single-ride tickets. If you're caught without a valid one, you will be fined (usually around €30). For details, see the individual Getting Around entries in the destination chapters.

Bicycle

From nuns to Jan Ullrich wannabes, Germans love to cycle, be it for errands, commuting, fitness or pleasure. Many cities have dedicated bicycle lanes, which must be used unless obstructed. There's no helmet law, not even for children, although using one is recommended, for obvious reasons. Bicycles must be equipped with a white light in the front, a red one in the back and yellow reflectors on the wheels and pedals. Also see Bicycle p763 and Cycling p737.

Bus & Tram

Buses are the most ubiquitous form of public transportation and practically all towns have their own comprehensive network. Buses run at regular intervals, with limited service in the evenings and on weekends. Some cities operate night buses along the most popular routes to get night owls safely back home.

Occasionally, buses are supplemented by trams, which are usually faster because they travel on their own tracks, largely independent of car traffic. In city centres, they sometimes go underground. Bus and tram drivers normally sell single tickets only.

S-Bahn

Metropolitan areas such as Berlin and Munich have a system of suburban trains called the S-Bahn. They are faster and cover a wider area than buses or trams but tend to be less frequent. S-Bahn lines are often linked to the national rail network and sometimes interconnect urban centres. Rail passes are generally valid on these services.

Taxi

Taxis are expensive and, given the excellent public transport systems, not recommended unless you're in a real hurry. (They can actually be slower than trains or shuttle buses if you're stuck in rush hour traffic.) Look up *Taxi Ruf* in the phonebook to call a taxi or ask about the nearest taxi rank. Taxis are metered and cost up to €2.30 at flag fall and €1.30 per kilometre; in some places higher night tariffs apply. See the Getting Around sections in the destination chapters for more information on taxis.

U-Bahn

The fastest and most efficient travel in large German cities is by underground/subway train, known as the U-Bahn. Route maps are posted in all stations and at many stations you'll be able to pick up a printed copy from the stationmaster or ticket offices. The frequency of trains usually fluctuates with demand, meaning there are more trains during commuter rush hours than, say, in the middle of the day. Buy tickets from vending machines and validate them before the start of your journey.

TRAIN

Operated almost entirely by the **Deutsche Bahn** (DB; ☎ 118 61 for reservations & information, €0.60 per min, ☎ 0800-150 7090 for automated timetable information; www.deutschebahn.de), the German rail system is justifiably known as the most efficient in Europe. A wide range of services and ticket options is available, making travelling by train the most attractive way to get around – sometimes even better than using a car. With 41,000km of track, the network is Europe's most extensive, serving over 7000 cities and towns.

All large (and many small) train stations in Germany have coin-operated left-luggage lockers (€1/2 for small/large lockers per 24 hours). Left-luggage offices (*Gepäckaufbewahrung*) are sometimes more convenient than lockers and charge similar rates.

For information on how to transport your bicycle by train, see Bicycle Transportation p763.

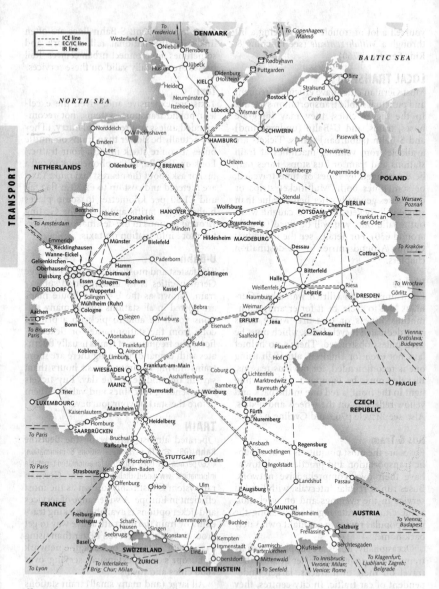

Classes

German trains have 1st and 2nd class cars, both of them modern and comfortable. Paying extra for 1st class is usually not worth it, except perhaps on busy travel days (normally Friday, Sunday afternoon and holidays) when 2nd class cars can get very crowded.

In both classes, seating is in compartments of up to six people or in open-plan carriages with panoramic windows. First class generally buys wider seats, a bit more leg-room and – on ICE, IC and EC trains – you can buy drinks and snacks right at your seat. When making seat reservations, you can choose from window or aisle seats, row seats or facing seats or seats with a fixed table. You can make and receive phone calls from any train.

On ICE trains you'll enjoy such extras as reclining seats, tables, free newspapers and audio-systems in your armrest. Newer generation ICE trains also have individual video screens in 1st class and electrical outlets at each seat.

All trains have smoking and nonsmoking cars and all but IR and most local trains are fully air-conditioned. Long-distance trains have a restaurant or self-service bistro.

NZ (night) trains have private one- to three-bed sleeper compartments, four- to six-bed couchettes (sleeping berths) and cars with reclining seats. If you have a rail pass, you only pay a supplement for either. Women can ask for a berth in a single-sex couchette when booking, but book early.

Costs

Though train travel in Germany generally offers good value, standard, non-discounted tickets are quite expensive. A one-way ICE train ticket from Munich to Berlin, for instance, costs €83.60 in 2nd class and €125.40 in 1st class, which can be the same or more than a cheap flight. Depending on how much travelling you plan to do, you can cut costs by buying a rail pass (see below) or by taking advantage of discount tickets and special offers. Always check www.bahn.de for the latest rail promotions.

SCHÖNES-WOCHENENDE-TICKET

The 'Nice-Weekend-Ticket' is Europe's finest rail deal. It allows you and up to four accompanying passengers (or one or both parents or grandparents plus all their children or grandchildren up to 14 years) to travel anywhere in Germany on *one day* from midnight Saturday or Sunday until 3 am the next day for just €28. The catch is that you can only use IRE, RE, RB and S-Bahn trains in 2nd class.

LÄNDERTICKETS

These are essentially a variation of the Schönes-Wochenende-Ticket, except that they cost €21, are only valid during the week and are limited to travel within one of the German states (or, in some cases, also in bordering states). For an extra €13, you also get to use IR and D trains (slower night trains).

Tickets & Reservations

Many big city train stations have a large *Reisezentrum* (travel centre) where you can buy tickets and ask staff to help you plan an itinerary (ask for an English-speaking agent). Smaller stations may only have a few ticket windows and the smallest ones aren't staffed at all. In this case, you must buy tickets from ticket machines. These also exist at bigger stations and are convenient if you don't want to queue at a ticket counter. Instructions are normally also provided in English. Both agents and machines accept major credit cards.

Tickets *can* be purchased on board (cash only) but, unless the ticket window where you boarded was closed or the machine broken, you must pay a surcharge of between €2 to €7.50.

A PRIMER ON TRAIN TYPES

Here's a quick lowdown on the alphabet soup of trains operated by Deutsche Bahn.

- **InterCity Express (ICE)** Long-distance, space-age bullet trains, they stop at major cities only; special tariffs apply and they're the most comfortable of the trains.
- **InterCity (IC) & EuroCity (EC)** Long-distance trains that are slower than the ICE but still pretty fast, they stop at major cities only.
- **InterRegio (IR)** Long-distance trains with more frequent stops than ICs.
- **RegionalBahn (RB)** Local trains, mostly in rural areas, with frequent stops, the slowest in the system.
- **Regional Express (RE)** Local trains with limited stops that link rural areas with metropolitan centres and the S-Bahn.
- **StadtExpress (SE)** Local trains primarily connecting cities and geared towards commuters.
- **Stadtbahn (S-Bahn)** Local trains operating within a city and its suburban area.

For trips over 101km, you can also buy tickets online (www.bahn.de) up to one hour before departure at no surcharge. You'll need a major credit card and a printer to print out your ticket. Present both your ticket and the credit card to the conductor.

Seat reservations for long-distance travel are highly recommended, especially if you're travelling on a Friday or Sunday afternoon, during holiday periods or in summer. The fee is a flat €2.60, regardless of the number of seats booked, and reservations can be made as late as a few minutes before departure.

Train Passes

BAHNCARD

A Bahncard may be worth considering if you plan a long stay or return trips to Germany within the one year of its validity. There are two versions: **BahnCard 25**, which entitles you to 25% off regular fares and costs €50/100 in 2nd/1st class; and **BahnCard 50**, which, you guessed it, gives you a 50% discount and costs €200/400. The latter only costs half-price if you're the partner of a card holder, a student under 27 or a senior over 60. It's available at all major train stations.

GERMAN RAIL PASSES

If your permanent residence is outside of Europe, you qualify for the **German Rail Pass**. It entitles you to unlimited 1st or 2nd class travel for four to 10 days within a one-month period. Sample prices are US$180/248/316 for four/seven/10 days of travel in 2nd class and US$260/358/458 in 1st class. The pass is valid on all trains within Germany and some KD Line river services on the Rhine and Moselle.

If you are between the ages of 12 and 25, you qualify for the **German Rail Youth Pass**, which costs US$142/180/216 and is only good for 2nd class travel. Two adults travelling together should check out the **German Rail Twin Pass** for US$270/372/474 in 2nd class and US$390/537/687 in 1st class. Children between six and 11 pay half the adult fares. Children under six travel free.

If you're already in Germany, five- and 10-day passes are available at select DB outlets, eg the Frankfurt airport or the EurAide offices in Munich (p331) and Berlin (p103).

In the US and Canada, the main agency specialising in selling the German Rail and other passes, as well as regular DB train tickets, is **Rail Europe** (☎ 888-382-7245 in the US, ☎ 800-361-7246 in Canada; www.raileurope.com). If you live in another country, contact your travel agent.

Rail Europe also offers the **German Rail 'n Drive** pass available for a minimum of two days of unlimited train travel plus two days of car rental during a one-month period. It costs €232/202 1st/2nd class for one person with an economy car rental. Two people travelling together pay €185/154 each.

Health

CONTENTS

Before You Go	**773**
Insurance	773
Recommended Vaccinations	773
In Transit	**773**
Deep Vein Thrombosis (DVT)	773
Jet Lag & Motion Sickness	774
In Germany	**774**
Availability & Cost of Health Care	774
Traveller's Diarrhoea	774
Environmental Hazards	774
Sexual Health	774
Travelling with Children	774
Women's Health	774

BEFORE YOU GO

While Germany has excellent health care, prevention is the key to staying healthy while abroad. A little planning before departure, particularly for pre-existing illnesses, will save trouble later. Bring medications in their original, clearly labelled, containers. A signed and dated letter from your physician describing your medical conditions and medications, including generic names, is also a good idea. If carrying syringes or needles, be sure to have a physician's letter documenting their medical necessity. Carry a spare pair of contact lenses and glasses, and take your optical prescription with you.

INSURANCE

If you're an EU citizen, an E111 form, available from health centres or, in the UK, post offices, covers you for most medical care. E111 will not cover you for nonemergencies, or emergency repatriation home. Citizens from other countries should find out if there is a reciprocal arrangement for free medical care between their country and Germany. If you do need health insurance, make sure you get a policy that covers you for the worst possible case, such as an accident requiring an emergency flight home. Find out in advance if your insurance plan will make payments directly to providers or reimburse you later for overseas health expenditures.

RECOMMENDED VACCINATIONS

No jabs are required to travel to Germany. The WHO, however, recommends that all travellers should be covered for diphtheria, tetanus, measles, mumps, rubella and polio, regardless of their destination.

IN TRANSIT

DEEP VEIN THROMBOSIS (DVT)

Blood clots may form in the legs during plane flights, chiefly because of prolonged immobility. The longer the flight,

---

MEDICAL CHECKLIST

All of the following are readily available in Germany. If you are hiking out of town, these items may come in handy.

- antibiotics
- antidiarrheal drugs (eg loperamide)
- acetaminophen (Tylenol) or aspirin
- anti-inflammatory drugs (eg ibuprofen)
- antihistamines
  (for hay fever and allergic reactions)
- antibacterial ointment
  (eg Bactroban; for cuts and abrasions)
- steroid cream or cortisone
  (for poison ivy and other allergic rashes)
- bandages, gauze, gauze rolls
- adhesive or paper tape
- scissors, safety pins, tweezers
- thermometer
- pocketknife
- DEET-containing insect repellent
  for the skin
- pyrethrin-containing insect spray for
  clothing, tents and bed nets
- sun block
- oral rehydration salts
- acetazolamide
  (Diamox; for altitude sickness)

the greater the risk. The chief symptom of DVT is swelling or pain of the foot, ankle or calf, usually but not always on just one side. When a blood clot travels to the lungs, it may cause chest pain and difficulty breathing. Travellers with any of these symptoms should immediately seek medical attention.

To prevent the development of DVT on long flights you should walk about the cabin, contract the leg muscles while sitting, drink plenty of fluids and avoid alcohol and tobacco.

JET LAG & MOTION SICKNESS

To avoid jet lag (common when crossing more than five time zones) try to drink plenty of nonalchoholic fluids and eat light meals. Upon arrival, get exposure to natural sunlight and readjust your schedule (for meals, sleep etc) as soon as possible.

Antihistamines such as dimenhydrinate (Dramamine) and meclizine (Antivert, Bonine) are usually the first choice for treating motion sickness. A herbal alternative is ginger.

IN GERMANY

AVAILABILITY & COST OF HEALTH CARE

Excellent health care is readily available and for minor self-limiting illnesses pharmacists can give valuable advice and sell over-the-counter medication. They can also advise when more specialised help is required and point you in the right direction.

TRAVELLER'S DIARRHOEA

If you develop diarrhoea, be sure to drink plenty of fluids, preferably in the form of an oral rehydration solution such as Dioralyte. If diarrhoea is bloody, persists for more than 72 hours or is accompanied by fever, shaking, chills or severe abdominal pain you should seek medical attention.

ENVIRONMENTAL HAZARDS
Heat Stroke

Heat exhaustion occurs following excessive fluid loss with inadequate replacement of fluids and salt. Symptoms include headache, dizziness and tiredness. Dehydration is al-

ready happening by the time you feel thirsty – aim to drink sufficient water to produce pale, diluted urine. To treat heat exhaustion drink water and/or fruit juice, and cool the body with cold water and fans.

Hypothermia

Hypothermia occurs when the body loses heat faster than it can produce it. As ever, proper preparation will reduce the risks of getting it. Even on a hot day in the mountains, the weather can change rapidly, so carry waterproof garments, warm layers and a hat and inform others of your route.

Hypothermia starts with shivering, loss of judgment and clumsiness. Unless rewarming occurs, the sufferer deteriorates into apathy, confusion and coma. Prevent further heat loss by seeking shelter, warm dry clothing, hot sweet drinks and shared bodily warmth.

SEXUAL HEALTH

Emergency contraception is available with a doctor's prescription in Germany. It is most effective if taken within 24 hours after unprotected sex. Condoms are readily available throughout Germany.

TRAVELLING WITH CHILDREN

Make sure the children are up to date with routine vaccinations, and discuss possible travel vaccines well before departure as some vaccines are not suitable for children under one-year-old.

If your child has vomiting or diarrhoea, lost fluid and salts must be replaced. It may be helpful to take rehydration powders with boiled water.

WOMEN'S HEALTH

Emotional stress, exhaustion and travelling through different time zones can all contribute to an upset in the menstrual pattern.

If using oral contraceptives, remember some antibiotics, diarrhoea and vomiting can stop the pill from working. Time zones, gastrointestinal upsets and antibiotics do not affect injectable contraception.

Travelling during pregnancy is usually possible but always consult your doctor before planning your trip. The most risky times for travel are during the first 12 weeks of pregnancy and after 30 weeks.

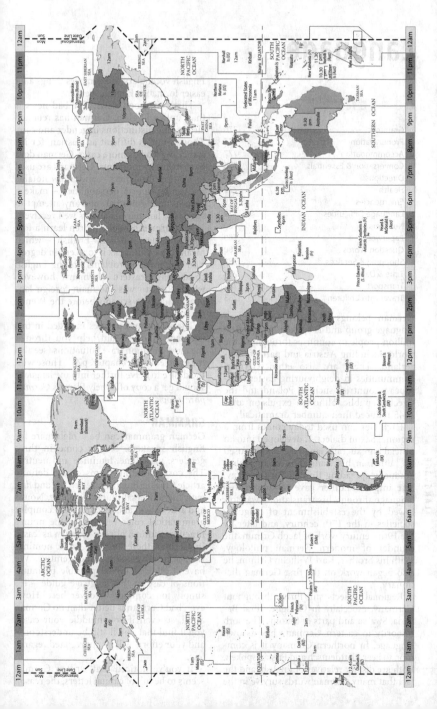

Language

CONTENTS

Grammar 776
Pronunciation 777
Accommodation 777
Conversation & Essentials 778
Directions 778
Health 779
Emergencies 779
Language Difficulties 779
Numbers 780
Paperwork 780
Question Words 780
Shopping & Services 780
Time & Dates 781
Transport 781
Travel with Children 783

German belongs to the Indo-European language group and is spoken by over 100 million people in countries throughout the world, including Austria and part of Switzerland. There are also ethnic-German communities in neighbouring Eastern European countries such as Poland and the Czech Republic, although expulsion after 1945 reduced their number dramatically.

High German used today comes from a regional Saxon dialect. It developed into an official bureaucratic language and was used by Luther in his translation of the Bible, gradually spreading throughout Germany. The impetus Luther gave to the written language through his translations was followed by the establishment of language societies in the 17th century, and later by the 19th-century work of Jacob Grimm, the founder of modern German philology. With his brother, Karl Wilhelm Grimm, he also began work on the first German dictionary.

Regional dialects still thrive throughout Germany, especially in Cologne, rural Bavaria, Swabia and parts of Saxony. The Sorb minority in eastern Germany has its own language. In northern Germany it is common to hear Plattdeutsch and Frisian spoken. Both are distant relatives of English, and the fact that many German words survive in the English vocabulary today makes things a lot easier for native English speakers.

That's the good news. The bad news is that, unlike English, German has retained clear polite distinctions in gender and case. Though not as difficult as Russian, for instance, which has more cases, German does have its tricky moments. Germans are used to hearing foreigners – and a few notable indigenous sports personalities – make a hash of their grammar, and any attempt to speak the language is always well received.

All German school children learn a foreign language – usually English – which means most can speak it to a certain degree. You might have problems finding English speakers in eastern Germany, however, where Russian was the main foreign language taught in schools before the Wende (change).

The words and phrases included in this language guide should help you through the most common travel situations (see also the Food & Drink chapter, p74). Those with the desire to delve further into the language should get a copy of Lonely Planet's *German phrasebook*.

GRAMMAR

German grammar can be a nightmare for English speakers. Nouns come in three genders: masculine, feminine and neutral. The corresponding forms of the definite article ('the' in English) are *der*, *die* and *das*, with the universal plural form, *die*. Nouns and articles will alter according to complex grammatical rules relating to the noun's function within a phrase – known as 'case'. In German there are four cases: nominative, accusative, dative and genitive. We haven't allowed for all possible permutations of case in this language guide – it's simply too complex to cover here. However, bad German is better than no German at all, so even if you muddle your cases, you'll find that you'll still be understood – and your efforts will be appreciated regardless.

If you've noticed that written German seems to be full of capital letters, the reason is that German nouns always begin with a capital letter.

PRONUNCIATION

It's not difficult to pronounce German because almost all sounds can be found in English. Follow the pronunciation guide and you'll have no trouble getting your message across.

Vowels

German Example	Pronunciation Guide
hat	**a** (eg the 'u' in 'run')
habe	**ah** (eg 'father')
mein	**ai** (eg 'aisle')
Bär	**air** (eg 'hair', with no 'r' sound)
Boot	**aw** (eg 'saw')
leben	**ay** (eg 'say')
Bett/Männer/kaufen	**e** (eg 'bed')
fliegen	**ee** (eg 'thief')
schön	**er** (eg 'her', with no 'r' sound)
mit	**i** (eg 'bit')
Koffer	**o** (eg 'pot')
Leute/Häuser	**oy** (eg 'toy')
Schuhe	**oo** (eg 'moon')
Haus	**ow** (eg 'how')
zürück	**ü** ('ee' said with rounded lips)
unter	**u** (eg 'put')

Consonants

The only two tricky consonant sounds in German are **ch** and **r**. All other consonants are pronounced much the same as their English counterparts (except **sch**, which is always as the 'sh' in 'shoe').

The **ch** sound is generally like the 'ch' in *Bach* or Scottish *loch* – like a hiss from the back of the throat. When **ch** occurs after the vowels **e** and **i** it's more like a 'sh' sound, produced with the tongue more forward in the mouth. In this book we've simplified things by using the one symbol **kh** for both sounds.

The **r** sound is different from English, and it isn't rolled like in Italian or Spanish. It's pronounced at the back of the throat, almost like saying a 'g' sound, but with some friction – it's a bit like gargling.

Word Stress

As a general rule, word stress in German mostly falls on the first syllable. In the pronunciation guides in the following words and phrases, the stressed syllable is shown in italics.

ACCOMMODATION

Where's a ...?
Wo ist ...?   vaw ist ...
bed and breakfast
eine Pension   *ai*·ne pahng·*zyawn*
camping ground
ein Campingplatz   ain *kem*·ping·plats
guesthouse
eine Pension   *ai*·ne pahng·*zyawn*
hotel
ein Hotel   ain ho·*tel*
inn
ein Gasthof   ain *gast*·hawf
room in a private home
ein Privatzimmer   ain pri·*vaht*·tsi·mer
youth hostel
eine Jugendherberge   *ai*·ne yoo·gent·her·ber·ge

What's the address?
Wie ist die Adresse?
vee ist dee a·*dre*·se
I'd like to book a room, please.
Ich möchte bitte ein Zimmer reservieren.
ikh *merkh*·te *bi*·te ain *tsi*·mer re·zer·*vee*·ren
For (three) nights/weeks.
Für (drei) Nächte/Wochen.
für (drai) *nekh*·te/*vo*·khen

Do you have a ... room?
Haben Sie ein ...?   *hah*·ben zee ain ...
  single
  Einzelzimmer   *ain*·tsel·tsi·mer
  double
  Doppelzimmer mit   *do*·pel·tsi·mer mit
  einem Doppelbett   *ai*·nem *do*·pel·bet
  twin
  Doppelzimmer mit zwei   *do*·pel·tsi·mer mit tsvai
  Einzelbetten   *ain*·tsel·be·ten

How much is it per ...?
Wie viel kostet es pro ...?   vee feel *kos*·tet es praw ...
  night
  Nacht   nakht
  person
  Person   per·*zawn*

May I see it?
Kann ich es sehen?   kan ikh es *zay*·en
Can I get another room?
Kann ich noch ein   kan ikh nokh ain
Zimmer bekommen?   *tsi*·mer be·*ko*·men
It's fine. I'll take it.
Es ist gut, ich nehme es.   es ist goot ikh *nay*·me es
I'm leaving now.
Ich reise jetzt ab.   ikh *rai*·ze yetst ap

LANGUAGE

MAKING A RESERVATION

(for phone and written requests)

To ...	An ...
From ...	Von ...
Date	Datum
I'd like to book ...	Ich möchte ... reservieren.
	(see the list under 'Accommodation' for bed and room options)
in the name of ...	auf den Namen ...
from ... (date) to ...	Vom ... bis zum ...
credit card	Kreditkarte
number	Nummer
expiry date	gültig bis ... (valid until)
Please confirm availability and price.	Bitte bestätigen Sie Verfügbarkeit und Preis.

CONVERSATION & ESSENTIALS

You should be aware that German uses polite and informal forms for 'you' (*Sie* and *Du* respectively). When addressing people you don't know well you should always use the polite form (though younger people will be less inclined to expect it). In this language guide we use the polite form unless indicated by 'inf' (for 'informal') in brackets.

If you need to ask for assistance from a stranger, remember to always introduce your request with a simple *Entschuldigung* (Excuse me, ...).

Hello.
Guten Tag. — goo·ten tahk
Grüss Gott. — grüs got
(in the south)
Hi.
Hallo. — ha·lo/ha·law

Good ... — Guten ... — goo·ten ...
 day — Tag — tahk
 morning — Morgen — mor·gen
 afternoon — Tag — tahk
 evening — Abend — ah·bent

Goodbye.
Auf Wiedersehen. — owf vee·der·zay·en
See you later.
Bis später. — bis shpay·ter
Bye.
Tschüss./Tschau. — chüs/chow
How are you?
Wie geht es Ihnen? (pol) — vee gayt es ee·nen
Wie geht es dir? (inf) — vee gayt es deer

Fine. And you?
Danke, gut. — dang·ke goot
... and you?
Und Ihnen? (pol) — unt ee·nen
Und dir? (inf) — unt deer
What's your name?
Wie ist Ihr Name? (pol) — vee ist eer nah·me
Wie heisst du? (inf) — vee haist doo
My name is ...
Mein Name ist .../ — main nah·me ist .../
Ich heisse ... — ikh hai·se ...
Yes.
Ja. — yah
No.
Nein. — nain
Please.
Bitte. — bi·te
Thank you (very much).
Danke./Vielen Dank. — dang·ke/fee·len dangk
You're welcome.
Bitte (sehr). — bi·te (zair)
Excuse me, ... (before asking for help or directions)
Entschuldigung. — ent·shul·di·gung
Sorry.
Entschuldigung. — ent·shul·di·gung

DIRECTIONS
Could you help me, please?
Können Sie mir bitte helfen? — ker·nen zee meer bi·te hel·fen
Where's (a bank)?
Wo ist (eine Bank).? — vaw ist (ai·ne bangk)
I'm looking for (the cathedral).
Ich suche (den Dom). — ikh zoo·khe (dayn dawm)
Which way's (a public toilet)?
In welcher Richtung ist eine öffentliche toilette? — in vel·kher rikh·tung ist (ai·ne er·fent·li·khe to·a·le·te)
How can I get there?
Wie kann ich da hinkommen? — vee kan ikh dah hin·ko·men
How far is it?
Wie weit ist es? — vee vait ist es
Can you show me (on the map)?
Können Sie es mir (auf der Karte) zeigen? — ker·nen zee es meer (owf dair kar·te) tsai·gen

left	links	lingks
right	rechts	rekhts
near	nahe	nah·e
far away	weit weg	vait vek
here	hier	heer
there	dort	dort

on the corner	an der Ecke	an dair e·ke
straight ahead	geradeaus	ge·rah·de·ows
opposite ...	gegenüber ...	gay·gen·ü·ber ...
next to ...	neben ...	nay·ben ...
behind ...	hinter ...	hin·ter ...
in front of ...	vor ...	fawr ...
north	Norden	nor·den
south	Süden	zü·den
east	Osten	os·ten
west	Westen	ves·ten

SIGNS

Polizei	**Police**
Polizeiwache	**Police Station**
Eingang	**Entrance**
Ausgang	**Exit**
Offen	**Open**
Geschlossen	**Closed**
Kein Zutritt	**No Entry**
Rauchen Verboten	**No Smoking**
Verboten	**Prohibited**
Toiletten (WC)	**Toilets**
Herren	**Men**
Damen	**Women**

Turn ...
Biegen Sie ... ab.   bee·gen zee ... ap

left/right
links/rechts   lingks/rekhts
at the next corner
an der nächsten Ecke   an dair naykhs·ten e·ke
at the traffic lights
bei der Ampel   bai dair am·pel

HEALTH
Where's the nearest ...?
Wo ist der/die/das nächste ...? (m/f/n)   vaw ist dair/
die/das naykhs·te ...

chemist
Apotheke (f)   a·po·tay·ke
dentist
Zahnarzt   tsahn·artst
doctor
Arzt   artst
hospital
Krankenhaus (n)   krang·ken·hows

I need a doctor (who speaks English).
Ich brauche einen Arzt (, der Englisch spricht).
ikh brow·khe ai·nen artst (dair eng·lish shprikht)
Is there a (night) chemist nearby?
Gibt es in der Nähe eine (Nacht)Apotheke?
gipt es in dair nay·e ai·ne (nakht·)a·po·tay·ke/

EMERGENCIES
Help!
Hilfe!   hil·fe
It's an emergency!
Es ist ein Notfall!   es ist ain nawt·fal
Call the police!
Rufen Sie die Polizei!   roo·fen zee dee po·li·tsai
Call a doctor!
Rufen Sie einen Arzt!   roo·fen zee ai·nen artst
Call an ambulance!
*Rufen Sie einen
Krankenwagen!*   roo·fen zee ai·nen
krang·ken·vah·gen
Leave me alone!
Lassen Sie mich in Ruhe!   la·sen zee mikh in roo·e
Go away!
Gehen Sie weg!   gay·en zee vek
I'm lost.
Ich habe mich verirrt.   ikh hah·be mikh fer·irt
Where are the toilets?
Wo ist die Toilette?   vaw ist dee to·a·le·te

I'm sick.
Ich bin krank.
ikh bin krangk
It hurts here.
Es tut hier weh.
es toot heer vay
I've been vomiting.
Ich habe mich übergeben.
ikh hah·be mikh ü·ber·gay·ben
I have diarrhoea/fever/headache.
Ich habe Durchfall/Fieber/Kopfschmerzen.
ikh hah·be durkh·fal/fee·ber/kopf·shmer·tsen
(I think) I'm pregnant.
(Ich glaube,) Ich bin schwanger.
(ikh glow·be) ikh bin shvang·er

I'm allergic to ...
Ich bin allergisch gegen ...   ikh bin a·lair·gish gay·gen ...
antibiotics
Antibiotika   an·ti·bi·aw·ti·ka
aspirin
Aspirin   as·pi·reen
penicillin
Penizillin   pe·ni·tsi·leen

LANGUAGE DIFFICULTIES
Do you speak English?
Sprechen Sie Englisch?
shpre·khen zee eng·lish
Does anyone here speak English?
Spricht hier jemand Englisch?
shprikht heer yay·mant eng·lish

Do you understand (me)?
Verstehen Sie (mich)?
fer-*shtay*-en zee (mikh)

I (don't) understand.
Ich verstehe (nicht).
ikh fer-*shtay*-e (nikht)

How do you say ... in German?
Wie sagt man ... auf Deutsch?
vee zagt man ... owf doytsh

Could you please ...?
Könnten Sie...?   *kern*-ten zee ...

  speak more slowly
  bitte langsamer sprechen   bi-te *lang*-za-mer *shpre*-khen

  repeat that
  das bitte wiederholen   das *bi*-te vee-der-*haw*-len

  write it down
  das bitte aufschreiben   das *bi*-te owf-*shrai*-ben

NUMBERS

1	*ains*	aints
2	*zwei*	tsvai
3	*drei*	drai
4	*vier*	feer
5	*fünf*	fünf
6	*sechs*	zeks
7	*sieben*	*zee*-ben
8	*acht*	akht
9	*neun*	noyn
10	*zehn*	tsayn
11	*elf*	elf
12	*zwölf*	zverlf
13	*dreizehn*	*drai*-tsayn
14	*vierzehn*	*feer*-tsayn
15	*fünfzehn*	*fünf*-tsayn
16	*sechzehn*	*zeks*-tsayn
17	*siebzehn*	*zeep*-tsayn
18	*achtzehn*	*akh*-tsayn
19	*neunzehn*	*noyn*-tsayn
20	*zwanzig*	*tsvan*-tsikh
21	*einundzwanzig*	*ain*-unt-tsvan-tsikh
22	*zweiundzwanig*	*tsvai*-unt-tsvan-tsikh
30	*dreizig*	*drai*-tsikh
31	*einunddreizig*	*ain*-und-*drai*-tsikh
40	*vierzig*	*feer*-tsikh
50	*fünfzig*	*fünf*-tsikh
60	*sechzig*	*zekh*-tsikh
70	*siebzig*	*zeep*-tsikh
80	*achtzig*	*akh*-tsikh
90	*neunzig*	*noyn*-tsikh
100	*hundert*	*hun*-dert
1000	*tausend*	*tow*-sent
2000	*zwei tausend*	tsvai *tow*-sent
one million	*eine Million*	*ai*-ne mil-*yawn*

PAPERWORK

name	*Name*	*nah*-me
nationality	*Staatsan-* *gehörigkeit*	shtahts-an- ge-her-rikh-kait
date of birth	*Geburtsdatum*	ge-*burts*-dah-tum
place of birth	*Geburtsort*	ge-*burts*-ort
sex/gender	*Sex*	seks
passport	*(Reise)Pass*	(*rai*-ze-)pahs
visa	*Visum*	*vee*-zum

QUESTION WORDS

Who?	*Wer?*	vair
What?	*Was?*	vas
Where?	*Wo?*	vo
When?	*Wann?*	van
How?	*Wie?*	vee
Why?	*Warum?*	va-*rum*
Which?	*Welcher?*	*vel*-kher
How much?	*Wie viel?*	vee feel
How many?	*Wie viele?*	vee *fee*-le

SHOPPING & SERVICES

I'm looking for ...
Ich suche ...
ikh *zoo*-khe ...

Where's the (nearest) ...?
Wo ist der/die/das (nächste) ...? (m/f/n)
vaw ist dair/dee/das (*naykhs*-te) ...

Where can I buy ...?
Wo kann ich ... kaufen?
vaw kan ikh ... *kow*-fen

I'd like to buy ...
Ich möchte ... kaufen.
ikh *merkh*-te ... *kow*-fen

How much (is this)?
Wie viel (kostet das)?
vee feel (*kos*-tet das)

That's too much/expensive.
Das ist zu viel/teuer.
das ist tsoo feel/*toy*-er

Can you lower the price?
Können Sie mit dem Preis heruntergehen?
ker-nen zee mit dem prais he-*run*-ter-gay-en

Do you have something cheaper?
Haben Sie etwas Billigeres?
hah-ben zee *et*-vas *bi*-li-ge-res

I'm just looking.
Ich schaue mich nur um.
ikh *show*-e mikh noor um

Can you write down the price?
Können Sie den Preis aufschreiben?
ker-nen zee dayn prais owf-*shrai*-ben

Do you have any others?
Haben Sie noch andere?
hah-ben zee nokh *an*-de-re

LANGUAGE

Can I look at it?
Können Sie ihn/sie/es mir zeigen? (m/f/n)
ker·nen zee een/zee/es meer *tsai*·gen

more	mehr	mair
less	weniger	vay·ni·ger
smaller	kleiner	klai·ner·tee
bigger	grosser	gro·ser

Do you accept ...?
Nehmen Sie ...?   nay·men zee ...
credit cards
Kreditkarten   kre·*deet*·kar·ten
travellers cheques
Reisechecks   rai·ze·sheks

I'd like to ...
Ich möchte ...   ikh *merkh*·te ...
change money (cash)
Geld umtauschen   gelt *um*·tow·shen
cash a cheque
einen Scheck einlösen   ai·nen shek *ain*·ler·zen
change some travellers cheques
Reisechecks einlösen   rai·ze·sheks *ain*·ler·zen

an ATM	ein Geldautomat	ain *gelt*·ow·to·maht
an exchange	eine Geldwechsel-	ai·ne *gelt*·vek·sel-
office	stube	shtoo·be
a bank	eine Bank	ai·ne bangk
the ... embassy	die ... Botschaft	dee *bot*·shaft
the hospital	das Krankenhaus	das *krang*·ken·hows
the market	der Markt	dair markt
the police	die Polizei	dee po·li·*tsai*
the post office	das Postamt	das *post*·amt
a public phone	ein öffentliches Telefon	ain *er*·fent·li·khes te·le·*fawn*
a public toilet	eine öffentliche Toilette	ain *er*·fent·li·khe to·a·*le*·te

What time does it open/close?
Wann macht er/sie/es auf/zu? (m/f/n)
van makht air/zee/es owf/tsoo
I want to buy a phone card.
Ich möchte eine Telefonkarte kaufen.
ikh *merkh*·te ai·ne te·le·*fawn*·kar·te *kow*·fen
Where's the local Internet cafe?
Wo ist hier ein Internet-Café?
vaw ist heer ain *in*·ter·net·ka·fay

I'd like to ...
Ich möchte ...   ikh *merkh*·te ...
get Internet access
Internetzugang haben   in·ter·net·tsoo·gang *hah*·ben
check my email
meine E-Mails checken   mai·ne ee·mayls *che*·ken

TIME & DATES
What time is it?
Wie spät ist es?   vee shpayt ist es
It's (one) o'clock.
Es ist (ein) Uhr.   es ist (ain) oor
Twenty past one.
Zwanzig nach eins.   tsvan·tsikh nahkh ains
Half past one.
Halb zwei. ('half two')   halp tsvai
Quarter to one.
Viertel vor eins..   *fir*·tel fawr ains
am
morgens/vormittags   mor·gens/fawr·mi·tahks
pm
nachmittags/abends   nahkh·mi·tahks/ah·bents

now	jetzt	yetst
today	heute	hoy·te
tonight	heute Abend	hoy·te ah·bent
tomorrow	morgen	mor·gen
yesterday	gestern	ges·tern
morning	Morgen	mor·gen
afternoon	Nachmittag	nahkh·mi·tahk
evening	Abend	ah·bent

Monday	Montag	mawn·tahk
Tuesday	Dienstag	deens·tahk
Wednesday	Mittwoch	mit·vokh
Thursday	Donnerstag	do·ners·tahk
Friday	Freitag	frai·tahk
Saturday	Samstag	zams·tahk
Sunday	Sonntag	zon·tahk

January	Januar	yan·u·ahr
February	Februar	fay·bru·ahr
March	März	merts
April	April	a·pril
May	Mai	mai
June	Juni	yoo·ni
July	Juli	yoo·li
August	August	ow·gust
September	September	zep·tem·ber
October	Oktober	ok·taw·ber
November	November	no·vem·ber
December	Dezember	de·tsem·ber

TRANSPORT
Public Transport
What time does the ... leave?
Wann fährt ... ab?   van fairt ... ap
boat	das Boot	das bawt
bus	der Bus	dair bus
train	der Zug	dair tsook

What time's the ... bus?
Wann fährt der ... Bus? van fairt dair ... bus
first	*erste*	ers·te
last	*letzte*	lets·te
next	*nächste*	naykhs·te

Where's the nearest metro station?
Wo ist der nächste U-Bahnhof?
vaw ist dair naykhs·te oo·bahn·hawf

Which (bus) goes to ...?
Welcher Bus fährt ...?
vel·kher bus fairt ...

metro		
U-Bahn	oo·bahn	
(metro) station		
(U-)Bahnhof	(oo-)bahn·hawf	
tram		
Strassenbahn	shtrah·sen·bahn	
tram stop		
Strassenbahnhalte-	shtrah·sen·bahn·hal·te·	
stelle	shte·le	
urban railway		
S-Bahn	es·bahn	

A ... ticket to (Berlin).
Einen ... nach (Berlin). ai·nen ... nahkh (ber·leen)
one-way		
einfache Fahrkarte	ain·fa·khe fahr·kar·te
return		
Rückfahrkarte	rük·fahr·kar·te
1st-class		
Fahrkarte erster Klasse	fahr·kar·te ers·ter kla·se
2nd-class		
Fahrkarte zweiter Klasse	fahr·kar·te tsvai·ter kla·se

The ... is cancelled.
... ist gestrichen. ... ist ge·shtri·khen
The ... is delayed.
... hat Verspätung. ... hat fer·shpay·tung
Is this seat free?
Ist dieser Platz frei? ist dee·zer plats frai
Do I need to change trains?
Muss ich umsteigen? mus ikh um·shtai·gen
Are you free? (taxi)
Sind Sie frei? zint zee frai
How much is it to ...?
Was kostet es bis ...? vas kos·tet es bis ...
Please take me to (this address).
Bitte bringen Sie mich bi·te bring·en zee mikh
zu (dieser Adresse). tsoo (dee·zer a·dre·se)

Private Transport
Where can I hire a...?
Wo kann ich ... mieten? vaw kan ikh ... mee·ten

I'd like to hire a/an ...
Ich möchte ... mieten. ikh merkh·te ... mee·ten
automatic		
ein Fahrzeug mit	ain fahr·tsoyk mit
Automatik	ow·to·mah·tik
bicycle		
ein Fahrrad	ain fahr·raht
car		
ein Auto	ain ow·to
4WD		
ein Allradfahrzeug	ain al·raht·fahr·tsoyk
manual		
ein Fahrzeug mit Schaltung	ain fahr·tsoyk mit shal·tung
motorbike		
ein Motorrad	ain maw·tor·raht

How much is it per ...?
Wie viel kostet es pro ...? vee feel kos·tet es praw ...
day		
Tag	tahk
week		
Woche	vo·khe

ROAD SIGNS
Gefahr	**Danger**
Einfahrt Verboten	**No Entry**
Einbahnstrasse	**One-way**
Einfahrt	**Entrance**
Ausfahrt	**Exit**
Ausfahrt Freihalten	**Keep Clear**
Parkverbot	**No Parking**
Halteverbot	**No Stopping**
Mautstelle	**Toll**
Radweg	**Cycle Path**
Umleitung	**Detour**
Überholverbot	**No Overtaking**

petrol (gas)
Benzin (n) ben·tseen
diesel
Diesel dee·zel
leaded
verbleites Benzin (n) fer·blai·tes ben·tseen
LPG
Autogas (n) ow·to·gahs
regular
Normalbenzin (n) nor·mahl·ben·tseen
unleaded
bleifreies Benzin (n) blai·frai·es ben·tseen

Where's a petrol station?
Wo ist eine Tankstelle?
vaw ist ai·ne tangk·shte·le

Does this road go to ...?
Führt diese Strasse nach ...?
fürt *dee*·ze *shtrah*·se nahkh ...

(How long) Can I park here?
(Wie lange) Kann ich hier parken?
(vee *lang*·e) kan ikh heer *par*·ken

Where do I pay?
Wo muss ich bezahlen?
vaw mus ikh be·*tsah*·len

I need a mechanic.
Ich brauche einen Mechaniker.
ikh *brow*·khe *ai*·nen me·*khah*·ni·ker

The car has broken down (at ...)
Ich habe (in ...) eine Panne mit meinem Auto.
ikh *hah*·be (in ...) *ai*·ne *pa*·ne mit *mai*·nem *ow*·to

I had an accident.
Ich hatte einen Unfall.
ikh *ha*·te *ai*·nen *un*·fal

The car/motorbike won't start.
Das Auto/Motorrad springt nicht an.
das *ow*·to/*maw*·tor·raht shpringkt nikht an

I have a flat tyre.
Ich habe eine Reifenpanne.
ikh *hah*·be *ai*·ne *rai*·fen·pa·ne

I've run out of petrol.
Ich habe kein Benzin mehr.
ikh *hah*·be kain ben·*tseen* mair

TRAVEL WITH CHILDREN

I need a ...
Ich brauche ...   ikh *brow*·khe ...

Is there a/an ...?
Gibt es ...?   gipt es ...
  baby change room
  einen Wickelraum   *ai*·nen *vi*·kel·rowm
  baby seat
  einen Babysitz   *ai*·nen *bay*·bi·zits
  booster seat
  einen Kindersitz   *ai*·nen *kin*·der·zits
  child-minding service
  einen Babysitter-Service   *ai*·nen *bay*·bi·si·ter·*ser*·vis
  children's menu
  eine Kinderkarte   *ai*·ne *kin*·der·kar·te
  (English-speaking) babysitter
  einen (englisch-   *ai*·nen *(eng*·lish-
  sprachigen) Babysitter   shpra·khi·gen) *bay*·bi·si·ter
  infant formula (milk)
  Trockenmilch für Säuglinge   *tro*·ken·milkh für *soyg*·ling·e
  highchair
  einen Kinderstuhl   *ai*·nen *kin*·der·shtool
  potty
  ein Kindertöpfchen   ain *kin*·der·terpf·khen
  stroller
  einen Kinderwagen   *ai*·nen *kin*·der·vah·gen

Do you mind if I breastfeed here?
Kann ich meinem Kind hier die Brust geben?
kan ikh *mai*·nem kint heer dee brust *gay*·ben

Are children allowed?
Sind Kinder erlaubt?
zint *kin*·der er·*lowpt*

Also available from Lonely Planet:
German Phrasebook

ont break.

Glossary

(pl) indicates plural

A

Abfahrt – departure (trains)
Abtei – abbey
ADAC – Allgemeiner Deutscher Automobil Club (German Automobile Association)
Allee – avenue
Altstadt – old town
Ankunft – arrival (trains)
Antiquariat – antiquarian bookshop
Apotheke – pharmacy
Arbeitsamt – employment office
Arbeitserlaubnis – work permit
Ärzte – doctor
Ärztehaus – medical clinic
Ärztlicher Notdienst – emergency medical service
Aufenthaltserlaubnis – residency permit
Auflauf, Aufläufe (pl) – casserole
Ausgang, Ausfahrt – exit
Aussiedler – German settlers who have returned from abroad (it usually refers to post-WWII expulsions), sometimes called *Spätaussiedler*
Autobahn – motorway
Autonome (pl) – left-wing anarchists
AvD – Automobilclub von Deutschland (Automobile Club of Germany)

B

Bad – spa, bath
Bahnhof – train station
Bahnsteig – train station platform
Bau – building
Bedienung – service; service charge
Behinderte – disabled
Berg – mountain
Bergbaumuseum – mining museum
Besenwirtschaft – seasonal wine restaurant indicated by a broom above the doorway
Bezirk – district
Bibliothek – library
Bierkeller – cellar pub
Bierstube – traditional beer pub
Bildungsroman – literally 'novel of education'; literary work in which the personal development of a single individual is central
BRD – Bundesrepublik Deutschland or, in English, FRG (Federal Republic of Germany): the name for Germany today; before reunification it applied to West Germany
Brücke – bridge
Brunnen – fountain or well

Bundesland – federal state
Bundesrat – upper house of the German Parliament
Bundestag – lower house of the German Parliament
Bundesverfassungsgericht – Federal Constitutional Court
Burg – castle
Busbahnhof – bus station

C

CDU – Christian Democratic Union
Christkindlmarkt – Christmas market; see also *Weihnachtsmarkt*
CSU – Christian Social Union; Bavarian offshoot of CDU

D

DB – Deutsche Bahn (German national railway)
DDR – Deutsche Demokratische Republik or, in English, GDR (German Democratic Republic): the name for the former East Germany; see also BRD
Denkmal – memorial
Deutsches Reich – German Empire: refers to the period 1871–1918
Dirndl – traditional women's dress (Bavaria only)
DJH – Deutsches Jugendherbergswerk (German youth hostels association)
Dom – cathedral
Dorf – village
DZT – Deutsche Zentrale für Tourismus (German National Tourist Office)

E

Eingang – entrance
Eintritt – admission
Einwanderungsland – country of immigrants
Eiscafé – ice-cream parlour

F

Fahrplan – timetable
Fahrrad – bicycle
Fasching – pre-Lenten carnival (term used in southern Germany)
FDP – Free Democratic Party
Ferienwohnung, Ferienwohnungen (pl) – holiday flat or apartment
Fest – festival
FKK – nude bathing area
Flammekuche – Franco-German dish consisting of a thin layer of pastry topped with cream, onion, bacon and sometimes cheese or mushrooms, and cooked in a wood-fired oven. Especially prevalent on menus in the Palatinate and the Black Forest.

Fleets – canals in Hamburg
Flohmarkt – flea market
Flughafen – airport
Föhn – an intense autumn wind in the Agerman Alps and Alpine foothills
Forstweg – forestry track
Franken – 'Franks', Germanic people influential in Europe between the 3rd and 8th centuries
Freikorps – WWI volunteers
Fremdenverkehrsamt/Fremdenverkehrsverein – tourist office
Fremdenzimmer – tourist room
FRG – Federal Republic of Germany; see also BRD
Fussball – football, soccer

G
Garten – garden
Gasse – lane or alley
Gastarbeiter – literally 'guest worker'; labourer from primarily Mediterranean countries who came to Germany in the 1950s and 1960s to fill a labour shortage
Gästehaus – guesthouse
Gaststätte, Gasthaus – informal restaurant, inn
GDR – the German Democratic Republic (the former East Germany); see also BRD, DDR
Gedenkstätte – memorial site
Gemütlichkeit – a particularly convivial, cosy ambience and setting, for instance in a pub, restaurant or living room
Gepäckaufbewahrung – left-luggage office
Gesamtkunstwerk – literally 'total artwork'; integrates painting, sculpture and architecture
Gestapo – Nazi secret police
Glockenspiel – literally 'bell play'; carillon, often on a cathedral or town hall, sounded by mechanised figures depicting religious or historical characters
Gründerzeit – literally 'foundation time'; the period of industrial expansion in Germany following the founding of the German Empire in 1871

H
Hafen – harbour, port
halbtrocken – semi-dry (wine)
Hauptbahnhof – central train station
Heide – heath
Heiliges Römisches Reich – Holy Roman Empire, which lasted from the 8th century to 1806; the German lands comprised the bulk of the Empire's territory
Herzog – duke
Heu Hotels – literally 'hay hotels'; cheap forms of accommodation that are usually set in farmhouses and similar to bunk barns in the UK
Hitlerjugend – Hitler Youth organisation
hochdeutsch – literally 'high german'; standard spoken and written German, developed from a regional Saxon dialect

Hochkultur – literally 'high culture'; meaning 'advanced civilisation'
Hof, Höfe (pl) – courtyard
Höhle – cave
Hotel Garni – a hotel without a restaurant where you are only served breakfast

I
Imbiss – stand-up food stall; see also Schnellimbiss
Insel – island

J
Jugendgästehaus – youth guesthouse of a higher standard than a youth hostel
Jugendherberge – youth hostel
Jugendstil – Art Nouveau
Junker – originally a young, noble landowner of the Middle Ages; later used to refer to reactionary Prussian landowners

K
Kabarett – cabaret
Kaffee und Kuchen – literally 'coffee and cake'; traditional afternoon coffee break in Germany
Kaiser – emperor; derived from 'Caesar'
Kanal – canal
Kantine – cafeteria, canteen
Kapelle – chapel
Karneval – pre-Lenten festivities (along the Rhine)
Karte – ticket
Kartenvorverkauf – ticket booking office
Kino – cinema
Kirche – church
Kloster – monastery, convent
Kneipe – pub
kommunales Kino – alternative or studio cinema
Konditorei – cake shop
König – king
Konsulat – consulate
Konzentrationslager (KZ) – a concentration camp
KPD – German Communist Party
Krankenhaus – hospital
Kreuzgang – monastery
Kristallnacht – literally 'Night of Broken Glass'; attack on Jewish synagogues, cemeteries and businesses by Nazis and their supporters on the night of 9 November 1938 that marked the beginning of full-scale persecution of Jews in Germany (also known as *Reichspogromnacht*)
Kunst – art
Kunstlieder – early German 'artistic songs'
Kurfürst – prince-elector
Kurhaus – literally 'spa house', but usually a spa town's central building, used for social gatherings and events and often housing the town's casino

Kurort – spa resort
Kurtaxe – resort tax
Kurverwaltung – spa resort administration
Kurzentrum – spa centre

L

Land, Länder (pl) – state
Landtag – state parliament
Lederhosen – traditional leather trousers with attached braces (Bavaria only)
Lesbe, Lesben (pl) – lesbian (n)
lesbisch – lesbian (adj)
lieblich – sweet (wine)
Lied – song

M

Maare – crater lakes in the Eifel Upland area west of the Rhine
Markgraf – margrave; German nobleman ranking above a count
Markt – market; often used instead of *Marktplatz*
Marktplatz – marketplace or square; often abbreviated to *Markt*
Mass – 1L tankard or stein of beer
Meer – sea
Mehrwertsteuer (MwST) – value-added tax
Meistersinger – literally 'master singer'; highest level in medieval troubadour guilds
Mensa – university cafeteria
Milchcafé – milk coffee, *café au lait*
Mitfahrzentrale – ride-sharing agency
Mitwohnzentrale – an accommodation-finding service that is usually for long-term stays
Münster – minster or large church, cathedral
Münzwäscherei – coin-operated laundrette

N

Nord – north
Notdienst – emergency service
NSDAP – National Socialist German Workers' Party

O

Ossis – nickname for East Germans
Ost – east
Ostalgie – a romanticised yearning for the GDR era, derived from 'nostalgia'
Ostler – old term for an *Ossi*
Ostpolitik – former West German chancellor Willy Brandt's foreign policy of 'peaceful coexistence' with the GDR

P

Palast – palace, residential quarters of a castle
Pannenhilfe – roadside breakdown assistance for motorists

Paradies – architectural term for a church vestibule or anteroom; literally 'paradise'
Parkhaus – car park
Parkschein – parking voucher
Parkscheinautomat – vending machine selling parking vouchers
Passage – shopping arcade
Pension, Pensionen (pl) – relatively cheap boarding house
Pfand – deposit for bottles and sometimes glasses (in beer gardens)
Pfarrkirche – parish church
plattdeutsch – literally 'low german'; a German dialect that is spoken in parts of northwestern Germany (especially Lower Saxony)
Platz – square
Postamt – post office
postlagernd – poste restante
Priele – tideways on the Wattenmeer on the North Sea coast
Putsch – revolt

R

radwandern – bicycle touring
Rathaus – town hall
Ratskeller – town hall restaurant
Reich – empire
Reichspogromnacht – see *Kristallnacht*
Reisezentrum – travel centre in train or bus stations
Reiterhof – riding stable or centre
Rezept – medical prescription
R-Gespräch – reverse-charge call
Ruhetag – literally 'rest day'; closing day at a shop or restaurant
Rundgang – tour, route

S

Saal, Säle (pl) – hall, room
Sammlung – collection
Säule – column, pillar
S-Bahn – suburban-metropolitan shuttle lines; Schnellbahn
Schatzkammer – treasury
Schiff – ship
Schifffahrt – shipping, navigation
Schloss – palace, castle
Schnaps – schnapps
Schnellimbiss – stand-up food stall
schwul – gay (adj)
Schwuler, Schwule (pl) – gay (n)
SED – Sozialistische Einheitspartei Deutschlands (Socialist Unity Party)
See – lake
Sekt – sparkling wine

Selbstbedienung (SB) – self-service (restaurants, laundrettes etc)
Soziale Marktwirtschaft – literally 'social market economy'; German form of market-driven economy with built-in social protection for employees
Spätaussiedler – see *Aussiedler*
SPD – Sozialdemokratische Partei Deutschlands (Social Democratic Party)
Speisekarte – menu
Sportverein – sports association
SS – Schutzstaffel; organisation within the Nazi party that supplied Hitler's bodyguards, as well as concentration-camp guards and the Waffen-SS troops in WWII
Stadt – city or town
Stadtbad, Stadtbäder (pl) – public pool
Stadtwald – city or town forest
Stasi – GDR secret police (from Ministerium für Staatssicherheit, or Ministry of State Security)
Stau – traffic jam
Staudamm, Staumauer – dam
Stausee – reservoir
Stehcafé – stand-up café
Strand – beach
Strasse – street; often abbreviated to Str
Strausswirtschaft – seasonal wine pub indicated by wreath above the doorway, also known as a *Besenwirtschaft*
Süd – south
Szene – scene (ie where the action is)

T
Tageskarte – daily menu or day ticket on public transport
Tal – valley
Teich – pond
Thirty Years' War – pivotal war in Central Europe (1618–48) that began as a German conflict between Catholics and Protestants
Tor – gate
trampen – hitchhiking
Treuhandanstalt – trust established to sell off GDR assets after the *Wende*
trocken – dry (wine)
Trödel – junk
Turm – tower

U
U-Bahn – underground train system
Übergang – transit or transfer point
Ufer – bank

V
verboten – forbidden
Verkehr – traffic
Verkehrsamt/Verkehrsverein – tourist office
Viertel – quarter, district
Volkslieder – folk song

W
Wald – forest
Waldfrüchte – wild berries
Wäscherei – laundry
Wattenmeer – tidal flats on the North Sea coast
Wechselstube – currency exchange office
Weg – way, path
Weihnachtsmarkt – Christmas market; see also *Christkindlmarkt*
Weingut – wine-growing estate
Weinkeller – wine cellar
Weinprobe – wine tasting
Weinstube – traditional wine bar or tavern
Wende – 'change' of 1989, ie the fall of communism that led to the collapse of the GDR and German reunification
Weser Renaissance – ornamental architectural style found around the Weser River
Wessis – nickname for West Germans
Westler – old term for a *Wessi*
White skins – skinheads wearing jackboots with white laces
Wiese – meadow
Wirtschaftswunder – Germany's post-WWII 'economic miracle'

Z
Zahnradbahn – cog-wheel railway
Zeitung – newspaper
Zimmer Frei – room available (for accommodation purposes)
Zimmervermittlung – a room-finding service, primarily for short-term stays; see also *Mitwohnzentrale*
ZOB – Zentraler Omnibusbahnhof (central bus station)

Behind the Scenes

THIS BOOK

The 1st edition of *Germany* was written by Steve Fallon, Anthony Haywood, Andrea Schulte-Peevers and Nick Selby. Andrea and Anthony also updated the 2nd edition, along with Jeremy Gray, and worked on the 3rd edition with Andrew Bender, Angela Cullen and Jeanne Oliver.

This 4th edition of *Germany* was prepared in Lonely Planet's Melbourne office. Andrea Schulte-Peevers again came on board, coordinating a skilled team of authors comprising Sarah Johnstone, Etain O'Carroll, Jeanne Oliver, Tom Parkinson and Nicola Williams.

THANKS FROM THE AUTHORS

Andrea Schulte-Peevers Major thanks to the leagues of people who've helped in the research of this book, including tourist office staff, friends and family. Extra big hugs to Kerstin and Marco Göllrich; Walter, Ursula, Judith and Oliver Schulte; Tina, Torsten, Timo and Thure Piltz; and Steffi, Jörn and Nele Gellert-Beckmann for being such constants in my life. Frau Renate Stenshorn of the Rhineland-Palatinate tourist office deserves a special mention for her extraordinary efforts. As usual, though, the biggest thanks go to David without whose love, support and patience this would be a most lonely planet for me indeed.

Sarah Johnstone Thank you to all the staff in the many tourist offices who patiently helped me along the way. Christine Lambert in Dessau, in particular, stands out as having been a brilliant help, and talking about Bauhaus with her felt

more like fun than work. I'm also grateful to old friends in Germany like Rainer and Irene Horn and new friends like Natalie Arends and Eva May for company and insider tips. Thanks to my mate Max for moral support, and I'm sorry I didn't have time to track down Kirstin or Peter. But my biggest debt this time undoubtedly is to coordinators Andrea, Suzannah and Birgit for their supreme patience and good humour in enduring late copy and emails regularly going astray. Thank you!

Etain O'Carroll Heartfelt thanks to the staff at numerous tourist offices around Bavaria who patiently answered all my questions, plied me with glossy brochures and filled me with enthusiasm for their local attractions. Special thanks to Katje Zunterer in Mittenwald for saving me from a parking ticket; Rupert Geiger in Oberammergau; Christine Harper in Berchtesgaden; Euraide in Munich; the ever-patient staff at Nuremberg tourist office for their assistance and good humour; Stefanie Lackmeier in Bad Tölz; Anje Gerle in Oberstdorf; and to the staff at the GAP, Regensburg and Würzburg tourist offices for their time, help and support. Back at home a big thank you to Peter and Sheila Baseby for all the background information and their sheer enthusiasm for all things Bavarian, Bernhard HG Schaefer for his observations and opinions over the years, Oda for keeping me sane through the long days of Felixisation, and to Tim Ryder for starting the project so well and his patience with the endless queries. Thanks also to Mark for all his support, and for putting up with the incredible mess on my desk – and his.

THE LONELY PLANET STORY

The story begins with a classic travel adventure: Tony and Maureen Wheeler's 1972 journey across Europe and Asia to Australia. There was no useful information about the overland trail then, so Tony and Maureen published the first Lonely Planet guidebook to meet a growing need.

From a kitchen table, Lonely Planet has grown to become the largest independent travel publisher in the world, with offices in Melbourne (Australia), Oakland (USA), London (UK) and Paris (France).

Today Lonely Planet guidebooks cover the globe. There is an ever-growing list of books and information in a variety of media. Some things haven't changed. The main aim is still to make it possible for adventurous travellers to get out there – to explore and better understand the world.

At Lonely Planet we believe travellers can make a positive contribution to the countries they visit – if they respect their host communities and spend their money wisely.

Jeanne Oliver First, I'd like to thank Maria Riesterer for sharing her local knowledge of the region and helping to make my research easier. A thousand thanks are also due to the staff at the various tourist offices throughout Baden-Württemberg who provided information and documentation freely and with a smile. I'm grateful to Angela Cullen for her fine update of the last edition and to Tim Ryder, the commissioning editor of this project, for his good grace. Our conscientious and patient coordinating author, Andrea Schulte-Peevers also deserves a round of applause for facilitating our work.

Tom Parkinson Thanks to all the people who helped me out along the way: Lena, Lotte, Martin, Holger et al in Marburg; Kristen, Troy and Ferdy, Craig and friends, Amanda and the laundry Yanks, and some bemused young musicians in Leipzig; Scott, Patrick, Evie and Kattel in Dresden; Arek in Görlitz; and Anne-K, Silvius and co in Herzberg. For extra hospitality I'm particularly indebted to Kurt and Sabine Hasenbach in Offenbach and fellow Sahara veteran Reinhard Straach, king of Herzberg. Special mention should also go to the many tourist offices around the country who fixed me up with accommodation and provided a rainforest-busting 35kg of brochures and information! In the UK, cheers to Jill at Mingo PR for providing Frankfurt sounds, and to former editor Tim Ryder for putting the job my way. Finally, special thanks to Kathryn Hanks for her valuable contributions in Mecklenburg, and Nina K, just because.

Nicola Williams Loving smiles of thanks to my parents-in-law, Christa and Karl Otto Lüfkens, whose family home in Krefeld has provided me with a wealth of eye-openers into German culture over the years (not to mention a brain-teasing lesson in the great German tradition of splitting trash between several dozen kitchen bins). Thank you too to Krefeld architect Werner Klinkhammer; Frankfurter-born Andreas Rogal; my co-authors Andrea Schulte-Peevers, Sarah Johnstone and Tom Parkinson for particularly invaluable input; and at home, to my very own new-generation Germans, Matthias and Niko Lüfkens.

CREDITS

Series Publishing Manager Virginia Maxwell oversaw the redevelopment of the country guides series with help from Maria Donohoe. Regional Publishing Manager Katrina Browning steered the development of this title. The series was designed by James Hardy, with mapping development by

Paul Piaia. The series development team included Shahara Ahmed, Susie Ashworth, Gerilyn Attebery, Jenny Blake, Anna Bolger, Verity Campbell, Erin Corrigan, Nadine Fogale, Dave McClymont, Leonie Mugavin, Rachel Peart, Lynne Preston and Howard Ralley.

This edition was commissioned and developed in Lonely Planet's London office by Tim Ryder, and taken on by Judith Bamber and Fiona Christie. Cartography for this guide was developed by Mark Griffiths. Overseeing production were project managers Charles Rawlings-Way and Andrew Weatherill, managing editor Brigitte Ellemor and managing cartographer Mark Griffiths.

Editing was coordinated by Suzannah Shwer with assistance from Pete Cruttenden, Sally Steward, Anne Mulvaney, Kristin Odijk, John Hinman, Adrienne Costanzo, Kate James, Danielle North and Emma Koch. Cartography was coordinated by Birgit Jordon and Natasha Velleley, with assistance from James Ellis, Tony Fankhauser, Michael Mammarella, Louise Klep, Huw Fowles, Karen Fry, Joelene Kowalski, Chris Lee Ack and Chris Tsismetzis. Vicki Beale laid the book out with help from Sally Darmody. John Shippick prepared the colour pages. The cover was designed by Daniel New and Yukiyoshi Kamimura. Quentin Frayne compiled the Language chapter.

BEHIND THE SCENES

THANKS FROM LONELY PLANET

Many thanks to the travellers who used the last edition and wrote to us with helpful hints, useful advice and interesting anecdotes:

A Kevin Abney, Melissa Agney-Zinsou, Sebastian Althen, Ian Andersen, John Arwe **B** PL Baas, Tom Bailess, Anne Baumeister-Eckersley, Gregory Becker, Madelien Bierema, Dorit Bockelmann, Steve Bratt, Sam Brkich, Raymond Brownell, Jessica Browning, Dorris Bruce, Julika Bruening, Emily Butler **C** Al Carlson, Peter Cerda, Carmen Chan, Lisa Cipelli, Robert Codling, Yvonne and Brendan Colley, Elisabeth Cox, John Cox, J Cravens, Lesley Croft, Dela Cruz **D** Roger Davis, Steffi Domagk **E** Thomas Edison, Robert Edmunds, Frank Eisenhuth, Cosima Ertl, Cathrin Eszbach **F** Deborah Fink, Mickie Folmar, Nick Fowler, Markus A Frank, Viola Franke, Anne Froger, Ralph Fuchs **G** Joshua C Gambrel, Wayne Geerling, Joseph Gillespie, Sophie Goodrick, M Grabautzky, Elena Grant, Michael Groth, Thomas Guenther **H** Horst & Debra Hagemann, Olivia Hall, Rolf Hampel, Mulle Harbort, Mike Harris, Henning Heerde, Adrian Hervey, Stacy Hoffinger, Mindy Huixing, Christopher Hunt, John Hyatt **J** F Jackson, Ronald Jahn, Rebecca Johannsen, Maurice Jonas **K** Ole Kampovski, Anil Kanji, Jennifer Kirchner, Dominik Klein, Wim Klumpenhouwer, Joachim Korner, Martin Koschmall, Toni-Ann Kram, Martin Krauskopf, Noriko Kumagai **L** Jane Larew, James Leitzell, YH Leung, David Lewis, Don Lowman, Ewan Lumsden, Paul Lyddon **M** Kyrill Makoski, Bruce Mansell, Barry Meldrum, Gunnar Merbach, Sarah Merrit, Jo Milne, Barry Moses, Laurent Mousson, Marcus Munkemer, Franklin Murillo, Jonathan Murphy, Tracey Murphy, Gabriela Muskova **N** Monica Naish, Howard & Heide Neighbor, Mark Nessfield, Deirdre Ni Dhea, Katarzyna Niemiec, Joe Nisbet, Yvette Norris, Joel Northcott **O** Elka (Alice) Olsen, Paul Ozorak **P** Alexander Paluch, The Pegasus Team, Ed Piekara, Barbara Pilling, Christopher Pope, Heidi Potts, John Preece, Giles Pritchard, Emma Pritchett **R** Peter Ratcliffe, Jean-Renaud Ratti, Bettina Rickert, Ronald Jan Rieger, Klaus Rohde, Kelly Ann Rooke, Graham Rowe, Jaroslaw Rudnik, Melissa Russel **S** Mary Saldanha, Kuros Sarshar, Bernard Sayer, Uta Scheller, Julia Scheunemann, Christoph Schwerdtfeger, Daniela Schwirz, Stephen Seifert, Erik Seiling, John Sharp, Lincoln Siliakus, Alexander Smith, Mike St John, Johannes Suechting, Gabriel Syme **T** Giorgio Tedeschi, Johannes Teverssen, Jeroen Thijs, Philipp Thomas, Cushla Thompson, Margaret Thresh, Mike Tobin, Michael Tung Yep **U** CCM Ubben-Verbraak **V** Gabriel Veilleux, Joyce Vermeer **W** Conor Waring, Christoph Wewer, Roy Wiesner, Jon Wilton, Mark Wojcik, Raymond Wu **Y** Andrew Young, Sit Yue Hai **Z** Fernando Zaidan, Holger Zimmermann, Attila Zsunyi, Angela Zwadle

ACKNOWLEDGMENTS

Many thanks to the following for the use of their content:
Mountain High Maps® © 1993 Digital Wisdom, Inc. and Deutscher Brauer-Bund e. V., Wasser- und Schiff-fahrtsamt Eberswalde, Berliner Verkehrsbetriebe (BVG) and Münchner Verkehrs- und Tarifverbund GmbH (MVV) for permission to use their material.

Index

A

Aachen 594-7, **595**
Abbe, Ernst 231
abbeys
  Abbey of St Liudger 601
  Benedictine Abbey 472
  Kloster Lorsch 555
  Messel 555
accommodation 734-7
  camping 735
  farm holidays 735
  holiday flats 736
  hostels 736
  hotels 736-7
  inns 737
  long-term rentals 737
  pensions 737
  private rooms 737
activities 737-9,
  see also individual activities
Adolf-Mittag-See 240
Ahr River 504
Ahr Valley 504-7
Ahrweiler 505
air travel
  air fares 756-9
  airline offices 755-6
  airports 755
  to/from Germany 755-9
  within Germany 763
Albers, Josef
  Josef Albers Museum 606
Albtal 476
AlliiertenMuseum 115-16
Alpirsbach 463
Alpspitze 382
Alster River 684
Alte Nationalgalerie 105
Altena 616
Altenahr 506
Alter Schwede (Wismar) 302,
  168-9
Altes Land 707
Altes Museum 105
Altmark, the 242-3
Altmühl River 404
Altmühltal Nature Park 404-5
Amalia, Anna 216, 217
Amrum 732
Andechs 357
animals 69-70, 71,
  see also bird-watching
Ankershagen 294
Apel, Heinrich 239
aquariums
  Kiel 712
  Sealife Speyer 501

archaeological sites, see Roman ruins,
  ruins
Archäologischer Park 576
architecture 55-9, 145, 147, see also
  individual styles and periods
art galleries & museums, see also
  museums
  Albertinum 171
  Alte Nationalgalerie 105
  Alte Pinakothek 336
  Anhalt Art Gallery 246
  Augusteum 674
  Augustinermuseum 469
  Ausstellungsgebäude
    Mathildenhöhe 554
  Berggruen Collection 114
  Berlin 137
  Bildergalerie 147
  Bomann Museum 647
  Brücke Museum 116
  DaimlerChrysler Contemporary 110
  Deichtorhallen 693
  Deutsche Guggenheim 104
  Galerie der Gegenwart 693
  Galerie Dresdener Kunst 171
  Galerie Eigen+Art 188
  Galerie Haus Dacheröden 205
  Galerie im Cranachhaus 251
  Galerie Junge Kunst 157
  Galerie Noah 373
  Galerie Waidspeicher 205
  Gemäldegalerie 109
  Graphikmuseum Pablo Picasso
    608-9
  Hackesche Höfe 107
  Hamburger Bahnhof 108
  Hamburger Kunsthalle 693
  Haus der Kulturen der Welt 108
  IM Pei Bau 104
  K20 Kunstsammlung am
    Grabbeplatz 571
  K21 Kunstsammlung im
    Ständehaus 571
  Kunst- und Ausstellungshalle der
    Bundesrepublik Deutschland 591
  Kunsthalle (Bremen) 623
  Kunsthalle (Düsseldorf) 571
  Kunsthalle (Emden) 675
  Kunsthalle (Karlsruhe) 456
  Kunsthalle (Kiel) 712
  Kunsthalle (Mannheim) 449
  Kunsthalle der Hypo-Kulturstiftung
    335
  Kunsthalle Erfurt 208
  Kunsthaus (Stade) 707
  Kunstmuseum (Wolfsburg) 664
  Kunstmuseum Bonn 591

  Kunstmuseum Walter 373
  Kunstsammlungen (Chemnitz) 182
  Kunstsammlung
    (Neubrandenburg) 292
  Kupferstichkabinett 110
  Ludwig Forum für Internationale
    Kunst 596
  Ludwig Museum (Koblenz) 509
  Lyonel-Feininger-Galerie 279
  Marburger Kunstverein
    Ausstellungshaus und Artothek
    559
  Martin-Gropius-Bau 111
  Municipal Gallery (Meersburg) 484
  Museum am Ostwall 604
  Museum de Bildenden Künste 186
  Museum Folkwang 599
  Museum für Gegenwartskunst 617
  Museum für Konkrete Kunst 408
  Museum für Moderne Kunst
    (Frankfurt-am-Main) 544
  Museum für Neue Kunst (Freiburg)
    469
  museum kunst palast (Düsseldorf)
    570-1
  Museum Ludwig (Cologne) 580
  Museum Moderne Kunst (Passau)
    419
  Museum Wiesbaden 556-7
  Museumsberg Flensburg 724-5
  Neue Nationalgallerie 109
  Neue Pinakothek 336
  Neues Museum (Nuremberg) 391
  Neues Museum (Weimar) 216
  Old Masters Gallery 172
  Pinakothek der Moderne 336
  Roselius Haus 622
  Schleswig-Holstein-Haus 288
  Sprengel Museum 637
  Staatliche Kunsthalle
    (Baden-Baden) 458
  Staatsgalerie (Stuttgart) 428
  Städelsches Kunstinstitut
    (Frankfurt-am-Main) 544
  Stadtgalerie (Saarbrücken) 531
  Tacheles 107
  Villa Hügel 600
Art Nouveau architecture
  Bremen 621, 622
  history of 57
  Kollegiengebäude I 469
  Mädlerpassage 188
  Ruhrgebiet, the 598
  Traben-Trarbach 523
  Weimar 216
arts 52-68, see also individual styles
  and periods

Artists' Trail (Deidesheim) 503
Aschaffenburg 365
ATMs 749
Attendorn 616
Audi Forum 408
Augsburg 371-5
August, Carl 215
Augustusburg 183-4
Autobahn 434, **767**
Autostadt 663-4

B
Babelsberg 149
babysitters 118
Bach, Carl Philipp Emanuel 59
Bach, Johann Sebastian
  Bach Memorial 190
  Bach Museum 185
  Bachhaus 225
  birthplace of 223
  home town of 184
  life of 149
  tomb of 189
  work of 59, 222, 648
Bacharach 513-14
Bad Doberan 301
Bad Dürkheim 503-4
Bad Harzburg 269-70
Bad Karlshafen 564, 645-6
Bad Kösen 260-1
Bad Lausick 194
Bad Neuenahr 505
Bad Neuenahr-Ahrweiler 504-6
Bad Schandau 179
Bad Tölz 358-9
Baden-Baden 457-61
Baden-Württemberg 423-90, **425**
Badische Weinstrasse 457
Baltic Sea 16
  tour of coast 16, **16**
Baltrum 680
Bamberg 396-9, **396**, 6
Barbarossahöhle 223
Bärental 473, 474
Barlach, Ernst
  Atelierhaus 291
  Gertrudenkapelle 291
  life of 290
baroque architecture
  Altes Rathaus (Bonn) 590
  Altstädter Rathaus 395
  Angermuseum 206
  Apelshaus 188
  Asamkirche Maria de Victoria 407
  Augustinerkirche (Mainz) 495
  Bad Karlshafen 645
  Barockhaus 199
  Benedictine Abbey 472

Blockhaus 171
Clemenskirche (Münster) 609
Dompropstei 480
Erbdrostenhof 609
Franziskanerkirche 358
Fulda 560
Görlitz 199
Haus zum Cavazzen 489
history of 53, 56
Kalvarienbergkirche 358
Ludwigslust ducal residence 290
Markgrafentheater 395
Markgräfliches Opernhaus 399
Marktkirche Zum Heiligen Geist 272
Michaeliskirche (Hamburg) 692
Michaelskirche (Munich) 335
Münster 607
Museum of Early Dresden Romanticism 169
Neues Palais 147
Peterskirche (Görlitz) 199
Rathaus (Bautzen) 197
Rathaus (Jena) 231
Rathaus (Lüneburg) 652
Rathaus (Neustadt an der Weinstrasse) 502
Rathaus (Rostock) 296-7
Rathaus (Speyer) 501
Rathaus (Tübingen) 438
Residenz (Würzberg) 360-2
Saarbrücken 530
St Peterskirche (Munich) 333
Schaetzlerpalais 372-3
Schloss (Münster) 609
Schloss Augustusburg 588
Schloss Elisabethenburg 230
Schloss Friedenstein 220
Schloss Nordkirchen 611
Siemenshaus 266
Statthalterpalais 206
Unteres Schloss 617
Walhalla (Osnabrück) 672
Zwinger 172
Basilica Vierzehnheiligen 403
basketball 135
Bastei 178-9
Battle of Teutoburg Forest, the 23, 24
Bauhaus
  Bauhaus Archive/Museum of Design 109
  Bauhaus Kolleg 244
  Bauhaus Museum 216
  Bauhausgebäude 244
  Dessau 243
  Haus am Horn 216
  history of 54, 57, 246
  Lyonel-Feininger-Galerie 279
  Martin-Gropius-Bau 111
  Meisterhäuser 244-5
  Ruhrgebiet, the 598
  Törten 245-6

Baumeister, Willi 54
Bautzen 196-8
Bavaria 317-422, **320-1**
Bavarian Alps 378-85, **7**, 168-9
Bavarian Forest 420-2
Bavarian Forest National Park 71, 421
Bayerisch Eisenstein 422
Bayreuth 399-402
Beatles, the
  history of 703
  Kaiserkeller 688
  museum 253-4
Beckenbauer, Franz 48
Becker, Boris 49
Beckmann, Max 55
Beck's Brewery 78, 623
beer 77-9, see also breweries
  Brauereimuseum (Lüneburg) 652
  beer gardens 82
Beethoven, Ludwig van
  Beethoven Haus 590
  Beethoven Memorial 590
  birthplace of 588
  work of 59
Befreiungshalle 416
Beilstein 525
Berchtesgaden 383-5
Berchtesgaden National Park 71, 383
Berchtesgadener Land 383-5
Bergen-Belsen 650-1
Berlin 87-141, **90**, **94-5**, **96-7**, **98**, **100-1**, **102**, **126-7**, **129**
  accommodation 119-24
  activities 116-17
  attractions 103-16
  Charlottenburg 113-15, 122-3, 127-8, 132-3, **102**
  clubbing 134
  discount cards 92
  drinking 129-32
  emergency services 92
  entertainment 132-6
  festivals 119
  food 124-9
  Friedrichshain 121-2, 126-7, 131, 132, **100-1**
  history 89-91
  Internet access 93
  Internet resources 93
  itineraries 91
  Kreuzberg 111-13, 121-2, 126-7, 131, 132, **100-1**
  maps 92
  medical services 93
  Mitte 103-11, 120-1, 124-6, 129-32, 130-1, **98**
  Prenzlauer Berg 120-1, 124-6, 129-32, 130-1, **126-7**
  Schöneberg 128-9, 131, 132-3, **129**
  shopping 136-8
  special events 119
  tourist offices 103

000 Map pages
000 Location of colour photographs

tours 118-19
travel to/from 138-9
travel within 139, **94-5**
Wilmersdorf 122-3, 127-8, **102**
Berlin Wall
  Berliner Mauer
    Dokumentationszentrum 112
  Checkpoint Charlie 111
  East Side Gallery 112
  history of 39, 40, 41, 89, 112
  Internet resources 40
  Wall Victims Memorial 112
Berlin Zoo 114
Berliner Dom 105
Berliner Unterwelten 118
Berlusconi, Silvio 44, 51
Bernau am Chiemsee 355
Bernkastel-Kues 522-3
Besenwirtschaft 432
Beuys, Joseph 55
bicycle travel, *see* cycling
Bierkeller 81
Biggesee 616
Bille River 684
Bingen 514-15
Bingen, Hildegard von 515, 516
Binz 314-15
birds 70, 294, *see also* bird-watching
bird-watching, *see also* birds
  Alpine 69
  Amrum 732
  eagles 513
  Hamburg Wadden Sea National
    Park 71
  Lower Oder Valley National Park 71
  Lower Saxony Wadden Sea
    National Park 71
  Müritz National Park 71
  Naturpark Elbufer-Drawehn 654
  St Goarshausen 513
  Schleswig-Holstein Wadden Sea
    National Park 71
  Vorpommersche Boddenlandschaft
    National Park 71
  Wutachschlucht 477
Birnau 485
Bismarck, Otto von
  biography of 30
  Bismarckhäuschen 668
  role in unification of Germany 30-1
Black Forest **455**
  Northern 454-62,
  Central 463-5
  Southern 466-77
  scenic drives 457
Blies Valley 535
Blomberg 358
Blomberg Mountain 358
Blumenthal 629
BMW
  BMW Museum 337
  factory 337

boating 739
  Bad Schandau 179
  Chiemsee 355-6
  Emden 676
  Freyburg 260
  Hamburg 695
  Hanse Sail Rostock 297
  Lindau 489
  Lower Oder Valley National Park
    161
  Munich 339
  Müritz National Park 294
  Oker Valley 268
  Poel Island 304
  Rostock 297
  Schwerin 288
  Stendal 243
  Stralsund 307
  Titisee-Neustadt 474
  Tollensesee 292
boat tours, *see also* cruises
  Brandenburg 149
  Lübben 153
  Lübbenau 154
  Niederfinow 162
  Rheinsberg 160
boat travel
  to/from Germany 761-3
  within Germany 764
Bochum 602-3
Bocksberg 268
Bode Valley 281
Bodensee 478-90
Bodenwerder 564, 645
Bonn 588-94, **589**
Bonndorf 477
borders, historical **36**
books
  animals 70
  architecture 57
  beer 78, 79
  food 75, 76, 83
  history 24, 30, 31, 32, 35, 37,
    39, 40
  music 59
  Nazism 32, 33
  plants 70
  politics 29
  theatre 68
  travel 84
  wine 80, 81
  WWI 31
  WWII 34, 35, 37
Boppard 511-12
Borkum 681
Bosch, Robert 426
Bottrop 606-7
Brahms, Johannes
  Johannes Brahms Museum 692
Brandenburg 142-62, **144**
  accommodation 149-50
  attractions 145-9

drinking 150
entertainment 150-1
festivals 149
food 150
tours 149
travel to/from 151
travel within 144, 151
Brandenburg an der Havel 151-3
  accommodation 152
  festivals 152
  food 152
  tours 152
  travel to/from 152
Brandenburg Concertos 149
Brandenburg Gate (Berlin) 53, 57,
  103-4, **136-7**
Brandt, Willy 39, 40, 64
Braubach 511
Braunfels, Stefan 59
Braunlage 270-1
Braunschweig 657-62, **658**
Brecht, Bertolt
  Bertolt-Brecht-Gedenkstätte 373
  Brecht-Weigel Gedenkstätte 107
  Brecht-Weigel-Haus 156
  work of 67
Breisach 471-2
Bremen 619-30, **621**, **624**
  accommodation 624-6
  activities 621-3
  attractions 621-3
  drinking 627
  entertainment 627-8
  Fairy-Tale Road 564
  food 626-7
  shopping 628
  travel to/from 628-9
  travel within 629
Bremen-Nord 629
Bremerhaven 630, **552-3**
breweries
  Alte Klosterbrauerei 403
  Beck's Brewery 623
  Dampfbier-Brauerei 420
  Dinkel Acker Brewery 429
  Fränkisches Brauereimuseum 397
  Friesisches Brauhaus zu Jever 677
  Klosterchenke Weltenburg 416
  Maisel's Brauerei-und-Büttnerei-
    Museum 400-1
Brocken mountain 273, 277, **168-9**
Brockenbahn 275
Brockenhaus 277
Brühl 588
Brussig, Thomas 64
Buchenwald 219
Buckow 156-7
bungee-trampoline 730
Burg Altena 616
Burg Are 506
Burg Eltz 525, **520-1**
Burg Hohenzollern 439-40

INDEX

Burglesum 629
bus tours 118
bus travel
    to/from Germany 759-60
    within Germany 764-5, 769
Busch, Wilhelm 63
business hours 739
Buxtehude 708

C
cable cars
    Eibsee-Seilbahn 379
    Schauinsland 470
    Thale 282
    Wiesbaden 556
Caesar, Julius 23
cafés 82
canoeing 739
    Altmühltal Nature Park 404
    Lower Oder Valley National Park 161
    Lübben 153
    Müritz National Park 71
    Rheinsberg 160
    Rügen Island 316
    Ulm 453
car racing 506
car travel
    Black Forest 457
    driving licence 766
    hire 766
    insurance 766-7
    road distance chart 765
    road rules 768
    to/from Germany 760
Caroline-Mathilde of Denmark 647
casinos
    Bad Neuenahr 505
    Baden-Baden 458
    Konstanz 480
castles & palaces
    Altes Schloss (Baden-Baden) 459
    Altes Schloss (Bayreuth) 400
    Altes Schloss (Meersburg) 483-4
    Burg Altena 616
    Burg Blankenstein 602
    Burg Bosselstein 526
    Burg Dankwarderode 659
    Burg Eltz 525
    Burg Falkenstein 280
    Burg Hohenzollern 439-40
    Burg Hülshoff (Havixbeck) 611
    Burg Katz 513
    Burg Klopp 514
    Burg Maus 513
    Burg Metternich 525
    Burg Reichenstein 514
    Burg Rheinfels 512
    Burg Rheinstein 514

Burg Sooneck 514
Burg Stahleck 513
Burg Vischering 611
Burgruine Landshut 522
Cyriaksburg castle 205
Dornburger Schlösser 234
Drachenburg 594
Ehrenbreitstein 509-10
Fallersleben Schloss 665
Grevenburg 523
Hambacher Schloss 502
Herzogsschloss 417
Hirschhorn Castle 445
Hohe Schloss 376
Jagdschloss Granitz 314
Japanisches Palais 171
Kaiserburg 389
Kaiserpfalz 266
Kurländer Palais 171
Landgrafenschloss 559
Landschaftsgarten Grosskühnau 248
Marksburg 511
Marmorpalais 148
Neue Residenz (Bamberg) 397
Neues Schloss (Bayreuth) 399-400
Neues Schloss (Meersburg) 484
Neues Schloss (Stuttgart) 428
Neues Schloss Schleissheim 357
Palais Boisserée 444
Palais Schaumburg 591
Pillnitz Palace 177-8
prince-electors' residence (Trier) 520
Reichsburg 524
Renaissance Altes Schloss
    Schleissheim 357
Renaissance Neues Schloss
    (Baden-Baden) 459
Residenz (Eichstätt) 405
Residenzschloss (Ludwigsburg) 435
Residenzschloss (Mannheim) 449
Saarbrücker Schloss 531
Schaetzlerpalais 372-3
Schloss (Augustusburg) 183
Schloss (Celle) 647
Schloss (Chemnitz) 182
Schloss (Dresden) 172
Schloss (Erlangen) 395
Schloss (Güstrow) 290
Schloss (Heidelberg) 443
Schloss (Jever) 677
Schloss (Karlsruhe) 456
Schloss (Kiel) 712
Schloss (Münster) 609
Schloss (Oldenburg) 674
Schloss (Schwerin) 288
Schloss (Tangermünde) 243
Schloss (Weilburg) 558
Schloss (Wolfenbüttel) 662
Schloss Augustusburg 588
Schloss Babelsberg 149
Schloss Bellevue 109
Schloss Benrath (Düsseldorf) 572

Schloss Charlottenburg 113-14
Schloss Ehrenburg 402
Schloss Elisabethenburg 230
Schloss Friedenstein 220
Schloss Gottorf 722
Schloss Heidecksburg 234
Schloss Herrenchiemsee 355
Schloss Hohenschwangau 375-6
Schloss Jägerhof 572
Schloss Johannisburg 365
Schloss Linderhof 381
Schloss Löwenburg 563
Schloss Luisium 248
Schloss Lustheim 357
Schloss Moritzburg 178, 254
Schloss Mosigkau 248
Schloss Neuhaus 614
Schloss Neuschwanstein 375
Schloss Nordkirchen 611
Schloss Nymphenburg 338
Schloss Oberstein 526
Schloss Oranienbaum 248
Schloss Ortenburg 197-8
Schloss Reinhardsbrunn 227
Schloss Rheinsberg 159
Schloss Rosenstein 429
Schloss Salem 485-6
Schloss Sanssouci 145
Schloss Schwetzingen 448-9
Schloss Stolzenfels 510
Schloss Thurn und Taxis 410-11
Schloss vor Husum 727
Schloss Weesenstein 177
Schloss Wilhelmsburg 228
Schloss Wilhelmshöhe 562-3
Schloss Wolfsburg 664
Schloss Wörlitz 247
Schlossberg (Quedlinburg) 279
Schönburg (Oberwesel) 513
Stadtschloss (Fulda) 561
    tours around 13, 17, 18, **13**, **17**, **18**
Unteres Schloss 617
Veitsburg 488
Veste Oberhaus 417
Wartburg 224-5
Wasserschloss 726
Wasserschloss Kemnade 602
Wernigerode Schloss 273
Willibaldsburg 406
Wittumspalais 217
Yburg castle (Baden-Baden) 459
cathedrals 17, **17**
    Albrechtsburg 180
    Berliner Dom 105
    Deutscher Dom 105
    Dom (Aachen) 595-6
    Dom (Bamberg) 397
    Dom (Braunschweig) 659
    Dom (Eichstätt) 405
    Dom (Fulda) 561
    Dom (Güstrow) 290-1
    Dom (Limburg) 558

Dom (Lübeck) 718
Dom (Magdeburg) 239
Dom (Mainz) 494-5
Dom (Paderborn) 613
Dom (Schwerin) 286
Dom (Trier) 520
Dom Maria Heimsuchung 372
Dom St Blasien 476-7
Dom St Marien (Erfurt) 207
Dom St Nicolaus (Stendal) 242
Dom St Nikolai (Greifswald) 309
Dom St Paul (Münster) 607
Dom St Peter (Osnabrück) 672
Dom St Peter (Regensburg) 410
Dom St Peter und Paul
    (Brandenburg an der Havel) 151
Dom St Petri (Bautzen) 197
Dom St Petri (Bremen) 622-3
Dom St Petri (Schleswig) 722-3
Dom St Stephan (Passau) 417-18
Dom St Viktor (Xanten) 575
Fairytale Cathedral 235
Frankfurter Dom 541-2
Französischer Dom 105
Hildesheimer Dom 655
Kaiserdom (Speyer) 500
Kaiserdom (Worms) 498
Kölner Dom 578-80
Münster (Ulm) 451-2
Museum am Dom (Würzburg) 362
tours around 13, 17, **13, 17**
Catholicism 27, 52
caves
    Atta-Höhle 616
    Marienglashöhle 227
    Rübeland Caves 275
Celle 646-50
Celtic fortress 281
Celtic people 23-4
cemeteries
    Alter Friedhof 592
    Dorotheenstädtischer Friedhof 108
    Heiliger Sand 498
    Historischer Friedhof 215
    Jewish cemetery
        (Frankfurt-am-Main) 545
CentrO Adventure Park 606
Chagall, Marc 495
Charlemagne 24, 25, 56, 62
Checkpoint Charlie 111
Chemnitz 181-3
Chemnitz River 181
Chiemsee 354-6
children, travel with 739-40
    activities 117-18
    babysitters 118 (Berlin)
    Fairy-Tale Park 443
    food 83
    Frankfurt airport 545
    German Doll & Bear Museum 512
    health 774
    Internet resources 319

Märchenwald 269
Munich 339
    Sea Life 480-1
    theatre 352
Chorin 162
Christmas markets
    Berlin 119
    Christkindlmarkt (Munich) 340
    Christkindlmarkt (Nuremberg) 391
churches
    Abdinghofkirche 614
    Alte Inselkirche 679
    Alte Kapelle 412
    Andreaskirche (Düsseldorf) 569
    Andreaskirche (Uhlbach) 434
    Asamkirche 335
    Asamkirche Maria de Victoria 407
    Augustinerkirche (Gotha) 221
    Augustinerkirche (Mainz) 495
    Augustinerkloster 207
    Barfüsserkirche 206
    Basilica Vierzehnheiligen 403
    Basilika St Johann 531
    Birnau 485
    Church of St John the Baptist 616
    Church St Ursula 580
    Church of Sts Cosmas and Damiani
        707
    Clemenskirche 609
    Damenstiftskirche 335
    Divi-Blasii Kirche 222
    Dom St Kilian 362
    Dreifaltigkeitskirche 199
    Dreikönigskirche 169
    Elisabethkirche 559
    Felsenkirche 526
    Florinskirche 509
    Franziskanerkirche 358
    Französische Kirche 148
    Frauenkirche (Dresden) 171
    Frauenkirche (Meissen) 180
    Frauenkirche (Munich) 335
    Frauenwörth Abbey 355
    Friedrichswerdersche Kirche 104
    Georgenkirche 225
    Gross St Martin 580
    Heiligen-Geist-Kirche (Wismar) 302
    Heiliggeistkirche (Flensburg) 725
    Heiliggeistkirche (Heidelberg) 443-4
    Heiliggeistkirche (Munich) 333
    Hofkirche 172
    Hugenottenkirche 395
    Jakobikirche (Chemnitz) 182
    Jakobikirche (Stendal) 242
    Jakobskirche (Rothenburg ob der
        Tauber) 366
    Jesuit church (Heidelberg) 444
    Jesuitenkirche (Paderborn) 613
    Johanniskirche (Saalfeld) 235
    Johanniskirche (Zittau) 201
    Kaiser-Wilhelm-Gedächtniskirche
        114

Kalvarienbergkirche 358
Karmelitenkirche 417
Katharinenkirche 718
Kirche Unser Lieben Frauen 622
Kloster Maria Laach 506-7
Kloster Unser Lieben Frauen 239
Klosterkirche 162
Konstantinbasilika 520
Konzerthalle CPE Bach 157
Kornmarktkirche 222
Kreuzkirche (Dresden) 171
Kreuzkirche (Zittau) 201
Lambertikirche 674
Liebfrauenkirche (Koblenz) 509
Liebfrauenkirche (Oberwesel) 513
Liebfrauenkirche (Ravensburg) 488
Liebfrauenkirche (Trier) 520
Liebfrauenmünster (Ingolstadt)
    408
Lorenzkirche 389-90
Ludwigskirche 531
Marienkirche (Berlin) 106
Marienkirche (Dessau) 246
Marienkirche (Dortmund) 604
Marienkirche (Flensburg) 725
Marienkirche (Frankfurt an der
    Oder) 157
Marienkirche (Greifswald) 309
Marienkirche (Husum) 727
Marienkirche (Lübeck) 717
Marienkirche (Mühlhausen) 222
Marienkirche (Neubrandenburg) 291
Marienkirche (Osnabrück) 672
Marienkirche (Rostock) 295
Marienkirche (Stendal) 242
Marienkirche (Stralsund) 306
Marienkirche (Zwickau) 195
Marktkirche (Hanover) 638
Marktkirche (Halle) 254
Marktkirche (Wiesbaden) 556
Marktkirche St Benedikti 278
Marktkirche Zum Heiligen Geist 272
Martinskirche 469
Michaeliskirche (Erfurt) 207
Michaeliskirche (Hamburg) 692
Michaelskirche (Fulda) 561
Michaelskirche (Munich) 335
Münster (Freiburg) 468
Münster (Konstanz) 480
Münster (Villingen-Schwenningen)
    466
Münster St Georg 369
Münster St Stephan (Breisach) 472
Neumünster 362
Nikolaikapelle (Soest) 612
Nikolaikirche (Berlin) 106
Nikolaikirche (Flensburg) 725
Nikolaikirche (Kiel) 712
Nikolaikirche (Leipzig) 188-9
Nikolaikirche (Potsdam) 148
Nikolaikirche (Rostock) 297
Nikolaikirche (Siegen) 617

INDEX

churches *continued*
Nikolaikirche (Stralsund) 306
Oberkirche 155
Orthodox chapel (Württemberg) 434
Parish Church (Eibingen) 516
Paulskirche (Frankfurt-am-Main) 541
Paulskirche (Schwerin) 286
Peterskirche (Bacharach) 513
Peterskirche (Erfurt) 207
Peterskirche (Görlitz) 199
Peterskirche (Lindau) 489
Petrikirche (Dortmund) 603
Petrikirche (Lübeck) 717
Petrikirche (Rostock) 297
Pfarrkirche Maria Himmelfahrt 358
Pfarrkirche St Katharinen 151
Pfarrkirche St Kornelius 598
Pfarrkirche St Michael 522
Pfarrkirche St Ulrich 503
Pfarrkirche Unsere Liebe Frau 388
Predigerkirche 206, 225
Reglerkirche 206
Reinoldikirche 603
Rochuskapelle 514
Russian Orthodox Church (Wiesbaden) 556
Russische Kirche (Baden-Baden) 459
St Andreaskirche (Eisleben) 256
St Andreaskirche (Hildesheim) 656
St Anna Kirche (Augsburg) 372
St Annenkirche (Eisleben) 256
St Georgenkirche (Schmalkalden) 229
St Georgskirche (Nördlingen) 370
St Gereon 580
St Gertraudkirche 157
St Hedwigskirche 104
St Jacobikirche (Göttingen) 668
St Jakobskirche (Straubing) 417
St Johannis (Föhr) 733
St Johanniskirche (Göttingen) 668
St Johanniskirche (Lüneburg) 652
St Lamberti Church (Münster) 609
St Lambertus Kirche (Düsseldorf) 569
St Maria & St Klemens Doppelkirche 592
St Maria im Kapitol 580
St Maria zur Höhe (Soest) 612
St Martin (Oberwesel) 513
St Michaeliskirche (Hildesheim) 656
St Nikolaikirche (Kalkar) 577
St Patrokli (Soest) 612
St Peterskirche (Mainz) 495
St Peterskirche (Munich) 333
St Petri (Buxtehude) 708

St Petri (Hamburg) 690
St Petri (Soest) 612
St Petri Pauli Kirche (Eisleben) 256
St Severin (Keitum) 730
St Stephanskirche 243
St Ulrich Kirche (Regensburg) 412
St-Gangolf-Kirche 520
St-Georgen-Kirche (Wismar) 302
St-Ignatius-Kirche (Mainz) 495
St-Marien-Kirche (Marburg) 559
St-Marien-Kirche (Wismar) 302
St-Nikolai-Kirche (Wismar) 302
St-Peter-und-Pauls-Kirche (Rothenburg ob der Tauber) 367
St-Stephan-Kirche (Mainz) 495
Sts Peter und Paul Kirche (Potsdam) 148
Schlosskirche (Augustusburg) 183
Schlosskirche (Friedrichshafen) 486
Schlosskirche (Lutherstadt Wittenburg) 250
Schottenkirche St Jakob 412
Sebalduskirche 388
Severikirche 207
Severuskirche (Boppard) 511
Stadtkirche (Celle) 648
Stadtkirche (Freudenstadt) 462
Stadtkirche (Jever) 677
Stadtkirche St Andreas 234
Stadtkirche St Marien (Lutherstadt Wittenburg) 250-1
Stadtkirche St Michael (Jena) 231
Stadtkirche St Peter und Paul (Weimar) 216
Stadtkirche St Wenzel 258
Stiftskirche (Aschaffenburg) 365
Stiftskirche (Baden-Baden) 459
Stiftskirche (Neustadt an der Weinstrasse) 502
Stiftskirche (Tübingen) 438
Stiftskirche St Cyriakus 280
Stiftskirche St Nikolaus (Comburg) 437
Suurhusen 676
Sylvestrikirche 273
Theatinerkirche St Kajetan 334-5
Thomaskirche (Leipzig) 189-90
tours around 17, **17**
Überwasserkirche (Münster) 607-8
Universitätskirche 395
Ursulinenkirche 417
Wigbertikirche 206
Wipertikirche 279
circuses
Cabuwazi 118
Circus Crone 352
classical music 62-3
Berlin 135
Berliner Philharmonie 110
Braunschweig 661
Cologne 587
Dresden 175-6

Düsseldorf 574
Erfurt 211
Festspiele Mecklenburg-Vorpommern 297
Frankfurt-am-Main 552
Göttingen 670
Hamburg 705
Händel Festival 668-9
Hanover 642-3
Heidelberg 447
Johannes Brahms Museum 692
Kreuzchor 171
Leipzig 192
Lübeck 720
Magdeburg 241-2
Munich 351
Schleswig-Holstein Music Festival 713
Stuttgart 433
Wagner Festival 401
Clausthal-Zellerfeld 272-3
climate 9, 740-1
clothing sizes 734
Coburg 402-3
Cochem 524-5
coffee 77, 83
Colditz 194
Colditz Escape Museum 194
Cologne 577-88, **578**, **583**, 8
accommodation 582-4
attractions 578-82
drinking 585
emergency services 577
entertainment 586-7
food 584-5
Internet access 577
medical services 577
shopping 587
travel to/from 587
travel within 587-8
Comburg 437
Communist Party 31
concentration camps
Bergen-Belsen 650-1
Buchenwald 219
Dachau Concentration Camp Memorial 354
Sachsenhausen Concentration Camp 158-9
consulates 744-5
contemporary art 54-5
Corinth, Lovis 53
costs 9-10
Cotta, Johann Friedrich
Cotta Haus 438
Cottbus 155
courses 741-2
credit cards 749
cruises 738
Attendorn 616
Berlin 118-19
Bremen 624

Emden 676
Hamburg 696
Hamelin 644
Heidelberg 444
Regensburg 413
Saar River 535
Saarbrücker 532
Stralsund 307
Wismar 303
culture 44–68
drink 83
food 83
Internet resources 44, 45
customs regulations 742
cycling
Altmühltal Nature Park 404–5
Bad Harzburg 269
Bavarian Forest National Park 71
Berlin 116–17
Danube Bike Trail 465
Elbetour Cycling Trail 653
Emden 676
German cyclists 49
Hamburg 695
Harz Mountains 264
hire 763
Internet resources 737
Jasmund National Park 71
Lahn Valley 558
Lake Constance 479
Lower Oder Valley National Park 71, 161
Max-Eyth-See 435
Mittenwald 381–2
Moselle Valley 517
Munich 339
Müritz National Park 71
Neubrandenburg 292
organisations 116, 117, 737
Passau 417
Poel Island 304
Rheinsberg 160
Rhine Valley 507–8
Romantic Road, the 359
routes 737, 763
rules 763, 769
Saale-Unstrut Region 257
Sauerland 615
Schierke 276
transport 763–4
Wernigerode 274

D
Dachau Concentration Camp Memorial 354
Dadaism 54
Daimler, Gottlieb 426
Danube Bike Trail 465
Danube Gorge 416
Danube River 407, 450, 453
Darmstadt 554–5
Deep Vein Thrombosis 773–4
Deidesheim 503

Demmler, Georg Adolph 57
Denmark 299, 312
Dessau 243–7
Dessau, Paul 60
Deutsche Alleenstrasse 313
Deutsche Uhrenstrasse 457
Deutsche Weinstrasse 502–4
diarrhoea 774
Dietrich, Marlene 64, 66
Dinkelsbühl 369–70
disabled travellers 743
discount cards 10, 743–4
Ditschard 506
diving 303
Dix, Otto 54, 55
Döblin, Alfred 63
Doldinger, Klaus 60
Dom, see cathedrals
Dom St Blasien 476–7
Dornburger Schlösser 234
Dortmund 603–5
Drachenfels 594
Dresden 165–77, 166–7, 170
accommodation 173–4
attractions 169–70
clubbing 176
drinking 175
entertainment 175–6
festivals 173
food 174–5
shopping 171
tours 172–3
travel to/from 176–7
travel within 177
drinks 77–81, 83
Droste, Annette Hülshoff von 484
Fürstenhäusle 484
Duisburg 606
Dürer, Albrecht
Albrecht-Dürer-Haus 389
Albrecht Dürer Monument 388
theory & practice of 52
Düsseldorf 568–75, 570, 8
accommodation 572–3
Altstadt 569–70
attractions 569–2
drinking 574
emergency services 569
entertainment 574
food 573–4
Internet access 569
Königsallee 571–2
Medienhafen 571
travel to/from 574–5
travel within 575

E
Eagle's Nest 384
East Frisian Islands 678–81
East Germany, see GDR
Eckerloch 276
economy 21–2, 39, 42–3
Ehrenbreitstein 509–10

Eibingen 516
Eichstätt 405–6
Eifel, the 504–7
Eifel mountains 509
Einstein, Albert 450
Eisenach 223–6, 224
Eisenman, Peter 59
Eisleben 256–7
Eisler, Hanns 60
Elbe River 165, 178, 180, 684
electricity 734
Elend 276
email services 747–8
embassies 744–5
Emden 675–6
emergencies, see inside front cover
Engels, Friedrich 29
Enlightenment, the 28–9
environmental issues 70, 72–3
Erfurt 204–12, 206, 208
accommodation 209–10
attractions 205
drinking 211
entertainment 211
food 210–11
tours 209
travel to/from 211–12
travel within 212
walking tour 206–9, 206
Erhard, Ludwig 37, 39
Erlangen 394–6
Ernst, Max 54
Essen 598–602
Ethnologisches Museum 115
Europa Park Rust 472–3
Europäischer Kulturpark Bliesbruck-Reinheim 535
European Economic Community (EEC) 37
European Union (EU) 42, 43
exchange rates, see inside front cover
expressionist art 54

F
Fairy-Tale Road 564, 643–6
Falkau 473
Fallersleben 665
farm museums
Hohenloher Freilandmuseum 437
Vogtbauernhof 463–4
Fassbinder, Rainer Werner 65
fax services 751–2
Federal Republic of Germany (FRG) history of 37–40
Feengrotten 234, 235
Feininger, Andreas 216
Feininger, Lyonel
Feiningerhaus 245
Lyonel-Feininger-Galerie 279
Feldberg 473–4
Fernsehturm 106
Ferropolis 248

INDEX

festivals 11, 745-6
  Africa-Festival 363
  Antikenfestspiele 521
  Bach Festival 190
  Bachtage 149
  Bingen/Rüdesheim 508
  Blühendes Barock 435
  Book Fair (Leipzig) 190
  Cannstatter Volksfest (Stuttgart) 430
  Carnival (Cologne) 581
  Christkindlmarkt (Munich) 340
  Christkindlmarkt (Nuremberg) 391
  Christmas markets 119
  Christopher Street Day 119, 130
  Dinkelsbühl's Jazz Festival 369
  Dippemess 546
  Domstufenfestspiele 207
  Dresden City Festival 173
  Dresden Music Festival 173
  Dürkheimer Wurstmarkt 503
  Erlanger Bergkirchweih 395
  Fasching 340
  Fasnacht (Mittenwald) 382
  Festspiele Mecklenburg-Vorpommern 297
  Festtage in der Staatsoper 119
  Filmfestival Potsdam 149
  fireworks festival (Hanover) 638
  fireworks festival (Heidelberg) 445
  Frankfurt Book Fair 546
  Frülingsfest 340
  Gallopp-Rennwoche 270
  Gäubodenfest 416
  Goat Festival 503
  Hafenfest 303
  Händel Festival 253, 668-9
  Hanse Sail Rostock 297
  Harzer Bergtheater 282
  Heidelberger Herbst 445
  Historischer Schäfertanz 367
  Historisches Festspiel 'Der Meistertrunk' 367
  Honky Tonk Pub Festival 190
  International Dixieland Festival 173
  International Film Festival 340
  International Jazz Festival 638
  Internationale Filmfestspiele 119
  Internationale Tourismusbörse 119
  Jakobidult 340
  JazzFest Berlin 60, 119
  Kammeroper Schloss Rheinsberg 160
  Karnival der Kulturen 119
  Kieler Woche 712
  Kinderzeche 369
  Kirsch Fest 258
  Koblenz to Braubach/Spay 508

  Kunsthandwerk Heute 546
  Kurt Weill Festival 246
  Loreley rock 508
  Love Parade 41, 119
  Maidult 340
  Maschsee festival 638
  Mittelalterfest 177
  Mozart Festival 363
  Musikfestspiele Potsdam Sanssouci 149
  Nördlinger Pfingstmesse 371
  Oberwesel 508
  Ökomedia International Environmental Film Festival 73
  Oktoberfest (Brandenburg an der Havel) 152
  Oktoberfest (Munich) 341, 8, 168-9
  Opera Festival 340
  Parade of the Sächsische Dampfschiffahrt fleet 173
  Potsdamer Schlössernacht 149
  Regensburger Bürgfest 413
  Reichsstadt-Festtage 367
  Rheinsberger Musiktage 160
  Rhine in Flames 508
  Riflemen's Festival 638
  Samba Festival 402
  sand sculpture festival 721
  Schleswig-Holstein Music Festival 713
  Schwedenfest 303
  Schwul-Lesbisches Strassenfest 130
  Siebengebirge 508
  Sommerfest 430
  Sound of Frankfurt 546
  Theatertreffen Berlin 119
  Tollwood Festival 340
  Wagner Festival 401
  wine festival (Freyberg) 259
  wine festival (German Wine Road) 502
  Zappanale 301
film 11, 34, 60, 64-6, 73
  Bavaria Filmstadt 339
  Deutsches Film- und Fototechnik Museum 503
  Deutsches Filmmuseum (Frankfurt-Am-Main) 544
  Filmmuseum (Potsdam) 148
  Filmmuseum Berlin 110
  Filmpark Babelsberg 149
  Internet resources 65
Fischer, Joschka 43
Fischmarkt (Hamburg) 691, 552-3
fishing 304
Flensburg 724-6
Föhr 733
Fontane, Theodor 160
food 74-87, 746
  books 75, 76, 83, 84, 85, 86

  customs 83
  Internet resources 75
  regional dishes 76-7
  sweets 76, 85
  vegetarian 82
  vocabulary 84-6
football 48-9, 135, 337,
  see also World Cup (football)
Franconia 385-409
Frank, Anne 650
Frank, Charlotte 59
Frankenstein 407
Frankfurt-am-Main (Frankfurt) 538-53, **542-3**, 520-1
  accommodation 546-8
  attractions 541-5
  Bahnhofsviertel 548
  Bornheim 550
  drinking 550-1
  emergency services 540
  entertainment 551-2
  festivals 546
  food 548-50
  Fressgasse 548-9
  Internet resources 540
  medical services 540
  Nordend 550
  Römerberg 549
  Sachsenhausen 549-50
  shopping 552
  tours 546
  travel to/from 552-3
  travel within 553
  Zeil 549
Frankfurt an der Oder 157-8
Frankfurt Book Fair 64, 546
Frankish Reich, the 24
Fraueninsel 355
Freiburg 467-71, **467**
fresco 52
Freudenberg 618
Freudenstadt 461-2
Freyburg 259-60
Friedrich, Caspar David 53, 315
Friedrichroda 227-8
Friedrichshafen 486-7
Fritsch, Wener 68
Fugger, Jakob
  Fugger Stadtpalast 372
Fulda 560-1
Füssen 375-8

G

Garmisch-Partenkirchen 378-80
Gaststätte 81, 83
gay issues 43, 47
gay travellers 130-1, 746
  Berlin 130-1
  Cologne 586
  Frankfurt-am-Main 551-2
  Hamburg 704
  Hanover 642
  Munich 350-1

GDR
  history & politcs of 37-40
  Internet resources 47
  museums 251
  Zeitgeschichtliches Forum 186-7
Gedenkstätte Bautzen 198
Gedser 299
Gendarmenmarkt (Berlin) 104-5
Gengenbach 464
geography 69
geology 69
German Democratic Republic, see GDR
German National Tourist Office
  (GNTO) 12
German phrases 776-83
German Wine Road 502-4
Gernrode 280-1
Gildehaus (Erfurt) 208, 136-7
Glasstrasse 420
Gluck, Christoph Willibald 59
Glücksburg 726
Goebbels, Joseph 33
Goethe, Johann Wolfgang von
  Goethe Gedenkstätte 232
  Goethe Haus (Frankfurt-am-Main)
    542-3
  Goethe Haus (Weimar) 213-15
  Goethe Museum (Düsseldorf) 572
  Goethe Nationalmuseum (Weimar)
    215
  Goethe plaque 438
  Goethe room 191
  Goethe trail 229, 229
  Goethehaus (Stützerbach) 229
  Goethes Gartenhaus 215
  life of 213
  statue 188
  work of 62, 67, 228, 232
Goethe Institut 12, 545, 741-2
  Haus der Frau von Stein 217
Goethewanderweg 229, 229
Goetheweg trail 277
Goetz, Rainald 68
Göhren 313-14
Görlitz 198-200
Goslar 265-8, 266
Gotha 219-21
Gothic architecture 52, 56
  Altstädtische Rathaus 152
  Blasterturm 488
  Dom (Magdeburg) 239
  Dom (Paderborn) 613
  Elisabethkirche 559
  Frauenkirche (Munich) 335
  Gewandhaus 488
  Görlitz 199
  Haus zum Walfisch 469
  Heiliggeistkirche (Heidelberg)
    443-4
  Kloster Chorin 162
  Klosterkirche 162
  Kreuzkirche (Zittau) 201

Kreuztor 408
Lambertikirche 674
Liebfrauenkirche (Trier) 520
Marienkirche (Dortmund) 604
Marienkirche (Lübeck) 717
Marienkirche (Neubrandenburg) 291
Marktkirche (Halle) 254
Marktkirche (Hanover) 638
Marktkirche St Benedikti 278
Münster (Villingen-Schwenningen)
  466
Nikolaikirche (Leipzig) 188-9
Petrikirche (Dortmund) 603
Pfarrkirche Maria Himmelfahrt 358
Pfarrkirche Unsere Liebe Frau 388
Rathaus (Goslar) 266
Rathaus (Mühlhausen) 222
Rathaus (Münster) 609
Rathaus (Stralsund) 306
Rathaus (Wernigerode) 273
St Georgenkirche (Schmalkalden)
  229
St Georgskirche (Nördlingen) 370
St Jacobikirche (Göttingen) 668
St Jakobskirche (Straubing) 417
St Johanniskirche (Göttingen) 668
St Lamberti Church (Münster) 609
St Maria zur Wiese 612
St-Gangolf-Kirche 520
Schlosskirche (Chemnitz) 182
Stadtkirche (Celle) 648
Stadtkirche St Andreas 234
Stadtkirche St Michael 231
Stadtkirche St Wenzel 258
Stadtmuseum (Saalfeld) 235
Stadtturm (Straubing) 416
Stiftskirche (Neustadt an der
  Weinstrasse) 502
Gothmund 718
Göttingen 564, 666-71, 667
Graf, Steffi 49
Grand Prix 49
Grass, Günter
  Günter Grass-Haus 717-18
  work of 64
Greenpeace 73
Greens, the 41, 42, 43, 72
Greifswald 293, 308-10
Grimm, Brothers 63
  Brüder-Grimm-Museum 563
  Town Musicians of Bremen 622
Grönemeyer, Herbert 62
Gropius, Walter 57, 111, 216, 244,
  245, 246
Grosz, George 54
Grüne Strasse 457
Guericke, Otto von 239, 240
Gursky, Andreas 55
Güstrow 290-1
Gutach 463-4, 477
Gutenberg, Johannes 27, 496
  Gutenberg Museum 495

H
Hackl, Georg 49
Hahnenklee 268-9
Hainich National Park 71, 223
Halle 253-5
Hallig Hooge 728
Halligen 728
Hamburg 682-708, **684**, **686-7**, **688**,
  690, **692**, **694**, **698**
  accommodation 696-700
  activities 695
  Alster Lakes 699, 701
  Altona 694-5, 701-2, **694**
  attractions 688-95
  Blankenese 695
  drinking 702-3
  emergency services 685
  entertainment 703-5
  festivals 696
  food 700-2
  Internet access 685
  Karolinenviertel 694
  Neustadt 699, **692**
  Övelgönne 694-5, 701-2
  Port of Hamburg 689-90
  Reeperbahn 688
  St Georg 698-9, 701, **698**
  St Pauli 688-9, 699, 701, **688**
  Schanzenviertel 694, 699, 701
  shopping 705
  Speicherstadt 691
  tours 695-6
  travel to/from 705-6
  travel within 706-7
  Universitätsviertel 699-700, 701
Hamburg Wadden Sea National Park
  71, 708
Hamburger Kunsthalle 693, **552-3**
Hamelin 564, 644-5
Hanau 564
Händel, Georg Friedrich
  birthplace of 253
  Händel Festival 253
  Händelhaus 254
Hannawald, Sven 49
Hanover 633-43, **636-7**, **552-3**
  accommodation 639-40
  activities 635-8
  attractions 635-8
  drinking 641
  emergency services 634
  entertainment 641-3
  festivals 638
  food 640-1
  shopping 643
  travel to/from 643
  travel within 643-4
Hanover trade fair 633
Hanseatic League, the 27, 305, 716
Harz Mountains 262-82, **264**
Harz National Park 71, 264, 269
Haslach 464

Havixbeck 611
Haydn, Joseph 59
health 773-4
heat stroke 774
Heckel, Erich 54
Heidelberg 440-8, **440-1**
 accommodation 445-6
 attractions 442-4
 drinking 447
 entertainment 447
 festivals 445
 food 446
 tours 444-5
 travel to/from 447-8
 travel within 448
Heine, Heinrich
 Heinrich Heine Institut 570
 life of 29
 parent's home 653
 work of 63
Helgoland 733
Helsinki 299
Hensel, Kerstin 64
Hermann, Judith 64
Hesse 536-65, **538**
Hesse, Hermann 63
Hiddensee Island 316, **311**
hiking, see also walking 738
 Altmühltal Nature Park 404-5
 Bad Harzburg 269
 Bad Schandau 179
 Baden-Baden 459
 Bavarian Forest National Park 421
 Berchtesgaden National Park 384
 Blomberg 358
 Bocksberg 269
 Boppard 511
 Braunlage 270
 Buckow 156
 East Frisian Islands 680
 Feldberg 473-4
 Garmisch-Partenkirchen 379
 Gernrode 280
 Goethewanderweg 229
 Goetheweg trail 277
 Hahnenkleer 269
 Hamburg Wadden Sea National
  Park 708
 Harz Mountains 264
 Harz National Park 264
 Harz-Gebirgslauf 274
 Hochharz National Park 264
 Kaiserstuhl 472
 Lahn Valley 558
 List 730
 Mittenwald 381-2
 Moselle Valley 517
 Müritz National Park 71, 294

000 Map pages
000 Location of colour photographs

Oberstdorf 382
organisations 264, 738
Passau 419
Rennsteig 223, 226
Rheinhöhenweg 508
Rhine Valley 507-8
Rothaarsteig 615
Rotweinwanderweg 504
Saale-Unstrut Region 257
St Andreasberg 271
Sauerland 615
Schierke 276
Tegelbergbahn 377
Thale 281, 282
Wanderdünengebiet 730
Wernigerode 274
Wutachschlucht 477
Zittau Mountains 201
Hildesheim 655-7
Hindemith, Paul 60
Hindenburg, Paul von 32
Hinterhermsdorf 179
Hirschsprung 473
historic buildings, see also individual
 architectural styles, castles &
 palaces, cathedrals, churches
 Alte Börse 188
 Alte Königliche Bibliothek 104
 Alte Staatsbibliothek (Berlin) 104
 Alter Klopstock 278
 Alter Schwede (Wismar) 302
 Altfriesisches Haus 730
 Bachhaus 225
 Bäckergildehaus 266
 Bartholomäuskapelle 614
 Befreiungshalle 416
 Borgerforeningen Hof 725
 Börse (Hamburg) 690
 Brückengasse Kloster Zoffingen
  480
 Brusttuch 266
 Bürgermeister-Hintze-Haus 707
 Carolingian Torhalle 355
 Chile Haus 692
 Citadelle Petersberg 207
 Dampfmaschinenhaus 148
 Fairy-Tale House (Celle) 648
 Festung Marienberg 362
 Friedenssaal 609
 Fürstenhaus 217
 Gildehaus (Erfurt) 208
 Gildehaus zur Rose (Quedlinburg)
  278
 Green House (Celle) 648
 Haus Börner 668
 Haus der Frau von Stein 217
 Haus Rüschhaus 611
 Haus zum Breiten Herd 208
 Haus zum Roten Ochsen 208
 Haus zum Sonneborn 207
 Haus zur Engelsburg 207
 Heiligen-Geist-Hospital 718

Heisingsche Haus 613-14
Historisches Kaufhaus 469
Hochzeitshaus 644
Hofbräuhaus 333
Hoppener Haus 648
Humboldt Universität 104
Jagdhaus Gabelbach 229
Junkernschänke 668
Kaufhaus am Brand 495
Konzilgebäude 479
Lederhaus (Ravensburg) 488
Ludwigslust ducal residence 290
Lutherhaus 225
Nassauer Haus 389
Neue Wache 104
Neues Gebäude 286
Nordfriesisches Museum Ludwig-
 Nissen-Haus 727
Ottonian Kaiserpfalz 614
Pfunds Molkerei 169-70
Pilatushaus 389
Pompejanum 365
Rattenfängerhaus 644
Reichstag (Berlin) 108
Residenz (Munich) 334
Römisches Haus 215
Schloss Cecilienhof 148
Schwedenspeicher 707
Spitzhäuschen 522
Staatsoper Unter den Linden 104
Stadtschloss (Weimar) 216
Statthalterpalais 206
Studentenkarzer 444
Tiergärtnertor 389
Westindienspeicher 725
Wulflamhaus 306
Zeughaus 104
history 23-43, 114
 Berlin Wall 39
 Bismarck, Otto 30-1
 books 24, 30, 31, 32, 35, 37, 39, 40
 Celtic people 23-4
 East Germany (GDR) 36-9
 Enlightenment, the 28
 Frankish Reich, the 24
 Jewish people 28-9
 Habsburg, house of 26
 Hitler, Adolf 31- 5
 Hohenstaufens, the 24-6
 Holocaust, the 34
 Internet resources 23, 24, 31, 34
 Nazi party 32-5
 recent events 41-3
 Reformation, the 27
 reunification 40
 Roman people 23-4
 Saxon people 24-6
 Terrible Time, the 26
 West Germany 36-9
 workers' movement 29
 WWI 31
 WWII 32-5

INDEX

hitching 760, 768-9
Hitler, Adolf 31-2, 33, 34, 89, 383, 724
Hochharz National Park 71, 264, 273, 274, 275
Hoetger, Bernhard 622
Höfer, Candida 55
Hohenloher Freilandmuseum 437
Hohenstaufens 24-6
Hohnstein 179
Höllental 473
Holm 722
Holocaust, the 34-5
    Buchenwald 219
    Dachau Concentration Camp Memorial 354
    Sachsenhausen Concentration Camp 158-9
Holy Roman Empire, the 25
Honecker, Erich 39, 40, 41
Horn, Rebecca 55
Hörschel 226
horse racing 136
horse riding 738
    List 730
    Poel Island 304
    Stendal 243
hot-air ballooning 297
House of Habsburg, the 26-7
Huch, Ricarda 63
Hunsrück Mountains 525-7
Husum 726-8
hypothermia 774

I

ice skating
    Berlin 117
    Oberstdorf 382
Idar-Oberstein 525-7
Iller River 453
Ilmenau 228
Imbiss 82
immigration 50-1
Industrial Heritage Trail 15, 598
industrial museums
    Deutsche Arbeitsschutzausstellung 604
    Deutsches Bergbaumuseum 602
    Eisenbahnmuseum 602
    Gasometer 606
    Zeche Zollverein XII 599-600
    Zollern II/IV Colliery 604
Ingolstadt 406-9
insurance
    car 766-7
    health 773
    travel 747
Internet resources
    air tickets 759
    architecture 57, 58
    art 53
    beer 78, 79
    Berlin 93
    Berlin Wall 40

culture 44, 45
East Germany 47
environmental issues 73
expats 12
film 65
food 75
Frankfurt Book Fair 64
Frankfurt-am-Main 540
Freiburg 468
German-language course 12
Goethe Institut 12
Heidelberg 442
history 23, 24, 31, 34
Hitler, Adolf 33
literature 63, 64
maps 12
Munich 322
music 60, 61
national parks & reserves 70, 72
news 67
Ostalgie 47
politics 42
religion 52
restaurants 82
Roman ruins 23
Rothenburg ob der Tauber 365
society 42
Sorb people 153
sport 49
Stuttgart 427
swimming 117
theatre 67
tourist office 12
TV 66
vegetarian travellers 82
wine 80, 81
women's issues 46
world facts 12
WWI 31
WWII 33
Iraqi War 22, 42
Isar River 336, 358
itineraries
    author's favourite trip 19, **19**
    Baltic Sea coast 16, **16**
    castles & palaces 17, **17**
    cathedrals & churches 17, **17**
    classic tour 13, **13**
    grand tour 14, **14**
    off the beaten track 15, **15**
    wine 18, **18**
    World Heritage Sites 18, **18**

J

Jahn, Helmut 59
Jahrtausendturm 239
Jasmund National Park 71, 315
jazz 60
    Berlin 135
    Dinkelsbühl's Jazz Festival 369
    International Jazz Festival 638
    JazzFest Berlin 60
    Lübeck 720

Munich 351
Völklinger Hütte 534
Jena 231-4
Jenaer Glasswerke 232
jet lag 774
Jever 676-8
Jewish history & culture 28-9
    Begegnungsstätte Kleine Synagoge 208
    Centrum Judaicum 107
    Document Neupfarrplatz 412
    Holocaust, the 29
    Jewish Cultural Museum (Augsburg) 373
    Jewish Museum (Braunschweig) 659
    Jüdisches Museum (Berlin) 111, **136-7**
    Jüdisches Museum (Frankfurt-am-Main) 545
    Jüdisches Museum (Worms) 498
    Jüdisches Museum Franken in Fürth 390-1
    Jüdisches Museum München 338
    Lappenberg 656
    memorial (Frankfurt-am-Main) 545
    Museum Judengasse (Frankfurt-am-Main) 545
    Otto Weidt Workshop 111
    pogroms 26, 28
    Raschi Haus (Worms) 498
    Synagogue (Celle) 648
    Worms 498-9
Johannisbad 195-6
Jonsdorf 201
Jork 707
Judaism 52
Jüdisches Museum (Berlin) 111, **136-7**
Jugendstil (Art Nouveau) 56
Juist 681

K

Kaiserstuhl 472
Kaiser-Wilhelm-Gedächtniskirche 114, **136-7**
Kalkar 577
Kaminer, Vladimir 64
Kampen 729-30
Kandinsky, Wassily 54, 57, 216, 245, 246
Kap Arkona lighthouse 316
Karl Marx diorama (Leipzig) 189, **136-7**
Karlsruhe 454-7
Kassel 561-5
Kästner, Erich
    Erich-Kästner-Museum 169
kayaking 739
    Altmühltal Nature Park 404
    Lahn Valley 558
    Lower Oder Valley National Park 161
    Rheinsberg 160
Keitum 730
Kepler, Johannes
    Kepler-Gedächtnishaus 412

Kiefer, Anselm 54
Kiel 711-14
Kinzig River 463
Kinzig Valley 463-4
Kirche, *see* churches
Kirchner, Ernst 54, 109
Kirnitzsch River 179
Kirnitzschtalbahn 179
Kirsch, Sarah 64
Klee, Paul
  exhibits of work 109
  work of 54, 55, 57, 216, 246
Klopstock, Friedrich Gottlieb
  Klopstockhaus 278
Kloster (Straslund) 308
Kloster Eberbach 516
Kloster Lorsch 555
Kloster Maria Laach 506-7
Klosterchenke Weltenburg 416
Koblenz 508-11
Kocher River 435, 436
Kohl, Helmut 40, 41
Kollwitz, Käthe
  Käthe Kollwitz Museum (Cologne)
  581
  Käthe-Kollwitz-Museum (Berlin)
  114
  work of 54
Kölner Dom 578-80, **520-1**
Königssee 384
Königstein 179
Königstuhl 315
Konstanz 479-82
Kornelimünster 598
Kraftwerk 60, 61
Krenz, Egon 40
Krupp Dynasty 600
Kulturforum (Berlin) 109-10
Kumpfmüller, Michael 64
Kunsthalle (Hamburg) 53, 54
Kunstmuseum (Bonn) 54
Kurfürstendamm (Berlin) 114-15
Kurtaxe (resort tax) 735
Kyffhäuser, the 222-3
Kyffhäuser Monument 222-3

L
Laboe 714
Lahn River 558
Lahn Valley 558
lakes
  Biggesee 616
  Chiemsee 354-6
  Fünf-Seen-Land 356
  Königssee 384
  Lake Constance 478-90, **478**
  Maschsee 637-8
  Max-Eyth-See 435

Mummel-see 461
Obersee 479
Starnberger See 356
Titisee 474
Tollensesee 292
Untersee 479
Windgfällweiher 473
Landschaftspark Duisburg-Nord 606
Lang, Fritz 64, 65, 148, 149
Langeoog 679-80
language 776-83
  food vocabulary 84-6
  Saxon dialect 169
League of Nations, the 31
legal matters 748
Leibl, Wilhelm 53
Leibniz, Gottfried Wilhelm 638
Leipzig 184-94, **186-7**, **188**
  accommodation 190-1
  attractions 185-8
  clubbing 192-3
  drinking 191-2
  entertainment 192-3
  festivals 190
  food 191
  travel to/from 193
  travel within 193-4
Lenbach, Franz von 336
lesbian issues 43, 47
lesbian travellers 746
  Berlin 130-1
  Cologne 586
  Frankfurt-am-Main 551-2
  Hamburg 704
  Hanover 642
  Munich 350-1
Lessing, Gotthold Ephraim
  Lessinghaus 662
  work of 67
Libeskind, Daniel 59, 111
libraries
  Alte Königliche Bibliothek 104
  Alte Staatsbibliothek (Berlin) 104
  Anna Amalia Library 217
  Herzog August Bibliothek 662
  Neue Staatsbibliothek 110
  Staatsoper Unter den Linden 104
Liebermann, Max 53
Limburg 558
Limes Road 23
Lindau 488-90
List 730
Liszt, Franz
  Liszt Haus 215
  music academy 217
literature
  10 best novels 11
  classical 54, 62-3
  contemporary 44, 45, 48, 52
  Internet resources 63, 64
  modern 63-4
  travel 10, 12

Loreley 512-13
Love Parade 41
Löwenberg 293
Lower Oder Valley National Park 71,
  161-2
Lower Saxony 631-81, **634-5**
Lower Saxony Wadden Sea National
  Park 71
Lübben 153-4
  accommodation 154
  activities 153
  attractions 153
  festivals 154
  food 154
  tours 153
  travel to/from 154
  travel within 154
Lübbenau 154-5
Lübeck 714-21, **715**, 6
  accommodation 719
  activities 716-18
  attractions 716-18
  drinking 720
  entertainment 720
  food 720
  tours 718-19
  travel to/from 720-1
  travel within 721
Lüdinghausen 611
Ludwigsburg 435
Ludwigslust 290
Lüneburg 651-4, **651**
Lüneburger Heide 646-54
Lüpertz, Markus 55
Luther, Martin
  Bible translation 62
  birthplace of 15
  church 207
  death mask of 254
  Eisenach 223, 225
  hymn singing 59
  Luther's Wedding festival 249
  Luthereiche 250
  Lutherhaus 225, 249-50
  Luthers Geburtshaus 256
  Luthers Sterbehaus 256
  Lutherstadt Wittenberg 248
  Reformation, the 27, 28,
Lutherstadt Wittenberg 248-53, **250**
Luxemburg, Rosa 'Red' 31

M
Mack, Heinz 54
Macke, August
  August-Macke-Haus 592
  birthplace of 588
magazines 51, 734
Magdeburg 238-42, **240**
Main River 539
Mainau Island 482
Main-Danube Canal 396
Mainz 493-7, **494**
Mangelsdorff, Albert 60

Mann, Thomas
  Buddenbrookhaus 717
  work of 63
Mannheim 449-50
maps 748
Marburg 558-60, 564
Marc, Franz 54
Märchenstrasse, see Fairy-Tale Road
Marcks, Gerhard
  Gerhard Marcks Haus 623
  work of 54
markets, see also Christmas markets
  Berlin 137
  Fischmarkt (Hamburg) 691
  Viktualienmarkt 335
  Weihnacht-Reiterlersmarkt 368
Märkische Schweiz 155-8
Marx, Karl
  Karl-Marx-Haus 521
  work of 29, 31
Maschsee 637-8
Max-Eyth-See 435
Mecklenburg Seenplatte 286-94
Mecklenburg-Western Pomerania
  283-316, **285**
medical services 774, see also health
medieval buildings
  Albrechtsburg 180
  Bacharach 513
  Bocksturm 672
  Burg Blankenstein 602
  Burg Klopp 514
  Burg Vischering 611
  Dreikönigenhaus 520
  Friedländer Tor 291
  Grevenburg 523
  Haus Degode 674
  Ingolstadt 406
  Kalkar 577
  Karlstor 335
  Lübeck 718
  Marienkirche (Flensburg) 725
  Marientor 258
  Martinskirche 469
  Neustädter Tor 243
  Nördlingen 370
  Oberwesel 513
  Rathaus (Greifswald) 309
  Rathaus (Oldenburg) 674
  Regensburg 409
  Rothenburg ob der Tauber 365-9
  Schloss (Augustustburg) 183
  tour of 13
  town wall (Ahrweiler) 505
  Treptower Tor 291
  Wasserschloss Kemnade 602
  Werden 601
  Wiekhäuser 292
  Xanten 575
Meersburg 483-5
Mein Kampf 32
Meiningen 230-1

Meissen 180-1, **136-7**
Meisterhäuser 244-5
Melanchthon, Philipp
  Melanchthon Haus 251
memorials
  Adenauer Memorial 591
  Aegidienkirche Memorial 638
  Beethoven Memorial 590
  Mahn- und Gedenkstätte
    Steinwache 604
  Memorial for the Victims of the
    Nazi Regime 569
  Memorial to the Murdered
    European Jews 104
  Soviet War Memorial 109
  Sowjetisches Ehrenmal 116
  Wall Victims Memorial 112
  Waterloo Memorial 638
  WWI memorial (Magdeburg) 239
Mendelssohn-Bartholdy, Felix
  Mendelssohn-Haus 186
  work of 59
Menzel, Adolph 53
Menzenschwand 476
Mercedes-Benz 426
  Mercedes-Benz Museum 429
Messel 555
metric conversions,
  see inside front cover
Metropolis 53, 148, 149
Mettlach 534-5
Miró, Joan 109
Mittelbau Dora 276-7
Mittenwald 381-2
mobile phones 752
modern architecture 57-9
  Allianz Arena 339
  Berliner Philharmonie 110
  Colorium 571
  DaimlerCity 110
  Fünf Höfe 335
  Grand Bateau 571
  Haus der Bürgerschaft 622
  Hundertwasserschule 251
  IM Pei Bau 104
  Mexican embassy 109
  Musical Instruments Museum 110
  Neue Staatsbibliothek 110
  Neuer Zollhof 571
  Neues Gewandhaus 189
  Neues Kanzleramt (Berlin) 108
  Neues Kranzler Eck 113
  Nordic embassies 109
  Sony Center 110
  Stadthaus (Ulm) 452
  Yenidze 169
modern art 63-4
  Lüftmalerei 381
Moholy-Nagy, László 246
monasteries
  Andechs 357
  Berg Oybin 201

Kloster Banz 403
Kloster Chorin 162
Kloster Eberbach 516
Schlosskirche (Chemnitz) 182
Mönchgut Peninsula 313-14
Mondrian, Piet 246
money 9-10, 748-9,
  see also inside front cover
Moselle Valley, the 516-25, **517**,
  520-1
motion sickness 774
motorcycle travel 760, 765-8
Mt Kandel 472
Mt Karwendel 382
Mt Merkur 459
mountain biking, see cycling
mountaineering 738
mountains, see individual entries
Mozart, Wolfgang Amadeus 59, 60
Muche, Georg
  Muche/Schlemmer Haus 245
Mühlhausen 221-2
Müller, Heiner 67
Mummel-see 461
Munch, Edvard 109
Münchhausen, Baron
  home town of 645
  Münchhausen Museum 645
Munich 319-54, **323**, **324-5**, **326**,
  328, **329**, **330**, **333**
  accommodation 340-4
  activities 339
  Altstadt 342, 344-5, 346, 348
  attractions 331-9
  clubbing 350
  drinking 347-9
  emergency services 322
  entertainment 349-52
  festivals 340
  food 344-7
  Haidhausen 345, **328**
  Ludwigsvorstadt 343-4, 345
  medical services 331
  Neuhausen 343, 345, 348,
    330
  Nymphenburg 343, **330**
  Schwabing 343, 345, 346, 349,
    329
  shopping 352
  tours 340
  travel to/from 352-3
  travel within 353-4
  Westend 343-4
Munich Agreement, the 33
Munich Putsch, the 32
Münster 607-10, **608**
Münster (Freiburg) 468
Münsterland Castles 610-11
Münter, Gabriele 54
Müritz National Park 71, 293, 294
Museum für Sepulkralkultur 563,
  520-1

INDEX

museums, *see also* art galleries
& museums, farm museums,
industrial museums, science &
technology
Abenteuer Museum 531
Ägyptisches Museum 114
Akademisches Kunstmuseum
(Bonn) 590
Albrecht-Dürer-Haus 389
AlliiertenMuseum 115-16
Altes Museum (Berlin) 105
Altona Museum/North German
State Museum 694
Alt-Rothenburger Handwerkerhaus
367
Angermuseum 206
Antikensammlungen 336
Archäologische Staatssammlung
337 (Munich)
Archäologisches Landesmuseum
(Konstanz) 480
Arithmeum (Bonn) 590
Atelierhaus 291
Automobilmuseum (Eisenach) 225
Automobilmuseum (Zwickau) 195
AutoMuseum 664
Bach Museum 185
Badisches Landesmuseum 456
Basilika St Kastor 509
Bauhaus Archive/Museum of
Design (Berlin) 109
Bauhaus Museum (Weimar) 216
Baumbachhaus 230
Bayerisches Armee Museum 408
Bayerisches Nationalmuseum
337
Beatles Museum 253-4
BMW Museum 337
Bodensee Natural History Museum
481
Brauereimuseum 652
Bröhan Museum 114
Buchheim Museum 357
Bunkermuseum 676
Buxtehude Museum 708
Carl Maria von Weber Museum 170
Carolingian Torhalle 355
Cathedral Museum (Fulda) 561
City History Museum (Leipzig) 188
City History Museum (Lübeck) 716
Deutsches Apothekenmuseum 443
Deutsches Architekturmuseum 544
Deutsches Edelsteinmuseum
(Idar-Oberstein) 526
Deutsches Film- und Fototechnik
Museum 503
Deutsches Filmmuseum
(Frankfurt-am-Main) 544

Deutsches Medizinhistorisches
Museum 407-8
Deutsches Salzmuseum 652
Deutsches Schifffahrtsmuseum
(Bremerhaven) 630
Deutsches Sport- & Olympia
Museum 581
Deutsches Technikmuseum 113
Deutsches Weihnachtsmuseum 367
Deutsches Zollmuseum 692
Dialog im Dunkeln 691-2
Diözesan Museum (Cologne) 581
Diözesanmuseum (Paderborn) 613
Diözesanmuseum (Regensburg) 412
Dom- und Diözesanmuseum
(Mainz) 495
Dommuseum (Brandenburg an der
Havel) 151
Dornier Museum (Meersburg) 484
Düppel Museum Village 117
Egyptian Museum (Leipzig) 187
Egyptology & Archaeology
Museum (Tübingen) 438
Eisenbahnmuseum 156
EL-DE Haus 581
Erich-Kästner-Museum 169
Erotic Art Museum (Hamburg) 689
Erotik Museum (Berlin) 114
Ethnological Museum (Dresden) 169
Ethnologisches Museum (Berlin) 115
Fachwerkmuseum Ständebau 278
Fälschermuseum 314
Feuerwehrmuseum 273
Film Museum (Düsseldorf) 570
Filmmuseum (Potsdam) 148
Filmmuseum Berlin 110
Fränkisches Brauereimuseum 397
Franziskaner Museum 466
Frauenmuseum 592
Friedensmuseum 504
Friesenmuseum 733
Fuggereimuseum 372
Fürstenbaumuseum 362
Fürstenhaus Herrenhausen-
Museum 636
Gäubodenmuseum 417
Gedenkstätte Deutscher
Widerstand 109
Gedenkstätte Goldener Löwe 225
Gedenkstätte und Museum
Sachsenhausen 159
German Doll & Bear Museum 512
Germanisches Nationalmuseum
(Nuremberg) 391
Glasmuseum 418-19, 420
Glyptothek 336
Goethe Museum 572
Goethe Nationalmuseum 215
Goslarer Museum 267
Grassi Museum Complex 187
Grube Samson Mining Museum 271
Gründerzeit Museum 118

Gutenberg Museum 495
Hällisch-Fränkisches Museum 436
Händelhaus 254
Harz Museum 273
Harzer Roller Kanarien-Museum 271
Haus der Geschichte
(Lutherstadt Wittenburg) 251
Haus der Geschichte der
Bundesrepublik Deutschland
591 (Bonn)
Haus Giersch Museum Regionaler
Kunst (Frankfurt-am-Main) 544
Heimatmuseum (Bad Tölz) 358
Heimatmuseum (Bingen) 514
Heimatmuseum (Borkum) 681
Heimatmuseum (Warnemünde) 300
Heimatstube 227
Heinrich-Schliemann-Museum 294
Herzog Anton Ulrich Museum 659
Hessisches Landesmuseum 554
Hetjens Museum (Düsseldorf) 570
Historisches Museum (Bamberg) 397
Historisches Museum
(Frankfurt-am-Main) 544-5
Historisches Museum (Hanover) 638
Historisches Museum (Regensburg)
412
Historisches Museum am Strom 514
Historisches Museum der Pfalz 500
Historisches Museum Saar 531
Hoffmann Museum 665
Hohe Lilie 258
Hugenottenmuseum 105
Hygiene Museum 170
Ikonen-Museum 544
Instrumenten Museum (Stuttgart)
428
Jahrtausendturm 239
Jewish Cultural Museum
(Augsburg) 373
Jewish Museum (Braunschweig) 659
Josef Albers Museum 606
Jüdisches Museum (Berlin) 111
Jüdisches Museum
(Frankfurt-am-Main) 545
Jüdisches Museum (Worms) 498
Jüdisches Museum Franken in
Fürth 390-1
Jüdisches Museum München 338
Juister Küstenmuseum 681
Jura-Museum 406
Kaiserburg Museum 389
Kasematten 171
Käthe Kollwitz Museum (Cologne)
581
Käthe-Kollwitz-Museum (Berlin) 114
Kestner Gesellschaft 638
Kestner Museum 638
Kleist-Museum 157
Klopstockhaus 278
Kloster Lichtenthal Museum 459
Kloster Unser Lieben Frauen 239

Kloster Zum Heiligen Kreuz 296
Kölnisches Stadtmuseum 582
König Albert Museum 182
Kröpeliner Tor 296
Kulturgeschichtliche Museum 671-2
Kulturhistorisches Museum (Marburg) 559
Kulturhistorisches Museum (Stralsund) 306
Kulturhistorische Museum des Jeverlandes 677
Kurpfälzisches Museum 444
Kutschenmuseum 183
Landesmuseum (Braunschweig) 659
Landesmuseum (Koblenz) 509
Landesmuseum (Münster) 608
Landesmuseum Mainz 495
Landesmuseum Oldenburg 674
Leistehaus 644
Lessinghaus 662
Liebieghaus Museum Alter Plastik (Frankfurt-am-Main) 544
Linden Museum 429
Lochgefängnisse 388
Luthers Geburtshaus 256
Luthers Sterbehaus 256
Mainfränkisches Museum 362
Maisel's Brauerei-und-Büttnerei-Museum 400-1
Märkisches Museum 106
Marstallmuseum 338, 411
Martin-von-Wagner Museum 362
Maximilian Museum 373
Medieval Torture Museum 516
Meeresmuseum (Stralsund) 306
Mercedes-Benz Museum 429
Mittelalterliches Kriminalmuseum 366
Mittelrhein-Museum 509
Mönchehaus Museum 267
Monchgüter Museum 313
Morgenstern Museum 630
Mosel-Weinmuseum (Bernkastel-Kues) 523
Motorradmuseum 183
Mühlenhof 609
Münsterland Museum 611
Museum Berlin-Karlshorst 116
Museum der Arbeit 693-4
Museum der Bildenden Künste (Leipzig) 188
Museum der Brotkultur 453
Museum der Stadt Boppard 511
Museum der Weltkulturen (Frankfurt-am-Main) 544
Museum für Angewandte Kunst (Cologne) 582
Museum für Angewandte Kunst (Frankfurt-am-Main) 544
Museum für Antike Schifffahrt (Mainz) 495

Museum für Europäische Gartenkunst (Düsseldorf) 572
Museum für Hamburgische Geschichte 692-3
Museum für Indische Kunst 115
Museum für Kommunikation (Frankfurt-am-Main) 544
Museum für Kunsthandwerk (Frankfurt-am-Main) 544
Museum für Kunsthandwerk (Leipzig) 187
Museum für Naturkunde 108, 182
Museum für Ostasiatische Kunst 115
Museum für Puppentheater 717
Museum für Regionalgeschichte & Volkskunde (Gotha) 220
Museum für Sepulkralkultur 563
Museum für Stadtgeschichte 469
Museum für Thüringer Volkskunde 205
Museum für Ur- und Frühgeschichte 469
Museum für Völkerkunde (Göttingen) 668
Museum für Völkerkunde (Hamburg) 693
Museum für Völkerkunde (Leipzig) 187
Museum für Vor- und Frühgeschichte (Saarbrücken) 531
Museum Heylshof 499
Museum Idar-Oberstein 526
Museum im Kulturspeicher 362
Museum im Zwinger 267
Museum Judengasse (Frankfurt-am-Main) 545
Museum Koenig 592
Museum Künstlerkolonie (Darmstadt) 554
Museum Mensch und Natur 338
Museum of Early Dresden Romanticism 169
Museum of Europäischer Kulturen 116
Museum of Pre-History & Early History 406
Museum of Pre- and Early History 113
Museum of Saxon Folk Art 169
Museum of the 3rd Dimension 369
Museum Prora 315
Museum Reich der Kristalle 336
Museum Schnütgen 581
Museum Thüringer Bauernhäusern 234
Museumsdorf Bayerischer Wald 420-1
Museumshafen Övelgönne 695
Musical Instruments Museum (Berlin) 110

Musikinstrumenten-Museum (Leipzig) 187
Musikinstrumenten- und Puppenmuseum 267
Narrenmuseum 464
Natural History Museum (Stuttgart) 429
Naturhistorische Sammlungen 172
Naturkundemuseum & Planetarium (Münster) 609
Naturkundemuseum (Düsseldorf) 572
navigation museum (Laboe) 714
Nibelungen Museum 499
Niedersächsisches Landesmuseum 638
Nietzsche Haus 258
Oberammergau Museum 381
Oberharzer Bergwerksmuseum 272
Oberhausmuseum 417
Ostfriesisches Landesmuseum 675-6
Panorama Museum 223
Paula Becker-Modersohn Haus 622
Pergamon Museum 105
Pommersches Landesmuseum 309
Porsche Museum 429
Puppen- und Spielzeugmuseum (Rothenburg ob der Tauber) 367
Rammelsberger Bergbau Museum 266-7
Raschi Haus (Worms) 498
Rathaus (Lutherstadt Wittenburg) 251
Rathaus (Wismar) 301-2
Red Dot Design Museum 599-600
Regional History Museum (Neubrandenburg) 291
Regional Museum (Xanten) 576
Reichsstadtmuseum 367
Reichstagsmuseum 412
Residenzmuseum (Munich) 334
Reuter-Wagner Museum 225
Rheinisches Landesmuseum (Bonn) 592
Rheinisches Landesmuseum (Trier) 520
Richard Wagner Museum (Bayreuth) 400
Richard Wagner Museum (Dresden) 170
Roemer- und Pelizaeus-Museum 656
Rokokomuseum 216
Romanisches Haus 261
Römermuseum 419
Römisch-Germanisches Museum 580
Römische Villa Museum 505
Röntgen Gedächtnisstätte 362-3
Rosgartenmuseum 480
Ruhrlandmuseum 599
Rum Museum 725

museums *continued*
Saarland Museum 531
St Annen Museum 718
Schabbellhaus (Wismar) 302
Schatzkammer der Residenz
   (Munich) 334
Schiffahrtsmuseum (Flensburg) 725
Schiffahrtsmuseum (Kiel) 712
Schiffahrtsmuseum (Langeoog)
   679-80
Schifffahrt Museum (Düsseldorf)
   569
Schifffahrtsmuseum (Rostock) 297
Schifffahrtsmuseum Nordfriesland
   727
Schleifmühle 288
Schleswig-Holsteinisches
   Freilichtmuseum 714
Schleswig-Holstein Landesmuseum
   722
Schloss Moritzburg 254
Schloss Museum (Wolfenbüttel) 662
Schlossbergmuseum (Chemnitz) 182
Schlossmuseum (Darmstadt) 554
Schlossmuseum (Gotha) 220
Schlossmuseum (Weimar) 217
Schokoladen Museum (Cologne) 580
Schott GlasMuseum 232
Schwarzwald Freilicht Museum 463
Schwarzwaldmuseum 465
Schwules Museum 130
Senckenberg Museum 555
Siegerlandmuseum 617
Siegfrieds Mechanisches
   Musik-kabinett 515
Sorbian Museum 198
Speicherstadtmuseum 692
Spicy's Gewürzmuseum 692
Spielzeugmuseum (Munich) 333
Spielzeugmuseum (Nuremberg) 389
Spielzeugmuseum (Trier) 520
Staatliches Museum (Schwerin) 288
Staatliches Museum Ägyptischer
   Kunst (Munich) 334
Stadt Museum (Wolfsburg) 664
Städtische Galerie im Lenbachhaus
   336
Städtische Museum (Zittau) 201
Städtisches Museum (Göttingen)
   668
Städtisches Museum (Güstrow) 290
Städtisches Museum
   (Ludwigsburg) 435
Städtisches Museum (Worms) 499
Städtisches Museum Simeonstift
   519-20
Stadtmauermuseum (Nördlingen)
   371

Stadtmuseum (Baden-Baden) 459
Stadtmuseum (Dresden) 171
Stadtmuseum (Erfurt) 205
Stadtmuseum (Ingolstadt) 408
Stadtmuseum (Kiel) 712
Stadtmuseum (Lindau) 489
Stadtmuseum (Munich) 335
Stadtmuseum (Münster) 609
Stadtmuseum (Nördlingen) 370-1
Stadtmuseum (Saalfeld) 235
Stadtmuseum Erlangen 395
Stadtmuseum Fembohaus 388
Stadtmuseum Göhre 231
Stadtmuseum im Frey-Haus 152
Stasi Museum (Berlin) 116
Stasi Museum (Leipzig) 187
Stiftsmuseum 365
Story of Berlin 114
Suermondt Ludwig Museum 596
Sylter Heimatmuseum 730
Tabak-und Kindermuseum 727
Theatermuseum (Düsseldorf) 572
Theatermuseum (Meiningen) 230
Thüringer Produkte Museum 207
Topographie des Terrors 111
Trachtenmuseum 464
Übersee Museum 623
Ulmer Museum 452-3
Universitätsmuseum für Bildende
   Kunst 559
Verkehrsmuseum 172
Waldmuseum 420
Wallraf-Richartz-Museum 580-1
Walpurgishalle 282
Weimar Haus 216
Weinbaumuseum (Meersburg) 484
Weinbaumuseum Uhlbach 434
Weinmuseum (Rüdesheim) 516
Wendisches Museum/Serbski
   muzej 155
Wikinger Museum 722
Wilhelm-Busch-Museum 637
Wine Museum (Deidesheim) 503
Wine Museum (Speyer) 500-1
Württemberg State Museum 428
Zeitgeschichtliches Forum 186-7
Zentrum für Aussergewöhnliche
   Museen 339-40
Zeppelin Museum 486
Zinnfiguren-Museum 267
Zucker Museum 118
Museumsinsel (Berlin) 105
music, *see also* classical music, jazz,
   opera
Choriner Musiksommer 162
contemporary 60-2
hip-hop 62
Internet resources 60
Musical Instruments Museum
   (Berlin) 110
Musikinstrumenten-Museum
   (Leipzig) 187

Musikinstrumenten- und
   Puppenmuseum 267
pop 55, 62
punk 61, 62
rock 62
techno 61
Zappanale 301
Muslims 52

N
Nahe River 526
national parks & reserves
Altmühltal Nature Park 404-5
Bavarian Forest National Park
   71, 421
Berchtesgaden National Park
   71, 383
Hainich National Park 71, 223
Hamburg Wadden Sea National
   Park 71, 708
Harz National Park 71, 269
Hochharz National Park 71, 264
Internet resources 70, 72
Jasmund National Park 71, 315
Lower Oder Valley National Park
   71, 161-2
Lower Saxony Wadden Sea
   National Park 71, 678
Müritz National Park 71, 293, 294
Nationalpark Bayerischer Wald 420
Ood Nature Reserve 732
Saxon Switzerland National Park
   71, 178-9
Schleswig-Holstein Wadden Sea
   National Park 71, 728
Vorpommersche Boddenlandschaft
   National Park 71, 304-5
NATO 38
Naturpark Elbufer-Drawehn 654
Naumburg 257-9
Nay, Ernst-Wilhelm 54
Nazism
art, banning of 55
books 32, 33
Dokumentation Obersalzberg 383-4
Dokumentationszentrum 390
Eagle's Nest 384
Haus der Wannseekonferenz
   Gedenkstätte 116
history of 32-3
Reichsparteitagsgelände 390
Neckar River 426, 437, 442
Neckar Valley 448
Neckarsteinach 444
Neisse River 198, 199, 201
neoclassical architecture
history of 57
Johanniskirche (Zittau) 201
Palais Schaumburg 591
Römisches Haus 215
neo-Gothic architecture
Alte Universitätsbibliothek 469
Burg Hohenzollern 439-40

Drachenburg 594
Rathaus (Erfurt) 208
Rathaus (Munich) 332-3
Rathaus (Saarbrücken) 531
Rathaus (Straubing) 416
Rathaus (Weimar) 217
Rochuskapelle 514
Schloss (Schwerin) 288
Schloss Reinhardsbrunn 227
neo-Nazism 43, 44, 51
Neubrandenburg 291-3
Neue Rathaus (Hanover) 635, **552-3**
Neuendorf 308
Neues Rathaus (Munich) 332-3
Neugraben 707
Neustadt an der Weinstrasse 502-3
Neustrelitz 293, 294
newspapers 51, 734
Niederfinow 162
Nietzsche, Friedrich
    Naumburg 257
    Nietzsche Archiv 216
    Nietzsche Haus 258
    school of 260
Night of Broken Glass, the 34
Night of the Long Knives, the 32, 33
Norderney 680-1
Nördlingen 370-1
North Frisian Islands 728-33
North Rhine-Westphalia 566-618, **568**
Northern Brandenburg 158-62
Nürburgring 506
Nuremberg 386-94, **386**, **388**
    accommodation 391-2
    attractions 388-91
    drinking 393
    entertainment 393-4
    food 392-3
Nuremberg trials 37
Nuremberg Trials Courthouse 390
Nussbaum, Felix
    Felix-Nussbaum-Haus 671

O
Oberammergau 380-1
Oberhausen 606
Oberhof 226
Obersee 479
Oberstdorf 382-3
Oberwesel 513
Oder River 310
Oderbruch 155-8
Oker River 268
Oker Valley 268
Oktoberfest
    Brandenburg an der Havel 152
    Munich 341, **8**, **168-9**
Ölberg 594
Oldenburg 673-5
Olympia Stadion 115
Olympics 48, 49, 50
    Olympiapark 337
Ood Nature Reserve 732

opera 59, 60
    Berlin 135
    Erfurt 207
    Hamburg 705
    Leipzig 192
    Markgräfliches Opernhaus 399
    Oper Bonn 593
    Opera Festival 340
    Semperoper 172, 175-6
Oslo 308
Osnabrück 671-3
Ostalgie 47, 65
Ostpolitik 39
Oybin 201

P
Paderborn 613-15
Pariser Platz (Berlin) 103-4
parks & gardens
    Belvedere Park 216
    Botanical Garden (Berlin) 115
    botanical gardens (Marburg) 559
    botanika (Bremen) 623
    Botanische Gärten (Göttingen) 668
    Botanischer Garten (Erlangen) 395
    Branitzer Park 155
    Charlottenburg Schlossgarten
        113-14
    Edelsteinminen Steinkaulenberg 526
    ega 205
    Englischer Garten 331, 336
    English Garden (Meiningen) 230
    English park (Putbus) 313
    Eremitage 400
    Fairy-Tale Park (Heidelberg) 443
    Gönneranlage 458
    Göttinger Wald 668
    Grosser Garten 170
    Herrenhäuser Gärten 636-7
    Hofgarten (Bayreuth) 399
    Hofgarten (Düsseldorf) 572
    Karlshöhe 429
    Lapidarium (Stuttgart) 429
    Ludwigslust ducal residence 290
    Neuer Garten 148
    Palmengarten 545
    Park an der Ilm 215-16
    Park Schönbusch 365
    Rosengarten (Bamberg) 397
    Rosenneuheitengarten
        (Baden-Baden) 459
    Rosensteinpark 429
    Sanssouci Park 145-8
    Schlosspark (Husum) 727
    Schlosspark (Meiningen) 230
    Stadtpark Rotehorn 239
    Tiefurt Park 216
    Tiergarten Park 108-9
    Weissenburg Park 429
    Wörlitz Park 247
Passau 417-20, **418**
passports 755, see also visas
Peasants' War 222

Peene River 310
Peenemünde 310
Pegnitz River 389
Penzlin 293
Pergamon Museum 105
Perl-Nennig 535
Phantasialand 588
photography 749-50
Picasso, Pablo
    Graphikmuseum Pablo Picasso 608-9
Pied Piper of Hamelin 644
Piene, Otto 54
Pillnitz Palace 177-8
Pink Floyd 41
Pirna 177
planetariums
    Carl Zeiss Planetarium (Stuttgart)
        429
    Naturkundemuseum &
        Planetarium (Münster) 609
    Planetarium Wolfsburg 664
    Zeiss Planetarium (Jena) 232
    Zeiss Planetarium Bochum 602
planning 9-12, see also itineraries
plants 70
Plattling 422
Poel Island 304
Poland 200
politics
    books 29
    Internet resources 42
    political parties 41-2, 42-3
    recent changes 21-2
Polke, Sigmar 54
population 48
Porsche Museum 429
Porzellan Manufaktur 180
postal services 750-1
Potsdam 144-51, **146**
Potsdamer Platz (Berlin) 110-11
Prien am Chiemsee 355
Prora 315
Protestantism 27, 52
public transport 769
Putbus 313

Q
Quedlinburg 277-80, **278**

R
Radebeul 178
radio 734
Rahn, Helmut 48
Rastatt 462
Rathaus (Quedlinburg) 277, **168-9**
Ravensburg 487-8
recycling 72
Red Wine Hiking Trail 504
Reformation, the 27
Regensburg 409-15, **411**
Reger, Max 230
Regnitz River 396
Reichenau Island 482-3

Reichenturm (Bautzen) 197
Reichstag (Berlin) 108
Reinhardt, Max 67
religion 52, *see also individual religions*
Remagen 504
Remarque, Erich Maria
   Erich Maria Remarque
      Friedenszentrum 672
   work of 63
Renaissance architecture
   Alte Oper 543-4
   Altes Rathaus (Chemnitz) 182
   Altes Rathaus (Leipzig) 188
   Burg Hülshoff (Havixbeck) 611
   Fürstenhof (Wismar) 302
   Gadenstedtsches Haus 273
   Gewandhaus 659
   Görlitz 199
   Haus Willmann 672
   Haus zum Breiten Herd 208
   Haus zum Roten Ochsen 208
   history of 56
   Kasematten 171
   Rathaus (Augsburg) 372
   Rathaus (Düsseldorf) 569
   Rathaus (Gotha) 220
   Rathaus (Güstrow) 291
   Rathaus (Paderborn) 613
   Rathaus (Saalfeld) 235
   Rathaus (Stendal) 242
   Rathaus (Zittau) 201
   Schloss Johannisburg 365
   Schloss Wilhelmsburg 228
   Schlossberg (Quedlinburg) 279
   Wasserschloss 726
Renaissance art 52
Rennsteig 223, 226-7
Residenz (Würzburg) 360, 362
restaurants 74, 81, 82, 83
Reuter, Fritz 291
Rheinsberg 159-61
Rhine River 479, 507
Rhine Valley 507-16, **507**
Rhineland, the 568-98, **568**
Rhineland-Palatinate 491-527, **493**
Riefenstahl, Leni 65
Riemenschneider, Tilman 52
Rilke, Rainer Maria 63, 629
Rinke, Moritz 68
rivers, *see individual entries*
rock climbing
   Fulda 560
   Munich 339
   Saxon Switzerland National Park 71
   Schierke 275
rococo architecture
   Andechs 357
   Basilica Vierzehnheiligen 403

history of 57
St Peterskirche (Mainz) 495
Scloss Sanssouci 145
Schloss Schwetzingen 448-9
Rohe, Ludwig Mies van der 57, 246
Roman ruins 14, 18, 23
   Amphitheater 520-1
   Archaeological Park (Boppard) 511
   Archäologischer Park (Xanten) 576
   Baden-Baden 459
   Barbarathermen (Trier) 521
   Cologne 582
   Internet resources 23
   Roman villa 535
   Roman wall (Regensburg) 412
   Trier 519
   Viehmarktthermen (Trier) 521
Romanesque architecture
   Abbey of St Liudger 601
   Abdinghofkirche 614
   Dom (Braunschweig) 659
   Dom St Paul (Münster) 607
   Gross St Martin 580
   Kaiserpfalz 266
   Nikolaikirche (Siegen) 617
   St Gereon 580
   St Maria & St Klemens
      Doppelkirche 592
   St Maria im Kapitol 580
   St Michaeliskirche 656
   St Ursula 580
   Stiftskirche St Cyriakus 280
Romans 23-4
   Romanisches Haus 261
   Römische Bäder 147
   Römische Villa Museum 505
   Römisch-Germanisches Museum
      580
Romantic Rhine, the 507-16
Romantic Road, the 359-78
Römerberg (Frankfurt-am-Main) 541,
   520-1
Röntgen, Wilhelm Conrad 362
Rostock 294-300, **296**
Rotes Rathaus (Berlin) 106
Rothaarsteig 615
Rothenburg ob der Tauber 365-9, **366**
Rotweinwanderweg 504
Rübeland 275
Rübeland Caves 275
Rudelsburg 261
Rüdesheim 515-16
Rudolstadt 234
Rügen Island 311-16, **311**, 7
Ruhr River 600
Ruhrgebiet, the 598-607
ruins
   Burg Ehrenfels 516
   Münzenberg 279
   Neue Felsenburg 178
   Schloss Drachenfels 594
Runge, Philipp Otto 53

running 117
Ryck River 308

S
Saale River 226, 257, 260
Saale Valley 231-5
Saaleck 261
Saalfeld 234-5
Saar River 534, 535
Saarbrücken 530-4, **532**
Saarland 528-35, **530**
Sachsenhausen Concentration Camp
   158-9
safe travel
   crime 742-3, 761
   hitching 760, 768-9
   road 768
sailing
   Kiel 711
   Lindau 489
   Titisee-Neustadt 474
St Andreasberg 271-2
St Blasien 476-7
St Goar 512
St Goarshausen 512-13
St Peter 472
Salzbergwerk 384
Sanssouci Park 145-8, **136-7**
Sauer, Heinz 60
Sauerland 615-17
saunas 739
Saxon people 24-6
Saxon Switzerland 178-9
Saxon Switzerland National Park 71
Saxony 163-201, **165**
Saxony-Anhalt 236-61, **238**
Schaabe 316
Schadow, Johann Gottfried 53
Schattenmühle 477
Schauinsland 470
Scheunenviertel (Berlin) 106-7
Schierke 275-6
Schiller, Friedrich von
   meeting with Goethe 232
   Schiller Haus 215
   work of 67
Schiltach 463
Schindler, Oskar 410
Schinkel, Karl Friedrich
   architecture of 57, 105, 114, 135,
      147, 148, 149, 200, 316, 590
   exhibit of work 104
Schlaun, Johann Conrad 56
Schleissheim 357-8
Schlemmer, Oskar 216, 246
Schleswig 721-3
Schleswig-Holstein 709-33, **711**
Schleswig-Holstein Wadden Sea
   National Park 71, 728
Schleswig-Holsteinisches
   Freilichtmuseum 714
Schliemann, Heinrich
   Heinrich-Schliemann-Museum 294

INDEX

Schloss, see castles & palaces
Schloss Charlottenburg 113-14
Schloss Herrenchiemsee 355
Schloss Moritzburg 178
Schloss Neuschwanstein 375, 168-9
Schloss Ortenburg 197-8
Schloss Salem 485-6
Schloss Sanssouci 145-8
    Chinesisches Haus 147-8
    Orangerieschloss 147
    Schloss Charlottenhof 147
Schloss Schwetzingen 448-9
Schlossplatz (Berlin) 105-6
Schluchsee 475-6
Schlüter, Andreas 52
Schmalkalden 228-30, 231
Schmidt, Helmut 40
Schmidt-Rottluff, Karl 54
Schneider, Simone 68
Schöna 177
Schönberg, Arnold 60
Schott, Otto 231, 232
Schröder, Gerhard 21, 42
Schult, HA 55
Schultes, Axel 59
Schulze, Ingo 64
Schumann, Robert Alexander
    birthplace of 194
    home town of 588
    Schumannhaus (Bonn) 592
    Schumann-Haus (Leipzig)186
    Schumann-Haus (Zwickau) 195
    work of 60
Schwäbisch Alb 436
Schwäbisch Hall 435-7
Schwangau 375-8
Schwarzwald-Bäder-Strasse 457
Schwarzwald-Hochstrasse 457, 461
Schwarzwald Panorama Strasse 472
Schwerin 286-90, **287**
science & technology, see also
    planetariums
    Centre of Aerospace Technology 623
    Deutsches Museum (Munich) 337-8
    Deutsches Museum Bonn 591
    Explora 545
    Flugwerft Schleissheim 357
    Forum der Technik 338
    Geosammlung 272
    Heinz Nixdorf MuseumsForum 614
    Historisch-Technisches
        Informationszentrum 310
    Mathematics and Physics Salon 172
    Museum of Minerology and
        Geology 172
    Neue Hütte 230
    Optisches Museum 232
    Phaeno Science Center 664
    Phänomenta 310
    Rieskrater Museum 370
    SiemensForum 336
    Spectrum science centre 113

    Technik Museum (Speyer) 501
    Universum Science Center 623
    Verkehrszentrum 338
sculpture 52
    Die Nanas 637
    GDR diorama 188
    Karl Marx diorama (Leipzig) 189
Seebrugg 474
Selke Valley 280
sexual health 774
Shelley, Mary 407
Sieben Jungfrauen 513
Siebengebirge 594
Siegen 617-18
Siegerland 617-18
skiing 9, 738-9
    Bavarian Forest National Park
        71, 421
    Berchtesgaden National Park
        71, 384
    Bocksberg 268
    Braunlage 270
    Feldberg 474
    Freudenstadt 462
    Fulda 560
    Garmisch-Partenkirchen 379
    Harz Mountains 264-5
    Karwendel 382
    Oberstdorf 382
    St Andreasberg 271
    St Blasien 476
    Torfhaus 277
    Winterberg 616-17
skinheads 742
soccer, see football
society 21-2, 42, 45-7, 50-1
Soest 611-13
Sommerrodelbahn 184
Sorb people 50, 153
spa towns
    Bad Dürkheim 503-4
    Bad Harzburg 269
    Bad Karlshafen 645-6
    Bad Kösen 260-1
    Bad Neuenahr 505
    Bad Schandau 179
    Bad Tölz 358-9
    Baden-Baden 457-61
    Glücksburg 726
    St Blasien 476-7
    Traben-Trarbach 523-4
    Villingen 466-7
    Wiesbaden 555-8
Space Park Bremen 623
Spartacus 31
spas 307, 739
    Bad Dürkheim 504
    Baden-Baden 459
    Carolus-Thermen 596
    Harz Mountains 265
    Kaiser-Friedrich-Bad 557
    Kaiserthermen (Trier) 520

Lüneburg 653
    Watzmann Therme 384
special events 745-6, see also festivals
Speicherstadt (Hamburg) 691-2,
    552-3
Speyer 500-2
Spiekeroog 679
Spielhaus Richtersche Villa 234
sport 48-50, see also individual entries
    Allianz Arena 339
    Berlin 135-6
    Diözesan Museum 581
    Internet resources 49
    Olympia Stadion 115
    Olympiapark 337
    Stadion Hamburg 695
Spreewald 153-5
Stade 707-8
Staffelstein 403
Stalin, Joseph 33, 37
Starnberg 356-7
Starnberger See 356
Stasi 37, 38
    Stasi Museum (Berlin) 116
    Stasi Museum (Liepzig) 187
statues
    Fräulein Maria 677
    Gänseliesel 666, 667
    Herkules 562
steam trains
    Bochum 602
    Chiemseebahn 356
    Gernrode 280
    Molli Schmalspurbahn 301
    Rasender Roland 313
    Zugspitzbahn 379
Stein, Peter 68
Steinau 564
Stendal 242-3
Stockholm 308
Storm, Theodor
    home town of 726
    Theodor-Storm-Haus 727
    work of 63
Stralsund 305-8, **305**
Strasse der Romanik 280
Straubing 416-17
Strauss, Richard 60, 172, 230
Stuttgart 425-34, **426**
    accommodation 430-1
    attractions 428-9
    drinking 432
    entertainment 432-3
    festivals 430
    food 431-2
    medical services 428
    shopping 433
    travel to/from 433
    travel within 433-4
surfing 339
Süskind, Patrick 64
Sweden 299, 312

swimming
Alpamare 358
Berlin 117
Blub Badeparadies 118
Chiemsee 355-6
Internet resources 117
Munich 339
Strandbad Wannsee 118
Sylt 728-32
synagogues
Alte Synagoge (Worms) 498
Begegnungsstätte Kleine
Synagoge 208
Celle 648
Neue Synagoge 106
Schwäbisch Hall 436
Synagoge Augsburg 373

T
Tallinn 299
Tangermünde 243
tax 735
taxis 769
telephone services 751-2
Teller, Jürgen 55
tennis 49, 136
Terrible Time, the 26
Tetraeder 606
Thale 281-2
theatre
Augsburger Puppenkiste 373
Baden-Baden 458
Berlin 133, 136
Berliner Ensemble 107
books 68
Braunschweig 661
Cologne 587
Deutsches Theater &
Kammerspiele 107
Dresden 176
Düsseldorf 574
Erfurt 211
Frankfurt-am-Main 552
Friedrichstadtpalast 107
Göttingen 670
Hamburg 705
Hanover 642-3
Heidelberg 447
history of 67-8
Internet resources 67
Konstanz 480
Leipzig 193
Lübeck 720
Ludwig II Musical 376
Magdeburg 241-2
Munich 351-2
Nuremberg 394
Puppentheater Berlin 118

Stuttgart 433
Waldbühne 115
Zaubertheater Igor Jedlin 117
theatres
Alte Oper 543-4
Altes Residenztheater (Munich) 334
Anhaltisches Theater 246
Deutsches Nationaltheater 217
Festspielhaus 400
Kulturpalast 171, 176
Markgrafentheater 395
Passionstheater 380
Semperoper 172
Staatstheater 155
Waidspeicher 207
theft 742
Theodor, Carl 568
Third Reich, the, see Nazism, WWII,
Thirty Years' War, the 27, 28, 367
Thuringia 202-35, **204**
Thuringian Forest 223-31
Tiergarten Park 108-9
time 752, **775**
tipping 734
Tischbein, Johann Heinrich 53
Titisee-Neustadt 474-5
Tollensesee 292
Tölzer Land 358
Topographie des Terrors 111
Torfhaus 277
tourist information 752-3
Town Musicians of Bremen 622
Traben-Trarbach 523-4
train travel 760-1, 769-72, **770**
rail passes 760-1, 772
to/from Germany 760-1
within Germany 769-72, **770**
tram travel 769
transport 755-72, **765**, **767**, **770**
travel insurance 747
travellers cheques 749
Travemünde 721
Treaty of Brest-Litovsk, the 31
Treaty of Versailles, the 31
Treaty of Worms, the 25
Trelleborg 299
Triberg 464-5
Trier 518-22, **519**, **520**
Tübingen 437-9
Tübke, Werner 223
Tucholsky, Kurt 63
TV 46, 47, 51, 66, 66-7
Twain, Mark 440

U
Uhlbach 434
Ulbricht, Walter 37
Ulm 450-4, **451**
unemployment 50, 51
Unesco World Heritage Sites 18, 53,
58, **18**
Bamberg 396-9, **396**
Dom (Aachen) 595-6

Kloster Lorsch 555
Messel 555
Middle Rhine Valley 507
Museumsinsel (Berlin) 105
Quedlinburg 277-80
Residenz (Würzburg) 360, 362
Schloss Augustusburg 588
tours of 16, 18, **16**, **18**
Trier 518-22, **519**
Wartburg 224-5
Wieskirche 378
Wilhelmshöhe 562
Wörlitz Park 247
Zeche Zollverein XII 599-600
Ungers, Oswald Matthias 59
universities
Bauhaus Universität 216
Collegium Majus 207
Freie Universität 115
Heidelberg 444
Humboldt Universität 104
Ludwig-Maximilian-Universität
332
Rostock 296
Universität Jena 232
Unstrut River 221, 257
Unter den Linden (Berlin) 104
Untersee 479
Usedom Island 310

V
van de Velde, Henry 216
Varus Disaster, the 24
Väth, Sven 61
Vegesack 629
vegetarian travellers 82
Veste Oberhaus 417
Villingen-Schwenningen 466-7
visas 753, see also passports
Vitte 308
Völkerschlachtdenkmal 187-8
Völklinger Hütte 534
Volkswagen 33, 194, 664
Gläserne Manufaktur 170
von Bülow, Hans 230
von der Vogelweide, Walther 59
von Klenze, Leo 57
von Uhde, Fritz 53
Vorpommersche Boddenlandschaft
National Park 71, 304-5

W
Wagenfeld, Wilhelm
Wilhelm Wagenfeld Haus 623
Wagner, Richard
Eisenach 225
home town of 184
Reuter-Wagner Museum 225
Richard Wagner Museum 170, 400
statue 189
Wagner Festival 401
work of 60
Walhalla 416, **168-9**

walking, *see also* hiking
　Amrum 732
　Bavarian Forest National Park 71
　Berchtesgaden National Park 71
　Buckow 156
　Hainich National Park 71
　Hamburg Wadden Sea National
　　Park 71
　Harz National Park 71
　Hochharz National Park 71
　Höllental 473
　Jasmund 71
　Lower Oder Valley National Park 71
　Lower Saxony Wadden Sea
　　National Park 71
　Lübbenau 154
　Müritz National Park 71
　Neubrandenburg 292
　Partnachklamm 379
　Saxon Switzerland National Park 71
　Sternhaus Ramberg 280
　Vorpommersche Boddenlandschaft
　　National Park 71, 304-5
Wallraf-Richartz-Museum - Fondation
　Corboud 580-1
Walther, Johann 59
Wangerooge 679
Wank mountain 382
Waren 294
Warnemünde 300-1
Warner Bros Movie World 606-7
Warnow River 294
Wartburg 224-5
waterfalls
　Lichtenhainer Wasserfall 179
　Radau Waterfall 269
　Römkerhalle 268
　Triberg 465
water sports 739,
　see also individual sports
Weber, Carl Maria von
　Carl Maria von Weber Museum 170
　work of 60
websites, *see* Internet resources
Weesenstein 177
weights & measures 734,
　see also inside front cover
Weilburg 558
Weill, Kurt
　Kurt Weill Festival 246
　Kurt-Weill-Zentrum 245
Weimar 212-19, **214**, **217**
　accommodation 217-18
　attractions 213-16
　drinking 219
　entertainment 219
　food 218-19
　travel to/from 219
　travel within 219
Weimar Republic, the 29, 30, 32,
　89, 212
Weinstrasse (Vineyard Road) 257

Weissflog, Jens 49
Wellem, Jan 568
　statue 569
Wende, the 40-1
Wenders, Wim 65
Wernigerode 273-5
Werra River 230
Weser River 621, 644
West Germany
　history of 35, 37-40
Westerland 729
Western Pomerania 305-10
Westerwald mountains 509
Westphalia 607-15
Wetterssteinspitze mountain 382
White Rose, the 35, 332
Wieck, Clara 60
Wiesbaden 555-8, **556**
Wieskirche 378
wildlife watching 69
Wilhelm, Otto Ludwig Friedrich 30,
　31, 376
Wilhelmshöhe 562
Wilson, Woodrow 31
Winckelmann, Johann 53
Windgfällweiher 473
windsurfing 730, 739
　Lindau 489
　Poel Island 304
　Sylt 729
　Titisee-Neustadt 474
wine, *see also* wine regions
　books 80, 81
　Dürkheimer Wurstmarkt 503
　festival 259
　glossary 81
　Hanse-Sektkellerei 303
　Internet resources 80, 81
　Kloster Pforta winery 260
　Mosel-Weinmuseum
　　(Bernkastel-Kues) 523
　regions 18
　Rotweinwanderweg 504
　Weinbaumuseum (Meersburg) 484
　Weinbaumuseum Uhlbach 434
　Weindorf (Stuttgart) 430
　Weinmuseum (Rüdesheim) 516
　Wine Museum (Deidesheim) 503
　Wine Museum (Speyer) 500-1
wine regions 80-1, **18**, *see also* wine
　Ahr Valley 504
　Freyburg 259-60
　German Wine Road 502-4
　Kaiserstuhl 472
　Meissen 180
　Moselle Valley 516-25, **517**
　Rhine Valley 507-16, **507**
　Saale-Unstrut Region 257-61
　Schulpforte 260
　Weinstrasse (Vineyard Road) 257
　Winterberg mountain 616-17
Wismar 301-4

Wissower Klinken 315
witches & warlocks 281
Witt, Katrina 50
Wittow 315-16
Wolf, Christa 64
Wolfenbüttel 662-3
Wolfsburg 663-6
women travellers 753-4
women's issues
　Frauenmuseum 592
　health 774
　Internet resources 46
work 754
workers' movements 29-30, 32
World Cup (football) 48, 51, 56, 115,
　339, 603, 642, 695
World Heritage Sites,
　see Unesco World Heritage Sites
Worms 497-500
Worpswede 629-30
Wurmberg 270
Württemberg 434-5
Würzburg 360-4, **361**
Wutach 477
Wutachmühle 477
Wutachschlucht 477
WWI 31, 89
WWII 33-5, 89, *see also* concentration
　camps, Hitler, Adolf
　books 34, 35, 37
　Haus der Wannseekonferenz
　　Gedenkstätte 116
　Internet resources 33
　White Rose, the 332

X
Xanten 575-6

Z
Zappa, Frank 301
Zeche Zollverein XII 599-600
Zeiss, Carl 231
Zella-Mehlis 231
Zeppelin, Ferdinand von 480, 486, 487
Zgorzelec 199
Zittau 200-1
Zittau mountains 201
Zollern II/IV Colliery 604
zoos
　Allwetterzoo (Münster) 609
　Berlin Zoo 114
　Frankfurt-am-Main 545
　Leipzig 187
　Münchener Tierpark Hellabrunn
　　338-9
　Schwerin 288
　Tierpark 282
　Wilhelma Zoo (Stuttgart) 429
Zugspitze 379
Züssow 310
Zwickau 194-6
Zwickauer Mulde valley 194
Zwinger 172, 6

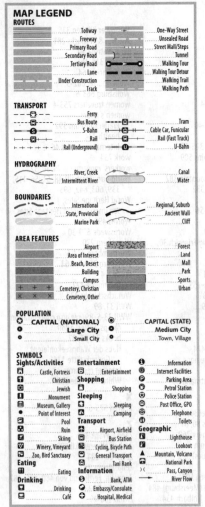

MAP LEGEND

ROUTES

Tollway	One-Way Street
Freeway	Unsealed Road
Primary Road	Street Mall/Steps
Secondary Road	Tunnel
Tertiary Road	Walking Tour
Lane	Walking Tour Detour
Under Construction	Walking Trail
Track	Walking Path

TRANSPORT

Ferry	
Bus Route	Tram
S-Bahn	Cable Car, Funicular
Rail	Rail (Fast Track)
Rail (Underground)	U-Bahn

HYDROGRAPHY

River, Creek	Canal
Intermittent River	Water

BOUNDARIES

International	Regional, Suburb
State, Provincial	Ancient Wall
Marine Park	Cliff

AREA FEATURES

Airport	Forest
Area of Interest	Land
Beach, Desert	Mall
Building	Park
Campus	Sports
Cemetery, Christian	Urban
Cemetery, Other	

POPULATION

CAPITAL (NATIONAL)	CAPITAL (STATE)
Large City	Medium City
Small City	Town, Village

SYMBOLS

Sights/Activities
- Castle, Fortress
- Christian
- Jewish
- Monument
- Museum, Gallery
- Point of Interest
- Pool
- Ruin
- Skiing
- Winery, Vineyard
- Zoo, Bird Sanctuary

Eating
- Eating

Drinking
- Drinking
- Café

Entertainment
- Entertainment

Shopping
- Shopping

Sleeping
- Sleeping
- Camping

Transport
- Airport, Airfield
- Bus Station
- Cycling, Bicycle Path
- General Transport
- Taxi Rank

Information
- Bank, ATM
- Embassy/Consulate
- Hospital, Medical
- Information
- Internet Facilities
- Parking Area
- Petrol Station
- Police Station
- Post Office, GPO
- Telephone
- Toilets

Geographic
- Lighthouse
- Lookout
- Mountain, Volcano
- National Park
- Pass, Canyon
- River Flow

LONELY PLANET OFFICES

Australia
Head Office
Locked Bag 1, Footscray, Victoria 3011
☎ 03 8379 8000, fax 03 8379 8111
talk2us@lonelyplanet.com.au

USA
150 Linden St, Oakland, CA 94607
☎ 510 893 8555, toll free 800 275 8555
fax 510 893 8572, info@lonelyplanet.com

UK
72–82 Rosebery Ave,
Clerkenwell, London EC1R 4RW
☎ 020 7841 9000, fax 020 7841 9001
go@lonelyplanet.co.uk

Published by Lonely Planet Publications Pty Ltd
ABN 36 005 607 983

© Lonely Planet 2004

© photographers as indicated 2004

Cover photographs by Lonely Planet Images: Renaissance-era mansion on the Romantic Road, Andrea Schulte-Peevers (front); Schloss Neuschwanstein in Fussen, Chris Mellor (back). Many of the images in this guide are available for licensing from Lonely Planet Images: www.lonelyplanetimages.com.

Printed through Colorcraft Ltd, Hong Kong.
Printed in China